THE GLORIOUS BEANEATERS OF THE 1890S

EDITED BY BOB LEMOINE AND BILL NOWLIN

ASSOCIATE EDITOR LEN LEVIN

Society for American Baseball Research, Inc.
Phoenix, AZ

The Glorious Beaneaters of the 1890s

Edited by Bob LeMoine and Bill Nowlin

Associate editor Len Levin

Copyright © 2019 Society for American Baseball Research, Inc.

Library of Congress Control Number: 2019919053

All rights reserved. Reproduction in whole or in part without permission is prohibited.

ISBN 978-1-970159-19-6

(Ebook ISBN 978-1-970159-18-9)

Front cover:

(top row, L to R): Tommy McCarthy, Jimmy Collins, Kid Nichols.

(bottom row, L to R): John Clarkson, King Kelly, Hugh Duffy.

All photographs are public domain. Collins is courtesy of Robert Edwards Auctions, and Nichols and Kelly are courtesy of the Library of Congress.

Back cover (top to bottom): Courtesy of Mark Souder, John Thorn, Boston Public Library, John Thorn

Book design: Rachael Sullivan

Society for American Baseball Research

Cronkite School at ASU

555 N. Central Ave. #416

Phoenix, AZ 85004

Phone: (602) 496-1460

Web: www.sabr.org

Facebook: Society for American Baseball Research

Twitter: @SABR

CONTENTS

PLAYERS

Jimmy Bannon
Thomas J. Brown, Jr. 13

Charlie Bennett
Paul Hofmann.................................16

Marty Bergen
Brian McKenna.................................23

Cliff Carroll
Alan Cohen.................................27

Boileryard Clarke
Matt Albertson.................................32

John Clarkson
Brian McKenna.................................36

Jimmy Collins
Charlie Bevis.................................45

Frank Connaughton
Joanne Hulbert.................................51

Cozy Dolan
Bob LeMoine.................................56

Hugh Duffy
Bill Lamb.................................61

Charlie Frisbee
Bill Nowlin.................................66

Charlie Ganzel
Chad Moody.................................70

Hank Gastright

Glen Sparks.................................76

Pretzels Getzien
Mike Huber.................................81

Billy Hamilton
David L. Fleitz.................................84

Joe Harrington
Seth Moland-Kovash.................................88

King Kelly
Peter M. Gordon.................................91

Fred Klobedanz
Mark S. Sternman.................................98

Ted Lewis
Rory Costello.................................102

Herman Long
Richard "Dixie" Tourangeau.................................105

Bobby Lowe
Richard "Dixie" Tourangeau.................................112

Tommy McCarthy
Bill Lamb.................................117

Bill Merritt
Bob LeMoine.................................122

Billy Nash
Richard "Dixie" Tourangeau.................................128

Kid Nichols
Richard Bogovich.................................134

Joe Quinn
Rochelle Llewelyn Nicholls..................................138

Jack Ryan
Matt Clever..................................146

General Stafford
Richard "Dixie" Tourangeau..................................149

Chick Stahl
Dennis Auger..................................154

Harry Staley
JW Stewart..................................158

Jack Stivetts
Gregory H. Wolf..................................164

Harry Stovey
Paul Hofmann..................................169

Jim Sullivan
Richard Bogovich..................................176

Billy Sullivan Sr
Trey Strecker..................................182

Marty Sullivan
Mike Huber..................................185

Fred Tenney
Mark S. Sternman..................................188

Tommy Tucker
David Nemec..................................192

Vic Willis
Daniel R. Levitt..................................195

George Yeager
Richard Bogovich..................................199

MANAGER

Frank Selee   *David L. Fleitz*..................................209

OWNERS

James B. Billings   *Charlie Bevis*..................................215
William H. Conant   *William H. Lyons*..................................221
Arthur Soden   *Brian McKenna*..................................227

BALLPARKS

South End Grounds   *Bob Ruzzo*..................................235
Congress Street Grounds   *Charlie Bevis*..................................244

GAMES

April 22, 1891: Beaneaters Start Championship Run in First Game in New Polo Grounds
Stew Thornley..249

April 27, 1891: Kid Nichols Shuts Out Phillies in Beaneaters' Home Opener *Richard A. Cuicchi*..........252

June 11, 1891: Beaneaters' Hot Bats Earn Series Split With Colts *Bill Mortell*..254

June 12, 1891: Kid Nichols Strikes Out 12 and has Game-Winning Hit *Kevin Larkin*.........................256

August 17, 1891: Kid Nichols One-Hits the Giants *Bill Lamb*..258

September 4, 1891: A Meeting with Grampa *Rob Nee*..260

September 28-30, 1891: The Clouded Finish: Beaneaters Take Over First Place *Lyle Spatz*....................262

October 1, 1891: Beaneaters Clinch Pennant Amid League Controversy *Richard A. Cuicchi*..................264

October 2, 1891: Beaneaters Win 18th Consecutive Game in Pennant Run *Richard A. Cuicchi*..............266

April 23, 1892 (doubleheader): Sweep Continues Strong Season Start for Beaneaters *Joel Rippel*........269

May 6, 1892: A "Long" Game *Mark Pestana*..271

July 4, 1892: Comeback Win by Boston Spoils Cincinnatti's Glorious Day *Joel Rippel*.........................273

July 11, 1892: A Close Victory, But Still a Laugher *Bob LeMoine*..275

August 5, 1892: Triple Play Helps Preserve a Shutout *Bill Nowlin*..277

August 6, 1892: Jack Stivetts No-Hits the Bridegrooms *Bill Nowlin*..279

September 19, 1892: Kid Nichols' Batting Feat *Eric Miklich*..281

October 1892: October 1892: The Split-Season Playoff *Terry Gottschall*..284

April 28, 1893: Beaneaters Open Season With Rout of Giants *Joel Rippel*...286

May 15, 1893: Home Opener In Front of Star-Studded Crowd *Jerrod Cotosman*................................288

May 19, 1893: The Home Run That Wasn't *John Zinn*..290

May 26, 1893: A Barrage of Batting *Mark Pestana*..292

July 22, 1893: "Tucker Hit Like A Fiend" and "Nichols Saved the Day" *Bill Nowlin*...........................295

August 19, 1893: Unsafe Passage *Andy Terrick*..297

September 20, 1893: "Proud Emblem to Wave Here Next Year – Spiders Bite the Dust in Cleveland"
Mark Souder...300

April 24, 1894: Baltimore Stuns the Champs, Scoring 14 Runs in the Ninth for the Win
Mike Huber..303

May 7, 1894: A Duel of Aces   *John Zinn*......305

May 15, 1894: "It Was a Hot Game, Sure Enough!"   *Terry Gottschall*......307

May 30, 1894: Four Home Runs for Bobby Lowe   *Charles F. Faber*......309

June 6, 1894: Crushed at Congress Street   *Andy Terrick*......311

June 18, 1894: The Bunker Hill Day Massacre   *John Bauer*......314

June 20, 1894: Congress Street's Glorious Finale   *Richard "Dixie" Tourangeau*......317

July 17, 1894: Stall and Feign and Pray for Rain   *Bob LeMoine*......319

July 20, 1894: Beaneaters Blast Giants 12-1 in First Game at South End Grounds after Fire
Mark S. Sternman......322

August 7, 1894: Jimmy "Foxy Grandpa" Bannon Slugs Two 3-Run Homers   *Michael R. McAvoy*......324

August 27, 1894: Charlie Bennett Charity Game   *Bob LeMoine*......327

September 18, 1895: A Cozy Shutout: Cozy Dolan Shuts Out the Orioles   *Kevin Larkin*......329

April 20, 1896: A Patriots' Day Hit Parade   *Gerard R. Goulet*......331

May 13, 1896: Playing Until Dark   *Bob LeMoine*......334

September 3, 1896: Boston Puts Their Batting Clothes On   *Richard Riis*......337

April 19, 1897: A Furious Comeback Falls Short   *David L. Fleitz*......339

May 31, 1897: Tenney Leads Memorial Day Parade With Six Hits   *Richard Riis*......341

June 21, 1897: Two-Way Threat "Kloby" Leads Boston to 11-6 Win over Brooklyn
Mark S. Sternman......343

August 6, 1897: An Unusual Brawl and a Wild Ending   *Gerard R. Goulet*......345

September 1, 1897: Utilityman Bob Allen's Big Day – As Bostonians Begin to Travel Underground
Bill Nowlin......348

September 24, 1897: Boston Rooters Flock to Baltimore to See Crucial Pennant Race Victory
Jerrod Cotosman......350

September 27, 1897: Good (Beaneaters) versus Evil (Orioles)   *Bill Felber*......353

September 29, 1898: Collins Grand Slam Helps Beaneaters Score Six Runs in Ninth to Beat Philadelphia
Brian M. Frank......355

October 11, 1898: Relieved Beaneaters Gain Title Again   *Ralph Peluso*......357

October 13, 1899: Kid Nichols' Masterful 3-hitter Caps 10 Straight Seasons with 21+ Victories
Mike Huber......359

OTHER

How Bostonians Became the Beaneaters *Mark Souder* 363

Slide, Kelly Slide *Joanne Hulbert* 368

1897: Last Gasp of the Temple Cup *Bill Felber* 371

King Kelly's Funeral *Peter M. Gordon* 373

Starts, Stops, and Streaks – A Modern Fan's Guide to the 1890s Baseball Schedule
Richard "Dixie" Tourangeau 376

Boston Beaneaters Spring Training in the 1890s *Bill Nowlin* 378

SEASONS

The 1891 Season: 18 Straight Down the Stretch *Jean-Pierre Caillault* 387

Boston Beaneaters of 1892 *Steve Hatcher* 394

1893: Summer 35-5 Stretch Garners Third Straight Flag *Richard "Dixie" Tourangeau* 400

The 1894 Season: No Four-Peat for Boston *Charlie Bevis* 403

The 1895 Season: Strictly for the Birds, Again *Bob LeMoine* 407

1896 Season: Another Pennant From a Birds-Eye View *Bob LeMoine* 410

1897: Boston's Crusade *Bill Felber* 413

1898: A Very Long Season Ends with Another Flag *Richard Riis* 419

1899: The Cracks Begin to Show *Richard Riis* 425

CONTRIBUTORS 430

INTRODUCTION

"LONG AGO WHEN THE TEAM WAS KNOWN AS THE BEANEATERS."

BY BOB LEMOINE

On Wednesday afternoon, June 17, 1953, at Milwaukee's County Stadium, Warren Spahn, one of baseball's greatest left-handed pitchers, was on the mound for the Milwaukee Braves to take on the visiting Philadelphia Phillies. While the veteran Spahn already had a celebrated career with four 20-plus-win seasons, this was only his third start in Milwaukee. Spahn had pitched in Boston for the previous decade for a franchise that dated back to 1871. The club had suddenly and unceremoniously announced its move to Milwaukee during spring training, ending 82 years of a National League club in Boston. While there was excitement in the Brew City over its new franchise, which would lead the NL in attendance and see a World Series title in 1957, there was the empty shell of Braves Field in Boston and the now-forgotten landmark where the South End Grounds once stood amid the roar of streetcars.

Probably few fans noticed the presence of a guest from Oregon who came to watch the Braves that day. He owned a walnut ranch out there, but Wisconsin was his home state, where he learned to play baseball in the cow pastures. He was Billy Sullivan Sr., a former major-league catcher famous for his time with the Chicago White Sox in the first decade of the twentieth century. Sullivan was of a small few still around who had played in the nineteenth century, and he had played for Boston in 1899. When he died in 1965, just a few days shy of his 90th year, Sullivan was the last living member of Boston's baseball dynasty of the 1890s.

"I'm a Braves rooter because I played with the Braves long ago when the team was known as the Beaneaters," Sullivan told Sam Levy of the *Milwaukee Sentinel*. Even after a half-century, those days were still fresh in his mind, including those of his battery-mate, Kid Nichols, who he said was the fastest pitcher he ever caught. "The Kid was one of the best," he said.

More than a century has passed since the "glorious Beaneaters" era of Boston's baseball history in the 1890s. Sullivan actually wasn't a major factor in that history, having played only 22 games for Boston in 1899 and not having experienced the pennant seasons of 1891-1893 and 1897-1898. The franchise now lives on in Atlanta, but it's doubtful you ever hear reference made to the Beaneaters. Their stories are largely forgotten by all but the serious follower of baseball history. Yet, while Boston would soon have a second baseball club that would capture the hearts of New England, never again would there be such dominance over a decade as the Beaneaters accomplished.

Nine of these players would one day become hall of famers. There was John Clarkson, whose mental health issues late in life overshadowed a truly remarkable pitching career which saw him win 327 games in a 10-year span. Kid Nichols was Boston's ace on the mound during the era. Despite seven seasons of at least 30 wins and 362 career wins he was "pushed into baseball's medieval past" in the words of historian Bill James. There were the "Heavenly Twins," Hugh Duffy and Tommy McCarthy, who roamed the Boston outfield with speed and grace. Yet, no one could top the speed of Sliding Billy Hamilton, whose career stats in walks, runs, steals and batting average still make the modern researcher shake their head. Jimmy Collins won pennants with both Boston franchises and has been dubbed by Charlie Bevis as "the patron saint of today's Red Sox Nation." Vic Willis was just a rookie when the Beaneaters dynasty was winding down, but his 25 wins helped propel them to the 1898 pennant and he enjoyed seven more seasons of at least 20 wins. And what can you say about King Kelly, baseball's true first superstar whose exploits on and off the field elevated the game into the world of popular culture? *Sporting Life* called Frank Selee "a thorough baseball general" and he exhibited his leadership in guiding these Beaneaters to five pennants throughout the 1890s.

If you're a baseball fan but don't recognize these names, you're not alone. The Baseball Hall of Fame itself seemed to forget these legends. They were part of a forgotten era as America steamed into the twentieth century. Fortunately, the game eventually remembered their names and their times. Some were inducted while in their golden years, but time ran out on others who never received the recognition they deserved. Now enshrined in the Hall, their stories live on, enabling a group of SABR researchers to delve deeper into who they were and what the game was like.

But we have to ask, what is a Beaneater?

"Beaneaters" was not even an official nickname for the team, but one coined by sportswriters, as Charlie Bevis wrote, "to drum up more interest among readers than by continuing to use the bland 'Bostons' term." Yet, the name stuck and the Beaneaters and the 1890s remain a distinct era in Boston's baseball history.

This book is the result of SABR researchers who believe the Glorious Beaneaters era of the 1890s is a story worth telling. We attempt to do so by telling the stories of the men who played for Boston and some of the interesting games they were involved in. "The tumultuous 1890s witnessed a player revolt against high-handed and monopolistic management," wrote baseball historian John Thorn, "epitomized by a cap on salaries, followed by a nearly ruinous contraction from three major leagues to one 12-team circuit. The national economy suffered a panic in 1893 and a sluggish recovery thereafter; baseball attendance dwindled; and the lack of postseason interleague competition after 1890 (as there had been since 1884) was sorely felt. The game was in a period of consolidation, or hibernation, or stagnation; one's perspective depended upon whether he were an owner, fan, or player." Legendary manager Connie Mack remembered that era firsthand as "a turbulent decade of the so-called roughhouse days in baseball. The Boston Beaneaters were ready for any fray, ever willing to take on the pugnacious Baltimore Orioles and give them a dose of their own medicine."

We hope this book will give you, the reader, an enjoyable journey into the 1890s and the era of the Glorious Beaneaters.

PLAYERS

JIMMY BANNON

BY THOMAS J. BROWN JR.

Jimmy Bannon, 1895 Mayos Cut-Plug tobacco card.
(public domain)

James Henry "Jimmy" Bannon was born on May 5, 1871, in Amesbury, Massachusetts. He grew up in Saugus, Massachusetts, where he played ball with his brothers Tom, George, and William. Tom Bannon also became a professional ballplayer and played two seasons with the New York Giants (1895, 1896). George and William never made it out of the minor leagues. Their parents, Patrick and Johanna (Conners) Bannon, were natives of Ireland. Patrick Bannon worked in a woolen mill at the time of both the 1870 and 1880 Censuses. There were 10 Bannon children at the time of the 1880 Census; James was the sixth-born.

Bannon played minor-league ball for the Lynn, Massachusetts, team in 1891 and the Portland, Maine, team in 1892. (Both teams were in the New England League.) In 1893 Bannon pitched for the College of the Holy Cross baseball team, which finished the season with an 11-5 record.[1]

Bannon also played in 1892 and 1893 for the independent Northampton (Massachusetts) team, which played exhibition games against the Boston Beaneaters before large crowds at the Driving Park, as well as against the Louisville Colonels and St. Louis Browns.[2]

Bannon's play as an outfielder and shortstop at Holy Cross had brought him to the attention of the Browns, and they signed him to a contract for the 1893 season. In his major-league debut, on June 15, 1893, he played right field in a 5-1 loss to the Boston Beaneaters. He played in 26 games for the Browns in 1893 and batted .336, with three doubles, four triples, and eight stolen bases. He also started one game on the mound for the Browns, pitching four innings in a loss in which he allowed 18 runs (10 earned).

Bannon played two games at shortstop early in his rookie season, committing seven errors in just two games, so manager Bill Watkins moved him permanently to the outfield. But he didn't improve his defensive skills there; he made eight more errors in 24 games. Yet the *New York Clipper* said Bannon "became popular with the Mound City [St. Louis] enthusiasts on account of his hard and timely batting. When [St. Louis Browns] President [Chris] Von der Ahe released him near the end of the season there was a storm of indignation, and his release was recalled, but it was finally decided to let him go for good, as Mr. Von der Ahe considered [Duff] Cooley, who was on his club's pay rolls, to be as good, if not a better player."[3]

According to the *New York Clipper,* several teams sent telegrams to Bannon expressing interest in him, "but somehow they did not reach him."[4] He learned of this upon returning to Boston, where he joined the Beaneaters for the 1894 season. He played in the outfield with future Hall of Famers Hugh Duffy and Tommy McCarthy. Bannon continued to hit well. He batted .336 with 130 runs scored and 114 runs batted in for the powerful Boston offense. But Bannon continued to struggle defensively. Although he led all National League outfielders with 43 assists, he was second in the league with 41 errors. (He did help turn 12 double plays, which was the NL record for most double plays by an outfielder in a season until Jimmy Sheckard of the Baltimore had 14 in 1899.)

One of the highlights of the season for Bannon came when he hit grand slams in consecutive games.[5] The first came on August 6 in a 15-7 win against the Washington Nationals. The next day he hit another in the Beaneaters' 19-8 win over the Philadelphia Phillies.

On May 15, 1894, the Beaneaters were playing the Baltimore Orioles at the South End Grounds, which *Sporting Life* had described as the "handsomest in the country." The structure had been repaired in the offseason, and workers had left sawdust and debris behind, under the right-field seats.[6]

After the end of the third inning, Bannon saw flames coming up through the right-field bleachers stands as he headed to the outfield and he ran to put it out. Wind caused the fire to flare up and Bannon tried without success to extinguish the fire with his feet. Soon, the right-field bleachers caught fire and eventually the outfield fence as well as the left-field bleachers went up in flames.

Quickly the fire spread from the ballpark to neighboring buildings. At least 12 acres were destroyed in the surrounding area and more than 1,900 people were made homeless by the fire,[7] which became known as the the Great Roxbury Fire of 1894.[8] The homeless Beaneaters moved to Boston's Congress Street Grounds, which had hosted Boston Players' League and American Association teams earlier in the decade.

After the season Bannon was offered a salary of $1,200 for 1895 by Beaneaters manager Frank Selee. Bannon initially refused to sign, claiming that he had earlier been offered a raise for the 1895 season.[9] He eventually signed on the condition that he receive the raise or be released from his contract.[10] The team signed him, raised his salary on June 1 and Bannon played the entire season with the Beaneaters.

Bannon continued to be a productive hitter in 1895, batting a career-high .347 with 74 RBIs. Several times during the season, he led the Beaneaters to victory. *Sporting Life* described one series where Bannon played a key role in consecutive wins for the Boston team: "If any one player owned a town, Bannon owns Boston. Few batting feats will compare with those of his last week. On Tuesday he made three hits. On Thursday he went to bat nine times and made eight hits, besides making a timely sacrifice. Friday morning, with Lowe on first base and St. Louis one ahead, he sent the ball over the left field fence, there being two out at the time and one man on base and the game was won. In the afternoon he made a home run again and hit safely every times [sic] he came to bat. On Saturday Cincinnati led in the seventh inning until he came to the rescue with another home run. Naturally he led the team in batting at the close of the week, both in singles and in totals. He made 13 hits in the four games."[11] During the season, Bannon was credited with hitting safely in 21 straight games.[12]

Bannon slumped badly in 1896. His batting average dropped to .253 and he had only 87 hits before the Beaneaters dropped him in August. His poor fielding may have also led the team to consider Bannon a liability. The *Boston Globe* commented that "good base running and line throwing do not altogether offset miserable fielding."[13] Playing in in the outfield as well as around the infield, he had 29 errors when he was released on August 18. *Sporting Life* wrote that the Pittsburgh team was interested in him but Boston did not immediately release their claim on Bannon. He never signed with another major-league team.[14]

In four years, Bannon played in 367 major-league games and batted .320. His fielding percentage was a meager .877 and he had made 98 errors as both an infielder and outfielder.

After being released by the Beaneaters, Bannon became a journeyman minor leaguer. He moved to a new team almost every year through 1910. He split the 1897 season between the Kansas City Blues (Western League) and Springfield Ponies/Maroons (Eastern League), and batted a combined .327 with 41 doubles and 66 stolen bases. Bannon started the 1898 season with Springfield, but later moved to the Montreal Royals in the same league. He was dropped near the end of the season, according to *Sporting Life.* There was speculation that the club didn't want to pay him since he was a "high priced man" due to his prior major-league experience.[15]

In February 1898 Bannon married Mary Elizabeth O'Brien in Lynn, Massachusetts. The couple had two children, Lucas and Lauretta.[16]

Bannon played for the Toronto Maple Leafs in the Eastern League from 1899 to 1902. He batted a career-high .341 in 1899 and stole 44 bases. He batted over .300 the next two seasons, too. But *Sporting Life* noted in May 1902 that Bannon was batting left-handed and that he had made the change on "account of the poor luck he had" at the plate during the prior season.[17]

Bannon played for the Columbus Senators in the American Association in 1903 but returned to the Eastern League in 1904, playing for a different team in the league every year until 1907.

Bannon's stops included the Newark Sailors, Montreal Royals, and Rochester Bronchos (two separate years). He never had the same hitting success that he experienced earlier in his career.

By 1908 Bannon's skills as a player had begun to decline severely. He spent the next three years playing in the Class-B New York State and New England Leagues. Each year saw Bannon playing in fewer games as he continued to see his batting average slide lower and lower.

Bannon managed teams in five different seasons before he quit professional baseball. His first job was managing the Columbus (Ohio) Senators in 1903. Bannon also spent two years as player-manager for the Montreal Royals as well as the Binghamton (New York) Bingoes of the New York State League. His greatest success as a player-manager came in 1908 when he managed the Bingoes to a second-place finish. He managed the Lawrence (Massachusetts) Colts of the New England League in 1910; his final stint as a manager was in 1911 with the Haverhill (Massachusetts) Hustlers, also of the New England League.

By the time Bannon finished his playing career, he had earned the nickname of Foxy Grandpa. As early as 1902, he was referred to by *Sporting Life* as the "white haired" Jimmy Bannon.[18] The *Wilkes-Barre Record* wrote on February 8, 1906, that "the gray haired youngster, known from coast to coast as Foxy Grandpa, will manage the Montreal club in the Eastern League. Bannon isn't as old as he looks by twenty years because his hair is prematurely gray."[19]

After he left baseball, Bannon bought the Rochester, one of the largest hotels in Rochester, New Hampshire.[20] He ran the hotel for many years before selling it and moving to New Jersey. Bannon was elected to the New Hampshire legislature in 1912. *Sporting Life* described his election as follows: "Coming from a progressive family whose members cannot be kept down because of dash, and energy, Jimmy goes to the legislature to learn new fields and new duties. His friends say that no one was more surprised than Bannon."[21]

Bannon died in March 24, 1948, at the age of 76. He was living in Glen Rock, New Jersey, at the time. He was buried in St. Mary's Cemetery in Rochester, New Hampshire.

NOTES

1. "2015 Holy Cross Baseball Record Book," goholycross.com/fls/33100/import_content/sports/m-basebl/archive_files/Record_Book/2015_Record_Book_w-out_All-Time_Results.pdf, accessed March 8, 2017.
2. "Northampton Baseball III: 1890's - Independent Baseball in Northampton," historic-northampton.org/highlights/baseball3.html.
3. "James Bannon," *New York Clipper*, November 16, 1895: 587.
4. Ibid.
5. John Tattersall, "The Grand Slam Story," research.sabr.org/journals/grand-slam-story, accessed March 9, 2017.
6. Bob Ruzzo, "Baseball Is Back: An Unexpected Farewell: The South End Grounds, August 1914," bostonbaseballhistory.com/an-unexpected-farewell-the-south-end-grounds-august-1914/, April 4, 2014.
7. Ibid.
8. "The Great Roxbury Fire of 1894," GoodOldBoston.Blogspot.com, May 12, 2013.
9. "Merry Montreal Will Not Lose Her Franchise in Eastern League," *Sporting Life*, March 23, 1895: 8.
10. "Hub Happenings: The Boston Team Work So Far Satisfactory," *Sporting Life*, May 4, 1895: 5.
11. "Hub Happenings: The Ex-Champions are Now Playing and Drawing Well," *Sporting Life*, June 8, 1895: 5.
12. "James Bannon."
13. "Baseball News and Comment," *Sporting Life*, May 16, 1896: 5.
14. "League Bulletin," *Sporting Life*, August 29, 1896: 5.
15. "Pittsburg Points," *Sporting Life*, September 17, 1898: 9.
16. The spelling may or may not have been the idiosyncratic rendering of Loretta by the census enumerator.
17. "The Populous East," *Sporting Life*, May 13, 1902: 8.
18. "Roused a Tartar," *Sporting Life*, November 22, 1902: 13.
19. *Wilkes-Barre Record*, February 8, 1906.
20. Albert Spink, *The National Game* (St. Louis: National Game Publishing Company, 1910), 27.
21. "Bannon's Rise," *Sporting Life*, November 23, 1912: 15.

SOURCES

In addition to the sources cited in the Notes, the author also utilized the Baseball-Reference.com and Retrosheet.org websites for box scores, player, team, and season pages, pitching and batting game logs, and other material pertinent to this biography.

CHARLIE BENNETT
BY PAUL HOFMANN

Charlie Bennett.
(Library of Congress)

When asked to name the best catchers of the nineteenth century, most baseball historians wouldn't have to name very many before they mentioned Charlie Bennett, a fan favorite who was admired for his intense toughness and true love of the game. He was one of the most durable and best defensive catchers during an era when catchers lacked the benefit of large padded catcher's mitts and modern protective equipment. He often played through injuries and took the punishment that resulted in battered hands, mashed fingers, and broken ribs in a manner that honored the game and the catching profession. In a similar manner, his dignified response to a tragedy that ended his career "elevated him to near-sainthood" among baseball fans across America.[1]

Charles Wesley Bennett was born in New Castle, Pennsylvania, on November 21, 1854. New Castle at that time was a town of just over 1,600 inhabitants and a stop on the Western Pennsylvania canal system. He was the eighth of 11 children born to Silas and Catherine (Nickols) Bennett. Silas, a native of Connecticut, was a tinner and operated a hardware store in New Castle. When not playing baseball, Charlie helped his father in his shop.

Bennett began his career in Organized Baseball with the Neshannock team in the Pennsylvania League. He played with the team from 1874 to 1876. It was said he "broke the directors because of the number of balls knocked into the river."[2] Originally an infielder who divided his time between second, third, and shortstop before becoming a catcher, Bennett recalled the genesis of this transition in a 1908 interview with sportswriter George R. Pulford.

"When we played Beaver I noticed that their catcher stood up close behind the bat. You know in those days the catcher used to stand back and take the ball on the bound. But this fellow stood up there and grabbed the ball barehanded, and our fellows didn't steal many bases.

"Well, we were playing one day after this, and our opponents stole bases right along. I told our catcher to go up behind the batter but he refused. 'Not me,' he replied. 'If you want to try it, go ahead. I think too much of my hands.'

"Well, I went behind the bat and caught out the game and no more bases were stolen. I like the position, because it kept me doing something all the time, and from then on I caught."[3]

At the end of the 1876 season, the 22-year-old Bennett, along with Nashannock teammates George Creamer and Ned Williamson, signed with the Detroit Aetnas.[4] Though originally an amateur club, the Aetnas began dipping into the professional ranks in the summer of 1876, bringing an end to one of the strongest strictly amateur clubs Detroit had known.[5]

The next two seasons Bennett played for the Milwaukee Grays. The Grays were part of the League Alliance before joining the National League in 1878.

Bennett made his major-league debut on May 1, 1878, against the Cincinnati Reds at Avenue Grounds in Cincinnati. He went 2-for-4 and scored a run in the Grays' 6-4 Opening Day loss. The next day the Reds best the Grays again as Bennett attempted to catch back-to-back games. However in the fourth inning, Bennett's hands gave out and he moved to center field.[6] Injuries hampered Bennett throughout the season.

The 23-year-old Bennett was still learning the position and was not the defensive standout he later became. On June 12 the Grays dropped a 1-0 10-inning decision to the Chicago White Stockings in a game during which Bennett made seven errors.[7] After the game, Bennett was released. At the beginning of July, before the Grays series with Boston, "Bennett was re-engaged" and spent the rest of the season with the team.[8]

Bennett played in 49 games, 35 as a catcher, and batted .245 with one home run and 12 RBIs. The home run came on July 25 off 18-year-old rookie right-hander John Montgomery Ward in Milwaukee's 7-1 win over the Providence Grays. The top of the ninth home run helped end Milwaukee's 14-game losing streak that extended more than a month. Milwaukee finished the season in last place with a dismal 15-45 record and disbanded early in 1879.

In late February of 1879 Bennett and Bill Holbert, a fellow catcher who had most recently played with the Louisville Grays, attempted to organize a new professional club in Milwaukee. The pair set out to raise $1,000 in capital from investors but within two weeks the club fell through and the money was returned to the backers. Bennett dropped the attempt, concluding that the baseball business in Milwaukee was a thankless job: "If you ever catch me undertaking such a task again here, you can just lift my head from my shoulders and use it for a football."[9]

With no prospects for baseball in Milwaukee, Bennett joined the Worcester Grays of the minor National Association, a team organized and managed by vagabond manager Frank Bancroft. With the additions of Bennett and backstop Doc Bushong, the Grays had two outstanding catchers. This was an asset during an era when catchers lacked the protective equipment and needed time to recuperate after catching a game. Bennett played in 42 games for Worcester and hit .328. Bushong played in 46 games and hit .290.

On June 2, 1879, Bennett played a key role in in the no-hit professional debut of left-hander Lee Richmond.[10] The last-place Worcester club sent Richmond, a 22-year-old star pitcher on the Brown University team, to the mound to face the National League-leading Chicago White Stockings. The White Stockings were 14-1 at the time. Bennett played first base and went 1-for-2 with a triple, scored two runs, and made what was described as "a remarkably fine foul catch" in support of Richmond.[11] The Grays shellacked the White Stockings, 11-0.

During the winter of 1879-80, Bancroft persuaded Bennett and some of his teammates to barnstorm through the Southern United States and Cuba. In late November the group, which included Bushong, George Wood, Lon Knight, Art Whitney, Chub Sullivan, Curry Foley, Arthur Irwin, and Tricky Nichols, made its way to Cuba. Calling themselves the Hop Bitters, the club became the first American professional team to visit Cuba.[12] The trip was a flop, both financially and otherwise. Only a few games were played and the Americans dominated their Cuban hosts. Bennett and the Hop Bitters arrived back in New Orleans at the end of December and continued barnstorming.

In 1880 Worcester was admitted to the National League and became known as the Ruby Legs. That season, Bennett played in 51 games, 46 as a catcher, and hit .228 with 18 RBIs. The team finished in fifth place with a record of 40-43, its highest finish in its three years of existence. The Ruby Legs' season included one notable highlight.

On June 12, 1880, Bennett's name was etched into the annals of baseball history when he caught major-league baseball's first perfect game. Richmond, who had tossed two National Association no-hitters in 1879, retired all 27 Cleveland Blues he faced in a 1-0 Ruby Legs victory at Worcester's Agricultural Fair Grounds. Years later Richmond, who left baseball for a career in education, said that Bennett was his favorite catcher to work with and "the best backstop that ever lived."[13]

While playing in Worcester, Bennett met Alice Spears, a young woman from Vermont. The couple married in 1882 and Alice would later play a key role in the development of the chest protector worn by catchers. According to Bennett, his wife was constantly worried about his safety as she watched him catch fastballs, block curves and fend off foul balls, all without the modern tools of ignorance. So the two set out to design something that would protect his rib cage and chest area. Bennett and his wife designed and made a "crude but very substantial shield … made by sewing strips of cork of a good thickness in between heavy bedticking material" that faintly resembled the modern catcher's chest protector.[14]

Fearful of being taunted by spectators for wearing such a cowardly apparatus, Bennett wore the protective device under his jersey. After testing his new invention, Bennett wore the chest protector in a regular game, and with the eyes of thousands of spectators gazing upon him he would let a fast one hit him square on the chest, the ball would rebound back almost to the pitcher much to the amazement of the fans and players who weren't onto the hidden cause.[15]

Years after his playing career ended, Bennett reflected on the evolution of the equipment and how it affected the position: "I remember the first gloves we had were padded across the palm, and the fingers were cut off at the second joint. Later on we used the big mitts, mask and breast protector, and catching became a cinch."[16] Indeed, mutilated hands, broken fingers, and cracked ribs were common injuries suffered by catchers during Bennett's era.

At the end of the 1880 season, Bancroft was hired to manage the new National League franchise in Detroit and took several Worcester players with him, including Bennett, third baseman Art Whitney, and outfielders George Wood and Lon Knight.[17] While the Wolverines finished above .500 only once in their first five years, the popular 26-year-old was entering his prime. He enjoyed the best years of his career in Detroit and soon became recognized as one of the game's early stars.

In his first season with the Wolverines, Bennett established himself as one of the best players in the National League with a MVP-caliber season. He played in 76 games, 70 as the catcher, and hit .301 with a team-leading 7 home runs, 64 RBIs, and a .476 slugging percentage. His home-run and RBI totals were the second highest in the National League. Defensively he was even better, leading all catchers with 418 putouts and a range factor of 7.19. He also established a major-league record for catchers with a .962 fielding percentage. Bennett's WAR rating for position players was 4.3, the second highest, as the Wolverines finished their inaugural season with a respectable record of 41-43.

According to baseball historian Peter Morris, Bennett took the first recorded "curtain call" in baseball on Opening Day of 1881. After hitting a home run off Buffalo's Jack Lynch, Bennett was "loudly applauded, and the crowd would not desist until he bowed in acknowledgment."[18] While the home run had little impact on the outcome of the game, the Wolverines lost 6-5, the fans' tribute to Bennett was a foreshadowing of the special relationship he would have with Detroit and its baseball fans.

Despite the team's surprising fourth-place finish and Bennett's immense popularity with Detroit fans, the Wolverines' star catcher was quickly growing disenchanted. Bennett, who wanted to play for a winner, later said that he was unhappy playing for the Wolverines during the franchise's early years. "During the next four years I wished many times I was out of Detroit, or rather out of that team," he said. "It was awful."[19]

Bennett continued to lead the Wolverines offense and enjoyed another fine season in 1882. In 84 games, 65 behind the plate, he again hit .301. He hit 10 triples and 5 home runs, drove in 51 runs, and had a .450 slugging percentage. Behind the plate, he led National League catchers in putouts (446) and range factor (7.94). Again, he was among the league leaders in WAR among position players (4.2) and helped the Wolverines finish above .500 for the first time.

Despite the team's modest improvement, Bennett contemplated leaving the Wolverines at the end of the 1882 season.

> Toward the end of the 1882 season, Bennett signed a preliminary agreement with the [Pittsburgh] Alleghenys of the American Association for his personal services for the next year. But then he had a change of heart, chose to stay in Detroit, and refused to sign the 1883 contract. The Alleghenys' principal owner, Harmar Denny McKnight, sued, seeking a federal court injunction compelling Bennett to sign a formal contract and restraining him from playing for Detroit. The court dismissed the charge, deciding in Bennett's favor that a preliminary arrangement did not amount to a final agreement; and, furthermore the contract that was presented for signature lacked mutually equitable terms between club ownership and the ballplayer.[20]

Perhaps Bennett's change of heart was related to the realization that the grass might not have been greener on the other side of the fence. The Alleghenys finished the 1883 season in seventh place in the American Association with a record of 31-67. Regardless of the reason why, Bennett's case was "baseball's first real case of contract litigation."[21]

The Wolverines were unable to build upon their first winning season and finished with a 40-58 record in 1883, dropping to seventh place. But it may have been Bennett's best all-around season. He played in a career-high 92 games and established career highs in average (.305), hits (113), and OPS (.825). He hit five home runs, the sixth most in the National League, and drove in 55 runs. In 72 games behind the plate, he led National League catchers with 11 double plays and a .944 fielding percentage. His career-high WAR of 4.9 ranked third among all position players.

Bennett's three-year performance between 1881 and 1883 (.302, 170 RBIs, .811 OPS) is impressive when one considers how grueling catching was in the early 1880s and the evolving nature of the game, which resulted in vast differences in players' performance.

Bennett experienced an offensive falloff in 1884 as the Wolverines continued their downward spiral. He caught a career-high 80 games and appeared in 90 overall. He finished the year with a .264 average, 3 home runs and 40 RBIs. The Wolverines finished a dismal 28-84, 56 games behind the National League champion Providence Grays. Bennett recalled, "I thought sometimes we were lucky to finish last. Every week I caught a new pitcher."[22] The revolving door of Wolverines pitchers may have contributed to Bennett's decline in fielding percentage and career-high passed balls.

After a decade-long absence from the game, bunting began to re-emerge in 1884, with Arthur Irwin and Cliff Carroll of Providence among the more adept practitioners of the art.[23] Not everyone was pleased about the bunt's return. Bennett was among those displeased. In a 1906 interview published in the *Detroit News Tribune*, Bennett said, "Bunting has destroyed base-running. There is no necessity for a runner to take chances like they did before the bunt came into general use. As a result, one of the finer points of the great game has become almost a lost art."[24]

Things hit rock bottom for the Wolverines at the start of the 1885 season. After opening with three straight wins against the Buffalo Bisons, Bennett and his teammates won only two of their next 28 and were buried deep in the National League cellar by the end of May. The team's fortunes began to turn in June after they acquired Sam Thompson and eight other players from the Indianapolis Hoosiers of the Western League.[25] From July 1, the team went 33-34 to finish the season in fourth place.

Bennett appeared in 91 games in 1885 and compiled a WAR of 4.5, the second highest of his career and fifth highest among position players, on the strength of his 42 extra-base hits and stellar defensive play. He finished the season with a .269 batting average, 5 home runs, and 60 RBIs.

In September of 1885, the Wolverines acquired the entire Buffalo roster when the Bisons disbanded. Among those acquired were Dan Brouthers, Hardy Richardson, Jack Rowe, and Deacon White. With a strong nucleus in place, Bennett was soon to realize his dream of playing on a winning team. The Wolverines' record improved dramatically in 1886. The team finished with an 87-36 record, 46 wins more than the previous year and good enough for a second-place finish, 2½ games behind the first-place Chicago White Stockings.

Bennett's offensive production dropped noticeably that year. However, he may have enjoyed the best defensive season of his career. In 72 games Bennett hit .243, his lowest average during his eight years with the Wolverines, with 4 home runs and 34 RBIs. Defensively, he played in 69 games behind the plate and compiled a defensive WAR rating of 2.0. He led all league catchers with a .955 fielding percentage and 13 double plays.

The 1887 season was the high point in the Wolverines' history as they captured their first and only National League pennant with a record of 79-45. Bennett, however, was limited to only 46 games as the toll of catching for more than a decade began to take its toll. He finished the season with a .244 average with 3 home runs and 20 RBIs.

Bennett's ability to play through pain was on full display during the Wolverines' 1887 World Series against the American Association champion St. Louis Browns. Initially ruled out of the series by a doctor who feared he would be in danger of having his thumb amputated if he caught another game, Bennett was determined to play. Playing with "a pair of hands that could hardly grip the bludgeon," Bennett performed admirably.[26] In 42 at-bats, he hit .262, had two doubles, a triple, five stolen bases, and a team-leading 9 RBIs. Behind the plate, he held Arlie Latham and the other Browns basestealers in check as the Wolverines won the series 10 games to 5.

In 1888, the 33-year-old Bennett snapped back and enjoyed one of his better all-around seasons. In 74 games he hit .264 with 5 home runs and 29 RBIs. However, it was on defense that he shined brightest. Despite being the eighth oldest player in the National League, Bennett complied the highest defensive WAR rating of his career (2.2), as he broke his own single-season major-league record with a .966 fielding percentage. The Wolverines were unable to repeat the success they enjoyed the previous year, despite bringing back the most feared lineup in baseball. The team finished in fifth place with a 68-63 record.

With high salaries owed the team's star-studded roster, gate receipts declining markedly, and debt mounting, the Wolverines folded in October 1888. On October 16, in an effort to recoup what cash they could, the club sold Bennett, Brouthers, Richardson, White, and Charlie Ganzel to the Boston Beaneaters for $26,000.[27]

Bennett was reported to have received a salary of $3,500 with the Beaneaters during the 1889 season, an enormous sum for that period, in part because of his ability to handle a pitching staff. During his five years with the Beaneaters, Bennett worked with legendary pitchers John Clarkson, Old Hoss Radbourn, and Kid Nichols. Bennett and Nichols were particularly close and remained friends for the remainder of their lives.

In his inaugural year in Boston, Bennett played in 82 games, all behind the plate, and hit a modest .231 with 4 home runs and 28 RBIs. He continued to pace National League catchers in fielding percentage with a .955 mark, 45 points higher than the league average for catchers and 18 points higher than Buck Ewing, who was considered the second-best defensive catcher of the era.

One thing that separated Bennett from most of his contemporaries was his ability to play through pain and injuries, especially to his hands. Jim Hart, the Beaneaters manager in 1889, said of Bennett's ability to play through pain:

> "He had more grit than any catcher I ever knew. A score of times when his hands were badly injured he would continue to catch, and the only way we would find out that he was hurt was to discover blood on the ball. I remember a game in Pittsburgh, the last one of the season in 1889 for the Boston club, when he refused to go out of the game until I simply refused to let him play any longer. Clarkson was pitching, and in the third inning he showed me the ball covered with blood. I called Bennett to the bench and asked to see his hands, and he refused to show them. Mike Kelly was playing right field, and I called him in to catch. Bennett wanted to catch the game out so much that he wouldn't give Kelly the mask or the pad. I sent him home after the game, and two weeks later Bennett's hands were so sore that he could hardly feed himself."[28]

Another account of Bennett's grit was cited by Peter Morris in his book *Catcher: How the Man Behind the Plate Became an American Folk Hero*:

> "Bennett declared that only a sissy would use a padded glove with the fingers and thumb cut off. During one of the games in which he figured a foul ball split the left thumb of Bennett's hand from the tip right down to the palm. The flesh was laid open right to the bone. A doctor who examined it immediately told Bennett that it would be necessary for him to quit the game until such time as the thumb healed sufficiently. The physician pointed out … that blood poisoning might set in which would cause him the loss not only of the thumb but perhaps a hand or an arm.

But despite all the doctor's caution Bennett remained in the game catching day after day with his horribly mangled finger. He kept a bottle of antiseptic and a wad of cotton batting on the bench and between innings would devote his time to washing out the wound."[29]

Despite Bennett's decreased offensive production, the catcher remained in high demand after the 1889 season. After being offered a contract by the Boston Reds of the new Players' League, Bennett was able to leverage the offer to sign a three-year contract to remain with the Beaneaters. The contract called for Bennett to receive a $6,000 signing bonus and a salary of $4,000 a year.[30]

News of Bennett's shrewd deal with the Beaneaters was applauded by the *Detroit Free Press,* which praised him for his consistent work ethic and ability to handle pitchers:

> "That Detroiters will rejoice in his good fortune goes without saying. No matter whether we had a tail end club or the world's champions, there was no difference in the quality of his work. Young and nervous pitchers under his wise counsel and steady influence became valuable men. Detroit is more his house than any other place and it matters not how far away he goes, we shall always regard him as 'our catcher.'"[31]

This was not a surprising commentary, given Bennett's popularity in Detroit and the fact that he played with the Wolverines for all eight of the team's seasons. He was one of only two players (the other was Ned Hanlon) to play for the Wolverines every season the franchise existed.

In 1890 Bennett played in 85 games and hit .214 with 3 home runs and 40 RBIs while leading all National League catchers in fielding for the third straight year with a .959 percentage. The Beaneaters, who were beaten out by the New York Giants by a single game in 1889, dropped to fifth place under first-year manager Frank Selee.

On August 12, Bennett hit a 12th-inning walk-off home run off Philadelphia left-hander Phenomenal Smith at Boston's South End Grounds. The home run gave the Beaneaters a 1-0 victory. At the time, it was only the third time in National League history that a 1-0 game ended with a walk-off home run.[32]

Bennett's 1891 season was nearly a carbon copy of the previous year, with one major exception. He hit .215 with 5 home runs and 39 RBIs, and for the fourth straight year led the league's catchers with a .960 fielding percentage. The difference this season was that the Beaneaters finally won the National League championship. Boston finished 87-51, 3½ games ahead of the White Stockings.

By 1892 the wear and tear of catching had taken a tremendous physical toll on Bennett. King Kelly, who took over as the team's number-one backstop that season, later commented on the effect catching had on Bennett's hands. Kelly said, "If I had hands such as Charlie Bennett, I wouldn't catch a game of ball for a whole church full of millionaires with their entire wealth stuffed in their pockets."[33] As a backup, Bennett played in only 35 games and hit .202 (13 points higher than Kelly) with one home run and 16 RBIs. The Beaneaters won 102 games on the way to their second consecutive pennant.

The 1892 season had a unique split-season arrangement, with Boston winning the first half and Cleveland the second. In the championship series against the Cleveland Spiders, Bennett went 2-for-7 with one RBI as the Beaneaters took the series, five games to none.[34]

Bennett shared the team's catching duties with Ganzel and Bill Merritt in 1893, appearing in 60 games behind the plate. Still one of the better defensive catchers, the 38-year-old veteran of 15 major-league seasons hit only .209 with 4 home runs and 27 RBIs as the Beaneaters rolled to their third consecutive title.

Bennett's baseball career came to a tragic end on January 10, 1894. He was on his way to a hunting trip with former Beaneaters teammate John Clarkson when his legs were crushed by a passenger train at a stop near Ottawa, Kansas. The accident occurred when Bennett stepped off the train to talk with an old friend who lived in the area. When the two friends said goodbye and the train started moving, Bennett turned to catch the railing of the train, but his foot slipped and went over the rail. Bennett pushed his right leg against the rail to push himself back, but it also slipped and went over the track.[35] The train's wheels ran over his left foot and right leg at the knee.

That evening, doctors at the North Ottawa Hospital amputated the 39-year-old Bennett's left foot just above the ankle and his right leg just above the knee.[36] Bennett's nephew, George Porter, whom he was particularly close to, recounted the tragic tale in a 1934 *Detroit Free Press* interview:

> "Five doctors worked on him. It was the blackest day of my life. His physical condition was so good that ten days later they were able to move him the 18 miles through zero degree weather to our home where we nursed him back to health."[37]

Amazingly, just three months after the accident, Bennett had regained much of his strength and began the process of learning to walk with prosthetic legs.

After a few months of convalescing, Bennett and his wife returned to Detroit and, along with a partner, opened a cigar store on Woodward Avenue. According to the *Detroit Free Press,* after his intentions were announced publicly, "Charlie received over 100 letters from a friend asking if the report be true. One lady wrote to Mrs. Bennett: If Charlie Bennett opens a cigar store in Detroit, all the ladies will commence smoking."[38] For some time the cigar store was profitable, but increased competition from large tobacco manufacturers eventually forced him to sell the business.

The loss of Bennett was a shock to Boston fans and provided a terrible blow to the psyche of the Beaneaters. Following three consecutive National League pennants, they finished the 1894 season in third place with a record of 83-49, eight games behind the pennant-winning Baltimore Orioles and five behind the second-place New York Giants. According to some newspaper accounts, the absence of Bennett was one of the reasons given for the team failing to win a fourth consecutive pennant.[39]

On August 26, 1894, the team held a benefit to help Bennett pay his medical bills. At one point bowed to the crowd and stood speechless and legless at home plate. The benefit was attended by the heavyweight boxing champion, Gentleman Jim Corbett, who briefly played in the contest. A crowd of 9,000 fans attended and Bennett was given the $6,000 gate.[40]

Never one to complain, Bennett handled his fate in the most optimistic and dignified manner possible. After all, he was fortunate to have survived such a horrible accident. He continued to hunt (from his buggy) and fish. In fact, he was doing so well getting around that during his visit to Boston for a benefit game the Beaneaters were hosting, former teammate and fellow catcher Charlie Ganzel proposed a race between the two. Bennett, known for his good sense of humor, said he was willing if he could have a 98⅓-yard head start.[41]

On April 28, 1896, the Detroit Tigers of the Western League opened their new ballpark, named Bennett Park in tribute to Bennett. A cannon brought from nearby Fort Wayne was fired to signal the start of the season and Bennett himself caught the ceremonial first pitch from Wayne County treasurer Alex McLeod.[42] Bennett caught the ceremonial first pitch for every Tigers home opener through 1926.[43]

In later years Bennett took up the hobby of painting china dishes. It was hard with his mangled fingers from catching, but "the perseverance that made him the greatest catcher base ball ever saw made it possible to master the art."[44] The former catcher's intricate creations eventually commanded "a ready market and good price."[45]

Bennett's 15-year major-league career ended with modest offensive numbers: a .256 batting average, 55 home runs, and 533 RBIs. During his eight-year stint in Detroit, Bennett hit .278 with 37 home runs and 353 RBIs. It wasn't until the long-term effects of catching with limited protection hampered his ability to grip the bat that his offensive numbers began to decline. Still, it was Bennett's defensive prowess that differentiated him from his catching peers.

When Bennett began his major-league career, the National League record for games caught in a season stood at 63. He eclipsed that mark in 10 different seasons. Altogether he played in 1,062 games, 954 as a catcher, which at the time of his accident was a major-league record that stood until 1897. He led in fielding percentage seven times and retired with a fielding percentage of .942, a major-league record for catchers that stood until 1896. His career total of 114 double plays and 5,123 putouts also stood as major-league records until 1900 and 1901, respectively. In 1983 Bennett was recognized by SABR's Nineteenth Century Committee as the best nineteenth-century catcher not in the Hall of Fame.[46]

Bennett's health began to deteriorate in early 1926 and in November he underwent surgery to remove a "superorbital abscess of the face."[47] He never fully recovered from the surgery. He died at his home in Detroit on February 24, 1927. Bennett was 72 years old. He was survived by his wife, Alice, who died in 1931. The couple had no children but always considered his nephew George and George's wife, Sarah, as their own children. He was buried at Woodmere Cemetery in Detroit.

SOURCES

In addition to the sources cited in the Notes, the author also relied on Baseball-reference.com and Retrosheet.org

NOTES

1. Richard Bak, "The Bittersweet Story behind Charlie Bennett's Park." Retrieved from detroitathletic.com/blog/2012/09/03/the-bittersweet-story-behind-charlie-bennetts-park/.

2. "The Boys Who Catch: Pen and Ink Portraits of the Receivers of the Country," *The Sporting News*, November 10, 1888: 5.

3. George R. Pulford, "Winter Journeys to the Homes of Celebrated Ball Players – Peerless Charlie Bennett," *Seattle Star*, January 4, 1908: 2.

4. George Creamer was a light-hitting (.215) second baseman who played seven seasons (1878-1884) for the Milwaukee, Syracuse, and Worcester teams in the National League and the Alleghenys of Pittsburgh in the American Association. Ned Williamson had a 13-year major-league career, including 11 seasons with the National League's Chicago White Stockings. The stocky

third baseman and shortstop established the single-season major-league record of 27 home runs. The record stood until 1919 when Babe Ruth hit 29.

5 "Record of the Aetnas: The Four Years' Career of the Club was a Brilliant One," *Detroit Free Press*, February 24, 1889: 7.

6 Dennis Pajot, *The Rise of Milwaukee Baseball: The Cream City from Midwestern Outpost to the Major Leagues, 1850-1901* (Jefferson, North Carolina: McFarland Publishing, 2009), 62.

7 Pajot, 66.

8 Ibid.

9 *Evening Wisconsin* (Milwaukee), as cited by Pajot, 70.

10 Left fielder Abner Dalrymple was the only Chicago batter to reach base, on a first-inning leadoff walk. Richmond pitched a second no-hitter later that year.

11 John R. Husman, "Lee Richmond's No-Hit Debut," in Bill Felber, ed., *Inventing Baseball: The 100 Greatest Games of the Nineteenth Century* (Phoenix: Society for American Baseball Research, 2013), 114.

12 Brian McKenna, "Doc Bushong," SABR BioProject. Retrieved from sabr.org/bioproj/person/5d4b5fe8.

13 E. Bates, "Improved Game: J. Lee Richmond, Once a Great Pitcher, Is One of the Few Veterans Who Concedes Advance Base Ball," *Sporting Life*, March 19, 1910: 12.

14 Maclean Kennedy, "Charlie Bennett, Former Detroit Catcher, Inventor of Chest Pad: Old-Time Star and Mrs. Bennett Made First One Out of Cork Sewed Between Bed-Ticking Strips," *Detroit Free Press*, August 2, 1914: 19.

15 Ibid.

16 Pulford.

17 John R. Husman, "Roger Connor's Grand Slam," in *Inventing Baseball*, 133.

18 Peter Morris, *A Game of Inches: The Stories Behind the Innovations That Shaped Baseball* (Chicago: Ivan R. Dee, 2010), 414.

19 "Poor Charley Bennett: The Afflicted Catcher Recites His Baseball Career," *Detroit Free Press*, June 23, 1894: 4.

20 James K. Flack, "Becoming a Contract Jumper: Deacon Jim McGuire's 1902 Decision," *Baseball Research Journal*, (Phoenix: SABR, Fall 2018): 113.

21 Patrick K. Thornton, *Legal Decisions*, 33; *Allegheny Base Ball Club v. Bennett*, 14 F.257 (W.D. Pa., 1882), law.resource.org/pub/us/case/reporter/F/0014/0014.f.0257.pdf, cited by Flack.

22 "Poor Charley Bennett: The Afflicted Catcher Recites His Baseball Career."

23 Morris, 55.

24 "Stories of Early Base Ball Days Told by Charlie Bennett, King of the Olden Catchers," *Detroit News Tribune*, March 11, 1906, cited in Morris, *A Game of Inches*, 56.

25 On June 15, 1885, the Wolverines acquired Thompson, Chub Collins, Jim Donnelly, Jim Keenan, Larry McKeon, Gene Moriarty, Dan Casey, Sam Crane, and Deacon McGuire from the Indianapolis Hoosiers of the Western League for $4,000 (only $2,000 was paid due to dispute).

26 "C.W. Bennett, Veteran Baseball Star Dies," *Detroit Free Press*, February 25, 1927: 2.

27 Ibid.

28 "Charlie Bennett: 'Our Catcher,'" Retrieved from Bless You Boys, blessyouboys.com/2018/3/8/17097104/charlie-bennett-our-catcher.

29 Peter Morris, *Catcher: How the Man Behind the Plate Became an American Folk Hero* (Chicago: Ivan R. Dee, 2009), 208-209.

30 "Sporting Matters: Some Facts in Relation to Bennett's League Contract Signature," *Detroit Free Press*, February 16, 1890: 6.

31 Ibid.

32 Lyle Spatz, ed., *The SABR Baseball List & Record Book* (New York: Simon & Schuster, Inc., 2007), 55.

33 "Charlie Bennett: 'Our Catcher.'"

34 The series lasted six games with one game ending in a tie. Officially, the Beaneaters beat the Spiders 5-0-1.

35 "Poor Charley Bennett: The Afflicted Catcher Recites His Baseball Career."

36 "A Tragic Close to a Brilliant and Long Career on the Diamond: Details of the Horrible Accident Which Cut Off Bennett's Legs and Livelihood – A Tribute to the Suffering Player – Sketch of His Career," *Sporting Life*, January 20, 1894: 3.

37 "Old Catcher Was Iron Man: Train Mishap Ended Bennett's Career," *Detroit Free Press*, September 30, 1934: 30.

38 "Charlie Bennett: 'Our Catcher.'"

39 Ibid.

40 "Nearly $6000: Benefit to Bennett Was a Grand Success; Catcher Bowed to 9000 Friends; Walked Out to Home Plate to Do It; Champion Corbett in the Left Field," *Boston Globe*, August 28, 1894: 1.

41 "Charlie Bennett in Town," *Boston Post*, August 26, 1894: 3.

42 Bak.

43 Jeffrey M. Samoray, "Tigers Celebrate Centennial at Same Site," *Detroit News*, April 28, 1996: 5E.

44 Pulford.

45 Ibid.

46 J.R. Husman, "Charles Wesley Bennett," in R.L. Tiemann and M. Rucker, eds., *Nineteenth Century Stars* (Manhattan, Kansas: Society for American Baseball Research, 1989).

47 "C.W. Bennett, Veteran Baseball Star Dies," *Detroit Free Press*, February 25, 1927: 1. An orbital abscess is an inflammation of eye tissues behind the orbital septum. It is most commonly caused by an acute spread of infection into the eye socket from either the adjacent sinuses or through the blood.

MARTY BERGEN

BY BRIAN MCKENNA

Marty Bergen was one of the finest catchers in the National League during his brief stint. His defense was admired throughout the league. As one sportswriter noted in 1898, "Martin Bergen is a kingpin of catchers, and without him the Bostons would be probably in second place or even lower down the ladder."[1] Although he was nothing special in the batter's box, the 5-foot-10, 170-pound Bergen had an extremely strong and accurate arm. He finished his career with a .265 batting average, 44 doubles, 15 triples, and 10 home runs in 344 games. Giants owner Andrew Freedman, for one, coveted his fine play and more than once approached Boston about trading the player.

Over the course of his short baseball career, Bergen became increasingly despondent and irrational, continually accusing his teammates of plotting against him and of doing things to harm him. There were numerous verbal altercations and even some physical ones between the catcher and the rest of the team. At times he jumped his club and returned home to the comfort of his family. Naturally, this didn't sit well with management and his teammates. He exasperated more than one manager. In April 1899, after Bergen's oldest son died, the ballplayer's mind started to stray from reality. By the end of the season, he was accusing his teammates of using his son's death against him. Bergen more than once threatened his teammates' lives and they were at their wits' ends in dealing with their unstable catcher. The players feared for their safety and hoped that he wouldn't return the following spring. As it turned out, they were right to be concerned. Bergen slaughtered his entire family that January and then killed himself

Martin Bergen was born on October 25, 1871, in North Brookfield, Massachusetts, to Michael and Ann, nee Delaney, Bergen. Michael and Ann were both born in Ireland, immigrating

Marty Bergen.
(McGreevy Collection, Boston Public Library)

to the United States in 1865 at the end of the Civil War. Michael supported his wife and six children working in a shoe factory. The Bergens' third child, Martin was the first son. His brother William (Bill) was the sixth child and only other boy. Like Marty, who was seven years older, Bill was a catcher, learning the trade from his elder brother. Although he was one of the poorest hitters in major-league history, Bill caught for Cincinnati and Brooklyn from 1901 to 1911, and both Bergen brothers were regarded as among the finest catchers of their time.

Marty grew up in North Brookfield, a small town in Worcester County about 75 miles from Boston. He played on his local independent club, known as the Brookfields. One of his teammates was Connie Mack, also a North Brookfield resident. In 1892 the 20-year-old Bergen joined Salem in the New England League, his first professional club. In 59 games at catcher he batted .247. After the regular season for several years to come, Bergen rejoined the Brookfields during the late fall. In 1893 he joined Northampton, Massachusetts, an independent club, and played three games for Wilkes-Barre in the Eastern League. At the end of that season, he was signed by the Pittsburgh Pirates, managed by his neighbor Mack.

In 1892 Harriet (Hattie) Gaines moved to North Brookfield from New York State after securing a position at a local mill. She soon met Bergen, and they were married on July 11, 1893. A few years later they purchased a small farm, called Snowball Farm, on Boynton Street. The couple had three children: Martin, born circa 1894; Florence born a year later; and Joseph a year or two after his sister.

In 1894 the Pirates assigned Bergen to Lewiston (Maine) in the New England League for seasoning. The practice of farming wasn't legal at that time in baseball history, thus the transfer became an issue and Bergen's contract with Pittsburgh was voided. He hit .321 in 97 games for Lewiston. At the end of the year he was drafted by both the National League's Washington Senators and the Western League's Kansas City Blues. Baseball officials assigned Bergen to Kansas City. However, club president and field manager Jimmy Manning soon became exasperated with his new catcher. Bergen was a moody sort who constantly expressed his displeasure. At one point in mid-season, Bergen walked away from the club for a week over some supposed slight while the team was in Minneapolis. In 113 games he batted a strong .372 with 188 hits and 118 runs scored. At the end of the year Marty was drafted by the Boston Beaneaters of the National League. He had been recommended to manager Frank Selee by pitcher Kid Nichols, a Kansas City native. Nichols had seen the catcher in a game during the 1895 season when he stopped at home during a western trip.

Before Bergen would join Boston, team owner Arthur Soden had to make a trip to North Brookfield to convince the sensitive player that he was valued and would be treated well by his new club. He played for Boston from 1896-99, catching 63, 85, 117, and 72 games during those four years. He gained a reputation as one of the finest catchers in the league. One *Sporting News* article described him as "the greatest throwing catcher that the game ever produced."[2] Connie Mack, a catcher himself, stated that Bergen was the only catcher he'd seen gun down a base stealer at second from his knees. From the get-go though, Bergen had trouble with his teammates. As one reporter explained in May 1896, "Martin Bergen, the young backstop…is unpopular with his fellow players on the Boston team. Bergen is a sullen, sarcastic chap, never associates with the players, and always nurses a fancied grievance. His disposition handicaps his playing talents."[3]

Boston was one of the top teams in the league during Bergen's stint behind the plate. They finished fourth in his rookie season. The next two years they copped the pennant, before finishing second by eight games in 1899. Kid Nichols, Boston's ace, explained how important the catcher was to the team, "Baltimore beat us the next three years, after we lost (catcher Charlie) Bennett. Then we got Marty Bergen from Kansas City and won the pennants again in 1897 and 1898."[4] Despite his catching abilities and the team's success, Bergen was often the topic of trade rumors because of his moodiness, melancholy, inability to mesh with teammates, and penchant for sulking and leaving the club. However, not all the trade rumors originated that way. New York Giants owner Andrew Freedman tried to work a trade for the catcher on more than a few occasions. At the time of Bergen's death, most within the game assumed that he would be playing for the Giants in 1900.

Even as a teenager, Bergen had showed signs of anxiety and stress. He would become moody, pout, and storm off if he felt that he wasn't getting his fair share of applause. In 1891, his first professional season, he engaged in a brutal fistfight with one of his teammates. During his time in Boston, Bergen had several run-ins with teammates and opponents. Newspapers commonly referred to his erratic behavior, describing him as "sullen and silent" and highlighting his moodiness, aloofness, and inaccessibility.

Near the end of the 1898 season, Bergen threatened his teammates after an altercation on the bench. He declared that he would "club them to death" at the end of the season.[5] He slapped teammate Vic Willis in a St. Louis hotel dining room. As the *Indianapolis News* noted via wire reports, "Martin Bergen, the eccentric catcher of the Boston team, is in trouble again… Bergen, always surly, often lets his temper get away from him, and makes breaks from which there is no provocation. He hit pitcher Willis in the face because he sat down at the same table in the dining room. The incident was hushed up at the time, but it is likely that Bergen will be traded before the opening of next season, as Selee says he has stood Bergen's crankiness as long as he can."[6] On July 20, 1899, the Boston team was traveling by train to Cincinnati. The men were having a good time playing cards, but Bergen sat withdrawn from his teammates. When the train stopped in Washington, D.C., Bergen hopped off, jumping the club and returning home to North Brookfield. On July 24, he told friends in the Massachusetts community that he would rejoin the ballclub at Louisville.[7] Another wire article described Bergen as, "the hardest man in the National League to manage."[8] The writer described Bergen as "the erratic catcher of the Boston club, who has deserted the club annually since his connection with it and always at a time when his services were most needed. His grievances are fanciful. Of a moody disposition he imagines that his fellow players are leagued against him and are intent on bringing about his downfall. The contrary is the case. Manager Selee and his players have treated the great backstop with unusual consideration."[9]

Boston Globe reporter Tim Murnane rode out to the Bergen farm to assess the problem and to coax the moody catcher into rejoining the Beaneaters. Bergen lamented that his teammates were hounding him and that at least four of them shouted, "Strike him out!" when he was at bat. He claimed his teammates and team owner Soden were avoiding him, and he was upset because manager Frank Selee wouldn't give him a day off to visit his family. He was also dismayed by the $300 fine he received for jumping the club. Furthermore, he didn't like the tone of a telegram he had received from Soden during his absence. Bergen then claimed he was injured and had to return home because only his lifelong friend and hometown physician, Dr. Louis Dionne, could care for him.[10] He finally rejoined the club a week and a half later.

Bergen registered numerous complaints about his teammates throughout the years. From the other perspective, Bergen's bizarre actions took a toll on his teammates. According to Harold Kaese in *The Boston Braves: 1871-1953*, by the end of 1899 some did not want him to return to the club, plus several were seriously concerned about their safety around the disgruntled player.[11] As the *Sandusky Star* noted, "It is now conceded that the Boston nine dropped out as a champion factor largely because of the trouble between the players and Martin Bergen, the catcher. Ever since Bergen's first desertion of the nine there has been a feeling of bitterness, intensified by the cordial reception that Bergen received when he returned to the team. The public did not understand the facts as well as the players, and the players felt aggravated that the misunderstanding had arisen."[12] As *Sporting Life* put it, "Marty Bergen is accused of creating dissention in the Boston team, which is the cause of the champions' recent defeats."[13]

When the team was at home in Boston, Bergen always spent the night at his farm. Neighbors said he would play with his children all day, rarely associating with others. Throughout the 1899 season Bergen pestered Selee for time off to return to his family. He would play a few games and then ask to go home. On April 24, 1899, Bergen's son Martin, 5, passed away from diphtheria while his father was out of town. After two weeks at home with his family, he rejoined the club, but he quickly descended into a downward spiral. Toward the end of the season he was estranged from his teammates. He claimed that they continuously and maliciously reminded him of his son, causing him a great deal of stress. Unhappy, Bergen jumped the club yet again at the end of September without a word and went home for a few days complaining of a sore hand.

Several sources report that Bergen suffered a broken hip at the end of the 1899 season. The story goes that this injury threatened his career and sent him into a depression, which spiraled into the tragedy of January 1900. However, this doesn't match the evidence. Bergen was bothered by hip problems throughout his career and he had an operation for an abscess on his right hip on January 28, 1899, the result of sliding into home near the end of the 1898 season, but that didn't stop him from playing the entire year. Nor were there stories about any excessive lingering effects during the 1899 season. Furthermore, he played the entire game on October 13, the next-to-last day of the season, and he was not injured and didn't play in the season finale. Bergen visited his doctor after the season ended without mentioning any significant hip troubles. The catcher was the subject of numerous trade rumors and that winter even hosted a sportswriter or two at his house. An injury was never mentioned by any of those parties. Surely an injured hip would have been at the center of any trade article about a catcher.

The hip surgery in January 1899 required him to be under anesthesia for four hours. His doctor and family noted that he never seemed to recover mentally from the operation. Most important to Bergen's frail state was the death of his five-year-old son. This was compounded by guilt over the fact that he was away from home at the time, on the road with the ball club.

Immediately after the 1899 season, Bergen talked with his physician and confidant, Dr. Dionne, who later told reporters that all seemed fine, but the doctor soon heard from family, friends, and neighbors that Bergen was acting "wild."[14] When the doctor visited, he found Bergen pacing in front of his house. It didn't take much prodding for the ballplayer to "open his heart" in a tearful rant. He confessed to Dionne that he had "strange ideas" and said he was afraid that he was "not right in the head."[15] Bergen admitted that he couldn't remember much about the past baseball season. All he remembered was that a man came up to him after his last game and congratulated him on a fine performance and gave him a cigar. Bergen was afraid to smoke the cigar because he believed it was poisoned. He was also concerned that Dionne and his wife were trying to poison him. He refused to take any medicine they gave him if he didn't first mix it himself.

Bergen believed the National League had found out that Dionne was his doctor and had paid Dionne to kill him. He described being frightened of his teammates, feeling that they were out to kill him. Bergen said he always sat sideways on the bench, in the clubhouse, and on trains in case his teammates decided to attack. He wished he had quit baseball so he could find some peace. He also believed that people in general, including the Boston team and other National League players, were plotting against him.

The doctor gave Bergen a bromide and told him to repeat the dosage in three hours. However, the doctor did give him some advice that seemed to work. Bergen chewed and sucked on tobacco constantly. The doctor suggested that he quit the habit as it was contributing to his nervousness and anxiety. Bergen did so and felt better for a time. Later Dionne had what he described as a nice, pleasant conversation with Bergen, who got up to leave the office and said, "This has been a pleasant talk, and it is strange how it has rattled me."[16] Bergen also confided in his pastor that he believed himself to be insane and feared his own actions. He asked for help, but none was forthcoming from his doctor, priest, family, or community.

On the night of January 18, 1900, a Thursday, the Bergen family ate a hearty meal and turned in. When Bergen's father found the bodies the following morning, the beds had been slept in. Some time in the early morning, Bergen arose and started preparing for the day. He removed the ashes from the stove, the home's primary heat source, indicating that the stove had cooled overnight. Bergen then placed paper in the stove for lighting though he hadn't yet retrieved wood from outside, as the inside pile was depleted.

Then, for some unknown reason, he snapped. Stressed and delusional, Bergen slaughtered his family. First he attacked his wife in the bedroom, hitting her multiple times in the head with the blunt side of an axe. She fell, dying on one of the beds. Bergen then whacked his son once with the sharp side of the axe. The boy died in the other bed. In the kitchen Bergen killed his daughter, smashing her multiple times in the head with the blunt end of the axe. Bergen then retrieved a razor and stood in front of a mirror in the kitchen. He sliced his own throat, nearly severing his head, and fell beside his daughter.

On January 20 the entire family was laid out in the Bergen home for family and friends to view. They were transported to St. Joseph's Church for the funeral ceremonies and interred North Brookfield's St. Joseph's cemetery.

After Bergen's deeds on January 19, 1900, Dr. Dionne repeatedly made comments that Bergen was "insane" and a "maniac."[17] The doctor believed that the situation was out of his control and out of his purview. Finally acknowledging Bergen's mental illness, Tim Murnane wrote that Bergen "was entitled to the undivided sympathy of the baseball public, as well as players and directors."[18] In the wake of the tragedy, North Brookfield made efforts to better educate professionals and the community about mental health issues.

SOURCES

Minor-league statistics provided by Ray Nemec. In addition to the Sources cited in the Notes, the author also consulted Ancestry.com, and the following newspapers: *Boston Daily Advertiser, Boston Globe, Cedar Rapids Evening Gazette, Chicago Tribune, Daily Iowa State Press* (Iowa City), *Daily Review* (Decatur, Illinois), *Fort Wayne News, Fort Wayne Sentinel, New York Times,* and *the Washington Post.*

Nack, William, "Collision at Home," *Sports Illustrated*, June 4, 2001: 74.

Thanks also to Cassidy Lent, Giammati Research Center, Baseball Hall of Fame, Cooperstown, New York.

NOTES

1. Charles E. Edwardes, "The Boston Team: How it Won the Championship," *North Adams Transcript* (North Adams, Massachusetts), October 17, 1898: 7.
2. E.J. O'Connor, "About August 15. Date When the Bostons Will Take the Lead," *The Sporting News*, July 29, 1899: 1.
3. "Base Ball Brevities," *Pittsburgh Press*, May 26, 1896: 5.
4. Sam Smith, "Nichols: "We Stayed In and Pitched," *Baseball Digest*, June 1951: 80.
5. Bill Felber. *A Game of Brawl: The Orioles, the Beaneaters & the Battle for the 1897 Pennant* (Lincoln, Nebraksa: University of Nebraska Press, 2007), 250; The *Boston Herald*, at Bergen's death, reported that before the close of the 1898 season "Bergen said in the dressing room of the club that after the season ended he would like to take a bat and drub some of the men from their heads down to their shoulders." See "Ball Players Feared Him," *Boston Herald*, January 20, 1900: 3.
6. "Base Ball Notes," *Indianapolis News*, October 15, 1898: 12.
7. "Bergen's Plans," *Boston Herald*, July 25, 1899: 4.
8. *The Sporting News*, July 29, 1899: 4.
9. Ibid.
10. Tim Murnane, "Bergen's Grievance," *Boston Globe*, July 26, 1899: 4.
11. Harold Kaese, *The Boston Braves 1871-1953* (Boston: Northeastern University Press, 2004), 97.
12. "Won the Pennant," *Sandusky Star-Journal* (Sandusky, Ohio), October 11, 1899: 1.
13. "News and Comment," *Sporting Life*, September 2, 1891: 6.
14. Tim Murnane, "Bergen's Insane Deed," *Boston Globe*, January 20, 1900: 1.
15. Ibid.
16. "Bergen's Madness," *Boston Herald*, January 20, 1900: 3.
17. Ibid.
18. "Bergen's Insane Deed," 3.

CLIFF CARROLL

BY ALAN COHEN

During the 1892 season while playing for St. Louis, Cliff Carroll had the misfortune of being fined by the club when a ball inadvertently rolled into his pocket. The incident, which occurred in the sixth inning on August 17 of that season, was his major claim to fame, although in his time he was a fair hitter, fielder, and stolen-base threat and had, in 1890, come back from exile to help lead the Chicago Colts to a second-place finish.

Hugh Fullerton, in *American Magazine*, reported on the errant-ball incident. In a game at St. Louis, Carroll charged a ball hit to the outfield by Brooklyn's Darby O'Brien, seeking to field it on the first bounce. The ball took a bad bounce and hit Carroll in the chest. He grabbed the ball and inadvertently shoved it into the handkerchief pocket on the front of his uniform shirt. The runner, noticing this, just kept on running and advanced to second base. At this point, Carroll ran toward the infield and fielder and runner raced toward third base. Try as he would, Carroll couldn't dislodge the ball and the runner scored. Team owner Chris Von der Ahe had pockets removed from his team's uniforms, and the rest of the National League followed suit.[1]

The game was not particularly close, with Brooklyn winning 11-3 and the Browns making 12 errors. Both George Gore and Bill Moran had committed errors early in the game and before Carroll's muff the score was already 6-0. The *St. Louis Post Dispatch* wrote, "Yesterday's exhibition baffles description. If the Browns had the jaundice, they couldn't have played yellower ball. It was an absolute burlesque on the game. The spectators jeered the players and managed to extract fun out of their attempts at playing." After the game, Von der Ahe fined Carroll and Moran

Cliff Carroll.
(Library of Congress)

$50 each for "general indifference and rotten playing."[2] At season's end, Carroll was made available in trade to Boston.

Carroll played in the National League for parts of 11 seasons between 1882 and 1893. Although not known as a power hitter, in 1890 and 1891 with the Chicago Colts he had seven home runs each year and finished in the top 10 in the league. He also has the rare distinction of homering at the same ballpark in the minors and majors. While with Providence in 1885, he hit a home run at Buffalo's Olympic Park on October 7 off Pete Conway in the opener of the last series at that venue. Of his 31 major-league homers, that was his only blast at Olympic Park. Carroll's career was temporarily on the downturn in 1888 and he wound up in the minor leagues, playing with Buffalo in the International Association. On June 23, 1888, he homered at Olympic Park in a 10-2 shellacking of Albany. Each of his two minor-league homers that season was at Olympic Park. He thus became the fifth player in Organized Baseball to homer at the same ballpark in the majors and minors.

Samuel Clifford Carroll was born on October 15, 1859, in Clay Grove, Iowa. He grew up in Bloomington, Illinois. His parents, John M. and L. Marie Carroll, had five children. Three sons came along before Cliff and his twin sister, Katy, were born. It was in 1867 that the family relocated to Bloomington.

John M. Carroll, who had been born in Baltimore on April 12, 1821, was a pillar of the community in Bloomington, operating a grocery store. But he suffered financial losses during the banking crisis of the early 1870s. He spent the last decades of his life in darkness as he went blind on December 25, 1876. He died on July 6, 1909, at the age of 88. Cliff's mother, who survived her husband, was born in Butler County, Ohio, on November 5, 1823. She was called Maria.[3] She lived to the ripe old age of 95, dying on November 18, 1918.

By 1877, Cliff had established his baseball credentials to the point where he became a member of Bloomington's semipro club. The *New York Clipper* tells us, "The members consider the nine the strongest they have ever had and would be pleased to hear from all Eastern clubs going West. They say they have splendid inclosed grounds and promise good terms." Among the team's directors was pitcher Charles Radbourn.[4] In 1878, he entered the professional ranks and made his way to Oakland, California, where his team won the California State championship. He continued to play in California through 1880, when he was suspended on one occasion for overdrawing his account with the team by $60.[5] He then made his way to the Nevada silver mines, but an old friend from his Bloomington days brought him to the attention of Providence Grays manager Harry Wright.

Carroll made his major-league debut with Providence in August 1882. He was the second player from Bloomington to be signed by Providence. Radbourn, his old teammate, had also become a major leaguer. The right fielder got into 10 games at the end of the season. Although he went only 5-for-41, he received plaudits for his fielding. After his first League game on August 3 against Cleveland, it was said that "Cliff Carroll, the new right fielder, showed up famously in the field."[6] An article in his hometown Bloomington newspaper noted, "(Carroll) has played his first three games without making an error, but for some reason, he does not loom up in his batting as of old."[7] In one of those games, on August 17, Carroll was in the outfield alongside his old pal Radbourn. Monte Ward was pitching and hurled an 18-inning shutout. Radbourn provided the only offense his team would need with an 18th-inning home run. It was the first career homer for Radbourn, who went on to hit nine homers to go along with his 309 wins on the mound. The win kept the Providence lead at three games. They took that lead into September but lost it when they were swept by Chicago in a three-game series. The Grays wound up finishing in second place. Carroll did not make an error in the field until October 11 in a postseason exhibition game against first-place Chicago.[8]

Carroll first gained unpleasant notoriety in 1883 while playing with Providence. During practice before the game, he picked up a hose and sprayed water onto a spectator named James Murphy. Mr. Murphy was not amused by this, went home, and came back carrying a gun. He took a shot at Carroll and missed, but struck Carroll's teammate Joe Mulvey.[9] Playing in 58 of his team's 98 games (he missed some time in May and June with a sprained ankle), Carroll batted .265 as the Grays finished in third place with a 58-40 record.

In 1884, Providence won the National League pennant with an 84-28 record and Carroll played in 113 games batting .261 with 23 extra-base hits and 54 RBIs. After the season, Providence accepted a challenge from the American Association champion Metropolitans of New York. The three-game championship was held at the Polo Grounds. In the first game, Carroll reached first base after being hit by a pitch, and came around to score as Providence won 6-0. He went 1-for-10 with two runs scored and an RBI in the three games. Radbourn, who had won 59 games during the regular season, was the only pitcher Providence needed. He pitched every inning and won each game as Providence swept the Mets for the championship.

It is for one deed during that 1884 season that Carroll is also remembered. Per teammate Arthur Irwin, Providence was playing at Boston. In the fifth inning of the game, Carroll reportedly came up with the idea of bunting the ball and laid down the first bunt. Of course, since it was the first (per Irvin), it had yet to be named. In the *Boston Herald*, per Irvin, the reporter said that Carroll "punted" the ball. Eventually, of course, "punt" became "bunt."[10] By the time the teams played on August 9, with Providence winning 1-0, the term "bunt" was being used. In the game of that date Carroll laid down a bunt in the eighth inning.[11] Actually the bunt had been part of the game since the 1860s and into the early years of the National Association, with Dickey Pearce and Tommy Barlow credited for its invention. However, the bunt had been not utilized for a decade when Carroll and Irwin brought it back into the game.[12]

The 1885 season was Carroll's last with Providence. He batted .232 while playing in 104 of his team's 110 games as the Grays finished in fourth place, Chicago and New York running away from the pack. Providence, with its 53-57 record, finished 33 games out of first place.

Carroll signed on with Washington in 1886 and spent two years in the nation's capital. But they were not without controversy. During the 1886 season, Carroll was fined $100, a hefty sum in those days, for his objections to team management using amateur pitchers.[13] He balked at re-signing for the following season unless the fine was rescinded by team President Walter Hewitt. Hewitt agreed, and cut a check to Carroll. However, before Carroll could cash the check, Hewitt stopped payment. This only made things worse. At the winter meetings, other owners prevailed on Hewitt to remedy the situation and he did.[14] In Carroll's first year with Washington, his batting average dropped to .229, but he did finish in the top 10 in stolen bases with 31 for a team that finished last with a 28-92 record.

According to an inaccurate accounting in Fred Lieb's *The Pittsburgh Pirates*, in 1887 Carroll was with the Pittsburgh Alleghenies, and was positioned at first base for a few games after first baseman Alex McKinnon became ill and died. Carroll was described by Lieb as a "good hit, no field outfielder." However, Carroll spent the entire 1887 season with Washington, batting .248 while appearing in 103 of his team's 126 games. But he was no longer the quality player he had been in his Providence days. The author may have confused Cliff Carroll with Fred Carroll who in 1887 batted .328 with Pittsburgh and made 62 errors, including 14 in 17 games at first base. He also made 27 as a catcher and 21 as an outfielder.

At the end of the 1887 season, in which Carroll lifted his batting average to .248 and had a career-high 40 stolen bases, he was released by Washington after the team finished the season in seventh place with a 46-76 record. By that time, "for lack of care of himself, he became almost valueless to the club, and was released."[15] The release was motivated by Carroll's drinking. While in Washington he owned a saloon for a time, and was his own best customer. The team thought Carroll was attending to business too closely, staying up late at night, and therefore released him.[16] He moved on to Pittsburgh in May 1888, as a replacement for John Coleman, who was ill.[17] He was with Pittsburgh for less than a month and got into only five games before overstaying his welcome. Carroll was released on June 4, 1888. His once highly regarded fielding skills had eroded. In his five games, all in the outfield, he made three errors in nine chances.

In 1888, after six seasons in the National League, Carroll went back to the minor leagues, playing with Buffalo in the International Association. Although he batted .282 with 22 extra-base hits and 27 stolen bases, his talents were no longer in demand. He spent the 1889 season out of baseball entirely, getting married to Addella Wood of Bloomington and tending to his farm.[18] A daughter, Bernice, came along on December 28, 1889. She was their only child. According to data in the 1920 Federal census, she married Thomas Armentrout, and they had four children.

At the urging of Old Hoss Radbourn in 1890, several teams in the newly formed Players League contacted Carroll about returning to baseball, but it was Cap Anson of the National League's Chicago Colts who signed Carroll to play for his team.[19] Carroll had accompanied Anson and the team in a world tour after the 1888 season.[20] In 1890, he signed with Anson's Colts and had the two most productive seasons of his career. Early in the 1890 season, it was reported that "Cliff Carroll, the fleet-footed left-fielder of the Chicago club, is under a pledge not to touch intoxicating liquors this season. This was his greatest failing as a ballplayer, and caused his retirement for a time from the diamond. But for the Brotherhood (as the Players League was also known), he would probably have never been given an opportunity to return to the profession. His brief retirement seems to have done him much good as he is playing splendid ball for the Chicagos. He is one of the finest fielders in the country, a good batter and a clever base-runner."[21]

Chicago, then called the White Stockings, had finished in third place in 1889 with a 67-65 record, 19 games behind the pennant-winning New York Giants. There were numerous changes in 1890. The team's name was changed to Colts. More importantly, there was a team overhaul. Anson brought on Carroll along with young pitchers Pat Luby (21) and Ed Stein (20). He also added second baseman Bob Glenalvin, shortstop Jimmy Cooney, and slugging outfielder Walt Wilmot. The changes worked.

In 1890, the Colts finished in second place with an 83-53 record. The team did not lack for offense, scoring 10 or more runs on 26 occasions. They went 23-6 in September but were unable to catch Brooklyn, finishing 6½ games behind the league champions. At the insistence of Anson, Carroll gave up switch-hitting and hit exclusively from the left side.[22] He batted a career-high .285 with seven home runs (fifth best in the league) and 65 RBIs. He stole 34 bases. On his own team, only Anson (.312) posted a higher batting average. Carroll had a team-leading 134 runs scored, second in the league, and he finished fourth in the league with 166 base hits. He led the league with 137 singles. His 215 total bases were ninth best in the league. He also flashed his glove in 1890, finishing fourth in outfield assists with 28.

Carroll also got on pitchers' nerves during games by switching sides of the plate while the pitcher was warming up. The rule restricting this practice did not go into effect until 1914.[23]

After returning to the major leagues in 1890 and enjoying his best season, Carroll played in the National League through 1893, finishing his career with the Boston Beaneaters, who won the National League pennant in 1893.

In 1891, he once again put up good numbers with the Colts, although some were not as good as those in 1890. His power numbers were on the ascendant as his extra-base hits increased from 29 to 35 and his 80 RBIs were second best on the team. However, his batting average slipped to .256. Carroll was 31 years old and did not fit into Anson's plans, as Carroll and Anson grew further apart as the season progressed.

In 1892, Carroll signed with the St. Louis Browns. His season was going well and he was on his way to a .273 batting average when his fielding mishap on August 17 placed him on the outs with team ownership.

Boston manager Frank Selee traded for Carroll before the 1893 season, sending Joe Quinn to St. Louis in exchange. He played the outfield for Boston as Bobby Lowe was moved to second base. Although Carroll's overall statistics for the season were not good, (he batted a disappointing .224, the worst average in the league of any hitter with 400 or more at-bats[24]), he was a key factor in his team's success. The 33-year-old patrolled left field in 120 of his team's 131 games. One of Old Cliff's best performances came on June 14, in the field and at the plate. Boston was playing St. Louis and in the second inning Carroll, playing in left field, made a spectacular catch. The *Boston Journal* mentioned:

"The pleasing feature of the game was 'Cliff' Carroll's rejuvenation. To him must be given the glory of making the best catch seen on the grounds this season. [Lew] Whistler hit the ball to the farthest corner of left field, but Carroll caught it while on the dead run toward the seats, though he fell after his great effort."[25]

Carroll's day was not complete. The Beaneaters trailed by two runs as they came to bat in the ninth inning. With none out and Billy Nash and Tommy Tucker on base, Carroll came up to bat. The *Boston Globe* tells us that:

"Carroll now had a chance to pay back an old grudge he owed Mr. Von der Ahe. First he fouled one [pitch] trying to sacrifice. Turning to [Hugh] Duffy, he nodded as much to say, 'Will I cut loose?' Duff answered, 'As you like.' The next instant, the ball was going on a line to center over (Steve) Brodie's head, two runs coming in and the score tied." After the double, Carroll advanced to third on a wild pitch and scored, with two outs, on a single by Tommy McCarthy.[26] Boston had an 11-10 win and remained tied for first place. The Beaneaters went on to win the pennant by five games. Carroll did not play in the major leagues after 1893. For his career, he batted .251 in 991 games, with 203 extra-base hits and 423 RBIs.

The hit-by-pitch statistic was not kept in the National League until 1887, but records indicate that Carroll was quite proficient at taking one for the team. On three occasions between 1887 and 1892, he finished in the top five in the league. In 1891 *Sporting Life* noted, "Cliff Carroll is winning games for Anson by letting pitched balls hit him. Cliff is too old and tough to feel anything short of a rifle ball."[27] In August 1897, Carroll remembered a few things while speaking with *Sporting Life*. "I think I have one distinction that no player of the present time is anxious to earn. I have been hit oftener by Amos Rusie than any other man. And even to earn a base, it's no joke to be hit by Rusie. When another pitcher hits a man, the man rubs himself; when Rusie hits anyone, the man usually goes to bed."[28] In addition to his farming interests, Carroll also operated a meat market in Bloomington, but sold the business prior to the 1892 baseball season.

In 1894, Carroll finished his career with Detroit of the Western League.[29]

After his playing days, Carroll farmed in Hoopeston, Illinois, before relocating to Linn, Oregon, in 1910, where he tended to a 280-acre fruit farm. While in Hoopeston, he was, according to an account in *Sporting Life*, "Regent and Ruling Monarch" and manager of a ballclub in the area.[30]

Carroll died in Portland, Oregon, on June 12, 1923, and is buried at Lincoln Memorial Park. He was survived by his wife and daughter. Largely forgotten to the baseball world at the time of his passing, he was eulogized in print. The following was printed in the *Oregonian*:

"Carroll was the most wonderful fielder whoever trod a diamond. He had Ty Cobb faded as a base stealer and run getter. He and Charley Radbourne [sic] were inseparable. Carroll was almost as much the vogue as a fielder as Radbourne was as a pitcher. He will be remembered by old timers as one who helped to give the game of baseball impetus in its infancy and his feats of that long-passed day imparted much of the glamour that has since made baseball the most popular sport in America."[31]

And the following (perhaps a bit overstating the case) appeared in his hometown *Bloomington Daily Pantagraph*.

"He owned a large collection of souvenirs and mementoes. Carroll, in addition to being a wonderful hitter and fielder ranked with the fastest men on the bases. One remembrance consisted of a pin representing a foot with two miniature wings to represent fleetness. The foot is of gold and the wings were set with diamonds. He was the greatest of his day and generation."[32]

SOURCES

In addition to the sources cited in the Notes, the author used Baseball-Reference.com, Ancestry.com, and:

Balinger, Ed F. "Cliff Carroll Claimed by Death: Was Pirate Star of Bygone Days," *Pittsburgh Daily Post*, June 22, 1923: 13.

NOTES

1 Hugh S. Fullerton, "Freak Plays That Decide Baseball Championships," *American Magazine*, May 1912: 118, reprinted in *Warren County* (Illinois) *Democrat*, May 23, 1912: 20.

2 "Comedy of Errors: The Browns Give a Fearful Exhibition of Poor Ball Playing," *St. Louis Post-Dispatch*, August 18, 1892: 12.

3 "John Carroll Obituary," *Weekly Pantagraph* (Bloomington, Illinois), July 9, 1909: 6.

4 "Shortstops," *New York Clipper*, May 26, 1877: 67.

5 "The Game in California," *New York Clipper*, July 10, 1880: 125.

6 "Sic Semper M'Ginnis," *Cincinnati Commercial Tribune*, August 4, 1882: 8.

7 "Amusements," *Bloomington Daily Leader*, August 12, 1882.

8 "Another Defeat for the Chicago Nine at Providence," *Boston Herald*, October 12, 1882: 3.

9 Don Doxsie, *Iowa Greats: Sixteen Major Leaguers Who Were in the Game for Life* (Jefferson, North Carolina: McFarland Publishers, 2015), 182-183.

10 Frank G. Menke, "Cliff Carroll First Player to Bunt Ball: Member of Providence Grays, in 1884, Paralyses Opponents and Fans with Unexpected Action," *Idaho Statesman* (Boise), February 19, 1921: 6.

11 "T'was a Good Game: And Providence Won It in the 11th Inning," *Boston Herald*, August 10, 1884: 2.

12 Peter Morris, *A Game of Inches: The Stories Behind the Innovations That Shaped Baseball* (Chicago: Rowman and Littlefield, 2010), 53-55.

13 "From the Capitol: Harsh Treatment of Players – Cliff Carroll's Suspension – Barr's Release, etc.," *Sporting Life*, August 11, 1886: 1.

14 "The Washington Club," *The Sporting News*, December 31, 1886: 1.

15 "They Play With Anson," *Chicago Tribune*, April 20, 1890: 28.

16 "Diamond Notes," *Cleveland Leader and Herald*, May 10, 1888: 3.

17 "On Tour With the Bostons: Some Observations of a Clipper Correspondent on Absurdities in the Rules," *New York Clipper*, May 19, 1888: 157.

18 "Player Carroll Married," *Daily Inter-Ocean* (Chicago), February 28, 1889: 2.

19 "Carroll to Play Again," *Kalamazoo Gazette*, February 9, 1890: 8.

20 Obituary, *Oregonian* (Portland), June 25, 1923: 11.

21 "Sporting Gossip," *Anaconda* (Montana) *Standard*. May 8, 1890: 6 (originally appeared in *Cincinnati Commercial-Gazette*).

22 "Winter Ball Talk," *Kansas State Journal* (Topeka), March 7, 1890: 7.

23 David Nemec, *The Great Encyclopedia of 19th Century Baseball* (New York: Donald Fine Books, 1997), 340.

24 Nemec, 499.

25 "A Close Call: Boston Won the Game Because the Umpire Did Not See a Trick by Glasscock," *Boston Journal*, June 15, 1893: 3.

26 "Pretty Finish – Boston Makes a Spurt in the Ninth Inning," *Boston Globe*, June 15, 1893: 9.

27 "News, Gossip, and Comment," *Sporting Life*, August 15, 1891: 2.

28 W.A. Phelon Jr., "Chicago Gleanings," *Sporting Life*, August 28, 1897: 11.

29 George V. Toohey, *A History of the Boston Base Ball Club* (Boston: M.F. Quinn, 1897), 226-227.

30 W.A. Phelon Jr. "Chicago Gleanings," *Sporting Life*, February 8, 1896: 5.

31 James H. McCool, "Blue Mountain League to Close Down for Harvest," *Oregonian*, June 25, 1923: 11.

32 "'Cliff' Carroll," Obituary in *Bloomington* (Illinois) *Daily Pantagraph*, June 18, 1923: 10.

WILLIAM JONES "BOILERYARD" CLARKE

BY MATT ALBERTSON

Boileryard Clarke was known throughout the major leagues for his booming voice that could be heard clearly all over the field. It served him well as both a catcher – a coach on the field – and as a college coach from the dugout. Clarke spent 55 years in baseball as both a professional player and collegiate coach, but during his later years was unclear about exactly when he took an interest in the game. "I can't recall where I picked up baseball," he told an interviewer, "I used to hook school to go watch the boys play baseball. Every time I hooked I used to get a licking which was pretty frequent."[1]

William Jones Clarke was born to John and Mary Clarke on October 18, 1868, in New York City. His father moved the family of 10 to St. Louis by 1880 and to Santa Fe by 1885 to help build an Indian school.[2] Census records listed Clarke's father as either a mason or a carpenter.

Clarke entered Brothers College in Santa Fe (now Santa Fe University of Art and Design), a Catholic school, sometime between 1886 and 1889. "I used to play ball with the priests there. … They told me I had a natural gift for the game," he recalled many years later. "It's a funny thing, though – there was never any thought in my mind that I would ever play for pay. I just wanted to play."[3] He joined the Aspen and Pueblo baseball teams of the Colorado State League in 1889. According to an interviewer, Clarke's "most prominent blurb used throughout interviews [was] 'it's not a matter of where you're going to play but how much you get to play. If you were getting $25 a month then, you were getting real money.'"[4] This can explain the road by which many Deadball Era players like Clarke took to the major leagues. After a season in Colorado, Clarke played for the Ottumwa club of the Illinois-Iowa League in 1890, went west

Boileryard Clarke.
(Courtesy of NYYFans.com Forum)

and played for the San Francisco Metropolitans in 1891 and the San Jose Dukes in 1892. "I caught every day," he said.[5] It was in California that Clarke's door to the major leagues opened.

A San Francisco acquaintance suggested that Clarke look into playing for the Baltimore Orioles of the National League in 1893. He had telegram offers from Louisville, Chicago, and Philadelphia as well but decided to sign with the Orioles. Clarke said, "It was a very fortunate move on my part because the Orioles (then in eighth place in a 12-team league) turned out to be a championship ballclub."[6] Clarke said he didn't care whether or not he played in Baltimore or California because any team would have signed him. "As I walked into the hotel when I arrived in Baltimore I remember seeing Mike Kelly, Bill Brown, and Ed Gunther sitting in the lobby." He said, "I thought my chances were practically nil" and told Heinie Reitz, "It doesn't look like we'll have much opportunity with all these big leaguers here."[7] Major-league clubs scoured America trying to find any talent that would help them win the pennant. Signing players from obscure minor leagues was typically cheap and worth a tryout during spring training or the season.

By February 1893, Baltimore's acquisition of Clarke was made public in the *Baltimore Sun*. "Clarke is a catcher of great promise," the *Sun* wrote. "He played 84 games last season in the California League. He ranked second in fielding, went to the bat 335 times, made 93 base hits, 24 sacrifice hits, 48 runs, stole 27 bases, and had a batting average of .277."[8] The 1892 Orioles finished in eighth place but manager Ned Hanlon began to make wholesale changes to the roster for the 1893 and 1894 seasons. He traded veteran Tim O'Rourke for Harry Taylor and a young shortstop named Hughie Jennings. Harry Stovey was released. Dan Brouthers and Willie Keeler were acquired. Only four players who were on the 1892 Orioles were still on the team in 1894: catcher Wilbert Robinson, infielder John McGraw, outfielder Joe Kelly, and pitcher Sadie McMahon. The Orioles went from consecutive eighth-place finishes in 1892 and 1893 to champions of the National League in 1894. From 1894 to 1898, the Orioles finished first in the National League three times and second twice, and won the Temple Cup twice.

While Clarke was in Baltimore he met and married Isabelle Taylor Thomas. Census records show that the couple were listed as living in Baltimore through at least 1920 despite Clarke's playing in Boston and coaching Princeton University's baseball team. While a member of the Beaneaters, Clarke opened a café and bowling alley with his brother, Stanton, on Fayette Street in Baltimore.[9] The Clarkes had two sons: Oscar Taylor Clarke, born March 21, 1899, and William Jones Clarke II, born in 1902, died in 1905. In 1922 the couple moved to Princeton full time and remained there until Clarke died in 1959.[10]

In 1897 Clarke and Robinson split catching duties but both missed about two weeks with injuries. Clarke, while idle, helped to coach the Princeton baseball team for their game with Yale. Evidently his tutelage helped as the Tigers defeated Yale 22-7. *Sporting Life* wrote in 1898 that Clarke considered coaching the Tigers in the spring, which the paper said "would benefit him as well as them, as he could get into fine throwing and batting trim by practice in the Princeton cage."[11]

Clarke served primarily as a backup to Wilbert Robinson in his six seasons with the Orioles (1893-1898) and slashed .259/.321/.330 with 349 hits, 50 doubles, 5 home runs, and 214 RBIs. He and Robinson virtually split catching duties in 1898. In 1899 Clarke signed with the Beaneaters. "The news that Boston had secured Baltimore's tried and true backstop was a decided surprise to the base ball world," commented *Sporting Life*.[12] Clarke was considered a coach on the field at the time. Manager Frank Selee said, "Clarke will give us a taste of his old time Baltimore coaching, of course, and it will doubtless prove as popular to the local cranks as it was unpopular when he was with Baltimore."[13]

Clarke proved to be popular with the Boston fans in his two seasons with the Beaneaters. He was a capable backstop who handled the pitchers well, called a good game, and played hard. "His throwing has been magnificent," wrote *Sporting Life*. "Clarke keeps the men going in good style, steadies his pitcher and never gives up when there is a chance in sight."[14] He suffered a broken hand late in the 1899 season against Chicago but hadn't realized the injury until he returned to Boston after the road trip. *Sporting Life* commented, "Bill was sadly missed by the patrons (in Boston). He certainly could not be charged with any lack of ginger."[15]

Clarke's first season in Boston was subpar even by backup-catcher standards. He played in 60 of the team's 152 games in 1899 and slashed .224/.270/.283 with only two home runs and 32 RBIs. Clarke had his best major-league season at age 31 when he slashed .315/.344/.359 with one home run and 30 RBIs. (His batting average was 59 points higher than his career average.) *Sporting Life* exclaimed in late June, "Catcher Bill Clarke has struck his gait and is putting up the finest kind of ball imaginable. … Boston made a better investment than was at first imagined when it secured this man. Bill has put to blush the critics that hinted he was not the real thing. He is strawberries and cream with a vengeance."[16]

On June 11, 1900, at the Sturtevant House in New York City, a new baseball union was formed, the Protective Association of Professional Base Ball Players, or Players' Protective Association. Clarke was one of the three Boston delegates to the meeting, indicating the degree of respect other players had for him.[17] The purpose of the union was to "counteract the despotic policies and grasping methods of the little coterie of ancient fossils who are gradually running the League and even the national game to death," *Sporting Life* said. "The players have at last learned that the only way to meet the League trust is with counter organization."[18]

At the meeting the players were addressed by Daniel Harris of the American Federation of Labor. Harris told them that their grievances, if handled properly, could be rectified without much trouble from the League. He said the union did not have to affiliate with the AFL immediately, or at all, but would receive the support of the AFL regardless. The delegates elected not to affiliate with the AFL at that time because they did not want to antagonize the League. This softer approach differed from that taken by the previous players' brotherhood and Players' League of 1885-1890. Officers were elected but not made public and a committee on bylaws was established. Each club chose one delegate to act as a representative of their club.

The Association reconvened on July 30 at the Sturtevant House. Clarke was elected treasurer.[19] In December Clarke told *Sporting Life*, "I hope … every player will stick and refuse to sign until the League gives us a proper recognition. The men have all pledged themselves to stand together, and I believe they will. We would look ridiculous indeed if we gave in at the very first clash. The magnates may think we are bluffing, but they will find out their mistake." He said that the organization was healthy financially because of its $5 initiation fee and $2-a-month dues during the season.[20]

In 1890 three major leagues totaling 24 teams competed against one another in a terrific baseball war. But the Players' League collapsed after the 1890 season and the American Association folded the following year, leaving the National League with a major-league monopoly. Baseball suffered. After the 1899 season the National League dropped the least profitable teams, Baltimore, Louisville, Cleveland, and Washington. In 1901 when organizer Harry D. Quinn seemed to have the league prepared to actually play ball that year.

Clarke was listed as a catcher on the Boston reserve list after the 1900 season but in early 1901 *Sporting Life* reported that he became part-owner and manager of the Baltimore Association club. "Clarke professes to be in the brightest hopes, says he will get his release from Boston for nothing," the paper said.[21] He told *Sporting Life* that a Baltimore resident had the necessary capital to establish a club in Baltimore but that he could not sign players because the Players' Protective Association forbade players to sign contracts at that time.[22] Unfortunately for Clarke and others involved, the league dissolved before ever taking the field, thanks in part to the newly organized American League. Clarke's career as a big-league owner and manager lasted a few weeks.

Tim Murnane of the *Boston Globe* reported in *Sporting Life* that the Beaneaters had planned to release Clarke before the 1901 season. He jumped to the upstart American League instead. Beaneaters director J.B. Billings made light of the move, saying, "I was wondering what we would do with him if we kept him."[23] Clarke played with Washington for four years, batting .251 over the period as a platoon catcher. Washington released him in 1905 and he signed with the New York Giants, joining former Baltimore teammate John McGraw. Clarke slashed .180/.241/.240 in 31 games. The 1905 season was Clarke's last in the major leagues; his contract was sold to Toledo of the minor-league American Association. He played for Toledo in 1906 and 1907, Minneapolis in 1908, and Albany in 1909 before retiring as a player. He acted as player-manager for Albany in 1909 and manager in 1910 but abruptly tendered his resignation to club president Charles M. Winchester in April 1911. Winchester said of Clarke, "His resignation came to me as a big surprise. ... I always considered Bill Clarke to be one of the most competent and capable managers in the country. His judgment of baseball players was excellent and he was always given a free rein to build up a team. ... Clarke in my estimation was a conscientious, honest ballplayer. He knew every department of the game and added prestige to the team."[24] *Sporting Life* wrote that Clarke was well liked and "his sterling qualities of manhood placed him high in the estimation of the fans. ... His famous 'W-e-o-o-w' while on the coaching line at first base will live long in the hearts of fans in this city."[25] Hence the nicknames Roaring Bill and Boileryard.

Throughout his career, Clarke was lauded for his baseball intelligence and ability to be a manager on the field. Since his time in Baltimore, Clarke helped train and coach the Princeton baseball team before going to spring training. He is listed as the manager in Princeton's records beginning in 1900 and served in that capacity in three stints: 1900-1917, 1919-1927, and 1936-1944.[26] In 1910 Clarke became Princeton's first paid coach.[27] *Sporting Life* noted in its April 29, 1911, issue that Princeton was anxious to sign him to a three-year contract worth $9,000. Clarke also worked as a scout for the Detroit Tigers in 1911 in addition to his duties as Princeton coach.[28] Clarke managed a group of YMCA baseball players in Europe in 1918 during World War I which would explain why 1918 was the only year between 1900 and 1927 that he did not coach the Princeton team.[29]

In 1915 Clarke co-wrote *Baseball: Individual Play and Team Play in Detail* with Fredrick T. Dawson.[30] The book's focus was baseball theory from the perspective of coaches and players. The authors wrote: "Although it is a sport which is widely followed, yet comparatively few players, and fewer spectators really understand it thoroughly. ... In the present work, the authors, after careful study based on personal experience, injury, and comparison, have formulated for the general public, including the amateur and professional player, the whole subject of baseball as it is played in the most advanced circles, namely, in the major leagues."[31]

Clarke and his wife moved to Princeton in 1922 and lived in the basement of their antique shop at 76 Nassau Street.[32] He retired as coach in 1927, but was rehired in 1936. He retired for good in 1944. Overall, Clarke's record at Princeton was 564-322-10 and only six of his teams failed to post winning records. He led the Tigers to Eastern Intercollegiate Baseball League championships in 1941 and 1942. On May 17, 1939, the Tigers played Columbia at Columbia's Baker Field in the first televised baseball game, won by Princeton 2-1. Clarke coached two future major leaguers, Moe Berg and Charlie Caldwell. During his last coaching stint with Princeton, in 1939, the university created the William J. Clarke Award, presented annually to the Princeton team's best player.[33] Princeton's baseball diamond, Clarke Field, is named after him.

The university honored Clarke with gala parties, for his 80th and 90th birthdays. Friends, alumni, former players, and former opponents joined in the festivities. Clinton W. Blume, a former player for the Colgate baseball team, told Clarke in a letter on his 90th birthday, "Besides having the admiration and respect of the men that played for you, you also had the respect and admiration of the opposing players."[34] In an article by Asa Bushnell in the October 1958 *Princeton Alumni Weekly*, Clarke reminisced on his 90 years and his time at Princeton. "Ninety years old today, still-spry Bill Clarke honestly believes his first baseball-induced fractured thumb was his 'luckiest break,'" Bushnell wrote. "That injury, suffered in the spring of 1897, brought him to Old Nassau."[35] Clarke remembered, "We'd been on a road trip. ... When we got back to Baltimore, the manager said I couldn't do anything to help our club for a while because of my thumb. He said Princeton University needed someone to straighten out its team – they were having a terrible time with the infield. I didn't even know where Princeton was ... but I agreed to give it a try."[36]

Princeton alumnus George H. Sibley in a letter to Clarke on his retirement, said, "I don't suppose that a man who has endeared himself as you have to the hearts of so many young men, an affection which abides with them always, realizes fully the lasting contribution you have made to the development of their characters."[37]

NOTES

1. *Super Sports Feature on Bill Clarke,* William J. Clarke, Faculty and Professional Staff files, Box 101, Princeton University Archives, Department of Rare Books and Special Collections, Princeton University Library.

2. Ancestry.com *and Super Sports Feature on Bill Clarke,* William J. Clarke, Faculty and Professional Staff files, Box 101, Princeton University Archives, Department of Rare Books and Special Collections, Princeton University Library.

3. Asa Bushnell, "Bill Clarke's 90th Birthday," *Princeton Alumni Weekly,* Vol. 59, No. 7, October 31, 1958: 5.

4. *Super Sports Feature on Bill Clarke.*

5. Ibid.

6. Ibid.

7. Ibid.

8. "Sporting News: Baltimore Base-Ball Players," *Baltimore Sun,* February 4, 1893: 6.

9. "Baltimore Bulletin," *Sporting Life,* July 15, 1899: 10.

10. *Super Sports Feature on Bill Clarke.*

11. "Oriole Perquisites," *Sporting Life,* January 15, 1898: 3.

12. "Hub Happenings," *Sporting Life,* March 11, 1899: 8.

13. Ibid.

14. "Hub Happenings," *Sporting Life,* May 7, 1900: 5.

15. "Boston Blue," *Sporting Life,* September 16, 1899: 10.

16. "Hub Happenings," *Sporting Life,* June 23, 1900: 4.

17. "Players Organize," *Sporting Life,* June 16, 1900: 4.

18. Ibid.

19. "Finely Shaped Up," *Sporting Life,* August 4, 1900: 5.

20. "Players' Points," *Sporting Life,* December 29, 1900: 2.

21. "Clarke Cheerful," *Sporting Life,* January 27, 1901: 5.

22. "Baltimore Bulletin," *Sporting Life,* March 2, 1901: 5.

23. "News and Comment," *Sporting Life,* March 23, 1901: 3.

24. "New York News," *Sporting Life,* April 29, 1911: 19.

25. Ibid.

26. "Baseball 2016 Record Book," goprincetontigers.com/documents/2017/3/2/BASE_Record_Book_2016.pdf.

27. "150 Years – Baseball," goprincetontigers.com/news/2014/11/22/209777562.aspx?path=baseball.

28. "Eastern League Events," *Sporting Life,* September 23, 1911: 13.

29. "Baseball History Up-to-Date," *Baseball Magazine,* July 1918: 279; "A Letter from Aix-les-Bains," *Baltimore Sun,* May 19, 1918: 15; Biographical Questionnaire for Princeton Coaches, Princeton University Library.

30. William J. Clarke and Fredrick T. Dawson, *Baseball: Individual Play and Team Play in Detail* (New York: Charles Scribner's Sons, 1915). books.google.com/books?id=BrRHAAAAIAAJ&lpg=PR3&ots=jbajYtmJBM&dq=Baseball%2C%20individual%20play%20and%20team%20play%20in%20detail%2C%20by%20W.%20J.%20Clarke%20...%20and%20Fredrick%20T.%20Dawson%20...%20with%20illustrations%20and%20diagrams.&pg=PR3#v=onepage&q&f=true.

31. Clarke and Dawson, v, viii.

32. *Super Sports Feature on Bill Clarke.*

33. "Baseball 2016 Record Book," goprincetontigers.com/documents/2017/3/2/BASE_Record_Book_2016.pdf.

34. Clinton W. Blume to William J. Clarke, March 24, 1958, William J. Clarke, Faculty and Professional Staff files, Princeton University Library.

35. Bushnell, "Bill Clarke's 90th Birthday."

36. Ibid.

37. George H. Sibley to William J. Clarke, August 3, 1944, William J. Clarke, Faculty and Professional Staff files.

JOHN CLARKSON
BY BRIAN MCKENNA

John Clarkson.
(Courtesy of National Baseball Hall of Fame)

More than a few contemporary baseball insiders viewed John Clarkson as the finest pitcher of the 19th century. He won 30 or more games in a season six times, including two of the top four all-time totals, 53 in 1885 and 49 in '89. In the 10-year period between August 1884 and July 1894, he amassed 327 victories in the National League, and then retired at the age of 33. Clarkson was recognized as half of the "$20,000 Battery," so called for the price Boston paid for the pitcher and King Kelly. Perhaps more recognize his name because he spent much of the last four years of his life in mental hospitals. Some even claim that the crazed former ballplayer mutilated his wife. Seemingly the Hall of Fame forgot his name entirely, overlooking his contributions until 1963.

John Gibson Clarkson was born on July 1, 1861, in Cambridge, Massachusetts, to a Scottish-born father, Thomas G. Clarkson, and an Irish-born mother, Ellen M. (Hackett) Clarkson. John had two younger sisters, Isabella and Helena, and four younger brothers, Arthur, Thomas, Walter, and Frederick. Arthur and Walter, also pitchers, followed John into the majors, as did two cousins from his mother's side of the family, Mert and Walter Hackett.

In contrast to most big leaguers of the era, John was born into a family of means. His father owned a prospering jewelry and watchmaking business in Boston. John attended local schools and trained in the jewelry business as a teenager. He was also attracted to baseball, perhaps influenced by a watchmaking co-worker of his father's and one of professional baseball's founding fathers, Harry Wright. At his high school, the Webster School, John made the baseball team as a catcher in 1878. During the season, he also made his debut in the pitcher's box. After high school he worked in the family trade and attended the local Comer's Business School. Because Clarkson hailed from the Harvard University area, false reports throughout his career said he was a graduate of the university. He was not, but his brothers Walter and Frederick did, and played baseball there.

Starting in 1880, John played amateur ball for the Beacons of Boston for a little over two years. He also played for the Hyde Park club at times. Clarkson was one of the Beacons' star hitters and eventually developed into the club's leading pitcher. The team played all comers, including major-league clubs, and

Clarkson soon gained a reputation as one of the area's leading hurlers. During his Beacon days he received some pitching tips from Boston Red Stockings pitcher Tommy Bond. In late April 1882, the Beacons played the Worcester Ruby Legs of the National League in an exhibition contest. Worcester manager Freeman Brown signed Clarkson soon after the game to help solidify his rotation, which had been a little shaky against some college squads that April.

A few days later, on May 2, 1882, 20-year-old Clarkson made his major-league debut, in a home game against Boston. It was the second game of the season, on a very cold and windy day that kept the crowd to only 400. Though he was hit hard, Clarkson pulled out an 11-10 victory, helped by a couple of doubles of his own. He started again three days later but lost to Hoss Radbourn and the Providence Grays, 17-2. The reviews after the contest were stinging, for example: "With Clarkson as pitcher today, the Worcesters were beaten by the Providence team with the utmost ease, they batting Clarkson for fourteen singles and two two-baggers in the sixth and seventh innings."[1] On the 11th, he pitched better but lost again, 4-0, to Tim Keefe of the Troy Trojans. The rebound was noticed: "Clarkson pitched for the Worcesters and was quite effective, no earned runs being scored off his pitching."[2] In three games he pitched, opposite three of the toughest hurlers of the early professional era, Bobby Mathews (Boston), Radbourn, and Keefe, he fared adequately if unspectacularly. Unfortunately, his shoulder was ailing and he was released before the end of the month, within a week or so of his final game. It appears that he sat idle the rest of the season.

After the 1882 season, Arthur Whitney, a Boston-Worcester area player, took over the Saginaw, Michigan, club of the Northwestern League. Whitney contacted Clarkson over the winter and signed him to a contract. At first Clarkson filled a utility role, playing every position but catcher. The club directors were unimpressed and soon discussed releasing the young player. Whitney then installed him on the mound and those thoughts dissipated. The move proved a success. Clarkson appeared in 21 games as pitcher for the club; his record is unknown, but the team challenged for the championship all season, falling just two games short of the title. Clarkson credited Whitney with turning his career around and solidifying his spot in professional baseball. Specifically, Whitney helped convert Clarkson to an overhand pitcher, spending hours working on his motion behind the team's hotel and at the ballpark. The overhand style was just about to become legal in the National League.

Clarkson returned to Saginaw in '84, posting a season that earned him accolades throughout the industry. In 45 games and nearly 400 innings pitched he accrued a 34-9 record with nine shutouts and a stunning 388 strikeouts and a 0.64 ERA – all by the middle of August. He hit .306 as well. He was regularly fanning upward of 10, 15 and even 19 batters a game. In five games pitched between June 30 and July 14, Clarkson racked up 73 strikeouts. This caught the eye of major-league managers. In early August, pitchers Jim McCormick and Jack Glasscock, along with catcher Fatty Briody, jumped the Cleveland National League club for Cincinnati of the Union Association. Manager Charlie Hackett tried to sign Clarkson to fill the void but the deal fizzled. Then, on August 14, the Northwestern League ousted the Saginaw club for nonpayment of dues and the club disbanded.

Now a free agent, Clarkson fielded offers from Boston, Chicago, and Cincinnati but signed with Cap Anson of the White Stockings around August 24. His first game with the club took place three days later, a 5-3 loss to Hoss Radbourn. The *St. Louis Globe-Democrat* wrote of Clarkson after the game, "His pitching is very effective . . . He is a good fielder and his playing today showed him to be a valuable addition to the nine."[3] Clarkson appeared in 14 games for the White Stockings, posting a 10-3 record. On September 30, he struck out seven straight New York Gothams batters, and 13 in all.

Clarkson, a 5-foot-10, 155-pound right hander, threw the three basic pitches, fastball, curve, and changeup. He relied heavily on curves, especially his drop curve, one that fell sharply, from a 12 o'clock to 6 o'clock angle. He could throw a sweeping rising curve as well. Billy Sunday said that Clarkson "could put more turns and twists into a ball than any pitcher I ever saw."[4] Teammates said he could put so much English on a billiard ball with his big hands that it would circle the entire table. Clarkson's fastball was a riser, generally sailing up through the zone. He liked to keep the batter off-balance, delivering the ball from a variety of arm angles, most often from sidearm, and trying to work the element of surprise. The *Brooklyn Eagle* wrote of his delivery, "Clarkson, of Boston, faces second base first, then quickly whirls around and throws the ball over the plate, startling the batter."[5] He wore a large, shiny belt buckle that he tried to shine in the batter's eyes. Umpires routinely had him remove it. Excellent fielding complemented his pitching talents. *Sporting Life* wrote, "Clarkson fields his position better than any other League pitcher."[6]

Clarkson possessed a good deal of pitching speed, but that wasn't his dominant weapon. Wrote the *Chicago Daily Inter Ocean*, "Clarkson is able to pitch every other day for the reason that instead of adopting (Amos) Rusie's method of firing the ball at the catcher with cannonball speed, he depends entirely upon head work, change of pace, and the fielders back of him. In this way Clarkson saves his arm, and is still ready for the finish."[7] Clarkson did in fact strike out a great many batters, but that wasn't his goal. He much preferred to cut down on his pitch count by having the batter put the ball in play for his fielders to do their job. Moreover, he was a master at working to a batter's weakness and at keeping him guessing. Sam Thompson, an outfielder with Detroit and Philadelphia, said, "I faced him in scores of games and I can truthfully say that never in all that time did I get a pitch that came where I expected it or in the way in which I guessed it was coming."[8] Cap Anson said, "In knowing exactly what kind of a ball a batter could not hit and in his ability to serve up just that kind of ball, I don't think I have ever seen the equal of Clarkson."[9]

Clarkson's forte was his control; he put the ball where he wanted. Teammate Fred Pfeffer, an infielder, defined this ability: "I stood behind him day in and day out, and watched his magnificent control, as confident of success, especially in tight places, as I would have been with the United States army behind me. There was Clarkson's long suit – he was master of control. I believe he could put a ball where he wanted it nine times out of ten. He had everything any pitcher ever had as well. His speed was something terrific, and he could throw any curve. However, his favorite ball was a drop something like the spitball of today, although he delivered it without the ointment necessary nowadays."[10] The *Chicago Tribune* noted more reasons for his success: "John Clarkson was a great pitcher, because he was a student of the game and relied upon his strategy and control rather than his physical strength, which never was great. He was naturally an athlete, possessed of plenty of speed, but used it in moderation and was of the style of pitchers represented in later years by (Clark) Griffith. Clarkson was one of the first to develop the 'jump' ball and as the pitching distance then was shorter than it is today he was able to use it with deadly effect. That, in connection with the drop curve which Clarkson also had perfectly under control, made him the best of his day."[11]

Part of Clarkson's strategy was to regularly pitch around the best hitters in the game. . One such example was against New York in 1885: "Clarkson pitched for us and showed more good judgment and foresight than I have ever seen any pitcher display in a ballgame. In the first inning, for instance, with (Orator) O'Rourke and (Roger) Connor – the heaviest batters in the League -- ... Clarkson sent them to first on called balls, and as a result caught O'Rourke napping at second, while Connor and (Buck) Ewing went out a moment later in a double play. ... In taking no chances against the heavy-hitting abilities of Connor and O'Rourke, Clarkson proved his ability to use his head as well as his hands in his work."[12]

Clarkson was also fortunate to work with some of the best catchers of the day. With Chicago, Silver Flint caught 148 of his games. King Kelly worked as the backstop in 73 of Clarkson's games with both Chicago and Boston. Charlie Bennett (119 games) and Charlie Ganzel (43) worked behind the plate in the bulk of his outings with Boston. Chief Zimmer (57 games) did the same with Cleveland. Years later Zimmer called Clarkson the greatest of all pitchers – and Zimmer caught Cy Young for nearly a decade.

Chicago White Stockings manager Cap Anson said that Clarkson "was peculiar in some things, however, and in order to get his best work you had to keep spurring him along, otherwise he was apt to let up, this being especially the case when the club was ahead and he saw what he thought was a chance to save himself."[13] Anson added, "Many regard him as the greatest, but not many know of his peculiar temperament and the amount of encouragement needed to keep him going. Scold him, find fault with him, and he could not pitch at all. Praise him and he was unbeatable."[14] Anson suggested that Clarkson was deeply affected by razzing and would falter on the mound amid abuse. Some of these broad accusations, though, don't seem to match up with the record books or day-in/day-out contemporary accounts.

Clarkson started 1885 coaching the pitchers at Dartmouth. He continued to train college squads throughout his baseball career and into retirement. It was a part of his winter conditioning. The only year he took off from coaching was 1886 and that was because of his impending marriage. He coached Harvard pitchers from 1887 to 1892. In 1890 he also worked with the hurlers at the Boston Athletic Association. In 1893 and '94 he worked out

John Clarkson, 1887.
(Library of Congress)

the staff at Yale. In '94 he also trained the Union College pitchers in Schenectady, New York. The following year he worked for the University of Michigan.

His talents went beyond baseball. In March 1885, Clarkson refereed a boxing match in Hanover, New Hampshire. It was a championship bout between a minor leaguer named Harmon and a Professor Craig. On train trips and in hotels throughout spring training and during the season starting in '85, Clarkson and King Kelly entertained their teammates with song.

By any measure Clarkson was the National League's most valuable player in 1885. He started 70 games, finishing all but two, and posted a 53-16 record in 623 innings. Those 53 victories are the most in a season after Hoss Radbourn's 59 the previous year. Clarkson tossed 10 shutouts and struck out 308 batters. All the numbers mentioned other than the loss total led the league.

From June 1 to 24, 1885, Clarkson won 13 consecutive games. On June 20, he shut out Buffalo, 5-0, on a one-hitter. It was one of his 10 straight victories over Buffalo that season. Clarkson pitched a no-hitter on July 27, a 4-0 win over Providence and Radbourn. The *Sporting Life* wrote, "Clarkson's work in the box last week was really remarkable. In one game he disposed of the Providence club without a hit…In another but four hits were made on him in fourteen innings and in the Philadelphia game also but four hits were made off him – a total of but eight hits in thirty-two innings. Wonderful."[15]

Chicago took the pennant by two games over New York that season; the rest of the league was at least 30 games behind the White Stockings. In the postseason championship series, the White Stockings tied the St. Louis Browns of the American Association, 3-3-1. Many modern researchers consider the postseason series that began in 1884 to be the first World Series, but the tie that year goes a long way at viewing the 19th-century postseason contests as mere exhibitions.

After the season, Clarkson barnstormed in St. Louis before returning to Chicago for the winter. He stayed in Chicago to split the distance with his girlfriend, Ella Moorhead McKenna. Ella, from Detroit, was born in May 1860. They met when he was with Saginaw. On March 4, 1886, the couple married. She traveled with the club that spring to Hot Springs, Arkansas, and back. Over the years she attended many games. It's probably good that she did since Clarkson attracted more than his share of women to the park. He was a good-looking Irishman with dark hair and bluish-gray eyes. And he was a bit of a dandy when it came to his attire, as the *Sporting Life* noticed: "All of the Chicago players dress well off the field but Clarkson is the bright particular dude of the team. He is very scrupulous about his dress, and there is considerable of the English in his style."[16] The *Detroit Free Press* said, "His uniform was always immaculate, his linen always possessed the fresh-from-the-laundry touch, he was always smoothly shaved, his manners were always faultless."[17] He also wore a silk handkerchief on the outside of his uniform.

In 1886, Clarkson won 36 games in 55 starts, striking out 313. On August 14 he defeated St. Louis, 5-2, for the 17th consecutive time, a record that still stands. Four days later, he fanned 16 Kansas City batters to set the club record. On August 23, Clarkson tossed a one-hitter over Detroit, losing a no-hitter in the eighth inning on a controversial hit by Deacon White. Chicago won the pennant by 2½ games over Detroit. Again the White Stockings faced the St. Louis Browns of the American Association in the postseason. This time St. Louis won, four games to two. Clarkson was 2-2 in four starts, winning Games One and Three. The series is memorable for the sixth and final game, a contest regarded as one of the finest of the era. Clarkson took the mound with his club down three games to two and took a 3-0 lead into the eighth inning, hoping to tie the series. However, the Browns pushed across three runs to even the score. In the 10th, St. Louis outfielder Curt Welch tried to steal home. He was seemingly caught but Clarkson's pitch to King Kelly went astray and Welch scored the winning run. Clarkson had apparently crossed up his catcher. It was known as the "$15,000 Slide" because of the winner-take-all agreement between the clubs. The Chicago players were drinking heavily during the series, some showing signs of drunkenness while on the field. Clarkson may not have been drinking during the day, but he was tearing it up at night. It was said that he was slotted to start Game Five but couldn't because of a hangover. It was the only time in seven tries that an American Association club won the postseason series between the two leagues.

Over the winter, Clarkson worked out daily with fellow Cambridge native Tim Keefe. The two pitchers were concerned about the new rules in 1887 that shrank the pitcher's box and lengthened the pitching distance to 55 feet 6 inches. It had been 50 feet when Clarkson debuted in 1882. Clarkson was also concerned about the loss of his catcher, King Kelly, who had been sold to Boston for $10,000. These matters didn't deter Clarkson, though; he led the league in most pitching categories again in 1887, amassing a 38-21 record in 59 starts. Detroit won the pennant, however. Clarkson defeated the Wolverines nine times, the most by one pitcher over an eventual pennant winner. As the end of the season neared, Clarkson negotiated a $200 bonus if the club finished in second place; but the White Stockings fell to third. After another fine year, he wanted a significant boost in income; he also wanted out of Chicago; more specifically, he wanted to play near his home. He declared, "My home is in Boston, and all the domesticities I have center there. I am anxious to have a house of my own, and to fit it up as a permanent residence."[18] As the season ended he met with club president Al Spalding and told him so, asking for a trade to Boston, and later sending follow-up letters reaffirming his desire. Clarkson's family was also pushing him to leave baseball and join the family jewelry business. (Another rumor, neither proved nor disproved, claimed that Clarkson and the White Stockings' shortstop, Ned Williamson, had had a falling-out and Clarkson vowed to never play with him again.)

Spalding had his own plans; he was having a fire sale. After getting the cash for Kelly, he was offering any of his men for the right price. He set the menu: $10,000 for Clarkson; $7,500 for Ned Williamson; $5,000 for Fred Pfeffer; $2,500 each for Mark Baldwin, Jimmy Ryan, and Dell Darling. The owner declared: "There is no player so good but that his equal can be found."[19]

Clarkson wanted a salary close to that of Bob Caruthers, a pitcher for St. Louis, who was making a reported $4,500. The *Sporting Life* took the pitcher's side: "Clarkson has pitched more games in the last two years than any other pitcher in the country. No wonder he feels sore when he considers that he is not paid as much as many players who are playing with weaker clubs and only pitch once a week or once in two weeks."[20] Clarkson also cited Henry Boyle, a pitcher for Indianapolis, who made $500 more than he did with a weaker team in a smaller market, with a lighter workload and less success.

Clarkson, or more likely some friends, approached Boston Beaneaters president Arthur Soden and asked him to work a trade. Soden offered the White Stockings $7,500 as early as September 1887. It wasn't enough; Spalding was holding out for more. Part of Spalding's negotiating stance was to declare that the club would rely on Gus Krock and George Van Haltren on the mound for the coming season if Clarkson chose to hold out. Clarkson was equally as adamant, in fact more so. In December he declared, "You can depend upon it that I will not play in the Chicago club next year under any circumstances. … I think it is about time that I should have something to say where I shall play. I will remain in Boston and work at my trade. I mean just what I say. I will not play in Chicago under any circumstances."[21] He threatened to sit out the season and join the family business if not traded. Spalding shot back that he would simply blacklist the player if he didn't report in the spring.

By February 1888, the entire White Stockings squad had signed except for their disgruntled ace. The deal was finally brokered on April 3, just before the exhibition season began. The *Boston Globe* headlined, "HE IS OURS: Ten Thousand Dollars for Another Beauty."[22] Clarkson was reunited with his backstop King Kelly; the pair was now known as the "$20,000 Battery." Two days later, on the 5th, 4,500 Boston fans showed up to see the battery in action, a high turnout for a blustery spring-training game in New England. The high dollar sales for the two players led in part to mounting dissatisfaction among players. A lot of money was being thrown around between the owners, but the reserve clause was helping to hold down salaries and personal freedoms as well. The prevailing players union, the Brotherhood of Professional Baseball Players, was busy solidifying its ranks in response to the disgruntlement. Clarkson joined his colleagues, pledged his support to the Brotherhood in early 1889, and paid his dues. Oddly, he did so at the urging of Boston Beaneaters director William Conant, who believed that the other men would play better behind him during the season if he did. According to *Boston Globe* sportswriter Tim Murnane, "The pitcher promised at the time that he would never hurt the Boston club."[23]

Clarkson started on Opening Day 1888, not ceding a hit until the sixth inning, and Boston won its first nine games, five of which were credited to their new ace. In all, he went 33-20 with a league-leading innings total (483 1/3) again. The club, though, finished in fourth place, 15½ games out.

Clarkson was appointed temporary captain in April 1889 amid fighting between the club directors, on the one hand, and player-manager John Morrill and King Kelly, who presented separate issues, most involving his alcoholism. Morrill was sold to Washington, where he became manager, and Jim Hart was brought in to manage the Beaneaters. It looked to be a bright year indeed. After spending all that money for Kelly and Clarkson, Boston tapped the failing Detroit Wolverines for Charlie Bennett, Dan Brouthers, Charlie Ganzel, and Hardy Richardson. The club went 18-4 in May to take a 3½ game lead in the standings. Clarkson didn't lose his second game until June 10, by which point he was 15-2. In the first game of a doubleheader on June 22 in Pittsburgh, Clarkson shut out the Alleghenys 5-0, allowing only five hits and striking out 12. In the seventh inning of the second game he was ejected while sitting on the bench. Pittsburgh manager Fred Dunlap noticed that Clarkson was signaling to his teammate, pitcher Bill Sowders, and informed the umpire. On July 12, Clarkson was pulled for some extra rest in the fifth inning despite leading 10-0 and tossing a no-hitter. Reliever Sowders gave up just one hit the rest of the way in the 13-1 defeat of Pittsburgh. On September 16, the Beaneaters started a 15-game road trip to finish the season. They stood a half-game behind the New York Giants in the standings. Clarkson and the club directors agreed that he'd pitch every game down the stretch for some extra compensation. Clarkson actually started 13 of those games, taking two games off, but that was done in consultation with club officials. It was a tactical error; the pennant slipped out of Boston's hands.

For the first time in major-league history, the pennant came down to the final day of the season (October 5). The Beaneaters were facing Pittsburgh, and the Giants were playing the Cleveland Spiders. Clarkson and Boston manager Jim Hart made waves by offering the Cleveland battery $1,000 if they defeated New York. The money would come from a previous promise by the *Boston Globe* to reward the local club if it copped the pennant. New York in turn offered a suit of clothes to the Pittsburgh players if they stopped the Beaneaters. Henry Chadwick, for one, found this all distasteful. Clarkson lost to Pittsburgh, 6-1, and New York defeated Cleveland to take the championship by one game over the Beaneaters. As would be the case for decades to come, the contenders played an uneven number of games: New York finished at 83-43; Boston, at 83-45. Drinking may have cost the club the pennant, as more than a few of the men imbibed heavily as the season and summer moved to a close. Clarkson won the pitching Triple Crown, leading the league in wins (49), strikeouts (284), and earned run average (2.73). He tossed eight shutouts. The 49 wins are the fourth highest total in major-league history. In the five seasons from 1885 to 1889, Clarkson posted a 209-93 record with 295 complete games, 2,716 innings pitched, and 1,365 strikeouts. For all this work and success Clarkson wasn't even listed among the top 20 earners of 1889 according to the *Spalding Guide*. He wanted his big payday.

With the growing unrest among players, 1889 was a contentious year. As the summer wore on, the players firmed up plans to organize a league of their own. The new league, the Players League, would operate in 1890 as a third major league, pulling most of the top players from the National League. The two leagues would compete head-to-head in virtually every National League city. Clarkson was hedging his bets on the new league, though. He was listed as a member of its Boston entry and had signed an agreement to sign a contract, though not an actual contract. He was also one of the first to purchase stock in the new Boston club. However, he soon started backtracking. After an interview with him, the *Chicago Tribune* called Clarkson "a shining mark in his profession, a Brotherhood man, and a signer with the rest of the Boston team to the agreement which now binds the players to the National Players' League."[24] But Clarkson added: "I shall also consult my own interests, do the best I can, and do not consider the agreement which I signed binding on me other than a promise that I would go with the other men if such a step is consistent and legal. … I am with the boys, and if it is for my best interests to go with them I shall do so. But I am not bound. The League people are entitled to a good deal of consideration at our hands."[25] His Brotherhood colleagues didn't see it the same way. Like the other ballplayers, Clarkson had agreed with and supported the union, attended meetings and voted. He even nominated King Kelly for an office. However, as the plans actually came into fruition, he needed to reevaluate his commitment. He was concerned that the new league wasn't well funded or organized and that it would fail, leaving the men to "scramble for old positions and loss of the best part of a season's earnings."[26]

Soon after the Brotherhood solidified its plans at a meeting on November 4 in New York, Clarkson departed with many of his teammates on a California barnstorming trip. In late November, Kelly headed to San Francisco to meet the Boston players and gain their signatures for the coming season. He was worried about some of the comments made by Clarkson and Hoss Radbourn; they seemed to be pulling away from the union. "Mike Kelly, who is deputed by the Brotherhood to sign players, arrived in the city yesterday," a press service report said. "He is rather disappointed at not being able to secure John Clarkson. Clarkson has been offered by the Brotherhood the same salary as he was getting from the League and Kelly offered to give him $500 out of his own pocket, but it wasn't enough."[27] Clarkson wanted more money, stating that he "must in justice to myself and family earn my money while I can."[28] Certainly this additional quote didn't win any friends: "I am looking out for myself as usual, and ain't bothering myself a great deal about anyone else."[29]

In secret, Clarkson started trading telegrams with Beaneaters owner Arthur Soden, and a deal was worked out. Soden said, "We paid John Clarkson $25,000 for three years. For simply signing his name to a contract we paid him $10,000. This is the largest salary that has ever been paid to a baseball player."[30] It was in fact a lot of money; no one had been guaranteed $25,000 before. Clarkson made the best deal possible, financially speaking. The pitcher also agreed to act as an agent for the Boston club. Soden gave him carte blanche to re-sign as many men as possible. He talked Pop Smith and Charlie Ganzel into re-signing with the club and approached several others, including Hardy Richardson and even Kelly. Clarkson also sent telegrams to and later visited Charlie Bennett's residence and signed him up as well.

Naturally this was in violation of the agreement Clarkson had made with the Brotherhood and most of his teammates and friends around the league. It wasn't received well, many believing that he previously sat in on their meetings solely to report back to Soden and the League. Fred Pfeffer recalled, "I never saw such a change in a man in my life. When I last saw him before that he was as strong a Brotherhood man as could be found and dwelt at length on the prospects of the Players League. Then he became an icicle. It chilled me through to hear him talk and I walked away from him."[31] Someone discovered that Clarkson was working as an agent for the League and sent a telegram to John Morrill, a secretary of the Brotherhood, in San Francisco. It read: "Clarkson is a traitor and is working for Soden. Show this to the boys and watch Clarkson."[32] He wasn't treated well after that and had a strained relationship with many for months to come, even years. For the rest of the barnstorming trip, many shunned Clarkson, blasting him for his duplicity. Kelly, once a good friend, apparently was among them. Their friendship never recovered.

On December 18, the Brotherhood met again to firm up the new league. The members expelled Clarkson and 14 others, officially blacklisting them. On January 11, 1890, the men returned to Chicago from San Francisco. The *Chicago Tribune* wrote, "The Brotherhood sentiment was strong in all excepting Clarkson, who did not move about with the others."[33] Hardy Richardson took the opportunity to publicly blast the pitcher, calling him out for his double-agent activities and disloyalty to his colleagues. The two didn't speak for many months. (One story during this period was that Ella Clarkson talked her husband into staying in the National League because the Boston directors offered her free tickets to games for herself and any friends.)

Boston dropped to fifth place in 1890 despite 26 wins from Clarkson. On April 19, he won 15-9 over Brooklyn even though he himself committed 10 errors, which were actually wild pitches. Sloppily, there were a total of 35 errors in the contest. The Players League folded after only one season and the men funneled back to their old teams. During the negotiations Monte Ward declared, "The talk of refusing to play with (Jack) Glasscock, (Jerry) Denny, Clarkson, or any of the deserters from our ranks is all bosh. Of course it is a bitter pill, but for the sake of peace and harmony we will swallow it."[34] That was merely the face of the union speaking publicly; the friction did not go away. Many of the men had issues with Clarkson and he was treated rudely and shunned by some for the rest of his career. Some observers claimed that a few of his teammates slacked off while Clarkson was on the mound, the very thing Conant, the Beaneaters director, feared previously. King Kelly for one refused to return to Boston, instead jumping to the American Association, in part because he didn't want to play with Clarkson and Charlie Bennett.

Both Clarkson and Kid Nichols won at least 30 games for the Red Stockings in 1891 and the club captured the pennant by 3½ games over Chicago. Clarkson presented a new look for 1892, shaving off his trademark mustache for a season or so. He started off shakily, posting an 8-6 record through 16 games. On May 6, he went toe-to-toe with Cincinnati and opposing pitcher Elton "Icebox" Chamberlain for 14 scoreless innings, giving up only four hits but walking six. Chamberlain surrendered only three hits and a walk. "Six times during the game for Boston and four for Cincinnati would a base hit have decided the contest," the *Boston Globe* wrote the next day.[35] The game was called at the beginning of the 15th inning "on account of the sun," as the umpire Jack Sheridan declared that it was beating in the batters' and pitchers' eyes. A sore arm kept Clarkson off the mound from May 15 to 25. On the 26th, he defeated Louisville 7-0 but lost a no-hitter with two outs in the ninth when Hughie Jennings placed a single. With a young Kid Nichols developing into an ace, Arthur Soden was looking to shed the expensive Clarkson but was a little hesitant to do so since he was still under the three-year contract for which the club had given him a significant signing bonus. Regardless, on June 30, 1892, Clarkson, whose record was 8-6 at the time, was given his unconditional release. The dismissal had as much to do with cutting costs as it did with Clarkson's shaky start and questions about the health of his arm. With the merger of the National League and American Association, only one major league operated in 1892. The owners were thus in a position to tighten their belt. They would soon implement system wide payroll cuts and institute a salary cap.

Cleveland owner Frank Robison wanted Clarkson, but his co-owners didn't. Robison pressed and got his way. It added to a rift among them though, which wasn't resolved until Robison bought the others out later in the summer. The Spiders signed the free agent on July 5. The payroll cuts hit just as Clarkson joined the Spiders; every man was required to sign a new contract at a lower rate. Clarkson's days of being the staff ace were over in Cleveland; that distinction belonged to the speedballer Cy Young. Clarkson did well, winning 17 games for the club and proving that his arm was holding up by pitching a total of 389 innings. He won his first game for the Spiders on July 9, an 8-2 victory over Tim Keefe. On September 21, he claimed his 300th major-league win, a five-hitter over Pittsburgh that the Spiders pulled out in the ninth inning, 3-2. Cleveland finished in second place, 8½ games behind Boston. Since there was only one major league, the top two teams faced off in a championship series. Boston won the series, five games to none, with one tie. Clarkson lost both of his starts. In Game Five, he blew a six-run lead and lost, 12-7.

Before the 1893 season, the pitching rubber was pushed back another five feet to the current distance of 60 feet 6 inches. It signaled the beginning of the end of Clarkson's effectiveness.

Though only 31 years old, he couldn't adjust adequately and won only 24 more games in 53 starts. He did, however, log the innings once again, a total of 445 2/3. Cleveland gave Clarkson a contract for $2,500, which was actually $100 over the salary cap. It was also $200 more than Cy Young was making. That didn't sit well with Young, and the club had to renegotiate with its ace. The next season, 1894, couldn't have started any worse for Clarkson. He planned a camping trip near Kansas City with his good friend and former batterymate Charlie Bennett. On the trip in early January, Bennett carelessly hopped off the train to speak with a friend. He slipped, fell under the wheels and lost parts of both legs.[36] The scene was bloody and horrifying. Clarkson was dramatically affected. He was already drinking heavily toward the end of his career, and the incident didn't help matters. Clarkson stayed with his friend for over a month, returning home on February 19 to take over the Yale pitching staff. He helped organize a benefit for the catcher later in the year.

Throughout his time in Cleveland, Clarkson clashed with his teammates and was said to be unhappy. Many of them were staunch Brotherhood supporters. A cynic might claim that some didn't play their best when he was on the mound. Cy Young, who wasn't a part of the Brotherhood struggle, later acknowledged Clarkson's help in refining his game. According to Young's biographer Reed Browning, "Clarkson showed Young how to improve his curve ball, advised him on ways to sharpen control, and prodded him to think about pitching strategy."[37] All these were lessons he had been imparting to college pitchers for years. Moreover, "Young declared unequivocally that Clarkson had helped him become a better pitcher."[38]

On July 12, 1894, Clarkson made his final major-league appearance, in a 20-10 shellacking by Philadelphia. The next day he was traded to Baltimore for another aging pitcher, Tony Mullane. Orioles manager Ned Hanlon was happy to make the trade for the pennant run, declaring, "Clarkson has not been satisfied in Cleveland and will show his appreciation of the change of base by demonstrating that he is still one of the best pitchers in the business. He has, beyond doubt, the easiest delivery of all the pitchers. His coolness in trying circumstances is proverbial. I have made many deals in my effort to build up a team, but none which gave me more satisfaction that when I traded Mullane even up for Clarkson."[39] The *Washington Post* was a little less enthusiastic about the repercussions of the trade: "It is an open secret that Clarkson has been dissatisfied in Cleveland and anxious to get away, while Mullane is never satisfied anywhere, so neither team has much the worst of the bargain."[40] The *Boston Globe* saw little for the Orioles to gain: "Perhaps John Clarkson may do better in Baltimore than Cleveland. But that remains to be seen. His work this season is decidedly of the passé order."[41] To Hanlon's dismay, Clarkson refused to join the Orioles, returned home to Bay City, Michigan, and retired. Mullane appeared in four games for Cleveland and was done as well.

For his career, Clarkson inserted a 328-178 win-loss record into the books and nearly 2,000 strikeouts. Before the mound was pushed back to 60 feet 6 inches in 1893, he fanned the second most batters, behind Tim Keefe. Clarkson failed to complete only 33 of his 518 starts. He also knocked 24 home runs, a number by far the most of any 19th century pitcher and a record that lasted for decades.

In September 1894, John and Ella Clarkson purchased a cigar store and manufactory at 103 Center Avenue in Bay City. They later opened a wholesale business on Fifth Avenue and a retail establishment in the Phoenix area. In 1904 they opened another cigar enterprise at Sixth and South Sherman Streets in Chicago. The latter three businesses proved unsuccessful. The decade after leaving baseball was for the most part spent managing his four business enterprises. John's brother Arthur moved to Bay City to help run the businesses after his professional baseball career ended. He initially worked as a clerk in the cigar store and then took over operations at the Phoenix location. Later, he opened a clothing store a few doors down from the cigar shop. During this time, John made infrequent trips to Boston to visit friends and family and to Detroit to check in with Charlie Bennett and Ella's family.

On the baseball end, Clarkson established, organized, managed, and occasionally pitched for an independent, amateur Bay City club in 1895. He tried to place a Bay City franchise in the Interstate League for 1897, but it was a no-go. Also in '97, Ban Johnson, president of the Western League, wired Clarkson offering the ex-pitcher a job as an umpire. Clarkson had actually worked four games during his major-league career, three of them behind the plate. However, he replied, "Many thanks, but I am out of baseball for good."[42] Through the rest of the decade, though, Clarkson teased reporters about a possible return to the majors but it was ultimately in jest. As late as 1904, a *Chicago Journal* writer wrote that Clarkson "looks as strong and agile today as he did fifteen years ago."[43]

In March 1905, Clarkson, then in his early 40s, was listed as the vice president of the Michigan State League and was set to manage the Bay City franchise. In May, Ella and Arthur summoned John's father to Bay City for a family conference. John had been in a "bad way for several months."[44] They decided to confine him to the Oak Grove Sanitarium in Flint, Michigan, for the "treatment of mental disorders," a nervous breakdown combined with depression and possibly paranoia which was certainly exacerbated by his excessive drinking.[45] He was said to live in the past more than the present, often recalling his baseball days as if they were yesterday. As the *Sporting Life* noted at the time of his death, "He seemed to have no memory at all for things of today, but talked clearly and lucidly of matters connected with the past."[46] King Kelly would have been surprised. He once described Clarkson as "a quiet, modest gentleman, and does less talking about baseball than any player in the country."[47] Clarkson returned home briefly in December 1905 but was soon transferred to the Eastern Michigan Asylum in Pontiac. At the time reports declared, "There are no hopes that his condition will improve." He had "completely broken down mentally and physically."[48]

After three months in Pontiac, his father brought him to the McLean Psychiatric Hospital in Waverly, Massachusetts, near the family home in Cambridge in March 1906. At the time Thomas Clarkson told reporters, "John is in a bad way, and he has been for the last two years. . . . Physically he is as well as he ever has been and this, of course, gives us encouragement. His mind wanders back to the old baseball days. His wife … came on with him and is now at our home. When he became sick she ran his business for some time, but is now closed out."⁴⁹

Ella moved in with her in-laws. Clarkson remained, for the most part, at McLean except for occasional furloughs during holidays and such. His family visited often. Eventually he lived with his wife and parents for stretches at a time. A report from Cambridge in February 1908 claimed that Clarkson "is looking well."⁵⁰ He was living with his family and often visited friends in Boston. He was even seen as a spectator at a ballgame that October. John was supposedly doing well at the end of the year. Ella visited Bay City and told reporters that her husband was improving and perhaps might leave McLean. That was perhaps wishful thinking. The truth is that the doctors saw little long-term hope for her husband.

In January 1909, Clarkson was living with his parents at their home on Wave Way Avenue in Winthrop, Massachusetts. He became ill with pneumonia and was readmitted to McLean. Both lungs were overtaken by the illness; Clarkson lapsed into a coma and died on February 4 at the age of 47. The death certificate listed the cause of death as lobar pneumonia of six days' duration. It also noted that Clarkson had suffered from a general paralysis for the past several years. John Clarkson was buried in the family plot at Cambridge Cemetery. He rests not far from Tim Keefe.

Unfounded rumors persist that Clarkson killed his wife. The fact is that after his death, she returned to Bay City and helped Arthur Clarkson in business. Bay City erected a ballfield soon after John's death and named it in his honor. In 1963 one of the top pitchers of the 19th century was finally inducted into the National Baseball Hall of Fame.

Too often reviewers have projected Clarkson's psychological problems at the end of his life back into his playing career. There may indeed have been some clues, but a lot has been read into little things, and too much has been interjected into the story long after the fact. Too many have taken liberties with supposed clues of mental instability during his playing career. There are no hints of significant mental difficulties in contemporary accounts before his entering a sanitarium, which, by the way, was more than a decade after his retirement from the game. Later claims that he was a loner, high-strung, moody, and depressed both on and off the mound were exaggerated in an effort to signify underlying troubles. Clarkson was calm and collected on the mound; he was noted as so time and again. He may have disliked being singled out for razzing at times but that is not abnormal. He may have needed coaxing at times but isn't baseball history littered with stories of catchers and managers giving pitchers pep talks? It's amazing how a pitcher can be so successful year in and year out, month-in and month-out and some claim he was still prone to "wilt" or "wither" on the mound.

Cap Anson made several comments about Clarkson's temperament at or near the end of the pitcher's life that some have used to trace his mental difficulties back as far as two decades before he actually was institutionalized. It's perhaps telling that these quotes don't show up in Anson's book *A Ball Player's Career*, which was published in 1900 before Clarkson had his breakdown. Anson chose to add these characterizations only after Clarkson's difficulties became known publicly. In the book, Anson talks about Clarkson needing encouragement throughout the game to keep him focused, but nowhere does he mention anything about the pitcher's fragile temperament.

It is clear, though, that Clarkson was a heavy drinker throughout his career. If it didn't start with the White Stockings, it certainly blossomed then. Quite a few of his teammates were heavy drinkers, including close friends George Gore, Billy Sunday, Jim McCormick, King Kelly, and Ned Williamson. There were also plenty of men to drink with on the Boston nine, Hoss Radbourn for one. Certainly whatever trials Clarkson had in his later life, he exacerbated them with two decades of alcohol abuse. Billy Sunday, who left baseball in part to escape the drinking influence, attributed Clarkson's health problems to smoking: "Cigarettes broke down his health. I have known him to smoke eight to ten boxes of them in a day. I used to room with John. The water would be stained with nicotine when he'd take a bath."⁵¹

NOTES

There is no relation between the author and Mrs. John Clarkson, the former Ella McKenna.

There is a persistent story that John Clarkson threw a lemon to the plate during one game to demonstrate to umpire Jack Kerins that it was too dark to continue play. The story suggests that Kerins called the pitch a strike, thus proving Clarkson's point. No date or even year is ever identified in the claim, suggesting that it has never been verified. Kerins was a substitute umpire for only one game in the National League, on September 6, 1888. At the time, Kerins was living in Indianapolis, his birthplace. The game he umpired pitted Pittsburgh against Indianapolis and didn't involve Clarkson. The story was introduced into lore by John McGraw at the time of the publication of his book *My Thirty Years in Baseball*. In an accompanying piece distributed by the Christy Walsh Syndicate in January 1923, McGraw claimed that the pitcher was "Clarkson, I think." In the story the catcher was Wilbert Robinson. While it's not impossible that those two were batterymates at some point during some postseason or preseason, it's more likely that the pitcher was merely misidentified 30 years later. If the lemon story in fact has merit and Kerins and Clarkson were participants, it surely would have taken place during an exhibition contest.

SOURCES

In addition to the sources cited in the Notes, the author also consulted numerous newspapers and databases, and the following publications:

Egan, James M. Jr. *Baseball on the Western Reserve: The Early*

Game in Cleveland and Northeast Ohio, Year by Year and Town by Town 1865-1900 (Jefferson, North Carolina: McFarland, 2008).

Fleitz, David L. *Cap Anson: The Grand Old Man of Baseball* (Jefferson, North Carolina: McFarland and Company, Inc., 2005).

Ivor-Campbell, Frederick, Robert L. Tiemann, and Mark Rucker, eds. *Baseball's First Stars* (Cleveland: The Society for American Baseball Research, 1996).

James, Bill, and Rob Neyer. *The Neyer/James Guide to Pitchers: An Historical Compendium of Pitching, Pitchers, and Pitches* (New York: Simon and Schuster, 2004).

Kusmierz, Marvin, "John Gibson Clarkson (1861-1909)," *Bay City Journal* website, September 2002.

Morris, Peter. *A Game of Inches: The Stories Behind the Innovations That Shaped Baseball, The Game on the Field* (Chicago: Ivan R. Dee, 2006).

Pearson, Daniel Merle. *Baseball in 1889: Players vs. Owners* (Wisconsin: Popular Press, 1993).

NOTES

1. "Providence-Worcester," *Inter-Ocean* (Chicago), May 6, 1882: 4.
2. "Troy 4, Worcester 0," *Chicago Tribune*, May 12, 1882: 6.
3. *St. Louis Post-Dispatch*, August 28, 1884: 8.
4. Elijah P. Brown, *The Real Billy Sunday: The Life and Work of Rev. William Ashley Sunday, D.D. The Baseball Evangelist* (Dayton, Ohio: Otterbein Press, 1914), 41.
5. "Base Ball Players Busy," *Brooklyn Daily Eagle*, November 25, 1888: 10.
6. "Notes and Comments," *Sporting Life*, October 21, 1885: 3.
7. "Sporting Odds and Ends," *Inter-Ocean*, July 22, 1891: 3.
8. John Clarkson, National Baseball Hall of Fame, baseballhall.org/hof/clarkson-john Date accessed January 4, 2017.
9. Jonathan Fraser Light. *Cultural Encyclopedia of Baseball* 2nd Ed. (Jefferson, North Carolina: McFarland, 2005), 198.
10. "Current Gossip of the Sporting World," *Harrisburg* (Pennsylvania) *Daily Independent*, February 9, 1909: 2.
11. "Clarkson, $10,000 Pitcher, Is Dead," *Chicago Tribune*, February 5, 1909: 10.
12. Harry Clay Palmer [Remlap], "From Chicago," *Sporting Life*, October 7, 1885: 5.
13. Adrian Constantine Anson, *A Ballplayer's Career: Being the Personal Experiences and Reminiscences of Adrian C. Anson* (Chicago: Era Pub Co, 1900), 130.
14. Harvey Frommer *Old Time Baseball: America's Pastime in the Gilded Age* (Lanham: Maryland: Taylor Trade Pub, 2005), 125.
15. "Notes and Comments," *Sporting Life*, August 5, 1885: 5.
16. "Notes and Comments," *Sporting Life*, July 14, 1886: 5.
17. Quoted in Fleitz, David L. *Ghosts in the Gallery at Cooperstown: Sixteen Little-Known Members of the Hall of Fame* (Jefferson, North Carolina: McFarland and Company, Inc., 2004), 112.
18. *Chicago Herald* story which ran in the *Freeport Journal-Standard* (Freeport, Illinois), October 14, 1887: 4.
19. "Doings on the Diamond," *Wilkes-Barre Sunday Morning Leader*, September 11, 1887: 6.
20. "Notes and Comments," *Sporting Life*, October 11, 1887: 3.
21. "Clarkson Dead Set Against Chicago," *Chicago Tribune*, December 10, 1887: 2.
22. "He is Ours," *Boston Globe*, April 4, 1888: 1.
23. Tim Murnane, "Conant After Omaha," *Boston Globe*, September 24, 1889: 5.
24. "Warring Baseballists," *Chicago Tribune*, November 12, 1889: 3.
25. Ibid.
26. "Nothing But a Name," *Evening Star* (Washington, D.C.), November 8, 1889: 7.
27. "Kelly in San Francisco," *Omaha Daily Bee*, December 4, 1889: 1.
28. "Chicago's Backers," *Sporting Life*, November 20, 1889: 5.
29. Quotation found in unidentifiable newspaper clipping.
30. Philip E. Shirley, "Alas, Poor Yorick!" *Sporting Life*, April 14, 1906: 9.
31. "Out-Door Sports," *Lawrence Daily Journal* (Lawrence, Kansas), February 12, 1890: 4.
32. "Triumvir of Traitors," *Saint Paul Globe*, (Minnesota) December 10, 1889: 5.
33. "Brotherhood Men Here," *Chicago Tribune*, January 12, 1890: 7.
34. "All In favor of Peace," *New York Times*, October 10, 1890: 3.
35. "Not a Run Scored," *Boston Globe*, May 7, 1892: 5.
36. "Bennett's Recovery Assured," *Boston Globe*, January 19, 1894:2; "Cut a Hot Pace," *Boston Globe*, February 20, 1894: 2.
37. Reed Browning, *Cy Young: A Baseball Life* (Amherst: University of Massachusetts Press, 2000), 29.
38. Ibid.
39. "Clarkson Will Join the Baltimores," *New York Times*, July 16, 1894: 8.
40. "Sporting News and Comment," *Washington Post*, July 16, 1894: 6.
41. "Base Ball Notes," *Boston Globe*, July 17, 1894: 2.
42. "Clarkson Would Not an Umpire Be," *Chicago Tribune*, June 15, 1897: 4.
43. Cited in the *Denver Post* article "May Still Be a Good One," March 17, 1904: 7.
44. "Base Ball Notes," *Washington Post*, May 12, 1905: 4.
45. "Needs A Rest," *Boston Globe*, May 7, 1905: 25.
46. "Clarkson's Passing," *Sporting Life*, February 13, 1909: 6.
47. Mike "King" Kelly, Michael J. Kelly, Gary Mitchem, and Mark Durr, *Play Ball: Stories of the Diamond Field and Other Historical Writings about the 19th Century Hall of Famer* (Jefferson, North Carolina: McFarland and Company, Inc., 2006), 62.
48. "John Clarkson Failing," *Boston Globe*, December 12, 1905: 7.
49. "Alas, Poor Yorick!" *Sporting Life*, April 14, 1906: 9.
50. "National League News," *Sporting Life*, February 29, 1908: 3.
51. Homer A. Rodeheaver, *Twenty Years with Billy Sunday* (Nashville, Tennessee: Cokesbury Press, 1936), 50. Cited in "A Short History of Baseball and Tobacco," in Peter Carino, ed., *Baseball/ Literature/Culture: Essays 2004-2005* (Jefferson, North Carolina: McFarland, 2006), 128.

JIMMY COLLINS

BY CHARLIE BEVIS

The initial third baseman enshrined in the Baseball Hall of Fame, Jimmy Collins was an outstanding fielder and above-average hitter during his 14-year major-league career in the Deadball Era. As the first manager of the Boston franchise in the American League, Collins gained widespread acclaim when he led the team to consecutive pennants in 1903 and 1904 and victory in the inaugural 1903 World Series.

Collins was a businessman in a baseball uniform. In an interview with the *Buffalo Evening News* just a few weeks before his death, he gave writer Cy Kritzer an encyclopedic recall of his salary levels as a ballplayer, practically gloating about once earning $18,000 in one year, but yet, as Kritzer related, "he couldn't recall once during the interview the size of his batting average in any one season."[1] It wasn't just about acquiring money, though. Collins used his baseball income to develop a real-estate business by building multifamily rental housing, which provided his income after his playing days.

James Joseph Collins was born on January 16, 1870, in the village of Suspension Bridge in Niagara Falls, New York, the second of four children of Irish immigrants Anthony and Alice Collins. The family moved in 1872 to Buffalo, where Anthony Collins worked as a policeman for three decades, rising to the rank of captain.

The Collins family first lived in Buffalo's Irish-American neighborhoods in the southern section of the city. Irish-Americans were then the distinct minority in Buffalo, as they tussled for economic and political power with the dominant German-Americans on the East Side and the native-born Americans on the West Side. Collins's father tutored him well in how to work

Jimmy Collins, 1897.
(Library of Congress)

effectively within the three ethnic groups that controlled life in Buffalo.

After receiving his early education in Catholic parochial schools, Collins attended St. Joseph's College in downtown Buffalo. Despite the use of "college" in its name, St. Joseph's was more like an advanced high school, more akin to a prep school today; its successor is a high school, St. Joseph's Collegiate Institute. Collins graduated from St. Joseph's in 1888 with a diploma in commercial studies, acquiring a business education that he put to good use in the coming years. After graduation Collins worked as a clerk in the Black Rock station of the Delaware, Lackawanna and Western Railroad, just a few blocks north of his parents' new residence on Niagara Street in Buffalo's native-born-American-dominated West Side.

The teenaged Collins honed his baseball skills by playing for amateur teams organized by the social clubs in Buffalo. In 1889 and 1890 he played outfield for the Socials, a team made up of Irish-Americans, which helped maintain ties to his old neighborhood. For the 1891 and 1892 seasons, though, Collins played third base for the North Buffalo team, based in the Black Rock section of the city, where he made the difficult decision to forsake his Irish-American ties with the Socials and forge new relationships with the men in his new neighborhood. Soon baseball changed his perspective on life and Collins abandoned his father's traditional Irish-American value that deified job security.

When Jack Chapman, the manager of the Buffalo minor-league team in the Eastern League, offered Collins the chance to play professional baseball in May 1893, he left his secure job with the railroad for the uncertain life of a ballplayer and what he hoped would be greater income potential in the future. After starting out at third base, Collins played mostly shortstop for Buffalo during the 1893 season, finishing with a respectable .286 batting average, but an erratic .863 fielding average. When Chapman put Collins in the outfield for the 1894 season to minimize his fielding lapses, his batting average improved to .352 (among the league's top 10 hitters) and he led the league with 198 hits.

In November 1894 the Boston ballclub in the National League paid $500 to obtain the services of the 5-foot-9, 178-pound Collins from the Buffalo ballclub as insurance should one of its outfielders stage a lengthy holdout in salary negotiations. Jimmy Bannon did hold out, so Boston manager Frank Selee put Collins in right field on Opening Day. After 11 games, though, the right-handed hitting Collins was clearly a less than adequate substitute for Bannon, as he was hitting barely .200 and had committed four errors. When Boston finally signed Bannon, Collins was expendable, so he was sold to the last-place Louisville team for $500 in a transaction characterized as a "loan" that was really a recall option.

Collins played in the outfield during his first few games with Louisville, before manager John McCloskey suddenly pressed him into service at third base midway through the May 31 game at Baltimore after the Louisville third baseman had committed four errors. The legend of Collins's first major-league game at third base, like so many baseball legends, grew over time so that the more recent retellings – that he told Baltimore's Hugh Jennings, "Bunt 'em down to me and I'll show you something," and then threw out four bunters in a row – bear only a partial resemblance to the 1895 facts.[2] The bunters Collins threw out were fewer than four and occurred two months later (on July 28) after he became the regular third baseman in mid-June.

Since Collins flourished at third base in Louisville, Boston decided to exercise its recall option in August to have him temporarily fill in for an injured infielder. Collins, however, balked at returning to Boston. The brash Collins looked to leverage the situation and get a better deal from Boston, telling baseball writers that if he couldn't stay with Louisville he'd retire from baseball and return to his railroad job in Buffalo. Boston relented and instead recalled Collins for the 1896 season.

After Boston traded its incumbent third baseman, Billy Nash, to Philadelphia in November 1895 to make room for Collins in the Boston infield, Collins showed tremendous chutzpah in his salary negotiation with Arthur Soden, the principal owner of the Boston ballclub. The strong-willed Collins thought the Nash trade gave him a negotiation advantage, so he held out for a higher salary until April 1896. Since the National League was a monopoly and the reserve clause in the player contract bound the player to a team until released, ownership had the upper hand in player negotiations. Collins learned a hard lesson that he had little leverage over ownership and finally agreed to a salary of $1,800 for the 1896 season. After performing well as the Boston third baseman in 1896, Collins was offered a salary increase to $2,100 for the 1897 season. Collins, however, felt he should be paid the unofficial salary maximum of $2,400. As he had been the year before, he was a holdout, but he eventually accepted Soden's offer, which was four times the $500 average pay of an American worker.

Continual disagreements over money soured Collins's relationship with the Boston ballclub and led to his highly publicized departure from the National League after the 1900 season. Collins had an easier time negotiating back home in Buffalo and in Louisville, where there was a more ethnically tolerant climate among the Irish-Americans, German-Americans, and native-born populations than the environment he found in Boston. There was a fundamental difference in ethnic relations in Boston, where the Irish didn't just clash with the native-born Brahmin aristocracy over political, religious, and economic issues but indeed were the underbelly of society. In the 1890s the Brahmins (Soden included) controlled virtually everything in Boston, and considered Irish-Americans like Collins as simply pawns in their world.

In 1897 during Boston's drive to the National League pennant, Collins matured into a graceful fielder and a consistent line-drive hitter who could find the outfield gaps. He became a fan favorite among the changing nature of the spectators at the South End Grounds, dubbed the Royal Rooters, who were middle-class businessmen that were displacing the gentlemanly crowd as ballpark spectators. In late September, more than 100 Rooters traveled to Baltimore to watch the Boston team play a crucial series there, where Collins, with a leech on his face to heal a swollen eye, led the team to victory in the series. Three days later Boston clinched the pennant.

While Collins finished the 1897 season with a .346 batting average, his real value was his ability to produce runs. Although the RBI statistic hadn't yet been invented, a retrospective determination indicates that Collins would have had 132 RBIs in 1897, second among all National League batters. With the regular season over, Collins moved on to the supplemental income opportunities of the postseason. After the anticlimactic rematch with Baltimore in the Temple Cup series, Collins played for the All-America Baseball Team in a cross-country tour with the Baltimore team, where he observed Boston manager Frank Selee as businessman turn a profit on the itinerant baseball venture.

Collins quietly negotiated a contract with Soden to be paid the $2,400 salary maximum for the 1898 season. After three years as a National League ballplayer, the 28-year-old Collins had reached the pinnacle of his profession. However, because the National League owners lengthened the baseball season by 22 games to play 154 games in 1898, Collins felt duped by Soden, since Collins actually received just a minimal pay increase on a per-game basis.

Boston went on to capture a second consecutive National League pennant in 1898, as Collins compiled a .328 batting average, seventh highest in the league, and led the league with 15 home runs. Collins, who didn't take kindly to having a boss, responded well to manager Selee's approach to leave the ballplayers alone to play the game, a managerial style Collins adopted in the future. By now Collins had developed a stellar reputation as baseball's best fielding third baseman, because he had a quick eye, good dexterity, extensive range, and a strong throwing arm. Collins covered a lot of territory at third base, not just bunts and groundballs but also snagging many pop flies in foul territory and in short left field.

At a team testimonial in October 1898, Selee received a $2,500 check from Soden to share with the players, as a "gratuity" for winning the pennant. It must have galled Collins to receive a "tip" as if he were a Pullman Car porter. It was one more signal to Collins that his income potential was very limited by working for the Boston ballclub. Indeed, he had no success in securing a salary increase for the 1899 and 1900 seasons.

During the winter of 1900 Collins made an investment to take advantage of the explosive future growth he saw in the nascent South Buffalo neighborhood, to which Irish-Americans had begun moving from the inner city. Collins purchased a house lot and made plans to construct a rental unit on it. This was the first of many properties Collins purchased as he planned to live off the rental income as a self-employed person during his post-baseball years.

Collins doubtless saw no benefits in a future with the Boston National League ballclub. Given the penurious ways of the Boston owners, he was likely to face a decrease in salary as age took its inevitable toll on his playing skills. He had no chance to succeed Selee as manager and had been passed over as captain. One ray of hope for Collins to get an increased salary was the formation of the Players Protective Association in 1900. Collins was one of Boston's player representatives in the fledgling players union, but he was also looking out for his own interests. After attending two union meetings that summer and seeing no action

Jimmy Collins in 1899, Imperial Cabinet
photo courtesy of Robert Edward Auctions.

on the compensation front, Collins took matters into his own hands.

In March 1901 Collins became the manager, captain, and third baseman of the Boston team in the new American League, which Ban Johnson had established as a second major league to compete against the monopolistic National League. Collins justified jumping leagues at the time by saying, "I have given the National league people my best efforts for several years past and often asked them for more money, knowing that I was worth it, but until now they have turned a deaf ear to all my requests. ...I saw a chance to better myself and took it."[3]

Since Collins was motivated by money and displeased with his history of salary negotiations with the Boston Nationals, he was willing to take the risk of switching over to the Boston Americans. The possible failure of the new baseball enterprise and of being blackballed by the National League were not big risks to the 31-year-old Collins; he could simply fall back on his real-estate venture and connections in Buffalo. Collins was not only pleased that he could be a manager in the American League, but he was also intrigued that former ballplayers could also be part-owners, as exemplified by Connie Mack in Philadelphia.

Collins was handsomely compensated for jumping leagues. His contract with the Boston Americans called for a $3,500 annual salary for three years, nearly a 50 percent increase over his $2,400 salary for the 1900 season, with no reserve clause to restrict his freedom to negotiate with other teams thereafter. This $10,500 package was a key aspect of the deal for Collins, so that he'd have additional capital to invest in his real-estate business. Charles

Somers, the owner of the Boston club, agreed to add a personal guarantee concerning the salary payments, to negate Collins's risk if Soden took legal action to try to enforce the reserve clause that he thought legally bound Collins to the National League ballclub. Collins was also a nominal owner of the Boston Americans, being awarded a few shares of stock in the club.

The timing of Collins's switch to the American League was impeccable from a cultural perspective, coinciding with the rise of Irish-American political power in Boston. John Fitzgerald, a member of the Royal Rooters, was a congressman in Washington (and soon would be mayor of Boston), while Patrick Collins became the second Irish-American mayor of Boston. From 1902 to 1905, two men named Collins were the toast of Boston among the city's Irish-American citizens: the mayor and the baseball manager.

Collins piloted Boston to a second-place finish in 1901 and to third place in 1902, while producing .332 and .322 batting averages, respectively, as the team's third baseman. Because the Royal Rooters followed Collins and transferred their loyalty, the Americans outdrew their rival Nationals at the ballpark, becoming the more popular team in Boston. Collins seized the opportunity to renegotiate his contract each year, nearly doubling his 1901 salary by the beginning of the 1903 season.

Collins was successful as a baseball manager because he extended to the baseball diamond his general contracting skills from his house-building activities in Buffalo, where he had to depend on highly skilled, motivated workers to build well-constructed houses for him. In this fashion, Collins adopted the same philosophy that his former manager, Frank Selee, had used during his five years with the Boston Nationals: find good ballplayers and let them do their jobs without interference. Because he was able to motivate his players through his on-the-field activities as a third baseman, Collins was more of a leader "among" men than a leader "of" men. It was the "we're all in this together" attitude that enabled Collins to win two American League pennants as player-manager and lead his team to victory in the first modern-day World Series.

Offsetting these positive attributes as manager, Collins had several flaws, primarily that he stayed too long with veteran players and failed to adequately mix in younger players to prepare the team for the future. His problem with handling aging ballplayers was compounded by his weakness in talent evaluation, which stemmed in large part from his inability to build an effective network of contacts to acquire new talent in that pre-farm-system era.

While he continued to perform as a third baseman in Boston for five more seasons, Collins focused more on the leadership functions of his job and his activities to improve the stature of the American League and its president, Ban Johnson. Two developments in 1903 elevated Johnson's gratitude to Collins for making the new league a success: the peace conference between the two leagues in January 1903 and the first modern-day World Series in October 1903. Both developments solidified Johnson's stature as an influential baseball executive, and they enabled Collins to enjoy several more years of financial prosperity as well as indulgence by Johnson as his reward for jumping leagues in 1901.

When the Boston Americans secured the American League pennant in September 1903, new Boston owner Henry Killilea and Pittsburgh owner Barney Dreyfuss agreed to play an interleague postseason series in October. The agreement provided for the owners to share revenue from the games, but did not include a provision to pay the ballplayers. Since the contracts of the Boston players expired at the end of September, Killilea had foolishly entered into a contract to play a postseason series without securing the services of the Boston ballplayers. Collins exploited Killilea's poor business judgment to negotiate a great deal for the ballplayers. They got not just 75 percent of Boston's portion of the shared revenue under the World Series agreement, but 75 percent of *all* of Boston's net revenue from the series.[4]

After Boston lost three of the first four games of the best-of-nine-games postseason series, Collins led the team, accentuated by the Royal Rooters' incessant singing of the song "Tessie," in a comeback to win the next four games to become the World Series champion. In the eyes of the sporting public, the victory over the National League established the legitimacy of the American League. At the time Collins believed these postseason games to be merely meaningless exhibitions to generate additional income, based on his experience in 1897 with the Temple Cup series and the All-America tour. However, he took advantage of the national belief that the 1903 World Series determined baseball supremacy. Indeed, the vast majority of his wealth garnered from major-league baseball between 1904 and 1908 was the direct result of his national acclaim from Boston's 1903 World Series victory.

After the World Series victory, Collins negotiated a new three-year guaranteed contract with Killilea, who was seeking to retain his services so he could sell the ballclub, which paid Collins a $10,000 annual salary and had a profit-sharing arrangement equal to 10 percent of the club's profits over $25,000.[5] In April 1904 John I. Taylor, the son of *Boston Globe* publisher Charles Taylor, became the new owner of the Americans. Collins's clash with the inexperienced Taylor led to a testy feud that eventually led to Collins's departure from the Boston Americans three years later.

Collins led an aging Boston team to a second consecutive pennant in 1904, in a neck-and-neck battle with the New York Highlanders in the first installment of the longstanding rivalry between the Boston Red Sox and New York Yankees. Unlike 1903, when Boston participated in the first modern-day World Series, the 1904 championship had no similar culminating event, as the National League champion New York Giants refused to play such a series. Although Taylor honored the profit-sharing provision in Collins's contract, the $8,000 payment on top of Collins' $10,000 salary stuck in the owner's craw.

An article in the *Boston Globe Magazine* in January 1905 portrayed Collins as an up-and-coming businessman. Accompanying the article was a portrait of Collins dressed in a suit, white shirt with raised collar, cravat loosely knotted at the neck, with a watch fob draped across his breast. He looked like any well-to-do Boston Brahmin, not a baseball player. Three photos of his rental properties in Buffalo were also included. "For several winters he devoted his time to looking after the new buildings he was erecting," writer Tim Murnane wrote of Collins's dedication to this business venture, "and even now with several fine pieces of real estate, he has planned for two more new houses."6 Collins was now more businessman than ballplayer, which accelerated Taylor's dislike for him.

Collins also displayed more hubris during the 1905 baseball season, indicating that he believed the Boston Americans were *his* team, not Taylor's. Collins had run the baseball operation for three years without any direct oversight by the ballclub's absentee out-of-town owners before Taylor became the owner, and had successfully engineered a second straight pennant-winning season in 1904 without Taylor's assistance. This was the dark side to the soft-spoken but ambitious Collins.

Taylor took a more active role in the team for the 1905 season, seeking to remedy the team's injury and age issues, not by providing the resources to Collins so that he could fix the situation, but rather by fancying himself as a recruiter of baseball talent to rescue the team on his own. Not only did Taylor's signings do nothing to improve Boston's chances for victory on the baseball field (the team finished in fourth place), they intensified Collins's smoldering animosity for Taylor. While hidden from the public during the baseball season, the feud spilled onto the sports pages in December.

In a late December meeting in Buffalo with Ban Johnson, Collins leveraged his favorable relationship with the American League president to push him to honor the verbal commitment made back in 1901 for Collins to eventually obtain an ownership interest in an American League ballclub. Johnson then exiled Taylor to Europe for a six-month vacation. The timing was perfect to take advantage of John Fitzgerald's becoming mayor of Boston in January 1906 as the city's first American-born Irish Catholic mayor, to increase the influence of the Royal Rooters among Irish-Americans and take advantage of transportation improvements (train connections and automobiles) that would bring suburban spectators to the Americans' Huntington Avenue Grounds.

Although Johnson temporarily assumed the role of Boston owner, Collins was the acting president of the Boston ballclub. To reflect his new duties, Collins extended his guaranteed contract for two more years, through the 1908 season. At the same time, he made his first investment in a baseball organization when he became a one-third owner of the minor-league Worcester, Massachusetts, club in the New England League.

With Taylor out of the way for the 1906 season, Johnson gave Collins a tryout as president. However, just when he was on the cusp on moving from the baseball diamond to the executive suite, three factors combined to derail Collins from achieving his ultimate goal in professional baseball. First, Collins discovered that he just wasn't good at the job of being an executive, which changed his relationship with the ballplayers. Second, the early success of his investment in the Worcester ballclub nudged him to modify his goal to be a minor-league owner rather than one at the major-league level. Third, Collins, a 36-year-old bachelor, looked to marry his longtime girlfriend.

Over a two-year span following consecutive American League pennants, Collins plummeted from revered hero to reviled bum. A 20-game losing streak in May 1906 sank the team into last place, where it stayed for the remainder of the season. On July 1 Collins abruptly left the team and made his fateful decision to stop performing all his duties for the Boston ballclub to focus on his personal future. He made just two brief returns to the team during the summer. On August 29 the front-page headline in the *Boston Globe* told the whole story: "Capt. Jimmy Collins No Longer at Helm: Indefinitely Suspended by Boston American League Club." After Collins' several absences without leave, Johnson used the term "desertion" in the press announcement.

Collins's decision to desert the Boston Americans was a disaster. He struck out at buying into ownership in the Buffalo and Providence ballclubs of the Eastern League, believing the asking prices to be too inflated to justify the investment. By December Collins was negotiating to return to Boston as its third baseman for the 1907 season, since he had a guaranteed contract to play through 1908 with the Boston Americans. Because Taylor, now back from his extended European vacation, was legally obligated to pay Collins whether or not he played, he agreed to take Collins back as a player, but not as manager.

During the winter of 1907 Collins secretly married Sarah E. "Sadie" Murphy before he left for spring training. The news of the marriage wasn't reported in the Boston newspapers until after he was traded on June 7 to the Philadelphia Athletics, when old friend Connie Mack agreed to take on Collins and his contract to bolster the A's infield to make a run at the pennant. By August Philadelphia had climbed from fourth place to first place, but then lost the pennant after a late September swoon. In August 1908 Mack excused Collins from the team's season-ending road trip so he could try out some minor-leaguers at third base to replace Collins in 1909, which gave Collins some time to contemplate his next step in baseball and enjoy some family time with his newborn daughter, Agnes.

For the 1909 season, Collins had to settle for being player-manager of the Minneapolis Millers in the American Association. Early in the season, however, Collins suffered an off-the-field tragedy when 8-month-old Agnes died in Buffalo. Collins returned to Buffalo to console his distraught wife, who was now four months pregnant, and made arrangements for Sadie to return to Boston so that she could be with her family for the next five months of her pregnancy. In early July Minneapolis moved into first place, but faded down the stretch to a third-place finish. Just before the season ended, Collins received word from Boston that his daughter Kathlyn had been born.

Now living with his family in Boston, not Buffalo, Collins sought a position near Boston. In October 1909 he was hired as the manager of the Providence team in the Eastern League, which was owned by Charlie Lavis, a former Royal Rooter. He lasted only a season and a half at Providence, being fired in June 1911; his passive managerial style didn't produce results in an era dominated by intimidating managers. Collins's hope to become the majority owner of a minor-league ballclub was dashed, as prices continued to skyrocket at what turned out to be a height of popularity of minor-league baseball. In January 1912 his daughter Claire was born and Collins sold his one-third interest in the Worcester ballclub and left Organized Baseball.

Settling into Boston was challenging for Collins. During his days as a popular player-manager, he had managed to navigate the ethnic stratification between Boston's Brahmin society and its Irish-American underclass. Now, as just another former ballplayer, he couldn't establish himself in business in the city. Collins was even rebuffed when he tried to become the baseball coach at an Irish-American institution, Boston College. In 1914 the family moved back to Buffalo, where Collins purchased a house in South Buffalo near his rental properties and settled into a quiet life as a real-estate mogul.

In 1922 Collins was appointed president of the Buffalo Municipal Baseball Association, in the wake of a corruption scandal in the Buffalo Parks Department, which sent to prison the former head of the city's amateur baseball leagues. Collins served 22 consecutive terms as president of the muni-league, during which he helped to expand the opportunity for thousands of youngsters to develop their baseball talents in the city-run amateur leagues, a vast improvement over the former system of social-club leagues in which Collins had played that could accommodate only a few hundred players.

As muni-league president, Collins's reputation as a great major-league ballplayer spread among a new generation of baseball fans and sportswriters in western New York. John Meahl, the commissioner of the Buffalo Parks Department, was not bashful about profusely praising Collins as baseball's "greatest third baseman of all time."[7] As a result of Meahl's promotional efforts, Collins's baseball reputation soon spread beyond regional newspapers into national publications. During the 1920s his name regularly surfaced as the third baseman picked for the various all-time teams selected by famous ballplayers and sportswriters. When *The Sporting News* published a long biographical sketch of Collins in 1933, the baseball weekly reinvigorated the fabled 1895 story about his exceptional fielding of bunts by the infamous Baltimore Orioles.[8] Ten years later this legend became the centerpiece of a campaign to put Collins in the Baseball Hall of Fame.

Collins's real-estate business reached its zenith of prosperity during World War I, before suburban flight in the 1920s changed the neighborhood, real estate prices peaked in 1926, and then mortgage defaults during the Great Depression resulted in property foreclosures. In 1927 Collins sold his home; he and his wife began renting apartments, before they moved in with their oldest daughter, Kathlyn. By 1935 Collins's real-estate business had imploded and he earned an income as an employee in the Buffalo Parks Department. Despite his financial reversals, Collins continued to gracefully serve as an ambassador for Buffalo athletics in his unpaid role as muni-league president.

Collins died on March 6, 1943, in Buffalo and was buried in Holy Cross Cemetery. Two months before Collins passed away, *Buffalo Evening News* sports editor Bob Stedler began a press campaign to have Collins elected to the Baseball Hall of Fame at the next BBWAA election in January 1945. Even with a heavy dose of electioneering by Stedler, Collins polled only 49 percent of the vote, far short of the required 75 percent. But that spring the Old-Timers Committee unanimously selected Collins for enshrinement in the Hall of Fame.

Jimmy Collins's legacy in baseball is much more than his batting and fielding exploits during the Deadball Era. As a star player, first manager, and the public face of the nascent Boston Americans, Collins put the franchise, valued by *Forbes* in 2012 at $1 billion, on a solid foundation. He delivered two pennants in the team's first four years and victory in the 1903 World Series, and thus should be remembered as the patron saint of today's Red Sox Nation.

SOURCES

In addition to the sources cited in the Notes, the author also consulted:

O'Connell, Fred. "Boston's Baseball Idol: Jimmy Collins, Manager and Captain of the World's Champion Club." *Washington Post*, September 11, 1904.

Stedler, Bob. "Jimmy Collins, Buffalo's Baseball Immortal, Dies," *Buffalo Evening News*, March 6, 1943.

NOTES

1. Cy Kritzer, "Late Jimmy Collins, the 'King of Third Sackers,' Became Hot Corner Star by Ability to Handle Bunts," *The Sporting News*, March 11, 1943.

2. Charlie Bevis, *Jimmy Collins: A Baseball Biography* (Jefferson, North Carolina: McFarland, 2012), 33-35.

3. *Boston Globe,* March 10, 1901.

4. Bevis, *Jimmy Collins*, 113, 120-121.

5. Ibid., 7.

6. Tim Murnane, "His Winter Pastime Collecting Rents," *Boston Globe Magazine* section. January 15, 1905.

7. *Buffalo Express*, December 6, 1922.

8. "Daguerreotypes: James J. (Jimmy) Collins," *The Sporting News*, July 27, 1933.

FRANK CONNAUGHTON

BY JOANNE HULBERT

Frank Connaughton,
Kansas City Daily Journal, January 11, 1897.

There are many ways to leave a mark on baseball history. Home-run records, ERA, RBIs, AVG – records that can be bested at any time. There are other ways too, some subtle and serendipitous, intentional or accidental, fleeting moments of bravado and incidents that changed the course of baseball history culminating with names emblazoned on plaques in Cooperstown and elsewhere. And then, history holds the story of Frank Connaughton.

Frank Henry Connaughton, son of Lawrence and Ellen, was born on New Year's Day 1869 in Clinton, Massachusetts, son of an Irish immigrant farmer in a town that had been baseball-mad ever since the game grew out of the rampant ballgame culture of Worcester County. Even today, Clinton claims – arguably – that its baseball field holds the record for longest continuous use, since 1878,[1] in Massachusetts. And it is likely the place where Frank took his first at-bats.

The players found around the Worcester County hill towns were signed by minor-league teams throughout New England and beyond. Frank's reputation as a steady, competent catcher connected him to several prominent amateur teams, leading to his first professional contract, with Woonsocket in 1891. Pawtucket of the New England League was his next engagement, in 1892; he stayed with the team until it disbanded and subsequently finished the year in Lewiston, Maine.[2] He traveled farther in 1893 when he signed with the Savannah team of the Southern League, and while there he earned a reputation as a very solid, useful utility infielder on second and third base, as well as his primary position as catcher. He was a fast, reliable baserunner and batsman, considered at the time as one of the best all-around players produced by the New England League.[3]

In January 1894 Connaughton's reputation paid off when he signed with Boston's National League club. He had also been of interest to Washington and the Kansas City club (Western League), where James Manning, proprietor, manager, captain, and second baseman, paid him the ultimate complement: "[H]e is a fine thrower and never drinks."[4] But Boston was close to home, which allowed him frequent contact with his family. There was one question: Could Connaughton play without a glove?

The wearing of gloves by players was an issue in 1890s baseball. Only the catcher and the first baseman traditionally wore a glove, but Connaughton could be found at second, third, and shortstop as well as behind the plate, and he had become accustomed to that handy adornment no matter which position he happened to be playing.

Connaughton's first appearance as a major-league player occurred on May 28, 1894. Boston needed to replace Charlie Bennett, who had suffered a devastating injury the previous January. As catcher Connaughton received a positive report, scored three runs, and put out four in a game won by Boston against Washington, a game described as "very bad"[5] despite individual players including Connaughton, doing brilliant work. His time with Boston was short-lived. True to the nature of the utility player, Connaughton was sent to the New England League in June, first to Haverhill and then to Brockton. He returned to Boston in July, and played shortstop, a position new to him at the time. He played well enough to receive positive reports from the writers after the game. By August the reactions were mixed and despite having proved to be a fine utility player at any position he was assigned to, creeping criticism appeared. "Connaughton had too many Joe Quinn moments before throwing the ball to get a base runner," reported the *Boston Globe*.[6]

Connaughton, the quintessential utility player, appeared in just 46 games in 1894, but he made good use of the time while there – "just the man Boston needed this year, and has fitted nicely in the time of need."[7] He certainly did what he could. On August 21, 1894, he scored five runs, placing him in good company along with Ed Delahanty, Bill Dahlen, and Billy Hamilton.

As Boston hobbled to the end of the season, Connaughton's future was in doubt. Despite moments when his skill and contributions highlighted game reports, his future with the team was rumored to be at an end, another promising player cast aside while the club looked for more talent. Connaughton was a versatile player as he fit in comfortably around the infield and at the catcher position. At the postseason meetings of 1894, owners debated whether to prohibit players from wearing gloves on the diamond. This feature, it was reported, had been "overdone" by such players as Lave Cross of Philadelphia and Connaughton, who had used catcher's gloves while playing at third base and shortstop. They allowed for the fact that it would have been unwise to abolish gloves altogether, as their use had prevented many hand injuries and therefore saved clubs the added expense of having players languishing on the injury list.[8]

Connaughton claimed that he was not bound to the Boston club, that he was in essence a free agent before such was defined, as he claimed he had signed with the team on condition that the reserve clause be stricken out of his contract.[9] Therefore, he claimed, he could sign with anyone he wanted and go anywhere he pleased. He was ultimately given the opportunity, but not on his terms. Along with Fred Tenney and Jimmy Bannon, Connaughton was "put on hold for the present."[10] In February 1895 Beaneaters President Arthur Soden received several offers for those players' services, as some clubs were willing to stipulate that they would be returned to Boston at any time their services might be desired.[11] One month later, Connaughton was signed by Kansas City of the Western League and did not appear in a Boston uniform again until 1906.

While in Kansas City, Connaughton crossed basepaths with other New England players who were also biding their time in the Western League before returning to more familiar grounds. He spent most of his time at shortstop and met up with Marty Bergen, who was holding down the catcher's position. Bergen was from North Brookfield, not far from Connaughton's home in Clinton. When Bergen was signed by Boston for the 1896 season, Connaughton spoke about him in the highest terms, and said that Boston would find in him one of the best men ever behind the bat. Bergen, according to Connaughton, was "a magnificent thrower and often got the runner out when it seemed impossible.[12]

Connaughton's western exile was short-lived. The National League's New York club drafted him. Connaughton was still on Boston's reserve list and the club still claimed the right to recall him back to Boston.[13] But under the National Agreement, the rules governing the major and minor leagues, New York could draft Connaughton at a price of $1,000. Would Frank Connaughton be worth it, inquiring minds wanted to know.[14]

In 1894, when a member of the Boston team, Connaughton appeared at shortstop in 33 games while Herman Long was disabled. His fielding percentage was ranked better than that of Dahlen, Long, Shorty Fuller, Fred Pfeffer, and [Joseph D.] Sullivan. His batting average, currently reckoned at .345, was better than many others. Boston let him go to Kansas City, wrote the *New York Herald*, "because they had a superfluity of players, and that club never pays unnecessary salaries."[15] New York considered Connaughton after he had spent a year at Kansas City, became an improved player both at the bat and at shortstop, and they hoped he would provide insurance so that in 1896, the Giants would not be found in a "helpless condition" should accidents and injuries plague the starting players, as was the case during 1895.[16]

There were a few skeptics among the New York sportswriters. The *New York Herald* reported that Connaughton was "weak on fly balls and cannot play while facing the sun. If that be so he will find it hard work at the Polo Ground."[17]

But Giants manager Arthur Irwin, when assessing his team after spring training, was effusive in his praise, and said, "That man Connaughton is a wonder. At bat? Well, say, he'll lead the team in less than a month, and you know what that means. Frank is also a good base runner and plays left field like a veteran. He is a wonderful strength to the nine, can hit a high or low ball equally well and should be one of the batting wonders of the year."[18]

Never again would Frank Connaughton receive such glowing predictions of his potential worth as a player. He still needed to prove he could outperform both Shorty Fuller – who ultimately appeared in only 18 games in 1896 – and Fred Pfeffer – who played only four games with New York before returning to Chicago – two obstacles to the advancement of his reputation and career in professional baseball. And yet, he outlasted them, with 88 games to his credit.

Despite those 88 games with the New York Giants in 1896, Connaughton had no significant impact with the team nor was he mentioned very often in the sports pages. He would enter the halcyon halls of memorable utility players – quickly cast aside, shuffled around the leagues and easily forgotten. Frank Connaughton returned to Clinton, Massachusetts, and married Emma Bateman on November 24, 1896, a woman he had met in Boston. The young couple moved in with his parents at 49 Oak Street, seemed intent on settling down, away from baseball, to domestic tranquility and all that could promise.

Wedded bliss was interrupted by Kansas City calling for Connaughton's return in 1897, but he hesitated before agreeing to the contract for his return to the shortstop position. By the start of the season he finally agreed, packed up his glove, bat, and his wife, and signed the contract upon their arrival in Kansas City in April. Not all went well for Connaughton or for the Kansas City team. He was accused of miserable fielding and blamed for the loss of the June 14 game with Indianapolis that should have been an easy win, according to critics.[19] The *Kansas City Journal* reported that at the July 18, 1897, game Connaughton "was in the game with a vengeance. He covered a world of ground and batted with his old time vigor. Out of nine times up he got six hits, two of which called for three sacks."[20] The Kansas City Blues had only three players who had started the season who were still there on July 30 – Jock Menefee, Frank Blanford,[21] and Connaughton, who showed no signs of slowing down. Connaughton did what he could and answered the critics in an August game in which he made four of the eight hits for the team and accepted nine chances out of 10 in the field.[22]

By January 1898, Connaughton made the difficult decision to retire from professional baseball and declined the offer to return to Kansas City. Perhaps it was the frustration of years of shuffling from one team to another, often against his will, or the inability to land a permanent position preferably closer to Clinton, Massachusetts, or perhaps it was the birth of his daughter that influenced his decision.

Connaughton took up the family profession managing his father's saloon, but there is something about baseball that keeps a tenacious hold on former players like him. Throughout New England, there was a robust minor-league culture with numerous teams making up myriad leagues with opportunities that lured many players aspiring to a professional career, and were also a place for professionals on their way down toward retirement as a place to give it one more try to stay relevant in the game or to at least indulge those baseball instincts that are so slow to dissipate.

In March 1898, Charlie Ganzel organized a meeting in Worcester to form a baseball league to be known as the Central Massachusetts Association of Base Ball Clubs, and Connaughton attended, representing the interests of the town of Clinton. By the end of the month, negotiations came undone, and Connaughton withdrew Clinton from the Association. He then just as abruptly decided to return to the Kansas City Blues. By September, after a disagreement with manager Jimmy Manning, he left the team and returned to Clinton, leaving a cloud of controversy in his wake. Manning called Connaughton's departure "a French leave,"[23] and denied he had agreed to a bonus in addition to his stipulated salary if the season proved to be a successful one financially. Furthermore, he asserted that Connaughton had already been paid more money than was rightfully due him.[24] Manning dubbed Connaughton "the Defector" and threatened to impose a fine, complained that the team had paid for Connaughton's medical bills when he was sick, and also that traveling expenses from Massachusetts were covered by the team, more than Connaughton should have expected. And this is how Manning and the Kansas City team were treated by this ungrateful player? Well, if another team were to sign Connaughton, Jimmy Manning vowed, "I promise I would leave the baseball business at the end of this season for all time."[25]

Was it collusion? Perhaps, but there was no rule against punishing a player this way as owners and managers were the ultimate dictators of who played and who were excluded. A Milwaukee correspondent reported that Connie Mack was "also making efforts to secure Connaughton from Jimmie Manning, but so far he has not succeeded. Manning feels he ought to punish Connaughton's uncalled for desertion just when he was most needed."[26] The *Boston Herald* then reported that Connaughton had sent a letter to John McGraw, stating he wanted to come to Baltimore, promoted his fine fielding and batting skills, and could fill in well at second base. McGraw, who had a high opinion of Frank's baseball record, made an offer to Jimmy Manning but was told Connaughton was not for sale at any price.[27]

In 1899 McGraw dropped his effort to secure Connaughton, and the Kansas City Blues, with Jimmy Manning still holding down the manager position, did not do well with Frank Connaughton missing from the roster. And yet, when the Milwaukee club inquired about the availability of Connaughton, Jimmy Manning adamantly refused to negotiate. "Connaughton will play in Kansas City or not at all this year. I sent him a contract, and if he does not like the terms he can remain idle, as I have determined to make an example of a player of this kind. Last year he tried to throw the championship away from Kansas City by deserting me at a critical point and now he will have to suffer."[28]

Connaughton returned to Clinton, secured a good position with the Clinton baseball team, and played ball there every Saturday. Instead of searching for another opportunity with a major-league team, he took on the team's manager position and worked on strengthening a local team that was still playing games in late November of 1899.

Buffalo came calling for the 1900 season, but Connaughton declined, saying he could not leave his saloon business in Clinton for a place so far away as Buffalo and that nothing could induce him to sign a baseball contract.[29] Instead, he joined the Worcester club of the Eastern League – closer to home and not an interference with his business interests in Clinton.

Major-league teams used the minor leagues as repositories, a place to park useful utility players whom they could call on to temporarily supplement their rosters for one or two games, or to reserve them without having to pay the players' salaries while they languished, hoping and waiting for the call back up. Many of these players make up the multitude of baseball players who appear in the baseball archives with only a handful of games making up their entire professional career. Here was where Frank Connaughton spent his years after the New York Giants and the Kansas City Blues, hoping for just another chance to wear a major-league uniform. Worcester's 1900 season enjoyed a mixed-up roster of has-beens and bright prospects. There was pitcher Fred Klobedanz on his way down from a career with Boston; Joe Rickert, formerly of Pittsburgh and later of Boston; fellow Clintonian catcher Malachai Jeddidiah Kittridge; Homer "Doc" Smoot, biding his time until St. Louis came calling in 1902; and Kitty Bransfield, between major-league contracts with Boston and Pittsburgh. All were waiting to see what baseball fortunes might come their way. During the early twentieth century the Worcester team, known as the Farmers, Ponies, Lambs, or the Riddles, provided baseball in Worcester, a city that had once been home to the Brown Stockings, a National League franchise from 1880 to 1882. Here Frank Connaughton found a home, albeit for a brief time. He left the team at midseason with the accusation hanging over him that he played poorly in an attempt to be released.[30]

Connaughton continued to operate his saloon during the baseball season of 1901 and he was arrested in July 1901 for operating a beer team that sold liquor to the workers of the Metropolitan Water System while they were constructing the Wachusett Dam in Clinton. He had been warned several times and was finally charged with breaking the law by driving his beer team through the forbidden district. The case was continued. He was convicted on the charge. He appealed. He lost. In March 1902, he was denied a liquor license.

In 1901 and 1902, Connaughton played for the Leominster team known as the Has-Beens, and returned to the Worcester Lambs in August, where in a game on August 13, 1902, the *Worcester Daily Spy* reported: "Ezekiel Hezekiah Wrigley and Francis Connaughton of Clinton were the other front rank men in the posse of swatstick swingers that riddled the carcass of Thielman with thorns. The King of Clinton cracked the ball four times in five chances, tearing off two-base bumps on two occasions."[31] In 1903 he was back the Worcester Riddles, an Eastern League team that suffered financial problems and allegedly weak hometown interest, and was sold and transferred to Montreal in midseason. The Riddles roster was made up of former major league players and many others passing them on their way up. Fred Applegate, the three-fingered pitcher; Joe Delahanty, brother of Ed; Reddy Grey, brother of writer Zane Grey; and George Hemming – "Old Wax Figger," who had played for five National League clubs before his semi-retirement at Worcester. Connaughton, shortstop, was part of this baseball fraternity, full of riddles, with a confounding history of sales, transfers, and wins and losses that spun the heads and pens of Worcester sportswriters and fans alike.

The years after Worcester sent Connaughton along a baseball career path that returned him to Haverhill in 1904, Harrisburg, Pennsylvania. in 1905, and back to Haverhill and Lawrence in 1906. While in Haverhill, the major leagues came calling again when the Boston Nationals needed a utilityman during the last month of the season to replace Al Bridwell, who had suffered a knee injury. He finished the season in "such good style, says he intends to be in the game next season and is eligible to sign with any club."[32] Once again Connaughton expressed his intent to exercise his freedom of choice and gave a firm nudge against the the reserve clause. The 1907 season found him instead in Lynn, Massachusetts, and in 1908 he returned to Lawrence and also coached the Tufts College baseball team. He returned to Haverhill again in 1909. He was found managing the Waterbury, Connecticut, team in 1910, and subsequently in Brockton in 1911. In 1912, while with the New Bedford team, Connaughton was credited with discovering Rabbit Maranville and launching him on his legendary major-league career.

By 1914, it seemed as though Connaughton had finally sworn off baseball. He was arrested in Clinton for hunting without a license near the Wachusett Reservoir, a charge he intended to appeal to a higher court. In 1915 he felt the call of the game still haunting him and seriously considered accepting a management position with a minor-league club "if the right sort of offer presented itself."[33] No one came calling.

Frank and his wife, Emma, settled into a new occupation in Boston by operating rooming houses at 48 Union Park and 159 West Newton Street in Boston's South End. The 1930 census showed Frank living at Union Park, and Emma living around the corner on West Newton Street. Emma died in 1936 and her obituary mentioned that she was "the wife of Frank H. Connaughton, the latter a member of the Boston National League Club in the 80's."[sic][34] Frank died on December 2, 1942, at Boston City Hospital after being struck by an automobile. The remainder of his obituary in the *Boston Globe* recounted Connaughton's discovery of Rabbit Maranville while Frank was playing second base for New Bedford. The obituary also mentioned how he imparted all the tricks he had learned with Boston, Kansas City, and other teams, and how the young New England Leaguer proved an apt pupil, and that he was so good, Connaughton urged the Boston Nationals to buy his release. Rabbit made good from the start and the Clinton King was elated.

NOTES

1. "Guinness Recognizes History of Fuller Field," *Worcester Telegram* October 5, 2007: 1.
2. "A Clever Short Stop," *Evansville Courier and Press*, July 19, 1895: 5.
3. "Boston's New Ball Players," *Boston Herald*, January 21, 1894: 22.
4. "Manning's Team," *St. Louis Republic*, January 23, 1894.
5. "Glaring Errors," *Boston Globe*. May 29, 1894: 7.
6. "Echoes of the Game," *Boston Globe*, August 4, 1894: 2.
7. Baseball Notes," *Evansville Courier and Press*, October 14, 1894: 10.
8. "Changes in the Rules," *St. Louis Republic*. December 18, 1894: 5.
9. Baseball Notes," *Cleveland Plain Dealer*, October 17, 1894: 3.
10. "Offers for Beaneaters," *Cleveland Plain Dealer*, February 15 1895: 3.
11. Ibid.
12. "Chat with Two Herald Callers," *Boston Herald*, October 20, 1895: 34.
13. "Baseball News and Gossip," *New York Herald*, October 10, 1895: 10.
14. "The Giants' Latest Acquisition," *New York Herald*, November 4, 1895: 9.
15. Ibid.
16. Ibid.
17. "Notes and Comments," *New York Herald*, January 31, 1896: 7.
18. O.P. Caylor, "New Yorks Are Home Again," *New York Herald*, April 2, 1896:7.
19. "Friend's Ill Luck," *Kansas City Star*, June 15, 1897: 3.
20. " Monday Morning Baseball Gossip," *Kansas City Journal*, July 19, 1897: 5.
21. According to the original article from the *Boston Herald* of August 30, 1897, he was "Frank," while Baseball-Reference states "Fred."
22. "Base Hits," *Boston Herald*, August 30, 1897: 5.
23. "He Quit the Team," *Kansas City Journal*, September 10, 1898: 5.
24. Ibid.
25. Ibid.
26. "Discipline for Connaughton," *St. Paul Globe*, March 26, 1899: 10.
27. "Thrown Balls," *Boston Herald*, March 10, 1899: 7.
28. "Discipline for Connaughton," *St. Paul Globe*, March 26, 1899: 10.
29. "Baseball Talk," *Buffalo Evening News*, March 20, 1900: 6.
30. "Cocking Main Near Clinton." *Worcester Daily Spy*. May 12, 1902: 4.
31. "Sebring Led Lambs in Batting Carnival," *Worcester Daily Spy*, August 14, 1902: 3.
32. "Doings in the World of Sport," *San Francisco Chronicle*, December 2, 1906: 27.
33. "Connaughton Feels Call of the Game," *Boston Herald*, January 16, 1915: 6.
34. "Mrs. E. Connaughton," *Boston Herald*, June 2, 1936: 15. The obituary writer mistakenly placed Frank's Beaneaters career a decade earlier than the 1890s.

COZY DOLAN[1]
(PATRICK HENRY DOLAN)
BY BOB LEMOINE

Cozy Dolan.
(Courtesy of John Thorn).

Harry "Cozy" Dolan was from Cambridge, Massachusetts, just across the Charles River from Boston and in the shadow of MIT and Harvard. The promising left-handed pitcher got the opportunity to pitch for the Boston Beaneaters in 1895-1896. He struggled on the mound, and then bounced around the minors before returning to the majors four years later as an outfielder. His nickname of "Cozy," according to the *Brooklyn Daily Eagle*, came from "his habit of taking things comfortably under all circumstances."[2] Dolan played for four teams in six seasons before returning to Boston. Contracting typhoid fever in 1907 while in spring training, Dolan died at the age of 34

Patrick Henry Dolan was born on December 4, 1872, to John and Ellen Dolan. John was listed as a furniture repairer in the 1880 US census. Patrick had an older brother, John, and a younger sister, Margaret. He began playing baseball in 1890 as a shortstop with the semipro Baldwins of Cambridge, made up of 18-year-olds.[3] In 1892 with the amateur Cambridge Reds Dolan played some third base but also "developed into a wonderfully clever pitcher" in the words of the *Cambridge Tribune*.[4] He played the following season with the semipro team in Weymouth, Massachusetts, making about $12 per game.[5] "Dolan was very successful last year," the *Boston Post* wrote of his 1893 season. "He is left-handed, with good curves and great speed."[6]

Dolan started with the Fall River (Massachusetts) club in the spring of 1894,[7] but early in the season[8] was transferred to

Portland, Maine, of the New England League. The *Worcester Daily Spy* commented, "Dolan, Portland's little left-handed pitcher, seemed to puzzle the Lewiston (Maine) batsmen" in a Lewiston 10-6 win on May 7.[9] Dolan received some major-league attention when the champion Boston Beaneaters paid a visit to Portland on May 11 for an exhibition game. Boston won easily, 9-3, but Dolan had limited the Beaneaters to one or two hits (depending on the account) and one run. "[Tommy] Tucker's coaching caught the crowd," the *Boston Herald* wrote, "and next to Dolan he was the hero of the hour."[10] "Dolan's work was fine and the crowd was very appreciative," wrote the *Boston Journal*, "especially in the second inning, when the youngster struck out Tucker, who had been keeping up a steady stream of comment and humor."[11] Dolan also shined with the bat, going 3-for-4 with a run scored and a steal of third. "Dolan was a puzzle" to Pawtucket batters in a 13-6 win on May 22.[12]

The Portland club struggled financially and the ownership gave players the option of taking a 20 percent pay cut or being released. Dolan at first refused the cut, but later changed his mind and stayed with the team.[13] But as the team limped along, Dolan drew more attention. Manager Mike Garrity "thinks he comes very near to having one of the best pitchers in New England "in young Dolan, the Cambridge boy, who is doing such clever work for the club," the *Herald* wrote. "Dolan has been very effective and has shut out both the Lewistons and Fall Rivers this year."[14] Portland did disband in early September, and Dolan finished the season at New Bedford.[15] His first start for New Bedford was September 6 when he "had splendid control of the ball and was very effective" in a 7-3 win at Fall River, according to the *Boston Journal*.[16] Dolan also briefly played for the Springfield (Massachusetts) club during the season. The unofficial statistics published in the *Boston Globe* listed Dolan as having a 20-15 record with a 1.86 ERA in 35 starts with 85 strikeouts, and 16 appearances without allowing a run.[17]

The Beaneaters signed Dolan in mid-September.[18] Boston catcher Jack Ryan, who was loaned to New Bedford for a few games, said Dolan had the best "drop ball" he had ever seen[19] and recommended him to manager Frank Selee. The long-armed lefty had some advantages in his windup. "His preliminary swing is high over his head and he gets a great drop to his curves and straight balls," wrote the *Globe*. "He watched the bases very closely, and fields his position in beautiful style."[20] Dolan "has great speed and is very accurate," wrote the *Boston Journal*, and "has a deceptive delivery, having a great command of the ball for a south paw twirler. He has a puzzling drop and a great change of pace."[21]

In a spring-training game in Charleston, South Carolina, Dolan held the Washington Senators to three hits in five innings.[22] He caught on with the Beaneaters and made his regular-season debut on April 26, 1895, in New York. Dolan was taking tickets at the gate, but was told to get dressed and get into the game.[23] He entered in the fifth inning with Boston trailing 9-0. "His work was superb from the start," the *Globe* commented, "and of the six hits made off him in the last four innings three were scratches."[24] Boston lost 14-3. Dolan was later "farmed out" to Portland when Boston went on a Western trip.

Dolan returned shortly, and in his first appearance before a Boston crowd, he scattered nine hits and defeated Pittsburgh 3-1 as old Cambridge friends cheered him on.[25] "[F]ull of ginger, both in fielding his position and while dancing them around the rubber," Dolan shut out St. Louis on three hits in a 6-0 win on September 9.[26] On September 18, with Baltimore in a pennant fight with Cleveland, the Orioles met Boston, which had fallen out of the race. Dolan shut out the eventual champions 8-0, allowing only three hits.[27] He finished the season 11-7 with a 4.27 ERA and three shutouts in 25 games.

In 1896 Dolan pitched in only six games, going 1-4 with a 4.83 ERA, and at the end of July was "farmed out" to Providence of the Eastern League.[28] J.C. Morse wrote in *Sporting Life* that Dolan was "useless about the whole of the season on account of overexertion with an unseasoned arm."[29] Still, Providence won the Eastern League pennant with Dolan and fellow Boston pitcher Ted Lewis contributing.

Released by Boston just before Opening Day in 1897,[30] Dolan was upset because major-league clubs had already finalized their rosters.[31] He bounced around the minor-league level for the rest of the season. He played briefly for the Reading (Pennsylvania) club, then was laid off without pay, and appealed to the National Board and National League President Nick Young. "He asks President Young to assist him in securing his release, as he is deprived of a means of livelihood."[32] Dolan then pitched exhibition games for Philadelphia of the Atlantic League, as management saw no reason to put him into championship games.[33] He also pitched for Millville of the South New Jersey League, and then went back to Springfield.

Dolan "is anxious to get a place in the [Springfield] outfield," wrote *Sporting Life* just before the 1898 season. "He says he has had enough of pitching, and would like to quit the box for good, and is of the opinion that he could hold his own."[34] He became the regular right fielder and team captain.[35] Dolan had two solid seasons at the plate with Springfield in 1897-98, batting .283 and .309, while going 9-4 and 9-8 on the mound. *Sporting Life* also noted that Dolan kept busy in the winter of 1898-99 by running Roughan's bowling alley in the Charlestown neighborhood of Boston.[36]

Dolan wanted to be solely an outfielder.[37] His wish was granted and he had a successful 1899 season in which he batted .295 for Springfield and pitched in only two games. He had a two-home-run game at Worcester on Labor Day.[38] He also played a few games for New Haven of the Connecticut League.

As 1900 dawned, Dolan found himself in Springfield once again. He was improving as an outfielder and at the plate. He batted .333 in 126 games, with 86 runs scored and 7 triples. His season included a 4-for-5 performance at Toronto in September.[39] His perseverance paid off as after four seasons he got another crack at the major leagues. In late September, the Chicago National League club, then referred to as the Orphans instead of the Cubs because of Cap Anson's departure, purchased Dolan's contract for the remainder of the season. He was given $250 down with $250 more in incentives, mainly if the management felt he was satisfactory. "Dolan has been regarded all through the season as the Springfield player most likely to graduate into the big league," wrote the *Springfield Republican*. "He has improved in all departments of the game. He is the most scientific hitter on the team and probably in the Eastern League. He has improved in judging fly balls and his throwing in from right-field could hardly be improved upon."⁴⁰ The *Chicago Tribune* said Dolan was "regarded as the best player in that [Eastern] league from the standpoint of brains. He is a tricky batter and baserunner, gets down to first base fast, beating out bunts, and is a fair batter, ranking over the .300 mark."⁴¹ Unofficially, Dolan finished fourth in hitting in the Eastern League with a .329 average.⁴²

Dolan debuted for Chicago on September 29, batting second and going 1-for-5 as the right fielder in a 10-7 loss to St. Louis.⁴³ In his 13 games in the outfield for the sixth-place club, Dolan made four errors, three of them in one game on October 8 in a 13-4 loss. He batted .271 for his brief stint.

The *Boston Herald* on March 5 noted that Dolan was coming back to the city for the 1901 season.⁴⁴ He would not be playing for the Beaneaters, but for the new Boston team in the newly formed American League. Teams were making a mad dash to either snatch talent or hold onto their own. The *Chicago Tribune* reported that Dolan was already under contract for the Orphans and "is the first player to actually jump a contract in the present war."⁴⁵ A few days later, however, Dolan acknowledged that he had not signed with Boston but "put his name to an agreement to sign" as a negotiating tactic. Chicago had still not paid him the back salary due from his Springfield contract, so Dolan was ready to jump leagues and return to Boston.⁴⁶

With his contract settled, Dolan batted cleanup for Chicago on Opening Day and stroked three hits in the team's 8-7 win over St. Louis.⁴⁷ He had two triples in a game on May 3 against Pittsburgh,⁴⁸ and batting leaders published in the *Chicago Inter-Ocean* on May 5 showed Dolan batting .308 in nine games (12-for-39).⁴⁹ But he still struggled in the outfield, in one instance muffing a fly ball that led to an inside-the-park home run on June 4.⁵⁰ The *Tribune* said Dolan "made his usual error" in a June 10 game.⁵¹

Dolan's time in Chicago grew short as his 10 errors in 82 chances gave him a ticket out of town, but the Brooklyn Superbas were quick to sign him.⁵² Brooklyn had won the pennant in 1900 and was hanging around the .500 mark in 1901. Dolan played much better in the outfield for Brooklyn, having a .967 fielding percentage compared with his .878 for Chicago. He batted .261 in 66 games. He even demanded a higher salary at the end of the season. "Dolan made his request with the easy grace and nonchalance which have earned him his sobriquet of 'Cosey,'" wrote the *Brooklyn Daily Eagle*, "and he upheld that nickname by expressing no surprise whatever when the management refused to accede to his demands."⁵³

At spring training in 1902, Dolan was asked to fill in at first base due to an injury. "Dolan is looking splendidly," the *Eagle* wrote. "He is not unacquainted with first base, as he played the position in Springfield two years ago."⁵⁴ Dolan became the regular center fielder and had a strong season, leading the National League in games played (141), at-bats (592), and plate appearances (640). He was fourth in singles (142) of his 166 total hits. He also had 24 stolen bases to go along with his .280 batting average and .324 on-base percentage. He patrolled the outside, mostly in center, with Wee Willie Keeler in right. Brooklyn was a good second-place team but was still 27½ games behind dominating Pittsburgh.

On the morning of August 24, 1902, Dolan married Frances M. Duffy of Chicago. The Superbas had a doubleheader that day and Dolan, perhaps inspired by wedding bliss, went 4-for-5 in their 7-2 win in the first game, a repeat of his performance at Pittsburgh the previous day. "The bride witnessed the two games from the grandstand and accompanied her husband to Pittsburgh,"⁵⁵ where the Superbas had a makeup game.

Dolan moved to Chicago, since Frances was there, and signed a contract to play for the American League's Chicago White Sox, owned by Charles Comiskey.⁵⁶ A reserve, he played 19 games at first base and four games in the outfield for the White Sox before being traded with second baseman Tom Daly to the Cincinnati Reds for second baseman George Magoon. "When we can get two such good men as Daly and Dolan in exchange for one, I believe in making the deal," said Reds President Garry Herrmann.⁵⁷ "I will be willing to be a party to the trade," Dolan said by "the long-distanced telephone" with Cincinnati manager Joe Kelley, "although I regret to leave Chicago for business reasons. If the terms I submitted to the Cincinnati Club are acceptable, there will be more money for me, and I hope to be given a regular position on the Reds."⁵⁸ Dolan was "prospering on the West Side

"COZY" DOLAN,
Boston National Right Fielder, Who Died in Louisville Last Night.

[Chicago] as a restaurateur," at 600 Madison, according to the *Cincinnati Enquirer*.[59]

Dolan's batting average jumped 28 points with the Reds (.288) and he found a home as the regular right fielder. The Palace of the Fans had a 450-foot right field in which the blazing sun caused problems. "Well, I got along pretty well with the sun out there," Dolan told the *Cincinnati Enquirer*. "But I'm ready to turn the field over to anybody else who wants it and take another."[60]

Before the 1904 season began, the Dolans celebrated the birth of their only child, John.[61] "I have been quite busy during the past week," Dolan wrote to the *Cincinnati Enquirer*, "and you know baseball was off my mind." He went on to jokingly write, "Both mother and son are doing fine, and I expect to send him to work next week. I am getting just a bit anxious for starting time to come."[62] Frances would bring young John to home games, "the youngest rooter in the Palace of the Fans," Ren Mulford Jr. wrote in *Sporting Life*.[63] Dolan batted .284 for Cincinnati with a .342 on-base percentage in 129 games, mostly in the outfield but with 24 games at first base. His six home runs ranked him third in the league.

Dolan's 1905 season fell apart in Cincinnati. Batting .234 in 22 games, he was released on June 2. Dolan blamed the Cincinnati sportswriters for his release and on that very night met *Cincinnati Enquirer* reporter Jack Ryder at the Grand Central Depot. Dolan attacked Ryder, who gave Dolan "an artistic trimming." Because this occurred on railroad property, there was an immediate warrant for Dolan's arrest. He paid his fine, and a few days later signed with the Beaneaters. He was going back to where his career began a decade earlier.[64] This was a much different Boston team, on its way to a horrible 51-103 season.

Dolan took over as Boston's starting right fielder, playing in 112 games and batting .275. A highlight of his season was getting five hits and seven RBIs in a doubleheader sweep of Brooklyn on September 18.[65] But he had an awful .931 fielding percentage for the season. He also took the mound for the first time in nine seasons at the major-league level, pitching four innings of relief. In 1906, Dolan was again Boston's starting right fielder. His batting average dropped to .248 but he played in all of Boston's 152 games, and pitched two games in relief. While statistics weren't compiled on a game-by-game basis, the *Globe* wrote that Dolan batted near .400 for the second half of the season.[66] His fielding percentage as an outfielder didn't improve, falling to .928, the worst in the league among outfielders. Off the field, Dolan moved to Wellesley, Massachusetts, where he opened a hotel and restaurant.[67]

In 1907 the Beaneaters were renamed the Doves, after new owner George Dovey. At the 1907 spring training in West Baden Springs, Indiana, Dolan developed severe chills. On March 16 he was hospitalized at the Norton Infirmary in Louisville with malarial fever. The team traveled on to Georgia. Dolan didn't respond to treatment, and then it was discovered that he had developed typhoid fever.[68] His wife, Frances, and his sister came to be with him, as did close friend Frank Chance of the Chicago Cubs. Dolan died in Louisville on March 29. Frances complained that he was being treated by surgeons instead of physicians and that her husband died of neglect.[69]

Boston canceled its remaining spring games and came home for the funeral. The Boston baseball community was already in a state of shock and grief; 24 hours earlier manager Chick Stahl of the Boston Americans had committed suicide.[70]

Beaneaters President George Dovey addressed the team, saying "the duty that devolves on us is to pay the last sad token of respect and esteem to our departed comrade."[71] "He was not only a model ball player," manager Fred Tenney said, "but a most lovable companion. It was a genuine pleasure to have such a one as he in the club, and I feel every one of us has sustained a deep personal loss in his death."[72] Tenney and other Boston players served as pallbearers, and the streets near the Dolans' home on Prospect Street in Somerville, outside Boston, "were crowded with people, most of them lovers of the national game to whom the face of 'Cozy' Dolan was long familiar," wrote the *Cambridge Sentinel*. As the procession moved toward St. Joseph Church in Somerville "the crowd stood with reverently bared heads, and tears dimmed many an eye."[73] Dolan was buried at St. Paul's cemetery in nearby Arlington.

NOTES

1. Not to be confused with another Cozy Dolan in baseball history. Albert James Dolan was also referred to as Cozy. He played from 1909 to 1922.
2. "A Billet Doux From 'Cozy'; Harry Dolan We Should Say," *Brooklyn Daily Eagle*, February 17, 1902: 17.
3. "Base-Ball," *Cambridge Tribune*, May 17, 1890: 8, May 17, 1890: 8.
4. "Sporting. Base-Ball," *Cambridge Tribune*, May 20, 1893: 1.
5. Ibid.
6. "They Want a Pitcher," *Boston Post*, January 21, 1894: 13.
7. "Fall River Nine for '94," *Boston Herald*, March 12, 1894: 8.
8. "New England League," *Boston Post*, August 28, 1894: 3; "Dolan Signed," *Boston Globe*, October 28, 1894: 14.
9. "Lewiston 10, Portland 6," *Worcester* (Massachusetts) *Daily Spy*, May 8, 1894: 7.
10. "The Bostons Visit Portland," *Boston Herald*, May 12, 1894: 2.
11. "Only Three Times," *Boston Journal*, May 12, 1894: 3.
12. "Portland 13, Pawtucket 6," *Worcester Daily Spy*, May 23, 1894: 7.
13. "Portland Players Cut Down," *Boston Herald*, August 3, 1894: 2.
14. *Boston Herald*, August 13, 1894: 8.
15. "Base Ball Notes," *Boston Journal*, September 5, 1894: 3.
16. "New Bedford 7; Fall River 3," *Boston Journal*, September 7, 1894: 3.
17. "Wins and Losses," *Boston Globe*, September 17, 1894: 2; "Fielding," *Boston Globe*, September 23, 1894: 15; "Dolan Signed."
18. "Put Outs," *Boston Herald*, September 15, 1894: 2.
19. "Dolan Signed."
20. Ibid.
21. "Will Pitch for Boston," *Boston Journal*, October 29, 1894: 3.
22. "Wins First Game," *Boston Globe*, March 22, 1895: 2.

23. Players took turns working the gate at the ballpark.
24. "Wipe Out Wilson," *Boston Globe*, April 27, 1895: 1.
25. "Good for Dolan," *Boston Globe*, June 8, 1995: 4.
26. "Due to Dolan," *Boston Globe*, September 10, 1895: 4.
27. "Dolan's Glory," *Boston Journal*, September 19, 1895: 3.
28. "Diamond Dust," *Springfield Republican*, July 29, 1896: 3.
29. J.C. Morse, "Hub Happenings," *Sporting Life*, March 13, 1897: 9.
30. "Dolan Released," *Boston Daily Advertiser*, April 20, 1897: 5.
31. "News and Comment," *Sporting Life*, May 1, 1897: 5.
32. "News and Comment," *Sporting Life*, June 26, 1897: 5.
33. Francis C. Richter, "Phillies' Per Cent," *Sporting Life*, July 24, 1897: 6.
34. "Hub Happenings," *Sporting Life*, February 5, 1898: 6.
35. "Another Change in the Team," *Springfield Republican*, August 19, 1898: 9.
36. Ibid.; The *Boston Post* frequently mentioned the Roughans and other bowling teams of the area, such as in the March 22, 1897, edition.
37. Jacob C. Morse, "Hub Happenings," *Sporting Life*, March 18, 1899: 9.
38. Jacob C. Morse, "Boston Blue," *Sporting Life*, September 16, 1899: 10.
39. "Items of Interest," *Sporting Life*, September 22, 1900: 7.
40. "Chicago Buys Harry Dolan," *Springfield Republican*, September 18, 1900: 12.
41. *Chicago Tribune*, September 27, 1900: 8.
42. "Eastern League Averages," *Washington Evening Star*, November 29, 1900: 10; other statistics list his average as .333.
43. "Cardinals Win One," *Chicago Tribune*, September 30, 1900: 11.
44. "Parent to Play Here," *Boston Herald*, March 5, 1901: 8.
45. "Is Dolan a Contract Jumper?" *Chicago Tribune*, March 6, 1901: 9.
46. "Case of Harry Dolan," *Boston Journal*, March 9, 1901: 7.
47. "Orphans Begin With Victory," *Chicago Tribune*, April 20, 1901: 4.
48. "Loftus' Men Lose Again," *Chicago Tribune*, May 4, 1901: 4.
49. "National League Records for April," *Chicago Inter-Ocean*, May 5, 1901: 10.
50. "Orphans Win at Last," *Chicago Tribune*, June 5, 1901: 8.
51. "Spider and Fly Game," *Chicago Tribune*, June 11, 1901: 8.
52. "Remnants Arrive in Boston," *Chicago Tribune*, June 19, 1901: 6.
53. "Two California Players Added to the Brooklyn Roster," *Brooklyn Daily Eagle*, October 15, 1901: 13.
54. "Keeler Gives Players First Hard Practice," *Brooklyn Daily Eagle*, April 3, 1902: 13.
55. "Dolan Married," *Brooklyn Daily Eagle*, August 25, 1902: 2; "Win and Lose With Chicago Orphans," *Brooklyn Daily Eagle*, August 25, 1902: 11; "Harry Dolan Dead," *Cambridge Chronicle*, March 30, 1907: 4.
56. "Cozy Dolan a White Stocking," *Chicago Tribune*, January 13, 1903: 8.
57. "Trade Daly and Dolan for Magoon," *Inter-Ocean*, June 12, 1903: 13.
58. "Dolan and Daly," *Cincinnati Enquirer*, June 13, 1903: 3.
59. "Disarmed," *Cincinnati Enquirer*, December 20, 1903: 10; "National League News," *Sporting Life*, October 17, 1903: 3.
60. "Disarmed."
61. "Harry Dolan's First Born," *Cincinnati Enquirer*, January 30, 1904: 3.
62. "'Cozy' Dolan's New Role," *Cincinnati Enquirer*, February 4, 1904: 4.
63. Ren Mulford Jr., "East's Big Guns," *Sporting Life*, July 4, 1904: 5.
64. "Harry Dolan Released," *Louisville Courier-Journal*, June 3, 1905: 9; "Arrested," *Cincinnati Enquirer*, June 4, 1905: 10; "Dolan Joins Boston and Street Comes as Loan," *Boston Journal*, June 6, 1905: 8; "Warrant for 'Cosy' Dolan," *Courier-Journal*, June 4, 1905: 20.
65. "Superbas Beaten in Both Games of Doubleheader," *Boston Journal*, September 19, 1905: 4.
66. "News of All Branches of Sport," *Boston Globe*, March 30, 1907: 6.
67. "Harry Dolan Dead."
68. "'Cozy' Dolan in Hospital," *Boston Globe*, March 18, 1907: 7; "Dolan's Death Follows Close Upon the Suicide of Captain Chick Stahl," *Boston Journal*, Match 30, 1907: 5.
69. "Outfielder Harry Dolan," *Sporting Life*, April 6, 1907: 5; "National League News," *Sporting Life*, September 7, 1907: 9.
70. The *Boston Journal* published an article that would be of interest for fans of the paranormal. While Dolan had been delirious and incoherent in his last days, he spent his last hours telling those at his bedside that Stahl was dead. The family and friends at Dolan's bedside had no knowledge of Stahl's suicide, and no one was there to tell this news to Dolan. They thought this was simply part of his delirium and did not realize until a day later that Stahl had indeed died. See "Talked in Delirium About the Death of Stahl," *Boston Journal*, April 6, 1907: 1.
71. "Team Starts for Home," *Boston Globe*, March 30, 1907: 6.
72. Ibid.
73. "Harry Dolan Buried," *Cambridge Sentinel*, April 6, 1907: 5.

HUGH DUFFY

BY BILL LAMB

For decades, Hugh Duffy was a franchise fixture in Boston, a small white-haired man who over the years had served the Red Sox as manager, scout, occasional first base coach and batting instructor, tryout camp supervisor, and all-around good will ambassador. To the younger Sox faithful, Duffy seemed to have been a club functionary forever. So when his obituary was published in October 1954, many were surprised to learn that Hugh Duffy had once been baseball's premier batsman. Some 60 years before his death, the little gent had set a single-season major-league batting record by posting a .440 batting average.[1] Although extraordinary, the mark was far from a fluke. During a 17-season playing career, Duffy had been an outstanding hitter, attaining yet another unique batting distinction: to this day, he is the only player in history to compile a .300+ career batting average in four different major-league circuits: National League (.326), Players League (.320), American Association (.336), and American League (.302). On top of that, he had also been a standout defensive outfielder, an accomplished base stealer, and an innovative baseball strategist. It was no wonder, then, that the likeness of Hugh Duffy came to be inscribed on a plaque at Cooperstown.

Like a host of other late-nineteenth century ballplayers, Hugh Duffy was the son of Irish Catholic immigrants. But his biography is shrouded by the non-existence of an official birth record,[2] and by Duffy's lifelong evasiveness about his age. As best as can be ascertained, Duffy was born on November 26, 1866, the oldest child of laborer Michael Duffy (c.1842-1902) and his wife, the former Margaret Egan (c.1838-1883). According to Hugh himself, he was born in Cranston, Rhode Island.[3] But most everything published during his lifetime put his birthplace

Hugh Duffy.
(McGreevy Collection, Boston Public Library)

as nearby River Point, one of the Pawtuxet Valley mill villages that now make up the town of West Warwick.4 Whichever the case, many years later one inquisitive journalist wrote, "At the church rectory of St. Anne's Church, Cranston, we uncovered the official fact that Hugh Duffy, son of Michael and Margaret, was baptized on November 28, 1866."5

A recent Duffy biographer portrays the family as close, affectionate, and religiously devout – but small-sized for an Irish Catholic clan of the times.6 National and Rhode Island censuses place younger daughters (Anna, born 1870, and Catherine, born 1874) in the household, and mention of nieces and nephews in Hugh's last will and testament suggests that at least one of them may have survived childhood, their non-appearance in subsequent census listings for the Duffy family notwithstanding.7 Little else is known is about his siblings. During Hugh's formative years, the family resided in River Point where Hugh was schooled locally. To census-takers in 1940, Duffy maintained that he had gotten through the second year of high school. But contemporaneous records place him in the work force by the time he had reached his early teens.8 Indeed, he may have begun working in the River Point mills by age 9.9 Although short in stature (5-foot-7), long hours of heavy lifting endowed young Hugh with broad shoulders and a powerful upper torso, physical attributes that he soon put to good use on the diamond.

Duffy's life in baseball followed a familiar trajectory. As a youth, he played in local sandlots, then graduated to action in faster venues. Originally a catcher, the righty-throwing and batting Duffy began playing semipro ball in 1884 with the River Point entry in the Rhode Island State Association, drawing down $5/week.10 The following year, he relocated to Jewett City in eastern Connecticut, working in a linen dye factory and playing for the company team for a reported $30/week, plus room and board.11 In 1886, Duffy worked and played for a company club in Winsted, Connecticut, his recompense rising to $50/week, again plus room and board.12 Late that year, Duffy entered the professional ranks, signing with the Hartford Dark Blues of the Eastern League. He debuted in an October 1 game against Newark. Starting at catcher and then moving to second base, he earned the distinction of being the only Dark Blues player not to commit a fielding miscue in a 24-8 drubbing. In all, Duffy saw action in seven Hartford contests, batting .278 (5-for-18) for a middling 40-48 club.

Duffy spent the 1887 season on tour of Massachusetts, as the clubs that he joined twice folded financially. He began the season with the Springfield Horsemen of the Eastern League, and was batting .350 in 17 games when the circuit abandoned play in late May. Duffy then moved on to the New England League, which he positively tore up. In 27 games with the unfortunately-named Salem Fairies, he batted a torrid .461. When Salem disbanded in early July, Duffy transferred to another New England League team, the Lowell Lions (or Magicians). With new acquisition Duffy leading the way (.475 BA, with 30 extra-base hits and 71 runs scored in 49 games), Lowell (71-33) surged from middle of the pack to the NEL pennant.

Duffy's scintillating stick-work had been closely observed by major-league agents, and soon a bidding war broke out for his services. A shrewd, hard-nosed businessman even as a 21-year-old, Hugh leveraged competitive interest in him into a handsome $2,000 contract (with a $500 advance) from the National League Chicago White Stockings. For the remainder of his long life, Duffy relished telling the story of his introduction to Cap Anson, the brusque, oversized field leader of the White Stockings. Taking his first look at the small, boyish-looking Duffy, Anson exclaimed, "What are you doing here? We already have a batboy." Anson was dumbfounded when informed that Duffy was the high-priced outfield recruit signed by the club's eastern agent, Boston sportswriter Tim Murnane, and walked away shaking his head.13 When the 1888 season got started, Anson ignored Duffy and left him on the bench for more than two months. But the departure of flycatcher Billy Sunday and the anemic bat of replacement Marty Sullivan finally prompted Anson to afford Duffy an audition for the right-field spot, and Hugh did not miss his chance.

On June 23, 1888, Hugh Duffy made his field leader take notice, going 2-for-6 at the plate and playing flawless defense in his major-league debut, a 12-1 thrashing of Pittsburgh. Pleased with the game's outcome, Anson left Duffy in the lineup, and the rookie continued to produce. By season's end, he was the club's everyday right fielder. In 71 games, Duffy batted .282, with 21 extra-base hits and 13 stolen bases. He had also played sound defense, recording 19 assists from his post in the pasture. And against the odds, Anson had taken a liking to him.

Cap Anson was a man firmly imbued with nineteenth-century prejudices, and Duffy's size, religion, and ethnic background were all to be counted against him in Anson's book. But Anson prized Duffy's talent, intelligence, sobriety, and seriousness, and, innate biases notwithstanding, invested time and interest in his young charge's development. Hugh responded with a standout sophomore campaign. Playing in all 136 of Chicago's games, Duffy batted .312, with 40 extra-base hits and 89 RBIs, and placed among league leaders in runs scored (144, second-best), base-hits (182, third), home runs (12, fifth), and stolen bases (52, seventh). But all was not well, for either the Chicago club or the National League. With a tight-fisted salary classification system recently imposed atop the hated reserve clause, players were in full rebellion by season's end. Soon thereafter, Duffy, like virtually all frontline NL players, bolted to the newly formed Players League for the 1890 season. And much to the chagrin of captain Anson and club boss Al Spalding, he joined the new circuit's local entry, the Chicago Pirates.

In his third major-league campaign, now 23-year-old Hugh Duffy became a bona fide star. In a circuit stocked with the game's very best players, Hugh stood out. He posted a .320 batting average and ranked among Players League leaders in virtually every offensive category. He topped the league in base hits (191) and runs scored (161); ranked second in extra-base hits (59) and total bases (280); third in stolen bases (78); fourth in doubles (36); and fifth in triples (16). Hugh also shined defensively, particularly with the arm. His 34 assists ranked second-most among PL outfielders.

The collapse of the Players League after its inaugural season left most players scrambling for new berths and at the mercy of their erstwhile employers. But not High Duffy. Pursuant to the reserve system, the rights to Duffy had reverted to the National League and its Chicago club. But Hugh, estranged from field leader Anson and with a hearty dislike of club boss Al Spalding, had no intention of returning to the Chicago fold. Instead, he ignored his reversion designation and negotiated a handsome new contract with the Boston Beaneaters, which Spalding promptly blocked, as was his prerogative with any National League team that attempted to secure Duffy without his assent. This turn of events prompted Duffy to approach the American Association which, having vitiated the National Agreement the previous year, was not obliged to recognize the player-reversion claims of National League clubs. In due course, Hugh signed with the AA's Boston Reds and, in the process, commenced an association with Hub City baseball that would span more than 60 years.

The year 1891 was a watershed for Hugh Duffy. Professionally, he had another banner year, batting .336 with an AA-leading 110 RBIs. He stole a career-high 85 bases, and achieved top-10 rankings in batting average, on-base percentage, slugging, runs scored, base-hits, steals, and home runs. Perhaps more important, the Reds, led by field captain Duffy, captured the Association flag, its outstanding 93-42 (.689) record eight and one-half games better than a St. Louis Browns club that featured an outfielder soon to loom large in Boston baseball and the life of Hugh Duffy: Tommy McCarthy. But with the AA now in its death throes, no postseason inter-league championship was conducted. Rather, for the second consecutive year, a major-league circuit folded, leaving Duffy, McCarthy, and their ballplaying brethren to fend for themselves.

For the moment, however, baseball was not Duffy's primary concern. Hugh had matrimony on his mind. In October 1891, he married the "Belle of the Pawtuxet Valley," the fetching (but consumptive) Katherine Gilland.[14] The happy couple immediately took up residence in River Point, but their union was brief and childless, constantly beset by concern over Katie's fragile health.

Another close but relatively brief union was formed late that year when both Hugh Duffy and Tommy McCarthy signed contracts to play the upcoming season for the National League Boston Beaneaters. The two men, soon to be dubbed the "Heavenly Twins," were hardly look-alikes. But they had much in common. Each was New England-born (although McCarthy was the older by three years) from the same ethnic/religious stock, short but sturdily-built men who batted and threw righty, were swift afoot, and played the same position, although Hugh would soon move over to center to leave right field to Mac. More important, they were both aggressive players endowed with keen baseball intelligence. In their several seasons together, Dufy and McCarthy would devise, refine, or popularize much of the game strategy of the 1890s. They also became lifelong friends and, for a time, partners in a popular Boston bowling alley/saloon.

Statistically, their initial season together was not impressive. While team-best, Hugh's .301 batting average was well beneath his previous marks, while McCarthy's .242 was below both National League (.250) and Boston (.245) norms for the 1892 season. Yet following each other in the batting order, they triggered a hit-and-run/stolen base-oriented offense that placed the Boston club second in runs scored (655) during that offensively-challenged season. And in the outfield the two developed defensive tactics (like close-in positioning and the trapped-ball double play) that ably supported the exceptional pitching (Kid Nichols, 35-16; Jack Stivetts, 35-16, and Harry Staley, 22-10) that paced the Beaneaters to a pennant-winning 102-48 record in the first season of play for the expanded 12-team National League. With Duffy (.462) and McCarthy (.381) showing the way, Boston then swept the Cleveland Spiders in six games (including one tie) of postseason pseudo-championship play.[15]

The following two years saw the Heavenly Twins at the pinnacle of their prowess. With the pitching distance elongated to the present 60 feet, six inches and the pitcher's box eliminated, league bats revived. In 1893, McCarthy posted a robust .346 batting average, but league-leading honors went to Duffy (.363), who also placed high in runs scored (147, second place) and base-hits (203, third). Boston (86-43), meanwhile, cruised to another National League pennant, but with the ill-received postseason competition of the previous year discontinued, most Boston players thereafter busied themselves playing lucrative exhibition matches. Hugh, however, passed on these paydays to attend to his seriously ailing wife. It was hoped that a winter stay on the warmer West Coast might restore Katie's health, but the sojourn proved to no avail. With the 1894 baseball season fast approaching, the couple began their return home to River Point, but Katie did not make it. Removed from the train and hospitalized in Blackstone, Massachusetts, Katherine Gilland Duffy died on March 31, 1894, age 25.[16]

A grief-stricken Hugh Duffy got an understandably late start on the 1894 campaign. But by the time that it was over, he had completed a season like few others in baseball history. Amidst a league-wide explosion in offense, Duffy batted .440, still the all-time major-league single-season batting average high. He also led the league in base-hits (237), doubles (51), home runs (18), extra-base hits (85), total bases (374), and OPS (1.196), while finishing second in RBIs (145), fourth in runs scored (160), and ninth in stolen bases (48).[17] Hugh also played excellent outfield defense, combining with McCarthy (who batted .349) to register 55 assists. But the Beaneaters' excellent 83-49 record was good for no better than third place that season. And the brief heyday of the Heavenly Twins was now approaching its end.

Although not comparable to his previous year's numbers, Duffy posted fine stats in 1895. He batted .353, with 9 home runs and 100 RBIs. He also scored 112 runs and stole 42 bases. But Tommy McCarthy, overweight, nagged by minor injuries, and flashing the bad attitude that would soon hasten his departure from the majors, was slipping (.290 in only 117 games). Mac's business partnership with Duffy was also headed toward dissolution. At the close of the 1895 season, Hugh had remarried, and new wife Nora Moore was lace-curtain Irish, not the type to humor saloon-keeping by her husband for long.[18] Within months, the Duffy-McCarthy business association was terminated.[19] The two, however, remained friends.[20]

McCarthy was sold to Brooklyn, and 1896 (.249 in 104 games) was his final major-league season. Boston and Hugh Duffy were also having difficulties. That season, the Beaneaters (74-57) fell to fourth place, while the name Duffy (.300/5/113) no longer appeared among NL batting leaders. But both rebounded strongly in 1897, with Boston (93-39) capturing the pennant and Hugh leading the NL in homers (11), while batting .340, with 129 RBIs and 130 runs scored. Boston dropped the postseason Temple Cup match in five games to the runner-up Baltimore Orioles. But that was no fault of Duffy's. He hit .524 (11-for-21) with seven runs batted in, a fitting capstone for what was his last truly outstanding major-league season.

The next two seasons Hugh posted respectable, if not Duffy-esque, numbers: (.298/8/108 in 1898; .279/5/102 the next year). His playing days, however, were clearly waning. A .304 batting average in an injury-plagued (only 55 games played) 1900 campaign brought his nine-season run as a Boston Beaneater to a close. The next year, he was among the multitude of NL stalwarts jumping to Ban Johnson's new major-league circuit, the American League. With Connie Mack and Tommy McCarthy, Duffy also served on the committee that located suitable playing grounds in Boston for the new league.[21]

Engaged as player-manager of the Milwaukee Brewers, Duffy was saddled with a hapless roster, one whose ablest player was its now-34-year-old skipper. Appearing in 79 contests, Hugh batted .302 for the last-place (48-89) Brewers. The league thereupon removed the franchise to St. Louis, but Duffy declined to accompany it. Instead, the "Duffmeier" (as admiring fans in the heavily-German city had nicknamed him) chose to remain in Milwaukee and take charge of the city's entry in the Western League, the Milwaukee Creams.

A close third (80-54 in 1902) and pennant-winning (83-49 in 1903) finishes by Milwaukee prompted the National League Philadelphia Phillies to make Hugh Duffy their manager for the 1904 season. His two-year stint with the Creams had demonstrated that, given first-rate playing talent to work with, Duffy could manage a ball club capably. But the mediocre Phillies were another matter. Hugh began his tenure by suffering through a 52-100 last-place season, but thereafter guided Philadelphia to consecutive, albeit non-pennant contending, first-division finishes. But that did not satisfy club brass, and Duffy was discharged at the close of the 1906 season, having compiled a cumulative 206-251 (.429) record at the Phillies' helm. Because he had made a handful of game appearances while the Philadelphia manager, Duffy's entry in the record book was slightly enlarged. But now his major-league playing days were behind him. In 1,737 games spread over 17 seasons, Hugh had batted .326, with 1,302 RBIs and 1,554 runs scored. His 550 extra-base hits included 106 home runs, seventh-highest for a player primarily from the 1893-1919 era. Duffy also stole 574 bases, and was an excellent outfield defender. On top of all that, he had joined with Tommy McCarthy to devise innovative game tactics, both offensively and in the field. In all, Hugh Duffy had enjoyed an exceptional playing career.

Although an intelligent, ambitious man, Duffy rarely pursued outside business opportunities. He was a baseball lifer, and the remainder of his long life was devoted to service to the game. In 1907, Dufy purchased an ownership interest in the Providence Greys of the Eastern League, and managed the club to three close-but-no-pennant finishes. He then sold out his Providence holdings to return to the majors, assuming the post of manager of the Chicago White Sox. Sox owner Charles Comiskey and Hugh were old friends – the two had been teammates on the 1890 Chicago Pirates – but Comiskey proved an impatient boss. Despite some modest improvement in club performance under Duffy's direction, Comiskey fired him at the close of the 1911 season. The termination embittered Duffy, and the friendship never recovered.[22]

In 1912, Duffy returned to Milwaukee to manage the Brewers of the Class-AA American Association for a single (78-85) season, his only non-winning campaign as a minor-league manager. He then went home to New England, where, as earlier in Providence, he became an owner-manager in Portland, a newly incorporated Maine franchise in the lower Class-B New England League. The club, named the "Duffs" in Hugh's honor, advanced steadily in league standings until it captured the pennant in 1915. When league president Tim Murnane, another longtime Duffy friend and his original pro baseball patron, reorganized the circuit into a new Eastern League, Duffy and his Portland club followed. The (81-37) Duffs finished the 1916 season a close second to the New Loudon (Connecticut) Planters. But following Murnane's unexpected death in February 1917, Duffy sold the Portland club. Shortly thereafter, he was engaged to fill a baseball coach vacancy at Harvard. But between the exigencies of World War I and differences with the university administration, his time with the Crimson was brief and unsuccessful.[23]

Duffy returned to the professional ranks in 1920, guiding the Toronto Maple Leafs of the Class-AA International League to a fine (108-46) season. He then got the call from the Boston Red Sox, becoming manager of a once dominant American League club then being divested of playing talent by its cash-strapped owner, Harry Frazee. The Red Sox were a non-contending (75-79) fifth-place finisher for Duffy in 1921. The next year, the club went a dismal 61-93 (.396) and plummeted to the cellar, beginning a decades-long occupation of the AL nether regions. Duffy was relieved of duty at season's end, and did not manage again.[24] But he remained on hand in Boston for years, serving the Red Sox as a scout, front office functionary, spring training instructor, occasional first base and batting coach, tryout camp supervisor, and good-will ambassador. In time, Hugh made the acquaintance of Sox all-time great Ted Williams. Although men of different generations and temperament, the two shared a mutual love of the art of batting and enjoyed a cordial relationship.[25]

In April 1945, baseball bestowed its highest accolade on Hugh Duffy: induction into the Hall of Fame via selection by the Veterans Committee.[26] That same month, he presided over the dubious tryout that the Red Sox accorded Negro Leagues star Jackie Robinson.[27]

In March 1953, an 86-year-old Duffy, still mentally alert and physically fit, reported to spring training, spending hours in uniform instructing Sox recruits on the fine points of batting.[28] But the end was now coming into view. Later that year, Nora Duffy died, bringing to a close a happy but childless 57-year marriage. Hugh, suffering from prostate cancer, succumbed to a fatal coronary at his home in the Brighton section of Boston on October 19, 1954.[29] He was 87. The High Requiem Mass at St. Columbkille Church in Brighton was packed with religious dignitaries, baseball big shots, and common fans alike. Internment alongside Nora at nearby Old Calvary [now Mt. Calvary] Cemetery in Roslindale followed. The long, productive lifetime of Hugh Duffy, a 19th-century star who had devoted himself to the game, was now a memory.

SOURCES

Sources for the biographical information provided herein include the Hugh Duffy file maintained at the Giamatti Research Center, National Baseball Hall of Fame and Museum, Cooperstown, New York; Donald J. Hubbard's *The Heavenly Twins of Boston Baseball: A Dual Biography of Hugh Duffy and Tommy McCarthy* (Jefferson, North Carolina: McFarland, 2008); *The Encyclopedia of Minor League Baseball,* Lloyd Johnson and Miles Wolff, eds. (Durham, North Carolina: Baseball America, Inc., 2d ed., 1997);and various of the newspaper articles cited below. Stats have been taken from Baseball-Reference and Retrosheet.

NOTES

1 This does not encompass the walks-as-base-hits inflated batting averages of 1887. Hugh Duffy's .440 batting average is one of various baseball records revised long after the fact. In 1894 and for some 90 years thereafter, the Duffy batting mark was recorded as .438.

2 As verified in a July 29, 1982 letter from Angelo B. Mendillo, III, Acting State Registrar of Vital Statistics, Rhode Island Department of Health, to John J. Duffy of Portsmouth, New Hampshire, contained in the Hugh Duffy file at the Giamatti Research Center.

3 See Henry McKenna, "Duffy's Birthyear Finally Uncovered," *Boston Herald,* September 3, 1944: "I was born in Cranston, Rhode Island and that's all I'll tell you," said Duffy. "I think a person's age is their private, personal business."

4 See e.g., *Boston Herald,* September 24, 1893; *Dallas Morning News,* October 5, 1897; *Trenton Evening Times,* June 20, 1919, and *Portland Oregonian,* March 20, 1938. The Duffy file at the Giamatti Research Center includes an undated circa 1889 profile of Hugh Duffy from the *NewYork Clipper,* file materials compiled by Hall of Fame statistician Ernie Lanigan, and the profile of Duffy published in the *Biographical Dictionary of American Sports,* all of which cite River Point as the Duffy birthplace. The Hugh Duffy profile in *Baseball's First Stars,* Frederick Ivor-Campbell, Robert L. Tiemann, and Mark Rucker, eds. (Cleveland: SABR, 1996), 54, provides conflicting birthplaces. The bio data box states that it was Cranston, the bio text by Rich Eldred names River Point.

5 See again, McKenna, *Boston Herald,* September 3, 1944. But given that River Point did not have its own Roman Catholic Church in 1866, many infants born into the faith would have been baptized in Cranston. Duffy's biographer takes no position on the point, observing only that Hugh's adolescence was spent living in River Point. See Donald J. Hubbard, *The Heavenly Twins of Boston Baseball: A Dual Biography of Hugh Duffy and Tommy McCarthy* (Jefferson, North Carolina: McFarland, 2008), 17.

6 Hubbard, 17.

7 Then again, such relations, like Hugh F. Moore, the nephew who completed a posthumous Hall of Fame questionnaire for Hugh Duffy in 1958, may have descended from the family of Hugh's second wife, Nora Moore Duffy. But biographer Hubbard states that the Duffy will makes express mention of blood relations, which implies that the child-less Hugh had siblings who later had children of their own.

8 The 1880 US Census describes the occupation of 13-year-old Hugh Duffy as "works in print shop." Later-day newspaper accounts of Duffy's youth maintained that he was operating a wrangle machine at a clothing factory in River Point as a 14-year-old. See e.g., the *Miami Herald* and *Belleville* (Illinois) *News Democrat,* June 19, 1911.

9 Per the 1875 Rhode Island census.

10 Hubbard, 18.

11 According to the Hugh Duffy obituary published in the *New York Times,* October 20, 1954.

12 Hubbard, 18.

13 As related by George C. Carens in "Every Day Thanksgiving for 86-Year-Old Duffy," *Boston Traveler,* November 25, 1952, and elsewhere.

14 Hubbard, 88.

15 Now without a rival circuit to provide competition, the "Big League" manufactured a postseason world championship series between the winner of the first half of the 1892 season (Boston) and the team with the best won-lost in the second half (Cleveland).

16 As reported in the *Boston Herald,* April 1, 1894. Massachusetts health records posited the cause of death as phthisis, a synonym for consumption or tuberculosis.

17 Until modern baseball record revisionists credited Sam Thompson with the six additional RBIs that brought his 1894 season total to 147, Duffy was considered a Triple Crown winner.

18 Think "Bringing Up Father," the long-running newspaper cartoon featuring the henpecked nouveau riche Irish-American Jiggs and his social-climbing wife Maggie. For more on Nora Duffy's influence on her husband's lifestyle, see Hubbard, 130-136.

19 Sans Duffy, McCarthy continued to operate the saloon for another 17 years. See Hubbard, 119-124.

20 At McCarthy's funeral in 1922, Hugh Duffy served as a pallbearer.

21 The site was promptly transformed into the Huntington Avenue Grounds, home of the Boston Americans (later Red Sox). For more detail, see Bill Nowlin, *Red Sox Threads: Odds and Ends from Red Sox History* (Boston: Rounder Books, 2008), 364-368.

22 For more on the Comiskey-Duffy relationship, see Hubbard, 177-178. Inheriting a middle-of-the-pack team, Duffy went 155-159 (.495) in his two seasons as White Sox manager.

23 Like many colleges, Harvard cancelled the baseball season upon United States entry into World War I in April 1917. The program resumed the following year, but Duffy had little success at Harvard. His teams went 8-21 (.276) in two seasons, and in 1920 he was replaced as baseball coach by former major leaguer Jack Slattery. From 1928 to 1930, Duffy was a more popular with school administrators but not overly successful baseball coach at Boston College.

24 In eight seasons as a major-league manager, Duffy had led his teams to a cumulative 535-671 (.444) record. He had more success in the minors, going 879-531 (.623) in 11 seasons, with pennant-winners in the Western League (Milwaukee, 1903) and the New England League (Portland, 1915).

25 In a late-life interview, Duffy related that just as Cap Anson had mentored him as a young batsman, he had passed along hitting tips to the young Williams. See George C. Carens, "Everyday Thanksgiving Day to 86-Year-Old Duffy," *Boston Traveler,* November 25, 1952.

26 A year later, old friend and teammate Tommy McCarthy was named a Hall of Famer by the Veterans Committee, as well. McCarthy's modest credentials have made him a controversial Cooperstown resident.

27 Sam Jethroe (who became National League Rookie of the Year in 1950 playing for the Boston Braves) and Marvin Williams also attended the tryout. Shortly thereafter, Brooklyn general manager Branch Rickey signed Robinson, initiating the racial integration of major-league baseball. Robinson was N.L. Rookie of the Year in 1947. The Red Sox, meanwhile, remained an all-white club until 1959.

28 See Gabriel Schechter, "Hugh Duffy: 68 Years in Baseball,"on-line at www.thenationalpastimemuseum.com/article/hugh-duffy-68-years-in-baseball. Duffy preached hitting the ball back up the middle.

29 As per the death certificate contained in the Hugh Duffy file at the Giamatti Research Center.

CHARLIE FRISBEE
BY BILL NOWLIN

Outfielder Charlie Frisbee was a switch-hitter who threw right-handed. His first year in the minors was as a catcher, but then he took up work in the outfield. He played two seasons in the majors, in the National League for the Boston Beaneaters in 1899 and for the New York Giants in 1900. After leaving baseball, he worked in a number of occupations.

Charles Augustus Frisbee was born in Dows, Franklin County, Iowa on February 2, 1874. His parents were both from the Eastern part of the country: His mother, Ellen (Young) Frisbee, was from New York and his father, Francis "Frank" Frisbee, was from either New York or, possibly, Pennsylvania. They had married in February 1871.

Frank Frisbee became a physician, after graduating from the Iowa College of Physicians and Surgeons at Keokuk in 1880. Charles was the oldest of their two children; daughter Laura Hannah Frisbee was born a few years later.

Charlie attended Grinnell College in Iowa and was a catcher for the team. In March 1896, it was announced that he had signed a contract to play in Oregon for the Portland baseball team in the four-team New Pacific League. Manager Bob Glenalvin was reportedly "very much tickled now because he signed Frisbee, his catcher, of whom he hears most flattering accounts. Frisbee bears the reputation in Iowa Falls, whence he hails, of being remarkably fast on the path. ... Frisbee is said to be a fine

Charlie Frisbee.
(public domain)

specimen of muscular development."[1] He was 5-feet-9 and listed at 175 pounds.

The Portland Gladiators finished first in the standings with a record of 19-9, but the league disbanded on June 15. Frisbee's record shows him playing in every game, batting .339 (40-for-118) with one home run, one triple, and eight doubles.

In 1897, Frisbee played right field, typically leading off, for the Quincy Little Giants of the Western Association, though he caught in 11 games. In 122 games, he hit .309 and the *Quincy Journal* reported that he might well be drafted by one of the National League clubs.[2]

Manager Jim Manning of the Kansas City Blues of the Western League had his eyes on Frisbee and on February 5, 1898, it was reported that he had acquired Frisbee from Quincy.[3] Frisbee played left field for the Blues, and had another excellent season. Portland had been ranked a Class-C team, Quincy in Class B, and Kansas City as Class A.

In May, Frisbee earned himself a small feature news story thanks to another effort. Members of the Kansas City team were standing outside the Mercer Hotel in Omaha around 7 P.M. when two horse-drawn carriages collided with each other. One of the horses spooked and bolted, a wheel collapsing and the phaeton overturning. Dr. Robinson's wife was trapped in the top, being dragged straight toward a telephone pole. Frisbee grabbed the reins with one hand and the saddle with another. Even though he couldn't get the horse to stop, he caused it to veer away from slamming into the pole and Mrs. Robinson was extricated uninjured. "Her nerve and Frisbee's clever work were both the subject of laudatory comment."[4]

Frisbee's season had indeed been a good one. In 138 games for the Blues, he hit for a .315 batting average in 549 at-bats. Kansas City finished in first place. Frisbee's average ranked him ninth in the league. In addition to his 173 base hits (quite a few of which were bunts for base hits), he sacrificed 32 times and stole 28 bases.[5]

On October 28, 1898, it was announced that manager Frank Selee of the Boston Nationals had drafted Frisbee from the Blues. His fielding percentage, however, was a disappointing .906.[6]

It was understood that Frisbee would receive a trial during spring training ("ante-season practice") and would be returned to Kansas City if he proved "too inexperienced for such fast company." The *Boston Globe* story said, "He is very popular, as well as being good in the field and at the bat. He is especially clever at sacrificing."[7] One of the considerations in Selee's mind was that Frisbee had experience in catching, and thus, if he made the grade, Boston would need to carry only Marty Bergen and George Yeager on the roster, freeing up room for another player.[8]

In March, Frisbee was assigned to the Worcester Farmers of the Class-A Eastern League. The *Washington Post* said the Worcester team "will be a genuine farm this year" and that Frisbee (and Yeager, also assigned there) "will be within easy call during the season."[9] But on March 22, the "dapper and trim outfielder" Frisbee reported to Beaneaters captain Hugh Duffy at Washington's Normandie Hotel. Selee said, "He's an athletic-looking youngster, and I know he's fast on his feet. That's what we want. Speed is becoming more of a factor in baseball every day."[10] When the season opened, however, Frisbee was with Worcester. He played very well and was not only hitting over .400 by May 23 but showed some remarkable fielding. A *Worcester Telegram* dispatch reported on two tie games against Montreal and said, "According to all accounts, it was Frisbee who saved each game by making a marvelous catch, once turning a complete somerset by tripping over a rope after getting the ball. But though Frisbee fell he did not drop the ball."[11]

On June 2, with the score tied 7-7 in the ninth inning Frisbee hit a long home run to deep center to beat Springfield at Worcester. On June 21, Selee sent a telegram summoning Frisbee to join the team at Pittsburgh – having come to the conclusion that the further usefulness of injured outfielder Billy Hamilton was in question. Frisbee was "considered the star all-round outfielder in the Eastern League"[12]

In his major-league debut, on June 22, Frisbee was 1-for-3 and played a good center field. Boston beat Chicago, 5-1, in Chicago. "Showed Up Well at the Bat and in the Field" read a *Boston Globe* subhead.[13] On July 13, it was reported that Hamilton was probably out for the season, "unable to put on a uniform. Meanwhile Frisbee is putting up a splendid game."[14]

Be that as it may, Hamilton did return and in early August, Frisbee was back with Worcester, on loan. He stayed with the team until the final day of the Eastern League season, September 5, having himself a four-hit game with a double and a home run (and a stolen base) in the final game. His .362 batting average led the Eastern League.

On September 11, Frisbee was back with Boston, and with Hamilton out due to a lame leg, he played center field again for the Beaneaters.

By season's end, he had played in 42 major-league games, with a batting average of .329 (the team average was .287). He showed some speed on the basepaths with 10 stolen bases. He scored 22 runs and drove in 20. His fielding left a lot to be desired, however; he made 11 errors in 88 chances (.875).

The year-end figures from the Eastern League showed Frisbee third in the league, with a .362 batting average in 71 games. The two men above him, however, had played in only 18 and 16 games respectively and thus the title was Frisbee's.[15]

At this point in Frisbee's career, something cropped up which the "Baseball Notes" writer for the *Washington Post* deemed an injustice to Frisbee, an injustice in the farming of ballplayers by "grasping magnates" in the game. "Frisbee was turned over to Tom Loftus, of the Grand Rapids team in the Western League, along with $1,000, in the deal for Backstop Sullivan."[16] This was catcher Billy Sullivan, who had hit .306 in 83 games for Grand

Rapids in 1899 and ultimately caught in 88 games for Boston in 1900. A deal had been struck in September. The "Notes" writer continued: "This exchange of dollars and one human being for a likely player gave Frisbee a right to file a large and vociferous wail, and he is backed in his grievance by Major league managers, who are desirous of signing so promising a player as the athlete who was relegated to the Grand Rapids farm. In other words, the Boston club handicaps the future of a player for the sake of experimenting with another, in the obscurity of a minor league. Frisbee may run to seed and his hopes of a future be blasted by the selfishness of grasping magnates."[17]

The *Boston Herald* was also highly critical of baseball's reserve system, calling it "tortured and twisted beyond endurance." Frisbee could have earned more on the free market than the $150 a month he was paid under the deal bringing him from Kansas City. Boston upped his pay to $200 when it sent him to Worcester, but "now he is farmed out to Grand Rapids without being consulted in the least. He must go to that place and must take just whatever amount of salary the Boston club chooses to pay him. The player is traded for and bartered just like a piece of merchandise. He does not receive a cent of the purchase price. …"[18]

Between 1899 and 1900, the National League planned to contract by four teams, from 12 to eight. One might think this would provide a surplus of available talent, because there was at the time no other league deemed a major league. Nonetheless, there were any number of contractual details to be attended to in ensuring equity and competitive strength for each of the teams. Even as late as mid-March, however, the formal work of consolidating into a league of eight teams had not yet been completed and an article referring to the New York Giants in the March 20 *New York Times* noted, "Nothing has yet been done to strengthen the New York team. The local club has not accepted the offer of the Boston Club to release Outfielder Frisbee and Pitcher [Charlie] Hickman. … [Giants manager Buck] Ewing spoke well of Frisbee, who he believes will develop into a good man, and his services will be accepted if better players are not forthcoming."[19] Had Frisbee not become Grand Rapids property?

So thought Loftus. Shown the story in the *Times*, he said, "[Arthur] Soden is getting liberal giving away my players. Frisbee belongs to the Grand Rapids club, and will go with the club to Cleveland."[20] That there actually was no longer a Grand Rapids club was a further confusing element; Cleveland was the successor club. Loftus had worked a deal to place Frisbee with the Cleveland club (formerly of the National League, now becoming part of the American League). President Ban Johnson of the new American League was in the process of "arranging to transfer Frisbee to Cleveland with the rest of his Grand Rapids team, and if Boston wishes a clear title to Frisbee Loftus will have to be consulted."[21]

Two days later, the *Chicago Tribune* reported, "From Boston comes the report that Frisbee and Hickman will play in New York this season, President Soden having accepted [New York Giants principal owner Andrew] Freedman's offer, the amount of which is not given out."[22]

Not so fast, said Tom Loftus. He wrote a "scorching letter" declaring that he owned Frisbee and that Soden had no right to make any deal involving him, and demanded that either Frisbee or Sullivan be returned at once to the Cleveland club.[23] *The Sporting News* backed up Loftus's claim, writing, "The rights of a minor-league club do not cease with a change of base."[24]

Frisbee's signed contract with New York was received, and he intended to play there. Soden said that Frisbee had only been loaned to Grand Rapids, and was not Loftus's property.[25] On April 7, Frisbee played center field in an intrasquad exhibition game at the Polo Grounds.

On April 12, a meeting of the American League owners was held in Chicago and all league business was concluded in just the one day. The Frisbee matter, however, was "discussed at great length" and all the correspondence reviewed. Their decision was that Frisbee was Cleveland property, and Cleveland agreed to pay the salary he was being given by New York. Ban Johnson was to take up the matter with Boston.[26] Frisbee played for New York in an April 14 exhibition game against Manhattan College, leading off and playing right field.

On Opening Day, Frisbee batted third and played in right during a 3-2 loss to Brooklyn. He singled in the game and was said to be "every bit the batter he is cracked up to be. He is good on bunt hits, and also showed himself capable of 'lining 'em out.'"[27] He didn't play much for New York, however, his final statistics showing him in only four games, 2-for-13 (.154), with three RBIs. His fielding was atrocious; he committed three errors in five chances, two of them on fly balls while New York was in Chicago.

But Ban Johnson hadn't given up on getting Frisbee for the American League, issuing another statement to that effect in mid-May.[28] His case was placed before the National Board of Arbitration. On June 16, the *Cleveland Plain Dealer* announced that the board had decided in favor of Cleveland. Frisbee played in 60 games for the Cleveland Lake Shores, but hit for only a .232 batting average – by far his worst season.

A knee injury in 1900 kept Frisbee out for the entire 1901 season. He was on the roster of the Rochester club but was simply unable to play "and remained quietly at home all the season, recuperating from his bad knee."[29] He spent the offseason working as a clerk in a general store in Alden, Iowa. A month before the season began, he quit work and devoted full time to training, dropping weight, and getting in shape.[30]

In 1902, Frisbee returned to Worcester. He definitely had his game back, batting .323 in 115 games. His fielding attracted some comment in the press: "Charlie Frisbee worked two more errors into his fat list of bungles. Fris foozles too often. After one year in private life, Fris has not been as emphatic a success as formerly, but there are other seasons ahead."[31]

Frisbee started the season with Worcester again in 1903, but became so ill in Toronto that he had to be hospitalized. His record for 1903 shows him batting .247 in 20 games for a combination of Worcester/Montreal, the team having moved to Montreal on June 21. On June 24, his contract was sold to New Orleans. There he joined the sick list once more; he played in 25 games, but hit only .202.

Charlie and Luella Florence (Catlin) Frisbee married on December 31, 1903, at Alden, Iowa.

In 1904, Frisbee signed with the Toledo Mud Hens. He played a full season, appearing in 149 games, and hit for a respectable .278 average. He played for Colorado Springs/Pueblo in 1905, but he moved on to Des Moines and then, in early July, the *Denver Post* said he had been named to manage the Burlington (Iowa) Flint Hills, in the Iowa League, giving him the opportunity to be closer to home.[32] He was the third of three managers; the team finished in last place. In 1906, Frisbee was named manager of the Waterloo team. Another controversy arose, with Burlington claiming him.[33] A lot was expected of Waterloo in 1906, but it was Burlington that finished first while Waterloo – Frisbee no longer at the helm – finished seventh.

To some degree, we are able to use census information to track Charlie Frisbee's career after baseball. He had lost both parents in 1905, his father dying on May 20 and his mother on November 17. At the time of the 1910 census, he and Luella were living in Alden, where he worked as a retail merchant in a lumber yard. The Frisbees had two children of their own, Nellie Naoma Frisbee (1905-2001) and Frank (1906-1985).

During the First World War, Charlie registered for the military draft. At the time he was working for the State Savings Bank in Goodell, Iowa. At the time of the 1930 census, the Frisbees lived in Concord Township, Hancock County, where Charlie was the postmaster. Naoma had left the home, but Frank – then 21 – was employed as a laborer in an oil station. The family had two female lodgers, a stenographer and a public-school teacher.

In 1940, the Frisbees lived in Garner, Iowa, where Charlie had his own real-estate firm. Frank had left the home, too, but Alfred Thompson, age 40, a sales clerk in a local drugstore, was a lodger in the home.

Luella Frisbee died in 1950. Charlie died on November 7, 1954, in Iowa Falls. He is buried in Alden Cemetery.

SOURCES

In addition to the sources noted in this biography, the author also accessed the *Encyclopedia of Minor League Baseball*, Retrosheet.org, and Baseball-Reference.com.

NOTES

1 "Mr. Chapman Goes Home," *The Oregonian* (Portland), March 13, 1896: 6.

2 As reported in "Sporting Notes," *Daily Register-Gazette* (Rockford, Illinois), October 4, 1897: 3.

3 "Meet Next Tuesday," *Daily Register-Gazette*, February 5, 1898: 3.

4 "Caught by Fielder Frisbee," *Omaha World-Herald*, May 11, 1898: 2.

5 See "Boston Has Drafted Frisbee," *Kansas City Star*, November 2, 1898: 3, for comment on Frisbee bunting for base hits, and for Manning's regret that Boston had drafted Frisbee. If major-league fielders were more on the lookout for bunts, he felt, Frisbee might not fare as well. Manning felt Frisbee could benefit from more development.

6 "Selee Drafts Two Players," *Boston Herald*, October 28, 1898: 3.

7 "Selee Has Drafted Frisbee," *Boston Globe*, November 3, 1898: 7.

8 "Tried to Get Farrell," *Washington Post*, February 17, 1899: 8.

9 "Experts on Worcester Team," *Washington Post*, March 16, 1899: 8.

10 "Beaneaters in Shape," *Washington Post*, March 23, 1899: 8. The *Rockford* (Illinois) *Republic* had said he was the state sprinting champion in Iowa. "Baseball Briefs," *Rockford Republic*, April 17, 1897: 2.

11 "Baseball Notes," *Boston Globe*, May 24, 1899: 5.

12 "Boston Needs Fielder Frisbee," *Washington Post*, June 22, 1899: 8.

13 "More Like It," *Boston Globe*, June 23, 1899: 5.

14 "Hamilton Out of the Game," *Washington Post*, July 14, 1899: 8.

15 "Records of the Players," *Hartford Courant*, January 12, 1900: 4.

16 "Baseball Notes," *Washington Post*, November 20, 1899: 8.

17 Ibid.

18 "Baseball Monopoly's Doom," *Boston Herald*, January 7, 1900: 20.

19 "That Baseball Snarl," *New York Times*, March 20, 1900: 9.

20 "Orphans Will Start South Today," *Chicago Tribune*, March 21, 1900: 9.

21 "Alliance to Be Binding," *Chicago Tribune*, March 21, 1900: 9.

22 "Freedman Serves Legal Notice," *Chicago Tribune*, March 23, 1900: 9.

23 "Manager Loftus Accuses Soden," *Chicago Tribune*, March 26, 1900: 4.

24 "Soden Criticised," *Boston Herald*, April 2, 1900: 8.

25 "Loftus Sends Protest to Soden," *Chicago Tribune*, March 29, 1900: 4.

26 "Magnates Quick Work," *Chicago Tribune*, April 13, 1900: 4. There may have been an assumption that Loftus would simply accommodate the wishes of the major-league clubs. See "Placating Freedman," *Boston Herald*, March 19, 1900: 6, in which it was suggested, for reasons unspecified, that Loftus "would doubtless relax his grip to accommodate the New York club."

27 "League Baseball Season Is Opened," *New York Times*, April 21, 1900: 9.

28 "Good Boy, Bob," *Boston Globe*, May 16, 1900: 5.

29 "Frisbee Again for Worcester," *Worcester Daily Spy*, March 21, 1902: 2.

30 "Frisbee With Friends Again," *Worcester Daily Spy*, April 9, 1902: 1.

31 "Sporting Notes," *Worcester Daily Spy*, September 1, 1902: 3.

32 "Frisbee's New Job," *Denver Post*, July 7, 1905: 11.

33 "Iowa League Affairs," *Daily Nonpareil* (Council Bluffs, Iowa), February 19, 1906: 8.

CHARLIE GANZEL

BY CHAD MOODY

"We are a baseball family, I guess," said Charlie Ganzel of his clan in a 1904 interview.[1] One of a bevy of family members who achieved success in baseball, Charlie was arguably the most prominent of the Ganzel brothers. Although he was a key contributor to five pennant-winning National League teams during the late nineteenth century, the part-time player seemed forever destined to play in the shadows of teammates who were among the biggest stars in the game. Nonetheless, media and peers recognized Ganzel throughout his career as being one of the finest catchers and most versatile players in the game.

Charles William Ganzel was born in Waterford, Wisconsin, near Racine, on June 18, 1862, to Charles Ganzel Sr. and Elizabeth Ganzel. His father worked as a carpenter and his mother was a homemaker. Both of Ganzel's parents emigrated in the mid-nineteenth century from Prussia (Germany) to the United States, where they started their family, which ultimately grew to include 10 children. Charles – whose nickname is often also spelled "Charley" – was the third oldest of the children, who included five sisters (Anna, Ida, Julia, Lizzie, and Minnie) and four brothers (Frederick, George, John, and Joseph). The Ganzels called the Racine area home until around 1883, when they relocated to Minnesota. After spending four years in the Twin Cities, Charles Sr. and Elizabeth again relocated the family – this time permanently – to Kalamazoo, Michigan. And with all but one of the Ganzel boys eventually spending notable time playing professional ball in Michigan, it is perhaps not surprising that the clan was known as the "first family of Michigan baseball."[2]

Ganzel's parents preached to their children the virtues of avoiding alcohol, and attributed to their espousal of clean living the

Charlie Ganzel.
(Spalding Collection, New York Public Library)

family's overall good health and athletic giftedness – particularly as it related to their sons. "The children of the elder Ganzels, especially the boys, are giants in size, all but one measuring over six feet one inch and weighing close to 200 pounds each," noted the *Detroit Free Press* before also highlighting that the boys were "naturally of an athletic turn."[3] Indeed they were athletic, as Ganzel and his four brothers all found success in baseball at various levels. Frederick, his older brother, had the promise of a professional career dashed by an ankle injury after playing years of independent ball, while younger brothers George and Joseph each made it to the minor-league level.[4] And John, the youngest and most successful of Ganzel's baseball-playing brothers, played for five big-league teams between 1898 and 1908 before spending two seasons as a manager in the National and Federal Leagues. "It is to the fact that they have never used liquor that the sons attribute their success on the diamond," wrote the *Detroit Free Press*, echoing the sentiments of the family's patriarch and matriarch.[5] In actuality, the success the sons achieved was perhaps driven more by genetics, as their father himself was reputedly at one time a noted player.[6]

Ganzel spent his formative years residing in a "little house" on the south side of Racine, where he "played ball on the prairies south of the city and on the [Racine College] grounds."[7] In 1880 the Third Ward baseball team was organized in Racine. Although comprising solely local players, the amateur club was "probably was one of the outstanding baseball outfits representing the city."[8] Ganzel, at the time in his late teens, honed his craft for the talented Third Ward club, along with his brother George. When not playing ball, he was employed as a painter, according to census information. Additionally, an 1887 news story reported that he also had spent time working in a blacksmith shop earning $1 a day.[9] In a show of respect for the native son, Ganzel was posthumously inducted into the Racine Athletic Hall of Fame in 1969.[10]

A 1914 newspaper article in Ganzel's file at the library of the National Baseball Hall of Fame and Museum indicates that his first foray into professional baseball came in 1882 with Grand Rapids of the Northwestern League. This is dubious, however, as that league did not begin play until 1883. More likely is that there was confusion with his brother John, who played for the Grand Rapids Bob-o-Links of the Western League at the beginning of his professional career. What is for certain is that upon his family relocating to Minnesota in 1883, Ganzel played for the semipro Minneapolis Brown Stockings. Although he later recalled that he manned first base for the team, newspaper box scores of the day indicate that Ganzel displayed early signs of the versatility that later became one of his hallmarks, as he frequently also bounced around to various infield and outfield positions.[11] And in a late-July game, he did some "pretty work" behind the plate, which was certainly a harbinger of things to come.[12] Comprehensive 1883 season statistics are not available for the right-handed batter and thrower; however, Ganzel was "considered one of the most certain players in the club."[13]

With the independent Minneapolis club seeking to join the fully professional Northwestern League for the following campaign, team ownership and management sought to stack their roster with "real ball players" in lieu of simply harvesting local talent.[14] This forced several of the old Brown Stockings to find new teams – including Ganzel. Latching on with the neighboring St. Paul club, the 21-year-old got his first taste of professional ball in 1884 competing in the Northwestern League. Ganzel began the season primarily playing first base for St. Paul, but also exhibited some solid play behind the plate in an early-season contest against Stillwater. "He has the stuff in him for a fine catcher," the *St. Paul Globe* presciently opined after this performance.[15] Despite finishing the season hitting .189 and being criticized by the press for his lack of speed, the burgeoning backstop was still regarded as being one of the best players on the team.[16]

In an interview two decades later, Ganzel reflected on his shift in positions during the season. "In 1884 I was with St. Paul as a first baseman, and in the middle of the season I started in to catch," he recalled. "This was mainly due to Elmer Foster, the pitcher. They had no one to catch him, and I broke in with him, and after that catching was my home position."[17] Ganzel employed an interesting technique to improve upon the inferior protective catching gear of the day. "In those days the insufficient protection of the gloves caused the hands to swell to double their usual size," he remembered. "I used to get a piece of beefsteak and put it inside of the glove. This served to moisten my hands and served also as a protection."[18]

Upon the conclusion of Ganzel's first professional season in baseball, another one immediately began. In September, the St. Paul club joined the Union Association – a fledgling (and ultimately doomed) major league – at the tail end of that league's 1884 campaign. Although the team played just nine games to wrap up the season, Ganzel's appearance in seven of those contests constituted his first big-league experience. "That year's playing was the hardest of my career," he later admitted.[19] And with the future of his St. Paul club being in doubt, Ganzel quickly sought opportunities to take his talents elsewhere.

In the fall of 1884, it was frequently reported that he had agreed to play for Kansas City in 1885.[20] Although it is possible Ganzel signed with Kansas City's Union Association club shortly before it (and the league) disbanded, more likely is that the reports were incorrect or speculative.[21] What is for certain is that Ganzel accepted an offer (that he recalled as $1,500) to join the Philadelphia Quakers of the National League for the 1885 campaign.[22] The 6-foot, 180-pound catcher's time in Philadelphia was disappointing, however. Appearing in less than one-third of the team's games in 1885, Ganzel featured a .168/.194/.208 slash line, and was relegated to being the club's third-string catcher behind Andy Cusick and Jack Clements. After rumors swirled of his involvement in a possible transaction with Washington during the offseason, he found himself back with Philadelphia for the 1886 season.[23] Things went from bad to worse, however. "In the spring of '86 I refused to report, owing to a cut of $100 in salary, for then there was no clause in the contract relating to cutting," Ganzel later recalled. "I was then living in Minneapolis and I received a letter from the club stating that unless I did report, my name would be blacklisted."[24] Under this coercion, he relented and reported to the Quakers – although he requested his release.[25] The admittedly dissatisfied catcher went hitless and played poorly behind the plate in one game before being granted his release.[26] Poor play aside, the team reportedly cut ties with him primarily because "the club had more catchers than it needed."[27] Corroborating this report, Philadelphia manager Harry Wright reportedly commented that Ganzel would be an asset to any team if given regular playing time.[28] Despite his difficulties in Philadelphia, Ganzel still considered Wright the finest man he had ever met.[29]

Although clubs in the American Association had rumored interest in securing his services, Ganzel remained in the NL upon signing with the Detroit Wolverines as a backup to star catcher Charlie Bennett in June 1886.[30] "Philadelphia has earned Detroit's sincere thanks. In Ganzel we have received a first-class catcher," the Detroit editor of *Sporting Life* asserted. "He is a jewel and will prove a splendid substitute for Charley Bennett."[31] Ganzel did not disappoint, making an impact with the club in his first appearance. "Ganzel had sat on the players' bench for two days and his appearance created a favorable impression. But few expected he would acquit himself in the superior manner in which he did," reported the *Detroit Free Press*. "He caught admirably and showed that he could throw by cutting off two attempts to steal second. His style is artistic, and the Detroit Club has in him a valuable addition to the nine."[32] Philadelphia media also took note of the immediate success of their local club's former backstop. "Ganzel did himself proud on Tuesday, his record for the afternoon being six put-outs, three assists, no error and one of the ten hits made by the home team," the *Times* (Philadelphia) reported. "Everybody here [Detroit] was happy over the new acquisition and the prophets, especially those who are without honor, went about predicting that Detroit's 'G.G.' battery ([Pretzels] Getzien and Ganzel), would soon do as good work as the 'B.B.' pair – [Lady] Baldwin and Bennett."[33] (The so-called prophets proved to be correct, as the future success of the "G.G." battery led the duo to become more famously dubbed the "Pretzel Battery" – owing to their German heritage.)[34] Building on his strong start with Detroit, Ganzel continued his fine play as a very capable backup to relieve the veteran Bennett. All told for Detroit in 1886, he played in 57 games, and hit a solid .272 with one home run and 31 RBIs to contribute to the Wolverines' second-place finish in the NL.

Although Detroit again slated Ganzel for a substitute backstop position as they headed into the 1887 season, the club gave him the opportunity to take on a much more prominent role with the veteran Bennett battling injuries.[35] Appearing as a catcher in 51 games – the most catching appearances on the club – Ganzel acquitted himself quite nicely. Despite featuring offensive statistics that were not overly impressive – he hit .260 with no home runs and 20 RBIs – his play behind the plate was widely lauded. In addition to calling Ganzel a "phenomenal catcher," the *Boston Globe* had this to say about the 25-year-old: "He has great reach, very large hands, and is an excellent back stop. No pitcher is too speedy for him and his long reach enables him to save a good many wild pitches."[36] The *New York Clipper* also offered a glowing review of Ganzel's second season with Detroit: "Last season [1887] he caught in nearly one half of the championship games his club played, and to his efforts, as much as any other man, is due the high standing the team was able to take in 1887."[37] By season's end, Ganzel was widely recognized as a key cog that helped lead the Wolverines to the NL pennant and a pre-modern World's Series championship over the American Association's St. Louis Browns. At the dignitary-filled banquet celebrating the champion Wolverines on October 24, team owner Frederick Stearns summed up Ganzel's significant contributions thusly: "The man who is the backbone of the nine, Bennett, could not join us till August, and nothing but his able ally and colleague, Ganzel, could save us."[38] For his efforts, Ganzel received a "handsome" gold watch and chain.[39] "I think that the Detroit champion team of 1887 was the best team ever got together," Ganzel opined in a 1904 interview.[40]

With Bennett returning to health – and lead catching duties – following an injury-plagued 1887 season, Ganzel nonetheless continued to add value to the Wolverines in the 1888 campaign by displaying versatility on the diamond. During the course of his 95 appearances, he played in the outfield and all four infield positions – in addition to providing his usual solid play as Bennett's backup. Labeled "one of the best all-round players in the country" by *Sporting Life*, Ganzel finished the season hitting .249 with one home run and 46 RBIs.[41] The *New York Clipper* praised his versatility: "This season [1888] Ganzel has proved himself a valuable all round player. Besides his excellent work behind the bat he has been filling the position of second baseman, during Hardie Richardson's absence, in a very creditable manner."[42] While Ganzel evolved into a super-sub, the Wolverines devolved into mediocrity due to injuries and team dissension. Resultant poor fan attendance coupled with a roster full of high-payroll stars caused fatal financial problems for the club.[43] Amazingly, Detroit ultimately went from being champions in 1887 to defunct after the 1888 season.

As Detroit prepared for its resignation from the NL shortly after the end of the 1888 season, a frenzy of sorts began as other teams attempted to procure many of its stars – with Philadelphia reportedly even offering to purchase the entire lot of Wolverine players.[44] The NL's Boston Beaneaters became the sweepstakes winner once the dust settled in October, however. For the sum of $30,000, Beaneaters director James B. Billings secured the services of five of Detroit's prized players: Ganzel, his backstop colleague Bennett, and three of the so-called "Big Four" – Dan Brouthers, Hardy Richardson, and Deacon White.[45] Were it not for the other member of the Big Four, Jack Rowe, being quickly dealt by Detroit to the Pittsburgh Alleghenys, Ganzel likely would have found himself moved elsewhere. Boston originally targeted Rowe in the deal; however, upon his lack of availability the club opted for Ganzel in his stead.[46] The magnitude of Boston's transaction – at the time called "the greatest deal in the history of baseball" by one publication – sent shockwaves through the game.[47] Similarly, the *Boston Herald* immediately proclaimed it to be "the greatest deal ever perfected in the history of the national game," under an optimistically titled headline: "Bostons Are the Champions: That Is, It Is Safe to Bet on It for the Season of 1889."[48] Although White eventually landed in Pittsburgh when his deal with the Beaneaters fell through, Boston was able to execute contracts with Ganzel (at a salary reported in the range of $2,500 to $3,500), Bennett, Brouthers, and Richardson for the 1889 season.[49] Reaction to the acquisition of Ganzel was favorable. "Ganzel is also considered one of the best catchers in the league," wrote the *Boston Herald*. "He is a remarkably fine thrower and he can stand any amount of punishment at the hands of pitchers."[50]

Picking up in Boston where he left off with Detroit, Ganzel was tagged to back up catcher Bennett for the 1889 campaign. Even in his role as a part-time player, the media wasted no time heaping praise on Ganzel. "Wherever we go all look with envy at our backstops," boasted the *Boston Herald* of Ganzel and his counterpart Bennett.[51] Too valuable to sit on Boston's bench solely as a backup receiver, however, Ganzel was given the opportunity to display the versatility he exhibited in Detroit a year earlier. "Charlie Ganzel would make a great fielder if ever there became need for him to take a position in the outfield," opined the *Herald* quite presciently in April. Over the course of the season he played in 73 of Boston's 128 games, primarily splitting time at catcher and outfield, while even making several appearances as an infielder. "Ganzel doesn't make much noise and his modesty rather obscures his brilliancy, yet he is becoming one of the great all-round players of the League," wrote *Sporting Life*.[52] Although lauded for his super-sub skills and called a "prime favorite here by his quiet and unassuming way of going about his business," offensively Ganzel finished the season with the second-place Beaneaters in typical middling fashion, hitting .265 with one home run and 43 RBIs.[53]

While Ganzel enjoyed a successful first season on the diamond with Boston, trouble had been brewing off the field in the NL during the 1889 campaign. The Brotherhood of Professional Base Ball Players – a players association originally formed in 1885 – grew increasingly disenchanted with perceived low pay and unfair treatment by team owners. This led to the Brotherhood's formation of the Players' League, to begin play in the 1890 season. This upstart major league succeeded in snaring a significant number of star players away from the NL and American Association to create a strong rival for these more established leagues. As Ganzel was a member of the Brotherhood and thus a likely candidate to jump ship as some of his teammates had done, desperate Players' League representatives went to the lengths of attempting to track him down in a remote area of California while he was on a hunting trip to hurriedly persuade him to sign a contract. Their search proved too late, however.[54] Ganzel – although supportive of the Brotherhood – had already signed with the Beaneaters reportedly as a "matter of honor," owing to a verbal agreement he made with the team committing him to a two-year deal when he originally signed.[55] Not all saw his actions as honorable; Ganzel received his share of criticism for not jumping to the Players' League. "Charley has lost many friends by his actions in this matter. The day will come when he will regret deserting his brothers," wrote one newspaper at the time.[56]

Ganzel did indeed honor his commitment to the Beaneaters, performing in his usual "quiet and gentlemanly manner" on the field for the 1890 campaign.[57] Despite being named team captain at the beginning of the season, he appeared in his fewest games since 1885.[58] Having a typically mediocre year at the plate, Ganzel still provided value in flexing between his normal backup catcher role and the outfield. With his contract fulfilled at season's end, rumors swirled that Ganzel might take over as skipper of Boston's Players' League club – even though some in the Brotherhood considered him a deserter for remaining in the NL for the 1890 season.[59] Any speculation was put to rest, however, when the Players' League folded after its one and only season.

Remaining with the Beaneaters, Ganzel continued as a model of consistency behind the plate, with the *Boston Globe* writing that he had "caught admirably" during his time in Boston.[60] Although still used in a backup role behind Bennett and megastar King Kelly in contributing to Boston's winning three consecutive pennants (1891-1893), Ganzel was deemed a "favorite with the players as well as the public."[61] And one newspaper later recalled how his skills as a backstop "lifted [future Hall of Fame pitchers] Kid Nichols and John Clarkson to greater heights of repute."[62] Possibly around this time period, he and Kelly – a noted trickster – were reportedly involved in a legendary play that spurred a rule change involving in-game substitutions. The November 28, 1894, edition of the *New Castle* (Pennsylvania) *News* provided Charlie Bennett's recollection of the event. "During a game one day, [Kelly] sat on the bench and Ganzell [*sic*] was behind the bat. A foul fly was popped up, out of Ganzell's reach, when quick as a flash Kel ran forward, ordered Ganzell out of the game, caught the ball, and then ordered the umpire to declare the batter out. He maintained with a great deal of force, that he had as much right to order Ganzell out of the game, while a ball was in the air, as at any other time during the progress of the game. However, the decision went against him," recalled Bennett.[63] Several versions of this story have been in circulation over the years, but whether the event actually occurred is still in question for lack of indisputable evidence.[64]

Ganzel finally got his opportunity to become Boston's unequivocal regular catcher in 1894 after a tragic accident that befell his longtime catching counterpart Bennett. In January Bennett – with whom Ganzel had maintained a "most pleasant" relationship – lost both legs after slipping under a train while attempting to board.[65] In reflecting on Bennett in a later interview, Ganzel called the venerable star "the greatest catcher who ever put on a glove."[66] Unable to fully capitalize on his opportunity as the club's regular backstop, however, Ganzel was released by Boston in midseason. "Charlie is a good fellow and has been an excellent player until this season, but his playing thus far has not been up to the standard we require, and after giving him all the opportunity in the world to better his play, which he has not done, he has been given his release," explained Beaneaters manager Frank Selee.[67] After Ganzel received offers from several teams – including one from Cincinnati that he seriously considered – Boston decided to re-sign him less than two weeks after releasing him. "Yes, we re-signed Charley because we really believe he will play good ball for us," said Beaneaters President Arthur Soden.[68] Soden's hunch proved correct, as Ganzel rebounded and arguably put together the best year of his career. The *Brooklyn Eagle* summed up Ganzel's season thusly: "The Boston club made no mistake when it got Charlie Ganzel back. He is playing in his old

Detroit form and that is saying a good deal."[69] In his 70 games, Ganzel hit .278 with 3 home runs and 56 RBIs – all career highs.

After another solid season in 1895 as the regular backstop for Boston where his play was described as "A 1," Ganzel found himself out of action for several weeks during the 1896 season with a serious leg injury suffered when he was spiked during a game against Washington in June.[70] Supplanted as the regular catcher by promising 24-year-old rookie Marty Bergen, Ganzel played in only 47 games in 1896 – his second fewest since his initial NL campaign. The acquisition of Bergen essentially spelled the end for the aging veteran, with Boston now in the midst of a rebuilding process.[71] Hanging on in a little-used backup role to Bergen for the 1897 season, Ganzel added one more NL pennant under his belt – his fourth with the Beaneaters and fifth overall – but did not enjoy his lack of playing time along the way. "Charlie Ganzel has not caught for so long even the bleacherites fail to recognize him when he appears in uniform to warm up the infielders or catch the pitching prior to the game. Charlie is sore at Selee for playing Marty Bergen continuously, and thinks he is given to playing favorites," wrote the *Washington Evening Times*.[72] Released by Boston after the 1897 season, Ganzel retired at age 35 after 14 seasons in the big leagues with a .259 career batting average, 10 home runs, and 412 RBIs in 787 games.

Ganzel remained in the Boston area after his retirement. He also remained very close to the game, playing for several local semipro teams, including the Carters of Franklin, Milford, Newburyport, and Worcester.[73] Ganzel also coached the Williams College squad for several seasons in the late 1890s and early 1900s, and occasionally could even be found umpiring in college, semi-pro, and big-league contests.[74] When not on the diamond, he had a successful business career as a traveling salesman in the garment industry. Ganzel was a member of the Freemasons, and volunteered his time with the young men's Makaria Bible class organization at Bethany Congregational Church in Quincy, Massachusetts.[75]

Ganzel also spent time raising a family with his wife, Alice, whom he had married in 1885. From 1885 to 1910, the couple had nine children: Arthur, Rupert, Gladys, Wesley, Lloyd, Charles, Foster, Alice, and John. One-year-old Arthur died in 1886, and 5-year-old Alice died in 1914 of diphtheria. "The only things I now have to live for are my wife and my Bible. And I still retain my faith in God," Ganzel confessed after the passing of his young daughter.[76] On a happier note, Ganzel's sons Wesley and Foster carried on the family's tradition of finding success in baseball. Wesley made it to the minor-league level. And Foster – better known as Babe – played two seasons with the Washington Senators. Babe's 1927 major-league debut – 43 years after his father's debut in the Union Association – resulted in the longest span ever between the first big-league games by a father and son.

Around 1912, Ganzel was diagnosed with cancer. The ensuing long battle with the disease included several surgeries and sapped the family's finances. In recognizing that Ganzel was "under sentence of death," Boston newspaper editors and baseball executives formed a committee to raise funds to assist the struggling family.[77] In a testament to Ganzel's popularity and character, over $1,000 was raised for a man called "one of the cleanest, gamest and most honorable players ever connected with baseball."[78] On April 7, 1914, "after one of the most stubborn fights any man had ever made against that most dreaded disease," Ganzel died of epithelioma of the lower lip and jaw – on his brother John's 40th birthday and only two months after his daughter Alice's death.[79] He was buried at Mount Wollaston Cemetery in Quincy.

SOURCES

In addition to the sources cited in the Notes, the author accessed Ganzel's file at the library of the National Baseball Hall of Fame and Museum in Cooperstown, New York; Ancestry.com; Baseball-Reference.com; Chronicling America; GenealogyBank.com; NewspaperArchive.com; Newspapers.com; and Retrosheet.org.

NOTES

1 "Detroit Team Was the Best," *Detroit Free Press*, April 3, 1904: 14.

2 Marty Appel, *Pinstripe Empire: The New York Yankees from Before the Babe to After the Boss* (New York: Bloomsbury, 2012), 26; Keith Howard, "The Ganzel Brothers: Baseball Legends," Kalamazoo Public Library, kpl.gov/local-history/biographies/ganzel-brothers.aspx, June 2015, accessed August 16, 2017.

3 "In This Family of Fifty-Two There Has Never Been a Death," *Detroit Free Press*, June 24, 1906: 18.

4 Ibid.

5 Ibid.

6 "Ganzel Family Reunion," *Racine Journal*, November 6, 1906: 1.

7 "Racine Boys Make Good in the Baseball World," *Racine Journal-News*, August 23, 1915: 6; "To an Old Time Star," *Racine Journal-News*, February 9, 1914: 9.

8 Peter Herman, "Baseball History of Racine Related," *Racine Journal-Times*, February 23, 1941: 8.

9 "Oshkosh Is Third," *Oshkosh* (Wisconsin) *Northwestern*, August 22, 1887: 3.

10 "Name 10 Athletes to 'Hall of Fame,'" *Racine Journal-Times*, May 9, 1969: 26.

11 "Detroit Team Was the Best."

12 "The Browns Have a Walk Away with the Hudsons – Score 25 to 5," *St. Paul Globe*, July 26, 1883: 6.

13 "The Red Caps Defeat the Brown Stockings in a Score of Three to Ten," *St. Paul Globe*, September 16, 1883: 6. The box score in this newspaper suggests that Charlie's brother George appeared in at least one game for Minneapolis in 1883. Because reports of the day tended to refer to players only by their surnames, it is possible that some of the highlights credited to Charlie above in fact belong to his brother. This is highly unlikely, however, due to Charlie's exploits for the Brown Stockings being well-documented, coupled with George's youthfulness at the time (he was 17 years old).

14 Stew Thornley, *Baseball in Minnesota: The Definitive History* (St. Paul: Minnesota Historical Society Press, 2006), 17.

15 "One for Stillwater," *St. Paul Globe*, April 28, 1884: 6.

16 "First of the Season," *St. Paul Globe*, June 10, 1884: 2; "Threshed Our Sister," *St. Paul Globe*, June 24, 1884: 3.

17 "Detroit Team Was the Best."

18 Ibid.

19. "Three Famous Old Players, Ganzel, Nash and M'Carthy, Now Boston Business Men," *Boston Post*, August 10, 1902: 6.

20. "Yesterday's Sports," *St. Paul Globe*, October 18, 1884: 5.

21. "News Summary," *Phillipsburg* (Kansas) *Herald*, November 8, 1884: 6.

22. "Three Famous Old Players, Ganzel, Nash and M'Carthy, Now Boston Business Men."

23. "Notes and Comments," *Sporting Life*, February 10, 1886: 5.

24. Ibid.

25. "Piling Up Victories," *Detroit Free Press*, June 16, 1886: 5.

26. "A Farce at Recreation Park," *Philadelphia Times*, May 29, 1886: 2.

27. "The Local Season," *Sporting Life*, September 29, 1886: 5.

28. "Base Ball Notes," *Philadelphia Times*, June 3, 1886: 3.

29. "Detroit Team Was the Best."

30. "Fresh Base Ball Gossip," *Philadelphia Times*, May 16, 1886: 2.

31. "At Home Again," *Sporting Life*, June 23, 1886: 1.

32. "Piling Up Victories."

33. "Detroit Wild Over Ball," *Philadelphia Times*, June 20, 1886: 11.

34. "Detroit, 10; St. Paul, 9," *Chicago Tribune*, April 20, 1887: 3; "Baseball's Honor Roll Has Famous Batteries," *Detroit Free Press*, September 12, 1909: 16.

35. Roy Kerr, *Big Sam Thompson: Baseball's Greatest Clutch Hitter* (Jefferson, North Carolina: McFarland, 2015), 64.

36. "The Champions," *Boston Globe*, October 11, 1887: 3.

37. Jean-Pierre Caillault, *The Complete New York Clipper Baseball Biographies* (Jefferson, North Carolina: McFarland, 2009), 257.

38. "Our Champions," *Detroit Free Press*, October 25, 1887: 4.

39. "A Grand Finale," *Detroit Free Press*, October 25, 1887: 2.

40. "Detroit Team Was the Best."

41. "Detroit Dotlets," *Sporting Life*, July 4, 1888: 5.

42. Caillault, *The Complete New York Clipper Baseball Biographies*, 257.

43. Kerr, 79.

44. "$30,000 for the Detroits," *Boston Herald*, October 10, 1888: 5.

45. "Bostons Are the Champions," *Boston Herald*, October 19, 1888: 5.

46. "The Detroit-Boston Deal," *Boston Herald*, November 13, 1888: 5.

47. "Sporting Matters," *Pacific Commercial Advertiser* (Honolulu), October 29, 1888: 2.

48. "Bostons Are the Champions."

49. "Base Ball Chat," *St. Louis Post-Dispatch*, November 16, 1888: 8; "A $50,000 Ball Club," *Philadelphia Times*, November 4, 1888: 14.

50. Jean-Pierre Caillault, *A Tale of Four Cities: Nineteenth Century Baseball's Most Exciting Season, 1889, in Contemporary Accounts* (Jefferson, North Carolina: McFarland, 2003), 7.

51. "Boston Is Rated Second," *Boston Herald*, April 15, 1889: 5.

52. "Notes and Comments," *Sporting Life*, July 3, 1889: 4.

53. "Hub Happenings," *Sporting Life*, May 22, 1889: 7.

54. Robert B. Ross, *The Great Baseball Revolt: The Rise and Fall of the 1890 Players League* (Lincoln: University of Nebraska Press, 2016), 121-123.

55. "'Spiders' in Town," *Boston Globe*, May 16, 1890: 7; "The Triumvirs' Big Trio," *Boston Herald*, December 13, 1889: 10.

56. "From Celeryville," clipped newspaper article from Ganzel's file at the library of the National Baseball Hall of Fame, January 29, 1890.

57. "Clubs the Policemen Favor," *Boston Herald*, April 6, 1890: 23.

58. "All Disabled," *Brooklyn Eagle*, March 19, 1890: 2.

59. "News Notes and Comments," *Sporting Life*, September 20, 1890: 5.

60. "The Champions of '92," *Boston Globe*, October 5, 1891: 11.

61. Ibid.

62. Associated Press, "Catching as Baseball Art Is No More; Ancients Were Far Better, Critic Says," *Battle Creek* (Michigan) *Enquirer*, July 8, 1929: 13.

63. "A Talk with Charlie Bennett," *New Castle* (Pennsylvania) *News*, November 28, 1894: 8.

64. Sarah Wexler, "'Kelly Now Catching': King Kelly and Baseball's Substitution Rules," *Hardball Times*, fangraphs.com/tht/kelly-now-catching-king-kelly-and-baseballs-substitution-rules/, December 4, 2015, accessed October 26, 2017.

65. "Detroit Team Was the Best."

66. Ibid.

67. "Catcher Ganzel Released," *Boston Advertiser*, July 25, 1894: 5.

68. "Ganzel to Remain," *Boston Advertiser*, August 6, 1894: 2.

69. "Base Ball Notes," *Brooklyn Eagle*, September 6, 1894: 4.

70. "Personal," *Sporting Life*, June 29, 1895: 6; "Badly Spiked," *Kalamazoo Gazette*, June 27, 1896: 1.

71. Bill Felber, *A Game of Brawl: The Orioles, the Beaneaters, and the Battle for the 1897 Pennant* (Lincoln: University of Nebraska Press, 2007), 44.

72. "Diamond Dust," *Washington Evening Times*, August 26, 1897: 6.

73. "On the Line," *Boston Herald*, June 30, 1900: 4; "Baseball Notes," *Boston Globe*, May 6, 1904: 5; "Lynn, 16; Newburyport, 0," *Boston Herald*, May 3, 1903: 7; "News in the Sporting World," *Springfield* (Massachusetts) *Republican*, April 15, 1898: 3.

74. "Baseball Brevities," *Pittsburg Press*, April 27, 1898: 6; "Hub Happenings," *Sporting Life*, March 24, 1900: 8; "Coaching Players," *Sporting Life*, April 12, 1902: 12; "Not a Run for Brown," *Boston Herald*, May 8, 1903: 9; "Lynn Now Leader of the N.E. League," *Boston Journal*, May 20, 1909: 9; "Giants Easy for Boston," *Brooklyn Eagle*, September 15, 1901: 8.

75. "Spokes from the Hub," *Sporting Life*, December 1, 1906: 3; "The Obit for Charlie Ganzel," The Deadball Era, thedeadballera.com/Obits/Obits_G/Ganzel.Charlie.Obit.html, accessed October 25, 2017.

76. "Minneapolis Globules," *St. Paul Globe*, October 12, 1886: 3; "Charlie Ganzel's Little Daughter Dies in Hospital," *Boston Herald*, February 15, 1914: 4.

77. "Famous Catcher Very Ill," *Boston Post*, January 7, 1914: 10.

78. "The Obit for Charlie Ganzel"; "Famous Catcher Very Ill."

79. "The Obit for Charlie Ganzel."

HANK GASTRIGHT

BY GLEN SPARKS

The photograph hanging on the wall of a Cincinnati area pizzeria inspired Russ Gastright to delve into some family history, specifically about the life and up-and-down career of a certain right-handed pitcher. A friend of Russ's spotted the photo, a team shot of the 1896 Reds. One player's name stood out.

"My friend, Mike Draznik, told me about a guy named 'Hank Gastright,'" said Russ, who grew up in northern Kentucky just across the Ohio River from Cincinnati. "I thought, 'Wow, I guess it's true. We really do have a major leaguer in the family.'"[1]

Russ had heard for years that one of his relatives played major-league baseball in the nineteenth century. His father, Bill, mentioned it several times. He played for the local team, the Reds, Bill said. But, what position did he play? How long did he play? Did he play for any team besides the Reds? The story was fuzzy. About 15 years ago, Russ began looking into the details. All because of that photo on the wall of a pizzeria. He wanted to fill in the gaps, on the field and off it.

First, Russ contacted a cousin in South Carolina who does genealogical research. Yes, she said, Hank Gastright is your great-great-uncle. Bingo! Russ began surfing the internet, writing letters to research libraries, and sending emails to historical societies, the Library of Congress, *The Sporting News,* and the National Baseball Hall of Fame. He collected newspaper articles and any other tidbits he could find about Hank, a 6-foot-2-inch, 190-pound hurler.

Hank Gastright enjoyed one big year in the major leagues and played seven total seasons (1889-94, 1896). He won 72 games, including 30 as a 25-year-old in 1890, although he never won

Hank Gastright, with Columbus.
(public domain)

more than 15 games in any other year. He also threw four of his six career shutouts in 1890, the only time he completed a campaign with a sub-3.00 ERA.

"What happened after that one big year? He was still young and at the peak of his strength and durability," said Russ, 64, who counted Reds stars Frank Robinson and Vada Pinson as two of his boyhood baseball heroes. "You get started with this search and you really can't stop. You want to know more about Uncle Hank."[2]

Henri Carl Gastreich was born on March 29, 1865, in Covington, Kentucky, the son of German immigrant Frederick and Swiss immigrant Catherine (Borgman) Gastreich. Frederick was born in 1832, Catherine in 1836. The couple married in 1855 and had 12 children, according to the 1910 US Census. (The Census also reported that only five of the Gastreich children were still living.) Frederick worked as a miller in nearby Newport, Kentucky.

Hank found work at a local mill as a teenager. The future big leaguer played for the Favorites, a semipro team, and signed with the Toledo Maumees of the Tri-State League in late 1888 One year later, the newly formed Columbus Solons (also called the Buckeyes) of the major-league American Association purchased Gastright's contract. (Hank eventually changed the spelling of "Gastreich" to "Gastright." Most newspaper accounts of his playing career use the latter spelling, as do his descendants.)

Columbus finished 60-78 in 1889, in sixth place in the eight-team league. First baseman David Orr jumpstarted the Solons' offense. He batted .327 and drove in 87 runs. Mark Baldwin led the pitching staff. He threw a league-leading 513⅔ innings, struck out 368 batters, and went 27-34.

Gastright, who made his major-league debut on April 19, 1889, started 26 games and relieved in six others as a rookie. He went 10-16 and posted a 4.57 ERA with 21 complete games. Bases on balls hurt him. Gastright walked 104 batters in 222⅔ innings.

Even so, Columbus manager Al Buckenberger liked what he saw. The kid had some talent. Buckenberger, though, feared that Gastright might jump to the newly formed Players' League. (Future Hall of Fame pitcher and infielder John Montgomery Ward helped organize the league, which attracted many National League stars but lasted just one season.) The skipper wanted to keep his young pitcher in Columbus, and the two negotiated into the late-night hours at the Grand Hotel in downtown Cincinnati. They finally agreed to a deal worth $2,500.[3]

Gastright rewarded Buckenberger's confidence in him. The second-year hurler won 30 games, lost 14 and sported a 2.94 ERA. He finished third among American Association pitchers in wins, seventh in ERA, and second (tied) in shutouts with four. Gastright completed 41 of his 45 starts, hurled 401⅓ innings, gave up 312 hits, struck out 199, and walked 135. He also hit 18 batters. The 24-year-old finished fifth in innings pitched during this rubber-armed era. (Sadie McMahon led the Association with 509 innings pitched with two teams.) Thanks in part to Gastright, Columbus vaulted ahead of several teams and finished in second place with a 79-55 won-lost mark.

The 1890 Solons relied on outfielder Spud Johnson to do much of the heavy hitting. He drove in 113 runs and batted .346 in his second big-league season. Third baseman Charlie Reilly smacked four home runs and catcher Jack O'Connor batted .324. Frank Knauss (17-12, 2.81 ERA), Elton "Ice Box" Chamberlain (12-6, 2.21 ERA, six shutouts), and Jack Easton (15-14, 3.52) rounded out the pitching staff.

Gastright, the Solons' ace, grabbed many of the sports-column headlines. A *Philadelphia Inquirer* reporter wrote, "Gastright pitched phenomenal ball and was almost faultlessly backed up" in a 7-3 Solons win on May 8.[4] Gastright also threw a solid game on June 19 against the Louisville Colonels. He won 7-1, allowing just the solo run in the second inning. "Columbus defeated Louisville hands down today," wrote the *Democrat and Chronicle*, "thanks to the wonderful pitching of Gastright and the hard hitting of the home team."[5]

In a July 15 home game against the Brooklyn Gladiators at Recreation Park, the Solons won a 16-2 laugher. A *Brooklyn Eagle* reporter grumbled about the Gladiators and reserved his compliments for the Solons' starting pitcher: "Gastright was in great form. Only three scattered hits were made off him."[6]

Gastright saved his best effort for a game late in the season. He hurled an eight-inning no-hitter at home against Toledo on October 12, winning 6-0 in front of about 4,000 fans. He struck out six and walked just one. Umpires were forced to call the game because of darkness. The *Daily Ohio State Journal* praised Gastright's masterpiece: "All hail, King Gastright, Ruler of the Realm of the Pig-skin," the writer exclaimed. "As for Gastright's superb work, no such pitching has been seen this or any other year."[7]

Columbus scored single runs in the first, fourth, and sixth innings and three more in the seventh. No Toledo runner reached third base. "You couldn't curve a dinner plate as much as Mr. Gastright curves the ball," the newspaper said. "Sometimes, it comes so swift that spectators in the grandstand have to tie themselves to their seats and hold their hats on."[8]

It looked as though Gastright had emerged as a major-league star. A *Wichita Daily Eagle* writer called him "one of the crack twirlers of the American Association."[9] The 1891 campaign, though, turned sour for both Gastright and the Solons. Columbus fell to 61-76, slipping once again to sixth place. Phil Knell, in his third season, took over as the team's top pitcher. He went 28-27 with a 2.92 ERA and 47 complete games.

Gastright dropped to 12-19. More telling, his ERA rose to 3.78, nearly a run higher than in 1890. He threw just 283⅔ innings, more than 100 fewer innings than the previous year, and walked 136. What went wrong? Russ Gastright thinks that the heavy workload from the 1890 campaign took its toll. "They wore him out," said Russ, still trying to figure out why his great-great-uncle's career took such a sudden downturn. "If he had promise, it was gone after that year."[10]

Gastright's Columbus career ended with the 1891 campaign. It had nothing to do with his frequent wild streaks. Rather, the American Association, which had been founded in 1882, went out of business after 10 seasons. Gastright, suddenly unemployed as a major-league pitcher, needed work. He signed with the Washington Nationals, who finished a woeful 44-91 in 1891 and were one of four AA teams (Louisville, Baltimore, and St. Louis the other three) that joined the now 12-team National League.

The 1892 Nats didn't fare much better than the previous year's team. They went 58-93 and ended up 10th. (The NL played a split-season format that year. Washington went 35-41 in the first half, good for fifth place, and dropped to last place in the second half with a 23-52 mark.) It probably wasn't any fun playing losing baseball during a hot, sticky summer in the nation's capital. At least Gastright missed much of the losing. He pitched in only 11 games and threw just 79⅔ innings, going 3-3 with a 5.08 ERA as a starter and reliever.

Next stop, Pittsburgh. Gastright signed a contract to play for the Pirates in 1893. It was a short stay. On the upside, he won three games and lost just one for a team (81-48) that finished in second place, thanks in part to three hitters (Jake Beckley, Denny Lyons, and Mike Smith) who each drove in over 100 runs. On the downside, Gastright had a 6.25 ERA. The bugaboo? Yes, too many baserunners. Gastright gave up a combined 113 hits and walks in just 59 innings. Pittsburgh released him in June. Gastright was once again free to look for a job.

The Boston Beaneaters gave him a shot, signing him in early July. Gastright had asked Beaneaters manager Frank Selee for a tryout, according to the *Boston Post*. Selee "always had a good opinion of Gastright … (who) always showed that he could pitch good ball. But he lost confidence in himself."[11]

The Beaneaters were coming off another successful season. They finished 102-48 in 1892 to capture their second straight pennant, 8½ games ahead of the second-place Cleveland Spiders, and defeated them and the great Cy Young in a postseason series.

Boston featured top hitters like Hugh Duffy, Tommy McCarthy, and Billy Nash, and complemented them with excellent pitching. Kid Nichols, who would win 361 games in a Hall of Fame career, was the team's workhorse and ace. Gastright blended in with a starting staff that included Jack Stivetts and Harry Staley in addition to Nichols.

The 1893 Beaneaters didn't match the 1892 squad's lofty record, but still went 86-43 and earned another pennant. Duffy batted .363 and drove in 118 runs. Nash knocked in a team-high 123 runs, while McCarthy brought home 111 runs and hit .346. Nichols hurled 425 innings and went 34-14, the third straight year that he won at least 30 games. (Nichols reached the 30-win plateau seven times in his 15-year career and topped the 400-inning mark five times.)

Stivetts finished 20-12, while Staley compiled an 18-10 mark. Gastright, for his part, went 12-4 with an elevated 5.13 ERA in less than a full season of work. He pitched in 19 games, starting 18. Over his 156 innings, he gave up 179 hits and walked 76 batters. (By comparison, Nichols walked 118 in his 425 innings.) Gastright struck out 27 batters and hit nine.

Clearly the Boston offense provided Gastright with plenty of run support. He led the NL with a .750 winning percentage (15-5 total won-lost mark) despite posting an overall ERA of 5.44 between his work with the Pirates and the Beaneaters.

Gastright hung in there and won games even if he didn't always win pretty. He gave up eight runs against the Louisville Colonels on September 8, but the Beaneaters scored 11, highlighted by a five-run third inning. The *Chicago Tribune* reported, "The Louisvilles batted hard all-through the game, but the lead which the Bostons gained in the earlier innings was more than the visitors could overcome. The contest was long drawn out and tedious."[12]

The *Boston Post* still lauded Gastright for his "masterly" pitching delivery. "Comments have been made on his great success. He wants the Bostons to win every game and, when not pitching, always helps the team by coaching," the paper said. On a personal note, the *Post* reported: "Gastright is very attractive. In his street clothes, he would be taken for a clergy man, an actor or a student. He is tall and well-built and a modest, unassuming fellow."[13]

An article in the October 14, 1893, edition of the *Allentown (Pennsylvania) Leader* labeled Gastright "one of the mysteries of the season," adding, "Last year, he was a 'floater,' being engaged and released on an average of once a month." Gastright began his tenure with Boston in a similar fashion, the writer explained. "When at last the Bostons gave him a trial, while Stivetts and Staley were almost useless, the other clubs (knew) that the champions were indeed in desperate straits. But here the unexpected happened. Gastright turned up in winning form."[14]

Once again, though, Gastright packed his suitcase when the season ended. The Beaneaters released him in April 1894 after a short salary dispute. Gastright told the *Cincinnati Enquirer* that Boston wanted to cut his salary, so he refused to sign a contract.[15]

The Brooklyn Bridegrooms came calling. Gastright joined a team that went 65-63 the previous season and featured top pitchers Brickyard Kennedy and Ed Stein. The May 18, 1894, edition of the *Brooklyn Daily Eagle* paid Gastright several compliments. "Gastright is a man of exemplary habits, does not drink nor use tobacco in any form," the paper said, adding, "He is quiet and gentlemanly on and off the field and is always in condition."[16]

Gastright pitched only one season in Brooklyn despite his clean living. He started eight games and relieved in eight others. Gastright ended the year with a woeful 2-6 won-lost record and a sky-high 6.39 ERA. The problem was simple and the same old story. He allowed way too many baserunners. In 93 innings, Gastright gave up 135 hits (13.1 hits per nine innings) and walked 55 (5.3 BB per nine innings).

Even so, he threw one of the best games of his career on June 1. The 29-year-old hurled a one-hit shutout against the Chicago Colts. Only three runners reached first base. The *Eagle* reported that Gastright "pitched phenomenal ball and deserves all the credit of his victory." His effort was, the *Eagle* decided, "a remarkable achievement for a pitcher in these days of heavy batting." After the final out, "Gastright was showered with congratulations."[17]

Usually, though, Gastright struggled during his time with Brooklyn. The *Eagle* offered some sympathy, especially after he lost a game late in June to the Senators. A reporter acknowledged that Washington "succeeded in knocking Gastright out of the box." On the other hand, "Few people, however, recognize the difficulties under which Gastright labored. Those who have seen the Washington ball grounds would see the difficulties in an instant. These grounds are the worst in the circuit." The writer even cut Gastright some slack over the pitcher's now-typical control problems. A stiff breeze had swirled through the park that day, according the article. "An eddying wind also interfered with Gastright's delivery and made it impossible for him to get the ball over the plate."[18]

Brooklyn, which ended the season at 70-61 and in fifth place, released Gastright in August. The *Eagle* reported on August 4 that "Gastright will sever his connections with the club's pay roll on Monday next."[19]

Illness prevented Gastright from pitching in 1895. He explained to the *Cincinnati Enquirer:* "I took the typhoid fever and that is the reason I did not succeed. I have entirely recovered, and I am sure that I am as good as I was before I took sick."[20]

According to the *Pittsburgh Press*, Gastright relaxed in his Kentucky home that spring and waited for a team to contact him. Apparently, he was a little picky. He didn't want to pitch for just any ballclub. "He has had some offers from clubs in both the eastern and western leagues, but turned them down," the *Press* reported.[21]

A *Cincinnati Enquirer* writer pushed the Reds to invite Gastright to spring training in 1896. "Fans will cheer even louder for a local guy to succeed on the baseball diamond," the newspaper asserted. "Nine out of 10 of the local enthusiasts want the Cincinnati Club to give Gastright a trial. .... Come on, Buck (Ewing, the Reds manager), give Henry a chance."[22]

Club officials finally relented and told the veteran hurler to join his new team in New Orleans. Gastright seemed thankful. He told the *Enquirer* that "it won't take me long to find out whether I am a has-been or not."[23] (At least one newspaper objected to this media pressure: "In Cincinnati, the newspapers forced the hiring of Henry Gastright," wrote the *Buffalo Enquirer*. "This kind of interference with the duties of a manager is the worst sort and always works harm."[24])

Injuries postponed Gastright's comeback attempt. He pitched in a few practice games, but soon hurt his back "slipping on a stone slab in the pitcher's box."[25] The mishap kept him off the field until early June. Finally, on June 5, Gastright took the mound again in a big-league game. Ewing asked Gastright to open the third inning against Brooklyn. Grooms hitters had knocked around Cincinnati starter Frank Dwyer. Gastright could not stop Brooklyn's attack. He gave up eight hits and six runs (three of them earned) in six innings. Cincinnati lost, 10-1.

The *Enquirer* on June 6, 1896, pleaded that the hometown ballplayer simply needed a little more time to shake off the rust. "After a pitcher has been out for a year and three months," it lectured; "it cannot be expected that he will jump in and pitch to championship form."[26]

Gastright never pitched another major-league game. He contracted dysentery and went home to recuperate. The Reds released him in late July. Gastright signed with the Hartford Blue Jays of the Atlantic League. With Hartford he posted a 13-7 record and a 2.34 ERA in 1897. Gastright waited for one more chance to pitch in the big leagues but never got the call.

Gastright left major-league baseball with a lifetime record of 72-63. Of his 72 wins, 30 came in 1890. Gastright played in 173 games over his career, 171 as a pitcher, one as an outfielder, and one as a pinch-hitter. He started 143 times, completed 121 games and recorded two saves. Gastright struck out 514 batters but walked 584. Over his 1,301⅓ innings, he gave up 1,337 hits, and retired with a 4.20 ERA.

Gastright never married. He lived with his widowed mother for many years and then with his brother Tony. He pitched for several amateur teams in Covington, reportedly did some umpiring, and served on the Newport, Kentucky, police department. Later, he worked as a miller for the Union Hay and Grain Company. In his last years Gastright suffered from poor health, living mostly at the Campbell County Infirmary.

The former big leaguer was 72 years old when he died on October 9, 1937, in Cold Spring, Kentucky, just a few miles from his birthplace. He is buried at St. Joseph Cemetery in Wilder, Kentucky. Several Gastright family members are buried nearby.

Russ Gastright has compiled several folders filled with newspaper clippings, statistical pages, letters from research librarians, and more, about his great-great-uncle. Even so, he still has plenty of questions. Did the former ballplayer follow his hometown Reds? Did he do any coaching? The ultimate prize for Hank would be to find a diary. Did Hank write one? "Hank was born March 29, 1865," Russ said. "Cy Young was born March 29, 1867. They played on opposing teams, but did they ever meet? Did they ever talk about sharing the same birthday? That would be cool to know."[27]

The topic of Hank Gastright comes up frequently when Russ gets together with his brothers. Having a former big leaguer in the family also is quite the conversation piece when he talks about baseball with friends. "I tell people that my great-great-uncle played in the major leagues and he even played for the Reds, though it was just for one game," Russ said. "At least he did have a few good seasons in the big leagues."[28]

SOURCES

The author thanks Hank Gastright's great-great-nephew, Russ Gastright, for his help in putting together this biography. Russ provided valuable information and feedback.

In addition to the sources cited in the Notes, the author also consulted baseball-almanac.com and baseball-reference.com.

NOTES

1. Author interview with Russ Gastright, November 22, 2017.
2. Author interview with Russ Gastright, December 19, 2017.
3. "Hugh Duffy with the Brotherhood," *Chicago Tribune,* January 3, 1890: 6.
4. "Gastright Pitched Phenomenal Ball," *Philadelphia Inquirer,* May 9, 1890: 6.
5. "Special Dispatch to Democrat and Chronicle," *Rochester Democrat and Chronicle,* June 20, 1890: 7.
6. "Keeping It Up," *Brooklyn Eagle,* July 16, 1890: 2.
7. *Daily Ohio State Journal* (Columbus), October 13, 1890: 1.
8. Ibid.
9. "Columbus' Crack Pitcher," *Wichita Daily Eagle,* January 21, 1891: 6.
10. Joe Heffron and Jack Heffron, *The Local Boys: Hometown Players for the Cincinnati Reds* (Covington, Kentucky: Clerisy Press, 2014), 80.
11. *Boston Sunday Post,* September 10, 1893: 15.
12. "Boston, 11; Louisville 8," *Chicago Tribune,* September 9, 1893: 7.
13. *Boston Sunday Post,* September 10, 1893: 15.
14. "The Pennant Winners," *Allentown* (Pennsylvania) *Leader,* October 14, 1893: 2.
15. Heffron and Heffron, 80.
16. "Pitcher Henry Gastright. The Latest Addition to Brooklyn's Ball Team," *Brooklyn Daily Eagle,* May 18, 1894: 6.
17. "Shut Out with One Hit," *Brooklyn Daily Eagle,* June 2, 1894: 5.
18. "We Are in Fourth Place," *Brooklyn Daily Eagle,* June 20, 1894: 5.
19. "A Game for Each Team," *Brooklyn Daily Eagle,* August 4, 1894: 5.
20. Heffron and Heffron, 80.
21. "Baseball Brevities," *Pittsburgh Press,* April 25, 1895: 5.
22. Heffron and Heffron, 80.
23. Ibid.
24. "Spiders' Makeup," *Buffalo Enquirer,* April 1, 1896: 8.
25. Heffron and Heffron, 81.
26. "Baseball Gossip," *Cincinnati Enquirer,* June 6, 1896: 2.
27. Interview with Russ Gastright, November 22, 2017.
28. Ibid.

PRETZELS GETZIEN

BY MIKE HUBER

In addition to being a pretty good pitcher and the first German-born player in the major leagues, Charles Getzien had one of the better nicknames in nineteenth-century baseball: Pretzels or Pretzel Twirler. Before becoming a Boston Beaneater, Getzien gained prominence as a star for the Detroit Wolverines of the National League, winning a championship with them in 1887. Getzien's surname was constantly misspelled (most commonly as "Getzein") by the press, but at least the reporters got "Pretzels" right.

Charles Friedrich Ludwig Getzien was born on February 14, 1864, to Carl and Wilhelmine Getzien. The Getziens had lived in the small north Prussian village of Kletzin[1] (today this is northeastern Germany) before coming to the United States. Both Carl and Wilhelmine (known to the family as Mina) were born in 1836 in Prussia. The family emigrated from Germany when Charles was a boy, although the exact year is unknown. According to the 1880 US Census, the family was living at 173 Cornell Street in Chicago.[2] Carl (he had changed his name to Charles upon arrival in America) was working as a day laborer. Mina stayed at home to care for their three children, Charles, aged 16 and employed as an errand boy; daughter Mina, 12, and Sophia, 8. Sophia was listed as being born in Illinois.

Getzien's professional baseball career started with the Grand Rapids (Michigan) Baseball Club in 1883. A right-handed pitcher, he was 14-12 in his inaugural season. A year later he was the pitching star of the team, producing a won-lost record of 27-4,[3] and that led him to sign with the Detroit Wolverines later in the 1884 season. On August 13, 1884, Getzien made his major-league debut. Facing the Cleveland Blues, Getzien struck out six

Pretzels Getzien.
(Library of Congress)

of the first eight batters he faced, but picked up 1-0 loss, falling to a former Grand Rapids teammate, John Henry, who was also making his NL debut. Cleveland scored an unearned run in the fifth inning when third baseman Joe Farrell muffed a popup.[4] Getzien came up short in his first eight decisions before finally gaining a victory on September 20 for the last-place Wolverines. Another of his Grand Rapids teammates was Edward Gastfield. Gastfield, a catcher, who also started in the Chicago City League and became Getzien's batterymate with Detroit.

Getzien earned the nickname Pretzels because of his "puzzling twisters."[5] According to *Sporting Life*, batters "describe the course of the ball from his hand to their bats as a 'pretzel curve.' In delivering his 'pretzels' 'Getz' faces third base with one foot in either corner of the lower end of the box. Bending the left knee slightly, he draws his right arm well back. Then, straightening up quickly, he slides the left foot forward with a characteristic little skip, and, bringing his arm around with a swift overhand swing, drives the ball in at a lively pace."[6]

The high point of Getzien's 1884 season occurred on October 1, when the 20-year-old hurler pitched a six-inning no-hit game.[7] In a game played at Detroit's Recreation Park, Getzien struck out 10 of the 19 batters he faced. He helped his own cause with a single in the seventh before rain forced the game to be called. In the second inning, Getzien walked Tom Lynch and Charlie Ferguson reached on an error. Lynch was erased on a double play, giving Ferguson, the Quakers' pitcher, "the honor of having been left on base."[8] Detroit won the contest, 1-0. Overall, Getzien's rookie season was a success. In 147⅓ innings, he allowed 118 hits while striking out 107. Although his record was 5-12 (Detroit's record was 28-84), Getzien's earned-run average was 1.95, third lowest in the National League.[9]

Getzien continued with the Wolverines for the next four seasons. In 1885 he completed all 37 of his starts, pitching 330 innings, but his ERA shot up to 3.03. He won only 12 games and lost 25. The next season, 1886, he posted an identical 3.03 ERA while winning 30 games and losing 11. Only 111 of the 222 runs he allowed were earned. In an article in September the *Detroit Free Press* detailed the success of Getzien's pretzel curves. Under the subheadline of "Our Sturdy German Twirler Does Good Work at Kansas City," readers discovered that "The Pretzel is all right. He went into the box to-day and pitched one of his finest, his curves circling around in the form of the delicious pastry from which Getz takes his sobriquet; all of which brings to the front the pleasing fact that the pot of Grand Rapids will do good work for the Detroit Club for the remainder of the season."[10]

In an article in 1915, *Baseball Magazine* described an 1886 game between the Wolverines and Washington Nationals:

> "The Nationals got onto Getzein in the fourth inning and batted him all over the field. In the fifth inning they kept up the slugging until Getzein said he was ill, and Manager [Ned] Hanlon wanted the Nationals to allow Getzein to retire, claiming that he was too sick to play. [Phil] Baker, captaining the home club, said he would call a doctor and have him examine Getzein, and if the latter was really sick he would probably allow the change to be made. Dr. Bond, who happened to be present, was called on, and he examined the pitcher, while the crowd guyed Getzein terribly. The doctor announced that he did not consider Getzein sick, only discouraged at the pounding he had received, and that he would be able to finish the game."[11]

In 1887 Getzien led the National League with a .690 winning percentage (29-13) with 41 complete games. He tied for the league lead (with Egyptian Healy) by yielding 24 home runs. At the beginning of September, *Sporting Life* wrote, "A surprise is in store for Charlie Getzien. His magnificent work for the club has excited the admiration of Detroiters to a high degree and they intend to express their feelings in a substantial manner. … An elegant two hundred dollar gold watch and chain [was] purchased, which will be presented to the sturdy twirler."[12] Another example of his prowess on the mound came in a game at Sportsman's Park against the St. Louis Browns of the American Association. This was Game 10 of the postseason series between the two teams. Getzien toyed with another no-hitter. According to the *Detroit Free Press*, "Up to and including the eighth inning only twenty-seven men went to the bat and not a clean hit had been scored. Not till the ninth did the world beaters succeed in getting a hit, and then they failed to score the much desired run."[13] A crowd of 10,000 "seemed to enjoy the way in which the Browns were larruped"[14] as Getzien and the Wolverines defeated the Browns, 9-0, enroute to winning the series, 10 games to 5.

Getzien's career with the Wolverines ended after the 1888 season. He pitched in 46 games, winning 19 and losing 25. Pete Conway became the ace of the pitching staff. Getzien posted a career-best 202 strikeouts, but the right-hander, now 24 years old, served up a career-high 411 hits in 404 innings. Stories appeared in the newspapers about a possible feud between Getzien and Wolverines manager Bill Watkins. After he gave up 21 hits to the Boston Beaneaters in a game in June, *Sporting Life* suggested that he may have lost his desire to pitch:

> The Getzein episode makes Detroiters weary. The Bostons have no license to make 21 hits off the Pretzel when he pitches his game. Either he was not in condition to pitch or he didn't try to. If the former was the case he is entitled to sympathy. If the latter, and he repeated his performance against the Kansas Citys a few years ago, when he deliberately tossed the balls to the plate and permitted the Cowboys to make 13 runs in one inning, why no one here [in Detroit] would mourn much if he was fined to the limit. What the merits of his quarrel with Watkins are of course are not known here. But Getzein is inclined to be very free with his tongue. Considering his fine treatment here it is time for him to get over his childish humors and do the best he knows how whenever called on.[15]

In any event, the so-called childish and free-tongued Getzien parted ways with Detroit before the next season began. He was sold to the Indianapolis Hoosiers on March 5, 1889. The *Free*

Press predicted, "When Getz loses his head among the Hoosiers, a circus with six rings will ensue."[16]

Two months before the sale, on January 17, 1889, Getzien married Rose Dibble of Grand Rapids, Michigan. She was the daughter of John and Lottie Dibble. The new couple had been living in Grand Rapids at the time of the marriage. In five seasons with the Wolverines, Getzien had pitched in 186 games, starting 185 of them and pitching 182 complete games. With the Hoosiers, he pitched in 45 games in 1889, starting all but one, but completed only 36. His earned-run average was 4.54. (The National League average was 4.02.) The Hoosiers ended the campaign in seventh place, 28 games behind the New York Giants, and 16 games under .500. The Indianapolis team folded after the 1889 season, and its players were placed "under league control."[17]

The Boston Beaneaters were the next club to sign Getzien, adding him to their roster on March 22, 1890. According to *Sporting Life*, "The Boston triumvirs got tired of negotiating with Detroit for Pitcher [Frank] Knauss, and settled the question by signing Getzien, late of Indianapolis."[18] Getzien put together a 10-game winning streak that season for the Beaneaters and had a 23-17 record. He shared the starting rotation with rookie sensation Kid Nichols and veteran John Clarkson. The trio won all of fifth-place Boston's 76 wins that season.

The next season, Getzien lost his spot in the Beaneaters' rotation, and Boston released the 27-year-old on July 16, 1891. He signed with the Cleveland Spiders in August and pitched in one game for them, allowing nine runs (eight earned) on 12 hits. He gave up one home run and four walks in the loss.

In 1892 Getzien began the season with the St. Louis Browns. He appeared in 13 games, pitching 108 innings. His control was gone. He allowed 159 hits and 31 walks, threw four wild pitches, and hit six batters. Getzien played his final major-league game on July 19. His record that season was a dismal 5-8, with an ERA of 5.67. In nine seasons in the National League, Getzien won 145 games and lost 139. He pitched 2,539 innings in 296 games, and finished his career with 277 complete games. Pretzels Getzien was out of major-league baseball before he celebrated his 29th birthday.

Getzien became a naturalized US citizen on October 12, 1892.[19] In 1894 *Sporting Life* reported, "'Pretzel' Getzien, the old League pitcher, is playing first base for a Chicago City League team."[20] He was still just 30 years old, but he never made it back to the National League.

After his playing days were over, Getzien and his wife moved to Chicago. According to the 1900 Census, he was working as an assistant grain-elevator inspector.[21] Census documents claim that he had come to the United States in 1865. Ten years later, according to the 1910 Census, Charlie and Rose had a nephew, Fred, living with them.[22] His immigration date was now listed as 1866, and he was still employed as an inspector of grain elevators in Chicago. By 1920, Getzien was now an "Inspector for the Board of Trade."[23] Some time after this, he took a job as a typesetter with the *Chicago Tribune*.[24]

Charles Getzien suffered a heart attack in 1932, at the age of 68, and died shortly thereafter, on June 19. He was buried at Concordia Cemetery in Forest Park, Illinois. His 145 wins still are a record for a pitcher born in Germany.

SOURCES

In addition to the sources mentioned in the notes, the author consulted baseball-reference.com and retrosheet.org.

NOTES

1 As of December 31, 2015, the population of Kletzin was 809. See "Bevölkerungsstand der Kreise, Ämter und Gemeinden in Mecklenburg-Vorpommern 31.12.2015". *Statistisches Amt Mecklenburg-Vorpommern* (in German), July 2016.

2 Year:1880; Census Place: Chicago, Cook, Illinois; Roll: 196; Family History Film: 1254196; Page: 211A; Enumeration District: 142; Image: 0062.

3 baseball-reference.com/bullpen/Charlie_Getzien.

4 "Sporting Matters: Detroit's Weak Batting Team Shut Out by the Cleveland Team," *Detroit Free Press*, August 14, 1884: 3.

5 "Notes and Comments: Chas. H. Getzien," *Sporting Life*, November 2, 1887: 3.

6 Ibid.

7 In 1991 major-league baseball clarified its definition of a no-hitter as "a game in which a pitcher, or pitchers, gives up no hits while pitching at least nine innings. A pitcher may give up a run or runs so long as he pitches nine innings or more and does not give up a hit." Before this clarification, Getzien's feat was considered a no-hitter.

8 "Sporting Matters: Getzien and Gastfield, With a Little Aid, Play a Wonderful Game," *Detroit Free Press*, October 2, 1884: 7.

9 Old Hoss Radbourn led the NL with an ERA of 1.38.

10 "Getzien Goes In: Our Sturdy German Twirler Does Good Work at Kansas City," *Detroit Free Press*, September 15, 1886: 8.

11 Wm. A. Phelon, "Baseball Customs Past and Present," *Baseball Magazine*, October 1915: 56.

12 "Getzien in Luck," *Sporting Life*, September 3, 1887: 1.

13 "The Browns Whitewashed: Getzien Holds the World Beaters Down to Three Actual Hits," *Detroit Free Press*, October 17, 1887: 5.

14 Ibid.

15 "Detroit Speculations," *Sporting Life*, June 20, 1888: 1.

16 "Sporting Notes," *Detroit Free Press*, March 12, 1889: 3.

17 "Transactions," baseball-reference.com/players/g/getzich01.shtml.

18 "Notes and Gossip," *Sporting Life*, April 5, 1890: 3.

19 Ancestry.com. Accessed January 18, 2017.

20 "Editorial Views, Notes, Comment," *Sporting Life*, May 19, 1894: 3.

21 Census document found on ancestry.com. Year: 1900; Census Place: Chicago Ward 15, Cook, Illinois; Roll: 262; Page: 5B; Enumeration District: 0429; FHL microfilm: 1240262.

22 Census document found on ancestry.com. Year: 1910; Census Place: Chicago Ward 15, Cook, Illinois; Roll: T624_257; Page: 16B; Enumeration District: 0724; FHL microfilm: 1374270.

23 Census document found on Ancestry.com. Year: 1920; Census Place: Chicago Ward 15, Cook (Chicago), Illinois; Roll: T625_324; Page: 2A; Enumeration District: 873; Image: 813.

24 baseball-reference.com/bullpen/Charlie_Getzien.

BILLY HAMILTON

BY DAVID L. FLEITZ

Billy Hamilton was the greatest base stealer and most prolific run scorer of nineteenth-century baseball, but few recognized his name when he gained admittance to the Hall of Fame long after his death. Bill James, who ranks Hamilton as the ninth-best center fielder of all time in his book, *The New Historical Baseball Abstract* (1999 ed.), remarked on the anonymity of the man called "Sliding Billy."

"Hamilton was completely invisible in the literature of the sport up to 1960," wrote James, "and was not elected to the Hall of Fame until 1961. He left no legend behind him, no stories, no anecdotes … Hamilton was eventually elected to the Hall of Fame purely on the overwhelming quality of his numbers. Even now, in books about nineteenth-century baseball, he is often not mentioned at all, and is never presented as a fully-formed character."[1]

William Robert Hamilton, the son of Scottish immigrants Samuel and Mary Hamilton, was born in Newark, New Jersey, on February 16, 1866. Billy was the first of two children, the other being his sister, Mary, born two years later. By 1870, the Hamilton family had settled in Clinton, Massachusetts, an industrial town in the hub of the New England textile industry. Clinton was a textile-producing town with several large factories that produced gingham, rugs, and carpeting. Samuel Hamilton found work in a textile mill. By the time Billy was 14 years old, he had quit school and joined his father in the mill.

A left-handed batter and a right-handed thrower, Billy excelled in the semipro leagues around Clinton as a teenager. He stood only 5-foot-6 as an adult, and weighed 165 pounds, but his thick, muscular legs made him appear heavier. Those powerful legs

Billy Hamilton.
(public domain)

became his greatest asset. He was an incredibly swift runner, and was usually the fastest man on the field in any game he played. He learned to use his speed to beat out bunts, steal bases, and cover large amounts of ground in the outfield. Billy was more interested in playing ball than in building a life as a textile worker, and he realized that his speed was his ticket out of the mill.

His first professional engagement came in 1887 with Lawrence of the New England League, a team that moved to Salem in mid-July to finish the season. The 1888 campaign found Billy in center field for Worcester, also an entry in the New England League. He batted .351, scored 76 runs, and stole 72 bases in only 61 games. His offensive prowess marked him as a future star, and in July of that year Worcester sold his contract to the Kansas City Cowboys of the American Association, one of the two major leagues in 1888. On July 31, Billy made his debut in right field against the Philadelphia Athletics, batting leadoff and going hitless against veteran pitcher Gus Weyhing, who pitched a no-hitter against the hapless Cowboys that day. The 22-year-old rookie played in 35 of Kansas City's remaining 58 games that season, batting .264 and stealing 19 bases for the last-place club.

Installed as Kansas City's regular right fielder and leadoff batter for the 1889 season, he posted a .301 average and a league-leading 111 steals. His totals cannot be compared to those compiled in the present day, since stolen bases then included advancing on fly balls and taking extra bases on errors. Still, Hamilton's 111 thefts, 20 more than the second-highest total in the Association that season, marked him as one of the rising stars of the game. Kansas City moved up a notch to seventh place, in large part due to the inept Louisville team falling behind them, but the ball club lost money and disbanded at season's end. On January 7, 1890, Kansas City sold Hamilton's contract to the Philadelphia Phillies for $5,000.

The Phillies (known as the Quakers prior to 1889) were harmed, as was nearly every other National League team, by the Players League revolt of 1890. Many of the 1889 Phillies had deserted the club and signed with the new league, though the team managed to retain such key performers as home run champion Sam Thompson, pitcher Kid Gleason, and catcher Jack Clements. Manager Harry Wright and team owners John I. Rogers and Al Reach filled the holes on the roster with minor-league imports and acquisitions from other teams. Wright installed Billy Hamilton as the left fielder and second-place hitter, with rookie center fielder Eddie Burke in the leadoff spot.

Hamilton displayed both his strengths and his weaknesses to the Philadelphia fans. On the basepaths, the 24-year-old Hamilton "tried to steal everything in sight, including the umpire," as one paper put it. His spectacular slides brought cheers from the fans and resulted in his nickname, "Sliding Billy." He had the go-ahead to steal at any time, not that he needed any encouragement. "Hamilton's work on the basepaths was spectacular; he delighted in stealing bases," said his outfield mate, Sam Thompson, years later. Thompson, who played a few games for the Detroit Tigers in 1906, claimed that Hamilton was "more daring and reckless" than Ty Cobb.[2] In mid-May, Hamilton and Burke switched places in the lineup, with Billy now batting leadoff.

Hamilton's speed and bunting skill kept his batting average above the .300 mark, but his fielding was sorely lacking. He led the league in outfield errors in 1890, and his fielding percentage of .882 was one of the worst in the league. He chased the ball well enough, but dropped many flies, while poor throws plagued him all season long. One Philadelphia sportswriter complained in May that Hamilton "omitted to close his hands properly at different times," after he committed two errors in a game against Brooklyn.[3] Despite these shortcomings, he batted .325 and led the third-place Phillies and the National League with 102 steals.

In 1891, the Players League refugees came streaming back to the National League following the demise of that circuit, and the best-hitting outfield in major-league history was complete with Ed Delahanty's return to Philadelphia's center field. "Big Ed" was a native of Cleveland who joined the Phillies in 1888 and jumped to Cleveland's Players League entry in 1890. He was a muscular, hard-hitting, right-handed batter, and while he was not much better in the outfield than Hamilton, he owned a stronger throwing arm. Sam Thompson, the right fielder, also was no defensive standout, but when he joined with Hamilton and Delahanty, Philadelphia boasted an offensive powerhouse no other National League outfield could match.

Hamilton's defensive play improved in 1891, with his error total dropping and his fielding percentage rising, but his main contribution to the Phillies was still on offense. He captured the league batting title with a .340 mark that year, while leading the circuit in hits (179), runs scored (141), and stolen bases (111). He was a disruptive force, particularly with his ability to frustrate opposing pitchers by fouling off their deliveries until he found one to hit or drew a walk. He was the ideal leadoff man, getting on base in more than 45 percent of his plate appearances that season, and putting himself in position to be knocked in by sluggers Delahanty and Thompson.

Though the Philadelphia pitching was too weak for the team to mount a serious challenge for the pennant, the offensive fireworks drew fans. The flashy Billy Hamilton was one of the most popular players on the team. In 1892, all three outfielders batted over .300, with Hamilton leading the way at .330. In 1893, after the pitching distance increased ten feet to the current 60' 6" standard, their batting averages soared. His outfield defense improved as well, and in 1893 Harry Wright, in his final season as manager, moved him to center field, and sent Ed Delahanty to left. Billy remained in center for the remainder of his major-league career.

Baseball scholars do not know how many times Sliding Billy was tagged out while trying to steal, as such statistics were not kept until the twentieth century. But newspaper accounts indicate that his rate of success was remarkably high. As *The Sporting News* reported in 1898, "[Hamilton] has got base stealing down to a science, and no player succeeds in the attempt so often in proportion to times attempted. His slide is wonderful, and often he gets away from the fielder when the latter has the ball in hand waiting to touch him."[4] They called it the "fadeaway slide," and while Hamilton may not have invented it, he was its most skilled practitioner. Billy's base-running exploits, while delighting fans, frustrated and embarrassed his opponents, and made him unpopular on the field. During one game against the Cleveland Spiders, third baseman Chippy McGarr became so angry with

Hamilton that he picked up the diminutive Phillie, carried him to the stands, and tossed him over the railing and into the seats.

If anyone still needed confirmation of Hamilton's value to the team, they received it in 1893. He was on his way to another outstanding season in early August, and the Phillies stood in second place after three double-digit drubbings of the Senators. Hamilton had complained of not feeling well, and his health grew worse as he tried to play despite fever and fatigue. On August 10, a doctor diagnosed Hamilton with a case of typhoid fever and ordered him out of the lineup. Billy played no more that season, and the Phillies fell out of the race, going 19-26 the rest of the way, and settling into fourth place.

Manager Arthur Irwin, who succeeded Harry Wright, scoured the minors for pitching prospects before the 1894 season started. But although Phillies displayed the most incredible hitting attack ever seen, with all their outfielders batting .400 or better, their mediocre pitching kept them back in third place. Thompson, who missed a month after finger surgery, hit .415 and drove in 147 runs; Delahanty batted .404, and substitute Tuck Turner turned in a .416 average. As for Billy Hamilton, he rode the crest of the offensive wave to score 198 runs, the highest total ever achieved in the major leagues, which has never been challenged seriously since. Hamilton also became the first player to reach base in more than half of his season plate appearances; his .521 on-base percentage stood as a record until Baltimore's John McGraw passed it four years later.

The official statistics at season's end gave Hamilton a batting average of .399 on 223 hits in 559 trips to the plate. He missed the .400 circle by one hit. Statisticians have since revised the numerical records of long-ago games, correcting errors and discrepancies, and determined that he actually had 225 hits in 558 trips, putting his average at .403. Though major-league baseball, and the Baseball Hall of Fame web site, still list his 1894 average at .399 (with 196 runs scored), the researchers at Retrosheet.org put Hamilton in the .400 class with his outfield mates.[5]

Hamilton's 1894 season was remarkable in many ways. From July 6 to August 2, he scored at least one run in 24 consecutive games for the hot-hitting Phillies. On August 31, he tied George Gore's 13-year-old major-league record with seven stolen bases, leading the Phillies to an 11-5 win over the Senators. He also compiled a 36-game hitting streak, the longest in Phillies team history until Jimmy Rollins matched the feat in 2005. But Hamilton quarreled with manager Arthur Irwin, with Irwin complaining to the papers that he was a "disorganizer." The Phillies finished nine and a half games behind Baltimore and seven in back of the Cleveland Spiders. Irwin was dismissed, and on November 14, 1895, in one of the worst trades in Philadelphia baseball history, the Phillies sent Hamilton to the Boston Beaneaters for third baseman Billy Nash, who replaced Irwin as manager of the ballclub.

Boston manager Frank Selee, seeking to replace the aggression of Tommy McCarthy (recently traded to Brooklyn), put Hamilton in the leadoff spot and gave him free rein on the base paths. His speed and enthusiasm energized the Boston lineup, and his .366 average and 153 runs scored led the Beaneaters to a fourth-place finish in 1896. In 1897, Selee promoted two young pitchers, Ted Lewis and Fred Klobedanz, to regular roles in support of the staff ace, Kid Nichols; suddenly Boston owned the best starting pitching in the league. Third baseman Jimmy Collins and first baseman Fred Tenney solidified the infield, while rookie Marty Bergen took over as the regular catcher. Boston was now the most balanced team in the National League. After a strenuous battle with the defending champion Baltimore Orioles, the Beaneaters won their first league title since 1893, making Hamilton a pennant-winner for the first time in his career.

Hamilton was now the centerpiece of a new all-star outfield, with Hugh Duffy in left and rookie Chick Stahl, who batted .354 and scored 112 runs, in right. Hamilton was a major contributor to the championship team, leading the league with 152 runs scored and 105 walks. On September 27, with the pennant on the line in the final contest of a three-game series with Baltimore, he swatted four hits, scored three runs, and stole two bases in a 19-10 win. That virtually sewed up the flag for Boston. The Beaneaters wound up winning the pennant by two games over the Orioles.

Hamilton loved playing for the Beaneaters, as Boston was only an hour by train from his home in Clinton. Billy had married a local girl named Rebecca Carr in 1888, and by 1896 they had three daughters: Ethel, Mildred, and Ruth. A fourth daughter, Dorothy, was born in 1904, completing the family. The Hamiltons made their home in Clinton for more than three decades, and he often took the train to Clinton on off-days during the season.

The Beaneaters repeated as champions in 1898, but Hamilton's legs were beginning to wear down. A sprained knee limited him to 110 games in a 152-game season; batted .369 and scored 110 runs. A more serious injury in 1899 — a tendon problem in his lower leg that developed after he wrenched his knee while sliding in early May — shortened his 1899 season and put his career in jeopardy. He played only 84 games, and saw his batting average fall to .310. His stolen base total dwindled to 19. At age 34, Hamilton managed to play the entire 1900 season without a serious injury, batting .333, but with only 32 stolen bases. Frank Selee still batted him in the leadoff slot, but his days of scoring more than a run per game were over. He was slowing down noticeably, and the Beaneaters fell to sixth place.

When the American League began play in 1901, most of the Boston stars bolted to the new circuit, leaving Selee with a shell of a team. Hamilton, however, turned down all offers and remained with the Beaneaters for one more season. He was now 35 years old, and his batting average sank below the .300 mark for the first time since 1888. He stole only 20 bases in 102 games for the seventh-place Beaneaters, and at the end of the season he requested and received his release.

Few observers paid attention to lifetime statistics and career records 100 years ago, but Billy Hamilton's numbers marked him as one of the greats. He retired as baseball's all-time leader in walks, a distinction he held until Eddie Collins passed him in 1922. His .344 career batting average is the eighth highest of all time, and his on-base percentage of .455 is surpassed only by Ted Williams, Babe Ruth, and John McGraw. Hamilton's career stolen bases, once recorded as 937 and later revised to 914, stood as a major league record until Lou Brock, who retired in 1979 with 938 steals (under different rules). During his 14 years in the majors, Billy scored 1,697 runs in 1,594 games, and his average of 1.06 runs per game is the highest figure ever recorded. Only three men (Hamilton and fellow nineteenth-century stars Harry Stovey and George Gore) scored more than one run per game during their careers, and no modern player has come close to matching the feat.[6]

Billy Hamilton was gone from the majors, but not from the game. In June 1902 he was hired to manage and play for the New England League team in Haverhill, Massachusetts. He remained with Haverhill for three seasons, playing on a part-time basis in 1902 and 1903, and becoming a full-timer in 1904. His 1903 team finished last, but he led the team to the pennant in 1904. At the age of 38, he won the batting title with a .412 average, and led the league in stolen bases and runs scored.

This success at Haverhill led to a position at Harrisburg in the Tri-State League, but disputes both with the team owners and players led to his ouster in mid-1906. The old ballplayer then returned to Haverhill, where he played and managed until 1908, winning another batting title. He spent the next two seasons with another New England League team, the Lynn Shoemakers, before he finally retired as a player after the 1910 campaign.

Hamilton spent the 1911 and 1912 seasons scouting for his old Boston team (who became the Braves in the early 1910s), and then managed for Fall River and Springfield in the New England League in 1913 and 1914. In 1916, he bought a part-interest in the Worcester ballclub and moved his family there, managing the team for one season. Billy sold his interest in the club in March 1917 and never returned to the game. He and wife, Rebecca, resided in Worcester for the rest of their lives. The old ballplayer obtained a position as a production foreman at a local leather manufacturing plant, where he worked until the early 1930s. He battled heart disease after his retirement from the factory. Mostly confined to bed for the last year of his life, Billy Hamilton died at home in Worcester on December 16, 1940, at the age of 74. His wife, who lived until 1957, survived him, as well as four daughters and two grandchildren.

On July 24, 1961, 21 years after his death, three of his children represented him at his Hall of Fame induction ceremony in Cooperstown.

NOTES

1 Bill James, *The New Bill James Historical Baseball Abstract* (New York: Free Press, 2001), 728.

2 Robert L. Tiemann and Mark Rucker (editors), *Nineteenth Century Stars* (Kansas City, Missouri: Society for American Baseball Research, 1989), 75.

3 *Brooklyn Eagle*, May 10, 1890.

4 *The Sporting News*, June 4, 1898.

5 This statistical information was obtained free of charge from and is copyrighted by Retrosheet. Interested parties may contact Retrosheet at http://www.retrosheet.org.

6 Ibid.

JOE HARRINGTON
BY SETH MOLAND-KOVASH

Joe Harrington, 1900.
(public domain)

A funeral Mass was celebrated for one of Fall River's favorite sons on Saturday, September 16, 1933, at the city's St. Louis Church. Bouquets and tributes were sent by many of his old baseball friends and fans. Joe Harrington had been born in Fall River, Massachusetts, and he died in Fall River, having played baseball for Fall River among many other stops along the way. His brief major-league career came in late 1895 and through the majority of the 1896 season with the Boston Beaneaters of the National League. His debut with Boston was special, as he hit a home run on September 10, 1895, becoming the first major leaguer to hit a home run in his first major-league at-bat.

Joseph C. Harrington was born in Fall River on December 21, 1869, to the 39-year-old Jeremiah and 36-year-old Mary (McCarty) Harrington. Jeremiah and Mary had been born in Ireland and were part of the great Irish migration to the United States in the middle of the nineteenth century. Fall River, south of Boston and just across the state line from Rhode Island, was the center of the American cotton textile industry at the time, boasting over 120 cotton mills. Jeremiah worked in one of the local cotton mills and Mary kept house. Joe came into the world as the youngest of seven. It was a hard life for the Harringtons as it was for many in those days: According to the 1870 census, Joe's three eldest siblings (ages 15, 14, and 12) had joined their father to work in the mill.

There would be no full-time life in the mill for Joe, however, as baseball beckoned. At the age of 21 in 1891, he joined the Woonsocket (Rhode Island) club of the New England League. He played in Woonsocket for two years, batting only .213 in 96 games (384 at-bats) in 1892,[1] before joining his hometown Fall River Indians for the 1893 campaign. At the age of

23, Harrington was among the youngest on this team but the right-handed batter and thrower led the team with a .333 batting average in nearly full-time play. During 1893, Harrington played exclusively at first base for the club, managed by fellow local Michael McDermott.

Statistical records for Fall River and the New England League do not exist for the 1894 and 1895 campaigns, but we do know that Harrington continued to play for the Indians through the end of the 1895 season and that his team won the New England League championship in both of his seasons, with the 1894 team being called "one of the best ever representing Fall River in the league."[2] He is presumed to have moved off first base and primarily to third base during the 1894 and 1895 seasons as he was celebrated as "star third baseman for several seasons in the old New England League" in his funeral announcement.[3] Upon his death, Harrington was not remembered as a great slugger but as a wonderful fielder:

> Joe Harrington was without question one of the greatest baseball players ever developed in Fall River, and in the opinion of veteran critics, he was the best third basemen ever to play in the New England league. As a fielder he had no faults, being able to go to his right or left without any apparent exertion and on bunts he had few surprises. His great arm, which enabled him to get the ball across the diamond with bullet-like speed, was sure death to any opponents who tried the bunting game.[4]

In Harrington's post-major-league return to the New England League, records were a bit stronger and he is recorded as playing 31 games at third base over two seasons. This reputation as a great New England League third baseman must have come from 1894 and 1895.

When the Fall River season ended in 1895, Harrington had earned a bigger chance. His contract was purchased on September 9 by the National League's Boston Beaneaters led by manager Frank Selee. On the morning of September 10, when Harrington was set to make his major-league debut, Boston sat at 62-49, in fourth place, 10½ games behind the eventual champion Baltimore Orioles. Harrington joined a team featuring future Hall of Famers including pitcher Kid Nichols, who finished the year at 26-16 with a 3.41 ERA; outfielder Tommy McCarthy, who was at the tail end of his Hall of Fame career; and outfielder Hugh Duffy, who was the team batting leader with an impressive batting average of .353, after record 1894 average of .440. Hall of Fame third baseman Jimmy Collins was also a member of the 1895 Beaneaters but he spent the bulk of the season on loan to Louisville.

The regular second baseman for Boston, Bobby Lowe, was out with an injury and many Beaneaters had covered second base for a stretch. Boston called on the 25-year-old Harrington to play second base and bat eighth in his first game, on Tuesday, September 10, against the St. Louis Browns before a sparse crowd of 1,000. The Beaneaters lost the game 8-4 before heading off to New York to play the Giants the next day. The *Boston Post* wrote of his debut:

> The Boston team was a trifle strengthened, as Joe Harrington of Fall River was secured to play second base. He filled Lowe's shoes, and both in fielding and at the bat he acted like Duffy. When he stepped to the plate in the first inning he was given a great ovation as he approached the rubber. He responded with a home run drive over the left field fence. Harrington has come to stay. He has the style and make-up of a natural ball player. When he stands up to the plate he reminds one of the Cleveland batters. He is not afraid and meets the ball squarely. His fielding was perfect, as he handled ground balls with ease.[5]

Harrington added two more singles later in the game to finish 3-for-4 with two runs scored. In the field he was credited with two putouts, five assists, and no errors. The *Post* assured its readers that Harrington would be back at second base for that afternoon's contest in New York.

Harrington had a scare less than a week later when he was injured in a traffic accident on the team bus after a doubleheader in Baltimore on September 14.[6] Despite early fears, he returned the Beaneaters lineup quickly. Harrington manned second base for 18 of the final 20 games of the team's season. He added one more home run and finished the season batting .277 and slugging .431 in his 75 plate appearances as the Beaneaters played out a 71-60 sixth-place campaign.

When the 1896 season opened, Harrington was a regular fixture for the Beaneaters, but at third base this time. In the offseason, the Beaneaters made a few transactions that cleared room for him. They traded regular third baseman Billy Nash to the Phillies for outfielder Billy Hamilton. Then they sold outfielder Tommy McCarthy to the Brooklyn Grooms and Jimmy Collins came back from the Louisville Colonels on his loan. Collins, who had split time between third base and the outfield for Louisville in 1895, was installed in Boston's outfield, clearing third base for Harrington. That arrangement did not last long.

Harrington played most of the games in the first half of the season, primarily at third base with a bit of shortstop and second base thrown in.[7] In that time, his defense was below average, with a range factor of 3.19 compared with the league average of 4.09. With below-average defense, his bat would have to carry the day and it did not. In 222 plate appearances in 1896, Harrington hit just .201 and slugged only .271. And so, on July 28, 1896 Harrington was released by the Beaneaters and Jimmy Collins was installed at third base.

After his release, Harrington played for many minor-league teams from the top-level Eastern League Syracuse Stars and Worcester Farmers to the New England League's New Bedford Whalers and his hometown Fall River Indians, to even lower-level teams in the Connecticut State League, including the Norwich Reds and Meriden Silverites. After splitting time between New Bedford and Meriden in 1904, Harrington hung up his spikes and moved home to Fall River.

Harrington never married and never had children, but remained close with his many nephews and nieces. He was a favorite of Fall River baseball fans throughout his life. In his 1933 obituary, a brief story was told about a benefit game for him held some years before:

> A few years ago a benefit game was staged here for Harrington and the money received as a result of the game helped to make Joe's last years happy. He never forgot the great turnout at the benefit game, which he attended himself, and for which he was always grateful to Fall River fans.[8]

Harrington was long forgotten as the first major leaguer to hit a home run in his first at-bat. But he was not forgotten by the baseball fans of Fall River, Massachusetts.

SOURCES

In addition to the sources cited in the Notes, the author also used Baseball-Reference.com and ancestry.com

NOTES

1 *Spalding's Official Base Ball Guide and Official League Book for 1893: A Complete Handbook of the National Game of Base Ball* (Chicago: A.G. Spalding & Bros, 1893), 142.

2 "Death Calls 'Joe' Harrington, Star of 'Little Old New England League,'" *Fall River Herald News*, September 14, 1933: 1.

3 "Funerals," *Fall River Herald News*, September 16, 1933: 6.

4 Death Calls 'Joe' Harrington."

5 "Tables Turned: This Time the St. Louis Team Won Out," *Boston Post*, September 11, 1895: 3.

6 "Lose Them Both," *Boston Post*, September 14, 1895: 4. A "bus" in the 1890s was, of course, a horse-drawn vehicle used to transport people.

7 In 1896, Harrington played 49 games at third base, four at shortstop, and one at second base. In his late-season 1895 call-up, all 18 of his games were at second base.

8 "Death Calls 'Joe' Harrington."

KING KELLY

BY PETER M. GORDON

Mike "King" Kelly was professional baseball's first matinee idol: the first ballplayer to "author" an autobiography, the first to have a hit song written about him, and the first to have a successful acting career outside the game. A handsome man with a full mustache and a head of red hair, Kelly through his fame helped change professional baseball from a pleasant diversion into America's most popular sport. At his peak Kelly earned the highest salary in the game. He spent every cent he made, and died almost penniless less than a year after he played his last professional game.

Michael Joseph Kelly was born on New Year's Eve, 1857, in Troy, New York, to Irish immigrants Mike and Catherine Kelly. Mike and Catherine had left Ireland during the 1840s to escape the potato famine. After landing in New York City, they moved 125 miles up the Hudson to Troy, at that time a bustling commercial town at the eastern terminus of the Erie Canal.

The United States in 1857 had 31 states and approximately 31 million people. Mike Kelly was born three years before Abraham Lincoln's election and the start of the Civil War. Baseball was largely an amateur sport in those days. Different forms of the game competed with one another and with cricket for players and fans.

In 1862, when Mike was 4 years old, his father joined the Union army and marched south with Troy's volunteer regiment, leaving Catherine to raise Mike and his older brother, James. Mike's father re-enlisted after the Civil War and the family moved to Washington, DC. Kelly told the story of what happened next in his autobiography, *Play Ball, Stories of the Ball Field:* "Ill health compelled my father to leave the army, and we moved

King Kelly, 1898.
(public domain)

King Kelly in 1897
(public domain)

to Paterson, N.J. My father's health didn't continue to improve any, and we had not been in Paterson very long before he passed over to the great silent majority. My mother followed him not long after."[1]

It's an indication of Kelly's character that, despite being orphaned at a young age, he stayed positive. The next passage states, "My boyhood days in Paterson were just the same as is usually spent by boys. In my more youthful days, out-door sports occupied most of my time after school-hours."

Mike found work at a coal factory, where his job was to carry a bucket of coal from the basement to the roof. Once that was done for the day, he could leave and spend his time doing what he most enjoyed – playing baseball. One of his best friends in Paterson was Jim McCormick, who also became a professional player, winning 265 games in the major leagues. The two played sports, performed amateur theatricals, and enjoyed life as much as possible in the Paterson of the 1870s. For Mike, his friend Jim, and many other boys in Paterson, that meant days of hard manual labor for a few dollars, and as much "outdoor sport" as they could find.

Paterson was home to several amateur clubs. In 1873, when Mike was 15, he was recruited to play on Paterson's top club, captained by Blondie Purcell, who later played on several teams in the National League. The Paterson club also included McCormick and Edward Sylvester Nolan, a pitcher so good he was known as "The Only" Nolan. By 1876 Kelly had become the starting catcher, with McCormick as pitcher. Their team, the Keystones, dominated local competition in the mid-1870s, but the haphazard nature of professional ball in the 1870s forced the best players to rely on luck to advance in their careers.

According to his autobiography, Kelly considered quitting baseball in 1877. He apprenticed himself to a weaver, but as he put it, "I was a crank [fan] on the game, and couldn't leave it if I wanted to."[2] Kelly joined a team in Port Jervis, New York, and then was contacted by the Columbus (Ohio) Buckeyes, a minor-league team. In all probability McCormick was responsible for scouting Kelly. Kelly was happy to sign his first professional contract, although he said that the players didn't always get the money they were promised. Kelly's batting average for his first year as a pro was only .156.[3] The Buckeyes lost money and disbanded on September 15.

The Buckeyes did play enough exhibition games against National League teams for those teams to evaluate talent, and the Cincinnati Red Stockings offered Mike a contract for 1878. Indeed, they thought enough of Kelly to make him one of their 10 reserved players. At the age of 20, Mike Kelly became a big-league ballplayer.

The Red Stockings signed Kelly as a catcher and an outfielder, but he played mostly in the outfield since the Red Stockings already had an established catcher, Deacon White. Mike played in 60 games, batted .283, and scored 29 runs. The Red Stockings, after having a losing record the previous year, finished over .500, only four games out of first place.

In 1879 Kelly became a star. He batted .348, third in the league. He was fourth in runs scored, third in hits, and third in triples. He also began to develop a reputation as a heady ballplayer, who took advantage of his superior "base ball brains."[4] In one game between Cincinnati and Cap Anson's Chicago White Stockings, Kelly stroked a double to left. After he rounded second, the ball came in to Chicago second baseman Joe Quest, who thought he tagged Kelly out. The umpire called Kelly safe, which led to a fervent argument at second base between the umpire and most of the Chicago players. Kelly, realizing that no one had called time, jumped up and came home to score, thus calling himself to the attention of Cap Anson.

Kelly had a great 1879 season, but the Cincinnati club didn't. The club reportedly lost $10,000, a significant sum for the time. Owner J. Wayne Neff simply released all of his players in September, saying he couldn't pay them.[5] This left Kelly free to seek other employment for the 1880 season, reserve clause or no.

After the 1879 season Kelly went on a California barnstorming trip with several other major leaguers, including Purcell and Anson. According to Kelly's autobiography, this fall trip made the players "a pocketful of money."[6] The California fans loved Mike's bantering on the field, his good-natured personality, and his "kicking" or baiting umpires. He performed so well that Anson asked him to join the Chicago club.

Kelly didn't get so excited by the prospect that he forgot to bargain for the best salary. He held out until Anson agreed to meet his figure. At the age of 22 Kelly was about to become one of the biggest stars on the first great professional team of the 1880s, the Chicago White Stockings.

When Kelly reported to Chicago on April 1, 1880, he was astounded to find that Anson expected him to lose 20 of his 170 pounds. Anson's hard training got Kelly and the rest of the team into shape for the season. It's hard to say whether Kelly did lose 20 pounds that year, because his reported height and weight for most of his career was 5-feet-10 and 170 pounds. There's no question that young Kelly and the other White Stockings did round into shape by the start of the 1880 season. The team got off to such a great start that soon all professional teams imitated the White Stockings' "spring training."

Chicago was the biggest city in the National League in 1880 and usually led in attendance. Owned by former player and entrepreneur Albert Spalding and captained on the field by the 28-year-old Anson, the White Stockings had the best management and financial resources, and assembled some of the best players available. In addition to Anson and Kelly, the team included Silver Flint, Ned Williamson, Abner Dalrymple, George Gore, Larry Corcoran, and Tom Burns. Flint was the team's regular catcher, playing without a glove, mask, or any equipment. Kelly played mainly in the outfield, and was the team's "change" catcher. Ever the innovator, Kelly adopted the use of the catcher's glove, mask, and chest protector to help him stay in the game.

Anson, in his biography, *A Ball Player's Career*, characterized Kelly in the 1880s as follows: "(Kelly) came to Chicago from Cincinnati, and soon became a general favorite. He was a whole-souled, genial fellow, with a host of friends, and but one enemy, that one being himself."[7]

Anson wrote about how he tried to reform Kelly's drinking habits and keep him in shape, but no matter how many times Kelly swore to give up booze and stay on the straight and narrow, he would always fall off the wagon. In the 1880s many ballplayers were notorious drunks, including Kelly's teammates Williamson, Gore, and Flint.

The White Stockings opened the 1880 season in Cincinnati, Kelly's former town, and Mike won the opener, 4-3, with a home run. It was to be his only home run of the season, but that was still 25 percent of the team's total of four. The White Stockings didn't need home runs to dominate that season. They finished with a 67-17 record, 15 games ahead of second-place Providence. Their .798 winning percentage remains a National League record. Part of that was due to on-field innovations devised by Kelly. He was an expert at the hit-and-run. He experimented with different methods of getting past infielders to the base. Kelly gets credit for inventing the hook slide, which in his era was called the Chicago slide.

In *Slide, Kelly, Slide*, a biography of Kelly, author Marty Appel quotes early baseball historian Maclean Kennedy about Kelly's baseball prowess. Kennedy saw Kelly play, and wrote, "There was never a better or more brilliant player. Colorful beyond description, he was the light and the life of the game. ... He was one of the quickest thinkers that ever took a signal. He originated more trick plays than all players put together. ... As a drawing card, he was the greatest of his time. Fandom around the circuit always welcomed the Chicago team, with the great Anson and his lieutenant, King Kelly."[8]

Kelly batted a respectable .291 in 1880. Gore, his teammate, won the batting title at .360, with Anson second at .337. Off the field Kelly became known as a fashion plate. He liked to frequent taverns and buy rounds for his friends. He loved the theater, attending both plays and vaudeville. It was to be a pattern throughout his brief life. Kelly made a great deal of money for his time, but spent every penny enjoying himself.

Anson kept the team intact for the 1881 season. Kelly again showed his ability to take advantage of situations by cutting, or deliberately running 15 to 20 feet inside third base during a game when the umpire's attention was elsewhere, to score the winning run in a 5-4 game on May 20 against Boston.[9] A writer at the game reported this, but it was certainly not the first or last time Kelly pulled that trick.

The 1881 pennant race was closer than 1880's, but Chicago still won going away with a nine-game lead. Anson won the batting title with a .399 average. Kelly and his teammate Dalrymple tied for sixth in the league with a .323 average. Kelly finished second in runs scored with 84 in 82 games.

After the season Kelly returned to Paterson and married his girlfriend, Agnes Hedifen, on October 25, 1881. They often spent the offseason at her brother's farmhouse in Hyde Park, New York.

In his autobiography Kelly called the 1882 White Stockings the greatest team he ever played on, and perhaps the greatest team of all time. They received their first strong challenge for the pennant from the Providence Grays, managed by Harry Wright. The race came down to a three-game series in Chicago in September. The White Stockings swept three close games from the Grays, and Kelly made the key play. As he slid into second as the first out of a sure double play, Kelly flung his hand up and pushed shortstop George Wright's arm so that the sure out turned into a two-base error. Afterward manager Harry Wright blamed the losses on "Kelly's infernal tricks."[10]

Kelly had a subpar year in 1883, hitting .255, and the White Stockings finished second to the Boston Beaneaters. In 1884 overhand pitching was allowed and averages went down, but

Frank O. Small painting.
(Courtesy McGreevy Collection, Boston Public Library)

Kelly hit a league-leading .354 and scored 120 runs. The White Stockings finished tied for fourth to the Providence Grays and the amazing Hoss Radbourn, who won 59 games. Kelly spent most of his time in the outfield but also played all the infield positions, caught, and even pitched in two games. He continued to invent plays. Running at third base in a close game against Detroit, he faked an injury to give Williamson, who was on second, a reason to come over and check on him. Kelly alerted Williamson that he would dash for home on the next pitch and for Williamson to be ready to follow right behind him. Detroit, astounded at Kelly's quick recovery, didn't think to throw the ball until he was close to the plate with Williamson right behind. Detroit catcher Charlie Bennett got the ball and was about to tag Kelly when Kelly opened his legs wide and Williamson slid through them and around Bennett to score because Bennett wasn't expecting it. Later, of course, the rules were changed so a runner would be called out if he passed the runner ahead of him.[11]

In 1885 the White Stockings were back on top. Owner Albert Spalding and Anson brought in Kelly's old friend Jim McCormick to pitch alongside future Hall of Famer John Clarkson, and the club moved into a brand-new park, the West Side Grounds. The White Stockings got off to a great start, and it appeared that the only thing that could stop them was Chicago's night life. Kelly wasn't the only drinking man on the team, others being Gore, Williamson, Flint, and a new young substitute outfielder, Billy Sunday. By midsummer the New York franchise earned its nickname Giants with a lineup that included John Montgomery Ward, Roger Connor, Buck Ewing, and Mickey Welch. The pennant was still in doubt when the Giants came to Chicago in late September for four games. Anson's men took three out of four. Kelly led all batters with seven hits in the four games, and scored five of Chicago's 25 runs. For the season he batted .288 and led the National League for the second straight year with 124 runs scored.

After the season the White Stockings played a series against the American Association champion St. Louis Browns for what was billed as the US Championship. Unlike a modern World Series, Spalding and Browns owner Chris Von der Ahe negotiated a 12-game traveling exhibition series with a top prize of $1,000 for the winning team. One game was in Chicago, three in St. Louis, and the rest in a variety of National League cities. The series was marred by poor umpiring, a controversial tie game, a potential forfeit, and poor play on both sides. At the end of the series, Spalding and Von der Ahe decided to count the disputed second game a forfeit for Chicago, because that enabled them to claim the shortened series as a tie between the teams, making each team 3-3-1. Neither owner would then have to pay the $1,000 purse. Kelly had a good series at the plate, hitting over .300, but made five errors.[12]

In 1886 the 28-year-old Kelly was arguably the biggest star in a star-studded National League. Newspapers and fans routinely called him King Kelly or The Only Kelly, a cherished sobriquet because of the large number of Irish immigrants in the United States at the time. Kelly responded to the adulation with his best season. He led the league in batting with a .388 average, led in runs scored for the third straight year with 155, and had 32 doubles, 11 triples, and 53 stolen bases.

During the 1886 season Spalding made a strong effort to curtail the excessive drinking of some of his stars, including Kelly, McCormick, and Williamson. At one point Spalding held back $250 from their pay, which they could earn back by staying sober. During the summer he had detectives follow the players, and fined some $25 for excessive drinking. Kelly at the time was paid at least $2,000 per season by the White Stockings, and had income from other business activities. The fines were significant, but nothing could curb Kelly's fondness for alcohol.

After a night of drunken revelry during the summer of 1886, Billy Sunday told his drinking buddies, "Goodbye. I'm going to Jesus Christ."[13] In his autobiography, Sunday wrote of how he was scared to tell his teammates he was reforming. The first man he saw at the park was Kelly, who said, "Bill, I'm proud of you. Religion is not my strong suit, but I'll help you all I can."[14] That statement sums up his character – generous to a fault, willing to help everyone, but unable to tame his own demons.

The 1886 pennant race was a tight battle between the White Stockings and the Detroit Wolverines. The race came down to the end of September, when Chicago prevailed. Immediately after the season, Anson and Spalding took the team to Washington, where they met with President Grover Cleveland. Kelly counted that as one of the greatest achievements of his life.

Again Kelly played all over the field – mainly outfield and catcher, but also first base, second base, shortstop, and third base. Once again St. Louis won the American Association pennant. This time Spalding and Von der Ahe agreed to make the series a best-of-seven, with the first three games in Chicago, the next three in St. Louis, and the final game, if necessary, on neutral ground. The winner was supposed to take the entire gate for the series; the loser would get nothing. Chicago took two of the first three games. Kelly didn't hit much, but made some heady plays at catcher, picking off the speedy Arlie Latham at second base on a dropped ball and tagging out Yank Robinson at home and holding on to the ball despite being spiked in the collision.

The series moved to St. Louis, but without starting pitcher Jim McCormick, who was said to have "rheumatism," forcing Anson to pitch third baseman Williamson one game. The Browns won Games Four and Five easily, but found Chicago pitcher John Clarkson in fine form for Game Six. Chicago went ahead 3-1, but St. Louis tied it up. In the bottom of the 10th, Clarkson gave up a single to Browns center fielder Curt Welch. The next batter singled and Yank Robinson sacrificed. With the winning run just 90 feet away, Clarkson tried to quick-pitch the batter and lost control. The pitch went far over Kelly's glove. Welch slid home with the winning run, in what came to be known as the $15,000 slide (even though some newspaper reports didn't mention a slide at all), since the Browns received all the gate receipts.

After this devastating loss, Anson and Spalding decided to clean house and get some players who would be better able to keep in training. The Boston Beaneaters believed Kelly would attract the numerous Irish population of the city, and were willing to pay the amazing sum of $10,000 to purchase his contract. They paid Kelly $5,000 in salary, which was listed as the $2,000 National

League maximum plus $3,000 for the use of his picture for advertising purposes.[15]

The record purchase price only increased Kelly's celebrity. Young Boston fans began following him around town, asking him to sign his name on a piece of paper. Kelly may not have been the first baseball player fans followed for an autograph, but as the most famous he can certainly be given credit for popularizing the practice.

Kelly also received extra income from endorsements. A "Slide, Kelly, Slide" model sled was tried, as was a Kelly-branded shoe polish. Reproductions of a painting of Kelly sliding head-first into second base in front of a cheering crowd replaced paintings of Custer's Last Stand and other scenes in Irish taverns throughout the city. In 1889 a song called "Slide, Kelly Slide," written by John Kelly (no relation) for vaudeville star Maggie Cline, became a hit, selling millions of copies of sheet music. Later, in 1892, when early recording techniques allowed for songs to be reproduced, "Slide, Kelly Slide" became America's first hit record.

Kelly justified the price of his sale from the start of the 1887 season. More than 10,000 fans packed the park for the Beaneaters' first few home games, and the team got off to a fast start. Reports of Kelly's high salary made people think he was rich, but as Kelly wrote at the time: "There are two classes of people whose wealth is always exaggerated by the great public. They are ball players and actors. There are a few rich ball players and a few rich actors, but they are few and far between. They find so many different ways of spending money, that it is very hard for them to save very much."[16]

Kelly knew whereof he spoke. He liked to spend money at the faro table, the track, and, of course, the saloons, where he preferred whisky to beer. Still, Kelly liked to boast that he "will never be broke."[17] He had a good year in 1887, hitting .322, scoring 120 runs (although he didn't lead the league) and stealing 84 bases. (That was the second year steals were an official statistic.) Boston finished fifth. The *Boston Globe* presented Kelly with a gold medal after the season inscribed to the "champion base stealer" of the Boston Base Ball Club.[18] That medal is now in the Hall of Fame.

Kelly continued his tricky play. He was said to drop his catcher's mask in front of home just as runners began to slide home to keep them from touching the plate. In the outfield he reportedly kept an extra ball in his pocket to use when a ball was hit over the fence to make it appear he had caught the ball. Perhaps the most repeated story was the time Kelly was on the bench in the bottom of the ninth with two outs. At the time the rules allowed a player to substitute himself into a game just by making an announcement. As the batter lofted a pop foul near the Boston bench, Kelly stood up and said in a loud, clear voice, "Kelly now catching." He caught the ball barehanded and won the game. (This writer was unable to find a specific game associated with this story. It was constantly repeated, and whether or not it was true, it was an example of the sort of play Kelly was capable of.) As Chicago sportswriter Hugh Fullerton wrote, "He was perhaps the most brilliant individualist the game ever knew."[19]

Kelly barnstormed through the West after the 1887 season, accompanied by his wife, Agnes. He made his first professional appearance on stage in Boston in a play called *A Rag Baby*. He received more than a minute of applause after he uttered his first line, and the play was a success. Kelly wrote, "Glad it was a success; glad that I lived through it."[20] He and a ghostwriter produced what was the first published autobiography of a ballplayer. Called *Play Ball: Stories From the Ball Field*, it was released in 1888, and sold for 25 cents.

Boston sent another $10,000 to Chicago in the offseason to purchase pitcher John Clarkson, and could boast in 1888 of its $20,000 battery, Kelly and Clarkson. However, this move did not bring the Beaneaters a pennant. The team jumped out to an early lead but faded, losing the pennant to the New York Giants. Kelly hit .318, third in the league, but his 85 runs scored and 56 stolen bases were both down from the previous season. As a catcher, he made 54 errors in 76 games and allowed 54 passed balls. In the winter of 1888 Spalding organized a world tour that pitted his Chicago team against a picked nine of the best players in the rest of the league. Spalding wanted Kelly, the biggest star in baseball, to join him. Kelly signed a contract to go on the trip, but backed out at the last minute, citing "business interests"[21] in New York. Perhaps he just didn't want to work again with Spalding and Anson; his reasons for skipping the trip were never made clear. He was back playing for Boston in 1889.

The Beaneaters fought bravely for the pennant until the last day of the 1889 season, finishing one game out. Kelly hit .294 and scored 120 runs in 125 games. His drinking may have made a significant difference for the team; he missed at least one crucial game down the stretch because he was too hung over to play.

After the 1889 season, simmering labor unrest between the owners and players broke into open warfare. The Players Brotherhood enlisted the help of some financial backers and formed the Players League, which attracted more than 100 players from both the National League and the American Association. The Players League had stars but not the financial acumen of the National League owners, who scheduled their games in direct competition with Players League games in their cities. Kelly was named captain and manager of the Boston Reds, the Players League franchise. As with everything else in his life, he exuded confidence. "I'm one of the bosses now," he said. "Next year we will be in command and the former presidents will have to drive horse cars for a living."[22]

But Kelly struggled with the business details of running a club. A sportswriter recalled seeing him wrestle with an account book. "This bookkeeping's hell, me boy," Mike told him.[23] However, on the field the Boston Reds sparkled. In addition to Kelly, the team had Dan Brouthers, Radbourn, Tom Brown, Bill Daley, and Hardy Richardson.

In June the Reds went to Chicago for a four-game series. Spalding met with Kelly, who told him that the Players League clubs were all losing money and that launching it was a "foolish blunder."[24] Spalding laid a check for $10,000 on the table and told Kelly he could have that check and a three-year contract at a figure he could name if he rejoined the Beaneaters. According to Spalding's memoirs, Kelly asked for a little time to think about it and went out for a walk. When he returned he said, "I've decided not to accept."

Spalding said, "What? You don't want the $10,000?"

Kelly said, "Aw, I want the $10,000 bad enough; but I've thought the matter all over, and I can't go back on the boys. And, neither would you."[25]

Spalding shook Kelly's hand, and then Kelly borrowed $500 from Spalding.

The Players League lacked the deep pockets of the National League and folded after its one season. Kelly's Boston Reds had the biggest attendance, and won the championship. Kelly hit .325 and stole 52 bases in what was his last all-around good year. As the players started looking for jobs for the 1891 season, Kelly found that neither Chicago nor Boston wanted him back. He ended up signing with Cincinnati's American Association franchise for $1,750 to play and manage the team.[26] No doubt the Cincinnati owners thought Kelly would draw a crowd. They named the team Kelly's Killers.

The Cincinnati team couldn't afford good players, and Kelly had to play any warm body. Attendance was poor, and after only five months in Cincinnati the franchise disbanded. Kelly moved to the Boston American Association franchise. After only eight days on that team Kelly accepted a better offer from the Beaneaters of the National League. This signing provoked another war between the American Association and the National League. Kelly didn't play much for the Beaneaters, but after his arrival they reeled off 18 straight wins and won the National League pennant, Kelly's seventh championship. After the season, Kelly and his wife joined the team on a European barnstorming tour.

The American Association dissolved after the 1891 season, with the National League absorbing four of the franchises. The 12-team league created a split season so that the first-half and second-half winners could have a championship series. Kelly was 34 during the 1892 season, and his skills were fading. He was never much for training, and was losing his speed and strength. He hit only .189 in 78 games, mostly at catcher. Boston won the first half and the Cleveland Spiders won the second half. The Beaneaters won the championship series, but without playing Kelly.

Kelly may not have expected to play baseball in 1893. He worked the vaudeville circuit during the offseason, talking about baseball and sometimes reciting that new poem "Casey at the Bat." Monte Ward, the former leader of the Players Brotherhood, was engaged to manage and captain the New York Giants, and decided to bring Kelly to the team. As usual, the fans were happy to see him. But Kelly wasn't in shape, and as a catcher had difficulty handling the swift pitches and puzzling curves of Amos Rusie. Ward ordered Kelly to dry out every morning in a Turkish bath to erase the effects of his nightly drinking, but it didn't seem to improve his skills.[27] The team's fourth-string catcher, he played in only 20 games and hit .269. The 35-year-old Kelly played in his last major-league game on September 2, when Ward sent him in as a substitute in the fourth inning of a game the Giants led 15-3. Kelly hit a single and scored a run, leaving him with a lifetime average of .307, 1,813 hits, and 1,357 runs scored. The Giants finished fifth. After the season Kelly and Agnes had a child. We don't know if it was a boy or a girl, but we do know that the baby was the reason Agnes stayed behind in Paterson when Kelly took ship for Boston in the winter of 1893-94 for a vaudeville engagement.

Kelly spent the winter booking vaudeville appearances, then signed on with an old friend, Albert Johnson, as captain and manager of the Allentown team in the Pennsylvania State League. Kelly smacked the league's pitchers for a .310 average. But the Allentown franchise dissolved on August 6. Johnson sent Kelly and some of the players to a team he owned in Yonkers, New York. There Kelly finished his professional baseball career, hitting .377 in 15 games. Perhaps for the first time in his life, Kelly received some derogatory press. Reporters wrote that he was old and out of shape. Yonkers reserved Kelly for the 1895 season, but he must have known that his career was winding down. He prepared for that by taking some offseason work with Mike Murphy's vaudeville act, appearing in a piece called "O'Dowd's Neighbors." They played a week at the Bijou Theater in Paterson before heading to Boston to play the Palace Theater, no doubt hoping to cash in on Kelly's continuing popularity. Kelly had spent every cent he earned in baseball, and if he was going to support his wife, his baby, and his fancy lifestyle, he would have to make big money in theater.

Kelly left New York City on Sunday, November 4, 1894, and traveled by boat to Boston. A snowstorm hit during the journey, and Kelly took ill. Some reports have Kelly catching cold because he gave his overcoat to a freezing man on the boat. When he arrived in Boston he had chills and fever and rested at a friend's house. Dr. George Galvin, former team doctor for the Beaneaters, saw Kelly at 2 in the afternoon, and found that he had difficulty breathing. By 4 P.M. on Monday, November 5, it was clear that pneumonia had set in, and Galvin moved Kelly to Emergency Hospital. It was reported that when Kelly came to the hospital the stretcher carrying him slipped to the floor, and he said, "This is my last slide."[28]

Kelly was given oxygen. His health was front-page news in the Boston papers, which reported on Wednesday night that he was improving. The snowstorm prevented Galvin from contacting Agnes until Thursday morning. She started for Boston, but did not make it in time. By Thursday afternoon it was clear that the pneumonia was winning. A priest from St. James Catholic Church administered the last rites. Around 6 P.M. on Thursday, Kelly roused himself to say, "Well, I guess this is the last trip."[29] At 9:55 P.M. on Thursday, November 8, 1894, King Kelly died at the age of 36.

Kelly's unexpected death was front-page news in every National League city. Agnes arrived on Friday afternoon and arranged to bury him in Boston, the city that loved him. By some estimates, 7,000 people attended Kelly's funeral on November 11. His song, "Slide, Kelly, Slide," was recorded by several artists on records, and remained a popular American tune into the 1920s. In 1945 he was elected to the Baseball Hall of Fame.

Kelly did as much as any other player to popularize professional baseball in the nineteenth century. His popularity transcended the game and became part of popular culture. He had a large effect on the game. It was said that half the rules in the baseball rulebook were rewritten to keep Kelly from taking advantage of loopholes. He played the game with gusto and looked for every edge he could get to win, and his teams won eight championships in 16 years. We are not likely to see a player like King Kelly again.

SOURCES

In addition to the sources cited in the Notes, the author also consulted the following:

Spalding, A.G. *Spalding's Base Ball Guide 1886* (Spalding Books, 1886), 18-67.

Voigt, David Q. *American Baseball: From Gentleman's Sport to the Commissioner System* (University Park, Pennsylvania: Penn State University Press, 1983).

Seymour, Harold. *Baseball: The Early Years* (New York: Oxford University Press, 1960).

Thorn, John. *Baseball in the Garden of Eden: The Secret History of the Early Game* (New York: Simon and Schuster, 2011).

Palmer, Pete, and Gary Gillette, eds. *The Baseball Encyclopedia* (New York: Barnes and Noble, 2004).

NOTES

1. Mike "King" Kelly, *Play Ball, Stories of the Ball Field* (Boston: Emery & Hughes, 1888, issued digitally in 2008), Chapter 2. (Online version used for this article offered only chapter numbers.)
2. Kelly, Chapter 3.
3. Marty Appel, *Slide, Kelly, Slide: The Wild Life and Times of Mike "King" Kelly* (Lanham, Maryland: Scarecrow Press, 1996), 198.
4. Appel, 29.A
5. Appel, 30.
6. Kelly, Chapter 4.
7. Adrian "Cap" Anson, *A Ball Player's Career* (Chicago: Era Publishing, 1900), 115-116.
8. Appel, 45.
9. Appel, 48.
10. Appel, 58.
11. Appel, 72.
12. Appel, 78-83.
13. Appel, 87.
14. William T. Ellis, *Billy Sunday, The Man and His Message* (Dayton, Oho: Thomas Manufacturing Co, 1914), Digital Edition, Chapter 4.
15. Appel, 103-104.
16. Kelly, Chapter 16.
17. Anson, 117.
18. Appel, 122.
19. Appel, 123.
20. Kelly, Chapter 17.
21. Appel, 135.
22. Mark Lamster, *Spalding's World Tour: The Epic Adventure That Took Baseball Around the Globe – And Made It America's Game* (New York: Public Affairs Press, 2006), 26.
23. Appel, 149.
24. Appel, 150.
25. Appel, 150-152.
26. Appel, 157.
27. Appel, 173.
28. Appel, 184.
29. Appel, 186.

FRED KLOBEDANZ

BY MARK S. STERNMAN

A 20-game-winning, power-hitting pitcher in the National League at the end of the nineteenth century who starred on a pennant winner, Fred Klobedanz had a brief but impactful major-league career bookended by sensational stints with several New England League squads.

A newspaper profile published near the end of his time in the majors provides a balanced portrayal of his pitching: "He does not at first impress one as being … very wonderful … but his delivery is more deceptive than it appears, and his effectiveness is due to his excellent command and his curve ball. He is … a fair … easy going sort of pitcher, and he has a knack of getting away … without being too severely punished."[1]

Born on June 13, 1871, to Siegmund and Charlotte (Klinzman) Klobedanz[2] and raised in Waterbury, Connecticut Klobedanz attended public school and played semipro ball from 1889 to 1891 before debuting with Portland of the New England League in 1892.[3] He got off to a fast start with his Maine team with shutouts on May 27[4] and June 2, the latter by a remarkable 31-0 score.[5]

In 1893 Klobedanz wanted more. More run support? No. Klobedanz and three teammates wanted their salaries paid up front rather than in arrears. If the players did not get paid, then they would not travel to their next game. An investigation ensued, Portland's management deemed Klobedanz the lead conspirator, "and it was decided to make an example of him by imposing a fine and suspension."[6]

This imbroglio ended Klobedanz's two years in Portland. He stayed in Maine, pitched one game for Lewiston of the New England League, and remained with that team for a brief time

Frederick Klobedanz.
(Courtesy of National Baseball Hall of Fame)

without pitching again because of the suspension imposed by Portland.[7] Moving south, Klobedanz spent the remainder of the season with Dover, New Hampshire, to complete an 1893 campaign in which he hurled for half of the New England League's six squads.

Home in Waterbury in 1894, Klobedanz faced his future team, the Boston Beaneaters, in a preseason game. He filled the box score. Klobedanz gave up 10 hits, walked 11, and threw four wild pitches. Batting fifth, he doubled and tripled. Ten Waterbury errors meant that Klobedanz yielded only four earned runs in a 17-6 defeat.[8]

The New England League expanded to eight teams in 1894, and Klobedanz joined a Massachusetts entry for the first time by playing for the Fall River Indians, where he swung a hot bat with a .325 average and 12 homers by mid-August.[9]

Klobedanz expanded his Fall River family in 1895. Brother William, a fellow pitcher, tried out for the Indians,[10] and Fred married Annie L. Durfee of Fall River on June 24.[11] Klobedanz enjoyed another stellar season. "In 1895 Klobedanz pitched against the St. Louis team at Fall River, and his work so impressed [St. Louis first baseman] Roger Connor that he offered a round figure for his release, but Fred refused to leave the city."[12] Late in the season before a game in which Klobedanz played first base and hit cleanup, he received "a handsome ebony bat, mounted with silver, by the Butchers and Grocers' Association ... for leading the batting list."[13] Klobedanz finished 1895 with a 28-9 record and a .377 batting average.[14]

Ten games into the 1896 NL season, Klobedanz again faced Boston. This time, his pitching impressed the Beaneaters. Klobedanz gave up three runs (two earned) in the second inning as Fall River won 4-3. "The big left hand twirler's great speed, curves and nice command, allowed the hard hitters of the National League only six hits, three being made in the first three innings," the *Boston Globe* noted.[15] Future Hall of Famers Billy Hamilton and Hugh Duffy graced the Boston outfield that day; with Nap Lajoie, Fall River had a future Cooperstown immortal in the lineup as well.

Klobedanz again performed at a high level for Fall River in 1896. On the hill, he went 25-6, a record boosted by a 14-game winning streak.[16] He batted .353 and slugged .600. Boston bought Klobedanz for $1,200, an impressive price considering that a fortnight earlier Lajoie and another player had gone to Philadelphia for $1,500.[17]

Klobedanz had a promising rookie year, both hitting and pitching. On September 2 he had five hits and gave up only six as Boston battered St. Louis 18-3 in the first game of a doubleheader.[18] On September 12 he became the first pitcher ever to yield a grand slam and then hit a go-ahead homer in the following half-inning, a feat matched as of 2018 only by Hal Jeffcoat and Madison Bumgarner.[19] Playing in 11 games with the Beaneaters, Klobedanz went 6-4 with a 3.01 ERA. He homered twice and slugged .488, a figure that, although achieved in limited action, topped the team.

Klobedanz had his biggest year in 1897, when he went 26-7. His .788 winning percentage led the National League. Boston went 93-39 to finish first. Kid Nichols, Jimmy Collins, Hamilton, and Duffy led the team in Wins Above Replacement, no surprise given that all four went on to the Hall of Fame. Klobedanz finished fifth in his first full big-league season, a campaign that started bumpily both on and off the field, but finished triumphantly.

The *Globe*'s baseball writer Tim Murnane had great fun with the wild "Kloby" in 1897. In April Murnane recounted, "Klobedanz was not in his best form and found more trouble in locating the rubber plate at times than a woman has in fixing her first baby for a photograph."[20] In May Murnane reported, "'Kloby' was of no more account than a muzzled telephone. The home plate was charmed and the Boston pitcher worked like a song and dance man to get the ball over now and then, but it wouldn't go. Think of nine base on balls and two men hit with pitched balls in less than six innings; this was 'Kloby's' record."[21] Indeed, Klobedanz walked 125 in 1897, tied with fellow Beaneater Ted Lewis for the sixth most in the NL. Kloby hit 23 batters, the fourth most in the league.

Playing a weak hand poorly, Klobedanz after the nine-walk game went on strike for the second time in his young professional career. Facing an arduous road trip to Pittsburgh, Cleveland, Chicago, St. Louis, Louisville, and Cincinnati, Klobedanz declined to go. "It so happened that he needed $75 in addition to what he had already drawn, and the club would not give it. ... 'Kloby' felt that he was justified in asking for the money, as he had signed for a very small figure – $200 per month."[22]

In response, Boston President Arthur Soden stated, "We have treated Klobedanz liberally, and propose to continue to do so. It may be that he will think better of his determination. Of course, this sulking and refusing to go on the trip ... is a very serious matter. ... I expect him to think it over and cool off, and see that he has made a mistake."[23]

Soden's supposition proved correct. Klobedanz rejoined the team in Pittsburgh, asking "to be put in at once in order that he could show ... that he was a pitcher, even if he did sulk on a question of salary once in awhile,"[24] and threw a four-hitter as the Beaneaters won 3-1.

Klobedanz spurred the Boston stretch drive. In August against New York, he "pitched one of the best games of his career," according to Murnane. "He was steady, giving but one base on balls and holding the hard-hitting visitors down to two single hits."[25] On September 30, with Boston holding a 1½-game lead over Baltimore with two games to go, Klobedanz pitched the clincher in a 12-3 win over Brooklyn.[26]

Just two months after his greatest year, Klobedanz again faced financial woes. "It was hoped by Kloby's friends that he would be in shape to hold out for a fair salary this season, but it looks like the same old story – short of funds and a hurry for advance money by taking a salary that he would kick at when the performance was under way next season," *Sporting Life* noted.[27]

Weeks later, Klobedanz, working at a Fall River bowling alley, signed a contract for the 1898 season that contained "a substantial raise,"[28] an anonymous characterization that could have come from Soden.

Klobedanz had better numbers nearly across the board in 1898 than he did in 1897 and finished his second and final full major-league season with a still good but less standout 19-10 record. His four-hitter at New York on July 5 failed to impress a denizen of the press box, who wrote that Klobedanz "did not seem to have … too much speed, nor did his curves appear very deceptive. From a seat behind the plate, the ball looked easy enough to hit."[29]

In 1899 Klobedanz won just one game in five starts before the Beaneaters dropped him. "Kloby was pitching fairly good ball, but was slow in fielding his position, and found much trouble in keeping in condition," the *Globe* wrote.[30] In a profile of Klobedanz, SABR member Bob Richardson wrote, "[He] was clumsy afield; his slow delivery made him easy prey for base stealers and tighter enforcement of the balk rule cramped his style."[31] Klobedanz also had an injury. "The player said he would probably go to Fall River and rest for a week or 10 days, and have a doctor treat his arm. He had a talk with manager [John] McGraw, and may consider an offer from Baltimore," the *Globe* said.[32]

Other teams talked up Klobedanz. In spite of reports that he would join Hartford of the Eastern League[33] or Chicago of the National League,[34] or find a place in the future American League,[35] none of these possibilities came true, perhaps because Klobedanz had run "afoul a labor union while working as a scene shifter, during the offseason, at the Park Theater [in Boston]. He acquired a reputation as a strikebreaker and was literally hounded from the field."[36] For whatever reason, Klobedanz drifted to Worcester of the Eastern League, where he went 55-40 from 1899 through 1901.

Returning to the New England League in 1902, Klobedanz began the first of three seasons with Lawrence, where he went 55-46 from 1902 through 1904. Pitching against inferior competition, Klobedanz had statistics surprisingly similar to those of his breakout Boston season:

	W	L	W-L%	G	IP
1897	26	7	.788	38	309⅓
1902	26	10	.722	39	320

Klobedanz attracted the attention of his former team while pitching in Lawrence, a city about 30 miles north of Boston. The 1902 Beaneaters had a top-heavy staff. Vic Willis, who would end up in Cooperstown, went 27-20 and threw 410 innings. Togie Pittinger also won 27, pitching 389⅓ innings. No other pitcher had a winning record for Boston save for an old-timer who made a cameo after more than one month of rumors about his return.[37]

On September 5 Klobedanz returned to Boston to face Pittsburgh, by far the best team in the 1902 National League, in the second half of a doubleheader. In a darkness-shortened game that got so out of hand that Honus Wagner made the second and final pitching appearance of his career, Klobedanz led the Beaneaters to a 12-1 rout. Besides giving up just one run, he went 1-for-2 with a double and a walk. Murnane praised Klobedanz for "making chicken feed out of the league champions"[38] in his final major-league game.

Klobedanz should have pitched for Boston again. After the doubleheader on September 5, the Beaneaters had twin bills against the Cardinals on September 10 and 11. Pegged to pitch against St. Louis, "he failed to show up."[39]

For the third time, Klobedanz joined a minor-league team for three seasons, pitching for New Bedford from 1905 to 1907, when he went 30-18. After his first year, Klobedanz made front-page news after a fireman rescued him and three others from a burning New Bedford hotel.[40]

In 1906 Klobedanz again had a contract snafu. Baseball's top echelons fined New Bedford $500 and discounted the results of a game against Lowell for playing Kloby in spite of a suspension against him for having played with an independent team.[41] The suspension seems to have lasted about 10 days, and Klobedanz resumed play pending an appeal.[42]

Klobedanz joined his seventh and final New England League team in 1908, when he went 0-3 with Brockton before the club released him on June 15.[43]

Kloby's legend outlasted his career. According to *Sporting Life*, "Klobedanz received a letter the other day which was written by Christy Mathewson, in which the famous pitcher asked if the records were true that once Larry Lajoie, king of the batters, was struck out four times in a nine-inning game by Klobedanz. 'It was when I was a member of the Bostons,' said Klobedanz when he finished reading the letter. 'Larry was then playing on the Philadelphia Nationals, together with Ed Delahanty. I was working in good shape that day and fanned Lajoie four times. … Every strikeout was the result of three healthy swings at the ball.'"[44]

A longer-lasting tale concerns a homer Klobedanz hit in an exhibition game, a story that made the Boston papers in both 1922 and 1937, long after his playing days had concluded. Not surprisingly, the second version, in the *Globe*, spins the more colorful yarn: "Gene Moore's … home run … the other day reminds the writer of a hit Fred Klobedanz made at the South End grounds in the late '90s. Fred lifted the ball so high and so far over the 25-cent seats in right field that the Boston and Providence players … dropped upon the ground in much amazement."[45]

At the age of 68 in 1940, Klobedanz died of cancer in Waterbury, his birthplace, where he had worked as a hotel clerk.[46] His tale serves as a microcosm of players from his era as opposed to today. Pitchers could hit, play other positions, and bat in spots other than last in the order. Neither clubs nor players regarded contracts as sacrosanct. The differences between the majors and minors, in terms of both pay and prestige, did not seem as wide as they do today. Kloby played a boy's game like a boy, following his whims up and down the professional ladder and back again rather than proceeding in a conventionally responsible fashion. Not the most reliable teammate, Fred Klobedanz stayed true to his own sense of priorities in carving out a uniquely interesting baseball career.

NOTES

1. "Frederick A. Klobedanz," *New York Clipper*, May 20, 1899.

2. The 1880 US Census reveals that the Klobedanz family came from Germany, where the father, Siegmund, was born in 1841, Charlotte in 1842, and their son Siegmund in 1866. Fred's father worked in cigar manufacturing. Fred's younger siblings (Willie, Charlie, and Emma), like him, were all born in Connecticut.

3. Joseph Anderson, Sara Johnson Prichard, and Anna Lydia Ward, *The Town and City of Waterbury, Connecticut, Volume 3* (New Haven: Price & Lee Company, 1896), 1106. Baseball Reference does not have data for Klobedanz prior to 1893 although the *Boston Globe* has game stories and box scores featuring him.

4. "McGuire's Wildness," *Boston Globe*, May 28, 1892: 5.

5. "Charge It to Smith," *Boston Globe*, June 3, 1892: 5.

6. "Big July 4 Attendance," *Boston Globe*, July 6, 1893: 5.

7. "Base-Ball Notes," *Boston Globe*, July 18, 1893: 2.

8. "Lampe Was Hit Freely," *Boston Globe*, April 10, 1894: 2.

9. "New England League Stars," *Boston Globe*, August 20, 1894: 2.

10. "Fall River Facts," *Sporting Life*, March 16, 1895: 8. Klobedanz's Charles pitched for the Waterbury Rough Riders in 1899, and for Derby in 1899 and 1900. "Connecticut League," *Sporting Life*, August 26, 1899: 9. Fred's sister had an unfortunate baseball connection involving George Prentiss, a Waterbury teammate of Charles. In 1899 Prentiss "was charged with bastardy – impregnating a woman out of wedlock – and [sought to get] out of the trouble [by marrying] the local woman involved: Boston Beaneaters pitcher Fred Klobedanz's 20-year-old sister, Emma. It appears … Emma had been a baseball fan … but it is unclear whether the two had met before … the season opener. As the *Bridgeport Herald* put it, 'It was after the first game that the alleged act making her a mother took place.' After consulting … a saloon keeper and co-owner of the Waterbury team, Prentiss decided to consent to the forced marriage, despite his being engaged to a woman back in Wilmington. … The husband and wife then went their separate ways: Prentiss back to his room downtown and she back to her parents' home on James Street. Emma filed divorce papers the following week." David Forrester, "George Prentiss," sabr.org/bioproj/person/a3bd6618 (accessed August 2, 2017).

11. Anderson, Prichard, and Ward, 1107.

12. George V. Tuohey, *A History of the Boston Baseball Club* (Boston: Miller Press, 1897), 166.

13. "Fall River Wins Again," *Boston Globe*, September 25, 1895: 3.

14. "Klobedanz Signed by Boston," *Boston Globe*, August 16, 1896: 4.

15. "That Stop over," *Boston Globe*, April 30, 1896: 5.

16. "The Deal Made," *The Sporting News*, August 22, 1896: 1.

17. "Hub Happenings," *Sporting Life*, August 22, 1896: 10. A more recent source asserts that Boston actually paid only $1,000 for Klobedanz. David L. Fleitz, *Napoleon Lajoie: King of Ballplayers* (Jefferson, North Carolina: McFarland & Company, 2013), 15. The August 16 *Globe* article on his signing said Boston offered $1,000 but the Fall River manager held out for $1,200.

18. T.H. Murnane, "Full of Batting," *Boston Globe*, September 3, 1896: 3.

19. "San Francisco Giants 2016 Game Notes," sanfrancisco.giants.mlb.com/documents/9/9/8/196503998/8.19.16_vs._NYM_bdhibyq8.pdf (accessed August 2, 2017).

20. T.H. Murnane, "First Victory," *Boston Globe*, April 29, 1897: 3.

21. T.H. Murnane, "Klobedanz Wild," *Boston Globe*, May 9, 1897: 6.

22. "Hub Happenings," *Sporting Life*, May 22, 1897: 9.

23. "Boston Player on a Strike," *New York Times*, May 11, 1897.

24. "Sulks No More," *Boston Globe*, May 13, 1897: 4.

25. T.H. Murnane, "Single Score," *Boston Globe*, August 11, 1897: 1.

26. "Bostons Win the Pennant," *New York Times*, October 1, 1897.

27. "Shiftless Klobedanz," *Sporting Life*, December 11, 1897: 4.

28. "Two Have Signed," *Boston Globe*, December 25, 1897: 3. Klobedanz had interesting offseason jobs. After the 1900 campaign, he worked for his father-in-law's draying business in Fall River. Draying involves driving a cart to haul goods. "Hub Happenings," *Sporting Life*, January 5, 1901: 6. He also refereed roller polo, a forerunner of roller hockey, after the 1903 season. "Roller Polo Notes," *Boston Globe*, December 4, 1903: 8. A recent account also says he did "winter carpentry for the teams he played for." William A. Moniz, "How a City Found Passion on Diamond," southcoasttoday.com/article/20150803/SPECIAL/150809992 (accessed August 2, 2017).

29. "On the Baseball Field," *New York Times*, July 6, 1898.

30. "Killen to Pitch for Boston," *Boston Globe*, May 12, 1899: 5.

31. Bob Richardson, "Frederick Augustus Klobedanz," in *Nineteenth Century Stars* (Kansas City, Missouri: Society for American Baseball Research, 1989), 73.

32. "Baseball Notes," *Boston Globe*, May 13, 1899: 4.

33. "Eastern League Results," *Boston Globe*, May 21, 1899: 4.

34. "Klobedanz to Chicago," *Boston Globe*, August 3, 1899: 7. Klobedanz signed a contract with Chicago but failed to report to the team. "Chicago Signs a New Pitcher," *Boston Globe*, August 7, 1899: 5.

35. "Rival Looms Up," *Boston Globe*, November 12, 1899: 22.

36. Harold Kaese, *The Boston Braves, 1871-1953* (Boston: Northeastern University Press, 2004), 98.

37. "Echoes of the Game," *Boston Globe*, August 1, 1902: 8.

38. T.H. Murnane, "Lose and Win," *Boston Globe*, September 6, 1902: 5.

39. Jacob C. Morse, "Boston Briefs," *Sporting Life*, September 20, 1902: 4.

40. "Klobedanz Is Rescued," *Boston Globe*, November 22, 1905: 1.

41. "Game Thrown out," *Boston Globe*, April 29, 1906: 13.

42. "'Kloby' Gets His Chance," *Boston Globe*, May 9, 1906: 4. Tim Murnane, the president of the New England League who allowed Klobedanz to resume playing, performed dual roles in both covering baseball in Boston and likely penning these unbylined articles on the case (see also "Klobedanz May Play," *Boston Globe*, May 9, 1906: 4).

43. "Pitcher Klobedanz Released," *Boston Globe*, June 16, 1908: 4.

44. "Klobedanz's Feat," *Sporting Life*, July 13, 1907: 9. Although the author believed this anecdote appeared apocryphal, the fact-checker of this article, SABR member Bob LeMoine, found an account of such a game in T.H. Murnane, "Two Victories Each," *Boston Globe*, May 5, 1897: 5. Thanks to LeMoine for the tip.

45. Sportsman, "Live Tips and Topics," *Boston Globe*, September 10, 1937: 26.

46. David Nemec, *Major League Baseball Profiles, 1871-1900, Volume 1: The Ballplayers Who Built the Game* (Lincoln: University of Nebraska Press, 2011), 110.

TED LEWIS

BY RORY COSTELLO

Ted Lewis, 1900.
(public domain)

Williams College is best known in baseball circles for two nonplaying alumni: the last independent commissioner, Fay Vincent (1960), and the blustery Boss himself, George Steinbrenner ('52). There hasn't been an Ephman in the majors since 1934, but Ted Lewis, "The Pitching Professor," was not just the finest ballplayer Williams ever produced – like Sir Thomas More, he was a man for all seasons. Educator, elocutionist, natural leader – Lewis embodied an array of talents but always retained a winning humility.

Horatio Alger could not have conjured up a life story like this, which has the power to make the most hardened cynic believe in ideals again. Edward Morgan Lewis was born on Christmas Day 1872 in Machynlleth, Wales. His parents were John C. Lewis and Jane L. (Davies) Lewis. When the boy was 8 years old, his family moved to Utica, New York, where they lived on the banks of the Erie Canal. Little Ted earned his first quarter delivering groceries for the local corner store (though he was docked if he broke a ketchup bottle), and scouted out other odd jobs, supplementing the immigrants' straitened budget.

It is an article of faith that Welshmen have wonderful voices and a love of poetry, and the Lewis family reinforced this tradition. The great American poet Robert Frost was a crony of Ted Lewis's for 20 years – even into their 60s, they played "singles" baseball or softball in the backyard whenever they got together. Frost read from Tennyson and Whitman at his friend's memorial tribute, and his address showed the profound influence of culture on character:

"He told me once – I was afraid that the story might not be left for me to tell – that he began his interest in poetry as he might have begun his interest in baseball – with the idea of victory – the 'Will to Win.'

"He was at an Eisteddfod in Utica, an American-Welsh Eisteddfod, where the contest was in poetry, and a bard had been brought in from Wales to give judgment and to pick the winner; and the bard, after announcing the winner and making the compliments which judges make, said he wished the unknown victor would rise and make himself known and let himself be seen. (I believe the poems were read anonymously.) The little 'Ted' Lewis sitting there beside his father looked up and saw his father rise as the victor. So poetry to him was prowess from that time on, just as baseball was prowess, as running was prowess. And it was our common ground."

Lewis worked as a bundle boy in a department store and as a surveyor's helper, studying borrowed textbooks by lamplight. With the $50 in personal savings he managed to put aside, the youth entered Marietta College in Ohio, which gave him the opportunity to meet his tuition payments by working as a letter carrier, hotel clerk, and janitor.

In the fall of 1893 sophomore Ted Lewis transferred to Williams, the small liberal-arts school nestled in the Berkshire Hills of western Massachusetts. He made a tremendous impression on his classmates, becoming president of the elite Gargoyle Society and winning the class cup in a walkover, receiving 32 votes while no one else got more than four. Lewis's accomplishments on the mound were certainly a part of his status. In 1895 he won all eight games in the Triangular League (which then consisted of Williams, Amherst, and Dartmouth rather than Wesleyan), and he followed up with six more in his senior year.

Baseball was the most popular sport at the college in those days, and the *Williams Weekly* was full of manly exhortations to give full voice while cheering. The souvenir scorecard from the 1896 Commencement Game against Amherst is another charming curio, with Captain Ted's photo on the front cover and official yells (Osky-wow-wow, Skimmy-wow-wow, Jimmy-wow-wow, W-O-W) on the back.

Lewis faced some most intriguing opponents besides Yale and Harvard. These included the original black pro team, the Cuban Giants, whose trip to the Purple Valley bears further investigation. Another was Louis Sockalexis, then the star center fielder for Holy Cross. A year before his briefly spectacular run with Cleveland, the Penobscot Indian "played a phenomenal game, catching and batting balls, whenever and wherever he pleased."

During his college days, Lewis also won the heart of hometown girl Margaret Hallie Williams with a move that would have left Sir Walter Raleigh in the dust. At a local game in Richfield Springs, New York, he had promised her that he would meet her at the grounds and usher her in. But Margaret arrived a little late, while Ted was facing the first batter. Yet when he spied his wife-to-be, he calmly dropped the ball, walked off the hill (making the captain think Lewis had gone "bughouse"), and saw to his escort duties. The gallant then returned to a huge hand from the crowd

Seeking money to further his studies, the graduate commenced his major-league career with the Boston Beaneaters. Frank Selee's club was the class of the National League in the 1890s, winning five pennants behind numerous Hall of Famers and near-greats.

Lewis was a key part of the last two titles, especially in 1898, when he led the league in winning percentage at 26-8. He also appeared in three games in the 1897 Temple Cup series, winning one, losing one, and allowing Boston to claw back from an early blowout into a near win with a strong effort in long relief. In 1904 *Boston Globe* sportswriter and old-time player Tim Murnane remembered Lewis as "a superb pitcher, with great curves and fine speed, both of which he used with rare judgment. He was a fine batsman for a pitcher and was a willing worker for his club."

The "good guy" Beaneaters had an ongoing battle with John McGraw's Baltimore Orioles, notorious for their ruffian tactics. "Parson" Lewis prefigured the fictional Yalie Galahad Frank Merriwell and McGraw's Mr. Clean with the Giants, Christy Mathewson. A leading example of Lewis's devotion to fair play came on August 24, 1901, when he helped rescue umpire Joe Cantillon from a mob of Boston fans who stormed the field. Tim Murnane stated, "It is doubtful if good, clean sport ever had a more earnest and successful practitioner than 'Ted' Lewis." Echoing these sentiments, Damon Hall, a close friend from Williams, said: "One might have supposed in those earlier days of professional baseball that a college graduate who did not drink, who refused to play Sunday ball, who said his prayers and read his Bible daily, who even asked his teammates to go to prayer meetings with him, would have been esteemed somewhat of a prig by the other members of the squad. Instead, they took him to their hearts."

Indeed, Ted had seriously considered entering the ministry but decided he could reach more young people through the classroom. While with Boston he found time to coach the Harvard nine. After jumping to the new American League in 1901 and playing with the very first Red Sox team (then known as the Americans, among other early names), Lewis retired from baseball to devote his full energies to teaching. His lifetime record was 94-64, with an earned-run average of 3.53 and a batting average of .223.

The Professor had earned his master's from Williams in 1899, and from 1901 to 1903 he taught elocution at Columbia. His alma mater then lured him back to teach oratory for eight years, during which he also lectured at the Yale Divinity School. In 1910 the Welsh community of Berkshire County formed a society, acclaiming Lewis as president. For many years he would return to North Adams on St. David's Day, March 1, to address his leek-waving brethren. (The only other major leaguer born in Wales was Jimmy Austin, who was one of Lawrence Ritter's subjects in *The Glory of Their Times*.)

Also in 1910, Lewis ran for Congress as a Democrat in a staunch Republican district, and missed pulling off an upset by just 736 votes. He said, "It may be that I am starting in on this campaign in the ninth inning with the score 9 to 0 against me. But if the odds are against me I'll play the game out, for you never can tell what a score you may make in the ninth."

The next year, however, Massachusetts Agricultural College in Amherst beckoned. Lewis soon proved how capable an administrator he was, being pressed into service as acting president in 1913-14 (when he made another unsuccessful bid for Congress, supported by pioneering muckraker Ray Stannard Baker). The dean of languages and literature again stepped into the breach in 1918-19 and 1924, finally accepting the position of president officially in 1926. It was through his efforts that the modest "Aggie" school was transformed into today's University of Massachusetts. Lewis felt uncomfortable with the political pressure there, however; there was an ongoing power struggle with the state government over funding and the authority of the Board of Trustees. Thus Lewis moved to the University of New Hampshire in 1927. But before he left, Massachusetts Agricultural College surprised its outgoing president by conferring upon him the honorary degree of doctor of laws.

Under the aegis of President Lewis, UNH, in Durham, New Hampshire, established a graduate school and broadened its infrastructure considerably, building the first women's dormitory. In Durham Lewis received many of his famous friends, including Robert Frost. He had first met the then-unknown poet, a fellow MAC professor, in 1916 – and the Eisteddfod veteran delivered the first public reading of Frost's verse. Forty years later, by then a grand American institution, Frost wrote about the 1956 All-Star Game for *Sports Illustrated,* also reminiscing about his pitching lessons from Lewis.

The UNH archives also show how Lewis knew and corresponded with US Presidents William Howard Taft (then chief justice of the Supreme Court), Calvin Coolidge (as vice president), Woodrow Wilson, and Franklin D. Roosevelt. There are letters from other well-known individuals in this special collection, including another chief justice, Charles Evans Hughes; polar explorer Richard Byrd; heavyweight boxing champion Gene Tunney; and Philadelphia Athletics manager Connie Mack.

Ted Lewis died at midnight on May 23, 1936, at the age of 63. His health had begun to fail about two years before, but even though the beloved "Prexy" was suffering greatly from liver cancer, he summoned up his old athletic reserves to climb the stairs to his office. In February he underwent an operation, and he rallied enough to make an appearance at UNH's Opening Day ballgame versus Bates – pitched and won by future major leaguer Bill Weir. The students again took heart, but Lewis relapsed shortly thereafter. He was survived by his widow, Margaret; his two sons, Edward W. Lewis and John B. Lewis; and his daughter, Gwendolyn (Mrs. Samuel W. Hoitt).

Lewis was laid to rest in the Durham Community Cemetery on May 26, with former Boston teammate Fred Tenney serving as one of the pallbearers. In a memorial tribute before the entire student body and faculty that afternoon, Robert Frost read his friend's two favorite poems, Tennyson's "In Memoriam" and Walt Whitman's "On the Beach at Night."

UNH sports teams still play today at the Lewis Fields, but this man's most fitting memorial might be the measured question he always posed to his colleagues: "Well ... what can we do to better the situation?"

QUOTES

on Ted Lewis the ballplayer, compiled by UNH alumnus Rich Eldred for his Lewis sketch in *Nineteenth Century Stars* (SABR 1988):

"Teddy Lewis will pitch good ball for the Boston Americans no matter how many others may croak."
— Wilbert Robinson

"When at concert pitch there are few better than Lewis."
— Tim Murnane, *Boston Globe*

"Lewis was steady as a minister should be.... Chicago's heaviest hitters went down before his speedy deliveries like corn stalks before a gale."
— Jake Morse, *Boston Herald*

"Parson Lewis is closing his career in a blaze of glory."
— *Boston Globe* after Lewis beat Nixey Callahan with a two-hitter in his final game

SOURCES

Ted Lewis File at National Baseball Hall of Fame and Museum, Cooperstown, New York.

Ted Lewis File at Williams College Alumni Association, Williamstown, Massachusetts. (Includes a typewritten manuscript of "Edward Morgan Lewis, Early Career" by his younger relative Hobart L. Morris Jr.)

Obituary, *New York Times*, May 24, 1936.

Online census records, 1910 and 1920.

"In the Loop," News for Staff and Faculty, University of Massachusetts at Amherst, May 18, 2004.

Online records, University of New Hampshire.

HERMAN LONG

BY RICHARD "DIXIE" TOURANGEAU

Herman Long.
(Library of Congress)

If there had been a draft in the baseball world of 1890, a Chicago-born shortstop likely would have been the number one selection by any of the 24 teams of the three major leagues operating that season. In his prime of the 1890s, and even before, as he made his way toward national stardom, the every-other-day mention of his exploits usually included some noteworthy feat that had amazed ballgame spectators. During his career he was charged with almost 1,100 errors, the most by any player ever, but that didn't seem to bother most onlookers, especially his own team's fans. As for his bat, it wasn't mentioned as frequently, but it was potent. In his first National League game, the phenom clouted two home runs, and when the decade was complete, he had slugged his way to the highest mark.

Herman C. Long was born in the Windy City on April 3, 1866, almost exactly a year after the Lincoln assassination.[1] He was the first child born into the German immigrant family of railroad laborer John (aka Johan Lange) and Fredericka Long. The father was from Mecklenburg-Vorpommern, Germany, a northern state on the Baltic Sea, and the mother from Prussia, according to the 1880 census. Both had come to America in 1863 and married in 1864. Through the years, census takers badly scribbled the simple last name a few times, it was transcribed as "Song" in 1900. There were at least six sons, Herman, followed by John, Henry, Fritz, George, and Charlie. Trying to track them is frustrating because of the common name and because Herman left home before age 20 to play ball so he is never listed in any Chicago city directory to help match addresses with any of the two dozen John Longs. His family's suspected address for more than 30 years was 497 West 16th Street, now near the corner of Canal Street. In the 1900 census the mother is listed as having had 10 children, but only five were then alive. At least four other children apparently died before the 1900 census as did son Henry in July 1896. He was a pitcher for Hagerstown (Maryland) and was fatally injured when he slipped while boarding a train.

Chicago newspapers carried almost no detailed information about the city's neighborhood leagues in the mid-1880s, so whatever reputation Long made for himself is unsubstantiated. There were city semipro teams starting in 1880 when Thomas Edward Barrett organized a league (president for 14 years and Cook County sheriff by 1902). Barrett's team was the Whitings and Long was on it before 1886. Other papers reported that he was also on the Diamonds roster. Whatever Long's accomplishments were, they got him invited 600 miles southwest to Arkansas City, Kansas, for the 1887 season. Arkansas City is directly south of Wichita, and four miles from the Oklahoma border at the junction of the Arkansas and Walnut Rivers. "Canal City" grew quickly in the 1880s because of its rail line and residents dreamt of it becoming a thriving metropolis and having a good ball team could enhance that fantasy. Club owners imported several players, including Long, to play in the four-team Kansas State League.

The *Arkansas City Daily Republican-Traveler* reported on May 14 that games would begin the following week and that its Chicago players would arrive the next night. The first two contests were against nearby Wellington, with Herman playing shortstop and then pitching in 7-6 and 4-1 wins. Long was proclaimed "a dandy" at short by the newspaper and "the best man in the box in Kansas" after his four-hitter in which he had three hits and scored.[2] He enjoyed notoriety right away with his fielding abilities as he played several positions. Small leagues often broke apart when one or more members folded or joined better circuits. Arkansas City was good but its financial foundation was shaky. In early August (after 40 games), Long was sold to Emporia (100 miles northeast), which had been in the same circuit but was moving up a notch to the eight-team Western League because St. Joseph, Missouri, dropped out. In his final game for AC, pitcher Long lost to Emporia, 6-5. His Emporia stint started on August 14, when he played center field, batted leadoff, and went 3-for-5 and scored as Emporia lost to Hastings, Nebraska, 8-6. Emporia (6-12) was a bit outclassed in its new environs and disbanded on September 9, after beating Kansas City 11-5 and 14-7. Long was 1-for-5, scoring three runs as the center fielder and then pitching the final Emporia win, going 3-for-6, (single, double, triple) scored thrice again while batting leadoff at the Kelso Park finale. During his entire Emporia employment, the *Evening News* printed glowing descriptions of Long's fielding and claimed that he was destined for a higher league.

On Monday, October 17, the name "Long" was in the *Chicago Tribune* box score for the last-place Diamonds in Chicago's eight-team City League, which played Sunday games. That Long pitched and caught in a 25-6 rout of the Stars, smacking two doubles and whiffing five.

When the 1888 baseball season opened, Herman was home in Chicago with the Maroons of the eight-club Western Association. Sam Morton was league president and owned the Chicago entry. In an April 16 exhibition, the Maroons beat Adrian "Cap" Anson's White Stockings, 6-5 in 12 innings. Long dazzled the crowd with his plays at shortstop and scored but was hitless batting cleanup.

Morton claimed Herman was "the best ballplayer Chicago ever produced."[3]

Long's multiple talents were soon enjoyed by a wider group of fans. He played all outfield positions, pitched a bit, and saw an occasional game at shortstop. Long's foot speed and basepath daring almost demanded that he be the leadoff batter. His best game as a Maroon was against St. Paul on Decoration Day (game two); he was 4-for-6, stole four bases, and scored thrice while batting second and playing left field in a 12-3 victory. The *St. Paul Globe* wrote after the game, "Sam Morton holds Long's release at a high figure but the chances are that he will soon pose in a league nine as a several-thousand-dollar beauty."[4] By then fans in each Association city expected to see Long perform some astounding feat, and only a few times were they disappointed.

With both teams hovering around the .500 mark, the Maroons dealt Long and third baseman Fred Lange to Kansas City Blues (Western Association) on July 10. The *Tribune* explained, "Now that Long, believed by many to be the star fielder of the country, has been sold, (White Stockings) President Albert Spalding and Captain Anson give it out that they wanted him. Owner Morton replied, 'The man who pays the money gets the plum.'"[5] In his final appearance for the Maroons, left fielder Long recorded no stat, a 0-for-all in a 9-6 win at Omaha (managed by Frank G. Selee). In his first game for the Blues on July 12 as leadoff batter and right fielder, Long singled, doubled, and scored as Charlie Nichols pitched his first game for Kansas City, a 4-1 win over first-place St. Paul. Nichols was obtained by Blues player-manager Jim Manning after his Southern Association Memphis club folded on June 30. Long would later play behind Kid Nichols for a dozen NL campaigns.

For another two weeks the Blues lingered around .500. On July 31 Manning switched Long to shortstop for the duration of the season. In a 12-inning gem at Exposition Park, Long had four hits, scored twice, batted home the winner, swiped four bases, and dazzled fans by preventing Milwaukee from scoring in the 10th with a great play. Hurler Park Swartzel won the 3-1 nail-biter. Then Long went 4-for-35 with 11 errors over the next eight games. In late August the Blues finally surged behind Nichols' pitching. From September 1 they were 31-3 but missed the Association pennant by .002 to Des Moines (which played five fewer games and beat them twice in the final week) because the rules said the best percentage took the flag. It was a wild finish as Kansas City owners paid Morton's Maroons $500 to play four October games in Kansas City instead of Chicago as scheduled. The Blues swept.

In 1889 Long (.275, 137 runs) went with the American Association Kansas City Cowboys under Bill Watkins and finished seventh. Billy Hamilton (.301, 144 runs) was his most talented teammate. Long opened the season in Louisville's Eclipse Park and in his first Association game had two hits, scored three runs, stole two bases, had six assists, whiffed twice, and made an error in a 7-4 win. In the four-game sweep for KC, Long was 4-for-13, scored seven runs, made 21 assists, had six steals, had four walks, made three errors, and homered off Thomas "Toad" Ramsey in a 14-9 win. The *Louisville Courier-Journal* needed no more evidence and claimed at the end of the series, "Long is the finest shortstop in the American Association."[6] In another week Long managed a five-hit, four-run game and then a four-hit, two-score performance. In a stretch of 15 games he made 25 hits and scored 28 runs. Near the end of the campaign, he scored in 12 straight contests. Rookie Long was charged with 128 errors that season but his play was still considered on a higher plateau. He was error-free in 57 games and in another 52 had only one miscue of the 136 games he played. The *Baltimore Sun* said after a twin-bill split on August 1, "In the second game … the general excellence of the field work of shortstop Long was noticeable. Even Long's two errors were brilliant. He stopped three or four safe hits, which robbed Baltimore of bases."[7] He topped AA shortstops with 335 putouts.

Before the 1890 season began, the baseball world was thrown into chaos by the establishment of the Players' (Brotherhood) League, a defiant move by a number of players to get better pay and not be tied to one team for however long any owner saw fit. Three eight-team leagues now needed talent and the searches began when the 1889 season closed as teams felt they could not be left out of the hunt. Several Boston players jumped to the PL and club President Arthur Soden hired Selee (of Western Association champ Omaha) to manage whatever revamped version of the Beaneaters he could assemble. Selee's pickups included Kid Nichols (Omaha), Bobby Lowe (WA Milwaukee), AA batting champ Tom Tucker (Baltimore), and Long. Kansas City stars Long and Hamilton were "wanted" players and both needed to first get officially released, but the price was high. To avoid a nasty contract rights squabble within the NL, the league's Committee on Players chose to have Boston and Philadelphia reps (both teams claimed Long and Hamilton) draw slips from a hat. Philly got Hamilton and Boston acquired the rights to Long and veteran first baseman Daniel Stearns. Quickly on January 4, Selee went to Chicago and happily got Herman's signature, while Stearns was never signed and stayed with Kansas City. A few days later Cowboys President John W. Speas told the press that Long's release was bought for $6,500 by Boston.[8] (Because of a prolonged illness, Speas, the Kansas City Distilling Co.-Monarch Vinegar magnate, took his own life with pistol and poison on June 3, 1909, only three months before Long passed.)

Nationally known for his uncanny fielding prowess, Herman debuted on Patriots Day (April 19) at the South End Grounds by launching two home runs in a 15-9 victory over Brooklyn, the eventual NL champion. Parisian Bob Caruthers and William "Adonis" Terry were the victims in the comeback win for John Clarkson. Not to disappoint defensively, Long had seven assists. Even more fans got to know Long on May 31, 1890, when that day's *New York Clipper* issue profiled his career previous to Boston.[9] When Boston first visited Chicago for a July Fourth doubleheader, Long's neighborhood admirers presented him with a solid ice pitcher and gold-lined mug during the morning game. Herman's triple/RBI/run ignited the rally to a 12-2 win but in the afternoon his two errors cost the 6-5 loss. The Beaneaters finished 76-57, fifth behind Brooklyn, and leadoff man Long hit .251/8 HR in only 101 games (injuries). He scored in 12 of his first 14 games, had two 10-game hit streaks before a lame back shelved him in late August when Boston was only three games out of first. Though still hurting, he was 4-for-30 in the season's final games, which dropped his average to .251. His 95 runs were second-most on the squad. An average-sized player at 5-feet-8, 160 pounds, Long was the only true lefty swinger on the Bostons during his first few seasons.

Economics closed down the PL and when the contract dust cleared for 1891, the Bostons fielded a solid contender. Ex-Beaneater, now also an ex-PL Boston Red, Billy Nash, was back at third base and imported slugging vet Harry Stovey, led the NL in HRs and triples. But it was Long, who missed only one game and topped his team in average, runs, walks, and steals (.282; 129, second in NL; 80; 60) and only Stovey had more extra-base hits. The Beaneaters took their first 1890s flag by 3½ games over Chicago's White Stockings despite losing the season series to them 7-13. *The Sporting News* used the same 1890 *Clipper* text and image of Long in explaining his career path in its July 18, 1891, issue.[10]

Continued success followed the Beaneaters and Long in 1892-93 as they won both pennants. He hit .280 and .288 while scoring 115 and 149 (tops) runs. It was in June-July 1892 that Long made 12 of his 19 career appearances in the pasture, as the unique split-season ended part one and began part two. A contract problem arose in March 1893, according to the *New York Sun*. On March 10, Long declared he would not play for Boston that season because his salary was cut (fewer games than 1892), saying, "The terms are out of all proportions to the work expected of me."[11] But a deal was apparently ironed out as Long opened the South End Grounds season by homering on the first pitch by Cannonball Ed Crane of the Giants. He also scored the final run in the 8-6 win, adding a third run, seven assists, and a steal. Most players' averages spiked in 1894 (second season of pitching distance at 60 feet 6 inches) and Long was in that group. For the next four campaigns he averaged .326/8 HRs/110 runs/30 steals but the Baltimore Orioles won three straight flags before Boston regained the title in 1897. The original "Flying Dutchman" enjoyed a memorable doubleheader on May 30, 1894. While cheering on his Keystone buddy, Bobby Lowe, who lofted four homers into the left-field bleachers in that day's second game at the Congress Street Grounds, Long (5-for-8) got into the record book as well by scoring nine runs of the combined 30 Boston tallied. He could not use Lowe's coattails as Bobby was leadoff man and Long batted second. In 125 years since, only Mel Almada (Washington, July 25, 1937, 6-for-9) scored nine times in a twin bill.

In July 1895, smack in the middle of the Beaneaters' 1890s swoon, two events involved Long. On July 17 he married Annie L. Hillock of Chicago (died March 1930) in their hometown. On that day comments by manager Selee were made known in the national press exposing trouble in the Hub family. "If I had anything to say about it (why didn't he?), I would put three players on the bench tomorrow. They are Hugh Duffy, Charlie Ganzel and Long. Whenever Ganzel is catching, Duffy is criticising his work and trying to hurt his standing with the club. Ganzel does the same to Duffy. Long has not spoken to Nash in some time. … All of the men play good ball individually but they don't work together."[12] Boston left in first place for a 26-game road trip (10-15, with one tie). The trip included four games in Cincinnati, where they lost three to the Reds, including a doubleheader on July 17, 12-1 and 6-1. Herman and bride Annie then waited for his club to arrive in Chicago for the next series. With Long back leading off, Boston scored one run again in a third consecutive game, the lowest output all season. This was a 2-1 loss to Clark Griffith.

Long displayed his amazing fielding abilities on September 24, 1897, in Baltimore. The difference in the season proved to be the last dozen games, Boston 8-4, Orioles 5-7. But Baltimore still had a chance on that afternoon, down 6-2 with the bases loaded in the eighth inning. Long leapt into the sky to grab a line drive by Jake Stenzel (.353), choking off that rally. To the chagrin of Orioles fans his performance was not complete. In the ninth the plucky Orioles scored twice and with two more men on base Long once again made a fantastic grab of a certain base hit by NL top batter Willie Keeler (.424),[13] a liner that Long caught, then flipped to Lowe at second, doubling off the runner to end the game, 6-4.

Even Long's tremendous reputation paled in the face of such clutch efforts. The teams split the next two games (Long was 9-for-14 in the three games) and Boston won the flag by two games after the Giants took two from the depressed Birds to end the season. In 1897's final Temple Cup matchup, Long hit .318 but his rival Baltimore shortstop Hughie Jennings hit .391 and the victorious Orioles averaged 10 runs in the final four games of the best-of-seven set (4-1). Boston finished out the 1890s decade and the nineteenth century by repeating as champs in 1898 but lost out to Brooklyn in 1899 and 1900. Long's bat plunged to .264/8 HR/88 RBIs/90 runs, over the three-year span, but his 12 circuit clouts in 1900 topped the NL.

Of all Selee's 1890s' selections, Herman lasted the longest, even longer than Selee himself and Lowe, who both left Boston after 1901. By then Long had a lame arm and a battered body from 12 NL seasons, hitting just .231 and .213 in 1902-03. Despite three injury-ridden years, he played 91 percent of Boston's 1890s games. Long's final series as a Beaneater and in the NL was a five-game set with the Giants in October 1902. Boston won the first four but Long was 0-for-16 with 24 assists and two errors. In the season finale, Giant Ironman Joe McGinnity won, 5-1, but loser Long had a single and five more assists. Completely out of character, Long and new manager Albert Buckenberger "showed up" second baseman Gene DeMontreville by yanking him from the game after his two errors in the meaningless game allowed New York to score three times. In a sour ending, the South End Grounds crowd heckled their longtime hero in his last appearance in Boston garb.

Long hit his final two career home runs that season, May 23 and June 3, both off Cardinal Ed Murphy, who led the NL by tossing seven gopher balls. But Murphy won both games, home and away, 10-6 and 11-9. Long's favorite long-ball targets over the decade were Jack Powell and Cy Young (four each). Cy split the four games while Powell lost three. Rookie Bert Abbey gave up Long's last three homers in 1892. Abbey (5-18, seven gopher balls) won two of those games. Long blasted three in a month off New York Giant Bill Carrick in 1900, two on consecutive September days, one being in the year's wildest game, a 14-14, 11-inning draw. On May 9, 1896, at Louisville, Long hit for the cycle off 264-win hometown legend Gus Weyhing, in a 17-5 victory (four runs, three RBIs).

Defensively, Long's best stat game was May 6, 1892, in Porkopolis. In the 14-inning, 0-0 epic duel between John Clarkson (8-6) and Cincinnati's Elton "Icebox" Chamberlain (19-23), Herman had five putouts, 14 assists and only one miscue. Those numbers were not equaled in the nineteenth century and only Tommy Corcoran managed 14 assists (two errors) in a nine-inning game in August 1903. In April 1982 Angels shortstop Rick Burleson made 15, but in 20 innings, three coming after frame 14. Neither had as many total chances. Showing some special longevity, by percentage Long was the best fielding shortstop in the NL in both 1901 and 1902, .946 each campaign. From 1889 through 1903, Long had 14 four-error games and one awful fiver, September 14, 1899 vs. St. Louis at the South End Grounds, in an 11-1 loss.

Only three weeks after the 1902 season ended, AL boss Ban Johnson raided the NL rosters and announced on October 26 the signing of 19 players including Long. Boston was shocked that Herman had decided to pack his bags and go to New York to the new Highlanders team (basically moved/stolen from Baltimore). He lasted until June, hitting .188 in 22 games. His arm was lame and he could not perform his shortstop duties in his accustomed manner. The Detroit Tigers picked him up, and manager Ed Barrow placed him at second base and made him captain. Long's fielding was inconsistent and he hit only .222 in 69 games. Detroit finished the season in pennant-winning Boston and New York. In his final Boston appearance (at the Huntington Avenue Grounds, across the multi-railroad tracks from the South End Grounds), second baseman Long was 4-for-6 off 20-7 Tom Hughes, a fellow Chicagoan, in a 6-6, 11-inning tie. He thrilled the crowd with five assists. Herman must have glanced over the track barrier once or twice, remembering when he was king for a decade only 500 feet away. Ending his only AL year at New York's Hilltop Park, where he started that April, Long was 0-for-6 in a win and then got three straight hits in two other games, the last being a pinch-hit single (run) in his (almost) final major-league at-bat in the ninth inning off rookie reliever Merle "Doc" Adkins, who was also playing his final major-league game. New York won 10-4, ending the season.

In 1904 Long was hired to play for and manage the American Association Toledo Mud Hens, which he did until June 24, when he (.242) resigned with the club in last place. The NL Phillies, managed by old teammate Hugh Duffy, offered him a contract that proved to be for one day, July 13. He went 1-for-4 off Patsy Flaherty (19-9) in the 11-0 trouncing at Exposition Park along the Allegheny River in Pittsburgh. He played second base and had four assists and an error in the worst shutout loss of the season for Duffy's last-place men. The *Pittsburgh Press* observed, "Long's whip is in poor shape."[14] That was his major-league finale.

Long's baseball salvation came on November 18 when he signed to manage and play for the 1905 Des Moines Underwriters in the six-team Western League. Midwest minor-league magnates "Pongo" Joe and Mike Cantillon were responsible for the perfect match as Long joyfully schooled his players each morning on the game's finer points and stayed healthy for most of the season (.307). In a lengthy piece on April 30 the *Des Moines Register* printed "Grosspapa" Long's philosophy: "In baseball there is 65 percent luck and 35 percent noodle work. Almost anyone can catch a ball and field it. Hitting is largely a developed gift, but the good ballplayer is the man who combines head work with all these and unless a man uses his head he will never make a first class ballplayer."[15] Des Moines edged the Denver Grizzlies by four games for the title. Denver was managed by Herman's longtime NL friend Big Bill Everitt. Long's best pupils were Claude Rossman (.357 tops), George Hogriever (122 runs, most), Albert "Lefty" Leifield (26-9, best), and Pete Manske (357 innings, most).. On September 28 the game was stopped by umpire Bob Caruthers (first home-run victim) and Long was presented with a diamond set ring on behalf of the players who acknowledged the credit he deserved for their capturing the pennant. The ring was engraved, "To Herman Long from His Friends in Des Moines, 1905."[16] Herman thought he had a chance at the Boston managerial job for 1906 and even visited the Hub as the 1905 season concluded. But it was not to be; old teammate Fred Tenney continued as manager.

There were levels of closure to Long's career in 1906, which started with the shocking April duo disasters of the San Francisco Earthquake shaking the headlines with Italy's deadly Mount Vesuvius eruption. He captained Ed Barrow's (last-place) Eastern League Toronto Maple Leafs for about 30 games (.247). By June 2 he was off to join Bill "Pa" Rourke's Omaha club in the Western League, where he played second base and hit .213 in 69 games. In his first game, on June 4, he (age 40 and captain) had a hit and four assists in a 2-1, 11-inning loss to Lincoln, Nebraska, at Omaha's Vinton Street Park. His final games occurred as summer faded to autumn on September 21-22. In another 2-1 loss to Lincoln, Long played shortstop and made four putouts, eight assists, and a double play (one error, 0-for-3) in the 65-minute game. Next day in a split doubleheader, he was 3-for-8, scored, had six assists and an error in each game at Lincoln. He didn't play in the final games (4-7) and Omaha sank to third place from second, finishing a game below .500. Long's baseball career ended in Lincoln. On October 2 Arthur Soden sold his (last-place) Boston NL team to Tenney, Roy Thomas, and a Philadelphia businessman. Everything familiar to Herman Long in 1890s baseball was then gone.

Long didn't have much good fortune after his Boston playing days ended. He and partner Frank A. Sanderson bought the Hawthorne Hotel saloon on Avery Street just off the Boston Common in December 1902 and within two years it was in bankruptcy. His wife, Annie (and daughter Harriett), loved her Chicago roots and refused to move to Denver with him for his final care. That estranged the couple. Long was never a muscular specimen and nearly 20 years of ultra-aggressive ballplaying took its toll. His health began to fade badly in 1907-08 but that didn't prevent him playing shortstop in an exhibition game in Chicago in April 1907 and a benefit in July 1908 for ChiTown billiard wizard Jake Schaefer (died 1910 in Denver). By 1909 Long was diagnosed with "consumption," the unstoppable white plague killer of the era. At the time Denver's clean, thin air was looked upon as a healthy option for those afflicted. His illustrious Boston manager Frank Selee went to the (Frederick W.) Oakes Home for Consumptives in spring 1909 and on July 5 he died there. Long was present to bid his friend and mentor a peaceful eternal rest and the newspapers reported that Long tearfully told Selee, "I'll soon be with you, Frank." Long entered the marvelous Oakes facility, a sprawling million-dollar complex on West 32nd Avenue between Eliot and Clay Streets, which was run mainly by an endowment and generous donations, got the same room Selee had and died there on September 16.[17] He is buried in Forest Park's Concordia Cemetery (Chicago) with most of his family.

Various obituaries said that Long had a "love of drink and misdirected generosity" and that he met death "friendless and penniless."[18] One thought was exaggerated and the other just false. Though he did lack any personal finances, his Oakes Home treatment was free. The next morning the *Denver Republican* remarked, "Since coming to Denver, Long has been cared for by the players of the baseball leagues of the country. When it was known he was not "flush" with money, the players sent funds to Bill Everitt and city clerk Burton F. Davis (treasurer/tobacconist), making the last days of Long full of rest and peace." Long's most important and best friend was the Mile High City's Everitt, the old Chicago infielder, who amassed a nice fortune from the Colorado Wrecking and Building Co. he owned. Everitt visited Long all through the fatal illness, making sure he was comfortable; they took walks when Herman was strong enough. *Sporting Life* made note of Big Bill's charitable efforts in its September 5, 1914, issue: "Everitt went to the front and stood good for all the expenses of shipping the short fielder to his native soil (Chicago)." He accompanied the casket personally via train.

Confusingly, a few newspaper datelines and wording have Long passing on September 16, while others say the 17th. The major daily Denver press agree on the 16th and that date appears to be correct. Ironically his biggest 1890s shortstop rival, Jennings, is shown dancing in many of those same papers because he is cajoling his Detroit Tigers to their third straight pennant as the season winds down. Rossman is with the Tigers while Leifield and Long's old Boston mate Vic Willis are with eventual World Series winner Pittsburgh.

Long's fielding abilities were a sensation from his first game in Arkansas City. Because he died young, most fans forgot about his spectacular diamond entertainment for a decade-plus. But Long has had some very important supporters, and they pop up time and time again during the early twentieth century. His name is always linked with Jennings of the 1890s Baltimores. They were the spitfire rivals, Jennings having a better batting average and smoother fielding technique, but Long is always seen as the more exciting player, covering more ground than any human should be able to and making plays that constantly astounded patrons. Both were game-day masters of encouraging teammates and ragging the opposition. At shortstop, Long was obsessed with getting to the moving white sphere no matter the consequences. To him, errors were out chances gone awry and seemingly most fans were oblivious as well to any negative impact. Few scolded him for his near-1,100 miscues. Jennings is in the Hall of Fame, while Long is not nearly mentioned as often as he should be for that honor. Some heralded shortstops like Jack Glasscock and Tommy Corcoran simply could not ever do what Long did weekly and Herman certainly was no slouch at the plate.

Hidden in the stats of the 1890s is the fact that Long hit the most home runs in the NL from 1890 to 1900. Slugger Ed Delahanty and willow wizard Hugh Duffy played in other leagues for a year or two while Long's NL career spanned those 11 seasons perfectly. Even if future Hall members Delahanty's (81 HR's, .351) and Duffy's (85, .330) complete totals were counted, Long is second (83). For the decade (1890-1899), he hit .293 and averaged 40 extra-base hits each season. In addition, Long posted hitting streaks of 23 games in 1895 and 26 games in June-July 1897. He had hit in 13 games previously and Emerson "Pink" Hawley of Pittsburgh prevented his having a 40-game streak (1897). In 1893 he scored in 20 consecutive contests. In the field Long's only real rival was Jennings but Hughie played only seven near-full seasons of the 11. Each shortstop averaged a shade under seven chances per game and Jennings's career shortstop fielding mark was .922, Long's .906.

After Long's death several sportswriters' remembrances shed light on how he played. The *Omaha Daily Bee* noted, "In his day Long was regarded as the king of shortstops. Long's greatest virtue was resourcefulness. As a heady, tricky player, he had few equals in his day. He was always ready with some surprise to spring in an emergency. Long was never rugged physically. ... He was one of those who elevated and magnified the greatness of baseball."[19] The *Buffalo Evening News* wrote, "Long was a peerless shortstop and ranked among the very best at that position, past or present. All points considered, he never had a superior. He not only was reliable, but made more than his share of brilliant stops and throws."[20] In January 1926, Jennings in his national column, Rounding Third, noted, "Long was a crack shortstop and one of the most sensational fielders of all time. He executed impossible plays."[21] In spring training 1924, Connie Mack was asked about shortstops and chose Jennings and Long (who broke Connie's ankle on a slide home in June 1893) as the best he saw. "(Long) was a phenom. He was a tremendously hard hitter and he played deeper short field better than anyone. Herman had a great arm and could play deep, cut off many a hit and beat the batter to first base because he had a whip of steel."[22]

Part of the *Kansas City Times* remembrance of Herman was, "Long was the father of a play which for years has been standard in every baseball league. With a man on first it was customary for the second baseman to cover second if the batter was righthanded."[23] It went on to describe that Herman changed that because he started to cover second base himself instead of Lowe. It faked out basestealers several times and onlookers were also astonished when he first did it.

John Henry Gruber, dean of *Pittsburgh Post-Gazette* sportswriters, who started his career in the 1880s and was official Pirates scorer for decades, penned a syndicated column in February 1914, "Players of Other Days, Herman C. Long." He wrote, "One of the most brilliant infielders the game ever produced was Herman C. Long, intelligent, quick-witted and speedy. His home position was at short, and his work at that station will bear comparison with that of the best in history."[24] An admiring biography followed.

Eleven years later, up popped William Blythe Hanna's accolades for Long on December 11, 1925, in the *New York Herald Tribune*. For seemingly no particular reason, Hanna, the longtime baseball and football expert of the New York sports pages, decided Long deserved a remembrance column. "Gleaned in the Field of Sport" was the venue. Hanna was blunt, "Herman Long was the best shortstop I ever saw. Glenn Wright of the Pirates, nor anyone else covered the ground Long did. ... Long, the 'Dutchman' as he was called, was the best shortstop and the most fiery. He was as sensational in his day as Babe Ruth or Ty Cobb. He was a player with a tremendous personal following, with the magnetism of King Kelly and commonplace in nothing. His vicious throwing and his fondness for first-ball hitting were two of his chief characteristics. As leadoff man he was one of the best because he was a good hitter or a good waiter as occurrences justified. He wasn't graceful, but he was the last word in energy."[25] James H. "Jimmy" Manning, the veteran player-manager of the Kansas City Blues in 1888, told of putting Long at short when his own arm went lame. Only exaggerating a bit, Manning recalled that after a short time he could not take his job back and he found that he didn't need a third baseman or second baseman because of what Long was doing.[26]

Most biased of all, and properly so, was Hall of Fame 300-game winner Charles Augustus "Kid" Nichols, an adversary in the minors and a Beaneaters teammate icon for a decade. It was believed that no one in baseball knew the original Flying Dutchman as well as Kid. As rookies in 1890, Nichols' first two career shutouts were each 1-0 nailbiters. Long scored both runs as well as tallying in four of Kid's five other shutouts that year. Nichols recalled, "No man fought harder to win games than Long, but with all of his aggressiveness he never quarreled with the players or umpires. A great many writers have compared him with Jennings as the stars at the midfield position, but I have always given the honors to Long. Jennings was more graceful and probably had more finish, but even with his noise he lacked Herman's ginger. Herman didn't worry about errors, he tore in after everything. He had a wonderful arm and it took a mighty speedy runner to beat out an infield hit when he handled the ball. Then, he was one of the most timely hitters in the business."[27]

Perhaps the most poignant comments came from a very unlikely source, Montana's *Butte Miner*. On September 21, four days after Long's passing, a lengthy nonbyline story appeared that was not copied from another news outlet. In part it said, "The death of Long removes one of the most notable figures that the national game ever produced. Long was one of the brainiest ball players, a pioneer of the class regarded as the greatest exponents of inside baseball – the men who think quickly. Frank Selee, perhaps the finest judge of players who ever lived, always regarded him as among the greatest ball players of all time. In the game he was the essence of ginger and off the field he was a gentleman. 'There might have been shortstops who fielded higher averages, but it is doubtful whether the game has ever known a short-fielder of greater all around value to his team,' long-time Michigan sportswriter Emerson W. Dickerson is quoted, 'and in this I do not except Hans Wagner. There was a reckless disregard of possible errors in Long's play which is sadly lacking in present-day players. In a season the Dutchman reached perhaps 50 balls which ordinary shortstops do not try for.' A testimonial benefit was given (for Long) about two years ago, when he broke down under the long strain of many years of play, a sufficient amount to make his remaining days comfortable. Yes, Herman Long of German descent and who spoke it fluently, was called the Dutchman way before John Honus Wagner arrived in 1897."[28]

In January 1911 Fred Tenney, a manager in Boston and New York and Long's old target at first base, wrote several articles for the *New York Times* on various baseball topics. One was about "Famous Shortstops" he knew. In part and with a possible bias, he wrote, "Long was far and away the best man from 1890 to 1894. He was the most marvelous ground coverer ever developed at that time. He seemed to know where a batter would hit the ball and always moved to that point. He made more spectacular plays than any man before or since. He was remarkably strong in handling thrown balls, and touching base runners and (on offense) was a wonderful base runner and run getter."[29]

Finally, an iconic adversary and keen analyst of decades worth of baseball players had this to say, from the grave. About a week after his death in 1934 the *Pittsburgh Press* ran an interview that had been done about three weeks before with this baseball legend. The byline read "Daniel" and his question was simply who were the best double-play combo – Tinker and Evers? "Hell no," came the gruff reply. "The greatest pair for making two out were Dutch Long and Bobby Lowe of the Boston Nationals. They were remarkable infielders and they played alongside each other for so many years that knew by instinct and habit what each would do in a given situation," observed John Joseph McGraw.[30]

In his 1994 classic *The Beer and Whisky League*, author David Nemec's peerless in-depth research illuminated a huge injustice to Long: "His play brought him more votes than all but seven other nineteenth-century players when the Hall of Fame conducted an initial poll in 1936. Long is the only finisher among the top 12 (now 14) in the first Old Timers' ballot who is not enshrined."[31]

At their Sun Trust Park in Smyrna, Georgia, the Atlanta Braves pay tribute to players from their entire history dating to 1871 in Boston. Along the Monument Garden walkway there's only one nineteenth-century player whose name/picture banner hangs from a 30-foot pillar among the many more modern Braves. It is Herman Long, who resides in the top 10 of many franchise categories; first in stolen bases (434), third in triples, fourth in runs and sacrifices, fifth in hits, sixth in RBIs, and eighth in games played. He was inducted into the Braves Hall of Fame in 2005.

SOURCES

In addition to the sources cited in the Notes, the author also consulted Ancestry.com, Harold Kaese's *The Boston Braves, an Informal History*, Dave Nemec's *Major League Baseball Profiles 1871-1900 Vol. 1*, David L. Porter's *Biographical Dictionary of American Sports: Baseball*, Baseball Reference.com, Long's player file from the National Baseball Hall of Fame Library, Baseball America's *Encyclopedia of Minor League Baseball*, Retrosheet.org, Sun Trust Park Memorial Garden (Atlanta Braves), and the following newspapers: *Baltimore Sun, Boston Globe, Boston Herald, Boston Evening Transcript, Buffalo Evening News*, Butte (Montana) *Miner, Chicago Tribune, Chicago Inter Ocean, Cincinnati Enquirer, Denver Post, Denver Republican, Des Moines Register, Detroit News*, Emporia (Kansas) *Evening News, Kansas City Star, Kansas City Times, Louisville Courier-Journal, New York Clipper, New York Herald Tribune, Omaha Daily Bee, Pittsburgh Press, Rocky Mountain News*, and *The Sporting News*.

NOTES

1 Throughout Long's career and 50 years beyond his death, almost all references to his birth say April 3. Then in June 1964, his nephew Dr. Clyde Hillock Jacobs corresponded with Baseball Hall of Fame librarian Lee Allen. Jacobs filled out a questionnaire about Long and wrote that his birth was April 13, 1866. Whether a simple error in family memory, a typo or something else, since that paper was placed on file, researchers have used the April 13 date as gospel. Dr. Jacobs was born in 1912 and admitted not knowing very much about Herman or his life, which was his reason for contacting the Hall Library. His posted September 17 death date was also incorrect.

2 "7 to 6" and "How Our Boys Play Well," *Arkansas City* (Kansas) *Daily Republican Traveler*, May 18 and 19, 1887: 5.

3 "Twelve Innings Played," *Chicago Tribune*, April 17, 1888: 6.

4 "On the Diamond – Turn About Fair Play," *St. Paul Globe*, May 31, 1888: 4.

5 "Western Association – Changes in Maroon Club," *Chicago Tribune*, July 12, 1888: 3.

6 "Another Game Lost – Notes," *Louisville Courier-Journal*, April 21, 1889: 5.

7 "Each Club Won a Game (Some Notable Points)," *Baltimore Sun*, August 2, 1889: 6

8 "Says Long Cost Boston Club $6,500," *Boston Globe*, January 10, 1890: 5.

9 *New York Clipper*, May 31, 1890: Vol. 38, No. 12: 185.

10 *The Sporting News*, July 18, 1891: Vol. 12, No. 9: 1.

11 "Long Refuses to Play for Boston," *New York Sun*, March 11, 189:, 4.

12 "Trouble in the Boston Team," *Chicago Tribune*, July 18, 1895: 4.

13 Per Retrosheet. The *Reach Guide* and the *Minor League Encyclopedia* each have his average at .432.

14 "Shutout for the Phillies – Baseball Notes," *Pittsburgh Press*, July 14, 1904: 12.

15 Tracy Garrett, "In the West with the Underwriters," *Des Moines Register*, April 30, 1905: 23.

16 "Des Moines Takes Second of Series," *Des Moines Register*, September 29, 1905: 7.

17 "Herman Long Is Out, Tuberculosis Tags Him," *Rocky Mountain News*, September 17, 1909: 8.

18 "Herman Long Dead," *Sporting Life*, September 25, 1909: 2.

19 "Judgments," *Omaha Sunday Bee*, September 19, 1909: 30.

20 "Famous Shortstop Passes Away," *Buffalo Evening News*, September 17, 1909: 60.

21 Hugh A. Jennings, "Rounding Third – Fielding with the Feet," *Des Moines Register*, January 2, 1926: 9.

22 S.O. Grauley, "Connie Mack Picks Jennings and Long," *Philadelphia Inquirer*, March 9, 1924: 18.

23 "The End to Herman Long," *Kansas City Times*, September 17, 1909: 4.

24 John H. Gruber, "Old Time Players – Herman Long," *The Sporting News*, March 5, 1914: 4.

25 William Blythe Hanna, "Gleaned in Fields of Sport," *New York Herald Tribune*, December 11, 1925: 27.

26 "Was a Great Ballplayer," *Kansas City Star*, September 17, 1909: 13.

27 Tannehill A. Mark, "Get the Brush – Baseball Notes," *Boston Globe*, June 3, 1903: 5.

28 "Herman Long Dead," *Butte Miner*, September 21, 1909: 3.

29 Fred Tenney, "Famous Shortstops Tenney Has Known," *New York Times*, January 22, 1911: 29.

30 Daniel [sic], "Double Play Kings? Long, Lowe Choice of McGraw," *Pittsburgh Press*, March 4, 1934: 19. "Daniel" was the byline affected by Dan Daniel, a longtime New York sportswriter.

31 David Nemec, *The Beer and Whisky League* (New York: Lyons and Burford, 1994), 169.

BOBBY LOWE

BY RICHARD "DIXIE" TOURANGEAU

Bobby Lowe, with Milwaukee in 1888. Old Judge cigarette card.
(Courtesy of National Baseball Hall of Fame)

Visiting Cincinnati hurler Elton Chamberlain was in Boston's Congress Street Grounds pitcher's box for the afternoon game of the May 30, 1894, Decoration Day doubleheader. "Icebox" had no-hit the champ Beaneaters the previous September in Porkopolis (in a game called due to darkness after seven innings) and he was about to face half the same lineup. Leadoff batter Bobby Lowe made the first out, leaving himself 0-for-7 for the day. In the third inning it was 2-2 when Lowe came up again. Baseball history then took a few turns at bat.

Robert Lincoln "Linc" Lowe was born in Pittsburgh on July 10, 1865, just short of three months after the assassination of President Abraham Lincoln. His parents were Robert L. Lowe, a railroad and blast-furnace engineer and Jane R. (Crahan) Lowe. In 1868 the family of seven moved 50 miles north to Union Township (also called West New Castle), the next locale west of burgeoning New Castle, an area where furnace-related jobs were numerous. They lived on Bluff Street, just across the Shenango River from New Castle, which gained city status in 1869. On December 6, 1878, tragedy struck the family when a newly repaired blast furnace at the Brier Hill Coal and Mining Co. in Youngstown, Ohio, exploded while being relit. Robert, project boss on the job for two weeks, died the next day from his horrific injuries.[1] (This was the same year teammate Billy Nash lost his mother.) To help support his mother and four siblings, teenager Bobby found work as a printer's devil at the *New Castle Courant*. There he met compositor Charlie Power, about five years older, who was also an amateur baseball player and team organizer. In the summer of 1881 city doctors and printers planned a friendly community baseball match and Bobby begged for a spot on Power's team. Appreciating Lowe's enthusiasm Charlie allowed the youngster to play despite the objections of the older boys. Bobby was the star, impressing everyone who played and watched. As the years passed, Lowe played for a succession of town amateur teams: the James P. Witherow Works (furnace equipment), the Archie Reeds (Reed was a jovial, celebrity railroad conductor), and finally the reborn and more talented Neshannocks (Indian name of largest nearby river), by then (1886) managed by Power. Lowe caught Charlie's pitches in most games but also was the change hurler.[2]

New Castle was already on the big-time baseball map because of native sons Joe Quest, an infielder for Chicago and Detroit, and Charlie Bennett, who by the 1880s was the nationally known catcher for the Detroit Wolverines. In 1887 Power and Lowe made their way to Eau Claire, Wisconsin, to play in the Northwestern League. Abe Devine, manager, was skeptical of Lowe's ability despite Power's insistence that Bobby was good enough to compete. On May 3 Lowe got his chance to play third base and Power pitched. Bobby homered in a 10-3 loss, scoring twice on three hits. In the following weeks he played some outfield and caught. Starting off 0-11, Eau Claire was destined for last place. Team injuries finally forced Lowe into the daily lineup and he performed beyond expectations. By June 21 manager Devine was fired (team at 7-27) and Quest took over after resigning from his National League umpiring slot. Bobby (.294) became a fixture at third base; Eau Claire finished 39-84. The league disbanded after concluding the season, with the four best teams moving to a better circuit.

Lowe was picked up by Milwaukee manager James Hart for 1888. The Western Association Brewers were a middle-of-the-pack club and Lowe, playing left field mostly, was batting about .280 when his mom suddenly died in New Castle on July 27. After taking 10 days off for family issues, he was 2-for-25 in his first week back and never really got untracked, hitting .246 by year's end. While he was in New Castle, Eau Claire was 1-8, scoring just 12 runs. In 1889 the old Boston NL star third baseman Ezra Sutton managed the Milwaukee club as Hart went to Boston to manage its NL entry. Sutton kept Lowe in the outfield but did move him to infield spots when injuries occurred. Ezra's Creams were marginal, 58-63, ending way behind Frank Selee's Omaha Omahogs, 83-38, led by pitcher Charlie "Kid" Nichols, 39-8. Lowe finished in the league's top 10 hitters of those players who appeared in more than half the games, leading his club at .315.

Twisted baseball fate guided Lowe's next move. Hart left Boston for England in an attempt by baseball's high powers to ignite some interest across the Atlantic. Boston, with a full roster in 1889, had finished only one game from the pennant claimed by New York despite John Clarkson's 49 wins. Omaha manager Selee was given the reins of Arthur Soden's Beaneaters for the chaotic 1890 season when the upstart Brotherhood (Players') League would be a third major employer along with the NL and the American Association. Underpaid players jumped to higher-bidding teams every day. Signing anyone was a formidable task as contract squabbles and lawsuits prevailed. NL Boston lost seven position players. Taking no chances on the possible fickleness of the PL, Lowe was the first to sign with NL Boston, in October 1889. Selee had seen him in the Western circuit and knew of his ability and character. Since Boston stalwart third baseman Billy Nash had skipped off to the PL Boston Reds, that position was open for Lowe. Another reason for his quick signing was that New Castle hero Charlie Bennett came to Boston in 1889 and now Bobby would get to play with him in the oldest, most stable league. But it all didn't matter for long, since Bobby got hurt in early May.

Rookie third sacker Lowe was ablaze in his first 10 NL games, leading the NL in hitting (.470) on May 2 when bad knees crippled him. What was thought to be just a short-lived injury to be cured with rest turned into almost no action for three months. Bobby tried to play twice in the outfield, even got hits, but weakness forced him to give up and sit on the bench. A lanky-looking player at 5-feet-10 and 150 pounds, Lowe saw action in only 52 games, managing .280 for the season. It was by far the fewest games the right-handed swinger would play during the 1890s. Boston finished fifth (76-57) behind champ Brooklyn but Selee had cleverly assembled a solid squad for future campaigns.

Baseball fans nationwide got their first education about Lowe on January 3, 1891, when the *New York Clipper* profiled him, explaining his background and route to the Beaneaters.[3] The exact same story and image were published by the *The Sporting News* in its July 25, 1891, issue (front page). When the financially doomed PL folded after one season, popular third baseman Nash was lured back to the South End Grounds and was given the captaincy as part of his "prodigal son" deal. Veteran Joe Quinn was at second so Lowe was relegated to a utility role over the next two seasons. Lowe could play any position well, but his bat soured. He hit .260 and .242, stats that were overlooked as Boston won the pennant both years, including a record 102 victories in 1892 thanks to a longer season. In 1893 the pitcher's box was moved back from 50 to 60 feet 6 inches and Bobby took advantage, hitting .298 with a team-high 14 home runs (third in the NL behind Phillies slugger Ed Delahanty's 19). Quinn was dealt to St. Louis for Cliff Carroll and Lowe settled in at second base, a place he'd call home for a decade. Post-1891, the AA also went defunct, and Boston's outfield had acquired the scoring punch of the Heavenly Twins, Hugh Duffy and Tommy McCarthy, who helped the 1893 squad win a third straight pennant. Nash, Lowe, shortstop phenom Herman Long, and first baseman Tommy Tucker gave the Beaneaters the best all-around infield in the League.

Omen-like tragedy struck the Boston franchise early in 1894. Beloved catcher and Lowe's hometown buddy Bennett was severely injured in a January railroad accident in Wellsville, Kansas. After speaking to a friend at the depot, he tried to reboard a slowly moving train leaving the station and slipped beneath the wheels. He survived but lost parts of both legs and his career was over. On a brighter personal note, before coming to Boston to start the season, Lowe on April 3 married Harriet "Hattie" Hughes, whose father, Benjamin, and brother Issac ran the Leslie Hotel and a café in New Castle. Almost simultaneously, Duffy was hit with the second tragedy when his wife died while returning from a March trip to visit Southern friends. More bad news awaited.

On May 15, in the 20th game of the season and only the fifth at home, the costliest event occurred when Boston's South End Grounds, "the architectural crown jewel of nineteenth-century parks," burned to the ground during a game with Baltimore.[4] Starting small under the right-field stands along Berlin Street, the soon unstoppable blaze took 200 Roxbury buildings with it. No one was killed but the Grounds' ornate witch-hat towers Grand Pavilion was history. The incident forced the Beaneaters to rent the unused PL/AA Congress Street Grounds for their next 27 home games.

Most batters finally caught on to the longer pitching distance in 1894, and the League average spiked to .309, the highest ever. Lowe joined the parade and enjoyed his best season (.346), but he had to settle for second place to the amazing Duffy in Beaneater hits, runs (158, fifth in the league), and home runs. Lowe's 212 hits placed him fourth in the NL. Duffy whacked 18 home runs (really 19, see the June 20 game account) to Lowe's 17 to snag that title.

Against the exceptional pitchers of the New York Giants, Rusie (pitching triple crown winner) and Jouett Meekin, runs were at a premium even at short-porched Congress Street, but after that the ballpark's penchant for big scores took over. Lowe was collared by both Giants and a few days later he was 0-for-6 against Cincy's Tom Parrott in the morning tilt of the Decoration Day twin bill, taken 13-10 by Boston. He and wife Hattie then had lunch at a North Station restaurant before returning to the Congress Street yard for the afternoon contest against Icebox Chamberlain. Elton was 2-2 there lifetime and got Bobby out as leadoff batter, but did give up two quick scores. In the third inning Lowe took his first historic swing and smashed a pitch over the left-field fence for a 3-2 lead, then repeated that before the inning concluded. His two home runs in the inning ignited the host Beaneaters to an 11-2 lead. Icebox had melted but was still in the box when, continuing his surreal groove, Lowe blasted his third round-tripper in the fifth, and in the sixth frame he and Keystone pal Long drove back-to-back circuit blasts. The roaring crowd saw Bobby once more that day; he singled in the seventh much to their good-natured dismay. Kid Nichols took the 20-11 victory and Lowe walked away with a single-game record of four home runs and 17 total bases, tied by Delahanty in 1896 but not surpassed until Milwaukee's Joe Adcock did so in 1954 at Ebbets Field (18 total bases). In appreciation of the entertaining afternoon power splurge, the jubilant patrons threw about $160 worth of coins on the field for Lowe to pocket. His worst and best games ever had come on the same day. Recounting the feat many times as the years passed, he claimed that all four clouts fell within 30 feet of each other.[5]

Ned Hanlon's Orioles eventually pulled away from the Beaneaters in September (20-3 to 14-11) and took the pennant, preventing a fourth straight Boston title. Selee's club had beaten Baltimore 8-4 in games but didn't crush the bad teams as often, finishing eight games behind Baltimore despite hitting .331 and plating the most runs (1,220). Lowe, as leadoff batter most of the season, led the NL with 613 at-bats and was second to Billy Hamilton of Philly in plate appearances. Good health, knees included, allowed Bobby to play all 133 games.

In 1895 the Beaneaters figured to bounce back, but it never happened. They pitched decently but hit .041 less, finishing fifth at 71-60-2. Lowe hit .297 and scored 102 runs, but Baltimore (87-43-2) took its second pennant. The Orioles defeated Boston in 10 of 12 games, the worst season series beating by one team of the decade over Selee's squad. By midseason Boston had dugout trouble as rumors abounded that cliques had formed. An offseason blockbuster deal sent third-base fixture Nash to Philadelphia

Lou Gehrig and Bobby Lowe, each of whom hit four homers in a game.
(Courtesy of John Thorn)

to play and manage the 1896 Phillies in exchange for bat wizard and flychaser Hamilton. McCarthy was then sent packing to Brooklyn for his final season. Lowe hit .320 but played in only 73 games due to injuries. Rookie Marty Bergen caught well (.269), phenom Jimmy Collins (.296) handled third base, and Hamilton was terrific (.366, 110 walks, 153 runs), but it was not enough to derail the Orioles express (90-39), which claimed a third straight flag. Rookie switch-hitter Dan McGann (.322) filled in for Lowe at second; it was his only year as a Beaneater.

Slugger Charles "Chick" Stahl (.354) came to Boston in 1897. He was the only major roster change as the Beaneaters tried to dethrone the thrice pennant-winning Orioles. The two rivals nearly matched each other in pitching and hitting and split their 12 games. Selee's squad did manage to outscore (1,025-964) and outhomer the Orioles. Boston edged Baltimore by two games for the pennant, thanks to the New York Giants beating Baltimore 7 of 12 times, while the Beaneaters whipped New York 8 of 12. Boston's team average was .319. Making up for catcher Bergen's .248 was pitcher-outfielder Jack Stivetts (11-4, .367). Lowe batted .309 and knocked home 106 runs while playing excellent defense behind Nichols' 31-11 record and that of Fred Klobedanz (26-7).

In 1898 Baltimore's hitting and pitching were a shade better than Boston's and they even scored more runs, but Boston won 102 games in the expanded schedule of 154 games and edged the Orioles to win the flag for a fifth time in the 1890s, this time by six games. The Beaneaters' average dropped to .290 despite Hamilton's topping the club at .369/110 runs. Lowe chipped in a decent .272/94 RBIs and led the club with 20 sacrifices. Bobby's fielding (.952) was second best in the league.

Ending the fabulous 1890s Gilded decade and the century, Lowe's average didn't change much with age, (.272 and .278), 88 and 71 RBIs, as the Beaneaters finished second to Brooklyn in 1899 before sinking to 66-72 in 1900 when their great pitching finally declined. In each of those years, Lowe was still a top-fielding second baseman while playing 279 games. The Beaneaters dynasty was all but over, and in 1902 three of the oldest South End Grounders moved on. Selee went to North Side Chicago to manage the Cubs and Lowe went with him to be a veteran presence. Nichols headed back to the Midwest, leaving Long as the longest-term Beaneater, but even he was gone by 1903.

In Chicago Lowe was made captain and played well (.248), replacing the retired Clarence "Cupid" Childs. Bobby was the fourth infielder when Frank Chance and rookies Joe Tinker and Johnny Evers (debut) took the field together for the first time on September 1, 1902. It was a bit depressing for Lowe to watch his new team hit just six homers all season. A broken kneecap allowed him only 32 games in 1903 (.267). He played mostly second base for Selee's Cubs in April, May, and half of June, but on the 13th his knees hurt terribly. It was diagnosed as water on the knee, and all thought rest would be helpful. On July 4, after three weeks off, Lowe got his last hit and run for Chicago at the West Side Grounds while making three errors in a 16-9 win over New York. Then doctors' X-rays discovered the real problem. Regretting the inevitable, Selee released his old soldier on July 18 so he might latch on to another club as a manager.[6]

Durand Clarence Packard, owner of Denver's Grizzlies of the Western Association, signed Lowe to pilot the team starting July 28 as manager Ed Barrow had departed. In his first series as manager, Lowe was pitted against old pitching-ace pal Nichols, who was manager-pitcher for Kansas City. In 1904 Lowe tried to catch on with the thrice-NL champ Pirates and spent March in Hot Springs, Arkansas, playing for the Pittsburgh Yanigans. Spring training improved his health and he signed a Pirates contract on April 14, only to be released on the 19th after one at-bat, a pinch-hit strikeout in a 6-5 loss at St. Louis. But Lowe had Tiger friends and he immediately went to Detroit, where a spot at second base awaited. On April 23 he started his first game of 140, and finished second among AL second basemen in fielding (.964) but hit just .208. He was again with New Castle legend Charlie Bennett, who was a Bengals coach.

On July 24 manager Ed Barrow had resigned. Owner William H. Yawkey (uncle of future Red Sox owner Tom Yawkey) and business manager Frank Navin chose Lowe as manager to finish the season. Detroit went 30-44 under Lowe. At age 39 in 1905, Lowe gave up managing and became the Tigers utilityman, playing all infield positions and some outfield in his 58 games (.193). Lowe remained with Detroit for another 58 games in 1906-07, hitting .214. Lowe claimed the major-league players' "hard luck" title in 1906. First a bout with malaria shelved him, followed by a torn fingernail and a sprained ankle, both topped by a broken nose from his own fouled bunt attempt in drizzly Philadelphia on August 25. That finished his season.[7]

In 1907 Lowe started the spring as baseball coach at the University of Michigan (11-4-1). He returned to the Tigers for 17 games, appearing only once before August 13. He subbed at third base mostly and pinch-hit twice. All of his final career hits, RBIs, and an error came in the club's final games on October 6, a doubleheader at St. Louis, as AL champ Detroit rested regulars for the World Series. Lowe knocked in runs in each first inning, first off rookie Bill Bailey and then off veteran Harry Howell, but the Browns won 10-4 and 10-3. Lowe hung around long enough to play with Ty Cobb and see the Tigers take the 1907 AL pennant under manager Hughie Jennings, his old Orioles adversary.

The 1908 baseball season saw Lowe in Grand Rapids, Michigan, managing the Central League's Wolverines. They finished 68-71 in fifth place behind Evansville. In 1909 he signed with Washington and Jefferson College, southwest of Pittsburgh, to coach that college squad. Off and on he was still there in 1914.

According to the 1910 census, Bobby and Hattie were in Detroit and he was listed as a "baseball traveler" as he scouted for the Tigers for a few years. Their residence then at 617 John R. Road is 300 feet from present-day Comerica Park. About 1922 Lowe found a comfortable position with the Detroit Public Works Department, where he was employed as an inspector of streets and sewers until retirement in the 1940s. Bobby's entire family – parents Robert and Jane, three sisters, Mary, Lida, and Olive, and brother, Charles, all died before 1900. His wife, Hattie, died in September 1947, and Lowe, suffering from crippling neuritis, passed away in Detroit at the Arnold Home for the Aged/Retired on December 8, 1951, three days after Shoeless Joe Jackson (Greenville, South Carolina). The Lowes are buried in north Detroit's Evergreen Cemetery, south of Woodlawn Cemetery near Palmer Park.

Lowe's notable diamond exploits are not limited to his four-homer outburst on May 30, 1894. He had a six-hit game and three five-hit games; in one of them he scored six runs (May 3, 1895, 27-11 versus visiting Washington). Over a five-year span, Lowe clouted four home runs off fellow Pittsburgher Addison Gumbert, equaling his four off the Icebox in four innings. Though his Decoration Day record gets the most attention, Lowe said that his second favorite game was as a Cub on June 22, 1902. In the longest game ever at the West Side Grounds, Chicago beat champ Pittsburgh 3-2 in 19 innings. Lowe helped tie the game in the ninth and won it 10 frames later with an RBI single off stalwart Charles Deacon Phillippe before a howling crowd of 10,000.[8] According to a list of home runs specifically hit by second basemen through 1900, compiled by era expert Dave Nemec, Lowe ranks second only to Chicago's Fred Pfeffer, 93 to 56, with McPhee at 53. Since Pfeffer and McPhee played mainly in the 1880s, by default Bobby Lowe is easily the premier Keystone slugger of the 1890s. Both Pfeffer and Lowe took good advantage of home-field short porches.

In March 1911 his ex-teammate and by then a respected manager, Fred Tenney, wrote in the *New York Times* that Lowe was the best all-around utility player of his era, able to handle any position smoothly as well as wield a solid bat.[9] Lowe's three grand slams came in successive years, off George Haddock in May 1893, Charlie Petty in May '94 and Ernie Beam in August '95. Of Bobby's 71 home runs, half were with men on base.

Considered a gentleman and exceptional baseball citizen, Lowe was ejected only twice in his career, never as Beaneater. On

August 13, 1902, Tom Brown expelled him for arguing a decision, and on July 22, 1904, ump Frank Dwyer didn't appreciate Lowe and Wild Bill Donovan bringing flaming newspapers on to the field in the 13th inning of a scoreless game in Washington to indicate they felt it was too dark to continue. While going from Hot Springs to Grand Rapids for the start of his 1908 managerial season, Linc and Hattie stopped in Fort Wayne to see the mother of former teammate Chick Stahl, who had committed suicide the year before.

Boston Braves captain and 1914 World Series champ (and future Hall of Famer) Johnny Evers penned the best evidence of Lowe's grand baseball citizen credentials. In a syndicated column in March 1915, Evers recalled 37-year-old Bobby on the Cubs in 1903 guiding 21-year-old Evers through the baseball wars. "Lowe was one of the best friends I had in baseball during my struggle to stick," Evers wrote. "He did everything he could for me. Lowe later went into the insurance business and I am glad to say that I took the first policy he ever wrote. He is now scouting for Detroit. Selee had been with him for 12 years in Boston and when it came time to give Bobby his release, Selee wouldn't do it. The Chicago club finally gave it to the veteran and a grand player passed out of the league. The members of the Cubs bought Lowe a diamond watch fob as a mark of esteem before he hung up his spangles for good. I want to say that I believe Bobby Lowe had more to do with me making good than any other man in baseball, with his kindly advice and valuable tips which he had gathered during his long experience. I was sorry to see him go."[10]

Lowe made his final appearance in a Boston uniform on September 11, 1922, at Braves Field. He was one of the Old Timers invited to a benefit game there for Children's Hospital. Some 20,000 fans saw about 40 stars of bygone days and Bobby was 1-for-1 in the 28-7 loss to the AL team. The *Detroit Free Press* ran a humorous anecdote in 1948 about Ty Cobb and his wife visiting the Lowes in Detroit in the late 1930s. The wives were in the living room when they heard commotion in the kitchen. Ty had told Bobby he developed a slide technique that enabled him to avoid any tag. Lowe tried to prove him wrong and the two retired teammates were wrestling on the floor before the ladies called a halt to the childish ruckus.[11] Bobby had the "guest of honor" head-table spot for the April 1938 Old Timers Association gathering to welcome the new season in the Motor City.

Because of his longevity as a Beaneater, Lowe is in the top 10 of several categories in the descendant Braves franchise history. He is fourth in stolen bases and fifth in hit by pitches, and ranks eighth, ninth or 10th in games, at-bats, runs, RBIs, average, hits, triples, and sacrifices. In the *Detroit Free Press,* New York sportswriter Whitney Martin composed an unexpected tribute to Lowe for the August 19, 1942, edition. His theme was great second basemen through the years and included elders Nap Lajoie, Bid McPhee, Charlie Gehringer and Rogers Hornsby. The headline read, "Speaking of Great Second Basemen, Don't Forget Lowe."[12] Bobby never received a single Hall of Fame vote.

SOURCES

In addition to the sources cited in the Notes, the author also consulted Ancestry.com, Baseball-Reference.com, Lowe's player file at the National Baseball Hall of Fame, *Baseball America's Encyclopedia of Minor League Baseball*, Retrosheet.org, and the following newspapers: *Boston Herald, Boston Post, Cincinnati Enquirer, Fort Wayne Daily News, Milwaukee Journal, New Castle* (Pennsylvania) *News, Pittsburgh Post-Gazette,* and *The Sporting News.* Thanks to David Nemec for supplying nineteenth-century home-run statistics.

NOTES

1. "Hot Blast Explosion," *Youngstown* (Ohio) *Vindicator,* December 13, 1878: 5.
2. "Brilliant Player – Story of How Bobby Lowe Was Discovered," *Boston Globe,* December 22, 1895: 15.
3. *New York Clipper,* January 3, 1891: 681.
4. John Pastier, "Constructing Paradise: the Evolution of the Ballpark," *Ballparks Yesterday and Today* (Edison, New Jersey: Chartwell Books, Inc., 2007), 13.
5. See Bob Latshaw, "4 Homers in One Game!" *Detroit Free Press,* March 23, 1947: 31, and "Bobby Lowe Dies at 83," *Boston Globe,* December 10, 1951: 10.
6. "Capt. Lowe Is Released," *Chicago Tribune,* July 9, 1903: 8.
7. "Bobby Lowe Claims the Hard-Luck Title," *Pittsburgh Press,* September 26, 1906: 14.
8. "Four Homers in One Game," *Detroit Free Press,* March 23, 1947: 31.
9. Fred Tenney, "Bobby Lowe Best Utility Player," *New York Times,* March 14, 1911: 9.
10. Johnny Evers, "Some More Inside History," *Honolulu Star-Bulletin,* March 3, 1915: 9.
11. Lyall Smith, "As of Today; Even Cobb Had His Moments," *Detroit Free Press,* May 9, 1948: C-1.
12. Whitney Martin (Associated Press), "Speaking of Great Second Basemen, Don't Forget Lowe," *Detroit Free Press,* August 19, 1942: 15.

TOMMY MC@RTHY

BY BILL LAMB

Tommy McCarthy, 1895 Mayo Cut-Plug tobacco card.
(public domain)

During a relatively short late-nineteenth century playing career, Tommy McCarthy forged a reputation as an inventive baseball strategist, a fine defensive outfielder, and a good, if not exceptional, batsman. A significant member of pennant winners in both the American Association and the National League, McCarthy lingered in memory as the lesser half of the Boston Beaneaters' celebrated "Heavenly Twins" outfield of the early 1890s. Fifty years after his major-league baseball days were over, McCarthy joined fellow Twin Hugh Duffy in the Hall of Fame as a member of the 10-man class selected by the Veterans Committee in 1946. Since that time, McCarthy's induction has served as a paradigm for Cooperstown critics, often cited as the foremost example of VC dilution of the standards for baseball immortality.

The subject of this critical commentary was born Thomas Francis Michael McCarthy in Boston on July 24, 1863, the eldest of seven surviving children born to Irish immigrant laborer Daniel McCarthy and his wife Sarah, nee Healy.[1] Young Tommy grew up in the Celtic enclave of South Boston, beginning his working life in a local clothing factory while still in grade school. His spare time was spent playing baseball on Boston sandlots. Following graduation from John A. Andrews Grammar School, McCarthy found work in local piano assembly plants and attracted attention pitching after-hours for company league teams.[2] In 1884, he was given a tryout by Tim Murnane, later a famed sportswriter but then player-manager of the Boston entry in the fledgling Union Association. Although signed by the Boston Reds as a right-handed pitcher, McCarthy made his professional debut as a right fielder, going hitless in a July 10 game against Chicago's Hugh Daily.[3] For the remainder of the season, McCarthy alternated between the outfield and the mound, pitching well against local semipro competition in exhibition games but without success in UA play, going 0-7 with a 4.82 ERA. Nor did the righty batter impress with the stick, hitting only .215 with little power in over 200 plate appearances.[4]

After the one-season UA folded, McCarthy was signed as an outfielder by the National League Boston Beaneaters. But again, he failed to hit, drawing his release in August after posting a paltry .182 BA in limited action. McCarthy finished 1885 playing for Haverhill in the Eastern New England League under manager Frank Selee, a pilot who would become a recurring presence during the McCarthy career. Tommy began the following season on the Haverhill roster, but after seven games his contract was purchased by Providence, only recently the NL champions but now demoted to the Eastern League. He batted .281 in 20 games for Providence before the franchise collapsed in June. The next stop on the 1886 McCarthy odyssey was Brockton of the New England League where a capable .327 BA in 76 games caught the eye of Harry Wright, then leading the Philadelphia team in the NL. Once acquired by the Phillies, however, McCarthy saw action in only eight games, hitting .185 in 27 at-bats.

The start of the 1887 season brought more of the same. McCarthy received little playing time in Philadelphia and was unproductive – a .186 BA in 73 plate trips – when he was in the line-up. By June, Tommy was back in the minors, sold to Oshkosh of the Northwestern League for $800. There, McCarthy finally blossomed as a ballplayer. Reunited with manager Frank Selee, McCarthy tore up the circuit. In 80 games, he hit .389 for Oshkosh, with 102 runs scored and 69 stolen bases. Aside from the patient tutelage of Selee, McCarthy may also have benefitted from the company of his wife during his stay in the Northwestern League. Like Tommy, the former Margaret McCluskey had been born in Boston of Irish-Catholic immigrant parents.[5] But little else is known of Margaret, including the date of her marriage to Tommy McCarthy. At the time, however, she was probably about 20 years old and already carrying the couple's first child, a daughter named Sarah (Sadie), born in Boston in January 1888.[6] McCarthy's sensational half-season in Oshkosh put him back on the path to the majors. When Oshkosh disbanded after its pennant winning 1887 season, he signed with the St. Louis Whites of the newly-organized Western Association. Once there, standout play in an 1888 preseason exhibition series with the St. Louis Browns of the AA prompted Browns player-manager Charlie Comiskey to purchase McCarthy's contract and slate Tommy for the team's vacant right-field post.

At age 24, Tommy McCarthy was about to embark on the nine-year major-league baseball run that would ultimately land him a place in Cooperstown. Despite the loss of stalwarts Bob Caruthers, Curt Welch, Dave Foutz, and Bill Gleason from an 1887 World Series championship team, the Browns were still a formidable lot. In addition to slick fielding first baseman Comiskey, the squad boasted AA batting titleist Tip O'Neill, feisty third baseman Arlie Latham, and 32-game-winner Silver King. During the 1888 season, the unproven new right-fielder contributed more than his share to the Browns' fourth straight AA crown, hitting a solid .274, with 107 runs scored. And the fielding and baserunning attributes that would win McCarthy lasting fame were also on early display. With the strong, accurate throwing arm that befitted a former pitcher, Tommy registered 42 assists from his outfield post. The speedy McCarthy was also a force on the base paths, credited with a career-high 93 stolen bases, fourth best in the AA. McCarthy continued his first-rate play in the postseason, but the Browns failed in their World Series defense, dropping a 10-game match to the NL champion New York Giants. Still, Tommy paced his mates with a team-high 10 runs scored in a losing cause.

McCarthy solidified his hold on the Browns' right-field job with an excellent sophomore season. He upped his batting average to .291, while leading the AA in plate appearances (656) and official at-bats (604). He also scored 136 runs, stole 57 bases, and chalked up 38 more assists from his outfield post. Despite the meddling of bumptious team owner Chris von der Ahe, the Browns recorded an outstanding 90-45 log for the 1889 campaign. But Brooklyn, paced by Browns expatriates Caruthers (40 wins) and Foutz (113 RBIs), edged St. Louis by two games for the AA crown.

The 1889 season had been played amid rising player discontent with major-league baseball management practices. Simmering resentment about the reserve clause and other restraints on player freedom of movement had been exacerbated by the adoption of a miserly salary classification scheme by NL team owners that year. Revolt came under the direction of John Montgomery Ward, the visionary star shortstop of the World Series champion Giants. Although Ward and his agents focused – with great success – on inducing NL stars to join the new league, the AA was not immune to player defections. And the Browns were particularly hard hit by jumping players. Abandoning St. Louis were Comiskey, O'Neill, Latham, and King, the very heart of the Browns team. Given his 1889 performance, Tommy McCarthy would have seemed a likely target of PL recruiters, as well. But McCarthy had already signed with the Browns for the 1890 season by the time that the new league began its player raids, and he would remain true to St. Louis. That loyalty was rewarded by Browns owner von der Ahe, who appointed the now 26- year-old outfielder his new player-manager for the coming AA pennant chase. In short order, McCarthy would come to rue his boss's favor.

With only remnants of the Browns championship array still in uniform, McCarthy's team got off to an indifferent 11-11 start. Mediocre play on the field was aggravated by the post-game carousing of some of McCarthy's charges, behavior that the new manager seemed unable to suppress. Displeased and impatient, von der Ahe summarily discharged McCarthy, replacing him with Jack Kerins and stepping off the parade of managerial changes that the mercurial team owner would inflict on the Browns that season.[7] To his credit, McCarthy did not let his travails as Browns field leader affect his play. Against the watered-down AA competition of 1890, Tommy had a breakout season, batting a career high .350 with 43 extra-base hits. He paced the league in plate appearances (625) and stolen bases (83), while ranking in the AA top five in runs (137), base-hits (192), homers (6), OBP (.430), and slugging average (.467). McCarthy also demonstrated his versatility, playing 33 games in the Browns infield.

The collapse of the Players League at season's end brought Comiskey back to St. Louis, where he reassumed the Browns helm. And the return of Tip O'Neill and the arrival of Dummy Hoy placed Tommy McCarthy back in a first-class outfield.

McCarthy was a major contributor to the Browns strong second-place AA finish in 1891, filling in capably at second, short, and third when not playing a sterling (29 assists) right field. He had a fine season offensively as well, batting .309 with 92 RBIs and 124 runs scored. McCarthy's power stats and stolen base (37) totals were down from the previous year but his ability to make contact with the bat was remarkable. In 629 plate appearances, he stuck out only 19 times.

The 1891 season brought to a close the 10-year existence of the American Association as a major league. The AA's demise precipitated expansion of the National League to a 12-club circuit and a scramble to sign desirable AA players. Tommy McCarthy availed himself of the opportunity to return home, joining the Boston Beaneaters. The move united McCarthy once again with mentor Frank Selee and made Tommy a teammate of the player who would become his fellow Heavenly Twin, business partner, and lifelong friend: Hugh Duffy. The two were remarkably similar – New England-born Irish Catholics of small physical stature (McCarthy: 5-foot-7,170 pounds; Duffy: 5-foot-7, 168 pounds) and feisty temperament (although Duffy was a far more virulent umpire baiter than McCarthy). Both were outstanding defensive outfielders who had the dexterity to play infield positions competently when called upon. Each man was swift afoot, with McCarthy being the more prolific base stealer while Duffy, a right-hand batter like McCarthy, was the decidedly better hitter of the two. Perhaps most important, both Tommy McCarthy and Hugh Duffy were aggressive and intelligent baseball men, devising or refining the diamond strategies that were the hallmark of major-league play in the 1890s. No less astute an observer than John Montgomery Ward credited McCarthy with invention of the hit-and-run play, used to great advantage with Duffy batting behind him.[8] McCarthy was also an early exponent of the outfield trap, employing that maneuver as well as the feigned misplay to throw out many an unwary baserunner. In addition, he was an expert stealer of opponents' signs.

The duo that would soon be dubbed Boston's Heavenly Twins did not make an overwhelming first impression on Beaneaters fans. In their inaugural season together, both registered undistinguished marks at the plate, Duffy hitting a subpar (for him) .301 while the McCarthy BA sank to .242. Key to the pennant captured by the 1892 Boston team was the stellar pitching of Kid Nichols and former Brown Jack Stivetts, each of whom posted a 35-16 log, and the adroit managing of Frank Selee. The Duffy and McCarthy bats would awaken, however, in the post-season. Hugh (.462) and Tommy (.381) charged the offense that carried the Beaneaters to a sweep of the second-half split-season champion Cleveland Spiders in a playoff match that attracted little fan interest. The pair's post-season heroics were a taste of things to come. The 1893 season would find Duffy and McCarthy on batting rampages – doubtless fueled in some measure by the elongation of the pitching distance to the present 60 feet, 6 inches and the elimination of the pitcher's box. Hugh would hit a league leading .363 and rank among NL leaders in runs, base-hits, and RBIs. Although limited by injuries to 116 games, McCarthy provided yeoman support: a .346 BA, with 107 runs scored, 111 RBIs, and 46 stolen bases. With McCarthy now flanking center fielder Duffy on the left rather than right and both men given to playing shallow, the pair continued the crafty outfield tactics that raised havoc with enemy baserunners.[9] Abetted by the strong work of teammates Herman Long, Billy Nash, Bobby Lowe, and Tommy Tucker, and with excellent pitching by Nichols, Stivetts, and Harry Staley, the Heavenly Twins paced the Beaneaters to the 1893 pennant, captured by five games over runner-up Pittsburgh. But without a viable formula, no post-season championship play was attempted that year.

At the close of the 1893 season, McCarthy and Duffy joined forces off the field as well, becoming co-proprietors of a Boston bowling alley/saloon. A convivial man not averse to having a drink, McCarthy enjoyed bending an elbow with the Beaneaters fans who patronized the establishment. But the venture did little to enhance his baseball skills and initiated the weight gain that would plague him for the remainder of his playing career, and life thereafter.[10] But no diminution in McCarthy's abilities was immediately detectible. The 1894 season would find the Heavenly Twins at the zenith of their on-field performance and public acclaim. In a year where a .310 batting average was the league norm,[11] Hugh Duffy hit a major-league all-time high .440, while leading the NL in hits, doubles, homers, and total bases. He also scored 160 runs and drove in another 145. While not comparable to Duffy's performance, McCarthy posted more than respectable offensive numbers himself, hitting .349, with career highs in home runs (13) and RBIs (126). He also scored 118 runs and stole 43 bases. But the offensive exploits of their Heavenly Twins was not enough to carry Boston to a third straight NL pennant. Rather, the Beaneaters fell to third place, eight games behind the tempestuous Baltimore Orioles of McGraw/Keeler/Jennings/Kelley/Robinson fame.

Although only 30 years old, Tommy McCarthy's best playing days were already behind him. The 1895 season would prove an unhappy one for McCarthy and the Boston club, which plummeted to sixth place. Out of shape and often in foul temper, McCarthy hit a mediocre .290 with only 17 extra-base hits. The former AA base stealing champ was also sluggish afoot, stealing only 18 sacks, while often playing a lackadaisical left field. Worse yet was McCarthy's behavior outside the lines. On various occasions, he voiced unseemly public criticism of manager Selee and team captain Nash. He also engaged Jack Stivetts in an ugly off-field confrontation.[12] In a relatively brief period, McCarthy wore out his welcome with the Beaneaters and he was placed on the trading block at season's end. His business partnership with Hugh Duffy was also drawing to a close. In November 1895, Duffy relinquished his interest in the Duffy & McCarthy establishment (but the two would continue their friendship).[13] In the meantime, Boston sold its contract for McCarthy's services to Brooklyn for $6,000.

After holding out in spring 1896, McCarthy reported to the Bridegrooms in poor physical condition, made little effort to get in shape thereafter, and proved a disappointment to Brooklyn. A lack of hustle in the field and on the bases was periodically noted in press coverage of McCarthy's play[14] and he underperformed with the bat as well, hitting only .249 with but 15 extra-base knocks. All in all, McCarthy's 1896 performance was roughly comparable to the dismal ninth-place finish of the Brooklyn team as a whole. The dissatisfaction of team management was reflected in the salary slash contained in the 1897 season contract sent to Tommy. Then, tragedy struck the McCarthy family. On February 26, 1897, Margaret McCarthy died of pneumonia, leaving her husband alone to raise their three young daughters. McCarthy thereupon rejected the Brooklyn contract, electing to remain in Boston.[15] For the next 15 years, he would support his family primarily with the income produced by his saloon.

Although his major-league career was now over, Tommy McCarthy did not sever the connection with baseball. He would stay involved in the game for the remainder of his life. In early 1899, McCarthy succeeded Jesse Burkett as coach of the Holy Cross College nine, guiding the team to a 19-5 record that season. The following winter, he served as public representative of Boston interests in a stillborn effort to revive the American Association.[16] McCarthy then returned to his coaching duties at Holy Cross, with his team posting a 19-6-1 log in 1901. After a three-year hiatus, McCarthy resumed his coaching duties in 1904-1905, the latter Crusaders team featuring future major-league standouts Bill Carrigan and Jack Barry. An on-field incident with an insubordinate Holy Cross pitcher named James Spring, however, prompted McCarthy to submit his resignation late in the 1905 season.[17] The following year, he took the reins of the Dartmouth team, combining his college coaching duties with a new found passion for golf.[18] After a successful first year at the Dartmouth helm, Tommy was approached about becoming the Boston Red Sox manager but he declined,[19] preferring to remain in the college coaching ranks. But McCarthy would have cause to regret his return to Dartmouth. Months after the conclusion of the 1907 season, the college administration publicly faulted McCarthy's failure to curb his players' appetite for summer pro ball and unceremoniously dismissed him from his coaching post.

Thereafter, Tommy began a varied scouting career, initially bird-dogging prospects for the Cincinnati Reds from 1909 to 1912. He sold his Boston tavern the following year and soon took up scouting for the Boston Braves. While still working for the Braves, he put in a final spring as coach of the Holy Cross team. The Crusaders' 10-8 record for 1916 closed the McCarthy college coaching log at a commendable 107-53-3 over seven campaigns.[20] In 1918, Tommy took his lone fling at managing a professional team, piloting the Newark Bears to a 64-63 fourth-place finish in the Eastern League. Midway through that season, the now 55-year-old McCarthy succumbed to the urge to insert himself into the action. In his final professional at bat, Newark pinch-hitter Tommy McCarthy rapped a sharp single – only to be thrown out trying for second.[21]

McCarthy took up scouting for the Boston Red Sox in 1920 but soon thereafter his health began to fail. He managed to fight off a case of double pneumonia during the winter of 1921-1922 but was diagnosed with cancer a few months later. Mac felt well enough to do a little scouting in spring 1922 but was thereafter confined to his bed. As word of his condition spread, arrangements were made for the playing of a Tommy McCarthy all-star benefit game in Fenway Park. Sadly, Mac would not live to see it. He died of stomach cancer at his Dorchester home on August 5, 1922, aged 59.[22] A stricken Duffy was among the pall bearers delivering the deceased to Old Calvary Cemetery in nearby Roslindale, where Tommy was laid to rest next to his wife. He was survived by daughters Sarah, Edith, and Margaret (Rita).[23]

After the funeral service, Hugh Duffy remembered his old outfield companion fondly, telling assembled reporters that McCarthy was "always a quick thinker, full of nerve and fast, with a wonderful arm. ... I have never seen anyone who could think or act as quick as he could."[24] But from there, the memory of Tommy McCarthy receded as baseball entered the Age of Ruth and embraced an entirely different way of playing ball. It was, therefore, largely unexpected when the Veterans Committee included McCarthy among those enshrined in the Cooperstown Class of 1946, an honor bestowed some 50 years after Mac had played his final major-league game. By Hall of Fame standards, Tommy McCarthy's measurable accomplishments, apart from steals (468) and outfield assists (266), are exceedingly modest: 1,273 major-league games played, 1493 hits, 732 RBIs, and a lifetime .292 batting average. This has made the McCarthy selection a prime complaint of Veterans Committee critics.[25] But as baseball scholar/author David Fleitz has observed, McCarthy was inducted "not for his statistical achievements but for his contributions to baseball strategy" and their impact on the game.[26] And it is on that basis that the likeness of Tommy McCarthy graces the walls at Cooperstown, his memory forever preserved with that of Ruth, Cobb, Jackie Robinson, and the other immortals.

NOTES

1. The primary source for the biographical details of this profile is Donald Hubbard, *The Heavenly Twins of Boston Baseball: A Dual Biography of Hugh Duffy and Tommy McCarthy* (Jefferson, North Carolina: McFarland, 2008). Hubbard gives Tommy's mother the first name Rose, without maiden name. The identification of Mrs. McCarthy as the former Sarah Healy is based on death certificate information supplied to the registrar by Tommy's daughter Sarah (Sadie). A copy of the Tommy McCarthy death certificate was obtained by the writer from the Giammati Research Center, Cooperstown, and its designation of Sarah Healy as the name of McCarthy's mother is adopted by the McCarthy entry in the *Biographical Dictionary of American Sports: Baseball*, Porter, D., compiler, rev. ed., 1995. An improbable coincidence arises if Sarah Healy was, in fact, the maiden name of Tommy McCarthy's mother. For the mother of McCarthy contemporary and fellow Hall of Famer George Davis was born Sarah Healy, as well. Unlike Mrs. McCarthy, however, Sarah Healy Davis was born in England, not Ireland, and emigrated as a child with family to Cohoes, New York, rather than Boston.

2. As per Hubbard, 15-19, and an unidentified news article in the Tommy McCarthy file at the Giammati Research Center.

3. In fact, only one Boston batter managed a hit off Daily in McCarthy's debut game.

4. The statistical information provided herein is from Baseball-Reference.

5. Hubbard, 39.

6. Ibid.

7. Kerins was succeeded by Chief Roseman, Count Campau, Joe Gerhardt, and McCarthy himself, who posted a 4-1 record in a brief encore as Browns manager that season.

8. According to Bill James, *The Bill James Historical Baseball Abstract* (New York: Villard Press, 1986), 47-48. See also the *Boston Globe*, August 8, 1922.

9. The infield fly rule was reputedly instituted, in part, as an antidote to this McCarthy/Duffy stratagem. See David Fleitz, *More Ghosts in the Gallery: Another Sixteen Little-Known Greats at Cooperstown* (Jefferson, North Carolina: McFarland, 2007), 63.

10. Toward the end of his major-league career, McCarthy weighed close to 200 pounds, adding the nickname "Pudge" to his sobriquets.

11. In 1894, Philadelphia outfielders Ed Delahanty, Billy Hamilton, and Sam Thompson each bettered the .400 mark, while part-timer Tuck Turner hit .418 in 347 at-bats. The Philadelphia team as a whole hit a torrid .350.

12. The 1895 Boston team was wracked with dissention, much of it breaking along religious lines. Catholics McCarthy, Duffy, and Tommy Tucker were reputedly in frequent conflict with Protestant teammates like Long, Lowe, and Stivetts.

13. Apparently, the recently-remarried Duffy's second bride did not approve of the saloon's clientele and sought to elevate Hugh's social standing by getting him out of the tavern-keeping business.

14. See e.g., the *Brooklyn Eagle*, July 11, 1896.

15. Despite McCarthy's retirement, Brooklyn kept him on the team's reserved list until 1902, as per *The Sporting News*, March 3, 1917.

16. See the *Boston Globe, Chicago Tribune,* and *Washington Post,* November 16, 1899-February 15, 1900, *passim*. The attempt to resurrect the AA is not to be confused with Ban Johnson's efforts to elevate his American (nee Western) League to major-league status.

17. As recounted in Hubbard, 163-164.

18. According to the *Washington Post,* October 25, 1906.

19. A natural athlete, McCarthy shot 80 in the first golf tournament that he ever entered. He went on to become the inaugural president of Scarboro Golf Club in Massachusetts and remained a club member until his death, as per the McCarthy obituary in the *Boston Herald,* August 5, 1922.

20. The McCarthy college coaching record further breaks down to 77-36-2 in five seasons at Holy Cross and 30-17-1 in two at Dartmouth.

21. Hubbard, 169.

22. As recorded on the McCarthy death certificate. Post-pneumonic abscess to the lung was listed as a factor contributing to McCarthy's passing. Biographer Hubbard suspects that McCarthy's demise was also hastened by sustained alcohol abuse.

23. After Margaret's death, McCarthy never remarried. The benefit game was played shortly after Tommy's passing, with the proceeds going to his daughters, as per the *Boston Globe*, August 14-15, 1922.

24. *Boston Herald*, August 5, 1922.

25. Critics include Bill James, James Vail, and Robert Cohen. Their critiques of the McCarthy enshrinement are excerpted in Dennis Corcoran, *Induction Day at Cooperstown* (Jefferson, North Carolina: McFarland, 2009), 45.

26. Fleitz, 63.

BILL MERRITT
BY BOB LEMOINE

Bill Merritt.
(Courtesy of Mark Pestana)

Bill Merritt was a backup catcher during the 1890s, appearing in 401 games in eight seasons with five major-league teams. Needed for his glove and throwing arm, Merritt could also at times find his way with the bat, even leading the league in hitting at various times during the seasons in which he played, despite a career batting average of only .272. Known as Billy in his hometown, Merritt always stayed close to his New England roots, playing, managing, and even owning a minor-league franchise. He was part of one pennant-winning team, the Boston Beaneaters of 1893, but spent most of his career with second-division clubs.

William Henry Merritt was born on July 30, 1870,[1] in Lowell, Massachusetts, to William and Mary (Cleary) Merritt, who had emigrated from Ireland. In 1872 the couple lost a daughter Josephine at only five days of life on April 19, then a daughter Elizabeth at just 17 days of life on May 2. At the 1880 census, Merritt's father, William, worked as a laborer. Other siblings included a sister Sarah, who worked at a woolen mill, a sister Isabella, who worked in a cotton mill, and a brother, Frank, who was listed without an occupation.

Merritt attended the Colburn and Edson schools in Lowell. He played baseball for a local team called the Burkes, believed to be from a Temperance Society named after a Father Burke.[2] Merritt later played college baseball for Holy Cross in Worcester, Massachusetts, 40 miles west of Boston. "He was a great favorite with the college boys," the *Boston Globe* wrote, "and especially with the ball team. He rapidly developed into a catcher after entering the school, and was a receipt of numerous professional clubs, but declined them and continued his studies."[3] In 1891 Holy Cross pulled off a major upset, defeating Harvard for the first time in their baseball history. The 3-2 win at Harvard on

June 10 was the result of strong pitching by John Stafford, base-running, and "the catching and throwing of Merritt," according to the *Worcester Daily Spy*. Students had "joy with a big J" and prepared a major celebration when the team returned to campus on the 11 o'clock train. "Students were sent to the city for fireworks, and the supply ran out so quickly another delegation was sent back for more." The crowd chanted, "Sis! Boom bah! Here we are! What did we do? We beat Harvard, three to two!" Players were hoisted on the shoulders of celebrating fans and probably no one who lived near campus got any sleep that night.[4]

Just as the Holy Cross season was ending, both Merritt and Stafford were signed by the Woonsocket (Rhode Island) club in the New England League.[5] "He [Merritt] is a heavy hitter," Brattleboro, Vermont's *Phoenix* newspaper commented, "a splendid back stop, and the best thrower in New England."[6] Merritt wouldn't stay long, however. The Chicago Colts came to Boston for a series in early August. Manager Cap Anson was in need of a catcher (he had tried five during the season and he himself caught a couple of games). According to a story years later, Merritt sought out Anson for a tryout wearing raggedy clothes and no shoes. While Merritt did meet Anson, the poverty details were made up. Merritt himself responded to the story in 1899:

"A most absurd story has been going the rounds about my debut in baseball. I don't know the person that wrote it up first, but if I did I promise you I would make it hot for him. I want it understood that I never walked up to Anson in Boston in my bare feet and poorly dressed. I always had good clothes to wear before I ever played base ball and I shall have them after I quit playing the game. In justice to myself and my parents who reside here in Lowell I want you to contradict the absurd and false story in your paper. If my parents should read that in the paper they would feel very much put out over it. When I asked Mr. Anson for a trial in Boston, my clothes were just as good and costly as Mr. Anson's."[7]

In any event, Merritt received a tryout for the August 8 game.[8] "He proved a find," wrote Chicago's *Inter Ocean*, noting that Merritt was "shifty and easy on his feet, a good backstop, and he throws to bases cleverly. Anson is greatly pleased with him."[9] Chicago was driving toward the pennant and on August 26 the "Woonsocket Wonder," as Merritt was called at the time, scored the go-ahead run in a three-run eighth to give Chicago a 9-8 win.[10] A streaking Boston team would eventually surpass the Colts, and Merritt's season was over after he batted .214 in 11 games.

Merritt was not given a contract by Chicago for 1892 and went to Columbus (Ohio) of the new Western League. He was batting .224 in 40 games when the league disbanded in the middle of July. By the end of the month he was playing for Memphis of the Southern Association.[11] Merritt batted only .167 in a dozen games but "has done remarkable back stop work in Memphis," according to the *Baltimore Sun*.[12] Before going to Memphis, however, Merritt had received a letter from Fred Pfeffer, manager of the Louisville Colonels of the National League, asking what his terms were to come to Louisville. Merritt responded, but the reply did not reach Pfeffer for three weeks, and in the meantime Merritt signed with Memphis. "The supposition," wrote the *Louisville Courier-Journal*, "is that Merritt handed the letter to someone to mail, who was desirous of keeping the man away from Louisville and therefore failed to post it for three weeks."[13]

Because the Southern Association was part of the National Agreement, under which competing leagues would honor one another's contracts,[14] the issue went before National League President Nick Young to arbitrate. It was a quick decision, and Louisville acquired Merritt around August 17. He spent the remainder of the season there. "Manager Pfeffer saw Merritt play in Chicago," wrote the *Courier-Journal*, "and knew what he was doing when he signed the man. Merritt is one of the quickest throwers in the country."[15]

"He is a ward worker," the *Courier-Journal* wrote of Merritt's first few days with the team. "He is a fighter from 'way back,' and never quits playing until the bats are packed up. He is a man of the best habits."[16] Merritt impressed his new team in his first game, on August 20, in a 4-2 win over Washington in which he scored a run and "nailed every man that tried to go down [to steal]."[17] Merritt played both games of a doubleheader with Chicago on September 28, the day after fire destroyed the grandstands of the original Eclipse Park. Temporary seating was in place, but a few fans of the 700 present had to scurry as smoldering debris kicked up another flame. Louisville split the doubleheader.[18] In 46 games (43 of them said to be consecutive[19]), Merritt batted just .196 and made 15 errors with a .940 fielding percentage for the ninth-place club. He signed with Boston in the offseason to be a backup to the aging Charlie Bennett.[20] In the offseason, *Sporting Life* noted that Merritt had a thriving wood and coal business in Lowell and "is a great favorite in the Spindle City."[21]

For a ballplayer in the nineteenth century to have his sketch and biography featured in the *New York Clipper* is probably the modern-day equivalent of being on the cover of *Sports Illustrated*. Such was the experience of Merritt, who was profiled in the February 25, 1893, edition with the description of being a "young and promising player" who "faces pluckily the swiftest and wildest pitching, and promises to excel as a catcher."[22] Merritt was impressive in the preseason. "Young Merritt promises to win golden opinions," wrote the *Boston Herald*. "He handles the bat well, and is a strong thrower and sure catch of pitched as well as foul balls."[23]

While he was needed for his glove, it was Merritt's bat that was being noticed early in the 1893 season. "Merritt's hitting was greatly enjoyed," the *Boston Herald* commented on his contributions in an 18-6 thrashing of Philadelphia on May 23. "This youngster does not try to see how near he can come to putting himself out of joint when he hits at a ball, but he meets it finely."[24] He certainly did that day, powering two home runs, the second of which "stirred the triumvirs," the nickname for the three Boston team executives Arthur Soden, William H. Conant, and James B. Billings, "to such an extent that they applauded until their hands burned. It would have been a good time to ask for an increase in salary."[25] The unofficial batting averages listed by the *Boston Herald* on June 12 showed Merritt leading the league at .490 (25-for-51) with four teammates batting over .300.[26] Boston was already 11 games up in first place when on August 28 Merritt singled in a game-tying run in the ninth inning in a game Boston won in the 10th.[27] While Boston surged, Merritt's batting average had fallen back to earth, possibly due to an injured finger that cost him a few weeks, but still was at an astounding .372, listed as 10th in the league, on September 5.[28] On September 5 a foul tip split his right hand open, and his season was over as he returned to Lowell to recover.[29] He finished the year batting .348 with 3 home runs and 26 RBIs in 39 games, and Boston easily won the pennant.

Merritt began the spring of 1894 holding out for more money, "and the directors do not seem to care much whether he signs or not, believing they are well enough equipped [with catchers]," wrote the *Boston Herald*.[30] Merritt eventually signed, but the team's outspoken captain, Billy Nash, took exception to this attitude by the triumvirs. "I am free to say, and so is every member of the Boston club, that catcher Merritt was shamefully treated in the matter of salary this year, after the way he played to bring the pennant to Boston last season. If they did not want to give him the figures he earned fairly and squarely in the estimation of press and players, why did they not let him go where he could do better? Surely the Boston club could afford to pay him as much as he could get elsewhere."[31] After playing in only 10 games, Merritt was released by Boston at the end of May because "President Soden said that the club was carrying too many catchers."[32]

On June 1 Merritt was signed by the Pittsburgh Pirates,[33] where he backed up player-manager and future Hall of Famer Connie Mack in his first year of a 53-year managing career. Merritt played in 36 games for the Pirates, six of them at first base or in the outfield, batting .275 with one home run. As Pittsburgh fell out of the pennant race, Merritt was let go on August 21.[34] He was quickly signed by the Cincinnati Reds, and, having just turned 24 that summer, was playing for his fifth major-league club in four years.[35] He batted .325 for the Reds in 30 games with a .956 fielding percentage as catcher. He remained with Cincinnati in 1895, batting .177 in 22 games. Merritt was released in June, and Mack, seeing him available, re-signed him for Pittsburgh, making him their starting catcher, replacing a suspended Tom Kinslow.[36] Merritt excelled in his role, batting .333 (27-for-81) in his first 24 games.[37] While he had a solid year at the plate (.285 for Pittsburgh with a .340 on-base percentage), his fielding suffered; his 25 errors were fourth-most in the league among catchers and he allowed 160 stolen bases, third-highest in the league. Merritt had a solid year for Pittsburgh again in 1896, catching in 62 games and playing at least two games at every infield position. He was fifth in the league in assists for a catcher and in throwing out 85 would-be basestealers. He had a similar year at the plate as he did in 1895, batting .291 in 77 games.

On January 6, 1897, Merritt married Nellie Veronica Riley of Lowell. As one would expect, his hometown paper, the *Lowell Sun,* made this a front-page story with all the details of the occasion as Merritt married "a charming daughter of old Ward 3. Music and song was heard and an elaborate wedding supper was served by the Page Company." His new Pittsburgh manager and Lawrence, Massachusetts, native Patsy Donovan was his best man. Donovan said it seemed the whole town of Lowell turned out, from the mayor to the policeman on the beat. The Merritts had "a tour of New York and the other large cities" for their honeymoon, and then returned to their new home in Lowell.[38]

Remaining with Pittsburgh, Merritt hit his only home run of 1897 in Boston to the cheers of the crowd.[39] In a 16-3 pounding of Baltimore on July 24, Merritt went 4-for-4 with a walk.[40] But management was disappointed with his "slow work" and in mid-August gave him a 10-day notice that his release was imminent if his performance didn't improve.[41] Apparently the warning lit a fire under the catcher and "he has been killing the ball recently," wrote the *Pittsburgh Press*, and "the club decided it could not afford to part with the chunky backstop."[42] He finished with a .263 batting average in 62 games. Perhaps there were other reasons for Pittsburgh's disdain for Merritt, since the team gave him a $500 bonus if he did not drink during the season.[43]

Merritt's time in Pittsburgh came to an end after the 1897 season. Released to the Kansas City Blues of the Western League, he refused to go. "When I get through with the National League," Merritt said, "I will quit the game. I would not leave my present position [clerk] at the Arlington Hotel for a berth in the Kansas City team."[44] In March the *Washington Post* commented, "Billy Merritt alleges that he is too speedy a member to be wasted in a minor league, and threatens to retire from the game unless Jimmy Manning, of Kansas City, to whom Billy was sold, takes the reef out of that $1,200 salary limit that is supposed to be a law in the Western League. Billy's backstop talents should command at least $1,800, so Billy claims, though Manning is $600 shy of Merritt's opinion."[45] A few days later the *Kansas City Journal* reported, "Saloonkeeper Billy Merritt says he will stay in Massachusetts and drink his own whisky before his will play ball in this city for a beggarly $200 a month."[46] The story hadn't changed by April. "Billy Merritt was assigned to that team, but still refuses to report and announced his retirement from baseball," the *Pittsburgh Post* reported on April 1.[47] He never did go to Kansas City; instead he played for a Lowell team, South Ends.[48] *Sporting Life* said in October that Merritt was doing well in the saloon business and didn't plan on returning to baseball.[49]

Oddly, in 1899 there was the expectation that Merritt was still going to play in Kansas City. "Manager [Jim] Manning expects to have Billy Merritt, the old leaguer, behind the bat. It is not expected that he will hold out another year," said one report.[50] Manning was attempting to trade Merritt to Boston for Charlie Frisbee, who had been farmed out to the Worcester (Massachusetts) club, but that trade never happened.[51] Things got even nastier by the end of August. "Merritt intends to bring suit against Manning for keeping him out of the game this season. He thinks he has a good case, as Manning's actions has [*sic*] prevented him from earning a good salary at ball playing. Merritt has notified Manning that he intends to sue him. He is acting under the advice of legal friends in Lowell."[52] Apparently no lawsuit was ever filed.

Boston did not have the services of any catcher on their roster for the last game of the 1899 season and gave Merritt one last hurrah. "Behind the plate stood William Merritt of Lowell, who has been out of the game for a year," the *Boston Globe* wrote about the rusty veteran. "Billy was fat as butter and displayed a porcelain wing. One time he chased a foul fly near to the fence and puffed like a flat boat stemming the Ohio River. Considering that he was out of condition the old leaguer was not half bad."[53] Neither team had anything at stake in the game, which was Merritt's final appearance in the major leagues.

At the 1900 census, Bill and Nellie lived in Lowell and he worked as a "liquor dealer." They had three children: sons Francis (Frank)

Joseph and William Anthony, and a daughter, Margaret, who died that year just shy of turning 7 months old.[54]

Merritt returned to the diamond in 1901 in his familiar surroundings of Lowell. With former major leaguer Fred Lake (who would later manage both Boston teams), Merritt organized the Lowell club in the New England League and the two alternated between playing catcher and first base. "With these seasoned old-timers behind the bat," wrote the *Lowell Sun*, "the younger players will be kept in line at all times."[55] Merritt spent 1901-1903 with Lowell, which won the pennant in 1903. The statistics we have available show Merritt batting .339, .276, and .280 in the three seasons.

In 1904 Merritt, dissatisfied with the club's pay offer, made a difficult decision to leave his hometown team and play for the Manchester (New Hampshire) club, also in the New England League. "While I would have preferred to play at home," Merritt confessed, "I did not feel like waiting the entire season for a settlement of affairs whereby I would be willing to go back to the Lowell team. It has been said that I was fussy and thought that the team could not get along without me, but I assure you I never felt that way, for I know too well that a ball player is only one man in a whole team and if he gets through or refuses to play there are plenty of good ones to take his place, and he is soon forgotten. It was never through any feeling of egotism that I refused to sign with the Lowells. It was simply because the money promised me as was promised the others for winning the pennant was not forthcoming."[56] Merritt mostly played first base for Manchester. In July he left Manchester for an opportunity to manage the New England League team in Nashua, New Hampshire. "Well, I guess I'll be with you boys," Merritt told the Nashua players awaiting his arrival.[57] But at the end of August, he resigned to "attend to his business interests."[58]

Merritt returned to Lowell as player-manager in 1905,[59] but the team disbanded for financial reasons in early August. The franchise was moved to Taunton, Massachusetts.[60] Merritt ended the season with the Manchester team, which had moved to Lawrence, Massachusetts. In 1907 Merritt was still playing locally when the Calgary (Alberta) team of the Western Canada League, which had been organized in Lowell, either fired its manager or saw him resign after one week. Merritt accepted the managerial job while the Canadian team was playing exhibitions in New England. But he was not satisfied early on. "Merritt does not think well of the Calgary bunch that was selected," wrote the *Winnipeg Free Press*, "and it is understood that an entirely new bunch will be picked up."[61] It was an unsuccessful stint, however, as he lasted only a month. "Manager Merritt donned a uniform for the first time in Calgary at last night's game," quipped the *Calgary Herald*, "and he looks very pretty, but he also looks as though the sacrificing of about half a hundredweight of fat would not hurt him a bit."[62]

Merritt returned to Lowell and umpired in the New England League.[63] He scouted and later managed the Lowell team in 1909,[64] then in 1910 became a scout for the Boston National League team, his former team later known as the Braves.[65] His old friend Fred Lake was the manager, but the reunion didn't last long. The team finished eighth and Lake retired, so Merritt also left and returned to Lowell to spend time in business. Merritt sent a letter seeking an umpiring position in the Eastern Association in 1913.[66] Little is mentioned of Merritt for over a decade, with the exception of his son Frank serving in France in World War I and receiving a Purple Heart.[67] At the 1920 census, Bill and Nellie were living in Lowell with both sons and Bill's 89-year-old father, William. Bill worked as a watchman in a cotton mill. His son Frank was an electrician and William was a plumber's apprentice.

Merritt got back into the game in 1929, purchasing the Salem (Massachusetts) franchise in the New England League and moving it to Lowell, which had been devoid of a team since 1926.[68] While there was a touch of nostalgia in Merritt's running his hometown team once again, the reality was that times had changed. By the end of May, the future of the club was in doubt. "Billy Merritt has had a woeful experience," wrote the *Lowell Sun*. "There's no denying it: Lowell has not supported inner-city league ball in the past and from the Lookout it looks as though this will be another entry on the dark pages. Merritt has been digging, with practically nothing coming in, and his private bank roll has been sadly depleted."[69]

The team was sold and moved to Nashua. "He staked all he had on the ill-fated Lowell franchise of the New England League," John F. Kenney wrote in the *Lowell Sun* in 1937. "We can remember him then, a hearty man beyond his fifties, to whom any true-blooded fan could warm up. He pushed his Lowell club vigorously … hoping … hoping it would click with the fans he felt sure would come through with support. Then, when the handwriting was seen on the wall, we could see the wound in Billy Merritt's heart. It wasn't altogether the financial loss. He could not understand why the game had not caught on as in the days gone by."[70]

At the 1930 census, the Merritts were living in their own home valued at $3,500 in Lowell. Bill worked as a salesman, and although we don't know his salary, they checked "yes" in the new category on the census: owning a radio set. In 1935 he sent a hand-written letter to National League President Ford Frick:[71]

> Dear Sir,
>
> I hear that a few of the old time ballplayers in my town (Lowell Mass.) received a complimentary pass for the ball games.
>
> I am the oldest ball player that played in the N.L. for over forty five years having started in Chicago in 1891 with Mr. Anson. Played in Louisville in 92 with Fred Pfefer and Johnny Chapton. Boston in 93-94 Buckenberger Pat Donovan and Connie Mack.
>
> And I done Scout for the Bostons Ame. in 1899 and with the Boston N. in 1910. If you have a pass to share I would

be glad to have one as I go to Boston very often and would like to see the games.

Yours truly,

William H. Merritt

18 Fairfield St.

Lowell Mass.

A letter was sent in response by an unknown person on behalf of Frick:

Dear Mr. Merritt:

Mr. Frick turned over your letter to me, and he and I were both very glad to hear from you, as we are to get in touch with all those fine men who battled for their teams back in the 90's.

Unfortunately, the way the league rules are at this time, your term of service in the league was not long enough to entitle you to a lifetime pass. However, Mr. Frick is hopeful of having the rule changed later this year to make it possible for us to include you in the select circle. I will keep your letter, and if this is done, you will receive your lifetime pass.

Cordially,

[no name given]

It is an interesting letter from Merritt. For one, if his handwriting is to be understood correctly, he claims to have scouted for the Boston Americans (future Red Sox) in 1899. This couldn't have happened because the club did not yet exist, as it was a charter member of the American League in 1901. Several obituaries mention Merritt scouting for both Boston teams, but if and when he scouted for the Red Sox is unknown. Players with 10 or more years of experience were given lifetime passes by the National League.[72] This action was taken at the National League winter meetings in December of 1934, which is why Merritt's letter in 1935 would say he knows of other old-time players receiving one. Babe Ruth famously received one for the National League, even though he played in the NL for only three months out of his long career.[73]

Merritt attended Braves Field on June 25, 1936, when the 60th anniversary of the founding of the National League was celebrated. Also attending were Boston legends George Wright, Tommy Bond, and Merritt's teammates Sliding Billy Hamilton, Fred Tenney, and Hugh Duffy.[74]

Bill Merritt died at St. Johns Hospital in Lowell after a brief illness on November 17, 1937, at the age of 67. The funeral was held on November 19 at his home in Lowell. Donovan, Merritt's old manager in Pittsburgh, and Jack Ryan, his old teammate in Boston, attended the service. Mass was celebrated at St. Margaret's Church, and Merritt was buried in the family lot at St. Patrick's Cemetery. Merritt was a member of the Elks and Eagles lodges as well as the Lowell Holy Cross Club. Besides his widow and two sons, Merritt was survived by three grandchildren.

SOURCES

In addition to sources listed in the Notes, the author was assisted by the following:

Baseball-reference.com.

"Billy Merritt Dies Suddenly," *Lowell Sun*, November 17, 1937: 1.

Retrosheet.org.

"Services for Billy Merritt," *Lowell Sun*, November 19, 1937: 1, 7.

"William Merritt. Ex-Ball Player Dead," *Boston Globe*, November 18, 1937: 15.

NOTES

1. Some records list his birth as July 30, 1869.
2. "University of Massachusetts Lowell Center for Lowell History Oral History Collection," retrieved April 25, 2017. library.uml.edu/clh/OH/WPOL/Rynne.pdf; "Talk of the Town," *Lowell Sun*, March 26, 1892: 8.
3. "Amateur Notes," *Boston Globe*, August 22, 1891: 3.
4. "Holy Cross Boys Happy," *Worcester Daily Spy*, June 11, 1891: 1.
5. "Base Ball Notes," *Boston Globe*, June 9, 1891: 5.
6. "Notes," *Vermont Phoenix*, July 31, 1891: 5.
7. Article of unknown origin marked 4/9/1899 in Merritt's Hall of Fame file.
8. "Base Ball Gossip," *Cincinnati Enquirer*, April 12, 1898: 5.
9. "Lost in One Inning," *Chicago Inter Ocean*, August 9, 1891: 2.
10. "Ten Won in Succession," *Chicago Tribune*, August 27, 1891: 7.
11. *Bay City* (Michigan) *Times*, July 23, 1892: 8.
12. "Southern League Stars," *Baltimore Sun*, August 16, 1892: 8; "Chat of the Diamond," *Philadelphia Inquirer*, August 20, 1892: 3.
13. "Base Ball," *Louisville Courier-Journal*, August 7, 1892: 20.
14. See "National Agreement," baseball-reference.com/bullpen/National_Agreement.
15. "Base Ball," *Louisville Courier-Journal*, August 21, 1892: 13.
16. Merritt Arrives," *Louisville Courier-Journal*, August 18, 1892: 6.
17. "Game After Game," *Louisville Courier-Journal*, August 21, 1892: 10.
18. "Played Amid Ashes," *Louisville Courier-Journal*, September 29, 1892: 5.
19. *New York Clipper*, February 25, 1893: 823.
20. "Bennett Has Signed," *Boston Post*, March 30, 1893: 3.
21. "Lines from Lowell," *Sporting Life*, December 24, 1892: 9.
22. *New York Clipper*, February 25, 1893: 823.
23. "The Bostons Are in New York," *Boston Herald*, April 27, 1893: 12.
24. "Much Like a Walkover," *Boston Herald*, May 24, 1893: 2.
25. Ibid.
26. "We Have the Leading Batsman," *Boston Herald*, June 12, 1893: 10.
27. "Merritt's Hit," *Boston Herald*, August 29, 1893: 3.
28. "Heavy Batters of the League," *Boston Herald*, September 5, 1893: 2.
29. "John's Brother," *Boston Herald*, September 6, 1893: 3; "From the Infield," *Boston Herald*, September 10, 1893: 4.
30. "Games in the South Missed," *Boston Herald*, April 9, 1894: 8.
31. "A Word from Nash," *Boston Herald*, April 22, 1894: 23.
32. "Merritt Released," *Lowell Sun*, May 25, 1894: 4; "Catcher Merritt Released," *Boston Journal*, May 25, 1894: 3.
33. "Merritt in Pittsburgh," *Pittsburgh Post-Gazette*, June 2, 1894: 6.
34. "Glasscock and Merritt Go," *Pittsburgh Post-Gazette*, August 22, 1894: 6.
35. "Only Laughed," *Cincinnati Enquirer*, August 24, 1894: 2.
36. "Merritt Is a Pirate Again," *Pittsburgh Post-Gazette*, June 23, 1895: 6.
37. "Unlucky Browns Here," *Pittsburgh Daily Post*, August 5, 1895: 6.
38. "Matrimonial," *Lowell Sun*, January 7, 1897: 1; "May Go to Atlanta," *Pittsburgh Press*, January 11, 1897; "Donovan Arrives," *Pittsburgh Post-Gazette*, January 11, 1897: 6.
39. "Red-Hot Finish by Pittsburgh," *Pittsburgh Daily Post*, June 6, 1897: 6.
40. "Donovan's Men Tear the Balls," *Pittsburgh Daily Post*, July 25, 1897: 6.
41. "Sporting Notes," *Pittsburgh Post-Gazette*, August 4, 1897: 6.
42. "Late Sporting News," *Pittsburgh Press*, August 13, 1897: 6.
43. "Pittsburg Points," *Sporting Life*, October 16, 1897: 7.
44. "Billy Merritt's Position," *Lowell Sun*, January 29, 1898: 2.
45. *Washington Post* article appearing in the *Kansas City Journal*, March 18, 1898: 5.
46. "Baseball Notes," *Kansas City Journal*, March 20, 1898: 5.
47. "Magnate Auten Backer of Anson," *Pittsburgh Post*, April 1, 1898: 6.
48. "South Ends 13, Emeralds 3," *Lowell Sun*, April 20, 1898: 2.
49. "News and Comment," *Sporting Life*, October 8, 1898: 5.
50. "Kansas City," *Topeka Daily Capital*, February 24, 1899: 2.
51. "Puffs from the Pipe," *Kansas City Journal*, April 15, 1899: 5.
52. "Baseball Notes," *St. Joseph* (Missouri) *Herald*, August 27, 1899: 7.
53. "Watch the Clock," *Boston Globe*, October 15, 1899: 7.
54. "Deaths," *Lowell Sun*, September 28, 1900: 3.
55. "Merritt Signed," *Lowell Sun*, April 16, 1901: 6.
56. "Billy Merritt," *Lowell Sun*, June 11, 1904: 5.
57. "Merritt Engaged," *Lowell Sun*, July 12, 1904: 5.
58. "Billy Merritt Severs His Connection with Nashua Team," *Lowell Sun*, August 27, 1904: 5.
59. "Lowell's Line-Up," *Sporting Life*, April 15, 1905: 3.
60. "Lowell Disbands," *Lowell Sun*, August 2, 1905: 1.
61. "Lethbridge Leaguers Here," *Winnipeg Free Press*, May 13, 1907: 6; "Western Canada Baseball 1907," attheplate.com/wcbl/1907_1.html.
62. *Calgary Herald*, May 30, 1907. Quoted in "Game Reports Western Canada League 1907." attheplate.com/wcbl/1907_1i.html.
63. "Boston Briefs," *Sporting Life*, March 21, 1908: 7.
64. "Lawrence Lines," *Sporting Life*, July 31, 1909: 18.
65. "Billy Merritt to Scout for Boston National Team," *Lowell Sun*, April 29, 1910: 44.
66. "News Items Gathered from All Quarters," *Sporting Life*, March 15, 1913: 6.
67. "Many Attend Merritt Rites," *Lowell Sun*, January 2, 1945: 3.
68. "N.E. League Meeting Here," *Lowell Sun*, March 12, 1929: 13; "Lowell Formally Entered in New England Loop," *Lowell Sun*, March 13, 1929: 14.
69. "From the Lookout," *Lowell Sun*, May 20, 1929: 15.
70. John F. Kenney, "The Lookout," *Lowell Sun*, November 18, 1937: 17.
71. Letters are from Merritt's file from the Giamatti Research Center at the Baseball Hall of Fame
72. "Herman Bell May Be Having Trouble Selling Himself," *Kansas City Star*, April 15, 1935: 12.
73. "N.L. Gives Babe Lifetime Pass," *Boston Herald*, September 5, 1935: 27.
74. " 'Bostons' Win Old-Time Game," *Boston Globe*, June 26, 1936: 29.

BILLY NASH

BY RICHARD "DIXIE" TOURANGEAU

Washington's Nationals opened their 1875 National Association season at their DC grounds. Defeated 8-2 by the defending three-time champ Boston Red Stockings, the teams then moved 90 miles to Richmond, Virginia, for the next two games, those being the first Association games ever played in "The South." Danbury, Connecticut, manufacturer/promoter Alfred P. Sturges had contracted a few teams to play in his wife's hometown throughout the season in an effort to draw large crowds for the probable not-so-competitive Washington club. The Richmond Fair Grounds (currently the Monroe Park area) was the site of the slaughters as the Stockings waltzed 22-5 and 24-0. Likely in the crowd was a 10-year-old boy, who lived only a few blocks away on West Clay Street and a well-to-do boot manufacturer, who was enthralled by the sport's spectacle. In less than 10 years the boot magnate fielded his own amateur team and the then teenager was a main cog on it. By 1891 the kid was captain of the champion Boston Beaneaters, the National League descendants of those Red Stockings he had watched with awe.

William Mitchell "Billy" Nash born in the ruins of Richmond on June 24, 1865, only two months after retreating Confederate troops strategically burned the city's main business section and President Abraham Lincoln had been assassinated. William M. was the second son of five children of policeman William Frederick Nash and wife Jeannette (Smith). In the ensuing years William F. changed jobs twice, according to city directories and the 1870 and 1880 census. Sgt. Nash had served in the Confederate Army's Parker Battery Quartermaster Unit from

Billy Nash, 1895 Mayo Cut-Plug tobacco card.
(public domain)

March 1862 to his attendance at the Appomattox Court House surrender.

Tragedy struck the family in 1874 when eldest son Albert Sidney died and again when mom Jeannette passed in March 1878 of an unrecorded illness. Single-dad William, whose service records say suffered post-war from bronchitis, bouts of typhoid and dysentery, was by then employed at the rebuilt Gallego Manufacturing Company. The Gallego Flour Mill complex was the largest in the country before it was torched as the final defiant act of the rebels as they escaped their beloved Confederate capital. Father Nash remarried in 1880 and with Emma Harris parented four more children. Eventually William F. started his own grocery business at 504 North Second Street where the first Nash brood had moved by 1879.

In 1882 teenager Billy was working for the Boschen Shoe Company when Henry C. Boschen decided his factory and city deserved a better baseball team than the one he organized and played for against local teams in the late 1870s. In March 1883 there was a reorganization notice in the *Richmond Dispatch* about forming a better club and Billy, possibly the youngest member at 17, held down the third-base slot.[1] Seeing the popularity of "base ball" growing, another group, the Virginia Base Ball Club, started its own team in June 1884, boldly drawing/stealing from the Boschens and upgrading further with out-of-state talent.

Nash was recruited with older Richmond-born players Jim Powell, Ed Glenn, and Ed Ford. The Eastern League allowed the Virginias entry but soon a few of its other clubs folded and the EL was in a shaky situation. When the American Association Washington Statesmen (12-51) succumbed to various problems, president William C. Seddon and his Virginians (28-30) escaped to that higher plateau to complete the Statesmen schedule. They were usually overmatched (12-30) but young Nash showed promise, as did their Kingston, New York, outfielder, Dickie Johnston. Players were at a premium since the Union Association, a third "major league," was in operation, so even mediocre talent was in short supply.

Nash hit just .199 but half his hits were for extra bases and his fielding was considered above average. The first five EL games were in Richmond and Philadelphia's Athletics trounced their hosts 14-0 to welcome them to the AA on August 5. Veteran Bobby Mathews kept Billy hitless. Next day Nash singled and scored off Billy Taylor, but Philly won 5-4. Then Brooklyn came to town and Nash contributed three runs, and an RBI from two hits (triple) off Adonis Terry as Richmond prevailed, 10-2. The Virginians then lost 9-2 and tied 5-5 to end its first professional home stand. In the loss Billy had a double, then tripled, scored twice, and plated a run in the tie. Richmond's one shining stint was later sweeping the host Pittsburgh Alleghenys, 10-5, 2-1, and 8-4. Billy scored five runs (3-for-12) but made five errors. On September 15 in St. Louis, Nash belted his first home run, off starter Dave Foutz. Browns reliever "Parisian" Bob Caruthers got the 7-6 comeback win.

Looking for a comfy niche in 1885, the Richmond club found itself back in the EL. Insurance man Thomas Alfriend was now team president and a few new players were added along with manager Joseph Simmons. Richmond was suddenly a powerhouse, repeatedly whipping all opponents. They were very good – in fact too good. By mid-July the first-place Virginians were so dominant that many fans stopped coming to boring, sure=win games and by mid-August players had to be sold to keep the franchise solvent. On August 18 they were 59-14. In his final week as a Virginian, Nash hit .333, with two home runs, with four singles in the season finale. On August 21, both Nash and Johnston (.329/16 HRs) were sold to NL Boston's Beaneaters for $1,250. Without its stars, the Virginias collapsed and lost the pennant by two games.

Beaneater president Arthur Soden and player-manager John Morrill likely knew of young Nash's abilities from exhibition games in April. Until then Boston's fans were used to only two third-sackers, Harry Schafer of the NA Red Stockings and initial NL squad, and then Ezra Ballou Sutton, who replaced him in 1877. Nash and Johnston finished up 1885's last 26 games starting on September 1, in a 2-0 win at Providence. Both had come from an apparent pennant cake-walk to Boston, which was having its worst season of the nineteenth century (46-66). In addition, Nash was being groomed to take over the position of a near diamond god, Sutton, then 35, who was leading Boston in six offensive categories and was second in triples.

The defending NL champ Providence Grays' Fred L. "Dupee" Shaw, a Boston boy, lost that 2-0 game but collared Nash. At his new South End Grounds home the next day, righty-swinging Nash (5-foot-8, 165 pounds) not only got his first two hits, but his sacrifice in the 11th inning knocked home the game-winning run to beat Charlie "Old Hoss" Radbourn, 4-3. Two more hits and being part of a rarely executed 5-3-5 double play with player-manager Morrill help crush Providence and Shaw, 11-1 the following afternoon. In his first 10 NL games Nash was 13-for-38 with 16 putouts, 17 assists, and only five errors. Boston fans were pleased with their Southern pickup and the team was 13-13 in those 26 outings. In a second Radbourn-hurled, 11-inning game, Nash had two hits, and the game-winning RBI before scoring on Sutton's insurance blast for a 9-6 victory.

By 1886 Sutton (.294), who began his career at the NA's creation in 1871, was playing four positions and because of age his batting prowess was in decline. Nash replaced him at third base in 1886. Morrill took his Bostons to Richmond for spring training and Nash and Johnston were welcomed back along with Edward "Pop" Tate. Boston beat Rochester, 14-2, in the first exhibition, and Nash was the only regular to go hitless. In five games he was 4-for-23 (.174). Boston improved but was still not a contender, though Nash posted a decent rookie campaign (.281). In Detroit on August 27, he hit his first NL home run, aiding Boston's 7-3 win.

On December 4, 1886, Nash got his first national notoriety as he was profiled in the *New York Clipper* as an outstanding new player who was taking over from the revered Sutton, who had 10 fine years with Boston. "Nash has a lively, dashing style, and his throwing is remarkably swift and accurate," said the *Clipper*.[2]

For the next three seasons Boston continued to improve by acquiring experienced players such as Chicago's Mike "King" Kelly. Then owner Soden raided Detroit for tandem-catching Charlies, Bennett and Ganzel, and infielders Dan Brouthers, and Hardy Richardson. Nash was now surrounded by solid talent on the diamond. He led the Beaneaters in RBIs in both 1887 and

1888. On July 16, Nash finally homered over the South End Grounds I fence, to help beat Indianapolis, 6-1. Boston could have won the NL flag in 1889 but was nipped by New York in the final four games when NY was 4-0, Boston 2-2.

The August 10, 1889, edition of *The Sporting News* detailed the career of Nash complete with pen and ink portrait.[3] Boston looked competitive for 1890 until the new Players League lured several Beaneaters to the rebel Boston Reds. Nash was a jumper, signing while on a December barnstorming tour in California. The PL Reds proved to be a relentless scoring machine (1,031 runs) thanks to ex-Beaneaters Richardson (.328, 16 HRs, 152 RBIs), Brouthers (.335), King Kelly (.325), Joe Quinn (.300), and Harry Stovey (.298, 12 HRs, 145 R), plus Tom Brown (.280, 149 R), and Arthur Irwin (.260). Nash hit only .275 but was third on the club with 94 RBIs and took 90 walks. His defense was also a factor as he led "hot corner" guardians in assists and DPs. More telling was that with a roster of noted stars it was Nash who captained the Reds when manager Kelly was absent. Boston (81-48) easily won the PL's only pennant. The Reds played at the newly constructed (for them) Congress Street Grounds, located downtown near Boston Harbor. Nash scored the winning run in the ninth inning of the Opening game on Patriots' Day, April 19, nipping Brooklyn 3-2. He also set the tone for the first 18 home games, getting at least one hit in each, 31-for-85 (.365) and scoring 20 runs. His first home run there was May 17, off Cleveland Infant John "Cinders" O'Brien, the 13-5 victor.

Financial chaos and other organizational problems eliminated the PL and put the AA on its last leg (1891). Meanwhile Soden's depleted NL Bostons had obtained a new manager, Frank Selee, and his eye for talent spied five solid players to fill his 1891 roster; Herman Long, Robert Lowe, Charlie Nichols, Steven Brodie, and Tom Tucker. Getting the popular, stable veteran Nash back to the South End Grounds II was a Soden-Selee priority and in the spring Nash signed with his old team and was made captain in the deal. Quinn also came back and they brought veteran slugger Stovey with them. Nash got $5,000 for each of the next three seasons and a bonus for signing. It was a grand start for Billy and his new bride, Rose Currier of San Francisco, whom he married on March 19, 1891.

Long (.281, 129 R) had the highest Beaneater average in 1891, and was nicely backed by Stovey and Nash. Despite both hitting just under .280 they each had 95 RBIs, placing second to Chicago icon Cap Anson's 120. Anson's White Stockings topped the NL into September but Boston's 18-0-1 spurt was too difficult for them to match. When the Beaneaters swept New York in consecutive South End doubleheaders on September 29-30, they clinched the pennant. Nash was 5-for-16 with no miscues. The Beaneaters led the NL in runs and ERA as John Clarkson won 33 and "Kid" Nichols, 30. The Beaneaters' only competition for city glory was King Kelly's AA Reds down at the harbor, winners of the final flag (93-42) of that League's 10-year existence.

With the AA's demise came changes in the 1892 NL. It gained four teams, absorbed from the AA and a longer, split-season schedule so that no one team could dominate the standings all year and curb general attendance in September. Hugh Duffy, Tommy McCarthy, and Jack Stivetts joined Boston, thus creating a powerhouse lineup with virtually no holes. They started the season with a 10-1 record and ended with a 14-2 flourish.

Though captain Nash hit only .260, he led the club once again in RBIs (95) as Boston won 102 games. The 100th victory (a first in NL history) was the 13th consecutive over Baltimore. In the 9-5 comeback, Nash had two hits, and scored. In the "World's Championship Series" against Cleveland (second-half winner) Boston swept five games after an opening scoreless tie versus Cy Young. Billy was 4-for-24, scored three runs, had 14 assists, no errors, while Duffy's 12-for-26 took Boston's batting honors. In the second game, the first win in Cleveland, Nash's RBI (of Duffy) proved to be the game-winning tally, 4-3.

Few changes were made to the 1893 Beaneater roster. Quinn was gone, Lowe moved from the outfield to second base and his space was filled by Cliff Carroll (.224). The 12-team NL campaign was cut to 132 games and there was no split-season. Boston looked to equal the 1880-1882 Chicago White Stockings who won three consecutive NL pennants. Starting at 10-10 they looked to be off their expected game. The defending champs improved, especially from mid-July to mid-August, when they reeled off a 24-2-1 mark, erasing most competition. Even finishing poorly at 5-11-1, they still cruised to a five-game edge over Pittsburgh. The team was tops in no major category, but was very solid in every aspect. Boston was second to Philadelphia in runs scored, 1,011 to 1,008. Nash had his best season hitting .291 with 123 RBIs (fourth) while scoring 115. At season's end he had the best fielding percentage of any third baseman (.923). The (Helen) Dauvray Cup resided in Boston for the third straight year, and was retired to the Beaneaters trophy case for that accomplishment.

Soden, Selee, and the Bostons appeared destined for a fourth consecutive title in 1894. No club had accomplished that except the National Association's Red Stockings (1872-75) and they did it in the same ballpark. But tragedy struck on January 9, when both of catcher Charlie Bennett's legs were mangled when he slipped under the wheels of his train after speaking to a friend at the Wellsville, Kansas (35 miles southwest of Kansas City) depot. Ganzel took over and the backup spot was given to Jack Ryan, a Massachusetts native. Otherwise standing nearly pat again, the Beaneaters only replaced failure Carroll with Jimmy Bannon (.336) in the left pasture. The pitcher's box had been moved from 50 to 60'6 in 1893 and most fans thought hitters would benefit immediately. But it took a year as the NL average was .280 then but spiked to .309 in 1894. Boston topped the field in runs (1,200) and home runs (103) and was in first place in late August. But a 10-10 finish while Baltimore won 18 straight and finished 20-3 in the month allowed Baltimore to dethrone the Hub's three-time champs.

The delayed pitcher's disadvantage enjoyed by most batters didn't affect Nash, he hit basically the same as always, .289, 87 RBIs, with a career-best 132 runs scored. In the field he took third-base honors again, leading in putouts, assists, DPs, and percentage (.933) while missing only one game. Each position scored 100-plus times for Boston. They beat Baltimore eight games to four in the season series but the Orioles crushed lesser opponents more often. Other than Bennett, the biggest loss of the year was the massive fire on May 15 that destroyed what, since 1888, was considered the most beautiful ballpark in the League, along with 200 other Roxbury buildings. Two other fires claimed the ballparks in Philadelphia and Chicago during the season. Proof of his popularity around the baseball world, Street and Smith's *New*

York Five Cent Library did a character sketch on Billy in June 1894.[4] Despite being a piece of pure fiction about Nash's life, it did put him in special company. The only two other baseball names on a list of 88 people profiled to that date were "King" Kelly and Yale Murphy.

Boston maintained its core lineup for 1895. But Tucker's bat was fading and much touted Fred Tenney had proven ready in late 1894. Pitchers Tom Lovett retired and Harry Staley went to St. Louis, leaving Jim Sullivan to back Nichols and Stivetts. When not much meshed, Boston finished fifth. The league average fell to .290 as did several Bean bat marks proportionately. By midseason when it was evident they were not real contenders to the rampaging, defending champ Baltimores (10-2 over Boston), there were rumors of a rift between some players. A Duffy-McCarthy clique and an "Unhappy Jack" were blamed and Nash was included. Mediocre team play didn't help, but in the midst of it all clutch Billy had a fine season. Playing every game he again paced the Beaneaters in RBIs (110) and home runs (10) while hitting .290. In the field he led third basemen in putouts and DPs (.881). With only 71 wins it was Boston's worst season of the 1890s.

Manager Selee knew changes were needed and on November 14, 1895, a blockbuster trade was announced, possibly the biggest of the nineteenth century, and arguably the worst. Captain Nash was shipped to Philadelphia for on-base wizard "Sliding Billy" Hamilton. Reasons stated: ineffective Arthur Irwin was let go as Phillies manager and it was thought Hamilton's bat was faltering. Nash was a solid baseball man, clever, level-headed, and widely respected. Philadelphia led the NL in hitting several times but never approached first place but now with Nash as manager they hoped to turn the tide.

Some thought it was a good deal for both teams, while other scribes questioned the basics. Hindsight proved Boston got the goods while Philly suffered. Things looked fine for the Phils for a few weeks, Nash got his team off to a 14-5 start but a few days later Billy was hit above the left eye by a (Boston-born) Tom Smith pitch in Louisville. He was out for a week but still managed the team. When he returned Philly won six straight. Meanwhile, Jimmy Collins (.279, .926 third base) was coming back to Boston from Louisville and he would soon launch his own (future) Hall of Fame career. Selee could afford to deal Nash and take a chance on Hamilton getting back his batting eye from 1894 when he hit .403 (fifth), while being tops in the NL in walks (128) and steals (100).

Nash broke his finger on August 10 against his old Boston mates and was out for the season, playing only 65 games (.247, .911 fielding). Philly finished 62-68 despite being second in scoring. Meanwhile, Hamilton hit .366 and scored 153 runs (second) for his new club. It was a personal disaster for the easy-going Nash as critics claimed he was soft on the players, but what hurt most was not contributing personally. For 10 years with Boston he had played in 97 percent of the games, hitting .281. On July 22 both the *Philadelphia Inquirer* and *Philadelphia Times* stated that Nash was being removed as captain in favor of catcher-coach Jack Boyle. In that era that decision also meant Billy also had been relieved of managerial duties. Following debacle losses in Pittsburgh, Nash was dispatched to follow the New England League's Fall River club to scout sluggers Phil Geier and Napoleon Lajoie. Nash was in search of young talent for Philadelphia, but when he returned in late July both papers again referred to him as manager.

George Stallings was brought in to manage the Phils in 1897. Nash was back at third and his fielding was a solid .919 but his hitting did not recover (.258, 39 RBIs in 104 games). Delahanty was good again (.377, 96 RBIs, 109 runs) and was aided well by near-rookie Nap Lajoie (.361, 127 RBIs, 107 runs) but Stallings had no pitching and ended at 55-77 in 10th place. Up in Beantown Hamilton regained form (.343; 152 runs, 105 walks, both tops), making the "Billy" trade look even worse. With Collins at third (.346, 132 RBIs, 103 runs) and Tenney at first (.318), the Beaneaters now had the best infield and outfield, after adding Chick Stahl (.354). They did to Baltimore what the Orioles did to them in 1894: broke the string of three straight pennants by edging the defending champs by two wins. Collins also swept honors for third-sack fielding while playing every game. The torch had been passed, Nash had been great, but Collins eventually would prove to be better.

Nash played only 20 games in 1898, finishing up on May 28 in Chicago. The Phils were 11-17 but ended 78-71 behind Lajoie and Delahanty. Nash concluded at .243, and .958 fielding, better than the other four third basemen the Phils employed. On May 27 Nash scored his last run (final hit) in an 8-2 loss to Clark Griffith and on May 28 he went hitless (but walked) in a 10-4 win. Nash committed the only Philly error that day behind Al Orth. *The Sporting News* front page of June 11 printed a June 2 letter from Philadelphia saying Nash was given the required 10-day notice of release soon after that game, but it was held in secret so that he could arrange a favorable deal for himself On July .[5] In the *New York Daily Tribune* of June 8, New York captain Bill Joyce remarked that he, "was after Nash of Philadelphia," and would sign him if Nash could secure his release.[6] But nothing materialized and that was it. Three weeks later Stallings was out as manager in favor of Bill Shettsline.

Because of two NL pals from the 1880s, Nash was beckoned to Buffalo, New York, during the offseason. Jack Rowe lived there and was selling cigars and managing the Buffalo Bisons Eastern League club. Shortstop Rowe (.286 career hitter) had played for 12 years, mostly with Buffalo and Detroit, and with Bison team owner, Alderman James Franklin, found himself in the baseball and meat businesses. He quit managing in 1898 and so the call went out. Nash answered it and applied to be player-manager. Knowing Billy well from the NL, Rowe likely recommended the move. The Bisons, also called the Pam-Ams by the local press because of the city's upcoming 1901 Pan-American Exhibition/World's Fair, were 6-6 when there was a very sudden falling out between Nash and English-born, wheeler-dealer Franklin. Nash handed in his resignation saying, "If I am going to manage a baseball team, I will do it my own way or not at all. Mr. Franklin could not see the matter in the same light as I did and so we decided to part company." Nash's contract gave him, "absolute control of the men and authority to hire and release such players as he sees fit."[7] In the four games he played at second base and shortstop, Billy was 4-for-12, had nine putouts, 12 assists and four errors

Both the *Buffalo Courier* and the *Buffalo Enquirer* thought Nash got a raw deal. The *Enquirer* noted, "...he is a hustling manager and a good judge of players, besides being popular with the boys.

The news of Billy's release will be a great disappointment to the Buffalo baseball public, for he has ever been a popular favorite both on the diamond in private life and has a host of friends in this city. He has been a consistent and vigorous player and has always handled his men in a manner satisfactory to the public."[8] The players called a meeting with Franklin and begged him to recall Nash and outside baseball people thought the adversaries would mend their differences and reconcile. They didn't.

Within a week Nash was called by the newly-formed Hartford, Connecticut, Indians to play with the Eastern League club managed by Billy Barnie. On May 18 Hartford beat host Toronto, 11-4, and Nash scored and had four assists. Then, despite the addition of Maine's Penobscot tribe hero Louis Sockalexis, the cellar dwellers lost four straight, with Nash committing two bad errors in one 8-7 loss. He was 2-for-19 (.105) and released on May 25. Hartford and Buffalo critics now thought Alderman Franklin was right after all.

Former Boston shortstop Sam Washington Wise was Nash's next Buffalo connection. Sam was a teammate from 1885 to 1888. An Akron, Ohio, native, Wise had moved to Buffalo to operate the Mansion House's (hotel) saloon. He and Billy were partners for more than a year at the turn of the century. Nash left in 1901 to become an NL umpire for one season, working 101 games. On May 17, he was involved in a dangerous melee at the Polo Grounds when he ejected three New York Giants. The Giants blew a chance to nail an Orphan-Cub baserunner at home. Both furious at the call, third baseman George Davis and catcher Jack Warner were thumbed, Warner kicking Nash bloody. Billy called for police action but 50 Tammany cops stood around laughing, according to the *Chicago Tribune*. Pitcher Luther Haden "Dummy" Taylor then adamantly complained about balls and strikes in sign language and was tossed as well.[9] Giants owner Arthur Friedman denounced Nash's actions and tried to get him fired but Billy held on to finish the year. Ump Nash never ejected any other ballplayers.

Following his umpiring stint, Nash's exact whereabouts are uncertain. There was a William M. Nash traveling salesman in Boston in the 1910 census, and he was the proper age. The 1920 census does nail him down in Norfolk, Massachusetts, being an attendant and watchman at the State Public Health (Pondville) Hospital there. Town directories show that he lived with his wife Rose in Wrentham, about 20 miles south of Boston, during the 1920s. After settling there, Nash coached high school baseball at nearby Foxborough for a year or two in the 'Teens.

Few ballplayers have had their simple deaths more fouled up than Nash. He and Rose were on a short vacation with her sister Carrie and husband Dr. William Charles Hassler to New York City on November 15, 1929. Dr. Hassler was a famous physician in San Francisco, a leader in combating the infamous flu epidemic of 1918-19 and then was top public health officer of that city. Leaving the wives in New York, he took Billy with him to East Orange, New Jersey, to check out a health facility and that's when Nash dropped dead of a heart attack. In the shock, sadness and confusion, several newspapers mixed up the two Williamses and published that "Dr. William" Nash had died suddenly. Even the *Boston Globe* and *Richmond Dispatch* believed the account and reported that the subject had received a medical degree after his baseball career. In its lengthy and detailed obituary, the *Globe* had him as a "former health officer in Wrentham."[10] In the *Richmond Quarterly* of Spring 1981, author Hiram T. Askew ("Billy Nash - First Richmond Baseball Great") did a fine writeup of Nash's career but he too had him with a medical degree at his death.[11] Rose kept his cremated ashes in Wrentham until she died in August 1937. Then a friend dutifully sent both urns to Rose's oldest sister, Ada, in San Francisco and they were placed in the Hassler Mausoleum at Woodlawn Memorial Park in Colma, California, where the entire Currier family is interred. Because of time lapse and distance, for about 60 years, Billy Nash's final resting place was unknown. An explanatory telegram from the J. T. Waterman Funeral Home files in Boston's Kenmore Square solved the mystery when unearthed as the twenty-first century began.[12]

Billy Nash was not a superstar like several teammates and many adversaries. His 10-season Beaneater average was a solid, but modest, .281. In fact, as nineteenth century expert Dave Nemec points out, he has the highest average for anyone that century who never hit .300.[13] Nash's yearly total of hits fits snuggly between 132 and 149, and despite those seemingly light numbers he averaged 93 RBIs and 100 runs a season. During Nash's Boston span of 10 seasons, the NL-PL hit .268 while his own teams averaged .279. On defense he was tops in putouts, DPs and had the highest fielding percentage four times each and assists twice. He hit about one home run per month, two of his 60 were grand slams. On August 9, 1894, his ninth-inning blast off Philly Jack Taylor iced an 11-2 victory for debuting rookie George Hodson. On June 4, 1895, Nash's big clout off Cincy's Bill Phillips, helped Boston win 12-5. Last home runs: for the Beaneaters, off New York Giant rookie Ed Doheny, a 13-5 loser, in his second start served up an South End Grounds solo on September 19, 1895; for Billy's career, St. Louis lefty Ted Breitenstein gave one up on May 29, 1896, at the Baker Bowl in a 10-6 Phillies' win.

Nash has three interesting accomplishments due to longevity and precise timing. He was the only player on the field in both Boston and Chicago to see Lowe (1894) and Delahanty (1896) each hit a record four home runs and a single in one game. Because of his span of seasons in Boston (1886-1895) he is the only player to have been in the last game at South End Grounds I, the opening game of South End Grounds II, the opening PL game at Congress Street, the last game at South End Grounds II, the last game at Congress Street (rented for a month in 1894), and the first game at rebuilt South End Grounds III. Nash played the most games at third base (1,127 NL plus 132 more for the PL Reds) for Boston in the 19th century. In Braves franchise annuals Billy still ranks ninth in runs and 10th in RBIs.

When Nash was on that 1896 scouting mission, he tracked the Fall River Indians and stars Geier (.381) and Lajoie (.429). Manager Charlie Marston at first declined to sell either player, hoping for higher bids, but low finances dictated a time limit. Nash outbid his old Boston boss Selee and took the prize players to Philadelphia. This was only a half season after Selee had traded Billy. The same monetary circumstances that had prevailed when

Boston obtained Nash and Johnston from Richmond in 1885 had come full circle in Billy Nash's baseball life.

SOURCES

In addition to the sources cited in the Noted, the author also consulted Ancestry.com, Baseball-Reference.com, Retrosheet.org, Nash's player file at the National Baseball Hall of Fame, the *Encyclopedia of Minor League Baseball*, and the book

Mayer, Scott P. and W. Harrison Daniel, *Baseball and Richmond, 1884-2000* (Jefferson, North Carolina: McFarland 2003).

NOTES

1. "The Ball Will Roll," *Richmond Dispatch*, March 27, 1883: 1.
2. *The New York Clipper*, December 4, 1886: 610.
3. *The Sporting News*, August 10, 1889: 1.
4. Billy Boxer, the Referee; Street & Smith's *"New York Five Cent Library,"* #86 Captain Billy Nash, June 23, 1894, New York, 2-15.
5. "Anson May Succeed Stallings," *The Sporting News*, June 11, 1898: 1.
6. "New York Shut Out," *New York Daily Tribune*, June 8, 1898: 10.
7. "Nash's Release," *Buffalo Evening News*, May 13, 1899: 6.
8. Hotspur's Daily Column of Sporting Gossip, "Release of Billy Nash a Surprise to Buffalo Fans," *Buffalo Enquirer*, May 13, 1899: 4.
9. "Rowdyism in New York Again," *Chicago Tribune*, May 18, 1901: 6.
10. "Old Time Ballplayer, Dr. Billy Nash Dies," *Boston Globe*, November 16, 1929: 8.
11. Hiram T. Askew, "Billy Nash: First Richmond Baseball Great," *Richmond Quarterly* 3, Richmond, Virginia, 1981, 34-36.
12. Joseph S. Waterman and Sons, Inc. Funeral Home, 497 Commonwealth Avenue, Boston, Western Union telegram of August 1937.
13. David Nemec, *Major League Baseball Profiles, 1871-1900, Volume 1* (Lincoln: University of Nebraska Press, 2011), 426.

KID NICHOLS

BY RICHARD BOGOVICH

Charles Augustus Nichols was born into a large family on September 14, 1869 in Madison, Wisconsin. His father was a butcher there for many years and briefly served as an alderman. For a few years before Charles was born, his half-brothers James and John were regulars for Madison's Capital Citys club, which was connected to the National Association of Base Ball Players.[1] After Charles arrived, the names of his brothers Will and George would also occasionally show up in newspaper articles about local baseball games, such as one during 1877 in which Will, about 19 years old, was the winning pitcher.[2]

Around 1881, Charles and most of his siblings moved with their parents to Kansas City, Missouri. By 1885 he was playing on the amateur Blue Avenue club with Will, George, and a future brother-in-law. They were crowned as champions at least once with Charles in the pitcher's box.[3] He also spent time with at least one other amateur club, Beaton's nine of nearby Armourdale, Kansas, and it was with them in 1887 when he reportedly came to the attention of the Kansas City Cowboys in the Western League as summer approached.[4]

June 14, 1887 was the date of his first pro game. Nichols ended up as the winning pitcher in a 7-6 outcome at Lincoln, Nebraska. It has been widely reported that Charles Nichols received the nickname "Kid" upon joining the club, when the older players either mistook him for a batboy or at least thought he looked more like one than he did a professional player. His weight at the time was estimated to be no more than 135 pounds.

Nichols made 29 more starts and finished the season with 18 wins. Oddly, the local management appeared to have little interest in resigning him, so he began the 1888 season in the Southern

Kid Nichols.
(Library of Congress)

League with the Memphis Grays. He had a record of 11-8 when the league disbanded in June, and in July he started pitching for one of two minor-league teams in Kansas City that year, the Western Association's Blues. He sparkled with a record of 16-2 and a league-leading ERA of 1.14.

Ownership in St. Joseph, Missouri, bought the Blues franchise but Nichols held out, insisting that he was free to sign elsewhere.[5] He prevailed, and in 1889 eventually joined the Omaha team led by Frank Selee. The Kid's record that season was 39-8.

Selee was hired to manage the NL's Boston Beaneaters for 1890 and wanted to take Nichols with him, but the Cincinnati Reds also claimed him, after Nichols reportedly rejected other offers from Chicago and St. Louis.[6] In the midst of this offseason confusion, on January 29, 1890, he married to Jane Florence Curtin (who often went by Jennie). They honeymooned in Omaha and stopped in Madison on their way to the East Coast.

On April 23, Nichols made his major league debut at home against Brooklyn. Nichols was the winning pitcher, but he didn't make too much of an impression until facing Amos Rusie in New York on May 12 as a Players' League game was taking place in an adjacent field. The two pitchers gave up almost nothing for the first nine frames, and as the game proceeded through extra innings, many fans watching the adjacent game supposedly were instead trying to watch the drama unfolding in the NL's Polo Grounds. The game ended in the 13th inning on a towering homer by slugger Mike Tiernan of the Giants off Nichols. This pitching duel was immediately put on a pedestal by journalists, and remains one of the most-discussed battles of the National League's early decades.

Nichols finished his rookie season with 27 wins against 19 losses. Kid and Jennie Nichols wintered in Boston, and on December 8 they celebrated the birth of their only child, Alice. Nichols won 30 games for the first time in 1891, and would reach that total in six of the next seven seasons. His seven 30-win seasons remains a major-league record.

In the process, he would help his team to three consecutive NL pennants, from 1891 to 1893. Baltimore then ran off their own streak of three pennants, and in 1897 the Beaneaters battled them down to the wire as the rough-and-tumble Orioles tried for a fourth straight title.

On September 21, Nichols suffered the worst inning of his major-league career, yielding 12 runs to Brooklyn in the first inning of a 22-5 loss. Three days later, with a razor-thin lead of half a game, Boston began a three-game series in Baltimore with only three more games left in the season afterwards. Nichols shook off his recent humiliation and was the winning pitcher in a 6-4 contest to open the series. Baltimore rebounded the next day with a 6-3 win, and Selee again turned to Nichols for the third game. The Beaneaters broke open a tie game with a three-run fourth to give Nichols a lead of 8-5. Boston exploded for nine more in the seventh, and Nichols then cruised to a final score of 19-10.[7] Though this game clearly wasn't anything like the many low-hit gems Nichols pitched throughout the season, half of Baltimore's runs came after the game was out of reach, and box scores indicated that only four or five of the 10 runs were earned.

Though Boston had three more games to play, in Brooklyn, and Baltimore hosted Washington for four to end the season, many newspapers declared the pennant to have been won, for all practical purposes. They were right. For the season's remaining days and for quite awhile thereafter, Nichols seemed to have the most praise heaped upon him of any single Beaneater.

In 1898, Boston added a fifth pennant in Nichols' first eight years as a major leaguer, to strengthen their case as the decade's top team. For the *New Bill James Historical Baseball Abstract*, the author developed a formula for determining the effect that a player had on individual pennant races throughout his career. He wasn't surprised by the first and second rankings. "There were six pennant races that clearly would have ended differently if Babe Ruth had been merely a good player, and Mickey Mantle also had a decisive impact on six," James wrote. "However, while you might have guessed the numbers one and two men on the list, the number three man was a pitcher who had a decisive impact on the pennant races of 1891, 1892, 1892, 1897, and 1898, Kid Nichols. Nichols won [at least] 30 games in all of those seasons—for teams that won pennants by relatively thin margins."[8]

At first glance, Nichols record of 21-19 in 1899 stands out like a sore thumb compared to all of his previous seasons with Boston, On the other hand, his ERA of 2.99 was better than in three of his previous years, including the pennant-winning season of 1893 when he won 34 games. Boston's daily newspapers tended to write off his low winning percentages as simple misfortune.

In 1900, Nichols was hampered significantly for the first time in his career by an injury, suffered in late April,[9] and he ended up with his first losing season as a pro, at 13-16. Still, his ERA of 3.07 was better than his 3.52 mark of the 1893 championship year and the next two seasons after that. The most notable difference in his performance was that his strikeouts dropped considerably from the previous season. Nichols rebounded somewhat in 1901, his final year with Boston, and finished with a record of 19-16.

Near the turn of the century Nichols spent the closing weeks of successive preseasons coaching collegiate players along the East Coast, at Amherst (1899), Yale (1900), and Brown (1901). He received an offer from Brown again for 1902, but in mid-December of 1901 a shakeup in the Western League provided Nichols an opportunity to co-own and manage that circuit's Kansas City club, which were known as the Blue Stockings under Nichols—while the Blues name shifted to a rival franchise across town in the newly formed American Association.

Nichols' squad fared better in its league's standings, but the AA club brought in opposing teams from much more populous cities and was apparently considered to offer fans higher quality play. Therefore, even though his club won the Western League pennant while the AA franchise barely had a winning season, the latter won the bitter battle of the box office by far.

Nevertheless, Nichols could derive considerable satisfaction not only as a manager but also as pitcher, proving that he wasn't washed up by winning 26 games on the mound and losing only seven with an ERA of 1.82. His top rival for the league's pitching honors was Mordecai Brown, who had one more win than Nick but also had 15 losses to go with an ERA of 2.22.

Nichols continued as player-manager in 1903, and with a week left in the season his Blue Stockings were in third place with had a record of 66-58. He wasn't pitching quite as well as in 1902 but remained a considerable asset with a record of 21-12 and an ERA of 2.51. However, as meager attendance continued in the Western League its season was abruptly cancelled because its franchises generally couldn't afford to play their final few games.[10]

In the end, the Western League surrendered Kansas City to the much more successful American Association, but Nichols ended up in a better situation for 1904 when a year-old rumor became reality, and he was named to manage the St. Louis Cardinals.

Kid Nichols took over a team that had finished dead last under Patsy Donovan in 1903, with a record of 43-94. After he pitched the Cards to victory on June 4 in his return to Boston, where fans greeted him warmly, his new team left town with a record of 18-18. Toward the end of the season Nichols had steered the Cardinals to a record of 75-73, but they lost their final games to finish 75-79, still a considerable improvement in one year. He fared even better as a pitcher, with a record of 21-13 and a career-best ERA of 2.02.

Though Nichols was widely held in high regard by teammates, opponents, and fans in other cities, and he didn't share most other players' fondness for alcohol,[11] he had experienced periodic contract disputes with Boston's owners and actually held out a few times. This strong will was apparently the cause of trouble for him early in the 1905 season. He got along well with only one of the Cardinals' co-owners, Frank Robison, but as Robison's health declined in 1905 his brother Stanley exercised more control as the other co-owner.[12]

After accumulating a record of 5-9, on May 3rd Stanley Robison relieved Kid Nichols of his managerial duties, though he was retained as a pitcher. About two months later, after compiling a record of 1-5 with an ERA of 5.40, Nichols was unconditionally released. In short order he was signed by a former Boston teammate, Hugh Duffy, who had become manager of the Phillies. The change of teams worked wonders for the second half of the season, and he rewarded Duffy's faith in him with an ERA of 2.27 to go with a record of 10-6. Nichols returned to the Phillies in 1906 but was suffering from pleurisy, a debilitating inflammation of the rib cage, and after four poor performances he retired.[13]

Kid Nichols won 361 games, lost only 208, and saved 17. He finished 95% of his career starts and was the youngest pitcher to reach 300 career victories.

By 1907, Nichols turned his attention to an activity that he had become very fond of more than a decade earlier, bowling. More often than not he would own or manage an alley or two for the rest of his life. Though he had no formal connection to professional baseball in 1907, at his bowling "academy" back in Kansas City he started presenting games on an electric scoreboard that used lights to depict action occurring elsewhere in the country (during an era before radio). On August 6 he even filed a federal patent application for his unique method of showing baserunners in motion.

Partway through the 1908 season, Nichols returned to professional baseball, in the state of his birth. In July he took over as manager of the woeful Oshkosh Indians in the Wisconsin-Illinois League. About a month into this stint his team played a 23-inning game in nearby Fond du Lac, which Oshkosh won, 4-2. Nichols guided Oshkosh to more wins than losses, 34 to 31. He put himself in 35 games during that half-season, but not many as a pitcher. His 3-1 record on the slab gave him career totals as a professional pitcher of 495 victories against 258 losses.

In 1909, Kid Nichols started playing semipro ball in Kansas City with Johnny Kling, among others. Kling was holding out after helping the Cubs to consecutive World Series crowns. To taunt Chicago's ownership, the popular catcher took Nichols and the rest of "Johnny Kling's All-Stars" to play semipro teams in the Windy City that summer. They did very well in Chicago, but not in their last game, on September 11. They faced the famous African-American team known as the Leland Giants, formerly the Chicago Union Giants. The most prominent player in the Leland lineup was future Hall of Famer John Preston "Pete" Hill. Kling's team scratched out only six hits, two by Nichols, who batted eighth ahead of pitcher Chick Fraser. Nick scored the only run for his club in a 6-1 loss.[14]

Early in 1910, Nichols he had a conversation with a teenager across the street from where he lived, Charles (eventually "Casey") Stengel. Stengel would go on to become a major league player but gained far more fame leading the Yankees to seven World Series titles in twelve years. He would consistently credit Nichols as one of his most important early influences.[15]

In 1911, Nichols led a baseball team in a game of some historical significance. A club from Keio University in Japan had spent three weeks playing collegiate teams in the U.S., and on May 12 they faced Nick's semipro team in Kansas City, augmented with players from other local squads, including one from Kling's. The Kansas City club, with Nick pitching, had the game in hand until Keio rallied for four runs in the eighth inning, on their way to a 7-6 victory.[16]

Kid Nichols reconnected with the major leagues that summer when he was hired by the Detroit Tigers to scout in the Texas League for a few months.

1913 was an eventful year for Nichols in several regards. On March 22 he and famous Cub Joe Tinker opened a movie and vaudeville house in Kansas City called the Diamond Theater.[17] (It's unclear how long they both maintained an ownership stake in it.) On August 5, the federal government awarded Nick a patent for his "Amusement Apparatus," almost six years to the day of when he had applied for it. Also, his daughter Alice and her husband made him a grandfather.

In 1915 and 1916, Kid Nichols managed the Missouri Valley College baseball team. Otherwise, for the better part of a decade his only regular association with baseball resulted from announcements about the electronic scoreboard.

That changed late in the summer of 1922 when he was invited to Boston for an old-timers' game. He pitched the first two innings for one squad and Cy Young did so for the other. Sadly, Nick was bashed for seven runs in the first frame, though he managed to escape the second inning unscathed.

A decade later, Kid Nichols received recognition as a key figure helping to launch an expanded Ban Johnson League in the area, for amateur ballplayers under the age of 21.[18] Nichols was drafted to train and coach the Franklin Ice Cream club in 1932. The enlarged league would produce many notable major leaguers, most prominently Mickey Mantle.

The next year, at the age of 63, Kid Nichols won the Kansas City bowling championship. Not much later, his beloved wife Jennie passed away.

Early in 1936, the inaugural class of the National Baseball Hall of Fame was announced, but Nichols suffered through years of barely registering in the voting. *The New Bill James Historical Baseball Abstract* explained the circumstances that contributed to this outcome. "Kid Nichols has been excluded from discussions about the greatest pitchers of all time, as much as anything, because of an accident of the calendar," James wrote. "Baseball exploded in popularity between 1905 and 1910, just as Nichols was leaving the game. Other things happened. Sports coverage by newspapers increased exponentially, and the wire services began to cover and report every game to a national audience. Nichols missed all that; his memory was pushed into baseball's medieval past almost before he got the clay out of his spikes."[19]

In 1939, shortly before turning 70, Kid Nichols had a chance to redeem himself in a second old-timers' game, again in Boston, a day after attending the All-Star game in New York. In a steady rain Nick pitched to five batters and finished his inning without allowing a run. A few years later, the first of his great grandchildren was born.

Sportswriters would periodically advocate for Nichols' election to the Hall of Fame, such as Grantland Rice,[20] and Nichols' contemporaries such as Cy Young were reportedly in his corner, but the biggest single boost to his consideration may have come in April of 1948 when a legend who was in many ways his exact opposite, Ty Cobb, loudly and repeatedly clamored for Nichols to join him at Cooperstown.[21]

Nichols and the late Mordecai Brown were approved for membership early in 1949, and that June he was inducted into the Hall. For four years he was able to bask in that glow, until his death on April 11, 1953, at the age of 83.

NOTES

1. Sam Smith, "Nichols: 'We Stayed In and Pitched,'" *Baseball Digest*, June 1951, page 76. See also the *Record Book on the Games of the Capital Baseball Club, 1866-1869*, in the archives of the Wisconsin Historical Society.

2. "Stoughton Scooped," *Wisconsin State Journal* (Madison), June 30, 1877: 4.

3. Nichols' descendants still possess a commemorative bat with engraved gold and silver plates for an amateur championship won by the "Blue Avenue Base Ball Club."

4. Ernest Mehl, "Sporting Comment," *Kansas City Star*, September 14, 1950.

5. "'Kid' Nichols an Old Timer," *St. Louis Republic*, May 17, 1903, Part IV, page 1.

6. "Diamond Stories," *Philadelphia Inquirer*, December 3, 1899: 13.

7. For a detailed account of this race, see Bill Felber, *A Game of Brawl: The Orioles, the Beaneaters and the Battle for the 1897 Pennant* (Lincoln: University of Nebraska Press, 2007).

8. Bill James, *The New Bill James Historical Baseball Abstract* (New York: Free Press, 2001): 978.

9. W. S. Barnes, Jr., "Boston's Worst Defeat," *Boston Sunday Journal*, April 29, 1900, section 2, page 1.

10. A primary source for information about Nichols' stint leading the Kansas City Blue Stockings was Dennis Pajot, *Baseball's Heartland War, 1902-1903: The Western League and American Association Vie for Turf, Players and Profits* (Jefferson, NC: McFarland & Co., Inc., 2011).

11. "Will Urge Players to Stand Together," *St. Louis Republic*, December 19, 1901: 7.

12. Dick Farrington, "Kid Nichols, Holder of Two 'Hidden' Major Hill Marks, Still Making His Way Via 15 Hours a Day at Age of 73," *Sporting News*, December 31, 1942: 11.

13. Nichols explained this around 1949 in a handwritten autobiographical document that is in possession of the National Baseball Hall of Fame.

14. "Klings Lost the Last One," *Kansas City Star*, September 12, 1909: 12.

15. For example, see Casey Stengel, as told to Harry T. Paxton, *Casey at the Bat: The Story of My Life in Baseball* (New York: Random House, 1962): 58-59.

16. See these articles in the *Kansas City Star*: "'Japs' Play Here Tomorrow," May 11, 1911: 11; "Kansas Beat Keio 10 to 8," May 12, 1911: 10; "Japs Use their 'Noodles,'" May 13, 1911: 13.

17. Advertisement, *Kansas City Star*, March 22, 1913: 4.

18. For example, see "Founders of Ban Johnson League See Idea Spreading over Nation," *Syracuse Herald* (New York), March 8, 1932: 15.

19. James, *The New Bill James Historical Baseball Abstract*: 852.

20. For example, see Grantland Rice, "Sportlight," *Ellensburg Capital* (Washington), January 23, 1948: 2.

21. For example, see Robert Moore, "Ty Cobb Plugs Pitcher Nichols For Baseball's Hall Of Fame," *Florence Times* (Alabama), April 2, 1948: 9.

JOE QUINN

BY ROCHELLE LLEWELYN NICHOLLS

Joe Quinn, 1888.
(Courtesy of R. Nichols)

Joe Quinn's 17 seasons between 1884 and 1901 marked the first appearance by an Australian in major league baseball. For 102 years, Quinn was the only player from "Down Under" to feature at the top level of American pro ball, and he remains the only Australian to manage in the major leagues. He played on the team with the best winning record in major-league history – the St. Louis Unions of 1884 – but in 1899, captained and managed the Cleveland Spiders to the worst win-loss percentage in big-league history. The little second baseman, who worked as an undertaker in the off-seasons, was enormously popular, both for his skill and earnestness on the diamond and his spotless reputation off it: in 1893, he was voted "America's Most Popular Player" in a *Sporting News* public poll. In an era characterized by a constant tug-o'-war for player services, Quinn was the glue that held together teams rent by ruthless owners, failing finances, and broken spirits. He often took the helm when no one else would, embodying the unique Australian quality of "having a go" even in impossible circumstances.

Joseph James Quinn was born on December 24, 1862, in the village of Ipswich, Queensland, in northern Australia.[1] His parents, Patrick Quinn and Catherine McAfie, were both refugees from the Irish Potato Famine. The son of an impoverished farmer in County Laois, Ireland, 17-year-old Patrick came to Australia on a one-way ticket in 1855, his passage subsidized under the British Assisted Immigration scheme.[2] Born in about 1830, Catherine was raised as a servant on a farm near Enniskillen in what is now Northern Ireland, and orphaned by the famine while still a teen.[3] Her ability to read and write allowed her to escape the county workhouse and find another servant's position in 1847; it took a further six years for her to save her fare to

Australia.⁴ Catherine and Patrick met in the small Irish enclave of Broulee on the New South Wales south coast in 1856; though she was eight years his senior, within weeks, they were married.⁵

In 1857, Patrick took his new bride to the Araluen goldfields near the modern-day Australian capital of Canberra, where their first son, Patrick Jr., was born.⁶ The diggings were destroyed by a monster flood in 1860, and the Quinns, who had failed to make their fortune at Araluen, now journeyed 600 miles north to Ipswich, chasing rumors of work on a new inland rail line.⁷ When Joe was born on Christmas Eve in 1862, the family was sweltering in a tent in a squatters' camp outside town, with only potatoes and feral goat for their Christmas dinner.⁸

Patrick Quinn made a paltry living laboring on Queensland's first rail line, which opened in July 1865.⁹ By that time, the state was gripped by drought, failing crops, and riots over unemployment. The Quinns escaped by walking all the way south back to the Irish settlement at Campbelltown, just west of Sydney. This was the harshest period of Joe Quinn's life. Founded as a British penal colony in 1788, Australia's convict era was now over, and prison labor was replaced in many cases by underpaid child workers. Joe Quinn was one of 37,000 Australian children who worked as factory hands, farm workers, and domestic servants in the year 1871 alone.¹⁰ He bent his small body for a few pennies a week, only attending school intermittently. There was no time or money for games and sports. But by 1872, when Quinn was 10 years old, his family was down to their last pennies. Hailstorms and wheat rust had decimated local agriculture and many families were bankrupt and unemployed.¹¹ Having not found their promised land in Australia, the Quinns took ship for the United States.

They settled in Dubuque, Iowa, after a journey of 11,000 miles by ship, stagecoach, and countless miles of painful walking.¹² A large Irish diaspora had settled in the village beside the Mississippi River after the post-Famine exodus, so much so the town became known as Little Dublin. Perhaps finally feeling at home after almost two decades of wandering, Patrick Quinn settled his family in a small house on Grandview Avenue, where he remained until his death in 1902.¹³

But in Dubuque, little changed for 11-year-old Joe Quinn. His family, still immigrants, still uneducated, faced the same grinding poverty, with the Australian farms now exchanged for Iowa's zinc mines.¹⁴ His father took a job in the Avenue Top mine and exaggerated Joe's age to get him a job underground too, shifting rubble and shoring up walls on just 50 cents a day.¹⁵

Thus far, sports had played no part in Joe Quinn's underprivileged life. In Australia, the game of baseball had existed only among American expats on the goldfields.¹⁶ But in Dubuque, "all the boys played," as Quinn said in a later interview.¹⁷ At 16 years old, Joe Quinn had struggled to integrate with these local children: he spoke differently, he was a dirty half-educated miner's boy who was beneath their contempt. In baseball, he at last found some common ground.¹⁸

Despite his late start in the game, Quinn clearly showed some natural ability. Within three years, in 1881, he was invited to join the local semi-pro team, the Dubuque Rabbits, playing alongside future Hall of Famers Charles "Hoss" Radbourn and Charlie Comiskey.¹⁹ Quinn played first base as understudy to Comiskey. He stood just 5-feet-7, and at 150 pounds, was hardly an intimidating presence for the oncoming baserunner – but Joe Quinn had become battle-hardened in the mines, and in this era of gloveless play, his tough hands were perfect for taking throws on bare palms.

On the national stage, unrest was high in professional baseball. The National League and American Association squabbled relentlessly over players, admission prices, and salaries. Players jumped back and forth between leagues searching for the best pay and conditions. In response, both leagues adopted the reserve clause, allowing clubs to indefinitely hoard their best five players. In 1883, reserve quotas were hiked from five to 11.²⁰ In response, St. Louis millionaire Henry Lucas established the Union Association, boldly snatching talent from the established leagues and the semi-pro ranks with lofty salaries and no reserve clause.²¹ Joe Quinn was engaged for Lucas's St. Louis team, the Maroons, for $2,000 – a sum that would have bought passage from Australia to the USA 50 times over.²²

Just before his departure from Dubuque in late 1883, Quinn took a night-time walk which nearly ended his baseball career. A section of rotten sidewalk gave way, sending him crashing down an embankment. Quinn was forced to sail down the Mississippi River for St. Louis with his broken arm in a splint, for which he later sued the City of Dubuque for $2,500 damages.²³ It was hardly the perfect preparation for the rough and rowdy world of professional baseball, where brawling, cheating, and hard drinking were a way of life and two good fists were often needed to earn a player a break, as Quinn himself later recalled.²⁴ The violence often included brutal victimization of rookies. Quinn gave up 70 pounds to some of his hulking teammates, who pitched balls at his head, tore his uniforms, and complained he was too small to play first base.²⁵

But Quinn's hard upbringing had instilled in him a fierce self-respect: he refused to retaliate, instead letting his play do the talking. In his major-league debut on April 26, 1884, against Altoona, he banged his first hit in pro ball over the shortstop's head and scored from third in the 9-3 victory. He then cemented his place in the team with an errorless four-game series at first base, St. Louis averaging 14 runs per game while the Pennsylvania outfit scored just 12 for the entire series.²⁶ One hundred and two years passed between Joe Quinn's debut and another Australian appearing in major-league baseball, when Craig Shipley lined up at shortstop for the Los Angeles Dodgers in 1986.

In 1884, St. Louis decimated the breakaway Union Association. Their 94-19 win-loss record remains unsurpassed in professional baseball. Quinn hit a respectable .270 and handled over 1,000 putouts at first base. He also appeared briefly in the outfield and at shortstop, as he would on occasion in years to come. However, the Union Association was so top-heavy it collapsed after only one season. While some baseball observers have questioned its classification as a major league,²⁷ as baseball's first attempt to protect the rights of professional players, it awoke in Joe Quinn a desire for justice which would shape many of his future choices.

What followed was two years of humiliation for the Maroons franchise as it joined the National League and was immediately blown away by the higher caliber of pitching and defense. The

Maroons finished the 1885 season dead last, and 1886 was little better. Quinn was shunted around the infield and then, because he had been timed sprinting 100 yards in under 11 seconds,[28] dispatched to right field, from where he was expected to throw runners out at first base. His batting average hovered around .220. By November 1886, the Maroons were bankrupt and out of the league.

With a scarcely-impressive three seasons behind him, baseball oblivion beckoned for Joe Quinn. But an opportunity came in Duluth, Minnesota, on the icy shores of Lake Superior. That Northwestern League club had lost its second baseman, John Ake, in a boating tragedy on the Mississippi, and were scrambling mid-season for a replacement.[29] The entire Maroons franchise had been sold to Indianapolis but, with a top-heavy list of infielders, Quinn had not played a single game, and owner John T. Brush agreed to sell his "extra fielder" to Duluth, despite Quinn having played just 15 games at second base in his entire professional career. Quinn could do nothing but "have a go," in the great Australian tradition.[30]

Joe Quinn had hit only one home run in his pro career. Now, in 1887, he slammed 11 and posted a .372 batting average. He was made captain, then manager, of the Freezers.[31] But squabbling board members and financiers were crippling the club. Quinn stood by his struggling team – even when management proposed selling him to raise capital, Quinn refused to desert his sinking ship and consent to the sale.[32] His loyalty, however, came to naught: the club finished seventh in the eight-team league and was disbanded.

Quinn returned to St. Louis for the winter of 1887-88, where he boarded in the Irish enclave known as the Kerry Patch.[33] Nineteenth-century players were paid only during the season, and many worked during the winters to keep their heads above water until next spring. There were showmen and preachers, trappers and teachers.[34] In 1886, under the wing of Kerry Patch mortician Thomas McGrath, Joe Quinn had become an apprentice undertaker.

The funeral business was dangerous as it was somber. Undertakers inhaled arsenic and mercury from embalming fluids, and were exposed to diseased corpses without the protection of face masks, gloves, or antiseptic.[35] Quinn's decision to enter the industry arose from a great fear of returning to his childhood destitution:

"I realized I only had a limited period as a player, and seeing all about me great stars doomed after their playing days to poverty and often starvation, I determined that when my time came, there would be no such story told about me."[36]

Quinn drove himself fiercely through the winters, working for McGrath and earning extra cash shoeing horses[37] and tending bar.[38] But while it was gloomy and hazardous, the association with Thomas McGrath had a special advantage for Joe Quinn. McGrath had four daughters, and one in particular caught Quinn's eye – Mary Ellen, a spirited girl with auburn hair and blue eyes, was six years his junior, and saw much in Quinn beyond the vile reputation many ball players had for drinking, fighting, and gambling. They were married on November 17, 1886, at St. Bridget's Catholic Church in St. Louis.

In 1888, Quinn signed with Des Moines in the Western Association to play second base for the Prohibitionists.[39] In this temperance heartland, teetotaler Quinn was their poster boy. On a diet of pork and corn, he filled out to over 170 pounds and helped himself to a .309 average in 77 games.[40]

Back in the National League, baseball's richest club, Boston, had a problem. In 1888, they had already tried and sacked three second-basemen, two of whom couldn't hit and one who fractured his skull falling off a tram.[41] The solution – tempt the Prohibitionists with $3,000 for the in-form Joe Quinn.[42] But once again, Quinn would not break his contract. The offer increased to $4,000; Quinn again refused. However, the Prohibitionists were in financial trouble, and in August, they handed over his contract.[43] Quinn was furious. It was a terrible realization that he was merely a commodity to be traded, and to have the public potentially perceive him as a greedy jumper was abhorrent.

Boston wanted Quinn before facing league-leaders New York at the Polo Grounds on August 27. In New York, Quinn faced such a riotous crowd of Giants fans that the overflow of their carriages had to be parked in center field. The game was titanic. The Beans took the lead in the third inning as speedy Dick Johnston hit safely, stole second, and came home on a Tom Brown hit which Giants outfielder Mike Slattery allowed to bounce. But the Giants equalized at the top of the ninth; two Boston hitters fell trying for the winning run – and with the crowd raising a din audible for miles, out of the dugout walked little Joe Quinn.

Giants pitcher Tim Keefe was on a 19-game winning streak; he had already struck out 10 that day. But Quinn looked Keefe straight in the eye and swung hard at the first pitch. The hit soared over center fielder Slattery's head to land among the carriages. Scrambling Giants fielders couldn't disentangle the ball before Quinn slid in for the winning run, the strangest inside-the-park home run of the year.[44]

In 1884, Quinn had been a part of baseball's first rebel league. As the 1880s drew to a close, insurrection again threatened professional baseball. Front and center was Boston crowd favorite Joe Quinn.

Since his dramatic debut for the Beaneaters, the Boston public had clamored to know the serious young man from "Down Under." Quinn had been taken under the wing of the team's greatest celebrity, Hall of Fame catcher Mike "King" Kelly, who guided him through the minefield of life in the spotlight. Kelly and Quinn were baseball's most improbable pairing. Unlike the sober Quinn, Mike Kelly loved nothing more than strong drink, fine food, and betting on horses. But he won two batting crowns in the 1880s, and his inventiveness required constant changes to baseball's rules.[45] Kelly's parents had died soon after he was born, and it was perhaps his lifelong quest for love and attention that drew the King to Quinn, whose modesty was the perfect foil for his own exuberance.[46] In the reflected glow of Kelly's brilliance, Quinn had thrived in his return to the big time. He hit .301 in 38 games in 1888 and recorded over 200 putouts at second base. Boston fans presented him with a gold-inlaid bat in September 1889, with which Quinn promised he would hit a home run.

The best he could do was a hard-hit single, but the crowd still raised the roof.[47]

But 1889 was a rollercoaster season for Boston, who lost the pennant to New York amid bitter infighting, much of which fans blamed on Kelly. The King's staunchest defender was Joe Quinn, even when he too was vilified:

"Some of my friends are sore on me for upholding Kelly. Well, Kelly acted like a gentleman when I first went to Boston. He could not do any more for his brother than he did for me."[48]

There was also ongoing unrest in the National League. Conflict over the reserve clause was inflamed by introduction of the Classification Rule to cap player payments. To the Brotherhood of Base Ball Players, the players union formed to fight the reserve clause, this attack on player rights could not go unpunished.[49] Quinn was privy to the union's secret plans to form a breakaway league in 1890.[50] On September 21, 1889, *The Sporting News* published a letter from a "leading Boston player" trumpeting the plan:

"We have concluded to start an association of our own and ask no more favor from the directors of the league…No matter what happens, do not mention my name in connection with this letter."[51]

Quinn admitted he had authored the letter, with the support of the Brotherhood.[52] Over 100 of the era's greatest players, including King Kelly, Hoss Radbourn, Charlie Comiskey, and Tim Keefe, now openly rejected the strictures of the reserve clause and prepared to join the rebel league.[53]

However, Quinn hesitated at the 11th hour. After his poverty-stricken childhood, he was suddenly nervous about litigation – he had saved hard throughout his career but now could lose everything if the National League's lawsuits against the Players' League succeeded.[54] But the ever-loyal Quinn did sign with the Boston Reds. And in the company of many of the game's greats, he enjoyed his best year on the diamond so far. He had 153 hits – including seven homers, his best single-season total in the majors – for an average of .301, well above the league average .274. He stole 29 bases (also a career high) and led the league in fielding percentage at second base (.942), the first time he did so.

"Joe Quinn is the most valuable second baseman in the Players' League. His sacrificing won many a game, he is among the leaders in batting, has the highest fielding average of the League and tries for everything. He has been a gold find."[55]

The Reds were the champions of the Players' League, which collapsed after its only season in 1890. Quinn returned to the Beaneaters and won a further two National League championships with Boston in 1891 and 1892. However, the 30-year-old was supplanted by younger infielder Bobby Lowe at the end of 1892. Not only did Boston let Quinn go – they sold him to one of the league's weakest teams, the St. Louis Browns.

The Browns had won four American Association pennants in the 1880s and had finished either second or third from 1889 through 1891. After joining the National League in 1892, however, the club spiraled downward into 11th place out of 12. The Browns needed a captain who would both lead the struggling team and liaise with the capricious owner, Chris Von der Ahe – a task requiring a hide as thick as the proverbial rhinoceros.[56] In February 1893, Joe Quinn arrived to captain and play second base for the Browns. *The Sporting News* observed:

"The selection is a wise one…Unlike many other professionals, he has never broken a contract or been charged with double-dealing of any kind. He is honest and upright and commands the respect of the fraternity at large."[57]

Quinn now took the greatest gamble of his baseball career. After years of being apprenticed to Thomas McGrath, Quinn bought his own business, a livery stable in the Kerry Patch. In the 19th century, livery and undertaking services worked symbiotically, with transport to and from the burial complementing the funeral services. Working during the playing season was unheard of for professional ball players, yet Quinn was now stabling horses, renting buggies, transporting the bereaved, and somehow fitting it all around his numerous duties on the ballfield.[58]

He managed, initially: in fact, in mid-May of 1893, Quinn and his Browns were actually leading the league.[59] The captain had laid down firm guidelines for the discontented squad:

"People will not patronize the sport if they are compelled to listen to the language of swell-headed toughs…If these offenses are repeated under me, you will quit ball-playing for all time."[60]

But it couldn't last. As the Browns began to slip back toward the cellar, Von der Ahe berated, fined, and suspended his players for every minor error. Morale crashed. Quinn himself was exhausted by practice, travel, and hours of extra labor in the stables. His batting average was under .240, and only fumbling third baseman Jack Crooks made more errors.

The one bright spot came on September 30, 1893, when the Browns, having lost their previous 10 games, crushed league-leaders Boston in both games of a doubleheader during which Quinn hammered eight hits.[61] This performance coincided with his decision to sell the Kerry Patch stables.[62] Quinn's pride was wounded at having to return to working for McGrath, but an unexpected reward came his way. In one of the worst seasons of his career with both bat (.230 average) and glove (.942 from 135 games), Quinn was voted "America's Most Popular Player" by *The Sporting News*, with its readership of 80,000. The award was proof that Quinn didn't need to play for a winning team or produced Hall of Fame numbers to be respected and admired. He wore the gold watch presented to him for the rest of his life, albeit tucked deep in a pocket lest it mar his sober image.[63]

Freed from the demands of his business, Quinn's 1894 form had been much improved. In partnership with new shortstop William "Bones" Ely, the pair were hailed the best infield duo in the league.[64] But it all came undone on the Fourth of July when Quinn, who had made three hits and turned three double plays against Washington, had his hand smashed by an errant pitch.[65] His absence saw the Browns began their familiar backslide, and Von der Ahe slashed all salaries as punishment. With his hand only half healed, Quinn hastily reinstated himself – but by August, the players had not been paid in months and finished the year in ninth place.[66] Despite his shattered hand, Quinn finished the year second in the league in fielding at second base

(.952), making just 34 errors in 106 games. The Browns finished the year ninth.

Between 1894 and 1898, the Browns had 13 managers, and the team's performances degenerated from the uncertain to the preposterous. The 1895 season was just eight weeks old when the yoke landed on the shoulders of Joe Quinn.

By late June 1895, Von der Ahe had already dispensed with two managers for the season. The Browns' performances had been so awful that fans were booing and whistling Handel's *Dead March* every time they took the field.[67] It seemed only Quinn could resist the slide toward the National League cellar, hitting .362 for the year. It was no romantic transition, however: the Browns lost their first seven games under Quinn's stewardship.[68] But on July 25, Quinn slammed four singles and a double against Brooklyn to drag the Browns out of another six-game losing streak,[69] and *Sporting Life* reported:

"The Browns are doing better, much better, under the direction of Manager Quinn. There is more harmony in the club, less chance for jealous differences, and when a few broken fingers and wrecked joints have got into normal condition, still better results may be looked for."[70]

It was the last good thing said about the Browns during Quinn's reign – they won only one of his remaining 11 games in charge. Quinn was still batting .347 but he cabled his notice as manager to Von der Ahe on August 4, insisting that the best way he could serve the club was to focus on playing.[71] Despite earning the respect of his men through his honesty and integrity, Quinn was never comfortable in the role of manager. Off the field, he was a loner, and he admitted he lacked the genuine connection with the players which distinguishes the captain from the general.[72]

Over the next 12 months, the Browns had a further seven managers and many players were sacked or traded for minor offenses. In July 1896, Von der Ahe issued the ultimate warning to the demoralized team: he traded their most consistent player, Joe Quinn, to Baltimore.[73] It was the crowning insult in the entire debacle – the man with the cleanest reputation in baseball was sold to its dirtiest team.

Despite winning National League championships in 1894 and '95, the Baltimore Orioles were just as well known for hustling, fighting, and outright cheating. Their star-studded roster included Hall of Famers John McGraw, Hugh Jennings, Joe Kelley, and Wee Willie Keeler, and Quinn now faced a major test of his integrity – how to earn the respect of his fractious new teammates without compromising his own pristine reputation. But Joe Quinn was no pushover. After years of maltreatment in St. Louis, he bloomed in the Baltimore hothouse. His batting average revived to .329 in 24 games as the bad Birds clinched the 1896 pennant. They had the best winning percentage in Baltimore major-league history with their 90-39 record.[74] Quinn recounted:

"If a man didn't get out and do battle, he didn't last long. The players were a rip-snorting lot and it took a good two-fisted fellow to make his own breaks."[75]

In 1888, Australians had been formally introduced to baseball when the Chicago White Stockings and American All-Stars played 12 games there as part of the Spalding World Tour. An ambitious return tour of the United States by Australian players was organized in 1897. But for all the players' enthusiasm, the self-financed Australian team was routinely humiliated by its American counterparts. By the time they reached Chicago, the Australian manager had fled with the meager takings and the players were broke and abandoned.[76] They scraped together cash for a final treat, watching Chicago entertain the visiting Orioles. They were warmly greeted by both teams after the game, including by Orioles infielder Joe Quinn, who they were astonished to learn was a native of Queensland and who the Australian *Argus* reported was "anxious for news from home."[77] Quinn's exploits had never reached the Australian media or his playing counterparts "Down Under," and this encounter was the only mention of Quinn in any Australian broadsheet of the era.

In early 1898, Joe Quinn was traded back to St. Louis to rejoin the hapless Browns, around the time the bankrupt club was bought by Cleveland street-car magnates Frank and Matthew Robison, who also owned the Cleveland franchise. Syndicate baseball – two clubs with one owner – is now illegal in professional baseball. But in the nineteenth century, it was common, and nowhere was it more disastrous than Cleveland in 1899. The Robisons dispatched Cleveland stars including pitcher Cy Young and .400 hitter Jesse Burkett to St. Louis to create a southern super-team, and made only an indifferent attempt to restock the Spiders with washed-up veterans and unblooded youngsters from the Browns.

The tone for the Cleveland Spiders' season was set from the first game, which, cruelly, was scheduled against St. Louis in the Robisons' new southern stronghold. 15,000 fans cheered the Browns as they stamped out their northern brothers, 10-1.[78] Cy Young was on the mound – he would win 26 games in 1899, more than his former team managed for the season. The Spiders then proceeded to set new records for futility in almost every aspect of the game, and their fans deserted them in droves. Lave Cross, perhaps the only good-quality player the Robisons had left in Cleveland, managed the team for the first 38 games of the 1899 season, winning just eight; his performances at third base, however, were good enough to earn him a ticket to St. Louis. Who better qualified to take over the rag-tag bunch than Joe Quinn?

One facetious report suggested Cleveland had the proper manager in Quinn: "a corpse in charge of an undertaker."[79] But the 36-year-old second baseman hauled himself up to his best season in five years, batting .281 and fielding at the top of the National League at second base.[80] The *Washington Times* wrote:

"He is batting and fielding as well as he ever did. If not better. He is a credit to the profession, and the game would be better with more of his kind."[81]

The Spiders did manage one hurrah for their long-suffering fans, whose average attendance was just 100 per game. On July 1, Cleveland defeated Boston 10-9, coming from 7-0 down at the start of the ninth inning. With the score tied in the 11th inning, Quinn stole second and crossed the plate with the game winning run.[82] It was sweet but short-lived: the Spiders then lost 14 games in a row.[83]

The Spiders split their July 18 doubleheader with Washington, Quinn putting in what the *Spalding Base Ball Guide of 1899* described as "the fielding performance of the season," making eight putouts and 14 assists without an error.[84] But his miserable troops could not follow suit: between August 25 and season's end, Cleveland won just one game and lost 40. They closed out the season the way they had started – dismally, thrashed by Cincinnati, who had already beaten them 14 times that season.

Joe Quinn was the last manager of the Cleveland Spiders, whose 20-134 record remains the worst in major league baseball history. The valiant Quinn led the team in batting at .286, and led the league in fielding at second base (.962), committing just 31 errors in 147 games. And teams continued to vie for his services. In 1900, Quinn had another stint in St. Louis of just 24 games; he then played 74 games in Cincinnati, where he made his final appearance in the National League in October 1900.[85]

Quinn appeared in the inaugural season of the American League with Washington in 1901. But the mediocre play of the Senators was too much, and Quinn sought his release in July.[86] It was the only time in his 17-year career that he purposely turned his back on a club.

But in 1902, an invitation to play back in minor-league Des Moines was more than he could resist. After the 1902 season, the team actually changed its moniker from the Midgets to the Undertakers to honor their 40-year-old captain, who had been the Western League's leading second baseman for the year.[87] Quinn closed the book on his professional baseball career with the Undertakers in September 1903, with five championships on his résumé.

By 1920, 58-year-old Joe Quinn, father of eight, had settled into the simple pleasures of life. In 1895, he had been made a full partner in Thomas McGrath's undertaking business, and though McGrath had died in 1907, McGrath & Quinn had continued to flourish in their gloomy trade. By 1920, the firm had moved into larger premises on Union Boulevard; three of Quinn's five sons had also followed him into the business.[88] Two of the boys, Joseph Jr. (b. 1893) and Clarence (b. 1894), had been enthusiastic sandlot ball players in St. Louis but had given the game up to work with their father.[89] But in 1920, Joe's fourth son, John Richard – known as "Scotty" – was invited to try out with John McGraw's New York Giants. Quinn adored the boy, both for his resemblance to his own father and for his passionate love of baseball. Scotty was born in 1897, the year the Orioles won the Temple Cup with McGraw and Joe Quinn sharing duties at third base. And now Scotty had a shot at becoming manager McGraw's new third baseman.

But in that terrible year, St. Louis was under siege from deadly Spanish influenza. On February 2, 1920, just days before Scotty's departure for New York, Joe's daughter Estelle came dashing, hysterical, into the funeral parlor and fetched him home. Scotty was already unconscious. Joe watched his son struggle for life for three days. On February 5, Scotty Quinn died.[90] Four of Joe and Mary Ellen Quinn's babies had been stillborn,[91] but this was different: a tragedy of such dreadful proportions that Joe never spoke of his son again.[92]

The impoverished boy who had once earned a living grubbing in the Iowa zinc mines had become one of St. Louis' most successful businessmen. But in 1937, life dealt Joe Quinn another blow – the loss of his wife of 51 years when Mary Ellen Quinn died from heart disease.[93] Quinn's own health began to decline. Suffering from myocarditis and the beginnings of dementia, he was hospitalized in February 1940, and never returned to his home at 1389 Union Boulevard. Quinn died on November 12, 1940, aged 77.[94] His funeral was arranged by his faithful sons. He was buried in the family plot at Calvary Cemetery in St. Louis beside his wife and his beloved Scotty.[95]

On May 4, 2013, Quinn was inducted into Baseball Australia's (virtual) Hall of Fame as an "Australian baseball pioneer…for many more to come."[96] However, accolades were not Joe Quinn's way. The only monument to his life, still standing in Calvary Cemetery, is appropriately unpretentious: it is marked only "Quinn."

This biography has been adapted from the full-length book by Rochelle Llewelyn Nicholls, *Joe Quinn among the Rowdies: The Life of Baseball's Honest Australian* (Jefferson, North Carolina: McFarland & Co., 2014).

NOTES

1. Queensland Registry of Births Deaths & Marriages. (2015). "Birth Registration: Quinn, Joseph James (Per Quinn, Patrick - Catherine Mcafie)", Department of Police & Justice, Queensland. [cited July 15, 2001]. Available.

2. From records of the ship *Matoaka*: "Matoaka [Passenger List]: Online Microfilm of Shipping Lists." (2012). New South Wales Government State Records. [cited July 7, 2012]. Available from: http://www.records.nsw.gov.au.

3. Vynette Sage (2009). "Enniskillen Workhouse Register: Dec 1845 – July 1847." Ireland Genealogy Projects. Available from: http://www.igp-web.com/fermanagh/Donated.htm. [cited December 12, 2012].

4. "Telegraph [Passenger List]: Online Microfilm of Shipping Lists." (2012). New South Wales Government State Records. [cited December 28, 2012]. Available from: http://www.records.nsw.gov.au.

5. Queensland Registry of Births Deaths & Marriages. (2015). "Birth Registration: Quinn, Joseph James (Per Quinn, Patrick - Catherine Mcafie)" "Department of Police & Justice, Queensland. [cited July 15, 2001]. Available.

6. "Australia Birth Index, 1788-1922: Patrick F. Quin." (2010). Ancestry.com. [cited July 1, 2012]. Available from: www.ancestry.com.

7. "Supreme Court, Brisbane. In the Insolvent Estate of the Moreton Bay Tramway Company," *Queensland Times, Ipswich Herald & General Advertiser* (Brisbane, , Queensland). February 17, 1863, 3.

8. "Municipal Council," *Queensland Times, Ipswich Herald & General Advertiser* (Brisbane). July 12, 1864, 3.

9. "Opening of the First Railway in Queensland (from Our Special Reporter)," *The Brisbane Courier*, August 1, 1865, 2-3.

10. Maree Murray, "Children's Work in Rural New South Wales in the 1870s," *Journal of the Royal Australian Historical Society*. 79 (3-4), 1993: 226-244.

11. "Distress in the Agricultural Districts," *The Sydney Morning Herald* (Sydney, New South Wales), March 9, 1864, 5.

12. The logs of 1872 passenger ships between the USA and Australia did not record the names of steerage passengers, but the year of the Quinns' arrival in the United States, 1872, is recorded in the 1900 United States census: Joseph J. Quinn (image no. 00620): "United States Census: City of St. Louis, Missouri - Division of St. Louis City." (1900). United States Census Office. [cited November 11, 2012]. Available from: www.familysearch.org.

13. "Patrick Quinn Is Dead," *Dubuque Telegraph-Herald* (Dubuque, Iowa), April 12, 1902: 3.

14. *Marble's Dubuque City Directory* (Dubuque, Iowa: Chas. A. Marble, 1881).

15. William Mott Steuart, *Special Report: Mines and Quarries* (Washington: Department of Commerce and Labor – Bureau of the Census, 1905), 450.

16. Joe Clark, *A History of Australian Baseball: Time and Game* (Lincoln, Nebraska: University of Nebraska Press, 2003), 12.

17. Dick Farrington, "Half a Century through Joe Quinn's Eyes: Union Star Recalls Birth of 'the Sporting News'", *The Sporting News* (St. Louis, Missouri). May 21, 1936: 9B.

18. Ibid.

19. Harold Seymour and Dorothy Seymour Mills, *Baseball: The Early Years* (New York: Oxford University Press. 1960), 102.

20. David Nemec, *The Great Encyclopedia of Nineteenth-Century Major League Baseball* (Tuscaloosa, Alabama: University of Alabama Press, 2006), 178.

21. Bill Borst, *Baseball through a Knothole: A St. Louis History* (St. Louis: Krank Press, 1980), 34.

22. Farrington, "Half a Century through Joe Quinn's Eyes"

23. "Notes and Comments," *The Sporting Life* (Philadelphia, Pennsylvania), April 22, 1885: 7.

24. Farrington, "Half a Century through Joe Quinn's Eyes"

25. "Washington Whispers," *The Sporting Life,* September 6, 1890: 13.

26. "Sporting: The Altoonas Again Defeated by Our Union Club," *The Republican* (St. Louis, Missouri), April 27, 1884: 3

27. Bill James, *The New Bill James Historical Baseball Abstract*. (New York: Simon & Schuster, 2010), 24-31.

28. "From the Mound City," *The Sporting Life,* March 24, 1886: 8.

29. "Joe Quinn," *Indianapolis Herald,* June 15, 1887: 3.

30. Rochelle Llewelyn Nicholls, *Joe Quinn among the Rowdies: The Life of Baseball's Honest Australian* (Jefferson, North Carolina: McFarland & Co., 2014), 61-75.

31. "Duluth's New Manager," *The Sporting Life,* August 31, 1887: 7.

32. "Sports, Limited," *Saint Paul Daily Globe* (St. Paul, Minnesota), February 8, 1888: 5.

33. Joseph M. O'Toole, *"My God, What a Life!"* (St. Louis: O'Toole, 1981), 13.

34. Seymour and Mills, *Baseball: The Early Years,* 332-333.

35. Robert G. Mayer, *Embalming: History, Theory, and Practice, Fifth Edition* (New York: McGraw-Hill Professional, 2011), 492.

36. Farrington, "Half a Century through Joe Quinn's Eyes."

37. "St. Louis Screed," *The Sporting Life,* October 27, 1886: 2.

38. "From St. Louis,". *The Sporting Life,* October 6, 1886: 4.

39. "A Talk with Joe Quinn," *The Sporting Life,* November 23, 1887: 3.

40. "Sporting Notes," *Boston Globe,* January 6, 1888: 6.

41. He had made his professional debut in 1872, the year Quinn arrived in America, with the Brooklyn Atlantics. Kathy Torres, "Jack Burdock," SABR Baseball Biography Project. Society for American Baseball Research. [cited May 5, 2013]. Available from: http://sabr.org/bioproj/person/834f6239.

42. "Hunting for Talent," *Saint Paul Daily Globe*, August 12, 1888: 6.

43. "The price of his release has not been made public, but it is well known that it was not less than $4,000. The Boston management is to be praised for its liberality and perseverance in bringing to a close this negotiation, which ranks with those that secured Clarkson and Kelly." From: "Boston's Latest: Joe Quinn, Their New Second Baseman, and His Record," *The Wichita Daily Eagle* (Wichita, Kansas), October 16, 1888, 7.

44. "Won by a Home-Run Hit," *New York Times,* August 30, 1888: 7.

45. "Baseball Stories by Joe Quinn; Outlook for the Cardinals in 1906," *St. Louis Republic* (St. Louis, Missouri), December 10, 1905: 6.

46. Peter M. Gordon, "King Kelly," SABR Baseball Biography Project. Society for American Baseball Research. [cited June 20, 2013]. Available from: http://sabr.org/bioproj/person/ffc40dac.

47. "Joe Quinn Gets a Bat," *Boston Globe,* September 13, 1889: 8.

48. "Joe Quinn in the Outfield," *The Sporting News,* April 12, 1888: 5.

49. Daniel M. Pearson, *Baseball in 1889: Players vs. Owners* (Bowling Green, Ohio: Bowling Green State University Popular Press, 1993).

50. Dean A. Sullivan, *Early Innings: A Documentary History of Baseball, 1825-1908*. (Ann Arbor, Michigan.: The University of Michigan Press, 1995), 197.

51. "The Great Scheme: The Plans of the Brotherhood Given in Detail," *The Sporting News,* September 28, 1889: 3.

52. David Stevens, *Baseball's Radical for All Seasons: A Biography of John Montgomery Ward* (Lanham, Maryland: Scarecrow Press, 1998), 91.

53. Alfred H. Spink, *The National Game,* (Carbondale, Illinois: Southern Illinois University Press, 2000 – reprint), 28-29.

54. "News, Notes and Comment," *The Sporting Life,* December 11, 1890: 5.

55. "Joe Quinn, the Champion Second Baseman," *Boston Globe,* October 11, 1890: 7.

56. J. Thomas Hetrick, *Chris Von Der Ahe and the St. Louis*

57. "J. Quinn," *The Sporting News,* February 11, 1893: 1.

58. St. Louis City Directory 1893-1894: *"United States City Directories, 1882-1901. Saint Louis, Mo. [Microform]."* (1990). Research Publications: Woodbridge, Connecticut.

59. "St. Louis Siftings – the Dedication of a New Park a Social Event," *The Sporting Life,* May 6, 1893: 3.

60. "The Browns in a Rather Crippled Condition," *The Sporting Life.* July 13, 1995: 10.

61. "Obituary: Joe Quinn," *The Sporting News,* November 21, 1940: 8.

62. The *Sporting Life* reported, "Capt. Joe Quinn has sold his livery stable business. Joe has a nice competence, and is of that steady, thrifty character that gives him the reputation of being one of the really substantial members of the profession": "St. Louis Siftings - Rumors as to the Make-up of the '94 Team," *The Sporting Life,* October 21, 1894: 5.

63. Farrington, "Half a Century through Joe Quinn's Eyes."

64. "St. Louis Siftings – Ready for the Great Fight of 1894," *The Sporting Life,* April 21, 1894: 6.

65. "Games Played July 4," *The Sporting Life,* July 14, 1894: 3.

66. "St. Louis Siftings," *The Sporting Life,* August 4, 1894: 4.

67. The *Dead March* is part of a three-act oratorio, "Saul," composed by George Frederic Handel in 1738. See also: "Baseball: Personal," *The Sporting Life,* June 8, 1895: 4.

68. "League-Association," *The Sporting Life,* July 6, 1895: 3.

69. "Obituary: Joe Quinn."

70. "St. Louis Sayings," *The Sporting Life,* July 27, 1895: 10.

71. "The Browns in a State of Demoralization," *The Sporting Life,* August 10, 1895, 11.

72. J. Thomas Hetrick, *Misfits! The Cleveland Spiders in 1899: A Day-by-Day Narrative of Baseball Futility.* (Jefferson, North Carolina: McFarland & Co., 1991).

73. "Joe Quinn Released: Der Cherman Pand Must Be Playing Madhouse Airs!," *New York World,* July 1, 1896: 3.

74. The .698 win-loss percentage of the 1896 Orioles bettered their 1894 effort by 0.003; the team won the National League pennant in both years, in addition to their 1895 triumph. The franchise was born in 1882 and spent its first nine seasons in the American Association before transferring to the National League. In 1899, the team franchise and that of the Brooklyn Superbas were co-owned by Baltimore owner Harry Van der Horst and Ned Hanlon – most of the star Baltimore players were shipped to Brooklyn and the denuded Orioles finished only fourth. They were one of four teams dropped by the National League as it downsized to eight teams for the 1900 season. Mark L. Armour and Daniel R. Levitt, *Paths to Glory: How Great Baseball Teams Got That Way.* (Washington, DC: Brassey's, 2004), 12-17.

75. W.J. Monaghan, "One of Baseball's Great," *St. Louis Globe-Democrat,* November 26, 1933: 6,14.

76. Clark, *A History of Australian Baseball,* 35.

77. Twister, "The Australian Base-Ballers," *The Argus* (Melbourne, Victoria), July 23, 1897: 5.

78. "The Farce Has Begun," *Cleveland Plain Dealer,* April 16, 1899: 1.

79. "Gossip of the Diamond," *Evening Times* (Washington, DC), August 12, 1899: 6.

80. "Cleveland Chatter – Cross' Men Broke Even with the Eastern Clubs," *The Sporting Life,* June 3, 1899: 4.

81. "Gossip of the Diamond," *The Times* (Washington, DC), July 19, 1899: 6.

82. "A Revival of Interest in the Forest City," *The Sporting Life,* July 8, 1899: 5.

83. "Games Played July 17," *The Sporting Life,* July 22, 1899: 3.

84. Henry Chadwick, *Spalding Official Base Ball Guide for 1899* (New York: American Sports Publishing Company, 1900), 145.

85. "St. Louis Sad over the Persistent Bad Luck of the Cardinals," *The Sporting Life,* June 16, 1900: 5; "The Passing of Quinn," *The Sporting Life,* September 29, 1900: 7.

86. "Notes About the Big and Little Ball Tossers," *St. Paul Globe,* April 7, 1902: 5.

87. Dennis Pajot, *Baseball's Heartland War, 1902-1903: The Western League and American Association Vie for Turf, Players and Profits* (Jefferson, North Carolina: McFarland & Co., 2011), 199.

88. "United States Census: City of St. Louis, Missouri - Division of St. Louis City." (1920). United States Census Office. [cited November 12, 2012]. Available from: www.familysearch.org.

89. Farrington, "Half a Century through Joe Quinn's Eyes."

90. John R. Quinn: "Missouri Death Certificates, 1910-1962." (2013). Missouri Digital Heritage. [cited April 28, 2013]. Available from: http://www.sos.mo.gov/archives/resources/deathcertificates/advanced.asp.

91. "Section and Lot Report for Calvary Cemetery," Catholic Cemeteries of the Archdiocese of St. Louis, 1988. [cited May 17, 2000]. Available from: http://archstl.org/cemeteries/content/view/91/233/.

92. Tom Hesemann, *"Re: Joe Quinn - Australian Born Major League Ball Player,"* E-mail to Rochelle Nicholls. April 20, 2000.

93. Mary Ellen Quinn: "Missouri Death Certificates, 1910-1962." (2013). Missour Digital Heritage. [cited April 28, 2013]. Available from: http://www.sos.mo.gov/archives/resources/deathcertificates/advanced.asp. and "Death Notice - Mary E. Quinn (Nee Mcgrath).". *St. Louis Globe-Democrat.* December 14, 1937: 5C.

94. "Missouri Death Certificates, 1910-1962." (2013). Missouri Digital Heritage. [cited April 28, 2013]. Available from: http://www.sos.mo.gov/archives/resources/deathcertificates/advanced.asp.

95. "Obituary: Joe Quinn."

96. *2012/13 Baseball Australia Annual Report* (Gold Coast, Australia: Baseball Australia, 2013), 59.

JACK RYAN

BY MATT CLEVER

Jack Ryan.
(Library of Congress)

Of all the factors that influenced the development of baseball in its infancy, perhaps the most overlooked is the Great Irish Potato Famine. The famine compelled hundreds of thousands of Irish to immigrate to the United States in the middle of the nineteenth century, including the parents of future Hall of Famers John McGraw, Mike "King" Kelly, Joe Kelley, and Roger Bresnahan. The Ryan family came from Counties Kilkenny, Kildare, and Tipperary in "the Motherland," first to St. John's, Canada, and then to Haverhill, Massachusetts. It was there that John Bernard Ryan was born on November 12, 1868.

Jack Ryan began playing ball "at an early age" and made his professional debut at 18 with Belfast, helping the team finish first in the Maine State League in 1887. In 1888 Ryan was the everyday catcher for the Dovers of the New Hampshire/Massachusetts League, and won another championship. For the 1889 season he was picked up by Auburn, which proved to be the best club in the New York State League that year. So in his first three seasons, Ryan was a part of three championship teams, although he wasn't around to see Auburn win the title. Late in that season he was picked up by the Louisville Colonels of the American Association, the worst team in the major leagues, who were on their way to an abysmal 27-111 record. But the following year, sure enough, the Colonels won the 1890 pennant. Their seven-game Championship Series against the NL champion Brooklyn Bridegrooms resulted in a deadlock – three wins apiece and one tie that was never completed. Ryan stayed with Louisville through 1891, during which "his accurate throwing arm was his chief point of excellence."[1] But perhaps because he had batted just .215 over his first 189 big-league games, Ryan was sold back down to Providence of the Eastern League for the 1892 season, and of course they became the league champion.

After Ryan hit .329 for Springfield in 1893, a tragic accident paved the way for Ryan to return to the majors. Boston Beaneaters catcher Charles Bennett slipped under a train that offseason and lost both of his legs. Backing up Charlie Ganzel, the 25-year-old Ryan played in 53 official games for Frank Selee's Beaneaters in 1894 and batted .269. "He had the confidence of his pitchers," wrote the *New York Clipper,* "and was a hard working, faithful player."[2] Selee brought Ryan back again in 1895 as Ganzel's backup, and gave him a chance to win the starting job in '96, but Ryan began the year in a 3-for-32 slump and soon found himself with the Syracuse Stars of the Eastern League. It was as a member of the Stars that Ryan made make his greatest contribution to the Beaneaters.

The Syracuse pitching staff included an inexperienced and unremarkable right-hander named Vic Willis. Ryan worked closely with Willis, and even built a freestanding wooden target to help the young pitcher develop his control.[3] After two years under Ryan's tutelage, Willis was one of the most dominant pitchers in the Eastern League (and helped Ryan win another championship). Primarily due to Ryan's repeated recommendations, the Beaneaters purchased Willis for the 1898 campaign, and so began his Hall of Fame career.

Ryan also caught the attention of a big-league club himself that offseason – the Bridegrooms, who drafted him out of the Eastern League. But Ryan once again found major-league pitchers much tougher than the bush leaguers, finished with a woeful .189 batting average, and was back in the minors in 1899 playing for the Detroit Tigers in Ban Johnson's Western League. The league itself was renamed the American League in 1900 but remained a minor league for one more season, during which Ryan filled a tremendous hole for the Tigers by playing 91 games at second base.

Ryan re-established himself in the majors with the St. Louis Cardinals from 1901 to 1903. But he batted only .203 in 226 games, and in 1904 was back in the minors with the Kansas City Blues of the American Association. He had a solid season for the Blues, and another for Columbus in 1905, but at age 37 drew little interest from the big-league clubs. Always one to take the initiative, Ryan composed a letter in February of 1906 to August Herrmann, owner/president of the Cincinnati Reds and one of the most powerful men in Organized Baseball, to inquire, "How is your club for catchers? I am trying to get some club to make a trade for me, and I wish to get with a club that comes east, as I am a man with three children and in playing with an American Association club I don't see them for six months. … Of course I have the name of an old-timer but I can assure you I will be in the game a great many more years, as I have always taken the best of care of myself and have never known the taste of any kind of liquor."[4]

Herrmann was not interested, however, and Ryan had no choice but to return to Columbus for the 1906 season, without his family. At least he was able to find employment back in the Eastern League for 1907, playing 2½ years for Buffalo before the Bisons sold him to the Jersey City Skeeters on July 4, 1909.[5] Jack Ryan was 40 years old that summer, and immediately upon acquiring him the Skeeters named him their manager, replacing 29-year-old first baseman Red Calhoun. Though he would continue as a part-time catcher through 1910, this transaction represented the beginning of Jack Ryan's second career in baseball – as a manager.

In January of 1911, Skeeters owner Bob Davis died, leaving the franchise in a state of uncertainty. Local lawyer James Lillis quickly began assembling a syndicate to purchase the ballclub and keep it in Jersey City. Lillis assured fans that he would be willing to spend money liberally to put a winning team on the field.[6] To prove it, he offered Ryan a three-year contract and full charge of the baseball operations, essentially making him both manager and general manager of the Skeeters.

Once again Ryan penned a letter to August Herrmann in Cincinnati, offering him a chance to join Lillis's group. Once again he failed to convince Herrmann, but with a dialogue now opened between the two men, they decided to make a trade. Ryan packaged his starting shortstop from 1910, promising 21-year-old Jimmy Esmond, to Cincinnati in exchange for light-hitting infielder Tommy McMillan. An injury to McMillan caused Ryan to regret the deal almost immediately, and on March 11 he penned another letter to Herrmann in Cincinnati to complain that "I am getting roasted for the way the deal for McMillan turned. … Now if there is any way to let me have Downey[,] see that I get him for that will be the only way I can square myself here."[7] Of course Herrmann wasn't about to simply give away the Reds' starting shortstop, so the issue dragged on, unresolved, into the summer. On June 28 Ryan wrote again, "As we have had to go to a big expense to get a short stop to take the place of McMillan I think that there is a little due to me. … Now I need a pitcher and if you are not going to use Jack Doscher is there any way you can let me have him? … I was not treated right in the McMillan matter and if you can do this for me I will deem it a great favor."[8] Even though Herrmann relented and sent his seldom-used left-hander Doscher to Jersey City as requested, the episode is indicative of the frustrations Ryan was feeling as the 1911 season dragged on.

In spite of his preseason promises, Lillis was either unwilling or unable to provide enough cash to keep the Skeeters competitive. During a home game at West Side Park one hot July afternoon, umpire Jack Doyle made a close call on a play at the plate, and ruled in favor of the visitors. An argument ensued, during which one of the Skeeters deliberately spiked Doyle, opening up a bloody gash on the top of his foot. No one in attendance was entirely sure which Skeeter had done it. Even Doyle was uncertain, amid all the chaos. League President Ed Barrow levied a $25 fine on Skeeters catcher Tony Tonneman, but Lillis was insistent that his manager had actually been the assailant. "I have a dozen witnesses, including a prosecuting attorney, who saw Ryan commit this unwarranted assault," Lillis claimed. "I paid Tonneman's fine because I knew he was innocent. I have an affidavit from Tonneman to the effect that Ryan told him to keep his mouth shut."[9] Whether Lillis really had such evidence, or whether he was just looking for a reason to get rid of Ryan, remains unclear. In either case, Lillis fired Ryan at the conclusion of the season, more than a month after the Doyle incident, and with two years remaining on his contract at $3,000 per year. Ryan announced that he would carry his case through the various baseball courts to the National Commission if necessary, and if that failed he would sue the club for damages and breach of contract. The dispute made headlines nationwide that winter, until the parties eventually settled in December for $3,500. "I have done what I could to drive Ryan out of the Eastern League," said Lillis.[10]

Just when he thought he had finally attained some semblance of stability for his family, Ryan was suddenly without a job for 1912. Still bitter about the Jersey City situation, he dreamed of a job from which he couldn't be fired. On February 24, 1912, *Sporting Life* reported that "since his exoneration of all charges at the last meeting of the league he has had several offers to take charge of minor league teams. He is endeavoring to secure a team of his own and may blossom out as a magnate before long."[11]

Instead Ryan accepted an invitation from Washington Senators manager Clark Griffith to return to the big leagues as a coach. He spent two years with the Senators, a competitive and colorful squad featuring baseball clowns Germany Schaefer and Nick Altrock, as well as legendary hurler Walter Johnson. The highlight of his tenure occurred in the final game of each season, when Griffith allowed his coaches to play a few innings. On October 4, 1913, at Griffith Stadium, Griffith himself took the mound to pitch the eighth inning, with Ryan behind the plate in a farce of a game in which the umpires allowed each team four outs in one inning.[12] Though no one took it seriously, the game was nonetheless official. Thus Ryan became the second player in major-league history (as of 2017 he's still one of only 29) to appear in a game in four different decades, and along with Griffith etched his name into the record books as part of baseball's oldest pitcher-catcher battery (with a combined age of 88 years).

A few months later, Ryan accepted the coaching job at the University of Virginia, one of the premier collegiate baseball programs in the nation, and held that post through 1916, then again in 1922. Through his friendship with Griffith, Ryan was able to schedule one or two exhibition games each spring against the Senators. After the collegiate season ended, Ryan managed to land gigs as an umpire in both the Central League (Class B) and Western League (Class A), beginning in 1916.

In the summer of 1922 Ryan got back into the dugout as manager of the Crisfield Crabbers in the Class-D Eastern Shore League in Maryland. In February 1923, incoming Red Sox manager Frank Chance hired Ryan as his pitching coach.[13] Ryan spent five years with the Red Sox before finishing his career in the Class-B New England League, first as the skipper of his hometown Haverhill Hillies in 1928 and then, finally, with the New Bedford Millmen in 1929. "Everyone in the league held him in tremendous respect," recalled former first baseman Jack Burns.[14]

After hanging up his spikes for good, Ryan continued umpiring amateur and semipro games in the Boston area. He also managed a bowling alley in the Jamaica Plain section of Boston until he had to be hospitalized with tuberculosis at age 83. He spent the last nine months of his life in the Boston Sanatorium until his death on August 21, 1952. He was survived by his wife, Marla, his daughter, Rita, and also by his cousin's grandson, Mike Ryan, who enjoyed a long career in major-league baseball as a catcher and coach for the Red Sox and Phillies from 1964 to 1995. But Mike said he had no memory of ever meeting Jack.[15]

Jack Ryan spent more than 40 years in the world of professional baseball, in various capacities. He debuted when catching equipment was primitive, when the pitcher stood just 50 feet from home plate, and before fouls were counted as strikes, yet he was still in uniform to see Babe Ruth swat home runs in Yankee Stadium. He is buried in St. James Cemetery in Haverhill.

SOURCES

In addition to the sources cited in the Notes, the author relied primarily on clippings from Ryan's player file at the National Baseball Hall of Fame Library in Cooperstown, New York.

NOTES

1 Unknown newspaper article dated November 11, 1890, in Ryan's player file at the Hall of Fame.

2 *New York Clipper*, March 12, 1898: 27.

3 David L. Fleitz, *Ghosts in the Gallery at Cooperstown* (Jefferson, North Carolina: McFarland, 2004), 210-211.

4 Jack Ryan, letter to August Herrmann, February 20, 1906, from Ryan's Hall of Fame player file.

5 Unidentified newspaper clipping in Ryan's player file at the Hall of Fame.

6 *Sporting Life*, February 18, 1911: 9.

7 Jack Ryan, letter to August Herrmann, March 11, 1911.

8 Jack Ryan, letter to August Herrmann, June 28, 1911.

9 *Rochester Democrat and Chronicle*, December 12, 1911: 21.

10 Ibid.

11 *Sporting Life*, February 24, 1912: 3.

12 Bruce Nash and Allan Zullo. *Baseball Hall of Shame* (New York: Simon & Schuster, 1989), 101.

13 James C. O'Leary, "Frazee Trades Russell and Reel to Senators for Catcher, Outfielder and All Around Player," *Boston Globe*, February 11, 1923: 14. See also "Claim Jack Ryan Will Act as Red Sox Battery Coach," *Boston Herald*, February 11, 1923: 19.

14 Roger Birtwell, "Hub's Ryan Extends Proud Mitt Legacy," *The Sporting News*, February 27, 1965: 9.

15 Ibid.

JAMES JOSEPH "GENERAL" STAFFORD

BY RICHARD "DIXIE" TOURANGEAU

Despite not having the longest of careers and being only slightly above average in talent, James Joseph "General" Stafford made more of his baseball-playing mileage than almost any other player who played mostly in the nineteenth century. He loved being on the field and kept at it no matter the number of times he was traded, injured, or released, or how many of his teams folded. The ballfields on which he performed spanned the entire nation. Though he was never close to being a star, his short-duration Beaneaters teammate Fred Tenney wrote of him in the *New York Times* in March 1911. Tenney's topic was those men he thought were marvelous utility players and he counted Stafford in his top handful.[1]

Stafford was born on January 30, 1868, in Thompson, Connecticut, just across the state line from the Central Massachusetts baseball hotbeds of Webster and Dudley. Town directories and the 1870 and 1880 censuses indicate that the Stafford family did not live very long in Thompson, if at all. Thompson and Dudley are adjacent rural communities of northeastern Connecticut and south-central Massachusetts, while Webster was the industrial metropolis, 15 miles south of Worcester. With shoe factories and four textile mills, it drew young men who craved employment. By the 1870s Samuel Slater's vast textile-mill complex and those of his competitors were running full blast thanks to the available water power of the French River flowing between Webster and Dudley. The 1850s Massachusetts game of "base ball" was swept away by the New York-rule style after the Civil War. As the 1870s played out, Webster's ballclubs became famous in the state as its talent pipeline was easy to follow: Individual mill department nines became entire-mill squads and finally they combined into

James Stafford.
(Courtesy of National Baseball Hall of Fame)

all-star teams playing for town honor and hefty wagers. It was in this environment that Stafford grew up.

Born to Irish immigrants Frank and Anne (Keegan) Stafford, James was the sixth of seven children. Of the four boys, the last born, John Henry Stafford, also played pro ball. Frank (born 1838) was a Dudley pioneer, coming to the United States in 1849 and marrying in 1859. He was a shoemaker and later worked in the woolen mills, normal jobs for any male resident. Webster's amateur teams of the early 1870s were exceptional. At least a half-dozen members reached the major-league level if only for a very short time. James and brother John followed them in the late 1880s, sometimes playing for shorthanded neighboring Connecticut towns. After throwing for Dudley's Nichols Academy and some local amateur teams, Jim caught on with his first pro club, Springfield (Massachusetts) of the Eastern League, in 1887. April 30 was his first game when the season opened at Ward Field in Hartford. He pitched and lost 13-8 but scored twice. On May 3 in Springfield, he lost to Hartford again, 14-9, but managed two hits (season .314) and scored again. Springfield was expelled from the six-team league on May 25 and Stafford (.298) joined Hartford and won his first game with them on May 28, 14-8. Hartford was a better club but by August 5 it also left the EL (36-24) because of turmoil. Combined, Stafford was 7-12. With a taste for the fast game, Stafford hooked up with Worcester of the New England League in 1888 and was 16-7 while batting .166. He returned to Worcester in 1889 (Atlantic Association) and helped the team win the pennant under Walter Burnham. Two of his teammates were Harry Lyons and future Hall of Famer Jesse Burkett. Stafford re-signed for 1890 (.260), still pitching (19-16, best fielding hurler) and playing outfield, whichever was needed. His brother John was 4-8 and .118 for Worcester. When the team (37-31) suddenly disbanded on July 29, he joined the last-place Buffalo Bisons of the talent-seeking Brotherhood (Players') League in late August. Stafford finished 3-9 and batted .143.

At 5-feet-8, 160 pounds, Stafford won his first outing at Brooklyn's Eastern Park, 10-9, thanks to Connie Mack's three hits and three runs. A righty batter and thrower, he then lost 8-6 in Philadelphia in 10 innings, as his defense bobbled a 6-1 lead. The *Philadelphia Inquirer* remarked, "Stafford has a deceptive drop-ball which was entirely too much for the home batsmen for the first seven innings."[2] His other wins were over Cleveland's Ed "Jersey" Bakley and New York Giant (PL) Hank O'Day, the future Hall of Fame umpire. Some of Stafford's Bison teammates besides Mack were Jack Rowe, Sam Wise, Bill "Dummy" Hoy, and James L. "Deacon" White, who was playing his farewell season.

Stafford's next adventure was with Lincoln, Nebraska (Western Association). The club disbanded August 20, after Stafford batted .280 and finished 7-3 in the box. In 1892 he trained west to Los Angeles to play for the Seraphs/Angels in the four-team, 172-game California League. The league had been the fiefdom of the Bay Area but by 1892 Stockton had been replaced by San Jose and Sacramento by Los Angeles. Stafford was signed in late February and the *Los Angeles Times* profiled him in March, while giving the new team's fans background info about the roster. His bat prowess and speed on the basepaths were both extolled, and the report claimed he "had great speed and good curves" as a pitcher.[3] Stafford was much admired for his pitching, fielding skills, and general demeanor. In his first four games in the box, he beat the other three squads, proving his worth from the outset. Los Angeles won the second half-season flag and then captured the December (4 through 16) best-of-11 postseason series with the San Jose Dukes (6-2-1). Batting second, shortstop Stafford (10-for-40, 2 runs, 5 RBIs, 13 errors) helped the Angels capture their first Pacific Coast championship. During the season he was 14-10 (1.47), while hitting .282 in 156 games.

In late February 1893 Stafford signed with the Augusta (Georgia) Electricians under George Stallings.[4] Augusta edged Charleston for the split-season first-half flag. By July 5 Stafford (.337), Les German, and Parke Wilson were sold for tidy sums, Stafford for $1,200. All went to the New York Giants. In his last Augusta games, on July 4, Stafford helped sweep Birmingham, 12-0 and 9-1, with two triples (4-for-11). The crowd gave him a rousing farewell. Without its stars, Augusta finished sixth at 51-39.

Quickly traveling north 500 miles, Stafford met with Giants player-manager John Montgomery Ward in Louisville at Eclipse Park on July 6. He was 3-for-5, and scored three runs in an 11-11 tie. With two outs in the ninth, he dropped a fly ball in right field, allowing the tying run. (Despite that beginning, he stayed with New York for four seasons, averaging .274.) The next day Louisville won again, 4-2. Stafford had another hit, made an error and threw home for a double play, cutting off another Colonels tally. Coincidentally it was the same afternoon that his brother John Henry Stafford was pitching his last four major-league innings (of only seven) for Cleveland in a 15-5 loss in Baltimore. In relief of George "Nig" Cuppy (aka Koppe), he allowed nine runs in four frames, six of them due to the bat of rookie Henry "Heinie" Reitz. John's first game was June 15 in Brooklyn, again relieving Cuppy. Walks, hits, and poor fielding allowed a 6-6 tie to become a 14-6 loss. In the game story the *Brooklyn Daily Eagle* sportswriter suggested that the poor performance was due to 1893's extra 10-foot pitching distance, which John Stafford was not used to while starring at Holy Cross College.[5]

On July 20 New York played in Boston after taking three of four games from them in New York. Jim Stafford went 3-for-19 in that series. Closer to his Dudley roots, he went 1-for-5 and scored but the Beaneaters clobbered Amos Rusie, 15-8. A combined 4-for-24 vs. Boston, he sat out the next two contests. After that Stafford suddenly found power, hitting five home runs before September, three on consecutive late August days. His first major-league clout came in an 11-10 Rusie victory. It was a first-inning, leadoff, inside-the-park roller off Pittsburgh native son Frank Killen (36 wins) and paved the way for the Exposition Park III slugfest. He hit another off Killen in New York on August 28 in a 3-2 loss. On August 29 he had three hits (home run) and scored thrice off Ted Breitenstein of the Browns in an 11-4 New York loss.

In the August 31 *New York Times*, a writer lamented Stafford's fielding lapses. "A muff of an easy fly ball by Stafford let in three runs. This man Stafford is a good hitter, a first-class baserunner, but is one of the poorest outfielders in the profession. He makes beautiful catches, does not shirk any balls, but his errors are charged against him on the most simple flies."[6]

In the February 17, 1894, issue of the *New York Clipper*, Stafford's portrait and biography revealed his playing history to the nation. It was a glowing list of some of his exceptional feats in every league in which he played – five hits in a Lincoln game, 18 defensive plays on 20 chances in a lengthy Los Angeles tilt, and a 330-foot throw to nail a runner at home while with Augusta.[7] However, because Giants regulars stayed healthy, Stafford played only 14 games (most between mid-May and mid-June) in 1894, batting just .217. Stafford was manager Ward's utilityman, playing mostly outfield but some infield whenever a mate was injured or playing poorly and needed a break. It was an important skill on teams with small rosters. Lack of playing time not only ruined his season but also any real involvement with the Giants finishing second to Baltimore and then beating the pennant winners in the postseason Temple Cup playoff. Stafford was a champion but had contributed very little.

Healthy in 1895, Stafford had his most productive NL season, hitting a solid .279 in 124 games while accomplishing career highs in hits (129), runs (79), RBIs (73), and steals (42). Since player-manager Ward retired in 1894, Stafford was the regular second baseman. That year he was struggling at about .210 in late May when a lame leg benched him for more than a week. Post-recovery, he hit above .300, including .406/21 runs/18 RBIs in August when he had two hit streaks of 13 of 14 games (one career high of 11 straight). Those two streaks were separated by an 0-for-14 drought in the cross-borough City of Churches, Brooklyn. Minus his .190 in 84 at-bats against the four best pitchers in 1895, Stafford hit .300. His fielding was more than adequate until mid-September, when 16 errors in 16 games got him moved to left field. The Giants crashed to ninth place (66-65) of 12 teams but Stafford had the distinction of scoring the winning run on September 27 against pennant-winner Baltimore, assuring his club of a winning campaign.

He was the fourth outfielder in 1896, hitting .287 in 59 games. His season was curtailed by one pitch from rookie Louisville Colonel no-control artist Charles "Chick" Fraser. Fraser broke Stafford's forearm on July 16. Fraser, who won the game 12-7 on three errors by Stafford's left-field replacement, led the league in walks and wild pitches, and placed second in hit batsmen. Stafford returned in September, getting 18 hits in as many games, ending the year going 3-for-5 against pennant-taker Baltimore, a 10-1 Jouett Meekin win. After seven games in 1897 the "General" was dealt to Louisville on May 13 for infielder Jim "Ducky" Holmes (.265). When rookie Honus Wagner arrived in Louisville in July, it was Stafford (.277/7 HRs) who was the regular shortstop (107 games), on occasion, ironically, behind the still-erratic Fraser. Stafford took some revenge on New York by hitting three home runs against them, two on Meekin tosses. On July 17 he hit one in each game as Louisville swept a doubleheader. He also had an RBI double and seven assists at shortstop for the near cellar-dwelling hosts.

After splitting near 50 games between second base and the outfield in 1898, Stafford (.298) was released by New York and signed by defending NL champ Boston. As the Giants had been in 1893, second-place Boston was in need of healthy players if they were going to repeat as pennant winners. Crafty Boston manager Frank Selee pounced on the opportunity to get Stafford to mend his injury-ridden roster. The move would put Stafford only 50 miles from his Dudley hometown.

Stafford played his first dozen of 37 games in right field, went 11-for-48, scored five runs, and the Beaneaters were 5-6-1. In total he hit a light .260 and fielded at .909 clip. He subbed for Chick Stahl and super batsman Billy Hamilton, who was not as good a fielder (.904). During the week-plus that Admiral George Dewey was taking over Manila and really ending the Spanish-American War, Boston won 11 straight games. Stafford had the game of his life on August 18 (the 10th victory) at the South End Grounds III. He was 4-for-4, scored three runs, stole a base, and had two RBIs. One hit was a home run off losing rookie reliever Walt Woods in a 10-0 thrashing of Chicago. Making the game even more one-sided, hosts Edward "Ted" Lewis and Charlie Hickman tossed a combined one-hitter. Stafford had three other four-hit games during his career. Boston went 23-4 in September to wilt the circuit and hoist another pennant, its fifth in eight years. Stafford was a champion again, and this time he played an important role.

Brooklyn fielded a fine club in 1899 as it had back in 1890, and this Superbas edition kept the defending champs at bay into August. While patrolling center field, Stafford had a great streak between mid-May and early June, hitting in 20 of 21 games (.364, 12 runs, 23 RBIs) as Boston was 17-4. In the mix was a four-hit game against Cincy lefty Bill Dammann (2-1).

Stafford's last two Beaneater round-trippers were the only three-run homers of his career; both came at the cozy South End Grounds. One helped defeat Emerson "Pink" Hawley, 8-2, on June 3, while the other was surrendered by Cleveland Spider Jim Hughey, the losingest pitcher (4-30) in the NL, on August 8, in an 18-8 romp. Stafford was subbing for shortstop Herman Long in the game and committed two errors. His final Boston at-bat was flying out as a pinch-hitter in the ninth inning on August 15 when Boston was shut out by Cincinnati's Brewery Jack Taylor, 1-0. On August 12, Stafford was notified (10-day release rule) and by August 22 Arthur Irwin's Washington Nationals had signed him to complete the season. His outfield defense had improved in Boston (.956), but for Washington he played all his 31 games in the infield and batted .246.

Stafford's 21st and last NL career blast was for the Nationals vs. Cincinnati on September 13. After the Nationals dropped a 14-4 game, second baseman Stafford's solo shot sealed a 6-3 win over rookie Emil Frisk of the Reds. His final NL appearances were in Boundary Field doubleheaders against visiting Baltimore and New York. He got a single and double off Harry Howell on October 9 and scored twice to help beat the Orioles 8-6 but was 0-for-2 in the shortened second game. New York's Charlie Gettig gave up Stafford's last hit, on October 12, while edging the Nationals 9-7. Ed Doheny collared Stafford (0-for-4) and most of the Nationals in game two, winning 5-4 in Stafford's final outing.[8]

General Stafford enjoyed the game too much to quit altogether, so in 1900 he joined up with the Providence Clamdiggers of the eight-team Eastern League, and stayed through 1901.

Under William Murray in 1900, the 'Diggers finished first, and Stafford at .269/5 HRs was the poorest "regular" hitter on the pennant club while playing third and the outfield. In 1901 he hit .265/5 HRs doing much the same. He missed only a half-dozen games in two seasons. Since Providence is less than 40 miles from Dudley, he was comfortably in reach of home cooking.

Stafford signed with Montreal's Royals in 1902, hit .259, and went back to Providence for his final pro season in 1903. He played third base, missed only one game, and hit .231 for the Grays, still the Clamdiggers to many league writers.[9] Stafford finished his pro career with a flourish. He got at least one hit in each of his last dozen games (.417, one 4-for-5 day vs. Rochester), and scored eight runs, aiding an 8-4 Clamdiggers finish. In his finale, on September 26 at Olympic Field in Buffalo (a neutral site), he played right field, and knocked in a run in a 4-3 win over Montreal. Finally, his 17-year baseball odyssey was over – except for one more exhibition game. The next afternoon, a Sunday, a few members of the Providence team who had not taken leave for their scattered homes squared off against the Riverpoints, a semipro group, at famed Rocky Point Park, 10 miles south of Providence. Stafford stayed to play third and center field and went hitless in the 6-3 defeat.

Finally making his Dudley home permanent, he eventually became the town-hall custodian, since the building was across the street from his house. In the latter 'Teens he was elected chairman of the Board of Assessors, a post he held until his death. Jim Stafford married schoolteacher Helen Jacobs in late 1920. They had one daughter, Harriet, in 1921. The General still played ball on occasion for town teams until about 1910. His obituary said he never spoke of his baseball exploits unless asked and then would entertain for hours. At the end of his NL career, there were widespread rumors that he was getting deaf and that that might have shortened his playing days.

On March 14, 1911, teammate Fred Tenney looked back on Stafford's career in a *New York Times* story he wrote about utility players. Tenney, by then a longtime manager, explained that Stafford was one of the best of such players in the 1890s as he could fill in at several positions (though he never caught a game) and hit well enough to avoid being a lineup detriment.[10] That's why Selee signed him in 1898 when Boston needed role players who could perform. Tenney related one (unproven) story of captain Hugh Duffy sending the General in to bat for Chick Stahl, who had two strikes already. On the first pitch Stafford got a hit that won the game. "While not a brilliant player," Tenney wrote, "Stafford was dependable, especially in tight places."[11]

James Joseph "General" Stafford died at Worcester's Memorial Hospital after an operation, from which his condition had been considered critical for weeks. Whatever the undisclosed ailment he suddenly contracted, it claimed him for eternity on September 18, 1923. The funeral was held in St. Louis Church, which his father helped build in the 1870s. Stafford is buried in Calvary Cemetery in Dudley with several members of his family. His last public appearance was at Braves Field in Boston on September 11, 1922, in a benefit for Children's Hospital. An all-star game was held between dozens of former star players from the nineteenth and early twentieth centuries. Stafford and Bob Emslie were the umpires.

As for his nickname, General, its true source is cloudy. Nineteenth-century player guru and peerless historian Dave Nemec, in his *Major League Baseball Profiles, 1871-1900*, (Volume 1, 2011), wrote, "One theory was that he was named after Confederate General Leroy Augustus Stafford, killed at the Wilderness."[12] But shedding some brighter light on this mystery was the *Louisville Courier-Journal* of July 17, 1896, while explaining his broken forearm. In the middle of the game story was the descriptive, yet out-of-the-blue side comment, "… the Cuban sympathizer …" referring to Stafford.[13] The Cuban War of Independence was into its second year and Stafford had taken a keen interest. If he talked or debated the war often enough with his less enthralled teammates, they likely gave him the nickname to poke fun at his obsession. By 1899 Boston sportswriters playfully demoted Stafford to "colonel." Nemec also points out that for more than 50 years most researchers knew nothing of James Joseph Stafford's existence. Someone finally filtered his NL stats away from Tar Heel-born Robert Lee Stafford, a 16-year minor-league first baseman of the 1890s, (.270), who was apparently named for a noted Confederate general. Dudley's General also paid his dues in the minors (757 games), but hit better in the major league (.274 to .269, 21 HRs to 19). He now has his proper place in baseball annals.

SOURCES

In addition to the sources cited in the Notes, the author also consulted Ancestry.com, Baseball-Reference.com, Retrosheet.org, Stafford's player file at the National Baseball Hall of Fame, *Encyclopedia of Minor League Baseball*, 2nd edition (Durham, North Carolina: Baseball America, 1997), and an array of publications including the *Atlanta Constitution, Boston Globe, Boston Herald, Boston Post, Buffalo News, Lincoln Journal Star, Los Angeles Herald, New York Herald Tribune, New York Sun, Providence News, Sporting Life, Webster Weekly Times*, and the *Worcester Telegram*.

NOTES

1. Fred Tenney, "Bobby Lowe Best Utility Player," *New York Times*, March 14, 1911: 9.

2. "Won in the Tenth," *Philadelphia Inquirer*, August 30, 1890: 3.

3. "Something About Stafford the Los Angeles Pitcher," *Los Angeles Times*, March 13, 1890: 8.

4. "Jottings from Augusta," *The Sporting News,* March 11, 1893: 4.

5. "A Fine Uphill Fight," *Brooklyn Daily Eagle,* June 16, 1893: 2.

6. "Home Runs Were Plentiful," *New York Times,* August 31, 1893: 3.

7. James J. Stafford, *New York Clipper,* February 17, 1894: 805.

8. By the weekend five other players he knew had their NL careers end. Old Augusta pal Parke Wilson, Jack Fifield, Dan McFarlan and Mike Roach, all of the Nats, and 1898 Boston mate Jack Stivetts were done.

9. Strangely the team did not play any home games after August 3, a 6-2 win over Montreal; then came 47 on the road. That was not the original April schedule, which had at least 12 games in Providence in September alone.

10. Tenney.

11. Ibid. Two other Beaneaters mentioned were Bobby Lowe (before settling in at the keystone sack in 1893) and Happy Jack Stivetts, a great hitting (.298/35 HRs) pitcher (203-132) who played 141 games in the outfield.

12. David Nemec, *Major League Baseball Profiles, 1871-1900*," Vol. 1 (Lincoln: University of Nebraska Press, 2011), 610.

13. "Hits and Errors," *Louisville Courier-Journal*, July 17, 1896: 6.

CHICK STAHL

BY DENNIS AUGER

Chick Stahl.
(Library of Congress)

Before committing suicide under mysterious circumstances in the spring of 1907, Chick Stahl forged a reputation as one of the best center fielders in the game over the course of a 10-year major-league career. A lifetime .305 batter, the left-handed Stahl could also hit with power, and often ranked among the league leaders in extra-base hits. Among his teammates, the popular Stahl "possessed a pleasing personality that endeared him to all that came in contact with him."[1] When the 34-year-old ballplayer killed himself on March 28, 1907, his Boston teammates were overcome with grief. "Stahl was a king among men," said catcher Lou Criger. "He was the squarest man I ever knew. He had only one fault – he was too generous. I never saw him go back on a friend or a deserving acquaintance. In fact, he was often bunkoed because he believed in the goodness of all mankind."[2]

Charles Sylvester Stahl was born on January 10, 1873, in Avilla, Indiana, the sixth child of Reuben and Barbara (Stadtmiller) Stahl, Catholics of German descent. During his early childhood, his father supported the growing Stahl clan as a peddler, but in 1885 the family moved to Fort Wayne, where Reuben found work as a carpenter. In an 1898 interview, Charles reported that he had 23 siblings. "We had just enough in our family to make a couple nines – eighteen boys and half a dozen girls."[3]

Young Charles attended Catholic school and developed his skills as a left-handed pitcher and outfielder on Fort Wayne's vacant lots and diamonds south of the railroads. After playing for Brunswick, a local amateur team, in 1889 the teenager pitched for the Pilsener club in the City League. Between 1889 and 1894, he also pitched for semiprofessional teams in Paducah, Kentucky; Decatur, Illinois; and Kalamazoo and Battle Creek, Michigan. He also worked in his father's carpentry business. His father wanted him "to tend store at Fort Wayne and give up baseball. But I took an inventory of the soft soap sale and the output of pickles to our customers, and I couldn't figure how I could turn out the revenue in the grocery business that came to me in baseball."[4]

In 1895, Stahl signed a professional contract with Roanoke of the Virginia League. At his own insistence, he became a full-time outfielder, and excelled at his new position, playing brilliantly in the field, posting a .311 batting average, and leading the league with 13 triples. His performance attracted the attention of the Buffalo team of the Eastern League, which drafted the young outfielder after the season. In 1896 Stahl continued to show improvement with his new team, finishing the year with a .340 average, 34 stolen bases, 52 extra-base hits, a league-leading 23 triples, and 130 runs scored. Based on Stahl's "splendid hitting and excellent fielding," Jimmy Collins, the star third baseman of the Boston Beaneaters, and Sam Wise, a former Beaneaters player, advised Beaneaters manager Frank Selee to draft him, and Selee did so.[5]

Selee planned to use Stahl in a utility role, but the 24-year old quickly became the club's starting right fielder. In 1897 he emerged "as the game's most outstanding frosh hitter."[6] Not only did he lead all rookies in 11 hitting categories, he also paced Boston with a .354 average, a mark that remains the franchise record for rookies. Stahl also topped the Beaneaters with a .499 slugging percentage, helping the Boston offense score more than 1,000 runs and capture the National League pennant. Another crown awaited Boston in 1898, and even though Stahl's average declined to .308, his fielding talents were highlighted in the sports pages. In one descriptive account, the *Washington Post* wrote "the soubrette fancier from Fort Wayne retrieved Tommy Leahy's fly in the eighth with the speed and celerity of a hound retrieving a jack rabbit."[7] The Beaneaters fell from first in 1899 but the Husky Hoosier (one of Stahl's nicknames) hit .351, produced career highs in hits (202), triples (19), home runs (7), total bases (284), walks (72), on-base percentage (.426), stolen bases (33), and runs scored (122). On May 31 he went 6-for-6 in a nine-inning game against Cleveland, "five of which [were] very long drives."[8]

Boston's fortunes tumbled in 1900 but Stahl still knocked in 82 runs, his second highest career total, and led National League outfielders with a .968 fielding percentage. In 1901 his teammate and best friend, Jimmy Collins, signed with the American League's Boston entry to become that squad's player-manager. Because of religious tension on the Beaneaters, the third baseman targeted talented Roman Catholic ball players to join the upstart club. Considered a devout Catholic as well as one of the National League's best outfielders, Chick fulfilled the criteria. Moving to center field, the intracity jumper became one of the Americans' main offensive threats while helping the squad to a second-place finish (.303 batting average, 105 runs scored, 72 RBIs). As for the character of 5-foot-10-inch, 160-pound athlete, it was demonstrated in a late August contest. After rookie umpire Joe Cantillon made a call that went against the home team, furious Boston fans assaulted him. Stahl and teammate Ted Lewis intervened, protecting Cantillon and escorting him off the field.[9]

Stahl coached Notre Dame's college baseball team from January to April of 1900 – leading them to a 15-2 record – he spent his offseasons primarily in Fort Wayne. On the evening of January 26, 1902, while he was walking with a friend in his hometown, Louise "Lulu" Ortmann, a 22-year-old stenographer, approached him. Described as "a very handsome girl," she reached for a revolver concealed in the folds of her dress, with the intent of killing him.[10] The local police superintendent, who had been tipped off that the infuriated woman was stalking Stahl, arrived just in time to disarm and arrest her. In accounting for her actions, Ortmann said she felt jilted by her "recreant lover."[11] "Mr. Stahl, on the other hand, had nothing to say" and dropped any charges.[12] This episode did not affect his 1902 season, as Stahl batted .323 with 92 runs scored and the Americans finished in third place.

In April 1903 Stahl injured his leg while sliding, and was limited to 77 games and a .274 average. Nevertheless, the Americans easily won the pennant. In the World Series against Pittsburgh, which Boston won in eight games, he was the only Boston player to hit .300, as he banged out 10 hits, including three triples, in 33 at-bats.

Stahl's health improved in 1904 and the outfielder returned to his old form with a .290 batting average, 27 doubles, and a league-leading 19 triples, as the Americans captured a second consecutive pennant. Stahl also showcased his glove during Cy Young's perfect game on May 5 against Philadelphia. After the game Young expressed his gratitude for Stahl's play on a sinking line drive off the bat of Ollie Pickering "that Chick caught around his knees after a long run from center."[13]

Along with many of his teammates, Stahl's play declined precipitously in 1905. He finished the year with a .258 batting average – by far the lowest of his career – and only 21 extra-base hits. The next season he improved to .286 with four home runs and 51 RBI, while leading American League outfielders in putouts and double plays. The Americans, however, won just 49 games, and Stahl became the acting manager in late August after the suspension of the increasingly disenchanted Jimmy Collins. One scribe wrote that Stahl was "the only man on the team who played his real game this season."[14] In what turned out to be his last major-league at-bat, he hit a home run off Tom Hughes of the New York Highlanders.

On November 14, 1906, Stahl married Julia Harmon at St. Francis de Sales Church in the Roxbury section of Boston. They had met at a church function and she was described as "a pretty little brunette" and accomplished musician.[15] Their honeymoon took them to Arkansas' Hot Springs and ended as guests of Jimmy Collins in Buffalo. The other significant event during this month was that Stahl, at the urging of owner John Taylor and with the approval of his closest friend Collins, accepted the manager's position for the coming season.

In 1907 the Chicks, as the team was nicknamed in deference to their manager (they wouldn't become the Red Sox until 1908), reported to Little Rock, Arkansas, for spring training. It soon became evident that Stahl's personality and the duties required of a manager were incompatible. On March 25, with the team in Louisville, Stahl abruptly resigned. Explaining his decision, he said, "This handling of a baseball team both on and off the field is not what it is cracked up to be. Releasing players grated on my nerves and they come so frequently at this time of the year that it made me sick at heart."[16] On March 27 the team arrived at West

Baden Springs, Indiana, where they were to play the next day. Having agreed to serve as acting manager until a replacement could be found, Stahl said in a telegram to his wife that night, "Cheer up little girl and be happy. I am all right now and able to play the game of my life."[17]

The next morning Stahl ate breakfast, checked the condition of the field, and returned to the hotel room to put on his uniform. Jimmy Collins, who shared the suite, saw Stahl go into the next room for a moment, then stumble back toward Collins and fall onto his bed. He had swallowed four ounces of carbolic acid, which had been prescribed for a sore on his foot. There are a number of variations, but Stahl's last words were, "I couldn't help it. I did it, Jim. It was killing me and I couldn't stand it, Jim."[18] In another version Stahl simply said cryptically, "It drove me to it."[19] Medical help arrived, but to no avail. Stahl suffered excruciating pain, dying in 15 minutes from poisoning. Since the death was ruled a suicide, a Catholic burial was denied. On March 31 the funeral rite, conducted by the Benevolent Order of Elks and the Fraternal Order of Eagles, took place at Stahl's mother's residence. The emotional state of the two women he had loved most "were pathetic in the extreme," according to one newspaper account.[20] "The young bride of a few months was almost prostrated and the grief of the aged mother of the deceased was pitiful to behold."[21] Five former teammates – Criger, Buck Freeman, Bill Dinneen, Freddy Parent, and Jake Stahl (no relation) – attended, but Collins was too distraught to be present. Stahl's body was conveyed to Lindenwood Cemetery "in one of the largest funeral corteges ever seen in Fort Wayne."[22] Thousands marched to the burial place, where Congressman James Robinson gave the eulogy.

Why did Stahl commit suicide? Initially, baseball-related stress was given as the reason, but soon other theories began to surface. Frederick P. O'Connell, the baseball editor of the *Boston Post*, contended that a nonbaseball factor had led to his suicide. He wrote, "a great trouble was generally admitted" which was known to many.[23] The truth was never known, as O'Connell developed pneumonia while in West Baden covering Stahl's funeral, and died there on April 21. Glenn Stout, a baseball historian who has written about the Red Sox, wrote that the "trouble" referred to a brief affair that Stahl had with a woman in Chicago in 1906 and its aftermath.[24] In March 1907 the woman, claiming she was carrying Stahl's child, threatened to blackmail him unless he married her. Unable to deal with the pressure and scandal, he ended his life. Stout cited another historian, Harold Seymour, who wrote, "There is reason to believe that a woman who asserted she was his pregnant wife hounded Chick Stahl into committing suicide."[25] Seymour provided no documentation. Stout also cited David Voigt, another baseball historian, who accepted the theory, referring to a 1959 quote from Al Stump, similar in content and with no identifiable source. In short, all of the historians provided an inconclusive theory based on questionable allegations.

The most significant contribution in examining Stahl's suicide came from baseball researcher Dick Thompson, who uncovered a crucial story in the *Fort Wayne Journal-Gazette* of March 30, 1907. In an article that ran with the headlines "MEDITATED SELF-SLAYING, CHICK STAHL HAD OFTEN TALKED ABOUT SUICIDE," and "BASE BALL PLAYER HAD ENTERTAINED DANGEROUS IDEAS ABOUT SELF-DESTRUCTION," the paper wrote that Stahl had suffered from depression and suicidal ideation since 1889. The paper quoted close friends "who were not surprised at his suicide."[26] Statements ranging from "Chick talked about killing himself several times" to "sometimes the slightest disappointment would sink him into almost a stupor of depression" appear to confirm that he suffered from clinical depression.[27]

This glimpse into Stahl's psyche helps us to understand his behavior. If his reputation as a womanizer was true, clinically, it is not unusual for a depressed person to self-medicate emotional pain through unbridled sexual activity. Also, since baseball was an integral dimension to Stahl's identity, his perceived failing as a manager could have intensified his depression. There is yet another element to the story. On March 30, 1907, a syndicated newspaper article related that David Murphy, an engineer in Fort Wayne, had committed suicide by swallowing carbolic acid. Stahl was described as "an intimate friend of Murphy," and the latter left a note that read, "Bury me beside Chick."[28] From a psychological perspective, this language and behavior strongly indicates that the relationship was not merely a platonic one. Was Murphy delusional, resulting in an unreciprocated sexual obsession? Or, if it was mutual, was this Stahl's "dark secret"?

Chick Stahl a strong Catholic faith. As one newspaper report after his death said, "Stahl never forgot his religious duties during the baseball season. Only a week ago last Sunday, Stahl did his Easter duty in Little Rock. He never missed mass if it was possible for him to attend."[29] To understand his behavior, it is important to realize that Jansenism, typically known for its ultra-rigid moral outlook and emphasis upon human nature as being corrupt, heavily influenced the nature of the Catholic Church during Stahl's lifetime. As a result, Stahl would have been exposed to teachings about God's love and forgiveness, countered by sermons regarding sins of the flesh and the fires of hell, with suicide being the ultimate sin. The unresolved conflict between his beliefs and behavior could have increased his inner turmoil and consequently his chronic depression. The healthy and unhealthy components of his persona were expressed during the last week of his earthly life, when he both fulfilled his Easter duty and committed suicide. As Thompson wrote, "I think O'Connell [the *Boston Post* writer] did know the truth, but the truth was not that Stahl was responding to a blackmail threat. It was that he was responding to his own haunted emotions."[30]

Speaking to his teammates after the ballplayer's death, Cy Young – named temporary manager in Stahl's absence – said, "It is mighty tough, boys. I never dreamed such a thing could happen. In fact, none of us could imagine Stahl doing away with himself. Players may come and go, but there are few Chick Stahls."[31]

An updated version of this biography appeared in *New Century, New Team: The 1901 Boston Americans*, edited by Bill Nowlin (SABR, 2013). The biography originally appeared in *Deadball Stars of the American League* (Potomac Books, 2006), edited by David Jones.

SOURCES

In addition to the sources cited in the Notes, the author also consulted Heritage Quest, various newspapers such as the *Boston Globe, Boston Post, Chicago Tribune, Los Angeles Times,* and *New York Times,* and the following publications:

Carroll, Charles. *Drugs in Modern Society* (Dubuque, Iowa: William C. Brown. 1989).

Carter, Craig ed. *The Sporting News Complete Baseball Record Book* (St. Louis: Sporting News, 2001).

Christensen, Chris. "Chick Stahl: A Baseball Suicide," *Elysian Fields*, vol. 20, n. 2, 20-32, 2003.

DeValeria, Dennis, and Jeanne DeValeria. *Honus Wagner* (Pittsburgh: University of Pittsburgh Press, 1998).

Gentile, Derek. *Baseball's Best 1000* (New York: Black Dog & Leventhal Publishers, 2004).

James, Bill. *All-Time Major League Handbook*. 2nd ed. (Morton Grove, Illinois: STATS, Inc., 2002).

Kinney, Jean, and Gwen Leaton. *Understanding Alcohol* (New York: Mosby, 1982).

Masur, Louis. *Autumn Glory: Baseball's First World Series* (New York: Hill & Wang, 2003).

Neft, David, Richard Cohen, and Michael Neft, editors. *The Sports Encyclopedia: Baseball 1999* (New York: Griffin, 1999.

Nemec, David, and David Zeman. *The Baseball Rookies Encyclopedia* (Washington: Potomac Books, 2004).

Palmer, Pete, and Gary Gillette. *The Baseball Encyclopedia* (New York: Barnes & Noble, 2004).

Reichler, Joseph. *The Baseball Encyclopedia*. 6th ed. (New York: Macmillan, 1985).

Reichler, Joseph. *The Great All-Time Baseball Record Book* (New York: Macmillan, 1981).

Seymour, Harold. *Baseball – The Golden Age* (New York: Oxford University Press, 1989).

Stout, Glenn, ed. *Impossible Dreams* (Boston: Houghton Mifflin, 2003).

Thompson, Dick. "Stahl's Suicide," in *Baseball Research Journal*, n. 28 (1999), 7.

Thorn, John, Pete Palmer, and Michael Gershman. *Total Baseball*. 6th ed. (New York: Total Sports, 1999).

Wesson, Donald. *Detoxification from Alcohol and Other Drugs* (Rockville, Maryland: U.S. Department of Health and Human Services, 1998).

Zoss, Joel, and John Bowman. *Diamonds in the Rough* (Lincoln: Bison Books, 2004).

NOTES

1. Unidentified clipping in Stahl's HOF file, April 6, 1907.

2. Bill James, *The New Bill James Historical Baseball Abstract* (New York: Free Press, 2001), 755. A slight variation of Criger's quote appears in the Fort Wayne *Journal Gazette,* March 31, 1907.

3. *Washington Post,* October 14, 1898.

4. Ibid.

5. Unidentified clipping in Stahl's player file at the National Baseball Hall of Fame, December 22, 1906.

6. Source of quote not located. *Sporting Life* refers to Stahl as "the hard hitting young outfielder of the Boston Club," July 3, 1897. In the August 14th, 1897 issue of the *Sporting Life* it is written that "the wonderful batting of Stahl, his strong stick work sending him to the top of the ladder, no small feat for a young man in his first year in the League." His .354 batting average remains the rookie record for this franchise (Boston, Milwaukee and Atlanta).

7. *Washington Post,* May 3, 1898.

8. Stahl's 6 hits were singles; source of quote not located. His greatest day in professional baseball occurred on August 12, 1895. Playing for Roanoke in the Virginia State League he went 7 for 7 including 2 triples and 2 home runs as recorded in *Sporting Life* August 17, 1895.

9. BaseballLibrary.com.

10. *Journal Gazette* (Fort Wayne, Indiana), January 27, 1902.

11. Ibid.

12. *Sporting Life,* February 8, 1902.

13. Source of quote not located. In Reed Browning's *Cy Young: A Baseball Life* (Amherst University of Massachusetts Press, 2000), 143, it is written that "Chick Stahl raced to grab a Texas Leaguer to center" as one of the key catches in the game.

14. Glenn Stout and Richard Johnson, *Red Sox Century* (Boston: Houghton Mifflin, 2000), 64.

15. *Sporting Life,* November 24, 1906; *Washington Post,* October 15, 1906.

16. *Journal Gazette,* March 29, 1907.

17. Ibid., March 30, 1907.

18. Dick Thompson, "In Name Only," *The National Pastime* 20, (2000): 55.

19. *Journal Gazette,* March 29, 1907.

20. Ibid., April 1, 1907.

21. Ibid.

22. Ibid.

23. Glenn Stout, "The Manager's End Game," in *Sports in Massachusetts: Historical Essays,* eds. Ronald Story and Martin Kaufman (Westfield: Institute for Massachusetts Studies, 1991), 132.

24. Ibid., 133.

25. Ibid., 134.

26. *Journal Gazette,* March 30, 1907.

27. Ibid.

28. *Evening Times* (Pawtucket, Rhode Island), March 30, 1907.

29. Frederick O'Connell, "Worried to Death." This article is found in Stahl's HOF file. It was syndicated and appeared in a St. Louis paper dated April 6, 1907. However, the original date of the article is March 31, 1907.

30. Thompson, 56.

31. Browning, 168.

HARRY STALEY
BY JW STEWART

Harry Staley.
(Library of Congress)

In the box, Beaneater Harry Staley pitched a mystifying curve, yet he often wrestled with his control and the barrage of temptations offered baseball stars. At his peak, the curves, the speed, and workhorse stamina helped the Boston Beaneaters to three straight pennants (1891-1893). "Staley wild" was an often-used phrase by the papers of the day while reports of reprimands and his frequent pitiful physical condition attested to his rowdiness and poor habits. Undeterred by his personal struggles and the numerous pitching rule changes during the 1890s, Staley won 72 games in his four years with the Beaneaters.

Henry Eli Staley was born on November 2, 1866, in Jacksonville, Illinois, to William and Emily Staley.[1] The Maryland natives were married in 1860. Emily gave birth to three daughters before Harry, then one more daughter, and two more sons by 1879. Harry grew up in Springfield, Illinois, and his family maintained a home there for the rest of his life. Staley's mother died in 1910, several months after Harry's untimely demise, while his coal-mining father survived to 1931.[2]

Staley began his baseball career with various amateur teams including the one from his hometown; his professional career began with the St. Louis Whites of the Western Association. The Whites acted much like the later farm teams with talent moving back and forth to Chris Von der Ahe's National League team, the St. Louis Browns. (Von der Ahe also owned the Whites.) According to *The Sporting News,* Staley "had no superior as a pitcher in the Western Association."[3]

A baseball-card portrait of Staley from his time with the Whites sits in the National Archives. The right-handed pitcher appears shorter than his stated 5-feet-10. His weight was listed as 175 pounds. His physique shows the athleticism of youth, though his trimness would disappear with age and bad habits. From illustrations in newspapers, his eyes are soft and dignified, but in the photo portrait the darkness and menacing intensity in his eyes is striking.

Von der Ahe's Western Association team was not financially sustainable, so he sold the club in June of 1888 along with most of its players to Indianapolis interests.[4] Staley and first baseman Jake Beckley, though, were sold to the Pittsburg Alleghenys for $4,500.[5] By June of 1888 Staley was pitching in Pittsburg alongside pitching stars James "Pud" Galvin and Ed Morris as well as the future evangelist Billy Sunday.

Staley's first recorded game with the Alleghenys came on June 23, 1888, an away game against the Chicago White Stockings. Staley closed, gave up three runs, and threw two wild pitches. The game was out of hand long before Staley stepped in the box and the team lost 12-1. His rough start would soon be forgotten. On June 30 before his new hometown crowd, Staley struck out four and limited the White Stockings to two earned runs in a 6-4 win.[6] *The Sporting News* credited Staley's pitching for the win, confirming its earlier prediction of excellence in Staley if he ever had "a club backing him up."[7] On July 10 Staley struck out eight Philadelphia batters; however, the Pittsburg bats were unable to hold up their end, leading to a 1-0 loss.[8] A week later, the rookie pitcher recorded his first shutout, against the Boston Beaneaters. He gave up no earned runs, walked only one, and hit one batter in the 4-0 victory.[9] For the rest of July, Staley maintained a steady stream of strikeouts and solid pitching performances.

Staley's trouble with control first appeared in August of 1888. In two games his wild pitches and walks led to defeats in close games against league leaders New York and Chicago.[10] Staley regained some control at the end of August, striking out five in a 9-2 victory against Chicago; however, at the end of the season he was "hit freely" by Washington and was described by the *Boston Globe* as "very wild."[11] Despite his late-season trouble, the Alleghenys pitching rotation of Ed Morris, Staley, and Galvin was described as "steady, reliable and effective."[12] Staley ended the season with a 2.69 ERA, two shutouts, and a 12-12 record, and was reserved by the Alleghenys for the 1889 season.[13]

The *Pittsburg Dispatch* thought highly of Staley's work in the box and declared that he would be a "first-class man" one day.[14] Yet rumors circled around the city of Staley's impending trade to Louisville. The Alleghenys manager, Horace Phillips, cited his "high opinion of Staley," and team owner William Nimick declared that he "wouldn't take thousands of dollars for Staley."[15] The stories continued as did negotiations behind the scenes into February, with the owner of the Louisville Colonels of the American Association stating that "Staley would make the Louisville club a valuable pitcher."[16] The *Pittsburg Dispatch* relayed the reasons for Staley's late-season struggles, according to manager Phillips: Staley had been "led astray" by his teammates, "led into bad company," and was not taking care of himself. Phillips heatedly protested the story, calling it and his statements wholly "fabricated."[17]

By the middle of February 1889, the trade rumors were gone. The team decided it needed Staley more than a good third baseman.[18] The reports on Staley's condition were promising. He apparently spent most of the winter with his family in Illinois and then traveled to Hot Springs, Arkansas, to ensure that he was healthy and in playing condition by spring. As the young pitcher improved his arm and defensive skills, the team worked to ensure that he and his other errant teammates stayed in playing condition. In March the Alleghenys dictated a set of behavioral standards for players to encourage them "to do right, morally and otherwise."[19] The concern for player morality and its effect on the game was shared by most teams of the day. The press was not optimistic for success.

Preseason matches showed Staley had improved in speed and defense, but walks and wild pitches still evidenced "a wildness" that observers feared would "prove costly."[20] The Alleghenys went 8-8 in their first four series. In a May 8 game against the White Stockings, Staley pitched well, yet his defensive abilities contributed more to the team's win. Staley stopped a hard-hit line drive in the ninth to protect Pittsburgh's 3-2 lead. The skillful stop left Staley's left hand battered and barely able to grip the ball. He finished the game by relying on the defensive work of his team. He pitched through May with a bruised hand. His usual skill was absent and he gave up more hits and scores than usual. Pittsburg's bats were productive, but could not keep up.[21]

As May turned to June, the Alleghenys slid further down the standings. Injuries had left Staley as the only experienced pitcher on the team, forcing him to work the box more often than usual. On May 31 owner Nimick awarded his team's workhorse a new suit of clothes in honor of his effort rather than any real success.[22] The team was 12-18. In a sentiment familiar to most team owners, Nimick asked for "patience and public encouragement."[23]

On June 29 Staley pitched a shutout against Philadelphia in front of the home crowd. The visitors "couldn't touch Staley," and the Alleghenys won 8-0. The second half of the season was no better for Pittsburgh, the team going 9-16 in July, but Staley's control and speed returned.[24] Staley's improvement also helped him work his way out of a fine imposed on him by the team in June for an unknown infraction during a road trip. Energized by his rediscovered command in the box, the players actively lobbied to have the fine returned.[25]

Staley continued to be in "excellent form" through the end of the season, while the Alleghenys put together several winning streaks in August and September, However, this burst of productivity could not remedy the record earned from May to July. Pittsburg ended up in fifth place, 25 games behind the first-place New York Giants. Staley won 21 games and lost 26 with a 3.51 ERA.

Staley was placed on reserve for the 1890 season; however, the rumblings between players and owners during 1889 were about to change his status. The Players' League grew out of the Brotherhood of Professional Baseball Players, established in 1885 to represent athletes and resolve conflicts with baseball ownership. The National League's abuses of the reserve clause and attempts to limit salaries as well as the absence of a system of redress for players increased tension with the owners.[26] Staley was an "enthusiastic supporter" of the Players' League, whose preparations to break away began during the summer of 1889.[27] Like many, he waited until December to officially sign with a Brotherhood team so as not to risk losing his last month's pay to the fury of his old bosses.[28] Staley signed with the Pittsburgh

Burghers as did most of his Alleghenys teammates, including "Pud" Galvin, Ed Morris, and Jake Beckley.

Staley was back in Hot Springs by January of 1890 with teammate Billy "Yank" Robinson. The pair undoubtedly took advantage of the spring-supplied "hydrotherapy" popular at the time to improve their condition and drop Staley's weight. Staley also worked on quickening his delivery, a specific assignment from his new manager, Ned Hanlon.[29]

By March, Staley was back in Pittsburgh and down to his playing weight. He was "enthusiastic about the Brotherhood's chances for success," but the Burghers posted a disastrous season and the Players' League succumbed to economic pressures and the machinations of the National League.[30] Staley managed 21 wins and a slightly better ERA, but he lost 25 and continued to show a game-losing wildness. In a July 8 game at Philadelphia, Staley gave up nine earned runs, and a week later he gave up seven against New York.[31] On July 26 He held Boston to just three hits until the end of the eighth with Boston leading 2-0. Pittsburgh scored three in the ninth, but Staley lost control in the bottom of the ninth and gave up two walks. The next batter hit a triple, scoring the runners and winning the game.[32] Staley received little support from his fielders, and batters had little trouble putting his pitches in play.

In August Staley's off-the-field carousing became public again. Seven members of the team were accused of drinking and violating team rules. Ed Morris was released from the team, his winning record unable to save him. Staley's infraction was his second offense and he received a heavy fine.[33] The fine and public reprimand apparently had good effect. Staley's strikeouts increased as his walks decreased. The *Boston Globe* reported him "in good trim" as he held the Beaneaters to just one hit per inning over six.[34] He hit two home runs in August, and despite his earlier struggles, the *Pittsburg Dispatch* proclaimed Staley "one of the best pitchers in the country today."[35] The Pittsburg Burghers finished 60-68 in sixth place. Rumors of players grumbling about manager Hanlon filled the *Pittsburg Dispatch*, and Staley was reported to be "tired of the Players' League."[36] In turn, the Brotherhood was not pleased with his off-field activities and told the pitcher he "must choose better companions if he wanted to stay with" the Burghers.[37]

The Burghers owner and his Players' League peers across the country began to merge with their National League counterparts across town in an attempt to save what remained of their investments.[38] In January of 1891, the Players' League wrapped up its last business, Staley was back in Hot Springs, and he signed with the new Pittsburg Pirates.[39] The team headed to St. Augustine, Florida, in April, but Staley showed up "a little heavy."[40] The 24-year-old pitcher struggled with his weight for the remainder of his career. Neither his pitching form nor waistline had improved by an April 23 game against Chicago, a 9-2 loss. A few days later, Staley and the Pittsburg offense gave the hometown crowd quite a show with a 17-6 victory over the Cleveland Spiders. Staley struck out eight, gave up no walks, and allowed only three earned runs. The Pirates, though, were headed to a last-place finish in 1891 and had "too many twirlers on their salary."[41] Aside from the Cleveland game, Staley's performances were lackluster. Pittsburg no longer wanted him, but interest remained in the rest of the league.

Brooklyn wanted Staley, and sportswriters reported the trade as a done deal.[42] Staley, however, said no. Unable to come to terms with the pitcher, the Pittsburg Pirates released him, and the Beaneaters swooped in and signed him. The acquisition was met with much fanfare in the Boston papers. They hailed him "an artist," "a handsome young athlete," and "the best pitcher in the business." Inexplicably the *Boston Globe* also mentioned his "good command" of the ball.[43] The Boston papers crowed about his 16 victories in his last 18 starts; however, the real number was 10.[44] The Phillies also took a look at signing Staley but withdrew, claiming he was an "undesirable man" with "uncertain habits."[45] Staley's notoriety as a winning pitcher was followed closely by his reputation for intemperance.

Four days after signing with the Beaneaters, Staley debuted in a home game against Cincinnati. He gave up two runs in the first, but shut out the Reds for the next eight innings giving Boston a 7-2 victory. According to the *Globe*, Staley's pitching performance "won his way into the hearts of all present."[46] In his next start, he also gave up two runs in the first, but this time Boston manager Frank Selee yanked him. John Clarkson relieved Staley but gave up eight more runs. The *Globe* howled at the "unfair movement" and the potential damage to Staley's confidence.[47] Clearly, the *Globe* was firmly in Staley's corner.

The summer of 1891 proved that the *Globe's* confidence was warranted. He held Brooklyn to just a double, a triple, and one run in an 8-1 win over the Grooms, pulling Boston up to second place.[48] Staley closed out June by holding Brooklyn to one run.[49] Staley's curves continued to "baffle" teams into July and August.[50] New York could manage only six scattered hits off him on July 27, the Phillies managed only eight in a 1-0 shutout on August 1, and only four Cincinnati players connected on August 5.[51] As Boston held on to second place, the *Globe* proudly crowed that visiting teams were helpless against Staley.[52] The Pittsburg press looked on in disgust at Staley's performance and the Pirates' own 33-52 record. "Certainly if there ever was a stupid transaction in baseball it was the releasing of Staley," wrote the *Pittsburg Dispatch*.[53]

As Staley and the Beaneaters entered September, they were firmly in second place behind the Chicago Colts. Two losses to the Colts put them seven games out. By the middle of September they were able to cut that to five, and then on September 18 the Beaneaters began a 17-game winning streak including four doubleheader sweeps. In a September 30 home game against the Giants, Staley shut out New York for six innings until "rupturing an artery" after being struck in the face by a batted ball in the sixth. It ended his season.[54] Despite losing Staley, Boston was now in first place and would remain there over the last three games of the season. As a Beaneater, Staley won 20 games and lost 8.

The 1892 Beaneaters lineup largely remained intact from the previous year including their pitching rotation. Staley, Kid Nichols, Jack Stivetts, and John Clarkson led the team to a 102-48 record and another championship. With the exception of a few days in July, Boston was in first place the entire season. Staley began the season in rare form, winning his first eight starts.⁵⁵ His first loss did not come until a 10-inning 3-2 loss to St. Louis in June.⁵⁶

August of 1892 brought trouble in the box. A 6-0 loss to Pittsburg featured dreadful fielding by Staley, one writer observing that he looked "like a man with wooden legs."⁵⁷ A week later he reportedly put "no life into his work" in a 6-1 loss to Cincinnati.⁵⁸ In September Staley was reportedly suffering from an arm injury, and there were no signs of improvement in his pitching by the end of the month.⁵⁹ In 1892 the National League experimented with declaring a champion for each half of the season. The two champions would then play a five-game series to determine the League champion. Staley pitched in the second game of the championship series, giving an "unsteady" performance that nearly lost the game if not for the Beaneaters' superb defensive work.⁶⁰ The Beaneaters were season champions, and despite the late-season injury, Staley ended with 22 wins and a 3.03 ERA.

Staley, Stivetts, and Nichols returned for the 1893 season after John Clarkson left the previous summer. While the Boston rotation remained steady, the rules of pitching changed dramatically. The modern pitcher's mound replaced the flat pitcher's box, raising the pitchers several inches above the batter. The distance between pitcher and home plate also was increased to the modern rule of 60 feet 6 inches. The two significant changes required a great deal of adjustment for pitchers, including Harry Staley.

The rule changes, however, were not the first hurdle for Staley. The pitcher failed to report to spring training on time.⁶¹ When he finally did appear, he was in poor shape. By May his condition was still substandard. The papers blamed the new pitching rules for his dreadful showing on May 2, but his weight and overall health did not help.⁶² The entire month of May 1893 was a disaster for Staley. He was "woefully out of trim" and it appeared his primary weapon, his curve, was gone.⁶³ In a 13-12 win over Washington, Staley gave up 16 hits in four innings before being pulled.⁶⁴ Rumors began to appear in the papers that a trade for better pitching was in the works.⁶⁵

June saw little improvement in Staley's pitching; however, on June 1, he had the greatest day of his career at the plate. In a 15-14 win over Louisville, Staley was responsible for nine Boston runs, with two home runs, a single, and two sacrifice hits. On the mound he was still in the wilderness, but his bat more than made up for it that day.⁶⁶ But a week later, Staley gave up 15 hits, walked six, and threw four wild pitches in an 11-9 loss to Cincinnati.⁶⁷ Plainly, Staley was still in need of conditioning or time to get accustomed to the new demands of pitching.

The *Boston Globe* reported on June 12 that Staley was living in Woburn, 12 miles from Boston, with the solid-hitting Boston shortstop, Herman Long. Their spare time was now spent with more subdued activities than the seductions offered by Boston.⁶⁸ About this time, Staley's fortunes on the mound began to turn. As June turned to July, his speed and control returned. In a 12-5 win over St. Louis on July 1, Staley gave up only three earned runs with two strikeouts. The victory put Boston in first place by one game over Philadelphia but the team slipped back into second by July 7.⁶⁹

The team struggled along with Staley at the beginning of the 1893 season. But despite giving up 16 hits in a 7-4 loss to Philadelphia in July, Staley's pitching largely regained its effectiveness as the Beaneaters charged into the final months of the season.⁷⁰ Once moving back into first place at the end of July, the Beaneaters never retreated, holding a lead of 13 games at one point but never less than five. The papers raved about the pitcher's performances. He was now in "prime condition," with his curves again mystifying the opposition.⁷¹ Staley ended the season 18-10 with a 5.13 ERA. His early-season struggles were evident in the much higher ERA and the eight games in which he was pulled off the mound.

Three straight pennants for the Beaneaters increased the monetary expectations of several players, and so the 1894 season began with Staley and four others holding out for more money. An abundance of pitchers and his poor showing in the spring of 1893 potentially left Staley's neck on the chopping block.⁷² By the beginning of April Staley and the team came to terms and another pitcher, Hank Gastright, was released.⁷³

Staley began the 1894 season poorly, and there was no recovery this time. The Beaneaters used him sparingly; he started only 21 games and finished 18. Staley finished 12-10 with a 6.81 ERA. His fielding was "miserable," and he began losing his control and speed late in games, giving up multiple hits. By July the press believed Staley was no longer a quality pitcher. He also gained weight over the summer, his body in no condition to play baseball. The press began referring to him as the "rotund Boston pitcher" and the "fat twirler."⁷⁴ According to the *Philadelphia Inquirer*, Staley became unpopular with the Boston sportswriters and the public because of what the public perceived as lackluster effort. The irascible Staley responded to the criticism by just giving up.⁷⁵ Boston finished in third place. To no one's surprise, the Beaneaters released Staley after the season.⁷⁶

Staley was not adrift for long. The St. Louis Browns signed him in January of 1895. Over the winter, Staley shrugged off the obnoxious end to the 1894 season and also shed about 50 pounds. St. Louis manager Al Buckenberger called Staley the "catch of the year," and owner Henry Killilea informed St. Louis fans "there is nothing the matter with his arm" and that "there is lots of good pitching in that fellow yet."⁷⁷ Clearly, these were the words of a promoter urging excitement in the face of his previous losing seasons.

Staley pitched mediocre ball for St Louis. His ERA for 1895, 5.22, was better than the previous year; however, he was routinely pulled from games as the other teams easily batted his pitches around the field. His weight and off-the-field activities made mediocre pitching worse and endeared him to no one. *The Sporting News* reported repeated "lushing" within the Browns lineup, with Staley one of the "chief offenders."⁷⁸

The Browns released Staley at the beginning of August. *The Sporting News* reported that he was struggling with rheumatism in his feet. There were rumors of offers from Philadelphia and Cincinnati, but they never materialized.⁷⁹ Between the pain in his feet, his weight, and his drinking, Staley's career in the major leagues was over.

Staley returned to Springfield and the bedside of his ailing brother shortly after his release. While he was there, a telegram arrived from Wheeling, West Virginia, seeking his help. The Wheeling

Mountaineers of the Class-C Iron & Oil League were five games back in their pennant race and needed the services of Staley, whom they considered a "crack twirler."[80] The team was led by Jack Glasscock, a former National League infielder. Glasscock had taken to recruiting older National League players for Wheeling, which the *Boston Globe* called a "last resort of the 'has-beens.'"[81] Staley came to terms with the team and the Mountaineers sent the pitcher a train ticket. Staley arrived on August 24 and stayed with the team through the end of the season. The Mountaineers won the pennant.[82]

Staley signed with the Toronto Canadians of the Eastern League and his former St. Louis manager Al Buckenberger for the 1896 season. His pitching was occasionally solid, but a lack of control continued to plague him. The team, which finished the season playing in Albany, New York, and with a winning record, brought Staley back for the next season. However, Staley continued to decline. At the end of August 1897 he had an 8-11 record with a team filled with younger and more successful pitchers. The team released him.

Staley found a spot on the Norfolk (Virginia) club of the Class-B Atlantic League for a brief time in 1898, but his pitching career was essentially over. He settled in Pittsburg after leaving the game and worked at a paper factory. In 1910 the 43-year-old pitcher checked into the Battle Creek Sanatorium in Michigan with a stomach ailment. Doctors attempted surgery on January 12, but Staley died after the procedure.[83]

The same six modest lines announcing his death on January 12, 1910, in his hometown newspaper ran in several other papers across the country. While Boston papers did not even mention his death, six years earlier the *Globe* gave a small tribute to the former Beaneater. It called him an "honest workman" who "left no enemies in the baseball fraternity."[84] Staley was a successful pitcher at a time of great upheaval in the game. He eagerly supported the idea of players' rights, struggled through the evolving pitching rules, and became one of many players struggling with off-the-field behaviors as the game tried to clean up its image with fans. Despite team and personal efforts to reform, Staley's curve and career succumbed to alcohol and the indulgences offered the stars of the game.

NOTES

1. 1870 US census, Sangamon County, Illinois, population schedule, Springfield, 531, William and Emily Staley; digital image, Ancestry.com, accessed November 25, 2017, ancestory.com.
2. Michigan, Death Records, 1897-1920, Emily Virginia Staley.
3. "Staley and Beckley," *The Sporting News* June 23, 1888: 1.
4. Peter Morris, *A Game of Inches: The Stories Behind the Innovations That Shaped Baseball* (Chicago: Ivan R. Dee, 2010), 358.
5. "Staley Signs With Boston," *Boston Globe*, May 27, 1891: 5; "Staley and Beckley," *The Sporting News*, June 30, 1888: 1. In the papers of the time period, Pittsburgh was spelled without the 'h.'
6. "Games of June 30," *The Sporting News* July 7, 1888: 2; Some sources credit him with one strikeout, some with five. Four is the number printed in the cited edition of *The Sporting News*.
7. "Staley and Beckley," *The Sporting News* June 23, 1888: 1.
8. "National League," *The Sporting News* July 21, 1888: 2.
9. Ibid.
10. "Pittsburg and Chicago Play Two Exciting Games," *Boston Globe* August 23, 1888: 5.
11. "Pittsburg, 7; Washington, 2," *Boston Globe* September 9, 1888: 5; "Washington, 8; Pittsburg, 3," *Boston Globe*, September 14, 1888: 5.
12. "Murnane's Message," *Boston Globe*, September 10, 1888: 8.
13. Baseball-Reference.com; "Reserved for Next Year," *New York Times*, October 19, 1888: 3.
14. "Sporting Review," *Pittsburg Dispatch*, January 13, 1889: 6.
15. "Baseball Matters," *Pittsburg Dispatch*, January 29, 1889: 6; "Staley Will Stay," *Pittsburg Dispatch*, January 14, 1889: 6.
16. "A Strange Story," *Pittsburg Dispatch*, February 10, 1889: 6.
17. Ibid.
18. "Sporting News," *Pittsburg Dispatch*, February 12, 1889: 6.
19. "They Must Be Good," *Pittsburg Dispatch*, March 12, 1889: 6.
20. "The Last Skirmish," *Pittsburg Dispatch*, April 23, 1889: 6.
21. "Easy Victory," *Boston Globe*, May 14, 1889: 5; "A Close Argument," *Pittsburg Dispatch*, May 16, 1889: 6.
22. "With Little Glory," *Pittsburg Dispatch*, June 1, 1889: 6.
23. "Not Losing Money," *Pittsburg Dispatch*, June 10, 1889: 6.
24. "Mickey's Measure," *Pittsburg Dispatch*, July 6, 1889: 6.
25. "Gone to the East," *Pittsburg Dispatch*, July 8, 1889: 6.
26. Harold Seymour, *Baseball: The Early Years* (New York: Oxford University Press, 1989), 221.
27. "A Break at Last," *Pittsburg Dispatch*, November 27, 1889: 6.
28. "Busy Brotherhood," *Boston Globe*, December 17, 1889: 8.
29. "Staley Heard From," *Pittsburg Dispatch*, February 18, 1890: 6.
30. "New Club Gossip," *Pittsburg Dispatch*, April 7, 1890: 6; "Pitcher Staley Arrives," *Pittsburg Dispatch*, March 20, 1890: 6.
31. "In Fourth Place," *Pittsburg Dispatch*, July 9, 1890: 6; "New York, 10; Pittsburg, 2," *Boston Globe*, July 19, 1890: 5.
32. "A Pitcher's Battle," *Pittsburg Dispatch*, July 27, 1890: 6.
33. "Released for Drinking," *Pittsburg Dispatch*, August 9, 1890: 6.
34. "'Kareless' Kilroy," *Boston Globe*, August 29, 1890: 5.
35. "It Was So Very Easy," *Pittsburg Dispatch*, September 30, 1890: 6.
36. "A Review of Sports," *Pittsburg Dispatch*, September 21, 1890: 14.
37. "Notes of the Diamond," *Wheeling Register*, October 12, 1890: 3.
38. Seymour, 244.
39. "Next Year's Teams," *The Sporting News*, January 24, 1891: 1; "Diamond Dust," *Wheeling Register*, February 1, 1891: 3; "An Inglorious End," *The Sporting News*, January 24, 1891: 1.
40. "A Call to Magnates," *Pittsburg Dispatch*, March 25, 1891: 6.
41. "Baseball Brevities," *New York Times*, May 23, 1891: 3.
42. "Staley Signs With Brooklyn," *Philadelphia Inquirer*, May 26, 1891: 3.
43. "Staley Signs With Boston," *Boston Globe*, May 27, 1891: 5.
44. Ibid.
45. "Couldn't Touch Staley," *Boston Globe*, August 6, 1891: 5.
46. "Off His Fodder," *Boston Globe*, May 31, 1891: 4.
47. "Tried Two Pitchers," *Boston Globe*, June 3, 1891: 5.

48 "Two Games for Boston," *New York Times*, June 18, 1891: 8.

49 "Brooklyn, 4; Boston, 1," *New York Times*, July 1, 1891: 3.

50 "Staley Unfathomable," *Boston Globe*, July 22, 1891: 5.

51 "Staley Puzzled Them," *Boston Globe*, July 28, 1891: 5; "Giants in Third Place," *New York Times*, August 2, 1891: 8.

52 "Couldn't Touch Staley," *Boston Globe*, August 6, 1891: 5.

53 "A Review of Sports," *Pittsburg Dispatch*, August 9, 1891: 18.

54 "Boston Takes Lead," *New York Times*, October 1, 1891: 6.

55 "Like a Ghost," *Boston Globe*, May 31, 1892: 16.

56 "Staley's First," *Boston Globe*, June 4, 1892: 5.

57 "Staley's Off Day," *Boston Globe*, August 20, 1892: 5.

58 "Kelly Weakened," *Boston Globe*, August 31, 1892: 5.

59 "Narrow Escape," *Boston Globe*, September 29, 1892: 5.

60 "Duffy's Batting," *Boston Globe* October 19, 1892: 2.

61 "Two Men Not Yet Signed," *Boston Globe*, April 2, 1893: 2.

62 "All Is Chaos," *Boston Globe*, May 3, 1893: 6.

63 "Out of Trim," *Boston Globe*, May 10, 1893: 5; "Three Straight," *Boston Globe*, May 18, 1893: 2.

64 "Boston's Day," *Boston Globe*, May 27, 1893: 6.

65 "Where Will Kelly Go?" *Boston Globe*, May 12, 1893: 5.

66 "Very Much in It," *Boston Globe*, June 2, 1893: 2.

67 "Dropped a Peg," *Boston Globe*, June 9, 1893: 3.

68 "Baseball Notes," *Boston Globe*, June 12, 1893: 9.

69 "Boston in First," *Boston Globe*, July 2, 1893: 7.

70 "Won the Third," *Boston Globe*, August 3, 1893: 2.

71 "Staley in Form," *Boston Globe*, August 11, 1893: 6.

72 "Tucker's Grievance," *Boston Globe*, March 25, 1894: 7.

73 "Boston's Ball Players," *Philadelphia Inquirer*, April 3, 1894: 3.

74 "Staley Slows," *Boston Globe*, September 9, 1894: 2.

75 'Chat and Comment," *Philadelphia Inquirer,* January 19, 1895: 4.

76 "Baseball Notes," *Washington Post*, December 30, 1894: 6.

77 "Pitcher Staley Signed by Browns," *Boston Globe*, January 9, 1895: 2; "Chat and Comment," *Philadelphia Inquirer,* January 19, 1895: 4.

78 "A Dead Issue," *The Sporting News*, June 9, 1895: 1.

79 "Henry E. Staley," *The Sporting News,* August 10, 1895: 5; "Baseball Notes," *Washington Post*, August 14, 1895: 6.

80 "Baseball Comment," *Wheeling Register*, August 20, 1895: 4.

81 "Baseball Notes," *Boston Globe*, September 11, 1895: 4.

82 "Baseball Comment," *Wheeling Register*, August 21, 1895: 4.

83 "Harry Staley Is Dead," *Kansas City Star* January 13, 1910.

84 "Harry Staley," *Boston Globe*, July 10, 1904: 36.

JACK STIVETTS
BY GREGORY H. WOLF

Jack Stivetts.
(public domain)

He threw a ball as fast as Amos "The Hoosier Thunderbolt" Rusie, hit the ball as "hard as any man in the league," and was versatile enough to play every position except catcher.[1] His name was Jack Stivetts. In an 11-year major-league career that began with the St. Louis Browns of the American Association in 1889, he won 203 games and batted .298. His greatest fame came in 1892, his first year with the National League Boston Beaneaters. That season Stivetts tossed the first no-hitter in franchise history, en route to winning 35 games, then helped lead the club to its second of three consecutive titles in an extraordinary performance in a postseason championship series. Here's the story of a forgotten nineteenth century hurler whose accomplishments deserve more recognition.

John Elmer Stivetts was born on March 31, 1868, in Ashland, Pennsylvania. His parents were German-speaking immigrants; father Adam Stibitz emigrated from the Kingdom of Bavaria as a 20-year-old and arrived in New York in January 1854; mother Emilie Kupfer left the Kingdom of Prussia in October 1853.[2] The Stibitz and Kupfer families soon thereafter settled in Ashland, in Schuylkill County, in hilly east-central Pennsylvania. The discovery of coal transformed the quiet rural village into a bustling boomtown, with population growing from about 200 in 1850 to almost 4,000 by the end of the decade. Like other immigrants with limited education and the additional challenge of a language barrier, Adam found work in the local anthracite coal mines. He and Amalia Cooper (Emilie's anglicized name) welcomed at least 12 children into the world from about 1859 to 1877, though not all survived infancy. They spoke German at home with their children. At some point after the 1880 US Census, the family changed its surname to Stivetts.

Had it not been for baseball, Jack, as he was called, was destined to spend his life underground in coal mines where he had already begun to work by the time he finished the eighth grade. Tall and sturdily built, Jack played town ball for Ashland, making a name for himself as both a pitcher and batter. His professional career began in 1887 when Ashland became one of eight founding members of the Central Pennsylvania League, whose teams played an imbalanced schedule of about 40-50 games. The following season, he moved to the Allentown Peanuts of the Central League. Though complete statistics are not available for Stivetts' first three professional seasons, he must have been a sensation in 1889 as a member of the York (Pennsylvania) club in the Middle States League. According to historian Robert L. Tiemann, Stivetts went 15-3 and yielded just one earned run in his last nine starts.[3] In an exhibition game against the St. Louis Browns (renamed the

Cardinals in 1900) of the America Association, Stivetts caught the attention of the club's player-manager, Charlie Comiskey, who supposedly secured his contract on the spot, in June 1889.[4]

Stivetts landed on the American Association's best team, which Comiskey had guided to the last four league titles. The Browns' success was also the product of their brash German-born owner, Chris von der Ahe, who knew little about baseball. A tireless marketer and self-promoter, von der Ahe helped establish the American Association as a major league to rival the National League by then-unconventional tactics, such as selling beer at games, playing on Sunday, and advertising the games to the average working man and not just high society. The Browns were once again engaged in a fierce pennant race with the Brooklyn Bridegrooms. The 21-year-old Stivetts was brought along slowly behind the team's two primary hurlers (also 21 years old), Silver King and Ice Box Chamberlain, who finished with 35 and 32 victories respectively. Stivetts, said *Sporting Life,* made a "good impression" in his debut, against the Cincinnati Red Stockings on June 26, yielding just one earned run and fanning nine in a 6-1 loss.[5] Four days later, he did "remarkable work" and showed "great speed" in notching his first win, 12-7 over the Louisville Colonels, whiffing nine.[6] When King complained of a sore arm on July 13 at Sportsman's Park in the Gateway City, Stivetts was the emergency starter, going the distance in the team's highest-scoring contest of the year, a 25-5 victory over the Baltimore Orioles. The Browns seemed destined to capture their fifth consecutive title before hitting a rough patch beginning with an extended road swing on August 30, losing 10 of 16 games, to fall 4½ games behind Brooklyn. Despite winning 13 of their last 14 games (one tie), the Browns finished in second place, two games behind the Bridegrooms. Stivetts (12-7) had the lowest ERA (2.25) among qualified pitchers in the league; however, his 191⅔ innings pale in comparison to King (458), Chamberlain (421⅔), and league leader Mark Baldwin (513⅔) of the Columbus Solons.

The Browns' chances to reclaim the title in 1890 were slashed in the offseason when Comiskey and King broke their reserve clause and jumped to the Chicago Pirates in the newly formed Players' League.[7] The league, an outgrowth of baseball's first union (the Brotherhood of Professional Base Ball Players), attracted many of the biggest stars in the sport, and placed yet further pressure on the two established major leagues, the NL and AA, to raise salaries. The loss of King and the early-season trade of Chamberlain enabled Stivetts to showcase his talents as one of the Browns' two front-line pitchers. Described by St. Louis sportswriter Joe Pritchard as the "lawn mower" for the way he made batters reach around for his fastball, Stivetts continued his ascendance as one of the circuit's top twirlers.[8] At 6-feet-2 inches and weighing 200 pounds, Stivetts cut an imposing presence on the mound; his heater and just enough wildness made him one of the most dangerous hurlers in the league. On April 27 he tossed a four-hitter to beat Columbus, 14-1, and punched out 12 with a ball that looked like a "fly speck" when it crossed the plate, thought the Solons manager Al Buckenberger.[9] Stivetts also emerged as a serious threat at the plate. On June 10 he tossed a complete game and whacked two home runs, including a game-winning grand slam in the ninth inning against the Toledo Maumees.[10] The Browns (77-58) finished in third place, winning less than 60 percent of their games for the first time since 1882, the inaugural season of the AA. By the end of the season, Stivetts' (27-21, 3.52 ERA in 419 innings and 41 complete games) name was plastered among the leader boards. He also rivaled Count Campau as the team's most feared hitter, slugging .500 with seven home runs, and played in the outfield or at first base in 13 games.

In the offseason, the Players' League collapsed and many of the top drawing cards returned to the AA in 1891, though not necessarily to their original teams. With Comiskey back as skipper and playing first base, the Browns flirted with first place until mid-August, when the Boston Reds pulled away and captured the pennant by 8½ games over the Browns. The team's biggest news item was Stivetts, and not only because of his work on the diamond. He once again placed in the top five in almost every significant pitching category, winning 33 games with a 2.86 ERA in 440 innings, and paced the circuit in strikeouts (259) and walks (232). He batted .305 and played 24 games in the outfield.

Known as "Happy Jack" for his carefree disposition and wide grin, Stivetts had an ornery and combative streak, especially when he drank too much alcohol. In late June 1891, he and roommate Joe Neale, who lived above a tavern across from Sportsman's Park at Grand and St. Louis Avenues, were hauled off to the police station in the middle of the night for their loud excessive behavior, but were not charged with an offense.[11] The *St. Louis Post-Dispatch* reported on August 20 that Stivetts got "very drunk" at a lawn party after the Browns game was rained out.[12] Never afraid to make his opinions known, Stivetts confronted von der Ahe, with whom he had a prickly relationship like many other Browns players. Von der Ahe ultimately called the police on Stivetts, who drew a short suspension from the owner. The big pitcher was hardly fazed by the incident or its results; "Der Boss," as von der Ahe liked to call himself, had suspended him other times for his "drunken carousals" and "disgraceful behavior," only to bring him back a game or two later when he was scheduled to pitch.[13]

Late in the season, rumors swirled that Stivetts had signed a contact with the NL's Boston Beaneaters for 1892. The American Association had been gradually imploding all season long, doomed by contract jumpers, an unwinnable financial struggle with the NL over quality players, and failure to win back the fans' trust after so many stars had bolted to the Players' League. At a meeting in Indianapolis in December, the AA and the NL agreed to merge. Clubs in St. Louis, Baltimore, and Louisville were admitted to the NL; the NL purchased the franchises in Chicago, Boston, Columbus, Milwaukee, and Washington, and their players were sold; and a new Washington team was awarded. The National League emerged as a 12-team monopoly.

Both the Browns and Beaneaters laid claims to Stivetts, who was awarded to the latter. The reigning NL champions already had two of the league's best pitchers, veteran John Clarkson and 22-year-old Kid Nichols, both of whom won at least 30 games in 1891; however, *Sporting Life* noted that "in short time [Stivetts] was acknowledged as one of the greatest pitchers in the league," which led to Clarkson's release.[14] Stivetts' season reads like a highlight reel. One day after playing in the outfield and belting a game-winning home run in the 12th inning of a scoreless game against the Brooklyn Grooms,[15] Stivetts took the mound against them on August 6 and tossed the first no-hitter in Beaneaters history. In what was described by the *Brooklyn Daily News* as the Grooms' "Waterloo defeat" in front of more than

7,000 spectators in Eastern Park in Brooklyn, Stivetts fanned six and walked five, and also scored twice in the 11-0 victory.[16] Stivetts started and won both games of a doubleheader against the Louisville Colonels on September 5, yielding just three runs. In the second game of a season-concluding doubleheader against the Washington Senators on October 15, Stivetts fired a no-hitter that was called after five innings so that the Beaneaters could catch a train from the nation's capital to Cleveland.[17] Stivetts (35-16) matched Nichols for the club lead in victories and tied for third most in the NL, completed 45 of 48 starts, logged 415⅔ innings, and fanned (180) just a few more than he walked (171). He also batted .296 and played in the outfield in 18 games.

Because of the NL-AA merger, league directors had established an experimental split-season format for the 1892 season and tentatively planned for a best-of-nine championship series. The plan worked perfectly as the Beaneaters won the first half and the Cleveland Spiders the second, setting the stage for the first-ever NL championship series, which commenced on October 17 in Cleveland. The Spiders were favored even though they finished with a worse combined record than the Beaneaters (93-56 to 102-48). The first game became "one the most evenly contested games that ever took place on the diamond," opined the *Cincinnati Enquirer*.[18] In one of the greatest pitchers' duels of the era, Stivetts and the 25-year-old Cy Young (in his third season, but already acknowledged as the best hurler in the league) battled for 11 scoreless innings, yielding just four and six hits respectively, before the game was called because of darkness and declared a tie. Two days later, the two hurlers squared off again, in Cleveland for Game Three, with Stivetts emerging victorious, 3-2. A rematch was scheduled for Game Five, on October 22 in Boston, but when Young complained of a sore arm, former Beaneater John Clarkson took the mound. The Spiders scored six unearned runs in the second inning, but Stivetts, gushed one reporter, "put on extra speed" thereafter while the Beaneaters whacked Clarkson to win, 12-7.[19] Kid Nichols beat Young in Game Six to give the Beaneaters the championship, winning five games and tying one. Stivetts' performance on the national stage secured his reputation: In 29 innings he yielded three earned runs, whiffed 17, and walked only seven. Despite the success of the series and the national excitement it generated, it was abolished after one season.

One of the most debated topics of the Hot Stove season was a major new rule instituted to increase scoring. The pitcher's box was replaced by a rubber plate, increasing the distance to home plate from 55½ feet (rear line of box) to 60 feet 6 inches on a flat surface. Sportswriters, players, and fans found no consensus regarding the effect the change would have on speedballers like Amos Rusie and Stivetts. *Sporting Life* opined that the new distance would make Stivetts' "drop ball more effective."[20] Without an adequate way to measure the speed of the ball, some thought hard throwers would be faster and those who struggled with control could become more dangerous. "I'm too young to die," quipped John Montgomery Ward about his prospects facing Rusie and Stivetts.[21]

The change in pitching distance had a dramatic effect on baseball in 1893. Scoring increased from 10.2 total runs per game to 13.2; batting averages improved from .245 to .280; and slugging percentage increased by 51 points to .379. While skipper Frank Selee piloted the Beaneaters to their third straight championship, Stivetts was described in *Sporting Life* as "not pitching ball as he did last season and is surely not in good form."[22] Like all moundsmen, Stivetts had to adjust to the new distance to the plate; however, several additional factors played a role in his reduced numbers (20-12, 4.41 ERA, and 14 fewer starts than a year earlier). Boston sportswriter J.C. Morse wrote that Stivetts "pitched a good part of the time as if there were something the matter with his arm";[23] and *Sporting Life* reported in May that Stivetts' "arm has not the movement characteristic of him and he has complained of arm pain."[24] He also battled with teammates, most notably star outfielder Hugh Duffy, who led the circuit in batting (.363). Their relationship was so toxic that *Sporting Life* noted that "it would seem to be in the best interest of harmony to let one of them go."[25] Both were still on the team the next season. Stivetts followed his own rules, such as going AWOL when the club was in Philadelphia in the early part of the season. Without permission he abandoned the club, for the second straight year, to visit his family in Ashland and drew criticism for not showing up for a game he was scheduled to pitch.[26] That wasn't the only time Selee had to find an emergency starter to replace Stivetts. On the club's season-ending 18-game road swing, Stivetts reportedly showed up in Cincinnati so intoxicated that he couldn't pitch. "[N]o doubt Stivetts indulgence in liquor has lessened his effect this season," declared sportswriter O. P. Caylor.[27]

Still considered among the fastest throwers in the league, Stivetts no longer piled up the strikeouts from the new distance to the plate. After averaging 218 punchouts per season leading up to the change, he averaged 80 in the next four seasons (1893-1896). On the positive side, he developed better control of his heater and curveball, and his walks per nine innings decreased each season from a high of 4.7 in 1891 to a better-than-league-average 2.7 in 1896. He had a peculiar delivery that disrupted the batter's timing. "[He] shakes his foot at the batter and his head at the second baseman just before delivering the ball," read one description.[28] The delivery was also called "erratic … requiring an artist to hold him."[29]

Early in the 1894 season, Stivetts was on the hot seat in more than one way. On May 15 a fire erupted in the wooden grandstand at the Beaneaters' home ballpark, the South End Grounds. As Terry Gottschall explained, the nine-alarm blaze swept through the ballpark and ultimately burned 12 acres and destroyed at least 200 buildings.[30] Stivetts, who had had training as a fireman, a lifesaving ability when working in coal mines, apparently rescued a disoriented elderly man in a building next to the ballpark by braving the flames and extracting him from the second story.[31] Stivetts, however, couldn't save himself from a poor start, further exacerbating his strained relationship with club management, which according to the *Boston Herald* threatened to suspend him.[32] On June 8, almost seven weeks into the season, Stivetts finally won his second game, but if anything, the burly hurler was streaky.[33] Eight consecutive losses were followed by 11 straight victories.[34] Tragedy struck the Stivetts family in August, when his 60-year-old father was crushed to death in a coal-mine accident.[35] Stivetts ended his season for the third-place Beaneaters by defeating the Pirates 8-1 in Pittsburgh and collecting four hits.[36] His 26 wins tied three others (including Cy Young) for fifth most in the league; he completed 30 of 39 starts and logged 338 innings. He yielded a league-most 27 round-trippers, the second of three times (1890 and 1896) he held that dubious distinction. While scoring increased to almost 14.8 total runs per game, Stivetts batted .328 (the team collectively hit .331, which ranked just third in the league) and slugged .533.

Dissension among Beaneaters players was palpable as the 1895 season commenced. Tensions erupted during spring training, when veteran Tommy McCarthy served as a special correspondent to a Boston newspaper.[37] Some of his more seasoned teammates felt insulted by the way he portrayed them in the press, and animosity grew. Two cliques formed: close friends McCarthy and Duffy on one side, and Stivetts and team captain Billy Nash on the other. The situation came to a head on May 16 in Louisville. In the crowded hotel restaurant, where players and other guests suppered, McCarthy punched the seated Stivetts, his former Browns teammate, causing a "disgraceful affair."[38] Notwithstanding that sucker punch, Stivetts didn't seem himself in 1895, thought Hub sportswriter J.C. Morse.[39] The hurler was beset by a series of maladies: a "small tumor" removed from his left eye (probably a cyst),[40] an injured arm from an exhibition game,[41] and finally malaria.[42] It was no surprise that the Beaneaters dropped to sixth place. Stivetts was still capable of "phenomenal speed" (such as in his two-hitter versus Rusie and the Giants on April 24);[43] however, he split his 34 decisions and logged 291 innings.

In 1896 Stivetts had a season commensurate with his previous three on the mound, going 22-14 and logging 329 innings as the Beaneaters finished in fourth place. Noteworthy was his production with the bat. He had often claimed that he enjoyed hitting more than pitching and voiced his frustration with his career lows in at-bats (158) and appearances as a position player (7) in 1895. Skipper Selee inserted the now 28-year-old into the field 18 times and the strategy paid dividends. Stivetts batted .347 (in 222 at-bats), trailing only future Hall of Famer Billy Hamilton, acquired in the offseason from the Philadelphia Phillies for Nash; and posted the highest slugging percentage on the team (.482). On June 12 Stivetts proved to be a double threat, going the distance in a 15-3 victory over the Reds in the Queen City, walloping two home runs among his four hits, and scoring four times.[44]

Given Stivetts' success at the plate, local and national media suggested that he'd be more valuable as a hitter. Selee, perhaps hedging his bets in case Stivetts' right arm failed, worked the hurler out at first and in the outfield during spring training, anticipating that the burly Pennsylvanian would play more in the field. In April Stivetts suffered a severely torn ligament in his right forearm.[45] That injury eventually ended his career as a twirler; however, it also enabled him to play more regularly in the field once he healed. After a brief demotion to Fall River (Massachusetts) in the New England League in mid-June, Stivetts pitched sparingly as the club's fourth starter, posting an 11-4 record and logging 129⅓ innings. Led by Kid Nichols, whose league-best 31 victories matched his average since debuting in 1892, Fred Klobedanz (26-7), and Ted Lewis (21-12), the Beaneaters emerged victorious in an exciting pennant chase with the Baltimore Orioles, capturing the flag by two games and setting a franchise record-high winning percentage (.705). Stivetts proved to be a valuable contributor. Making a career-high 29 starts as a flychaser, plus two at both first and second base, Stivetts led the team in batting (.367) and slugging (.533) in 199 at-bats.

With the emergence of Klobedanz and Lewis, Stivetts was converted to a full-time fielder in 1898; however, he lacked a natural position. Not fast enough to replace outfielders Duffy, Hamilton, or Chick Stahl, each of whom batted at least .340 in 1897, and not adroit enough with the glove to be a full-time infielder, Stivetts took on the role as a super-utility player, making appearances in the outfield and at first, second, and shortstop. His average dipped to .252, the result of a series of hand injuries. With rumors of his impending trade to the St. Louis Browns, Stivetts injured his thumb in late July, prematurely ending his season.[46] He left the club and returned home to Ashland to recuperate. When he received word that he had been traded to the Browns for pitcher Kid Carsey, Stivetts refused to return to the club and its owner von der Ahe, whose stadium had burned down in April.[47] The trade nullified, Stivetts was eventually sold outright to the Browns in mid-August.

Stivetts had a change of heart about the Browns in the offseason when Frank and Stanley Robison purchased the club, on the verge of financial collapse, from von der Ahe. Stivetts never donned the uniform of the Perfectos, the club's new name; rather, he was transferred to the Cleveland Spiders, also owned by the Robison brothers. In an obvious conflict of interest, the Robisons transferred the Perfectos' least productive players to the Spiders, which they ran like a circus show, side-project (they finished with the worst record in major-league history, 20-134). Stivetts lost all four of his decisions, batted .205, and was given his outright release on June 17.

So ended Stivetts' professional baseball career. He returned to his family in Ashland, where lived for the remainder of his life. He had married local Margaret Ann Thomas on June 30, 1886, and together they raised six children (five daughters and a son) born between 1889 and 1907. Like his father, Happy Jack ended up in a coal mine, but in a less dangerous role as a carpenter. He had also worked delivering beer during his playing days. Just 31 years old, Stivetts wasn't finished with baseball. For the next decade, he played semipro ball for a number of local teams, flashing the heat that propelled him to the majors where he had posted a 203-132 slate and logged 2,887⅔ innings. When Ashland's most famous citizen could no longer pitch, he managed and umpired in local leagues.

Jack Stivetts died on April 18, 1930, from a heart attack after falling down a stairwell.[48] He was 62 years old. Like his parents, he was buried in Ashland's Brock Cemetery.

SOURCES

In addition to the sources cited in the Notes, the author also accessed Retrosheet.org, Baseball-Reference.com, SABR.org, *Sporting Life* via the LA84 Foundation, *The Sporting News* archive via Paper of Record, and the player's file from the Baseball Hall of Fame in Cooperstown, New York.

NOTES

1. *Sporting Life*, July 21, 1894: 2.
2. Information about the Stivetts family is from US Census reports via Ancestry.com
3. Robert L. Tiemann, "John Elmer Stivetts," *Nineteenth Century Stars*, Robert L. Tiemann, Joseph Overfield, L. Robert Davids, Richard Puff, eds. (Phoenix: Society for American Baseball Research, 2012.)
4. "Base Ball Topics," *Philipsburg* (Montana) *Mail*, December 15, 1899: 2; and "Stivetts Hailed as 'Peer of Living Pitches' by Baseball World of '89." [untitled and undated article from players' file, Baseball Hall of Fame].
5. *Sporting Life*, July 1, 1893: 3.
6. *Sporting Life*, July 10, 1893: 3.
7. The official name was the Players' National League of Professional Base Ball Players.
8. Joe Pritchard, "St. Louis Stiftings," *Sporting Life*, May 3, 1890: 9.
9. *Sporting Life*, May 8, 1890: 13.
10. *Sporting Life*, June 14, 1890: 13
11. "He Stored Them," *St. Louis Post-Dispatch*, June 29, 1891: 2.
12. "Stivetts Suspended," *St. Louis Post-Dispatch*, August 20, 1891: 8.
13. "O'Neil Answered," *Sporting Life*, December 5, 1891: 10.
14. *Sporting Life*, October 29, 1892: 9.
15. "Umpire Lynch Did It," *Brooklyn Daily Eagle*, August 6, 1892: 3. 5
16. "Not a Hit off Stivetts," *Brooklyn Daily Eagle*, August 7, 1892: 8.
17. *Sporting Life*, October 22, 1892:4.
18. "Superb World's Championship Battle," *Cincinnati Enquirer*, October 18, 1892: 2.
19. "Out In Front. Cleveland Gets The Best of It," *Cincinnati Enquirer*, October 22, 1892: 6.
20. "Lucid Interval," *Sporting Life*, December 31, 1892: 3.
21. "We Plead Guilty," *Sporting Life*, November 20, 1892: 9.
22. *Sporting Life*, May 18, 1893: 2.
23. J. C. Morse, "Hub Happenings," *Sporting Life*, March 31, 1894: 5. [Date is partially missing from the paper].
24. *Sporting Life*, May 18, 1893: 2.
25. "Cincinnati Chips," *Sporting Life*, December 30, 1893: 2.
26. "A Timely Suggestion for Boston," *Sporting Life*, May 6, 1893: 2.
27. O. P. Caylor, "The Pennant Winner," *Akron Daily Democrat*, October 7, 1893: 5.
28. *Sporting Life*, September 16, 1893: 2.
29. J. C. Morse, "Hub Happenings," *Sporting Life*, January 20, 1895: 5.
30. Terry Gottschall, "May 15, 1894: 'It was a Hot Game, Sue Enough'," SABR Games Project. https://sabr.org/gamesproj/game/may-15-1894-it-was-hot-game-sure-enough
31. "Stivetts A Hero," *Sporting Life*, October 20, 1894: 4.
32. Boston Herald as quoted in *Sporting Life*, June 2, 1894: 1.
33. *Democrat and Chronicle* (Rochester, New York), June 9, 1894: 11.
34. Tiemann.
35. "Stivetts' Father Killed," *Evening Herald* (Shenandoah, Pennsylvania), August 24, 1894: 1.
36. *St. Louis Post-Dispatch*, September 28, 1894: 7.
37. "Internal Dissensions," *Sporting Life*, March 28, 1896: 2.
38. "'Striking' lack of Harmony," *Sporting Life*, May 25, 1895: 3.
39. J. C. Morse, "Hub Happenings," *Sporting Life*, August 31, 1895: 7.
40. *Sporting Life*, June 8, 1895: 4.
41. J. C. Morse, "Hub Happenings, *Sporting Life*, July 27, 1895: 6.
42. J. C. Morse, "Hub Happenings," *Sporting Life*, August 31, 1895: 7.
43. Wm. F. H. Koelsch, "New York News," *Sporting Life*, May 4, 1895: 3.
44. *Pittsburgh Daily Post*, June 13, 1896: 6.
45. J. C. Morse, "Hub Happenings," *Sporting Life*, May 1, 1897: 1.
46. J. C. Morse, "Hub Happenings," *Sporting Life*, August 6, 1898: 19.
47. "Jack Stivetts Sold," *Buffalo Commercial*, August 20, 1898: 4.
48. Bill Lee, *The Baseball Necrology* (Jefferson, North Carolina: McFarland, 2009), 382.

HARRY STOVEY
BY PAUL HOFMANN

Harry Stovey.
(Courtesy of National Baseball Hall of Fame)

There exists a long list of forgotten nineteenth-century baseball stars who played during the game's formative stages and under relative anonymity besides being a name in a newspaper. While the game was fundamentally the same, it was evolving in an era that saw many rule changes and ballparks with vastly varying dimensions. There were no bright lights or television, and record-keeping was inconsistent. One of the greatest players of the nineteenth century was Harry Stovey.

Stovey was "one of baseball's first dual threats" in the judgment of Matt Kelly at the Baseball Hall of Fame.[1] He possessed a rare combination of power and speed that set him apart from other nineteenth-century players. He was also an innovator on the basepaths, introducing sliding techniques to the game that had never before been seen. Yet, despite the enshrinement of many of his contemporaries in the Baseball Hall of Fame, Stovey remains a forgotten star who, more than 120 years after his playing career ended, continues to be overlooked by those guarding the gates of Cooperstown.

Harold Duffield Stow was born on December 20, 1856, in Philadelphia.[2] He was the eighth of nine children born to John and Rachel (Duffield) Stow (or Stowe by other accounts).[3] The Philadelphia almanac that year lists John's profession as a watchman. Census and other records identify him as a shoemaker. The Stows and Duffields traced their origins to England and both sides of the family had long histories in the United States dating back to at least the early eighteenth century. The Stows had notable Philadelphians in their family tree.

Harry Stow was a direct descendant of an earlier John Stow, a Philadelphia founder who along with his partner John Pass, is credited with recasting the Liberty Bell after it cracked. At Stow's foundry on Second Street, the bell was broken into small pieces, melted down, and cast into a new bell. The two founders found that the metal was too brittle, and augmented it by about 10 percent, using copper. The bell was ready in March 1753, and Norris reported that the lettering (which included the founders' names and the year) was even clearer on the new bell than on the old.[4] The Stow surname, along with the surname Pass, appears on the upper rim of bell. This is significant as it is one of a few pieces of evidence that point to the proper spelling of the family's surname.[5]

While relatively little is known about Harry's early childhood and education, his early life was certainly shaped by the events surrounding the Civil War. Philadelphia during the Civil War was an important source of troops, money, weapons, medical care, and supplies for the Union.

The Stow family resided in the eastern section of the Kensington District, a working-class community known for its large Irish Catholic and English-American communities.

The Stows, like many of the area families, contributed to the war effort. Harry's older sisters worked in Kensington's wool mills and his older brother John joined the 90th Regiment of Pennsylvania Infantry, a unit made up entirely of volunteers from Philadelphia.[6] It was also during this time that Harry lost his older brother Edwin. On June 14, 1862, Edwin unexpectedly died of an intussusception, a bowel obstruction, at the age of 13.

Harry loved baseball from an early age and as a youngster he spent what his parents considered an abnormal amount of time playing the game, and the more he played, the better he got.[7] In fact, his mother abhorred the game and strongly disapproved of Harry playing. Her hope was that Harry would dedicate his time to learning a trade. When he was not on the sandlots the adolescent Stovey, like many of his contemporaries, learned a trade. He apprenticed and was trained as a cooper.[8]

Stovey began his ballplaying career as a pitcher with the Defiance Club of Philadelphia in 1877 in the League Alliance. In an effort to conceal his ballplaying from his mother, Harry played under the name of Stovey to avoid the name Stow being used in accounts of local baseball games.[9] After enjoying success with Defiance, Stovey joined the Philadelphia Athletics club, which had been expelled from the National League at the end of the 1876 season and also was in the League Alliance.

He spent the next two seasons playing minor-league ball for the New Bedford Clam-Eaters under their nomadic manager, Frank Bancroft. Stovey took a liking to New Bedford and a young woman named Mary Walker. Stovey and Mary were married in July of 1879 and New Bedford would become Stovey's adopted home.[10]

In 1880 Bancroft was hired as manager of the National League's Worcester Ruby Legs and took Stovey along with him. Stovey made his major-league debut on May 1, 1880. Two-and-a-half months later, on July 17, he hit his first major-league home run when he connected off the Cleveland Blues' Jim McCormick, who led the National League with 45 victories that year. On September 21 Stovey collected four hits, including two home runs, off right-hander Mickey Welch as the Ruby Legs routed the Troy Trojans, 17-2. Four of Stovey's six home runs that year came at the expense of Welch.

Splitting time between first base and the outfield, the 23-year-old right-handed-hitting Stovey enjoyed a productive rookie campaign. While his .265 batting average may not have been that awe-inspiring, Stovey did lead the league with 14 triples and tied Boston's Jim O'Rourke for the lead in home runs with six. He also added 21 doubles, sixth most in the league, and finished second in the league in runs scored (76) and total bases (161).

Early in 1880 Stovey and his wife welcomed their first daughter, Elizzia, who would go by Lizzie. During the offseason, Stovey supported his young family by working as the night clerk at the Bancroft House in New Bedford.[11] The Ruby Legs manager, who had interests in the local theater and entertainment industry, had opened the Bancroft House to meet the needs of "managers, agents, and [theater] companies visiting New Bedford."[12] Bancroft would apply the same skills and abilities that made him successful in the theater industry – specifically his ability to recognize new trends – to the growing popularity of baseball.

The Ruby Legs finished in fifth place during their first season. However, the team was struggling financially. The club's board of directors concluded that a professional manager like Bancroft was not worth the investment.[13] Bancroft found employment as manager of the National League's newest team, the Detroit Wolverines, in 1881. The move signaled the start of precipitous decline for the Ruby Legs' fortunes in Worcester.

With Bancroft no longer at the helm, a rift occurred between player-manager Mike Dorgan and star pitcher Lee Richmond, who a year earlier had authored major-league baseball's first perfect game. The conflict caused Richmond to quit the team. On August 17 with the team in seventh place with a 24-32 record, the Ruby Legs suspended Dorgan (who immediately signed with Bancroft's Wolverines) and named Stovey manager for the remainder of the season. The Ruby Legs were 8-18 under Stovey and finished the season in last place, 23 games behind the pennant-winning Chicago White Stockings.

Stovey's power numbers dipped slightly in 1881. He finished the year with a .270 batting average, 25 doubles, 7 triples, and 2 home runs. His OPS dropped from .742 the previous year to .696. It was the last year his OPS would dip below .750 until 1892. Defensively he appeared in more games at first base than he did in the outfield.

Throughout his career it was often said that Stovey had sure hands and a strong, accurate arm with great range. Statistically, he was an above-average first baseman. He finished in the top four in the league in range factor from 1881 to 1885 and in the top five in fielding percentage during the same years. As of 2019, his 165 career outfield assists place him in the top 100 all-time.

The 1882 season was the final one for Stovey and the Ruby Legs in Worcester. The team continued its free fall in the National League standings and finished in last place with an 18-66 record. Things got so bad that the team's regular-season finale at the Agricultural County Fair Grounds on September 29 drew a crowd of just 25 patrons, an improvement over the day before, when they drew just six.[14]

Despite playing for poor teams – the Ruby Legs had a meager .361 winning percentage during their three NL seasons – Stovey continued to develop into one of the game's most exciting young players. He improved his batting average to .289 and scored 90 runs as his reputation as a daring baserunner grew. He also hit five home runs, which tied him for fourth best in the circuit.

After Worcester disbanded, Stovey was lured back to Philadelphia by Athletics owners Lew Simmons, Billy Sharsig, and Charlie Mason, who reportedly offered him a salary of $2,000, a 60 percent raise over what he was earning with the Ruby Legs.[15] His signing was a coup for the American Association. Philadelphia was one of the cities in which the Association was in direct competition with the National League and the articulate, well-mannered, handsome, and home-grown 5-foot-11, 175-pound Stovey gave them a decided advantage in winning the hearts and loyalties of Philadelphia baseball fans over the cellar-dwelling Quakers of the National League.

Stovey and fellow National League imports Lon Knight and pitcher Bobby Matthews joined an Athletics team that went 41-34 and finished in second place in the American Association's inaugural season. The 26-year-old Stovey quickly established himself as the game's premier baserunner and power hitter, proving to be the offensive sparkplug the team needed to win the Association championship. Stovey led the league in runs scored, doubles, home runs, total bases, and slugging percentage. He was also considered the best baserunner in the game.[16]

In fact, Stovey was an innovator on the basepaths. He is credited with inventing sliding pads to protect the often bruised and scraped hips he suffered while sliding on the crudely manicured nineteenth-century fields. He is recognized as one of the first baserunners to slide feet-first into bases and mastering the technique of the pop-up slide, a revolutionary method of going into a base that put added pressure on the defense.[17] However, Stovey's aggressive sliding led to many leg injuries during his career.

Despite his aggressiveness on the basepaths, Stovey was often referred to as "Gentleman Harry" for his clean play. Alfred Henry Spink, author of *The National Game*, wrote of Stovey in 1910: "He always slid feet first but was not 'nasty' with his feet in the way of trying to hurt the baseman, as some of his imitators were."[18]

According to Edward Achorn in *The Summer of Beer and Whiskey*, on the 1883 American Association season, Stovey and many of the Athletics were banged up as they limped toward the finish line for the Association pennant. Stovey was suffering from a sprained ankle that "had turned him into a sad parody of himself on the base paths."[19] Achorn chronicled the last half-inning of the Athletics' pennant-clinching victory on September 28 in which Stovey fittingly scored the pennant-winning run. The Athletics and the Louisville Eclipse were tied, 6-6, and right-hander Guy Hecker was on the mound as the Athletics came to bat in the bottom of the 10th inning.

> Now Harry Stovey pulled a bat from the box at the end of the bench and limped to home plate. … Hecker, either wary of Stovey or incapable of controlling his pitches at this point, kept the ball away from the plate, finally walking the batter. When an exhausted Hecker followed with a wild pitch, Stovey hobbled down to second base – not quite scoring position, this time, given the runner's lame ankle.
>
> Captain Lon Knight stepped to the plate. Throughout the pennant stretch he had repeatedly made clutch plays that kept the Athletics alive. Now he ripped a single to left field.
>
> Stovey barely made it to third.
>
> It was up to Mike Moynahan. He had enjoyed a fine day, going 2-for-4 at the plate and making nine assists at shortstop, with only one error. Hecker held the ball, stared at the plate, took a run and fired. Moynahan swung and connected. At the crack of the bat, left fielder Pete Browning and center fielder Leech Maskrey dashed for the ball as it shot between them. Harry Stovey who led the American Association with 109 runs scored stumbled home, wincing, with number 110.[20]

When the team returned to Philadelphia, a great victory celebration was held. At a banquet each Athletic player was presented with a gold badge bearing his name and the inscription "Athletic Base Ball Champions of 1884" (denoting their reign until the end of the next season).[21] Mason, one of the Athletics owners, also presented Stovey, whose "extraordinary grace and drive had sustained the club during its crucial final six weeks," with a gold watch and chain to commemorate his leadership.[22]

Stovey, who became the first major leaguer to hit 10 home runs in a season, set the single-season home-run record with 14 during the Athletics' championship run, out-homering five of the other seven Association teams.[23] However, his record lasted only one year. In 1884 Ned Williamson and three of his Chicago White Stockings teammates (Fred Pfeffer, Abner Dalrymple, and Cap Anson) surpassed Stovey. Williamson nearly doubled Stovey's mark with 27.[24]

There was more to Stovey's year than setting home-run records and contributing to a championship season with his hometown Athletics. In 1883 he and Mary welcome their second daughter, Susan. Two years later a third daughter, Harriett, was born.

Building on his success of the previous year, Stovey enjoyed an even better season at the plate in 1884. One highlight of the season came on August 18 when Stovey had three triples and two singles in the Athletics' 20-1 thrashing of the Baltimore Orioles. Two of his triples came in the eighth inning. He was the third major leaguer to hit two triples in an inning.[25]

In 104 games played that season (all at first base), Stovey hit .326 with 22 doubles, a league-leading 23 triples, 10 home runs (second to Cincinnati's John Reilly who clouted 11), and 83 RBIs. He also recorded a career-high .545 slugging percentage. Despite his offensive output, the Athletics failed to defend their Association title. The team finished in seventh place with a 61-46 record in the 13-team league, 14 games behind the champion New York Metropolitans.[26]

After the disappointing finish in 1884, the first real signs of unrest among the Athletics' triumvirate ownership group became apparent. In November Lew Simmons announced that he was taking over as field manager in 1885 because the team had lost $20,000 in 1884. He blamed Stovey for the team's slump. Simmons cited an incident in which he asserted that Stovey arrived at the ballpark too drunk to play, a common-enough claim in the 1880s. In fact, there were numerous reports of heavy drinking among the Athletics, and the owners expressed concerns about almost all their players. The club imposed rules that among other things addressed the problems of hard living associated with the team and the American Association.[27] However, the upstanding Stovey was never linked to the social ills that plagued the Athletics.

But co-owners Sharsig and Mason were quick to come to Stovey's defense, praising him for his performance on the field and his leadership. Stovey defended himself in a letter to *Sporting Life*. The letter read:

Dear Sir:

In your last issue you published an interview with Lew Simmons, in which that individual expresses himself altogether too freely concerning the occurrences of the past season, and in which he particularly singles me out as an "awful example." Permit me to say that Mr. Simmons is so bold in his utterance because he knows I am at a safe distance and cannot just now defend myself, and he embraces the opportunity to assail me. I wish to say that the scaffold accident did really happen at the time mentioned, and that 1 was really injured by the falling of the same can be easily proven. I was not intoxicated, as Mr. Simmons states, and I beg that you will do me the favor to publish this public contradiction. I shall shortly have a personal interview with my "*friend*" Mr. Simmons, concerning this matter.

He says he is going to be the manager next season, and further that he will make the boys play ball or he will fine and expel them. I think he is "shooting off his mouth" altogether too previously, and a short experience will convince him that that is not the way to get good work out of his men, for they cannot and will not play with any heart under apprehension of being fined for every error they make. In my estimation he will make what I may call, in the expressive slang of the day, a "dub" of a manager; and I will frankly state right here that I would prefer my release to playing under him. Trusting that I have not encroached too much upon your valuable space,

I remain. Very truly yours,

HARRY D. STOVEY[28]

The end result was that Stovey was appointed manager-captain for the 1885 season and Simmons was, albeit temporarily, relegated to low man on the ownership's totem pole.

Stovey established two significant milestones in 1885. In a game on July 16 at Sportsman's Park I, Stovey hit the 45th home run of his career, off the Browns' Jumbo McGinnis. The two-run clout made him the major-league career leader in home runs. On September 28 Stovey hit his final home run of the season, and the 50th of his career, off Pittsburgh Alleghenys rookie hurler John Hofford. Stovey was the first player to hit 50.

Stovey finished the season batting over .300 for the third consecutive year. Playing in a league-leading 112 games, the Athletics' player-manager finished with a .315 average, 130 runs scored, 27 doubles, 9 triples, 13 home runs, and 75 RBIs. His runs scored and home run totals led the Association. With Stovey at the helm, the Athletics finished in fourth place with a 55-57 record, 24 games behind the champion St. Louis Browns. Stovey never managed a major-league team again and finished his big-league managerial career with a 63-75-2 mark.

On the last day of the 1885 season, Stovey's older brother John Jr., who had served in the Union Army during the Civil War, died. John, who was unmarried, was buried in Cedar Hill Cemetery, where Stovey's parents and his sister Sarah would later be buried.[29]

Desperate to remain competitive in the American Association and with their crosstown National League rivals, the Athletics made another managerial change. Co-owner Simmons, who a year earlier blamed Stovey for the team's troubles, emerged as the new manager to start the 1886 season. The team was mired in sixth place with a 41-55 record before co-owner Sharsig stepped in to lead the team to a 22-17 finish over its last 39 games. The team finished in sixth place.

Stovey's offensive production dipped in 1886. Splitting time between center field, right field, and first base, he batted .294 with 28 doubles, 11 triples, and 7 home runs. But the 29-year-old Stovey led the Association with 68 stolen bases in the first in which stolen bases were an official statistic.

For 1887 the Athletics turned to Stovey's first manager at Worcester, Frank Bancroft. The addition of Bancroft had little impact on team's success. The Athletics had a record of 26-29 and were in fifth place when the manager was fired and replaced by Mason, the third Athletics owner to manage the team in as many years.

Stovey enjoyed a relatively productive year. In 124 games, the majority in the outfield, he batted .286, scored 125 runs, hit 31 doubles, and stole 74 bases. He hit only four home runs and before the end of the season he was passed by Detroit Wolverines first baseman Dan Brouthers as the leader in career home runs. It was the only season in which Stovey didn't lead the American Association in at least one major offensive category.[30]

On August 2 Stovey lost another member of his family. John Sr., Stovey's father, succumbed to a heart attack at the age of 77.[31]

The Athletics' revolving door of managers continued as Sharsig returned to guide the team in 1888. Stovey was the everyday left fielder for the 81-52 Athletics, who finished in third place 10 games behind the St. Louis Browns. Stovey finished with a .287 batting average, 127 runs scored, 25 doubles, a league-leading 20 triples, 9 home runs, 65 RBIs, and 87 stolen bases. On May 15 he hit for the cycle in a 12-3 victory over Baltimore Orioles.

That season the strong-armed Stovey participated in a long-distance throwing contest sponsored by the *Cincinnati Enquirer*. Stovey's heave of 123 yards 2 inches on the fly was good enough for second place, behind Ned Williamson,[32] who won the competition with a throw of 133 yards 11 inches.[33]

The Athletics repeated their third-place finish under Sharsig in 1889, a season that was one of Stovey's finest. Playing all 137 games in left field, he batted .308 and recorded career highs in runs scored (152), doubles (38), home runs (19), and RBIs (119). (His home-run total was considered a greater accomplishment by many baseball historians than Williamson's 27 in 1884.) Stovey regained the record for career home runs when he slugged his 80th and 81st against Lee Viau at Cincinnati's League Park on August 13. Stovey joined Charley Jones as the only players to hold the career record for home runs at two different times.

War broke out in major-league baseball after the 1889 season when the Brotherhood of Professional Base Ball Players announced the creation of the Players' League for the 1890 season. Stovey was a hot commodity and was courted by the new league's Boston Reds. He found the prospect of playing closer to his wife's hometown of New Bedford too appealing to pass up and signed with the King Kelly-managed Reds, ending his seven-year stint in the Association.

Despite playing only seven of the circuit's 10 campaigns, Stovey's 76 home runs and 883 runs scored are the most in American Association history. He also ranks in the top 10 of nearly every other category, including games played, batting average, slugging percentage, total bases, hits, and stolen bases.

Stovey was the Reds' everyday right fielder in 1890 and hit .298 with 26 doubles, 13 triples, and 12 home runs, the third highest total in the Players' League behind Hardy Richardson (16) and Roger Connor (14). He drove in 88 runs, scored 145 runs, and had a career-high 97 stolen bases, helping the Reds to an 81-48 record as the team finished in first place 6½ games ahead of the Brooklyn Ward's Wonders and captured the Players League championship. On September 3 Stovey became the first player to hit 100 home runs when he hit one off former Athletics teammate Jersey Bakley in Boston.

After the collapse of the Players' League after the 1890 season and the subsequent ratification of the new National Agreement, it was presumed that Stovey would return to the Athletics and resume his record-setting Association career. The new National Agreement stated that "everyone was supposed to return to the teams that had reserved them in 1889."[34] However, an administrative error on the part of the Athletics left Stovey and former Athletics teammate Lou Bierbauer unprotected and declared free agents.

Stovey opted to accept the National League's Boston Beaneaters' offer of $4,200 a season, the highest salary of his career.[35] The Beaneaters, led by manager Frank Selee, were coming off a fifth-place finish in 1890 and were confident the aging star could help them capture the National League championship.

On April 1, 1891, three weeks before the start of the season, Stovey and his wife welcomed their fourth daughter, Rachel. The infant, who also had a twin sister who was stillborn, did not survive infancy and died on June 6.

Despite the loss of his infant daughter, Stovey played a key role in the Beaneaters' run to the National League Pennant – his third championship team in three different leagues. Stovey was primarily used as a corner outfielder (39 games in left field and 96 games in right field). In 134 games he hit .279 with a league-leading 20 triples, 16 home runs, 271 total bases, and a .498 slugging percentage. He had a team-leading 95 RBIs and 57 stolen bases.[36] It was the last great season of Stovey's career.

Stovey started the 1892 season in one of the worst slumps of his career, and on June 20 he was released by the Beaneaters. At the time of his release he was hitting an anemic .164 with no home runs and 12 RBIs. Nearly three weeks later, the 35-year-old Stovey was signed by the last-place Baltimore Orioles. On July 21 he repeated his 1884 feat of hitting three triples in a single game during a 10-3 victory over Pittsburgh. In 74 games with the Orioles, Stovey rediscovered his hitting stroke and batted .272 with 4 home runs and 55 RBIs.

Stovey also started the 1893 season slowly. After hitting only .154 in eight games, he was released by Baltimore. Three days later, on May 25, the 35-year-old Stovey signed with Brooklyn Grooms. In 48 games with the Grooms, he hit .251 with one home run and 29 RBIs. Time and injuries had taken its toll on the one-time slugger. On June 8 he hit the final home run of his career in the Grooms' 7-6 victory over the Browns. It was his 122nd career home run, the major-league high. He played in his last major-league game on July 29.

Stovey's record lasted until 1895. Stovey was third on the list all-time home run list (behind Roger Connor and Sam Thompson) as late as 1920, the year Babe Ruth began to single-handedly usher in the live-ball era.

His major-league career behind him, Stovey was reunited with King Kelly when he played briefly for Allentown in the Pennsylvania State League. Then he became the player-manager for New Bedford of the New England League.

After retiring from baseball, Harry Stovey ceased to exist. The ex-player resumed use of the name he was born with, Harry D. Stow. In 1895 he joined the New Bedford police force and served for 28 years. While patrolling his beat along the city's waterfront one day in 1901, Officer Stow spotted a seven-year-old boy who had fallen between two piers and was struggling in the water. He dived in and saved the boy's life.[37] Soon afterward he was promoted to sergeant for bravery and became a captain in 1915. In 1922 his wife of 43 years, Mary, died. He retired from the police force in 1923.

Stovey died at his daughter's house in New Bedford on September 20, 1937. He was 80 years old. He is buried in New Bedford's Oak Grove Cemetery next to his wife and two of his daughters, Harriet and Rachel. At the time of his death, few New Bedford residents knew that Officer Stow was Harry Stovey, one of the greatest baseball stars of the nineteenth century.

Whether or not Stovey belongs in the Hall of Fame has been a topic of conversation among baseball historians for years. In 1936 he received six votes for the Hall of fame, the only year he appeared on the ballot. He outpolled both Kid Nichols and Jim O'Rourke, both of whom were later inducted into Cooperstown.[38] In 1983 a poll of SABR's nineteenth century research committee voted Stovey and Pete Browning as the two players of that era most deserving to be in the Hall (excluding those already enshrined).[39]

In 2011 SABR members selected Stovey as the Overlooked 19th Century Base Ball Legend.[40]

Statistically, a strong case can be made for Stovey's enshrinement in the Hall of Fame. In addition to being an early home-run king — Stovey finished in the top four in home runs 10 times, leading the league in five of those seasons — he was one of the early game's great doubles and triples hitters. Stovey finished his 14-year major-league career with 348 doubles and 176 triples. He had 912 RBIs, an impressive number considering he often batted in the leadoff position early in his career.

As of 2019, Stovey's 509 stolen bases ranked 35th all-time. However, no stolen-base statistics exist for the first six years of his career.

Stovey is also one of only three players to have played in a minimum of 1,000 games and averaged more than one run scored per game. Billy Hamilton and George Gore are the others.[41] Stovey scored 1,495 runs in 1,489 games, including nine seasons of 100 or more runs scored.

Throughout his career it was often said that Stovey had sure hands and a strong, accurate arm with great range. Statistically, he was an above-average first baseman. He finished in the top four in the league in range factor from 1881 to 1885 and in the top five in fielding percentage during the same years. As of 2019, his 165 career outfield assists placed him in the top 100 all-time.

Modern sabermetrics provide a less definitive case for Stovey's inclusion in the Hall of Fame. His black-ink and gray-ink scores of 56 and 210, respectively, are favorable.[42] Stovey led his league in important offensive categories more than 20 times, including extra-base hits five times, runs scored and triples four times, slugging percentage and total bases three times, stolen bases twice, and doubles and RBIs once. However, his WAR scores are less definitive. Stovey's career WAR of 45.2 and seven-year peak WAR of 31.1 are considerably below the average of the 20 left fielders in the Hall of Fame as of 2019. The average career WAR and seven-year peak WAR for left fielders are 65.5 and 41.6, respectively.

Stovey's omission from the Hall of Fame may also be a consequence of revisionist history. Early scoring rules differed and box scores and game accounts offered comparatively little information by today's standards. Later baseball historians went back and revised the American Association's statistics, resulting in a lowering of many of the jaw-dropping statistics that were once attributed to Stovey.[43] This, coupled with the fact that the Association, though recognized as a major league, was considered inferior to the National League, may be one reason why Stovey has yet to be elected to the Hall of Fame.[44]

Regardless of whether or not Stovey is eventually enshrined in Cooperstown, he should be remembered as one of the early game's great power hitters and an innovative baserunner who helped revolutionize the national pastime.

SOURCES

In addition to the sources cited in the Notes, the author also relied on Baseball-reference.com and Retrosheet.org.

NOTES

1. Matt Kelly, "19th Century Star Harry Stovey," baseballhall.org/discover-more/stories/pre-integration/stovey-harry Retrieved March 3, 2019.

2. Edward Achorn, *The Summer of Beer and Whiskey*. (New York: Public Affairs, 2006), 76.

3. US Census Records lists the family as both Stow and Stowe. Some records include the family as both Stow and Stowe in the same census. There may have been other children at some point, but nine appear in census records.

4. "CAST: Liberty Cast and Recast." Retrieved from castartandobjects.com/blog/2017/7/4/liberty-cast-and-recast

5. Harry first appeared in US Census Records in 1860 with the surname Stow. The surname on the family headstone in Oak Grove Cemetery in New Bedford, Massachusetts, is Stow. Unhappy with the sound of the bell, Stow and Pass recast the bell as second time in June 1753.

6. "United States Civil War Soldiers Index, 1861-1865," database, *FamilySearch* (familysearch.org/ark:/61903/1:1:FS3M-L28 : 4 December 2014), John P. Stow, Corporal, Company E, 90th Regiment, Pennsylvania Infantry, Union; citing NARA microfilm publication M554 (Washington: National Archives and Records Administration, n.d.), roll 119; FHL microfilm 882,454.

7. Buddy Thomas, "Stovey: City Man Changes the Game," *New Beford Standard-Times*, April 8, 2006. southcoasttoday.com/article/20060408/news/304089946.

8. A cooper is a person trained to make wooden casks, barrels, vats, buckets, tubs, troughs, and other staved containers.

9. Matt Kelly, "19th century star Harry Stovey." Retrieved from baseballhall.org/hall-of-famers/pre-integration/stovey-harry.

10. There are multiple records of the Stoveys' marriage. One lists the date as July 21 and others as July 23.

11. "Diamond Dust Early Blown," *Boston Globe*, January 16, 1881: 2.

12. Benjamin McArthur, *Actors and American Culture, 1880-1920* (Philadelphia: Temple University Press, 1984): 7-11, cited by Charlie Bevis in "Frank Bancroft," SABR BioProject. Retrieved from sabr.org/bioproj/person/48535bb7.

13. Charlie Bevis, "Worcester Nationals ownership history," Retrieved from sabr.org/research/worcester-nationals-ownership-history.

14. Philip Lowry, *Green Cathedrals* (New York: Walker & Company, 2006), 243.

15. Achorn, 77.

16. Stolen bases did not become an official statistic until 1886.

17. Peter Morris. *Game of Inches: The Stories Behind the Innovations that Shaped Baseball. New, Revised and Expanded One-Volume Edition*. (Chicago: Ivan R. Dee, 2010), 188.

18. Alfred Spink, *The National Game* (St. Louis: National Game Publishing Company, 1910), 186.

19. Achorn, 226.

20. Achorn, 226-227. Some accounts of the game report that Stovey scored the winning run on a wild pitch. According to his obituary in *The Sporting News*, he single-handedly sealed the championship for the Athletics in the final game of the season against Louisville when, in the 10th inning, he singled, stole second, went to third on an infield out, and scored on a wild pitch thrown by pitcher Guy Hecker.

21. Achorn, 240.

22. Ibid.

23. William McNeil, *The King of Swat: An Analysis of Baseball's Home Run Hitters from the Major, Minor, Negro and Japanese Leagues* (Jefferson, North Carolina: McFarland & Company, Inc., 1997), 36.

24. Williamson's 27 home runs in 1884 were largely attributed to the fact that in White Stocking Park (a.k.a. Lake Front Park), the field's dimensions were

24. 180 feet down the line to left, 280 feet to left-center, 300 feet to dead center field, 252 feet to right-center, and 196 feet down the line to right. The right-handed-hitting Williamson hit 25 of his 27 home runs at White Stocking Park and never hit more than nine home runs in any other season.

25. As of 2019 only 11 major-league players had hit two triples in one inning. The feat was most recently accomplished by the Colorado Rockies outfielder Cory Sullivan on April 9, 2006.

26. The American Association expanded to 13 teams for the 1884 season. The league contracted back to eight teams in 1885 and then played its final two seasons (1890 and 1891) with nine teams.

27. Paul Hofmann, "Jud Birchall," SABR BioProject. Retrieved from sabr.org/bioproj/person/8ab5cdb7.

28. Harry Stovey, "Harry Stovey Expresses Himself," *Sporting Life*, December 3, 1884: 3.

29. "Pennsylvania, Philadelphia City Death Certificates, 1803-1915," database with images, *FamilySearch* (familysearch.org/ark:/61903/1:1:JNLH-M3F : March 8, 2018), John P Stow, 09 Oct 1885; citing 797, Philadelphia City Archives and Historical Society of Pennsylvania, Philadelphia; FHL microfilm 2,070,684.

30. John Shiffert, *Base Ball in Philadelphia: a History of the Early Game* (Jefferson, North Carolina: McFarland & Company, Inc., 2006), 132.

31. "Pennsylvania, Philadelphia City Death Certificates, 1803-1915," database with images, *FamilySearch* (familysearch.org/ark:/61903/1:1:JKS5-M3X : 8 March 2018), John P. Stow, 02 Aug 1887; citing 257, Philadelphia City Archives and Historical Society of Pennsylvania, Philadelphia; FHL microfilm 2,078,809.

32. George Tuohey, *A History of the Boston Base Ball Club: A Concise and Accurate History of Base Ball from Its Inception* (Boston: M.F. Quinn & Co., 1897), 217.

33. "Baseball Records: Long Distance Throwing," *World Almanac 1892*: 227.

34. Shiffert, 153.

35. Thomas. After his retirement, Stovey claimed he never earned more than $2,400 per year playing baseball.

36. Billy Nash also recorded 95 RBIs to tie for the team lead.

37. Achorn, 245.

38. David Nemec, *The Beer and Whiskey League: The Illustrated History of the American Association – Baseball's Renegade Major League*, (New York: Lyons & Buford, Publishers, 1994): 238.

39. Lew Lipset, "Grandpa Was Harry Stovey," *The National Pastime*, Vol. 4, No. 2 (Cooperstown, New York: Society for American Baseball Research, Winter 1985): 84.

40. "Overlooked 19th Century Base Ball Legends." Retrieved from sabr.org/overlooked-19th-century-baseball-legends. Browning was selected in 2009 and Deacon White, who was elected to the Hall of Fame in 2013, was selected in 2010.

41. Gabriel Schechter, "Harry Stovey: Forgotten Five-Tool Star," The National Pastime Museum, May 9, 2013. Retrieved from thenationalpastimemuseum.com/article/harry-stovey-forgotten-five-tool-star.

42. The Black-Ink Test is named so because league-leading numbers are traditionally represented with **Boldface** type. The score is a measure of how often a player led the league in a variety of "important" stats. Similarly, the Gray-Ink test measures a player's appearance in the top 10 of the league in "important" stats. It is important to note that Stovey played during an era when 8 to 10 teams were typically the norm. These two comparative measures disadvantage modern players who played in 14- to 16-team leagues.

43. For decades after his retirement, Stovey was credited with having a career batting average of .321 and setting the single-season stolen-base record of 156 in 1888.

44. Schechter.

JIM SULLIVAN

BY RICHARD BOGOVICH

"Being Irish, he had an abiding sense of tragedy, which sustained him through temporary periods of joy." This remark has been credited (dubiously) to the Irish poet William Butler Yeats, a contemporary of Boston pitcher Jim Sullivan. This saying could apply to Sullivan starting in the mid-1890s, when he experienced deep sorrow repeatedly. At least relatives who survived him could look back on a few of his 26 wins for the Beaneaters as sunbursts in a span of sadness.

Daniel James Sullivan was born to Irish immigrants in Charlestown, Massachusetts, on April 25, 1867.[1] His parents, Timothy and Margaret (Desmond) Sullivan, had seven children, based on censuses. Margaret outlived four of her children.

Timothy Sullivan's occupation in the 1870 census was mariner, and classified ads from 1886 to 1889 indicate he recruited for the US Navy.[2] He also had a liquor operation, based on city directories. On at least two occasions, police raided it, in 1876 and 1889.[3]

Among the few available details of Jim Sullivan's youth is his participation in legendary fights with snowballs (and maybe stones) starting in the winter of 1875-76, when he was 8½ years old. "Twenty-five years ago and for several succeeding years, when the winters were long and cold, the Mystic river, between Charlestown and Chelsea, was a famous battle-ground where the boys from Chelsea and Charlestown fought decisive conflicts," recalled the *Boston Globe* in a lengthy article.[4] Perhaps that combat contributed to his pitching skill. In the 1880 census he was a student, as were his four oldest siblings, ages 8 to 15. In 1885, at the age of 18, he was presumably the "D.J. Sullivan" who helped direct a concert and dance celebrating the 10th

Jim Sullivan.
(public domain)

anniversary of the St. Mary's Young Men's Catholic Temperance Society.[5]

One profile of Sullivan in 1895 said his pitching career began in 1887 in the city's Temperance League, but two years later that same paper gave the year as 1888 and specified that his team represented the aforementioned St. Mary's organization.[6] In actuality, in May of 1888 the *Boston Globe* had announced the formation of such a team, and named D.J. Sullivan as its pitcher. The *Globe*'s coverage of a St. Mary's game in mid-June mentioned a Sullivan as their pitcher, and J. Sullivan was likewise in a box score in late July.[7] In April of 1889 the *Globe* reported that pitcher "Sullivan of St. Mary's of Charlestown, '88, joined the St. Stephen's Temperance Association team of Boston."[8]

In mid-1889 a tour by the St. Stephen's team took them 400 miles northeast into Canada, during which they played eight games. On July 11, 22-year-old Jim Sullivan pitched in St. John, New Brunswick, against a local team called the Shamrocks. He struck out 20 or 21 batters and had three fielding assists in an 11-4 victory.[9]

He soon joined that team, and continued to impress. "Sullivan, formerly of the St. Stephens in the Temperance league, is pitching great ball for the Shamrocks of St. John, N.B.," the *Boston Herald* reported in early September. "Last week he pitched against the heavy hitting Socials of Halifax, and his side won by a score of 19 to 2, Sullivan striking out 18 men." The opposing pitcher was "Flynn, formerly of the Chicagos," presumably Massachusetts native Jocko Flynn, in which case the Shamrocks crushed a former National Leaguer who had had a 23-6 record for the White Stockings just three years earlier.[10]

A city directory for 1889 listed Daniel J. Sullivan as living with his parents in Charlestown, at 100 Water Street. The family had lived there since at least 1874. His occupation in 1889 was upholsterer, but the New Brunswick League went professional in 1890 and the Shamrocks rejoined it, with Sullivan in tow.[11] Because the league's four teams aggressively imported talent, at least five of his teammates were also future major leaguers. One of them, fellow pitcher and future Beaneater Frank Sexton, reportedly received $150 a month. The Shamrocks officially won the pennant but only after their unruly fans essentially drove a rival team out of the league.[12]

Before the 1891 season, Sullivan got a tryout with Frank Selee's Beaneaters, probably thanks to Fred Lake, a catcher with the New Brunswick League's Moncton team in 1890. Lake was scheduled to attend spring training with the Boston Reds of the American Association but on March 9 Selee signed Lake away from them.[13] Sullivan was practicing with the Beaneaters in Boston by the end of March but wasn't signed until April 3, the day after a home exhibition game against Brooklyn, the reigning NL champion.[14] He pitched the middle three innings before 6,155 fans. Sullivan walked his first opponent, Mike Griffin, but quickly escaped a potential jam. "He got in the way of a hotshot from Smith's bat, which was dangerous to face. He succeeded in deflecting it to [Joe] Quinn and a corking double play resulted," reported J.C. Edgerly of the *Globe*. Sullivan yielded two runs in his third inning but still received acclaim. "Young Sullivan made an excellent showing," wrote Edgerly. "He was cool and had good command of the ball." The *Boston Journal* elaborated: "Sullivan might have been excused, on the score of nervousness, if he had been a little wild and unsteady, but he carried himself like a veteran, showed excellent command of the ball, with some puzzling curves, watched the bases sharply, and was an unexpected success in batting, while he did some running and sliding which, if he keeps it up, will make him a valuable man to have on the bases." As a batter, box scores showed him with two singles and a stolen base. "Sullivan surprised everybody by the excellent exhibition he gave," concluded the *Boston Herald*.[15]

Sullivan's major-league debut occurred at home against the Phillies on April 28, three days after his 24th birthday. Regrettably for him, the poise he had displayed against Brooklyn was absent. After eight innings Boston led 11-2, so Sullivan entered for the final frame. He first faced Al Myers, who singled. Sullivan walked the next two batters. A fly out scored a run, and then he walked the opposing pitcher. The next batter singled, and the main difference among newspaper accounts was whether the seventh and last batter Sullivan faced, Billy Shindle, also reached by a base hit or by Sullivan's muff covering first base. Very quickly the score was 11-6, and Kid Nichols relieved to retire the side for Sullivan. "It was his first baptism in a league game, and the strain was a little too much, although it was very plain that the umpire [Tim Hurst] was a little hard on him," commented the *Boston Post*. "He had speed and good curves but he could not gauge the plate."[16]

Sullivan didn't pitch again for Boston in 1891. Three days later he and Lake played for the Morrills, sponsored by former Beaneaters player and manager John Morrill's sporting-goods business, but it was unclear whether they had been loaned or released. "Kirmes and [Edward] Sullivan of the Morrills have signed with Salem. Sullivan and Lake, the 'pony battery' of the Boston leaguers, will join the Morrills at Burlington and play in their place," the *Globe* announced, referring to the location of the University of Vermont. The next day that paper printed a box score of the Morrills' 10-9 loss to the Vermont collegians in which Sullivan pitched and Lake also played.[17]

As of March 2019, Sullivan's baseball-reference.com entry showed him with Rochester of the Eastern Association in May of 1891, but that was actually former American Association pitcher Tom Sullivan;[18] by May 8 Jim had agreed to join the Clyde team in the Rhode Island State League (RISL). The Clydes reportedly had signed him in the winter only to have the Beaneaters intervene.[19] With the Clydes he was reunited with former Shamrocks teammate Joe Sullivan, who was said to be his cousin.[20] However, before Jim settled in with the Clydes, on May 14 the Sullivans and at least two Clyde teammates played for another Boston team, the Lovells, in Woonsocket, against that city's RISL team.[21] Another of his Clyde teammates was Dan Penno, who had been a member of the Boston Resolutes of the National Colored League in 1887 and also played with the Cuban Giants.[22]

RISL games were played on Saturdays but on Sunday, July 19, Sullivan was one of seven Clyde players in an exhibition game against the Providence Grays of the Eastern Association. Though the Grays won, 7-3, Sullivan struck out 10 of them. He clearly made an impression: "The Providence management are after Jim Sullivan, the Clyde Club's crack pitcher, and he should be signed," reported *Sporting Life*. "He was with the Boston Leaguers the first of the season, has good speed, fine command and a cool head. He is worth several M.J. and William Sullivans." That remark disparaged two Providence pitchers ("M.J." being Mike Sullivan) but became moot when Providence soon disbanded.[23] Sullivan remained with the Clydes, and they won the RISL championship with a record of 15-3.[24]

More significantly, on September 1 Sullivan returned to the majors, back in Boston. The Columbus Solons of the American Association faced the first-place Reds, and the visitors gave Sullivan a trial by fire.[25] He pitched a complete game but the Reds won, 9-5. As of this writing baseball-reference.com credits Boston with only four earned runs. The *Boston Journal* wrote that Sullivan "did as well as could be expected in an opening game and facing heavy batters. His chief weakness is his wildness, for he fields his position well in the main." The *Boston Post* commented that Sullivan "gave a creditable exhibition." The paper quickly added that Columbus catcher Tom "Dowse gave him poor support."[26]

After the RISL season concluded, Sullivan and his catcher, Linville McKie, let it be known they were a battery for hire. For example, on September 12 they helped the Marions of Brookline shut out the Beacons of Hingham, and Sullivan struck out 15 batters.[27] One newspaper said the duo was promised "a trial by the veteran manager, Harry Wright of the Philadelphia National league club, in the spring."[28]

Sullivan instead opened the 1892 season with Indianapolis of the Western League. He started 22 games and had a good earned-run average of 2.64 but his record was 6-18. Things were bad for the club early. At the beginning of May, manager Billy Harrington complained publicly about his roster, for which he blamed some committee's drawing. In particular, he blasted former major leaguer Moxie Hengel. "He would not get sober," Harrington asserted. "At St. Paul he coaxed out young Sullivan, our best pitcher, and got him full as a Thanksgiving turkey." In hindsight, it was foreshadowing when Harrington added, "Sullivan is a crack pitcher when he is well, but he is sick now."[29]

He recovered quickly enough, because after the league disbanded in mid-July, one Boston paper wrote that "Jim Sullivan was the mainstay of the Indianapolis team all the season. Sometimes he was called on to go in the box two games in succession and he cheerfully did so, and pitched winning ball nearly all the time." He may never have received the $108 owed to him when the league folded.[30]

Providence of the Eastern League soon signed him, and his debut on August 4 against Binghamton was described in the *Boston Herald* as "one of the sharpest and most exciting struggles of the season. Jim Sullivan pitched in magnificent style, and his work won the game." He yielded two hits to Binghamton's leadoff hitter, rookie Willie Keeler, but gave up only four more while striking out seven. Sullivan overcame five errors by his new teammates to prevail, 4-3.[31] Over his eight weeks with Providence his workload at least matched his stint with Indianapolis, and his ERA sparkled at 1.14, but he ended up with another losing record, at 8-12.

Before winter the NL's Washington Senators announced signing both Jim and Joe Sullivan for the 1893 season. However, Providence continued to hold Jim in reserve as the regular season approached, and Washington declined to pay whatever Providence asked for his release.[32] His statistics in 1893-94 are incomplete, but during one game he was "presented with a large and elegant bouquet" by admirers, reported the *Herald*. "In the middle of the bouquet was a small cabbage in which was secreted a gold ring with a cameo setting."[33]

In contrast to Sullivan's first two seasons with Providence, in 1894 they battled for their league's pennant, and he was a major contributor. For example, in August he fended off one of their top rivals, the Syracuse Stars, with a 3-1 complete-game victory during which he scattered six hits. Providence did indeed win the pennant, and manager Billy Murray called Sullivan the best pitcher in the Eastern League. As a swift outcome, the Beaneaters reacquired Sullivan for their 1895 squad.[34]

Sullivan notched his first NL win in his first start, at home on May 3, 1895, against Washington. The Senators gradually piled up 11 runs but Boston amassed a staggering 27 and led 17-6 after five innings. All things considered, sportswriter Tim Murnane said, Sullivan "did good work" and overcame "a hard deal from umpire [Tim] Keefe. The Charlestown boy used good judgment and had good control."[35]

The 1895 and 1896 seasons proved to be Sullivan's fullest in the NL and were fairly similar for him. He was securely entrenched in the bottom half of Boston's pitching rotation, won 11 games each season, and had ERAs not much higher than the staff as a whole.[36] He hit his only NL home run on August 17, 1896, over the left-field fence of the South End Grounds in a 5-4 win over Brooklyn. The best start of his career came exactly one month later, on the road against the formidable Baltimore Orioles. Sullivan held the pennant winners hitless until there were two outs in the seventh inning, when Steve Brodie beat out a bunt toward third base. Sullivan triumphed with a two-hit, 2-0 shutout.[37]

Outside of baseball, Sullivan experienced alternating emotional extremes from 1895 through 1899. Each year brought both great sorrow and great joy. In mid-1895 his older brother Charles died at about 30. At the beginning of 1896, Jim married Mary McMahon, of Charlestown. In October his father died, but about two months later Jim and Mary celebrated the birth of a daughter, Helen. In November of 1897 his frequent teammate Joe Sullivan died at the age of 27, and in March of 1898 baby Helen died at 15 months old. In early 1899 Jim and Mary welcomed son Francis into the world, but in the middle of that year his sister Agnes died at the age of 19.[38]

In the midst of this five-year span fell the bittersweet baseball season of Jim Sullivan's career: He experienced the amazing 1897 pennant race, but circumstances minimized his participation. Still, he did contribute to the championship early and late during the season. On May 7 he won, 4-0, at home against Washington, his second and last NL shutout. On August 12, as the pennant race with Baltimore, Cincinnati, and New York intensified, Sullivan started on the road against New York. The game was tied 1-1 after nine innings, and each team scored three more in the 10th. Boston scored in the 12th inning, and Sullivan had an impressive complete-game win.[39] In between those milestones, he pitched sparingly. A column in *The Sporting News* alluded to a reason, asserting that if Sullivan "had the endurance of a strong man there would not be a better pitcher in the whole land." Sportswriter Jacob Morse later provided context: "Jim Sullivan has not been in the best of trim this year," he wrote. "He caught cold while down South [during spring training], and that knocked him out, so that since then he has not been in form to pitch with the best results." Sullivan, though, insisted that he was in good shape.[40] He proved it in that 12-inning marathon, but hadn't previously "been in condition to pitch a half a dozen games this season," sportswriter Walter Barnes commented afterward. "A full game seemed to be testing the endurance of the invalided Sullivan," he concluded.[41] That season, at least, the 5-foot-10 pitcher weighed a mere 155 pounds.[42]

Sullivan pitched a few more times during the season's final two months, including in relief on September 22, the game before Boston's dramatic three-game series in Baltimore. Selee didn't take Sullivan to Baltimore. Also left behind were catcher Charlie Ganzel, whose wife had just given birth, and Charlie Hickman, who pitched only twice in regular-season games.[43] Nevertheless, Sullivan contributed advice that presumably resonated, because Jacob Morse brought it up two years later: "In 1897 when the championship was fought to the last ditch pitcher Jim Sullivan, of the Bostons, wired 'Kid' Nichols, of the Bostons, to Baltimore: 'Use both sides of your head.'"[44] Nichols won the first game and muddled through the third successfully, and soon enough Boston had the pennant. From a statistical standpoint, Sullivan was worthy of being called a champion. Despite being seeing far less action than during the previous two seasons, he had his only sub-4.00 ERA, while his 1.315 walks plus hits per inning pitched (WHIP) was bettered only by Nichols on the staff.

A few days before that decisive series in Baltimore, Sullivan had announced that he would spend the offseason in Asheville, North Carolina. In October it was rumored he was facing consumption, the disease which claimed Joe Sullivan. Jim admitted such fear was his reason for wintering in North Carolina.[45] His plan worked, at least in early 1898. "The players were delighted to find such a complete change in Jim Sullivan" when the Beaneaters reassembled for spring training in March, reported Tim Murnane.[46]

Sullivan pitched three times over the regular season's first three weeks, the third being a start at home on May 6 against New York. He lasted only two innings, and it proved to be his major-league finale. Within the week he was released due to ill health.[47]

By late July Sullivan was pitching weekly for a club in Laconia, New Hampshire, as it was forming a state league with teams in nearby cities.[48] On August 27 he was signed anew by Providence manager Billy Murray. First up was a start against Ottawa two days later, which was tied 1-1 after nine before Sullivan's team won it in the 12th. A *Sporting Life* columnist noted that "his sickness of last winter still shows its effects on him. This game was a hard test, but Sullivan, with the exception of one inning, kept the hits well scattered, struck out five men and did not give a base on balls."[49] Sullivan pitched well in three more Eastern League games.

He was in good spirits after the season and remained on good terms with the Beaneaters, as he demonstrated in a gathering held on November 1: "An event unique in the annals of base ball was the banquet tendered the owners of the Boston club ... and the base ball writers, by the players of the club, at the United States Hotel," wrote the *Herald*. "There was fun without limit, the humorists being out in force, and Jimmy Sullivan, formerly of the Bostons, was a side-show in himself."[50]

In early 1899 Frank Selee was asked to provide a Beaneater to coach the University of Maine's players for the coming season, and he recommended Sullivan. Hugh Duffy coached Boston College's team and obtained some help from Sullivan. That set up a friendly rivalry in May, when Jacob Morse reported that Sullivan's Maine team beat Duffy's, 7-6.[51]

That same month Sullivan signed with Manchester of the New England League, and he debuted with them at home on May 26 but pitched only the first inning. He was one of three relievers on June 1, but then was idle until June 24. With Fred Lake as his catcher, he shut out Pawtucket, 12-0, scattering six hits.[52] By all accounts, that was Sullivan's final game as a professional ballplayer.

In July Sullivan was back in Boston working at Tommy McCarthy's bar on Washington Street, and late in the year he was on the staff of local politician John R. Murphy.[53] In early 1900, when New Englanders and the sporting world were horrified to learn that Marty Bergen murdered his family and committed suicide, Jim Sullivan revealed that Bergen had threatened to kill him and Hugh Duffy about two years earlier. "And when I think of it now it looks as though Martin meant what he said," Sullivan concluded.[54]

In May of 1900, Sullivan was suddenly a source of baseball commentary. On one occasion he faulted most of Boston's current roster. "Capt Duffy is the only aggressive player in the bunch," he asserted. Later he expressed doubt about pitchers intentionally beaning batters: "I have often tried to burn one of those boys with a speedy one when they were trying to get their base without hitting, but found it impossible, and yet I have hit players when trying to keep the ball away," he told Tim Murnane.[55]

At the end of that month he was mentioned in local papers again for the somber reason. "The friends of Jim Sullivan, the ex-Boston pitcher, who is in a bad way on account of a serious sickness, are passing around the hat," wrote the *Boston Post*, which then told readers where financial contributions could be made. A month later, Worcester players contributed $39, and a month after that Providence sent a check for $90. By the end of August, Brooklyn players added $100, and the Beaneaters added $170 from exhibition games in Syracuse and Lynn. In October, *The Sporting News* reported that Sullivan had received $610 from various sources.[56]

In mid-1901, Sullivan went to Europe to rest for a few weeks, and afterward it was said he looked well when he was spotted at Boston's American League ballpark.[57] However, Daniel James Sullivan died at home on November 29, 1901, at the age of 34. Among the pallbearers at his funeral were former Boston teammates Duffy, McCarthy, Cozy Dolan, and Herman Long. One Boston paper said Sullivan "was light in build, but very nervy, had great curves and almost perfect control of the ball, and was generally looked upon as one of the 'headiest' and most scientific pitchers in the country." *The Sporting News* identified the cause as "consumption, which left him so weak that he could not pitch for the last couple of years." The newspaper concluded its brief tribute by saying he was a very fine fellow."[58]

SOURCES

In addition to the sources cited in the Notes, the author consulted Baseball-Reference.com.

NOTES

1. There is broad agreement among sources that his birthday was April 25, including his findagrave.com entry, but a few put the year as 1869. The 1900 census, for one, confirmed that he was born in April of 1867, not 1869, and he was listed as three years old in the 1870 census. During the early years of his baseball career, there were multiple pitchers named Sullivan in New England and first names often weren't used on newspapers' sports pages, so mentioning his Charlestown residency was one way to distinguish him. Charlestown was a separate municipality when he was born but was annexed by Boston in 1874.

2. Many of his naval recruitment ads gave only the family's address, but "T. Sullivan" was the contact specified in classifieds in the *Boston Globe* on April 23 and May 31, 1889. His longtime connection to the sea was also illustrated by his ad under "Yachts, Boats, Etc." *Boston Globe*, May 7, 1889: 7. He announced the sale of "the best whaleboat in Boston."

3. "Municipal Courts – Oct. 21," *Boston Post*, October 23, 1876: 4. "Liquor Raids," *Boston Globe*, November 18, 1889: 3.

4. "Fierce Contests," *Boston Globe*, January 29, 1901: 10.

5. "Concert and Dancing," *Boston Globe*, October 8, 1885: 2. His future best man, William T. Graham, was president of the Temperance Society at the time of this concert and dance. See "Pitcher Sullivan Married," *Boston Globe*, January 16, 1896: 5.

6. "Players of the Boston League Team, 1895," *Boston Post*, March 31, 1895: 13. "Now for the Temple Cup," *Boston Post*, October 3, 1897: 2.

7. "Medals for Charlestown Tossers," *Boston Globe*, May 14, 1888: 3. "Temperate Young Men," *Boston Globe*, June 19, 1888: 2. "St. Stephens, 8; St. Marys, 4," *Boston Globe*, July 29, 1888: 4.

8. "St. Stephen's Organize," *Boston Globe*, April 29, 1889: 4.

9. Sullivan's strikeout total was reported as 21 in "Base Ball Notes," *Bangor (Maine) Daily Whig & Courier*, July 13, 1889: 3. His total was instead reported as 20 in "Base Ball Gossip," *Boston Globe*, July 12, 1889: 3. The total was likewise stated as 20, with the additional detail about fielding assists, in "Base Ball Notes," *Boston Globe*, July 14, 1889: 6.

10. "Around the Bases," *Boston Herald*, September 5, 1889: 5. Four teams belonged to the New Brunswick League during its three years of existence, from 1888 through 1890, but at least toward the end of 1889 it was only a three-team circuit and the Shamrocks weren't members, according to "Base Ball Notes," *Bangor Daily Whig & Courier*, September 10, 1889: 3. Instead, after the St John A.A. club won the league's 1889 pennant they played the Shamrocks in a provincial championship series. Several overviews of Sullivan's minor-league days said the Shamrocks won the series but that wasn't true, according to "Local Matters," *Bangor Daily Whig & Courier*, October 5, 1889: 3.

11. Baseball-reference.com lists the 1890 New Brunswick League among minor circuits "which decided not to sign the National Agreement," at baseball-reference.com/bullpen/Non-Signatory_19th_Century_Leagues. Assessing Jim Sullivan's performance that year is complicated by the fact that the Shamrocks recruited another pitcher with that surname, as reported in "Base Ball. M.S.C., 23; Bowdoin, 17," *Bangor Daily Whig & Courier*, May 12, 1890: 3. He was "Joseph Sullivan, of South Boston. Sullivan has pitched in several Quincy, Mass., clubs and has a record of 19 winning games out of 23 pitched by him last year." However, on August 22, for one, it was explicitly Jim Sullivan who hurled a complete-game loss for the Shamrocks in Halifax against the Socials of that city. See "Base Ball Games," *Bangor Daily Whig & Courier*, August 25, 1890: 3.

12. Colin D. Howell, *Northern Sandlots: A Social History of Maritime Baseball* (Toronto: University of Toronto Press, 1995), 65-70. See also Brian Flood, *Saint John: A Sporting Tradition 1785-1985* (Saint John, New Brunswick: Neptune Publishing Company, 1985), 79. Joe Sullivan was one of Jim's teammates who later played in the National League; both of these books incorrectly said the two were brothers. In addition to Sexton, other 1890 Shamrocks who later played in the majors were Abel Lizotte (often "Lezotte"), Bill Merritt, and John O'Brien.

13. "Boston Baseball Players," *Boston Post*, March 10, 1891: 8.

14. Sullivan was mentioned among Boston pitchers in "Preparing for Fast Day," *Boston Globe*, March 29, 1891: 7. See also "They'll Play Great Ball," *Boston Herald*, April 1, 1891: 7.

15. J.C. Edgerly, "Boston on Top," *Boston Globe*, April 3, 1891: 1. "Striker Up," *Boston Journal Supplement*, April 3, 1891: 1. "Boston, and Easily," *Boston Herald*, April 3, 1891: 1. (On page 7 the latter paper contradicted itself, and the other two dailies, by saying Kid Nichols gave up Brooklyn's only two runs rather than Sullivan.) There wasn't any Smith in the box scores; it's possible Edgerly was thinking of Brooklyn's former shortstop, Germany Smith. The *Journal*'s account suggests the double-play ball was hit by either Adonis Terry or Oyster Burns. Sullivan's immediate signing was reported in "Base Ball Notes," *Boston Globe*, April 4, 1891: 3.

16. "Played Like Novices," *Boston Post*, April 29, 1891: 2. See also "Six Straight Games," *Boston Advertiser*, April 29, 1891: 8, "The Ball Field," *Boston Journal Supplement*, April 29, 1891: 1, and T.H. Murnane, "Still Another," *Boston Globe*, April 29, 1891: 9. As of this writing, Sullivan's baseball-reference.com entry, baseball-reference.com/players/s/sulliji01.shtml, shows his debut incorrectly, as April 22 instead of April 28; it also specifies that he faced eight batters whereas newspaper accounts documented seven.

17. "Base Ball Notes," *Boston Globe*, May 1, 1891: 3. Baseball-reference.com lists an Edward F. Sullivan on the roster of Salem in the New England League in 1891. See also "University of Vermont, 10; Morrills, 9," *Boston Globe*, May 2, 1891: 12.

18. "Nine to Three This Time," *Rochester (New York) Democrat and Chronicle*, May 13, 1891: 10. See also "Sporting Brevities," *Buffalo Times*, May 5, 1891: 1. In fact, another Buffalo paper explicitly rebutted earlier reports that Rochester signed Jim rather than Tom – see "Baseball Notes," *Buffalo Express*, May 9 1891: 6.

19. "Pawtuxet Valley Park," *Pawtuxet Valley Gleaner* (Phenix, Rhode Island), May 8, 1891: 1.

20. "Personal," *Sporting Life*, May 25, 1895: 4. "News and Comment," *Sporting Life*, October 30, 1897: 2. Conversely, Jim, Joe, and Mike Sullivan were also deemed to be unrelated in that same weekly: See J.C. Morse, "Hub Happenings," *Sporting Life*, November 13, 1897: 10.

21. "Woonsocket, 17; Lovells, 0," *Boston Globe*, May 15, 1891: 5. Early that season, at least, the Lovells had another pitcher named Sullivan, who pitched for that team on the same early April day when Jim Sullivan hurled three innings against Brooklyn.

22. "Pawtuxet Valley Park," *Pawtuxet Valley Gleaner*, July 3, 1891: 8. See also Robert Cvornyek, "The Color of Baseball: Race and Boston's Sporting Community" in *Black Ball: A Negro Leagues Journal*, volume 6 (2014): 73.

23. "Pawtuxet Valley Park," *Pawtuxet Valley Gleaner*, July 24, 1891: 5. "Clyde's Pitcher Wanted by Cheney," *Rhode Island Pendulum* (East Greenwich), August 7, 1891: 5. What Cheer, "Poor Providence," *Sporting Life*, August 8, 1891: 5. "Miscellaneous," *Boston Journal*, August 14, 1891: 4.

24. Sullivan also had a successful year as a batter, according to team statistics published after the season, showing him with a batting average of .303. See "Pawtuxet Valley Park," *Pawtuxet Valley Gleaner*, September 25, 1891: 1.

25. *Sporting Life* may have caused confusion by stating that Columbus "tried pitcher Sullivan, late of Providence, who pitched a couple of games for the Athletics." That clearly described Mike Sullivan, not Jim. See "Boston vs. Columbus at Boston Sept. 1," *Sporting Life*, September 5, 1891: 4. However, multiple sources in New England made it clear that the Columbus pitcher was indeed Jim Sullivan: "Boston, 9; Columbus, 5," *Boston Journal*, September 2, 1891: 3. "They Came Near Winning," *Boston Evening Transcript*, September 2, 1891: 5. "Still Winning," *Boston Advertiser*, September 2, 1891: 2. "Only a Good Finish," *Boston Post*, September 2, 1891: 8. "Pawtuxet Valley Park," *Pawtuxet Valley Gleaner*, September 4, 1891: 5. Thanks go out to SABR member Rick Huhn for searching Columbus newspapers at a library there.

26. "Boston, 9; Columbus, 5," *Boston Journal*, September 2, 1891: 3. "Only a Good Finish," *Boston Post*, September 2, 1891: 8.

27. "Marions, 6; Beacons, 0," *Boston Globe*, September 13, 1891: 2. There was a general announcement about their availability in "Base Ball Notes," *Boston Globe*, August 31, 1891: 5. The two were expected to play two games for the Melrose team during September, as reported in "Amateur Base Ball Gossip," *Boston Globe*, September 2, 1891: 5. Later in the month there were to serve as the battery for the Amesbury team, according to "Base Ball Notes," *Boston Globe*, September 16, 1891: 5.

28. "Pawtuxet Valley Park," *Pawtuxet Valley Gleaner*, October 9, 1891: 8.

29. "What Harrington Says," *Indianapolis Journal*, May 3, 1892: 3.

30. "Base Ball Notes," *Boston Globe*, July 18, 1892: 3. Jacob C. Morse, "Boston Briefs," *Sporting Life*, August 6, 1892: 9.

31. "The Eastern League," *Boston Herald*, August 5, 1892: 5.

32. The dual signing was widely reported throughout November. For example, see "Latest News by Wire," *Sporting Life*, November 5, 1892: 1. The inability of Washington and Providence to reach an agreement was also covered extensively. See, for instance, Ned Kay, "Providence Plans," *Sporting Life*, April 15, 1893: 16. This even touched off a minor debate about the reserve rule, when the *Buffalo Courier* quoted and rebutted a *Boston Post* complaint three days earlier about the rule's harm

to players. The *Courier* countered that without the rule "the minor leagues would soon go out of existence." – "Around the Bases," *Buffalo Courier*, April 16, 1893: 8.

33 "Grounders," *Boston Sunday Herald*, September 17, 1893: 32. Possibly making it difficult to compile Sullivan's statistics for 1893 was the fact that during the season Providence also had pitchers Dennis Sullivan and William Sullivan on its roster.

34 "Stars Couldn't Hit Sullivan," *Buffalo Courier*, August 6, 1894: 10. J.C. Morse, "Hub Happenings," *Sporting Life*, October 20, 1894: 5.

35 T.H. Murnane, "Show No Mercy," *Boston Globe*, May 4, 1895: 9.

36 Specifically, in 1895 he was 11-9 with an ERA of 4.74, while the staff's was 4.25. In 1896 he slid to 11-12 but lowered his ERA to 4.03, but the staff did likewise, to 3.78.

37 "Bridegrooms," *Boston Journal*, August 18, 1896: 8. "Full of Twists," *Boston Globe*, September 18, 1896: 5.

38 "Death of Charles F. Sullivan," *Boston Globe*, June 10, 1895: 3. "Pitcher Sullivan Married," *Boston Globe*, January 16, 1896: 5. "Charlestown," *Boston Globe*, October 12, 1896: 3. J.C. Morse, "Hub Happenings," *Sporting Life*, February 20, 1897: 11. "Joseph D. Sullivan," *Boston Journal*, November 3, 1897: 2. "Deaths," *Boston Globe*, March 16, 1898: 9. "Deaths," *Boston Globe*, July 19, 1899: 7. Massachusetts birth records prior to 1916 include a Francis Sullivan born to Daniel J. Sullivan and Mary C. McMahon on January 30, 1899. Not surprisingly, the five funerals were relatively private affairs, except for Joe Sullivan's. In addition to Jim Sullivan, the baseball fraternity was represented by the likes of Tommy McCarthy, Cozy Dolan, Toby Lyons, and Mike Sullivan, according to "Many Floral Tributes," *Boston Herald*, November 6, 1897: 2.

39 Bunker Hill, "Four Straight," *Boston Advertiser*, May 8, 1897: 8. "Pennant Ball," *Boston Globe*, August 13, 1897: 7.

40 "Is a Deserter," *The Sporting News*, May 15, 1897: 5. J.C. Morse, "Hub Happenings," *Sporting Life*, July 24, 1897: 9. On a different page in the latter issue it was reported that Sullivan displayed some atypical hostility about his situation: "Pitcher Jim Sullivan and catcher Ganzell [*sic*] were sent home from Pittsburg by Manager Selee. Sullivan is indignant over not being given a chance to pitch, claiming to be in good condition, and wants his release. See "News and Comment," *Sporting Life*, July 24, 1897: 5.

41 W.S. Barnes Jr., "This Is a Clincher," *Boston Morning Journal*, August 13, 1897: 1.

42 George V. Tuohey, *A History of the Boston Base Ball Club* (Boston: M F. Quinn & Co., 1897), 160.

43 "Off for Baltimore," *Boston Advertiser*, September 23, 1897: 5.

44 Jacob C. Morse, "Hub Happenings," *Sporting Life*, September 9, 1899: 8. As a very small consolation for not being taken to Baltimore, Sullivan pitched the final innings in the last game of the underwhelming postseason Temple Cup series. See "Orioles' Cup," *Boston Globe*, October 12, 1897: 3.

45 "Echoes of the Game," *Boston Globe*, September 19, 1897: 4. "News and Comment," *Sporting Life*, October 9, 1897: 5. "News and Comment," *Sporting Life*, October 30, 1897: 2.

46 T.H. Murnane, "Ready to Begin," *Boston Globe*, March 21, 1898: 9.

47 "Met the Spurt," *Boston Journal*, May 7, 1898: 7. "News and Comment," *Sporting Life*, May 14, 1898: 5.

48 "Baseball Notes," *Boston Globe*, July 20, 1898: 2. "Players' Bench," *Boston Post*, July 21, 1898: 3.

49 "Jim Sullivan With Providence," *Boston Globe*, August 28, 1898: 2. Rhody, "Providence's Pet," *Sporting Life*, September 10, 1898: 13.

50 "Boston Players' Banquet," *Boston Sunday Herald*, November 6, 1898: 35.

51 "Sporting Notes," *Boston Globe*, February 16, 1899: 3. Two years earlier Sullivan had similarly been engaged by Brown University. See "Happy Jack Egan," *The Sporting News*, March 13, 1897: 2. "Open Season with Brown," *Boston Globe*, March 19, 1899: 16. Jacob C. Morse, "Hub Happenings," *Sporting Life*, May 20, 1899: 3.

52 "Manchester 8, Cambridge 5," *Boston Globe*, May 27, 1899: 4. "Manchester 21, Taunton 17," *Boston Globe*, June 2, 1899: 4. "New England League," *Boston Journal*, June 25, 1899: 2. For Sullivan's finale, former major leaguer Alex Ferson was credited with "curing" Sullivan's pitching arm in "Baseball Notes," *Boston Globe*, June 27, 1899: 4.

53 Jacob C. Morse, "Hub Happenings," *Sporting Life*, July 22, 1899: 7. Jacob C. Morse, "Morse's Missive," *Sporting Life*, November 11, 1899: 8.

54 "Awful Shock to Many Friends," *Boston Globe*, January 20, 1900: 3.

55 "Baseball Notes, *Boston Globe*, May 19, 1900: 9. T.H. Murnane, "Baseball Veterans," *Boston Globe*, May 27, 1900: 35.

56 "Players' Bench," *Boston Post*, May 30, 1900: 3. "Baseball Notes," *Boston Globe*, June 30, 1900: 3. "Baseball Notes," Boston Globe, July 31, 1900: 4. "Baseball Notes," *Boston Globe*, August 26, 1900: 4. "Contributes $170 to Sullivan Fund," *Boston Globe*, August 31, 1900: 5. Hi Hi, "Several Changes," *The Sporting News*, October 13, 1900: 2.

57 "Baseball Notes," *Boston Globe*, July 21, 1901: 4. "Baseball Notes," *Boston Globe*, August 21, 1901: 4.

58 "Profusion of Flowers," *Boston Globe*, December 2, 1901: 5. "Won Fame on the Diamond," *Boston Herald*, November 30, 1901: 4. Hi Hi, "Jumps Once More," *The Sporting News*, December 7, 1901: 3. His death certificate shows the cause as pulmonary tuberculosis, a disease widely associated with consumption, and that he had been suffering for six months. The *Herald* and at least one Boston paper said Sullivan was survived by a widow and *two* children. Massachusetts birth records for daughter Helen and son Francis are accessible online, but confirmation of a third child remains elusive. Jim and Mary lived with her mother in the 1900 census, but Francis was their only child. Therefore, an additional child would have been born later in 1900 or in 1901. In the 1910 census Mary was reported to have borne three children, two still living. Nevertheless, only "Frank," age 11, was living with her. The solution to the mystery may be the household in 1910 that included Jim's three surviving siblings. All three were single, and neither sister had ever given birth. Living with them was William Sullivan, age 9, "nephew" of the head of the household, Jim's sister Mary. If William wasn't the illegitimate child Jim's brother Timothy, he was quite likely Jim's son being raised by close relatives.

BILLY SULLIVAN SR.
BY TREY STRECKER

Billy Sullivan.
(Library of Congress)

Though "never very strong in stick work," his Deadball Era contemporaries believed that Billy Sullivan's "brilliant performances behind the bat ... more than offset his weak hitting."[1] Although his paltry .213 lifetime batting average is the second worst all-time (next to Bill Bergen) among players with at least 3,000 at-bats, Sullivan developed a reputation as a brainy backstop with an uncanny ability to handle pitchers. Described by Ty Cobb as the best catcher "ever to wear shoe leather," Sullivan was "the best man throwing to bases in the American League," and "no man in the business [knew] more about getting the best work from a pitcher and holding an infield together."[2] Sullivan also revolutionized the way his position was played; he is credited as the first catcher to position himself directly behind the batter and as the inventor of an inflatable chest protector.

William Joseph Sullivan was born on a farm near Oakland, Wisconsin, on February 1, 1875, the son of Irish immigrants. He first displayed his potential as a ball player at Fort Atkinson High School, where he starred in the infield. As a high school student, Sullivan played shortstop until an accident disabled his team's regular catcher. Without any previous experience, the young Sullivan was put in to catch, where his work behind the bat attracted the attention of the local town team's manager. Afterward, he caught for an independent team in Edgewater, Wisconsin, before he broke into the professional ranks with the Western Association's Cedar Rapids Bunnies in 1896. The next year, the 5-foot-9, 155-pound right-hander played for Dubuque in the same league, managed by Joe Cantillon. Purchased from Dubuque by Tom Loftus, Sullivan worked behind the plate for Columbus (Ohio) of the Western League in 1898. The next year he was transferred with his team to Grand Rapids, Michigan, where he hit .306 in 83 games before being sold to the Boston Beaneaters at the end of the season. Catching 66 games for Boston in 1900, Sullivan slugged eight home runs, fifth in the National League. It was the only time in his career he would make the top 10 in any hitting category.

Before the 1901 season, an offer of $2,400 enticed him to jump to the White Sox, where he caught the American League's first game as a major league, Chicago's 8-2 victory over Cleveland on April 24, 1901. Despite his impressive hitting for the Beaneaters in 1900, once in American League company Sullivan's offense quickly disappeared, as it did for most of the era's backstops. He batted .245 in his first season with the White Sox, a pedestrian average that would prove to be the highest of his American League career. From 1903 to 1912, he never batted higher than .229 in any season, and finished as low as .162. His abysmal hitting was coupled with a shortage of power and an inability to get on base via other means; for his career he finished with a .254 on-base percentage and a .281 slugging percentage. Sullivan was particularly dreadful in his only postseason appearance. In the 1906 World Series against the Chicago Cubs he went hitless in 21 at-bats, including nine strikeouts. However, he caught every inning of every game and guided his pitchers to a collective 1.33 ERA in the Sox' six-game victory.

Somehow, the White Sox seemed a better team with the scrappy, resourceful Sullivan in their lineup. With Sullivan as their primary catcher, the White Sox won two pennants (1901 and 1906) and narrowly missed two others (1905 and 1908) while never finishing lower than fourth place. By contrast, in the two seasons in which he was injured, 1903 and 1910, the club finished in the second division both times, more than 30 games out of first place. During his years in uniform, Sullivan was particularly important in steadying Chicago's stalwart pitching rotation, which included the likes of Ed Walsh, Doc White, and Nick Altrock. Four times a league-leader in fielding percentage, Sullivan placed himself directly behind the batter. In 1908 Sullivan was issued a U.S. Patent for an inflatable, contoured chest protector, which protected his body better and, thanks to hinging, allowed more freedom of movement than the normal model.

On October 24, 1905, Sullivan married Mary Josephine O'Sullivan, who had emigrated from Ireland five years earlier. The marriage lasted 24 years until her death in January 1930. A clean-living player who didn't swear, drink, or smoke, Sully replaced Fielder Jones as Chicago's playing manager in 1909, piloting the club to a 78-74 record and a fourth-place finish. It was Sullivan's only season as manager; the next year, Hugh Duffy took the helm and Sully returned to catching full time.

On August 24, 1910, Sullivan caught three baseballs thrown by Ed Walsh off the top of the Washington Monument as a publicity stunt, duplicating Washington catcher Gabby Street's feat from two years earlier. Contemporary reports estimated that the balls sped at 161 feet per second toward Sullivan's pancake mitt. Remarkably, despite gusty winds, Sullivan caught three of the eleven balls Walsh threw. Following the stunt, Sully declined to attempt to catch a ball dropped from an airplane, saying he "might as well try to stop a bullet."[3]

Sullivan was often sidelined by injuries. An errant foul tip broke his throwing hand in 1901. The next year he required an emergency appendectomy. He was hit by a pitched ball in 1904 and knocked unconscious. During the 1906 pennant chase, he re-injured his throwing hand. Perhaps the most serious injury Sullivan faced was a battle with the blood poisoning he contracted in 1910, after stepping on a rusty nail during a spring training trip. Following the dubious advice of a quack physician, he received a nearly-lethal dose of turpentine and almost lost a leg before receiving appropriate medical care. "This Sullivan man is a real hero," the *Atlanta Constitution* wrote after the 1908 campaign. "He begged permission to catch the final game in Cleveland although two rows of stitches had been removed from his right thumb only the day before... The nature of his injury must have made his work agony, but he stuck to his job."[4]

In 1912, with Sullivan's performance and endurance declining, young backstop Ray Schalk emerged as his successor. Sullivan spent the 1913 and 1914 seasons as a Sox coach, assisting manager Nixey Callahan, teaching Schalk, and managing the B squad in spring training. Chicago owner Charles Comiskey had promised Sullivan lifetime employment with the team as a reward for his years of service, but broke that promise on February 15, 1915, when he unconditionally released the shocked Sullivan. After trying and failing to land a job as an AL umpire, Billy joined the Minneapolis Millers -- managed by his old skipper Cantillon -- where he coached, batted .215, and caught 105 games of "fine ball" as they won the American Association pennant. Released by Minneapolis at the end of the year, he only appeared in a single game as a player-coach with Detroit in 1916.

At the end of the 1916 season, the 41-year-old Sullivan accepted his release and retired to a twenty-acre apple, walnut, and filbert farm outside Newberg, Oregon, where he spent the rest of his life with his wife, Mary. During the 1917 season, Sully attempted to catch on with Portland of the Pacific Coast League and Seattle of the Northwestern League, but he was unsuccessful.

Upon his retirement, Sullivan paid tribute to four of the foremost pitchers he caught. According to Sully, "Kid Nichols, of the old Boston Nationals, possessed the greatest speed; Ed Walsh was the peer of the spit ball pitchers; Jim Scott tops all the curve ball experts, and for all-around mixing and slow ball delivery there never was a man who excelled 'Doc' White."[5]

Although his son Joseph, a second baseman and captain on the University of Notre Dame team, turned down an offer from the White Sox in order to pursue a law career, his son, Billy, Jr., began his own 12-year major-league career with the White Sox in 1931, playing with Chicago, Cincinnati, Cleveland, the St. Louis Browns, Detroit, Brooklyn, and Pittsburgh. When Billy caught for Detroit in the 1940 World Series, the Sullivans became the first father and son to have played in the Fall Classic. Baseball dopesters frequently remarked that if Billy, Sr. could hit like his son, and if Billy, Jr. could field like his father, they would be "the best catcher in the history of the game."[6]

Following Mary's death in 1930, Sullivan married Myrtle Nash in June 1933 and the couple enjoyed many years together. Sullivan died of a heart ailment on January 28, 1965, only eight days after the death of his Chicago batterymate Nick Altrock, and just four days shy of his 90th birthday. Survived by Myrtle, he was buried in St. James Catholic Cemetery in McMinnville, Oregon.

NOTE

This biography originally appeared in David Jones, ed., *Deadball Stars of the American League* (Washington, D.C.: Potomac Books, Inc., 2006).

SOURCES

Baseball-reference.com.

Billy Sullivan's clipping file at the National Baseball Hall of Fame

Brown, Warren. *The Chicago White Sox*. New York: Putnam, 1952.

Lindberg, Richard C. *The White Sox Encyclopedia* (Philadelphia: Temple University Press, 1997).

Spalding's Baseball Guide.

Spink, Alfred H. *The National Game*, 2nd ed. (Carbondale: Southern Illinois University Press, 2000).

NOTES

1. Mike Shatzkin, ed., *The Ballplayers* (Gettysburg, Pennsylvania: Arbor House Pub. Co., 1990), 1058.
2. David Lee Poremba, *The American League: The Early Years* (Charleston, South Carolina; Arcadia, 2000), 105.
3. Peter Morris, *Catcher: The Evolution of an American Folk Hero* (Chicago: Ivan R. Dee, 2009), 252-53.
4. "Billy Sullivan A Game Player," *Atlanta Constitution*, October 11, 1908: C4.
5. Sam Weller, "Passing of Sullivan," unidentified February 1915 newspaper clipping in Sullivan's player file at the National Baseball Hall of Fame.
6. "Billy Sullivan, Sr., Catcher On Hitless Wonders, Dead," *The Sporting News*, February 13, 1965: 26.

MARTY SULLIVAN

BY MIKE HUBER

Marty Sullivan.
(Library of Congress)

Marty Sullivan was a ballplayer who, at his prime, "was second to no left fielder in the country," according to Hall of Famer Cap Anson.[1] In his five-year major-league career, Sullivan played for four different teams, compiling a .273 lifetime batting average.

Martin C. Sullivan was born in Lowell, Massachusetts, on October 20, 1862, the third child of Michael and Mary Ellen Sullivan, Irish Catholic immigrants. Mike Sullivan was a leather currier, and his wife stayed home raising the children: Marty and his sisters Mary, Margaret, Marcella, Lizzie, and Kate, and brother Francis. By 1880, Mike had died has passed away, and Mary Ellen was raising the children as a widow.

As a boy, Sullivan was "the envy of his schoolmates on the ball field."[2] His first professional team was the short-lived X.Q.Z. team, with whom Sullivan signed on as a catcher. In 1884 he signed with the Mathew Temperance team, one of the strongest amateur teams in Massachusetts. His first professional club was the Concord, New Hampshire, team, as a catcher in 1885. He spent the 1885-86 winter playing in San Francisco, and afterward, he returned east and played for the Boston Blues.

On September 26, 1881, the 18-year-old Sullivan married Bridget Hogan. In 1885, Bridget gave birth to a son, Martin Charles Sullivan. Tragedy struck the family in 1887, when young Martin died of brain disease.[3]

Tim Murnane, a former major-league player, was a sportswriter for the *Boston Globe* and "assumed an unofficial role with the New England League"[4] as an indirect publicist. He also acted as a scout for Cap Anson and the Chicago White Stockings. If Murnane saw any talent in players in the New England League, he would send them Anson's way. The first ballplayer Murnane signed was Sullivan, the catcher for the Boston Blues. After the 1886 season, Sullivan signed with Chicago.[5] Anson converted the backstop into an outfielder, and in 1887 Sullivan played 115 games for the White Stockings as an outfielder. He debuted on April 30, going 1-for-4 with a run scored in a 6-2 loss to Pittsburgh. Sullivan tripled in the ninth inning and scored on a passed ball. He also pitched one game that season, going 2⅓ innings, giving up six hits and a walk while striking out one. Anson was the team's star, batting .347, but the 24-year-old Sullivan was fourth in average on the team, at .284. (The league batting average was .269.) He led the team in triples (16) and was third in hits (134), and the swift outfielder stole 35 bases. But the rookie also made 36 errors in the outfield.

In the winter of 1888-89, the White Stockings made a round-the-world barnstorming tour. During the tour, assembled by Albert Spalding, "the Chicago and All-America teams played 53 games of four innings and upwards."[6] Sullivan played left field for the Chicago squad. The two teams traveled westward across America, then to Australia, Ceylon, Egypt, Italy, France, England, Scotland, and Ireland, before returning to the United States and playing their way from the East Coast back to Chicago. Their games started on October 20, 1888, and finished on April 20, 1889. The success of the tour is summed up in this excerpt from the *Melbourne Sportsman*: "The best evidence offered that Melbournites were pleased and interested in the exhibition lies in the fact that the crowd of nearly ten thousand people remained through not only nine but twelve innings of play, and then many of them stayed to see a four inning game between the Chicago team and a nine composed mainly of our local cricket players, who made a very creditable show, considering the strength of the team they were playing against, and the fact that they were almost utter strangers to base ball."[7] One of the highlights had to be playing on the sands in front of the Pyramid of Cheops on February 9, 1889, and then climbing the Sphinx, to the horror of the locals.

Sullivan played 75 games for Anson and Chicago in 1889, all in the outfield. His batting average fell to .236, but his fielding percentage increased by 80 points. Had he played in more games, his fielding percentage of .927 would have been eighth-best in the National League.

Sullivan was released by the White Stockings on April 24, 1889. Six days later, he signed with the Indianapolis Hoosiers of the American Association. The *Indianapolis News* said he left Chicago because of a "disagreement with Anson."[8] Sullivan was expected to be in Indianapolis in time for a game on May 1 against the White Stockings, but he delayed leaving his home in Massachusetts in a dispute over advance money.[9] After three days Sullivan was still a no-show. So, the fans were told, "Sullivan may delay reporting all he pleases but he can't play with any other club, and he is not drawing salary, in which there is some comfort."[10]

On May 4, it was reported that "if Sullivan ever gets here, he will likely be assigned to center."[11] He finally arrived on the evening of May 6, in time to play on the 7th against Pittsburgh. It was worth the wait: "A base on balls and two home runs, besides acquitting himself satisfactorily in the field, marked Martin Sullivan's appearance with the Indianapolis team yesterday, and it was good enough for a player of greater pretensions."[12] Sullivan, playing right field, knocked the ball over the left-field fence in the fourth inning. He added a two-run shot, again over the left-field fence, an inning later. For the game he was 2-for-3 with a walk, two runs scored and three runs batted in. After Sullivan's second home run, "a shower of silver was thrown to him from the grand stand, and he realized several dollars by his successful work."[13] In 69 games with Indianapolis, Sullivan batted .285 with 50 walks, well above the team batting average of .278 and the league average of .266.

In addition to roaming the outfield, Sullivan also played five games at first base, and he was more than adequate as a fielder. With the Hoosiers, Sullivan was a fan favorite. "If he will take proper care of himself his popularity will continue. But it rests with himself," the *Indianapolis News* wrote on August 19.[14] Three days later, on the 22nd, Sullivan played his last game for Indianapolis, against the Cleveland Spiders. The next day, he and Cleveland's Chief Zimmer umpired the game, but he would no longer be part of the Indianapolis lineup. On September 12 Sullivan was released by the sixth-place Hoosiers. According to the *Indianapolis News*, "some such disposition of his case has been anticipated ever since [Paul] Hines was replaced at first."[15] By putting Sullivan at first base and then using him as an umpire, the Hoosiers seemed to be telling him that they had no room for him on the team. The Indianapolis team finished the season in seventh place at 59-75.

The 1890 season began with Sullivan playing left field for the Boston Beaneaters, under manager Frank Selee. On Opening Day before 3,882 spectators, he had two hits, a stolen base, and two runs scored in a 15-9 win over the Brooklyn Bridegrooms. The Beaneaters finished in fifth place and Sullivan batted .285 in 121 games, third-best on the team. Sullivan drew 56 walks and drove in 61 runs.

The next season, Boston took the National League pennant. With John Clarkson, Kid Nichols, and Harry Staley accounting for 83 of the team's 87 victories, the Beaneaters finished the season 3½ games ahead of the Chicago Colts (née White Stockings). Despite a nine-game winning streak earlier in the month, Boston finished June with a record of 30-27, and Selee's squad was in third place. Sullivan wasn't leading the charge, batting just .224 in 17 games. He had scored 15 runs, but had only 15 hits. On May 1, he hit a home run and scored twice in a 13-6 loss to Brooklyn, but otherwise there is little record of him in the box scores. He was released on July 12.

Sullivan signed with the Cleveland Spiders on August 14. He played only game for the Spiders, getting an RBI single. He was 1-for-4 at the plate and played right field for the entire game. His obituary in the *Lowell Sun* said he was injured in the game, a close contest won by Cincinnati. Sullivan, "while running from first to second base during the game, injured one of his feet very seriously and suffered with it to the time of his death."[16]

Released by Cleveland, Sullivan returned to his hometown of Lowell. He had played in 398 games for four teams, with a .273 batting average and 220 RBIs.

In the 1892 Lowell City Directory, Sullivan is listed as a "baseball player."[17] A year later he was working as a clerk in Lowell's Washington Tavern.

Sullivan died on January 6, 1894. At the time, he was living at the family home, at 350 Suffolk Street in Lowell, and working as a laborer. The official cause of death was phthisis or pulmonary tuberculosis. News of his death at the age of 31 was on the front page of the *Lowell Sun*, his hometown paper, which wrote that "his popularity was not confined to his native city but extended to all the large base ball centers in the country where during his base ball career he had by his magnificent playing and gentlemanly conduct on and off the field, made hosts of friends, and admirers."[18] The obituary stated that Sullivan was survived by his mother, a sister, and two children.

NOTES

1. "Martin Sullivan Dead," *Lowell Sun*, January 8, 1894: 1.
2. Ibid.
3. Correspondence with Richard Tourangeau, February 4, 2017.
4. Charlie Bevis, *The New England League: A Baseball History, 1885-1949* (Jefferson, North Carolina: McFarland & Company, Inc., 2008), 56.
5. Murnane's most famous signing was Hugh Duffy, a star in the New England League and later a Hall of Fame player for the Chicago White Stockings, Boston Beaneaters, and Philadelphia Phillies.
6. "1888-89 World Tour of Base Ball," found online at chicagology.com/baseball/1888worldtour/.
7. Ibid.
8. "Ball Notes," *Indianapolis News*, May 1, 1889: 4.
9. Ibid.
10. "Ball Notes," *Indianapolis News*, May 3, 1889: 4.
11. "Ball Notes," *Indianapolis News*, May 4, 1889: 8.
12. "An Up-hill Game," *Indianapolis News*, May 8, 1889: 4.
13. "Ball Notes," *Indianapolis News*, May 8, 1889: 4.
14. "Base Ball Notes," *Indianapolis News*, August 19, 1889: 4.
15. "Base Ball Matters," *Indianapolis News*, September 14, 1889: 8.
16. *Lowell Sun*.
17. Correspondence with Richard Tourganeau, and ancestry.com. Lowell, Massachusetts, Directories.
18. *Lowell Sun*.

FRED TENNEY

BY MARK S. STERNMAN

For decades, baseball historians ranked Fred Tenney behind only Hal Chase among great fielding first basemen. A self-professed originator of the 3-6-3 double play, Tenney also developed the style of playing deep and well off the bag, as modern first basemen do. One observer wrote that he "reaches his hands far out for the ball, and stretches his legs, so that he is farther out from the bag on every throw than any other first baseman in the league."[1] With his unconventional methods that soon became the norm, the first sacker led the National League in putouts in 1905 and 1907-08 and in assists each year from 1901 to 1907, setting a major-league record with 152 in 1905 that lasted until Mickey Vernon topped it in 1949.

A left-handed hitter, Tenney bunted masterfully and place-hit exceptionally, batting over .300 seven times en route to finishing with a .294 average.[2] His performance in an exhibition game illustrates Tenney's offensive approach. "His first time up, the rival shortstop crowded second. Tenney said, 'You're too far over. I'll hit the ball through the hole.' The shortstop laughed, so Tenney singled through the hole. His next time up, the shortstop played in the hole. 'Now you're too far the other way. I'll hit the ball over second base.' ... Tenney promptly singled over second."[3]

Grandson of a former Massachusetts state treasurer and son of a Civil War veteran,[4] Frederick Tenney was born in Georgetown, Massachusetts, on November 26, 1871. Fred's nickname, the Soiled Collegian, came from his aggressive playing style and his degree from Brown University, where he caught in spite of his southpaw status. Celebrating with classmates on June 15, 1894, Tenney recalled, "Shortly after midnight ... Frank Selee, manager of the Boston nationals, [phoned]. He asked me to help him out:

Fred Tenney.
(McGreevy Collection, Boston Public Library)

His regular catchers were disabled. I … told him I would leave on the 10 o'clock train from Providence. I rejoined the party, which broke up about 4 o'clock, and then turned in for a few hours' sleep."[5] That afternoon he made his NL debut, catching the entire game even though a foul tip fractured the forefinger of his throwing hand in the fifth inning.[6] The Beaneaters offered him a contract despite the injury, shocking Tenney, who had at first did not believe the offer.[7] The rookie rejoined the team a month later, after his finger mended, demonstrating his offensive potential by batting .395 in 27 games.

In his second season, Tenney changed both his positions and his marital status. Distrusting Tenney's arm, Selee in 1895 played Tenney more in the outfield than at catcher. On October 21 Tenney married Bessie Berry.[8] While Tenney's plate appearances doubled annually, from 100 in 1894 to 200 in 1895 and again to 406 in 1896, he still struggled defensively. In 1897 Selee moved Tenney to first base,[9] a shift that kept him in the lineup full time for the first time and completed an outstanding infield with Bobby Lowe at second, Herman Long at short, and Jimmy Collins at third. After his career, Tenney credited Selee for being "the first manager to put a very active, comparatively small man on the bag. … The active man at once changed all ideas and without being accused of egotism, I believe, I can easily say my advent introduced an entirely new school of first basemen."[10]

In 1897 the Beaneaters won the first of two consecutive pennants with a 93-39 record, and Tenney batted .318 while participating in a trio of the most memorable games of his career. On May 31 Boston beat St. Louis 25-5 as "Tenney gave one of the most scientific batting exhibitions ever witnessed at the South End Grounds, six hits in eight times at bat … [which] were … a double to left, a line single to center, a safe bunt to third, a well-placed single to right, a bunt to first base and a short liner to left."[11]

In a much closer contest, with the Beaneaters leading Baltimore by just 1½ games on June 25, Boston trailed the Orioles 9-8 with two outs and the bases loaded in the ninth. Facing a two-strike count, Tenney doubled to drive in the tying and winning runs. The Boston fans not only carried him off the field, but "insisted on remaining to see Tenney come out in street dress, and a handsome collection was taken up and handed to the nervy player as he came to the club room. Then several more cheers went up, and the crowd wandered home."[12]

That season Tenney also started what he claimed was the first-ever 3-6-3 double play, against Cincinnati with Claude Ritchey at the dish with a runner on first. "He hit one down the first base line," said Tenney. "I ran it, grabbed it and threw to second for the force out. In that instance, I was not far from first base, so got myself to take the throw from Long for the double play. The crowd didn't grasp it momentarily. … Then everybody seemed to get the significance of the play at the same time, and you never heard such a wild cheer."[13]

Tenney had two more productive years in 1898 and 1899. In the former, he set a career high in doubles with 25 while batting .328; in the latter, he set career highs in several categories including triples (17), batting average (.347), and total bases (265).

Off the field, Tenney took on extra domestic responsibilities after Bessie gave birth to Barbara on July 4, 1899, and Ruth on December 8, 1901.[14]

Often injured in 1900 and 1901, Tenney played in only 112 and 115 games before having arguably his finest offensive season in 1902, when he led the NL with 29 sacrifice hits and finished in the top 10 in batting average (.315), on-base percentage (.409), walks (73), and runs (88). Tenney set these marks in spite of an epic confrontation with Pittsburgh player-manager Fred Clarke. "Clarke called me names, then I twisted his nose, and he kicked me in the stomach," remarked Tenney about the incident, which prompted a fine and a 10-game suspension.[15]

The St. Louis, Cleveland,[16] and Detroit Americans attempted to lure Tenney to the junior circuit in 1901 and 1902; the Tigers offered to raise his $2,500 salary to $7,000 per year for two years.[17] But Tenney stuck with the Nationals, mainly because of his friendship with longtime Boston co-owner Arthur Soden; the club reciprocated by naming Tenney captain in 1903 and manager in 1905. Fred learned of the latter appointment shortly before spring training when Soden asked him to clean out former manager Al Buckenberger's desk. Tenney received no additional pay but would get a bonus if the club broke even financially.

With a three-year record of 158-295 in his first stint as Boston manager, Tenney lasted mainly because the owners cared more about dollars than victories. Tenney served as first baseman, field captain, manager, and even business manager, handling baggage, hotels, and receipts, going into the stands to retrieve balls, and taking tickets on Sundays (for most of his career he refused to play on the Sabbath).[18] In 1905 the *Boston Traveler* reported that Tenney was on the verge of signing William Clarence Matthews, an African-American middle infielder from Harvard.[19] Tenney, who also coached at nearby Tufts College during the offseason,[20] presumably had seen Matthews perform and felt comfortable playing alongside a fellow Ivy Leaguer, but Boston ended up not signing the talented player and continued its losing ways.

Both Tenney and Boston sagged as the Beaneaters finished last for the first time in 1906. "Tenney has fallen off in play, and no wonder, with all the duties he is called on to perform as business manager and all-round utility man from first base to the turnstile," said the *Boston Globe*.[21] On August 7 Tenney and umpire Bill Klem made front-page news[22] with a fracas over unused baseballs. Accounts differ, but as Klem prepared (or declined) to return extra balls after the game, Tenney started searching Klem's pockets, whereupon the two exchanged punches, leading to what *Sporting Life* called "the most turbulent scene ever witnessed on a [Boston] ballfield."[23] Tenney received a two-game suspension but earned his bonus and became a part-owner of the penny-pinching franchise.

The 1907 season saw the Beaneaters become the Doves, named after club President George Dovey, and Tenney played on Sundays for the first time, but these two developments could not prevent a 16-game losing streak in August. After the 13th straight loss, a reporter observed, "Tenney looks drawn and worried. Pretty good reason to, with the team all out of ginger."[24] Boston finished seventh at 58-90, a poor record by any standard that nevertheless serves as the top mark of Tenney's tenure as Boston manager. A 1907 cartoon depicted Tenney on tiptoes reaching for a balloon marked "6th Place," an impossible dream for a Tenney-led team.[25] In September, Dovey asserted that Tenney would remain with Boston in 1908 and continue as manager.[26] Three months later, the Doves sent Tenney to the Giants in an eight-player trade; Tenney kept his stock in the Boston franchise while playing for New York, a conflict of interest that remained unresolved. Summing up Tenney's Boston tenure, noted baseball scribe Tim Murnane of the *Boston Globe* asserted, "Tenney played fine ball, but several of the players, it is said, informed Mr. Dovey that they would not return to Boston if they were forced to work with him."[27]

Free of management duties, the 36-year-old first baseman enjoyed his last productive season in 1908. "He is like wine – he improves with age," wrote W.S. Farnsworth in the *New York Evening Journal*. "He is not only playing a grand game, but his coaching is making the youngsters, [Al] Bridwell and [Larry] Doyle, the spiciest pair ever to cavort around the keystone corner. … And his great ability to 'stretch' has given Arthur Devlin the greatest fielding season he has had since joining the Giants. With his swatstick, too, Tenney has a record to be proud of."[28] Tenney led the NL in runs (101) and ranked second in walks (72). He also started 156 of 157 games at first base (the Giants played three ties), but the one game he missed with an injury[29] allowed Fred Merkle his day of infamy, ultimately costing the Soiled Collegian his only chance at a World Series.

Battling leg woes in 1909, Tenney batted a career-low .235 in just 101 games and was released by the Giants.[30] He was the player-manager for Lowell of the New England League in 1910 and the Boston Nationals in 1911. He returned to Boston at the insistence of the team's new management, which otherwise would not buy his shares of stock.[31] With a record of 12-41 in mid-June, the 39-year-old first baseman remained as manager but lost his field captaincy to Johnny Kling.[32] Tenney proved terribly consistent as a skipper. Three of his four Boston teams lost at least 102 games. The 1911 edition proved the worst with 107 defeats. Kling became manager in 1912; because Tenney had a two-year contract, however, he was paid not to manage in 1912, an ironic conclusion to a managerial career that initially saw him manage without additional compensation.

After initially joining a shoemaking business in Lynn,[33] just north of Boston, and spending five years away from the game, Tenney returned, again in a hybrid role, by helping to purchase an International League team in Jersey City and moving it to Newark.[34] At the age of 44, he played in 16 games, batted .318, and quit the game for good after a year.

Tenney worked in Boston for the Equitable Life Insurance Society for more than three decades. When friends introduced him as "the best first baseman who ever lived," he typically replied, with a smile, "Thank you, but you gentlemen understand that there is only one first baseman – Mr. Chase."[35] At least as far back as 1901, Tenney had written for outlets like *Baseball Magazine*, the *Boston Sunday Post*, and the *New York Times*, and he picked up the pen again in his post-baseball career, typically praising pre-Deadball Era stars without denigrating latter-day players. Newspapers also featured his caricatures of players and fans at spring training.[36]

Fred Tenney died at age 80 on July 3, 1952, at Massachusetts General Hospital in Boston, a few miles from where the South End Grounds had once stood, where he had effectively and faithfully roamed the right side of the infield for so many seasons.

Note: An earlier version of this biography appeared in Tom Simon, ed., *Deadball Stars of the National League* (Washington, D.C.: Brassey's, Inc., 2004).

NOTES

1. Bill James, *The New Bill James Historical Baseball Abstract* (New York: The Free Press, 2001), 461. The quotation comes from an 1897 *Chicago Daily News* article.

2. Tenney ranks third among first basemen with 277 sacrifices. Lyle Spatz, "Leaders in sacrifice hits," email to deadball@egroups.com, January 11, 2001. Less impressively, Tenney also shares the record for most errors in a game by a first baseman since 1900 with four, a mark he set in the first game of a doubleheader on July 12, 1905. Thanks again to Spatz for this information provided in emails sent to deadball@egroups.com on April 12, 2001, and to the author on August 17, 2017. Tenney made three errors in the second inning alone. "Game and Game," *Boston Globe*, July 13, 1905: 8.

3. Harold Kaese, *The Boston Braves, 1871-1953* (Boston: Northeastern University Press, 2004), 83.

4. An article in Tenney's Hall of Fame file that has neither a date nor a newspaper name reports that Fred's paternal grandfather, Moses, born on June 18, 1808, married Mary Ann Northend. A member of the notorious Know-Nothing Party, Moses Tenney represented Essex in the Massachusetts State Senate and served as treasurer of the Commonwealth of Massachusetts from 1856 to 1861. Moses and Mary had a son named Charles, the father of Fred. "Four Generations of the Tenney Family." Charles married Sarah DeBacon on January 16, 1868.

5. J.D. McGlone, "Fred Tenney, Pioneer Left-Handed First Baseman, Found Way from Brown to Big League as Catcher," *Providence Evening Bulletin*, February 29, 1932.

6. Recounted Tenney's teammate Hugh Duffy: "It was a bad injury and Fred was out for weeks. Charlie Ganzel, one of our injured catchers, took Fred to a hospital in a cab, and on the way Fred apologized that he hadn't done a better job." Frederick G. Lieb, "Tenney First of Fancy Dans at No. 1 Bag," *The Sporting News*, October 30, 1946: 11.

7. Fred Tenney, "How Tenney Broke into Baseball," *New York Times*, March 21, 1910.

8. David L. Porter, editor, *Biographical Dictionary of American Sports* (Westport, Connecticut: Greenwood Press, 2000), 1528. They had at least three daughters; near the end of his life "Tenney lived with one of his married daughters, Mrs. Martha Chase, at Holliston, Mass." "Fred Tenney Dies; Rated Among Top First Basemen," *The Sporting News*, July 16, 1952: 22.

9. Selee managed Chicago after leaving Boston. With the Cubs, Selee still thought highly of Tenney, but liked his own Frank Chance even more. Stated Selee, "Tenney is a remarkable player, but I think Chance is the better first baseman. Now, mind you, I do not wish to be understood as saying anything derogatory to the Boston star, and, while in my judgment Chance has him beaten as a first sacker, I could easily find a place for the Boston man on the Chicago team." "Baseball Notes," *Boston Globe*, July 7, 1904: 7.

10. Fred Tenney, "Selee Brought Out Best First Basemen," *New York Times*, January 29, 1911.

11. T.H. Murnane, "Batting Record Made," *Boston Globe*, June 1, 1897: 5.

12. T.H. Murnane, "Glorious Climax," *Boston Globe*, June 26, 1897: 7.

13. "Baseball's Double Play Supreme: Fred Tenney's Idea," *Boston Evening Transcript*, December 24, 1931.

14. M.J. Tenney, *The Tenney Family or the Descendants of Thomas Tenney of Rowley, Massachusetts 1638-1904* (Concord, New Hampshire: Rumford Press, 1904), 614.

15. "Tenney and Clark [sic] Suspended," *Boston Globe*, May 17, 1902: 5. Rather than hold a grudge, Clarke repeatedly sought to obtain Tenney, according

to "Is After Fred Tenney," *Boston Globe*, June 16, 1904: 8, and "Want Fred Tenney on Pittsburg Team," *New York Times*, November 19, 1909.

16 "They Are After Tenney," *Boston Globe*, May 25, 1902: 4.

17 Telegram from Detroit Tigers President S.F. Angus to Fred Tenney, September 11, 1902.

18 According to the *Cincinnati Post*, "Tenney's reason for not playing on Sundays is that his contract does not call for Sunday games." "They'll Play Sunday," *Boston Globe*, May 23, 1904: 3. "Boston should either get a team that plays Sunday ball or cut out play on that day. To exempt the captain from duty and compel most of the others to play is not helping the team any – Cincinnati Enquirer." "Baseball Notes," *Boston Globe*, August 31, 1904: 7.

19 Karl Lindholm, "William Clarence Matthews," sites.middlebury.edu/karllindholm/william-clarence-matthews/ (accessed August 3, 2017).

20 "Tenney coached the Tufts College baseball team before … spring training in 1904. This was a common practice of the time." Norman Macht email to author, November 29, 2000. Tenney also coached at Brown and Dartmouth, according to an unattributed and undated clip in his Hall of Fame file headlined "Fred Tenney Has a Life-Time Pass."

21 "Baseball Notes," *Boston Globe*, June 4, 1906: 5.

22 "Tenney and Klem Clash," *Boston Globe*, August 8, 1906: 1.

23 "Tenney's Temper," *Sporting Life*, August 18, 1906: 10.

24 "Baseball Notes," *Boston Globe*, August 15, 1907: 5.

25 *Boston Globe*, August 29, 1907: 5.

26 "Tenney to Stay Here," *Boston Globe*, September 28, 1907: 5.

27 T.H. Murnane, "Big Deal Made by Joe Kelley," *Boston Globe*, December 14, 1907: 1.

28 W.S. Farnsworth, *New York Evening Journal*, August 26, 1908.

29 "Fred Tenney is playing solely on his nerve. His feet are in very bad shape, and his back is lame. Every time he stoops it is pain. But [New York manager John] McGraw had enough of Merkle … and called on Tenney for his brains. A one-legged man with a noodle is better than a bonehead," Gym Bagley, *New York Evening Mail*, September 25, 1908. "Tenney had some skin torn off his back and a plaster had been placed there to protect it. A trainer took the plaster off and tried to rub the tender skin, with the result that Tenney missed the only game of the long campaign," Joe Nutter, "A Long Brown for Fred Tenney '94," *Providence Evening Bulletin*, January 23, 1941.

30 "Giants Ranks Reduced," *New York Times*, May 10, 1910.

31 "Tenney owned $10,000 worth of stock in September 1907," according to "Baseball Notes," *Boston Globe*, September 3, 1907: 9.

32 The awkwardness of this abnormal arrangement seemed apparent at the time. "Tenney continues to manage the team, but it looks from the side lines as though Kling would have more to say than Tenney in a short time. Just what arrangement [Boston owner William] Russell made with Kling has not been published. It may be that Kling will be made manager as soon as Tenney's contract expires," A.H.C. Mitchell, "Boston Bulletin," *Sporting Life*, June 24, 1911: 3.

33 "Fred Tenney in Shoe Business," *New York Times*, June 1, 1912.

34 W.J. M'beth, "Jim Price and Fred Tenney Secure Newark," *Sporting Life*, February 26, 1916: 8.

35 Harold Kaese, "Tenney Pioneered Art of Playing First Base," *Boston Globe*, July 8, 1952: 10. Perhaps Tenney simply returned the compliment that Chase had given him a decade earlier. When injured, Chase had watched Tenney play against the Giants and later recalled, "I was really impressed … and it wasn't until then that I realized how flattering the 'second Fred Tenney' tag-line was to me. I was amazed by his footwork and his catlike reactions to a pitcher's throw trapping a runner off the sack. Tenney clamped the ball on the player with lightning speed on throws from the pitcher or catcher." Lester Grant, "Hal Chase, Who Plunged from Glory to Gloom, Recalls Greatest Thrills and Players of His Days on the Diamond," *The Sporting News*, September 25, 1941: 6.

36 Tenney had sketched players during his career and had studied under artists in Providence. "Fred Tenney Is an Artist," *Pittsburgh Press*, March 31, 1905: 22.

TOMMY TUCKER
BY DAVID NEMEC

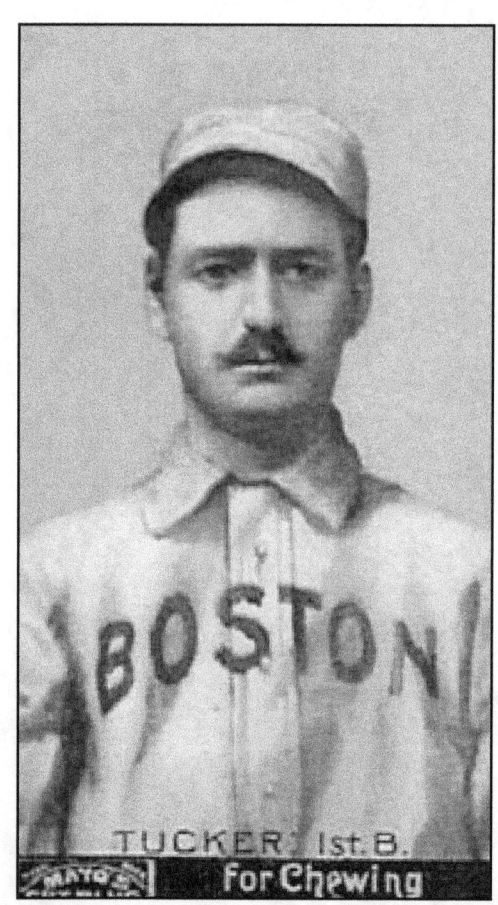

Tommy Tucker, 1895 Mayo Cut-Plug tobacco card.
(public domain)

Tommy Tucker's career highlight came in 1889, when he hit .372, becoming the first switch-hitter to win a major-league batting title. But scant attention was paid to such arcane matters then; he was a household name during his time not because of anything he accomplished on the diamond, but because a nursery rhyme bearing his name *(Little Tommy Tucker)* had yet to lapse into obscurity.

Through the 1892 season, approximately the halfway mark in his career, the right-handed throwing first baseman owned a .297 composite batting average. The increased pitching distance the following year heightened batting averages across the board for the rest of the 1890s. In every case but one, position players at or near the midpoint of fairly lengthy big-league careers increased their lifetime BAs after 1892, often by as many as 50 points, as was the case with Ed Delahanty. The lone exception was Tucker, who actually hit 13 points *less,* or just .284, in the second half of his major-league sojourn. He finished at 290.

If his hitting decline were not burden enough, he also grew increasingly unpopular among fellow players with each passing year. His nicknames – "Foghorn," "Noisy Tom," and "Tommy Talker" – provide an initial clue. By the time he took his last throw at first base in a major-league game in 1899, few indeed were sorry to see him go.

Thomas Joseph Tucker was born in Holyoke, Massachusetts, on October 28, 1863. His parents were Patrick and Mary (née McMannis) Tucker, both of whom were born in Ireland. Tommy was the second of their six children. He was preceded by a sister named Delia and followed by John, Timothy, Rosa, and Joseph. Patrick Tucker, who worked in a cotton mill, died in an accident in 1874. As of the 1880 census, the four oldest children worked in a paper mill while their mother kept house. In all likelihood Tommy, as the eldest male child, went to work at that trade soon after his father's untimely death and never finished school.

Tucker played for a semipro team representing his home town in 1882-83.[1] He turned pro in 1884 with the Holyoke entry in the minor league Massachusetts State Association. He began the following season with Springfield of the Southern New England League before moving to Newark of the Eastern League. Returning to Newark in 1886, he hit .281 and was acclaimed the best all-around first baseman in the loop. Baltimore manager Billy Barnie fired weak-hitting Milt Scott (.481 OPS in 137 games in 1886) and replaced him with the fancy-fielding switch-hitter.

On November 23, 1886, in Holyoke, Tucker married Theresa Powers (whose parents also both came from Ireland). It's notable that Tucker's occupation was still listed as paper worker.

In his big-league debut on April 16, 1887, at Baltimore, the 5-foot-11-inch, 165-pound Tucker batted cleanup for the Orioles and went 1-for-3 while swinging from the left side in an 8-3 win over Philadelphia's vaunted rookie right-hander Ed Seward.[2] He followed his outstanding rookie season in 1887 by leading the Orioles in home runs and RBIs in 1888, and then topped the American Association in batting in 1889.

Baltimore resigned its AA membership that fall and pirated most its players and team colors into the minor league Atlantic Association prior to the 1890 season. Tucker tied himself in knots, according to several items that winter in *Sporting Life*, and made himself look utterly foolish over whether to jump to the rebel Players League. He finally signed a personal services contract allowing Baltimore to sell him to any team he wanted, and wound up going to the Boston National League entry for $3,000.

Whether it was a change to the National League brand of ball or playing for a better caliber of team, he evolved almost immediately into a very different sort of player than he had been with Baltimore. Always an aggressive, in-your-face type – he led his league five times in being hit by pitches – he became downright fractious, perfecting a trick on wild pickoff throws to first base of falling heavily on top of the runner to prevent him from advancing. His language, particularly when he was acting as a base coach, grew increasingly vulgar and his off-field antics began putting him into frequent skirmishes with Boston manager Frank Selee. On September 21, 1893, Tucker showed up drunk for a game at Cincinnati but nonetheless insisted on playing. When Selee refused to put him in the lineup and wrote in Charlie Ganzel's name at first base, Tucker verbally abused the manager to the extent that he finally had to be dragged out of the park by the police.[3] That same season Tucker came under severe criticism from the Cleveland papers for his "dirty" play after Spiders catcher Chief Zimmer suffered a broken collarbone on July 12 when he tried to dive back into first base on a pickoff attempt, and Tucker blocked him off the bag with both knees.[4]

The following year, on May 15, 1894, at Boston's South End Grounds, Tucker and Baltimore's John McGraw helped launch the city's "Great Roxbury Fire" when they got into a savage fight on the field in the third inning after Tucker slid hard into third base and McGraw kicked him in the face. Prior to the start of the inning, a group of boys had unwittingly set a small bonfire amid some rubbish beneath the right-field stands. The conflagration in its initial stages could easily have been stomped out, but it was ignored by the crowd – who were caught up in the fracas on the field and its aftermath – until the end of the inning. By then the flames had reached such severity that they forced stoppage of the game and ultimately burned down not only most of the ballpark, but portions of over 200 buildings nearby, resulting in a loss "variously estimated at from $300,000 to $1,000,000" and leaving some 1,900 Bostonians homeless.[5] The damage to South End Grounds was so extensive that the park was closed for 10 weeks while it underwent reconstruction; in the interim the Beaneaters played at Congress Street Grounds

Tucker's most infamous moment in a road game also took place in 1894, at Philadelphia. On July 17, Boston tried in vain to delay a game during the eighth inning after Philadelphia had taken a prohibitive 12-2 lead. Boston had been ahead 2-1 at the end of the last fully played inning, the seventh, and wanted Umpire Bill Campbell to call the game because of the light rain that had begun falling before the eighth was completed. As per the rule, had Campbell done so the score would have reverted to the end of the seventh frame, and Boston would have won. After Philadelphia was able to circumvent Boston's delaying tactics and end its turn at bat by having Sam Thompson purposely miss second base on his return to first on a long foul ball, Boston refused to continue and Campbell forfeited the game to Philadelphia. Soon after he did so, several fans, in the opinion of the *Boston Globe*, seemed to have had a "preconcerted plan to attack Tucker, for they fairly swarmed around this player" when he attempted to return to the Boston bench to retrieve a sweater he had forgotten. Reports conflict as to whether he sustained a broken cheekbone in the fracas or merely a severe bruise before Philadelphia players and police helped get him away from his assailants.[6]

Following years of trying unsuccessfully to trade his quarrelsome first baseman, Selee finally gave up hopes of obtaining a decent player in return and sold him to Washington for around $2,000 on June 3, 1897.[7] Tucker seemingly thrived on the change of scene, hitting .338 for the D.C. club to post a composite .333 mark that season, his highest since winning the AA batting title eight years earlier. But Washington officials must have sensed that the revival was illusory, for they took a significant financial hit in order to get rid of Tucker. When they could not get waivers on him to send him to a minor-league team, they sold him to Brooklyn on March 5, 1898, for $800.[8] The 34-year-old first sacker lasted less than four months in Brooklyn before being peddled to last-place St. Louis on July 18.[9] *The Sporting News* commented that Browns manager Tim Hurst "thinks well of Tucker, but many experts are of the opinion that Tom is on the downgrade and is but little if any above the minor league standard."[10] Yet, just a few months earlier, catcher Aleck Smith had said Tucker was "one of the greatest first basemen I ever saw. You don't have to figure how you can get the ball in Tommie's pocket. All you have to do is shut your eyes and bang away in the direction of first base any old way."[11]

The next spring, when St. Louis and Cleveland consolidated under syndicate ownership, Tucker was shipped to the Forest

City entry along with the rest of St. Louis's dregs. He played in 1899 as if he were sleepwalking in between dodging all hard-hit balls that were sent his way (according to several sources), compiling an abominable .593 OPS and scoring just 40 runs in 127 games for the equally abominable Spiders. He was axed a full month before the season ended after he went 0-for-2 in an 8-2 loss to the Phillies' Red Donahue at Philadelphia on September 13.[12]

Shunned by all remaining clubs when the National League lopped off four teams at the close of the 1899 season, Tucker spent 1900 batting a lackluster .277 for Springfield of the Eastern League. Following two more undistinguished seasons in the Connecticut State League, he left the game to work at his original trade in Holyoke paper mills.

At the time of his death in a hospital "after a long illness" on October 22, 1935, in Montague, Massachusetts, a town some 30 miles north of Holyoke, his son Raymond was a political journalist in Washington.[13] Still, from all accounts, although Tucker had two successful children, and some of his grandchildren are alive today, life for him never had anywhere near the same flavor after he left baseball.

Tucker's .372 mark in 1889 still stands as the season record for a switch-hitter. In addition he is #3 on the all-time hit-by-pitch list and held the record from 1893 to 1901 when Hughie Jennings passed him. An interesting task awaits future researchers: determining whether Tucker hit better from the left or right side of the plate. Most batsmen in the nineteenth century experimented at one time or another during their careers with switch-hitting, but few remained switch-hitters throughout. Tucker stands alone among nineteenth-century hitters with lengthy careers, not only in that his batting fell off markedly after the pitching distance was lengthened in 1893, but also because he apparently never tried to determine if he might have been better served by batting only from one side of the plate.

This biography is an expanded version of one that appeared in David Nemec's *Major League Baseball Profiles: 1871-1900* (Bison Books, 2011) vol. 1.

SOURCES

In assembling this biography I made extensive use of the *Boston Globe*, *Sporting Life*, *The Sporting News*, the late David Ball's groundbreaking nineteenth century Trade Log, David Funk's blog "All Funked Up" and the Washington Post for details of Tucker's professional baseball career. His family background came from ancestry.com.

NOTES

1 *New York Clipper*, March 29, 1890.

2 *Sporting Life*, April 27, 1887: 2.

3 *Boston Globe*, September 22, 1893: 6. In the same game Cincinnati second baseman Bid McPhee wore a glove for the first time in his career.

4 *Sporting Life*, July 22, 1893: 1. See also "On the Diamond," *Cleveland Leader*, July 16, 1893: 15.

5 *Sporting Life*, May 19, 1894: 1; *Boston Globe*, May 16, 1894: 1; David Funk blog, "All Funked Up," May 15, 2015.

6 David Nemec and Eric Miklich, *Forfeits and Successfully Protested Major League Games* (Jefferson, North Carolina McFarland & Company, Inc., 2014), 78.

7 David Ball Trade Log

8 Ibid.

9 Ibid.

10 *The Sporting News*, July 23, 1898: 3.

11 *Cincinnati Enquirer*, May 24, 1898.

12 *Boston Globe*, September 14, 1899: 7

13 *Sporting Life*, April 27, 1887: 2.

VIC WILLIS

BY DANIEL R. LEVITT

Vic Willis.
(Library of Congress)

As a rookie in 1898, Vic Willis won 25 games as a key member of the pennant-winning Boston Beaneaters, one of the top teams of the nineteenth century. Eleven years later in his penultimate season, Willis again won over 20 games as a member of the world champion Pittsburgh Pirates, one of the top teams of the Deadball Era. In between he pitched well enough to finish with 249 wins in only a 13-year career. A big man for his time at 6-foot-2, 205 pounds, Willis pitched with an overhand delivery and was known as a great strikeout pitcher. In 1995, nearly a century after his major-league debut, the Veterans Committee voted the hurler nicknamed the "Delaware Peach" into the Hall of Fame.

Victor Gazaway Willis was born on April 12, 1876 in Cecil County, Maryland. Soon afterward his family moved just across the state line to Newark, Delaware, where his father James supported the family as a carpenter, and his mother Mary ran the household. In Newark, Willis grew up playing baseball, starring on his school team at Newark Academy and later for Delaware College. By the time he was 18, Willis was playing semiprofessionally around the state of Delaware.

In 1895 as a 19-year-old Willis first entered organized baseball by joining the Harrisburg club in the nearby Pennsylvania State League. His workload piled up rapidly as he pitched in 16 of the team's 37 games. The Harrisburg club folded in June, but Willis had gained some recognition and quickly caught on elsewhere--less than two weeks later he signed with Lynchburg in the Virginia League.

Overall, Willis pitched capably in 1895 despite the forced midseason relocation, and the next year he moved up to Syracuse of the Eastern League for the 1896 season. Willis battled illness nearly the entire year, but fought through it for a while to achieve a record of 10-6 by late July. Eventually the illness got the better of him, and on July 31 he left the team for the rest of the season to recuperate.

He returned to Syracuse healthy in 1897 and finished the season 21-16 as Syracuse won the league championship. Syracuse realized they had a budding star and hoped to sell him for $2,000, a fairly high price for the time. They ultimately settled for $1,000 and catcher Fred Lake from Boston. The major-league club developed its interest in Willis from the recommendations of Providence manager Billy Murray and Syracuse catcher Jack Ryan, previously a catcher in Boston.

In 1898 Willis joined the National League's Boston Beaneaters, fresh off their fourth pennant in seven years. Willis was expected to help the team immediately, with one sportswriter commenting: "The 'Wolf' as he is termed ought to be a great winner for Boston," and he further described the big right-hander as having good control, a change of pace, and a sweeping curve.[1] The *Boston Sunday Journal* reported that "Willis has speed and the most elusive curves. His 'drop' is so wonderful that, if anyone hits it, it is generally considered a fluke."[2]

Willis saw his first action April 20 in a mopup role in Baltimore when he entered the game in the sixth with the Beaneaters behind, 10-3. Willis showed some first-game jitters and over the final three innings he gave up eight runs while walking three and hitting two Oriole batters. Nine days later, in his first start, Willis pitched better and won 11-4 in a complete game. Willis surpassed even his high spring expectations by following up this first victory to finish 25-13 for the pennant winning Beaneaters.

The 23-year-old Willis followed up his superb rookie campaign with one of the best seasons of his career. He won 27, lost only 8 and finished second in ERA while pitching 342 innings. That year he led the league in allowing the fewest hits per game; a feat helped by hurling his only no-hitter on August 7. In the sixth inning of that game Washington pitcher Bill Dinneen hit a ball that took a bad hop and just eluded Boston third baseman Jimmy Collins. Fortunately for Willis this ball was scored an error and his no-hitter was preserved. After the season in February 1900 Willis married Mary J. Minnis, a union that would lead to two children, a girl and a boy born 15 years apart.

Years later Boston first baseman Fred Tenney recollected the team's pitchers and fielders working in harmony, even if the outcome was not always as anticipated:

"I remember once Vic Willis was pitching for Boston and Jesse Tannehill was at the bat. Long [shortstop Herman] saw as Willis wound up that he was going to give Tannehill a low ball and Tannehill could wallop that kind. He was apt to paste them hard to right field.

"'No, no; don't give him that,' cried Long, but Willis was just letting the ball go and Long darted across the diamond in front of the second baseman as fast as his legs could carry him. He knew that Tannehill was apt to slam the ball to right field, and he wanted to head it off. There were two strikes on Tannehill, and as luck would have it he missed this one and struck out. Long described a circle, came up to Willis from the direction of first base, grabbed him by the hand and exclaimed, 'that's the way to pitch, old boy!'"[3]

Despite a subpar 1900 season, Willis was still regarded as a top hurler, and in 1901 Boston paid him a $2,400 salary. At the end of the nineteenth century the National League's magnates adopted a salary maximum of $2,400. For the top players, however, teams often supplemented this salary with additional payments, both above and below the table. Willis' teammate, star pitcher Kid Nichols earning $2,400, held out prior to the 1899 season after winning the 1898 pennant because the team offered only $235 per man as a championship bonus.

In 1901 the American League challenged the National as a major league, and the completion between the leagues for ballplayers bid up salaries. As some of his teammates were leaving for greener pastures in the AL, Willis reportedly agreed to jump to the American League's Philadelphia Athletics but soon changed his mind. Other star National League hurlers saw their salaries jump from the American League threat: Noodles Hahn leapt to $4,200, Christy Mathewson reportedly made $5,000, and Joe McGinnity $3,000. That year Willis turned in another good season with a 20-17 record and finished fourth in ERA while pitching over 300 innings.

In 1902 Willis responded sensationally to an incredible workload: he completed a league-high 45 games, the modern (since 1901) NL record; hurled 410 innings, the second-highest total in modern NL history; and led the league in strikeouts with 225. On May, 29 against New York Willis struck out a league-high 13 Giants; that only 450 spectators saw this game highlights how far this franchise had fallen in the new century from its recent championship days. Additionally, Willis was used in several key relief situations, and he has been retroactively credited with a league-high three saves.

The American League came calling again during the 1902 season. Detroit Tigers president Sam Angus met Willis in the Victoria Hotel and offered a large cash downpayment on a two-year contract of $4,500 per season. Naturally tempted by the cash and salary, Willis initially accepted, but again later reneged after Boston reportedly matched the offer. His services remained in dispute until after the season when he was awarded to Boston as part of the peace settlement between the two leagues.

Over the next three years Willis won only 42 games while toiling for the rapidly deteriorating Beaneaters. In 1904 when Willis finished with a league-high 25 losses, his 18 wins represented 33% of his team's 55 victories. He also proved an excellent fielder that year and recorded 39 putouts, a modern NL record that would stand for nearly a century. Willis, who years later would complain about the team's fielding ability, probably figured the only way to get some outs was to make them himself. His grandson remembered Willis saying: "those outfielders couldn't catch a flyball with a peach basket."[4]

Prior to the start of the 1905 season the now anemic Boston club offered a salary of only $2,400. Willis expressed displeasure with his drastic salary cut by threatening to jump to an outlaw league in Pennsylvania. He eventually rejoined the Beaneaters but may have wished he hadn't. In 1905, with the league's worst offense supporting him, Willis again led the league with 29 losses, the most ever in modern baseball. Not surprisingly, after this frustrating season Willis again flirted with the outlaw league.

This time, however, the Pirates rescued the Willis from the hapless Beaneaters. Pittsburgh owner Barney Dreyfuss surrendered three players in the trade for Willis: new third baseman Dave Brain, first baseman Del Howard and pitcher Vivian Lindaman. After the trade Willis sent a letter to Dreyfuss acknowledging his unhappiness on the Beaneaters and expressing his approval of the trade, and added: "Don't believe those tales you hear about my being all-in. Wait until you see me in action for your team and then form your opinion of my worth to your team. I assure you that I am delighted to be a Pirate and that I will do my best to bring another pennant to the Smoky City."5 Dreyfuss reportedly restored Willis' $4,500 salary as well.

Willis started strongly for his new club pitching three straight shutouts early in the 1906 season. Now with a winning franchise again, Willis would win 21 to 23 games a year over his four years with the Pirates without ever losing more than 13 while consistently pitching around 300 innings a year. During his stint with the Pirates, Willis hurled the two one-hitters of his career.

The famous 1908 National League pennant race came down to the last game of the season for the Pirates. On Sunday October 4, the Pirates faced the Cubs in Chicago's old West Side Park in front of 30,247 fans, the most to have ever seen a baseball game up to that point and 6,000 more than had ever previously crowded into that park. A win for the Pirates and they would win the pennant; a loss and they would, for all intents and purposes, be eliminated.

Pirates manager Fred Clarke selected the well-rested Willis to start against the Cubs' Three-Finger Brown, another future Hall of Famer. Brown was on his way to an excellent 29-9 record but this would be his third game in six days. The Cubs jumped out to a 2-0 lead as the Pirates managed only three hits through the first five innings. The Pirates scored two in the sixth to tie the game. In the bottom of the sixth with two out Joe Tinker doubled and Willis and Clarke chose to intentionally walk catcher Johnny Kling to face Brown. Unfortunately for Willis and the Pirates, Brown singled in Tinker with the go ahead and winning run. The Cubs later added two insurance runs including another RBI from Brown and won the contest, 5-2.

In January of the following year, amid rumors of a salary dispute, Willis announced that he had decided to retire from baseball and claimed he could make more money back in his hometown of Newark, Delaware. By the time the season rolled around, however, Dreyfuss had brought Willis back into the fold

In mid-1909 Willis again pitched in one of the highest attended games to date—the grand opening of Forbes Field, one of the first concrete and steel stadiums. On June 30, amid great fanfare and the closing of many businesses at noon, 30,000 plus spectators including numerous baseball and Pennsylvania dignitaries packed the new stadium. The *Reach Guide* gushed on the unveiling: "Never, perhaps, in the history of the Old World or New--not excluding the assemblages in the Roman and Grecian amphitheaters and stadiums--was a scene more spectacular presented...."6 Willis started for the Pirates, once again against the Cubs, and pitched a four hitter. But the team lost 3-2 in a game Dreyfuss obviously wanted very much to win: "What a shame we had to lose that one. I'd have given my share of the gate to have won on this day."7

Unlike the previous season, in 1909 the Pirates gave their opponents no opportunity for late season heroics by winning 110 games and outdistancing the second-place Cubs by 6 1/2 games. Willis played a key role by winning 22 and losing only 11, winning 11 consecutive games over one stretch during the season. In the World Series against the Tigers, Willis pitched in just two games, the only World Series appearances of his career. He relieved Howie Camnitz in the third inning of Game Two, and Ty Cobb promptly stole home. Willis gave up three runs over his 6 1/3 innings in relief as the Tigers won the game, 7-2.

With the Pirates up three games to two, Clarke gave Willis the Game Six start and a chance to win the Series. Despite being staked to a three run lead in the first inning, Willis could not hold the lead. Clarke pulled him after five innings with Detroit ahead, 4-3. Although the Pirates ended up losing Game Six, they came back to win Game Seven and the World Series two days later.

Despite his fine 1909 season, the Pirates waived Willis before the 1910 season amid allegations of disciplinary problems with manager Clarke during the previous summer and World Series. The chronically second-division St. Louis Cardinals claimed Willis, and *The Sporting News* reported that he "should have a year or two of high-class work left in him if he will behave himself."8 Willis won only nine games for the seventh-place Cardinals, and just prior to the end of the season the team asked waivers on Willis.

During the offseason St. Louis sold Willis to the minor-league Baltimore Orioles of the Eastern League. Although some doubt existed whether Willis would report to the minors, he told the *Baltimore Sun*: "I feel very much satisfied to play in Baltimore."9 Despite this apparent sale, both the Cubs and Reds put in a waiver claim for Willis. These waiver claims were ruled to be valid; St. Louis President Stanley Robison had mistakenly believed his waivers were good until the opening of the next season and consequently had to return Baltimore's check. Willis ended up being awarded to Chicago for the $1,500 waiver price, but elected to retire rather than report to the Cubs.

With his playing career now over, Willis retired to his hometown of Newark where he purchased and operated the Washington House Hotel. Willis remained active in baseball, managing semi-pro and coaching at the youth and college level. He also spent time enjoying golf and raising bird dogs. Vic Willis was 71 when he died in Elkton, Maryland, on August 3, 1947, the victim of a stroke.

SOURCES

Many sources were consulted in preparing this biography. The most useful were *The Sporting News* (many issues), Harold Kaese's *The Boston Braves* (Putnam, 1948), Fred Lieb's *The Pittsburgh Pirates* (Putnam, 1948), Lois P. Nicholson's *Maryland to Cooperstown* (Tidewater, 1998), Stephen Cunerd's article, "Vic Willis: Turn of the Century Great," from SABR's 1989 *Baseball Research Journal*, several annual *Reach Guides*, Dennis DeValeria and Jeanne Burke DeValeria's *Honus Wagner* (Henry Holt, 1996), and Vic Willis's file at the National Baseball Hall of Fame library.

NOTES

1   *The Sporting News*, February 12, 1898.

2   "Has Elusive Curves," *Boston Sunday Journal*, July 2, 1899.

3   "It's Done by Instinct," *Fort Wayne Daily News*, January 28, 1911.

4   Vin Mannix, "Persistence Pays Off for Grandson," *Florida News*, March 20, 1995.

5   *The Sporting News*, January 16, 1906.

6   "The National League's Showplace," *The Reach Official American League Baseball Guide for 1910*, (Philadelphia: A.J. Reach Company, 2010), 126.

7   Frederick G. Lieb, *The Pittsburgh Pirates* (Carbondale, Illinois: Southern Illinois University Press, 2003), 133.

8   *The Sporting News*, February 24, 1910.

9   "Sporting News in Tablet," *Fort Wayne Daily News*, January 12, 1911.

GEORGE YEAGER

BY RICHARD BOGOVICH

George Yeager.
(Courtesy of Rich Bogovich)

"A ball player entertains thousands of people who go to see him at the ball grounds. But he also entertains millions who read about him in the newspapers," wrote Olympic athlete and nationally syndicated journalist Robert Edgren toward the end of baseball's Dead Ball Era.[1] As one newspaper commented, George Yeager was "one of those quick thinking players … always ready to grasp at anything to keep the crowd in good humor."[2] However intentionally, Yeager also found many ways to enliven the nation's sports pages. Often, though, his conduct caused consternation for umpires, management, and crowds during away games.

George J. Yeager was born in Cincinnati to Henry and Anna (Leistner) Yeager on June 4, 1874.[3] Henry was a Cincinnati native and Anna was an immigrant from Germany. Cemetery records indicate that Henry served in the Ohio Volunteer Infantry during the Civil War. In the 1880 census George had three sisters and in the 1900 census three younger siblings were still living with their widowed mother. Anna had 14 children but only six were living at that point. The youngest was his only surviving brother, Robert.

Based on city directories, George grew up west of downtown within a mile of the Ohio River. The 1880 census specified that Henry worked at a distillery. George attended school, and the 1940 census indicated that the highest grade he completed was eighth. In 1890 George Yeager had a separate entry in a city directory for the first time. His occupation was "mach. hand" and two years later it was spring maker. In 1893 he was listed as a ballplayer.

One team on which Yeager played was the Shamrocks. It was the only Cincinnati-area team mentioned in a *Boston Herald* profile of him a few years later.[4] In 1891 one of their pitchers whom Yeager caught was Tom Sullivan, a recent major leaguer.[5] That season Yeager also caught former Beaneater Dick Conway, and one newspaper article implied that the Shamrocks had several former NL players.[6] The Poplar Stars were the other Cincinnati team with which Yeager was most strongly associated, primarily by Hugh Fullerton, a founder of the Baseball Writers' Association of America. In 1906 Fullerton drew attention to the Poplar Stars among teams that produced multiple professional ballplayers, including Yeager and Barry McCormick.[7]

According to the *Cincinnati Enquirer*, George Yeager began his professional career with a club in Celina, Ohio, about 100 miles north of Cincinnati. The *Herald* profile said he was with that team starting in 1892.[8] A box score in late September of 1892 showed Yeager batting cleanup for Celina and playing second base. He did likewise in mid-October against none other than the Cincinnati Reds, in Celina before 5,000 fans, and managed one of his team's four hits while being shut out by Ice Box Chamberlain.[9]

Yeager, who was just 18 years old, continued with Celina in 1893. One box score in June had him batting second and playing second base again, but on July 2 he was the catcher in their first loss of the season, which was covered by Chicago, Indianapolis, and Cleveland newspapers.[10] He soon saw additional duty behind the plate for Celina.[11] At the beginning of August, the Celina team united with three others to form the Northwestern Ohio League, with each club to play 16 games to determine a regional champion.[12] By then Yeager had returned primarily to second base. He reportedly considered himself a better infielder than catcher, and preferred to play second base barehanded. In any case, he displayed enough power that season to be given the nickname "Home Run."[13]

In April of 1894 Yeager became the starting catcher for a team in Chambersburg, Pennsylvania.[14] The club won its first game, at home on May 4 against a nine from a nearby college. Yeager was both acclaimed and scolded in Chambersburg's newspaper: "He is one of the best catchers Chambersburg has ever had but he should confine himself to catching and not abuse the umpire as he did yesterday," advised the paper. "Chambersburg is not accustomed to this and Yeager's popularity as a catcher will be seriously impaired unless he learns to talk less and, when he does talk, in a more gentlemanly manner."[15]

On May 12 he was involved in a fistfight that was big news locally. Around midnight a number of men were gathered at Lewis Forney's cigar shop. A man named George Gruse tried to persuade a local named Charles Grove to fight Yeager. Ultimately Gruse challenged Yeager himself. "Yeager, it may be remarked here, gave Gruse a very severe beating," wrote the *Valley Spirit* in its lengthy coverage. Forney threatened to use a baseball bat on anyone who interfered. Thus, when it appeared Grove was about to swing a beer bottle at Yeager, Forney struck. Grove sustained a skull fracture and vomited blood for hours.[16] Forney was charged with assault and battery but Yeager also had to face authorities in a local courtroom. His case was dismissed because no complainant appeared.[17]

Yeager resumed his catching duties, including on May 18 and 24 against a team from the Carlisle Indian School.[18] Within a few weeks he jumped to a team that had been in the Connecticut State League, representing New Haven. His first game with them was on June 28.[19] The league had disbanded around the middle of the month but the New Haven team was already in turmoil at the beginning of June when players' salaries were cut from $50 per month to $2 per game.[20] High points during Yeager's brief stay with New Haven included getting to test himself against the Springfield (Massachusetts) Eastern League team on July 3 and a complete-game win the next day, 10-4, as a *pitcher* against a team from nearby Meriden.[21]

Before the middle of July Yeager was back with Chambersburg, and in a game on July 13 he had four hits, including a homer and double. Nevertheless, his return lasted only about 10 days. "George Yeager, catcher for the Chambersburg club, has been released and left to-day for his home in Cincinnati," a Carlisle newspaper reported on July 23. "Umpires in the valley towns will now feel perfectly safe since George has gone."[22]

In less than a week Yeager was playing professionally with the Brockton (Massachusetts) team of the New England League.[23] On August 2 he was already making enemies. "Yeager, the Brockton catcher, did a mighty mean trick … with the apparent intention of injuring the umpire," said a newspaper. Yeager allegedly made no effort to catch one fastball and instead bent down to let it sail past him, though the ump dodged it. "This was a disgraceful performance and Yeager deserved severe punishment," the account concluded.[24]

Yeager's best game with Brockton might have been at home versus Pawtucket on August 22, when he went 4-for-4 with two doubles and three runs scored. Three days later the Brockton club disbanded, and Yeager was immediately signed by Pawtucket.[25] When the New England League's season concluded about two weeks later, Pawtucket didn't hesitate to include Yeager among 15 players it reserved for the next season.[26] The *Pawtucket Tribune* said he was "the fun maker of the team since he joined it and never failed to keep the boys in good humor." As players dispersed after their final game and he went to catch a train, the *Tribune* reported, he "bid his friends adieu as follows: 'The boy stood on the railroad track. He did not hear the bell. Farewell!'"[27]

During that offseason George Yeager said goodbye to bachelorhood. According to Kentucky marital records, he married 19-year-old Tillie Stadtlander on March 11, 1895, in Newport, just across the Ohio River from Cincinnati. In the 1893 and 1894 Cincinnati city directories, she was a laundress living with her parents.

Yeager continued with Pawtucket. Early success included home games on May 4 when he had five hits, including a double and two homers, and on June 8, when he hit a two-out grand slam. Later in June he was singled out by sportswriters for a very different reason when he was ejected from a road game for throwing a broom at the umpire. At home on July 8 one daily reported he was fined $10 by a different umpire "for insolent language and threatening with the bat." Three days later he was back to making news for a good reason, when he went 5-for-5 in a home game.[28]

Yeager received some high praise from sportswriters in Boston. For one, Tim Murnane of the *Globe* considered him ready for the National League. Another endorsement was more specific:

"Those managers who are searching for catching talent for next year would do well to look over Yeager of the Pawtuckets, who has been playing phenomenal ball this season," wrote the *Herald*. "He is not only a hard hitter, but is represented as being a magnificent thrower to bases."[29]

When the New England League's season ended on September 7, Yeager was in the top 10 for batting average, with a mark of .360. In 94 games he scored 99 runs. In 78 of those games he played catcher, and his 102 assists led the league (19 more than the runner-up), but his .912 fielding percentage was the lowest among regulars at the position.[30]

Right after the regular season, the circuit's top two teams, Fall River and New Bedford, were half of a temporary league of sorts that had historical significance. They were joined by an independent club in Newport, Rhode Island, plus a trailblazing African-American nine, the Cuban Giants, which featured future Hall of Famer Frank Grant. Each team was to play at least 11 games. Fall River immediately recruited Yeager to beef up its lineup. The first time Yeager faced the Cuban Giants was on September 13 in a 16-9 win for Fall River.[31]

Yeager returned for a third season with Pawtucket in 1896. On May 20 he added to his career tally of ejections, but that time, at least, his manager joined him. Little more than two weeks later, he was back to making news for the best of reasons when he homered twice in an 11-inning game won by Pawtucket. During the first half of August Yeager was insubordinate and thus fined "$25 for giving unsolicited advice to his manager," as the *Boston Herald* put it, and toward the end of the month he became so angry catching Pawtucket's pitcher during a game that he was ordered to switch positions with their right fielder.[32]

What surely mattered more was Yeager's offense. In 98 games he scored 113 runs, stole 36 bases, hit 24 homers, batted .345, and slugged .604.[33] As a result of this output, Yeager was purchased by the Boston Beaneaters on September 5. Two days later, just before leaving to join Boston, he celebrated dramatically in the second game of a three-team doubleheader. In the seventh inning his team trailed by a run when he stepped up to bat with the bases full. A fan clamored for "a farewell home run," and Yeager proceeded to hit the very first pitch over the left-field fence for a decisive grand slam.[34]

Before appearing in a regular-season Beaneaters game, he played in several exhibitions.[35] Yeager then made his major-league debut, at the age of 22, on September 25, 1896, in Washington before 3,786 fans. "Tom Tucker was out of condition, so Yeager covered first base," noted the *Boston Globe*. "His work was equal to the best efforts of Tucker, and he played the bag as though he belonged there regularly." He batted fifth, and his team led by just one run in the seventh inning when he faced Doc McJames, a future 20-game winner. Yeager singled and eventually scored an insurance run that helped Boston prevail, 6-3. He batted once late in the next day's game and that was his final action for 1896.[36]

In mid-February of 1897 it was announced that Yeager had signed a contract to continue with Boston.[37] Shortly thereafter the *Boston Post* quoted him at length:

"I signed as a catcher," said Yeager, "and I have heard nothing to the contrary. However, I am willing to play anywhere or do anything to help the team. I am going to use part of my advance money in getting into condition. I realize that this is my chance. I have been in a minor league for three years, and this is my first opportunity to get to the front."[38]

At the start of the regular season, Yeager's height and weight were logged as 5-feet-8½ inches and 175 pounds.[39] An early highlight came when the Beaneaters first played the Reds, in his hometown on May 27. He was the starting catcher, and though he was the only player in Boston's lineup to go hitless that day, he was cheered "lustily" at one point just for reaching first base on a force out. Still, the best display by the "faithful adherents of the house of Yeager" came earlier in the contest. "When he first went to bat they sent out to their idol a six-foot stand of flowers and a diamond ring," reported the *Globe*.[40]

Yeager soon achieved a milestone, in a home game vs. St. Louis on June 1: He hit his first major-league home run, off Bill Kissinger. His only other homer that season came on June 28. Two days later disaster struck. Boston hosted Brooklyn, and in the fourth inning rookie pitcher Jack Dunn collided with Yeager during a play at the plate. Yeager suffered a broken bone on the back of his catching hand, and one Boston paper immediately declared that he would be out for at least three weeks.[41]

Yeager ended up spending about five weeks back home in Cincinnati and rejoined the Beaneaters around August 3. At first he only coached baserunners, and the *Globe* teased that he "waltzed around the coaching lines like a dancing master on his benefit night." By August 18 he still hadn't played, and at that point he was loaned to Providence in the Eastern League.[42] In 11 games for the Grays, he hit .286. A month later Yeager returned to the Beaneaters in the thick of a remarkable pennant race, and he quickly made a big splash in a crucial win at home against New York on September 18. As the *Herald* noted, "Yeager got his base every time he came to the bat – twice on balls and twice on hits." One of those hits was a triple. He tripled again in a win against Brooklyn three days later.[43] Those were his primary contributions toward taking the championship from Baltimore in the season's final weeks.

Yeager spent all of 1898 with the Beaneaters. One early result was his inclusion in an overview of players' quirks and traits. Readers of the *Globe* learned that he spent "most of his leisure time in reading scientific books," foreshadowing his career change a decade later.[44] Much more substantively, he was subjected to a lengthy assessment by the *Herald* in early June. That daily wrote in part:

"Yeager has shown great improvement in his work this season. He handles himself far better behind the bat than he did last season. He throws far more accurately and easily, and it is a lucky base runner who can get to second on him if he gets but half a show from the pitcher. In his hitting Yeager has greatly improved. He faces the pitcher with a great deal of confidence. Yeager is a far better man than many a catcher working regularly in the league today."[45]

About a week later, the *Herald* noted that Yeager had hit safely in eight of his first nine games; his batting average was .323.

On August 8 the paper mentioned that he had again hit safely in eight of his nine most recent games.[46] Alas, Yeager entered a rough stretch later that month. At home on August 22, he was playing first base against Cincinnati when a rally-ending ground-out was undone after one of the Reds insisted Yeager didn't have a foot on the bag. He protested the changed call and was ejected. In Chicago two days later, he tried to field a sharply hit grounder only to have it strike him in the eye, which necessitated a hospital visit. Then at home on September 5 he broke a small bone on the back of his throwing hand in the first inning of a doubleheader and was projected to miss a week.[47]

Yeager returned at the start of a doubleheader at home on September 26 against Brooklyn. He came to bat with the bases jammed in the first inning and received an ovation, then responded by singling in two runs.[48] Boston never relinquished its early lead and won both games to increase its lead in the standings over second-place Baltimore to 4½ games with 14 games remaining. Boston clinched the pennant soon enough, and Yeager was again a champion. He played in 68 games and hit .267.

The regular season lasted until October 15 and Yeager wasn't feeling well, so he left for home immediately. The next evening he visited the *Cincinnati Enquirer*, which printed an extensive interview. He sang the praises of starting catcher Marty Bergen, then described tension within the team as a whole:

"After a losing game with that Boston team it was an easy matter to get a fight. All you had to do was look for one, and you would get it. They took defeat so much to heart that after a losing game everybody was ready to fight. That game of ours never knew what it was to let up. They played just as hard when they were 10 runs in front as they did when they were 10 runs behind."

He also volunteered insights about his team's use of secret signals: "We have very few signs. I'll risk the remark that no team in the league had as few signs as the Bostons. We all understood each other."[49]

On March 2, 1899, the Beaneaters purchased catcher Boileryard Clarke from Baltimore, and soon there was speculation that manager Frank Selee would farm out Yeager to Worcester in the Eastern League. This soon became reality. "Manager Selee has told George Yeager that he has decided to let him go to Worcester this spring," wrote Tim Murnane. "Yeager seems perfectly willing to go there to play first base and catch a few games at the same salary he is receiving in Boston."[50]

Opening Day for Boston was on April 15, 1899, and 10 days later Yeager was back with the team, albeit fleetingly. Bergen was away due to the death of one of his children, so Yeager caught in a loss at Philadelphia on April 25 and two days later batted against them once.[51] Yeager was promptly returned to Worcester. In 90 games for that club he accumulated 26 doubles, 12 triples, 5 home runs, and 11 stolen bases, with a .316 batting average.

Despite his impressive performance, in Worcester on September 4 Yeager was removed by his manager for "insolence."[52] This kind of behavior again mattered little, because he rejoined Boston by September 8 to pinch-run for Billy Hamilton in the last inning of a loss. The next day he subbed for Hamilton in most of game in which Boston was one-hit by Doc McJames. That proved to be his last game ever for the Beaneaters.[53] Yeager's major-league career eventually continued, but his father didn't live to see it. Henry Yeager died on November 9, 1899.[54]

Yeager joined Milwaukee of the American League for 1900, the season before that circuit was considered a major league. After 25 games he was hitting a lofty .388 when he suffered another substantial injury on May 26 in Detroit. While batting during the second inning he dropped to the ground to avoid being beaned by a pitch. He had to be carried off the field after sustaining what was described as badly torn ligaments in his left knee.[55] He was still recuperating when Milwaukee released him in early July.[56]

Yeager continued in the American League in 1901, except with Cleveland. He made his regular-season debut in the team's second game, on April 25, as catcher.[57] He played 39 games with Cleveland, hit only .223, and was released on July 27. He returned to the National League, with Pittsburgh, on August 4. In 26 games his average improved, to .264.

During the following winter Yeager signed with the New York Giants. However, *Sporting Life* reported that he had recently "devised a most successful filter for the dark waters of the Ohio, and has met with such excellent success that he is putting in all his time at the filter manufacturing business just now, and is not giving base ball much thought." In fact, Yeager helped patent that water filter.[58] About a month later he also received atypical newspaper attention for his ability to communicate via sign language. He was quoted in detail about having had a deaf-mute roommate during one of his minor-league stints, and as a result he quickly befriended Luther Taylor, deaf pitcher of the Giants.[59]

After 39 games Yeager had a .204 average and the Giants released him on July 17, 1902. A week later the American League's Baltimore Orioles signed him. He hit .184 in 11 games for them and was released on August 7. It turned out that his final major-league game was on August 5 in a loss at St. Louis. Ironically – for someone with a history of early exits from games due to his temper – he didn't enter the game until the eighth inning because starting catcher Aleck Smith was ejected for arguing a call despite having full justification for doing so, the *St. Louis Republic* conceded.[60]

Yeager soon joined Minneapolis of the minor-league American Association and in 35 games he hit .328. He continued with them in 1903, and on May 13 he was named captain and manager.[61] Toward the end of August he made headlines nationwide at the end of a game in Toledo during which he challenged the umpire and at one point flung a ball over the fence. A group of boys harassed him after the contest, and he threw the broom used for sweeping the plate at one of them. When fans nearby saw the 10-year-old take a tumble, they reportedly went after Yeager with stones and clubs. Policemen rescued him but charged him with assault and battery.[62] Regardless, that season was a good one for Yeager at bat as he averaged .310 in 106 games.

On the other hand, Minneapolis finished near the bottom of the AA with a record of 50-89,[63] and in 1904 Yeager played for another team in that circuit, Columbus. He played in 123 games for the Senators and hit .249. In 1905 he had short stints with two more AA teams, Toledo and St. Paul. In June he umpired an AA game in Louisville. Locals disapproved of his called third strike that resulted in a loss to St. Paul, and as he left the grounds he was whacked over the head with a beer bottle, punched in the face by a second fan, and struck with a baseball by a third.[64] Less than a week later he jumped to Montgomery of the Southern Association.[65]

Yeager rejoined Minneapolis in 1906 and played in 78 games. In May he was coaching baserunners and added to his career total of ejections, and in midseason he received some attention when a teammate popped a foul near Minneapolis's bench during a game. Yeager tried an old trick of rattling the bats to distract the fielder who tried for a putout, and the ploy worked.[66]

In 1907 and 1908 Yeager played for Des Moines in the Western League. It was apparently between those two seasons that he completed a degree in veterinary medicine, after which he was occasionally called Doc Yeager.[67] As of 2019 baseball-reference.com listed a "Yeager?" on the roster of the Peoria Distillers of the 1908 Illinois-Indiana-Iowa League; that was George's later team that season.[68] Yeager played for St. Paul a second time in 1909, but by early August his role was reduced to advance scout due to what basically became a career-ending injury. Fittingly, shortly before that it was reported that he had been "cutting up boyish pranks all the time."[69]

A 1909 Cincinnati city directory identified Yeager as a ballplayer but in the 1910 census his occupation was veterinarian. That census also revealed that he and Tillie had had a baby at some point, though by then the child was deceased. Records of the cemetery where George and Tillie are buried do not include a child of theirs.[70]

Not surprisingly, being a veterinarian in Cincinnati didn't keep Yeager away from baseball entirely. By mid-1911 he had been signed to umpire in the local Saturday Afternoon League.[71] City directories continued to list him as a veterinary surgeon through 1918 but by 1920 he was clerking in a yardmaster's office for the Baltimore & Ohio Railroad. He remained in that field for the rest of his life. During 1931 and 1932, when he was past the age of 55, he was among numerous players invited to participate in old-timers' games at Redland/Crosley Field, though he wasn't named in coverage after they were played.[72] Yeager died of a cerebral hemorrhage on July 5, 1940. He was survived by his wife and his brother Robert. Tillie died in 1944.[73]

How does one sum up George Yeager's personality as a baseball player? Newspapers happened to do that late in his professional career. For example, at least two shared the *Decatur Review*'s assessment in 1908 that he had "much of the earmarks of a rowdy."[74] Much more recently, in one book baseball historian David Nemec called Yeager "an extreme extrovert who yammered unremittingly about himself" and in another summed him up as "egomaniacal."[75] Yeager probably would have preferred the summation one paper employed just before his final season in the high minors: "comedian."[76]

SOURCES

In addition to the sources cited in the Notes, the author consulted Baseball-Reference.com.

NOTES

1. Robert Edgren, "R. Edgren's Column," *Evening World* (New York City), July 2, 1918: 10.

2. "Weather Too Chilly," *Cleveland Leader*, April 11, 1901: 6.

3. His marriage license, draft registration card during World War I, Social Security application in 1937, and death certificate all agree that he was born in 1874, though the latter showed June 5 as the date. Other sources put his birth a day earlier, on June 4, 1873. For example, see George V. Tuohey, *A History of the Boston Base Ball Club* (Boston: M F. Quinn & Co., 1897), 158.

4. "League Games Now," *Boston Herald*, April 18, 1897: 17. See also Jack Ryder, "Passing of the Millcreek Bottoms," *Cincinnati Enquirer*, January 1, 1905: 8.

5. "The Shamrocks Still Winning," *Cincinnati Enquirer*, July 27, 1891: 2. This article specified that "Sullivan, late of the Kansas Citys," had hurled a one-hitter, and the paper also mentioned his stints with Columbus, Atlanta, and Birmingham, all of which applied to Tom Sullivan. His catcher, "Yaeger," had two doubles and a single. "Jaeger" was another spelling in coverage of Shamrocks games during 1891.

6. "Shamrocks Beaten by Peru Again," *Indianapolis Journal*, September 6, 1891: 5. In September of 1891 another local team, the Elliotts, had a catcher named Yeager for at least one game, according to "Base Ball Gossip," *Cincinnati Enquirer*, September 23, 1891: 2.

7. Hugh S. Fullerton, "Base Ball on the Lots," *Washington Evening Star*, October 22, 1906: 9. Hugh S. Fullerton, "Ball Players Like Rain," *Chicago Sunday Tribune*, June 9, 1907: II, 4. Jack Ryder, "Passing of the Millcreek Bottoms," *Cincinnati Enquirer*, January 1, 1905: 8. The Poplar Stars apparently were under the age of 20, at least in 1891, according to "Gossip," *Cincinnati Post*, April 14, 1891: 4. In the 1907 article Fullerton wrote vividly about a game during April of an unspecified year in which Yeager, McCormick, and the rest of the Poplar Stars played "against Jake Stenzel's team. This was before Jake ever broke into fast company." The site was the Liberty Street bottoms ballpark along Mill Creek, very close to where Yeager grew up. The Ohio River had caused extensive flooding nearby, and late in the game someone on Stenzel's team hit a fly to left field just as a surge from the creek pushed the left-field wall inward dramatically. As a result, what might have been an easy out instead cleared the field of play. The umpire reportedly ruled it a game-tying homer and then declared the game over due to the wet grounds. (Because it was an amateur game, it may not have been reported on by any Cincinnati newspapers in the immediate aftermath.) Given that Stenzel began his minor-league career in 1887 and made his NL debut in 1890, it seems very unlikely he and Yeager ever played amateur ball together. Regardless, Fullerton wasn't off base by associating that ballpark with Yeager; two years earlier a Cincinnati journalist did as much when the ballpark was being phased out, and he named additional major leaguers who honed their skills there in addition to Yeager.

8. "George Yeager," *Cincinnati Enquirer*, July 9, 1940: 9. "League Games Now," *Boston Herald*, April 18, 1897: 17.

9. "Snapped," *Lima* (Ohio) *Daily Times*, September 30, 1892: 8. This game ended prematurely when the opposing pitcher broke his arm while throwing. "Big Turn-Out," *Cincinnati Enquirer*, October 17, 1892: 2. See also "Baseball," *Cincinnati Post*, October 17, 1892: 4.

10. "On the Diamond," *Delphos* (Ohio) *Weekly Herald*, June 22, 1893: 3. "Sports Here and There," *Chicago Daily News*, July 3, 1893: 2. "Muncie, 6; Celina, 1," *Indianapolis Journal*, July 3, 1893: 3. "Other Games. Celina's First Defeat," *Cleveland Leader*, July 3, 1893: 3.

11. For examples, see "Celina Won," *Cleveland Leader*, July 5, 1893: 6; "Celina, 12; Findlay, 8," *Daily Inter Ocean* (Chicago), July 13, 1893: 4.

12. "Another Base Ball Infant," *Cleveland Plain Dealer*, August 3, 1893: 5. The other three cities were Columbus Grove, Delphos, and Findlay. The article noted that nearby Fort Wayne, Indiana, might provide a fifth team in the circuit and thus cause the league's name to change.

13. For additional examples of Yeager in box scores at second base, see "On the Diamond," *Delphos Weekly Herald*, July 20, 1893: 3, and August 3, 1893: 2; "Seventh Inning," *Elwood* (Indiana) *Daily Press*, August 21, 1893: 1. See also David Nemec, *Major League Baseball Profiles, 1871-1900, Volume 1: The Ballplayers Who Built the Game* (Lincoln: University of Nebraska Press, 2011), 288.

14. "Work on the Ballfield," *Valley Spirit* (Chambersburg, Pennsylvania), April 25, 1894: 1. David Nemec said that Yeager spent part of 1894 with Celina. Because Yeager had stints with four other clubs documented herein, it's difficult to envision when Yeager would have had time to return to Celina.

15. "7 to 2," *Valley Spirit*, May 9, 1894: 8. The opposing team was from Franklin and Marshall College of Lancaster, Pennsylvania.

16. "His Head Broken," *Valley Spirit*, May 16, 1894: 5. See also "Hit by a Base Ball Bat," *Hagerstown* (Maryland) *Daily Herald and Torch Light*, May 15, 1894: 4.

17. "With the Policemen," *Valley Spirit*, May 23, 1894: 6. Forney was charged with assault and battery but fled, only to be returned from Illinois. In August he was one of seven prisoners who escaped the local jail while awaiting trial. See "Franklin Has a Leaky Jail," *Philadelphia Times*, August 21, 1894: 1.

18. "A Tie Game," *Valley Spirit*, May 23, 1894: 8. "A Victory," *Valley Spirit*, May 30, 1894: 3.

19. "Base Ball Gossip," *Harrisburg Star-Independent*, June 27, 1894: 5. "New Haven 6, Willimantic 2," *New Haven* (Connecticut) *Morning Journal and Courier*, June 28, 1894: 1. "New Haven 15, Edgewood 8," *New Haven Morning Journal and Courier*, June 29, 1894: 1.

20. "At Savin Rock Shore," *New Haven Morning Journal and Courier*, June 18, 1894: 4. "Players' Salaries Cut," *New Haven Morning Journal and Courier*, June 5, 1894: 2.

21. "Eleven to Eight," *New Haven Evening Register*, July 4, 1894: 3. "New Haven Wins a Game," *New Haven Evening Register*, July 5, 1894: 3.

22. "Some Fresh Baseball Notes," *Valley Spirit*, July 11, 1894: 8. "Undines Defeated," *Carlisle* (Pennsylvania) *Evening Herald*, July 14, 1894: 1. "By-By, Yeager," *Evening Sentinel* (Carlisle, Pennsylvania), July 23, 1894: 3.

23. "Thirteen-Inning Tie Game," *Boston Herald*, July 28, 1894: 2.

24. "Another Easy Victory," *Bangor* (Maine) *Daily Whig and Courier*, August 3, 1894: 3. However, six months later that same paper characterized Yeager very differently when it believed that the local team had signed him. "He made a good impression when playing in this city," according to "Base Ball Notes," *Bangor Daily Whig & Courier*, February 1, 1895: 3.

25. "Brockton 14, Pawtucket 6," *Boston Globe*, August 23, 1894: 3. "Brockton Team Gives Up," *Boston Herald*, August 26, 1894: 4.

26. "Baseball Notes," *Boston Globe*, September 11, 1894: 2. The next day that paper published New England League fielding statistics (excluding catchers) and batting statistics. Column headings for the batting statistics were omitted, but context clues indicate that the first four columns were for games, runs, hits, and total bases. If so, as a batter for Brockton and Pawtucket combined Yeager played in 37 games, scored 25 runs, had 39 hits good for 48 total bases, and a batting average of .260. Five days later the paper published additional statistics for batteries, and in 27 games as catcher for Brockton and Pawtucket he had 158 putouts, 56 assists, 21 errors, 11 passed balls, and a fielding percentage of .911. See "New England Baseball," *Boston Globe*, September 12, 1894: 2, and "New England League Work," *Boston Globe*, September 17, 1894: 2.

27. "Made 'Home' Runs," *Pawtucket* (Rhode Island) *Tribune*, September 17, 1894: 1. The article implied that Yeager was catching a train back home to Cincinnati, but three days later he was the umpire for a game hosted by the New England League's champs in Fall River, Massachusetts. See "Those Exciting Intercity Games," *Boston Herald*, September 21, 1894: 2.

28. "Main Clubs All Beaten," *Boston Herald*, May 5, 1895: 4. "The Field of Sport," *Portland* (Maine) *Daily Press*, June 10, 1895: 2. "Lewiston, 6; Pawtucket, 4," *Boston Journal*, June 20, 1895: 3. "Slater's Home Run," *Portland Daily Press*, July 9, 1895: 3. "Pawtucket Made 32 Runs," *Boston Herald*, July 12, 1895: 2.

29. "Personal," *Sporting Life*, August 3, 1895: 2. "Around the Bases," *Boston Herald*, August 31, 1895: 8. Most of the Herald's assessment was lifted verbatim in "News and Comment," *Sporting Life*, September 7, 1895: 2.

30. "New England Ball Players," *Boston Herald*, October 8, 1895: 8.

31. "Base Ball," *Newport* (Rhode Island) *Mercury*, September 7, 1895: 1. "Champion Fall Rivers Beaten," *Boston Herald*, Sept 8, 1895: 7. "Fall River, 16; Cuban Giants, 9," *Boston Herald*, September 14, 1895: 8.

32. "Leaders Lost," *Boston Journal*, May 21, 1896: 4. "Over the Fence," *Boston Herald*, June 6, 1896: 3. "New England League Tips," *Boston Herald*, August 13, 1896: 8. "Base Ball," *Bangor Daily Whig & Courier*, August 28, 1896: 1.

33. To help put his slugging percentage in perspective, only seven times during the 1890s did a major leaguer record a higher figure. See baseball-reference.com/leaders/slugging_perc_season.shtml; all of the occurrences were from 1894 to 1896.

34. "Bought Another Catcher," *Boston Globe*, September 6, 1896: 4. Macque, "Pawtucket Pets," *Sporting Life*, September 12, 1896: 13.

35. "Seven in Seventh," *Boston Globe*, September 9, 1896: 9. "Down They Go," *Boston Post*, September 12, 1896: 3. "Boston Loses," *Boston Post*, September 15, 1896: 3. "Heavy Hitters Fooled, *Boston Globe*, September

24, 1896: 9. The exhibition games were in Fall River; Orange, New Jersey; Wilmington, Delaware; and Paterson, New Jersey.

36 "Due to Stivetts," *Boston Globe*, September 26, 1896: 2. "Failed to Hit Stivetts," *Washington Times*, September 26, 1896: 3. "Senators Lost the Last," *Washington Times*, September 27, 1896: 7. In contrast to the latter, the *Globe*'s box score credited Yeager with a sacrifice hit and thus no time at bat. See "Landed Fourth," *Boston Globe*, September 27, 1896: 4.

37 "The Boston Team," *Boston Post*, February 16, 1897: 3. The Post certainly expected this, as indicated in "General Sporting Gossip," *Boston Post*, January 3, 1897: 19. See also "Baseball Notes," *Boston Globe*, January 18, 1897:3.

38 "General Sporting Gossip," *Boston Post*, February 21, 1897: 8.

39 "League Games Now," *Boston Herald*, April 18, 1897: 17. In later years nasty or snide remarks were occasionally made about Yeager's weight, such as in "Sporting Notes," *Worcester* (Massachusetts) *Daily Spy*, May 13, 1901: 3. At one point he weighed 207 pounds, according to "Wore Out Grass Running Bases," *Minneapolis Journal*, May 17, 1904: 14. However, his weight was listed as 190 in "Statistics of the Des Moines Champs," *Denver Post*, April 6, 1907: 9.

40 "Biff and Run," *Boston Globe*, May 28, 1897: 9.

41 "All Three," *Boston Daily Advertiser*, July 1, 1897: 4. Details of Yeager's major-league home runs are provided at baseball-reference.com/players/event_hr.fcgi?id=yeagege01&t=b.

42 "Baseball Gossip," *Cincinnati Enquirer*, August 1, 1897: 2. "Baseball Notes," *Boston Globe*, August 10, 1897: 3. "Echoes of the Game," *Boston Globe*, August 20, 1897: 3. "Chipped Diamonds," *Evening Telegram* (Providence, Rhode Island): August 20, 1897: 6.

43 "Easy for Boston," *Boston Herald*, September 19, 1897: 4. "Yellow Ball," *Boston Globe*, September 22, 1897: 7. Yeager also saw action during the postseason Temple Cup series won by Baltimore. In particular, in the last game, on October 11, he went 3-for-4. He tripled in the ninth inning and then scored the Beaneaters' final run of 1897. See "Boston Loses," *Boston Journal*, October 12, 1897: 3.

44 T.H.M., "Baseball Notes," *Boston Globe*, May 1, 1898: 8. The author was Tim Murnane.

45 "Yeager's Work," *Boston Herald*, June 5, 1898: 13.

46 "On the Bleachers," *Boston Herald*, June 13, 1898: 5. "On the Rubber," *Boston Herald*, August 8, 1898: 8. On both pages there were team statistics a few columns to the right.

47 W.S. Barnes Jr., "Their Lucky Escape," *Boston Journal*, August 23, 1898: 7. Ren Mulford Jr., "Western Dogs o' War Astir," *Cincinnati Post*, August 25, 1898: 2. "Baseball Notes," *Boston Globe*, September 6, 1898: 9. See also "Senators' Helping Hand," *Washington Times*, September 6, 1898: 6.

48 "Two Games at South End," *Boston Globe*, September 26, 1898: 7.

49 "Baseball Gossip," *Cincinnati Enquirer*, October 17, 1898: 4. The paper consistently misspelled his surname as Yaeger.

50 "Baseball Notes," *Boston Globe*, March 15, 1899: 4. T.H. Murnane, "Sunday Run," *Boston Globe*, March 27, 1899: 5.

51 W.S. Barnes Jr., "Ragged Work," *Boston Journal*, April 26, 1899: 3. T.H. Murnane, "Bad Licking," *Boston Globe*, April 28, 1899: 3. See also a second article by Murnane on the same page, "Boston Uncomfortable." Barnes reported that early in the game on April 25 Yeager was injured near the elbow of his throwing arm by a foul tip, and that it hampered him all game.

52 "Worcester Drops Two," *Boston Globe*, September 5, 1899: 9.

53 "Echoes of the Game," *Boston Globe*, September 9, 1899: 4. On the same page see also T.H. Murnane, "Without a Run," though Yeager's name didn't appear in the accompanying box score. For a description of the one-hit loss see T.H. Murnane, "Hoodoo Reigns," *Boston Globe*, September 10, 1899: 5.

54 "Frosted Fan Food," *Cincinnati Post*, November 10, 1899: 2. Anna Yeager lived until late 1922, according to "Death Notices," *Cincinnati Post*, November 29, 1922: 13.

55 "Milwaukee 4-Detroit 2," *Cleveland Plain Dealer*, May 27: 16. "Slug Hard Take Game," *Milwaukee Journal*, May 28, 1900: 10.

56 "Yeager Released by Milwaukee," *Pittsburgh Press*, July 2, 1900: 5. On July 20 it was announced that the Omaha club of the Western League had signed him, but his name didn't appear in any of their box scores until August 2 – as the umpire in a game against Sioux City. According to one Omaha daily, that same day their local team had released "Tim Hurst Yeager," alluding to the famous umpire known for fairness but also a very short temper. See "New Men for Omaha Nine," *Omaha Evening World-Herald*, July 20, 1900: 8. "Base Ball Gossip," *Evening World-Herald*, August 2, 1900: 8. For the box score of the game in which Yeager umpired, see "Rourkes Slug the Soos" on page 7 of the latter paper.

57 "Team Not in Condition," *Cleveland Leader*, April 26, 1901: 6.

58 "News and Gossip," *Sporting Life*, April 12, 1902: 5. See also David Nemec, *Major League Baseball Profiles, 1871-1900, Volume 1: The Ballplayers Who Built the Game* (Lincoln: University of Nebraska Press, 2011): 289.

59 "Baseball Notes," *Washington Evening Times*, May 16, 1902: 3.

60 "Browns Take Series from Unlucky Birds," *St. Louis Republic*, August 6, 1902: 8.

61 "Yeager Is Manager," *Minneapolis Journal*, May 14, 1903: 16.

62 "Yeager Makes Himself Obnoxious," *New Orleans Item*, August 30, 1903: 1. This story went out via the Hearst News Service. See also "Yeager Yanked," *Sporting Life*, September 5, 1903: 5.

63 "Lose the Last Game," *Minneapolis Journal*, September 22, 1903: 8.

64 "Yeager Is Assaulted," *Minneapolis Tribune*, June 12, 1905: 3.

65 "A Few Foul Tips," *Montgomery Advertiser*, June 16, 1905: 10.

66 Frank E. Force, "On the Inside," *Minneapolis Tribune*, May 10, 1906: 8. Frank E. Force, "On the Inside," *Minneapolis Tribune*, July 1, 1906: 35.

67 "Yeager Reports," *Des Moines Daily News*, April 3, 1908: 14. See also Ren Mulford Jr., "Mulfordisms," *Sporting Life*, April 10, 1909: 11. Mulford named Frank "Noodles" Hahn as pro baseball's other Doctor of Veterinary Science.

68 "With Ball Players," *Rock Island* (Illinois) *Argus*, June 30, 1908: 3. "Peoria Gets Big Leaguer, *Dubuque* (Iowa) *Daily Times-Journal*, July 1, 1908: 7.

69 "Line 'o Dope," *Rock Island Argus*, August 5, 1909: 3. "Around the A.A. Circuit. The 'Old Doc' Quite a Kid," *Kansas City Star*, June 24, 1909: 9. The latter quoted the *Indianapolis Star*.

70 See springgrove.org/geneology-search.aspx.

71 "New Umpires Signed," *Cincinnati Enquirer*, July 12, 1911: 8.

72 Jack Ryder, "Old-Time Ballplayers to Cavort Once More over Redland Diamond," *Cincinnati Enquirer*, August 9, 1931: 31. Tom Swope, "Old-Timers Will Gather at Cincinnati for Game," *The Sporting News*, August 20, 1931: 3. Jack Ryder, "Heroes of Past Cavort Once More on Redland Diamond," September 6, 1931: 15. "Former Red," *Cincinnati Enquirer*, August 4, 1932: 2-3. Jack Ryder, "Old-Timers Presence Inspires Rixey, Who Blanks Bucs," *Cincinnati Enquirer*, August 22, 1932: 9.

73 "George Yeager," *Cincinnati Enquirer*, July 9, 1940: 9. His cause of death was specified on his Ohio certificate of death. Details of Tillie's death are accessible via springgrove.org/geneology-search.aspx.

74 "The Same in Springfield," *Illinois State Journal* (Springfield), August 18, 1908: 6. *Dubuque* (Iowa) *Daily Times-Journal*, August 19, 1908: 5.

75 David Nemec, *Major League Baseball Profiles, 1871-1900, Volume 1: The Ballplayers Who Built the Game* (Lincoln: University of Nebraska Press, 2011), 288. David Nemec, *The Rank and File of 19th Century Major League Baseball: Biographies of 1,084 Players, Owners, Managers and Umpires* (Jefferson, North Carolina: McFarland & Company, Inc., 2012), 94.

76 "Grand Stand Chatter," *Jonesboro* (Arkansas) *Daily News*, April 10, 1909: 2.

MANAGER

FRANK SELEE

BY DAVID L. FLEITZ

Frank Selee.
(Courtesy of National Baseball Hall of Fame)

A small, mild-mannered, prematurely bald man with a prominent mustache, Frank Selee looked more like an insurance underwriter than a baseball manager, especially in team photos next to his strapping young athletes. Nevertheless, he was one of the most successful field leaders of his era, directing the Boston Beaneaters to five National League pennants between 1891 and 1898. Later, he assembled the Chicago Cubs team that won four pennants and two World Series titles during the following decade. Selee, whom *Sporting Life* described in 1893 as "a manager who is a thorough baseball general … who knows what should be done and how to do it, and is able to impress his advice upon the men under his control,"[1] was elected to the Baseball Hall of Fame in 1999, 90 years after his death.

Frank Gibson Selee was born in Amherst, New Hampshire on October 26, 1859, the oldest child of Nathan and Annie Selee. Nathan Selee had taught school before becoming a Methodist preacher one year before the birth of his first son. In 1864, Nathan moved the family to Melrose, Massachusetts, about eight miles north of Boston. Frank played the outfield for the main town team in Melrose, the Alphas, though he possessed more enthusiasm than talent. While in his early twenties, he decided to focus his talents on organizing, not playing, the game.

In 1884, he left a job at a watch company to organize the new Waltham team in the Massachusetts State League. He signed players and raised $1,000 to provide the playing field with seats and a fence. Despite Frank's hard work, the Waltham franchise collapsed after a few months, and he and several of his players moved to Lawrence to finish the season. He played the outfield a few times that year, and those contests represent Frank Selee's entire professional playing career.

In 1885 and 1886, Frank managed at Haverhill in the New England League. He was hired by Oshkosh of the Northwest League in 1887, and convinced the team owners to sign outfielder Tommy McCarthy, who had won the batting title for Brockton, and pitcher Tom Lovett, a 32-game winner for Newburyport and Lynn.

Frank also took a chance on William (Dummy) Hoy, a speedy 24-year-old former shoemaker from rural Ohio. Hoy, who was deaf (the nickname "Dummy" was not considered a pejorative at the time), played for Oshkosh in 1886, but batted only .219. Selee retained Hoy for the 1887 season and devised ways to make it easier for him to play. As an 1888 article explained, "[Hoy] is left handed, and when he bats a man stands in the captain's box near third base and signals to him decisions of the umpire on balls and strikes by raising his fingers."[2] This may have been the first use of ball-and-strike signals on the baseball field; it was years before umpires adopted the practice. Hoy played centerfield and batted .367, while McCarthy hit .345. Frank won his first pennant over Jim Hart's Milwaukee club.

The directors of the Omaha club in the Western Association offered Frank a reported $3,000 to move his Oshkosh team *en masse* to Omaha. Tom Lovett made the move to Nebraska, but McCarthy and Hoy advanced to the major leagues and left Frank with holes in his lineup. Though Lovett won 30 games, Omaha finished in fourth place in 1888, with a 55-48 record. Lovett then left to join Brooklyn of the American Association, but Frank identified another outstanding pitching prospect. Charles (Kid) Nichols was an 18-year-old right-hander who had posted a 16-2 record for Kansas City in 1888. Kansas City won the Western Association pennant that year, then joined the American Association and decided not to sign Nichols for the 1889 campaign. Selee hired Nichols and installed the slender teenager as the team's premier starting pitcher.

Nichols posted an incredible 39-8 record and led Omaha to the Western Association pennant, Frank Selee's second as a manager. Omaha's 83-38 record and .686 winning percentage were the best in all of organized baseball that year. The National League's Boston Beaneaters signed Nichols to a contract for the following year, while William Conant, one of the three Boston club owners, persuaded the other two Triumvirs (as the papers called them) to hire Selee as well. In late 1889 Selee, who lived year-round in Melrose, became the manager of the nearby Boston ballclub.

Most of Boston's stars, except for pitcher John Clarkson and catcher Charlie Bennett, had jumped to the new Players League, leaving the Beaneaters short of talent. However, nearly every other National League team was in the same predicament, and the exodus removed several strong-willed and hard-drinking veterans from Selee's roster. Mike (King) Kelly, the most popular player in the game, had undermined Jim Hart's authority as manager in 1889, and Kelly's jump to the rival league left Selee free to manage with no interference from the game's biggest star.

Selee, the son of a minister, was not a drinker, in contrast to almost all other managers of his day. Frank was a soft-spoken man who relied on preparation, not force, to lead his players. "If I make things pleasant for the players, they reciprocate," Selee once explained. "I want them to be temperate and live properly. I do not believe that men who are engaged in such exhilarating exercise should be kept in strait jackets all the time, but I expect them to be in condition to play. I do not want a man who cannot appreciate such treatment."[3] He transformed the Beaneaters from a wild, hard-drinking crew into a team that relied on intelligence and execution to win games.

Kid Nichols stepped in as a starting pitcher, and Selee persuaded the Triumvirs to sign Milwaukee second baseman Bobby Lowe and Kansas City shortstop Herman Long. Long became a star at shortstop, Nichols won 27 games as a rookie, and Lowe filled in ably as a utility man. While Kelly and the Boston Players League squad won the pennant in the rival circuit, Selee brought the Beaneaters home in fifth place in the National League during his first season.

The Players League collapsed after one season, and third baseman Billy Nash and right fielder Harry Stovey returned to the Beaneaters. These stars solidified Selee's lineup and boosted Boston into the pennant race in the early stages of the 1891 season. By August, the Beaneaters stood alone in second place behind Cap Anson's Chicago squad, but later that month King Kelly returned to Boston and provided the spark that Selee's club needed. Chicago defeated Boston twice in mid-September, but then Selee's men ran off an 18-game winning streak (including one tie) and finished the race three games in front of Chicago. In Frank Selee's second season as Boston manager, he won the team's first league championship since 1883. When the American Association collapsed that winter, the Beaneaters acquired two future Hall of Famers, outfielder Hugh Duffy and the star of Selee's Oshkosh pennant-winners, Tommy McCarthy.

Team chemistry was paramount to Selee, and the manager made sure not to sign anyone who might disrupt the harmony of the ballclub. Reflecting upon his Boston experience, Selee once said, "It was my good fortune to be surrounded by a lot of good, clean fellows who got along finely together. To tell the truth, I would not have anyone on a team who was not congenial."[4] King Kelly was a behavioral nightmare and a hard drinker, but by the end of the 1891 season the Beaneaters were Selee's team and not Kelly's.

Kelly's presence electrified the fans and the local sportswriters, but he batted only .231. The next year, Kelly batted .189 as a part-time player. John Clarkson, too, was fading; he won 33 games in 1891, but when he complained of a sore arm in early 1892, the Beaneaters released him and replaced him with Jack Stivetts, another signee from the defunct Association. Stivetts and Nichols posted identical 35-16 records in 1892 as the Beaneaters won 102 games, becoming the first team in history to win 100 in a season.

The 1892 campaign marked the first and last instance (until 1981) of a split-season pennant race. Boston easily won the first half, but the Cleveland Spiders rallied in mid-season and won the second. In the end, Boston handily defeated Cleveland in their October matchup. Jack Stivetts and Cleveland's Cy Young battled to an 11-inning scoreless tie in the first game, but Selee's team won the next four contests and captured their second pennant in a row.

Selee valued players with brains as well as brawn, and trusted his men to make the right decisions. "He was a good judge of players," said Bobby Lowe. "He didn't bother with a lot of signals, but let his players figure out their own plays. He didn't blame them if they took a chance that failed. He believed in place-hitting, sacrifice-hitting, and stealing bases. He was wonderful with young players."[5] Under Selee, the Beaneaters refined the hit-and-run to a science. Monte Ward watched the Boston team with amazement. "I have never, in my twelve years' experience on the diamond, seen such skillful playing," said Ward in 1893. "The Boston players use more head-work and private signals than any other team in the country."[6]

Selee moved Bobby Lowe from the outfield to second base in 1892, and Lowe teamed with Herman Long to form a keystone combination that stayed together for nearly 10 years. In 1893, Selee's men held off the Pittsburg Pirates and won their third pennant by a five-game margin. The Boston dominance ended in 1894, when injuries, holdouts, and the emergence of the Baltimore Orioles drove the Beaneaters to a third-place finish, eight games behind.

Selee convinced the Triumvirs not to tear the team apart, but to refine it. He kept Long and Lowe at short and second, but sent third sacker Billy Nash to Philadelphia for outfielder Billy Hamilton. On a trip to Buffalo, Selee noticed a young third baseman named Jimmy Collins and brought him to Boston. Collins stumbled early on, and the Triumvirs demanded that Selee get rid of the youngster, but Selee farmed him out to Louisville for more experience. In 1895 Selee brought Collins back to Boston, where the young man completed the new Boston infield.[7]

Hugh Duffy remained, but Tommy McCarthy began to slow down in his mid-thirties, so Selee released his longtime favorite and put Hamilton in center, with Duffy in left and newcomer Chick Stahl in right. The pitching staff featured Kid Nichols, Jack Stivetts, and two new faces, left-hander Fred Klobedanz and right-hander Ted Lewis. The career of catcher Charlie Bennett ended in a train accident in 1894, but Selee found a talented replacement in Marty Bergen. The Orioles won three pennants in a row from 1894 to 1896, but the revamped Beaneaters stood ready to challenge again for the flag in 1897.

Selee's retooled ballclub jumped out to an early lead, but Baltimore stayed close all season long. In mid-September the two teams met in a three-game series to decide the pennant. Nichols won the first game for Boston. Lewis lost the second, and set the stage for one of the greatest games of the nineteenth century. On September 25, 1897, more than 25,000 people packed the Baltimore ballpark and watched Kid Nichols stagger to a 19-10 win over the Orioles. This victory virtually clinched Selee's fourth pennant and established Boston once again as the dominant team of the National League.

Jack Stivetts' mound career was crippled in 1898 by a sore arm, but Selee located another outstanding young pitcher. Vic Willis was a tall curveball specialist who posted a 20-17 mark for Syracuse in 1897, and Selee convinced the Boston owners to buy the pitcher's release for $3,000. Willis impressed the Boston observers with his overhand curve, but he needed work on his control, so Selee hired Jack Ryan, a retired catcher, who built a wooden target for Willis to practice against. Before long Willis began to get his pitches over the plate, and he joined the rotation in May. Willis posted a 25-13 record in able support of Nichols (31-12) and Lewis (26-8), and Selee's Beaneaters rolled to their fifth pennant in eight years.

The core of the team began to unravel in 1899. Nichols fell to a 21-19 record, Hamilton slowed down due to leg injuries, and stars such as Lowe, Long, and Duffy all were showing their age. The Brooklyn Dodgers ran away with the 1899 pennant as the fading Bostons held second place. Selee tried to rebuild, but management balked at spending money for minor-league players, and Selee had no choice but to play his aging stars. The club suffered another blow when catcher Marty Bergen committed suicide in January 1900, and left the Beaneaters short behind the plate. After a fourth-place finish in 1900, several Boston stars jumped to the new American League and doomed the Beaneaters to a sixth-place finish in 1901. At season's end, the Triumvirs hired Al Buckenberger to replace Selee.

Jim Hart, the man Selee replaced as manager of the Beaneaters in 1890, was the general manager of the National League Chicago Orphans and contacted Selee almost immediately after Selee's firing hit the newspapers. In no time, Selee signed a contract to succeed Tom Loftus as manager of the Chicago ballclub.

Once again, Selee built a team by studying young players and finding places for them to fit in. Frank Chance, who joined the club in 1898, was a good-hitting catcher but struggled with his defense, especially his throwing. Selee put the better-fielding Johnny Kling behind the plate and transferred Chance to first base. Selee brought Bobby Lowe with him to Chicago, but Lowe relinquished the second base position to an intense young man from Troy, New York named Johnny Evers. During spring training, Selee looked at a dozen shortstops before giving the job to Joe Tinker. He had created the most famous double play combination of all time: Tinker to Evers to Chance.

Selee's infusion of youth gave the Chicago ballclub the identity it needed. On May 27, 1902, the *Chicago Daily News* stated, "Frank Selee will devote his strongest efforts on the team work of the new Cubs, this year." That sentence turned the Chicago Orphans into the Chicago Cubs, a name the team still carries more than 100 years later.

The Cubs improved to within one game of .500 in 1902 and jumped to 82-56 and a third-place finish in 1903. After that season, Selee pulled off one of his most daring trades, sending 20-game winner Jack Taylor to St. Louis for a young right-hander from Indiana named Mordecai Brown. They called him "Three-Finger" Brown because his pitching hand was severely injured in a childhood accident, but he could throw unusual curveballs, and Selee saw Brown as a future star. Selee, as usual, was correct; Brown soon became Chicago's primary starting pitcher.

"To make a success," Selee once wrote, "a baseball manager must enter into his work with every bit of energy he can command."[8] By the early 1900s, Selee's poor health made him unable to apply his usual energy to the task of building another baseball team. He contracted a severe cold during the last series of the 1902 campaign, and by mid-October was diagnosed with pleurisy. He recovered, but his lungs remained weak, and he traveled to Colorado to spend the winter breathing the healthy mountain air. Selee spent the rest of his tenure with the Cubs battling health problems. In late 1904, he returned to Colorado to rejuvenate his weakening lungs.

The Cubs advanced to second place in 1904 and prepared to challenge for the league title in 1905, but Selee was not destined to be its leader. He fell ill during spring training at Santa Monica, California. He offered to give up the reins of the team, but Jim Hart convinced him to stay, so Selee opened the 1905 season as manager. His condition grew worse, and before long he developed both appendicitis and lung congestion. He stopped taking road trips, leaving Frank Chance in charge while he stayed in Chicago and sought medical attention. In July 1905, Selee received the bad news that he was suffering from tuberculosis; on July 28 he took a leave of absence. Frank Chance, who had been elected captain of the team earlier that season, succeeded him on an interim basis.[9]

Selee expected to return to the Cubs, but in the fall of 1905 Hart, who was ill himself, sold his interest in the Cubs to a group of Cincinnati and Chicago businessmen. Selee considered putting his own syndicate together to buy the team, but his health worsened again, and during the winter he severed his connection with the club. Chance became the full-time manager. Selee could only watch as Chance led the Cubs to three consecutive pennants and two World Series titles.

In late 1905, Selee moved to Denver, Colorado, hoping that the environment would restore his health. He could not stay away from the game, however, and in 1906 he bought an interest in the Pueblo team of the Western League. Despite his declining physical state, Selee managed the team for three seasons but never finished higher than fifth in an eight-team league. He sold the team after the 1908 campaign when his physical condition became precarious.

In 1909, he entered a sanitarium, the Rev. Frederick W. Oakes Home for Consumptives in Denver, where he died on July 5. He was 49 years old and left a widow, Mary, but no children. Frank's parents, who were still living, brought his body back to Massachusetts, and buried him in the town cemetery in Melrose.

NOTES

1. *Sporting Life*, September 23, 1893: 2.

2. Article by unknown writer, dated 1888, in *Silent World*, published by the Pennsylvania School for the Deaf.

3. Harold Kaese, *The Boston Braves* (New York: G. P. Putnam's Sons, 1948), 55-56.

4. Frank G. Selee, "Twenty-One Years in Baseball," *Baseball Magazine*, December 1911: 55.

5. Kaese, 55.

6. *Spalding's Official Base Ball Guide*, 1896. Reprinted in Dean A. Sullivan, ed., *Extra Innings: A Documentary History of Baseball, 1825-1908* (Lincoln, Nebraska: University of Nebraska Press, 1995).

7. In 1894 Selee also signed Fred Tenney, a left-handed catcher from Brown University, who by 1897 would replace the veteran Tommy Tucker at first base.

8. Selee, *Baseball Magazine*, December 1911: 56.

9. *Chicago Tribune*, July 29, 1905. The *Tribune* report made it clear that Chance was the interim, not the permanent, manager of the Cubs for the rest of the 1905 campaign.

OWNERS

JAMES B. BILLINGS

BY CHARLIE BEVIS

For 30 years from 1885 to 1904, J.B. Billings was treasurer and part-owner of the Boston baseball club in the National League. In addition to overseeing the club's financial affairs, he handled most of the contract negotiation and communication with the ballplayers. Billings was most famous for paying $10,000 to the Chicago ballclub in 1887 to release star player Mike Kelly so that Billings could sign Kelly to a contract to play for Boston.

James Bartlett Billings was born on February 21, 1837, in Lowell, Massachusetts, the oldest of three children of John and Adeline Billings.[1] His mother died in 1848, and several months later his father married Elizabeth Fifield, who became stepmother to Billings and his two sisters.[2] In the textile-dominated economy of Lowell, his father worked for a variety of businesses as a clerk, an apprentice businessman in the parlance of that era. By 1847 his father was the proprietor of his own business, a livery stable, which he soon expanded into an express company that shipped goods via the Boston & Lowell Railroad.[3] Billings witnessed the ups and downs of business ownership, as his father's enterprise failed by 1853 and he returned to being an employee for other business owners.[4]

Following in the business footsteps of his father, 18-year-old Billings worked as a clerk at the Franklin Bookstore in Lowell.[5] In 1856 he moved to Boston, where he worked as a bookkeeper for shoe companies with offices in the central business district.[6] He married Maria Braman on October 27, 1860, in nearby Cambridge.[7] They had one child, George B. Billings, born in 1864.[8] After seeing demand for footwear soar during the Civil War, Billings ventured out on his own in 1863 to start his own

J.B. Billings,
Boston Globe, March 16, 1913.

shoe company, Billings & Baldwin, in partnership with David Baldwin.[9]

In 1864 Billings dissolved the partnership with Baldwin and formed a new partnership with George B. Clapp.[10] For the next 17 years they operated Clapp & Billings, a shoe manufacturer with its main office in Boston and factories located in the outlying towns of Marlborough and Rockland.[11] The 1864 formation of Clapp & Billings was very timely. The demand for mass-produced footwear accelerated after the Civil War, which led to the movement to replace the disjointed system of small shops, staffed by artisans who made shoes by hand, with the centralized factory system in which industrial machines, manned by less-skilled workers, did the bulk of the work to build shoes.[12] Clapp & Billings took advantage of the first mechanical advancement in the nascent shoe industry, the McKay sole-sewing machine, which "did in one hour what a journeyman [shoemaker] did in 80 hours."[13] Billings and Clapp were soon rich men.

By 1870 Billings almost universally went by the initials "J.B." rather than his given name James, to signify that he was a prosperous businessman. He also moved his family into a home at 19 Hancock Street in the fashionable Beacon Hill neighborhood, where wealthy men typically resided in Boston.[14] After his successful investment in the emerging shoe industry, Billings became an investor in professional baseball. By 1876 he had purchased several shares of stock in the Boston Base Ball Association, the formal name of the corporation that operated the Boston ballclub.[15] It was a good time to invest in baseball, since share prices were depressed. Similar to the shoe industry a decade earlier, professional baseball in the nascent National League of 1876 faced an uncertain environment as control was shifting from ballplayers to club ownership. Billings believed "that a baseball investment would prove profitable" if the ballclub could be operated with sound business practices.[16]

As a member of an ad hoc committee of stockholders in December 1876, Billings participated in an audit of the Boston ballclub's financial situation.[17] The dismal fiscal performance during the 1876 season resulted in the dismissal of club President Nicholas Apollonio and the subsequent election of Arthur Soden, who went on to serve as president for three decades. Billings was also a member of an audit committee to review the financials of the 1877 season.[18]

In 1880 the Clapp & Billings partnership was dissolved, with "both men going out of business with handsome fortunes" after selling the Rockland factory.[19] While Clapp retired to a life of leisure, Billings remained in the shoe business by continuing to operate the Marlborough factory.[20] Billings soon purchased an opulent brownstone home at 362 Marlborough Street in the elite Back Bay neighborhood of Boston, which had recently been created via landfill of the Charles River tidal basin to be the nouveau place for wealthy Bostonians to reside.[21]

Billings now decided to devote more time to the business affairs of the Boston ballclub, where his financial skills and shoe-industry experience with industrialized labor could enhance the value of his investment in the ballclub. Over the four-year period from 1881 to 1884, Billings gradually changed from a passive investor in the Boston ballclub to an active management role, as the ownership structure evolved to consolidate power for the 1885 baseball season into the hands of three individuals: Soden, Billings, and Bill Conant.

At the annual stockholder meeting in December 1880, Billings was elected to be one of three new directors for the 1881 baseball season, as there was a wholesale shakeup of the five-man board, with Soden and Allan J. Chase the only holdovers.[22] One casualty was Fred Long, who was replaced as treasurer by Chase. Billings exerted his influence to limit the ballclub's disclosure of financial information. The last public disclosure of the club's profitability occurred at the December 1881 stockholder meeting.[23] Only gate-receipt information was provided at the December 1882 stockholder meeting.[24]

Between 1880 and 1883, Billings increased his stock holdings in the ballclub through purchases from men who held just one or two shares, which he bought at low prices since there was little demand for these shares. He did so in concert with Soden, as the two men "set about securing a controlling interest in the club."[25] Conant, who was elected a director for the 1882 season, accumulated stock on his own.

By the time of the annual stockholder meeting in December 1883, Billings was one of a four-man combine that controlled a majority of the shares of stock, along with Soden, Conant, and an unidentified man, who most likely was Chase.[26] No financial information at all was released at the 1883 meeting. "A call was made for the report of the treasurer, but, as attested by the certificate of a physician, that gentleman was sick," the *New York Clipper* reported on the absence of Chase, adding that "four gentlemen control the stock, and it is their desire to keep the financial condition secret."[27]

During 1884 the fourth man in the 1883 majority combine sold out to the threesome of Billings, Soden, and Conant to effectuate their takeover of the Boston ballclub. The final straw was no doubt the squabble over pricing of season tickets, as pressure increased for business practices to trump caring for dedicated fans (who paid higher prices) and minority stockholders (who no longer received them free).[28] There is no public indication what Billings and his two compatriots promised the fourth stockholder of the combine (likely Chase), but he probably was handsomely rewarded for selling, since it allowed the threesome to control all decisions related to the ballclub.[29]

By the December 1884 stockholder meeting, the trio of Billings, Soden, and Conant collectively controlled the majority of stock and thus rendered the minority stockholders powerless to stop the trio from executing their ideas.[30] They elected themselves to be the only officers of the ballclub, as Billings became treasurer to replace Chase, and downsized the directorate from five members to just the three officers. The new three-man board of directors immediately approved a $2,500 stipend for each officer and authorized the spending of up to $100,000 to purchase the land underneath the South End Grounds.[31]

The trio of Billings, Soden, and Conant became known as the triumvirs, the Roman Empire terminology for members of a three-man authority that shared power. Each of the three triumvirs owned roughly one-third of the ballclub.[32] However, when it came to big decisions, not even Soden as president had unilateral authority, since "the triumvirs have an iron-clad rule that when two of the trio agree that settles any question under discussion."[33] In one example from 1889, reportedly "Soden actually shed tears when the other two, Billings and Conant, outvoted him and released [John] Morrill," who was the longtime field manager of the team.[34]

As the treasurer, Billings handled the finances of the ballclub. One of the first big expenditures he faced was how to pay the

$100,000 to purchase the land underneath the South End Grounds. The decision was to pay $35,000 in cash and borrow the remaining $65,000 through a mortgage on the property.[35] This was one of the last numbers publicly revealed from the ballclub's financial ledgers, since Billings strongly believed the finances of the ballclub should remain private. "We don't want the affairs of the association spread before the world. That would not be a business way of doing things," Billings told the *Boston Globe* in 1887. "The financial standing of a concern is its own business and not for the public."[36] Billings didn't bother to attend the annual stockholder meetings until the last public one in 1887, when they were discontinued after a judge dismissed the minority-stockholder suit to obtain an accounting.[37]

Billings, though, was not bashful about spending money in his early years as treasurer, when he would often open up his "famous checkbook," as the sportswriters termed his spending habit. "Landing big stars was fun for J.B. Billings a few years ago when he roamed the country loaded with his famous checkbook," Tim Murnane reminisced in 1905. "Mr. Billings loved a winner and was willing to pay the price."[38] Today, his business perspective would be called the need to spend money to make money.

The first exorbitant use of the famous checkbook came in February 1887 when Billings instigated the acquisition from the Chicago club of Mike Kelly, who was one of baseball's most talented players of that era. "When I went to see Soden and Conant and told them about [the idea], it seemed like a good joke to them, for they rather laughed at it. They didn't believe anybody could get Kelly away from Chicago," Billings told the *Boston Globe*.[39] It took $10,000 to convince Chicago to release Kelly. After arriving at a mutually agreeable salary with Kelly, Billings said, "Good things come high, but we must have them."[40]

The $10,000 investment to acquire Kelly was initially successful, as attendance at the South End Grounds nearly doubled to more than a quarter of a million spectators during the 1887 season. When the triumvirs decided to build an opulent new grandstand to attract even more paying customers, Billings faced his next big financial challenge as treasurer, when the actual construction costs nearly tripled the $25,000 initial projected cost.[41] The solution advocated by Billings was to spend even more money by purchasing another star ballplayer to make sure the new grandstand was filled for all games. In April 1888 Billings paid another $10,000 to the Chicago ballclub to secure the release of pitcher John Clarkson.[42]

In his quest to sign star players from other teams, Billings operated more like a general manager in the modern-day free-agent era than the prevailing nineteenth-century model of owner-operator who searched for promising young talent.[43] Technically, Billings did sign free agents, most often by paying a steep price to a club owner to release the desired player (not directly overpaying the player as done today) and a few times on the open market when players were freely available after a team disbanded. As for grooming younger talent, Billings said in 1887: "This raising of colts is an expensive business. I prefer to buy them all ready for the track."[44]

Billings also negotiated the salaries of existing ballplayers to play with Boston the following season. He had his strongest relationships with the players during the 1880s. "The players on the nine all like him," the *Boston Globe* wrote about Billings in 1888, "but I do hear it rumored occasionally that they love to visit him for the purpose of getting his autograph to a little check."[45] However, there was no doubt that "the signing of the star players is now left almost wholly in his hands."[46]

Despite the good intentions of Billings, the $20,000 spent to acquire Kelly and Clarkson failed to generate a championship for Boston in either 1888 or 1889. Even worse, attendance did not increase at the ballpark in those two years. "Treasurer Billings was found seated in his office with a friend. The reflex of the year could be seen easily. Straws best show how the wind blows," the *Boston Globe* reported in July 1888. "The $20,000 bid for players, the $70,000 [grand] stand, the bad ball playing and diminished gate receipts could all be seen in the cigar which the genial holder of the finances was smoking. It was supported by a toothpick to insure its being burned to the last shred."[47] Frustrations exploded during the 1889 season, when Billings, disgusted at a string of losses on the road, dashed off a telegram to the club's field manager: "You are disgracing Boston. You are being hissed in Music Hall [at the telegraphic recreation of games]. ... Your work is costing us thousands of dollars."[48] The demoralization that this telegram caused among the ballplayers cost the team the pennant, as they finished one game behind the champion New York Giants.

The timing of this telegram could not have been worse, since, unbeknownst to the triumvirs, most of their ballplayers were contemplating leaving the team to play in 1890 for the Boston team in the new Players' League. Billings could not hold the team together after the 1889 season, as most of the players bolted to the Players' League team. After publicly failing to induce several players "to bid goodbye to the brotherhood and return to their old love," Billings could only convince two players to stay, Clarkson and catcher Charlie Bennett.[49] To bail out Billings, the other triumvirs brought in Frank Selee to be the manager of the team for 1890. Selee rebuilt the team with replacement players (including Kid Nichols) whom he had observed when he was a minor-league manager. While the Players' League disbanded after just one season, its Boston team transferred to the American Association for the 1891 season, before going out of business when that league merged into the National League for the 1892 season.

The two years of intense competition for baseball fans in Boston severely impacted the finances of the National League ballclub. The free-spending Billings lost the confidence of his fellow triumvirs as Selee used the cheaper, younger players to win three consecutive National League championships from 1891 to 1893. Billings maintained a low public profile, as his son, George, now handled many of the lower-level financial tasks, such as distributing paychecks to the ballplayers.[50] Billings also needed to devote much more of his time to his shoe business, which began a downturn in 1891 and struggled in 1893 due to the national economic depression.

In March 1894 Billings went bankrupt when his shoe business failed due to "poor collections, losses in the manufacturing department and shrinkage in profits during the past three years."[51] The company's $99,000 in liabilities greatly exceeded its $66,000 in assets and "there appears to be no equity in the debtor's residence nor in his baseball stock."[52] Billings had no equity in his Marlborough Street home because he had sold it to Soden for $25,000 in June 1893 to raise money to keep his business afloat.[53] Hoping to be repaid with a business upturn, Soden did not register the deed until four days before the public announcement of the business failure.[54] Billings had no equity in his baseball stock because he had used it as collateral for a loan made by Soden and Conant to provide additional funds to try to salvage his shoe business.[55] The business failure was quickly settled, as the creditors accepted 55 cents on the dollar.[56] Billings was now a minority owner of the Boston ballclub, since "instead of owning an equal portion of the stock, he now owns only one share, enough to entitle him to hold the office of treasurer."[57]

Although Soden now owned the house at 362 Marlborough Street, Billings and his wife continued to live there until Soden sold the property in July 1897.[58] This timing correlates with when Billings paid off his remaining debt to Soden and Conant, since Billings had borrowed more money from them to try to save his shoe business than the value of his loan collateral, his stock in the ballclub. Billings worked as the treasurer for the ballclub to repay this debt, when in 1897 "the profits of the club have been so great that Billings was able to pay back all he owed."[59]

As a minority owner, Billings was still considered a triumvir, but he now had little influence in the future direction of the Boston ballclub. The triumvirs kept their 2-out-of-3-votes rule for business decisions, to access the knowledge and opinion of Billings, but in practice Soden and Conant functioned as a veto-proof, two-man alliance. In general during the 1890s, the ballclub pursued a policy of fiscal restraint, with no more big-money player acquisitions like the ones Billings had engineered in the 1880s. He did do some bird-dogging for young players, but his larger role with the triumvirs was to vet manager Selee's proposed player signings, such as third baseman Jimmy Collins in the fall of 1894.

Billings continued to add value to the ballclub through his relationships with the ballplayers. For example, "Director J.B. Billings made an effort to convince Tommy Tucker that his work was appreciated by the owners of the club," when the first baseman had complained to sportswriters about club management.[60] However, there was little for Billings to do in salary negotiations, since many Boston players made the $2,400 salary limit that the National League strictly enforced during the 1890s. His treasurer responsibilities were also diminished, since William Rogers was brought in as assistant treasurer in the mid-1890s.[61]

When Billings was now mentioned in the sports pages, it often was about his reaction to the outcome of a game, such as "Director Billings was the most disappointed man in town last night, and what he thought would not look well in print."[62] In contrast to his fellow triumvirs, Billings faithfully attended most games at the South End Grounds and he often attended the telegraphic recreation of road games at the Music Hall.[63] However, Billings maintained such a low profile after his 1894 bankruptcy that George Tuohey, in his 1897 book about the Boston ballclub, wrote just a five-line biography of Billings, which was one-tenth the size of the biography of the club's groundskeeper.[64]

After Boston won consecutive pennants in 1897 and 1898 with the low-budget approach, Soden and Conant quashed all proposals by Billings to bring in big stars as a money-making opportunity. "Mr. Billings is in favor of putting out good money for one or more catchers," one writer noted in 1899, adding that Billings believed "it pays to have one or two stars each season."[65] Reflecting the waning influence of Billings, however, Selee "found Messrs. Soden and Conant in no hurry about going after star players … [since] the triumvirs, with the exception of director Billings, are for taking plenty of time."[66]

The beginning of the end for Billings was the botched salary negotiation with Jimmy Collins for the 1901 season. When he learned that Collins was rumored to be jumping to the Boston team in the new American League, Billings traveled to Buffalo, New York, to meet with Collins at his home. Billings was said to have offered Collins a $5,000 annual salary (twice his pay in 1900), but he wasted his time, because he misjudged why Collins was considering an American League offer. Collins signed a three-year guaranteed contract with an annual salary of $3,500 to be not only the third baseman but also field manager and part-owner (with a few shares of stock in the club), with no ties to the team following the third year.[67] Billings and the triumvirs completely misjudged the leadership potential of Collins (they passed him over as team captain for 1901) as well as the impact Collins would have with the American League team, which immediately captured the allegiance of most Boston baseball fans.

After the phenomenal success of the Boston Americans in 1901, Soden began to actively search for a buyer of the stock in the Boston ballclub.[68] Since most of the value of the stock in the ballclub was in the real estate it owned, Soden transferred ownership of the South End Grounds in 1902 to the Columbus Avenue Trust, whose trustees were Charles Soden, George Billings, and Conant.[69] In this manner Soden sought to maximize the value of the baseball team and its franchise in the National League, which were now the only items tied to the shares of stock in the ballclub. Secondarily, this transaction effectively transferred the ballpark asset to the next generation of two of the three triumvirs. Although no longer a significant stockholder in the ballclub, Billings was compensated for a share of the ownership of the South End Grounds, since his son was a trustee of the Columbus Avenue Trust.[70]

In 1904, when no realistic buyer for the ballclub surfaced, Soden forced Billings out of the ownership group, presumably by purchasing his one remaining share of stock.[71] Initially, there was no official announcement of his "retirement," just the conspicuous absence of his signature on the paychecks of the ballplayers. Only when Billings failed to attend the game on July 5 was there an official announcement that Soden would now be treasurer.

When the ballclub was finally sold in November 1906, Billings received nothing from the $75,000 payment by the Dovey brothers to acquire its stock; his son George did benefit from this sale, through the $200,000 mortgage that the Columbus Avenue Trust granted to the Dovey brothers when they acquired the South End Grounds in a no-cash transaction.[72] With the club under new ownership, the National League granted an honorary life membership to both Soden and Conant, but not to Billings, whom the League did not consider to be one of the owners at the time of the sale.[73]

Billings and his wife spent their retirement years living with their son George and his family in George's house in the Jamaica

Plain neighborhood of Boston.74 Billings died there on March 15, 1913, and is buried at the Mount Auburn Cemetery in Cambridge.75

NOTES

1. "Death Takes J.B. Billings," *Boston Globe*, March 16, 1913: 14. No birth record can be located for Billings. His birth was not recorded in *Vital Records of Lowell, Massachusetts, to the End of the Year 1849* (Salem, Massachusetts: Essex Institute, 1930).

2. Death records for Lowell in 1848 in the Massachusetts State Archives (Volume 38, Page 62); marriage records for Lowell in 1848 in the Massachusetts State Archives (Volume 38, Page 51).

3. *Lowell City Directory*, 1847: 65 and 1851: 27; federal census records for 1850 for John Billings, Lowell, Middlesex County, Massachusetts.

4. *Lowell City Directory*, 1853: 53, 1855: 32, and 1859: 42.

5. *Lowell City Directory*, 1855: 32.

6. *Boston City Directory*, 1856: 37, 1860: 51, and 1862: 42.

7. Marriage records for Cambridge in 1864 in the Massachusetts State Archives (Volume 136, Page 56).

8. "George B. Billings Dies at Home Here," *Boston Globe*, January 29, 1935: 19.

9. *Boston City Directory*, 1864: 39.

10. "Business Changes," *Boston Daily Advertiser*, May 30, 1864: 1; *Boston City Directory*, 1865: 39.

11. Obituary of George B. Clapp, *Boot and Shoe Recorder*, November 28, 1894: 69; John Galluzzo and Donald Cann, *Rockland Through Time* (Charleston, South Carolina: Fonthill Media, 2014), 3, 74-75; Susan Alatalo, *Marlborough* (Charleston, South Carolina: Arcadia, 2003), 7, 54-56.

12. Mary Blewett, *Men, Women, and Work: Class, Gender, and Protest in the New England Shoe Industry, 1780-1910* (Urbana: University of Illinois Press, 1988), 146-147; John Commons, "American Shoeworkers, 1648-1895: A Sketch of Industrial Evolution," *Quarterly Journal of Economics*, November 1909: 64.

13. Commons, "American Shoeworkers": 73.

14. *Boston City Directory*, 1870: 91.

15. "The Boston Base Ball Association," *Boston Globe*, December 8, 1876: 5.

16. George Tuohey, *A History of the Boston Base Ball Club* (Boston: M.F. Quinn, 1897), 176.

17. "The Boston Base Ball Association," *Boston Globe*, December 8, 1876: 5.

18. "Base Ball," *Boston Globe*, January 7, 1878: 8.

19. Obituary of George B. Clapp, *Boot and Shoe Recorder*, November 28, 1894: 69.

20. *Marlborough Directory*, 1885: 22 and 1887: 31.

21. Suffolk County Registry of Deeds, Book 1596, Page 323, cited in "362 Marlborough," *Back Bay Houses*, website providing genealogies of houses sponsored by Neighborhood Association of the Back Bay, accessed February 11, 2017, backbayhouses.org.

22. "Sporting News," *Boston Globe*, December 16, 1880: 1; "The Boston Baseball Association," *New York Clipper*, December 25, 1880: 317.

23. "Boston Base Ball Association," *Boston Globe*, December 22, 1881: 6; "The Annual Meeting," *New York Clipper*, December 31, 1881: 676.

24. "The Boston Club," *New York Clipper*, December 30, 1882: 661.

25. Tuohey, *A History of the Boston Base Ball Club*, 174.

26. "The Annual Meeting of the Boston Base Ball Association," *Boston Globe*, December 20, 1883: 2.

27. "Boston Baseball Gossip," *New York Clipper*, December 29, 1883: 693.

28. "The Boston Association and the Sale of Season Tickets," *Boston Globe*, February 17, 1884: 6; "The Base Ball Season Ticket Scheme Modified," *Boston Globe*, March 12, 1884: 4.

29. Silence was likely also part of the deal. No newspaper account can be located about Chase discussing his four years as ballclub treasurer, let alone the takeover of the ballclub by the triumvirs. At his death in 1933, Chase's obituary noted only that "Mr. Chase had been an ardent devotee of baseball." ("Allan J. Chase," *Cambridge Chronicle*, December 15, 1933: 6).

30. "Boston's Baseball Club," *New York Times*, December 18, 1884: 3; "Boston Base Ball Association," *Boston Globe*, evening edition, December 17, 1884: 1; "From the Hub," *New York Clipper*, December 27, 1884: 651.

31. Ibid.

32. A shareholder accounting published in 1887 indicated that Billings and Conant each owned 23 shares and Soden owned 22 shares, out of 78 total shares ("Again the Triumvirs," *Boston Globe*, December 22, 1887: 8).

33. "One Team Enough," *Boston Globe*, December 12, 1887: 8.

34. "What Is It?" *Boston Globe*, August 10, 1902: 33.

35. "Diamond Dust," *Boston Globe*, February 8, 1885: 6.

36. "Against the Triumvirs," *Boston Globe*, November 13, 1887: 3.

37. "Again the Triumvirs," *Boston Globe*, December 22, 1887: 8.

38. "Murnane's Baseball," *Boston Globe*, October 29, 1905: 36.

39. "Kelly, the King, Coming to Boston to Play Ball This Season," *Boston Globe*, February 15, 1887: 1.

40. Ibid.

41. "Diamond Points," *Boston Globe*, August 19, 1887: 8; "New Players Needed," *Boston Globe*, December 14, 1887: 9.

42. "He Is Ours; Pitcher John Clarkson Signs with Boston," *Boston Globe*, April 4, 1888: 1.

43. Mark Armour and Daniel Levitt, *In Pursuit of Pennants: Baseball Operations from Deadball to Moneyball* (Lincoln: University of Nebraska Press, 2015), 3-14, 279-280, 389-390.

44. "One Team Enough," *Boston Globe*, December 12, 1887: 8.

45. "Soden, Billings and Conant Working for Players," *Boston Globe*, April 1, 1888: 6.

46. "Triumvirs Are Hustling," *Boston Globe*, January 15, 1890: 8.

47. "Will Talk It Over," *Boston Globe*, July 26, 1888: 5.

48. "The Billings Telegrams," *Boston Globe*, August 10, 1889: 5.

49. "Triumvirs Are Hustling," *Boston Globe*, January 15, 1890: 8.

50. "Joy Turned to Grief," *Boston Globe*, April 23, 1892: 5; "Col. George Billings Well Known to the Ball Tossers," *Boston Globe*, December 10, 1893: 9.

51. "Business Embarrassments," *Boston Daily Advertiser*, March 9, 1894: 8.

52. "Business Failures," *Boston Globe*, March 22, 1894: 7.

53. "Real Estate," *Boston Globe*, March 11, 1894: 12.

54. Suffolk County Registry of Deeds, Book 2183, Page 569, cited in "362 Marlborough."

55. "Treasurer Billings Fails in Business," *The Sporting News*, March 17, 1894: 1.

56. "Accepted 55 Percent," *Boston Globe*, April 1, 1894: 23.

57. "Broken at Last: The Famous Boston Triumvirate Now Dissolved," *Sporting Life*, March 17, 1894: 4.

58. Suffolk County Registry of Deeds, Book 2453, Page 228, cited in "362 Marlborough."

59. "Is a Klondike: Boston's Triumvirs' Profits in 1897 $125,000," *The Sporting News*, February 26, 1898: 5. Apparently by 1894 the triumvirs were distributing the ballclub profits to themselves, rather than let them accumulate in the treasury, as was the original 1885 arrangement.

60. "Look Well and Strong," *Boston Globe*, April 3, 1894: 5.

61. "William Rogers Passes Away in New York," *Boston Globe*, April 22, 1905: 8.

62. "Baseball Notes," *Boston Globe*, September 29, 1895: 5.

63. "Hub Happenings," *Sporting Life*, July 17, 1897: 10.

64. Tuohey, *A History of the Boston Base Ball Club*, 175.

65. "League Magnates," *Boston Globe*, February 26, 1899: 29.

66 "Not Very Bright," *Boston Globe*, January 14, 1900: 21.

67 Charlie Bevis, *Jimmy Collins: A Baseball Biography* (Jefferson, North Carolina: McFarland, 2012), 85-86.

68 "Soden Ready to Sell Out," *Boston Globe*, January 11, 1902: 1; "Boston Club For Sale," *New York Times*, January 12, 1902: 10.

69 "Boston National Baseball Grounds Transferred," *Boston Globe*, April 8, 1902: 11; "Ball Ground Transfer," *Boston Post*, April 8, 1902: 3; "Realty of Boston National Club Valued at $205,000," *Boston Globe*, April 22, 1905: 3.

70 The percentage of ownership in the South End Grounds that was allocated to Billings was not publicly reported.

71 "Triumvirate Broken: Director J.B. Billings of Boston Club Out," *Boston Globe*, July 7, 1904: 7.

72 "Deal for Boston National League Club Completed," *Boston Globe*, November 29, 1906: 9.

73 "Honored by League: Diplomas Presented Messrs Soden and Conant," *Boston Globe*, August 21, 1907: 9.

74 Federal census records for 1910 for 22 Burroughs Street, Boston, Suffolk County, Massachusetts.

75 Death records for Boston, Massachusetts, in 1913, page 461. Mount Auburn Cemetery records show Billings is buried on Eagle Avenue, Lot 5861.

WILLIAM H. CONANT

BY WILLIAM H. LYONS

William Conant,
Boston Globe, October 25, 1926.

William H. Conant, Arthur H. Soden, and James B. Billings were the majority owners of the Boston Nationals[1] from its difficult early years, through its ascendancy to the position of one of the best teams in the National League, to its eclipse after the entry of the American League team in Boston in 1901. Held in high esteem by many of the owners of the other National League teams, in large part because they provided financial support in times of crisis, these three were also called misers and worse.[2] They spent unprecedented amounts of money to acquire the rights to star players and to build a ballpark that in its prime was the envy of other teams in the National League, yet they were unwilling to spend money on player salaries except in times of crisis, and refused to spend much to rebuild or maintain the ballpark after a fire in 1894. In 1906, when Conant and Soden sold the team and the ballpark, they received both lavish praise and stinging criticism. Examination of Conant's part in this story reveals these same dichotomies. As outgoing as Soden was retiring, Conant "enjoyed a big cigar and a drive behind a frisky span [of horses]."[3] Conant was willing to spend lavishly in some circumstances,[4] yet stories abound, some perhaps apocryphal, of his stinginess.[5]

William Henry Conant – in later years Uncle Bill Conant – was born in Bridgewater, Massachusetts, on March 15, 1834, to Ira and Lucy Conant.[6] Ira was a farmer. Although William may have worked on the family farm when he was younger, in 1855, when he was 21, he was living in North Attleboro, Massachusetts, with his older brother, Ira, and working as a clerk in Ira's "country store."[7] By 1860, William had started a hoop-skirt manufacturing and sales business.[8]

On May 2, 1860, William married Isadora "Dora" Shepardson in Attleboro, Massachusetts. Dora was born in Waterbury, Connecticut, on January 13, 1839, to George W. and Juliette Richards Shepardson. The newlyweds lived in Attleboro at the time of their marriage but by 1868 had established a home in Boston at 16 Rollins Street in the South End. They moved twice within Boston, finally moving to adjacent Brookline in 1904.

William and Dora had three children, William A., Fannie Dora, and Charles H. Conant.

By 1865, William's hoop-skirt business was located on Washington Street in Boston. His brother Ira joined him in the business, which they operated under the name Conant Bros. from 1867 through 1872 and as A.K. Young & Conant Manufacturing Co. in 1873 and 1874. A.K. Young had operated a separate hoop-skirt manufacturing business in Boston, and his addition to the Conant business name suggests that he first became a part-owner of the Conant Bros. business and then acquired the business when William and Ira started a different business.

The hoop-skirt business provided a living for William and Dora for about 14 years. When women's fashions changed, they started a new business initially known as the Gossamer Rubber Clothing Co. Over the years, the business had several locations in Boston and one in Framingham, about 30 miles west of Boston, Their partnership continued until Ira's death in 1895. Thereafter, William was the sole owner of the business, known as W.H. Conant Gossamer Rubber Co., until his oldest child, William A. Conant, became first an employee and then a co-owner of this business. Exactly when this business ended is not clear, although the *Boston Globe* listed ads for the sale of the business in June and July 1914.[9] The 1910 US Census lists William H. and William A. Conant as rubber manufacturers. The 1920 Census lists William A. Conant as a real-estate manager and William H. Conant as having no occupation. In 1914 the *Boston City Directory* lists father and son as owners of W.H. Conant Gossamer Rubber Co. but the1916 edition contains no business listing for either father or son, suggesting that they either ended or sold the business between 1914 and 1916.

Although there are no public financial records for the gossamer-rubber clothing business, that business provided William and his family with a very comfortable living.[10] Dora traveled in Europe in 1889 with their younger son, Charles. William owned at least three horses, a pair named Right Fielder and Left Fielder, and an iron-gray gelding.[11] From 1900 onward, William and Dora had domestic help living with them.

When the National League was formed in 1876, the Boston entry organized as a Massachusetts business corporation named Boston Base Ball Association.[12] The corporation was what now would be called a close corporation, meaning that a relatively small number of shares were issued,[13] and those shares did not trade on any established market. Soden initially bought 15 shares for $15 a share at the urging of his friend George B. Appleton. "Before the 1877 season started, Soden and his friend James B. Billings, a shoe and leather man, owned a majority of the stock," Harold Kaese wrote in his history of the Braves.[14] Conant initially became involved by employing an agent, identified by two sources as Captain Jones, to acquire single shares of stock from individual shareholders. Kaese refers to "an emissary named Captain Jones."[15] George V. Tuohey refers to "Captain Jones, who has followed the game since its opening in this city" and notes that "[i]n the [1870s] the stock went begging. It could be bought for as low as $15 a share, and some shares went for even less than that."[16] The identity of "Captain Jones," although apparently known to both Kaese and Tuohey, is a mystery today.

From 1876, when Soden was first elected a director at the corporation's annual meeting, through the 1880 annual meeting, when Billings become a director, to the 1881 annual meeting, when Conant became a director,[17] these three men accumulated stock ownership and power in the corporation. At the 1884 annual meeting, when Billings, Soden, and Conant owned the majority of the stock, the shareholders voted to reduce the board of directors from five members to three and elected Billings, Conant, and Soden as the directors, Soden as president, Billings as treasurer, and Conant as general manager.[18] At that point, these three essentially controlled the corporation and the team.

Why would successful businesspeople like Billings, Conant, and Soden invest in professional baseball? All three had a strong interest in game and Conant and Billings enjoyed generally good relations with the players.[19] Nonetheless, the 1876 Boston Nationals were not a success on the field, finishing the 1876 season in fourth place at 39 wins and 31 losses. Neither was the Boston team a financial success, losing, according to David Quentin Voigt, $777.22 in 1876.[20] Although the Boston team finished first in 1877 and 1878, the $2,230.85 loss for 1877 more than tripled the 1876 loss and the $1,433.31 loss in 1878 was more than double the 1876 loss.[21] The losses increased in 1879 ($3,346.90) and 1880 ($3,315.90).[22] National economic problems – a depression at its worst in 1878 – did not help, nor did the League's problems with drinking, gambling, and brawling.[23] Notwithstanding these financial issues, Billings, Conant, and Soden believed that they could put their experience as successful business owners to work making professional baseball in Boston profitable as well as entertaining for the public.[24] The application of what they considered good business practices, however, often generated controversy.

Their drive to improve the financial health of the team began with cuts in player salaries, advertising, clubroom upkeep, and travel expenses.[25] These cuts were not popular with the players, and manager Harry Wright's inability to deal with the problems caused by cuts in the travel budget may have caused his dismissal.[26]

In 1882 the directors announced that shareholders would no longer receive complimentary tickets to all home games. Many of the minority shareholders signed a petition objecting to the decision and stating that they had purchased their stock with an understanding that they would be entitled to the tickets.[27] After the directors refused to change their decision, a detailed letter to the editor of the *Boston Globe* appeared on April 16, 1882, stating the arguments for complimentary tickets.[28] Although the letter did not present very persuasive legal arguments, the anger of the shareholders was understandable even if the decision made financial sense.[29]

In 1884, after Boston had won the 1883 National League pennant, the directors raised the price of a season ticket from $20 to $30. A petition signed by 33 shareholders and former season-ticket holders asked the directors to reconsider the increase, to no avail. The directors decided to have two types of season tickets. The first, selling for $30, would entitle the holder to a specific grandstand seat. The second, selling for $20, would entitle the holder to general admission but not to the grandstand, although the holder could pay an extra fee for admission to the grandstand.[30]

The directors were notorious for severely limiting player salaries, and Conant was perhaps the toughest of the three on this issue. For example, Michael "Kid" Madden, a star pitcher originally acquired by Conant, visited Conant in early 1888 to discuss his contract for that year. During the 1887 season, Conant gave Madden $25 each time he won a game and $100 for winning the final two games with New York.[31] Thus, Madden likely assumed Conant would agree to a favorable contract for 1888. When Madden named his figure, "[i]t nearly knocked the solid Conant off his feet. When he had sufficiently recovered his breath to allow him to talk, he gasped: 'What is the size of your hat? Mike, you must be crazy. We have talked it over, and we have decided just what we will pay you. We will pay you just for next season, and when you get ready to sign let me know.'"[32] Madden signed for $2,000, the salary offered by Conant, but jumped to the Boston Players' League team in 1890.

Although the directors were usually tightfisted with player salaries, they nevertheless spent very large amounts of money to purchase the rights to players. Kaese credits Billings, Conant, and Soden with starting the practice of buying players. The purchases of Mike "King" Kelly in 1887 and pitcher John Clarkson in 1888, both from Chicago, are the two most prominent examples. Chicago received $10,000 each for these players. Billings apparently pushed for the acquisition of Kelly, but all three directors agreed on the acquisition of Clarkson.[33] Despite being willing to pay $10,000 to purchase the rights to Kelly, the team paid him only a $2,000 salary, the League maximum. Kelly had made it clear that he expected $5,000 to play for Boston, and extracted an additional $3,000, ostensibly for his portrait.[34] Later, in response to raids by the Players' League, Conant rebuilt the team by purchasing rights to players. When it came to attempts by other teams to purchase players reserved by Boston, however, Conant was generally unreceptive.[35] Further, once the challenge of the Players' League had ended, Conant decided that paying for players' releases was a bad practice, which the National League should prohibit.[36]

The Boston Nationals finished first in 1891, 1892, and 1893. This success, which suggested that the team was very profitable, prompted the players in 1894 to grumble about their salaries. Instead of quietly investigating this problem, Conant demanded that star left fielder Tommy McCarthy tell him if he had been spreading information about the team finances.[37] McCarthy reportedly affirmed to Conant that "he had, as had every other player on the team."[38] As *Sporting Life* noted, "[a] little diplomacy [from the owners] would set things right, but this is a business to which Director Conant would be very, very new."[39]

In the midst of the turmoil over salaries, a terrible fire destroyed virtually all of the South End Grounds.[40] The team temporarily moved to the Congress Street Grounds, where the Players' League and American Association teams had played. Although some argued that the Nationals should remain there, the team rebuilt the South End Grounds, but in smaller and less expensive form. The new grandstand did not include an upper deck because, Conant pointed out, the old upper deck "was only patronized on great occasions."[41]

The Boston press tried to link a tragic event to alleged reputed stinginess of the Conant and his partners. Martin Bergen, the Boston catcher from 1897 to 1899, apparently suffered from a mental illness.[42] On January 21, 1900, he killed his wife and two children before taking his own life. A *Sporting Life* article argued that the directors drove Bergen to kill because his meager salary made it impossible to provide for his family.[43] Tim Murnane responded that "[t]he Boston magnates did everything for him that they did for the other men, and, in fact, a great deal more, and are in no way to blame for any misfortune that overtook the player."[44]

Relations between the directors and the minority shareholders were also difficult. Lack of financial transparency proved a problem for the Boston Base Ball Association almost from its formation in 1876. At the first annual meeting, in 1876, the shareholders raised questions about finances and appointed a three-person committee that included J.B. Billings to audit the treasurer's accounts.[45] Ironically, as treasurer, Billings, supported by Conant and Soden, limited the release of financial information. At the 1883 annual meeting of the association, the bylaws were amended to require the treasurer to report to the directors and not to the shareholders,[46] a practice acceptable under Massachusetts law at the time.

At the 1885 annual meeting, the directors obtained approval to amend the bylaws to permit payment of compensation to the corporate officers (Billings, Conant, and Soden), prompting minority shareholder George H. Lloyd to request a treasurer's report from President Soden. Soden responded that he knew of no such report and that the treasurer (Billings) was in New York. Lloyd then sought to force disclosure of the 1883, 1884, and 1885 treasurer's reports, as well as other financial information, but the directors refused.[47]

In 1887 shareholders John C. Haynes, Charles C. Carey, Julian B. Hart, and Frederick E. Long asked a court to compel Billings, Conant, and Soden to provide a financial accounting.[48] Billings, no doubt expressing the feelings of Conant and Soden, stated: "We don't want the affairs of the association spread before the world. That would not be the business way of doing things. The financial standing of a concern is its own business and not for the public."[49] Because the minority shareholders did not (and likely could not) allege fraud by Billings, Conant, and Soden, the court concluded that "it was a hard situation, but there was no opportunity for the court to act unless there was an allegation of fraud."[50]

In addition to the problems caused by a lack of financial transparency, the directors faced three challenges from competing baseball teams placed in Boston prior to 1901. Conant played a significant role in two:

(1) Players' League – The Brotherhood (1890). Although some National League owners thought the Brotherhood revolt would come to nothing, Conant realized that the players were serious.[51] The Boston Nationals lost multi-position player Kelly, left fielder Hardie Richardson, and first baseman Dan Brouthers, as well as third baseman Billy Nash, second baseman Joe Quinn, outfielder

Dickie Johnston, pitcher Charles "Old Hoss" Radbourne, center fielder Tom Brown, pitcher Bill Daley, and pitcher Mike "Kid" Madden.[52] Conant took the lead in buying a replacement team that brought Boston success in 1891, 1892, and 1893.[53] He bought first baseman Tommy Tucker from Baltimore for $3,000, utility player Bobby Lowe from Milwaukee for $700, shortstop Herman Long from Kansas City for $6,300, and pitcher Kid Nichols for $3,500 from Omaha.[54] Conant had personally scouted Nichols, who became the backbone of the pitching staff of the Nationals' pennant-winning teams in 1891, 1892, and 1893. Conant was also instrumental in persuading pitcher John Clarkson to remain with the Nationals by offering a large salary increase (reportedly $7,000 a year). Clarkson in turn persuaded catcher-outfielder Charlie Ganzel to stay.[55] In the end, although the Boston Players' League team, managed by Kelly, finished first, the league disbanded after the 1890 season.[56]

(2) American Association (1891). The Association placed a new team in Boston in 1891. The team, the Boston Reds, played at the Congress Street Grounds. Mike Kelly, unsigned by either the Nationals[57] or the Boston Reds, agreed to manage and serve as captain of Cincinnati's American Association team. After the Cincinnati team decided to move to Milwaukee, Kelly requested and obtained his release.[58] Kelly then signed a contract with the Reds but Conant, who always thought very highly of him, induced Kelly to jump back to the Boston Nationals, despite Soden's opposition.[59] Both the Nationals and the Reds won their league championships, but the 1891 season proved the end of the American Association.

After offyears in 1894, 1895, and 1896, the Nationals won their fourth and fifth pennants of the decade in 1897 and 1898. But the glorious finish to the 1890s did not foreshadow success at the beginning of the twentieth century. After withstanding challenges from Boston teams in the Union Association, Players' League, and American Association, the directors of the Boston Nationals were unable to meet the challenge posed by the Boston Americans of the new American League.

Conant badly miscalculated the success the new league would have in signing players. He expected to keep pitcher Bill Dinneen, third baseman Jimmy Collins, left fielder Chick Stahl, and pitcher Kid Nichols for the 1901 season, regardless of whoever else he might lose to the American League.[60] Although Nichols and Dinneen remained with the Nationals, two key players, Collins and Stahl, did not. The first Boston defector was outfielder Hugh Duffy, who jumped to Milwaukee. Conant made no effort to persuade Duffy to stay: "He's about through as a player. We'll let him go in peace."[61] The devastating loss was Collins, who had promised to stay with the Nationals, but signed with the Boston Americans as player-manager for $4,000. Conant attempted to prevent the defection, sending Billings and manager Frank Selee to persuade Collins not to jump. Conant claimed he had authorized payment of up to $5,000 to Collins, but not only did Collins sign with the Americans for $4,000, he also persuaded Stahl, right fielder Buck Freeman, and pitcher Ted Lewis to go with him. Unable to replace the talent that had defected to the Americans, the Nationals did the best they could with the players they had left – which is to say a fifth-place finish. The Boston Americans battled for the American League pennant, finishing second to the Chicago White Sox by four games. Kaese argued that "[i]f they had been offered enough money, Collins, Lewis, Stahl, and Freeman would have remained with the Beaneaters. In Collins, the Triumvirs surrendered all the assets they had for this fight. Their one chance as to make the newcomers look like minor leaguers by comparison. Instead, the newcomers made the Beaneaters look like minor leaguers. ..."[62]

In April 1902, in a move likely intended to facilitate the ultimate sale of the team, the Boston Base Ball Association sold the South End Grounds and associated land to a real-estate trust called the Columbus Avenue Trust. The trustees of the trust were Charles A.R. Soden (son of Arthur Soden), George Billings (son of J.B. Billings), and Conant.[63] After the transfer, the Association became a tenant of the trust and paid rent for the use of the grounds.

In July 1904 Billings sold his remaining stock interest to Conant and Soden. "On July 4, an order was issued to the effect that [Arthur] Soden would act as treasurer of the club and that [William J.] Rogers would be his assistant."[64] Although Conant denied that Billings had retired (or been forced out),[65] from that point onward, Soden and Conant controlled the team.

After rumors of their interest in selling the team had circulated for several years, on November 28, 1906, Conant and Soden sold their stock in the Association to George B. Dovey. The real-estate trust sold the South End Grounds property to Dovey at the same time. Conant and Soden received $75,000 in cash and the trust accepted a promissory note for $200,000, secured by a mortgage on the South End Grounds, bearing a 3 percent interest rate.[66] *Sporting Life* summed the outcome of the sale for Conant and Soden: "One can see, therefore, that both the former owners need have no apprehension at all about their financial future. Each is rated at near the million mark."[67]

At its 1906 winter meeting, the National League feted Conant and Soden. They were the guests of honor at a gourmet dinner in the Waldorf-Astoria in New York City on December 12, 1906. League President Harry Pulliam, New York Giants President John T. Brush, and sportswriter Francis C. Richter spoke, giving Conant and Soden effusive praise for their long service to the League and the game. At the conclusion of the dinner, Conant and Soden received silver loving cups and honorary lifetime League memberships. Not long after the gathering *The Sporting News* carried a biting response to this praise: "Wasn't it the selfish management, the refusal to treat public and press with decent courtesy, the unwillingness to spend a few dollars for repairs to the dilapidated South End Grounds, to say nothing of the persistence with which they refused to strengthen their team when the American League came into Boston, that caused the public to go over to the Huntington Avenue grounds by the thousands while the Triumvirs' lot was deserted?"[68] The author asserted that Conant and Soden did not provide free tickets for players' wives, reneged on a promise to pay an injured player's medical bills, and refused to allow the manager to disburse cash to the players while the team was playing away from home. He concluded: "When Soden and Conant stepped down, it was the best thing that ever happened for the old organization . ..."[69]

After the sale, Conant maintained an active interest in baseball. He attended both Boston National and Boston American League home games.[70] When he wintered in Florida, he attended spring-training games in St. Petersburg. On May 8, 1925, the Nationals, by then known as the Braves, played the golden jubilee game that celebrated the founding of the National League. Although Soden remained at home following his doctor's advice, Conant, despite bad weather, attended the game with his son, William.⁷¹

Soden's death on August 14, 1925, upset Conant. "[Conant's] decline dated from that time and his condition became such that the Winter trip to Florida was abandoned," the *Boston Globe* said.⁷² Conant died at the Hotel Brunswick, in Copley Square in Boston, where he had been living for several years, on October 23, 1926, at age 92.⁷³ He had been widowed since Dora died on March 28, 1912. Both are buried at Forest Hills Cemetery in Boston.

Conant left $250,000 to his hometown of Bridgewater for the purpose of establishing a hospital. Conant made the gift by an Indenture of Trust dated June 4, 1925, as amended, between himself and Boston Safe Deposit and Trust Company as trustee. The William H. Conant Hospital Trust continues to this day as a nonprofit charitable foundation. The trust's primary purpose is to support the William H. Conant Community Health Center in Bridgewater.

NOTES

1. Referred to in this chapter as the Boston Nationals, but also known during this period as the Red Stockings, Reds, and Beaneaters.

2. "Billings was not a bad guy, but those other two, Conant and Arthur Soden, were the type of blackguards that even Charles Dickens would have rejected as character models for his novels as too one-dimensionally bad." Donald J. Hubbard, *The Heavenly Twins of Boston Baseball – A Dual Biography of Hugh Duffy and Tommy McCarthy* (Jefferson, North Carolina: McFarland, 2008), 87.

3. Harold Kaese, *The Boston Braves* (New York: Putnam, 1948), 23.

4. For example, spending thousands of dollars to buy the rights to rebuild the Boston Nationals during the battle with the Players Union.

5. A batter "fouled ten in succession over the back wall at Boston, and not one of them came back. As each ball went over, Conant … moaned in agony. After seven had gone, he wept aloud, and the tenth found him in spasms, his hands contracted nervously over a wad of dollars. Two more balls, at $15 the dozen … would have killed him then and there." "One on Conant," *Sporting Life*, May 18, 1900: 5.

6. Ira Conant died on February 19, 1871, at age 71, in Bridgewater. Massachusetts. Lucy Conant died on August 6, 1889, at age 87, in Bridgewater. *Boston Globe*, August 7, 1889: 8. Ira Conant and Lucy Leonard were married in Bridgewater on November 24, 1822. Vital Records of Bridgewater, Massachusetts to the Year 1850, Volume II –Marriages. The 1840 US Census stated that two members of the Conant household were employed in agriculture. The 1850 and 1860 US Censuses stated that Ira Conant was a farmer.

7. That census lists Ira M. Conant, age 28, as head of the household that included Mary P. Conant, Ira's spouse, their son George, age 3, and William H. Conant, 21.

8. See victoriana.com/Victorian-Fashion/crinoline.htm.

9. *Boston Globe*, June 28, 1914: 30; July 1, 1914: 13; and July 8, 1914: 13.

10. "When [hoop skirts] went out of fashion, [William H. Conant] manufactured rubber goods, from which he made a fortune." Kaese,

23. As with the hoop-skirt business, we have no information about how Conant treated the workers involved in producing the garments.

11. "Slipping Over the Road, Fast Trotters, Many Men, Few Women Face the Cold Winds Upon the Brighton Sleighing Ground," *Boston Globe*, January 4, 1887: 6.

12. "The Boston Baseball Association," *Boston Globe*, December 8, 1876: 5; "Boston's Club Unsold," *Sporting Life* November 11, 1905: 5.

13. Images of some stock certificates can be found on the internet. See, e.g., worthpoint.com/worthopedia/1883-boston-base-ball-association-25179879 (Certificate 124, J. B. Billings, 1 share, dated June 4, 1884); sterlingsportsauctions.com/1888_boston_base_ball_association_stock_certificat-lot45904.aspx (Certificate 140, Arthur H. Soden, 1 share, dated March 16, 1888); and scripophily.net/bobabaasbore4.html (Certificate 91, W.H. Conant, 1 share, dated December 16, 1881). Billings confirmed that the Association originally issued 150 shares of stock. "Against the Triumvirs," *Boston Globe*, November 13, 1887: 3. "[T]here are only 78 shares today – the 64 we [Billings, Conant, and Soden] own and the 14 scattering ones. … When the 150 shares were originally issued there was an assessment of 50 cents on $1. Later there was a second assessment of 20 cents on a dollar. When the third and last assessment of 30 cents was made it was paid on 78. The holders of the other 72 shares preferred to forfeit them rather than pay the assessment." Ibid.

14. Kaese, 22.

15. Ibid.

16. George V. Tuohey, *A History of the Boston Base Ball Club* (Boston: M.F. Quinn & Co., 1897), 176.

17. "The Boston Base Ball Association," *Boston Globe*, December 8, 1876: 5; "Boston Base Ball Association – Annual Meeting," *Boston Globe*, December 16, 1880: 1; "Boston Base Ball Association," *Boston Globe*, December 22, 1881: 2.

18. "Boston Base Ball Association," *Boston Globe*, December 17, 1884: 1. At the same meeting, the shareholders voted to purchase the South End Grounds property from the Estate of Barnabas Hammett "for a price not exceeding $100,000." Ibid.

19. Kaese, 23: "[Conant] was closer to the players than Soden, but not as close to them as Billings. Conant frequently travelled with the club, and often scouted the minor leagues."

20. David Quentin Voigt, *American Baseball: From the Gentleman's Sport to the Commissioner System* Volume 1 (University Park, Pennsylvania: Penn State University Press, 1983), 76. "Most clubs lost money for the first year; probably only Chicago showed a profit." Harold Seymour, *Baseball The Early Years* (New York: Oxford University, 1960, reprint 1989), 86.

21. Voigt, 76.

22. Ibid.

23. Voigt, 79-81.

24. At the 1881 annual meeting of the Boston Base Ball Association, the report of the board of directors closed "with the opinion that the corporation ought to be run on business principles to make it a success." "Boston Base Ball Association," *Boston Globe*, December 22, 1881: 2.

25. For details, see Voigt, 77.

26. Ibid.

27. "Dissatisfied Boston Stockholders," *Boston Globe*, April 2, 1882: 2.

28. "No Season Tickets for the Stockholders of the Boston Base Ball Association," *Boston Globe*, April 5, 1882: 4; "Those Season Tickets," *Boston Globe*, April 16, 1882: 8. The letter was signed "Justice."

29. The author asserts an oral promise of season tickets in perpetuity, and states: "The claim that nothing can be found in the articles of association or constitution and by-laws of the corporation giving the right the shareholders demand, may possibly be true, but do they find anything there denying that right?" The fact that the articles, constitution, and bylaws say nothing about the right to tickets does not help an argument based on an oral promise. The writer argues that the directors could be liable for denying the stockholders access to the home games, at best a legally dubious proposition. The letter also speaks of "antagonizing so large a majority of [the Association's] shareholders," but the

writer must mean number of shareholders, not number of shares. By 1882, Billings, Conant, and Soden collectively owned a majority of the shares.

30 "The Base Ball Season Ticket Scheme Modified," *Boston Globe*, March 12, 1884: 4.

31 "'The Kid' Signs a Contract," *Sporting Life*, January 11, 1888: 3.

32 Ibid.

33 Kaese, 46-47, 49.

34 Kaese, 47.

35 "Mr. Conant said it was amusing to hear of the clubs that expected to get Stivetts, Long, Lowe, and other men under reserve to Boston, when they knew it was simply impossible to get them at any price." "Conant Not Worried," *Boston Globe*, January 5, 1894: 2.

36 "The League Getting in Line Against the Sales System," *Sporting Life*, January 31, 1891: 1.

37 "The Boston Row," *Boston Globe*, March 19, 1894: 3.

38 Ibid.

39 Ibid.

40 "Boston's Ill Luck," *Boston Globe*, May 19, 1894: 1.

41 "The Boston Fire," *Boston Globe*, May 26, 1894: 3. "It will not be nearly as costly as the old structure. In this connection it may be said that only last year Director Billings was anxious to have the insurance increased $10,000, but this was not only opposed by Director Conant, but the latter was willing to allow as much of the insurance to drop, but it was, luckily, not done."

42 "Bergen's Insane Deed," *Boston Globe*, January 20, 1900: 1, 3 (referring to his aberrant behavior during the 1899 season).

43 "Bergen's Crime," *Sporting Life*, February 17, 1900: 2.

44 Ibid.

45 "The Boston Base Ball Association," *Boston Globe*, December 8, 1876: 5.

46 "The Annual Meeting of the Boston Ball Association," *Boston Globe*, December 20, 1883: 2.

47 "Boston Base Ball Association," *Boston Globe*, December 17, 1885: 1. Soden, Billings, and Conant voted themselves each a $2,500 salary for the year.

48 "Against the Triumvirs," *Boston Globe*, November 13, 1887: 3. Details of the claims asserted by the plaintiffs appear in "A Pooh-Bah Trio – Calling the Triumvirs to Account," *Boston Globe*, October 6, 1888: 1.

49 "Against the Triumvirs," *Boston Globe*, November 13, 1887: 3.

50 Ibid. Modern corporation law would grant minority shareholders reasonable access to the type of financial information the plaintiff sought.

51 "Bound to Fight," *Boston Globe*, November 1, 1889: 2 ("I was not surprised because I was under the impression … that the men were up to something."). When asked if the National League would fight, Conant responded: "Why certainly. We have nearly $50,000 lying idle with [National League President] Nick Young at Washington and that will help the weak clubs out. Boston, New York, Chicago, and Philadelphia have the pluck to stick it out, and we must help the other clubs." Ibid. The earliest challenge came in the form of the Union Association in 1884. Although the Boston Unions had several popular former Boston Nationals players – including pitcher Tom Bond, catcher Lew Brown, shortstop Walter Hackett, and first baseman Tim Murnane – their on-field performance (a lackluster fourth-place finish) was not sufficient to win fans from the Boston Nationals. Kaese, 38. Kaese states that Merton Hackett played for the Boston Unions, but it was Walter Henry Hackett, brother of Merton Hackett, who played for the Unions.

52 Kaese, 56.

53 The Boston Nationals finished fifth in 1890, in large part because of a series of accidents to key players John Clarkson, Herman Long, Bobby Lowe, and Patsy Donovan.

54 Kaese, 57.

55 "Where Was That Bomb?" *Boston Globe*, December 18, 1889: 3.

56 Robert R. Ross, *The Great Baseball Revolt – The Rise and Fall of the 1890 Players League* (Lincoln and London: University of Nebraska Press, 2016), 197.

57 The Boston Nationals did not claim Kelly on their reserved list. Marty Appel speculates that the Triumvirs may have concluded that Kelly's best days as a player were behind him. Marty Appel, *Slide, Kelly, Slide – The Wild Life and Times of Mike "King" Kelly Baseball's First Superstar* (Lanham, Maryland: Scarecrow Press, 1999 reprint), 156.

58 Appel, 162.

59 "They Are After Kelly," *Boston Globe*, June 10, 1891: 3; "War of Pitchers," *Boston Globe*, July 3, 1891: 5; Appel, 163-164.

60 "Conant's Ideas," *Sporting Life*, December 15, 1900: 8. Conant's omission of shortstop Hermann Long from this list struck one writer as a mistake. Ibid. Long, however, did not jump to the American League and played for the Nationals in 1901.

61 Kaese, 100. Conant's judgment appears sound, at least in hindsight – Duffy played in 79 games as player-manager for Milwaukee in 1901, batting .308. Thereafter, he played 18 games in 1904, 15 games in 1905, and one game in 1906, all for Philadelphia in the National League.

62 Ibid.

63 "Boston National Baseball Grounds Transferred," *Boston Globe*, April 8, 1902: 11.

64 William J. Rogers died suddenly, at age 45, on February 16, 1905. He had been the team's assistant treasurer for many years and became treasurer in the fall of 1904. "End Came Suddenly," *Boston Globe*, April 22, 1905: 7. His death was a shock to Conant and Soden and may have contributed to their decision to sell their interests in the team. See also "Triumvirate Broken: Director J.B. Billings of Boston Club Out," *Boston Globe*, July 7, 1904: 7.

65 Ibid.

66 When James Gaffney built Braves Field in the Allston section of Boston in 1915, the note and mortgage were paid so that the old South End Grounds could be sold. "To Retain Pre-Eminence in Ball Parks," *Sporting Life*, January 9, 1915: 2.

67 Francis C. Richter, "Dovey's Doings," *Sporting Life*, October 20, 1906: 3.

68 *The Sporting News*, February 2, 1907: 1.

69 Ibid.

70 See, e.g., *Boston Herald*, September 25, 1919: 14 (Conant attended a doubleheader at Braves Field between the Braves and the Giants).

71 "Veterans of Boston Teams of 70's at Golden Jubilee Celebration," *Boston Globe*, May 8, 1925: 8.

72 "Soden Funeral to Be Held Sunday," *Boston Globe*, August 15, 1925: 8; "'Uncle Bill' Conant Dead, Funeral Tomorrow," *Boston Globe*, October 25, 1926: 22.

73 Ibid.

ARTHUR SODEN

BY BRIAN MCKENNA

Arthur Soden
(public domain)

Arthur Soden was like many nineteenth century capitalists: He had a near single-mindedness when it came to the bottom line. He saw baseball as a business, pure and simple, though he did admit later in life that he had a fondness for the game. Controlling costs and expanding revenues were his priorities. The well-being and opinions of his players, minority stockholders and even the fans, to an extent, were not. To Soden, employees were necessary for production only. The fact that they were human beings with demands of their own only complicated the issue. The only thing he detested more than employee relations was labor's attempts to unionize.

The Boston franchise was riding high during the National Association years, copping pennants from 1872-75, sometimes by wide margins. Their dominance, in part, led to the formation of the National League in 1876. The club's profitability took a dramatic dip in the new league. In 1877 Soden and his associates took over an indebted Boston franchise. They tightened the belt hard, shocking the players and even the fans. It worked. Soon the franchise was among the most lucrative in the game. Pennants, eight by the end of the century, and profits followed.

Soden himself was among the most influential executives in baseball. He was a league director within his first year at Boston's helm and served as interim National League president for a season after the death of William Hulbert. Today, he is mainly known as the father of the reserve clause. He was also a driving force that helped the National League weather its challengers, the Union Association, Players League and American Association. The National League could have used his diligent guidance during the American League challenge but Soden's interest in the game was waning by then and his club was reeling financially.

Arthur Henry Soden was born on April 23, 1843, in Framingham, Massachusetts in Middlesex County, the only child of Samuel S. Soden and Ferona S. Johnson. The Sodens were married on December 28, 1841. Samuel was a partner in Bradbury, Soden & Company, a popular Boston publisher of books and magazines. He died when Arthur was just a year or two old. Ferona remarried in October 1848 to a Vermont farmer named Solomon

Clement. The family lived in Hartford, Vermont, for a few years before settling in Framingham. Solomon and Ferona had one daughter, Mary Q., eight years younger than Arthur.

In his late teens Arthur found work as a wholesale druggist and pharmaceutical supply salesman. At age 20, Soden was drafted into the Union Army during the Civil War, joining Company A, 22nd Massachusetts Infantry Regiment on July 13, 1863. On May 1, 1864 he was promoted to hospital steward. One of his tent mates described their living conditions: "I am now living with Soden, Hospital Steward, in a nice wall tent made of ponchos; we have nice bunks, covered with fly netting and filled with straw; we have a tin pail, wash basin, and everything comfortable, from the 'Sanitary' canned stuff, wines, etc."[1] After the 22nd was mustered out Soden joined the 32nd Regiment until he was discharged on November 1, 1864. Soon after returning from the war, he married another Framingham native, Mary Elizabeth Simpson, who was a year younger, in 1865. They settled in West Newton, Massachusetts, about 11 miles outside Boston. They lived there the rest of their lives and had three children. Unfortunately, only one, Charles, survived childhood. In 1867 Soden helped form Chapman and Soden Company, a roofing service and material supply business located in downtown Boston, initially on Water Street. He drove into the city for work with brown-bag in tow six days a week for the next six decades.

Soden was interested in baseball from his youth, playing amateur ball into his thirties. On July 16, 1874, about two dozen professional ballplayers, mainly from the Boston and Philadelphia squads, left the United States for Liverpool, England, on an international baseball and cricket tour organized in part by Al Spalding, who had made the trip over the previous winter to scout locations and size-up interest. About eighty fans accompanied the ballplayers; Soden was one of them. He even appeared in a game for Boston, playing center field on August 13 or 14 at the Kennington Oval in London. The Boston club, owned by Nicholas T. Apollonio, dominated the National Association, taking four pennants starting in 1872. After the fourth pennant the NA was tossed aside in favor of the upstart National League in 1876. That year, or perhaps a little earlier, one of Soden's friends, George B. Appleton, sold him three shares of stock in the Boston National League club for $45. The club dropped to fourth place in the new league, exacerbating existing financial woes. By the end of 1876 Apollonio sold out. After some boardroom bickering and maneuvering, Soden, J.B. Billings, a shoe factory owner, and William Conant, a manufacturer of hoop skirts and later rubber goods, took control of the club.

Soden became president, Billings was named treasurer and Conant accepted the position of secretary. The trio, known as the Triumvirs after the ancient Roman rulers, would oversee club operations for the next thirty years. By the mid-1880s they controlled about 65% of the stock. The club quickly bounced back on the field, taking pennants in both 1877 and '78. Soden and company gained a firm grip over expenditures; in fact, they cut expenses so deep the players and fans yelped. As Soden noted, "Common sense tells me that baseball is played primarily to make a profit."[2] He cut the players' meal money and booked them into shabby hotels on the road. As biographer Rich Eldred outlined in *Baseball's First Stars*, the men were forced to man the turnstiles, cut the lawn and wrestle fans for foul balls. They were also charged for uniform-cleaning costs while on the road, on top of the standard uniform fee. They were required to clean their own uniforms when at home.[3] Cuts went so deep that Boston offered its players an incentive if they made their shoelaces last for two years instead of one. Tight-fisted and penny pincher are but a few of the nicer things many called the Triumvirs. Salaries were cut as well; for example, star shortstop George Wright was forced to accept a $500 reduction for 1878. When the players threaten an upheaval over the ratty hotels, Soden fired manager Harry Wright because he wasn't forceful enough with the players.

The club made the players' wives pay full price for tickets and virtually did away with the concept of free passes. The press area was eliminated to make room for more paying customers. The Triumvirs themselves could be found manning the ticket booths during big paydays. Soden toted his lunch to the office each day and often dipped into his own pocket to cover team expenses. Clubroom upkeep dropped from $1,626 in 1875 to $551 in 1880. Travel expense likewise fell $4,000 a year over that time to $2,813. Payroll dropped 20 percent from 1877 to 1880 to an average of $1,377 per man. The cutbacks worked. The team lost $3,316 in 1880 but profits started to soar in 1881, posting $2,850 in the black that year. Soon profits were averaging over $30,000 a year. After the finances stabilized the Triumvirs voted themselves a yearly salary of $2,500 each. They also took steps to block the smaller stockholders from sharing the profits. In December 1885 the lesser shareholders called for an investigation of the club's finances, since Soden hadn't issued a financial statement in three years. The Triumvirs used their controlling interest to outvote them. They also refused to issue dividends, which ultimately forced the smaller shareholders to sell out one by one in disgust.

Virtually from the time he took over the Boston club, Soden became a leading force in league affairs. He was perhaps National League president William Hulbert's most trusted adviser in business matters. At the end of 1877 Soden became a league director and remained so until he retired in 1906. When Hulbert passed away in April 1882, Soden was named interim National League president until A.G. Mills was elected in November. Perhaps Soden's biggest accomplishment as president was pushing for the return of New York City and Philadelphia among the league's franchises. The two least-populated cities, Troy and Worcester, were pushed out to make room.

He was chairman of many league committees and a leader in National League circles for three decades. He was a dominant voice at meetings. During the early years Soden was a strong advocate against gambling and game-fixing. He was also the stabilizing force during the National League challenges with competitors in 1884, 1890 and 1891, among other years. Longtime National League president Nick Young asked Soden from time to time to help other league franchises financially. He once loaned the New York Giants $60,000. During the battle with the Players League, Giants owner John Day demanded $80,000 from National League coffers in July 1890 to help steady his club. He threatened to sell out the Players League if the money wasn't remitted. Soden purchased $25,000 in Giants' stock, as did Chicago owner Al Spalding. Indianapolis owner John Brush forgave a $25,000 loan in return for stock and a few others pitched in. Day was left with less than a $20,000 stake in the Giants. The New York stock remained in possession of the Soden family until 1928.

As respected as Soden was by his colleagues, few players had much nice to say about him. That was by design. He preferred to remain aloof from the players, wanting nothing to do with them. As one writer put it, Soden was "somewhat to the severe and reserved in his manner" in order to inspire "awe."[4] Conant and Billings dealt with the players. Soden never traveled, not once, with the team. This is not to say that he didn't like baseball; he did. He sat through every home game until the last out. Conant traveled with the men and handled matters while the club was away. As Boston sportswriter Tim Murnane noted, "Not one in three of the men who have played on the Boston team…ever spoke a word to Mr. Soden."[5] To Soden, the ballplayers were mere employees, a means to an end. He didn't want to get attached to anyone or compromised by association. He was a decision maker and capitalist, typically unconcerned with the welfare of his workers like most businessmen during the nineteenth century. He may have even viewed them as pampered and overpaid. As he once said, "When a player ceases to be useful to me I will release him," no sentiment about it.[6] A favorite move of Soden and his colleagues was to place a "troublemaking" player on the blacklist if he rocked the boat too frequently or harshly—from the owner's perspective, of course. A famous case involved the blackballing of Charley Jones in 1880 when he requested his back pay at an inappropriate time. Jones was fined for his troubles and tossed out of the league, never to return.

Before the 1879 season, Boston stars Jim O'Rourke and George Wright jumped to Providence. Providence won the pennant with Wright as its manager. In response, Soden fumed, "What man in his right mind will invest money in this kind of business? Today he has some assets. Tomorrow he has none."[7] Others league owners felt the same way. On September 29 the six owners of the National League agreed in a secret meeting in Buffalo to respect each other's rights to five players.[8] Thus, a reserved player couldn't sign with or play for another team. Originally called the "five men rule," the reserve clause was born; it survives in revised form today. Eventually all players would be held in reserve. Soden is generally credited with this innovation, but it was essentially the end result of many collaborations and communications between the magnates. The reserve clause marks Soden's lasting fame in baseball history. It was an obvious attempt to eradicate bidding wars for players and to limit an individual player's options and hence his leverage during salary negotiations. The reserve clause reigned unchecked for nearly a century.

In 1883 Boston won the pennant and emerged as a profitable franchise. After the success, Soden expanded the ballpark to accommodate more seating. In November 1885 Soden announced that he had personally purchased the failing Providence franchise and all its players for $6,600. It was later revealed that he was acting as an agent for the league with the other clubs sharing the cost. For his efforts and money, Soden selected pitcher Hoss Radbourn and 21-year-old catcher Con Daily for the Beaneaters.

Boston continued to do well at the box office despite falling to a succession of fifth-place finishes from 1885-87. In February 1887 Boston decided to open its coffers to get back in the pennant race. At Billings' suggestion, Soden purchased King Kelly, one of the game's first superstars, from Chicago for $10,000. The sale took the baseball public by storm. Many didn't believe such a price would or could be paid for a ballplayer. It was twice the known figure paid for any player in the past. The check was prominently displayed in a store window to prove to the public that in fact the money exchanged hands. The sale sparked a controversy on another front. Adding to the complaints of the new Brotherhood of Professional Baseball Players, Kelly was sold without receiving a percentage of the price. A year later, in April 1888, Chicago again took $10,000 from Boston, this time for Hall of Fame pitcher John Clarkson. Clarkson and Kelly became known as the "$20,000 battery." In October Boston spent more than $30,000 to buy Charlie Bennett, Charlie Ganzel, Dan Brouthers, and Hardy Richardson from the failing Detroit club. In 1889 Soden offered $7,500 for Jack Glasscock but was turned down by Indianapolis. In 1890 he purchased Herman Long for about $6,000. The money proved well-spent as Boston challenged for the pennant during the summer of 1889, losing out by one game to New York, and making a profit of $100,000. Sportswriter Tim Murnane estimated that the Triumvirs made a profit of around $300,000 for the club during the 1880s. It all collapsed in 1890 when Kelly, Brouthers and Richardson jumped to the new Players League organized by the Brotherhood. Clarkson threatened to jump, but stayed with Soden for a three-year, $25,000 deal. The Beaneaters dropped to fifth place. The Players' League lasted only one season, but the challenge hit every club in the pocketbook, as did the merger between the National League and American Association the following year. The peace talks between those two leagues were almost derailed when Soden swooped in and stole King Kelly from the American Association's Boston Reds in August 1891, offering him perhaps as much as $25,000 through 1892 as claimed by biographer Rich Eldred.

Boston rode high during the 1890s, taking five pennants from 1891-93 and 1897-98. With the folding of the American Association the National League split its season in 1892. Boston won the first half and challenged Cleveland for the second half—but Soden thought the Boston players weren't challenging hard enough. He believed they were tanking the second half in order to guarantee a playoff check. He cancelled the postseason but later recanted. Boston won the series 5-0-1, drawing 30,000 paying customers. Baltimore and Boston ran neck and neck in 1897. The exciting pennant race netted about a $125,000 profit for the Beaneaters, as the Boston club was called. By the late 1890s, Soden started stepping back from baseball. Previously he never missed a game. More and more he was taking extended vacations to go fishing and relax with family and friends.

As a capitalist, Soden was staunchly anti-union. He vehemently declared, "I do not believe in labor organizations or unions."[9] This stance worked well in the end for the league during its fight with the Brotherhood of Professional Baseball Players at the turn of the 1890s. When the players threatened to strike during the summer of 1890, Soden countered that he would bring in strikebreakers to quash the rebellion. However, the players used the resentment as a driving force during the American League's uprising a decade later.

A new union, dubbed the Protective Association of Professional Baseball Players, was officially formed in the summer of 1900. The most vigilant and vocal of the batch was vice president Clark Griffith, who had been pushing for unionization since 1897.

The pitcher elected himself the "official bomb thrower" in the fight against the owners.[10] Griffith first set his sights on Soden, who had refused to give him two passes during a recent series in Boston. At the end of the year he got his opportunity. On December 13, 1900, the National League owners rejected all demands made by the players. The union kept its cool. It drew up a petition requesting another hearing and handed it to Nick Young to give to committee chairman Soden. The union received no reply to the petition but Griffith and union president Chief Zimmer decided to attend the December 15 league meeting anyway.

Waiting to be heard, they were forewarned by Young that "They (the owners) aren't going to give you a thing."[11] The meeting adjourned with Griffith and Zimmer still waiting to present their case. Afterward sportswriter Tim Murnane approached Soden at the hotel bar, with Griffith and other players present, Soden innocently replied that he hadn't received such a petition. Then tauntingly, he casually pulled it from his breast pocket and snidely asked, "Can this be it?"[12] Some reports suggest that he and Griffith nearly came to blows. Irate, Griffith supposedly wired American League president Ban Johnson, "Go Ahead: You can get all the players you want."[13] Thus, sparked in part by Soden's callousness, many within the union broke from the National League and stocked the American League with proven, experienced talent.

The interloping American League sent the National League reeling, especially in Boston, where Ban Johnson relocated his Buffalo franchise. During the battle for talent the Beaneaters lost third baseman Jimmy Collins, right fielder Buck Freeman, catcher Boileryard Clarke, left fielder Chick Stahl and pitchers Bill Dinneen and Ted Lewis. All had been starters on the 1900 squad; all except Clarke went to the cross-town Americans. The Americans also added the great Cy Young. They won A.L. pennants in 1903 and '04, while the Beaneaters sank to the second division. The fans, now tired of the parsimonious Triumvirs, switch allegiances in droves. From 1901-05 the Red Sox attracted 2.1 million paying customers, the Beaneaters only a third as many.

National League executives were thrown into disarray by the American League's encroachment. In July 1901 Soden and fellow owners John Brush, Frank Robison, and Andrew Freedman met in private. They formed on paper what they called the National Baseball Trust. They wanted the National League set up as a holding company for its eight franchises. The four unilaterally assigned themselves percentages of the stock in the new enterprise. Freedman, representing the Giants, would take 30 percent and the others would each get 12 percent. That would only leave a third of the stock for the other four clubs; naturally, this didn't go over well. The trust plan was eventually defeated but not before it caused a great deal of animosity and chaos in the National League at a time that it needed its concerted efforts to stave off the advancing American League.

With the trust defeated and the American League gaining steam the Natural League sought a change at the top. Al Spalding made a strong bid to replace Nick Young as National League president; however, in the end Soden, Brush and Cubs president Jim Hart were appointed as a three-man committee to head the league. They were called the Board of Control or Executive Committee. In truth the committee rarely met; Brush made unilateral decisions as de facto head of the league. During this time Brush took over the Giants from Freedman and waged a spirited battle against the American League. But the other owners were looking to make peace with the new major league. Brush and Soden were the two National League leaders who wanted to continue the fight.

As noted, the Beaneaters were quickly becoming the "other team" in Boston. Profits dwindled dramatically. Billings sold out in 1904 to Conant and Soden. The latter two soon looked for a buyer as well. The deal was consummated in November 1906. George and John Dovey, John Harris and Fred Tenney purchased the club for $75,000 plus an overpriced $200,000 mortgage on the ballpark and grounds. The National League threw Soden and Conant a festive dinner party in appreciation of their 30 years of service.

Soden may have retired from baseball but he continued working. Outside his daily responsibilities at Chapman & Soden, which he ran with his son, he was the president and part-owner of the Street Railway Company, Columbus Avenue Trust and Mount Mansfield Electrical Railroad Company. He was also a part-owner and director in Commercial National Bank of Boston, Bay State Hardware Company, Clark Manufacturing Company, and Pioche Mining and Development Company, among others. Needless to say, Soden was a wealthy man. In December 1907 he purchased an electric railroad about 11 miles in length in Vermont. Soden was a frequent contributor to Boston College. Outside his contributions over the years, his will also bequeathed $145,000 to the institution, which was used to purchase a building named in his honor, among other investments. Outside business Soden loved chess, fishing, and expensive cigars. As president of the Boston Chess Club, he often hosted large competitions with both national and international competitors. He planned his vacations around fishing, often taking off for fishing holes throughout New England. He purchased a summer home on Lake Sunapee in New Hampshire.

Throughout his career Soden was known for his unquestioned integrity. At the end of 1908 he became entangled in a messy personal squabble. A Boston broker named Frederick Small accused Soden of having an affair with Small's second wife, Laura. He made wild allegations that Soden had drugged both him and his wife one night and claimed to have 50 love letters penned by the millionaire.[14] In February 1909 Small filed an alienation of affection lawsuit against Soden for $500,000, the largest such suit filed in U.S. history. Soden refused to acknowledge the claim, leaving it uncontested. It was settled by an arbitrator in May 1911 for $10,000. The arbitrator openly asserted that he believed that the Smalls were working a con but he couldn't prove it. Giving credence to that theory, Small was later convicted and executed for killing his third wife five years later for insurance money.

Into 1925 Soden, 82, still trekked to work at 150 Oliver Street in Boston, from Newton, six days a week with his son. Arthur Soden took an extended vacation that summer and died at his summer home in Sunapee on August 13, 1925. He was interred at Newton Cemetery.

SOURCES

In addition to Ancestry.com and a number of additional newspapers, the author also consulted

Bell, David, "Nineteenth Century Transactions Register," August 2004.

Caruso, Gary. *The Braves Encyclopedia* (Philadelphia: Temple University Press, 1995).

Dewey, Donald and Nicholas Acocella. *Total Ballclubs: The Ultimate Book of Baseball Teams* (Wilmington, Delaware: Sports Media Publishing, Inc., 2005).

Nemec, David. *The Great Encyclopedia of 19th Century Major League Baseball* (New York: Donald I. Fine Books, 1997).

Parker, John Lord. *Henry Wilson Regiment: History of the Twenty-second Massachusetts Infantry, the Second Company Sharpshooters, and the Third Light Battery, in the War of the Rebellion* (Boston: Press of Rand Avery Company, 1887).

Pearson, David Merle. *Baseball in 1889: Players vs. Owners* (Bowling Green, Ohio: Popular Press, 1993).

Porter, David L. *Biographical Dictionary of American Sports: Baseball* (New York: Greenwood Press, 1987).

Roer, Mike. *Orator O'Rourke: The Life of a Baseball Radical* (Jefferson, North Carolina: McFarland and Co., 2005).

Riess, Steven A. *Touching Base: Professional Baseball and American Culture in the Progressive Era, Second Edition* (Champaign, Illinois: University of Illinois Press, 1999).

Solomon, Burt. *Where They Ain't: The Fabled Life and Untimely Death of the Original Baltimore Orioles. The Team that Gave Birth to Modern Baseball* (New York: Doubleday Books, 1999).

Zimbalist, Andrew. *Baseball and Billions: A Probing Look Inside the Big Business of Our National Pastime* (New York: Basic Books, 1994).

NOTES

1. Robert Goldthwaite Carter, *Four Brothers in Blue: A Story of the Great Civil War from Bull Run to Appomattox* (Norman, Oklahoma: University of Oklahoma Press, 1999), 475.

2. Curt Smith, *Storied Stadiums* (New York: Carroll and Graf, 2003), 30.

3. Rich Eldred, "Arthur H. Soden," *Baseball's First Stars* (Cleveland: SABR, 1996), 153.

4. "More Money and Less Talk," *Boston Herald*, October 31, 1887: 8.

5. "President Soden," *Sporting Life*, August 8, 1891: 4.

6. Robert F. Burk. *Never Just a Game: Players, Owners, and American Baseball to 1920* (Chapel Hill, North Carolina: The University of North Carolina Press, 1994), 144.

7. Harold Kaese, *The Boston Braves: 1871-1953* (Boston: Northeastern University Press, 2004), 30.

8. Peter Morris. *A Game of Inches: The Stories Behind the Innovations That Shaped Baseball, The Game Behind the Scenes* (Chicago, Ivan R. Dee, 2006), 465.

9. Burk, *Never Just a Game*, 144.

10. *Pittsburgh Post*, December 14, 1900: 6.

11. Brian McKenna, *Clark Griffith: Baseball's Statesman* (lulu.com, 2010), 95.

12. Harry Casey, "The Story of Baseball (Part III)," *Baseball Magazine*, April 1912: 28.

13. Eugene C. Murdock. *Ban Johnson: Czar of Baseball*. (Westport, Connecticut: Greenwood Press, 1982), 46.

14. "Soden Must Pay $10,000," *New York Times*, April 28, 1911: 1.

BALLPARKS

THE SOUTH END GROUNDS (BOSTON)
BY BOB RUZZO

Boston's South End Grounds.

THE END OF THE BEGINNING

When the Boston Braves left the field at the South End Grounds on Tuesday, August 11, 1914, the glorious opening chapter of professional baseball in Boston passed into history without notice. After a frustrating 13-inning, 0-0 tie with the Cincinnati Reds, all that mattered that day was that the Braves had fallen a half-game behind the second-place St. Louis Cardinals in their quest to track down John McGraw's league-leading New York Giants.[1]

There would always be another game tomorrow, although the forecast for the next day's contest seemed somewhat dubious for Boston cranks contemplating a trip via the Tremont Street streetcar to the city's South End. Fans of the franchise had been making a similar journey for decades, first by horse-drawn car, then by electric streetcar.[2]

For the South End Grounds, the third iteration of a ballpark on the same city block, however, tomorrow never came. Major-league baseball was never again played on the 4½ acre site.[3]

With Wednesday's game postponed because of rain, the Braves left town the next day on an extended road trip, never to return to the location that served as their home for longer than any other facility in the more than 140-year history of the franchise. Upon their return to Boston in September, Fenway Park, less than two years old and still sparkling, beckoned. After the Braves started the following season in Fenway with the permission of their American League cousins, in August 1915, Braves Field would become the team's new home.

Over the course of the South End Grounds' more than 43 years of service, baseball, the nation, and the city of Boston had all changed dramatically. At the South End Grounds, these forces of change were marked both on the field and in the stands.

Today, many aspects of the first National Association of Base Ball Players game at the site on May 16, 1871, between the Boston Red Stockings and the Troy (New York) Haymakers would seem bewildering, if not downright amusing.[4] The pitcher stood in a box some 45 feet from home and delivered the ball by means of a straight-armed submarine style motion to a batter who could both call for his preferred pitch height and, if he didn't like them, foul pitches with impunity. His catcher had no mask and typically stood several feet behind home, hoping to "[catch] the ball on its first bounce." The pitcher wore no glove; neither did any of his fielders.[5] This was baseball as the game was played by the first of its "major" professional leagues in a largely agrarian nation six years removed from a debilitating Civil War.

Over the next four decades the sport transformed itself, reflecting the fluidity of a country entering a dynamic new age of industrialization. Despite many detours along the way, by August 1914 the game had taken on nearly all of its fundamental character, as the flickering celluloid images of that era primitively attest.

At the same time, the city of Boston was growing exponentially, swelling its ranks from 250,526 (seventh largest in the country) to 670,585 (fifth) in 1910.[6] Immigrants of every stripe filled its streets, particularly the baseball-mad Irish, who during this time transformed City Hall from a bastion of Yankeedom into a virtual Irish colony.

During this era of chaotic change, Boston's baseball franchise was a source of stability and success. Indeed, for most of this period, baseball had one constant. Boston was its king.

And the South End Grounds were figuratively, and for six sweet years literally, its palace.

The South End Grounds: Home of the Braves (and the Red Stockings, Red Caps, Rustlers, Beaneaters, and, while we're at it, even the Doves)

Having seen their various amateur baseball squads suffer ignominious defeats at the hands of the professional Cincinnati Red Stockings in 1870, Boston baseball enthusiasts sprang into action after the Red Stockings disbanded once their 87-game winning streak was snapped by the Brooklyn Atlantics. In January 1871 a corporation known as the Boston Red Stockings Club was capitalized to the tune of $15,000. Ivers W. Adams was selected president, but more importantly, George and Harry Wright were recruited to put the team together, a task that they (Harry in particular) accomplished with ultimately alarming success. Harry persuaded a number of former Cincinnati teammates to join him in Boston, but his true ten-strike was signing pitcher Al Spalding from the Forest Citys.[7]

The grounds for this new team were located along the border between Boston's South End and the newly annexed town of Roxbury, which had become part of the city of Boston in 1868.[8] The site was rectangular in shape, bounded on the east by Berlin Street (which was later incorporated into Columbus Avenue), and by the tracks of the New York, New Haven, and Hartford Railroad (Providence Division) to the west.[9] The railroad proved to be a harsh neighbor. "Passing trains could be counted on to periodically rain smoke and cinders down on the third base patrons and on the field itself," a baseball historian has written. "If the wind was right and the traffic was heavy, games were halted in order to allow the haze generated by the trains to clear."[10]

A Providence and Boston Railroad roundhouse was situated to the north of the playing field, and Camden Street lay beyond that. The southern perimeter was marked by a narrow passage known as Walpole Street, giving rise to the frequently used alternative appellation for the park: The Walpole Street Grounds.

South End Grounds
(Courtesy of John Thorn)

"Although a concession stand was in evidence from the beginning, rest rooms were not."[11] The park was also known as the Union Baseball Grounds, Boston National League Base Ball Park, or the Boston Base Ball Grounds.

Whatever name was used, the playing grounds were unusual in shape. Left field (250 feet) and right field (255 feet) were extremely close to home plate, and a compensatingly huge center field (450 feet) gave the park many of the characteristics of the bathtub-shaped Polo Grounds. It was said the park was "like a bowling alley. It only had one field: center."[12]

The grounds were at first leased from the railroad and its associated structures were quite simple. "The pavilion looked like a big volunteer fireman's carnival booth."[13] This covered seating area "was of simple design and resembled many of the parks of the era. The main grand stand was quite boxy, containing approximately twenty five rows of seats under the cover of the overhanging roof. The roof was held up by six supports."[14] "Four rows of primitive box seats and a smaller wooden bleacher section sat in front of the grand stand behind a three foot wooden fence."[15] Fifty cents brought admission to the grandstand, while a quarter was all that was required to sit in the uncovered "bleaching seats" that paralleled the basepaths. Standing room was plentiful, particularly in the generous confines of center field. At first the park was surrounded by a 12-foot-high wooden fence. Two ticket booths stood guard on Walpole Street, directly across the street from the groundskeeper's house.[16]

In these rather modest surroundings, the Red Stockings successfully began their professional odyssey in a match against a picked nine on April 6, 1871, before a packed house. "[A] full five thousand persons ... the largest number ever assembled before in these grounds" were on hand, with some standing on top of the fence and others watching from rooftops.[17] With Spalding pitching, the professionals defeated the opposition 41-10, thereby establishing two long-term local institutions: on-field success and inventive attempts to avoid paying the entrance fee.

With Spalding leading the way, the Bostons swept to four consecutive National Association titles between 1872 and 1875. In his signature season of 1875, Spalding posted a record of 54 wins and only five losses. Boston's one-sided dominance of the National Association was a major factor in its eventual collapse.

William A. Hulbert of Chicago became the driving force behind the newly formed National League.[18]

A SHIFT IN THE BALANCE OF POWER

At its core, this change represented a massive shift in power from players (in the National Association of Base Ball Players) to clubs and their owners (in the National League of Base Ball Clubs). Hulbert was also the driving force in luring Spalding along with three other Boston star players to Chicago: second baseman Ross Barnes, former catcher turned outfielder/first baseman Cal McVey, and catcher Deacon Jim White. When these "Four Seceders" came to Boston on May 30 for their first game in Chicago White Stocking uniforms, the *Boston Globe* reported that there had "never been so great a crowd at any base ball match ever played in this country, certainly not in this city."[19] The crowd of between 10,000 and 12,000 spectators, which the *Globe* described as "almost appalling," literally tore down the fences at the South End Grounds, according to one account.[20] The Four Seceders won that day, 5-1, and their defection led to a pennant for Chicago and a frustrating fourth-place Boston finish (a mere eight games over .500, landing the team in the middle of the eight-team field) in the National League's inaugural season.

The consequences of the passage of power to the owners were reflected quite clearly at the South End Grounds. By 1876 the presidency of the Boston club was vested in the hands of Nathaniel Taylor Apollonio, who was not shy about endorsing an exciting new method of protecting the security of the gate. In a postcard ad for the Washburn & Moen Manufacturing Co. of Worcester, Massachusetts, the Red Stockings president sang the praises of that company's barbed-wire fence. Installing it atop the wooden fencing "increased the size of [the] gate from $400 to $500" on the first day it was utilized.[21] Interestingly, the postcard ad also features opaque screening strung along the first-base side above the perimeter fencing in an apparent effort to thwart nonpaying spectators watching from "wildcat bleachers" on neighboring rooftops. The battle against these so-called "dead heads" was well and truly under way. It would escalate to near epic proportions in the years to come.

THREE CHEERS FOR THE TRIUMVIRS?

On-field success in the form of a pennant returned with impeccable timing to Boston in 1877, coinciding as it did with the rise of the so-called triumvirate (typically shortened to Triumvirs) of Arthur H. Soden, James B. Billings, and William H. Conant to power. According to franchise historian Harold Kaese, "Boston's threesome wielded fully as much power in the National League as their predecessors did in the Roman League and they survived to live considerably longer and happier lives."[22] At first, Boston's fans could also not have been happier, as the Triumvirs brought immediate successive pennants with them to power and secured, during the span of their collective careers, a total of eight championships.

The Triumvirs, however, had a schizophrenic quality about them. They were innovative and, upon occasion, more than willing to open their collective wallets in pursuit of glory. A prime example was the acquisition of slugger and speedster Michael "King" Kelly from Chicago in 1887 for the astounding sum of $10,000. The following season Kelly was joined by pitcher John Clarkson, a fellow refugee from Chicago. This so-called "$20,000 battery" was showcased in the magnificent brand-new grandstand built by the Triumvirs.[23]

Although team president Soden is forever remembered as the originator of the hated reserve clause, his game-changing, free-spending approach to the practice of buying big player contracts is virtually forgotten. Truth be told, this is due to the fact that the Triumvirs were notorious penny-pinchers. "Complimentary tickets were virtually unknown," and "players were encouraged to enter the stands and wrestle fans for foul balls."[24] On one occasion Soden "ripped out the press box to make room for more paying customers. Players' wives had to buy tickets to get in."[25]

Even worse, when it came to public relations, the Triumvirs were profoundly inept. For example, when team profits declined from $120,000 in 1897 to $90,000 in 1898, team treasurer Billings lamented: "We lost thirty thousand dollars last year." In 1905 president Soden told manager Fred Tenney: "We don't care where you finish so long as you don't lose money with the team."[26] Ironically, when other teams in the League did lose money, Soden frequently provided the cash to keep other teams (and the league) afloat.[27]

Nonetheless, the relationship between fans and ownership soured over time, resulting in a "sorry exit" when the team was sold in 1906.[28] Before that occurred, the South End Grounds and its surrounding environs experienced a roller-coaster ride of highs and lows.

SULLIVAN'S TOWER

Despite, or perhaps because of, their team's successes on the field, the Triumvirs were in an almost constant battle against outlaw "dead head" spectators attempting to avoid the price of admission. The rooftops of the adjoining city streets presented an economic opportunity for enterprising individuals who were amenable to hosting large groups of visitors. At the forefront of this band of hardy entrepreneurs was one Michael Sullivan, who lived behind right field on Berlin Street, near Burke Street. His "roost," more commonly known as Sullivan's Tower, was constructed level by level over time in lockstep with the efforts of the Triumvirs to block the view. Sullivan's Tower was "an architectural monstrosity"[29] that grew over time into a Boston landmark.[30] In the view of many, "Sullivan's Roost was as much a feature of a National League game in Boston as the contest itself."[31] In its day, Sullivan's Tower was as prominent and well known as the CITGO sign in modern-day Boston; in fact, one lyrically inclined fan penned a poem in tribute to the tower that was published in the *Boston Globe*.[32]

The tower had originally been built "upon the roof of a stable, but [was later] strengthened and braced and made a separate structure."[33] The passage by the state legislature of Chapter 374 of the Acts of 1885 gave new teeth to the authority of building officials to address issues of public safety in structures of all types. Thus empowered, local officials visited or "raided" (in Sullivan's view) the edifice. Efforts to declare it unsafe under the new law failed, however, and a subsidiary effort to challenge the lack of a permit for its construction met with a similar lack of success.[34] Ironically, at one point, the *Boston Globe* reported that Soden's rather poorly constructed fence "was either blown down or helped down," and that same morning a satisfied Sullivan was observed perched on his grandstand smoking a pipe.[35] Soden quickly rebuilt.

In 1887 an adventurous *Globe* reporter paid over his 15 cents and made the trek up Sullivan's Tower. The story unfolds: "At first it was an obscure staging, modestly peeping over Mr. Soden's fence. Mr. Soden's fence was raised a few feet one day, and the next day another story had been added to Mr. Sullivan's staging." And so, on (and up) it went.

At 80 feet in height, the roost was more than double the height of the surrounding buildings. The staging was "honestly built of good timber enough of which has been employed in its construction to amply satisfy the most exacting of building inspectors," and thus compared favorably to Mr. Soden's rebuilt fence, which, incredibly, was nearly as high as Mr. Sullivan's Tower, and not nearly as well constructed. "If both were let alone the roost would be standing a dozen years after the pickets of the fence had been blown to the four winds by the blasts of springtime."[36]

As time went on, and levels were added, the viewing platform of Sullivan's Tower diminished in size. Nonetheless, it is difficult to credit accounts that "as many as 500 fans climbed [Sullivan's Tower] to see a game."[37] By 1887 the most recent "addition" to the roost, while adding eight feet of height, cut the viewing platform in half from its earlier 30 feet square. About 30 spectators were present for the late-season game attended by the *Globe* reporter, in a year in which the Bostons finished fifth.

SOUTH END GROUNDS II: THE GRAND PAVILION

The end of the 1887 season brought the curtain down on the first iteration of the South End Grounds. In September the Triumvirs announced plans to build a new facility on the site at Walpole Street.[38] The initial cost estimate was reported as $25,000.[39]

The decision was long overdue. The old familiar grounds were the only site "unchanged since the beginnings of the National Association"[40] and Soden had promised to rebuild the "shoddy grounds" as far back as the conclusion of the 1883 season, when a surprising pennant run had set new attendance records.[41]

It was worth the wait. Designed by Philadelphia architect John Jerome Deery, the new grounds consisted of an elaborate two-tiered, curving grandstand, complete with a series of towers featuring conical "witches caps."[42] The Grand Pavilion, as it came to be called, "resembled a medieval castle or fairground."[43] The *Boston Herald* proclaimed it a "grand stand unequaled for beauty and convenience in the country."[44]

The grandstand was almost never built as originally conceived. Although architect Deery assured the Triumvirs during their negotiations that the cost "would not exceed $35,000," hard cost estimates were considerably higher and, upon opening, "the actual cost [was] reported at [$]70,000." Nonetheless, the

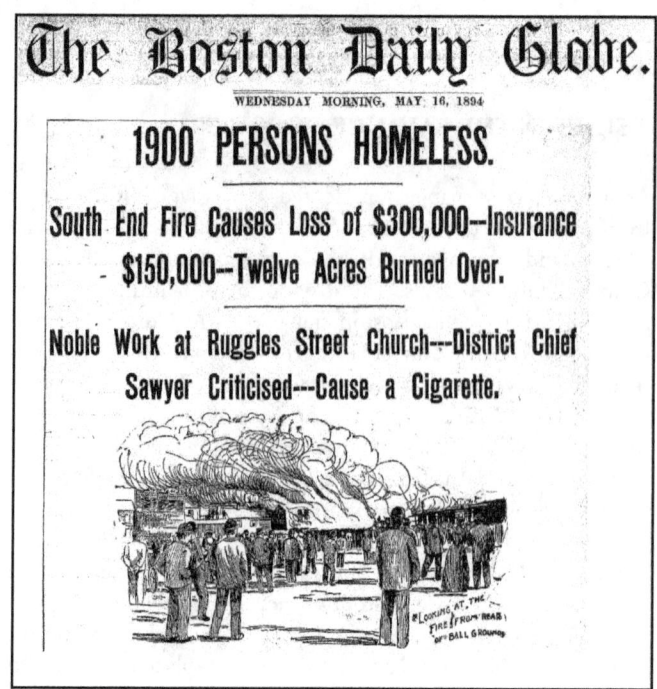

Boston Globe, May 15, 1894.

Herald reported that "the idea of abandoning the plan of having a new stand was not entertained for a moment." The question was whether to forge ahead or to build a less elaborate and less expensive structure instead. Not surprisingly, the *Herald* claimed it had influenced the outcome directly by pressuring the Triumvirs through the publication in mid-September 1887 of an elaborate description of Deery's master plan, complete with three drawings.[45] Just days prior, the *Globe* had publicized its estimate that the Triumvirs had made $100,000 during the 1887 season alone.[46]

Pressured or not, the Triumvirs went ahead despite the enormous costs. Optimism for the coming campaign abounded. In early April the *Boston Globe* published a cartoon entitled "Winning Cards" featuring a poker hand containing Clarkson, Kelly, and the new grandstand as three of the cards, predicting: "With this combination, the Boston Nine should be able to win a pennant and make a small fortune for the Triumvirs."[47]

The semicircular grandstand seated 2,800 persons. The lower tier accommodated 2,072 in nine sections labeled "A" (third base) through "I" (first base). Ample provision was made for "reporters and telegraphers" behind home plate. The home clubrooms were located on the first-base side, while the visitors were perched on the third-base side.

The balcony sat an additional 772 in seven sections.[48] Approximately 2,000 seats were also available in each of the two bleacher sections in left field and right field.[49] A *Boston Herald* account indicated that restaurants were located "on the extreme ends of the pavilion." "Toilet rooms were provided for the ladies with all the modern improvements." A concerted effort was made to keep the patrons of the grandstand separate from those sitting in the bleachers. The restaurants were configured so that both grandstand and bleacher patrons could be served "without in any way interfering with each other and neither can any patron of the outside seats obtain, by any subterfuge, admission to the pavilion through the restaurants."⁵⁰

The ballpark was visually imposing. The "witches caps" sat upon four tulip-shaped columns, two at each end of the curving grandstand.⁵¹ From Walpole Street, the full majesty of the edifice was evident. At either end sat large square brick towers with bays on the corners of their upper reaches. In between rose the central 82-foot brick and terra-cotta tower. The lower 40 feet of the tower were brick, while the upper reaches were made of terra cotta. Ticket offices were located on either side of the central tower. The Triumvirs also completed efforts to widen Walpole Street in order to improve access which provided "a good comfortable entrance" to the ballpark.⁵² "While the park was complimented on its architecture … [it was] criticized for its lack of comfort and poor sight lines."⁵³

After a lengthy season-opening road trip, Opening Day festivities on May 25, 1888, were a noteworthy affair, notwithstanding the 4-1 loss to Philadelphia. "Boston's upper crust, a big slice of the lower crust and a mighty congregation of the intermediate" were on hand.⁵⁴ Dignitaries in attendance included former Governor Ames, who thought the game was "more amusing than a session of the Legislature," and the mayors of both Boston and Cambridge, numerous other elected officials, and the spouses of the famed members of the "$20,000 battery." Nearly 15,000 fans were in attendance, more than doubling the new park's 6,800-person seating capacity. The chill east wind made some spectators miserable, "but still it was a great game – for the management."⁵⁵ The season held true to this form, with the Beaneaters finishing fourth but drawing more than an estimated 300,000 paying customers to the new grandstand, bringing smiles to the faces of the Triumvirs.⁵⁶

Those smiles truly blossomed in 1891 when second-year manager Frank Selee of Melrose, Massachusetts, and his talented roster, including Clarkson, Kelly, and pitching star Kid Nichols, took the first pennant in eight seasons home to Boston. It was the first of three consecutive pennants for the Bostons. Attendance, which had slipped as low as 147,539 in 1890, had climbed back to 193,300 by 1894.⁵⁷ While their success on the field could not be imitated, the short-lived (one year) Boston franchise of the upstart Players League had, in 1890, taken a cue from the Grand Pavilion. The club "spared no expense in planning for the new pavilion for their Congress Street Grounds" since any "baseball park [was] now incomplete without a grand pavilion," in the view of the *Boston Globe*.⁵⁸

As 1894 dawned the Triumvirs were indeed baseball's kings, ruling from their grand castle. What could possibly go wrong?

THE GREAT ROXBURY FIRE OF 1894

As visually striking as the Grand Pavilion was (despite its poor sightlines and uncomfortable seats), its tenure as Boston's home grounds was brief and its end spectacular. Constructed of wood, it is unsurprising that its end came by fire. Indeed, 1894 saw a series of fires at ballparks in Baltimore, Chicago, and Philadelphia as well as Boston. Some believed that "the fires were being set deliberately, and some went so far as to hint that Sabbatarians" were to blame, seeing in the fires a conspiracy to stop Sunday baseball, which the National League had sanctioned in 1892.⁵⁹

No such conspiracy was at work in the South End, although the precise cause of the fire on May 15, 1894, was (and perhaps remains) a matter of some dispute. The *New York Times* believed the fire was caused by "some small Roxbury boys" who had "set themselves up as rivals to Mrs. O'Leary's cow."⁶⁰ The *Boston Herald* concurred in this probability.⁶¹ The more widely accepted account, appearing in the *Boston Globe*, told of a carelessly disposed match falling upon sawdust and timbers beneath the stands.⁶²

A rotting portion of the center-field bleachers had been removed during the offseason and workers had left sawdust and debris behind, under the right-field seats.⁶³ Curiously, the detailed description of the careless smoker was provided by 14-year-old James Laskey who had, in the two nights following the fire, not returned home. He had been "bunking out … just to see how it would seem."⁶⁴ Just as remarkably, the *Boston Herald* noted that the "bleachers were boarded underneath and there was no interstices, so that it would be an impossibility for a person to drop a match or cigar to the ground."⁶⁵ Despite the somewhat questionable veracity of this youthful witness, Laskey's account was embraced by most. As a result, "all theories and suspicions of incendiarism [were] wiped from the minds" of property owners and city officials.⁶⁶

The fire began during a league match between Boston and Baltimore, in the third inning. Noticing the flames, Boston right fielder Jimmy Bannon tried to stomp out the fire with his feet. He was unsuccessful. The wind apparently shifted and "the fire roared to life."⁶⁷ The game was halted. The fire would dictate that day's winners and losers.

Within an hour, 12 acres were destroyed, 1,900 people were made homeless and the grandstand, "the handsomest in the country" in the opinion of *Sporting Life,* had been forever lost in the second worst fire in the history of the city of Boston.⁶⁸ The Triumvirs chided the Boston fire department (and police) for a slow response to the danger. Indeed, the *Boston Herald* concluded that there was one reason for such an extensive loss: "Somebody Blundered."⁶⁹ John Haggerty, the groundskeeper, tried valiantly to sound the alarm and appeared to be "the only man who acted with any sense," perhaps befitting a man whose home lay across Walpole Street from the burning grounds.⁷⁰

The franchise faced a crisis on two fronts. The immediate need to find a place to continue the still-young season was solved starting the next day by the use of the Congress Street Grounds. Located near a pier in South Boston, these were the former home grounds of the city's Players League and American Association teams.⁷¹

The second problem was more complicated. The Grand Pavilion and its associated facilities were worth $75,000, according to Triumvir Conant, but according to a list of insurance claims published two days later, the facilities were insured for only $45,000.⁷² The Triumvirs were severely criticized for underinsuring the Grand Pavilion and for the consequences that this underinsurance portended for the rebuilt ballpark.

In point of fact, the Triumvirs were hardly unique in their plight. Initial estimates (subsequently revised upward) pegged total losses from the fire at $300,000, only half of which was insured. The city of Boston lost both a school and a fire department "hose house" in the blaze. Neither the school nor the hose house was insured. According to one H.R. Turner of the Niagara Insurance Company, the fire, while "deplorable from a humanitarian standpoint," would "hardly be felt by the insurance companies," due to small tenement houses in the area. Very few "of these occupants carr[ied] any insurance." Then, in a statement callous enough to have come from one of the Triumvirs, he concluded: "The fire could not have happened in a locality more advantageous for insurance interests."[73]

One thing was certain. The long-running competition between the Triumvirs' fence and Sullivan's roost was over. "[T]he fire played no favorites. It leveled them both."[74]

While the criticism of Triumvir penny-pinching with insurance colors the subsequent discussion of the disappointing results of their rebuilding effort, a plausible case for caution could be made. In 1894 the country was in the midst of a severe recession following the Panic of 1893; indeed, employment would not return to 1891 levels until 1900. As a result of "the disruption in the financial system, some nonfinancial businesses found it difficult to obtain the funds they needed to meet payrolls and were forced to suspend operations."[75]

Thus, the Triumvirs – who after all had been willing to spend the money to construct the Grand Pavilion despite horrendous cost overruns – may have pulled back on their reconstruction efforts due to their lack of faith in the ability of *other* enterprises to keep paying (and employing) potential fans.

A more pointed – and irrefutable – criticism of ownership appeared in *Sporting Life*. The weekly chastised the Triumvirs for failing to properly police up the months-old debris in the area, and for even more egregiously failing to provide for a fire hydrant or a fire hose to be maintained on site. This "'pennywise and pound foolish' method of management" left the club unprepared for the preventable tragedy that unfolded.[76]

South End Grounds III: Is It Better to Burn Out Than to Fade Away?

The combination of a lack of insurance proceeds and a lack of confidence in the overall economy produced a rebuilt ballpark on a smaller scale than its majestic predecessor. What was impressive was that it was built at a breakneck pace. The Bostons defeated New York in the rebuilt grounds before 5,206 fans on July 20, barely two months after the fire.[77]

The new grandstand was a modest, single deck structure with "twin spires ... suggestive of the Churchill Downs racetrack"[78] and a seating capacity of 900. The number of bleacher seats was increased to compensate for this shortcoming. "[T]he only stands in the outfield were a small set of bleachers in [right field] called the pie bleachers because they were triangular shaped, like a piece of pie."[79] "Although not as impressive as the old building, the new park had more comfortable seating and better sightlines."[80] Its seating capacity was approximately 5,000.[81]

Within a year the inadequacy of the rebuilt grounds had become apparent and the push to upgrade the facility began. In 1895 two iron wings were added, bringing the grandstand's seating capacity to 2,300.[82]

The addition was timely; the Beaneaters rebounded to win consecutive pennants in 1897 and 1898, ending the three-year dominance of the Baltimore Orioles.[83] Thereafter, the team's fortunes receded and in 1906 the Triumvirs sold the team to George and John Dovey, who had partnered with a "theatrical man named John Harris."[84] It was a poor investment decision for the new owners. The Beaneaters finished last for the first time in franchise history in 1906, the South End Grounds were in disrepair – "an ugly little wart" in the words of one description – and there was a new team in town.[85]

Five years earlier, the American League's Boston team [as of the 1908 season, known as the Red Sox] had, through the maneuverings of Connie Mack, among others, taken up residence literally on the other side of the tracks. The Huntington Avenue Grounds, built in 1901, were bordered by the New York, New Haven, and Hartford Railroad on the east, a mirror image to the South End Grounds' western boundary. The American League "park was new, neat, and larger than the South End Grounds, of which the public had grown weary."[86] The price of admission was half that at the National League park. Little wonder, then, that on the date of the upstart league's inaugural home opener, they outdrew the Nationals substantially. With the benefit of at least 70 "jumpers" from the National League, by 1902 the American League was outdrawing the National League by some 300,000 fans.[87] Among the fans attracted to the new Boston team was saloonkeeper Michael "Nuf Ced" McGreevey. McGreevey (and his Royal Rooters) had originally been supporters of the Beaneaters, and a version of the slogan for his Third Base Saloon had adorned the left-field wall at the South End Grounds.[88]

The Dovey brothers' major contribution to the physical facility at Walpole Street was the construction of new outfield bleachers for the 1908 season, although they had also supplied a new scoreboard the year before.[89] A 40-foot-wide strip across the outfield was dedicated to the new seating, with an open space retained in the vicinity of the flagpole in center field. Overall seating capacity grew to 11,000.[90] When George Dovey died suddenly, his brother John ultimately took his stead, but soon the team was sold to a syndicate headed by William H. Russell. In less than a year Russell, too, was dead and the "Doves" who had briefly become the "Rustlers" were again in search of new ownership.

In December 1911 the team was sold to a new troika of leaders, headed this time by Tammany Hall hard-charger James E. Gaffney, the club's treasurer. The franchise soon acquired a new nickname – derived from the term "Sachem," which was used to describe the leader of Tammany Hall – the Braves.

Gaffney immediately set out to improve the tired South End plant.[91] Based on the recommendations of co-owner John Montgomery Ward, a series of changes to the configuration of the South End Grounds were put through. Given the permanence of its urban boundaries, the grounds had always retained its rectangular configuration. *Green Cathedrals* reports its dimensions at LF 250 (1894), LC 445, Deepest LC 450, CF 440, Right Center 440, RF 255.[92] The addition of outfield bleachers in 1908 decreased the straightaway left-field, left-center-field and center-field dimensions by between 38 and 43 feet.[93]

Ward's changes involved removing the left-field bleachers, adding another section to the grandstand and shifting the diamond toward right field to bring "the foul line over the left-field fence at a distance of 350 feet or more than 100 feet farther down the field than at [the] present time."[94] However, the 1912-1914 left-field dimension is reported in other reputable sources as 275 feet. The 350-foot distance description quoted above was provided by Tim Murnane of the *Boston Globe*, himself a former ballplayer, and has the ring of authenticity. The contemporary accounts of the *Boston Post* and the *Boston Herald* confirm that this indeed was the plan.[95]

The record nonetheless is not perfectly clear. *Sporting Life* first reported in February that "the task of changing around the old South End Ground is greater than was at first supposed" and then in March reported "that the fielding space is increased about 15 feet."[96] Murnane tells a different story. His Opening Day 1912 account reported that all 10,000-plus spectators "enjoyed the many changes made at the park, the transformation giving about 25 percent more room for hitting."[97] Finally, Harold Kaese, author of the seminal history of the franchise in Boston, also reports a 350-foot left-field distance in 1912.[98]

In right field, what was happening was indisputable. The firm of Waitt and Bond, manufacturer of the well-known Blackstone cigar, erected a modern cigar factory (reputed to be the world's largest) at 716 Columbus Avenue.[99] The factory building, which still stood in 2013, loomed over the grounds from the opposite side of the street. Kaese wrote that Jay Kirke, a powerful left-handed hitter whose fielding was less than graceful, often launched fly balls in that direction, frequently followed by the sound of tinkling broken glass. Eventually the factory was closed and a new facility opened in New Jersey.[100]

Gaffney also made numerous cosmetic improvements to the Grounds, painting the entire plant "green with crimson trimmings" so that the facility "altogether present[ed] a very attractive appearance."[101] "The walks to the field seats on either side of the field [were] relaid in blue stones" improving the park's appearance so much that "[o]ld time patrons of the park [would] not know the place. … More money [was] spent on decorations than the Triumvirs ever spent in their lives on such things."[102]

Gaffney was in a state of perpetual motion. In the fall of 1913, he acquired a parcel at Columbus Avenue and Walpole Street that would allow for the existing grandstand to be demolished, the playing field to be enlarged, and a new modern grandstand erected.[103] In mid-January of 1914, Gaffney was reported to be returning to Boston the next week to review bids for a new concrete grandstand.[104] He also installed a new scoreboard in deep center field at the start of the 1914 season.[105]

Standing on the threshold of a major financial commitment to the four-decades-old location, Gaffney hesitated. The fateful, wonderful miracle season of 1914 began.

THE END OF DAYS

It was success that ultimately spelled the end of the South End Grounds. The maniacal climb of the Miracle Braves flooded the facility beyond its capacity. By early August 1914, Red Sox president Joseph Lannin, who had only just previously acquired a small stake in the Braves franchise, put Fenway Park at the disposal of the Braves without charge.[106] Gaffney, ever the cagey politician, initially accepted only for Saturday and holiday game days.[107] Upon their return from the road, the Braves played a Labor Day morning-afternoon doubleheader against the Giants in Fenway. Nearly 75,000 attended the two games, and the Braves never returned to the South End.[108] For the 1914 season, the combination of access to Fenway and a baseball miracle for the ages lifted Braves attendance to 382,913, first in the National League.[109]

Gaffney never looked back. Frustrated by an undersized facility plagued by "clouds of smoke from the locomotives [that] interfered with the play and the comfort of the spectators,"[110] he scoured the Boston area for sites that would accommodate his vision of a playing field unencumbered by urban boundaries. He found just such a location on the site of a former golf course, bounded ironically by the same harsh neighbor – the railroad – that he had fled the South End to avoid.

When Gaffney's Braves moved from the Walpole Street facility, they were obliged to sell the grounds subject to an "iron bound agreement" that the land could not be used for baseball, an effort to block the grounds from falling into the hands of the Federal League.[111] And so the Braves left the familiar confines of the South End, despite the fact that to that time "[m]ore championships [had] been won on those old grounds than on any other in the world."[112]

Taking the grass from their infield with them, the Braves moved on. Moving to the expanse of Braves Field, however, "was like moving from a modern three bedroom apartment into a nineteenth century mansion."[113] The franchise was never the same, appearing in only one World Series in nearly four decades in Allston.

Today the site of the old South End Grounds barely countenances a memory of its storied past. The railroad is still there, in the form of the Southwest Corridor, and Columbus Avenue and the old cigar factory both have tales that they could tell. Now owned by Northeastern University, most of the field is occupied by surface parking and a garage. But if one goes just north beyond the garage, in the area where the old railroad roundhouse once stood south of Camden Street, there lies a trio of modest playing fields. Two of the fields are framed by small wooden stands and a larger array of concrete and aluminum seating sits there quietly as well, providing at least a distant echo to the cheers from the bleaching boards of the late 19th century.

NOTES

1. J.C. O'Leary, "13 Zeros Apiece," *Boston Globe*, August 12, 1914, 7.

2. In 1896, Chickering Station on Camden Street was closed. Prior to that time, the station was also heavily trafficked by baseball fans.

3. Ronald M. Selter, *Ballparks of the Deadball Era* (Jefferson, North Carolina: McFarland & Company, 2008), 20.

4. This was the date of the first National Association match. The first match between the Red Stockings and a picked nine took place on April 6 of that year and is described below.

5. Harvey Frommer, *Primitive Baseball* (New York: Atheneum, 1998), 61-68 (describing changes in the game from the mid-1870s to the new century).

6. census.gov/www/through_the_decades/fast_facts (retrieved June 15, 2013).

7. Harold Kaese, *The Boston Braves 1871-1953* (Boston: Northeastern University Press, 2004), 5, 7.

8. Sam Bass Warner, Jr., *Streetcar Suburbs, The Process of Growth in Boston (1870-1890)* (Cambridge: Harvard University Press, 1962), 41.

9. Alan E. Foulds, *Boston's Ballparks and Arenas* (Lebanon, New Hampshire: Northeastern University Press, published by the University Press of New England, 2005), 8. (The New York, New Haven, and Hartford Railroad leased the Old Colony Railroad in 1893, which by that time included the Boston and Providence Railroad.)

10. Bill Felber, *A Game of Brawl* (Lincoln: University of Nebraska Press, 2007), 60.

11. Foulds, *Boston's Ballparks and Arenas*, 8-9.

12. Michael Benson, *Ballparks of North America* (Jefferson, North Carolina: McFarland & Company, 1985), 39.

13. Benson, *Ballparks of North America*, 39.

14. Foulds, *Boston's Ballparks and Arenas*, 8-9.

15. Benson, *Ballparks of North America*, 39.

16. Foulds, *Boston's Ballparks and Arenas*, 8-9.

17. Kaese, *The Boston Braves*, 9.

18. Hulbert's bold maneuvering to establish the National League is described in detail in Michael Haupert's fine SABR biography, at sabr.org/bioproj/person/d1d420b3.

19. *Boston Globe*, May 31, 1876, 1.

20. Kaese, *The Boston Braves*, 19.

21. Michael Gershman, *Diamonds: The Evolution of the Ballpark* (Boston: Houghton Mifflin Company, 1993), 29.

22. Kaese, *The Boston Braves*, 22. The First Triumvirate of Rome was a political alliance between Gaius Julius Caesar, Marcus Licinius Crassus and Gnaeus Pompeius Magnus (Pompey the Great). Crassus died in battle approximately seven years into the alliance, whereupon Caesar and Pompey fought a civil war. The survivor, Caesar, ultimately was assassinated on the Senate floor.

23. *Sporting Life*, April 11, 1888, 1.

24. Kaese, *The Boston Braves*, 47, 23-24.

25. Benson, *Ballparks of North America*, 39.

26. Kaese, *The Boston Braves*, 113, 111.

27. Brian McKenna's SABR biography of Soden makes for entertaining reading on the extraordinary life of this Triumvir. sabr.org/bioproj/person/a1b2e0d0.

28. Besides their own miserliness and constant financial clashing with the team's human capital [the players], the Triumvirs' demise was hastened by poor on-field performance and the introduction of competition in the form of the American League in 1901.

29. Kaese, *The Boston Braves*, 68.

30. Peter Morris, *A Game of Inches: The Stories Behind the Innovations that Shaped Baseball: The Game Behind the Scenes* (Chicago: Ivan R. Dee, 2006), 429.

31. *Lewiston* (Maine) *Evening Journal*, July 29, 1914, 9.

32. *Boston Globe*, July 10, 1889, 5.

33. *Boston Globe*, August 1, 1885, 3.

34. *Boston Globe*, August 20, 1885, 4.

35. *Boston Globe*, August 19, 1887, 8.

36. *Boston Globe*, September 5, 1887, 4.

37. Donald Hubbard, *The Heavenly Twins of Boston Baseball* (Jefferson, North Carolina: McFarland & Company, 2008), 109.

38. *Boston Herald*, September 16, 1887, 5.

39. *Boston Globe*, August 19, 1887, 8.

40. Foulds, *Boston's Ballparks and Arenas*, 13.

41. Kaese, *The Boston Braves*, 37.

42. Unlike Fenway Park, which has evolved into a double-deck structure, the Grand Pavilion was designed and built as a two-tier facility, the only such structure in Boston baseball history.

43. Foulds, *Boston's Ballparks and Arenas*, 15.

44. *Boston Herald*, May 25, 1888, 5.

45. *Boston Herald*, May 25, 1888, 5.

46. *Boston Globe*, September 12, 1887, 8.

47. *Boston Globe*, April 8, 1888, 1.

48. *Boston Globe*, May 25, 1888, 5.

49. Lowry, *Green Cathedrals*, 108.

50. *Boston Herald*, May 25, 1888, 5; for a fascinating discussion with Tom Shieber of the Baseball Hall of Fame describing the Classic Ballpark Tours interactive exhibit featuring the South End Grounds, see: Paul Ferrante, "Travel Back in Time to Boston's South End Grounds," August 20, 2012, sportscollectordigest.com. Retrieved June 24, 2013.

51. Lowry, *Green Cathedrals*, 43.

52. *Boston Globe*, May 14, 1888, 8.

53. Foulds, *Boston's Ballparks and Arenas*, 15.

54. *Boston Post*, May 26, 1888, 2.

55. *Boston Globe*, May 26, 1888, 4.

56. Tim Murnane, "Hub Happenings," *Sporting Life*, October 3, 1888, 7.

57. Baseballalmanac.com/teamstats/roster. Retrieved July 15, 2013.

58. *Boston Globe*, February 23, 1890, 22. For an excellent history of the Congress Street Grounds, readers are directed to Charlie Bevis's ballpark biography of that facility, at SABR.org/bioproj/park/33169c79.

59. Gershman, *Diamonds: The Evolution of the Ballpark*, 53. Sunday baseball in Boston would remain controversial for decades.

60. *New York Times*, May 16, 1894, 1.

61. *Boston Herald*, May 16, 1914, 1.

62. "Was a Match," *Boston Globe*, May 18, 1894, 1.

63. Foulds, *Boston's Ballparks and Arenas*, 19.

64. *Boston Globe*, May 18, 1894, 1.

65. *Boston Herald*, May 17, 1894, 3.

66 *Boston Globe*, May 18, 1894, 1.

67 Paul Ferrante, "The Most Beautiful Ballpark Ever?" August 9, 2012, sportscollectordigest.com. Retrieved June 24, 2013.

68 *Sporting Life*, May 26, 1894, 3.

69 *Boston Herald*, May 16, 1894, 1.

70 *Boston Post*, May 16, 1894, 3.

71 Philip J. Lowry, *Green Cathedrals* (New York: Addison-Wesley, 1992), 108.

72 *Boston Globe*, May 18, 1894, 4.

73 *Boston Globe*, May 16, 1894, 5.

74 Kaese, *The Boston Braves*, 68.

75 Mark Carlson, "Causes of Bank Suspensions in the Panic of 1893," Federal Reserve Board (2002), federalreserve.gov/pubs/feds2002/200211pap.pdf. Retrieved June 11, 2013.

76 *Sporting Life*, May 26, 1894, 5; *Sporting Life*, June 2, 1894, 1.

77 Foulds, *Boston's Ballparks and Arenas*, 19.

78 Felber, *A Game of Brawl*, 60.

79 Selter, *Ballparks of the Deadball Era*, 18.

80 Foulds, *Boston's Ballparks and Arenas*, 19.

81 Selter, *Ballparks of the Deadball Era*, 18.

82 Tim Murnane, "Building Iron Wings," *Boston Globe*, January 13, 1895, 16.

83 Frommer, *Old Time Baseball*, 107.

84 Kaese, *The Boston Braves*, 115.

85 Kaese, *The Boston Braves*, 101, 113.

86 Kaese, *The Boston Braves*, 101.

87 Frommer, *Old Time Baseball*, 60.

88 Gershman, *Diamonds: The Evolution of the Ballpark*, 75.

89 Kaese, *The Boston Braves*, 115.

90 Tim Murnane, "Bleachers in Center Field," *Boston Globe*, January 7, 1908, 5.

91 Gaffney also once and for all provided the team with an enduring nickname. He chose the name Braves in deference to the Sachem, the symbol of his Tammany Hall. Previously, the franchise had been known as the Red Stockings, Red Caps, Rustlers, Beaneaters, and the Doves, as well as simply the Boston Nationals.

92 Lowry, *Green Cathedrals*, 109.

93 Selter, *Ballparks of the Deadball Era*, 20.

94 Tim Murnane, "Ward's Field Changes to Be Put Through," *Boston Globe*, January 20, 1912, 7. By the end of July 1912, John Montgomery Ward had sold his stake in the team, resigning as its president. Gaffney became the new president of the franchise.

95 *Boston Post*, January 20, 1912, 13; John J. Hallahan, "To Make Over South End Park," *Boston Herald*, January 20, 1912, 6.

96 *Sporting Life*, February 12, 1912, 7; March 30, 1912, 3.

97 Tim Murnane, "Boston Braves Play to 10,264," *Boston Globe*, April 12, 1912, 1.

98 Kaese, *The Boston Braves*, 129.

99 *Moody's Manual of Railroads and Corporation Securities: Volume 2* (New York: Poor's Publishing Company, 1921), 728.

100 Kaese, *The Boston Braves*, 125-6.

101 *Boston Globe*, March 26, 1912, 6.

102 *Sporting Life*, April 6, 1912, 7.

103 *Sporting Life*, October 18, 1913, 2.

104 *Sporting Life*, January 17, 1914, 14.

105 *Sporting Life*, April 25, 1914, 7.

106 *Sporting Life*, November 29, 1913, 3.

107 *Sporting Life*, August 8, 1914, 3.

108 *Sporting Life*, September 26, 1914, 8.

109 baseball-reference.com. Retrieved June 5, 2013.

110 A.H.C. Mitchell, "The World's Champions," *Sporting Life*, December 26, 1914, 3.

111 Tim Murnane, "Baseball Exit for South End Grounds," *Boston Globe*, December 20, 1914, 15.

112 *Sporting Life*, December 26, 1914, 3.

113 Kaese, *The Boston Braves*, 173.

CONGRESS STREET GROUNDS (BOSTON)

BY CHARLIE BEVIS

The Congress Street Grounds in Boston had a short but illustrious history during its seven-year existence from 1890 to 1896. In the two years that the grounds were used on a full-time basis for major-league baseball, the facility hosted pennant-winning Boston ballclubs in the 1890 Players League and the 1891 American Association. The Boston club in the National League also played 27 games there in 1894 while its burned-down South End Grounds were being rebuilt.

In early December 1889, the directors of the Boston club in the newly formed Players League signed a lease to play the team's games at a new ball grounds to be built on Congress Street extension, across the Fort Point Channel from downtown Boston. At that time, the Congress Street Grounds were located between Farnsworth Street and the tracks of the New York and New England Railroad.[1] Today, buildings at 368 and 374 Congress Street, between Thomson Place and Boston Wharf Road, stand on the land once occupied by the ball grounds.[2]

In 1889 Congress Street was the only thoroughfare that spanned the Fort Point Channel to connect the central business district of Boston with the relatively undeveloped South Boston section of the Boston waterfront, which was sparsely occupied save for a railroad yard and a few buildings. The Boston Wharf Company, which owned the land and sought to develop it, used the Congress Street Grounds as a promotional device to attract businessmen from downtown Boston to view the area and consider locating a warehouse or manufacturing facility there.

Boston Wharf Company built the Congress Street Grounds and leased it to the Boston Players' League club. This approach

Congress Street Grounds.
(Courtesy Project Ballpark.)

was consistent with the firm's general business philosophy, as espoused by company treasurer Joseph B. Russell, son of company president Charles T. Russell. "We prefer by far to make long ground leases," the younger Russell said in 1887. "It has been our custom to erect buildings for any reliable tenants, and also to sell land at reasonable terms on time."[3] Boston Wharf Company had its company architect, Morton Safford, design an ornate pavilion for the grandstand at the grounds.[4] In the Classical Revival style that he'd use for many Boston Wharf Company buildings, Safford designed a double-decker facility, 200 feet long and 62

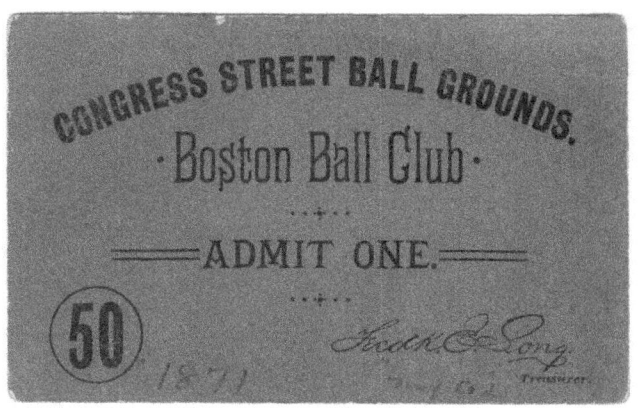

feet wide, with four entrances and two towers, each topped by a flagpole.

The grandstand was designed to seat 4,000 people, with bleachers along the left- and right-field lines to hold another 6,000.[5] After a reported 20,000 people tried to gain entrance to a preseason game on the Fast Day holiday on April 3, 1890, additional bleacher seating was erected in center field to accommodate another 5,000 people.[6] This raised the total seating capacity of the Congress Street Grounds to 15,000 spectators.

The leased grounds covered 200,000 square feet of land in a rectangle 640 feet in length (north toward the harbor) and 350 feet wide (east-west along Congress Street).[7] Home plate was located on the Congress Street side, with batters facing north toward the waterfront. The center-field fence was 385 feet from home plate, according to a contemporary *Boston Globe* report, which omitted distances to the left- and right-field fences.[8] Two sketches published by the *Globe* indicate a short distance from first and third bases to the end of the bleachers at the respective foul lines.[9] The distance from home plate along the left-field line was pegged at 250 feet by Philip Lowry in his seminal book *Green Cathedrals*.[10]

Since the grounds were a half-mile (and a 15-minute walk) from the central business district in downtown Boston, and no public transportation served the area near the grounds, private firms operated land barges to transport people from the business district to the ball grounds. Tickets to the games could be purchased downtown at two sporting-goods stores, John F. Morrill on Bromfield Street and John P. Lovell Arms Company on Cornhill Street. Businessmen could tell if a game was to be played by looking across the channel to see if flags were flying atop the grounds.

The first regular-season game at the Congress Street Grounds was played on April 19, 1890, when Boston defeated Brooklyn before a reported crowd of 10,000. The Boston team, led by the popular Mike "King" Kelly, proved to be quite an attraction, regularly outdrawing the crosstown rival National League club (if newspaper accounts can be believed). Boston captured first place in the Players League and raised the league pennant at the Congress Street Grounds on October 11, 1890, at an exhibition game with the New York club of the Players League

After the Players League dissolved following its sole season in 1890, the directors of the Boston club acquired a franchise in the American Association for the 1891 season. Boston finished in first place in that league as well, and raised the pennant during its last home game of the season on October 3, 1891. When the American Association merged with the National League before the 1892 season, the existing Boston club in the National League bought out the owners of the Boston Association club to regain its monopoly position in the Boston baseball market.

For the Boston Wharf Company and the Russell family, the two seasons of major-league baseball at the Congress Street Grounds served the business purpose. Demand rose to locate manufacturing and warehouses in the area around Congress Street, so the Boston Wharf Company could line up tenants to lease the new buildings on the drawing board. While Safford designed, and Boston Wharf Company constructed several buildings on Congress Street between 1892 and 1895, Massachusetts politicians debated where to locate a second publicly owned central train terminal (to mirror the recently built North Station) to replace the crazy-quilt system of privately owned terminals scattered south of downtown Boston.

The main athletic events staged at the Congress Street Grounds in 1892 were Gaelic football and Irish hurling matches played by young men who lived in the predominantly Irish-American neighborhood of South Boston. The New England AAU track and field championship took place at the Congress Street Grounds on June 11. One of the few baseball games at the grounds was played on September 8 by amateur teams representing the Boston and New York shoe and leather trades.

Professional baseball returned briefly to the Congress Street Grounds in 1893 when the Manchester, New Hampshire, club in the minor-league New England League transferred to Boston. The club played its first game in Boston on July 17. However, the New England League games were poorly attended, with small crowds of 400 to 600 people. After the August 4 game, the club gave up playing home games and played on the road for the remainder of the season.

In the spring of 1894, the Boston club in the National League temporarily used the Congress Street Grounds, under a one-month lease with the Boston Wharf Company, after the club's South End Grounds facility burned down on May 15.[11] Boston's groundskeeper, John Haggerty, worked the next few days to get the grounds into reasonable shape for an extended homestand beginning on May 21. Besides improving the field conditions, Haggerty had to borrow hundreds of chairs from other organizations to put in the grandstand, since the Boston Wharf Company had sold the folding chairs to the Philadelphia club.[12]

Home runs became an immediate phenomenon at the grounds, which one historian called "a long ball valhalla in its phoenix month of glory in 1894."[13] During the 27 games played in 1894 at the Congress Street Grounds, 86 home runs were stroked; the pace of more than three per game greatly exceeded the league's season-long average of less than one homer per game. Bobby Lowe hit four homers over the left-field fence in one game, on May 30, to enter the record books as the first major leaguer to hit four homers in one game, although the achievement was tainted by the short distance to the fence.

In his effort to remake the Congress Street Grounds into an acceptable playing field, Haggerty likely reoriented the field more toward Boston Harbor to shorten even more the distance from home plate to the left-field fence. Ron Selter, who re-creates ballpark dimensions by studying home-run data, city maps, newspaper sketches, and extant photographs, has estimated the distance to the left-field fence in 1894 to be 225 feet, shorter by 15 feet from his estimated distance of 240 feet in 1890 and 1891.[14]

Before the last professional baseball game at the Congress Street Grounds was played on June 20, 1894, between Boston and Baltimore, the *Baltimore Sun* decried the plethora of "fake" home runs stroked there: "The left field fence in Boston is so short that any long fly to left field sails over it … [and] would not fall within forty feet of the left field fence at Union Park [in Baltimore]."[15] Gaelic football returned as the main event at the Congress Street Grounds. One of the last baseball games was played on the grounds on the Bunker Hill Day holiday, June 17, 1895, between Holy Cross College and a team from South Boston.

Charles and Joseph Russell of the Boston Wharf Company were very politically connected (Joseph's brother William was governor of Massachusetts 1891-1894). The Russell family was able to influence the location of the new central train terminal to be at the intersection of Summer Street and Atlantic Avenue, right across Fort Point Channel from the company's land. In 1896 the Massachusetts legislature passed a law establishing Southern Union Station (now known simply as South Station) at that location and also authorized the extension of Summer Street across the channel, which conveniently connected the train station to the undeveloped land owned by the Boston Wharf Company on the other side of Fort Point Channel.

On May 23, 1896, the Congress Street Grounds were rented by a group to demonstrate a hot-air balloon ascension, which attracted 3,000 people. The *Boston Globe* wistfully noted: "The old grand stand from which so many exciting ball games have been seen was awakened by the shouts and tramping of legions of small boys, who swarmed over it like ants over the dome of their dwelling."[16] One of the last athletic events at the grounds was a Gaelic football game on June 17, 1896, between the O'Connells of South Boston and the Quinsigamonds of Worcester. The New England Firemen's Union Muster on September 23, 1896, may have been the last event held at the grounds before they were torn down.

In August 1896, the City of Boston approved the extension of A Street across Congress Street toward Boston Harbor, to traverse the land underneath the Congress Street Grounds; in 1900 this road was renamed Pittsburgh Street (now Thomson Place).[17] With heightened business prospects due to the new South Station train terminal, the Boston Wharf Company dismantled the Congress Street Grounds during the fall of 1896, constructed the A Street extension, and built warehouses on the land where the ball grounds had been located. Many of those buildings built in the 1890s still stand today, sporting a distinctive Boston Wharf Company marker to indicate their century-old heritage. These 100-year-old warehouses on the former site of the Congress Street Grounds have been remodeled into buildings that house luxury residences and upscale retail businesses, as part of the redevelopment of the Fort Point Channel area into the trendy Seaport District adjacent to the Boston Convention and Exhibition Center.[18]

NOTES

1. G.W. Bromley & Company, *Atlas of the City of Boston*, 1891, South Boston, Plate 30.
2. Boston Landmarks Commission, "The Fort Point Channel Landmark District," 2004: 47-50.
3. "Growth of the Boston Wharf Company," *Boston Globe*, June 19, 1887: 13.
4. Douglass Shand-Tucci, *Built in Boston: City and Suburb, 1800-2000* (Amherst: University of Massachusetts Press, 1999), xxiii.
5. "Congress Street Front of New Brotherhood Grand Stand," *Boston Globe*, February 23, 1890: 22.
6. "Congress Street Grounds," *Boston Globe*, April 14, 1890: 8.
7. "New Grounds of Players' League Club," *Boston Globe*, December 11, 1889: 5.
8. "Congress Street Front of New Brotherhood Grand Stand."
9. "New Grounds of Players' League Club" and "Congress Street Front of New Brotherhood Grand Stand."
10. Philip Lowry, *Green Cathedrals: The Ultimate Celebration of Major League and Negro League Ballparks* (New York: Walker & Company, 2006), 25.
11. "Grounds for the Present," *Boston Post*, May 16, 1894: 5.
12. "Philadelphia Pointers," *Sporting Life*, March 24, 1894: 3; "New England News," *Sporting Life*, April 7, 1894: 3.
13. Richard Tourangeau, "Remembering the Congress Street Grounds," *The National Pastime*, 2004: 78.
14. Correspondence with Ron Selter, July 13, 2015.
15. "Boston's Fake Home Runs," *Baltimore Sun*, June 20, 1894: 6.
16. "Small Riot: Wild Scene at Congress St. Ball Grounds," *Boston Globe*, May 24, 1896: 1.
17. *A Record of the Streets, Alleys, Places, Etc. in the City of Boston* (Boston: City of Boston, 1910), 368.
18. Thomas Palmer, "Rebuilding the Past: Transforming Old Warehouses into Luxury Condos Is More Than Cosmetics," *Boston Globe*, June 18, 2007: E1; Matthew Reed, "The Rise of the Seaport," *Boston Magazine*, online, July 2012.

GAMES

BEANEATERS START CHAMPIONSHIP RUN IN FIRST GAME IN NEW (NEW) POLO GROUNDS

APRIL 22, 1891: BOSTON BEANEATERS 4, NEW YORK GIANTS 3, AT THE POLO GROUNDS, NEW YORK

BY STEW THORNLEY

The Atlanta National League team traces its history through two previous cities and several nicknames. The franchise was a charter member of the National League in 1876, as the Red Stockings (or Reds, since Cincinnati reclaimed their original name), which also had played five seasons in the National Association prior to that, winning the last four pennants in that organization.

With some of its National Association players still on the roster, the Red Stockings of the National League continued their winning ways, taking two of the first three pennants. Boston finished first again in 1883 but then, often nicknamed the Beaneaters, went through a drought the rest of the decade.

The 1891 Boston team had hopes for improving on the 76-57 record of the previous year, which was good for only a fifth-place finish. The Beaneaters opened their quest on Wednesday, April 22, in New York in what was a new stadium for the National League.

New York also had an entry in the National League in 1876, but its team, the Mutuals, were expelled for not completing their schedule. And it really wasn't a New York team; the Mutuals played their games at the Union Grounds in the still-separate city of Brooklyn. The Union Grounds had another National League tenant in 1877, a team that had moved from Hartford, Connecticut, and retained the name Hartford Dark Blues. New York fans were understandably reluctant to support a team still identified with a city in a neighboring state, and the Hartford team disbanded after the 1877 season.

When the major leagues returned to New York, it came in the form of two teams: the Metropolitan, which played in the American Association, and a National League team that eventually adopted the nickname Giants. Both teams played on a long field to the north of Central Park that had been used for polo. The Polo Grounds, as this and other stadiums in New York became known, initially had diamonds at opposite ends, sometimes with games going on at the same time.

The Giants outlived the Metropolitan and won the World's Series in 1888.[1] However, it also marked the final games on the original Polo Grounds. Early in 1889 New York City decided to move ahead with plans to extend 111th Street, which at this point had been interrupted by the Polo Grounds between Fifth and Sixth avenues, through the site occupied by the Giants.

The Giants opened 1889 as an itinerant bunch, playing first in New Jersey and then on Staten Island before owner John B. Day found a site just off the Harlem River in the southern half of Coogan's Hollow in Manhattan, beneath the 155th Street viaduct and along Eighth Avenue. Day was concerned about confusion that might be present with fans as the team prepared for its third home of the season. He knew that New Yorkers associated the name Polo Grounds with his baseball team, so—to send an unambiguous message as to where the Giants would be headquartered—he christened the quarters the New Polo Grounds.[2]

In 1890 the National League had a neighbor in New York as a new league—the Brotherhood of Professional Base Ball Players—formed. Backers of the New York team in what became the Players' League leased the northern section of Coogan's Hollow and built a stadium, Brotherhood Park, next to the Polo Grounds.

The Players' League lasted only one season, and the Giants moved into the northern space, carrying the name Polo Grounds with them again.

The Giants prepared for the 1891 season with a final exhibition tuneup in Albany, where a new stadium brought out a large crowd, and the same happened the next day in New York.

For Opening Day, the Boston and New York players assembled at 1:00 PM at Wall Street and Broadway and "were driven to the grounds in tallyho coaches. The line of parade was crowded with people, and the players got a royal reception all along the line, and also when they appeared at the grounds."[3]

The teams did not play in a brand-new stadium—it had already been used for a season under a different name—but it was the first game with the name Polo Grounds. Attendance of between 15,000 and 20,000 was predicted, and the *New-York Daily Tribune* reported that "several wagers were made yesterday that the crowd would exceed 20,000."[4]

Although the attendance didn't reach that mark (it was 17,835), a huge crowd was on hand. Before the game, Giants who had remained with the National League team lined up on one side of the field with those who had gone to the Players' League on the other. The two sides then came together to indicate that past differences were settled and that they were one team again.

The game began at 4:00, the Giants batted first, and they took the lead as George Gore reached base on an error and later scored on a sacrifice bunt by Jim O'Rourke.

Boston tied it quickly in the first as Herman Long hit a long fly into the overflow crowd in left and made it all the way around the bases. Exactly what happened on the play is subject to the newspaper reports and rules of the time. The *New York Times* description: "Long hit the ball to deep left field amid the spectators. It was a 'blocked ball,' and before it could be handled by [pitcher Amos] Rusie in his position and sent home Long had scored. It was a close call, however." The *Boston Globe* reported, "Herman Long opened well for Boston by hitting the ball into the crowd in left field and scoring, as Rusie failed to remain in his position to receive the dead ball on the return."[5]

The play was scored as a triple by Long and an error on Rusie. Quizzed on what may have transpired on the play, John Thorn, the historian of Major League Baseball, wrote, "My guess about the 4/22/91 incident is that Long made three bases cleanly on the ball hit into the overflow crowd and that when the ball was returned to the infield Rusie was not in the box to receive it—an error that permitted Long to continue homeward."[6]

The score continued to seesaw as well as the pattern of players following a bad play with a good one—or vice versa.

The Giants took the lead in the third, with Roger Connor singling home O'Rourke, who had gotten aboard when Marty Sullivan lost his fly ball to left in the sun. Sullivan got the run back in the bottom of the fourth as he led off with a walk, stole second, and scored when Mike Tiernan dropped Billy Nash's two-out fly to right.

The game stayed tied until the ninth when Rusie grounded to short and was safe on first when Long's throw was wild. Rusie went to second on a passed ball (an error charged on the play to catcher Charlie Bennett, one of five made by the Beaneaters that day), and scored on Gore's single to left.

Gore undid the good of his hit in the bottom of the inning. Boston had two on and one out when Herman Long sent a fly to center. "Gore started after it, and to the great discomfiture of the vast throng he lost his footing and fell," reported the *Times*.[7]

The *Boston Globe* provided a different perspective: "Long came up with his long bat and hit the ball hard, but it sailed high and George Gore started to get under it, having plenty of time. He misjudged, however, and then made a muff of it, high over his head, the ball rolling along the field as Gore lay in a heap on the ground, having tangled himself up in reaching for the ball."[8]

The *New York Tribune* had a more scathing slant: "In plain English he [Gore] tried to win applause by making a difficult play out of an easy one, and his bungling caused him to make an error and lose a game in the last inning."[9]

The newspapers differed on whether Gore was charged with an error or Long credited with a triple; in either case, two runs scored to give Boston a 4-3 win. The *Boston Globe* account treated the final play as an error on Gore rather than a triple, but it appears based on the opinion of the *Globe* writer. Other reporters give Long a triple, albeit a dubious one, and it appears from them that the official scorer did not charge Gore with an error.

The pitchers were a pair of future Hall of Famers. John Clarkson of the Bridegrooms was nearing the end of his career while Amos Rusie was in the early stages of his. Both pitchers would be credited with more than 30 wins in 1891.[10] Boston won its first six games, finished 87-51, and went on to win the National League pennant for the first of three straight seasons. And five pennants in eight years.

For the remainder of their time in New York, through 1957, the Giants remained on this field. However, the wooden grandstand burned in 1911 and was rebuilt with a steel and concrete structure. The Polo Grounds name remained and is as synonymous with the National League team in New York as is the name Giants.

NOTES

1. The 1888 World's Series between the Giants and St. Louis Browns of the American Association, was set at 10 games. The fifth game, on October 20, was the final game on the original Polo Grounds. The Giants won that game and went on to win the series, six games to four. Until the Atlanta Braves closed Atlanta-Fulton County Stadium with a World Series game in 1996, the Polo Grounds on 110th Street was the only stadium to finish its history with a World's/World Series game.

2. "A New Baseball Field: The Giants Will Play Games in This City Again: Grounds Secured on the West Side of Town in a Convenient Place," *New York Times,* June 22, 1889: 2; "The Giants New Grounds: A Home for Them on Manhattan Island at Last," *New York Tribune,* June 22, 1889: 7.

3. "The Ball Is Set Rolling," *New York Daily Tribune,* April 23, 1891.

4. "To Open the Baseball Season," *New York Daily Tribune,* April 22, 1891.

5. Boston Defeats New-York: Over 17,000 Persons Witness the Opening League Game: The Giants Looked Like Winners to the Ninth Inning, but Lost by an Accident—Brooklyn Defeats Philadelphia. *New York Times,* Thursday, April 23, 1891: 2; "Grand Send Off: League Teams Begin the Battle for the Pennant: Over 17,000 People See the Game in Gotham: Boston Plays in Luck and Wins in the Ninth." *Boston Globe,* Thursday, April 23, 1891: 1.

6. Email correspondence between author and John Thorn, December 31, 2016.

7. "Boston Defeats New-York: Over 17,000 Persons Witness the Opening League Game: The Giants Looked Like Winners to the Ninth Inning, but Lost by an Accident," *New York Times,* April 23, 1891: 2.

8. "Grand Send Off: League Teams Begin the Battle for the Pennant: Over 17,000 People See the Game in Gotham: Boston Plays in Luck and Wins in the Ninth," *Boston Globe,* Thursday, April 23, 1891: 11.

9. "The Ball Is Set Rolling," *New York Daily Tribune,* April 23, 1891.

10. Clarkson is listed with a 33-19 record and Rusie a 33-20 record in 1891 by baseball-reference.com; these numbers have changed through the years. The win in the opener was the 221st of Clarkson's career (according to the baseball-reference.com accounting). Clarkson is now credited with 328 pitching victories in his career. The Thompson-Turkin baseball encyclopedia, 1963 edition, had each with 34 wins in 1891.

KID NICHOLS SHUTS OUT PHILLIES IN BEANEATERS' HOME OPENER

APRIL 27, 1891: BOSTON BEANEATERS 5, PHILADELPHIA PHILLIES 0, AT SOUTH END GROUNDS, BOSTON

BY RICHARD A. CUICCHI

In the spring of 1891, Boston Beaneaters pitcher Kid Nichols worked out with players from the Kansas City Blues team in Kansas City of the Western Association, where he had gotten his professional start in 1887 as a 17-year-old. One of the daily newspapers reported on his prediction for the 1891 season: "He says the 'bean-eaters' are going to win the pennant and then he and Herman Long will come out west for a world's championship series and show how it was done."[1]

Nichols' prophecy would turn out to be true, but his wasn't the only optimism being felt at the beginning of the season.

The *Boston Post*'s buildup of Boston's home opener on April 27 expressed hopefulness for the Beaneaters, who had swept the New York Giants in four games to start the 1891 season. New York was considered a favorite to win the pennant, so Boston gained a measure of confidence on the season's outlook from that first series. Based on those initial games, the Beaneaters were already being characterized as a hard-playing ballclub.[2]

Boston manager Frank Selee managed the Beaneaters to only a fifth-place finish in 1890, his first season with them. However, part of the new optimism for the club was also attributed to their acquisition of infielders Joe Quinn and Billy Nash and outfielder Harry Stovey in the wake of the Players' League collapse following the 1890 season.

The Beaneaters' home opener against the Philadelphia Phillies was a festive event attended by 7,559 fans, including Massachusetts Governor William Russell, Boston Mayor Nathan Matthews Jr., and numerous other city officials, as well as several military dignitaries.[3]

Selee started Nichols against the Phillies. The 21-year-old right-hander had acquired his nickname because of his youth and slender build when he began his professional career.[4] He had been discovered by Selee at Omaha, and when Selee got the job in Boston in 1890, he brought Nichols with him.[5] As a National League rookie in 1890, Nichols became one of the starters for the Beaneaters and won 27 games. In 1891 he was paired as one of Boston's primary starters with John Clarkson, a future Hall of Famer, and newcomer Harry Staley, who was acquired on May 27.

The Phillies had taken three of four games from Brooklyn to start the 1891 season. Manager Harry Wright used inexperienced right-hander John Thornton as his starting pitcher in this contest.

Boston wasted no time getting the scoring started in the bottom of the first when Herman Long singled to left and advanced to second on an unsuccessful pickoff attempt in which first baseman Ed Delahanty muffed the ball. Long scored on Harry Stovey's double to the left-field fence. Thornton snuffed out further scoring by picking Stovey off at second base and then retiring the side on a strikeout and fly out.

The Phillies attempted to mount their own rally in the top of the fourth inning. After Billy Shindle fouled out, Delahanty hit a terrific drive over third base. Sam Thompson hit a groundball to shortstop Long, who let the ball get though him in an anxious attempt to execute a double play, allowing Delahanty to advance to third. Al Myers followed with another groundball to Long, who was successful in completing the double play this time and ended the threat.

Boston added a run in the bottom of the fourth inning on a couple of Phillies fielding mistakes. Stovey got a single past first base and took second when outfielder Thompson bobbled the ball. Tommy Tucker sacrificed Stovey to third base. After Marty Sullivan grounded out to shortstop Bob Allen, Quinn hit an easy fly ball to outfielder Billy Hamilton, who dropped it, allowing Stovey to score the Beaneaters' second run.

The Phillies threatened to score again in the top of the seventh on leadoff walks to Myers and Jack Clements. But Nichols proceeded to strike out Ed Mayer, Allen, and Thornton in succession.

Boston didn't rest on its laurels, adding two more runs in the bottom of the seventh. With two outs, the Beaneaters scored on singles by Steve Brodie, Nash, and Nichols, to build a 4-0 lead.

In the bottom of the eighth inning, Stovey hit a tremendous fly into the furthermost corner in left field for a triple. According to the *Boston Post*, another foot would have put the ball "over on the railroad."[6] Sullivan's fly ball to Thompson scored Stovey.

The Phillies made one more attempt to put runs on the board in the top of the ninth inning. After Thompson grounded out, Myers hit a hard single back up the middle that narrowly missed Nichols. Clements followed with a single to left field. But then Mayer hit a groundball back to Nichols, who started a double play that squashed the potential rally and ended the game, 5-0.

Nichols pitched a solid game, yielding only five hits and three walks while striking out five. In the only three innings in which the Phillies had their best chances to score, Nichols was aided by double plays in two of the innings and helped himself in the other situation by striking out the side after allowing two baserunners. Nichols wound up winning 30 games in 1891.

The Phillies' Thornton wasn't hit that hard, but Boston's hits came in bunches. He gave up four earned runs on nine hits and didn't walk any batters. He struck out two. In its game summary the next day, the *Boston Post* declared that Thornton had pitched a respectable game, observing, "Thornton will surely be heard from later."[7] However, 1891 turned out to be the only full season in Thornton's three-year major-league career. He played for several minor-league teams before retiring from the game in 1906.

The Phillies committed four errors in the game, but only Hamilton's miscue affected the outcome.[8] Boston's Steve Brodie had one of the best defensive plays of the game when he chased down Thompson's towering fly ball and caught it running at full speed while facing the center-field fence.[9]

Boston ended the season winning 18 of its last 20 games (there was one tie), including 18 consecutive winning decisions, and overcame the Chicago Colts to capture the National League pennant even though Chicago had held a 6½-game lead on September 15. Boston would claim four more league titles during the 1890s.

Was Nichols just being braggadocious before the season in his first-place prediction, or did he perhaps have some type of premonition? In any case, the team's outstanding start to the season, including the shutout victory over the Phillies, put them on a good path that ended in winning fashion with their first National League flag since 1883.

SOURCES

In addition to the sources cited in the Notes, the author also consulted the following:

The source for all game details came from a box score and game summary in the *Boston Post*, April 28, 1891: 1-2.

Baseball-Reference.com.

Voigt, David. *The League That Failed* (Lanham, Maryland: Scarecrow Press, Inc., 1998).

NOTES

1. Richard Bogovich, *Kid Nichols: A Biography of the Hall of Fame Pitcher* (Jefferson, North Carolina: McFarland & Company, Inc., 2012), 45.

2. "Boston to Open the Season with Philadelphia Today," *Boston Post*, April 27, 1891: 8.

3. "Gov. Russell's Reception," *Boston Globe*, April 28, 1891: 1.

4. Jonathan Light, *The Cultural Encyclopedia of Baseball* (Jefferson, North Carolina: McFarland & Company, Inc., 1997), 831.

5. David Pietrusza, Matthew Silverman, and Michael Gershman, eds. *Baseball: The Biographical Encyclopedia.* (New York: Total Sports Illustrated, 2000), 506.

6. "Five Straight, Now," *Boston Post*, April 28, 1891: 2.

7. Ibid.

8. The *Boston Globe* said the Phillies committed three errors in the game.

9. "Five Straight, Now."

BEANEATERS' HOT BATS EARN SERIES SPLIT WITH COLTS

JUNE 11, 1891: BOSTON BEANEATERS 14, CHICAGO COLTS 6, AT SOUTH END GROUNDS, BOSTON

BY BILL MORTELL

The fourth-place Boston Beaneaters hosted the Chicago Colts at the South End Grounds for the finale of a four-game series on June 11, 1891. The Colts appeared to have no trouble in winning the first two games of the series, taking the opener 5-3 and the second game, the following day, by 9-7. In the third game, a sharp turn of events had the Beaneaters blanking the first-place Colts, 13-0. That win gave the Beaneaters the opportunity to gain a split in the series.

And win they did, with room to spare. The game was played in weather described by the *Chicago Tribune* as "fearfully hot." The paper commented that the 2,761 spectators "suffered considerably."[1]

The Colts named right-hander Ad Gumbert as their starting pitcher while the Beaneaters countered with another righty, Harry Staley. Gumbert went on to win 17 games in 1891, but was not at his best on this day. The Beaneaters' Staley was a worthy opponent, and a proven stalwart on the mound, in his third of four consecutive seasons of winning at least 20 games. Gumbert was a younger brother of Billy Gumbert, who pitched for Pittsburgh and Louisville from 1890 to 1893. He was also a grand-uncle of pitcher Harry Gumbert, who won 143 games in his 15-year National League career in the twentieth century.

Boston took a 3-0 lead in the bottom of the second inning. Bobby Lowe, who would three years later ensure his permanent spot in the record books by hitting four homers in a game,[2] slammed one to left to start the scoring.

The Colts tied the score in the top of the fifth inning, with two bases on balls and a home run by Jimmy Ryan.

The Beaneaters quickly responded in their half of the fifth, taking advantage of a leadoff walk to second baseman Joe Quinn, followed by errors by Cap Anson and catcher Malachi Kittridge that led to three runs and a 6-3 lead that was only the beginning. It was decidedly downhill for the Colts the rest of the game.

In the sixth Boston scored twice more on three hits, and continued its run production in the seventh with three runs coming from a combination of two hits, a walk, and three more Chicago errors. The *Tribune* told its readers, "From this on the game was devoid of interest and dragged to a close."[3]

In his seven innings, Gumbert gave up 13 hits and five walks. His relief pitcher, Pat Luby, was touched for five hits and three walks. So the Colts pitchers yielded 18 hits and eight walks in this one-sided battle. The Colts defense, or lack thereof, certainly contributed to the bad news with eight errors, including three by catcher Kittridge.

Boston's Bobby Lowe undoubtedly produced the most base hits in the game, but the scribes who reported his accomplishments did not agree on just how productive he was. Three newspapers (*Chicago Herald*, *Lower Worcester Daily*, and *Boston Journal*) wrote that Lowe had six hits in six at-bats. Three other papers (*Chicago Tribune*, *Boston Globe*, and *Boston Advertiser*) credited Lowe with five hits in six at-bats.

Tim Murnane's account in the *Globe* sheds light on Lowe's hit total for the day. In his fourth at-bat, Murnane wrote, Lowe "hit a fast one at third baseman Bill Dahlen that was sent wide of Anson. Some of the scorers gave it a hit, but it was stretching base ball rules and the *Globe* had to score it a misplay by Dahlen."[45]

Errors were frequent in the game and some of the newspapers did not agree on how many miscues actually occurred. Of six observed newspaper descriptions of the game, two papers reported eight Colt errors, three reported nine, and one reported 10 errors for the Chicagoans. They also disagreed on the number of Boston errors: one paper reported only one Boston error, two papers said two errors, and three papers scored three errors for the Beaneaters.

In the four-game series that concluded with the 14-6 win over the Colts, the Beaneaters salvaged a split. The Colts recovered from their disastrous performances of the last two games, and appeared headed toward a first-place finish at season's end. Not to be. Although the Colts held first place continuously from July 21 through September 29, they collapsed and lost their final four games of the season, allowing 50 runs in those losing efforts. The Beaneaters, not to be denied, won 25 of their final 33 games, to finish 3½ games ahead of the second-place Colts. Both teams had performed unusually well in the final two months of the season. The Colts and Beaneaters met 12 more times after June 11 game and the Colts won nine of those matches.

As for the June 11 game, the *Chicago Tribune* reported that Colts shortstop Jimmy Cooney was not at the ballpark but rather in Cranston, Rhode Island, "leading a fair maiden to the altar."[6] Jimmy, a native of Cranston, wed Ella Ann Dunham and that union resulted in four sons, two of whom (Jimmy and Johnny) went on to play major-league baseball.

By any measure, it was a subpar performance by the Chicago defense. The *Globe* said the Colts "played more like a Jim Crow team."[7] The *Chicago Herald* noted that "Chicago fielding at times was 'very yellow.'"[8] The *Boston Advertiser* commented, "Never did the Chicago team field more poorly that the one which played Bostons yesterday."[9] The *Chicago Tribune*, possibly in sympathy with the Colts, blamed pitching for the team's poor showing, not commenting on the play of the defense.

Author David Fleitz's SABR biography of Cap Anson mentions that many former Players' Leaguers hated Colts manager Anson for his attitude toward them.[10] He named Hugh Duffy and George Van Haltren as two who refused to return to Chicago, costing Anson much-needed talent. In the 1891 season, there were rumors that Boston opponents threw games to keep the pennant out of Anson's hands.

Boston went 18-1-1 in its last 20 contests. Anson wrote in his autobiography that "a conspiracy was entered into whereby New York lost enough games to Boston to give the Beaneaters the pennant."[11] Anson believed that the Giants and other rival teams cheated him out of the league championship in 1891. He didn't seem to mention the errors his team committed on June 11, however.

SOURCES

In addition to the sources cited in the Notes, the author consulted Baseball-Reference.com.

NOTES

1 "New York Even With Us," *Chicago Tribune*, June 12, 1891: 6.

2 Lowe accomplished the feat on May 30, 1894, in the second game of a morning-afternoon two-game set before a Memorial Day crowd at Boston's Congress Street Grounds. It should be noted that Lowe's home-run total for the entire season was 17, so four in a single game was a significant achievement. Lowe's afternoon heroics followed his 0-for-6 record in the morning game.

3 "New York Even."

4 T. H. Murnane, "Gumbert Was a Mark," *Boston Globe*, June 12, 1891: 5.

5

6 "New York Even."

7 Murnane.

8 "Gumbert Was a Mark," *Chicago Herald*, June 12, 1891: 7. Note: The *Chicago Herald* and *Boston Globe* pieces did indeed bear the same headline, but the stories themselves were different.

9 "Gumbert's Curves," *Boston Advertiser*, June 12, 1891: 8.

10 David Fleitz, "Cap Anson," SABR Baseball BioProject; sabr.org/bioproj/person/9b42f875.

11 Adrian Constantine Anson, *A Ball Player's Career: Being the Personal Experiences and Reminiscences of Adrian C. Anson* (Chicago: Era Publishing Co, 1900), 295.

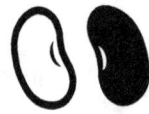

KID NICHOLS STRIKES OUT 12 AND HAS GAME-WINNING HIT

JUNE 12, 1891: BOSTON BEANEATERS 5, PITTSBURGH PIRATES 4, AT SOUTH END GROUNDS II, BOSTON

BY KEVIN LARKIN

In the history of major-league baseball, 24 pitchers have won 300 or more games. At the top of the list is Cy Young with 511 wins, and tied at 300 wins are Lefty Grove and Early Wynn. The oldest pitcher to win his 300th game was Phil Niekro, when he was 46 years old. The youngest pitcher to win his 300th game was Charles Augustus "Kid" Nichols, who won it on July 7, 1900, when he was just 30 years old.[1]

Nichols began his career on April 23, 1890, playing for the Boston Beaneaters. On June 12, 1891, he was on his way to his first 30-win season. He took the mound for the Beaneaters versus the Pittsburgh Pirates at the South End Grounds II in Boston. Boston (21-21) was in third place in the National League, 4½ games behind the first-place New York Giants. Nichols was opposed on the mound by Pirates right-hander Mark Baldwin, whose 33 wins had led the National League in 1890. That year had been the second in his own string of four consecutive 20-win seasons.

Boston batted first and sent up only three batters. Pittsburgh took a 1-0 lead in its first inning, even though Nichols ended up striking out the side.[2] (In fact, seven of Pittsburgh's first nine outs were strikeouts by Nichols.[3]) The Pirates scored their first-inning run on a hit, a passed ball, a wild throw, and a missed third strike.[4]

Boston scored a run in the second inning when third baseman Bill Nash hit a line drive that center fielder Al Maul lost sight of in the deep outfield grass.[5] By the time the ball was retrieved, Nash had crossed the plate with a home run.[6]

The Pirates might have added one on the second but with runners on first and second and one out, third baseman Doggie Miller tried to steal third. He beat the throw but over slid the bag and was tagged out.

The Beaneaters scored another run in the third inning. Catcher Charlie Ganzel led off with a single. Nichols bunted for a single, putting runners at first and second with no outs. Pittsburgh first baseman Jake Beckley picked up Herman Long's bunt and threw to shortstop Charlie Reilly, covering second. Reilly was upended by Nichols and Ganzel crossed the plate. However, Ganzel was sent back to third base and Nichols was called out. Reilly was out of the game and was replaced by Jocko Fields. Harry Stovey, the next batter, singled and Ganzel scored.

In the fourth inning, Boston added another run for a 3-1 lead when Tommy Tucker walked, stole second base, and was driven in by Ganzel's single.[7] There was no scoring the next two innings, but in the seventh Boston added a fourth run when Ganzel led off with a triple and scored on Nichols' fly ball.

The eighth inning almost proved fatal to the Beaneaters. Nichols hit leadoff batter Tun Berger, and when a groundball by Fields bounced off second baseman Joe Quinn's foot and bounded into right field, there were men on second and third base with no outs. Nichols struck out pitcher Baldwin on three pitches, but right fielder Fred Carroll hit a double to center field that scored both runners and made it a one-run game, 4-3.

The next batter, Pirates first baseman Jake Beckley, had struck out three times, but this time struck a groundball between shortstop and third base that neither shortstop Herman Long nor third baseman Billy Nash could get to. That ball scored Carroll with the run that tied the game at 4-4.

The Beaneaters came to bat in the top of the ninth with the score still tied. Tommy Tucker hit a fly ball to center fielder Carroll. Carroll muffed the ball, and Tucker reached second. Shortstop Fields bobbled Ganzel's grounder but Tucker, who broke late for the plate, was trying easily thrown out trying to score. Up came Nichols, who had figured in scoring opportunities earlier for the Beaneaters. Nichols was quickly down two strikes, but then hit a groundball past the shortstop to give the Beaneaters a 5-4 lead.

For Pittsburgh in the bottom of the ninth, Berger reached first, but Nichols added two more strikeouts to his total and sealed the victory.

Each pitcher had allowed seven hits, but Nichols had struck out 12 while Baldwin had struck out none.

Nichols ended the season with 30 victories and 17 defeats. It was the first of seven seasons in which he won 30 or more games.

Pitcher Nichols and catcher were the stars of the win for the Beaneaters. Ganzel had three hits, scored two runs, and drove in one. Nichols struck out 12, including Jake Beckley three times and Pete Browning twice. Nichols also drove in what proved to be the winning run in the ninth inning.

The two clubs featured a total of five players or managers who would be elected to the Baseball Hall of Fame. For the Pirates, catcher Connie Mack was elected as a manager in 1937, first baseman Jake Beckley was elected in 1971, and outfielder Ned Hanlon was elected as a manger in 1996. For the Beaneaters there was the pitching duo of Nichols (elected in 1949) and John Clarkson (elected in 1963), both of whom won over 300 games (Nichols with 361, and Clarkson with 328).[8]

The Beaneaters, managed by Frank Selee, were tough all year, and finished the season in first place with a record of 87 wins and 51 losses. The Pirates, at 55-80, wound up in last place, 30½ games behind the Beaneaters.

NOTES

1   baseball-almanac.com.
2   *Pittsburgh Daily Post*, "So Near and Yet So Far, After Winning the Game in the Eighth, Carroll Loses It in the Ninth," June 13, 1891: 6.
3   *Boston Post*, "Boston League Wins," June 13, 1891: 8.
4   *Pittsburgh Daily Post*.
5   T.H. Murnane, "Nichols Had His Inning," *Boston Globe*, June 13, 1891: 5.
6   Ibid.
7   Ibid.
8   Baseballhall.org.

AUGUST 17, 1891: KID NICHOLS ONE-HITS THE GIANTS

BOSTON BEANEATERS 3, NEW YORK GIANTS 0, AT THE POLO GROUNDS, NEW YORK

BY BILL LAMB

With both clubs vying for the National League pennant lead and their respective staff aces scheduled for duty, the August 17 match between the Boston Beaneaters and the New York Giants shaped up to be an exciting, hard-fought contest. Monday-morning newspapers showed the 1891 season standings tightly bunched, with the Chicago White Stockings (56-39) clinging to a one-game lead over Boston (53-38) and New York (50-36) another half-game back. To get his club off on the right foot in the three-game series at the Polo Grounds, Beaneaters manager Frank Selee would lead with right-hander Charles "Kid" Nichols, a beardless youngster backing up the previous year's 27-win rookie season with a standout sophomore campaign. New York, nominally managed by Jim Mutrie but actually led by captain-catcher Buck Ewing, would counter with burly fireballer Amos Rusie, another right-hander and arguably the circuit's most intimidating hurler.

As was their right, the homestanding Giants elected to bat first, and some of the 3,776 fans in attendance had barely settled into their seats when Nichols set the Giants down in order to begin the action. Rusie followed suit in the bottom of the first. The game's pattern had now been established. Over the initial five innings, Rusie dominated Beaneaters batsmen, allowing only two hits while fanning eight. But Nichols was even better, matching Rusie strikeout-for-strikeout and holding the Giants hitless. Having shown his fastball early, Nichols began tantalizing New York hitters with off-the-plate breaking pitches. And much to the disgust of the local press corps, the Giants chased them. "They hit at balls continually several feet wide of the plate," complained the *New York Times*,[1] while a wire-service account of the game observed that "The Giants had the blind staggers and struck at balls which they could not have reached with a telephone pole."[2]

After Nichols had posted his seventh straight hitless inning, a scoreless deadlock was broken in the Boston half of the frame. Rusie contributed to his own eventual downfall by walking leadoff batter Billy Nash. Steve Brodie then legged out a slow roller to short. With two on and no outs, Tommy Tucker sent a bounder to the right of Giants first baseman Roger Connor, who knocked the ball down and then tossed it to Rusie covering first as Tucker sped for the bag. A close call by lone umpire Tim Hurst went in Boston's favor, loading the bases.[3] The game outcome turned on a hot shot hit by Joe Quinn that went between Connor's legs into right field. Two runs scored on the error while Tucker took third. He then scored the inning's final tally on a sacrifice bunt by catcher Charlie Bennett.

Suddenly down three runs, New York attempted to rally. But all the Giants could manage was breaking up Nichols' no-hit bid. An eighth-inning single "of scratch order"[4] by Connor spared New York that indignity. Otherwise, Nichols' pitching had been flawless. In the course of a 3-0 one-hitter in which no Giants baserunner got as far as second base, he had struck out nine or 10 enemy batters, while walking none.[5] In the eyes of the Boston press, Kid had "pitched a phenomenal game,"[6] while even the partisan *New York Herald* acknowledged that Nichols had staged "a magnificent exhibition of box work."[7]

The umpire, Tim Hurst, was officiating in the first year of a 16-year major-league career. The game was completed in 1 hour and 33 minutes, according to the box score published in the next day's *Boston Globe*. One oddity of the game: Boston shortstop Herman Long and left fielder Bobby Lowe each played the game for Boston wearing Giants uniforms. The *Globe* reported, "Their baggage had not been delivered at their hotel before they left, and they had to borrow odds and ends."[8]

The clubs split the remaining two games of the series but were soon headed in opposite directions. Notwithstanding a yeoman's effort by Amos Rusie (33-20 and 500⅓ innings pitched), the Giants faded to a distant third-place finish, 13 games out. Meanwhile, Boston, behind the pitching of 30-game winner Kid Nichols, overtook Chicago for the first of three consecutive National League titles.

For Nichols, it was also the first of seven seasons in which he won 30 or more games; in 1949 he was named to the National Baseball Hall of Fame. Rusie, too, was inducted into the Hall of Fame, in 1977.

NOTES

1 *New York Times,* August 18, 1891. The *New York Tribune* lamented that "Nichols was throwing to men whose common sense seemed to have been left at home, and whose 'lamps' needed burnishing."

2 See, e.g., the *Cleveland Plain Dealer,* August 18, 1891.

3 The scoring decision on the play was not uniform. Next-day box scores published in the *Boston Daily Advertiser, Boston Journal,* and *New York Herald* credited Tucker with a base hit [as did the box score in *Sporting Life,* August 22, 1891]. Boxes in the *Cleveland Plain Dealer, New York Times, New York Tribune,* and *Washington Post* charged Connor with an error, as did *The Sporting News,* August 22, 1891

4 *New York Times,* August 18, 1891.

5 The box scores published in the *Boston Daily Advertiser, Boston Globe, New York Herald,* and *Sporting Life* all showed nine strikeouts, while those published in the *Boston Journal, Cleveland Plain Dealer, New York Times, New York Tribune, The Sporting News,* and *Washington Post* all showed 10.

6 *Boston Daily Advertiser,* August 18, 1891.

7 *New York Herald,* August 18, 1891.

8 "With a Solitary Hit," *Boston Globe,* August 18, 1891: 5.

A MEETING WITH GRAMPA

SEPTEMBER 4, 1891: CHICAGO COLTS 5, BOSTON BEANEATERS 3, AT WEST SIDE PARK, CHICAGO

BY ROB NEE

As the calendar turned to September in 1891, the Beaneaters headed to Chicago for a series with the Colts. This matchup between the league's top two teams produced one of the most memorable games of the season thanks to Chicago's legendary captain. Boston arrived trailing the Colts in the standings by six games and with other concerns as well. Herman Long would play the first game against the advice of his physician, having been diagnosed with bronchitis just days before in Cincinnati.[1] Mike Kelly also entered the series with an injured right hand. He attempted to play through it. However, the first ball hit to him in game one caused him to reinjure the hand and miss the rest of the contest as well as the entirety of game two.[2]

After falling to the Colts in the first game of the series thanks to some poor pitching by John Clarkson, the teams met again on September 4 in front of 3,500 fans at West Side Park.[3] The *Boston Globe* described the weather as "entirely too cold for comfort."[4] However, it was the antics of Cap Anson that made this contest of particular note. Anson played the entire game dressed as an old man complete with "pale horse-tail whiskers and bald wig."[5] The *Globe* wrote, "Anson created a sensation by appearing on the field with flowing whiskers of snowy whiteness and long hair. He played the game throughout in this disguise and the crowd seemed to enjoy the sight."[6] It's not as if baseball's all-time leader in hits, runs, and RBIs since 1886 would need to go out of his way to draw attention to himself. Rather, Anson's behavior was in reaction to the press coverage he would routinely get. For some time, newspapers had been focusing on Anson's long experience when referring to his play. As Leonard Washburne noted in the *Daily Inter-Ocean*, "It seems that some of the newspapers have fallen into the habit of calling Mr. Anson "Old Anse" and "Uncle" and "Grand pa."[7] The newspaper went on to add that the press had even gone so far as to "have printed pictures of him that look like the Santa Claus in a dry goods window."[8] Anson decided to have some fun with the idea. Washburne described the scene at West Side Park that day:

"It was a day off for that merry rogue Mr. Anson. He did not make a hit. He just fooled around and fondled his whiskers and conversed laughingly with the people on the bleachers. He pranced up and down in the box and dared Mr. Nichols to wipe off his beard. His eyes twinkled like stars in the frosty night and when there was no one else handy to talk to he prattled to himself."[9]

The game itself pitted Kid Nichols, who had never beaten the Colts, against Vinegar Tom Vickery, and although Anson did not get a hit, he did figure prominently in several key plays. Both pitchers prevented any scoring until Chicago broke through in the eighth inning.

Boston was unable to capitalize on two scoring opportunities early in the game. The first of these occurred in the third. With one out, Herman Long doubled off the left-field wall. Harry Stovey then hit a ball to Fred Pfeffer at second base that was mishandled. Stovey was able to reach first safely on the play.

Both Stovey and Long were thrown out in a botched double-steal attempt. Schriver threw out Stovey at second and an alert Pfeffer then threw home to get Long at the plate for the second out, and essentially ended the threat.

The fourth inning provided another opportunity for Boston to break through. Bobby Lowe led off by doubling along the left-field foul line. Billy Nash attempted a sacrifice back toward Vickery, whose throw to third was late and both runners were safe. Nash later took second on a passed ball. This set up one of the pivotal plays of the game which involved Chicago's disguised captain. Tommy Tucker came to the plate with one out and runners at second and third. He hit a grounder "toward Grampa's waving beard"[10] at first base. Old Man Anson was able to tag out Tucker and throw home in time to get Lowe at the plate for a double play. A second chance had been squandered.

Boston, having failed to take advantage of a pair of doubles in the third and fourth innings, depended upon Nichols to hold Chicago in check. He was successful up until the eighth. The Colts' bats came to life in the top of that inning. Fred Pfeffer started off with a single past Joe Quinn. Vickery then sacrificed him to second. Pop Schriver drove a ball to right field that was handled by Steve Brodie for the second out. Jimmy Ryan then stepped to the plate and drew a walk, giving the Colts their second baserunner. This brought up Walt Wilmot, who took the first pitch from Nichols for a strike and missed the second. Things looked manageable for Boston with two outs and two strikes on the batter. However, Wilmot smacked the third offering over the South Wall in left field. The Colts now led 3-0 and weren't done yet. Bill Dahlen followed Wilmot's blast with a single past Tucker at first and proceeded to steal second base. The whiskered Anson then came up and flied to center for what should have been the third out. However, Bobby Lowe "got sun in his eyes"[11] and muffed the play, allowing Dahlen to come around and score another run for Chicago to make it 4-0. Nichols then got Cliff Carroll to fly out to Stovey in left field to end the threat.

The Colts added to their lead when they returned to bat in the ninth. Jimmy Cooney led off by hitting a ball to Stovey in left field that was muffed. He was able to make it to second before the ball made it back in. Pfeffer sacrificed Cooney to third and Vickery struck out to make two outs. Schriver came up next and hit a ball into center field that scored Cooney and made the score 5-0. Nichols then struck out Ryan for the third out.

The Beaneaters came to the plate in the ninth needing five runs. Bobby Lowe got them off to a good start by singling up the middle. Billy Nash followed suit with single to left. Steve Brodie then came up and was able to force Pfeffer to take an out at first and allow the baserunners to advance one bag. Tucker then hit a triple to center field scoring both Lowe and Nash. Boston now trailed 5-2. Joe Quinn then grounded to Cooney which allowed Tucker to come home from third. It was now 5-3. However, Kid Nichols struck out to end the game, and Boston's rally fell short by a whisker … or two.

The Beaneaters were ultimately undone by their failure to take advantage of early opportunities and timely hitting on the part of the Colts. The *Boston Globe* summarized that "Chicago won by opportune batting and two damaging muffs by Stovey."[12] And as important as the result would prove to the pennant chase, Washburne was correct to observe that "Mr. Anson's whiskers dwarfed the game."[13]

SOURCES

In addition to sources listed in the Notes, the author also used the following for background information:

Fleitz, David. "Cap Anson," SABR BioProject. sabr.org/bioproj/person/9b42f875.

"Hits Were Scarce: Boston Wins From Chicago by Narrow Margin," *Boston Globe*, September 6, 1891: 4.

"Kelly's Popcorn: Presented to Him on the Field of Battle," *Boston Globe*, September 1, 1891: 5.

"Bostons Couldn't Win; Cincinnati Reds Left Them Far Behind," *Boston Globe*, September 2, 1891: 5.

"In McGinty's Class: As He of Song, so Bostons Went Down," *Boston Globe*, September 3, 1891: 5.

Spatz, Lyle. *Bad Bill Dahlen: The Rollicking Life and Times of an Early Baseball Star* (Jefferson, North Carolina: McFarland & Co., 2004).

NOTES

1. "Downed Again: Boston Leaguers Fall Easy Prey to Colts," *Boston Globe*, September 4, 1891: 5.
2. Ibid.
3. "Bostons Not in It: Anson's 'Colt's' Easily Down Them," *Boston Globe*, September 5, 1891: 5.
4. Ibid.
5. "His White Whiskers. Grampa Looking Young Again," *Chicago Herald*, September 5, 1891: 7.
6. "Downed Again."
7. Leonard Washburne, "Boston Falls Again. Another Victory Securely Packed and Labeled by Uncle," *Daily Inter-Ocean*, September 5, 1891: 2.
8. Ibid.
9. Ibid.
10. "His White Whiskers."
11. "Boston Falls Again."
12. "Bostons Not in It."
13. "Boston Falls Again."

SEPTEMBER 28–30, 1891: THE CLOUDED FINISH: BEANEATERS TAKE OVER FIRST PLACE

BY LYLE SPATZ

When first-place Chicago hosted second-place Boston on September 4, 1891, the Colts' lead over the Beaneaters was six games. Colts manager Cap Anson was so confident of winning the pennant that he entertained the crowd by wearing a white flowing beard throughout the game. The Colts' 5–3 victory increased the lead to seven games.

Ten days later it was down to 4½ games as the Colts prepared to face the Beaneaters in a final three-game series between the contenders. Chicago won the first two games, raising the lead back to 6½ games. A reporter at the *Chicago Daily Tribune* told his readers, "The good captain's men are champions and no mistake."[1]

Moreover, the scheduled pitchers in the third game indicated another likely win for Chicago. For Frank Selee's Beaneaters it was Charles "Kid" Nichols, 0–9 lifetime against Chicago; and for Anson's Colts it was Bill Hutchinson, already with eight wins against Boston this season.

But strong pitching by Nichols, together with seven Colts errors led to a Beaneaters victory. Following a tie, the challengers embarked on a 17-game winning streak that would not end until the final day of the season. Boston's 16th consecutive victory, on October 1 against Philadelphia, clinched the pennant.

Fifteen of Boston's 18 wins were against Philadelphia, Brooklyn, and New York, the league's other Eastern teams. Boston's spectacular late-season success against its regional neighbors led to a serious postseason accusation by Chicago president James Hart. Hart charged that the Eastern teams had conspired to ensure that Boston, not Chicago, won the pennant. He alleged that players in the National League as a whole did not want the Colts, a team with the league's lowest payroll, to be its champion.

Additionally, Hart believed that resentment against Anson still existed for his opposition to the Brotherhood-inspired Players League, many of whose former members were back playing in the National League. Adding to the mix was the animosity Giants manager Jim Mutrie harbored toward Anson over his refusal to play a postponed contest on an open date of the Giants' choice.

Hart pointed to several instances during the streak where suspect fielding plays contributed to Boston victories. He focused mainly on the Beaneaters' five games against the Giants on September 28–30. The series took place at Boston's South End Grounds and included back-to-back doubleheaders. The Beaneaters, of course, won all five games, the first four by huge margins: 11–3, 13–8, 11–3, 16–5, and 5–3.

Hart pointed out the Giants had arrived in Boston for this very crucial series without their two best pitchers, Amos Rusie and John Ewing. Also absent were first baseman Roger Connor and second baseman Danny Richardson. And, Hart added, those Giants who played did so in such a casual manner that *Sporting*

Life's comment that "the New Yorks beat all records for indifferent and rocky playing," was typical of the reaction by the press.[2]

The New York papers were normally fully supportive of the that the Giants openly stated they would do whatever was necessary to see that Boston won the pennant.[4]

Despite the seemingly overwhelming evidence to the contrary, owners Arthur Soden of Boston and John Day of New York denied any wrongdoing, and the league dismissed all charges.[5] However, to this day both Boston's 17-game winning streak and its 1891 championship remain clouded with suspicion.[6]

This essay was originally published in Inventing Baseball: The 100 Greatest Games of the 19th Century *(2013), edited by Bill Felber.*

The 1891 stretch run

Date	Boston	Chicago	Difference
Sept. 16	Chicago 7-2	@ Boston 2-7	Chicago 5½
Sept. 17	Pittsburgh 7-7	@ New York 1-3	Chicago 5
Sept. 18	Pittsburgh 9-3	@ New York 3-9	Chicago 4
Sept. 19	Pittsburgh 11-3	@ New York 0-8	
		Pittsburgh 11-2	Chicago 2½
Sept. 21	Brooklyn 6-1	@ Cincinnati 5-4	Chicago 2½
Sept. 22	Brooklyn 3-0	@ Cincinnati 4-1	Chicago 2½
Sept. 23	Brooklyn 5-1	@ Cincinnati 9-0	
		Brooklyn 9-2	Chicago 2
Sept. 24	Philadelphia 5-2	Pittsburgh 7-4	Chicago 2
Sept. 25	Philadelphia 6-3	Pittsburgh 4-4	
		(forfeit to Chi)	Chicago 2
Sept. 26	Philadelphia 8-6	Pittsburgh 6-6	Chicago 1½
Sept. 28	New York 11-3	@ Cleveland 2-4	Chicago ½
Sept. 29	New York 13-8	@ Cleveland 14-13	
		New York 11-3	Tied
Sept. 30	New York 16-5	@ Cleveland 5-12	
		New York 5-3	Boston 1½
Oct. 1	@ Philadelphia 6-1	Cincinnati 1-6	Boston 2½*
Oct. 2	@ Philadelphia 5-3	Cincinnati 16-17	Boston 3½
Oct. 3	@ Philadelphia 3-5	Cincinnati 9-15	Boston 3½

*Clinched pennant

On November 11 the league held a hearing at the Fifth Avenue Hotel in New York to consider Hart's charges. Hart offered two more alleged items of testimony in addition to the previous evidence presented. He claimed that 10 days before the Boston-New York series, umpire Jack McQuaid had told the Chicago players that the Beaneaters would sweep the series. And, Hart added, several Cincinnati players had told certain Colts players

NOTES

1. *Chicago Daily Tribune*, September 16, 1891.
2. *Sporting Life*, October 3, 1891: 3.
3. *New York Evening Telegram*, September 30, 1891.
4. *Chicago Daily Tribune*, November 12, 1891.
5. Day was allowed to be present at the entire meeting, while Hart was allowed in only to testify.
6. For a full discussion of Boston's winning streak and the controversy it engendered, see Robert L. Tiemann's "The Forgotten Winning Streak of 1891" in SABR's 1989 *Baseball Research Journal*: 2-5.

BEANEATERS CLINCH PENNANT AMID LEAGUE CONTROVERSY

OCTOBER 1, 1891: BOSTON BEANEATERS 6, PHILADELPHIA PHILLIES 1, AT PHILADELPHIA BASEBALL GROUNDS

BY RICHARD A. CUICCHI

The Boston Beaneaters made a remarkable run in September 1891 to overtake the Chicago Colts, and they ultimately clinched the National League pennant on October 1 amid Chicago's protests that Boston had gained an unfair advantage with the help of other teams in the league.

The Colts had held the league lead for most of the season, never more than 4½ games behind when they weren't in first place. The team was led by Cap Anson, who had been the player-manager of the franchise since 1879, with five National League pennants to his credit.[1]

The Beaneaters went on a 16-game winning streak that started on September 16 when they were 6½ games out of first place behind the Colts. (During the streak there was a tie game on September 17.) Boston took sole possession of first place on September 30. Then on October 1 the Beaneaters, 1½ games ahead of second-place Chicago, defeated the Philadelphia Phillies, 6-1. With only two games left in the season, the win clinched their first pennant since 1883.

Philadelphia, managed by Harry Wright, was 17½ games behind Boston when the teams faced off on October 1. The Phillies boasted an outfield of Sam Thompson, Ed Delahanty, and Billy Hamilton, all future Hall of Famers. Twenty-four-year-old Kid Gleason was their best pitcher. (He would become a full-time infielder later in his career.) However, left-hander Duke Esper drew the starting pitcher assignment against the Beaneaters.

Boston's manager was Frank Selee, who was in his second season at the helm. He gave the ball to 29-year-old veteran John Clarkson, a control specialist who was the staff's ace.

The *Boston Globe* reported that the contest was played before 1,000 fans at the Philadelphia Baseball Grounds. It was the first of a three-game series to end the season.

Neither team was able to push across runs in the first three innings. One of the highlights of the game was Boston's five double plays, with shortstop Herman Long involved in all of them. Two of the twin killings occurred in the first and second innings.

In the top of the fourth inning, Boston broke the scoreless tie with four runs. Billy Nash led off with a single and scored on Tommy Tucker's triple. Joe Quinn grounded out to shortstop Bob Allen, who was able to hold Tucker at third base.

Charlie Bennett drew a walk and Clarkson reached first base on a third strike muffed by catcher Jack Clements. Long hit a sharp grounder to Allen, who misplayed the ball, and Tucker scored the second run. Harry Stovey's single to right field scored Clarkson and Long. Charlie Ganzel ended the inning with an out to Allen.

In the bottom of the fourth, Philadelphia mustered its only run of the game when Delahanty reached base on first baseman Tucker's error on a throw by Long. After stealing second base, Delahanty scored on Al Myers' hit.

Long aided the Beaneaters' defensive efforts with his third double play in the fifth inning.

Boston scored two more runs in the top of the sixth, facilitated by two Phillies errors. With Bobby Lowe and Stovey on base, Ganzel delivered a two-run single.

Long participated in two more double plays in the sixth and seventh innings. The game was called at the end of the seventh due to darkness with a final score of 6-1.

For just a seven-inning affair, the game was sloppily played, as Boston issued six walks and committed three errors, while the Phillies accounted for six walks and four errors. Boston's five double plays and the Phillies' errors were key factors in the final score.

Clarkson went the distance for Boston, giving up six hits in recording his 33rd win of the season. He went on to record a career 328-178 won-lost record, which earned him a bronze plaque in the National Baseball Hall of Fame.

Esper yielded only six hits but was plagued by his teammates' four errors in the two innings Boston scored its runs. His record for the season ended at 20-15.

The Beaneaters' victory clinched their first of three consecutive pennants. They captured five league championships during the decade under Selee.

The second-place Chicago club suffered a huge disappointment as the season concluded. They had played superbly from July through September, losing only nine games each month, while winning 17 in July and 16 in both August and September. The Colts were in first place from July 21 through September 29. However, their season came down to their final four games, all of which they lost. They wound up 3½ games back of Boston.

Chicago had bitter feelings toward Boston about how the Beaneaters won the pennant. Chicago's ownership contended that the Eastern clubs in the league colluded with Boston to allow the Beaneaters to win the pennant.[2] They believed there was jealousy of the Chicago team and a conspiracy by former players of the ill-fated Players' League in 1890 to undermine Anson's drive for the pennant.[3]

Chicago President Jim Hart and Anson were so convinced of collusion that they sent a telegram to National League President Nicholas Young requesting proof that there was consent by two-thirds of the teams in the league for Boston to play doubleheaders with Pittsburgh on September 19, Brooklyn on September 23, and New York on September 29 and 30. (Boston won all eight of those games.) Chicago asserted that Boston scheduled the doubleheaders toward the end of the season to make up for previously postponed games, thereby providing opportunities to collect additional wins. Chicago hadn't taken the same approach; at the end of the season, Boston had indeed played three more games than Chicago. Chicago believed Boston independently arranged the makeup games with its opponents. Chicago's ownership wanted those extra games voided if the required leaguewide consent wasn't obtained. However, Young said he had no authority to declare any game voided and the teams' presidents would have the final say. The Cleveland club later reported that it had given consent for the doubleheaders in question and believed the other clubs would reply similarly.[4]

Chicago further claimed that the New York team had manipulated its pitching assignments, holding back its best pitchers, in games with Boston. It was said that Cleveland was inspired by promise of a reward from Boston should the Beaneaters defeat Chicago in their final series.[5]

In the end the league took no action against Boston or other teams, and nothing ever came of Chicago's assertions. However, reactions in several newspapers across the country indicated a belief that the New York club had truly been a culprit in the situation, and thus baseball's integrity had been damaged.[6]

Anson maintained for the rest of his life that he was unfairly targeted by former players of the Players' League who obstructed his chances of winning the National League championship in 1891.

SOURCES

In addition to the sources cited in the Notes, the author consulted the following:

Baseball-Reference.com.

"Still They Win: Boston Getting a Firmer Hold on Pennant," *Boston Globe*, October 2, 1891: 5. (All game play-by-play details and box-score information were obtained from this source.)

NOTES

1 The Chicago franchise was named the White Stockings from 1876 to 1889. Beginning in 1890 they became the Colts and eventually the Cubs in 1902.

2 "Bowed Down With Sorrow: The Chicago Team Sorely Aggrieved at the Loss of the Pennant," *Chicago Tribune*, October 2, 1891: 6.

3 When National League players jumped to the rival Players' League formed in 1890, Anson was one of their vocal critics. His role in squashing the new league angered many of his former players, and this carried over into the 1891 season.

4 "Another Pennant: It Is Assured to the Boston Leaguers," *Boston Daily Advertiser*, October 2, 1891.

5 "Plot Against Chicago," *Chicago Tribune*, October 1, 1891: 6.

6 "The Soiled Pennant," *Chicago Tribune*, October 4, 1891: 13.

BEANEATERS WIN 18TH CONSECUTIVE GAME IN PENNANT RUN

OCTOBER 2, 1891: BOSTON BEANEATERS 5, PHILADELPHIA PHILLIES 3, AT PHILADELPHIA BASEBALL GROUNDS

BY RICHARD A. CUICCHI

On the heels of clinching the National League pennant the day before, the Boston Beaneaters defeated the Philadelphia Phillies on October 2, recording a team-record 18th consecutive win on the back of star hurler Kid Nichols.[1] However, their league title came under a cloud of suspicion with Boston being the benefactor of alleged thrown games by the New York Giants during the preceding series, on September 28-30.

The Chicago Colts looked like certain pennant winners going into September. They led Boston in mid-September by 6½ games with 16 games remaining. However, on the 16th Boston began a remarkable stretch of 18 consecutive victories, not losing until their last game of the season. (The streak excluded a tie with Pittsburgh on September 17.) At the same time Chicago went 6-9 (not including a tie), with one of the wins coming on a forfeit by Pittsburgh.[2]

When the Beaneaters swept the New York Giants in a five-game series September 28-30 (including two doubleheaders), they took the league lead from Chicago and never relinquished it. Upset with the dismal end of their season, the Colts complained publicly that some of the Beaneaters victories were a direct result of the Giants benching their stars Buck Ewing, Roger Connor, and Amos Rusie in several of the contests.[3]

The Beaneaters had been improved by several key moves by manager Frank Selee. In 1890 Selee brought Nichols with him from Omaha (Western Association) and added Bobby Lowe. Then he added outfielder Harry Stovey and infielders Joe Quinn and Billy Nash for the 1891 season after the rival Players' League folded following the 1890 season.

In what might have been called the "Battle of the 'Kids,'" Boston's game with Philadelphia on October 2 was played before 912 fans at the Philadelphia Baseball Grounds.[4] Selee put the 22-year-old Nichols on the mound for his 48th start of the season, while 24-year-old Kid Gleason took the hill for his 44th start for Phillies manager Harry Wright. In that era, it was not uncommon for teams to use only two or three regular starting pitchers during the entire season, accounting for the high number of games pitched by each.

The scoring began in the top of the first inning when Philadelphia's Sam Thompson reached base on second baseman Quinn's wild throw and scored after Ed Delahanty singled. Thompson scored while Delahanty was being run down between the bases.

In the top of the second inning with two outs, the Phillies scored again when Kid Gleason doubled and went to third on Billy Hamilton's bunt single. Hamilton allowed himself to be caught between the bases, allowing Gleason to score.

Boston countered with a score in the bottom of the second frame when Nash walked, advanced to second on a passed ball by Jack Clements, and scored on a double by Tommy Tucker. Philadelphia led 2-1.

In the fourth inning, Philadelphia got on the board a third time. Jerry Denny reached first base on Nash's error. After Bob Allen doubled, William Brown's sacrifice fly scored Denny. In the bottom of the fourth, the Beaneaters got their second run on singles by Steve Brodie and Nash and a sacrifice hit by Tucker, making the score 3-2.

Boston evened the score in the fifth inning when Herman Long got on base on a force out. On Long's stolen-base attempt, substitute Philly catcher Bill Gray's effort to throw him out wound up in center field. When outfielder Delahanty fumbled the ball trying to retrieve the errant throw, Long circled all the bases to score their third run.

Boston added two more runs in the bottom of the seventh inning. Charlie Bennett drew a base on balls and advanced to second on a passed ball. Nichols doubled to score Bennett and scored himself when Tucker hit a ball to the outfield terrace. In attempt to go all the way home, Tucker was thrown out at the plate.

With no runs being added by either team in the eighth and ninth innings, the final score stood at 5-3.

Only three runs between both teams were earned, as the game was marred by numerous errors and miscues, particularly by Philadelphia, whom the *Philadelphia Inquirer* characterized as suffering from "very bum fielding."[5]

Both Nichols and Gleason had decent showings on the mound. In recording his 30th victory, Nichols gave up nine hits and two walks, while striking out three.[6] Gleason yielded seven hits and three walks, as he recorded two strikeouts. He took his 22nd loss of the season against 24 wins for the season.

Boston finished the season 3½ games ahead of Chicago.

Nichols was also a critical part of the Beaneaters' four additional pennant-winning teams in the 1890s. He had seven seasons of 30 or more wins with Boston and compiled 361 wins during his 15-year career. He was inducted into the Baseball Hall of Fame in 1949 after being elected by the Old Timers Committee.

Gleason eventually gave up pitching and became a full-time infielder from 1895 through 1906. He was the manager of the 1919 Chicago White Sox when they were accused of fixing games in the World Series against the Cincinnati Reds.

After the 1891 season a special National League committee summoned the Giants management group to a formal inquiry to investigate charges that they had thrown late-season games allowing Boston to take the pennant. When the Giants seemingly offered plausible reasons for key players' absences, the committee upheld the Beaneaters' championship title.[7]

The *Boston Globe* reported that Selee believed his team won the league championship on its own abilities, crediting his team with faithful work.[8]

The Boston Reds, champions of the rival American Association, urged its league president, Zach Phelps, to issue a challenge to the National League to allow the champions of the two leagues to play a world championship series. The series had become an annual postseason tradition between the two leagues since 1884.[9] Phelps proceeded with the challenge to N.E. Young, president of the National League, who declined it. Young responded that it would be a violation of the National Agreement, of which the two leagues had been participants, to play such a postseason series.[10]

Upon receiving notice of the National League's refusal, Phelps declared that the Reds were entitled to carry the "World's Championship Flag" for the 1892 season.[11] However, the American Association merged with the National League that year, and the Boston Reds franchise ceased to exist.

The National League title by the Beaneaters in 1891 was the first of five under manager Selee in the 1890s.

SOURCES

In addition to the sources cited in the Notes, the author also consulted the following:

Boston Post, October 3, 1891: 8.

Boston Globe, October 3, 1891: 5.

The source for all game details came from a box score and game summary in the *Philadelphia Inquirer*, October 3, 1891: 3.

NOTES

1. *2016 Atlanta Braves Media Guide*, 452. (The 18-game winning streak still stands as the record for the franchise, which includes the Boston team known as the Red Stockings, Beaneaters, Doves, Rustlers, Bees, and Braves; the Milwaukee Braves; and the Atlanta Braves.) In 2017 the Cleveland Indians' 22 consecutive victories generated some discussion around the baseball world. Cleveland surpassed the 21-game streak of the 1935 Chicago Cubs, but was still shy of the 1916 New York Giants' streak of 26. However, the Giants' streak included a tie game, so the phrase "consecutive wins" was a cause for dispute. The issue is beyond the scope of this article, but the 1891 Boston club's 18-game winning streak also included a tie game.

2. Richard Bogovich, *Kid Nichols, A Biography of the Hall of Fame Pitcher* (Jefferson, North Carolina: McFarland & Company, Inc., 2012), 51.

3. Ibid.

4. The *Boston Post* indicated the attendance was 912, while the *Boston Globe* reported 9,021. It seems unlikely that the latter attendance is correct, since the attendance on the day before was reported by the *Globe* as 1,000.

5. *Philadelphia Inquirer*, October 3, 1891: 3. The *Boston Globe* and *Boston Post* reported the number of earned runs by both teams as four.

6. The *Boston Globe* and *Boston Post* reported the number of hits yielded by Nichols as 10.

7. David Voigt, *The League That Failed* (Lanham, Maryland: Scarecrow Press, Inc., 1998), 36.

8. "Won on Its Merits," *Boston Globe,* October 5, 1891: 5

9. The first such series was actually held in 1882 but was canceled in 1883.

10. *Boston Globe*, October 10, 1891: 2.

11. "President Phelps Claims the Title for Boston Reds," *Boston Globe*, October 12, 1891: 5.

SWEEP CONTINUES STRONG SEASON START FOR BEANEATERS

APRIL 23, 1892: BOSTON BEANEATERS 11, BALTIMORE ORIOLES 7 (FIRST GAME); BOSTON BEANEATERS 19, BALTIMORE ORIOLES 9 (SECOND GAME), AT SOUTH END GROUNDS, BOSTON

BY JOEL RIPPEL

There was a lot of change after the 1891 season. The National League had grown from eight to 12 teams with the acceptance of four American Association teams as the Association folded as a major league.

One thing didn't change for the expanded National League – the Boston Beaneaters remained the best team in the League. The Beaneaters, who won the League title in 1891 with an 87-51-2 record, were expected to repeat as champions.

Going into their first homestand of the 1892 season, the Beaneaters were 3-1. The first nine days of the season had been disrupted by poor weather. After opening with a 14-4 victory at Washington, the Beaneaters played just once (an 11-5 victory over the Orioles in Baltimore on April 16) over the next six days.

The Beaneaters split two games in Philadelphia before returning to Boston for their home opener on April 21. The game was threatened by rain and played in less than ideal conditions. A crowd of 3,825 turned out for the Beaneaters and Orioles, who had created the first controversy of the season before leaving Baltimore the day before.

Leading 6-5 in the sixth inning of their game with the New York Giants, the Orioles refused to finish their game, saying they had to catch a train for Boston. The Giants claimed they had not been notified by the Orioles and protested. Umpire Jerry Mahoney ruled the game a forfeit to the Giants.

The Orioles, who had finished fourth in the American Association in 1891 with a 71-64-4 record, made it Boston in time for their first road game of the season. Opening Day was a big event for the defending National League champions and the city of Boston.

"Despite the rain, however, Governor William E. Russell and staff, Mayor Matthews and the board of aldermen and councilmen, over one-half of the Massachusetts senate and fully 100 members of the house, besides clergymen, pastors and lawyers of note, occupied prominent seats in the grand stand. Indeed, the Massachusetts legislature adjourned at noon to attend the game."1

The Beaneaters edged the Orioles, 7-6, to improve to 4-1. The loss dropped the Orioles to 1-5. Another rainout the next day forced the teams to schedule a doubleheader on April 23.

The doubleheader would test the patience of the local cranks before the Beaneaters emerged with a sweep via 11-7 and 19-9 victories.

A newspaper account of the doubleheader succinctly summed up the day's proceedings: "The champions took four hours and 20 minutes practice at the South End grounds yesterday, having the Baltimore team to fill the role of punching bag. The home team put up by far the best game, and by reason of their superior headwork, have two more victories on their string."2

While the games weren't long by twenty-first-century standards – game one was played in 1 hour and 58 minutes and the second game was played in 2 hours and 10 minutes – they were likely tedious for the crowd of 4,326. The teams combined for 25 errors, nine in the first game and 16 (12 by the Orioles) in the second game.

In the first game, Jack Stivetts made his pitching debut for the Beaneaters. Stivetts, who had spent the previous three seasons with the St. Louis Browns of the American Association, signed with Boston during the offseason and bolstered a pitching staff that included future Hall of Famers John Clarkson and Kid Nichols. When not pitching, Stivetts played in the outfield.

Stivetts, a 24-year-old right-hander, allowed just five hits, walked six, hit a batter, and had to weather five errors by his defense in the victory. The Orioles scored three runs in the first inning, but Stivetts settled down with four scoreless innings as the Beaneaters scored six in the fourth and two in the fifth to take an 8-3 lead. After the Orioles scored two in the sixth, Boston scored three in the seventh to open an 11-5 lead. The Orioles scored two in the seventh. None of the Orioles' runs were earned.

Stivetts finished strong, retiring the Orioles in order over the final two innings. "It was one, two, three (in) order in the eighth and ninth, Stivetts putting on steam and mowing them down with ease," reported the *Boston Globe*.3

The Beaneaters took control with their six-run fourth inning. Shortstop Herman Long opened the fourth with a double and future Hall of Famer Hugh Duffy reached on an error. Bobby Lowe hit a grounder to third baseman George Shoch, who threw to home to get Long, but Long returned to third base safely to load the bases. A single by Tommy McCarthy brought in the first two runs. After a sacrifice moved the runners up, Charlie Bennett's line drive to center field scored two more runs. Stivetts closed out the inning's scoring with a two-run single.

The Beaneaters added two runs in the fifth on a single by Lowe, a double by McCarthy and a wild pitch.

In the Orioles' subsequent at-bat, Lew Whistler hit a leadoff triple, but Lowe made a running catch in left-center field of a line drive and threw out Lew Whistler, who had tripled to lead off the inning, at home.

The Beaneaters final three runs came on two walks, a sacrifice, a single by Tommy Tucker and a double by Joe Quinn.

McCarthy, in his first season with the Beaneaters after four seasons with the St. Louis Browns, had three of Boston's 11 hits.

In the second game, the Beaneaters combined 13 hits with the Orioles' fielding problems to earn the victory. Only five of Boston's 19 runs were earned.

"Baltimore out batted Boston in the second game, but fielded miserably. Boston's base running was an important winning element in both games."4

After a five-minute break between games, Lowe got things started in the second game (the Beaneaters batted first) with a two-run home run to left. But the Orioles scored four runs in their half of the first on a walk, error four singles and a double to take a short-lived 4-2 lead.

The Beaneaters quickly added six runs in the second on singles by Quinn, Tucker, and Clarkson, a walk, a hit batsman, and two errors.

Tucker added a double in the Beaneaters' three-run eighth inning, and singles by Duffy and Billy Nash highlighted their three-run ninth inning.

Nash had four hits and Duffy, who had hit .336 in 1891 for the American Association champion Boston Reds, had three hits to lead the Beaneaters offense. The Beaneaters stole seven bases – three by Duffy and two by Nash – while Orioles starter George Cobb walked seven.

The Orioles had 15 hits off Clarkson, who was making his third start of the season. But only two of Baltimore's nine runs were earned. Clarkson, who was 33-19 with a 2.79 ERA in 47 complete games for Boston in 1891, also walked seven.

Shoch and George Wood each had three hits for the Orioles.

After the doubleheader, the Beaneaters went on the road and won four more games to stretch their winning streak to eight games. They were 11-2 in the first month of the season.

SOURCES

In addition to the sources cited in the notes, the author also consulted Newspapers.com and Retrosheet.org.

NOTES

1 "Sporting News," *Brooklyn Daily Eagle*, April 22, 1892: 1.

2 "Double Dirge," *Boston Globe*, April 24, 1892: 4.

3 Ibid.

4 "Baltimore Pushed Further Down the Line," *Brooklyn Daily Eagle*, April 24, 1892: 7.

A "LONG" GAME

MAY 6, 1892: BOSTON BEANEATERS 0, CINCINNATI REDS 0 (14 INNINGS), AT LEAGUE PARK, CINCINNATI

BY MARK PESTANA

The Beaneaters' first Western road trip of 1892 began in the final days of April. Two games apiece in St. Louis, Chicago, and Louisville preceded their season debut in Cincinnati on Friday, May 6. Losses in St. Louis and Chicago had brought Boston's record to 14-3.

The Reds, at 10-8, had lost three of their last five games, including two in a row to visiting Brooklyn immediately prior to Boston's arrival.

Two upper-echelon hurlers faced off before a crowd of slightly over 1,900 in Cincinnati's League Park. In the box for Boston was the great John Clarkson, who in the seven seasons from 1885 to 1891 had topped 30 wins six times, including individual years of 53 and 49 victories. Now, at 30 years old, his star was in the descendant: The 1892 season was to be Clarkson's last with a winning record (25-16).

Elton "Icebox" Chamberlain, winner of four of his first six starts, took the ball for the Queen City nine. A 32-game winner for St. Louis three years earlier, Chamberlain was only 24 but already in his seventh major-league campaign. With Tony Mullane, he formed an essentially two-man rotation that had started all but three games for the Reds to this point.

Little offense was mounted in the early innings, none of Boston's first nine batters reaching base, while the Reds, despite a Beaneater error and three walks doled out by Clarkson, could not get a man to second safely. Arlie Latham, beneficiary of a base on balls in the third, tested King Kelly's throwing arm and was gunned down handily.[1]

Boston first showed signs of life in its half of the fourth. Herman Long led off with a double and made third on Hugh Duffy's sacrifice. But Harry Stovey struck out looking, Tommy McCarthy grounded out, and Long was left hanging 90 feet from home.

In the fifth, with two outs, Reds catcher Jerry Harrington and hurler Chamberlain reached on a walk and an error respectively, but the inning ended on a fine play by shortstop Long, who was on his way to an outstanding day in the field. In its half, Boston came even closer to scoring. Bobby Lowe reached on a miscue by shortstop Germany Smith and was sacrificed to second by Kelly. The next batter, Joe Quinn, drove one to right-center, and Reds center fielder Eddie Burke gave chase. Lowe, thinking it looked good for a hit, took off from second. Two nights earlier, Burke and Harrington had crossed paths with Reds pitcher Billy Rhines at a local saloon and, fueled by a goodly intake of liquid spirits, the three held an intramural brawl in an alley outside the establishment. When Captain Charlie Comiskey learned of the late-night fracas, he slapped Burke and Harrington with $100 fines, and Rhines – who was characterized as the aggressor – with a suspension.[2] But Burke was up to the task now, snaring Quinn's drive on the run and then doubling up Lowe at the plate.

The home team's first hit finally came in the sixth inning: a single by right-fielder Jocko Halligan. But the safety was wasted, as the next batter, Burke, struck out, and Halligan, attempting to steal on the pitch, became the second victim of King Kelly's strong right arm.

Boston stranded men at second in the seventh and eighth innings. Bid McPhee singled in the Cincinnati eighth and got to second on Stovey's error, but another snappy assist by Long on a ball off Latham's bat ended the threat.

Both teams had good chances in the ninth inning but came up short. In the Reds' half, veteran outfielder Tip O'Neill came to the plate with two outs. He was one of the most consistent hitters of the nineteenth century, batting over .300 in each of the seven previous seasons and twice leading his league. At age 34, however, O'Neill was nearing the end of his string, and it was showing. Assessing his performance in Cincinnati's May 5 loss to Brooklyn, the *Cincinnati Post* sneered: "O'Neill played his usual chump game. Take him out, Captain Comiskey, and try Burke."[3]

O'Neill waited out Clarkson for a base on balls, and Comiskey himself now had an opportunity to break the deadlock. The captain lofted a fly to center, and it looked as though Duffy would easily squelch the Reds' hopes. To the surprise of all, though, the ball went through Duffy's hands. Had O'Neill obeyed the cardinal rule of running hard on any hit ball with two outs, the Reds would have had the game in hand. But it wasn't so. One paper said O'Neill "stopped at third when he might easily have gone home,"[4] another, that he "jogged around to third."[5] At any rate, with men now on first and third, Germany Smith grounded to the ubiquitous Long, and the Reds' best chance evaporated.

A relieved Hugh Duffy led off Boston's half[6] and, atoning for his muff, singled to left – only the second Boston hit of the game. Stovey, not having his best day either in the field or at the plate, grounded out to Chamberlain, with Duffy taking second. McCarthy's groundout landed Duffy on third, but the threat died there when Lowe lined out to outfielder O'Neill.

The next potential icebreaker came in the Boston 11th when Clarkson led off with a double to right. This brought up the top of the order and, in the *Boston Globe*'s felicitous terminology, "it was 20 to 1 that Boston would have shortcake for supper."[7] But Long fouled to Harrington, Duffy's bid for an infield hit erased Clarkson at third, and Stovey went out on an infield fly.

Chamberlain replicated Clarkson's feat by leading off the 13th inning with a double, Cincinnati's fourth and final hit of the day. Attaining third courtesy of McPhee's sacrifice, he watched helplessly from there as Latham's liner to left was snared by Stovey.

With one out in the bottom of the 14th, Duffy reached on an error and stole second. He could go no farther, though, as Stovey and McCarthy flied to O'Neill and Halligan for the final two outs of the game.

The game was called before the 15th inning could begin, but not really on account of darkness, though it was so reported in some papers. The *Springfield Republican* explained: "Finally the sun sank so low that it shone directly into the umpire's face, and as he could not see the ball he called the game."[8]

Player-turned-sportswriter Tim Murnane reserved extraordinary praise for the play of Beaneaters shortstop Herman Long, declaring in the *Boston Globe*, "His work in this game has never been equalled in the history of base ball."[9] In the game, Long made good on 19 of 20 chances, tallying 14 assists and 5 putouts, and sharing in two double plays.

Above all, though, this was one of the best pitching duels of the nineteenth century. "Chamberlain and Clarkson," effused the *Boston Journal*, "were at their best and gave magnificent exemplifications of the art of pitching."[10] Indeed, Clarkson, the future Hall of Famer, in surrendering four hits and six walks in 14 innings. was actually outdone by Chamberlain, who allowed but three hits and one walk to the mighty Beaneaters. The time of this epic scoreless battle should strike a chord of envy in jaded modern fans accustomed to enduring three, three-and-a-half, or four-hour games as a matter of course. When Umpire Sheridan rang down the curtain after 14 innings, the time of the game went into the books as 2 hours and 20 minutes.[11]

SOURCES

In addition to the sources cited in the Notes, the author also consulted the following:

Baseball-Reference.com.

Retrosheet.org.

Nemec, David. *Major League Baseball Profiles: 1871-1900, Volumes 1 & 2* (Lincoln, Nebraska: Bison Books, 2011).

_____. *The Great Encyclopedia of 19th-Century Major League Baseball* (New York: Donald I. Fine Books, 1997).

NOTES

1 "Not a Run Scored," *Boston Globe*, May 7, 1892: 5.

2 "Fighting Drunk," *Cincinnati Post*, May 5, 1892: 1.

3 *Cincinnati Post*, May 6, 1892: 7.

4 "A Wonderful Game," *Boston Journal*, May 7, 1892: 3.

5 "Not a Run Scored."

6 At this time, the home team did not automatically bat last, but could choose to go to bat first if so desired.

7 "Not a Run Scored."

8 Springfield (Massachusetts) *Republican*, May 7, 1892: 8.

9 "Not a Run Scored."

10 "To a Standstill, One of the Greatest Pitchers' Games on Record," *Boston Journal*, May 7, 1892: 3.

11 "Not a Run Scored."

COMEBACK WIN BY BOSTON SPOILS CINCINNATI'S GLORIOUS DAY

JULY 4, 1892: BOSTON BEANEATERS 7, CINCINNATI REDS 6 (SECOND GAME OF DOUBLEHEADER), AT LEAGUE BALLPARK, CINCINNATI

BY JOEL RIPPEL

The Cincinnati Reds and the city of Cincinnati were looking forward to the arrival of the defending National League champion Boston Beaneaters for a holiday doubleheader.

A newspaper headline said: "Big Bostons. They will be here To-Day. The Two Fourth of July Battles. Can the Reds Give the Leaders Two Falls?"[1]

In the middle of an 18-game road trip, the Beaneaters arrived in Cincinnati on a roll. They had won 12 of their previous 14 games and brought a league-best 47-18 record into the third meeting of the season between the two teams.

The host Reds, who had finished in seventh place in the eight-team National League in 1891, were playing solid baseball as well. They had gone 5-1-1 over their prior seven games to improve to 36-26-2.

Baseball fans turned out in force for the doubleheader. The first game was the sixth game of the season between the two. In early May the teams met twice in Cincinnati, with the first game ending in a 0-0, 14-inning tie and the Beaneaters winning the next day, 3-2. In mid-June the Reds visited Boston for a three-game series, with the Beaneaters winning two of three.

"The early trains brought in a great crowd of excursionists from surrounding cities and towns, and before 9 o'clock there was a human stream drifting toward the Cincinnati Park," wrote the *Cincinnati Enquirer*. "Every seat in the park was occupied, and they were standing up all the way around when Umpire (Bob) Emslie came on the lot and called play.[2]

The Reds continued their recent strong play with a 9-5 victory over the Beaneaters in the first game. The Reds scored five runs in the first inning to open a 5-1 lead. The Beaneaters scored three runs in the third inning and one run in the seventh inning to forge a 5-5 tie. But the Reds regained control with a run in the bottom of the seventh and three runs in the eighth inning.

The standing-room crowd of 9,678 for the first game grew larger for the separate-admission second game. The crowd of 10,861 for the second game – the doubleheader's combined attendance of 20,479 was the largest for a single day in Cincinnati history

– saw the Reds fall one out short of "the most glorious base-ball Fourth in the history of Cincinnati."³

The Reds jumped on the Beaneaters early in the second game, scoring six runs in their first three times at bat to open a 6-0 lead. Through six innings, the Reds led 6-1 and were on the verge of a victory and sweep, which "up to the closing inning, looked to be a moral cinch."⁴

The Beaneaters started their comeback in the seventh with four runs off Reds starter Frank Dwyer. The comeback began rather quietly when leadoff hitter Bobby Lowe was hit by a pitch and Charlie Bennett reached first on an error when Reds third baseman Arlie Latham, "who played a very rocky game in both contests, fell down on an easy play."⁵

Consecutive singles by Jack Stivetts, Tommy McCarthy, and Hugh Duffy and sacrifices by Herman Long and Tommy Tucker helped the Beaneaters pull within one run, 6-5.

Reds manager Charlie Comiskey brought in pitcher Elton "Ice Box" Chamberlain in the eighth inning. Chamberlain retired the Beaneaters in the eighth to maintain the Reds' slim lead. Stivetts, the Beaneaters pitcher, led off the ninth inning with a single – his third hit of the game. Chamberlain struck out McCarthy and then appeared to have the dangerous Duffy, who had four hits in the game, struck out. But the third strike got away from Reds catcher Henry "Farmer" Vaughn and Stivetts advanced to second base. Long followed with a single to drive in Stivetts with the tying run. Long then stole second and came home on a single by Tucker.

Stivetts retired the Reds in the ninth inning to close out the Beaneaters' stunning comeback victory.

A Cincinnati newspaper account of the game lamented, "It isn't yet clear how we lost it. One run was all that stood between us and a fitting climax to a day of brand sport. No one at the outset really expected the Reds to throw down the visitors in succession. There is scarcely a team in the League that has accomplished that feat, but after winning one game and having the other on easy avenue, with a lead of 6 to 0, it was heart-breaking to lose it. To lose such a game was enough to make a person rent the ambient air with a few choice expressions that might not pass muster in polite society."⁶

The account said, "Artistically, no two worse games of ball have played at the local park this season. The score shows that no less than an aggregate of twenty-three errors were made by the two teams in the two games."⁷

Latham, whose error contributed to the Beaneaters' comeback, had five errors in the doubleheader, as did Long, the Beaneaters' shortstop.

Despite that, the account concluded, "While there was plenty of misplays, the games were just the kind to suit the crowd. Both were full of lively hitting, hustling base-running and fast playing all around. Both games were of the scrappy up-hill kind people like to see. They were both fought down to the bitter end. The Bostons won the second game against great odds."⁸

The dramatic doubleheader split helped the Beaneaters maintain their hold on first place. Eight days later, the Beaneaters finished the first half of the National League schedule in first place with a 52-22-1 record, 2 games ahead of the second-place Brooklyn Bridegrooms (51-25-1). The Beaneaters were 28-12 on the road in the first half of the season.

SOURCES

In addition to the sources cited in the Notes, the author also consulted Newspapers.com and Retrosheet.org.

NOTES

1 "Big Bostons," *Cincinnati Enquirer*, July 4, 1892: 2.
2 "Near It," *Cincinnati Enquirer*, July 5, 1892: 2.
3 Ibid.
4 Ibid.
5 Ibid.
6 Ibid.
7 Ibid.
8 Ibid.

A CLOSE VICTORY, BUT STILL A LAUGHER

JULY 11, 1892: BOSTON BEANEATERS 3, CHICAGO COLTS 2, AT SOUTH SIDE PARK, CHICAGO

BY BOB LEMOINE

In 2013, eight Boston Red Sox players stopped shaving during the season as a show of team unity. "It's a bonding element," manager John Farrell said of his team, which was headed to a World Series title. "You have to have ways to have fun sometimes. It takes the focus off the daily grind."[1]

More than a century earlier and long before the Red Sox, the Boston Beaneaters were a team that knew how to have fun. They too would win a championship, and they decided to "take the focus off the daily grind" and have a little fun one day in Chicago.

The first half of the 1892 season was drawing to a close in the experimental split-season format. Boston had already clinched the pennant for the first half and had little to play for on July 11 at Chicago. While a modern baseball team in a meaningless game could call up minor leaguers and see how they perform at the major-league level, in 1892 Boston simply *performed*. The performance was literally laughable, as the players wore beards and red noses, and dressed themselves in comedic costumes.

"During the morning," wrote the *Boston Post*, "they cleared out several masquerade costume shops and appeared on the field in rigs that were a cross between a Salvation Army captain outfit and a penitentiary suit. Besides they had whiskers."[2] Actor Eddie Foy, a star in vaudeville theaters at the time, assisted the players with their makeup.[3]

The game itself was a pitchers' duel between Boston's Kid Nichols and Chicago's Bill Hutchinson. But more focus was on the pageantry. Boston "appeared in impossible costumes," wrote the *Boston Journal*. "[King] Kelly, [Hugh] Duffy, and [Tommy] McCarthy wearing false whiskers, and the entire team being clothed in some check suits of the loudest pattern."[4] The *Chicago Daily Inter-Ocean* said Boston was "attired in a species of base-ball make-up which strongly suggested a collection of penal servitude habits from the various penitentiaries of the country. The players' faces were hidden behind hideous whiskers and preposterous mustachios, surmounted by caps of every conceivable shape and device."[5] A comment from the press box likened their uniforms to Coney Island bathing suits.

King Kelly, as he often did, got the first and the last laughs of the day. It was no surprise the comedic Kelly came up with the plan, but then he also doubled to center in the eighth, scoring McCarthy with the go-ahead run, and Boston won 3-2. Kelly even had the gall and the time to stop at first base on his way by and tell Chicago's Cap Anson that the Illinois-Iowa League was looking for talent and he should "transfer his team into company of its own speed."⁶

The *Chicago Tribune* found no humor in these antics, reporting that the Beaneaters "appeared in the roles of buffoons," with "costumes being ridiculous and absurd."⁷ Chicago fans were used to Kelly's clowning and "it was not hard to pick out the author of this coarse and vulgar attempt at humor. Kelly, try as he may, can be nothing but coarse in anything he attempts of this kind. People who go to see baseball pay to see a game. When they want to see buffoons they go to a circus where clowns are paid to make fools of themselves for the public delectation."⁸

The *Boston Globe*, however, was more complimentary to their team dressed as "antiques and horribles" with Kelly being "made up as an English dude." ⁹

Kelly explained his scheme very simply. "Let us make up as old men and beat Anson's Colts," he suggested to the team, "and the boys all thought it a bright idea."¹⁰

NOTES

1. Peter Abraham, "Red Sox' 'Beard Bonding' Symbolic of Attitude Adjustment," *Boston Globe*, October 2, 2013. Retrieved February 1, 2017. bostonglobe.com/sports/2013/10/02/beards/BAQGj2IcEckzCq5Z0Piy3N/story.html.
2. "Neither Could Bat," *Boston Post*, July 12, 1892: 3.
3. "In New Uniforms," *Boston Globe*, July 12, 1892: 5.
4. "Boston, 3; Chicago 2," *Boston Journal*, July 12, 1892: 3.
5. "Conquered by Kelly," *Daily Inter-Ocean* (Chicago), July 12, 1892: 6.
6. Ibid.
7. "New Men Were Tried," *Chicago Tribune*, July 12, 1892: 7.
8. Ibid.
9. "In New Uniforms."
10. Ibid.

TRIPLE PLAY HELPS PRESERVE A SHUTOUT

AUGUST 5, 1892: BOSTON 2, BROOKLYN 0 (12 INNINGS), AT EASTERN PARK, BROOKLYN

BY BILL NOWLIN

When the 1892 season ended, the Boston Beaneaters had prevailed again and taken the pennant. The Brooklyn Bridegrooms – sixth-place finishers in 1891 – gave them a battle for the flag in 1892, finishing just 2½ games behind Boston for the first half of the season.

At the close of play on August 4, however, the Cleveland Spiders were in first place in the second-half standings by one game over Brooklyn, and Brooklyn held a half-game lead over Boston. For the year as a whole, Boston was up two over Brooklyn. The two teams had battled, but the Beaneaters had been tenacious and had dropped as low as second place on only four days during the season. Boston had just finished an 18-game homestand, playing Brooklyn on August 5 in the first game of a 25-game road trip.

Brooklyn manager Monte Ward asked right-hander George Haddock to pitch. Haddock had overcome a disastrous 9-26 season for Buffalo in 1890, pitching for Arthur Irwin's Boston Reds (American Association) in 1891 and posting a record of 34-11 with a 2.49 ERA that was less than half of his 1890 mark. When the Reds folded, he was secured by Brooklyn. He was 29-13 (3.14) for Brooklyn in 1892, winning the most games on the staff. And he pitched a whale of a game on August 5, going the distance through 12.

Boston's Frank Selee entrusted the game to Kid Nichols. This was Nichols' third season in the majors; he never won fewer than 20 games in his first nine seasons. He was coming off a 30-17 season, and wound up 1892 topping that, 35-16 (2.84 ERA). Nichols held the edge over Haddock on August 5, but it was a scoreless battle through 11 innings.

The *New York Herald* allowed as how Brooklyn should have won the game, 1-0, after the regulation nine but that "an unfortunate decision at the plate in the fourth inning deprived [left fielder Darby] O'Brien of a run and allowed [King] Kelly's men to complete a triple play."[1]

Haddock held Boston to only three hits all game long. Brooklyn had seven hits (or six, or eight – accounts differ.) Brooklyn had "outbatted and outfielded their bean eating rivals but luck was all the other way."[2] The *Herald* was critical of umpire Tom Lynch who, the newspaper claimed, "marred his usually good work by allowing the Boston players to indulge in tactics that were very close to rowdyism."[3]

The game was won in the top of the 12th when Haddock hit Boston first baseman Tommy Tucker for the second time in the game, and left fielder Jack Stivetts followed with a home run. Stivetts, normally a pitcher, played outfield in 18 games during 1892. Bobby Lowe had suffered a fractured arm and Stivetts filled in for him in left.

Threatening weather had kept the Eastern Park crowd down to a reported 2,287. Because the game was so close, the spectators were "kept at the highest pitch of excitement" throughout the

2-hour, 125-minute game.[4] The triple play in the fourth followed a walk to Tom Daly and a single by O'Brien. Catcher Con Daily bunted and reached on an error by his Boston counterpart, catcher King Kelly. That loaded the bases. Haddock came to the plate. He hit a "short bounder" to Boston third baseman Billy Nash, who fielded the ball and threw to Kelly to force Daly at home plate. Kelly threw to first baseman Tucker, retiring him. O'Brien kept running around third, so Tucker fired the ball home and the umpire called him out at the plate "amid a storm of hisses."[5]

Stivetts's home run was hit in the gap between right field and center. Shortstop Long and pitcher Nichols had the other two hits for the Bostons.

The Bostons tried to take advantage of Tom Daly playing third base instead of the usual Bill Joyce, and three times in the first inning hit the ball to Daly, who handled each ball well.

The *Brooklyn Eagle* came down hard on Lynch, titling its game account, "Umpire Lynch Did It."[6] The paper allowed that those present "witnessed one of the finest exhibitions of ball playing this year … a first class treat." It noted that catcher King Kelly was battered about by balls striking him on the hand, the arm, and both legs, but he played with pluck and even, bantering with the crowd, predicted the triple play: "Just you hold your horses, now," he declaimed, "here's where we cut 'em off with a triple play."[7]

Kelly, the *Eagle* reported, "kept his tongue wagging all through the game." The paper's correspondent detailed the injuries he suffered and reported extensively on the banter by various players throughout the game. The game account arguably presents a colorful picture of what baseball of the day was like. Kelly was repeatedly referred to as "the king."

As to the fourth-inning triple play, the *Eagle* called it "phenomenal" and "the finest ever seen at Brooklyn," also noting that Brooklyn manager Ward "kicked at the decision which made O'Brien out, though he was not in position to see the play." It did, however, report that Boston manager Selee, Stivetts, and left fielder Lowe (present, despite his arm injury) "all … were certain that Darby [O'Brien] was safe and expressed their opinions accordingly."[8]

The *New York Times* wrote, without any rancor, that "every person on the ground" thought Kelly had failed to tag O'Brien at the plate, observing dispassionately, "If the decision was incorrect and the Bostons failed to make the triple play, then Umpire Lynch was responsible for the loss of the game."[9]

From the sixth to the 12th inning, neither team made a base hit except for a 10th-inning single by a Brooklyn batter. As the 12th inning began, it was starting to get a little dark and Kelly called out, "Come, boys, let's finish this up. I want my supper awful bad and I'm tired of this." After Tucker was hit by the ball, Kelly shouted out, "Now, Tucker, old boy, look sharp, and we'll win the game right here." Then, as Stivetts stepped in, he yelled, "Here's our heavy weight pitcher, and he's just the man to do the job!"[10]

The *Boston Globe* led its account saying, "Jack Stivetts covered himself with glory at Eastern Park, Brooklyn, this afternoon."[11] With Tucker on first base in the 12th, "the sturdy pitcher … picked up a flat bat, but after knocking a couple of foul balls concluded to change to his old reliable wagon tongue."[12] He struck the next pitch: "it flew on a line between [center fielder Mike] Griffin and [right fielder Oyster] Burns and before either of these speedy men could get the ball and return it to the pate, Jack had crossed the rubber."[13]

The *Globe's* account singled out both third basemen for exceptional fielding, and noted that the pitchers' duel was so well appreciated by the small crowd that "the spectators gave each of the twirlers a round of applause after every inning."[14] There was considerable detail reported, but no mention of Lynch or question raised about his call in the fourth inning. The *Globe* wrote that the play was "loudly applauded."

Attending the game from Boston was irrepressible fan Arthur "Hi Hi" Dixwell, whose cries of "Hi! Hi!" punctuated each Boston play. He passed out a box of Reina cigars after the victory.

The Brooklyn loss dropped the Bridegrooms to third place in the second-half standings, a half-game behind Boston rather than a half-game ahead.

For Stivetts, the home run was one of three he hit in 1892. He was a good-hitting player with a career .302 batting average in National League play.

NOTES

1   "A Hard Game to Lose," *New York Herald*, August 6, 1892: 8.

2   Ibid.

3   Ibid. There was no reference to anything akin to rowdyism in the other newspaper accounts, though the next day one newspaper expressed the thought that Kelly's banter with the fans could be deemed rowdy.

4   "The Home Teams Defeated," *New York Tribune*, August 6, 1892: 10.

5   Ibid. The characterization "short bounder" comes from the *Brooklyn Eagle* account. The *Times* called it a "sharp grounder."

6   "Umpire Lynch Did It," *Brooklyn Eagle*, August 6, 1982: 3.

7   Ibid.

8   Ibid.

9   "Twelve Innings Played," *New York Times*, August 6, 1892: 3.

10 "Umpire Lynch Did It."

11 "Saved the Day," *Boston Globe*, August 6, 1892: 5.

12 Ibid.

13 Ibid.

14 Ibid.

JACK STIVETTS NO-HITS THE BRIDEGROOMS

AUGUST 6, 1892: BOSTON 11, BROOKLYN 0, AT EASTERN PARK, BROOKLYN

BY BILL NOWLIN

The day after Jack Stivetts beat Brooklyn, 2-0, with a two-run homer in the 12th inning, he took the mound for Beaneaters manager Frank Selee and threw a no-hitter, the first in franchise history.

Stivetts was primarily a pitcher, but he'd played left field on August 5 since Bobby Lowe was out with an injured arm. With Stivetts taking the mound on August 6, the winning pitcher from the 5th – Kid Nichols – took over in left field.

Brooklyn Bridegrooms President Charles Byrne was not amused at some of the goings-on during the August 5 game. First of all, he reminded umpire Tom Lynch that King Kelly's repeated interchanges ("rowdy talk") with spectators was specifically banned under league rule 60 – no player was allowed to converse with spectators. Byrne wanted the rule enforced, but the issue was moot because Kelly, his body battered by balls in the Friday game, took the day off, the catching for Boston done by Charlie Ganzel.[1] Byrne also more or less told Boston's most vocal uberfan, Hi Hi Dixwell, to shut up. The *Brooklyn Eagle* reported that General Dixwell "had a seat on the grand stand yesterday but nobody knew it."[2]

The attendance for the Saturday game was almost triple the day before, some 7,107.

Stivetts was the show – in addition to his work on the mound, he doubled, tripled, and (according to some accounts) stole home, accounting for four of Boston's 11 runs. It was far from a perfect game. Stivetts's work wasn't flawless. He walked five Brooklyn batters, and there were four Boston errors. Only once did a Bridegroom get as far as third base, but no one scored. It was second baseman and team captain Monte Ward, who walked, stole second, and advanced to third on an error.

Third baseman Billy Nash was singled out for particular praise by the *Boston Globe* correspondent. "He made marvelous stops and brilliant throws, and the bottled-up enthusiasm of the spectators found an outlet in cheering his good work."[3] As it happens, Nash was the only one on the Boston team who was unable to get a base hit, but he "more than made up for his poor luck at the bat by great fielding."[4]

The first run of the game came in the third inning when Boston second baseman Joe Quinn singled to left, taking second when starter Ed Stein threw errantly hoping to pick him off. Right fielder Tommy McCarthy singled to right field, and Quinn scored. Center fielder Hugh Duffy tripled to left field, and McCarthy scored.

Brooklyn got two men on base with a walk and an error, but didn't score. In the fourth, first baseman Tommy Tucker singled, and then the pitcher Stivetts – batting seventh in the order

– tripled him home with a drive to left field. He then scored on a fly ball hit by Quinn.

The Bostons had scored twice in the third, twice in the fourth, and once more in the fifth.

By that time, it was clear that Stein (who had a very good 27-16 season, with a team-best 2.84 earned-run average) was off his game, so he departed and rookie Brickyard Kennedy took over. (Both Brooklyn pitchers were right-handed.) Kennedy didn't fare any better. The *Globe* wrote, "The bean eaters went at him with the same dash and vigor that they had displayed in touching up Stein."[5]

Indeed, the first batter Kennedy faced was Tucker, who singled to center field. Stivetts then doubled, driving in the sixth run of the game. Quinn singled, putting runners on first and third. He was thrown out trying to steal second, while Stivetts crossed the plate. The first four batters had base hits. In all, Boston scored four times. They added two more in the eighth, drawing two bases on balls, McCarthy scoring on Herman Long's single and Duffy scoring on a fly off Ganzel's bat.

It's interesting that the *Eagle* reported, "The Bostons did not play near as well as they did on Friday," but – the paper correctly continued – "the pitching of Stivetts made up for every shortcoming, while they had no difficult in punishing the home pitching, backed up as it was by poor fielding."[6] The Brooklyn batters simply could not cash in. The second inning saw the leadoff man, Oyster Burns, reach first base when Kid Nichols dropped a fly ball in left field. Stivetts struck out the next three batters, "a lamentable exhibition of how not to bat runners round."

The Brooklyn cranks showed their impartial appreciation of Stivetts' work. "He had to doff his cap in response to the applause that greeted his achievement."[7]

By the sixth inning, a special report to the *Cleveland Leader* asserted, "The spectators … were cheering the Bostons and greeting the Brooklyns with mock applause."[8]

The *New York Herald* opined that Brooklyn didn't come close to seeing a base hit drop in, "every ball hit out from the plate going directly to a fielder. … There were also several dumb plays on the Brooklyns' side."[9]

All in all, the *Eagle* summarized, "Brooklyn did not make the ghost of a hit." Furthermore, they had dropped further in the standings. "Two shut outs on two successive days for the home team is something phenomenal."[10] And not in a good way, for Bridegrooms fans.

NOTES

1 "Not a Hit Off Stivetts," *Brooklyn Eagle*, August 7, 1892: 8.

2 "Just before the game the general and Mr. Byrne had an interesting conversation in which the old war horse from the Hub was told in most emphatic terms that if he wished to get off any of his 'Hi His' he would have to hire a boat on Jamaica bay, row quickly to Barren Island and there shoot off his jaw to his heart's content. It is needless to say that General Dixwell preferred to curb his enthusiasm rather than brave the dangers of the isle de smell." Ibid.

3 "On His Mettle," *Boston Globe*, August 7, 1892: 4.

4 "Record for the Year," *Boston Journal*, August 8, 1892: 3.

5 "On His Mettle."

6 "Not a Hit Off Stivetts."

7 Ibid.

8 "Mad Spectators," *Cleveland Leader*, August 7, 1892: 7.

9 "Giants and Grooms Exchange Places," *New York Herald*, August 7, 1892.

10 "Not a Hit Off Stivetts."

KID NICHOLS' BATTING FEAT

SEPTEMBER 19, 1892: BOSTON BEANEATERS 14, BALTIMORE ORIOLES 11 (EIGHT INNINGS), AT UNION PARK, BALTIMORE

BY ERIC MIKLICH

After the collapse of the American Association at the conclusion of the 1891 season, the National League absorbed four clubs and swelled to 12 teams. It was decided at the annual meeting in New York in November of 1891 that the 1892 season would be divided into two halves with the winner of the first half playing the winner of the second, if two different clubs filled those positions, to determine a champion.

Although Boston (52-22-1) finished in first place at the conclusion of the first half of the season, 2½ games in front of Brooklyn, the Beaneaters limped into Baltimore in late September for the start of a five-game road trip. The Orioles were simply an awful club. They would finish the season 46-101, last out of 12. At the end of the first half they were 20-55, 32½ games behind the Bostons.

Nursing a 33-21-1 second-half record, the Beaneaters were experiencing some internal conflict. Billy Nash, the team captain and third baseman, failed or refused, depending on the source, to make the five-game road trip due to a "sick relative."[1] More likely, Nash was perturbed about relinquishing the captaincy to legend Mike "King" Kelly. Kelly caused trouble the entire season, which was not unusual for him. From 1889 to 1891, Kelly suited up for five teams in three leagues. He was not the star player he once was. His batting showed the effects of a superstar who once was, and his fielding was almost nonexistent due to his frequent time on the bench. His deficiencies were certainly the result of his drinking and carousing. Kelly caused further ill feelings when he openly predicted that Brooklyn, which finished just behind Boston at the conclusion of the first half, would be the second-half season champion.[2] Kelly proved that his oddsmaking were as good as his play, with Brooklyn finishing third in the second half.

Nash spent seven of his eight seasons in Boston, including the 1890 season with the city's entry in the Players' League. He had developed into one of the game's best third basemen. Four Boston players, all captains at one time on other teams, had thrown their support for Nash early in the season.[3] Nash resigned as captain and manager Frank Selee promoted Kelly to the role, hoping that it would quell his disruptive presence.[4] This theory is in line with allowing a convicted bank robber uninhibited access to the vault at the community bank.

From the start of the season, Kelly claimed that his contract stipulated that he was to be the team captain.[5] In 1891 Kelly played in 16 games for the Bostons of the National League (NL) and four for the Bostons of the American Association (AA), both top finishers in their league. Kelly played in 78 games for the

Beaneaters in 1892; however, he was ineffective, hitting .189 as the team's only regular to hit less than .200.

On September 19 at Baltimore, Selee was forced to put starting pitcher Jack Stivetts in left field and assign left fielder Bobby Lowe in to fill Nash's position at third base.[6] (Although Stivetts was part of the three-man Boston rotation, he was a regular substitute in the outfield.)

Slated to start the road trip opener was Boston's budding star, 22-year-old Charles "Kid" Nichols. He had joined the Beaneaters in 1890. He won 27 and then 30 games in his first two seasons. Nichols would amass a career-high 35 wins in 1892 and on this day the switch-hitter would have a very productive day as a batter.

In front of 804 spectators at Union Park in Baltimore, Boston took a 1-0 lead after the first inning against starter George Cobb. Nichols held Baltimore scoreless through four innings. In the top of the fifth inning, Boston posted nine runs, eight of them as the result of five singles, two doubles, and a bases-clearing triple by Nichols. In the Baltimore sixth, Cub Stricker ended the inning by smashing a grounder to Nichols, who stopped the ball with his pitching hand. Nichols hopped around the box in pain before throwing to first baseman Tommy Tucker for the final out. An ineffective Cobb was replaced by part-time starter Tom Vickery to begin the sixth inning. Boston proceeded to add four more runs on a grand slam by Nichols to increase its lead to 14 runs and Nichols' RBI total in the game to seven.

In the sixth Nichols surrendered singles to the first two Baltimore batters. He removed himself from the box and switched positions with left fielder Jack Stivetts. Stivetts was not at his best; he surrendered 11 runs over three innings. Amid Baltimore's torrid comeback, darkness saved Boston as umpire Billy Lynch called the game after eight innings. The Beaneaters were 14-11 winners.

Boston would finish the second half three games behind first-place Cleveland, setting the stage for a best-of-nine playoff. Boston won the series five games to none, including a tie in Game One with Nichols winning Games Four and Six.

Nichols' record for RBIs for a pitcher stood for less than a year and was broken by another Beaneaters pitcher, Harry Staley, who plated nine on June 1, 1893.

BALTIMORE

	AB.	R.	BH.	TB.	PO.	A.	E.
Shindle, 3b	5	3	2	2	0	4	0
Van Haltren, cf	5	1	2	2	1	0	1
Sutcliffe, 1b	5	2	2	2	11	0	1
Stovey. lf	5	1	2	3	1	0	0
O'Rourke, ss	3	0	1	1	0	1	1
Ward, rf	5	0	1	1	0	0	0
Gunson, c	4	1	1	1	7	0	0
Cobb, p	2	0	0	0	1	2	0
Vickery, p	2	2	2	2	0	0	0
Stricker, 2b	3	1	0	0	3	2	0
Totals	30	11	14	13	24	9	4

BOSTON

	AB.	R.	BH.	TB.	PO.	A.	E.
Long, ss	5	3	2	3	1	3	1
McCarthy, rf	5	0	1	2	0	0	0
Duffy, cf	5	1	3	3	3	0	0
Bennett, c	4	1	2	3	1	1	0
Stivetts, lf, p	4	1	2	2	3	1	0
Lowe, 3b	4	2	2	2	2	0	1
Quinn, 2b	5	2	3	3	4	2	1
Tucker, 1b	5	2	2	3	9	0	0
Nichols, p, lf	5	2	2	1	7	1	0
Totals	42	14	19	27	24	8	3

	1	2	3	4	5	6	7	8	
Boston	1	0	0	0	9	4	0	0	– 14
Baltimore	0	0	0	0	0	3	3	5	– 11

Earned Runs – Boston, 6; Baltimore, 6. First base on errors – Boston, 3; Baltimore, 3. Bases on errors – Baltimore, 3; Boston, 5. Left on bases – Baltimore, 6; Boston, 7. Two-Base Hits – Long, Bennett, McCarthy, Stovey. Three-Base Hits – Nichols, Stovey. Home-Runs – Nichols. Sacrifice Hits – Quinn, Stricker. Stolen Base – Van Haltren (2). Sacrifice Hits – Stricker, O'Rourke, Quinn. Double play – O'Rourke, Stricker and Sutcliffe; Stivetts and Quinn. First base on balls – By Cobb, Bennett, Stivetts; by Vickery, Lowe; by Nichols, O'Rourke; by Stivetts, O'Rourke, Stricker. Struck out – By Cobb, McCarthy, Bennett, Nichols (2); by Vickery, Nichols; by Nichols, Cobb. Wild pitch – Cobb. Passed ball – Gunson. Time – 2:10. Umpire – Lynch. Attendance – 804.[7]

Of the four box scores used to create this one, no two were exactly the same. In fact, they were all vastly different, as was frequently the case in the nineteenth century. There was a discrepancy in many categories and some box scores were more detailed than others. The information gathered for this game was, at times, merely educated guesses. It cannot be said with the utmost confidence that that what is compiled is precisely what occurred on September 19, 1892.

SOURCES

In addition to the sources cited in the Notes, the author also consulted the *Baltimore Sun*.

NOTES

1. *Boston Globe*, September 20, 1892: 5.
2. Donald Hubbard, *The Heavenly Twins of Boston Baseball* (Jefferson, North Carolina: McFarland Company Inc., 2008), 93.
3. Hubbard, 91.
4. Hubbard, 93.
5. Hubbard, 91.
6. *Boston Globe*; September 20, 1892: 5.
7. Box score compiled from *New York Times* (9/24/1892), *Chicago Tribune* (9/20/1892), *Washington Post* (9/20/1892), and *Boston Globe* (9/20/1892).

OCTOBER 1892: THE SPLIT-SEASON PLAYOFF

BY TERRY GOTTSCHALL

Major-league baseball faced a serious crisis in the early 1890s. Players rebelling against the reserve clause had created the independent Players' League to challenge the existing National League and the American Association in 1890. The ensuing season, in which three major leagues competed for fans and revenues, weakened baseball overall. The Players' League folded after a single season, the American Association neared insolvency in late 1891, and even the venerable National League languished.

National League and American Association representatives found a solution when they met in Indianapolis in December 1891 and agreed to consolidate the two leagues. The new organization combined the eight National League teams with four American Association franchises to create what *Sporting Life* editor Francis Richter called the "big league." In order to accommodate more teams, league directors decided to expand the standard 140-game season to 154 games, and they established a split-season format. Hoping that a different team would win each split-season, the directors tentatively planned a postseason "world championship series."

The Indianapolis agreement also needed to reconcile significant differences between the two organizations. The new league established a standard 50-cent admission, but allowed the former American Association teams to charge their traditional "two bits" – 25 cents. Likewise, former AA ballparks could sell alcohol (the Association had acquired the nickname Beer and Whiskey League) forbidden at teetotaling National League grounds, and could schedule games on Sunday, violating the long tradition of blue laws in National League cities.[1]

The 1892 season began on April 12 with more than 40,000 fans turning out. The Boston Beaneaters quickly moved into first place, with the Brooklyn Bridegrooms and the Cleveland Spiders competing for second. When the first half ended on July 13, Boston (52-22) led second-place Brooklyn (51-26) by 2½ games. *Sporting Life* attributed Boston's success to pitching, baserunning, and teamwork. The report described Cleveland (40-33), which finished fifth, as "one of the best-balanced teams in the League, being equally strong in batting, fielding and base-running, well-handled and aggressive."[2]

When the second half of the season began, on July 15, Boston started slowly while Cleveland, Brooklyn, Philadelphia, and Cincinnati dominated. Cleveland broke away from the pack at the end of the month, remaining solidly in first for the remainder of the season. Although Boston (50-26) made a late-season run, the Spiders (53-23) finished the second half on October 15 with a three-game lead.[3] The dual champions enabled a best-of-nine "world's championship series" to begin, with the teams playing three games each in Cleveland, Boston, and, if necessary, New York.[4]

Both teams engaged in a bit of trash-talking. When Boston manager Frank Selee complained that late-October weather would lead to postponed games and reduce attendance, Cleveland's player-manager, Patsy Tebeau, suggested that "the Beaneaters fear the humiliation of possible defeat."[5] Tebeau termed the cold weather a "dodge … simply an excuse to avoid playing Cleveland."[6] Selee responded that "the Boston players are willing to go for broke on their ability to beat the club that has been 'easy' for [us] all year."[7]

Bettors made the Spiders the early favorite based on their pitching staff. Cy Young had gone 36-12 with a 1.93 earned-run average, while rookie George "Nig" Cuppy had a 28-13 record with a 2.51 ERA. Meanwhile, fans attributed Boston's second-half decline to the poor performance of aging superstar Mike "King" Kelly. Described as "one of the biggest failures of the base ball season," Kelly batted only .189, well below his career .308 average.[8]

The series began in Cleveland on Monday, October 17, as more than 6,000 fans watched the two teams play to a 0-0 tie. *Sporting Life* described the game succinctly: "It was altogether a pitchers' battle and not a run had been scored, when, after the eleventh inning, the game was called owing to darkness."[9]

	R	H	E
Cleveland	0	4	1
Boston	0	6	0

Batteries: Young (CLE) vs. Stivetts (BOS)

Boston, choosing to bat first, edged Cleveland, 4-3, in the second game, on October 18. The Beaneaters' center fielder, Hugh Duffy, led Boston to victory with a double and two triples, while the Spiders sent "the ball time and again into some fielder's waiting hands."[10]

	R	H	E
Boston	4	10	2
Cleveland	3	10	2

Batteries: Staley (BOS) vs. Clarkson (CLE)

Boston won Game Three, 3-2, in an excellent contest whose "agony was not over until the last man was out."[11]

	R	H	E
Cleveland	2	8	0
Boston	3	9	2

Batteries: Young (CLE) vs. Stivetts (BOS)

The series moved to Boston's South End Grounds, where the Beaneaters won Game Four, 4-0, on Friday, October 21.

	R	H	E
Cleveland	0	7	2
Boston	4	6	0

Batteries: Cuppy (CLE) vs. Nichols (BOS)

The Spiders started strong in Game Five on Saturday, October 22, scoring six runs in the top of the second inning. But Boston came back to win, 12-7.[12]

	R	H	E
Cleveland	7	9	4
Boston	12	14	3

Batteries: Clarkson (CLE) vs. Stivetts (BOS)

Both league rules and state laws required the two teams to take Sunday off before playing Game Six on Monday, October 24. A Cleveland victory would have moved the series to New York for the next game, but Boston won, 8-3.

	R	H	E
Cleveland	3	10	4
Boston	8	11	5

Batteries: Young (CLE) vs. Kid Nichols (BOS)

Sporting Life provided an apt description for the series: "The Clevelands put up a stiff game and fought every inch, but they [played] against a team that has proved their superiors in all the points of the national game."[13] Cranks also ignored manager Selee's fear of bad weather as more than 32,000 attended the series' six games.

League directors nonetheless decided to abolish the split-season format and cut the season back to 132 games for 1893. The "big league" itself continued through the 1899 season, when the league dropped four teams. A true World Series would not return until 1903 with the advent of the American League.[14]

This essay was originally published in Bill Felber, ed., Inventing Baseball: The 100 Greatest Games of the 19th Century *(Phoenix: SABR, 2013).*

NOTES

1. "The Revolution," *Sporting Life*, December 19, 1891: 1.
2. "The Record," *Sporting Life*, July 16, 1892: 3.
3. "The Season's End," *Sporting Life*, October 22, 1892: 4.
4. "The Big League," *Sporting Life*, September 24, 1892: 2.
5. "Tebeau Talks," *Sporting Life*, October 8, 1892: 11.
6. Ibid.
7. "20/3," *Sporting Life*, October 15, 1892: 3.
8. "Editorial Views, News, Comment," *Sporting Life*, October 22, 1892: 2. Both Baseball-reference.com and Retrosheet give King Kelly's BA as .307, not .308
9. "The World's Championship Series," *Sporting Life*, October 22, 1892: 4.
10. "Boston Wins the Second Game," *Sporting Life*, October 22, 1892: 4.
11. "Boston Wins Again," *Sporting Life*, October 22, 1892: 4.
12. "The World's Series," *Sporting Life*, October 29, 1892: 3.
13. Ibid.
14. "The Big League," *Sporting Life*, October 8, 1892: 2.

BEANEATERS OPEN SEASON WITH ROUT OF GIANTS

APRIL 28, 1893: BOSTON BEANEATERS 9, NEW YORK GIANTS 2, AT THE POLO GROUNDS, NEW YORK.

BY JOEL RIPPEL

Even in the nineteenth century, Opening Day was a much-anticipated event.

When the Boston Beaneaters and New York Giants were rained out in their 1893 season opener, the *New York Sun* wrote: "The postponement of yesterday's game as a consequence of bad weather was undoubtedly one of the severest disappointments ever suffered by New York cranks."[1]

Fans were looking forward to the matchup between the two-time defending National League champion Beaneaters and the improved New York Giants.

"For a month past, the cranks have been preparing for the happy day when the New Yorks would again meet the champion Bostons and take a trifle of the conceit out of the men from the Hub," said the *Sun*.[2]

Adding to the interest in the game was a rule change, instituted for the 1893 season and described by one newspaper as "the new rule, which places the pitcher several feet further from home plate."[3]

In an effort to create more offense, the pitcher's box was replaced by a raised mound and rubber slab. Before the rule change, the pitcher could have his back foot anywhere along the four-foot back line of the box, which was 4 by 5½ feet on flat ground and 55½ feet from home plate. Even with the change, in today's game we still hear the expression "The pitcher was knocked out of the box," even though the box disappeared over 100 years ago. The change would require a pitcher's back foot to be in contact with the rubber, which was 60 feet 6 inches from home plate.

The hometown *New York World* said the rule change "will give the New Yorks something of an advantage over the majority of the clubs in the League, inasmuch as almost all of the Giants are strapping big fellows and as speedy as any pitchers in the profession. It is this matter of speed that will tell in the coming race."[4]

After the 24-hour rain delay, an announced crowd of 15,000 – according to the *Boston Globe*, the largest to that point in time for an Opening Day in New York and one of the largest ever to see a major-league game – gathered to watch the Beaneaters and Giants get the season underway.

Beaneaters leadoff hitter Herman Long, who had batted .280 with six home runs in 1892, stirred the crowd – which was standing 10 deep around the outfield – on the first pitch of the game. Long drove Silver King's offering over the left-field fence, but just outside the foul line. Long followed with line drive past Giants second baseman Monte Ward for a single. After a fly out, Hugh Duffy singled past short with Long stopping at second. Long and Duffy then manufactured the Beaneaters' first run of the season.

"Duffy led well off first and (catcher Jack) Doyle threw sharply to (first baseman Roger) Connor. Then spry little Duffy began to hop back and forth, while Ward, Connor and (shortstop Shorty)

Fuller tried to corner him. Meantime, Herman Long was making tracks for third which he reached. Duffy was dodging back and forth like a pendulum. Connor was nearly on top of the little fellow, but he wriggled away and started for second. Connor threw to Fuller, and Long, who had been edging toward home, made a rush. Fuller sprinted after Duffy, and touched him, but Long scored the first run with a dive and slide to the plate."[5]

Staked to a 1-0 lead, Kid Nichols took the mound for the Beaneaters. The 23-year-old Nichols was beginning his fourth season with the Beaneaters. Even though Nichols had won 30 and 35 games, respectively, in the Beaneaters championship seasons in 1891 and 1892 season, Giants fans were apparently happy to see him.

The *New York World* said, "When Nichols took up a position in the box, the great crowd of spectators waxed exceedingly glad. 'He is a weak youth,' they argued, 'and he surely cannot stand the increased pitching distance.' They did not know the 'Kid.'"[6]

The 5-foot-10, 175-pound right-hander opened his season with three scoreless innings before the Giants got on the scoreboard with a run in the fourth inning.

Nichols hit Giants leadoff hitter Eddie Burke in the back with a curve. Burke, who was hit by a pitch 25 times in 1893, stole second and went to third on a sacrifice by Mike Tiernan. Burke scored on Ward's infield hit, "although (second baseman Bobby) Lowe committed an error of judgment in throwing to first instead of to the plate."[7]

After the Beaneaters went in order in the fifth, the Giants took a 2-1 lead. Third baseman George Davis led off for the Giants with a triple to left-center. Davis scored on Harry Lyons' single up the middle.

The momentum was short-lived for the Giants, as the "sixth inning brought a deluge of woe and desolation. Nobody knows whether King had let up or let down."[8]

Tommy McCarthy led off with a single to center. After Billy Nash popped out, Tommy Tucker and Lowe followed with singles. Lowe's hit scored McCarthy with the tying run. Charlie Bennett followed with a double to left-center to score Tucker, who had won the American Association batting title in 1889 with a .372 batting average (the first switch-hitter to win a major-league batting title), and Lowe and give the Beaneaters a 4-2 lead.

Nichols, who had hit two home runs in his first three seasons with the Beaneaters, followed with a long home run to left-center to make it 6-2. King secured the final two outs of the inning, but his day was finished after six innings.

The Beaneaters added three runs in the eighth inning. Giants reliever Ed Crane retired the first two Boston hitters and got two strikes on Long. Long then swung at a wide curve and missed, but the ball got past Doyle, and Long reached first base. Singles by Cliff Carroll, Duffy, and Nash, and a walk to McCarthy combined for the three runs.

Nichols closed with four scoreless innings – retiring the Giants in order in the ninth – to finish with a five-hitter for the first of his 34 victories in 1893. He walked one and struck out one.

The *New York World* wrote, "The sum and substance of the defeat of the New Yorks lies in their failure to bat. They could not touch the Boston pitcher at any stage of the game."[9]

Duffy and McCarthy each had three hits for the Beaneaters, who outhit the Giants, 14-5. All nine in the Beaneaters batting order had at least one hit.

"The Bostons won the game with the stick and in the field," commented the *Boston Globe*. "Tucker, Carroll and McCarthy were full of red pepper on the field and on the coaching lines, while Duffy, McCarthy and Lowe used the stick at salary-limit style, with something to spare."[10]

Davis and Lyons each had two hits for the Giants.

Despite the Opening Day success, the Beaneaters got off to a slow start in 1893. The Giants rebounded to beat Boston 15-6 the next day, and two weeks into the season the Beaneaters were just 5-7.

The Beaneaters eventually got on a roll, going 57-20 in June, July, and August en route to their third consecutive title.

SOURCES

In addition to the sources cited in the Notes, the author also consulted Newspapers.com and Retrosheet.org.

NOTES

1   "Unhappy Baseball Cranks," *New York Sun*, April 28, 1893: 8.

2   Ibid.

3   "These Games Will Count," *New York World*, April 27, 1893: 12.

4   Ibid.

5   "Beaten, But Not Crushed," *New York Sun*, April 29, 1893: 8.

6   "Baseball's Big Revival," *New York World*, April 29, 1893: 10.

7   "Beaten, But Not Crushed."

8   "Baseball's Big Revival."

9   "Beaten, But Not Crushed."

10 "Giants Go Under," *Boston Globe*, April 29, 1893: 5.

HOME OPENER IN FRONT OF STAR-STUDDED CROWD

MAY 15, 1893: BOSTON BEANEATERS 8, NEW YORK GIANTS 6, AT SOUTH END GROUNDS

BY JERROD COTOSMAN

The stars of Massachusetts came out to the South End Grounds as the Boston Nationals opened their 1893 home schedule. It was Monday, May 15, 1893, and around 8,000 fans braved the ominous clouds to see the defending champions face the New York Giants. The grandstand was awash in local dignitaries including mayors, state senators, and other public servants, the crown jewel of which was Governor William Russell. The governor was cheered by the masses and showed a deft politician's touch by purchasing a scorecard from a small boy selling them.[1] Other attendees of note, including John Quincy Adams, the former president's grandson, and the well-known rooter Arthur "Hi Hi" Dixwell, filed in and took their seats for the start of the contest.[2]

Boston had played its first 13 games on the road and had won six of them. The Giants' record was 5-8. The second division was unfamiliar territory for the local nine and even the raising of the 1892 pennant seemed desultory as the flag just hung limply since "there was no breeze and the incident lost most of its charm."[3] The champions took the field marching behind Baldwin's Cadet Band and stopped at home plate to bow to the fans in the grandstand.[4] They were wearing new white uniforms with bright red stockings, which contrasted with the Giants' outfits of bluish gray flannels with black stockings.[5]

Boston ace Kid Nichols retired the first batter and then waited for the governor and his party to take their seats before giving up a double to Silent Mike Tiernan.[6] However, the Giants failed to score when Roger Connor flied to left. In the bottom of the first, Herman Long provided a jolt of excitement for the crowd. Boston's star shortstop crushed an offspeed pitch from Ed Crane beyond the left-field fence for a home run. A few batters later, umpire John Gaffney held up the game to present third baseman Billy Nash with a gold locket compliments of the Continental Clothing Company.[7] Alas, if Nash was inspired, he had no chance to show it as Tommy McCarthy was thrown out trying to steal second to end the inning.

For a while it seemed one run would be all the support Nichols needed as he held the opposition scoreless while pitching out of several jams. George Davis doubled in the second but was tagged out in a rundown as he tried to score on a groundball. The Giants next threatened in the fourth when Connor walked and Davis drove the ball to deep left-center field. Cliff Carroll retreated to the depths of the grounds and made a fine catch near the fence. The next two batters went out to strand another runner.

But New York struck in the fifth when Harry Lyons bunted safely and Crane helped his own cause with a single. Eddie Burke then drove in Lyons with a base hit, and a sacrifice moved the runners up. Giants captain John Montgomery Ward grounded to Long, who threw out the man attempting to score. When Ward tried for second on the play, the throw from catcher Charlie Bennett was wild and Burke came home with the go-ahead run. George Davis followed with a single to make the score 3-1, but the Giants would not enjoy the lead for long as their defense fell apart in the home sixth.

Crane was in trouble from the start of the inning as McCarthy singled and Nash doubled, causing General Dixwell to take up his trademark "Hi Hi" cheer.[8] Tommy Tucker grounded to first but Connor fumbled the ball long enough for McCarthy to score. Bobby Lowe hit a ball to short and it appeared Nash was hung up off third, but a bad throw by shortstop Shorty Fuller left everyone safe and the game tied. Crane had been betrayed by his defense and now contributed to his own demise by walking Bennett and Nichols, loading the bases and bringing up Long.

The Boston shortstop's at-bat was not as dramatic as his first one, but it was more productive. He hit a hard shot to third. Davis made a fine stop and threw home trying for the force, but the ball hit the speeding Lowe in the shoulder and rolled all the way to the fence. Instead of a tie game with two out, it was now 6-3 and Carroll made it 7-3 with another hit. Boston had put up six runs in the sixth on a trio of Giants errors and had taken control of the game.

It was 8-4 by the ninth and the Giants tried to make the most of their last at-bat against the tiring Nichols. Crane batted for himself and beat out a bunt. Burke lined to Duffy in center and Tiernan singled sharply to right. McCarthy charged the ball and threw wildly to the infield, allowing Crane to come home and Silent Mike to reach third. Ward had a chance to cut further into the lead but he popped up to Long at short and then Connor singled to right. McCarthy made his second bad decision of the inning by trying to get the man at the plate and Tiernan was easily safe as the batter took an extra base on the throw.

The rooters became anxious; the score was 8-6 and the Giants' hottest hitter was coming to bat. George Davis was off to a torrid start, already had a pair of hits off Nichols, and had been robbed of another by Carroll's fine catch in the fourth. The *New York Times* would have him unofficially leading the National League in batting with a .468 average at the end of the day.[9] Now he took the measure of the Boston hurler and drove a ball deep to center, where Hugh Duffy ran it down for the final out. Boston was back to .500 and ready to resume another pennant chase while the dejected Ward was left to vow, "We are due to win a game tomorrow and nothing will stop us."[10]

NOTES

1 "Play Ball," *Boston Globe*, May 16, 1893: 1.

2 "Play Ball," *Boston Globe*, May 16, 1893: 6.

3 "Boston 8, New York 6," *New York Sun*, May 16, 1893: 4.

4 "Bostons Show Their Mettle," *Boston Post*, May 16, 1893: 5.

5 "On Home Grounds," *Boston Herald*, May 16, 1893: 1.

6 "Bostons Show Their Mettle."

7 "On Home Grounds," *Boston Herald*, May 16, 1893: 1.

8 "On Home Grounds," *Boston Herald*, May 16, 1893: 2.

9 "Giants Defeated Again," *New York Times*, May 16, 1893: 3.

10 "Play Ball," *Boston Globe*, May 16, 1893: 6.

THE HOME RUN THAT WASN'T

MAY 19, 1893: BROOKLYN BRIDEGROOMS 5, BOSTON BEANEATERS 4 (12 INNINGS), AT SOUTH END GROUNDS, BOSTON

BY JOHN ZINN

Discerning Beaneaters fans had a choice on Friday, May 19, 1893. Should they skip that afternoon's game with the Brooklyn Bridegrooms because of the threatening weather or risk getting wet to see their heroes take on Ed Stein, the young season's hottest pitcher? A 27-game winner the prior year, Stein, after dropping his first start, had won five straight including a victory over Boston just a week earlier. But the Brooklyn pitcher wasn't just winning games; he was dominating opponents, allowing Boston just three hits and throwing a one-hitter against Philadelphia.[1]

Stein's mound opponent was Jack Stivetts, a 35-game winner the year before, but just 3-3 thus far in 1893, including being "batted all over the field" in one start and suffering a "cannonading" in another.[2] Although some of Stivetts's problems may have been caused by the lengthening of the pitching distance to 60 feet 6 inches, sportswriter O.P. Caylor believed excessive drinking was the reason the Boston pitcher had "not been so effective this season."[3] Although Boston fans had both the weather and a matchup between two pitchers seemingly going in opposite directions as excuses to stay away, an estimated 2,500 turned up for what the *Boston Journal* called a game "which for real pleasure and excitement may not be equaled this season."[4]

Fortunately, the rain held off and the game developed into a pitchers' duel with both hurlers in command, not necessarily of their pitches, but definitely of the opposing batters. Stivetts was wild, to put it mildly, walking eight over the first eight innings, but the Boston pitcher didn't allow a single hit or permit a runner to advance beyond second base. Beaneaters batters were equally ineffective against Stein, registering only one hit through eight innings, and the game headed to the ninth scoreless and almost hitless.[5] But any fan disappointed by the lack of scoring would soon get more than his share of offensive fireworks.

Tom Daly began the Brooklyn ninth by reaching first on a "pretty bunt."[6] Next up was Danny Richardson, who "hit an easy bounder" to Stivetts, but the Bridegrooms got lucky when the Boston pitcher "grabbed at [the ball] like a blind man, and after fumbling awhile, threw it over first base.[7] Instead of what Tim Murnane, writing in the *Boston Globe*, thought should have been a double play, Brooklyn had men on second and third and none out. Doubtless cursing himself while bearing down at the same time, Stivetts got Tommy Corcoran to ground to third baseman Billy Nash, who threw Daly out at home. The Boston pitcher wasn't, however, so fortunate with Con Daily, who doubled, driving in Richardson and again putting runners at second and third with just one out. Next up was Stein, who grounded out to Tommy Tucker at first base, but when Tucker tried to throw out Richardson at home, the baserunner collided with Boston catcher Charlie Ganzel, allowing not just Richardson but also Daily to score. Stivetts got the final out without further incident, but the damage was done and the Beaneaters trailed 3-0 as they came to bat for what was likely the last time.[8]

Considering the Beaneaters had done nothing with Stein for eight innings, it was no surprise that "the home patrons began to file out of the grounds."[9] But even if the fans had given up, that wasn't the case with the Boston team, which Murnane said "always plays the string out." After Tommy McCarthy walked, Nash "sent the ball over the left field fence" and the Bostons were within one run.[10] Or were they? Although he was obviously entitled to score, Nash wasn't required to do so and according to the *Journal*, he elected to remain at third to "possibly make Stein unsteady."[11] It seems a strange strategy, but although the *Brooklyn Daily Eagle* claimed Nash's hit didn't leave the park and he was held at third, the Boston papers were clear that Nash chose to remain there rather than score. Whether his presence rattled Stein is debatable, but no one could argue with the result when Tucker "cracked one against the right field fence," driving in Nash and putting himself in scoring position.[12] A few minutes later Tucker scored on Tom Daly's throwing error, tying the game and leading fans to "cut as many other 'monkey-shines' as the most partisan college student."[13] Although the Beaneaters threatened to win the game right then and there, they failed to score and the game headed to the 10th.[14]

Stivetts's lack of control continued to plague him, helping the Bridegrooms load the bases, although Murnane attributed "much of the blame" to the calls of umpire John Gaffney.[15] Although Boston was fortunate to limit the damage, Brooklyn scored once, putting the Beaneaters' backs against the wall again. Fortunately for Boston and its fans, Nash was up third in the inning. Although two were out and none on, the Boston third baseman didn't disappoint, again homering over the left-field wall. This time he didn't stop at third, tying the score and earning an ovation that "has seldom been equaled on the [Boston] grounds."[16] Tied at 4-4, the game remained that way through a scoreless 11th and headed to the 12th with both starters still on the mound. If he didn't have enough problems with his lack of control, Stivetts was betrayed by the Boston defense when Cliff Carroll muffed Oyster Burns' fly ball, supposedly because, as Murnane cruelly put it, he was afraid "to dampen his feet in the wet grass."[17] After a sacrifice, Tom Daly singled in Burns and Brooklyn once again took the lead.

At this point, it was unlikely anyone expected Boston to go quietly and they weren't disappointed. Stein did nothing to help himself when he threw away Carroll's grounder, but somehow the Beaneaters batter made his second mistake of the inning and "lost a chance to make second base." Next up was future Hall of Famer Hugh Duffy, who managed only "a measly little grounder," forcing Carroll at second. After McCarthy went out, Boston's last chance was fittingly in the hands or bat of Nash, who "came up smiling" to "a ringing old shout" from the crowd. That roar was probably nothing compared to the sound when Nash hit the third pitch over the left-field fence, but sadly for him and Boston, it was foul by five feet. With masterful understatement, Murnane said, "Stein looked worried." Tempting the baseball gods by putting the winning run on base, Stein walked Nash, but got away with it when Tucker made the final out.[18]

After 12 innings of baseball drama, the *New York Sun* understandably believed "everybody, players included, felt weak," but the paper thought Boston had "no reason to feel down in the mouth."[19] Back in Brooklyn, the *Eagle* bragged that the win, the second straight over the defending champions on their home ground, was "indeed a triumph."[20] But if the paper, the Brooklyn club, or its fans thought this was a sign of a successful season, they were wrong because the Bridegrooms would finish in a sixth-place tie with Cincinnati, while Boston would win the pennant. A few days later, Stein won his seventh straight game, but it was downhill from there as he went 12-14 the rest of the season. Stivetts would continue to experience mixed success in 1893, winning 20 games, a far cry from his 35 victories the year before. Nash hit eight more home runs in 1893, but it is doubtful that he enjoyed any as much as the two on that May afternoon even though they came in a losing effort.

NOTES

1 "A Hot Game, Forsooth!" *Brooklyn Daily Eagle*, May 20, 1893: 3.

2 *Philadelphia Inquirer*, May 7, 1893: 3; *Daily Evening Bulletin* (Haverhill, Massachusetts), May 11, 1893: 1.

3 *Evening Herald* (Shenandoah, Pennsylvania), October 7, 1893: 3; Peter Morris, *A Game of Inches: The Story Behind the Innovations That Shaped Baseball* (Chicago: Ivan R. Dee, 2010), 27.

4 "Twelve Innings," *Boston Journal*, May 20, 1893: 3; *Baltimore Sun*, May 20, 1893: 6.

5 "Twelve Innings."

6 T.H. Murnane, "Bungling Work," *Boston Globe*, May 20, 1893: 6.

7 Ibid.

8 Ibid., "Twelve Innings"; "A Hot Game, Forsooth!"

9 "Twelve Innings."

10 Murnane.

11 Ibid.; "Twelve Innings."

12 "Bungling Work."

13 "Twelve Innings."

14 "A Hot Game, Forsooth!"; "Twelve Innings"; Murnane.

15 Murnane.

16 "Twelve Innings."

17 Murnane.

18 Ibid.

19 *New York Sun*, May 20, 1893: 4.

20 "A Hot Game, Forsooth!"

A BARRAGE OF BATTING

MAY 26, 1893: BOSTON BEANEATERS 13, WASHINGTON SENATORS 12, AT SOUTH END GROUNDS, BOSTON

BY MARK PESTANA

It had been a rough opening month for the defending National League champions. Although they never dipped more than two games below .500, they had not risen more than two games above .500 either. After a 7-5 loss on May 25 to the visiting Washington Senators, the Boston Beaneaters were lingering in fifth place in the NL, their record a mediocre 12-11.

For the second match of their series with Washington, Harry Staley was tagged to start for Boston. Thus far, the Beaneaters had relied mainly on a two-man rotation of Kid Nichols and Jack Stivetts, with Staley getting the call about every fourth or fifth game. A consistent, if unspectacular hurler, Staley was in his third season with Boston and had four consecutive 20-win seasons behind him.

The Washington club included a number of former Boston players, the most notable of whom was player-manager James "Orator" O'Rourke. At the age of 42, O'Rourke was not just the Senators' manager but also a full-time player, splitting most of his time between left field and first base and appearing in 129 of the team's 130 games. O'Rourke had played six seasons in Beantown, dating back to the days of the National Association's Boston Red Stockings.[1] The 1893 season was to be his final tour in the major leagues, but he was not there for merely sentimental reasons or in deference to his seniority: his 95-RBI total would top the Washington team.

O'Rourke called upon Al Maul to do the hurling duties. The 27-year-old Maul had performed in six prior major-league seasons, but had logged only one full year: 1890, when he pitched 31 games and went 16-12 for Pittsburgh of the Players' League. By the end of the 1893 campaign, he would amass a career-high 297 innings. Maul began 1893 with three straight victories but was winless in his last four appearances.

The Spring skies were overcast in Boston but a barrage of batting fireworks soon lit up the South End Grounds. The home team claimed first at-bats and went right to work. Shortstop Herman Long led off with a hit and, after Cliff Carroll's sacrifice, scored on a single by Hugh Duffy. Duffy tarried not long on the basepaths, as the next batter, Boston-bred Tommy McCarthy, hit a triple deep into left field. Team captain and third sacker Billy Nash plated McCarthy with a double and scored himself on Tommy Tucker's bounding single.

Bobby Lowe's fly to left was captured by O'Rourke for the second out, bringing to the plate third-string catcher Bill Merritt. The 22-year-old from the northern Massachusetts mill city of Lowell was enjoying his third start in four days. He had already displayed some heavy hitting in his limited playing time, notably a two-homer performance in the May 23 win over Philadelphia. From the eight spot in the lineup, with two outs and Tucker on first, Merritt launched a blast over the left-field fence. The *Daily Advertiser* reported, "The popular belief in the grandstand was that it fell down the smokestack of a passing locomotive."[2] With the Beaneaters holding a 6-0 lead, pitcher Staley completed the circuit of the batting order and ended the Boston half with a fly out to right.

The Washingtons did not wilt in the face of a six-run deficit. Leading off was right fielder Paul Radford. A Bay Stater by birth, the versatile and well-traveled Radford had begun his major-league career with the pennant-winning Beaneaters in 1883 and more recently had played on the American Association's 1891 champion Boston Reds.[3] He drew a base on balls from Staley, and took second on Dummy Hoy's groundout. O'Rourke was up next and quickly cut the Boston lead to four with a home run to left. Sam Wise, a veteran of seven years in Boston uniforms dating back to 1882, followed with a strikeout. But then the floodgates opened, as Staley failed to retire any of the next six batters. Five singles and a walk produced another four Washington runs, tying the score at 6-6 before Hoy flied out to end the carnage.

Each team added a run in the second inning, the Beaneaters stringing together a single, a walk, and a fly out to produce theirs. The Senators' resulted from two singles and an error,[4] with outstanding catches by McCarthy in left and Carroll in right perhaps preventing greater damage.[5] In the third, three singles, including one by Staley, gave Boston another run and an 8-7 lead.

Two scoreless half-innings ensued before the Senators renewed their abuse of Staley in the bottom of the fourth. Wise led off with a single, and was followed at bat by first baseman Henry Larkin. Now in his 10th and final season, Larkin was one of the most consistently heavy hitters in the majors, usually appearing among the leaders in doubles, triples, homers, and slugging percentage. With Wise waiting at first, Larkin showed off his power, knocking the ball over the left-field fence to give Washington a one-run edge.

Catcher Charley "Duke" Farrell was next up. Like Radford, he was a Bay State native and an alumnus of the 1891 AA Boston champs. Unlike Radford, Larkin, and O'Rourke, Farrell was nowhere near the end of his string; he would in fact play five years into the twentieth century. After wearing Staley down with a few fouls, including one that dropped embarrassingly between Nash and Merritt as they chased it down the third-base line, Farrell made it back-to-back round-trippers, putting the ball in almost the same spot as Larkin's. Joe Mulvey then reached base with one of his four hits in the game. Another Boston-area native, rookie shortstop Joe Sullivan, made the first out of the inning, and Maul followed with the second. But Radford joined the home-run derby, driving the third four-bagger of the inning over the left-field fence. Hoy made the third out, but the Senators led 12-8.

Staley's day was finished; Jack Stivetts assumed pitching duties in the fifth. Neither team scored in that inning, but the Beaneaters rallied in the sixth. O'Rourke replaced Maul with southpaw Duke Esper in that inning.[6] Esper had made only four pitching starts but, like Maul, would eventually log a career-high innings-pitched total by the end of the season and, dubiously, would top the NL with 28 pitching losses.

Herman Long began the Boston attack with his fourth straight hit, and Carroll followed with a safety. Duffy then made the score 12-11 with a three-run blast that disappeared, like every one of the game's five previous homers, somewhere over the left-field fence. Bases empty now, McCarthy doubled. Nash was put out on a close play at first, but the speedy Little Mac managed to score from second on the play, and the game was tied.

Washington got a single off Stivetts in the bottom of the sixth, but that was all. The home team took the lead in the seventh when, with two outs, Duffy drew a walk from Esper, took second on a passed ball, and scored on McCarthy's third hit of the day.

From the bottom of the seventh through the top of the ninth, Stivetts and Esper held their respective lines. In the ninth the Senators threatened. Leadoff batter Mulvey doubled deep to left. Tim Murnane in the *Globe* wrote, "Six inches more and the ball was over."[7] After an out, Esper bid fair to help his own cause with a single that advanced Mulvey to third. Top of the order, Radford up, already with two hits. He got hold of a Stivetts pitch and lined it into center. But Duffy had no problem snaring it and, with Mulvey tagging from third, sent a bullet toward the plate, where catcher Merritt stood waiting. Duffy's throw was true, Merritt's tag on Mulvey made it a double play, and the Beaneaters escaped with a 13-12 win.

The audience of 2,000[8] had witnessed quite a slugfest, the two teams producing 36 hits and an amazing (for the era) six home runs.[9] A note in the *Globe's* summary asserted, "While the crowd enjoyed the hitting, the game was too long."[10] The official game time was recorded as 2 hours 20 minutes.

SOURCES

In addition to the sources cited in the Notes, the author also consulted Baseball-Reference.com, Retrosheet.org. and the following:

Nemec, David. *Major League Baseball Profiles: 1871-1900, Volumes 1 & 2* (Lincoln, Nebraska: Bison Books, 2011).

_____. *The Great Encyclopedia of 19th-Century Major League Baseball* (New York: Donald I. Fine Books, 1997).

NOTES

1. At least one source gives him another nickname, "Judge." "Fusilade of Hits," *Boston Daily Advertiser*, May 27, 1893: 2.

2. "Fusilade of Hits."

3. Radford logged 900 games as an outfielder, nearly 500 at various infield positions, and even a handful as pitcher, while serving on nine teams in 12 years.

4. The *Boston Globe* credited Washington with three singles, but the *Advertiser* attributed the run to a McCarthy "fumble."

5. Tim Murnane called McCarthy's "one of the greatest catches ever seen at the grounds ... equalling the best work of the never-to-be-forgotten Andy Leonard." "Boston's Day," *Boston Globe*, May 27, 1893: 6.

6. The *Globe* reported that Esper entered the game in the seventh inning, while both the *Daily Advertiser* and the *Boston Journal* had him in the box for the sixth. Since two box scores show Esper with two at-bats in the game and the second of those was definitely in the ninth, the first must have been in the Washington sixth. As the Senators' half of the sixth followed the Beaneaters' half and as Esper most likely entered as the pitcher before going to bat; the accounts of the *Advertiser* and *Journal* appear correct on this point.

7. "Boston's Day."

8. This figure is per the *Advertiser's* report; the *Springfield Republican* of May 27 put it at 1,750.

9. The box scores in both the *Washington Post* and the *Washington Evening Star* of May 27, 1893, claimed there were seven homers, attributing one to Tommy Tucker, but no other reports bear this out. A contributing factor to the general home-run explosion was, of course, the increase in pitching distance that went into effect in 1893. Previously, the pitcher worked from a box whose front boundary was 50 feet from the center of home plate; beginning in 1893, the box was replaced by a rubber slab planted 60 feet 6 inches from home. The pitcher being required to keep one foot on the rubber was another boon to batters. Murnane wrote, "Capt. O'Rourke claims that it is not the five-foot extra that is making the heavy batting, but the fact that the pitcher is confined to the one-foot rubber plate." ("Boston's Day.")

10. "Boston's Day."

"TUCKER HIT LIKE A FIEND" AND "NICHOLS SAVED THE DAY"

JULY 22, 1893: BOSTON BEANEATERS 13, NEW YORK GIANTS 8, AT SOUTH END GROUNDS, BOSTON

BY BILL NOWLIN

The victory this day brought the Beaneaters to within a half-game of first place, just behind the Phillies. The Giants were in 10th place in the 12-team National League, 14½ games out of the lead. Though still in July, the game was the last matchup between the two teams in the 1893 championship season.

The Saturday afternoon game pitted two future Hall of Famers against each other, Kid Nichols for Boston and Amos Rusie for New York. Nichols was working his way toward a 34-14 season. Rusie wrapped up 1893 with a 33-21 record. But neither of them had started the game.

Pitching first for Boston was Harry Staley, who ultimately finished the season 18-10 despite a 5.13 earned-run average. He gave up two runs to the Giants in the top of the first. Center fielder Jack Doyle started things off with a single to left field off Staley. He was forced at second. After another out, third baseman George Davis posted his first of five hits in the game, driving in Giants manager and second baseman Monte Ward. Roger Connor singled home Ward and the Giants had a quick 2-0 lead.

Mark Baldwin had beaten Boston and Nichols, 4-1, on July 17. He'd beaten Boston again, 11-3, over Harry Staley in the second game of the July 19 doubleheader. This day he did not fare as well. He gave up seven runs in the bottom of the first inning. Herman Long walked and Bobby Lowe singled. Hugh Duffy sacrificed but was safe on an error and the bases were loaded with nobody out. Tommy McCarthy singled in two, to tie the score. Tommy Tucker and Charlie Ganzel both singled, and Staley doubled, and it was 7-2, Boston, after the first frame.

This prompted Boston super-crank Arthur "Hi-Hi" Dixwell to crow, making things "very disagreeable" for New York's lead rooter, "big fat Judge Cullom."[1]

After the first inning, Rusie took over for Baldwin.

This was no routine game in midseason. As T.H. Murnane wrote in the *Boston Globe*, "There were no smiles exchanged and the members of both teams played as if the pennant was at stake and this game would decide it."[2] The heat and humidity was fierce; a front-page lead story on the weather in the next day's *Sunday Globe* described an "over-baked and blistered city."[3]

Some 5,296 spectators made their way to the South End Grounds. It was, Murnane wrote, "large and the most enthusiastic of the season." After Umpire John Gaffney gave the word, the battle began. The crowd was not uniformly one of backers of the Beaneaters. Murnane observed that "at least one-third of the spectators … cheered the New York boys at every chance."[4]

New York scored twice more in the third, and Boston added one to their score, making it 8-4 – but the New Yorkers scored four times to tie it in the top of the fourth. Cullom stood from behind the visitors bench and yelled and yelled until Dixwell waved that the battle was on.

The *Boston Journal* wrote that "the man who did not have his fill of ecstasy and despair in quick alternation had no blood in his veins."[5]

The Beaneaters pushed two more runs across in the bottom of the fourth, and never looked back. That's when manager Frank Selee brought Nichols on. The *Philadelphia Inquirer* game story declared, "Nichols Saved the Day."[6]

Nichols shut down New York, allowing only Davis to reach base – twice: once on an infield single to third base and once on a single to left field in the top of the ninth.

"Rusie was hit hard at times and his support was poor," reported the *New York Times*.[7] The Beaneaters added another run in the fifth and two more in the eighth, and the final score was 13-8 in Boston's favor.

Davis was 5-for-5 on the day. For Boston, Murnane wrote, "Tucker hit like a fiend," going 4-for-5, and Ganzel was 3-for-3 at the plate.

Murnane devoted a full paragraph to praising the officiating of umpire Gaffney, saying that it was a "pleasure" to see such a well-umpired game.

The game lasted, according to the box scores, exactly two hours. In the matter of doubles, some box scores – such as the ones that ran in the *Inquirer* and the *New York Times* – show Tucker as having four doubles in the game. The hometown *Boston Globe*, however, showed him with just two.

Boston won the season series between the two clubs, eight games to four. The Beaneaters finished in first place, five games ahead of second-place Pittsburgh. The Giants climbed in the standings, while falling further out of first. They finished in fifth place, but were 19½ games behind Boston. So many other teams had simply performed worse, dropping further in the standings.

SOURCES

In addition to the sources cited in the Notes, the author also consulted Retrosheet.org.

NOTES

1 T.H. Murnane, "Coming Our Way," *Boston Globe*, July 23, 1893: 7. Digby Bell and Sam Crane joined Cullom in pulling for the Giants.

2 Ibid.

3 "Not a Hot City," *Boston Globe*, July 23, 1893: 1.

4 Ibid.

5 "A Game for Cranks," *Boston Journal*, July 24, 1893: 5.

6 "Nichols Saved the Day," *Philadelphia Inquirer*, July 23, 1893: 3.

7 "New-Yorks Sadly Trounced," *New York Times*, July 23, 1893: 6.

UNSAFE PASSAGE

AUGUST 19, 1893: BOSTON BEANEATERS 13, PITTSBURG PIRATES 10 (FIRST GAME), AT SOUTH END GROUNDS, BOSTON

BY ANDY TERRICK

The 1893 season for the Boston Beaneaters began in a mediocre manner, but after 20 games the team's wins consistently outnumbered its losses. By the time of the summer solstice, the team was battling for the lead in the National League. A road trip begun in late June achieved only mixed results through most of the following month, yet the Beaneaters managed to return home on July 20 a mere 1½ games behind first-place Philadelphia. And that was the point when Boston became nearly unbeatable. Between July 20 and August 18, the Beaneaters overtook Philadelphia in the standings, winning 24 out of 27 games, a torrid pace that the Phillies couldn't match. In fact, by August 18, Philadelphia no longer even held second place, having been overtaken by their cross-state rivals from Pittsburg. The Pirates had a fantastic beginning to their season, but like Boston, a road trip started in June didn't go the way they wanted. Unlike Boston, a return home didn't signal an instant turnaround. The Smoky City club lost a total of 18 games both at home and on the road during the month. After a 22-16 walloping at the hands of Brooklyn on June 30, the team in July regained its winning ways of April and May, claiming victory in 33 out of its next 43 games. The Pirates' offense led the way, accruing double-digit run totals in almost half of those 43 games.

A matchup between Pittsburg and Boston originally set for Friday, August 18, was called off because of inclement weather.[1]

So the two hottest clubs in the league were scheduled to play a doubleheader on Saturday, August 19, at the South End Grounds. Pittsburg was still 7½ games behind Boston, but with more than a month remaining in the season, a couple of victories against the leaders would go a long way toward closing that gap

The pitching matchup for the opener was Hank Gastright for Boston vs. Red Ehret for Pittsburg. Gastright was a former member of the Pittsburg staff, but had been cast off near the end of their disastrous June stretch; his poor showing in an 18-5 loss to Philadelphia led to his release.[2] Ehret was a reliable workhorse who ranked high on the list of hurlers with fewest walks per game in 1892, but he also led the league in hit batsmen that year, sharing the distinction with Phill Knell and teammate Mark Baldwin. In 1890 Ehret's Louisville club outpaced Gastright and his Columbus teammates to win the American Association pennant, thereby making that season's (thanks to the Players' League) talent-diluted World's Series.[3] Louisville was matched against the National League's Brooklyn squad, and Ehret contributed by pitching two victories in the inconclusive series. As a member of the Association runner-up Solons, Gastright had notched 30 victories. Both men knew what it was to be an integral member of a successful team.

In the opening game's first inning, neither team scored. When the Pirates came up in the top of the second, their offensive prowess started to show. Gastright got out of the inning only after facing the entire Pittsburg batting order. The visitors piled up five runs, and held a commanding lead.

That notion, however, changed quickly. In the bottom half of the inning, the first batter, Billy Nash, walked. Immediately, Boston players must have sensed something about a weakness in Ehret's state of mind, because it was reported that the next batter up, Tommy Tucker, "had a juicy lemon and began coaching."[4] Essentially, the team started using verbal warfare to psych out the opposing pitcher.

Tucker made it to first base by way of a single, while the next batter, Cliff Carroll, patiently earned a walk. Charlie Ganzel was hit by an errant pitch and, based on numeric evidence, this would suggest a run was forced in. However, no mention of scoring would happen in the *Boston Globe's* recap until the next batter, pitcher Gastright, also walked.[5] The loss of control and gain of dismay led Ehret to hit another batter, Herman Long, in the elbow, which sent home yet another run for the Beaneaters. With three runs in and the bases loaded, Pittsburg manager Al Buckenburger removed Ehret from the game, calling on William "Adonis" Terry to pitch relief. Terry had been a promising youngster who had twirled two no-hitters for Brooklyn's AA entry in the 1880s,[6] and he became a serviceable veteran. He was a bright spot during Pittsburg's unremarkable 1892 season with an 18-7 record. Terry's unusual moniker, "Adonis," likely had to do with his looks.[7]

The first batter Terry faced, Boston second sacker Bobby Lowe, was hit with a pitch, bringing in the fourth Boston run.

Hugh Duffy came to the plate next, and Terry walked him, too, an event that tied the game. Tommy McCarthy's at-bat provided a rare occurrence of actual bat-related contact for the inning when he flied out to left field. The reprieve for anyone updating the scoreboard was short-lived, however, as Nash came up a second time and swatted a single, scoring two more runs. Tucker's second at-bat of the inning resulted in another hit by pitch, which loaded the bases again. Carroll hit safely, too, knocking a single that drove in the eighth and ninth runs of the inning. Pittsburg's inning of inept pitching finally ended when Ganzel popped out.

Even after the deluge of Boston runs, the game was not decided. Both clubs scored a run in the third inning, followed by a fourth when, thanks in part to Gastright's throwing error, Pittsburg scored three more times. With his team holding on to a narrow 10-9 lead, Boston manager Frank Selee pulled Gastright in favor of Kid Nichols. Pittsburg tied the score in the sixth inning when outfielder Mike Smith traveled around the bases via a single, steal, wild pitch, and Louis Bierbauer's single.

Boston was not yet done producing runs, either. In the sixth inning, some small ball along with a missed catch by Patsy Donovan helped the home club claim another run. Two more were tacked on in the eighth, and after a scoreless ninth, Boston's victory was complete, by a 13-10 score. Nichols had little time to enjoy his successful relief appearance; he was scheduled to start the second game of the twin bill. In seven innings of work, he allowed 13 hits and five runs in a tied game that was called due to darkness.

Reaction after the off-target Saturday opener was embittered on the Pittsburg side. Both Ehret and Terry claimed umpire Tom Lynch's calls were highly suspect during the disastrous second inning, that he had missed calling strikes on pitches that should have sent a couple of the Boston batters back to the bench.[8] Their thoughts echoed prior commentary alleging Lynch's favoritism toward Boston,[9] though the duo remained mum in regard to their control issues and the four batters they hit in the second inning. Coincidentally, a sobering reminder of what errant pitching had the potential to do occurred the next day at a ballpark in the Chicago area, when an amateur player, Peter Hyland, died after being struck on the back of the head while at bat.[10]

The *Pittsburg Dispatch* quoted Buckenberger on the doubleheader in its Monday edition. Like his pitchers, the manager voiced a negative opinion on Lynch's umpiring. But he minced no words about the poor performance of his own starter, saying that Ehret "failed completely," continuing, "If (Ehret) had pitched only half as good as he can pitch, we would have won the first game."[11]

The season was far from over, but Boston's win (and the tie) on the 18th placed the Beaneaters a substantial nine games ahead in the standings. That gap eventually increased to 13. Only after a successful September for Pittsburg (19-4) in conjunction with a woeful late-month road trip by Boston (a journey that did include at least one victory in Pittsburg, where Kid Nichols and company had to flee the ballpark to avoid a stoning[12]) did the race return to a single-digit difference. But five games back was as close as Pittsburg could get, and Boston held on to win its third pennant in a row.

SOURCES

In addition to the sources cited in the Notes, the author consulted baseball-reference.com, retrosheet.org, and sabr.org.

NOTES

1. "In Good Position," *Pittsburgh Chronicle Telegraph,* August 19, 1893: 2.
2. "Killen and Gastright," *Pittsburgh Chronicle Telegraph,* June 29, 1893.
3. sabr.org/gamesproj/game/april-19-1890-debut-players-league.
4. "Wild Pitching," *Boston Globe,* August 20, 1893: 7.
5. Ibid.
6. nonohitters.com/2016/02/24/adonis-terry-threw-2-brooklyn-no-nos-died-101-years-ago-today/.
7. Terry's biography is at sabr.org/bioproj/person/e519508d.
8. "The Boston Struggle," *Pittsburgh Chronicle Telegraph,* August 21, 1893: 2.
9. "Base Ball Gossip," *Pittsburgh Chronicle Telegraph,* July 6, 1893.
10. Robert M. Gorman and David Weeks, *Death at the Ballpark: More Than 2,000 Game-Related Fatalities of Players, Other Personnel and Spectators in Amateur and Professional Baseball, 1862-2014* (Jefferson, North Carolina: McFarland & Company, Inc., 2015), 16.
11. "Buck Explains It," *Pittsburg Dispatch,* August 22, 1893.
12. Norman L. Macht, *Connie Mack and the Early Years of Baseball* (Lincoln: University of Nebraska Press, 2007), 100.

"PROUD EMBLEM TO WAVE HERE NEXT YEAR – SPIDERS BITE THE DUST IN CLEVELAND"

SEPTEMBER 20, 1893: BOSTON BEANEATERS 9, CLEVELAND SPIDERS 6, AT LEAGUE PARK, CLEVELAND

BY MARK SOUDER

The first frost would not arrive in Cleveland for another six days. Two thousand fans officially attended the pennant-clinching game against the defending champion Beaneaters. The attendance, slightly above average, was pretty respectable for a fall Wednesday afternoon game in northern Ohio when the home team's pennant chances were long gone.

Because the Spiders departed from baseball history in such an ignominious way in 1899, with their 20-134 record still being the worst in major-league annals, it is easy to forget that they were once a very good team.

In 1892 Cleveland had narrowly lost to Boston in a playoff between the split-season champions. While a team with Cupid at second, Virtue at first, and Patsy at third – not to mention Chief Zimmer at catcher who was not an Indian from Cleveland or anywhere – deserves to be good, any team with Denton True Young was going to be competitive.

Cy as he was called, was not quite as good in 1893 as he had been in 1892, winning only 34 games (which was still nearly half the team's wins). Having pitched the day before and with Cleveland headed for a third-place finish, Cy was not on the mound this day. Instead, Cleveland debuted a rookie who just arrived from the Buffalo Bisons of the Eastern League.

Chauncey Burr Fisher was from Anderson, Indiana. His nickname was Whoa Bill. His brother Thomas Chalmers Fisher, eight years younger, made his major-league debut in 1904 as a member of the Boston Beaneaters.[1] Chauncey Fisher was only 21, and already had pitched 416 innings that year for the combination of the lower-level Easton Dutchmen of the Pennsylvania State League and Buffalo. So he wasn't exactly a fresh arm.

Facing off with Fisher was 25-year-old Jack Stivetts. He was no slacker either, having pitched over 400 innings in each of the previous three seasons, though he was comparatively rested for this game since he hurled only 300 innings in 1893. Stivetts had been the Beaneaters' co-ace until the younger Kid Nichols moved ahead of him as the team's top pitcher in 1893.

Archrival Cleveland would rather have had Boston clinch its third championship in a row somewhere other than League Park, so the Spiders were determined to put up a fight. During the game the proceedings from Brooklyn's defeat of Pittsburgh were posted so, as one reporter noted, "The champions figured that if they won they would have the pennant in their fingers, so they went after it, and how they did go."[2]

The *Boston Globe*'s game article proclaimed: "Pennant Comes to Boston, Cleveland Put Up Grand Ball But the Bostons 'Got There.'" In other words, two pretty tired pitchers engaged in a hard-fought gritty game of "scientific baseball."[3]

The *New York Clipper*'s summary of Boston's triumph at the week's end stated and restated the same point. Boston was not an "aggregate of stars" but a "well-balanced body of team workers." The Beaneaters didn't work to "advance their own records" and their manager, Frank Selee, was "clever and shrewd." Even more bluntly, the *Clipper* wrote that "ball players are not as a rule gifted with over much brain power" so Selee basically had to outsmart the opponents.[4]

Timothy Murnane had been a decent ballplayer but earned even greater fame for his 30 years as a sportswriter for the *Globe*.[5] In both his year-end summary and the game summary, Murnane used the term "scientific ball," stating that "the exhibition of fine scientific work, both in the field and at the bat of the Boston players, has been a revelation to the baseball patrons, not only in Boston, but in each of the 11 other cities in the League."[6] Murnane included detailed statistics highlighting that Boston did not have the league leaders in the traditional hitting categories. The team utilized bunts, stealing bases, good fielding, solid pitching, and timely hitting to win games. His 1893 analysis was almost like a SABR conference presentation in 2017.

The September 20 game was not untypical of the season. Neither team could get a run across the plate for the first five innings. In inning six the relative floodgates opened as ballplayers were jamming the bases.

Boston scored three runs in the top of the sixth. Billy Nash, the team captain, was one of the Beaneaters' sluggers. He finished eighth in the NL with 10 home runs in 1893. In this game, Nash was Boston's primary slugger, hitting two doubles to go with the team's flood of singles. But Nash also understood so-called "scientific" baseball. He led off the sixth inning by drawing a walk. Then he stole second, and Boston was on its way.

Next up was Tommy Tucker, a mini-celebrity because of his name. For example, the *Boston Post* reporter couldn't resist, when noting that Fisher was debuting in this game, writing that "Cleveland wanted to try him on Boston because they thought if he could stand Tommy Tucker crying for his supper, he could stand anything."[7] Tucker earned his supper, beating out a bunt.

Then Chief Zimmer allowed a passed ball, which sent Nash to third and Tucker to second.

Charlie Ganzel grounded out to Cupid Childs at second, holding the runners. Pitcher Stivetts, batting seventh instead of ninth in the order, hit the ball to shortstop Ed McKean, who "fired the ball home to catch Nash."[8] Zimmer, who was not having a good inning, dropped the ball. 1-0, Stivetts to first base. The next Boston batter, Cliff Carroll, bunted, scoring Tommy Tucker. 2-0, Stivetts to second. Charlie Bennett stuck out but then shortstop Herman Long singled, scoring Stivetts. Suddenly it was 3-0 on a single, two bunts, a passed ball, an error by the catcher, and a stolen base.

Cleveland slugged its way right back into the game. The first batter made an out, but the next singled and went to second on a poor throw by Boston second baseman Bobby Lowe. A single scored Cleveland's first run. Spider Ed McKean doubled, moving the runner to third. Then Virtue came to the plate. Jack, as he was known, knocked both runners home with a double. 3-3. Third baseman-manager Patsy Tebeau followed, doubling in Virtue. Chief Zimmer partly redeemed himself with a hit to tally Tebeau. The teams headed to the seventh inning with Cleveland leading, 5-3.

But the rookie pitcher Fisher was obviously worn down. Nash hit a two-bagger. Tucker knocked him home with a single; then Ganzel doubled in Tucker. Carroll singled and Ganzel scored to regain the lead for the Beaneaters at 6-5. And they weren't done. A fly ball to left field by Bennett was dropped by Jesse Burkett, scoring Carroll. Then Long's single sent Bennett crossing the plate, which made it 8-5. Cleveland scored in bottom of the seventh to come within two runs but would score no more.

John McGraw, Wee Willie Keeler, and the famed Baltimore Orioles made so-called "scientific baseball" famous over the next few years. It was a combination of small ball as practiced by the Beaneaters, but also aggressive cheating. Boston was not above cheating either.

In the top of the eighth inning, Billy Nash doubled again. A bunt by Tommy Tucker moved him to third, but then Nash tried to score. Tucker threw his arms around pitcher Fisher as he covered first base on the bunt play, which prevented Fisher from throwing the ball to the catcher at home plate. It was the final run of the game.

As an interesting side note to the game, the *Boston Globe* reporter opened his game summary by stating that "on the merits of the game Cleveland ought to have won." He noted the Spiders' costly errors on Zimmer and Burkett but then added "[along] with some of the kind of umpiring that Hurst has done this summer."[9]

"Hurst" was Timothy Carroll Hurst, the game's umpire. Hurst was a bit pugnacious, for example hitting Kid Elberfeld in the jaw with his mask during a dispute and spitting on Eddie Collins, but generally he was just verbally combative.[10] While the *Globe* reporter was sarcastic about Hurst's umpiring skills, he concluded his game coverage by stating that Boston would have won the game anyway.

While John McGraw would have bragged about Tucker's grabbing the first baseman, not explaining the cheating away, this third consecutive championship by the Beaneaters was indeed classic scientific baseball before Baltimore made scientific baseball famous.

NOTES

1. "Chauncey Burr Fisher," Sports Legends, Madison County (Indiana) Historical Society website, mchs09.wordpress.com/sport-legends/

2. "Not This Time – Bostons Tangle Spiders in Their Own Web – The Errors Were Costly," *Boston Post*, September 21, 1893: 3.

3. "Pennant Comes to Boston; Cleveland Put Up Grand Ball but the Bostons 'Got There,'" *Boston Globe*, September 21, 1893: 10.

4. *New York Clipper*, September 30, 1893: 485.

5. Charlie Bevis, "Timothy Murnane," SABR Biography Project, sabr.org/bioproj/person/b2017f67.

6. T.H. Murnane, "Three-Time Winners, Graphic Story of How Boston's Baseball Stars Climbed from the Ninth Place in the Great National Race to the Championship Pennant," *Boston Globe*, September 24, 1893: 28; "It Is Ours – Proud Emblem to Wave Here Next Year – Boston Wins Base-Ball Pennant – Spiders Bite the Dust at Cleveland," *Boston Globe*, September 21, 1893: 10.

7. "It Is Ours."

8. "Not This Time."

9. "Pennant Comes to Boston."

10. Rich Huhn, "Tim Hurst's Last Call," in Morris Levin, ed., *The National Pastime: From Swampoodle to South Philly* (Phoenix: Society for American Baseball Research, 2013.)

BALTIMORE STUNS THE CHAMPS, SCORING 14 RUNS IN THE NINTH FOR THE WIN

APRIL 24, 1894: BALTIMORE ORIOLES 15, BOSTON BEANEATERS 3, AT ORIOLE PARK III

BY MIKE HUBER

Just about every kid who has ever played baseball has had the dream about coming to bat in the ninth inning with his team down by a run or two and being the hero. The *Baltimore Sun* described this dramatic game with the same fairy-tale-type approach: "It was the beginning of the ninth inning. Mighty Boston was Baltimore's adversary and the score was 3 to 1. The three runs belonged to the visitors. Pent-up enthusiasm was at fever-heat and the 8,400 spectators were on the tiptoe of expectation, for it was the Oriole's [sic] last chance to turn defeat into victory. And they did it."[1] It seemed as if each Orioles batter played the hero, until the Beaneaters just gave up.

The Orioles had just swept three home games from the New York Giants to open the 1894 season. The defending champion Beaneaters had likewise swept the Brooklyn Bridegrooms. (The first game was played in Boston and the next two in Brooklyn.) In this contest, Baltimore, the home team, batted first. Jack Stivetts pitched for Boston and Sadie McMahon for Baltimore. Each pitcher had been the Opening Day victor. According to the *Boston Globe*, "What promised to end in a well-played game wound up in a burlesque."[2]

The first eight innings of the game between these top two contenders were close and exciting. Boston pushed across two runs in the second inning as Tommy Tucker singled, Jimmy Bannon reached on an error, Charlie Ganzel and Stivetts sacrificed the runners, and Bobby Lowe doubled. Baltimore answered with a solo run in the fourth when Joe Kelley singled, stole second, and scored on a single by Heinie Reitz. Stivetts and Lowe hit back-to-back doubles in the seventh inning for another Boston run. Both teams played with purpose and professionalism. The crowd was anxious that their Orioles might lose.

There was some cleverness in the third inning. With one out, Willie Keeler batted with Wilbert Robinson on second and John McGraw on first. Keeler lifted a routine fly ball to left field and the runners stayed near their bases, but left fielder Tommy McCarthy "purposely muffed the ball [and] with lightning quickness he picked it up and sent it to [Billy] Nash, who touched third and threw to Lowe on second" for a double play.[3] Beaneaters first baseman Tucker remarked, "That's a new one on you" to the Baltimore players as he passed them coming off the field.[4]

And then came the dramatics. According to the *Lowell Sun*, "Boston showed the white feather in the last inning and allowed Baltimore to win in a canter."[5] The excitement of the ninth inning started when Baltimore's third-base coach, Boileryard Clarke, in an effort to distract both Stivetts and umpire Tim Hurst, "walked out to the bleachers and raised his hands like a 'pop concert' leader, and a volume of sound filled the air, every man, woman and child yelling for all he or she was worth."[6] At first, Stivetts did not seem moved, but "Hurst became rattled at the awful noise."[7] Stivetts pitched to his catcher Ganzel's mitt, but Hurst kept calling them balls, and the crowd kept getting louder. After Kelley drew a walk, Ganzel "made a vigorous protest"[8] and was fined 10 by the umpire. Reitz then stepped into the batter's box, "holding his bat on his shoulder without the least idea of striking at the ball."[9] He also walked on four straight pitches, at which point Stivett threw his cap to the ground. Hughie Jennings then stroked a single to short center, driving in Kelley. This brought the crowd to its feet. The first three pitches to Robinson were called balls, bringing thunderous roars from the crowd. With the third called ball, Stivetts again "acted like a wild man [and] he threw his cap upon the ground."[10] The Boston team gathered around home plate, offering Stivetts time to compose himself. Umpire Hurst then ordered Stivetts back to the mound. When he didn't comply, both the Beaneaters hurler and catcher were fined. A moment later, Stivetts was ejected.[11]

Beaneaters manager Frank Selee brought Kid Nichols on in relief. However, "he was refused the privilege of a little warming-up work by two big policemen, and went in cold and stiff."[12] Nichols threw one pitch, but it was wide, and Robinson trotted to first with an RBI walk. Suddenly the game was tied. Baltimore pitcher McMahon singled past Tucker at first, and two more runs scored. McGraw followed with a single, driving in Robinson. Then, according to the *Baltimore Sun*, the Beaneaters just quit; "the fielders acted like wooden soldiers when the Baltimore players sent the ball into their territory, and Nichols tossed the ball like a school boy."[13] Keeler singled, plating McMahon and McGraw, and advanced on a wild pitch. Steve Brodie tripled to the right-field fence and Dan Brouthers singled to left. One base hit followed another and the Baltimore squad batted around without making an out, scoring eight times.

Then, as Yogi Berra once said, "It was déjà vu all over again."[14] Kelley and Reitz once again reached via the base on balls. By now, the Baltimore fans were concerned that Boston would refuse to retire the side and the inning would be lost, due to darkness, giving the victory to Boston, so "the Baltimore players were loudly admonished by the spectators to be put out purposely."[15] Jennings popped out to second, but Robinson singled, driving in two more runs. McMahon laid down a sacrifice bunt, advancing Robinson to second, but Reitz held up at third. McGraw drew a walk to load the bases again. Keeler grounded back to Nichols, who threw wildly to first and two more runs came in. Keeler went to second on the error and then stole both third and home. The embarrassment finally ended when Brodie popped out to Nichols on the mound. The Beaneaters did nothing in the bottom of the ninth, making "no effort to get runs."[16]

Seventeen Baltimore players had batted in the final frame, scoring 14 runs. Had the Beaneaters batted first, the game could have been decided with a walk-off 4-3 victory for the Orioles. Instead, every Orioles player managed at least one hit and one run scored in the game. McGraw, Kelley, and Robinson led the Orioles offense with three hits each. McMahon pitched a good game, limiting the Beaneaters to three runs on eight hits, with the only strikeout of the game. Lowe shined for Boston with three hits, all doubles. There were eight sacrifices in the game. Amazingly, according to the *Baltimore Sun*, only four of the Orioles runs were earned.[17]

The two teams played again each of the next two days. Boston won both games, 6-3 and 13-7. For the season, Boston beat Baltimore eight of 12 matches, but the Beaneaters finished 1894 eight games behind the eventual champion Orioles.

SOURCES

In addition to the sources mentioned in the Notes, the author consulted baseball-reference.com and retrosheet.org. The author sincerely thanks Lisa Tuite of the *Boston Globe* for her assistance with providing sources.

NOTES

1   "A Game From Boston: Something Dropped in the Ninth Inning, and Then, Oh, My!," *Baltimore Sun*, April 25, 1894: 6.

2   "Yelled Like Mad: Crowd Tried to Rattle Jack Stivetts," *Boston Globe*, April 25, 1894: 5.

3   *Baltimore Sun*.

4   Ibid.

5   "Badly Punished," *Lowell Sun*, April 25, 1894: 8.

6   *Boston Globe*.

7   Ibid.

8   Ibid.

9   Ibid.

10 *Baltimore Sun*.

11 According to the *Boston Globe*, Boston pitcher Jack Stivetts and umpire Tim Hurst both hailed from Ashland, Pennsylvania. The *Globe* commented that it was "strange to say that every time that Tim umpires a game where Stivetts is pitching there is always trouble, and the Boston players claim that Mr. Hurst is not particularly stuck on his old townsman."

12 *Boston Globe*.

13 *Baltimore Sun*.

14 This Yogism is attributed to Yogi Berra (date unknown). It is inscribed on the walls of the Yogi Berra Museum & Learning Center, Little Falls, New Jersey.

15 *Baltimore Sun*.

16 *Boston Globe*.

17 According to the *Boston Globe* and the *Lowell* (Massachusetts) *Sun*, Baltimore had six earned runs.

A DUEL OF ACES

MAY 7, 1894: NEW YORK GIANTS 1, BOSTON BEANEATERS 0, AT THE POLO GROUNDS, NEW YORK

BY JOHN ZINN

Although the Beaneaters' May 7 game at the Polo Grounds against the New York Giants came early in the 1894 season, it would have been hard to find a more attractive matchup that year. Not only was the weather "ideal," the starting pitchers were two of the game's best, Charles "Kid" Nichols for Boston and Amos Rusie for the Giants. According to the *New York Tribune*, the two were "unlike as can be in physical and mental development." Rusie was a "big, good-natured" fellow with "the speed of the wind and genuine snake like curves," while his Boston counterpart, although "more delicate-looking," had "plenty of speed, curves and superb control," not to mention "plenty of gray matter under his cap."[1] Both pitchers were coming off 30-win seasons, but while Nichols was off to a fast start at 4-0, Rusie was only 1-3 thus far in 1894.

On this day, however, Nichols was operating at a disadvantage because of the absence of Herman Long, Boston's starting shortstop. Long was out of the lineup due to his muff, not of a baseball, but rather "his inability to catch the unlighted end of a lighted cigar in his mouth" a few days earlier.[2] Instead the stogie hit the foolhardy Long in the eye, fortunately doing no permanent damage, but causing injuries sufficient to keep him out of that day's game. Filling in was future Hall of Famer Hugh Duffy, with pitcher Jack Stivetts taking Duffy's place in the outfield.[3] In spite of the game's obvious box office appeal, attendance was limited to somewhere in the 3,500-to-7,500 range, not even 50 percent of the capacity of the Polo Grounds.[4]

Any fan who wanted to see some scoring had to be in his seat when Boston batted in the top of the first. After Rusie retired the first two batters without incident, he got ahead 0-and-2 on Stivetts before walking him, a mistake the New York *Sun* labeled both inexcusable and fatal.[5] Even so, Rusie and the crowd must have thought the Giants were out of the woods when Tommy McCarthy hit a "towering fly" to John Montgomery Ward, the Giants shortstop and manager.[6] Ward, however, "muffed it as if it had been a burning meteor," putting Stivetts on third and McCarthy on first.[7] After that, the *Evening World* declared, Ward "moved through the game trancelike." Unfortunately for Rusie and the Giants, that began with the very next play.[8] Having tested the New York defense and found it wanting, McCarthy broke for second, drawing a throw from Giants catcher Charles "Duke" Farrell. Stivetts then took off for home and Ward compounded his earlier error with a throw that appeared to be "aimed at the upper tier of the grand stand."[9] Reprieved by the Giants leader's second consecutive miscue, Stivetts gratefully "fell upon the rubber [home plate] like a ton of coal," with a run that Tim Murnane, writing in the *Boston Globe*, claimed "loomed up as big as the Brooklyn bridge."[10]

Although Boston repeatedly put men on base, Nichols' offensive support was limited to that first-inning run. The Beaneaters' best opportunity to increase their lead came in the eighth when they had men on second and third and only one out, but Billy Nash was thrown out at home to kill the rally. All told, Boston stranded 11 runners over the course of the game.[11] After recounting the visitor's missed opportunities, O.P. Caylor, writing in the *New York Herald*, told his readers, "Now I'll [tell] you about the Giants batting, and it will not take much space to recite it," especially since New York had only one hit in the first five innings.[12] The Giants fans reportedly did everything they could to bring their heroes luck, but as the *Sun* noted, all their "mascots and lucky charms were dead letters."[13] However, the Giants' fortunes revived in the bottom of the eighth when Eddie Burke hit a triple with one out, arriving at third "breathless but prouder than all the kings of Ireland."[14] All it would take to tie the game was a fly ball from Farrell, but the New York catcher grounded to shortstop. At least, however, he found the weak link in Boston's makeshift defense and was rewarded when Duffy fumbled the ball. But Burke stayed where he was, setting up a debate between Caylor in the *Herald*, who thought "certainly he could have scored" and the *Tribune* reporter, who labeled such criticism "foolhardy."[15]

In any event, the Giants still had the tying run 90 feet away with only one out and Rusie at the plate with a chance to help his own cause. The Giants pitcher responded with a "low liner" to right which Jimmy Bannon took on the run and made "a beauty" of a throw that Boston catcher Jack Ryan took on one hop and "cracked Mr. Burke on the back."[16] Although Boston had dodged that bullet, the Giants still had one more chance. With one out in the ninth, Yale Murphy reached on an error and then headed to second on the second pitch to Ward, perhaps anticipating a hit-and-run. It was the end of a not particularly good day for the future Hall of Famer as Caylor claimed, "Ward didn't do a thing, but stood still," and Murphy was easily thrown out at second. Sarcastically summing up the two men's performance as "great team work that!" Caylor's comment also pretty much described the Giants' lost afternoon.[17] Needless to say, Ward and the final Giants hitter went out without further incident and the Giants left the field "with a beautiful coat of Boston whitewash."[18]

Neither pitcher had cause to be ashamed of his day's work. Rusie had allowed only six hits, but was betrayed by Ward's two egregious errors, not just in one inning, but on two consecutive plays. After praising Rusie's performance, the New York media was quick to criticize the rest of the team with Caylor colorfully noting that the Giants resembled a "balky team of horses, (making) believe they were trying to pull a loaded wagon out of the dirt."[19] Turning to Nichols, the *Sun* recalled predictions that the Boston pitcher would no longer "be a puzzle" because he had done too much pitching in California over the winter. Based on this performance, the paper suggested, all other pitchers should emulate him since Nichols "could not have been hit safely with a snow shovel."[20] Somewhat grudgingly (and ungraciously), Murnane, in the *Boston Globe*, acknowledged Rusie's effort as "excellent work," but rated him "a poor second to our own Kid Nichols, who pitched one of the greatest games of his life."[21] More sportsmanlike was the *Boston Journal*, which characterized Nichols' performance as one of the "most notable exhibitions of steady and effective pitching in his triumphant career" without denigrating Rusie in the process.[22]

Although the *Journal* thought the "great pitchers' battle" was "a game of a season," surprisingly the New York papers couldn't even agree on whether or not it had been a good game. The *Tribune* believed those in attendance had seen "a contest which will linger long in the memory of every one there," but Caylor in the *Herald* caustically claimed that with only minor exceptions, the Giants "didn't play intelligently enough to distinguish themselves from the lower order of animals which eat grass for a living."[23] Better days were ahead, however, for both Rusie and the Giants. The rival aces hooked up twice more during the season and Rusie emerged the winner both times on the way to winning 36 games, four more than Nichols. Perhaps even more impressively, the Giants finished ahead of Boston for the first time since 1889, just three games behind first-place Baltimore.

NOTES

1 "Boston Scored One Little Run," *New York Tribune*, May 8, 1894: 4.

2 "New Yorks Whitewashed," *Sun* (New York, New York), May 8, 1894: 4.

3 O.P. Caylor, "Rusie Pitched a Great Game," *New York Herald*, May 8, 1894: 13.

4 Caylor; "New Yorks Whitewashed"; "Ward's Wretched Error," *New York Evening World*, May 7, 1894, Fourth Edition: 1; "Boston Scored One Little Run"; Philip J. Lowry, *Green Cathedrals: The Ultimate Celebration of Major League and Negro League Ballparks* (New York: SABR and Walker & Co, 2006), 151.

5 "New Yorks Whitewashed."

6 Caylor.

7 "New Yorks Whitewashed."

8 "Baseball Chat," *Evening World*, May 8, 1894 Fourth Edition: 1.

9 Caylor.

10 "New Yorks Whitewashed"; T.H. Murnane, "Battle Royal," *Boston Globe*, May 8, 1894: 7.

11 Caylor; "Oh! John!," *Boston Journal*, May 8, 1894: 3.

12 Caylor.

13 "New Yorks Whitewashed."

14 "Ward's Wretched Error."

15 Caylor; "Boston Scored One Little Run."

16 Murnane.

17 Caylor.

18 "New Yorks Whitewashed."

19 Caylor.

20 "New Yorks Whitewashed."

21 Murnane.

22 "Oh! John!"

23 "Oh! John!"; "Boston Scored One Little Run"; Caylor.

"IT WAS A HOT GAME, SURE ENOUGH!"

MAY 15, 1894: BALTIMORE ORIOLES 3, BOSTON BEANEATERS 3 (STOPPED IN THIRD INNING), AT SOUTH END GROUNDS

BY TERRY GOTTSCHALL

Nineteenth-century baseball often suffered game delays, suspensions, and even cancellations due to weather or dusk. But a game between the Baltimore Orioles and Boston Beaneaters on May 15, 1894, at Boston's South End Grounds concluded prematurely for a more life-threatening reason: fire. "It was a hot game, sure enough," the *Boston Globe* reported.[1] *Spalding's Guide* for 1895 described the game in equally brief terms: "Baltimore vs. Boston stopped by fire (3rd inning), 3–3."[2]

The South End Grounds, constructed in the city's Roxbury section in 1888, was considered one of the most beautiful ballparks of the time, with striking twin spires rising from each corner of the Grand Pavilion. A *Boston Globe* reporter audaciously asserted that the Boston Tea Party, the battle of Bunker Hill, and Paul Revere's ride would "fade into nothingness" when compared to the park's beautiful "cathedral-like grand stand."[3] The double-decked area seated approximately 2,000 in the lower deck and 800 in the upper deck, while bleachers along each foul line provided seats for another 2,600 cranks.[4] But like all ballparks of the era, it was built largely of wood, making fire a constant threat. Indeed, similar fires would damage the ballpark in Chicago and destroy the one in Philadelphia on consecutive August days that same season.

Unexpected fireworks first broke out on the field. As the Beaneaters' Tommy "Foghorn" Tucker slid into third, the Orioles' John McGraw kicked him in the face. Although the umpire broke up the ensuing brawl, Tucker nursed his sore jaw while awaiting an opportunity to avenge his injury.

That opportunity didn't come because with the Orioles at bat in the next inning, Boston right fielder James "Foxy" Bannon spotted a fire under the right-field bleachers. He rushed over to the stands and tried "to stamp out the flames with his feet." At first, most fans ignored the fire, preferring to watch the fiery Tucker in anticipation that he would "get even with the young Baltimore sport." The Beaneaters expected the game to resume momentarily "as the visitors were acting very fresh, especially catcher Wilbert Robinson, who kept shooting off his big mouth at a lively rate."

But a sudden, powerful gust of wind spread the fire, causing the "blackened and exhausted" Bannon to give up his "gallant efforts." Panicking fans "in the 25-cent bleachers rushed out on to the field, breaking the fence and tumbling over one another to get away from the heat."

The conflagration swept swiftly around the outfield fence to the left-field bleachers, then up the line to the grandstand, setting "the whole pavilion ablaze [with] the fire running wizard-like up to its highest tower." Witnesses later estimated that the fire destroyed the South End Grounds in less than 45 minutes, leaving the "jagged cornice of the east end of the grandstand, and that charred and broken, as the only relic remaining of the big pavilion."

The fire's rapid spread caused consternation among the players. They quickly returned to their locker rooms to grab their clothes but then had to change outside "in the open field." John Haggarty, the Beaneaters equipment manager, saved the team's bats and uniforms but lost four dozen balls when he could not find the key to the storage closet. He also reported that the fire had destroyed the team's championship pennant from 1893, but promised fans that "the Bostons would win another pennant just as good." Catcher Charlie Ganzel bravely saved the team's large photograph from the pavilion's foyer but lost three suits of clothes when his boarding house across the street burned down. Another player cut his hand severely while trying to help fans out of the burning ballpark.

Boston firefighters sent requests for assistance to fire stations 20 miles from the blaze. The nine-alarm fire caused no fatalities, but burned more than 12 acres, destroying about 200 buildings valued at more than $300,000. A total of 1,900 people were left homeless.[5]

The *Globe* initially blamed the fire on two young fans who it was said had set fire to an empty peanut bag and then dropped it underneath the bleachers. But Fire Marshal Edward J. Flynn, citing the eyewitness account of 14-year-old Jimmy Lasky, who had sneaked into the bleachers to avoid paying the 25-cent admission, said an adult fan had carelessly tossed away a cigarette that had set fire to trash underneath the bleachers.

Municipal officials cited the team's miserly ways for the destruction of the South End Grounds and the ensuing Roxbury fire. The city had installed a hydrant on the grounds, but team owners had failed to pay the fee necessary to have the water turned on. "If this is true, it would appear for the sake of saving $15, the grand stand, worth $80,000, was imperiled," the *Globe* remarked.[6]

Team directors moved the next day's game to the Congress Street Grounds, where other Boston teams had played in previous seasons. Fear of fire failed to deter a crowd of 2,000 who watched Boston defeat Baltimore, 10–8.[7]

The team built a new ballpark at the South End site. But because inadequate insurance coverage meant the owners had less money to invest, it had a smaller, one-story grandstand. Contractors also used more steel and brick to provide both "comfort [and] safety for the patrons of the game." When the new grounds opened on July 20, more than 5,200 fans watched Boston defeat the Giants.[8]

The Bostons did not, however, get their replacement pennant at season's end. It went to the other fire-stricken team that day, the Orioles, who outlasted the Giants by three games. The burned-out Beaneaters faded to third.

This essay was originally published in Bill Felber, ed., Inventing Baseball: The 100 Greatest Games of the 19th Century *(Phoenix: SABR, 2013).*

NOTES

1 "Editorial Points," *Boston Globe*, May 16, 1894: 6.

2 Henry Chadwick, ed., *Spalding's Base Ball Guide and Official League Book for 1895* (New York: American Sports Publishing, 1895), 32.

3 "Editorial Points," *Boston Globe*, May 26, 1888: 1. All otherwise unattributed quotations in this article come from this *Boston Globe* article.

4 Alan E. Foulds, *Boston's Ballparks & Arenas* (Boston: Northeastern University Press, 2005): 13.

5 "1900 Persons Homeless," *Boston Globe*, May 16, 1894: 1.

6 "Dread Doubt," *Boston Globe*, May 17, 1894: 5.

7 "Lively Batting," *Boston Globe*, May 17, 1894: 5.

8 "Bat Like Fiends," *Boston Globe*, July 21, 1894: 2.

FOUR HOME RUNS FOR BOBBY LOWE

MAY 30, 1894: BOSTON BEANEATERS 20, CINCINNATI REDS 11, AT CONGRESS STREET GROUNDS, BOSTON

BY CHARLES F. FABER

Fans arriving for the second portion of the Boston Beaneaters' morning-afternoon Memorial Day twin bill with Cincinnati on May 30, 1894, had reason to anticipate a pleasant afternoon. It was warm and sunny, with a breeze blowing from the south and southwest.[1] Beyond the pleasant conditions, their three-time defending National League champions had won four straight (including the morning game) and six of their last seven.

The crowd of 8,500 did indeed cheer their heroes on to a fifth straight victory. But beyond that, they witnesssed an unprecedented achievement. Bobby Lowe, the team's popular second baseman, that afternoon became the first major-league player to hit four home runs in a game.

The crowd for the afternoon portion of the split-admission holiday twin bill was much larger than the 3,000 who had showed up for the morning game, won by Boston in a 13–10 slugfest. Kid Nichols, on his way to his fourth straight 30-victory season, started for the home team in the second game. But the Reds treated Nichols roughly, with Bug Holliday's first-inning home run over the leftfield fence giving the visitors a 2–0 lead. Cincinnati hurler Elton "Icebox" Chamberlain, winless since the season's second game, disposed of Lowe leading off the home half of the first, but a walk followed by hits by Tommy McCarthy and Billy Nash knotted the score at 2–2.

Boston took the lead in the bottom of the third on Lowe's first home run, a line drive that cleared the left-field fence. The rest of the Beaneaters took it from there. Herman Long was hit by a pitch, Hugh Duffy sacrificed, McCarthy singled, and Nash walked, loading the bases. Tommy Tucker hit a fly to right field for the second out, but Jimmy Bannon, Jack Ryan, and Nichols followed with consecutive singles. Lowe, who had started the rally with his first home run, climaxed it with his second, again clearing the left-field fence. The champions produced nine runs off Chamberlain that inning, taking an 11–2 lead.

The Reds attempted to get back into the game in the fifth when Dummy Hoy and Jack McCarthy singled, Arlie Latham connected for a double, and Holliday drove them in with his second home run. That made the score 11–6. But in the home half of the inning, Lowe clouted his third round-tripper, this one easily clearing the left-field fence. That tied the major-league record for home runs in a game, held by six players.

Already leading 12–6, Boston added five more runs in the sixth. Nash walked, Tucker was hit by a pitch, and Bannon singled. That brought up Lowe again, and he etched his name in the record books by hitting his fourth home run, the ball again sailing over the left-field fence. The crowd, aware that it was witnessing an exceptional exhibition, cheered Lowe wildly, some throwing coins at him. Teammates helped the player gather the loot, which was later found to total $160. Long followed that blast with one of his own.

Neither Lowe nor his teammates were through yet. In the seventh inning, bases on balls to Tucker and Bannon and hits by Nash, Ryan, and Lowe scored two more runs. Lowe's fifth hit, a single, gave him 17 total bases for the game, another National League record and one that stood for more than 60 years until it was broken by Joe Adcock on July 31, 1954. In the eighth inning Boston scored its 20th and final run on a single by Long and a double by McCarthy.

Trailing 20–6, the Reds mounted a ninth-inning comeback against Nichols that produced five runs, including two more home runs, by Farmer Vaughn and Jimmy Canavan. The latter's carried into the top of the center-field bleachers. Amazingly, for a game that saw 31 runs scored, 33 hits, nine bases on balls, and two hit batsmen, both Chamberlain and Nichols pitched a complete game.

In recent years, some have questioned whether Lowe's accomplishment was aided by the fact that the game was played at the Congress Street Grounds—a facility abandoned by the Boston Reds when the American Association ceased play in 1891—rather than the Beaneaters' usual home, the South End Grounds. That park had burned in the Great Roxbury Fire just two weeks earlier. The fences at Congress Street Grounds were generally much closer than at South End Grounds.[2] Those on the scene, however, saw it differently. "His home runs were on line drives far over the fence, and would be good for four bases on an open prairie," wrote the *Boston Globe's* Tim Murnane in his account of the game the following day.[3]

Two years after Lowe accomplished his batting feat, Philadelphia slugger Ed Delahanty duplicated it in Chicago. But not until Lou Gehrig in 1932 did any of the great 20th-century sluggers hit four home runs in one game. Just a few weeks after Gehrig did so, photographers in Detroit, where the Yankees were playing, arranged for the famed slugger to pose with a plain-looking, 66-year-old, 20-year Detroit city employee with whom the Yankee powerhouse had something in common. The city employee was Bobby Lowe. As reported in the newspapers of the time, Gehrig's first question upon meeting the small, quiet man was, "Did you really hit four home runs in a single game?"[4]

Yes, he did.

	AB	R	H	TB	PO	A	E
Boston							
Lowe, 2b	6	4	5	17	2	2	1
Long, ss	3	5	2	6	2	4	2
Duffy, cf	5	0	1	1	1	0	0
T. McCarthy, lf	6	2	3	4	3	0	0
Nash, 3b	4	3	3	3	0	1	0
Tucker, 1b	2	1	0	0	10	2	0
Bannon, rf	4	2	2	2	1	0	0
Ryan, c	5	2	2	3	5	0	0
Nichols, p	5	1	1	1	3	2	0
Totals	40	20	19	37	27	11	3
Cincinnati							
Hoy, cf	5	1	1	1	3	0	1
J. McCarthy, 1b	5	2	2	2	9	0	1
Latham, 3b	4	3	2	4	0	3	2
Holliday, lf	4	3	2	8	1	1	0
McPhee, 2b	5	0	2	2	4	5	0
Vaughn, c	5	1	2	5	3	3	1
Canavan, rf	5	1	1	4	2	0	0
Smith, ss	5	0	1	2	1	5	1
Chamberlain, p	5	0	1	2	1	0	0
Totals	43	11	14	30	24	17	6

Cincinnati	2	0	0	0	4	0	0	5	-	11
Boston	2	0	9	0	1	5	2	1	x	20

Earned runs, Boston 7, Cincinnati 8. Two-base hits, T. McCarthy, Ryan, Latham 2, Chamberlain, Lowe, Smith. Home runs, Holliday 2, Lowe 4, Long, Vaughn, Canavan. Stolen bases, Long, Duffy, Nash 2, Hoy, Latham. Sacrifice hit, Duffy. First base on balls, Long 2, Tucker 3, Nash 2, Latham. Struck out, Bannon, Ryan, T. McCarthy, Vaughn, McPhee, Chamberlain. Hit by pitched ball, Long, Tucker, Vaughn. Umpire, Swartwood. Time, 2:10. Attendance, 8,500.

This essay was originally published in Bill Felber, ed., Inventing Baseball: The 100 Greatest Games of the 19th Century *(Phoenix: SABR, 2013).*

NOTES

1. *North Adams* (Massachusetts) *Daily Transcript*, May 31, 1894.

2. The dimensions at Congress Street Grounds were 250 feet to left field and 400 feet to center field. The South End Grounds dimensions were 250 feet to left field, 445 to left center, 500 feet to center field, 440 feet to right center and 255 feet to right field. See Philip J. Lowry, *Green Cathedrals* (New York: Walker & Company, 2006), 25. Lowry does not give the dimensions to right field at Congress Street Grounds.

3. T. H. Murnane, "Cheered Bobby," *Boston Globe*, May 31, 1894: 13.

4. Bobby Lowe File, A Bartlett Giamatti Research Library, National Baseball Hall of Fame and Museum.

CRUSHED AT CONGRESS STREET

JUNE 6, 1894: PITTSBURG PIRATES 27, BOSTON BEANEATERS 11, AT CONGRESS STREET GROUNDS, BOSTON

BY ANDY TERRICK

Less than one calendar year since winning the National League pennant, the 1894 Boston Beaneaters had been dealing with a couple of issues. The team was playing well through the beginning of June, almost exactly as well as they had been playing at that point in the prior season, but things were slightly different this time around. The clubs from Baltimore, Pittsburg, and Cleveland were sitting higher in the NL standings on June 6, with Philadelphia and Brooklyn right below. This provided a contrast to June 6, 1893, when only Pittsburg was ahead, and third and fourth position were a few games back. Aside from having lost a competitive step to some opponents since the previous year, the Beaneaters had to deal with the literal loss of a major asset: their ballpark. During a game against Baltimore in early May, a small fire that had begun under the bleachers at the iconic South End Grounds escalated into a full-scale conflagration.[1] In what was eventually dubbed "The Great Roxbury Fire," flames had quickly turned the ballpark (and many nearby buildings) into ashes and rubble.

The team was rendered homeless, and needed somewhere to play while its place was being rebuilt, so it took up temporary residence at the Congress Street Grounds. Congress Street had been the Players' League, then American Association teams home in 1890 and 1891, but since 1891 it had been used only intermittently for baseball, and only on a minor-league level. Presenting what seemed an indication of either neglect or as a general insight into the struggles of nineteenth-century ballpark maintenance, one writer described the park's field simply as "rough."[2] Slightly more expansive than the South End Grounds in some ways,[3] Congress Street's dimensions held one eye-catching exception: The left-field fence was about 125 feet beyond third base, or just 250 feet from home plate.[4] One reporter believed that most home runs hit there "would be easy outs on any other grounds in the country."[5] The quirk in distance may have aided Bobby Lowe in becoming the first major leaguer to hit four home runs in one game. It may not have been the preferable stadium to play at, but the team did hold a 9-2 record there.

It was here that the Pittsburg Pirates came for a three-game series from June 4 to 6.

Pittsburg's prior season had been its best yet in the National League. Surviving a rough stretch during June, the Pirates set team records for total hits, total runs, and, more importantly, total wins. They finished the year as runners-up, five games behind Boston. Going into the 1894 season, there was a great deal of optimism among the Pirates that 1894 would be their year to attain the pennant.[6] After an inconsistent beginning of the season, the team reached first place by late May. The Pirates were in a three-way tie for first with Baltimore and Cleveland after games of June 2, but after splitting the first two games of the Boston series, they fell back to second, tied with the Spiders.

For the rubber match between the clubs on the 6th, Boston manager Frank Selee gave the pitching duties to a young, green southpaw named Henry Lampe. A small amount of relief work against Baltimore just before the Roxbury disaster was the extent of Lampe's NL experience. About 2,000 fans showed up to witness what would be his first start.[7]

A scoreless first inning was followed by a burst of runs in the second for both sides. Boston started by logging two scores through the contributions of a walk to Billy Nash and singles by Jimmy Bannon and Charlie Ganzel. Pittsburg's counter in the bottom of the inning was the only home run hit that season by Connie Mack, a hit that scored three runs after it flew over the left-field fence.[8] Boston's third-inning response comprised a double by Hugh Duffy and a single by Tommy McCarthy, which evened the score at 3-3.

Pittsburg's bottom of the second inning was but a slight warmup for what happened in their half of the third. It began well for Boston, as Lampe struck out the first batter he faced, Jake Beckley. However, the next batter, Jake Stenzel, hit a home run beyond left field. After that, Denny Lyons legged out a double, and he was followed by singles by Jack Glasscock and Louis Bierbauer, the latter scoring Lyons. Lampe bested Mack by forcing him to fly out to McCarthy. With two outs, a crucial opportunity presented itself for Boston to end the inning while keeping the damage to a minimum. Lampe's pitching nemesis that day, Tom Colcolough, hit a grounder toward Herman Long, but when Long attempted to field the ball, it "bounded badly away," and all runners reached base safely.[9] Frank Scheibeck contributed to Pittsburg's effort with a single, driving in Bierbauer. Patsy Donovan then hit a ball in the direction of Bobby Lowe. Lowe was another fielder having an off day, as he mishandled the ball and failed to get Donovan out, allowing Colcolough to score. Tim Murnane in the *Boston Globe* criticized the unfortunate defensive duo in the next day's recap, saying, "Long and Lowe are fielding about as well as some of the glass arm boys are pitching."[10] Beckley's double brought in Scheibeck and Donovan. Then Stenzel brought Beckley and himself back to the dugout with his second home run of the inning, increasing Pittsburg's lead to 12-3. Lyons followed by hitting a home run to nearly the same spot beyond left field as Stenzel's. Another chance to end the inning came and went for Boston when Glasscock hit a grounder at Tommy Tucker, Tucker's throw to first was fumbled by the embattled Lampe, and the runner was called safe. Bierbauer caused further consternation to the home fans as he hit his team's fourth home run of the inning (also to left field). By the time Mack flied out to end the inning, Pittsburg held a 15-3 lead.

At this point, Selee had seen far too much of his young pitcher's abilities. The fans likely agreed; they gave Lampe an "ovation" during his at-bat in the fourth, which one can only figure was of the mock cheer variety.[11] In the bottom of the fourth, Tom Smith replaced Lampe. Smith was making his big-league debut. It showed. In the fourth inning, Pittsburg logged nine more runs through a variety of methods: four walks, one hit batsman, one single, two doubles, an error by Long, and another home run over the left-field fence (Scheibeck's second and last of a 390-game major-league career). Once the fourth inning ended, the pace of scoring slowed down … somewhat. Pittsburg mustered only three additional runs for the remainder of the game. Meanwhile, Boston logged a bevy in the fifth (a Lowe homer over the left-field fence), sixth, and ninth innings off Colcolough. However, it wasn't enough to come close to Pittsburg's total.

In the end, the 27-11 final score was brought about by a number of key factors. The strong offense of the visitors, the poor fielding of the home team, the novice pitchers, and the ballpark's unique field dimensions all played roles in the drubbing that took place. The *Globe*'s story on the game wondered why Selee didn't opt for one of his team's three capable pitchers who sat on the bench with better (or in this case, some kind of) experience. Pittsburg's seven home runs in a game weren't matched again by the franchise until 1947, when the team was led by the power numbers of Ralph Kiner and Hank Greenberg.[12] Pitcher Tom Smith played in one more Beaneaters game before being released on June 20. As for Henry Lampe, called by Murnane "in a class by himself, one of the very weakest men ever presented in a league game," his stint with the team was over.[13] He was released the day after the game. The next few years saw both Lampe and Smith return to the major leagues with various clubs, but they toiled mostly in the minors. Coincidentally, once their ballplaying careers were over, they each became Boston city policeman.[14] As for the Congress Street Grounds and its abbreviated dimensions, the Beaneaters' tenure there lasted two more weeks. During the 27 games they played there, teams hit a total of 86 home runs, including a game-winning, send-off blast by Hugh Duffy on June 20.[15] After a 23-game road trip that wrapped up in the middle of July, the team moved back to a rebuilt South End Grounds.

SOURCES

In addition to the sources in the notes, the author consulted baseball-reference.com, retrosheet.org, and sabr.org.

North Adams (Massachusetts) *Daily Transcript*, May 31, 1894.

The dimensions at Congress Street Grounds were 250 feet to left field and 400 feet to center field. The South End Grounds dimensions were 250 feet to left field, 445 to left center, 500 feet to center field, 440 feet to right center and 255 feet to right field. See Philip J. Lowry, *Green Cathedrals* (New York: Walker & Company, 2006), 25. Lowry does not give the dimensions to right field at Congress Street Grounds.

T. H. Murnane, "Cheered Bobby," *Boston Globe*, May 31, 1894: 13

Bobby Lowe File, A Bartlett Giamatti Research Library, National Baseball Hall of Fame and Museum.

NOTES

1. sabr.org/gamesproj/game/may-15-1894-it-was-hot-game-sure-enough.
2. T.H. Murnane, "Lampe Goes Out," *Boston Globe,* June 7, 1894: 3.
3. Robert D. Ross, *The Great Baseball Revolt: The Rise and Fall of the 1890 Players League* (Lincoln: University of Nebraska Press, 2016), 130.
4. "Base Ball Notes," *Pittsburgh Chronicle Telegraph,* June 6, 1894; Philip J. Lowry. *Green Cathedrals: The Ultimate Celebration of Major League and Negro League Ballparks* (New York: Walker & Co, 2006), 25.
5. "Diamond Flashes," *Baltimore Sun,* June 20, 1894, cited in Richard Tourangeau, "Remembering the Congress Street Grounds," *The National Pastime,* 2004: 78.
6. Norman L. Macht, *Connie Mack and the Early Years of Baseball* (Lincoln: University of Nebraska Press, 2007), 101-102.
7. "Was Simply Awful," *Pittsburgh Dispatch,* June 7, 1894.
8. Tourangeau, 76.
9. Murnane.
10. Ibid.
11. "Charleston's Boy," *Pittsburgh Chronicle Telegraph,* June 6, 1894.
12. baseball-almanac.com/box-scores/boxscore.php?boxid=194708160PIT.
13. Murnane.
14. Tourangeau, 76.
15. sabr.org/bioproj/park/33169c79.

THE BUNKER HILL DAY MASSACRE

JUNE 18, 1894: BOSTON BEANEATERS 24, BALTIMORE ORIOLES 7, AT THE CONGRESS STREET GROUNDS, BOSTON

BY JOHN BAUER

Bunker Hill Day, commemorating the Revolutionary War battle, arrived in Boston on Monday, June 18, 1894. For those in search of sporting entertainment as the calendar crept toward the first day of summer, two National League contenders would play a morning-afternoon doubleheader at the Congress Street Grounds. The host Boston Beaneaters, winners of the previous three NL pennants, held a record of 30-15 that was only good enough for second place. The Beaneaters trailed the 28-10 Baltimore Orioles, the surprise of the still-young season. Since joining the NL in 1892 from the defunct American Association, the Orioles had been a second-division club with finishes of 12th and then eighth. Manager Ned Hanlon, however, had fostered a family atmosphere[1] within an 1894 lineup that was the NL's youngest by average age. His infield of Dan Brouthers, Heinie Reitz, Hughie Jennings, and John McGraw was "all that could be desired";[2] however, the newcomers to the heights of the championship standings also spawned resentment among those who felt the Orioles did not belong among the class of elite clubs.[3]

The Bunker Hill Day doubleheader was the start of a four-game series. On the preceding Saturday, Boston finished a three-game home sweep of the Louisville Colonels, the series attracting sparse crowds to Congress Street. The Beaneaters' days at that ballpark appeared to be numbered with the brick grandstand at the South End Grounds expected to be complete by mid-July.[4] The Orioles had defeated St. Louis, 12-5, in Baltimore on Saturday. Making their way by train to Boston, they stopped at Newark for a Sunday match against Ironsides, the semipro champions of New Jersey. The Orioles defeated New Jersey's finest semipros, 11-3, but the effort and the evening train ride to Boston may have contributed to the debacle that awaited them in the opening game of the twin bill.

Under the "boiling hot sun" of midmorning, a sparse crowd reported to be 2,066 occupied the stands for the series opener. Jack Stivetts received the pitching assignment for the home team. While one commentator believed Kid Nichols and Tom Lovett were the "only [pitchers] under contract who can be depended upon,"[5] Stivetts would join Nichols as one of the workhorses for the 1894 Beaneaters. Lovett would be released within weeks and would not appear in another NL game. Hanlon handed the ball to veteran right-hander Tony Mullane. The 36-year-old had been an effective hurler through the 1892 season, but his abilities were fading fast. He struggled in 1893, joined Baltimore in June of that season, and was traded to Cleveland on July 13 for future Hall of Famer John Clarkson.[6]

The story of the June 18 game really begins and ends with the first inning. The Orioles faced a Boston defense that "has been very good of late."[7] Willie Keeler and Steve Brodie got on base in the top of the first, but didn't score. Boston had a much different inning, and the Beaneaters' frame "was one of the most terrific fusillades of singles, doubles and home runs."[8] Bobby Lowe led off with a single and Herman Long also singled to right field, putting runners at the corners. With Hugh Duffy at the plate, Mullane threw a wild pitch and Lowe scored while Long took second. With the game's first run in, "[t]he crowd was waxing warm with enthusiasm but was totally unprepared for what was to come."[9] Duffy drew a walk. Tommy McCarthy doubled, and Billy Nash and Tommy Tucker hit back-to-back singles. With four runs now across, Jimmy Bannon swatted the ball over the left-field fence, also bringing home Nash and Tucker, making the score, 7-0. Charlie Ganzel flied out to Brodie in center field for the first out, but Stivetts resumed the hit parade with a solo shot, also over the left-field fence, for a 8-0 Boston advantage; Stivetts hit a career-high eight round-trippers in 1894.

Mullane began his second tour through the Boston lineup by hitting Lowe with a pitch. Lowe stole second with Long batting, and crossed the plate on Long's single past third base. Duffy launched a Mullane pitch deep into the outfield, and the ball struck the top of the fence and bounced over. Boston's third home run of the inning extended the lead to 11-0. The inning was far from over. Mullane walked McCarthy before striking out Nash for the second out. Consecutive walks to Tucker, Bannon, and Ganzel scored McCarthy and left the bases loaded for Stivetts. The Beaneaters hurler singled, and Lowe did the same to start Mullane's third trip through the order. Long and Duffy then walked, the latter pass forcing in another run. With the bases still loaded and the score 16-0, McCarthy's grounder forced Duffy at second for the inning's third out. The Beaneaters' first inning consumed 40 minutes[10] and witnessed 22 men coming to the plate; there were 16 runs, 11 hits, 7 walks, and a hit batsman. The Orioles' chances appeared so hopeless that catcher Wilbert Robinson removed himself from the game. Initially, it was believed he might be injured. Rather, Robinson did not wish to "stay there a week" through Mullane's ineffectiveness, opting to be fresh for the afternoon game.[11] Boileryard Clarke assumed catching duties for the remainder of the game. With the sun creating a warm atmosphere, there was "little fight left in either team after [Boston's] remarkable hitting streak."[12]

Still, the scoring was far from complete. Tucker singled with one out in the Boston second; two batters later, Stivetts's single drove him in for a 17-0 advantage. Baltimore made a modest dent in Boston's lead in the top of the third. Long made a great play from the shortstop position on McGraw's grounder for a leadoff out, but Keeler and Brodie drew walks and Brouthers singled to score Keeler for the first Orioles run. Joe Kelley drove the ball deep into center field for a run-scoring double as Brodie crossed the plate for a 17-2 score. For the stocky Cambridge-born Kelley, the afternoon was something of a homecoming and Boston fans were favorably disposed toward the local boy.[13] Reitz "banged a hot one that caromed off Nash"[14] at third and scored Brouthers. The third inning ended at 17-3 when Long snared a liner off the bat of Jennings and doubled Kelley off second base. The fourth and fifth innings proved scoreless, but Baltimore scratched another run through singles by Jennings, Mullane, and McGraw in the top of the sixth. It was 17-4, Beaneaters.

The Beaneaters' half of the sixth provided "another picnic."[15] Mullane issued his 10th walk of the game, to Duffy, who went to third on Nash's double. Tucker also doubled to score both baserunners for a 19-4 lead. Bannon singled, Ganzel reached on Reitz's muff at shortstop, and Stivetts and Lowe hit back-to-back doubles for three more Boston runs and a 22-4 advantage. Mullane was finally relieved of his misery, with Bert Inks taking over pitching duties for the Boston seventh. The Beaneaters added two more runs in that inning. Duffy and Frank Connaughton (who had replaced McCarthy in the third inning) hit consecutive singles, and Tucker's double scored them both. Boston now led 24-4.

There was little the league leaders could do at this point to make the score respectable. The combination of a "well-placed bunt"[16] and a bad throw from Stivetts permitted McGraw to claim second base in the eighth. Brodie's single to right scored McGraw. For the ninth inning, Tom Smith took the ball from Stivetts. Dubbed a "new college find,"[17] the young left-hander had made his Beaneaters debut on June 6 and this day was his second and last of the season. His appearance "showed speed and curves, but lacked command."[18] As a result, Baltimore added two consolation runs. Kelley singled and took second on a wild pitch. Jennings was hit by a pitch before Clarke's drive past Connaughton scored both baserunners. Smith walked McGraw and Keeler to load the bases, but Brodie flied out to Duffy to end the game at Boston 24, Baltimore 7.

For all of the runs scored by Boston in the opener, the club finished the day in the same position as it started. After scoring four in the first inning of the second game, Baltimore maintained a lead until the end, winning 9-7. While the day ended in a split result, the Beaneaters had served notice that they would not surrender their pennant without a fight.

SOURCES

In addition to the sources cited in the Notes, the author also consulted baseball-reference.com.

NOTES

1. Albert Mott, "Baltimore Bulletin," *Sporting Life*, June 30, 1894: 4.
2. Ibid.
3. Ibid.
4. "Caught on the Fly," *The Sporting News*, June 23, 1894: 3. The grandstand had burned down on May 15 in a ruinous fire that spread beyond the ballpark and destroyed 200 neighborhood homes. While the grandstand was being rebuilt, the Beaneaters played home games at the Congress Street Grounds, home to Players' League and American Association teams in 1890 and 1891.
5. "Leaders to Meet," *Boston Globe*, June 18, 1894: 6.
6. Clarkson would never register an appearance with the Orioles.
7. "Batting Better Than Ever," *Boston Globe*, June 18, 1894: 6.
8. "League Leaders," *Boston Daily Advertiser*. June 19, 1894: 2.
9. "Had Both in Hand," *Boston Journal*, June 19, 1894: 5.
10. "Orioles Lose and Win," *Baltimore Sun*, June 19, 1894: 6.
11. "Diamond Flashes," *Baltimore Sun*, June 19, 1894: 6.
12. "Had Both in Hand."
13. "Leaders to Meet."
14. "Orioles Lose and Win."
15. Ibid.
16. T.H. Murnane, "They Quit Even," *Boston Globe*, June 19, 1894: 7.
17. "Orioles Lose and Win."
18. Ibid.

CONGRESS STREET'S GLORIOUS FINALE

JUNE 20, 1894: BOSTON 13, BALTIMORE 12, AT CONGRESS STREET GROUNDS, BOSTON

BY RICHARD "DIXIE" TOURANGEAU

Hugh Duffy strode to home plate in the bottom of the ninth inning. His Bostons trailed 12-11 but Bobby Lowe stood on third and Herman Long was on second after his clutch double. It was another roller-coaster thrill ride for the 2,100 fans in attendance but this was special, as it would be the last official National League game to be played at the Congress Street Grounds. The Beaneaters had rented the old home ballyard of the champ Players' League Reds (1890, home 48-21) and champ American Association Reds (1891, 51-17) because their magnificent South End Grounds was turned into ashes on May 15 along with 200 other Roxbury structures. Reborn over one hectic weekend and improved during the subsequent four weeks of play, the neglected winningest park in Boston baseball history (.726) was brought back to useful life for Hub fans, but the end was two outs away.

Appropriately, the much-despised Baltimore Orioles were the opposition on Wednesday, June 20, 1894. Ned Hanlon's crew was the opponent when the conflagration occurred and they were now in first place, looking to dethrone the three-time NL champion Beaneaters. Baltimore (30-11) was considered an upstart adversary to Boston (31-17). Rehabbed Congress Street had the second double-decked grandstand in Boston; the multi-witch-hat towered South End Grounds Pavilion (1888) was the first. When Boston Wharf Co. architect Morton D. Safford was contracted to design a PL facility, the SEG II was the natural model for it. In addition, the Congress Street locale was downtown, near Boston Harbor, nearly four miles away from the annoying sooty railroad smoke at Berlin and Walpole Streets. Because of short distances down both lines (250 to 275 feet), it was a hitter's heaven and a hurler's hell. Through 26 post-fire games, Boston's record there was 19-7; they averaged almost 11 runs per contest but allowed 9. During the monthlong span, Boston had clobbered Cincinnati 20-11 on May 30, behind Lowe's record four home runs, and pasted Baltimore, 24-7, on June 18. Not immune themselves, the hosts fell 22-8 to Cleveland Spiders star Cy Young on June 1 and were humiliated, 27-11, by Pittsburgh on June 6 when desperation substitute pitchers Henry Lampe and Tom Smith failed terribly by allowing seven Pirates fence clouts in one afternoon.

Some aspects adding to the ninth-inning drama on June 20 evolved from previous episodes. The starters were John "Sadie" McMahon for Baltimore and "Happy Jack" Stivetts for the locals. They had history, especially within the 1891 AA season. Jack was with St. Louis and McMahon with Baltimore before it was absorbed by the NL in 1892. They were two of the stellar workhorses of the Association's final campaign, McMahon topped the doomed circuit with 35 wins, Stivetts amassed 33 (third). They were one-two in appearances and games started, McMahon threw 503 innings (most). Stivetts led the AA in both walks and strikeouts, and despite his being near the top in hits and runs given up, McMahon's 2.81 ERA was fourth-best. Delaware native McMahon led the AA with 36 victories in 1890.

Now in 1894, Stivetts lost to McMahon in April in Baltimore. Sadie also beat Charlie "Kid" Nichols twice, the day before the fire (last victory recorded at the South End Grounds II) and just two days before the epic in progress. Nichols had an 8-0 record at Congress Street before the 9-7 defeat. Stivetts won the season opener at SEG II easily over Brooklyn and then was just horrible, losing eight straight (allowing 96 runs), before rebounding by winning four. On June 1 he had eight of the Beaneaters' 12 losses. Meanwhile, McMahon was cruising at 12-3, winning 10 of his last 11 starts. This was the sixth and last game in Boston between the rivals and Baltimore had won three of the five. Up to that date, McMahon was 5-3 lifetime at Congress and Stivetts had a 7-5 mark. Jack's four wins there in 1894 were backed by 66 Beaneater tallies.

Few fans outside of the Fort McHenry area liked the rude, crude, rough-and-tumble style of Orioles play led by belligerent John McGraw and his instigator pal Hughie Jennings. So every game soon became a ferocious grudge match. Congress Street's swan song seemed lost after seven innings with Sadie ahead 7-5, in what was a near pitcher's duel at the harborside launching pad. The daily slugfest had not begun — yet. Second batter Herman Long (four hits) smacked a home run in the first but Baltimore took hold of the game in the third frame with four runs and added two more in the fourth. In the eighth McMahon suddenly lost his stuff completely and Boston smacked five hits, including Tommy McCarthy's bases-clearing double (of his four hits), to surge ahead, 10-7. The crowd was ecstatic but Happy Jack instantly turned into April-May Jack and "lost his nerve and went to pieces."[1] After a Long fumble (ruled a hit), a second Dan Brouthers double to go with his triple that day, a hit batsman, and two walks, two runs had scored and the bases were still packed. Beaneaters manager Frank Selee had seen enough and with captain Billy Nash called on Tom Lovett to relieve. Lovett was 5-1 at Congress Street, but was bedraggled by fatigue. His first pitch short-hopped the plate and rolled to the backstop fence, allowing two runs. Then Wilbert Robinson's flyout brought home Jennings. On two hits the Orioles had gone ahead 12-10. Lovett steadied and got two more flies, ending the rally.

Catcher Jack Ryan grounded out to start the bottom of the ninth. Things looked bleak but local boy Frank Connaughton batted for Lovett and check-swung on what should have been a third strike. Umpire Bob Emslie allowed him to walk to first. The pesky old gal of a ballyard had set the stage, she was not about to host a sad finale. Then NL home run leader (13) Bobby Lowe, who had belted one off McMahon two days before, doubled, and according to only the *Boston Herald*, scored Connaughton. Many in the depressed crowd heading to the exits stopped cold and turned instantly into a screaming mob as Long, who also crushed a McMahon pitch two days previous, as well as in the first inning, also doubled. To make sure the sharp hit was not caught, Lowe hesitated going to third and did not score. This is where the other newspapers had Connaughton reach home. In any case it was 12-11.

Up came Duffy. Thus far he had only an infield single but had launched two home runs the day before off Bill Hawke, another Delaware-born Oriole, in Boston's 13-8 loss. Back in April 1891 as a member of the AA champ Reds, Duffy lofted a McMahon ninth-inning toss into the left-field seats, but McMahon had a comfy 12-5 lead that afternoon. This time the situation was a bit more intense. McCarthy, the other "Heavenly Twin," was on deck with four hits already so McMahon decided to pitch to Duffy. His smooth swing put the ball into the air and eventually it drifted into the left-field bleachers. Game over at 13-12. Some members of the crowd swarmed the field and carried Duffy around the infield while others gleefully cursed the shocked, exiting Orioles. The short-lived Congress Street Grounds encore had gone dark on its own terms of grandeur.

The Beaneaters would then leave town on a monthlong road trip enabling carpenters to continue to rebuild, at much less cost and minus any ornate design, the SEG III along what was a straightened and lengthened Columbus Avenue. Familiar Berlin Street was erased from all maps.

For ticket holders of the historic game just ended, it would be a great memory, but for twentieth- and twenty-first-century researchers the game's scorebook outcome is a little frustrating. Because of the rules of the day, Duffy was not officially awarded a home run, a second run scored or an RBI beyond Long's touching of home plate. The *Boston Globe*, *Post* and *Journal* each gave him a box-score single, while the *Daily Advertiser* and *Herald* gave the hero a double in their boxes. Most headlines exclaimed that he hit a "home run."[2] The *Baltimore Sun* listed a round-tripper in its box for Duffy along with a second run scored but it took a definite run away from Lowe to keep the tally at 13. The *New York Clipper* told of the home run in text but did not include it or any double in its stat box. The *Herald* was very meticulous in detail about the whole game and was the only paper to briefly explain the final scoring. "Although Duffy's hit was a home run, he gets credit under the rules for a two-baser only, as only that was necessary to send in the run that won the game."[3] The box score followed. The *Globe* reported that Duffy had stopped at second, likely knowing the rule and because he was surrounded by the celebrating mob who stopped his progress halfway around the bases.

SOURCES

In addition to the sources cited in the Notes, the author also consulted Baseball-Reference.com, Retrosheet.org, and the following newspapers: *Boston Globe, Boston Post, Boston Courier, Boston Advertiser, Baltimore Sun,* and *New York Clipper.*

NOTES

1 Tim Murnane, "Duffy's Homer," *Boston Globe*, June 21, 1894: 2.

2 See, for instance, "Duffy's Home Run," *Boston Journal*, June 21, 1894: 3.

3 *Boston Herald*, June 21, 1894.

STALL AND FEIGN AND PRAY FOR RAIN

JULY 17, 1894: PHILADELPHIA PHILLIES 11, BOSTON BEANEATERS 2, AT THE HUNTINGTON GROUNDS, PHILADELPHIA

BY BOB LEMOINE

Unlike most other sports, baseball has no clock, so a team never has to "beat the clock" as well as an opponent. There are very few times when actual minutes are measured instead of outs in baseball. When a relief pitcher is not yet ready to come into a game, a manager will come out to the mound to stall for time to give him more throws in the bullpen. Or in a rarer instance, if a team is trailing big early in the game and rain is in the forecast, it may stall in any way it can in the hope that the rain will start and the game be called off. This was the case on July 17, 1894, when Boston visited Philadelphia in a strange game that led to a riot on the streets of Philadelphia.

Boston, winner of the pennant the previous three seasons, was in a tie for first with Baltimore. Philadelphia was in fifth, 7½ games behind. Harry Staley took the mound for Boston while Philadelphia counted on the right arm of Jack Taylor. Boston manager Frank Selee was absent for reasons unknown today, so captain Billy Nash was in charge. Dan Campbell, a Philadelphia native, was umpiring his first National League game.[1]

Philadelphia batted first and took an early lead. Sliding Billy Hamilton walked and stole second. Boston players Tommy Tucker, Bobby Lowe, and Nash "raised a big howl"[2] to Campbell over the call. Campbell warned them, fined Lowe and Tucker, and threatened to eject Tucker. Tucker, however, "kept up a tirade of abusive language, which aroused the ire of the seven thousand spectators."[3] Hamilton scored on Ed Delahanty's fly ball.

The score was 1-0 into the fourth, when Boston tied the score. Herman Long singled. Hugh Duffy flied out, but Tommy McCarthy reached on a single, with Long moving to third. Long scored on a double steal.

The game remained tied into the seventh. Boston's Nash singled, stole second, and went to third on a muffed third strike. Staley popped out, but Lowe singled, and Boston led 2-1. What was a close, exciting contest descended into disarray from this point forward.

In the top of the eighth, Hamilton tripled to left center. Bill Hallman walked and stole second. Delahanty grounded to Tucker, well off the base at first. Tucker fielded, but neither Lowe nor Staley covered first, giving Delahanty the base as Hamilton scored the tying run. Delahanty stole second and scored with Hallman on a single by Sam Thompson. Philadelphia now led 4-2. Lave Cross walked and Jack Boyle beat out a bunt single to load the bases. Joe Sullivan hit a towering drive to left field. McCarthy, in an attempt to decoy the runners, stood dead still as if ready to catch it. The plan didn't work as the bases cleared when the ball sailed over his head and Sullivan was now at third.

Sullivan came home with another run on a groundout, and Philadelphia led 8-2.

"Then the circus proper began," the *Boston Globe* wrote.[4] Boston players knew their only real chance was for the "ominous sounds of thunder in the heavens"[5] to bring rain. In that case the game would end with the final score reverting back to the previous inning, and Boston would win, 2-1. Taylor hit a pop fly to left that McCarthy, Long, and Nash let drop. Taylor wound up on second, and tried to get himself put out by literally walking to third and then home. Boston players just watched him go. Hamilton then grounded between third and short with a true seeing-eye single, as Long and Nash both watched it go by. Hamilton made second, walking the entire way. He scored when Nash got out of the way of Hallman's hit. Hallman turned it into a walking inside-the-park home run.

Philadelphia tried to find other ways to get themselves out. Delahanty was called out on a foul strike when he stepped out of the batter's box. Boston players gathered around Campbell to argue. Thompson grounded to first, just past Tucker, who dodged the ball. Cross singled and Thompson was called out for cutting across the infield, missing second base. Nash and Boston players complained that Thompson should have been safe. Nash was, in the words of the *Philadelphia Inquirer*, "acting like a crazy man, jumping around and abusing the umpire, the spectators and the Philadelphia players and management, while Nash and Lowe were laying down the Boston law of 'how to play dirty ball' to the umpire."[6]

"Probably 20 minutes were frittered away in this fashion," the *Globe* reported, "during which the enraged spectators manifested their displeasure by groans and hisses."[7] Boston players left the field and refused to take their turn at bat. Campbell eyed his watch and, after allowing 30 seconds[8] for Boston to get to the plate, had seen enough and called the game to the Phillies.

"Then followed a scene as was never before witnessed on a ball field in this city," wrote the *Globe*.[9] Angry fans swarmed the field. Tucker had forgotten his glove at first base and went back to retrieve it. Fans circled him and he was given "the shoulder" by someone. "This was the spark that kindled the fire," in the words of the *Globe*.[10] Someone punched Tucker on the left cheek. Only the crowd kept him standing. The police broke through the mob and with the help of Philadelphia players, including Boyle and Mike Grady "fighting like Trojans,"[11] they literally tossed Tucker over the crowd and under the pavilion, where the door to the Boston dressing room was. In front of the door was Sergeant Eglof "and his 250 pounds avoirdupois was a bulwark not easily overcome," wrote the *Inquirer*, "and while he kept the mob at bay the doors were closed."[12]

The crowd, 1,500 by the *Globe's* estimate, was so thick that omnibuses and trolley cars on Broad Street were stopped. In the dressing room, the Phillies owner, Colonel John I. Rogers, and Nash had an "exciting colloquy" in the dressing room. Rogers promised that the National League would take action against the Boston players, while Nash blamed the Phillies.[13]

Lieutenant Wolf and reserve police officers arrived from the 22nd Precinct to get the players out of the park. The police formed a double line for the team to get to the coach at 15th and Huntington. The team got aboard and rode down Broad Street, with two policemen each on the front and back. Fans hurled rocks at the coach. An officer named Welker jumped off the coach to detain a 14-year-old brick thrower. Walker dragged him into a nearby store and "smacked the lad in the face, and he in turn was given a lively hustling by the crowd, during which the little offender made his escape."[14] The coach driver, seeing the distracted crowd, rumbled off.

The police arrested William Leonard and Lewis Sailor for the Tucker assault, but they were discharged for lack of evidence.[15] "The riotous scenes which ensued were traceable entirely to the ruffianly conduct of the visiting players," the *Inquirer* wrote. Selee telegraphed National League President Nick Young, blaming the incident on Philadelphia and requesting that the game not count in the standings.[16] Young took no action.

The *Boston Journal* thought there would be consequences felt in the game for years to come. "The National Pastime, a game which the American youth hardly out of his swaddling clothes is taught to play – has received a smirch which will take years to efface. … [U]pon those who a patronage is worth cultivating – those, whose presence at a ball game lends it both dignity and popularity, the effect will be demoralizing."[17] The *Times* of Philadelphia, placed blame on the National League since "in all the cases of rowdyism and disgraceful conduct that has transpired on the diamond during the year not a single word has gone forth from headquarters bent on putting an end to it."[18]

Tucker was involved in yet another incident at the team hotel after the next day's game. Players were standing in front of the Hotel Hanover when a man reached over the railing of a passing trolley car and punched Tucker in the mouth. Tucker and Jimmy Bannon chased the trolley and told a police officer to arrest his assailant. Instead, Tucker was ordered back to the hotel. He refused, became hostile to the officer, and spent the night in jail. He was released just in time to get on the train back to Boston.

"I don't know why it is that the people of Philadelphia pick on me the way they do," Tucker said.[19]

SOURCES

In addition to the sources cited in the Notes, the author also consulted Baseball-Reference.com, Retoroshet.org, and Felber, Bill. *A Game of Brawl: The Orioles, the Beaneaters & the Battle for the 1897 Pennant.* (Lincoln, Nebraska: University of Nebraska Press, 2007), 19-20.

NOTES

1. Campbell was installed by chief of umpires Harry Wright to replace Billy Stage after Stage was hit in the head by a foul ball and would later resign; "Tom Tucker Assaulted," *Washington Evening Star,* July 18, 1894: 11; Peter Morris, "Billy Stage," SABR BioProject sabr.org/bioproj/person/6c4a9372.

2. "Disgraceful Riot on the Ball Field," *Philadelphia Inquirer*, July 18, 1894: 1.

3. Ibid.

4. "Ends in Fight," *Boston Globe*, July 18, 1894: 2.

5. "Disgraceful Riot."

6. "Disgraceful Riot."

7. "Ends in Fight."

8. "Ball Players Face a Riot," *Philadelphia Times,* July 18, 1894: 1.

9. "Ends in Fight."

10. Ibid.

11. "Ball Players Face a Riot."

12. Ibid.

13. "Disgraceful Riot," 3.

14. Ibid.

15. "A Smirch. Riot on the Base Ball Field at Philadelphia," *Boston Journal,* July 18, 1894

16. "Both Were to Blame," *Boston Journal*, July 18, 1894: 8.

17. "A Smirch."

18. "Base Ball Comment," *Philadelphia Times,* July 22, 1894: 22.

19. "Tucker Meets His Waterloo," *Philadelphia Times,* July 19, 1894: 1; "Tommy Tucker Locked Up," *Philadelphia Inquirer,* July 19, 1894: 3.

BEANEATERS BLAST GIANTS 12-1 IN FIRST GAME AT SOUTH END GROUNDS AFTER FIRE

JULY 20, 1894: BOSTON BEANEATERS 12, NEW YORK GIANTS 1, AT SOUTH END GROUNDS

BY MARK S. STERNMAN

The Boston-New York baseball rivalry did not originate with the Red Sox and the Yankees clashing in American League contests. Diamond hostilities between the two cities predate the birth of the junior circuit. Heading into play on this July 1894 day in Boston, the 12-team National League clearly had an upper quartile in a trio of teams that all played better than .600 ball. The first-place Baltimore Orioles led the way, trailed closely by the second-place Beaneaters and the third-place New York Giants.

The mound matchup appeared compelling with two star pitchers at the height of their prowess. Both regularly won at least 20 games. For the home team, Jack Stivetts took the hill. In his rookie season, he led the American Association with a 2.25 ERA. From 1890 through 1893, Stivetts won 27, 33, 35, and 20 games for the Association's Browns and the Beaneaters. Those impressive stats, however, seemed somewhat small when compared with those of his mound opponent, Amos Rusie, the Hoosier Thunderbolt. For New York from 1890 through 1893, Rusie won 29, 33, 32, and 33 games, or 12 more than Stivetts did over the same span. But the old hoodoo appeared to afflict Rusie when he pitched against the club from the Hub. Noted the *Boston Globe,* "[H]e has won just one game from Boston since he has been with New York. Luck is dead against the big pitcher against the [Beaneaters]."[1]

And on this particular day, the Beaneaters had an unusual home-field advantage that might have inspired them. A bit more than two months earlier, the South End Grounds was destroyed in a fire "started by a cigar or cigarette dropped among old peanut shells"[2] during a Baltimore-Boston game, when Boston's Tommy Tucker and Baltimore's John McGraw … got into a savage fight … after Tucker slid hard into third base and McGraw kicked him in the face. … The conflagration in its initial stages could easily have been stomped out, but it was ignored by the crowd – who were caught up in the fracas on the field and its aftermath – until the end of the inning."[3]

The faithful Boston fans eagerly returned to their old stamping grounds, renovated after the fire, "and a large crowd turned out to greet them," noted the *New York Times*. "The heat was so intense that the cozy little grand stand, with a seating capacity of only 900, was totally inadequate to accommodate those who wished to witness the game from a sheltered position."[4]

Even against a pitcher as imposing as Rusie, the bats of the Beaneaters soon proved as hot as the weather. The Hoosier

Thunderbolt looked sharp early, wrote the estimable baseball scribe Tim Murnane: "It is doubtful whether Amos Rusie ever had greater speed, and the way he shot the ball through space … in the first inning made it seem impossible for any man to meet the ball with anything like accuracy."[5]

Boston's half of the second inning made this notion seem preposterous. Tucker singled. Jimmy Bannon singled. Billy Nash hit a three-run homer to put the Beaneaters up 3-0. Backup catcher Jack Ryan singled and scored on a triple by Stivetts that gave him a 4-0 lead. A multitalented player who appeared at every position other than catcher over the course of his 11-year career, Stivetts would slash his way to a .328/.369/.533 season in 1894 and smack seven triples.

Bobby Lowe plated his pitcher with a groundball to New York's Shorty Fuller, who made a throwing error that made the score 5-0 and placed Lowe on second. At 5-feet-6, Fuller today seems less exceptional for his lack of height than for the frequency of his miscues. (He made 73 in 1894, a substantial total but far short of the career-high 92 he made in 1892, his first season in New York.) Herman Long doubled Lowe home to put Boston up 6-0. Hugh Duffy, who would hit .440 in 1894, singled. Long and Duffy both scored, too, the latter on errors on the same play by Rusie overthrowing second and George Van Haltren doing the same with his return heave to George Davis at third base. The Beaneaters had tallied eight runs in the inning thanks to a bounty of Boston hits and a trio of errors by the Giants.

A bad day for New York got worse in the fourth inning when the Giants had runners on first and second and what looked like a single became instead a rare 7-4-5 double play. Tommy McCarthy in left field charged a liner and whipped it to Lowe for a force out at second base. Lowe relayed the ball to Nash at third who tagged out the runner from second. Murnane marveled, "It would be impossible to make a more daring and yet brilliant play on a ball field."[6]

Duffy, who in addition to his amazing batting average would lead the National League in 1894 with a career-high 18 homers, smashed a round-tripper in the fourth to put Boston up 9-0. Known as the Heavenly Twins, McCarthy and Duffy put on a celestial performance both at the plate and in the field.

Heaven could wait in the seventh when Duffy appeared to throw out New York player-manager John Montgomery Ward at third base. Nash's error attempting to apply the tag let the ball get away and enabled Ward to score an unearned run. Even though the move paid off, manager Ward should have chastised player Ward for his overly aggressive baserunning given the large deficit his team faced.

The Beaneaters got that run back plus two more in the seventh to make the final score 12-1. The rally consisted of McCarthy's triple, doubles by Tucker and Bannon, and, atoning immediately for his error, an RBI single by Nash.

In spite of the rout, both pitchers hurled complete games (amazingly, only five pitchers appeared for the Giants in 1894, when Rusie finished second in the NL with 444 innings pitched). While the more renowned Rusie got rocked, Stivetts superbly pitched a seven-hitter, a feat especially impressive in the offensively charged 1894 season, when the National League as a whole had a .309 batting average, and its teams averaged 7.4 runs per game. "Jack Stivetts," the *Globe* commented, "pitched a game … that would win every time."[7]

Beating New York always makes Boston fans feel grateful; doing so during the first game back at a beloved ballfield made an easy victory even more gratifying than usual.

NOTES

1 "Echoes of the Game," *Boston Globe*, July 21, 1894: 2.

2 Harold Kaese, *The Boston Braves, 1871-1953* (Boston: Northeastern University Press, 2004), 67.

3 David Nemec, "Tommy Tucker," sabr.org/bioproj/person/c54e887d (accessed August 8, 2017).

4 "Giants Badly Beaten," *New York Times*, July 21, 1894.

5 T.H. Murnane, "Bat Like Fiends," *Boston Globe*, July 21, 1894: 2. The descriptions of the plays in this game derive from Murnane's detailed account.

6 Murnane. The *Times* described the play thusly: "McCarthy worked his trap-ball trick when New York had a good chance to score in the fourth inning, and retired the side."

7 "Baseball Notes," *Boston Globe*, July 21, 1894: 2.

JIMMY "FOXY GRANDPA" BANNON SLUGS TWO 3-RUN HOMERS

AUGUST 7, 1894: BOSTON BEANEATERS 19, PHILADELPHIA QUAKERS 8, AT THE SOUTH END GROUNDS

BY MICHAEL R. MCAVOY

On a fine weather day, August 7, 1894, Boston met Philadelphia at home for the first game in a three-game series.[1] Boston's Jimmy Bannon had demonstrated a power streak in recent games.[2] On August 2 at New York, he hit a home run to left-center.[3] At home on August 6, he hit one against Washington.[4] The Quakers arrived in Boston as literal survivors. During their practice on August 6, they watched their home grandstand and bleachers burn.[5] The Boston club – the reigning champion – was in first place at 56-30.[6] Philadelphia was at the bottom of the first division, 43-38. Frank Selee managed the Beaneaters, and Arthur Irwin, the Quakers.[7] A crowd of 3,416 was present to watch the league's best hitting club.[8] Tim Murnane of the *Boston Globe* observed that the pavilion was composed almost entirely of women.[9]

The game began with the Quakers at bat. Boston pitcher Kid Nichols walked Billy Hamilton, then Jack Boyle bunted to first baseman Tommy Tucker to advance Hamilton. Notably, Nichols covered first base to earn the putout.[10] Hamilton scored on Lave Cross's single to left, and Cross advanced to second base on the play at the plate.[11] Third sacker Billy Nash "beautifully stopped" Ed Delahanty's drive, which trapped Cross between Nash and shortstop Herman Long. Delahanty advanced to second during the play. Nichols walked Sam Thompson. Bill Hallman's fly dropped into short center between the fielders to score Delahanty and place Thompson at second. Dick Buckley grounded out to shortstop for the third out. Philadelphia was ahead by two runs.

In Boston's half, Jack Fanning, newly acquired from New Orleans in the Southern Association, faced leadoff hitter Bobby Lowe. With a full count, Lowe "shot" a single past third base, then stole second. Long tripled to left-center to score Lowe. Hugh Duffy walked. Tommy McCarthy singled to left to score Long and move Duffy to second. Tucker went out, second baseman Hallman to Boyle, and Duffy advanced to third and McCarthy to second. Nash singled to left and Duffy scored. Nash took second on a passed ball. When Fanning walked Bannon, manager Irwin "blew his dog whistle" and brought in Kid Carsey.[12] Nevertheless, the runs continued. McCarthy and Nash scored on Charlie Ganzel's single to left. Bannon scored on Carsey's wild pitch, which advanced Ganzel to third. Nichols singled "in the right place" to score Ganzel.[13] Again at the top of the order, Lowe hit to shortstop Joe Sullivan to force out Nichols. To end the inning, Long was forced on a hit to Sullivan. The crowd "howled themselves so hoarse that quietness reigned the remainder of the game."[14] Boston led 7 to 2.

In the second, friends of Charlestown native Joe Sullivan presented him with a gold-headed cane, a large leather suitcase, and a huge floral wreath in the shape of a horseshoe, in which "Good Luck" was inscribed.[15] Instead, Sullivan hit to short for a force out. Nichols walked Carsey. Hamilton and Boyle flied out. Duffy led off Boston's half with a home run over the left-field fence.[16] McCarthy hustled out an infield hit to Cross, who made a great stop but a low throw. Carsey walked Tucker. Nash attempted a sacrifice bunt, but bunted out a fly to Carsey. Bannon drove a ball to Cross, forcing Tucker at second but moving McCarthy to third. Carsey threw to Boyle at first to hold Bannon, and McCarthy stole home.[17] Ganzel drove a ball long and high into left field where Delahanty dropped the ball to score Bannon.[18] Nichols struck out.

Boston was up 10-2. In the top of the third, Nichols covered first base for the putout when Tucker fielded Thompson's hit. The bottom of the third featured no Boston runs. The *Boston Globe* noted Duffy's "falling down badly" in the game the day before and the *Boston Herald* noted that he had to leave this game in the seventh inning due to a "lame leg."[19] .

In the fourth inning, Hallman doubled to left, where he was stranded. In Boston's half, Carsey hit Tucker with a pitch and walked Nash. Then Bannon homered and the crowd "went wild."[20] Ganzel flied out to Hallman at second. Nichols grounded out to Sullivan at short. Cross threw poorly to first on Lowe's hit, but he was then caught in a rundown play by Carsey, Boyle, and Hallman. Boston led, 13-2.

When Bannon took his position in right, fans provided him with a great reception. The *Boston Journal* noted that Bannon was the "idol of the 25 cent bleachers in far right field," and added, "It was a novel sight to see the receptions the 'little old man' got from his henchmen in right."[21] Furthermore, "Bannon was the hero of the game, and was busy tipping his cap to liberal applause every time he made a good catch, and after each of his timely home runs."[22]

Philadelphia scored two more in the fifth. Hamilton ran out an infield grounder.[23] On Boyle's grounder, Long touched second base to force Hamilton and threw to Tucker to complete the double play. With two out, Cross doubled and Delahanty singled. Thompson doubled to center to score Cross and Delahanty.[24] Hallman was forced out, Nichols to Tucker.

In Boston's fifth, Long flied out to Hamilton. Then Carsey loaded the bases when he walked Duffy, threw a wild pitch to move him to second, walked McCarthy, and watched as Hallman "fumbled" the ball on Tucker's hit.[25] Nash sacrificed to Delahanty to score Duffy and move McCarthy to third. Bannon homered to left again. Ganzel flied out to center. It was 17-4, Boston.

In the top of the seventh, Frank Connaughton replaced Duffy in center and Philadelphia scored two runs. Hamilton singled, then was forced out at second on Boyle's grounder.[26] Delahanty got on base. With two outs and two men on, Connaughton misplayed Thompson's triple, a long fly to center and the longest hit of the game.[27] Hallman recorded an out on a foul ball hit to the catcher, Ganzel. Boston's lead narrowed to 17-6. In the Philadelphia eighth, Buckley made first when Long threw wide from short. Sullivan hit to Nash and forced out Buckley, but Sullivan hustled to make first on the throw. Carsey drove a ball into Nichols' pitching hand, sending Sullivan to second. Nichols continued to pitch with a hurt hand.[28] Tuck Turner, who substituted for Hamilton, hit a hard grounder to Long, who threw to Nash at third to tag out Sullivan. Boyle flied out to Bannon.

In the Boston half, Ganzel singled on a long hit to center field and advanced to second on Carsey's wild pitch. Nichols and Lowe went out. Long hit a home run over the left-field fence to score two more runs.[29] Connaughton flied out to Delahanty in left. Boston's lead increased to 19-6. In the ninth, Philadelphia scored twice more. Delahanty and Thompson singled and Buckley walked. Sullivan singled to score two runs. Pitching with an injured hand, Nichols struck out the next two batters, including Carsey, for the last out.[30]

The game lasted 2 hours 5 minutes, Boston scored 19 runs on 14 hits, and made one error, and Philadelphia scored eight runs on 15 hits, but made seven errors. The game featured four home runs, the pitcher covering first for two putouts, a steal of home, and excited spectators. Notably, Jimmy Bannon provided the game's highlights with two three-run homers and good fielding. The Boston club hit Philadelphia's pitchers hard, as Fanning walked two and Carsey, "ragged" and "wild," walked four. The *Boston Journal* said Philadelphia played "dazed" and "in a trance." Cross made four of their six errors. The Beaneaters "were full of ginger, and never played a better game in their lives," wrote the *Philadelphia Inquirer*. "The fielding was brilliant and strong, often times reaching the height of phenomenal. ... Everyone used their gray matter and the base running was never excelled."[31] Ganzel praised Nichols as the finest fielding pitcher, who covered first base for two putouts.[32]

SOURCES

The game summary is primarily from "Champions Lost No Time," *Boston Herald*, August 8, 1894: 2. Where the game summary differs from the *Boston Herald*, the source is identified.

NOTES

1. In the 10th game of their 12-game season series, the Beaneaters trailed the series four wins to five losses. This was Philadelphia's first visit to Boston for the 1894 season.

2. After spending his rookie campaign with the 1893 St. Louis Browns, the 22-year-old Bannon signed with Boston for 1894, to play mostly in right field alongside future Hall of Famers Hugh Duffy and Tommy McCarthy. Bannon had a very good sophomore season. He played in 128 games, scored 130 runs, hit 29 doubles, 10 triples, and 13 home runs, drove in 114 runs, and stole 47 bases. He had a .336 batting average, .414 on-base percentage, and .514 slugging percentage. In right field, he led the majors with 43 assists, while recording 41 errors, one off the leader. Standing only 5-feet-5 but listed at 160 pounds, Bannon had nicknames including "Little," "Old Man," "Kid," and "Foxy Grandpa." The *Boston Post* described him as "swarthy and rosy-cheeked and gray-locked." After his release in 1896, Bannon continued to play in the minors until 1910. Bannon died on March 24, 1948, at the age of 76. "Fun With Philly," *Boston Post*, August 8, 1894: 3.

3. *New York Clipper*, August 11, 1894: 361.

4. *New York Clipper*, August 11, 1894: 362.

5. The source of the fire was believed to be a lighted cigarette discarded carelessly by an "urchin" who had snuck into the park to watch his heroes practice. The recent weather had been very hot and dry. A pile of rubbish served as tinder so the wooden stands were quickly engulfed in flames. The fire leapt across the street to the railway stables. The more than 1,000 horses in the stables were safely evacuated. The loss to the club owners was $80,000, with $60,000 covered by insurance. The home season schedule was to end on September 8, and the Quakers would play out their home games at the University of Pennsylvania grounds. "Ball Field Again," *Boston Post*, August 7, 1894: 6.

6. Baltimore and New York finished a close 1-2. Boston was third, eight games behind, at 83-49, then Philadelphia.

7. The *Boston Post* noted that Irwin "prances and dances on the coaching lines." "Fun With Philly," *Boston Post*, August 8, 1894: 3. However, it was not to be. "Irwin sat on the players' bench, and was very quiet. It was not his coaching day, and the crowd lost the fun they anticipated." Tim Murnane, "Each Have Five," *Boston Globe*, August 8, 1894: 5.

8. For the Quakers, three players were hitting over .400 and six others batted better than .300. "Heady Ball," *Boston Journal*, August 8, 1894: 3.

9. The *Boston Herald* noted a "small forest of umbrellas" in the 25-cent section.

10. Murnane, "Each Have Five."

11. The *Boston Journal* credited Cross with a double. "Heady Ball," *Boston Journal*.

12. Murnane, "Each Have Five"; The *Boston Post* recorded a more colorful account, "And thereat, Arthur Irwin, who is actually getting fat, swore terribly, until there was an azure hue, and, beckoning to a small youth, who answered to the family name of Carsey, bade him to supplant the tall young man, he of the anguished countenance." "Fun With Philly," *Boston Post*, August 8, 1894: 3. Baseball-reference lists 31-year old Fanning at 5-feet-9, and 22-year-old Carsey at 5-feet-7.

13. "Heady Ball," *Boston Journal*.

14. Ibid.

15. Ibid.

16. The *Boston Herald* noted, "How a hard hit over the fence, foul or fair, does arouse the spectators!"

17. The *Boston Journal* declared, "[McCarthy's theft of home] was the most daring piece of base running of the season, and was justly applauded," and recorded that Bannon stole second base. "Heady Ball," *Boston Journal*.

18. Murnane in the *Boston Globe* did not mention McCarthy's theft of home and recorded that McCarthy and Bannon scored on Ganzel's double. Murnane, "Each Have Five."

19. Murnane, "Feel Easy Now," *Boston Globe*, August 7, 1894: 5; "Champions Lost No Time," *Boston Herald*, August 8, 1894: 2.

20. "Heady Ball," *Boston Journal*.

21. Ibid.

22. Murnane, "Each Have Five."

23. The *Boston Journal* stated that Hamilton bunted, then Tucker caught Boyle's fly and Hamilton was caught off the bag on the throw. "Heady Ball," *Boston Journal*.

24. Murnane recorded that Thompson singled.

25. The *Boston Journal* and the *Boston Globe* record Hallman's action at second base a "fumble."

26. Murnane, "Each Have Five."

27. "Heady Ball," *Boston Journal*. The *Globe*'s Murnane mentioned that both men reached on singles and scored on the triple. Murnane, "Each Have Five."

28. Ibid.

29. Long's home run hit "was one of the longest hits seen this year." "Heady Ball," *Boston Journal*.

30. Murnane, "Each Have Five."

31. "Beaten by the Hubites," *Philadelphia Inquirer*, August 8, 1894: 3.

32. The game summaries made special note of Nichols covering first base for Tucker, when Tucker was drawn away from the base to field the ball hit by the batters. "Heady Ball," *Boston Journal*.

CHARLIE BENNETT CHARITY GAME

AUGUST 27, 1894: BOSTON 16, PICKED NINE 12, AT SOUTH END GROUNDS, BOSTON

BY BOB LEMOINE

"His hearty 'glad to see you,' and the warm grasp of the hand were the same as of old," wrote the *Boston Globe* reporter who shook hands with Charlie Bennett. His eyes "twinkled merrily" during the interview at the apartment of Kid Nichols on Tremont Street in Boston.[1] But this was not the same Charlie Bennett everyone remembered. The once great catcher had been crippled in January of 1894 when he slipped while boarding a train in Ottawa, Kansas, and was run over,[2] losing parts of both legs, requiring double amputation. "Only his strong constitution, made near perfect by his outdoor work and constant training, saved his life," wrote the *Detroit Free Press*, which had witnessed his career with the Detroit Wolverines from 1881 to 1888.[3]

It was now August and Bennett was tired from the long train ride from Michigan, but was able to enjoy some relaxing moments with his wife and former teammates Nichols and Charlie Ganzel and their wives. He had been fitted with artificial limbs in early June[4] and was said to simply resemble someone suffering from rheumatism.[5] But while this was not the same Charlie Bennett physically, his friends still cherished the time with the old catcher who had "stored away an inexhaustive [*sic*] fund of stories of the game and its kings."[6]

Bennett was in town as Boston held a charity game on August 27 against a squad of college players. The proceeds were going to Bennett. The *Boston Post* said tickets for the game were "selling like hot cakes."[7]

The former catcher saw 9,000 cheering fans come to pay tribute to him. "It was a trifle too cool for the greatest enjoyment," wrote *Sporting Life*, "but it did not deter the friends and admirers of Boston's crippled catcher from turning out in large numbers."[8] It must have been a moment that those who witnessed it would never forget, as Bennett made his way to his usual position "[w]ith the aid of his crutches and artificial limbs," wrote Tim Murnane in the *Boston Globe*. "He walked out to the home plate just before the ball game, and there, surrounded by the members of both teams, bowed to the spectators on the bleachers and in the pavilion until the grounds fairly shook with the cheers."[9] He was overcome with emotion, the *Boston Daily Advertiser* noted, as "his eyes were filled with tears, the corner of his mouth twitched, and his lips trembled with emotion."[10]

Gentleman Jim Corbett, the champion boxer of the day, donned the uniform of Boston's Jack Stivetts (who was away following the death of his father)[11] and went out to play left field for the Beaneaters. He was not afraid to get Stivetts's uniform dirty as he ran the bases and scored a couple of runs. But his biggest contribution of the day came via a $50 check to Bennett while he himself asked for no travel expenses or compensation for his services. "That shows that he isn't mean," the *Post* wrote.[12] Some familiar Boston ballplayers of yesteryear were also on hand: John Morrill, Harry Schafer, Art Whitney, George Wright and his brother Sam, and Dupee Shaw. King Kelly, a player-manager in one last hurrah in the minor leagues, sent a telegram showing that his sense of humor was fine: "Bennett can't play ball, but he can play cricket, as he has stumps. Put us down for $25."[13]

The game began at 2:30 P.M., and the crowd roared when Corbett was the first man to the plate. He swung the bat but looked more like a boxer, and struck out against Frank Sexton, formerly of Brown University and now with the New Bedford club.[14] Bobby Lowe doubled, Herman Long, Tommy McCarthy, and Tommy Tucker all singled and Boston led 2-0.

The score remained that way until the fourth when the Picked Nine vaulted ahead with four runs. Guys named Upton, Cotter, Ranney, Abbott, and Steere sliced hits off Boston pitcher Harry Staley. Boston fielders were also sloppy as Billy Nash's throw was wide and Jack Ryan dropped a throw. When the dust settled, the Picked Nine had scored four runs in the third and eight in the fourth, for a surprising 12-2 lead after four.

Boston stormed back to tie the game in the sixth. Had Sexton stayed in the game, *Sporting Life* believed, the Picked Nine would surely have won the game. But a pitcher named Dowd came in and "the champions didn't do a thing with him but roll up ten runs."[15] Corbett was hit by a pitch, Long, McCarthy, Tucker, and Nash singled, Jimmy Bannon doubled, and Ryan doubled. Ten runs had scored and suddenly it was a 12-12 game. Boston added one in the seventh, and in the eighth Lowe reached on an error and Frank Connaughton homered. Boston added another in the eighth for a 16-12 lead and the eventual win. The Beaneaters even gave up their turn at bat in the ninth. Boston had scored 14 unanswered runs to get the victory.

When the game ended, the crowd rushed on the field "to get a good look at Bennett." Bennett had watched the game from a large chair in the grandstand and "the ovation tendered him when some of his friends lifted him to their shoulders nearly took the roof off the structure," wrote the *New York Sun*.[16]

There were more events after the game. Fred Tenney, McCarthy, Nichols, and Bannon competed in races against each other and later Nash and Lowe had throwing competitions. High jumps were also conducted. After the festivities the players retired to the clubhouse, where Duffy and Long served as a reception committee. Refreshments were served,[17] and Bennett expressed his gratitude for the day. Mrs. Bennett mentioned, probably quietly to some of the guests, that Charlie had suffered more than he was letting on but had worked hard to look his best on this occasion. "The whole affair was handled in a first-class manner," Murnane wrote.[18]

Bennett sent a thank-you letter to the *Boston Globe* which was published on August 29. In it he thanked everyone in Boston from the players to the fans and sportswriters "who have shown such magnificent generosity to me in my misfortune by giving me so flattering a testimonial." He added that he "never shall be able to repay the manifold kindnesses which have been showered upon me from all sides."[19]

Bennett remained in Boston at the Nichols residence until September 6, then returned to his home in Detroit, where he had many friends, but "not any more than he has right here in Boston," Murnane wrote.[20]

It wouldn't be the last time Bennett would be on the field accepting the applause of a crowd. On April 28, 1896, a new ballpark was opened in Detroit at the corner of Michigan and Trumbull Avenues. Both teams lined up on the field, and the crowd began to cheer. The *Detroit Free Press* described the scene: "Charley Bennett, the idolized catcher from the palmy days, came out from the stand leaning on the arm of Charley Snyder, who was the star catcher of the American Association in the exciting days of twelve years ago. They walked to the plate and the players reverently doffed their caps." The ceremonial first pitch was thrown and Charlie caught it "as easily as he could handle one," the *Free Press* remarked. "The cannon boomed, the ceremony was over, and cheer after cheer went up for the man whose name the park bears."[21]

The ballpark was remodeled and renamed over the years to Navin Field, Briggs Stadium, and eventually Tiger Stadium until its demolition in 1999. But it began as Bennett Park.

Bennett's name has often appeared on a ballot for SABR's "Overlooked 19th Century Baseball Legend" voting.[22] He wasn't overlooked that day at the South End Grounds, however, in what the *Boston Journal* called "a splendid tribute to a ball player whose personal character made him an honor to his calling."

NOTES

1 "Same Old Charley Bennett," *Boston Globe*, August 27, 1894: 2.

2 "Charley Bennett Maimed," *Detroit Free Press*, January 11, 1894: 2.

3 "Poor Charley Bennett," *Detroit Free Press*, June 23, 1894: 4.

4 "Charley Bennett's Benefit," *Boston Globe*, August 26, 1894: 3.

5 "Same Old Charley Bennett."

6 "Poor Charley Bennett."

7 "Baseball Talk," *Boston Post*, August 25, 1894: 3.

8 "Bennett's Benefit," *Sporting Life*, September 8, 1894: 6.

9 T.H. Murnane, "Nearly $6,000," *Boston Globe*, August 28, 1894: 1.

10 "Nearly 9000 Persons," *Boston Daily Advertiser*, August 28, 1894: 8.

11 "Baseball Talk."

12 "Benefit Big," *Boston Post*, August 28, 1894: 3.

13 Ibid.

14 David Nemec, *Rank and File of 19th Century Major League Baseball: Biographies of 1,084 Players, Owners, Managers and Umpires.* (Jefferson, North Carolina: McFarland, 2012), 73; Sexton would play all seven games of his major-league career for Boston in 1895.

15 "Bennett's Benefit."

16 "Charlie Bennett's Benefit," *The Sun*, August 28, 1894: 4.

17 "Benefit Big."

18 Ibid.

19 "Charley Bennett's Thanks," *Boston Globe*, August 29, 1894: 1.

20 Murnane.

21 "17 To 2!!" *Detroit Free Press*, April 29, 1896: 6.

22 In 2015, Bennett was included on the ballot with a brief summary: "Bennett was one of the greatest catchers of the Nineteenth Century, starring for Detroit and Boston of the NL. He was a powerful hitter who often ranked among the leaders in homers and slugging percentage while finishing in the top 10 in bases on balls six times. His defense was stellar and he was a leader on the field." sabr.org/latest/announcing-finalists-2015-sabr-overlooked-19th-century-base-ball-legend, retrieved January 24, 2017.

A COZY SHUTOUT: COZY DOLAN SHUTS OUT THE ORIOLES

SEPTEMBER 18, 1895: BOSTON BEANEATERS 8, BALTIMORE ORIOLES 0, AT SOUTH END GROUNDS III, BOSTON

BY KEVIN LARKIN

From 1883 until 1906, the Boston entry in the National League was often known as the Beaneaters. They finished first in the league standings in 1883, 1891-1893, and 1897-1898. The team had such well-known players as Tommy McCarthy, Old Hoss Radbourn, John Clarkson, and Jimmy Collins, as well as their manager, Frank Selee, all of whom were elected to the Baseball Hall of Fame.

In this great era of baseball, many of the players played multiple positions. One of those players was Patrick Henry "Cozy" Dolan. Besides playing right field and first base, Dolan sometimes pitched.

On September 18, 1895, Dolan was on the mound as the Beaneaters prepared to play the Baltimore Orioles. Baltimore was led by Ned Hanlon and similarly boasted a plethora of future Hall of Famers like Wilbert Robinson, Hughie Jennings, John McGraw, Willie Keeler, Joe Kelly, and (briefly) Dan Brouthers as well as Hanlon.

The game was the fourth in a four-game series between Boston and the first-place Orioles, with Baltimore winning the first two games and Boston taking the third. Baltimore was leading the second-place Cleveland Spiders by 2½ games in the National League standings, while Boston was mired in seventh place, 15½ games behind the Orioles.

Dolan was opposed on the mound by the Orioles' staff ace, Bill Hoffer, who finished the year with a record of 31 wins and six losses.

It had rained the morning of the game and the grounds were in sad shape. Managers Hanlon and Selee had met at around 1 P.M. and had almost agreed to call the game off. However Selee changed his mind and telephoned the Orioles, telling them to come and play.[1] The morning rain put the field in poor condition and kept many fans away.[2] The game should never have taken place, in the opinion of the *Baltimore Sun,* as the steady rain made the playing field better suited for a convention of ducks than for a baseball game.[3]

Boston outfielder Jimmy Bannon led off the game with a single and advanced to second on a single by Herman Long. Both scored on a double by Hugh Duffy, and Duffy then scored on a single by Billy Nash, giving Boston a 3-0 lead.

There also was some excitement in the Baltimore half of the first inning when the Orioles loaded the bases on a hit batsman, a force out, a single, and then a walk. Orioles outfielder Steve Brodie then came to the plate. Brodie, who had a style of play that made him a favorite of both his teammates and the fans,[4] hit a ball just in front of home plate. Boston catcher Jack Ryan picked up the ball, stepped on home plate, and then threw to first for a double play. Brodie claimed it was a foul ball and began to argue the call vehemently. He "used language that didn't sound well," swung his fists at umpire Miah Murray and tore the mask off his face; Murray fined Brodie $25 and ordered him from the field. Brodie refused to leave but was finally removed by the police and the game resumed.[5]

For Boston, the second inning was almost a repeat of the first. Ryan opened the inning with a hit, Dolan reached on an error, and Bannon drew a base on balls to load the bases. Long hit a groundball to Kid Gleason who was playing a deep second base, but not so deep that he could not throw out Ryan, who tried to score from third base. There was one out and the bases were still loaded when Duffy hit a single that plated two runs. Fred Tenney drew a base on balls, then Nash hit a ball to deep right that scored Long. Tucker drew the third base on balls of the inning and that scored Duffy with the inning's fourth run.

The Orioles went down in order in the third inning, then manager Hanlon pulled Hoffer with a disgusted grunt and put in Duke Esper to see if he could stem the tide of Beaneater runs.

Esper made it easy for a while but in the fifth inning, Dolan and Jack Ryan both got hits and added another run to the Beaneaters total.

The Beaneaters scored three runs in the eighth inning. Duffy walked, Tenney got a hit, and Nash's sacrifice left the Beaneaters with two men on base and one out. Joe Harrington then stepped up to the plate and hit a home run to put three more runs on the board for the Boston nine. Then Ryan and Bannon singled and Dolan walked. Long flied out to center field, at which point umpire Murray called the game because of darkness.[6] The score reverted back to the previous inning, so Harrington's blast and the three runs didn't count. Nevertheless, Boston had an 8-0 victory.

The Orioles' loss reduced their margin over the Cleveland Spiders to 1½ games. The Spiders had five games left on the schedule, three with Pittsburgh and two with Louisville. Baltimore had 11 games left, three with Brooklyn and four each with Philadelphia and the New York Giants.

The Orioles went 8-2 with one tie in the 11 games, and finished 3 games ahead of Cleveland. Boston won six of its final 10 games and finished in a tie for fifth place with the Brooklyn Bridegrooms, 16½ games behind Baltimore.

After the 1895 season, Dolan pitched in only 10 more games, winning one and losing six. He played in the major leagues as an infielder and outfielder until 1906, appearing in a total of 830 games. He should not be confused with the Cozy Dolan (Albert) who played from 1909 until 1922. That player was banned for life by Judge Kenesaw Landis for his part in a bribery scandal during the 1924 season.

SOURCES

In addition to the sources cited in the Notes, the author consulted the Baseball-Reference.com and Retrosheet.org websites.

NOTES

1. "Is This Base-Ball?" *Baltimore Sun,* September 19, 1895: 6.
2. The attendance was said to be 500. T.H. Murnane, "Kept Guessing," *Boston Globe,* September 19, 1895: 4.
3. "Is This Baseball?"
4. William Akin, "Steve Brodie," SABR Biography Project, sabr.org, accessed April 23, 2017.
5. "Hit the Umpire," *Boston Post,* September 19, 1895: 3.
6. "Kept Guessing."

A PATRIOTS' DAY HIT PARADE

APRIL 20, 1896: BOSTON BEANEATERS 21, BALTIMORE ORIOLES 6, AT THE SOUTH END GROUNDS

BY GERARD R. GOULET

A combination of fine weather, a state holiday,[1] the largest recorded crowd at the South End Grounds to date, and serious Boston batting made the Beaneaters' 1896 home opener an event to be remembered for some time, although not for the quality of the baseball.

In 1896 the South End Grounds in its third iteration had a capacity of 6,800. Remarkably, the paid attendance for the home opener was 18,033, including a large enough number of women to be remarked upon in the Boston and Baltimore newspapers, and an additional 21 nonpaying boys taking in the game from the branches of the old tree outside the grounds behind first base.[2] According to Tim Murnane of the *Boston Globe*, "not more than twice before [had] so many people seen a baseball game in Boston," and the numbers attending on those two occasions had only been estimates.[3] Of even greater significance, it was reported that the Beaneaters ownership closed the gates 15 minutes before the 2:30 P.M. scheduled start and "refused to admit thousands of people who pushed and crowded in the street."[4] Moreover, many who did get in but could see nothing returned to the ticket office for a refund. In all, it was estimated that fully 5,000 were turned away.[5] Nevertheless, given the nearly threefold disparity between the seating capacity of the ballpark and the number of spectators who had paid for the privilege of viewing the game, many stood throughout the contest, with great throngs impinging on the corner infielders to such an extent that the police were called in to keep them back and force them to sit.

By the time team captains Hugh Duffy (for Boston) and Wilbert Robinson had come to agreement with umpire Tom Lynch on a special ground rule for baseballs hit into the crowds, the game had been delayed a full 15 minutes in starting. The rule agreed upon was that only one base would be allowed on any kind of hit into the crowd, but that a runner would be allowed to come home from second base. Although the rule made sense under the circumstances, it "robbed the game of its most attractive features, brilliant catches in the outfield."[6] As a result, all of the hits amassed by the two teams were singles. As the *Baltimore Sun* reported, "Naturally there was not much enthusiasm to see the players walk the bases on hits that went over the heads of the fielders into the crowd. It wasn't much like baseball."[7]

This verdict was not really apparent until the bottom of the third inning. At that point, the teams were tied, 4-4, with neither team showing to advantage in the field. Baltimore had scored two unearned runs in the top of the second inning without the benefit of a hit when left fielder Billy Hamilton, second baseman Bobby Lowe, and shortstop Herman Long each muffed flies. But Boston put the game away in its half of the third inning.

Captain Duffy led off with a single to left. Jimmy Collins placed one to right field and Duffy went around to third as Collins was caught attempting to go to second on fine throws by right fielder Willie Keeler and third baseman Jim Donnelly. Jimmy Bannon singled to center, scoring Duffy. After Tommy Tucker's hit to short right and Marty Bergen's infield hit, Kid Nichols walked with the bases loaded, forcing in Bannon. Hamilton then bunted to pitcher Sadie McMahon, whose error allowed Tucker to score. Long's hit scored Bergen and Nichols. Hamilton and Long advanced a base on Robinson's passed ball and both scored on Lowe's single to left. Lowe was thrown out attempting to steal second. Duffy's second plate appearance of the inning resulted in a walk. Collins reached first on a slow hit to the hapless McMahon, sending Duffy to third. Duffy scored on Robinson's unsuccessful attempt to catch Collins stealing second. Fortunately for Baltimore, Collins was caught napping shortly thereafter, allowing the frame to close with "only" eight runs plated, baserunning having accounted for all three of the outs.

Although comfortably ahead at that point, Boston was not quite finished demonstrating its batting prowess. The Beaneaters had been able to score only a single run off relief pitcher George Hemming in the fourth inning, but Boston treated him as poorly in the fifth as it had his predecessor in the third, tallying seven runs, all earned, on 10 hits, with Duffy and Collins each collecting two and, of the remaining seven batters, all but Bergen reaching safely, "each batter hitting into the crowd and trotting to second, while his predecessor walked across the plate."[8]

The rest of the game was anticlimactic with the exception of the final two innings when Boston manager Frank Selee unveiled Willard Mains, who had been drafted from Lewiston (Maine) of the New England League.[9] While Mains walked four batters over two innings, he allowed none of them to score and his unorthodox crossfire delivery, coming as if from third base, was a real crowd pleaser. In fact, if one merely read the first sentence of the *Boston Post's* account of the game ("Mains of Maine was the hero of the opening game on the South End grounds yesterday afternoon"[10]), one would have been seriously misled into thinking that the game had been a pitching gem rather than a slugfest. In the final analysis, but for the two half-innings of heavy Boston batting, the teams were fairly evenly matched, particularly in the field, with numerous errors committed by the two clubs, not to mention four passed balls, two wild pitches, and a hit batsman.[11]

While the quality of play left a lot to be desired, the forum did give the fans a first look at the new Boston players. Collins, at third base, was not really new to the team, having played briefly in 1895 before being loaned to the Louisville Colonels for the balance of the season. Nevertheless, interest in his prowess at the corner was keen; he was facing the unenviable task of replacing the popular Billy Nash, who had captained Boston's 1895 squad and had patrolled third base for the Bostons for more than 1,100 games over the previous decade. According to all accounts, Collins acquitted himself quite well, particularly in the field. Hamilton, acquired in the transaction that sent Nash to Philadelphia, replaced Tommy McCarthy, who was sold to Brooklyn after a poor year in 1895 that was exacerbated by an irritable temperament that wore on his teammates. Despite one rather grievous error, Hamilton did well at the plate. The other two newcomers, Bergen at catcher and Mains, were crowd pleasers, the former for the accuracy of his arm in cutting down would-be basestealers and the latter, although wild, for his unconventional pitching form. All in all, the fans left the field contented with this first glimpse of their team's offseason acquisitions.

In addition to focusing on the newcomers, the fans cheered on the locals from both teams and had ample time to pick out celebrities from the crowd. Cambridge native Joe Kelley, who had played briefly for Boston as a teenager in 1891 and was now playing for Baltimore, received a hand from the crowd when he first stepped to the plate.[12] Amesbury native and Holy Cross alumnus Bannon had many friends in attendance from the Saugus area. Around 50 fans from Holyoke were there in support of hometown hero Tucker, and North Brookfield's Bergen also had a crowd cheering him on from the western part of the state.[13] The Boston sportswriters also recognized a number of past Boston players from all four of the other leagues that had fielded Boston teams. Murnane, who had managed the Union Association's Boston Reds in 1884, spotted center fielder Mike Slattery and star pitcher Dupee Shaw as well as George Wright, the '84 Boston Reds owner and the star shortstop of Boston's first professional team, the Red Stockings. Murnane also mentioned sighting John F. Morrill, who had played infield for the Boston National League team from 1876 through 1888 as well as two final games with the Boston Reds of the Players League in 1890. Three players from the 1891 Boston Reds American Association team, Tom Cotter, George Haddock, and Jack McGeachey, also took in the festivities, as did Tommy Bond, who had amassed 123 victories for the 1877-1879 Beaneaters teams. One late arrival, Dr. Tom Gunning, who caught for the Beaneaters from 1884 to 1886, rode the Boston bench along with his wife in order to view the game.[14]

The *Brooklyn Daily Eagle* described Baltimore as having met a Waterloo. The lopsided win for last year's sixth-place team over the league's champion was certainly an unexpected result, tempered only slightly by the record take of $4,500 in proceeds for the visiting team.[15] That the Boston victory was not an aberration was amply demonstrated over the next two weeks as Boston, although outscored 36-25, defeated Baltimore in three of five games over that period.

SOURCES

In addition to the sources cited in the Notes, the author also consulted baseball-reference.com and retrosheet.org.

NOTES

1. This was the third annual celebration of Patriots Day, initially proclaimed by Massachusetts Governor Frederic Greenhalge on April 19, 1894, to commemorate the anniversary of the Battle of Lexington and Concord in the American Revolution and the first bloodshed of the Civil War.

2. "Echoes of the Game," *Boston Globe*, April 21, 1896: 2.

3. Timothy Murnane, "Out in Batting Togs," *Boston Globe*, April 21, 1896: 1.

4. Ibid.

5. "Notes of the Game," *Boston Post*, April 21, 1896: 3.

6. Murnane: 2.

7. "Alas, the Champions," *Baltimore Sun*, April 21, 1896: 6.

8. "Orioles Badly Beaten," *Brooklyn Daily Eagle*, April 21, 1896: 12.

9. The game was called as 6 P.M. approached after eight innings of play to allow the Baltimore team to catch transportation home to play the Beaneaters there on the following day.

10. "Boston Won," *Boston Post*, April 21, 1896: 1.

11. According to the *Boston Globe*, "[T]he ballplayers claim that the South End grounds is the poorest infield in the league; one on which it is impossible to judge a ground ball." The scribe for the *Baltimore Sun* was more inclined to attribute the cause of the sloppy fielding to "[t]he immense throng in the rather small Boston grounds pressed so near to the players as to embarrass them and to draw their attention from their work."

12. *Boston Globe*, April 21, 1896: 2.

13. *Boston Post*, April 21, 1896: 2

14. Fall River's city physician, Dr. Gunning had recently earned non-baseball notice for his participation as an assistant at the autopsies of Lizzie Borden's ill-fated parents, Andrew and Abby.

15. *Boston Globe*, April 21, 1896: 2.

PLAYING UNTIL DARK

MAY 13, 1896: BOSTON BEANEATERS 10, CHICAGO COLTS 4 (11 INNINGS), AT WEST SIDE GROUNDS, CHICAGO.

BY BOB LEMOINE

"Timothy Keefe, umpire, cold-bloodedly gave a game of baseball to Boston yesterday," wrote the *Chicago Tribune* about a weird game with Boston in the Windy City on May 13, 1896.[1] While the *Tribune* slammed the umpire, its rival Chicago newspaper the *Inter Ocean* placed no blame on Keefe but called the game "the funniest series of absurdities ever seen on a ball field."[2] The *Boston Globe* had no problem with Keefe, but declared, "Seldom has a baseball crowd at the league grounds manifested its anger so vehemently."[3] No matter what the interpretation, this early-season contest did not factor into the 1896 pennant as both teams finished well behind Baltimore. At the time, however, only 4½ games separated nine of the 12 teams in the National League. Chicago was only 1½ games behind and Boston two games behind the surprising Philadelphia Phillies.

Two veteran pitchers took the hill as Boston's Jack Stivetts opposed Chicago's Adonis Terry. Keefe, in his third year as a National League umpire, had won 342 games in his 14-year pitching career, retiring as a player in 1893. Cap Anson, in his 21st year as Chicago's player-manager, was not in the lineup this day, but quickly made his presence felt.

Boston batted first. With one out, Billy Hamilton singled to left and went to second on Herman Long's walk. Hugh Duffy lined a single to right, scoring Hamilton. Long scored as he and Duffy manufactured a double steal and shortstop Bill Dahlen threw wide to the plate. Charlie Ganzel then hit a grounder to Dahlen, who made another error when his wild throw pulled George Decker off the bag at first. Duffy scored, and Boston led 3-0. Chicago countered in the bottom of the inning with two runs. Shortstop Long mishandled a grounder by Bill Everitt, who scored on Dahlen's triple. Dahlen scored on Bill Lange's groundout.

The Beaneaters' 3-2 lead remained that way until their sixth inning. Ganzel singled and took second when a thundering Duffy was thrown out at the plate. Ganzel scored "like an exploded bottle of 'Anson's ginger ale'"[4] on Tucker's single and Boston led 4-2.

The Colts had only one hit off Stivetts when they batted in the bottom of the sixth. Everitt lined a shot down the third-base line. As Everitt rounded first, Tommy Tucker "threw his arms around his neck and the two spun around together," the *Tribune* reported. Enraged, Everitt pulled himself out of the embrace and was ready to go at it with Tucker. Keefe came running in to intervene when the ball was thrown in to second baseman Bobby Lowe, who tagged Everitt, still locked up with Tucker. "You're out!" cried the huffing Keefe as "the crowd broke into loud denunciations of the manifestly unfair decision," the newspaper wrote.

"Three thousand people saw the interference; only the umpire did not see it, though when he ran up to them the men were locked in each other's arms and standing not two yards from first base." Players gathered around Keefe to argue but he was "deaf to reason or argument," according to the *Tribune*.[5]

Play continued as Dahlen clobbered a drive "into the new seats in right field"[6] and Keefe awarded him a triple. Anson went nuts. "In vain did he uplift his hands, stamp the ground and bellow"[7] as he argued that it was a home run. Keefe's ruling was that a hit into the empty seats was a ball in play and "would count for what could be made,"[8] since the outfielder had a chance to retrieve it. If the seats were occupied the ball would have been ruled a home run. The crowd was even more irate now. The *Boston Globe* noticed "one fat man [who] waddled down the main aisle of the grand stand and pleaded with those about him to go on the field and do violence to Keefe."[9] Fortunately, no one did such. Dahlen did not score, so the game remained 4-2. Fans continued verbally assaulting Keefe and Tucker for the remainder of the game.

The score remained 4-2 as Chicago batted in the bottom of the ninth. Lange made first on a screaming liner that Stivetts couldn't corral, then made it to third on a bloop single to center by Jack Ryan. Harry Truby lofted a high fly to Hamilton in center. Both runners tagged, Ryan taking third and Lange scoring. Decker grounded out to first with Ryan scoring the tying run. The game was now 4-4 after nine innings.

Boston players insisted that the game had to end in a tie because they needed to catch a train for Pittsburgh, but Anson refused the request. Hamilton singled and stole second base as Long interfered with catcher Tim Donahue's throw. In the confusion, Hamilton took third. Long and Lowe were retired on grounders and Hamilton held at third. Duffy and Ganzel walked to load the bases, but Boston did not score as Terry got out of his "ticklish business."[10] Chicago was blanked in its half of the 10th. Both pitchers were still strong, the *Inter Ocean* surmising, "Both Stivetts and Terry held to their cunning as closely as a half done griddle cake sticks to a bald head."[11] But they were just getting started.

In the 11th, Joe Harrington, Stivetts, and Jimmy Bannon reached on hits for Boston and they all scored on Hamilton's triple. Anson now realized his only path to victory was in the setting sun. The game would be called and revert back to the 10th-inning tie. Anson felt he could protest the game with Nick Young in the National League office because of the interference play and the "home run" non-call.[12] He ordered his team to stall and wait for darkness.

Hamilton scored when Long's grounder went by a motionless Dahlen. Long stole second and third without any effort, then scored on Donahue's bad throw. Chicago players began to tie their shoes, one right after the other. Donahue "succeeded in finding more things to do, besides catch, than any man on the diamond," the *Inter Ocean* wrote.[13] He tied his shoes (wishing he was a quadruped, in the *Inter Ocean's* opinion), got a drink of water, and then hunted for a handkerchief to wipe his mouth. Then he conveniently forgot where he put his mask. "It seemed strange," the *Inter Ocean* wrote, "that a big hard mask could disappear on a level field, but that one had."[14] Donahue was going to investigate the grandstand when it was discovered hiding in a corner. Terry couldn't find the ball. After five minutes it was recovered but players had a hard time getting it back to him, overthrowing each other for a few minutes.

Terry finally was finally ready to pitch and lobbed the ball in. The Boston hitter connected and made a modern-day "Little League home run" as Chicago fielders kept throwing the ball all over the place. They probably were watching the sun set because six more Boston batters scored in similar fashion. Keefe refused to call the game for darkness; instead, he had enough of this foolishness and turned to the crowd. "This game is given to Boston by a score of nine to nothing," he bellowed, giving the regulation score for a forfeited game. The crowd roared angrily and Anson approached Keefe, protesting the game.

If Anson had allowed the Boston team to go and catch their train, the game would have been a tie, and none of this would have happened. "There are black and blue spots on his anatomy where he has kicked himself since those rash words," wrote the *Inter Ocean*.[15] "Anson is the same old child on the diamond," commented the *Boston Journal*.[16] While the game was ruled a 9-0 forfeit, for records purposes it was a Boston 10-4 win. No matter what gripes Anson had, the game was not overruled by Young, and Keefe was not disciplined.

Nearly 70 years later, Tim Keefe was posthumously inducted into the Baseball Hall of Fame for being one of the greatest pitchers of the nineteenth century. His umpiring career, however, ended two months later. "Once a great pitcher," John B. Foster in *Sporting Life* wrote, "but the game got away from him. The players, with few exceptions, no longer respected his authority, and life would have been more or less miserable constantly."[17]

Boston players grabbed a "later and slower train," according to the *Boston Post*. "They are sore over the loss of two games here [in Chicago]."[18] But they won the series finale, odd as it was.

SOURCES

In addition to sources listed in the Notes, the author also used the following for game information:

Bevis, Charlie. "Tim Keefe," SABR BioProject. Retrieved May 7, 2017. sabr.org/bioproj/person/6f1dd1b1#sdendnote66sym

NOTES

1. "Umpire Keefe Wins It," *Chicago Tribune*, May 14, 1896: 4.
2. "Wished for Night," *Inter Ocean*, May 14, 1896: 4.
3. "Anson's Idea," *Boston Globe*, May 14, 1896: 4.
4. "Wished for Night."
5. "Umpire Keefe Wins It."
6. Ibid.
7. "Anson's Idea."
8. "Umpire Keefe Wins It."
9. "Anson's Idea."
10. "Wished for Night."
11. Ibid.
12. At least in the opinion of the *Inter Ocean*.
13. "Wished for Night."
14. Ibid.
15. Ibid.
16. "Played Baby," *Boston Journal*, May 14, 1896: 4.
17. John B. Forster, "Brooklyn Budget," *Sporting Life*, July 25, 1896: 6.
18. "Anson Quits," *Boston Post*, May 14, 1896: 3.

BOSTON PUTS THEIR BATTING CLOTHES ON

SEPTEMBER 3, 1896 (FIRST GAME): BOSTON BEANEATERS 28, ST. LOUIS BROWNS 7, AT SOUTH END GROUNDS, BOSTON

BY RICHARD RIIS

It was the third doubleheader in as many days for the weary Boston Beaneaters. Shortstop Herman Long, nursing a badly bruised arm after being hit by a pitch in the opening game of the previous day's twin bill, was relegated to the bench, and first baseman Tommy Tucker, who'd played every game so far this season, was out nursing a sprained wrist. Juggling his lineup, manager Frank Selee shifted team captain and regular left fielder Hugh Duffy to shortstop in place of Long, and installed backup catcher Charlie Ganzel at first. Dan McGann was slotted at second base in place of Bobby Lowe, who'd been in and out of the lineup while recovering from a broken collarbone. "Happy Jack" Stivetts, whose ability with the bat earned him an occasional game in the outfield when he wasn't scheduled to pitch (Stivetts would hit .347 with three home runs in 1896), took Duffy's spot in left field.

"It was lucky for the Bostons that they had their batting clothes on," remarked one journalist in attendance, "for they presented a nine in the field which on paper was one of the weakest that has represented them for years."[1] With two pitchers and two catchers in the game and Duffy roaming the infield, it must have seemed a patchwork squad to even the most fervent of the 2,500 faithful at South End Grounds that afternoon.

Selected by Selee to start for Boston was right-hander Jim Sullivan, who had pitched three-plus innings of relief in a loss to Louisville two days before. Browns manager-baseman Tommy Dowd tapped journeyman right-hander Bill Hart, on his way to an NL-leading 29 losses, to start.

The Beaneaters, exercising the home team's prerogative, chose to bat first. Billy Hamilton and Fred Tenney opened the game with singles, and Duffy walked to load the bases. Ganzel's fly out to left brought in Hamilton, and after Stivetts grounded out to first, McGann's long single drove in Tenney and Duffy, staking Boston to a 3-0 lead. The Browns struck back in their half of the inning when Dowd doubled, then stole third and scored on veteran first baseman Roger Connor's single.

Third baseman Jimmy Collins led off the Boston second inning with a single. Sullivan doubled, scoring Collins, and Hamilton and Tenney singled, bringing in Sullivan. Duffy lined the ball over the left-field fence for a three-run homer, and the Beaneaters found themselves up 8-1. Sullivan made quick work of the Browns in the bottom of the inning, striking out two.

Boston scored a run in the third inning, driving Hart from the game, and another in the fourth off reliever Bill Kissinger. Marty Bergen's double, Collins's triple, and a single by Sullivan gave Boston two more runs in the fifth. Dowd gave the Browns a fleeting lift by depositing a pitch over the left-field fence in the bottom of the fifth to notch a second run for St. Louis.

In the seventh, Bergen led off for Boston with a sharp single. Collins poked a single to right. After Sullivan went down swinging, Hamilton and Tenney each singled, bringing Duffy up to the plate once again with the bases full. Swinging on the first pitch, Duffy drove the ball over the fence for a grand slam. "As it went sailing out over the tracks, it looked as safe as Old Glory flying over Fort Warren," waxed sportswriter Tim Murnane of the *Boston Globe*. "It was the finest hit made on the Boston grounds this season."[2] After Ganzel was put out, Stivetts banged a triple, Bergen singled for his second hit of the inning, and Collins doubled for his. Sullivan was retired once again for the third out.

With the score now 20-2 for Boston, some in attendance thought the Browns had suffered enough. "There were those among the spectators so surfeited with home runs, three-baggers, doubles and a legion of singles that they wanted the game called," observed one writer.[3] Appeals of "Enough!" came from the grandstand. When the Browns were sent down meekly once again in the bottom of the inning, captains Duffy and Dowd appealed to umpire Hardie Henderson to call the game so as to allow the second game to get underway. Henderson declined.

Had the arbiter agreed to call the game, Boston's offensive juggernaut would have gone unrecorded, as the first game of a doubleheader must be played to its conclusion to count as official. "It's not a bad idea for both captains and managers to know the rules," sportswriter and former major leaguer Tim Murnane admonished, "as it often keeps them out of trouble."[4]

Boston tagged the Browns for four more runs in the top of the eighth on singles by Hamilton, Tenney, Ganzel, Bergen, and Collins, and a triple by McGann. The Browns finally stirred in their half, scoring three runs on singles by left fielder Joe Sullivan, right fielder Klondike Douglass, Connor, and center fielder Tom Parrott, and McGann's muff on a throw by Collins.

The unstoppable Beaneaters put up four more runs in the ninth on singles by Tenney and Duffy, a double by Bergen, and McGann's second triple of the game. St. Louis tallied a futile pair on singles by Kissinger and Douglass, and a muffed fly by McGann off the bat of Connor to close out the most lopsided game of the season for either club. The final score: a rout for Boston, 28-7.

Boston tagged Browns pitching for 33 hits. Hart and Kissinger were "batted all over the lot until the players were almost exhausted by leather hunting," wrote the *Boston Post*.[5] Four Beaneaters – Hamilton, Tenney, Duffy, and Bergen – each collected five base hits, while Collins stroked six. It was Duffy, though, who took the individual batting honors. "The little Captain's batting was something worthy of verse," declared the *Boston Journal's* writer. "Hamilton, Tenney, and Bergen were as successful as he, and Collins saw him one better, but Duffy far excelled any of his mates in hitting for totals."[6] In making five hits, Duffy stroked two home runs, two singles, and a triple to drive in seven runs. He would add three singles in the second game to go a combined 8-for-10.

Duffy also fielded flawlessly at shortstop, "his stops and throws being of a sensational sort."[7] His defensive play pleased the crowd almost as much as his hitting, and Duffy was given a hand time and again as he came in from the field. "I may have my troubles yet," Duffy remarked at one point on his way to the bench but in handling 10 chances in the unfamiliar position, he registered two putouts and eight assists in the game.[8]

For the Browns, Connor made four hits and Dowd three, a single, a double, and a home run.[9]

With Stivetts moving from the outfield to the pitcher's plate and hurler Charles "Kid" Nichols inserted in left field, Boston won the second contest, 8-3, the game called after six innings on account of darkness.

SOURCES

In addition to the sources listed in the Notes, the author also consulted the *Cleveland Plain Dealer*, *Pittsburgh Press*, *St. Louis Post-Dispatch*, *St. Louis Republic*, *The Sporting News*, and the *Washington Evening Star*.

NOTES

1. "Bostons Eclipse League Batting Records," *Boston Journal*, September 4, 1896: 9.
2. T.H. Murnane, "33 Hits for 52," *Boston Globe*, September 4, 1896: 9.
3. "Bostons Eclipse League Batting Records."
4. Murnane.
5. "Hit the Ball," *Boston Post*, September 4, 1896: 3.
6. "Bostons Eclipse League Batting Records."
7. "St. Louis Cyclone," *Boston Daily Advertiser*, September 4, 1896: 8.
8. "Bostons Eclipse League Batting Records."
9. As is sometimes the case with nineteenth-century box scores, the newspaper accounts differed on statistics. The *Globe* listed St. Louis with 14 hits (Connor credited with three), while the *Journal* listed 13 hits (Connor credited with four hits). Duffy was also credited with seven assists by the *Globe*, but eight by the *Journal*.

A FURIOUS COMEBACK FALLS SHORT

APRIL 19, 1897: PHILADELPHIA PHILLIES 6, BOSTON BEANEATERS 5, AT SOUTH END GROUNDS, BOSTON

BY DAVID L. FLEITZ

At the start of the 1897 season, the Boston Beaneaters set out to regain the National League crown. Winners of three league titles earlier in the decade, the Beaneaters suffered through injuries, aging of key performers, and a ballpark fire in 1894 as the Baltimore Orioles built a new championship team. The Orioles, managed by Ned Hanlon, surpassed the Beaneaters and won three titles of their own from 1894 to 1896. Boston manager Frank Selee, who in 1896 led the club to a fourth-place finish, was determined to build another champion.

Right-hander Kid Nichols, a perennial 30-game winner, anchored the pitching staff, but the rest of the rotation needed help. Jack Stivetts won 22 games in 1896, but suffered from chronic arm pain and was no longer able to take the mound in a regular turn. Stivetts was a fine hitter, though, and found more playing time in the outfield. Jim Sullivan, 11-12 in 1896, was mediocre, so Selee promoted two youngsters, right-hander Ted Lewis and lefty Fred Klobedanz, to regular roles. Lewis and Klobedanz had limited experience, but the Boston manager saw both as future stars.

In the outfield, captain Hugh Duffy remained from the championship days, and speedy Billy Hamilton was the top leadoff man in the game. Right field, however, was a problem area, as Jimmy Bannon fell off so sharply that Selee released him and gave his roster spot to a rookie named Charles "Chick" Stahl. Stahl began the campaign on the bench. Second baseman Bobby Lowe and shortstop Herman Long gave the Beaneaters a solid keystone combo, while third baseman Jimmy Collins was headed for stardom in his third season. Veteran Charlie Ganzel and second-year player Marty Bergen took care of the catching.

Perhaps the key addition to the Boston lineup was Fred Tenney, who had joined the club in 1894 as a catcher but spent most of the 1896 campaign in the outfield. Selee was dissatisfied with veteran first baseman Tommy Tucker, a behavioral problem who had often clashed with his manager. Tucker's best days were behind him, so the manager toyed with the idea of moving Tenney to first. Though Tenney was only 5-feet-9-inches tall, this was the position the Brown University product was born to play. "Tenney's way is far different from that of other first basemen," wrote a *Chicago News* reporter in 1897. "He reaches his hands far out for the ball, and stretches his legs, so that he is farther out from the bag on every throw than any other first baseman in the league."[1] On Opening Day, however, Tucker manned the first sack while Tenney played right field.

The Boston club had won six National League titles in their history, but their opponents, the Philadelphia Phillies, had captured none since joining the league in 1883. Still, the Phillies harbored championship aspirations of their own. They possessed the most powerful offense in the game, led by hard-hitting outfielders Sam Thompson and Ed Delahanty. The Phillies also counted on a big season from the best young player on the club, a rookie first baseman named Napoleon Lajoie. A strongly built 22-year-old from

Rhode Island, Lajoie had impressed the Philadelphia fans in a 39-game trial in 1896.

The Phillies, a hard-drinking team known for their curfew-breaking exploits, began the season with a strict disciplinarian at the helm. Philadelphia management hired a 29-year-old former outfielder, George Stallings, to keep the players on the straight and narrow. Stallings was a sharp-tongued perfectionist, often sarcastic and cutting in criticizing his men. *The Sporting News* called him "the gentleman whose mouth is always in a state of volcanic eruption,"[2] and it remained to be seen how the Phillies would respond to his leadership. Stallings was also keen to improve a pitching staff that had allowed more than five earned runs per game in 1896. Pitching was a perennial problem for the Phillies, and the team had finished in eighth place in 1896 despite scoring more runs than every other club except the Orioles.

On Monday, April 19, 1897,[3] a state holiday celebrated in Massachusetts as Patriots Day, more than 14,000 Bostonians squeezed inside the South End Grounds. The club erected rope barriers in the outfield and along the sidelines to house the overflow. Outside, another several hundred fans milled around, unable to gain entry. On this day, the Beaneaters and Phillies had the attention of the baseball world all to themselves, as the rest of the teams did not begin their schedules until Thursday of that week. It was, according to an optimistic headline in *Sporting Life*, "The Brilliant Opening a Happy Augury of a Successful Season Artistically and Financially."[4] The crowd settled down to watch the duel between Boston's Kid Nichols and Philadelphia right-hander Al Orth.

While Orth breezed through the Boston lineup, allowing no hits in the first four innings, Philadelphia scored in the fifth. Sam Gillen led off with a single and Billy Nash, after a failed sacrifice attempt, singled down the first-base line as Gillen reached third. Orth, a good-hitting pitcher, then drove in the first run of the 1897 season with a bloop hit. Two groundouts scored Nash, and the Phillies led, 2-0.

Boston finally hit safely off Orth in the bottom of the fifth, when Lowe singled with two outs but was stranded on first. Hamilton singled and stole second in the sixth but advanced no farther. By the time Lajoie scored the third Philadelphia run in the eighth, Orth had allowed only three Boston hits.

The Phillies tacked on three more runs in the ninth. With Orth and Bill Hallman aboard with singles, Lajoie belted his third hit of the day, a line drive over the left-field fence for a three-run homer, the first in the National League in 1897. This blow put the Phillies ahead 6-0, and the game appeared to be over.

However, Orth faltered in the bottom of the ninth, and the Beaneaters nearly pulled out a victory. Manager Selee sent Chick Stahl, his rookie outfielder, to bat for Nichols. Stahl, in his major-league debut, worked Orth for a walk. Orth retired Billy Hamilton, but Fred Tenney drilled a single to right. Stahl raced for third as Sam Thompson's throw from the outfield had him beaten easily, but third baseman Nash dropped the ball as Stahl slid into third safely.

Herman Long, who committed three errors that day (his "fingers were all thumbs," according to *Sporting Life*[5]), then flied out to Delahanty in left, scoring Stahl. Duffy singled to score Tenney. Collins and Lowe followed with singles, loading the bases with two out. This brought Tommy Tucker to the plate, and the veteran first sacker drove a liner to right that nearly tied the game. The ball hit the top of the fence, inches from going over, and Tucker made it to second for a double while all three runners crossed the plate. The score was now 6-5, with the potential tying run on second.

Charlie Ganzel, the ninth batter of the inning, could have tied the score with a safe hit, but he batted a weak grounder to Gillen, who threw to Lajoie at first to end the game. The Phillies had escaped with a win in George Stallings' managerial debut. "The visitors," said the Boston correspondent to *The Sporting News*, "played the better ball and deserved to win."[6]

After the loss on Patriots Day, the Beaneaters went on the road and won only one of their next seven games (with one tie), dropping to last place by the end of April. Still, Chick Stahl, who may have impressed Selee with his daring baserunning in the opener, found more playing time and emerged as one of the game's brightest rookie stars. Before long Selee placed Stahl in right field, moved Fred Tenney to first base, and shifted Tommy Tucker to the bench. So successful was this arrangement that Tucker appeared in only three more games before Selee sold him to Washington in early June. Tenney and Stahl sparked Boston's climb up the standings, and a 17-game winning streak in June boosted the Beaneaters into first place. They held the lead until mid-September, lost it briefly to the surging Orioles, then rallied to win the pennant.

The Phillies, in the meantime, were unable to build on their Opening Day victory. Napoleon Lajoie emerged as a major star in his first full season, batting .361 and leading the league in slugging percentage, but the players quickly grew tired of their sarcastic new manager. Torn by dissention and their annual pitching woes, they finished the 1897 season in 10th place. Stallings was fired after a poor start in 1898, and not until 1915 would the Phillies finally win their first National League title.

NOTES

1 Mark Sternman, "Fred Tenney," sabr.org/bioproj/person/40c98ad2.

2 *The Sporting News*, July 3, 1897: 5.

3 This was also the date of the first Boston Marathon, which was run a few hours earlier.

4 *Sporting Life*, April 24, 1897: 2.

5 Ibid.

6 *The Sporting News*, April 24, 1897: 2.

TENNEY LEADS MEMORIAL DAY PARADE WITH SIX HITS

MAY 31, 1897: BOSTON BEANEATERS 25, ST. LOUIS BROWNS 5, AT SOUTH END GROUNDS, BOSTON

BY RICHARD RIIS

It was a cold, wet day in Boston. The morning half of the Memorial Day twin bill had been canceled because of a downpour, and the afternoon contest seemed in doubt until the rain tapered off shortly before game time. Although the outfield grass was soaked and slick and the basepaths muddy, the attendance-challenged Browns were anxious to get at least one game in and collect their visitor's share of revenue from an anticipated holiday crowd.[1] To the club's chagrin, only 2,500 Bostonians braved the wet chill to pay their way into the South End Grounds, and by the time the game was over, the Browns were likely wishing it had rained all day.

After dropping both ends of a doubleheader in New York on May 29, the beleaguered Browns arrived in Boston deep in last place with a record of 6-25. Less than a week before, player-manager Tommy Dowd had been relieved of command and replaced by Hugh Nicol. So far Nicol had fared even worse than Dowd, losing his first three games, albeit with a team beset by illness and injury. Third baseman Fred Hartman had gone down with a sprained ankle, and second baseman John Houseman, picked up earlier in the month from a Chicago city league when veteran Lou Bierbauer was suspended for jumping ship, was bedridden with an undisclosed ailment. Adding tragedy to misfortune, pitcher Duke Esper had received a telegram with news of the death of his child and boarded a train for home. Stitching together a patchwork lineup, Nicol shifted Dowd from center field to second, placed catcher Klondike Douglass at third, and put reserve backstop Ed McFarland behind the plate. Pitcher Bill Hart, who'd played a few games in the outfield over five major-league seasons, was stationed in center field. Pitching for the Browns was seldom-used left-hander Bill Kissinger. By contrast, the healthy Beaneaters, despite stumbling out of the gate by losing five of their first six (with one tie), and under .500 as recently as May 15, had caught fire and won 16 of 23 behind a solid offense that propelled the club into fourth place.

Boston's "Happy Jack" Stivetts, winner of 20 games or more in six of the last seven seasons, including a high of 35 in 1892, had reported this season overweight and ineffective. After a 10-5 loss to Baltimore in his first start, Stivetts was sent home to get back in condition. He rejoined the team three weeks later, playing right field. (A good hitter, Stivetts hit .367 that year.) Stivetts pitched in relief on May 18, then went down with a sore arm. Manager Frank Selee, satisfied that Stivetts was now fully mended, gave the right-hander the nod to start.

The skies still threatened as the game got underway. "It took several tons of sawdust and a good lot of muscle," reported Tim

Murnane, to get the field in passable shape to play.² Exercising their option as the home team to bat first, the Beaneaters took a quick lead in the first inning. First baseman Fred Tenney doubled to left-center, and, perhaps slowed by the mud, advanced only to third on a double to left by shortstop Herman Long. Center fielder Hugh Duffy grounded to third baseman Douglass, who threw Tenney out at the plate, but a single by right fielder Chick Stahl brought in Long with Boston's first run. Boston added another run in the second to go up 2-0.

The Browns, hitless in the first, pounced on Stivetts in the bottom of the second. McFarland opened with a single. First baseman Morgan Murphy grounded to Long, who forced the runner at second. Stivetts walked Monte Cross. Kissinger smacked a double, driving in two runs to tie the game. Dowd reached first on a wild throw by Long, and left fielder Dan Lally smacked a single, scoring Kissinger and Dowd, to give the Browns a 4-2 lead.

In the third inning, the skies opened again and the rain fell hard. Umpire Hank O'Day, after giving some consideration to calling the contest, elected to wait out the rain. With the field further saturated and the basepaths a quagmire of mud and soaked sawdust, the game finally resumed with a walk to Duffy, a triple by Jimmy Collins, and a single by catcher Charlie Ganzel to knot the game at 4-4.

Boston grabbed the lead for good in the fourth when Tenney led off with a bunt single, Long doubled and Duffy walked to load the bases. Kissinger was pulled and right-hander Roy Evans, making only his second appearance with the Browns after being recruited from the Western League, was handed the ball. Stahl greeted the rookie with a double, clearing the bases, then scored on a subsequent out at first.

Tenney opened the fifth with a single, Long bunted safely, and Duffy walked to load the bases. Stahl forced Long at third, but Dowd's wild toss home permitted Tenney to score. Bases still loaded, second sacker Bobby Lowe bounced one back to pitcher Evans, who tossed to the plate for the force out. Collins singled, scoring two more runs, before the Browns could shut down the Beaneaters.

The defensive play of the game occurred in the St. Louis half of the fifth. With one out, McFarland reached on a double, and Murphy walked. Stivetts then lost control of the wet ball. A diving Ganzel knocked down the pitch and fired to Tenney at first to catch Murphy.

From this point, the Browns threatened but once, putting a single run across the plate in the seventh inning, while the Beaneaters continued poking drives that had Browns defenders skating across the slippery outfield grass, and pushing bunts into the mud for base hits. Boston tallied four runs in the sixth on a walk and five singles, then batted around in the seventh for five more runs on another walk and five more singles. Boston tacked on five more runs in the eighth on singles by George Yeager, who replaced starter Billy Hamilton in center field, Tenney, Long, rookie catcher Mike Mahoney, his only major-league hit, and a double by Duffy.

Boston put up its only scoreless inning in the ninth, then mercifully retired the Browns to end the game. The final score: a staggering 25-5 victory for the Beaneaters.

In the sloppy proceedings, St. Louis logged six errors, handing Boston 11 unearned runs, while the Beaneaters made but two. The field conditions were no less tricky for baserunners. As Murnane observed, "At times the boys cut some highly interesting hieroglyphics as they went waltzing around the slippery base paths."³

Regardless, the Boston juggernaut saw Stahl and Duffy cross the plate five times each; Collins and Long four. Of the Beaneaters' 24 hits, Long collected five and Collins four. Duffy banged out only two hits but walked four times. But the batting star of the game was, by all measures, Tenney.

"Fred Tenney gave one of the most scientific batting exhibitions ever witnessed at the South End Grounds," reported Murnane, "six hits in eight times at bat, including five in succession."⁴ Tenney spread his hits in every direction, doubling to left, singling once to center and twice to right, and bunting safely to first and third.

Winning pitcher Stivetts pitched all nine innings for Boston, giving up 12 hits, walking four and striking out four; Kissinger took the loss for St. Louis. Evans, battered for 14 runs in five innings of relief, was given his release after the game.

Beginning with this game, the Beaneaters went on a tear, winning 17 games in a row before dropping one, 7-4 at Brooklyn, on June 22. The club would seize first place the next day and, but for falling briefly behind the Orioles in mid-September, would remain there for the rest of the season.

SOURCES

In addition to the sources listed in the notes, the author also consulted the *Boston Post*, *St. Paul Daily Globe*, *The Sporting News*, and the *Washington Evening Times*.

NOTES

1 "Alas and Alack, That It Did Not Rain All Day Monday," *St. Louis Republic*, June 1, 1897: 5.

2 T.H. Murnane, "Batting Record Made," *Boston*, June 1, 1897: 21.

3 Ibid.

4 Ibid.

TWO-WAY THREAT "KLOBY" LEADS BOSTON TO 11-6 WIN OVER BROOKLYN

JUNE 21, 1897: BOSTON BEANEATERS 11, BROOKLYN BRIDEGROOMS 6, AT EASTERN PARK, BROOKLYN

BY MARK S. STERNMAN

After a 2-1 loss at Cincinnati May 29, Boston's record dropped to 17-12, a good mark but one that left the team in fourth place, five games out of first. The defeat concluded a 17-game road trip after which the Beaneaters returned home for 16 games. Home cooking helped; the Bostonians' big bats boomed as the Beaneaters scored 10 or more runs in eight of the games and swept the homestand. Boston had climbed to second place, just a game behind first-place Baltimore and returned to the road with a 16-game winning streak.

Boston had strong pitching to complement its mighty offensive attack. Three pitchers split 111 of the team's 135 starts. Ace Kid Nichols led the way; he won 31 games in 1897, the sixth of the last seven seasons in which he won at least 30. Fred Klobedanz, at 26 only one year younger than Nichols but with much less big-league experience, would start for the Beaneaters to open the road trip. Often called Kloby in the papers, Boston's lone lefty on June 21 pitched his first game ever in Brooklyn against another southpaw, Harley Payne. Like Kloby, Payne had debuted in the National League in 1896 after a long apprenticeship in the minors. He pitched to John Grim, giving the Bridegrooms an excruciatingly named battery of Payne and Grim, an ominous pairing that foretold the outcome of the game for Brooklyn fanatics.

Neither pitcher showed much stuff in the early part of the game. With two outs in the first inning and Fred Tenney on first via a single, Hugh Duffy, Jack Stivetts, and Bobby Lowe all added singles to put the Beaneaters up 2-0. Great credit went to Stivetts for keeping the rally going. The team's fourth starting pitcher, Stivetts also pitched in at first base, second base, and all three outfield slots. With future Hall of Famers Billy Hamilton, Duffy, and Jimmy Collins as teammates, Stivetts, albeit in only 61 games, had Boston's best slash line in 1897 at .367/.417/.533.

His offensive prowess notwithstanding, Stivetts failed to impress a New York reporter, who characterized the 29-year-old as "an overgrown boy on the verge of long trousers,"[1] a cutting comment perhaps best explained by his 6-foot-2 height.

Thanks to shoddy defense by some of Boston's stars, Brooklyn came back quickly in the bottom of the first. Both Collins and Hamilton made throwing errors to give the Bridegrooms runners on the corners. John Anderson doubled home two runs; with two outs, Jim Canavan doubled to plate one more. Brooklyn led 3-2 after the first inning of play.

Unable to enjoy the pleasure of the lead, Payne suffered in the second frame. George Yeager singled. A great hitting pitcher who finished 1897 with .324/.363/.466 marks, Kloby doubled, and Yeager came around to tie the score. Augmenting the attack from the top of the order, Hamilton singled, Tenney bunted for a hit, and Herman Long's single was muffed, and he wound up at third. Boston now led 6-3. Long scored on Duffy's fly to right, upping the Beaneaters' lead to 7-3.

Reprising his extra-base power, Kloby tripled in the third off Chauncey Fisher, who came on in relief for the Bridegrooms. Hamilton knocked in his hurler with a single, putting Boston up 8-3.

The Beaneaters added two more runs in the sixth on singles by Long and Duffy, and an error by center fielder Mike Griffin on "a fairly easy long, high drive,"[2] one of Griffin's 17 errors in 1897. Leading all NL outfielders in fielding percentage five times in his career and "often called the finest center fielder of his era,"[3] Griffin committed more miscues in 1897 than he had since 1889.

Trailing 10-3, Brooklyn got back on the board in the bottom of the sixth. With a runner on, Grim singled, and Fisher hit the second and last triple of his five-year career to knock in two runs and pull the Bridegrooms to within 10-5. A Brooklyn wag found Fisher's mop-up effort the most redeeming feature of the game from the losing perspective. "Although the visitors hit his slow delivery rather heavily at times, they were unable to score with the frequency that their hits called for, and it is quite possible that Fisher might have won the game" had he started it, commented the Brooklyn Daily Eagle.[4] Fisher yielded four runs over his seven innings of work.

Brooklyn scored another run in the seventh to close to 10-6. Anderson singled, stole second, went to third on Yeager's throwing error on the steal, and crossed the plate on Billy Shindle's single. The team leader in RBIs with 105, the 36-year-old Shindle set a career high in this category in his second-to-last season. Shindle's total placed him 10th in the NL. Boston, by contrast, had three players with more RBIs: Collins finished second in the NL with 132 (by far the most he would ever have), Duffy third with 129, and Lowe tied for ninth with 106.

Adding insurance, Boston got the final run of its 11-6 win in the ninth on back-to-back hits by batterymates Yeager (a single) and Kloby (a double). The latter not only won the game on the mound, but went 4-for-5 with three extra-base hits, moving beat writer Tim Murnane to swoon, "Klobedanz gave one of the finest exhibitions of batting I ever saw"[5] in a milestone game.

The Beaneaters' 17th consecutive win, along with the New York Giants' sweep of Baltimore in a doubleheader, vaulted Boston into first place for the first time all season, by a half-game margin.

The *Boston Globe* reported exuberantly, "The opinion prevails almost unanimously among league men that Boston will win the pennant this season."[6] Betting on the conventional wisdom would have paid off as Boston finished the 1897 season with a 93-39 record, two games up on 90-40 Baltimore.

NOTES

1 "Base Ball Notes," *Brooklyn Daily Eagle*, June 22, 1897: 4.

2 "Boston Takes the Lead," *New York Times*, June 22, 1897. Taking a contrary view, the *Brooklyn Daily Eagle* scribe claimed, "It was a difficult ball to catch and Mike could have let it go as a hit without any fear of receiving any criticism. And because he showed that nothing is so difficult but that it is worth trying for he receives a howl of disapproval." "Base Ball Notes," *Brooklyn Daily Eagle*, June 22, 1897: 4.

3 Scott Fiesthumel, "Mike Griffin," sabr.org/bioproj/person/45f87fcd (accessed November 15, 2017).

4 "Boston Takes the Lead," *Brooklyn Daily Eagle*, June 22, 1897: 4.

5 T.H. Murnane, "At the Top," *Boston Globe*, June 22, 1897: 1.

6 "Baseball Notes," *Boston Globe*, June 22, 1897: 4.

AN UNUSUAL BRAWL AND A WILD ENDING

AUGUST 6, 1897: BOSTON BEANEATERS 6, BALTIMORE ORIOLES 5, AT THE SOUTH END GROUNDS

BY GERARD R. GOULET

As the morning of August 6 dawned, the Boston Beaneaters, losers in the previous day's contest, enjoyed a slender two-game lead over the Baltimore Orioles. Two strong pitchers, Boston's

Fred Klobedanz and Baltimore's Arlie Pond, were facing each other. Each team had lost 27 games to this point in the season, but Boston had won four more games than Baltimore. Given the tightness of the race, this series between the two teams was viewed as crucial to both. As a result, the Boston fans, some 9,000 strong, were not only entertained by the result; they also had the relatively rare experience of observing two athletic contests for a single admission price – one professional baseball game (in the eyes of some, two distinct games) and one amateur boxing exhibition. Moreover, the name that was as prominent in the headlines of the day as that of any player was that of the umpire, Tom Lynch.

The fact that two distinct games appeared to have been played over the course of the nine innings was evidenced by the box score. Baltimore had all the advantage for the first four innings; the fifth inning served as an intermission of sorts; and Boston held sway from innings six through nine. The game was also entirely differently described in the newspaper accounts. The *Boston Globe*'s T.H. Murnane touted the excitement of the great come-from-behind victory and Boston left fielder Hugh Duffy's magnificent throw to cut Baltimore pinch-runner Joe Quinn down at the plate for the final out.[1] Baltimore's scribes, on the other hand, viewed their team as having been robbed by an incompetent umpire who inexplicably chose this day to favor the home team.[2]

Then came the prizefight at the close of the eighth inning when umpire Lynch, having taken verbal abuse from Baltimore's Jack Doyle to his limit,[3] did the unmentionable and struck Doyle after fining him. This resulted in Doyle striking back, joined by Joe Corbett (heavyweight champion Gentleman Jim's brother) and a general outpouring of players from both teams until police were able to restore order.

Even after the game was over, the frenzy continued. As the Baltimore team was being driven back to its hotel, the hometown fans followed the horse-drawn coach and pelted it with mud until John McGraw seized a bat, stepped down from the coach, and single-handedly drove the mob away.[4]

None of this late-inning and postgame excitement could have been predicted at the game's midpoint, when Baltimore led 5-0. Interestingly, the score could have been far more lopsided in Baltimore's favor had the Orioles not squandered a golden opportunity in the first. Boston chose to bat first and its half of the inning was unremarkable. McGraw then led off the game for Baltimore with a single. After Willie Keeler popped to shortstop Herman Long, Hughie Jennings took a pitched ball to his hip and reached base. Long then made a great stop in deep short to hold Joe Kelley to an infield hit and prevent McGraw from scoring. The bases were now full and there was only one out. But Jake

Stenzel, swinging at the first pitch, grounded to second baseman Bobby Lowe, who threw quickly to Long, who relayed to first baseman Fred Tenney, completing the double play and denying Baltimore a chance to score.

Boston failed to score again in the second, but Baltimore had better luck in its half of the inning. Pond doubled after Doyle had walked and the Orioles plated two runs on McGraw's two-out single. The visitors could not add another, however, as McGraw's aggression backfired when he was caught stealing second. Boston went down in order in the top of the third, but two more Baltimore runs were added in the bottom half of the inning when Keeler reached safely and, after Duffy robbed Jennings of a hit, scored on Kelley's home run, his second in as many days. Boston's offensive futility continued in the fourth, but Baltimore plated its fifth run on McGraw's fly ball. The Orioles were denied further scoring when Kelley flied out with the bases loaded. Neither team scored in the fifth.

The tide turned in the sixth. Although the Baltimore players had tried to break up Klobedanz by calling him vile names,[5] he shut every Oriole batter down over the next four innings except for a bunt single by Pond in the sixth and Jennings's hit in the ninth.

Meanwhile, Boston scored two runs in the sixth, one in the seventh, and three in the eighth. In the sixth, with Jack Stivetts on third, Tenney on first, and one out, Duffy doubled in Stivetts. Tenney then scored on a fly out but Duffy was stranded at third when Jimmy Collins, who had walked, was erased attempting to steal second in what was described by the *Post* writer as a "piece of stupid base running."[6] The *Baltimore Sun* reporter protested that the scoring should never have occurred, claiming Duffy should never have been on base but had reached second "after he had been fairly struck out."[7] Then "Duffy was touched off second by two yards, as admitted by Boston scorers, but was called safe."[8] Neither the *Boston Post*[9] nor Murnane in the *Globe* said anything at all about the play.[10]

According to the *Sun*, these were the first two of five alleged bad calls by umpire Lynch, four before the fight and one after.[11] The third disputed call occurred in the seventh when Baltimore claimed that Marty Bergen had hit into a double play. However, Lynch called him safe at first, and Bergen scored on a single by Stivetts. There was apparently a fourth disputed call but what that may have been was unclear from the *Sun's* account. In any case, whether there had been three or four disputed calls to this point is largely irrelevant. According to the *Post*, "Doyle had been using his tongue to the limit on Lynch all afternoon"[12] and continued without letup thereafter until he was ejected.

After the fisticuffs, Jerry Nops relieved Pond, the fans pelted, and almost hit, Kelley with bottles, and Boston went down without scoring, but with maximum excitement. With two out, Duffy hit safely, stole second, and went to third on the wild throw to second. Then, while Nops was winding up, Duffy had home stolen but lost it when Stahl hit the ball simultaneously for the third out. The last of the ninth presented Baltimore, only one run down, with an opportunity to force extra innings, if not pull out a victory. With one out, McGraw rapped a sharp grounder to Long and went tearing down the first-base line, smashing viciously into Tenney. Long's throw rolled to the stands and McGraw took advantage of the situation to make his way to second. Quinn was pressed into service to run for McGraw, who had injured himself on the play. Keeler then weakly fouled out. At this point, it was all up to Jennings. He did not disappoint, driving Klobedanz's third offering on a line into left field. There Duffy charged the ball and fired it to Bergen. Quinn had run on contact and the ball and Quinn arrived at home plate simultaneously. This was the final disputed call. Here again, there was no agreement among the scribes. The Boston writers lauded Duffy's fine throw.[13] The *Sun* and manager Hanlon saw the play quite differently.[14]

EPILOGUE

In the aftermath of the game, the plight of the umpires was a main topic in the succeeding week.[15] Beaneaters President Arthur Soden indicated that he would have policemen on the ground for the third game between the two teams and that they would be instructed to arrest any ballplayer using profane language.[16] Lynch, who had telegraphed his resignation to National League President Nick Young but was convinced to withdraw it by the latter,[17] admitted to being in the wrong in striking Doyle first, "but he went so far in his remarks that I simply could not stand it. This was not the first time in the game that he grossly insulted me and I had repeatedly warned him."[18] Murnane clearly sided with Lynch in his reaction: "A deaf and dumb man might not have acted as did Mr. Lynch, but unfortunately deaf and dumb men are not eligible for positions as umpires. If such men as Doyle are allowed to utter foul language with impunity, and to apply obscene epithets to those doing their best to decide plays and balls and strikes as they see them, the time will soon come when no person above the grade of garroter can be secured to umpire a game."[19] From Murnane's perspective, "Men like Doyle have killed the game in Cleveland, and will in any city they are allowed to live in."[20] But Baltimore manager Ned Hanlon continued to suggest that there was some dishonesty afoot when he was quoted as saying, "[T]his man Lynch is at heart a Boston man, and I know it."[21] He also said, "I know pretty well when a man makes an honest mistake, and I believe this was another case like that of [Jack] Sheridan in Cincinnati."[22] Sheridan had resigned at the end of July and umpire Tim Hurst, who had inadvertently harmed a Cincinnati fan with a thrown beer glass on August 4,[23] was arrested, charged with assault with intent to kill, and required a writ of habeas corpus to allow him to return to umpiring duties.[24] Such was the bleak state of affairs that served as an immediate backdrop to Boston's victory.[25]

NOTES

1. "Exciting to the Last," *Boston Globe*, August 7, 1897: 1,7.

2. "The Baltimore Champions have a reputation for 'kicking' at umpires, but not until today have their protests ever ended in blows, although some of the players have at times been struck. Their propensity to object to decisions has been grossly exaggerated all over the League circuit, but it is true that protests from Hanlon's men are not unusual. Nor is it remarkable that they should protest when they believe that they have all the umpires prejudiced against them. The howl has gone up all over the circuit ever since 1894, 'Don't let Baltimore win.' The howl has been louder this year than ever, and the umpires have given Baltimore unusually rough treatment. Lynch has been one of the very few men on the staff who has heretofore given the Orioles fair treatment. It was all the more surprising that he should suddenly change today and by a series of decisions that seem impossible for a man of Lynch's judgment, practically snatch from them a game that they had won." "Fight on the Diamond," *Baltimore Sun*, August 7, 1897: 6. A more balanced view of the Orioles' aggressive tactics can be found in Bill Felber, *A Game of Brawl; The Orioles, the Beaneaters & the Battle for the 1897 Pennant* (Lincoln: University of Nebraska Press, 2007).

3. "As Doyle was passing the plate, he began to abuse umpire Lynch. After calling him a vile name Lynch ordered him out of the game. Doyle stood his ground and continued to abuse the umpire loudly enough for people in the stand to hear. Several of the visiting players gathered around the little umpire. Doyle pushed up against Lynch and repeated the vile name three times," *Boston Globe*, August 7, 1897: 7.

4. "Disgraceful Fight on the Boston Baseball Grounds," *Boston Post*, August 7, 1897: 8.

5. *Boston Globe*, August 7, 1897: 7.

6. Ibid. The stupidity was laid at the feet of Duffy in both Murnane's account in the *Globe* and that of the *Sun*'s reporter, both writers appearing to fault Duffy for his failure to try to steal home on the play. *Boston Globe*, August 7, 1897: 7, *Baltimore Sun*, August 7, 1897: 6.

7. *Baltimore Sun*, August 7, 1897: 6.

8. Ibid. This statement about the Boston scorers is not corroborated in any other account.

9. "There was a prolonged kick on calling Duffy safe as the decision was exceedingly close. Jennings and all the hard fighters surrounded Lynch, but it did not faze him," *Boston Post*, August 7, 1897: 8.

10. *Boston Globe*, August 7, 1897: 1,7.

11. *Baltimore Sun*, August 7, 1897: 6.

12. *Boston Post*, August 7, 1897: 8.

13. "The heralded line throws to the plate laid to the credit of Louis Sockalexis, the Indian, of Cleveland, which have been so frequent this season, cannot be compared with Duffy's throw from left field to the plate, which beat Baltimore in the greatest up-hill fight of the season yesterday afternoon by 6 to 5." *Boston Post*, August 7, 1897: 8. According to the *Globe*'s Murnane, Quinn was out by several feet. *Boston Globe*, August 7, 1897: 7.

14. "Jennings then singled to left field and Quinn crossed the plate, but Lynch called him out and left the field hurriedly. Quinn slid and was lying flat on the plate when he was touched by Bergen, to whom Duffy had thrown the ball. Bergen was standing right behind the plate, and when he reached down, touched Quinn on the chest, almost under his chin. He could not possibly have done so had not Quinn been on the plate." *Baltimore Sun*, August 7, 1897: 6.

15. "Now for Clean Ball," *Boston Globe*, August 8, 1897: 7; "Tough Week for Umpires," *Boston Globe*, August 9, 1897: 3. In addition, there were multiple articles and opinion pieces in the August 7, 1897, issue of *The Sporting News* at pages 1, 4, and 6 and in the August 14, 1897, issue at pages 1, 4, and 5.

16. *Boston Globe*, August 7, 1897: 7.

17. "Now for Clean Ball," *Boston Globe*, August 8, 1897: 7.

18. "Lynch's Statement" *Boston Post*, August 7, 1897: 8.

19. "Echoes of the Game," *Boston Globe*, August 7, 1897: 7.

20. *Boston Globe*, August 7, 1897: 7. This is likely a reference to the Cleveland Spiders and their manager, Patsy Tebeau, the notorious reputations of which, collectively, were the equal of those of the Orioles of the period. A flavor of the era can be gleaned from Richard Scheinen, *Field of Screams: The Dark Underside of America's National Pastime* (New York: W.W. Norton & Company, 1994), 55-67, and of Tebeau himself at pages 75-79. See also Harold Seymour, *Baseball: The Early Years* (New York: Oxford University Press, 1989), 289-292.

21. *Boston Globe*, August 8, 1897: 7.

22. *Baltimore Sun*, August 7, 1897: 6. This appears to be a reference to a celebrated incident earlier in the year when McGraw was called out at home in a one-run loss to Cincinnati, umpired by Jack Sheridan. "Baseball Gossip," *Cincinnati Enquirer*, May 21, 1897: 2. McGraw was ejected again the following day. In that case, Hanlon had wired to President Young that Sheridan had intentionally robbed Baltimore of the game with Cincinnati and promised to submit affidavits attesting to Sheridan's bias against Baltimore. *Baltimore Sun*, May 22, 1897: 6.

23. "Bang!" *Cincinnati Enquirer*, August 5, 1897: 2.

24. *Boston Globe*, August 7, 1897: 7.

25. In fact, Young was having such difficulty recruiting umpires at this stage that he resigned his federal clerical position in the office of Auditor for the War Department which he had held for decades so he could devote all his time and energy to his duties as league president, including, in particular, those related to the umpire question. *Boston Globe*, August 8, 1897: 7; *The Sporting News*, August 14, 1897: 4.

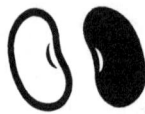

UTILITYMAN BOB ALLEN'S BIG DAY – AS BOSTONIANS BEGIN TO TRAVEL UNDERGROUND

SEPTEMBER 1, 1897: BOSTON BEANEATERS 7, CHICAGO COLTS 4, AT SOUTH END GROUNDS, BOSTON

BY BILL NOWLIN

Baseball wasn't the only thing on the minds of Bostonians on September 1, 1897. That was the day that the first subway system in the United States began operations. Motorman James Reed drove the first car, bearing about 150 people and departing Park Street station at 6:02 A.M. Conductor Gilman Trufent collected the 5-cent fares. Before the day was over, tens of thousands of people had paid their fares and tried out the new subway; the *Boston Globe* pegged the figure at "between 200,000 and 250,000."[1] The *Boston Daily Advertiser* calculated 75,000.[2] Aboveground, grievously overcrowded Tremont Street was now passable again with so many of the streetcars traveling unimpeded underground.

But there was also a very big game scheduled for the Boston Ball Grounds at 3:30 that afternoon. One could take in both events. The local nine, dubbed the Beaneaters by many, had won three pennants in a row from 1891-93, but had now fallen short three years and finished fourth in 1896. Yet as August closed, they were tied with the Baltimore Orioles – in fact, a little behind in percentage points. Baltimore was 72-32 (.692) and the Bostons were 74-34 (.685). On August 31 Boston had hosted the Chicago Colts, the game ending in an 8-8 tie.

Boston had been behind from the start of the season through June 19, reaching first place for a day on June 21. They dropped back a game on the 22nd, but on the 23rd they pulled ahead in the standings for good. They held that lead until the game on August 31, when they dropped into a tie. There were 24 games left on the schedule. Every one of them was going to count.

The Colts were 24 games behind the leaders, ensconced in sixth place in the 12-team National League. They were led by Cap Anson, who managed and played first base. Captaining the Boston team was Hugh Duffy. The Colts and Beaneaters had gone at it earlier in the season, Boston winning five of their first six meetings, but then dropping all three games in Chicago in early July. With the tie game on August 31, Boston was 5-4-1.

Starting for Boston was pitcher Ted Lewis. He'd been 1-4 in his first season, 1896, but the right-hander was on his way to a 21-12 season in 1897. Chicago countered with Danny Friend, a lefty the same age as Lewis (24). Friend was in his second full season;

he had been 18-14 (4.74) in 1896, and would finish 1897 at 12-11.

Former bank clerk Bob Allen was arguably the star of the day. He had turned 30 in July and after five years with the Phillies was out of baseball in 1895 and 1896. He played shortstop in 32 games for Boston in 1897, including the September 1 game. Regular shortstop Herman Long was "on the hospital list."[3] Allen was asked to bat seventh in the order.

Boston won the game, but the *Globe* overlooked Allen in its lead, concluding, "[T]o Capt. Duffy belongs the credit of saving the game for Boston."[4] In a subhead, the paper acknowledged that Allen's batting was "the feature of the game."

Neither team scored in the first inning, first baseman Anson making all three putouts for the Colts. In the second, Jimmy Callahan tripled for Chicago, over Duffy's head in left field, but was left stranded. Duffy drew a walk in the bottom of the second, took second base on a groundout by Jimmy Collins, and then scored when Allen singled. Chicago tied it up with a one-out double by pitcher Friend followed by shortstop Bill Dahlen's single.

Chick Stahl singled to lead off Boston's the fourth, but was forced at second by Duffy's bunt hit a little too hard. Collins doubled to right field, putting men on second and third. Allen then singled between third and short, driving in both baserunners. Fred Lake flied out to short, Lewis singled, and Billy Hamilton drew a walk. The bases were loaded and Fred Tenney got a "scratch infield single"[5] which scored Allen. Bobby Lowe grounded out to the end the inning, but it was 4-1 Boston.

And Boston added two more in the fifth. In the top of the inning, Chicago got two men on base but Lewis worked his way out of the jam. In the bottom of the inning, Collins drew a walk and then trotted home when Allen hit a home run over the fence in left field. Boston got a couple more men on base (Lake and Lewis both singled), but no more scored.

Lewis walked the first batter in the top of the sixth, then Callahan singled, and catcher Malachi Kittridge drew a one-out walk to load the bases. Friend flied out to the catcher. Lewis might have gotten out of the inning, but third baseman Bill Everitt singled past second base to drive in two. It was now 6-3, still in Boston's favor.

When center fielder Bill Lange singled to start off the seventh and Anson "dropped a lucky one into left field,"[6] Hugh Duffy made a move, calling in Kid Nichols to relieve Ted Lewis. Lange scored on an out, but only the one run came home. It was 6-4. The move to replace Lewis was unpopular with some fans, who hissed when Duffy came up to bat. The *Boston Journal* wrote that "several hundred began to hiss like silly geese."[7] But, wrote the *Globe*'s Tim Murnane, "Four-fifths of the spectators applauded the little captain who had the brains and the nerve to take a chance and save the day." After all, Murnane continued, "The time to change the pitcher is before the game is lost."[8]

Why this hissing? The *Journal* said it was the "shoestring gamblers" who reacted for "the most mercenary of motives, they had placed their paltry dollars on Chicago, and they feared that Duffy had played a card which would deprive them of possible small winnings."[9]

The *Journal* observed that three times Lewis skirted bigger problems, and – while he might have escaped the seventh, too, had Lowe executed a possible double play, what it called his "record of unsteadiness holds."[10] Three times he'd loaded the bases, but escaped more serious damage, noted the *Chicago Tribune*, crediting the timing of Boston's batters: "it was opportune hits that piled up the runs for Boston."[11] Umpire Lynch, the *Tribune* wrote, made a couple of controversial calls, both going against the Colts.

Nichols helped give his team an insurance run in the eighth, hitting a ball off the top of the left-field fence for a double. With two outs, Tenney hit a short one that dropped into center despite Lange's valiant effort at a catch. Nichols scored.

After Lange reached on a slow roller to third base in the top of the ninth, Nichols retired the next three batters, though Jimmy Ryan sent one deep to the flagpole in center before Hamilton snared it. The game ended with a 7-4 win, in 2:03 before 4,150.

In the second inning, Bob Allen had singled in Duffy. In the fourth inning, he singled in both Duffy and Collins. And in the fifth inning, he hit the two-run homer. He was credited with 34 RBIs in 1897, but five of them were from this one game.

The *Boston Journal* featured Allen's accomplishments under the headline "Bob Allen's Day," noting his fielding as well as his batting, doing more than might be expected of a utilityman.[12]

Murnane rightly concluded, "The absorbing topics of the day were the opening of the subway and Bob Allen's batting."[13]

NOTES

1 "Every Car Crowded," *Boston Globe*, September 2, 1897: 1.

2 "Big Crowds Thronged the Newly Opened Subway," *Boston Daily Advertiser*, September 2, 1897: 1.

3 "Allen's Hitting," *Boston Daily Advertiser*, September 2, 1897: 8.

4 T.H. Murnane, "No Change for Better," *Boston Globe*, September 2, 1897: 5.

5 Ibid.

6 Ibid.

7 "Bob Allen's Day," *Boston Journal*, September 2, 1897: 1.

8 T.H. Murnane.

9 "Bob Allen's Day."

10 Ibid.

11 "Hit at Proper Time," *Chicago Tribune*, September 2, 1897: 4.

12 Ibid.

13 T.H. Murnane.

BOSTON ROOTERS FLOCK TO BALTIMORE TO SEE CRUCIAL PENNANT RACE VICTORY

SEPTEMBER 24, 1897: BOSTON BEANEATERS 6, BALTIMORE ORIOLES 4, AT ORIOLE PARK

BY JERROD COTOSMAN

Boston players and Royal Rooters in front of Eutaw House in Baltimore 1897.
(McGreevy Collection, Boston Public Library)

Several hundred loyal Boston rooters blew their tin horns, banged their noisemakers, and cheered themselves hoarse against the roar of 12,000 Oriole fans. They had followed their team to the showdown series of the 1897 pennant race and had come prepared for a party unlike any other. The trip seemed such a unique and spectacular thing that Boston's competing newspapers vied to shower the travelers with trinkets like special medals and documented their movements with columns of newsprint.[1]

Two series remained in the season but these three games between the two contenders would surely decide who took the flag. The teams had stalked each other throughout the spring and summer and now fall had arrived with scarcely a hair's breadth separating them. On the morning of Friday, September 24, the defending champion Baltimore club had a winning percentage of .707, .001 better than the trailing Beaneaters. The Orioles had taken three straight pennants but had never been in a fight like this and the often ambivalent Baltimoreans had rallied to the cause and shown up in droves.

Hundreds of fans had lined up to buy tickets to the first game at 75 cents per reserved seat. Precautions such as limiting purchases to two seats at a time unless the patron was known to team management were taken to discourage scalpers. Yet so great was the demand that all manner of tricks were used to get around those very precautions. The age-old dodge of finding small boys to wait in line was applied and men were desperate enough to try disguising themselves by switching coats and hats. Baseball fever was raging and even a heavy downpour on the 23rd could not dampen the fans' spirits.[2]

Game day dawned fair and clear and soon Oriole Park was filled as the swelling crowed spilled over the stands and onto the field, necessitating special ground rules for balls hit into the throng.[3] Then disaster struck the Beaneaters as the teams warmed up. Nineteenth-century infields were a far cry from the pristine diamonds of the future and a grounder hit a rock and struck Boston's Jimmy Collins over his left eye.[4] The blow opened up a cut that quickly swelled and impaired his vision. Faced with the loss of his star third baseman, manager Frank Selee sent a boy to a nearby druggist for leeches that drained the wound and left Collins able to see and play.[5]

Boston's Kid Nichols and his 29-11 record faced Oriole Joe Corbett, who had posted a 24-6 mark, but Baltimore initially appeared to have the future Hall of Famer on the mound. Orioles third sacker John McGraw led off for the home nine and drew a walk on five pitches. Willie Keeler fouled out to Collins at third but McGraw stole second and scored on Hughie Jennings's single to left. Joe Kelley belted a ball over Hugh Duffy's head in center and Jennings scored. Four batters in and it was already 2-0. But Nichols stemmed the tide by getting Jake Stenzel to foul out and striking out Jack Doyle. Baltimore had missed a chance to score more runs and that theme continued throughout the day.

McGraw singled to lead off the third and Keeler bunted him over, but was thrown out at first on a fine play by Collins. The runner was stranded as neither Jennings nor Kelley could bring him in. Stenzel opened the fourth with a liner to center that Billy Hamilton tried for and missed as the ball shot through his legs, and the Orioles center fielder motored in to third. But when the runner broke for home on Doyle's slow roller, Collins gunned him down at the plate. Doyle took off for second and Marty Bergen nailed him stealing, and another threat had passed.

Meanwhile Corbett had retired the first 10 Boston hitters. Fred Tenney was number 11 and he walked after taking a pair of strikes. Bobby Lowe then doubled to center for the Beaneaters' first hit and Doyle muffed Chick Stahl's grounder, allowing the run to score. Corbett managed to escape further damage, but the magic of the first three innings was gone. Like a skilled boxer, Boston began to jab away, scoring enough to control the game but never delivering a knockout blow.

The visitors tied the game in the fifth when Herman Long singled and Bergen doubled him home. Nichols failed to get down a bunt and Corbett rallied to fan Hamilton. The Baltimore pitcher had a chance to wriggle off the hook but he walked Tenney again and, after getting two strikes on Lowe, he crossed up catcher Wilbert Robinson and the Beaneaters second baseman placed the ball along the right-field line to make it 3-2.[6]

By this time Nichols had settled in and easily retired the Orioles in the fifth and sixth innings. The jubilant Boston fans produced ditties like the popular "Hit her up, hit her up, hit her up again! B-o-s-t-o-n!" which was repeated incessantly.[7] The Beaneaters hurler helped his own cause by singling to lead off the seventh and benefited from sloppy Orioles fielding when Corbett threw Hamilton's grounder into the crowd and then compounded the error with a wild pitch. Nichols scored and Hamilton took third and then scored on Tenney's safe bunt. Corbett survived the inning but was replaced by Arlie Pond, who would give up another run but finish the game.

Baltimore bats finally came alive in the bottom of the eighth. Hamilton muffed Pond's liner and McGraw walked, but Keeler swung at a 3-and-0 pitch and popped to second.[8] Jennings then hit a sharp grounder but luck frowned on the Orioles as it hit Pond, who was called out. Nichols pitched carefully to Kelley and walked him, loading the bases for Stenzel. The Baltimore center fielder already had a triple and he rocketed a ball that seemed destined for left-center field and a sure two runs until Long made a leaping grab to end the inning. The Boston rooters howled in delight and showered the shortstop with silver coins as he returned to the bench.[9]

Boston stranded a pair of runners in the top of the ninth and took a 6-2 lead into the bottom of the frame when the Orioles made one last charge in the gathering twilight. Doyle led off with a single and went to third when Heinie Reitz matched him. Robinson hit another to drive in a run and Joe Quinn batted for the pitcher. Nichols got him to fly to center to briefly quiet the crowd. Up stepped John McGraw. The Baltimore third baseman already had a hit and a pair of walks, and had stolen two bases. Now he slashed another single and Reitz trotted home to cut the lead to 6-4.

It was loud in Oriole Park and the fans roared as Keeler came to the plate. A man who would hit .424 could not have too many bad days but this was one of Wee Willie's. He had popped to Collins in the first, been thrown out by the Boston third sacker on a bunt attempt in the third and hit another popup in the eighth. Even his leadoff base hit in the sixth was spoiled when he was caught stealing second by Bergen. Now he stood in as the winning run in the heat of the pennant race against a laboring Nichols. The Boston hurler wound up and released a curve which the impatient Keeler swung at and lined toward short. Long took in the ball and continued on to second to step on the base and double off Robinson for the final out as the stunned home fans fell silent.

The 6-4 decision flipped the top spots in the standings and left the Beaneaters with a .007 lead. They had outplayed the defending champions by stellar fielding and timely hitting, and now needed only to split the remaining two contests to be in the driver's seat for the pennant. The Boston rooters were anything but subdued as they marched back to their rooms at the Eutaw Hotel. The *Baltimore Sun* huffed, "Several hundred Boston 'rooters' were in attendance, and were hilarious at the result of the game, but it will be well for them to remember that 'he who laughs last laughs best.'"[10] At least for one night, it was the Beaneaters doing the laughing.

NOTES

1. Bill Felber, *A Game of Brawl* (Lincoln: University of Nebraska Press, 2007), 222-223.
2. "They Are Ready for It," *Boston Globe*, September 24, 1897: 2.
3. "On the Baseball Field," *New York Times*, September 25, 1897: 4.
4. "Boston Now Leads the Race," *Boston Journal*, September 25, 1897: 1.
5. Felber, 225.
6. "Outplayed by Boston," *Baltimore Sun*, September 25, 1897: 6.
7. "Boston Now Leads the Race."
8. "On the Baseball Field."
9. Felber, 228.
10. "The Ball Field," *Baltimore Sun*, September 25, 1897: 4.

GOOD (BEANEATERS) VERSUS EVIL (ORIOLES)

SEPTEMBER 27, 1897: BOSTON BEANEATERS 19, BALTIMORE ORIOLES 10, AT UNION GROUNDS, BALTIMORE

BY BILL FELBER

More than a battle for the 1897 National League pennant, the contest played out at Baltimore's Union Grounds was a living, breathing metaphor. To the 30,000 fans who literally broke down the park's gates and walls to see it, and to the thousands nationally who followed telegraphed accounts in locations as distant as Los Angeles, it was the real world playing out of the eternal struggle of good vs. evil.

Few confused the assigned roles. Virtually across the nation outside Baltimore itself, the Orioles were the embodiment of all that was wrong with baseball. Led by third baseman John McGraw, shortstop Hughie Jennings, first baseman "Dirty Jack" Doyle and right fielder Wee Willie Keeler, the team managed by Ned Hanlon had since 1894 terrorized the rest of the league, sweeping to three successive pennants by both skill and intimidation. "The dirtiest ball ever seen in this country," Boston sports writer Tim Murnane lamented of the Orioles' style.[1] A reporter in New Orleans, commenting on a spring training exhibition, had characterized McGraw as having adopted "every low and contemptible method that his erratic brain can conceive to win a play by a dirty trick." [2]

Though hardly saints themselves, the Beaneaters—three-time champions from 1891–93 before being dethroned by the Orioles—assumed the mantle of fan favorites once it became clear in 1897 that either they or the Orioles would win the pennant. Between August 27 and September 26, they combined to win 39 of 49 decisions (three games ending in ties), neither team ever leading the other by more than one game in the standings. A fated schedule ordered the clubs together for three games the final week in Baltimore. As the series opened, the Orioles held a one percentage point lead over Boston, although thanks to having played three more games the Beaneaters were actually a half game ahead in the standings.[3] The frantic first two games did nothing to resolve the tension. Boston won 6-4 on Friday behind ace pitcher Charles "Kid" Nichols with a throng of 13,000 overflowing onto the field. Another 14,000 turned out Saturday, again spilling onto the field and climbing atop the outfield fence, to watch the Orioles win 6-3 and draw the race back into a virtual deadlock. The illegality of Sunday baseball merely ensured that the drama would build one more day.

Despite the fact that Monday was a work day, fans overwhelmed the tiny baseball grounds to witness the decisive game. The attendance is commonly estimated at 30,000—easily surpassing the previous record for any game—but the truth is that nobody knows how many people watched. Fans broke through the outfield gate and knocked down part of the fence to get access.

Others stormed the turnstiles, erected seats on the roofs of houses across the street, or perched themselves on telegraph poles.

A delegation of more than 100 fans from Boston— the genesis of the famed "Royal Rooters"—showed up complete with a brass band to challenge the home team's noise advantage. Thousands more crowded the streets of Boston's "Newspaper Row" to "watch" on large play-by-play boards in a scene repeated on smaller scales in cities across the country. Nichols, already a 30-game winner, returned to the rubber on two days' rest as did the Orioles' Joe Corbett, who was seeking his 25th victory.

But chance had it in for Corbett. The game's fourth batter, Chick Stahl, lined a drive off his hand that jammed several fingers. Hanlon was forced to remove his ace. The Beaneaters got a run out of that first inning, but Keeler's base hit led to two Oriole runs in the bottom half of the inning. The lead changed hands three more times by the end of the third inning, which ended with the score tied at 5-5. In the Boston fourth, Billy Hamilton, the era's premier baserunner, singled and stole second, Fred Tenney walked, and Bobby Lowe singled to drive Hamilton across. Chick Stahl followed with a single that produced Tenney, and an error by Wilbert Robinson allowed Lowe to score an eighth run.

Bill Hoffer, whose 22nd victory had been Saturday's complete-game triumph, pitched scoreless ball from that point through the sixth. But by the beginning of the seventh inning Hoffer had worked 13 innings in less than two days against the league's best offense, and he was exhausted. What ensued turned the top of the seventh into one of the most productive (or, depending on your perspective, disastrous) half innings ever played.

Hugh Duffy opened for Boston with a solid base hit. Jimmy Collins drilled a fastball into the crowd in right field for a ground-rule double, and Dutch Long's double into the crowd in center scored both runners. When three more hits produced three additional runs, Hoffer did what in 1897 was the unthinkable: He motioned to team captain Robinson and manager Hanlon to relieve him. Both men ignored the gesture, imploring Hoffer to continue. He did, but by the time the slaughter had ended with Long's second double of the inning, nine Boston runs crossed the plate. The champion Orioles were, for the first time since 1893, effectively unseated.

When Nichols retired the last Baltimore batter and the final score 19-10 score was posted, a remarkable scene ensued. Although the Baltimore and Boston fans had exchanged epithets all season long, they now joined on the field in a series of mutual salutes. Their bands serenaded each other with renditions of "Yankee Doodle," "Dixie," "There'll Be a Hot Time in the Old Town Tonight," and "Maryland, My Maryland."[4]

The nation treated the outcome as something of a purgative for what were widely perceived as the game's ills. "Never was interest keener in America's great national game than it is today," said the *Boston Globe*.[5] The outcome put Boston a game and a half in front with just three to play; two victories in Brooklyn the following weekend formalized the pennant that ended the pennant run of the 19th century's most feared and despised team at three.

This essay was originally published in Inventing Baseball: The 100 Greatest Games of the 19th Century *(Phoenix: SABR, 2013), edited by Bill Felber.*

NOTES

1 T. H. Murnane, "The Champions," *The Sporting News*, June 30, 1894: 2.

2 Charles Alexander, *John McGraw* (Lincoln: University of Nebraska Press, 1988), 39.

3 The Orioles had four games remaining on their schedule compared to Boston's three. Due to travel problems, rained-out Orioles games in Cleveland and Louisville had not been made up.

4 "Boston On Top," *Baltimore Sun*, September 28, 1897: 6.

5 "Editorial Points," *Boston Globe*, September 28, 1897: 6.

COLLINS GRAND SLAM HELPS BEANEATERS SCORE SIX RUNS IN NINTH TO BEAT PHILADELPHIA

SEPTEMBER 29, 1898: BOSTON BEANEATERS 11, PHILADELPHIA PHILLIES 10, AT SOUTH END GROUNDS

BY BRIAN M. FRANK

The Boston Beaneaters entered their three-game series with the Philadelphia Phillies in a foul mood. Their frustration stemmed from a disappointing loss to the Brooklyn Bridegrooms the day before. The entire City of Boston seemed upset by the fact that Beaneaters manager Frank Selee had decided to start Vic Willis against Brooklyn just one day after he'd pitched a complete-game victory over them. Selee reasoned that since Philadelphia had been successful against Willis in the past, he'd use him against Brooklyn and save his other pitchers for the Phillies.[1] Unfortunately, Willis did not have his best stuff pitching on back-to-back days and the tired pitcher lasted just four shaky innings. Tempers boiled over during the game when Boston captain Hugh Duffy was ejected. Despite a comeback attempt in the ninth when Boston loaded the bases, Brooklyn hung on to win, 5-2. Kid Nichols pitched the final five innings, partly defeating the purpose of trying to save Boston's top arm for the Phillies. Tim Murnane of the *Boston Globe* wrote, "After the game everyone looked warm under the collar. Manager Selee came in for severe criticism from the directors and players for pitching Willis."[2] The *Boston Post* criticized the manager's decision to start Willis, writing that Selee had acted with "anxiety for the future without any regard for today."[3]

The loss snapped Boston's eight-game winning streak and cut the Beaneaters' lead over the second-place Baltimore Orioles to four games.

The displeasure over the loss to Brooklyn carried over to the next day, as the Beaneaters opened their series with the Phillies. The *Boston Traveler* reported, "Both the crowd and the team were out for the game, and there was plenty of ginger. They were sore at the loss of Wednesday's game and were ready to kick at anything."[4] This was the atmosphere at Boston's South End Grounds as the Beaneaters sent right-hander Fred Klobedanz to the mound to face Phillies right-hander Al Orth.

The Beaneaters jumped out to a first-inning lead when Bobby Lowe singled to right field, bringing home Billy Hamilton. Later in the inning, Lowe was gunned down at the plate on a great relay throw by Phillies second baseman Napoleon Lajoie for the third out.

The Phillies wasted little time jumping all over Klobedanz's pitches. In the second inning, Phillies pitcher Orth "sent a long fly down right center, which (Billy) Hamilton muffed, letting in two runs."[5]

Duff Cooley singled home Orth as center fielder Hamilton launched a wild throw home, and the Phillies increased their lead to 3-1.

Billy Lauder launched his second home run of the season in the third inning, a three-run shot over the left-field wall, to put Philadelphia up 6-1. That would be it for Klobedanz, who the *Boston Journal* noted had been saved for the Phillies, but "had proved to be just their 'mutton.'"[6] Ted Lewis was brought in to pitch the fourth, and the first batter to face him, Duff Cooley, lined one deep to center field. As the *Boston Traveler* told it, "Hamilton started back for it and the ball just hit the tip of his fingers. Then it rolled clear to the fence behind the flagstaff and Cooley tore home."[7] The *Boston Journal* wrote that the inside-the-park home run, the first of the season at the South End Grounds, was due to "slow fielding" by Hamilton, while the *Boston Evening Record* reported that Hamilton was playing with a bad knee, which helped explain his poor defensive play.[8]

The Beaneaters came back with a run in the fourth, but Philadelphia answered in the top of the fifth when Billy Lauder singled, and two wild pitches later scored the Phillies' eighth run of the game. Later in the inning, Boston right fielder Chick Stahl kept another run from scoring when he threw from the right-field fence to nail Ed McFarland at the plate, on a play that the *Boston Traveler* said was "a beauty, but the crowd was so sore at the way the game was going that they didn't appreciate it at all."[9] In the bottom half of the inning, Boston picked up a run when Hamilton tripled and was driven home by Herman Long to cut the lead to 8-3.

Both teams picked up a run in the seventh and eighth innings. Boston's run in the eighth came when Jimmy Collins picked up his third hit of the day, belting his league-leading 14th home run over the left-field fence to cut the Phillies lead to 10-5.

The Beaneaters entered the ninth inning trailing by five runs. With angry fans filing out of the ballpark, Boston was in danger of losing its second straight game and having its lead in the standings shrink even more. Hamilton led off the Beaneaters' ninth with a single to center. Fred Tenney followed with another single, "and the crowd woke up."[10] Herman Long hit a sharp grounder to third baseman Lauder that could have been a double play, but Lauder "fumbled the ball" and all hands were safe.[11] Lowe then lined a single to left, scoring Hamilton, while Tenney "mindful of the runs behind him, took no chances and very properly held at third."[12]

With the bases loaded, Jimmy Collins, already 3-for-4 with a home run, stepped to the plate as the game's tying run. The *Boston Evening Record* described the scene:

> Somebody shrieked out the discovery that a home run would tie the game, and the bleachers and stands fairly seethed with excitement. Five thousand eyes were on Collins, who by the way, leads the league in home runs, but the grand little player was cool as an iceberg and took his time. Two balls he fouled trying to get the range. Then he met one fair, and with a report like a pistol shot the ball sped over the fence while the spectators went simply crazy with excitement over the unexpected turn in affairs.[13]

As the crowd celebrated, a rattled Orth walked Chick Stahl. After Marty Bergen sacrificed Stahl to second, Hugh Duffy moved him to third on a groundout to shortstop Monte Cross and a "splendid pickup" by first baseman Klondike Douglass.[14] Pitcher Ted Lewis came to the plate with two outs and the winning run at third base. Lewis hit a high fly to shallow left field that left fielder Ed Delahanty, center fielder Duff Cooley, and shortstop Monte Cross all converged on to no avail. The crowd went wild as Stahl crossed the plate with the winning run. The *Boston Journal* described the chaotic celebration:

> Hats were hurled into the air as if their owners did not care if they never came back. Men hugged and whacked their neighbors, whether strangers or not, and neighbor passed it along. A thunder of incoherent shouting filled the air. Sober and staid citizens yelled like demons in a crescendo of pleasure when the climax came and the Bostons had won the game. A kodac (*sic*) picture of any one of three-quarters of the spectators would be damning evidence against sanity.[15]

The hero of the day was Jimmy Collins, who went 4-for-5, with two home runs, including the game-tying grand slam, and five runs batted in. After the game, the *Boston Evening Record* noted that in value to his team, Collins "ranks with the greatest players in the league. That may be trite, but it is true."[16]

After a frustrating two days, Collins's late-game heroics quickly turned a disheartened crowd into a jubilant frenzy. The Beaneaters had accomplished what they failed to do the day before, complete a dramatic ninth-inning comeback. The *Boston Evening Record* summed up the ninth inning perfectly, writing that the Beaneaters' improbable rally was "one of those things in baseball that make the game the national sport."[17]

NOTES

1 W.S. Barnes Jr., "A Game Thrown Away," *Boston Journal*, September 29, 1898.

2 Tim Murnane, "Too Much Willis," *Boston Globe*, September 29, 1898.

3 "Cost Hub a Game," *Boston Post*, September 29, 1898.

4 "Baseball Notes," *Boston Traveler*, September 30, 1898.

5 Murnane, "Fancy Finish," *Boston Globe*, September 30, 1898.

6 Barnes, "Overcame Long Lead," *Boston Journal*, September 30, 1898.

7 "Jim Collins Was the Hero," *Boston Traveler*, September 30, 1898.

8 Barnes, "Overcame Long Lead"; The Sportsman, "From Diamond, Track, Turf, Court and River," *Boston Evening Record*, September 30, 1898.

9 "Baseball Notes," *Boston Traveler*.

10 Murnane, "Fancy Finish."

11 Barnes, "Overcame Long Lead."

12 "Collins the Hero," *Boston Evening Record*, September 30, 1898.

13 Ibid. The actual attendance was 2,500 and both the *Globe* and *Traveler* noted that a large number of fans had left before the ninth-inning rally.

14 Barnes, "Overcame Long Lead."

15 Ibid.

16 The Sportsman, "From Diamond, Track, Turf, Court and River," *Boston Evening Record*, September 30, 1898.

17 Ibid.

RELIEVED BEANEATERS GAIN TITLE AGAIN

OCTOBER 11, 1898: BOSTON BEANEATERS 14, WASHINGTON NATIONALS 5, AT BOUNDARY FIELD, WASHINGTON, DC

BY RALPH PELUSO

As the skies darkened over the nation's capital, the spirit of the brave sportsmen from Boston brightened. The scoreboard-watching Beaneaters breathed easier when the young man serving as scoreboard operator removed the 12-by-16-inch placard noting the innings. The temporary gap caused players to pause. Beaneaters players elbowed each other and stared. Then an "F" appeared. The game over. Stunned, many in the dugout wondered, could this be? The second game of the Baltimore-New York Giants doubleheader had gone final, the game cut short by darkness and Baltimore on the losing end of the abbreviated six-inning contest, 6-2. A sense of relief filled the air. All the Boston team needed was to maintain the lead in their game. A victory against the Senators would clinch a Boston pennant for the second straight year. The ultimate prize dangled well within reach. Although they led through three innings, the Beaneaters' margin was tenuously narrow – just two runs. As the season barreled toward conclusion, there was a collective recollection of the prior year's late-September series between the two dynasties. The 1897 games, filled with anger and fistfights, perhaps haunted team captain Hugh Duffy. The Beaneaters controlled their destiny. Without a postseason tournament, the team that finished first in the regular season was crowned champion.

The game in Washington had been close to that point. The Nationals elected to bat first and leadoff batter Jake Gettman, the center fielder, singled to left-center. He ran all the way to third base on a wild pitch, and scored on Kip Selbach's fly ball to Duffy in left field. It was 1-0, Washington.

Boston came back with two runs in the first, and another one in the bottom of the second. The score stood 3-1 after the first three innings.

A collective burst of energy emerged, as the close game was broken apart in the top of the fourth. The visitors' relentless lineup, which featured three future Hall of Famers – third baseman and league-leading home-run hitter Jimmy Collins, and outfielders Duffy and Billy Hamilton – took over the game. Boston pounded nine runners across home plate in the frame. Ted "Parson" Lewis, an afterthought to a rotation that included Hall of Famers Charles Augustus "Kid" Nichols and Vic "The Delaware Peach" Willis, kept the Nationals from scoring until the top of the seventh, but Boston added one run in the seventh and another in the eighth.

The game did not end without a late show of life. In the ninth inning, playing in notably dark conditions, Washington's Jud Smith and Duke Farrell got things started with base hits. Both were plated by a screaming line drive that cleared the head of a frantically racing Hamilton. Gettman made the last out. A hard hit sent the ball to shortstop Herman Long, who knocked it down and made the routine toss to first baseman Fred Tenney. Many fans in Washington were happy the season ended. The 55-101 Senators had performed like an imitation of a baseball club.[1]

The steady pitching of Lewis held the Senators to five runs on seven hits; in the process he captured his 26th win of the season. Lewis increased his league-leading winning percentage to .765, an exclamation point to the finest season of his professional career. In the end the Beaneaters dominated in every phase of the game, soundly thumping the Senators, 14-5.

Boston's formidable lineup victimized Kirtley Baker with a 20-hit assault including four doubles and two triples.[2] Each starter collected at least two hits except weak-hitting backup catcher George Yeager, who went hitless. Tenney led the way with four hits, including a triple.[3] Sliding Billy Hamilton and Collins followed with three hits apiece. Hamilton swiped a base and led Boston with three runs scored.

It was the next-to-last home game of the season in Washington, and ladies' day, but, fed up with the home team's incompetence, fans shouted obscenities and other caustic remarks from the stands. One fan quipped, "Say, dose fellas wouldn't never be run in for playing base ball."[4] The fans had plenty to jeer about. Although the home team scorer charged the inept Senators with seven miscues, fans doubted the accuracy. The legitimacy of five or six other balls marked as hits raised questions and eyebrows. Indeed, both box scores from the *Boston Journal*'s W.S. Barnes Jr.'s and the *Boston Globe*'s Tim Murnane showed 11 errors for Washington.[5] All in all, the *Evening Star* of Washington called it "about as sorry a spectacle as could be imagined."[6]

The *Times* of Washington dubbed it "an atrocious burlesque," writing, "The local boys could not have hit a watermelon with a base [sic] fiddle; so far as fielding was concerned, they could not have stopped a rolling pumpkin with a dog catcher's net. … Among the infielders it appeared to be a contest as to which one could outshine the others in rank mishaps."[7] The *Times* box score showed 10 errors for Washington. There was no disagreement over the final score.

Although the Beaneaters hit Baker's offerings all over the field, team malaise did contribute to the one-sidedness of the affair. During the ignominious fourth inning, the Beaneaters did manage to pound out seven hits, but thanks to the abysmal performances of Frank Gatins, Doc Casey, and Jud Smith, five other hitters got on base through fielding lapses. The trio played as though they desired a very short afternoon. The sole error for Boston was captain Duffy's miscue on a catchable soft fly.

The game took two hours.

When the final out was recorded the curtain closed on a very disappointing campaign for Washington. For the Beaneaters, smiles finally emerged. The team had endured another season-long bitter battle with Baltimore. Unlike the nasty final stretch of 1897, this year the team was more entangled with each other throughout the heat of the race. Duffy and other players repeated their motto, "All is forgiven." Winning does cover plenty of sins. And win the Beaneaters did – winning 18 of 21 as the season closed. Handshakes, hugs, and admiration abounded. There were, however, "no antics and no shouts of triumph. It was more a spirit of contentment that pervaded the Boston camp." One player, who was unnamed, averred, "Now we would be happy, if a good-sized check came our way."[8]

Duffy commented, "I think Boston had the greatest team ever organized."[9] The pitching trio, led by Nichols, Willis, and Lewis combined for 82 wins. For Nichols, with 31, it was his third straight year earning 30 or more victories.

The 152 games Boston played in 1898 were 17 games more than in 1897.

The dean of Boston sportswriters, Tim Murnane, commented, "No ball team ever played more earnestly than Boston did this season, and the victory is one more argument for clean, honest baseball. It is a victory that should make New England proud of [Frank] Selee and his men."[10]

NOTES

1 Though the team name was formally the Nationals, newspapers in both Washington and Boston called them the Senators.

2 Some accounts have 19 total hits.

3 Some accounts have two hits.

4 "Boston Is Secure," *Washington Evening Star*, October 12, 1898: 7.

5 W.S. Barnes Jr., "Champions," *Boston Journal*, October 12, 1898: 7.

6 "Boston Is Secure."

7 "A Baseball Burlesque," *Times* (Washington DC), October 12, 1898: 9.

8 Barnes.

9 T.H. Murnane, "Boston Again Champion," *Boston Globe*, October 12, 1898: 9.

10 Ibid.

KID NICHOLS' MASTERFUL 3-HITTER CAPS 10 STRAIGHT SEASONS WITH 21+ VICTORIES

OCTOBER 13, 1899: BOSTON BEANEATERS 1, PHILADELPHIA PHILLIES 0, AT SOUTH END GROUNDS III

BY MIKE HUBER

For 10 straight seasons, one pitcher in the National League was the model of winning consistency: Kid Nichols. During the decade of the '90s (1890s, that is), Nichols won 297 games for the Boston Beaneaters. On October 13, 1899, he won his final game of the decade, marking a record of at least 21 victories per season for 10 consecutive years, causing the *Boston Globe* to headline its account of the game, "Nichols Pitches Best Game of Ball That Has Been Seen for Long Time."[1]

The Beaneaters' right-hander faced off against southpaw Wiley Piatt and the Philadelphia Phillies on the next-to-last day of the season, before a Boston home crowd of about 1,100. This was billed as "the decisive game of the season,"[2] and a "grand game played by crackerjacks, one playing for shekels and the defeated champions still fighting for second place"[3] in the National League. Boston, at 94-56-1, was one game ahead of Philadelphia (93-57-2). The Phillies owner had offered the team $2,500 for a second-place finish.[4] The *Philadelphia Inquirer* called the outcome "one of the most stubbornly contested and brilliantly played games ever played on the Boston or any other diamond."[5] Nichols had won his 20th game on October 4, by a score of 6-4 over the New York Giants, but he lost his next start (the one prior to this game). In 1898, Piatt, playing in his rookie season, had won 24 games for Philadelphia, and he was trying to match that total in this game.

In this masterpiece, Nichols struck out five and walked only one. He displayed "fine speed, sharp curves and a jump to his high ball."[6] All three hits he allowed were singles. His opponent, Piatt, allowed only four hits and no walks. Of the two pitchers, "Nichols was hit far the harder, even if the ball did not roll safely."[7] A few fly balls lingered in the air, aided by the wind, permitting Beaneaters outfielders to catch them.

In the bottom of the sixth inning, Marty Bergen batted with one out and hit a solid double into right field. After Nichols grounded out, Bergen came around to score on a single by Billy Hamilton, who "picked out a good one and shot it past [shortstop Monte] Cross."[8] Hamilton was caught stealing to end the inning. In eight other innings, Boston would get only two other baserunners to second base.

The Phillies had two chances to put a run on the board, and the first came in the fourth inning. Cross drew a base on balls from Nichols, the only free pass of the game, and advanced to second on a sacrifice by Ed Delahanty. A passed ball permitted Cross to scamper to third. Nichols bore down and struck out Pearce

Chiles and Nap Lajoie. The Phillies were then retired in order for four straight innings, but in the ninth, with one out, Elmer Flick singled to center and was forced out at second on a grounder by Cross. That brought up Delahanty, the "leading batsman in the league,"[9] who singled to right field, enabling Cross to motor to third. Delahanty stole second base, and suddenly the Phillies had runners at second and third. Chiles stepped into the batter's box, and after working the count to 2-and-2, he stepped out, called out on strikes. The game was over and Nichols and Boston had secured a 1-0 victory.

The Beaneaters finished the 1899 campaign by winning 14 of their last 20 games, but it was not enough to catch the Brooklyn Superbas, and Boston ended up eight games back, in second place in the National League. Even though they lost the final game of the season, 6-1, to the Phillies, Boston still held a one-game advantage over Philadelphia in the final standings.

The *Globe* wrote that "Charlie Nichols pitched a phenomenal game and was given grand support by the champions."[10] He retired the Phillies in order in six of the nine innings. Nichols had been the star of the Beaneaters for 10 years. As a 20-year-old rookie, he won 27 games and led the league in shutouts with seven. From 1896 to 1898, he won 91 games to lead the league each season in victories. His winning percentage was .663 for this decade. In his first 10 years with Boston, the future Hall of Famer averaged 49 starts and 400 innings pitched per season.[11] Even though the mark of 21 wins seems low in comparison to other seasons, Nichols' ERA of 2.99 was admirable. Further, "Boston's daily newspapers tended to write off his low winning percentages as simple misfortune."[12]

NOTES

1 "Shut Out Again," *Boston Globe*, October 14, 1899: 16.

2 "Phillies Outlucked: Great Pitchers Battle," *Philadelphia Inquirer*, October 14, 1899: 7.

3 "Shut Out Again."

4 "Phillies Outlucked."

5 Ibid.

6 "Shut Out Again."

7 "Phillies Outlucked."

8 "Shut Out Again."

9 Ibid. In 1899, future Hall of Famer Delahanty led the league in average (.410), hits (238), doubles (55), runs batted in (137), and slugging percentage (.582), as well as OPS (1.046).

10 Ibid.

11 From 1890 to 1999, Nichols pitched 3,996⅔ innings.

12 Rich Bogovich, "Kid Nichols," sabr.org/bioproj/person/2ad88b62.

SOURCES

In addition to the sources mentioned in the Notes, the author consulted baseball-reference.com and retrosheet.org. The author sincerely thanks Lisa Tuite of the *Boston Globe* for her assistance with providing sources.

OTHER

HOW BOSTONIANS BECAME THE BEANEATERS

BY MARK SOUDER

An 1890 beanpot medallion.
Collection of Mark Souder.

Most baseball fans, and nonfans for that matter, would consider Beaneaters to be among the most interesting major-league team nicknames with longevity (i.e., multiyear usage as opposed to short-term fad). In 1883 the Boston NL team became unofficially recognized by various sportswriters as the Beaneaters, though like most major-league teams they were generally referred to by their city name.

The Red Stockings (i.e., Red Sox, Reds) nickname began in professional baseball in Cincinnati. The Braves nickname was a gift to Boston by New York City Tammany Boss Charles Murphy's business partner and close ally James Gaffney when he bought the Boston NL team. Unlike the other nicknames,

Beaneaters is the truly original Boston baseball nickname because Boston and beans have long been associated. The nickname evolved informally because Boston was universally recognized as Beantown.[1] Eventually the city promoted itself with assorted symbols of the bean. In fact, they still do as is symbolized by everything from Boston Hard Rock Café beanpot pins to the annual Boston Beanpot Tournament featuring four local college hockey teams.

To understand why the Bostons became the Beaneaters requires some understanding of what is called "bean migration" and how Boston became associated with beans. More specifically, how Boston baked beans became the most geographically identified beans in the world, rivaled only by the lima bean.

WHY ARE BOSTONIANS ASSOCIATED WITH BEANS?

Boston is not the home of beans in the Americas. Bean migration is more about when various beans are noted in print than their actual appearance on earth. In 1551 the term "kidney bean" was first used in England so the English bean wouldn't be confused with common beans from the Americas, such as the lima bean, which migrated into the American colonies from what is believed to be Peru through Guatemalan distributors.[2]

When the first European settlers migrated to the Boston region, the beans had long ago arrived. While beans were not noted in the first "thanksgiving" feast between the natives and the Pilgrims (only venison, fowl, and maize are named), there is little doubt that beans were served, since it was a common staple that accompanied maize in the natives' diet.[3] Beans often get shortchanged in publicity. The Pilgrims soon adopted beans and beanpots as their own, largely for spiritual reasons: They could be prepared on Saturday so cooking did not have be done on their Sabbath Day.

While beans were in Boston before it was Boston, they were everywhere else as well. So how did beans become a worldwide association with the city of Boston? While there were a number of villages named Beantown, the Beantown most often referred to in the nineteenth century was in Maryland. But by the 1880s Boston was referred to as Beantown. Nearby Beverly complained about being neglected since it had the largest beanpot manufacturer, and occasionally had been referred to as the city most associated with beans such as in an 1839 *New Orleans Picayune*, article[4], but it was Boston that had a bean style named after it: Boston baked beans.

Before focusing on how Boston became the bean capital and why in 1883 the media began calling the baseball team the Beaneaters, a bit of bean history further explains an important role of Boston in American history and why Americans across the land easily associated Boston with baked beans. In marketing terms, it is cognitive resonance. In other words, people already associated beans with Boston, thus Boston (including baseball) marketed the term successfully because it already resonated with a logical association.

First one must understand what Boston baked beans are. The essential characteristics of baked beans are white beans, which are baked, including bits of pork, and then are cooked in a sauce of tomato, molasses, and corn syrup – or even maple syrup in the Quebec version. The cooking in the sauce turns the white beans brown. The original Boston version utilized molasses, as did most variations in New England.

While this explains the product, since it was widely produced in New England and Canada, how did Boston become the original focus of the baked beans, so associated with baked beans internationally that Boston baked beans are still a common term regardless of their origin? The simple answer has two parts: Both Boston's port and the related rise of manufacturing, both for canned goods and pottery production.

Long-distance travelers needed to preserve food. France is notable in bean history, as in most gastronomic history. Napoleon is credited with stating that "an army marches on its stomach," though it is attributed by some to Frederick the Great.[5]

What is true for armies, who are generally on land, is even truer for navies. Boston was a vital port in early America, home of the best harbor closest to England. Its importance is illustrated by the frigate Constitution, known as Old Ironsides, the the oldest commissioned naval vessel still afloat, and is preserved in Boston at the old Charlestown Navy Yard.

Beans were a poor man's protein substitute for meat. Meat was often "salt pork" and "dried beef" ("salt beef"). Boston, as the heart of New England, thus became the center for beans as well as cod and dried beef, which could be preserved for seafaring men. New England was also America's original manufacturing center to a large degree because of Boston and other regional ports such as Newport, so materials to store the items as well as cook them also centered on Boston.

The small white beans called haricot beans are the preferred bean for Boston baked beans, though other white beans can be used. Haricot beans are generally referred to as navy beans because of their ubiquitous use by the navy.

Molasses imported to Boston from the Caribbean was the key ingredient that improved the taste of the canned navy beans. Molasses was heavily used for rum, the favored drink of the era. Samuel Adams was an importer, but despite the eponymous beer, it is not clear that Adams brewed beer or rum. But he likely imported molasses and certainly imported malt. Sam Adams was at least a "maltster."[6]

But the real breakthrough was in canning. Boston canneries were the first to invent a can that preserved the beans. (The beanpots were not hard to make.) The key canning firm was Henry Mayo & Co. of Boston, which was the first producer of baked beans in cans (notwithstanding Van Camp's claim).

The company experienced a setback when, after receiving the silver medal for the best baked beans in the world at the Paris World's Fair in 1878, Henry Mayo was awarded a contract from the French government for 100,000 dozen cases. The company attempted to fill it, but the French government canceled the contract and Henry Mayo & Co. was awash in canned goods. It began national advertising, which greatly advanced the close tie of Boston to baked beans, but the firm went belly-up six years later.[7]

The world's first distinctively marine exhibition, the International Maritime Exhibition, was held in Boston in 1889-90. One of the exhibits was by Potter & Wrightington. It featured ship's supplies including "Boston baked beans, Boston brown bread and Boston codfish balls." A publication on the exhibition stated that "the firm of Potter & Wrightington is so old and well-established, and so widely recognized for the superiority of their goods, that they need no introduction to the people of the United States."[8]

An advertising card for Potter & Wrightington Boston Baked Beans (Old South Brand) says, "For SUPERIOR excellence our brand received highest prize at Berlin, 1880, OVER all Boston competitors."[9] A late nineteenth-century ad for Van Camp's of Indianapolis advertises "Boston Baked Pork & Beans" featuring two children each holding a can labeled baked beans. They look as though they could be Pilgrims but are actually Ludwig & Lena, patterned after the German Hansel & Gretel. Though Henry Heinz of Pittsburgh arguably popularized the German craze for baked beans beginning in 1910, Potter & Wrightington of Boston had received the highest prize in Berlin for baked beans 30 years earlier. The point is that identification with Boston was the key to selling pork & beans.

As one tracks bean migration and evolution, the confluence of multiple factors resulted in Boston's international association with baked beans: 1) the rising power of the US Navy; 2) the leadership of Boston in canning as well as pottery firms that led in beanpot manufacturing; 3) Boston bean firms winning major international bean awards beginning at the Paris World's Fair in

1878; and 4) the rising importance of advertising in developing national brands.

The 1890s weren't just glorious years for the Boston Beaneaters in baseball. The years from 1890 to 1907 were the peak years of Boston being the world's bean capital. The bean era of Boston began with the Grand Army of the Republic annual encampment being held in Boston in 1890 and ended with Boston's Old Home Week celebration in 1907.

Any veteran with an honorable discharge from the US military was eligible for membership in the GAR. It was a potent political organization after the Civil War. Five presidents were members of the organization. During the latter part of the nineteenth century the Republican Party refused to run a candidate without the GAR's endorsement.[10]

The annual encampments began in the founding year of 1866. Boston held its first in 1871, when the membership was small. When the GAR next returned to Boston, in 1890, the Civil War Union Colonel Benjamin Harrison was president, and the organization hit its membership peak of 409,489 members.[11] Boston didn't roll out a red carpet, but did present several thousand ornamental beanpots marked "Beverly Pottery" to attendees. E.B. Stillings & Co. sold metal tokens featuring a tag labeled "Dept. Mass. G.A.R" with a beanpot connected by a chain on a card stating that the souvenir was "officially endorsed."[12] There were other variations as well. It further solidified the association of Boston, baked beans, and beanpots across the nation. The items still command significant dollars today among Civil War collectors.

The bean decade of the 1890s was topped off when in 1896 an ornamental beanpot was placed on the top of the clock in the gallery of the Common Council chambers in Boston City Hall.[13]

As the century turned, baked beans and history continued their close association with Boston tourism. Singular or multiple beanpots were included with various Boston sites like Faneuil Hall, Paul Revere's home, and famous churches on postcards mailed by tourists. Functional beanpots were sold, mini-beanpots were tourist collectibles, as were paperweight copper beanpots featuring Faneuil Hall and other scenes.

As the twentieth century began, the GAR was beginning a steep decline in membership as Civil War veterans died and memories became more distant. President William McKinley, assassinated in 1901, was the last of GAR member presidents. Still, the national encampment's return to Boston in 1904 resulted in another proliferation of beanpot souvenirs. It is not insignificant that it is estimated that in 1904 approximately 94 percent of baked beans were still baked at home by housewives in beanpots.[14]

In 1907 the city of Boston held a celebration called Old Home Week marketed mostly to attract former residents. Almost all postcards and city materials featured at least one beanpot, or at least a small beanpot logo stamped on whatever piece of advertising material was utilized.

After 1907 Boston's focus on baked beans had declined enough that in 1908, when the Dovey brothers purchased the Beaneaters and dressed the team in white uniforms, the media nicknamed them the Doves.

Production of canned beans had shifted from Boston as other manufacturers expanded while Boston's declined (e.g., Van Camp's, Heinz, Bush). Nevertheless, Boston did not totally abandon its association with beans. Boston Baked Beans, the candy covered peanuts, were invented in Pittsburgh in the early 1930s but the only connection the candy has with the baked navy beans in molasses is that peanuts and beans are both legumes.[15] In 1993 the Massachusetts Legislature declared the baked navy bean the official bean of Massachusetts.[16] (It is the only state to have an official bean and one of the few to even have a designated state vegetable.) And since the Beanpot college hockey tournament is an annual Boston attraction, the city has not totally lost its beans.

RED STOCKING TO BEANEATER BASE BALL

In 1871, when professional baseball first arrived in Boston, the Paris World's Fair of 1878 was still seven years away and Boston was still getting its promotional "bean legs." Besides, teams were commonly referred to by their city's name, which was featured on the uniform or by the first letter (e.g., "B"). Beyond the name of the city, the teams often were referred to by the color of their stockings. In 1878, for example, the National League was particularly unimaginative. The six teams were the Cincinnati Red Stockings, Boston Red Stockings, Chicago White Stockings, Providence Grays, Milwaukee Grays, and Indianapolis Blues.

The entire "naming" problem beyond America's largest cities (Boston, New York, Brooklyn, Philadelphia, and Chicago) was complicated by the coming and going of teams in every league. A Wolverine would briefly appear and then vanish. Some teams would be named after some variation of the most prominent player or the owners. There were even variations of that phenomenon. For example, when Cap Anson was dropped as the manager of the Chicago team, they were commonly known as the Orphans.

The first Boston baseball nickname, the Red Stockings, is the granddaddy of all baseball names since two teams still carry it: Cincinnati in the National League and Boston in the American League. Writers shortened the names to Reds and Red Sox over the years, but those names still refer back to the Red Stockings. The 1869 Cincinnati Red Stockings were the undefeated champions of baseball. When the club's George and Harry Wright resettled in Boston in 1871, they brought the team's name to the first professional major league, the National Association. The Boston Red Stockings dominated baseball during the National Association era. Cincinnati went back down to club-level amateur ball. The transplanted nickname carried such legendary baseball status that it stuck in Boston, at least until Cincinnati re-emerged as a baseball power.

In 1876, when the National League was founded, both Boston and Cincinnati were the Red Stockings. After the 1880 season, Cincinnati was tossed out of the National League over its failure to support NL policy banning beer and Sunday baseball. (The

Cincinnati Red Stockings re-emerged in 1882 as part of the American Association.)

The NL had a huge problem. While the Providence Grays and Buffalo Bisons were established teams, the Troy Trojans and the Worcester Ruby Legs struggled. The AA had what the NL needed: New York, Brooklyn, Philadelphia, St. Louis, Cincinnati, and Pittsburgh.

The Cincinnati Red Stockings of 1882 compiled the highest winning percentage of any Cincinnati team in history, including the Big Red Machine of the 1970s. They were again the dominant Red Stockings.

The year 1882 is a bit confusing in Boston baseball nickname history: Some historians refer to the team as the Red Stockings, but a few cite Red Caps as an alternative name. A Cincinnati newspaper made a Boston Bean-eaters reference in May 1880, though it attached it to the entire city in a headline after an earthquake shook the Boston area.[17]

In June 1880 the *Chicago Inter-Ocean* noted that "two bean-eaters died at home plate," referring to baserunners in a Cleveland-Boston game.[18] In 1881 and 1882, the *Cincinnati Enquirer* often called the Boston baseball team the "bean-eaters." The *Detroit Free Press* also began using the Bean-eater nickname to refer to the Boston team.[19]

What is clear is that after Cincinnati's dominant AA championship season of 1882, Boston abandoned the Red Stockings nickname the Wrights had brought with them from Cincinnati.

Newspapers increasingly referred to them as the Beaneaters since not only had Cincinnati powerfully re-emerged with the moniker Red Stockings, but then joined the NL in 1890. The Red Stockings (e.g., Reds) name was also claimed by Boston teams in the Players' League (1890) and the championship Boston franchise in the AA beginning in 1891 (once Cincinnati had joined the NL). While modern marketers utilize the nickname Beaneaters on baseball cards, uniforms, and other materials, the nickname does not seem to appear in primary sources other than in news coverage or informal references. Perhaps it was because the nickname was not universally adored.

In 1882, as Boston baseball transitioned to Beaneaters, a headline on the front page of the *New York Tribune* exclaimed: "Shooting His Companion Because He Was Called A 'Boston Bean-Eater.'" The word was not intended as a compliment. The article began: "A shooting affray that came near to a fatal termination for one of the participants and endangered the lives of many people not engaged in it …" Two men, referred to as "confidence men" and apparently intoxicated, began arguing when the New Yorker referred to the Bostonian as a "Boston bean-eater." The reporter noted that when the Boston man "fully comprehended the meaning of those words, he shifted his stick into his left hand while with the right hand drew a large revolver and fired with a deliberate aim at the gray-haired, bare-headed man."[20]

If this were the end of this story, it would be fascinating enough, but it dragged on as a mini-press war between the two cities that was enjoyed in faraway places. A story a month later in distant Jamestown, North Dakota, quoted the *Boston Journal* as responding to the New York media by asserting that the shooter "may at some time have lived in Boston, but he was not – could not have been a Bostonian in the deepest and most glorious meaning of the word. Clearly a man who considers himself insulted by being called a 'bean eater' can have none of the commendable local pride which distinguishes the citizens of this favored metropolis."[21]

Because beans were used as a cheaper, healthy substitute for meat, the term was used as both descriptive and a derogatory reference to the poor. It also could be used to convey that a person was "cheap," substituting beans for meat when they could have afforded meat. Had the term come from a *Puck* satire, baseball historians might have assumed that the Beaneaters were named after penny-pinching Beaneater owner Arthur Soden.

And then there is the rather uncomfortable issue of flatulence. While it provided some occasional sarcasm from newspaper writers, the fact is that other alternative Boston names associated with the city would also have been uncomfortable at times. The early canners who made baked beans famous were also known for clam chowder and fishballs. The Boston Chowderheads or Boston Fish Balls would not have improved the situation. Had they chosen to be named after a product of co-owner William Conant's factory, the Boston Hoopskirts would have provided much mirth.

When Beaneaters was emerging in 1883 as the universal nickname for the Boston baseball team, Boston baked beans were rising in their national fame. Boston firms won awards for their baked beans in Paris in 1878 and Berlin in 1880. The first widespread advertising of baked beans had recently begun. The baseball team nickname did not occur as an isolated event but rather simultaneously with Boston merchants' promotional push for Boston baked beans.

How much the name change to Beaneaters inspired the Boston team to greater success in 1883 is debatable but they posted a 63-35 record and won the championship of the National League. To quote Johnny Cash's song, "I know if papa was here right now he'd sure be pleased, And papa, if you can hear me look at them beans."[22]

With all due respect to the Boston Red Sox' transplanted Cincinnati name and the Boston Braves' borrowed symbol from New York's Tammany Hall, there is no more appropriate name for a Boston team than the Beaneaters. If being a beaneater was good enough for the world boxing champion, it was good enough for baseball. In 1882 a bout between American boxing champion John L. Sullivan (also known as the Boston Strong Boy) and English champion Tug Wilson was headlined "Bean-Eater and Briton."[23]

It was also politically correct. The 1907 celebration of Boston Old Home Week, which featured Boston baked beans and beanpots in most promotions, was planned and staged when the Boston mayor was John F. Fitzgerald, aka Honey Fitz. He was later chairman of the Boston Royal Rooters and the grandfather of John Fitzgerald Kennedy. Honey Fitz clearly was a bean man. There can be no clearer Bostonian political stamp of approval than that.

NOTES

1. "It is for baked beans that Boston came to be known as Bean Town. The Puritan Sabbath lasted from sundown on Saturday until sundown on Sunday, and baked beans provided the Puritans with a dish that was easy to prepare. The bean pot could be kept over a slow heat in a fireplace to serve at Saturday supper and Sunday breakfast. Housewives too busy with other chores were able to turn the baking of the beans over to a local baker. The baker called each Saturday morning to pick up the family's bean pot and take it to the community oven, usually in the cellar of a nearby tavern. The free-lance baker then returned the beans with a bit of brown bread on Saturday evening or Sunday morning." Brett Howard, *Boston: A Social History* (New York: Hawthorn Books Inc., 1976), 126-127.

2. Maricel A. Presilla, "Lima Beans' History is Ancient, Exalted," *Pittsburgh Post-Gazette*, July 1, 2007. post-gazette.com/food/2007/07/11/Lima-beans-history-is-ancient-exalted/stories/200707110267; aggiehorticulture.tamu.edu/archives/parsons/publications/vegetabletravelers/beans.html.

3. Megan Gambino, "What Was on the Menu at the First Thanksgiving?," Smithsonian.com, November 21, 2011. smithsonianmag.com/history/what-was-on-the-menu-at-the-first-thanksgiving-511554/.

4. "Out of Beans, or the Half Mast Flag," *New Orleans Times Picayune*, June 20, 1839: 2.

5. oxfordreference.com/view/10.1093/oi/authority.20110803095425331.

6. "11 Things You Probably Didn't Know About Sam Adams," mentalfloss.com, n.d. mentalfloss.com/article/60927/11-things-you-probably-didnt-know-about-sam-adams.

7. Roger M. Grace, "Cans of Baked Beans Produced on Mass Scale in 1878," *Metropolitan News-Enterprise* (Los Angeles). The silver medal note is on a Henry Mayo & Co advertising card owned by the author.

8. John W. Ryckman, compiler and editor, *International Maritime Exhibition, Boston, 1889-90*, Press of Rockwell and Churchill, 325.

9. "Old South Brand Baked Beans, Potter & Wrightington; Packers of Canned Fish, Poultry, Beans, Soups &c., 197 Atlantic Ave. & 118 to 128 Commerce St., Boston, Mass." Advertising card with drawing and additional copy on the reverse side (author's collection), date unknown but does note, "For Superior excellence our brand received highest prize at Berlin, 1880, OVER all Boston competitors."

10. https://ohiohistorycentral.org/w/Grand_Army_of_the_Republic. Accessed November 20, 2019.

11. http://www.treasurenet.com/forums/civil-war/73486-national-encampments-grand-army-republic.html. Accessed November 20, 2019.

12. Card: "Officially endorsed by Dept. Mass. G.A.R.; E. B. Stillings & Co., Sole Manufacturers, 55 Sudbury Street, Boston." Attached is a small metal badge with "Dept. Mass. G.A.R." on it with small chains holding a beanpot labeled "Beans" (author's collection).

13. http://www.celebrateboston.com/architecture/old-city-hall.htm . Accessed November 20, 2019.

14. Jeffrey L. Cruikshank and Arthur W. Schultz, *The Man Who Sold America* (Boston: Harvard Business Review Press, 2010), 101.

15. Marjorie from Missouri, "Boston Baked Beans," oldtimecandy.com, n.d. oldtimecandy.com/walk-the-candy-aisle/boston-baked-beans/.

16. https://statesymbolsusa.org/symbol-official-item/massachusetts/state-food-agriculture-symbol/baked-navy-bean . Accessed November 20, 2019.

17. "Boston Bean-eaters Shaken by an Earthquake," *Cincinnati Daily Star*, May 14, 1880: 1.

18. "Boston vs. Cleveland," *Inter Ocean* (Chicago), June 29, 1880: 8.

19. For example, in 1881 the *Cincinnati Enquirer* used Bean-eaters for the Boston NL team in May, June, July, and August. Examples in 1882 include "May 1st will settle Wise's career as a Boston bean-eater," section titled "Base-Ball," *Cincinnati Enquirer*, April 23, 1882: 13, and "Boston Bean-Eaters Down the New Yorkers," *Cincinnati Enquirer*, April 25, 1882. Other newspapers had also begun referring to the Boston team as the bean-eaters: a front-page headline in the *Detroit Free Press* on May 2, 1882, proclaimed that "The Bisons, Bean-eaters and Clam-eaters Beat Chicago, Worcester and Troy." "Clam-eaters" refers to the Providence team, generally referred to as the Providence Grays. This is a great example of the fluidity of team nicknames.

20. "A Quarrel Between Confidence Men," *New York Tribune*, November 13, 1882: 1.

21. *Jamestown* (North Dakota) *Weekly Alert*, December 8, 1882: 6.

22. Concluding lyrics of the song "Look at Them Beans" from the Johnny Cash album *Look at Them Beans*, 1975.

23. "Bean-Eater and Briton," *Black Hills Weekly Times*, Deadwood, South Dakota, July 22, 1882: 1.

SLIDE, KELLY, SLIDE

BY JOANNE HULBERT

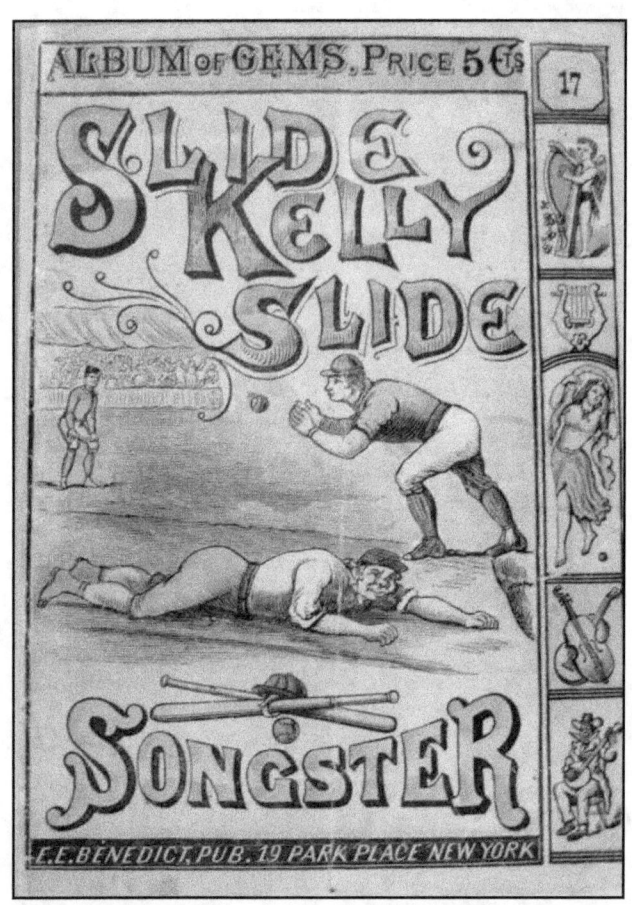

(Public domain)

About 3,000 people were present at the Brotherhood Base Ball Grounds when the championship pennant for 1890 was presented to the Boston Club. Colonel Charles H. Taylor made the presentation speech, complimenting the team upon the high standard of their work during the season. Mike Kelly received the pennant, made no set speech, and immediately hoisted the banner while the band played the music of "Slide, Kelly, Slide." A five-inning game was played by the champions and the New York Club. Boston featured all three of their batteries, while O'Day and William Brown pitched and caught for New York throughout the game.[1]

> I played a game of base-ball, I belong to Casey's nine,
>
> The crowd was feeling jolly, and the weather it was fine;
>
> A nobler lot of players I think were never found,
>
> When the omnibuses landed that day upon the ground.
>
> The game was quickly started, they sent me to the bat,
>
> I made two strikes, says Casey, "What are you striking at?"
>
> I made the third, the catcher muffed and to the ground it fell,
>
> I run like a divil to first base, when the gang began to yell.[2]

Mike "King" Kelly need not say any words to the assembled audience. The song said it all for him. A song that despite its seemingly admonishing tone reflected the regard the cranks held for this player who embodied all the good – and sometimes the less reputable side – of the national pastime, and he had captured the affection of another man who owned the Kelly name.

(Chorus)

Slide, Kelly, slide, your running's a disgrace,

Slide, Kelly, slide, stay there, hold your base;

If some one doesn't steal you and your batting doesn't fail you,

They'll take you to Australia, slide, Kelly, slide.[3]

How the song came to be written brings up the history of another Kelly – James W. Kelly, an Irish comedian and author of popular songs during the last decades of the nineteenth century. He was born in Philadelphia in 1854 and was called "a mirth provoker."[4] He was described as "having a wonderfully expressive face, a musical voice of limited range, which he knew how to use to the best advantage, and that mother wit, said to be one of the distinguishing traits of the Celtic race, from which he sprang. Though not a musician, he had a natural ear for melody, and composed the airs of all his own songs."[5] Parodies were his most reliable formula, and he carried over themes and cadences that ended up in other of his renditions. Why he was so smitten with King Kelly could be chalked up to being his namesake, or King Kelly deserved a stirring ballad to complement his outsized image on the baseball diamond. King Kelly needed no introduction to the cranks across the country. "Slide, Kelly, Slide" immediately became a favorite on the vaudeville circuit and was also a financial gold mine for the publisher, Frank Harding, who purchased James Kelly's interest in it. Harding published 27,000 copies of the words and music, and Henry Wehman, the Park Row publisher who secured the right to print the words, sold 40,000 copies of it. James Kelly probably made more money out of this composition than any of his other popular songs.[6] At the height of his career, James W. Kelly was the highest-paid performer on the variety stage, receiving as much as $400 per week. The Boston Vaudeville Club paid him regularly $100 for a single performance. Unfortunately he did not possess many frugal habits – "being a hail fellow well met, his large earnings were dissipated with the rapidity with which they were made."[7] He died on June 26, 1896, at his mother's home in New York City of an attack of acute gastritis at the age of 42.

'Twas in the second inning they called me in, I think,

To take the catcher's place while he went to get a drink;

But something was the matter, sure I couldn't see the ball,

And the second one that came I broke my muzzle, nose and all.

The crowd up in the grand stand they yelled with all their might;

I ran towards the club house, I thought there was a fight;

'Twas the most unpleasant feeling I ever felt before,

I knew they had me rattled when the gang began to roar:[8]

(Chorus)

James Kelly wrote 15 comic songs. His most popular along with "Slide, Kelly, Slide" were "Come Down, Mrs. Flynn" and "Throw Him Down, McCloskey," a ballad that celebrated a popular boxer of the time and the chorus of this song hinted at the rhythm and cadence of his most famous song:

"Throw him down, McCloskey," was to be his battle cry –

Throw him down, McCloskey, you can lick him if you try,

And future generations, with wonder and delight,

Will read on histr'y's pages of the great McCloskey fight.[9]

The tragic demise of King Kelly in 1894 and also that of James W. Kelly in 1896 did not spell the end of the song. The cranks kept up the chorus "Slide, Kelly, slide!" at baseball games. Soon the phrase found its way into the American slang dictionary – another addition bequeathed by baseball. The phrase turned up in odd and interesting places. An apocryphal tale relates that as King Kelly was carried into a Boston hospital on a stretcher that toppled over, tossing him to the ground, he weakly lamented, "This is my last slide."[10]

Ultimately, any person with the name Kelly was fair game to have the phrase used to their advantage. Any report of icy sidewalks or any warning of uncertain footedness conjured up the warning: 'Slide, Kelly, slide!" Fred C. Kelly, a *Cleveland Plain Dealer* columnist, wrote about the burden the name Kelly placed upon him, and how it soured him on playing baseball as everyone insisted he "slide!" – when he didn't want to.[11] But what was it that connected Mike King Kelly with the "slide"? The story and the legend of Mike Kelly lived on long after his death. James J. Corbett, in his syndicated column "In Corbett's Corner," reminisced in 1919 about Kelly and his connection to the slide. Corbett called it a stunt, that Kelly had perfected the head-first slide, a tactic that was considered either brave or foolhardy, and was discouraged by managers as potentially injurious.[12]

In 1907 at a preseason meeting in New York City, a new rule was adopted that if one baserunner passed another in an attempt to score while the other was being "tagged" out, the runner who passed would be declared out – all this thanks to an incident made famous by Mike Kelly. The new rule was calculated to prevent such stunts as the world-renowned slide pulled off by Kelly when he was a member of the Chicago team during a game in Boston in 1885.

"It happened in the last half of the ninth inning, when the score stood 1 to 0 against Chicago. Kelly was on first base and Ed Williamson was on second, and Anson knocked a fly ball out into right field. At the instant the fielder caught the ball both Kelly and Williamson made a dash for second and third. The ball was simply returned to the second baseman, but Kelly slid in and beat it by a hair. When Kelly arose from the ground and saw Billy Sunday at bat, he grabbed his arm, and pretending to be writhing in agony, he signaled to the umpire to call time. Then he called to Ed Williamson to come and pull his arm. While Ed was doing so, Kelly whispered to him as follows: "Say, Ed, when the pitcher throws the ball in, I'm going to start for third. This will draw the ball down to catch me, and then you make a dash for the plate and I'll be right behind you. By the time you get near the plate the catcher will be waiting for you with the ball, but get as near as you can to the plate, then open your legs wide and I will try to slide in."¹³ At the appointed time Kelly dashed for third. The ball was shot down to that base, and then Ed made for home, while the third baseman sent the ball back to the catcher. Kelly by this time had rounded third and was right behind Williamson, for whom the catcher was waiting with outstretched arms. When within a few feet of the plate, Williamson halted, suddenly spread his legs wide apart, and as the catcher jumped forward to tag Ed, Kelly slid between Williamson's legs and had his fingers on the plate before the catcher knew what had happened. Chicago made another run in the 10th inning, and this won the game.¹⁴

Kelly turned to the crowd and shouted: "It's all over! The game's won! You can't get it back! Open the gates and go home!"¹⁵ He laughed, and at first the crowd was enraged and protested he didn't touch third base. Sam Wise yelled, "He cut the bag by 5 yards!" But then a great cheer arose from the crowd of 10,000 for the trickiest ballplayer who ever walked the diamond. This trick was original with Kelly, and many players have since tried it.¹⁶

As baseball stories go, the tale of Kelly's slide spread across the land. The feat quickly became material for the song, as no one had ever heard of such a ploy to score a run, but James W. Kelly saw a lucrative opportunity by exploiting that move and the phrase and song "Slide, Kelly, Slide!" live on forever in baseball history.

> They sent me out to centre-field, I didn't want to go,
>
> The way my nose was swelling up, I must have been a show;
>
> They said on me depended victory or defeat,
>
> If a "blind man was to look on us, he'd know that we were beat.
>
> Sixty-four to nothing was the score when we got done,
>
> And everybody there but me said they had lots of fun;
>
> The news got home ahead of me, they heard I was knocked out,
>
> The neighbors carried me in the house, and then began to shout:¹⁷
>
> Slide, Kelly, slide, your running's a disgrace,
>
> Slide, Kelly, slide, stay there, hold your base;
>
> If some one doesn't steal you and your batting doesn't fail you,
>
> They'll take you to Australia, slide, Kelly, slide.¹⁸

NOTES

1 "Mike Kelly Receives the Pennant," *Philadelphia Inquirer*, October 12, 1890: 3.

2 "Slide, Kelly, Slide." Copyright, 1889, Frank Harding. Words and Music by J.W. Kelly.

3 Ibid.

4 "Exit J.W. Kelly, the Famous Rolling Mill-Man Responds to the Final Call," *Philadelphia Inquirer*, June 27, 1896: 1.

5 Ibid.

6 "John W. Kelly's Songs," *Duluth News-Tribune*, July 7, 1896: 6.

7 "Exit J.W. Kelly," *Philadelphia Inquirer*, October 12, 1890: 3.

8 "Slide, Kelly, Slide."

9 "John W. Kelly's Songs."

10 "Greatest of All," *Oregonian* (Portland), December 29, 1907: 7.

11 Fred C. Kelly, "The Burden of a Name," *Cleveland Plain Dealer*, August 23, 1911: 4.

12 James J. Corbett, "In Corbett's Corner," *Macon (Georgia) Telegraph*, January 19, 1919: 10.

13 "Runners Did Not Pass Each Other," *St. Louis Post-Dispatch*, April 5, 1907: 16.

14 "Kelly's Slide Home," *Dallas Morning News*, March 31, 1907.

15 "How Kelly Cut Third," *Philadelphia Inquirer*, July 18, 1897: 18.

16 Ibid.

17 "Slide, Kelly, Slide."

18 Ibid.

1897: LAST GASP OF THE TEMPLE CUP

BY BILL FELBER

The 1897 Temple Cup series opened on October 4 in Boston exactly one week after the conclusion of the two teams' dramatic pennant-deciding series. The Beaneaters had won that series, which was played in Baltimore, two games to one, taking the third and deciding game in front of an estimated 30,000 spectators.

But because the Cup series was by then widely viewed as more an exhibition than a true championship contest, enthusiasm waned quickly among fans of the competing entries. In part this reflected leaguewide questions regarding the importance of the Cup. In two of three previous iterations, the runner-up had defeated the League champion, the only exception being the 1896 Orioles, who beat runner-up Cleveland. Rumors of pot-splitting, effectively watering down teams' motivation to win, also damaged credibility.

In both 1895 and 1896, responding to the growing sense of disinterest, Chicago owner James Hart had introduced a motion at the League's winter meeting to terminate the competition and return the Cup to its donor, William Temple, a Pittsburgh businessman.

Boston fans who attended the series opener on October 4 at the South End Grounds had little motivation to look forward to the series. Their team, after all, had already won what was perceived to be the defining test, the regular-season championship. Still, an estimated 10,000 showed up that Monday afternoon, most apparently motivated by a desire to salute the new champions.

What those fans saw was a far cry from the championship enthusiasm the two teams had so recently displayed against each other. The clubs combined for six errors, eventually leading to several unearned runs In the next morning's *Globe*, longtime writer and former player Tim Murnane described it as "a weak affair."[1] Boston ace Kid Nichols, a 31-game regular-season winner, pitched listlessly for six innings, allowing 14 Orioles hits. But Baltimore's Jerry Nops was equally bad. In gathering darkness, the Beaneaters scored the tying and go-ahead runs in the bottom of the eighth and won 13-12.

The relatively dissolute play appeared to turn off fan bases already predisposed against investing emotionally in the series. One sure intimation that the contestants were not investing their hardest labors came when Beaneaters manager Frank Selee declared Nichols out for the remainder of the series. The next afternoon, only 6,000 took the trouble to watch Orioles ace Joe Corbett meet Boston's Fred Klobedanz.

Like the first game, it was a loosely played affair. The two teams combined for 33 hits and numerous errors. The teams traded six-run innings in midgame, and Corbett proved his own best offensive friend, delivering four hits. Heinie Reitz's fifth-inning home run knocked Klobedanz out and lightly-used veteran Jack Stivetts finished up.

If any enthusiasm for the series remained in Boston after that second-game defeat, it was fully drained early in Wednesday's third game. Only about 5,000 bothered to attend, watching the Orioles take a quick 8-0 lead and win 8-3 in a game called after seven innings because of darkness.

Editors of the *Globe* effectively captured the increasing ennui surrounding the event even in the Boston baseball hotbed, eliminating front-page coverage and consigning its reporting to the middle of the fifth page in smaller headline type than it gave Harvard's victory over Bowdoin. "Rather Tired," the headline writer wrote of the performance, which included nine bases on balls to Baltimore batters. Said Murnane, "The long season's grind has told on the boys and they seem anxious to quit."[2]

In an effort to pick up some spare change, the two teams played exhibitions in Worcester and Springfield, Massachusetts, on their way down to Baltimore to resume the series on Saturday, October 9. The Orioles won both those games as well. When they arrived at Baltimore's Union Grounds, however, they found enthusiasm far, far less intense than it had been for the concluding game of the regular season's decisive series less than two weeks earlier. The *Baltimore Sun* barely took notice of the series' resumption on game day and devoted just six inside paragraphs to a story played midway down the sports page the following Monday (with no edition on Sunday).

Another dozen unearned runs, created by a half-dozen errors, marred the fourth game, which was decided when Baltimore tapped Boston starter Stivetts for a half-dozen runs in the first inning and five more in the second. The Orioles eventually won 12-11 before what was merely described as a "small" crowd.

That put Baltimore in position to clinch retention of the Cup by taking the series' fifth game on Monday, October 11. As if anybody cared; only an estimated 700 Baltimoreans showed up to take in the potential decisive game. Baltimore broke a 2-2 tie with three runs in the third inning and breezed home behind Wizard Hoffer, 9-3. As in previous games, Boston's absence of true investment in the outcome could be seen on the mound, where manager Frank Selee entrusted pitching duties for the "do or die" game to Charlie Hickman and Jim Sullivan. Hickman was a 21-year-old rookie with a total of 7⅔ innings of mound work under his belt; Sullivan had gone 4-5 in 13 appearances during the regular season.

Among those less than enchanted with the play was the cup's donor, William Temple. Informed of the result, he asked the League to investigate "the charges that the Baltimore and Boston players this year agreed to an equal division of the receipts in face of the League's explicit conditions about 60 percent to the winner and 40 percent to the loser." If chicanery was uncovered, he added, "I shall ask that the offenders be blacklisted."[3]

The *Sun*'s reporter all but conceded the truth of Temple's allegation. "It is pretty certain … that most, if not all, the players on both sides privately made such an arrangement among themselves," the reporter asserted.[4]

League officials ignored Temple's demand for an inquiry. But one month later at that winter's annual meeting, faced with the obvious and growing lack of interest in the event, they voted 10 to 2 to terminate the Cup series and return the trophy to Temple.

NOTES

1 T.H. Murnane, "One of Them," *Boston Globe*, October 5, 1897: 8.
2 T.H. Murnane, "Rather Tired," *Boston Globe*, October 7, 1897: 5.
3 "Mr. Temple's 'Kick,'" *Baltimore Sun*, October 13, 1897: 6.
4 Ibid.

KING KELLY'S FUNERAL

BY PETER M. GORDON

On November 9, 1894, the *Boston Globe* reported, "At 9:55 PM last night, King Kelly heard the decision of the Great Umpire from which there is not appeal."[1] The best loved ballplayer of the nineteenth century was dead.

Even after he retired from major-league baseball in 1893, Mike "King" Kelly was arguably America's biggest sports star. He was the first ballplayer to have a hit song ("Slide, Kelly, Slide") written about him. Some writers believe Kelly was the model for the Mighty Casey in the poem "Casey at the Bat." Baseball Hall of Fame historian Lee Allen said, "Kelly was, in his day, as popular a figure as Babe Ruth would later be, and there was hardly a boy in the land who did not follow the daily doings of The King."[2]

When Kelly was at his peak, he was the highest-paid player in the game. He bragged that he would never be a pauper. However, by November 1894, one year after his retirement and after spending a year playing for a minor-league team in Allentown, Pennsylvania, the King was broke. A *Boston Globe* reporter wrote, "[H]is money went like the mist before a noonday sun, for it came easy and he thought it would last."[3]

The Cincinnati Reds signed Kelly in 1878. He had his first great year for the Reds in 1879, batting .348, but the financially-stripped club released all its players after the season. Albert Spalding and Cap Anson brought Kelly to Chicago to join the White Stockings for the 1880 season. In Chicago Kelly became a national star, soon called "King" Kelly or "The Only" Kelly. His fans lived in every city. Kelly's Irish heritage helped him become particularly popular in Boston. In 1887 the Boston franchise payed the princely sum of $10,000 to bring Kelly to Boston.

Kelly also managed the Boston entry in the short-lived Player's League.

In 1893 an out-of-shape and 34-year-old Kelly managed to play only 20 games for the New York Giants. It's fair to say that his lack of playing time and diminishing skills didn't diminish the great affection of Kelly's fans.

When Kelly was at the height of his fame as a ballplayer he made extra money during the offseason by appearing in stage shows and vaudeville. Kelly loved attending the theater and enjoyed the company of actors almost as much as he did other ballplayers during his storied career.

Kelly's Boston fans loved him, and producers expected them to turn out in great numbers to see him on stage. Kelly needed money to support his wife, baby boy, and lavish lifestyle. In 1894 acting offered Kelly the only reasonable opportunity to earn a salary approaching what he earned in baseball.

Kelly took a ship from New York City to Boston to start his tour. Cold winds blew and snow fell during his trip. Kelly walked the deck in this weather. He felt sympathy for a stowaway discovered by the crew, and Kelly gave his best suit to the ship's bursar as security to cover the man's fare. Over time, stories grew that Mike gave that stowaway his winter coat, which left Kelly with no defense against the snow and cold winds that assailed the boat as it sailed from New York to Boston.[4]

During his life Kelly was famous for his generosity, even to strangers. As Cap Anson, Kelly's White Stockings manager, said, "He was a whole-souled, genial fellow, with a host of friends, and but one enemy, that one being himself."[5]

Losing control of his best suit should not have significantly impaired Kelly's health. Even his famed drinking would not have brought on pneumonia. Still, one can imagine a drunk Kelly roaming the deck of his ship in a snowstorm, forgetting to button his winter coat or perhaps not even wearing one. After all, Mike Kelly never thought anything bad would happen to him.

No matter what the cause, Kelly took ill on the passage. When he arrived in Boston, he was too ill to appear on stage. He rested at a friend's house, hoping the chills and fever would go away. When they did not, Kelly's friends summoned Dr. George Galvin, former team doctor for the Beaneaters. He saw Kelly at 2 P.M. on Sunday, November 4, and found he had difficulty breathing. By 4 P.M. on Monday, it was clear that pneumonia had set in, and Galvin moved Kelly to Boston's Emergency Hospital. It was reported that when Kelly came to the hospital the stretcher carrying him slipped to the floor, and he said, "This is my last slide."[6]

Doctors gave Kelly oxygen. News organizations around the country kept his fans updated on his condition. On Wednesday many papers reported that he was improving. Despite the encouraging reports, Dr. Galvin contacted Kelly's wife, Agnes, to tell her to hurry to Boston. Agnes had friends and family watch their four-month-old baby and took the first train she could. She thought she was coming to help nurse her husband to health, and was astonished to find out when she arrived on Friday, November 9, that Kelly was gone.

As a reporter from the *Boston Evening Record* put it, "[H]is mind had been wandering all day."[7] Father Hickey from St. James Catholic Church administered the last rites. Around 6 P.M. on Thursday, Kelly roused himself to say, "Well, I guess this is the last trip."[8] Kelly lingered until 9:55 P.M., and then died.

A former teammate, the evangelist Billy Sunday, did not attend the funeral, but for years afterward in his temperance sermons would say Kelly "died a drunkard and was buried in a pauper's grave."[9] While it was true that Kelly died a pauper, he was not buried in a pauper's grave. Kelly was an Elk, and the Boston chapter of the Benevolent and Protective Order of the Elks made sure he was laid to rest in style.

Elks chapter members who wanted to remain anonymous paid the stowaway's fare to the steamship company and recovered Mike's best suit to bury him in.[10] They felt it was important to send Kelly out in the style that he lived – in his best clothes, in front of a large audience.

They succeeded. Kelly's body lay in state at the Boston Elks Hall on Sunday, November 11. Admirers sent so many flowers, according to the *Boston Globe*, that only "a narrow path" could be excavated to allow mourners to view the body.[11] Playwright Charles Hoyt and vaudevillian Eddie Foy sent wreaths. Cap Anson sent a pillow of roses, as did the members of the Actors Protective Union. Albert G. Spalding, owner of the White Stockings during Kelly's greatest years there, did not attend, but sent a white flower arrangement in the shape of a baseball with violets representing the laces. Reporting on the "grand" flower arrangements filled many column-inches in the Boston papers that week.

Over 5,000 mourners filed through the rooms of the Elks Hall to pay their last respects to their baseball hero. Thousands more stood in the street outside St. James Church when Kelly's funeral Mass was conducted later that day. The crowd in the streets was so large that carriage drivers found it difficult to drop mourners close to the church for the funeral. The crowds spilled back from the church steps down Heyward Place and Washington Street as far as anyone could see. Not a few women and children, and many men in the crowd, wept.

The *Boston Post* reported the day after the funeral, "Safe at Home is Michael J. Kelly. ... Now the sturdy form that used to electrify the crowds at the ball grounds are but memories." The *Post* reporter described the lines of fans waiting to view Kelly's body as a "never ending procession."[12]

Sweet-scented flowers surrounded Kelly's casket in the Elks lodge and on the way to the burial. Father Hickey, who had administered Kelly's last rites, led the Mass. Kelly's widow, Agnes, and his brother "Honest John" Kelly were the only family members who attended. Pallbearers included Beaneaters manager Frank Selee, Captain William M. "Billy" Nash, and players Tommy McCarthy and Hugh Duffy. Cincinnati's Morgan Murphy, F.L. "Red" Donahue from Kelly's last team, the Allentowns, and Elks Charles A. Kelly and Dennis P. Sullivan also came. Other attendees included Andy Leonard, a member of the 1869 Red Stockings, Boston players Herman Long, P.H. "Cozy" Dolan, and Fred Doe, Baltimore Orioles star Joe Kelley, and former stars Tommy Bond and Harry Schafer.

So many floral tributes filled the nave of the church that it took one large open wagon and two carriages to transport all the flowers to the burial. It was a closed-casket funeral. A large photo of Kelly in his prime sat on top of the coffin.

Fans also lined the streets on the way to Mount Hope cemetery. Several sources estimated the crowd outside the church and on the way to the cemetery at 7,000, which made Kelly's funeral one of the largest for any major-league star before Babe Ruth's in 1948. When the procession reached the grave site, Boston Elks Exalted Ruler William H. Blossom conducted the Elks funeral rituals with Leading Knight Sidney Sprague and chaplain John Waterman.

The hymn "Simple Yet Beautiful" was sung. Elk Tom Henry played "The Lost Cloud" on the coronet while the casket was lowered into the earth. Five thousand people who followed the procession stood and watched the funeral rites with uncovered heads.[13]

One week after the funeral, on November 18, the *Boston Post* announced the formation of the Kelly Fund, to raise money for Kelly's family.

Kelly left her nothing, and she had no means of support. The *Boston Globe* reported that the fund had raised $372 as of that day, including a $25 gift from DeWolf Hopper, famous for his vaudeville recitations of "Casey at the Bat," and a $10 gift from

Connie Mack. That amount was less than half of what Kelly earned in a month at his peak, but at least it was something.[14]

Agnes returned to Paterson, New Jersey, where her money soon ran out. She supported herself as a seamstress until her eyes went bad. A sister who lived in New Brunswick took her in, and Agnes lived with her sister until her death in 1937. It's not clear what happened to her son. This writer was unable to find a record of him outside of the mentions in contemporary accounts. It's probable that the baby died before adulthood; it's hard to believe he would have let his mother move in with a sister had he lived into the twentieth century and could support her.[15]

Kelly's fine funeral would remain the last ceremony the baseball world would give him. When he was elected to the Baseball Hall of Fame in 1944, because of World War II no induction ceremony was held. (An induction ceremony was held in 2013 for Kelly and others who never received a formal induction because of the wartime restrictions.

SOURCES

In addition to the sources cited in the Notes, the author also consulted:

Appel, Marty. *Slide, Kelly, Slide: The Wild Life and Times of Mike "King" Kelly* (Lanham, Maryland: Scarecrow Press, 1996).

Kelly, Mike "King." *Play Ball, Stories of the Ball Field* (Boston: Emery & Hughes, 1888, issued digitally in 2008).

Thorn, John. *Baseball in the Garden of Eden: The Secret History of the Early Game* (New York: Simon & Schuster, 2011).

Tiemann Robert L., and Mark Rucker, editors. *Nineteenth Century Stars: 2012 Edition* (Phoenix: SABR, 2012).

The Hall of Fame file on King Kelly contains a great deal of contemporaneous accounts of his career and funeral.

Thanks to the Baseball Hall of Fame Library and the Boston Public Library.

NOTES

1. "Death of Kelly," *Boston Globe*, November 9, 1894: 1.
2. baseballhall.org/hof/kelly-king.
3. "Funeral Report," *Boston Globe*, November 12, 1894: 5.
4. Joe Buchicio, *The Evangelist* (Albany, New York): 10A. Undated article from Kelly's Hall of Fame file.
5. Adrian "Cap" Anson, *A Ball Player's Career* (Chicago: Era Publishing, 1900), 115-116.
6. James A. Cox, "When Fans Roared 'Slide, Kelly, slide!' at the Old Ball Game," *Smithsonian Magazine*, October 1982, 130.
7. *Boston Evening Record,* November 9, 1894.
8. *Boston Post*, November 10, 1894: 3.
9. Joe Vila, "Setting the Pace," from Mike Kelly's Hall of Fame file – no page or publication listed.
10. Joe Buchicio, *The Evangelist.*
11. *Boston Globe*, November 12, 1894: 5.
12. *Boston Post*, November 12, 1894: 3.
13. The funeral coverage relies upon reports in the local papers, the *Boston Globe*, the *Boston Post*, and the *Boston Record*. The coverage was remarkably similar.
14. *Boston Globe*, November 18, 1894: 5.
15. Alfred P. Cappio, *The Story of Michael J. Kelly, The King of Baseball* (Passaic County Historical Society, 1962), 18. This publication may have relied on local sources in Paterson and Passaic County, New Jersey.

STARTS, STOPS, AND STREAKS – A MODERN FAN'S GUIDE TO THE 1890S BASEBALL SCHEDULE

BY RICHARD "DIXIE" TOURANGEAU

Baseball continued to deal with several scheduling issues in its final decade of the nineteenth century. In 1890 owners had to deal with the confusion and pure animosity provided by a third circuit, the Players' League, to go along with the National League (1876) and the American Association (1882). The latter two had coexisted, usually cordially, for eight years and had even played against one another in "World's Series" competition since 1884. In 1890 the three leagues were each made up of eight clubs, hoping to play 140 games (20 against the other seven cities in each circuit). Each league started within a day or two of April 19, and the PL and NL ended by October 4, the AA by October 15. Only the second-place AA Columbus Solons (79-55-6) actually played 140 total games, all six ties being squeezed into September-October.

Come 1891, the PL had dissolved and most things were back to normal, 140 games starting in mid-April and ending by October. The Beaneaters were one of two clubs to play 140 games, yet there was one game they didn't play in Philadelphia, a late July rainout that was never rescheduled. They tied New York in a classic 4-4 duel between Amos Rusie and host Charlie "Kid" Nichols that went 10 innings before dark set in, and deadlocked with Pittsburgh, 7-7, another unresolved game, so Boston took the season series 16-3-1. Boston was 15-5-1 versus the New York Giants.

When the AA broke up after 1891, that prompted a big change in the NL 1892 schedule. Four teams were absorbed (making 12 total for the NL), and the schedule was revamped so that the teams played each other 14 times for 154 total games. In hopes that some interest would not be lost late in the season by a runaway pennant race, the campaign was split: the winner of the first half to play the winner of the second half at the season's conclusion. Boston took the first half and probably should have won the second half as well, but Cleveland came along and made the campaign interesting and provided fodder for a "postseason" series matchup. To accommodate these extra games the year started a week earlier (April 12) and finished later (October 15). Big winner Boston (102 wins total) played 17 doubleheaders, the same as last-place Baltimore (46 wins).

Complaints about awful spring weather and October boredom forced changes so the schedule was tweaked again for 1893. The dozen teams would play one another only 12 times, cutting way back to 132 games, and the split-season idea was abolished. Teams began on April 27-28 and ended before October 1. Pennant winner Boston (86 wins) played 11 doubleheaders while lowly Washington (40) endured eight. In general, this schedule remained intact for another four years until 1898, when League owners suddenly decided to generate additional revenue with more games. For both 1898 and 1899, the teams played 154 games, 14 apiece against one another. In 1898 the pennant-snatching Beaneaters (102-47) played 12 doubleheaders while the bedraggled St. Louis Browns (39-111) managed 26 twin bills, seven in its nine days of October play. All teams started by April 20 and ended by October 10. To end the decade and century, the NL went back to eight teams playing 20 games against one another (140) in 1900.

In terms of starting each 1890s campaign, the Beaneaters had a selfish lock on the April 19 date, to join in with the Patriots Day celebration (officially beginning in 1894) in the city of Boston. Seven times in 11 years that was Opening Day in the Hub, though for six years they did begin on the road. The season's end at their "cozy confines" of the South End Grounds was on a wide range of dates from September 6 to October 14 through the 1890s. It was normal for the Beaneaters to begin on the road and come home for just Patriots Day and then be on the road again. In 1896 they played 27 road tilts bookending three at South End Grounds, Patriots Day included. For 1898 it was two on the road, host Patriots Day, and then 11 more away, followed by 1899's three away games, Patriots Day and 13 more out of town. April 19 was that important to their gate. The years 1890-94-95-97-1900 produced a favorable schedule, which had them open the season at the South End Grounds.

Homestands and road trips fluctuated greatly during that decade. Such things were uneven at best and sheer madness at worst.

In 1891 Boston had back-to-back 20-game stretches, home and away, and late in the year they were away for 19 and then home for 26. The longest homestand of the decade was 34 games in 1893 followed by 33 in 1897 and 29 in 1896. Boston traveled the longest in 1897, 30 straight games worth, and in 1895, 26. It was not until 1898 that the length of trips and comfortable home stays were scaled down to under 20. The wildest lack of team travel occurred in 1893, when only three homestands of 34, 17, and 14 games balanced off four lengthy road trips. By 1899 there were 10 shorter cuts of both, preparing twentieth-century fans for what became normal to them.

SOURCE

Retrosheet game logs for each season.

BOSTON BEANEATERS SPRING TRAINING IN THE 1890S

BY BILL NOWLIN

"Spring training is almost as old as baseball itself. The best evidence points to spring training first taking place in 1870, when the Cincinnati Red Stockings and the Chicago White Stockings held organized baseball camps in New Orleans. Other baseball historians argue that the Washington Capitals of the National League pioneered spring training in 1888, holding a four-day camp in Jacksonville. In either case, the roots of spring training history go deep, and the specific origins really don't matter. By 1900, spring training was firmly established as a baseball ritual, with most American and National League teams heading out of town so players could train and managers could evaluate."[1]

On March 24, 1890, the Boston Reds of the Players' League played a game against the University of Virginia team in Charlottesville, winning by a score of 14-4 but at the same time achieving recognition for the new team. The National League and other clubs that were organized under the National Agreement had tried to squelch the upstart league. Indeed, wrote Tim Murnane in the *Boston Globe*, those clubs had "tried to intimidate the collegians here into not playing with the brotherhood clubs." The manager of the university team said, "We will allow no one to dictate to us as to who we shall play."[2]

The Boston team had arrived from Richmond at 2:00 P.M., changed into their uniforms at the hotel, and played before 1,800 spectators. They had been working out in Richmond for about a week beforehand.[3] The crowd was said to be "the largest crowd ever gathered to witness a ball game."[4]

Back in Richmond, the Reds played a game on April 1 against the New York club of the Players' League (also named the New York Giants), winning 12-1 before 1,500. Both teams left for New York at 7:13 that evening, bound for separate destinations in Massachusetts, New York to play in Holyoke and Boston to play in Worcester.[5]

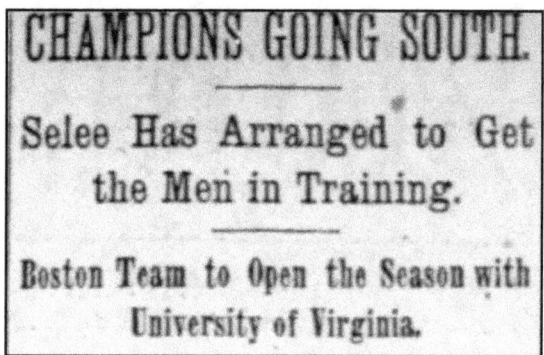

Boston Globe,
February 11, 1982

Frank Selee's Beaneaters stayed close to home, though the February 16 *Boston Herald* wrote, "Manager Selee will arrange more games for this vicinity in the spring than usual."[6] The first eight of the team to report gathered at the YMCA on March 18, planning to start practice in the gymnasium of the Y. on the 19th.[7] The league schedule was released a few days later. The team held a practice game in Boston on April 1, playing at the South End Grounds against the Boston Athletic Club. It was their first game of the year.[8]

On Fast Day, the Players' League team and the National League team both played in Boston, with the Players' League team outdrawing the NL team.[9] Selee ascribed that to curiosity, and a special appeal being made to laboring men to support the Players' League, but didn't expect there to be any true threat to National League dominance.[10] Selee's men made preseason appearances in Washington and Baltimore, prepared to play, but rain prevented playing actual games.

1891

Selee was manager of the Beaneaters for the full decade of the 1890s. The team had finished in fifth place in 1890. In this year, 1891, they finished first.

He arranged preseason games against Baltimore on March 28, 30, and 31. The *Daily Inter Ocean* of Chicago added, "It is probable that the Boston league team will go someplace in the vicinity of Richmond, Va., around March 20, and indulge in two weeks' outdoor practice before the Fast day games."[11]

There was, however, no Southern trip. As the *Boston Journal* reported, "The League team will not go South, as originally intended, but will take its practice at home, playing local clubs until the opening of the regular season. With good weather the club can get as much practice here as in the South, and the Southern trip would be a losing one financially in any event. Manager Frrank Selee is strong in his belief that the club is a winning one, and is hopeful of the best of results."[12] He may have forfeited a $300 deposit paid to secure a signed contract with the manager of the University of Virginia team.[13]

Selee arranged to play three games against Harvard, two of them at the South End Grounds, after Fast Day and before the start of the season.[14] On Fast Day itself, April 2, the Bostons hosted the 1890 champion Brooklyns for a 2:00 P.M. game. Selee's Beaneaters had worked out the day before at their home park. The first game against Harvard was on April 4; the next two four were on April 8, 10, 13, and 15.

Other games arranged in the spring were to be against the John F. Morrills on April 6, with games on the 11th in Fitchburg, the 14th in Portland, the 16th in Meriden, the 17th and 18th at New Haven, the 20th at Lynn, and the 21st at Worcester.[15]

1892

In 1892 the Beaneaters trained in the South, with the arrangements being announced on February 10. The plan was for all to meet in Boston on March 21 and train in Charlottesville until April 1. They planned to play against the University of Virginia nine every day. On April 2, they were to play New York at Richmond, followed by games against Waterbury on April 4, against Yale at New Haven on April 6 and 7, against Brown at Providence on April 8 and 9, and against Princeton on April 11. Of the plan to go South and play games, the *Boston Globe* said, "The management has acted wisely in sending their great team to a place where the boys can work off the superfluous flesh gained by several months' rest."[16] Manager Selee had reportedly been courted with offers from a number of communities from as far away as Florida. Some of the men had been with the 1890 Players' League team during their visit to Charlottesville.

Six left Boston on the New York & New England Railroad at 3:00 P.M. on March 22. Others came to Charlottesville from other locations. A number of conversations among the players and ownership before the train left Boston were recounted in the March 23 *Globe*.[17] They played their first practice game against the University of Virginia on March 24. The park in which they played was a mile and a half from their quarters, and with morning and afternoon practices or scrimmage games, that meant six miles of walking for the men. A number of the players took a roundabout route that gave them an extra five miles of walking. The *Boston Herald* correspondent wrote, "Manager Selee is delighted by the spirit shown by his men in this preliminary work. He says he never saw men so anxious to get right down to fighting trim. He firmly believes in the efficacy of outdoor work, and is supported in the view by his men. Not a member of the Boston team believes in gymnasium work. It is far more dangerous and risky to the limbs than outdoor practice."[18]

Some of the games were lopsided, of course, such as the 20-3 drubbing given the university team on March 29. Nash had three

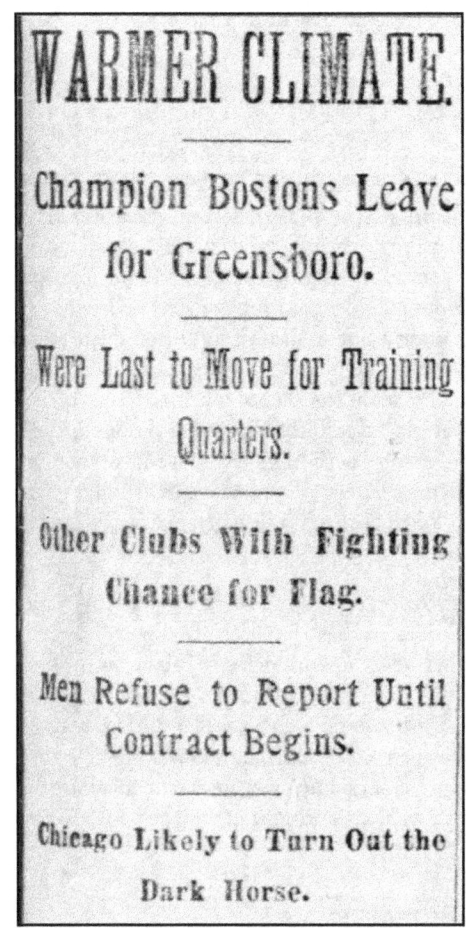

Boston Globe
March 20, 1898

home runs in the game. In 1892, the Beaneaters finished in first place again.

1893

In 1893 Selee started later. Players were ordered to report to the South End Grounds at 10:00 A.M. on April 1. They started outdoor practice at once, and on April 5 planned to play Brown University at Providence, with the same two teams coming to Boston for the Fast Day game on April 6. On April 7 and 8, Boston was to play at New Haven and on April 10 at Bridgeport. It was Hartford on April 11, Princeton on April 12, and at Petersburg, Virginia, on April 12 and 13. Richmond was April 15, and then the Bostons would remain at Charlottesville from April 16 through the 26th.[19] The schedule had not yet been formalized, and the time in Charlottesville might have been shortened, but indeed the first championship game was held in New York on April 28.

As it happened, snow prevented the two games against Brown from being played. On a chilly April 10, the game against Yale was held, with around 1,000 spectators, Boston winning, 8-5.[20] The game at Richmond was deemed a "farce," with Boston scoring 10 runs in the first inning against the city league champion team of Richmond, which played so "wretchedly" that playing against them provided little in the way of helpful competition.[21]

Boston won 86 regular-season games and lost exactly half as many (43); they finished first in the standings for the third year in a row.

1894

In 1894 the players were asked to report to the South End Grounds on April 2. The first preseason game was set for the very next day, in Providence.[22] "Not a player who showed up was fat or out of condition," wrote the *Globe*, "and manager Selee will not need the patent steam tubs of Arthur Irwin's."[23] Hugh Duffy's wife had died due to illness, almost on the eve of reporting. And weather in the Northeast was a hindrance; on April 3, it was simply "too cold" to practice outside.[24] The April 6 game against Yale was played in bitterly cold conditions and ended in a row, with the umpire declaring New Haven had won, 5-3, due to interference on the part of Boston captain Billy Nash, while Boston argued it had been a 5-5 tie when play was suspended due to the argument.[25]

It was said that by forgoing some degree of practice in the South in 1894, the team might have put itself at a disadvantage, the New England weather being unconducive.[26] They won in Waterbury, 13-0, on April 10. After the team arrived in New York, two games next planned for Princeton were canceled due to weather. Most of the players wanted to head back to Charlottesville to get in a week's work, but Selee said he had games scheduled for Brockton and Fall River, and then Springfield, and he couldn't get out of the obligations.[27] Though "too chilly for good ball playing," they got in the game against Springfield, winning 15-6.[28]

In championship play, Baltimore finished first, with the New York Giants second. Boston placed third, eight games back.

1895

There was no hesitation in 1895. The team was ordered to report much earlier, in New York on March 16, and to travel from there to Charleston, South Carolina, for spring training.[29] It was actually in Columbia that they were based, and they played their first game against a local team on March 19. There was a game planned for March 20 against Washington but it was rained out. On March 21, in Charleston, Boston beat the Washington ballclub, 8-4. A number of the players went to tour Fort Sumter. On the 26th they played in Savannah and, although Washington scored six runs in the first inning, Boston scored five – and put the game away with 12 runs in the fifth inning. On March 28 Selee's men played an intrasquad game, Colts vs. Regulars, on the grounds of Converse College in Spartanburg with women comprising most of the audience.[30] The weather had been good enough, but the trip had still placed them in some less than desirable circumstances. In general, it was felt that "the hotels are execrable."[31]

On March 29 they had to lend five players to the local team in Greenville, but they got in a game, winning narrowly, 6-5. When they arrived in Charlotte, North Carolina, on March 31, they were greeted by 300 people at the depot, and another large crowd met them at their hotel. It was the fields of play that were subpar.

Selee summed up the Southern trip to date: "I am perfectly satisfied with the work done by the team thus far and with the exception of a few lame arms the team is doing nicely. There are only one or two men overweight and should the good weather continue, the team will surely be able to do themselves justice at the end of the week. I am glad to know that we have at least reached a place where my men can do some field work. Every city we have visited thus far has had poor accommodations for grounds, and the players were afraid of doing themselves more harm than good, but I know they have worked faithfully and I must say they are in excellent condition, all things considered."[32]

On April 1 some 1,200 people turned out. The Charlotte field was the best to date, and they beat the University of North Carolina, 17-3. The next day's game, against the local Charlotte team, was rained out. The schedule saw the team head to Portsmouth, Norfolk, Richmond, Princeton, New Haven, and Springfield, with no games played at all in the Boston area prior to the season.

The Beaneaters finished in fifth place.

1896

There wasn't a chance the team was going anywhere other than Charlottesville in 1896. In speaking with Joe Kelley of the Baltimore team, Tim Murnane wrote, "The Boston brotherhood team was the first to go there, as the university of Virginia was the only college team at that time who would take a chance to play a brotherhood club, owing to the national agreement. That team won the pennant.

Manager Selee told Tim Murnane, "The next season the Boston association club went to Charlottesville and won the championship. Then for two years I took the league team to that place for spring practice, and each year we pulled off the pennant. Ed Hanlon got in ahead of me for 1894, and Baltimore got their practice there and won the championship.

"Last season none of the clubs visited this southern practice grounds and Baltimore won the flag. I went down there at the close of the season last year and made all my arrangements for grounds and hotels. And this spring the boys will start in for the championship from the old lucky starting place."[33]

A new pattern was being set for spring training. Every National League club except Washington was planning to go south – Jacksonville, New Orleans, Hot Springs, and Galveston among the destinations.

The Beaneaters planned to play the university nine, then have games against Richmond, Portsmouth, and Norfolk, head north via Princeton, and then play a number of games – mostly in in New England – at Fall River, Paterson (New Jersey), Melrose, Bridgeport, Derby (for "Harry Wright Day" on April 13), Newton, Providence, Brockton, Middletown, and Newport before heading south via Wilmington and opening the regular season in Philadelphia.

Their first workout had been on March 20 and the lack of a trainer or physical therapist was noted. "A mistake was made in not following the example of other league clubs in having a man accompany a team to rub the pitchers down, and attend to their wants. This has got to be a necessary thing nowadays. So much depends upon the pitchers that they should be surrounded with every convenience, and no greater convenience can be found than one of these 'rubbers.' The Philadelphias, the Brooklyns, and the New Yorks all have such men with them on their southern trips. A pitcher cannot look out for himself as a rubber can, and the expense of carrying such a man is a trifle compared with the results achieved."[34]

The university team had been working out for more than a month and put up a good showing in the first game of Boston's spring, a 12-7 win for the professionals. Hugh Duffy's team of regulars beat the second-string Roustabouts, 22-1, in a six-inning March 26 game umpired by Selee.

If Charlottesville was meant to ensure good luck, it didn't take; the Beaneaters finished fourth. They'd actually been shut out in Norfolk, 5-0, but after just six innings when the local umpire hurriedly called off the game because of what had reportedly been only a very few raindrops.[35] The Beaneaters' record of 74-57-1 saw them 17 games behind the first-place Baltimore Orioles.

1897

The plan was to train at Augusta, Georgia, in 1897 but Selee found that the Philadelphia team had secured an option there before he could act. He held one himself for the grounds at Hot Springs. The deal he ultimately signed, however, put the team in Savannah.[36] This year, they took a boat south, departing from Lewis Wharf, Boston, on March 18 on the Nacoochee. They arrived on the 21st, several of them having been quite ill from seasickness on the voyage south, including manager Selee.[37] Despite damp and cold conditions endured by some at the team hotel, by the time they arrived in Charleston on April 4, they were reportedly in good condition.

Stops included Norfolk, Richmond, Princeton (a close 3-2 win), Elizabeth, Middletown, a two-game day with games at Winsted and Torrington (both in Connecticut), and Springfield.

Boston reclaimed its place atop league standings with a record of 93-39 (with three tie games).

1898

Greensboro, North Carolina, was the choice for 1898, the selection made on January 25. The team planned to play five intrasquad games and then begin to take on opponents. Boston was the last of the 12 teams to head south, and it was a quirk of the contracts at the time that they were dated to be effective as of April 15, so there was no way to insist that players report before that date.[38] Fortunately, most of them wanted to get in shape and hone their skills.

On March 23 the Yannigans beat the Regulars by an astounding 15-3. The next day Boston beat Augusta, 18-3, in four innings before the rains came. They played an intrasquad game at Winston-Salem on March 26. There was rain on the 29th and 30th. There was an intrasquad game at Danville on April 1. Rain prevented a game against the university team at Charlottesville. They won a 10-inning game against Richmond, 8-7, on April 8.

The Lancaster, Pennsylvania, team beat the Beaneaters 7-3 on April 12. While stopping at York the night before, Billy Hamilton gave his opinion on spring training: "Spring training is only valuable to me so far as it enables me to cultivate my batting eye. If a man takes good care of himself during the winter he is ready in a jiffy to field, but it takes time to get back your batting skill. I never hit hard at the ball in the spring, and I think it a mistake to swing too hard in the beginning. I take things easy and work myself by degrees to the proper point. All I want to do is to satisfy myself that I can meet the ball just right. Our players are all right as far as fielding is concerned, but we need batting practice badly, and I hope we will get it in these games with the Pennsylvania clubs."[39]

The schedule was a longer one. The Beaneaters placed first, with 102 wins against 47 losses. There were again three tie games.

1899

Seemingly never content to train in the same place twice, the Beaneaters chose Durham, North Carolina, as their springtime home in 1899. The team offered $35 a week, plus expenses, to entice players to come for training, and once again were one of the last teams to head south, but the enticements were not enough and a number of players – some of whom had other business interests – elected to report later.[40]

On Sunday, March 27, after most of the players attended church in one part of town or another, they left at 2:30 P.M. for a five-mile hike and jog. Selee stuck to his guns; he "never allows his men to do gymnasium work of any kind, maintaining that the only place a player can get into proper condition is in open air. … There are fine baths at the college gymnasium here, but Selee refused to allow his players to go near the institution."[41] They played Trinity College at Durham (and won by scores of 11-4, 17-4, and 20-1), and had been planning to play the University of North Carolina at Chapel Hill, but after a few days of rain decided to cancel the visit, Selee seeing "the long drive over a waste of time."[42] They beat Norfolk, 11-0, but then heavy rain prevented a game in Richmond. They had gotten in their work, though, and on April 15 were in Brooklyn for the start of the 1899 season. The Beaneaters won that game, 1-0, in 11 innings. The Brooklyn Superbas got their revenge, however, and beat out Boston for the pennant, an eight-game margin separating the first- and second-place teams.

BOSTONS IN TRAINING

We add here a first-person account of the Beaneaters during spring training 1899.

BOSTONS IN TRAINING AT DURHAM NC

From the *Boston Journal* of April 23, 1899

It is interesting to note the methods of different ballplayers in the preliminary spring practice. The veteran, confident in his prowess, begins very slowly, while the colt, ambitious to show his mettle, starts off at a much more rapid gait. The veteran nurses himself along, the colt often has to do some serious nursing afterward, because he did not use his muscles cautiously at the start.

A staff correspondent of the *Journal* accompanied the Bostons South this spring and remained with them during their stay at Durham N.C. The merits of any place as a training ground for ball players are so dependent on the weather that a place which might be decided a failure one year would be a success the next. Judging solely on results Durham was a success, for certainly the Bostons never started North after two weeks' limbering up in such splendid physical condition. This state of affairs would not have been predicted at the close of the first week at Durham. It rained four days of that week, and what was equally discouraging was the absence of about a third of the players. Then came the reaction. The weather improved and the belated players began to report, and most of them showed that they had already been doing some work, so that they would soon be on a par with the first comers.

Frank Selee was so well pleased with the results attained that he asked for a refusal of the grounds at Trinity Park for next spring. The weather at Durham was tempered just enough with the cool breezes of the north to make the players go slowly in practice. Manager Selee contends that so long as the weather is sufficiently warm to permit the playing of base ball without discomfort it is better to train his men somewhere in the Middle South than to take them far South. They are then less likely to be affected by the changed conditions once they come North.

There was one drawback about the college ball grounds at Trinity Park. It had a "skin" diamond, an in fact there was not a blade of grass in the entire area. The soil was a mixture of sand and clay which was either heavy and muddy or hard, almost flinty, in the infield so that the ball was soon fuzzy or "wingey" as the ball players term it. A ball in this condition is extremely difficult to throw. It is heavy and does not carry well. For this reason the Bostons favored their arms and trained their eyes, both on the field and at the bat. Their heavy hitting in the games following their departure from Durham proved the wisdom of their judgment.

There was one feature of the sojourn. It could be declared a success in point of comfort. The ban of the ball players' visits South have been the hotels. The players found the Carrolina Hotel very much to their liking. Manager Selee had looked the ground over last December, a precaution which past experience had made necessary.

The daily routine of the players in training varied according to the weather. They rose at 8 o'clock each morning and at 10 started for the grounds, a mile and a half away, on foot and dressed for play. On the first day the morning practice did not last much more than half an hour, but this time was gradually extended to an hour and a half and more. A fast walk or slow jog back to the hotel followed this warming-up. Then a bath and a rubdown found the player very nearly ready for lunch. At 2:30 in the afternoon the morning program was repeated, except that often, instead of practice, there was a game with the Trinity College nine. Some days the condition did not favor playing at Trinity Park, especially in the first week, and on these days Manager Selee led his men in long walks across the country or along the road towards Chapel Hill. The genial manager often set the pace and always proved to be a stayer.

The Journal correspondent took with him to Durnam a camera that had seen service in Cuba. He had never snapped a kodak in his life and he had about as much knowledge of its working as the average citizen has of the partition of China. He had been told not to face the sun, and to do several things in sequence. In his innocence he attempted to take snap shots of the players in rapid action. He had been told that if someone had snapped a camera on him when he was scurrying after a fielder who was either running down a grounder or chasing a fly the Journal might now publish a series of comic pictures worthy of our funniest weeklies. The Journal man "got in" a little training on his own account shooting his camera at fleet-footed ball players, and he flatters himself that, whatever his failures artistically, his aim was good. The picture of Duffy catching a line fly was taken under hazardous conditions. The camera fiend thought he saw a good opportunity to catch Boston's "Little Corporal" when Klobedanz lined out a fly. The fellow with the kodak tried to judge a fly and adjust his camera at the same time. The scene must have been ludicrous, for at the time the camera was snapped the Journal man was running backward as fast as he could move his legs in order to avoid a collision.

The pictures of Lowe and Frisbie at second, of Klobedanz in the box in a game and of manager Selee and others at the players' bench were taken by Mr. George R. King, a well-known expert photographer of this city who was in Durham during the second week of the Bostons' stay there. None of the parties in the Selee group knew they were being photographed, so that the Boston Manager's appearance with a catcher's mitt on his left hand and a seater tied around his neck was not improvised for the occasion.

If the players had any one object to Durham as a place of training, it was its lack of opportunity for amusement during the leisure hours. Time dragged heavily, especially at night. There were practically no public amusements. There was little to do other than sit about the hotel, to read or to write letters. There was not a billiard table in town, so far as the players could discover. There were several pool tables and a nickel-in-the-slot machine which proved a better winner than several players who stacked up against it. The Carrolina (by the way this spelling with two r's is correct, as the name is a combination, the owners name and the name of the State) had no billiard or pool room and no bar. It was therefore difficult for the boys to go wrong. As Manager Selee expressed it, there was nothing to do but tend strictly to business. A visit to one of the leading factories was very interesting and Uncle Moses Hester's sermon to some of the players on Easter Sunday was almost as a minstrel show but a darky cake walk in a dimly-lighted tobacco warehouse was disappointing as a disturbing element interfered every time the walkers made a beginning. George Yeager discovered a boot black who could execute a buck and wing dance and George billed him for a number of matinees on the hotel piazza. If the Bostons go to Durham next spring Manager Selee will have to manufacture diversions to keep his men from being homesick.

Note: on the following page, the Journal printed a full page of photographs.

NOTES

1. springtrainingonline.com/features/history.htm.
2. T.H. Murnane, "Wings on a Ball," *Boston Globe,* March 25, 1890: 5.
3. "Twelve to One," *Boston Globe,* April 2, 1890: 2.
4. "Champions Going South," *Boston Globe,* February 11, 1892: 2.
5. "Bostons Play a Fine Game," *Boston Herald,* April 2, 1890: 2.
6. "Signs of the Season," *Boston Herald,* February 16, 1890: 16.
7. "Boston Base Ball Club," *Boston Journal,* March 18, 1890: 1.
8. "Bostons Play a Fine Game."
9. For more on Fast Day, see Joanne Hulbert, "Fast Day – Boston's Original Opening Day," in Bob LeMoine and Bill Nowlin, eds., *Boston's First Nine: The 1871-75 Boston Red Stockings* (Phoenix: SABR, 2016), 196-199. It was traditionally observed on the first Thursday of April.
10. "Boston's Seventeen," *The Sun* (Baltimore), April 10, 1890: Supplement 2.
11. "Sporting Scraps," *Daily Inter Ocean* (Chicago), February 20, 1891: 6.
12. "Will Not Go South," *Boston Journal,* March 27, 1891: 4.
13. "Stricker Has the 'Grippe,'" *Boston Herald,* March 29, 1891: 2.
14. "The Boston N.L. Nine to Play Harvard," *Boston Daily Advertiser,* February 26, 1891: 8.
15. "Spring Games of the League Nine," *Boston Herald,* April 4, 1891: 10.
16. "Champions Going South."
17. T.H. Murnane, "Champions Go South," *Boston Globe,* March 23, 1892: 10.
18. "The Champions in Training," *Boston Herald,* March 26, 1892: 10.
19. "Coming of the Champions," *Boston Herald,* March 29, 1893: 2.
20. "Yale Played Well," *Boston Daily Advertiser,* April 11, 1893: 8.
21. "Just Play for the Bostons," *Boston Herald,* April 16, 1893: 6.
22. "Ordered to Report," *Boston Globe,* March 18, 1894: 10.
23. "Look Well and Strong," *Boston Globe,* April 3, 1894: 5.
24. "Base Ball Notes," *Boston Globe,* April 4, 1894: 2.
25. "Champions Caught Napping," *Boston Herald,* April 7, 1894: 7.
26. "Games in the South Missed," *Boston Herald,* April 9, 1894: 8.
27. "Canceled Both Games," *Boston Globe,* April 12, 1894: 2.
28. "Champions Play in Springfield," *Boston Herald,* April 15, 1894: 4.
29. T.H. Murnane, "Boston Going South," *Boston Globe,* March 10, 1895: 24.
30. "Own the Town," *Boston Globe,* March 29, 1895: 2.
31. "Regular Ice-Water Pitchers," *Boston Herald,* March 28, 1895: 3.
32. "Bostons in Dixie's Land," *Boston Journal,* April 1, 1895: 8.
33. T.H. Murnane, "Signing Champions," *Boston Globe,* February 9, 1896: 17.
34. "Bostons Take the Field," *Boston Herald,* March 21, 1896: 12.
35. T.H. Murnane, "Tell It Softly!" *Boston Globe,* April 7, 1896: 2. Selee later hired a "female massage operator" to work on the pitchers' arms. See "Base Ball Notes," *Wilkes-Barre Times,* April 3, 1896: 5.
36. "Sure of Grounds," *Boston Globe,* January 22, 1897: 10.
37. "Arrive Alive," *Boston Globe,* March 22, 1897: 3.
38. "Warmer Climate," *Boston Globe,* March 20, 1898: 17.
39. "Boston Nine in Good Trim," *Boston Herald,* April 11, 1898: 10.
40. T.H.M., "Avoid the South," *Boston Globe,* March 20, 1899: 9.
41. "No Gymnasium Work Allowed," *Pawtucket Times,* March 27, 1899: 2.
42. "Boston's First," *Boston Globe,* April 1, 1899: 2.

THE GLORIOUS BEANEATERS

Boston Journal,
April 23, 1899

SEASONS

THE 1891 SEASON: 18 STRAIGHT DOWN THE STRETCH

BY JEAN-PIERRE CAILLAULT

At the close of the 1890 baseball season the upstart Players' League had died, the result of its owners bailing out on the players, leaving the National League and the American Association as the only remaining major leagues. And the climate surrounding those two leagues was far from peaceful.

In Boston, in particular, there was open disagreement, as the Association wanted to place, for the first time in its 10-year history, a team in the Hub city. The AA expected that a Boston team would be able to sign to contracts for 1891 many, if not most, of the players who had played for the Boston Reds, the champions of the defunct Players' League.

The NL Boston Beaneaters' President, Arthur H. Soden, stated that he would not object to an AA team in Boston, but thought that both clubs would lose money. What Soden, and the other two-thirds of the Triumvirs (as the three men who owned the Beaneaters – President Soden, Director William Conant, and Treasurer James Billings – were known) were hoping to get, though, were some concessions from the Association in exchange for accepting an AA team in Boston. Namely, they wanted some of the players from the previous season's Boston Reds roster: second baseman Joe Quinn, third baseman Billy Nash, and outfielder Hardy Richardson.[1]

The Triumvirs had run the Beaneaters franchise for several years. "Soden first got involved with the Beaneaters when he bought three shares of stock, at $30 per share, in the Boston League Base Ball Club back in 1876. Buying stock in a ball club then was

1891 Boston scorecard, AA, with Bill Daley
(Courtesy of John Thorn)

done simply to help the game, as a dividend was never thought of. He became president of the club in 1878."[2]

"Messrs. Billings and Conant, who are equal partners in the Boston league club, were baseball enthusiasts simply, until Mr. Soden got them to take stock. Mr. Billings became interested along about '79, while Mr. Conant came to the front in '83, the year Boston pulled off the league pennant for the last time."[3]

In January of 1891, the AA announced that it would indeed place a team in Boston.[4] Then, in early February, the Beaneaters made a shocking announcement – they had signed outfielder Harry Stovey, a longtime AA star and one of the main cogs in the previous season's Boston Reds Players' League championship team.[5] This signing, along with that of second baseman Lou Bierbauer by the NL's Pittsburgh club, caused an uproar throughout baseball.

The AA's Philadelphia club, the Athletics, claimed that they owned the rights to Stovey and Bierbauer, since they had been under contract when they jumped to the Players' League in 1890. Now that the Players' League no longer existed, the Athletics claimed that the two players should return to Philadelphia under the rules of the reserve system in place under the so-called "national agreement" between the two major leagues (and the Western League, a high minor league).[6]

Meanwhile, Director Conant of the Beaneaters was discussing the possibility of getting superstar catcher Mike "King" Kelly to return to the team after his one-year hiatus with the Boston Reds.[7] Kelly had played with the Beaneaters from 1887 to 1889 and was idolized by all of the baseball fans in Boston. Kelly was considered by most people in baseball to be the sport's biggest drawing card and, possibly, its best manager and motivator, too, so getting him back was a high priority.

Then, in mid-February came a blitz of announcements that would shape the course of baseball in 1891 and beyond. On February 14 the National Board, the governing body overseeing all affairs of the leagues participating in the national agreement, ruled that Stovey was awarded to the Boston League club and Bierbauer to Pittsburgh (causing the team forevermore to be known as the "Pirates"). Soden was quoted as saying, "We have a perfect right to sign Stovey and will insist that he remain with us. Mr. Stovey would not play Sunday games, and was anxious to play with the league, and he was just the man we wanted."[8]

The next day it was revealed that Allen W. Thurman, president of the American Association and one of the voting members of the National Board, had, shockingly, voted for the ruling favoring the League.[9] (Thurman was summarily dismissed as AA president, replaced by Louis Kramer.[10]) Two days later, there was an announcement that Kelly would captain the Association's new Cincinnati club, permitted to go there by the management of the Boston Reds.[11] And then the following day, National League President Nick Young received official notification from the AA of its withdrawal from the national agreement, precipitated, of course, by the ruling of the National Board.[12]

This set up a "war" between the two leagues that would have a major impact on the possibility of a world's series between the champions of the Association and the League at the end of the 1891 season and, more importantly, set the stage for the ultimate demise of the Association and the League's monopoly and syndication of major-league baseball throughout the remainder of the nineteenth century.

In early March the Beaneaters acceded to the financial demands of Billy Nash (reportedly $5,000 for each of the next three seasons plus a signing bonus of $2,500) and signed him as their third baseman and captain.[13] And in late March the members of the team started slowly trickling into town to begin preparing for the season. The Beaneaters used the YMCA gym on Boylston Street when the weather was bad and practiced at the South End Grounds when the weather was pleasant.[14]

Boston planned a big preseason exhibition game for Fast Day (April 2), the Beaneaters hosting John Ward's Brooklyn AA team, known as "Ward's Wonders."[15] More than 6,000 fans came to the South End Grounds and saw the League team whip Brooklyn, with Stovey hitting a home run and stealing a couple of bases in his Beaneaters debut.[16] The regular season was still weeks away, and, wrote the *Boston Globe,* "it was a very cold day, but it was Fast day, the bell had rung, the umpire was all ready to shout 'play ball,' and another season of the glorious old sport was about to begin."[17]

Tim Murnane, the *Globe*'s prominent sportswriter, saw the Reds as heavy favorites to win the American Association pennant, but in the National League he thought the Giants were the best team, with Chicago and Brooklyn not far behind. As for the local team, Murnane said, "How about Boston? Oh, the Bostons can play ball, but I am a few chips shy when putting the team down for pennant winners. If the men should all work together, without an eye for individual records, they will most likely get into the first division."[18]

Boston opened its National League season on Wednesday, April 22, in New York, where the heavily favored Giants hosted the Beaneaters in front of a huge crowd of 17,000. The game was a close pitchers' duel between Boston's veteran ace John Clarkson and the Giants' young, fireballing Amos Rusie. The Beaneaters won in the ninth inning, 4-3, on a fly ball hit by shortstop Herman Long that Giants center fielder George Gore misplayed.[19] Three days later, Boston had completed a four-game sweep of the stunned Giants and stood tied for first place with the Cleveland Spiders.

On Monday, April 27, a large crowd of 7,500 showed up at the South End Grounds to see Boston's first home game of the season. The story was the lead on the *Boston Globe* front page and even included an illustration of Massachusetts Governor William Russell arriving at the game.[20]

The Beaneaters' young ace, Kid Nichols, threw a five-hit shutout and Stovey hit two doubles and a triple as Boston beat Philadelphia, 5-0.[21] Boston ended up only splitting that four-game series with Philly, but they were still in first place, a game ahead of three other teams.

The Beaneaters then split four games in Brooklyn, but were still tied for first place with Cleveland, a half-game ahead of Chicago. Murnane expressed his strong opinion that the team was already in desperate need of an additional pitcher, as third starter Charles

"Pretzels" Getzien, who had pitched well for the Beaneaters in 1890 and for Detroit previously, had declined rapidly and was simply not capable of filling in adequately when Clarkson and Nichols needed rest.[22]

There was a lot of excitement in the Hub at the beginning of May, as King Kelly's "Killers" visited the Reds at the Congress Street Grounds, while Buck Ewing's Giants came to the South End Grounds, hoping to gain some revenge on Boston for having swept New York in their season-opening series.

The Giants won two out of three, as Boston tried out new pitchers John Kiley and Cyclone Ryan during the series (neither of whom ever pitched in the majors again). On May 10, as the Beaneaters prepared to travel for a long trip out West, where they were scheduled to play four games against each of the four Western teams, they found themselves in second place, one game behind Cap Anson's Chicago club.

John Clarkson pitched Boston to a series-opening win in Chicago, aided by Stovey's fourth-inning homer that was "hit far over the outer wall among the bitter weeds."[23] Despite a sterling second game from Stovey (another homer, plus three assists, throwing out runners at second, third, and home), the Colts pounded Kid Nichols.[24] The two teams split the next two games, too, so the Beaneaters still trailed by one game when they left Chicago for Cincinnati.

The last-place Cincinnati team called on "Old Charley" (also called "Old Hoss") Radbourn to beat his former team twice in the series (Radbourn had pitched for Boston for four years before jumping to the Boston Reds of the Players' League). The Beaneaters, having lost three of four in Cincinnati, then lost three of four in Cleveland, with Cy Young outdueling Kid Nichols in one game that was controversially called because of darkness, causing captain Billy Nash to make "a vigorous protest, but it was of no avail."[25]

As the Beaneaters finished up their road trip in Pittsburgh, their need for additional pitching was made all the more clear during the three games with the Pirates, as Nichols and Clarkson won their games, but new pitcher Charles Brynan lasted but one inning and never pitched in the major leagues again.[26]

On May 27, in what turned out to be a critically important move, Boston obtained from the Pirates 24-year-old Harry Staley, a workhorse who had started nearly 50 games and pitched around 400 innings in each of the previous two seasons.[27] It is worth noting that Pittsburgh's record on this date was 15-12, putting them in second place, three games behind Chicago. They would finish last. And the Beaneaters on that day were in fifth place, closer to cellar-dwelling Cincinnati than to first place Chicago.

Decoration Day (now called Memorial Day) on May 30 marked the first notable holiday of the season, celebrated with doubleheaders in both leagues. At the South End Grounds, 4,000 people attended the morning game, while 10,000 saw the afternoon game.

The Beaneaters swept their two games from Cincinnati, Staley winning his Boston debut in the first game, while Clarkson beat Radbourn in the second. The *Boston Globe* report gushed about Staley's work "in the box," but was especially nostalgic about Radbourn and his mid-1880s glory days with the Providence Grays:

"The real sendoff of the game was given to Old Hoss Charley Radbourn as he walked from the bench to take his position in the box before the game," wrote the *Globe*. "'Rad' tipped his cap and handled the ball nervously as the crowd cheered. The bronzed old warrior of the diamond felt the blood come to his cheek when he stood on the spot he had made famous but a few years back when he was the main stay of that Rhode Island champion team in the stubborn contests with the Bostons when games lengthened out in to 14 and 16 innings and the score of both teams seldom reached five in all.

"The day as a whole was a base ball success, from the jingle of the half dollar and the merry tick of the turnstile to the smile of the honest face of William Nash."[28]

At the end of May, the National League standings saw Boston in a five-team logjam, 3½ games behind first-place Chicago.

In early June Harry Stovey missed five games to be at home with his family, tending to his two-month-old daughter,[29] who died on June 6 (her twin was stillborn on April 1).[30] The Beaneaters lost three of those games and were 4½ games back when Cap Anson's first-place Chicago Colts made their first visit to the South End Grounds.

"Anson is willing to wager anything, from a chew of tobacco to a dress suit, that his Chicago nine can beat any team in the league for a place, and with a little odds will take his team for a pennant winner," wrote the *Globe*. "The Chicago team has always been the leading attraction in this city, and the next four games will be a test of the drawing power of our league team this season. [Bill] Hutchinson and Clarkson will most likely do the pitching. Hutchinson is looked on as a wonder, and is doing half the pitching for his team."[31]

The attendance at the South End Grounds totaled 12,000 for the four-game series, which the two teams split, Hutchinson and Clarkson each winning one of their two duels.

The New York Giants, meanwhile, were surging. By mid-June, after having swept four games from visiting Chicago, including a Saturday game in front of a record 22,289 fans at the Polo Grounds, to run the Colts' losing streak to six games, the Giants had won 15 of 16 and were in first place, four games ahead of Chicago and 4½ ahead of Boston.

On June 17 Boston hosted a doubleheader to celebrate Bunker Hill Day, but the cold, wet weather kept the attendance down to about 2,000 for each of the games at the South End Grounds. The Beaneaters beat visiting Brooklyn's "Ward's Wonders" twice, Nichols and Staley picking up the wins.

Although Cincinnati's "Kelly's Killers" were playing .500 ball in the Association and drawing decent crowds, there was talk of Mike Kelly coming back to Boston. Chicago's Anson was quoted as saying the Bostons should never have let him go, since Kelly was "one of the greatest ball players in the business and the best drawing card that Boston ever had. It was a big mistake to let him leave the league. With Kel in the Boston team the crowds at the South End grounds would have been just double."[32]

The *Cincinnati Commercial Gazette* reported on what it saw as Boston's motive: "By getting Kelly away from Cincinnati they would serve a double purpose in breaking up the association club in this city and in adding to their own team one of the most popular players that ever set foot on a ball field. Capt. Kelly today is rated as one of the greatest players in the profession, and he hasn't an equal as a drawing card."[33]

With nothing but rumors about Kelly swirling, the Beaneaters wrapped up their long homestand winning 13 and losing 7, tied for second place with Chicago, 2½ games behind New York. They then left, on June 21, for Philadelphia, embarking on a 3½-week road trip in which they would visit every other team in the league.

Boston won its first game on the trip with Clarkson handling the imposing Phillies' lineup that included future Hall of Fame outfielders Billy Hamilton, Sam Thompson, and Ed Delahanty, but the Beaneaters then lost the next three in Philly.

They then moved on to another showdown with the Giants in New York. The first scheduled game was rained out, but Clarkson beat Rusie in the second game in front of a large Saturday crowd of more than 7,000. With no Sunday game scheduled, as usual in the NL, Roger Connor and Jim O'Rourke each got three hits off Clarkson on Monday and the Giants beat Boston to split their two games.

The last day of June saw Stovey suffer the ignominy of striking out five times in one game, against Brooklyn's George Hemming, becoming only the second player ever to do so (the first was the Buffalo Bison's Oscar Walker in 1879).[34]

At the end of June the Beaneaters were in third place in the National League, 4½ games behind first-place New York and 3½ behind second-place Chicago.

The Beaneaters played their July 4 holiday doubleheader in Pittsburgh, in front of crowds of more than 5,000, and came away with two wins, Clarkson and Staley beating Silver King and Mark Baldwin. The Giants also won twice on the road, winning in Cincinnati, while the Colts, playing at home in front of crowds of 6,682 and 11,117, lost both ends of their doubleheader against visiting Brooklyn.

There were still plenty of rumors going around about the Beaneaters reacquiring Mike Kelly, especially since Boston manager Frank Selee was said to be disgusted with first baseman Tommy Tucker's play, both hitting and fielding. Murnane thought that Tucker was not putting up the game that was expected of a man getting a salary of over $4,000. Director Conant, "a warm friend" of Kelly's, and manager Selee wanted Kelly back, but President Soden and Treasurer Billings were not keen on his return.[35]

By the middle of July, the National League pennant race had narrowed down to three contenders: New York, Chicago, and Boston. And the second-place Colts, having just lost two of three at home to the first-place Giants, welcomed the third-place Beaneaters for a three-game set. Chicago won the first game easily, with Ad Gumbert shutting out Boston, but each of the next two games went to extra innings before the Beaneaters succumbed. The last game was described as the most exciting of the season. Boston had taken a two-run lead in the top of the 12th inning, but in the bottom of the inning, with two on and two out, a pop fly fell just in front of Stovey, whose throw to the plate "went against the stand, all three men scoring and the game was won before the crowd realized what had happened."[36] And with that sweep, at the midpoint of the NL season, Chicago jumped back into first place.

The Beaneaters' long 3½-week road trip, during which they won 10 games and lost 10, was finally over. "Staley, Nichols, and Clarkson were the back bone of the team, Kid Nichols doing phenomenally good work in the box," wrote the *Globe*.[37] With the exception of a brief series in Philadelphia scheduled for the end of July, Boston would be welcoming all of the other NL teams at the South End Grounds over the next month.

After getting swept in Chicago, Boston bounced back during the last two weeks of July and the first week of August, winning 10 of 13 games and jumping into second place ahead of New York and trailing Chicago by only 1½ games, just in time for Cap Anson's team's visit to the Hub city.

The first game, on Thursday, August 6, played before a South End Grounds crowd of more than 5,000 fans, ended in the 13th inning when Nichols hit a Chicago batter with the bases loaded, forcing in the winning run. The loss dropped Boston back into third place.

The next day the Colts, behind their workhorse pitcher Hutchinson, won in extra innings again. The Beaneaters finally won on Saturday, in front of nearly 9,000 enthusiastic fans: "It was one of the old-time crowds that witnessed the game yesterday at the South End grounds," the *Globe* noted. "About every seat in the pavilion and on the bleachers was taken."[38]

By the middle of August, with Boston having concluded its long homestand by winning four of its last five games, and with Chicago losing two of three in New York, the National League race was as tight as it could be, with the Colts in first place, a half-game ahead of the second-place Beaneaters, and one game ahead of the third-place Giants.

Boston then left for its last long road trip of the season, a three-week tour of every NL city but Philadelphia.

At their first stop, in New York, the Beaneaters took two of three from the Giants, permanently relegating the Giants to third place in the NL pennant race. During their next stop, in Brooklyn, Harry Stovey again fell to the curse of Brooklyn's George Hemming, striking out against him four times, almost equaling the five times Stovey fanned against Hemming back at the end of June. While on the next leg of their road trip, in Pittsburgh, there was a big headline on the front page of the August 26 edition of the *Boston Globe*:

"Kelly Jumps. Will Play with Boston League Team."[39]

Mike Kelly signed a contract that would pay him $25,000 from that date to the end of the following season. It was the "largest salary ever paid to a ball player."[40]

Director Conant said, "Well, the King is home again. He's back with the club he first started with in Boston. He has cost a good deal of money, but he is worth it, and he is the greatest drawing card in the base ball profession. Just imagine the people who will go to see him in Chicago when he gets there."[41]

There were, not surprisingly, major repercussions to this announcement. Coincidentally, representatives of the National League and American Association were meeting in Washington to try to hammer out a new national agreement, but the news about Kelly caused Association President Kramer to call a halt to the conference. "Breach is widened" was the subheadline in the *Globe*.[42]

And *Globe* columnist Tim Murnane couldn't resist making this snide remark: "If Mike Kelly has signed with the league he will probably play with one arm, as he took an oath some time ago that he would cut off his right wing sooner than sign with the league."[43]

Overshadowed by the controversial news about Kelly signing with the League and his reappearance in the Beaneaters' lineup beginning with the games in Cleveland, the Beaneaters won only half of their games over the last two weeks of their road trip, and fell from a half-game back of the Colts to five games back when they arrived in Chicago for a three-game series in early September.

In the first game between the two remaining NL pennant contenders, Chicago walloped Boston, 10-1, Bill Hutchinson limiting the Beaneaters to just two hits.[44] The next day, "Anson created a sensation by appearing on the field with flowing whiskers of snowy whiteness and long white hair. He played the game through in this disguise and the crowd seemed to enjoy the sight."[45] And Chicago won again, expanding its lead over Boston to a seemingly irretrievable seven games. The Beaneaters managed to salvage a small sense of pride by beating the Colts in the last game of the series, wrapping up their 19-game road trip with 10 wins and 9 losses. They then headed home, where they would host all of the League's teams at the South End Grounds over the last four weeks of the season.

Despite being so far behind Chicago in the standings, "Manager Selee said that nothing would please him more than to see the Boston league and association teams playing a series for the world's championship this fall. This would please the patrons of base ball in this part of the country more than any other thing the magnates could do."[46]

The Labor Day doubleheader at the South End Grounds was rained out, but the Beaneaters played back-to-back doubleheaders against visiting Cleveland over the next two days, winning three of four. They then swept three games from visiting Cincinnati, reducing Chicago's lead to 4½ games as the Colts arrived in Boston for their last visit.

In front of a large Monday crowd of more than 6,000 at the South End Grounds on September 14, Chicago's "Cannon-ball Willie" Hutchinson beat the Beaneaters again, holding them to just three hits for his 42nd victory of the season. Chicago won again the next day, John Clarkson getting roughed up by the Colts. Chicago had extended its lead to 6½ games and the *Boston Journal* said, "The Bostons might as well at once give up all hope of winning the championship this year. In the first place there are too few games to play to catch up with Anson; in the next place, they must play a far better game than they have shown of late to be able to cope with any team of the ability of the Chicagos."[47]

When Boston finally beat Chicago on September 16, Nichols beating Hutchinson, little did anyone know that the Beaneaters had begun what would turn out to be the most remarkable pennant-grabbing stretch-run sprint in baseball history.

After having a tied game called on account of darkness, Boston won three straight from Pittsburgh at the same time that New York was sweeping three from Chicago, Giants workhorse Amos Rusie winning two of the games.

The Beaneaters then took four in a row from visiting Brooklyn, followed by a three-game sweep of Philadelphia. The Colts pretty much kept up, winning all five of their scheduled games. Chicago's 1½-game lead looked somewhat tenuous, but as they headed into the last week of the season, the Colts' final two series would be with sub-.500 teams: fifth-place Cleveland and tail-ender Cincinnati. Boston, meanwhile, would have to face two teams with winning records: the third-place Giants and the fourth-place Phillies.

Then came the controversial series that would forever cast a shadow over the accomplishments of the 1891 Boston Beaneaters team. The New York Giants came to the South End Grounds a bit battered and lackadaisical after having been eliminated in the pennant race. In the first game of the series, the Giants sent 23-year-old Roscoe Coughlin to the pitcher's box to face the Beaneaters. Coughlin was making only his fifth start of the season. Star first baseman Roger Connor and starting catcher Dick Buckley were not in the lineup for the Giants as they were pummeled by the Beaneaters, 11-3. The skepticism about the integrity of the Giants' effort began right in Boston, as the Reds' "Billy Joyce was at the South End grounds yesterday and said: 'I wonder if that's the team [Jim] Mutrie [manager of the Giants] would put against the Reds for $1,000? Why, that crowd of Giants couldn't beat nine schoolboys.' "[48]

Chicago, meanwhile, lost to the Spiders, with Cy Young beating Bill Hutchinson, so the Colts' lead was down to a half-game.

More than 5,000 fans showed up for Tuesday's doubleheader, as they saw the Beaneaters easily take both games from the Giants. Although New York had aging veteran Mickey Welch pitch the first game, its pitcher for the second game was Mike Sullivan, who was making his first-ever start for the team. Connor and Buckley were still missing from the Giants' lineup, while Bobby Lowe and Harry Stovey led a barrage of hits against both Welch and Sullivan as Boston won, 13-8 and 11-3.[49] Even Tim

Murnane was disappointed in the way that the Giants were playing, writing, "The same teams play two games this afternoon, and the Giants should put a little more life into their work if they wish base ball to hold its present high standing among outdoor games."[50]

Chicago won a wild back-and-forth game in Cleveland, 14-13, winning in the bottom of the ninth inning, but the Colts and Beaneaters were now in a virtual tie, Chicago leading by the smallest of margins in winning percentage (.626, 82-49 for the Colts vs .624, 83-50 for Boston).[51]

On the last day of September, more than 4,000 fans came to the South End Grounds to see Boston's last home games of the season. The Beaneaters again won both games of a doubleheader, beating New York 16-5 and 5-3, running their winning streak to 16 games. Although Connor returned to the Giants' lineup, star outfielder Hardy Richardson was absent, and the Giants started Coughlin in the first game and Sullivan in the second, a far cry from aces Amos Rusie (33-20 for the season) and John Ewing (21-8). And Chicago was again beaten by Cy Young, so, for the first time since early May, the Beaneaters moved into sole possession of first place, 1½ games ahead of the slumping Colts. The *Globe* effused, "The Boston league team wound up the season of '91 at the South End grounds yesterday by taking two games from New York and going to the front in the greatest struggle known in the history of base ball."[52]

President James Hart of the Chicago club was irate. That same day, Wednesday, September 30, he wrote to National League President Nick Young asking whether prior consent had been given for Boston to play all of those doubleheaders it had played recently at the South End Grounds (September 19 with Pittsburgh, September 23 with Brooklyn, and September 29 and 30 with New York). According to Hart, consent had to have been granted by six clubs prior to the games having been played. If consent had not been given, then Hart wanted the games "declared void and thrown out of the championship table and the decision made public in tomorrow morning's papers."[53]

The *Globe* reported that Hart later said: "Public sentiment is running high, and it seems to favor the idea that the Eastern clubs are not playing as well as they might. I have no accusations to make against anybody, but I will say that things do look suspicious."[54]

On October 1, the Beaneaters clinched the pennant, with Clarkson beating the Phillies for Boston's 17th consecutive win. In Chicago, meanwhile, in front of only 2,000 resigned fans, "Cincinnati won from Anson's men today partly because [Tony] Mullane was in wonderful form and partly because the Chicagos manifestly played like men fighting for a lost cause. All of their ginger is gone, and the game was as dreary a thing as one could wish to see, particularly after the score board had announced another Boston victory."[55]

Two days later, there was a report from Chicago that "President James A. Hart of the Chicago club today received a telegram from Nick Young, telling him that every club but Chicago had given its consent to the extra games played by the Boston club lately.

"When he received this, Mr. Hart resolved on his course of action at once. On Monday he will forward to President Young formal charges of crookedness on the part of New York in their last games with Boston. 'I shall probe the matter to the bottom,' was Mr. Hart's parting shot."[56]

The following day the headlines on the front page of the *Globe* lauded the Beaneaters: "The league champions of 1892 will hail from Boston. It has been some time since Boston pulled off the league pennant, although they have made a good fight for the last three years. This year it looked almost impossible to overtake Capt. Anson's Chicago team, but the boys set about the task three weeks ago, and the magnificent work they did from that time until Chicago was passed and the pennant landed was never surpassed in this country.

"To Capt. William Nash and Manager Frank Selee belongs the most credit for bringing the honor to this city. Selee got out all the play there was in his men, and saw they needed a pitcher, when Staley was secured."[57]

As for the possibility of the two Boston champions playing a series to decide the world's championship, an article from Washington stated that NL President Nick Young had received a dispatch from AA President Zach Phelps saying, "The pennant club of the Association hereby challenges the pennant club of the League to play a series of three, five, or seven games for the world's championship."[58]

The Reds, who featured future Hall of Fame sluggers Dan Brouthers and Hugh Duffy, led all of major-league baseball in runs scored. The Beaneaters, meanwhile, allowed the fewest runs in the NL, thanks to their star pitchers John Clarkson (33-19, 2.79), Kid Nichols (30-17, 2.39), and Harry Staley (20-8, 2.50). What an incredible series it would have been for the Hub — a baseball version of the irresistible force versus the immovable object!

However, the series never occurred, as President Young replied to Phelps, "I hold in my possession an agreement called the national agreement, which was solemnly signed by three parties, one of which was your association. I sincerely regret that the breaking of that agreement by your association renders such a series of games as you propose impossible."[59]

Two days later, on October 12, the *Globe* published a letter to the Boston Reds club from President Phelps, saying that he had challenged the NL champs to a world's series, but they declined. He also said that the club itself challenged the Boston NL club and they declined. He then mocked the NL's excuse of using the national agreement. "There can, of course, be no agreement except there be at least two parties thereto, and the league alone is now party to what they are pleased to call the 'national agreement.'"[60]

The next day the committee assigned to investigate the charges brought against the New York Giants by President Hart of the Chicago club submitted its final report, exonerating all involved. The report concluded that the Giants' poor showing was attributable to their crippled condition. The committee thus determined that the charges of deliberate bad faith were unfounded and the committee regretted that full credit for having won the championship in such spectacular fashion was withheld from Boston as a result of the charges made by Chicago.[61]

The season of 1891 was arguably the city of Boston's greatest in its long, rich major-league history. The controversy surrounding the existence of two teams in the city, the weaving throughout the season of the story of favorite son Mike "King" Kelly, the unprecedented stretch run, pennant-grabbing, 18-game winning streak of the Beaneaters, and the unresolved argument as to which team was better, the American Association champion Reds or the National League champion Beaneaters, all made the season among the most memorable ever.

NOTES

1 "League Men Object," *Boston Globe*, January 14, 1891.
2 T.H. Murnane, "He Loves the Game," *Boston Globe*, August 1, 1891.
3 Ibid.
4 "Untangling the Tangle," *Boston Globe*, January 16, 1891.
5 T.H. Murnane, "Two Stars Sign," *Boston Globe*, February 6, 1891.
6 T.H. Murnane, "Pick of the Stars," *Boston Globe*, January 18, 1891.
7 Ibid.
8 T.H. Murnane, "War Declared," *Boston Globe*, February 15, 1891.
9 T.H. Murnane, "Base Ball War," *Boston Globe*, February 16, 1891.
10 "Kranmer [sic] at the Helm," *Boston Globe*, February 19, 1891.
11 "In War Paint," *Boston Globe*, February 18, 1891.
12 "Kranmer [sic] at the Helm."
13 "Big Money Got Him," *Boston Globe*, March 8, 1891.
14 T.H. Murnane, "Experts at Practice," *Boston Globe*, March 26, 1891.
15 T.H. Murnane, "How They Pitch," *Boston Globe*, March 30, 1891.
16 J.C. Edgerly, "Boston on Top," *Boston Globe*, April 3, 1891.
17 Ibid.
18 T.H. Murnane, "Murnane Sizes Them Up," *Boston Globe*, April 20, 1891.
19 "Grand Send Off," *Boston Globe*, April 23, 1891.
20 "Five Straight," *Boston Globe*, April 28, 1891.
21 Ibid.
22 T.H. Murnane, "Trying Point Reached," *Boston Globe*, May 4, 1891.
23 T.H. Murnane, "One on 'Anse,'" *Boston Globe*, May 12, 1891.
24 T.H. Murnane, "Hoss and Hoss," *Boston Globe*, May 13, 1891.
25 T.H. Murnane, "When Hits Would Tell," *Boston Globe*, May 23, 1891.
26 T.H. Murnane, "Costly Experiment," *Boston Globe*, May 27, 1891.
27 "Staley Signs With Boston," *Boston Globe*, May 27, 1891.
28 "Off His Fodder," *Boston Globe*, May 31, 1891.
29 "Tried Two Pitchers," *Boston Globe*, June 3, 1891.
30 Jean-Pierre Caillault, personal notes for future biography of Harry Stovey.
31 "Chicago Today," *Boston Globe*, June 8, 1891.
32 T.H. Murnane, "They Are After Kelly," *Boston Globe*, June 19, 1891.
33 Ibid.
34 Joseph L. Reichler, *The Great All-Time Baseball Record Book* (New York: Macmillan Publishing, 1981), 92.
35 T.H. Murnane, "Wanted 'King Kel' Back," *Boston Globe*, July 4, 1891.
36 "Played Twelve Innings," *Boston Globe*, July 17, 1891.
37 "On Their Native Heath," *Boston Globe*, July 18, 1891.
38 T.H. Murnane, "Anson Was Merciful," *Boston Globe*, August 9, 1891.
39 J.C. Edgerly, "Kelly Jumps," *Boston Globe*, August 26, 1891.
40 Ibid.
41 Ibid.
42 T.H. Murnane, "Breach Is Widened," *Boston Globe*, August 26, 1891.
43 T.H. Murnane, "New Agreement Needed," *Boston Globe*, August 26, 1891.
44 "Downed Again," *Boston Globe*, September 4, 1891.
45 "Bostons Not in It," *Boston Globe*, September 5, 1891.
46 "Leaguers at Home," *Boston Globe*, September 8, 1891.
47 "Both Beaten," *Boston Journal*, September 16, 1891.
48 "Base Ball Notes," *Boston Globe*, September 29, 1891.
49 T.H. Murnane, "Won Both in a Canter," *Boston Globe*, September 30, 1891.
50 Ibid.
51 Ibid.
52 T.H. Murnane, "Forged Ahead," *Boston Globe*, October 1, 1891.
53 "'Things Look Suspicious,'" *Boston Globe*, October 1, 1891.
54 Ibid.
55 "Still They Win," *Boston Globe*, October 2, 1891.
56 "President Hart's Action," *Boston Globe*, October 4, 1891.
57 "Champions of '92," *Boston Globe*, October 5, 1891.
58 "League Club Cannot Play," *Boston Globe*, October 10, 1891.
59 Ibid.
60 "Champions of the World," *Boston Globe*, October 12, 1891.
61 "Exonerate All," *Boston Globe*, October 14, 1891.

BOSTON BEANEATERS OF 1892

BY STEVE HATCHER

The Beaneaters, 1892
(McGreevy Collection, Boston Public Library)

The result of the prior year's conflict between the two major circuits ended with the demise of the American Association.[1] It was also the death of a favorable two-league balance for all concerned. Specifically, that meant the interleague rivalry both on the diamond and through the turnstiles that previously produced the ballplayers' edge in the market. For the first time since 1881, the only operating major league left in baseball was the National League.

The league's new name was now officially the National League and American Association of Professional Base Ball Clubs, which suggests a merger. It was not a merger but an absorption of the Association's four most desirable clubs, Louisville, Washington, St. Louis, and Baltimore. The League, after 16 years, had evolved into a nice blend of six Eastern and six Western members in roughly the same Northeastern quarter of the nation that major-league baseball would represent for the next 66 years.[2]

The Triumvirs (Arthur Soden, James B. Billings, and William H. Conant) were in a windfall position since recent events left the Beaneaters (or Bean-eaters, or Bean Eaters, or even Reds in rare instances) as the sole major-league team in the Boston area. Actually, Charles A. Prince, owner of the Boston Reds of the American Association, had desired to leave baseball in any event and agreed to the League's terms without much difficulty.

One of the first monopolistic moves that the owners undertook was to limit each club to 15 players, an increase of one from the previous five years.[3] Manager Frank Selee's roster was basically a mirror of last October's club except for three remarkable gains. The first was Jack Stivetts, the stocky right-handed 33-game winner for the St. Louis Browns of a year earlier. Happy Jack, as he was called, was downhearted playing for Chris Von der Ahe, owner of the Browns, and signed with Boston for 1892 one month before the end of the 1891 season.[4] Von der Ahe also lost his brilliant right fielder, Tommy McCarthy, to the Boston triumvirate and vainly demanded some sort of redemption from their organization. Von der Ahe's redemption was achieved to his own peculiar satisfaction when he sent two constables to Tommy's room at the Lindell Hotel in St. Louis on April 30 and seized his watch and chain to force satisfaction of a claim for $300 advance money given by the Browns' owner. McCarthy paid $19.50 to get his timepiece returned; Von der Ahe then signed Boston's recently released Steve Brodie, whom McCarthy replaced.[5] McCarthy was a hometown boy, born in South Boston on July 24, 1863, and had played 40 games for the Beaneaters back in 1885. Manager Selee had managed McCarthy with Oshkosh of the Northwestern League in 1887.[6] The Beaneaters also signed "Humpty Dumpty" Hugh Duffy, the center fielder at the Congress Street Grounds, where the Boston Reds played, and the only one of Prince's athletes who signed to play at the South End, a player the Boston directors had coveted for years. Duffy, who was the spring season coach for the Brown University team in Providence, was "looking fine as silk" after shedding about 12 pounds.[7] The outfield duo of Duffy and McCarthy became forever known as the Heavenly Twins.[8]

To heighten fan interest, the League-Association reintroduced a split-season format. With an expanded 154-game schedule, the champions of the first 77 games were to meet the winner of the second 77 in a best-of-nine series for the world's championship.[9]

The "Spring Programme" arranged by manager Selee began on March 31 at Charlottesville, Virginia, with two or three games against the University of Virginia nine. The team also played games in Richmond, Virginia, and Naugatuck, Connecticut, near Waterbury. The schedule concluded with games against Yale University, Brown University, and finally Princeton University on the way south to Washington.[10]

The regular-season opener was played on April 12 at National Park in Washington on a bitter cold day before 6,000 to 7,000 spectators, overflowing the grandstand and bleachers.[11] The Beaneaters, behind a 13-hit attack, trounced the Senators, 14-4, scoring six times in the seventh inning. Selee's lineup included Herman Long at short, Duffy in center, Harry Stovey in left, Tommy McCarthy in right, Captain Billy Nash at third, aging Mike "King" Kelly catching, Australian Joe Quinn at second, switch-hitting Tommy "Foghorn" Tucker at first, and 30-year-old John Clarkson in the box.[12]

With essentially this same Opening Day lineup, Boston surged to the forefront with the power and purpose of 400 stampeding buffalo (which was about all that remained of the species in 1892). Selee's nine won 12 of their first 15 matches.

His battery troupe alternated between catchers Mike Kelly, 37-year-old Charlie Bennett, and Charlie Ganzel, and pitchers Kid Nichols, Jack Stivetts, and Harry Staley, who together with Clarkson completed what appeared to be the first great starting rotation of four.

The Beaneaters won 15 of their first 18 matches, almost entirely on the road, before losing two in a row against the Cleveland Spiders at League Park on May 9 and 10. One of the more interesting games during that stretch was a scoreless 14-inning tie at Cincinnati's League Park on May 6 between Clarkson and Icebox Chamberlain of the Reds. Both hurlers completed what they started in the 2-hour 35-minute marathon. The pitchers' duel also extended to the bat, as the two boxmen both connected for two-base hits.[13]

The two victories on Decoration Day (Memorial Day) drew 3,687 fans to the morning game at the South End, while the afternoon game drew 7,367.[14] The morning contest featured John Clarkson versus Cy Young and the Spiders in an exciting 10-inning duel cleanly played for the first nine innings. The game was decided in the 10th by two walks, Young's miscue, and singles by Kelly and Stovey for a 4-0 triumph. If we ignore the five-run fifth that Cleveland fashioned, the afternoon match was a cakewalk for the Beaneaters, as the cranks were entertained to a 12-6 victory. King Kelly was the star with a double, two singles, and brilliant catching, helping Harry Staley win his eighth straight game.[15]

After Stivetts completed the three-game sweep of Cleveland by outpitching the Spiders' Nig Cuppy on May 31 by a score of 2-1, Boston found itself with a 4½-game lead over the second-place Chicago Colts, and stood 27-9.

The individual statistics as of June 9 placed Duffy ninth in batting at .320, but Boston was only eighth with a .234 average. Stivetts was first in the long-forgotten average earned-runs-per-game-by-opposition at 0.91. The Bostonians ranked just fifth in fielding average with a .934 average.[16] The early numbers and facts supported Cap Anson's claim that the Beaneaters were lucky. Even Stivetts wondered how the club kept winning despite a lack of hitting. His guess was that winning can be attributed to pitching and baserunning.[17]

In June, the club won 18 of 27 matches behind the tandem of Nichols winning eight of nine games, and Stivetts who won seven of eight while pacing the league in batting. Nichols, with two straight shutouts on June 22 and 24, had a string of 23 scoreless innings before giving up a run in the first inning at New York on June 27. Staley, with his effective "drops," started just four games, with meager run support. Boston had improved to 45-18 with a 5½-game lead over Brooklyn with just 12 days to go before the end of the season's first half.

June was a month of adjustments as club owners cut their squads to 13 in an effort to help defray the $130,000 indebtedness owed to the four frozen-out clubs of the American Association. Boston's two casualties were genial Harry Stovey and John Clarkson. Stovey, hitting just .164 over 38 games, was given the usual 10-day notice on June 20 for his release effective July 1.[18] His lackluster performance possibly resulted from what was described as a case of vertigo, or sore side, or some other undescribed ailment along with a strained hip early in the season; nonetheless, the 35-year-old landed a job with the hapless Baltimore Orioles on July 9 and managed better personal results.[19] John Clarkson was released on June 30 when his sore arm recurred.[20] His record up to his discharge was eight wins and seven losses. In one grand fling to the winds, the Triumvirs unloaded two of their oldest players and their heavy contracts as well.

For Clarkson it was especially thankless. Handsome John piled up 149 victories during his 4½ years with the Beaneaters, placing him second only to Albert Spalding in the 22-year history of the club. He was also the club's last 40-game winner (1889).

The loss of Clarkson was more than made up for by the singular efforts of Stivetts, the most valuable player on the squad. Not only did he match Nichols' record of 35 wins and 16 losses, Jack helped himself offensively with three homers and a .296 batting average, second best on the team.

Stovey's replacement in left field was Bobby Lowe, 26 years old, who was usually placed sixth or seventh in the batting order during the second half. Manager Selee, however, had no choice but to settle on his three remaining boxmen for the rest of the year, a simple task considering the lack in quality, depth, and endurance that the other managers were faced with. Clarkson's last game as a Beaneater came on June 28 in an 8-1 defeat at the hands of Timothy Keefe and the rising second-place Phillies at their cavernous Huntingdon Grounds in Philadelphia. Clarkson eventually landed with the Spiders of Cleveland and lost all three of his starts against his former club, all against Staley.

Near the end of the first half, Billy Nash, under a two-year contract, decided that the rigors of being captain detracted too much from his performance on the baseball diamond. It didn't help that he missed several games because of an injured hand with the first-half flag on the line.[21] Kelly, with all his savvy and experience, was awarded the position, this time without John Morrill, his old nemesis, to oversee his off-field antics.[22]

On July 11, new captain King Kelly had his gang take the field sporting beards in all sorts of ridiculous uniforms of ethnic varieties at Chicago's West Side Park, much to the dismay of Cap Anson and the Chicago reporters. The masquerade was in retaliation for Anson appearing at the South End with a set of long whiskers. Aside from the display, Boston won the match, 3-2, behind Kid Nichols.[23]

Billy Nash and Frank Selee guided their crew to a record of 52 wins and 22 losses to take the first-half title or pennant by 2½ games over Brooklyn. The Beaneaters defeated the Bridegrooms four out of seven times during the half.

The figures for the first half, which ended on July 13, showed that Stivetts was the top hitter in the league at .382, but with just 102 at-bats. For the twenty-first-century fan, the more acceptable leader was Oyster Burns of Brooklyn with a .366 average based on 262 at-bats. Among everyday players with an acceptable number of at-bats, Hugh Duffy was Boston's top batter and fourth overall in the League-Association with a .333 average. Herman Long was third on the club at .296 and Tucker was fourth with a .266 average, which placed him 44th in the league. Apart from Stivetts, the Beaneaters pitchers collectively hit .159 with eight long hits. Fielding was mixed as Ganzel led all catchers in fielding average (.980), and pitcher Staley had committed just one error so far.[24]

The Bostons got off to a wobbly start in the second half, losing to St. Louis in the opener, 20-3, on July 15, as Nichols gave up 20 hits in the most lopsided defeat of the year. Their second-half record stood at 8-6 on July 31, which was good for a fifth-place tie but only a single game behind three teams in first.

Some of their troubles could be attributed to pesky injuries. Bennett had been knocked out in one game. Ganzel's leg was incapacitated, unfit for duty, leaving poor-hitting Kelly to do all the catching. Long was suffering from an aching arm, resulting in a number of errant throws. And then there's the familiar blame directed at the umpiring, particularly Tim Hurst, the long-serving arbiter.[25]

August was not much better as Selee's crew managed a 14-11 record for the month and 22-17 for the half, rising to second place, but a distant seven games behind the surging Cleveland Spiders. The month featured four shutouts, two by Harry Staley. On August 5 Nichols pitched a 12-inning shutout against Brooklyn at Eastern Park that was finally decided when Tucker was hit by a pitch followed by a clean two-run homer by Stivetts, playing left field. The 6-foot-2 right-hander himself hurled an 11-0 no-hitter the next day against the Bridegrooms, marred a tad by five walks. It was the first in franchise history and the first one by friend or foe in Boston. On August 8 Staley pitched a four-hit whitewash of the Senators, a 7-0 victory at Boundary Field a.k.a National Park in the nation's capital. Boston pitchers threw three consecutive shutouts and 33 consecutive innings without giving up a run.[26] Notwithstanding Stivetts's pitching, off the field he was the center of unrest on the club that may have contributed to their subpar play so far in the second half, bringing manager Selee to the brink of trading his star to Cincinnati in exchange for Tony Mullane.[27]

Four players made appearances in just one game for Boston during the season. The first was catcher Joe Daly, the 23-year-old brother of Tom Daly of the Brooklyn Bridegrooms. Daly began the year with Columbia of the four-team South Atlantic League that went belly-up in late July. His one appearance for the Beaneaters came in relief of Kelly on August 13 against Philadelphia.[28] A fortnight later, handsome Lee Viau, recently released by Louisville, was signed and pitched one game on August 27, a nifty five-hit, 8-1 triumph over his former teammates at Eclipse Park. Selee changed his lineup for the match by placing Lowe in the leadoff spot and moving each player down a notch.[29]

On August 15, one month into the second half, the Bostons found themselves in third place, 2½ games behind Cleveland after Staley shut down John Clarkson and the Spiders, 5-0. Staley allowed only two hits, a double by Chief Zimmer and a single by Clarkson. Despite missing an entire week, left fielder Bobby Lowe was the topmost hitter on the club for the second half with a .313 average, followed by Billy Nash at .305.[30]

The determined Hubites steamrolled over the remainder of the second half, winning 28 out of 37 matches, and finishing three games behind the Spiders in second place. Under King Kelly's field leadership, the Beaneaters won 50 out of 76 decisions that still prompted some observers to accuse Boston of coasting in the second half. The Beaneaters, in any case, made history and became the first team to pass the century mark in one season, amassing 102 victories overall and a .680 winning percentage.

As a point of interest, John Clarkson's younger brother, Arthur, a blond 26-year-old right-hander nicknamed Dad at some point in his career, was plucked from the Philadelphia bench and/or the Troy Trojans where he had pitched 390 innings. He started one game for Boston and defeated Amos Rusie and New York, 3-1, in the second game of a doubleheader on October 8, a seven-inning affair.[31] The only other player to appear for Boston in one game was catcher Dan Burke, formerly of the Brockton Shoemakers, on October 1, after Kelly hurt his finger the previous day.[32]

Part of Boston's improvement over the 1891 season was due to the team's consistency on the road. There was no missing the fact, however, that Boston only did what the other seven National League seniors had done. The four hapless remnants of the Association were picked to pieces by the gang of eight and finished 9th, 10th, 11th, and 12th.

For good measure, Stivetts added a five-inning, 6-0 no-hitter against Washington at Boundary Field in the second game of a doubleheader on October 15, the final game of the regular season. It was also the last regular-season no-hitter hurled from the literal "box" of the pitcher.

There was a rumor or possibly a consideration that the world's championship would not be played, but played it was to the satisfaction of Boston's and Cleveland's populace. The series would consist of three games in Cleveland, three in Boston, and three in New York if necessary.[33]

The much-anticipated first game was played at League Park in Cleveland on October 17 before 6,000 spectators including League President N.E. Young, and several League umpires.[34] The crowd was blessed by a marvelous pitching battle between Jack Stivetts and Cy Young, backed by several extraordinary defensive gems and a pitching struggle for the ages as Stivetts battled Young in a scoreless tie that went 11 innings until darkness prevented its conclusion. Both teams had opportunities to score. Duffy in the fourth inning and Lowe in the fifth were the only Beaneaters to reach third base. For the Spiders, Jesse Burkett took a chance during a discussion between Quinn and the umpire and dashed for home.[35] Quinn threw a perfect throw to catcher Kelly and Burkett was tagged out one foot from the plate.[36]

The next day Harry Staley held the Spiders to three runs on 10 hits and bested John Clarkson, 4-3, before 7,500 spectators at League Park. The batting hero for the Beaneaters was Hugh Duffy with a double and two triples. Down 4-2, the Spiders had a chance to tie in the ninth inning when catcher Chief Zimmer banged a two-out triple that hit the top of the left-field fence, over 350 feet from home plate, scoring Jack O'Connor who singled. However, Clarkson – hitting just .139 for Cleveland – hit the ball hard to Staley, who fumbled momentarily before recovering and tossing the ball to Tucker at first to end the game.[37]

Game Three was played at League Park on October 19 before 7,500 fans on a clear, balmy afternoon. It was a rematch between Young and Stivetts in the box, as both struggled through the first couple of innings. For the Spiders, Cupid Childs led off with a smash past Nash at third base for a single; Burkett followed with a double to left, putting men on second and third. Ed McKean then drove both runners home with a one-out single to center. The Spiders never scored again. In Boston's half of the first inning, Herman Long singled, but was forced out by McCarthy, who then stole second. With two out, catcher Charlie Ganzel singled to right, scoring McCarthy. In Boston's half of the second inning, Bobby Lowe singled to left and was advanced to second base by Tucker's sacrifice. Light-hitting Quinn lifted a fly ball to left field that Burkett misjudged, giving the second baseman a gift double and Boston's second run and tying the game, 2-2. The teams failed to score until Boston's half of the eighth inning when Stivetts doubled and then scored on McCarthy's single for what turned out to be the winning run. Cleveland mounted a threat in the ninth as Jimmy McAleer got to third where he "died."[38]

The two contestants then changed their base of operations and two days later, on October 21, the series continued at Boston's South End Grounds before 6,547 spectators, enjoying the cool but fair weather. For the first time the Beaneaters appeared in blue stockings instead of their familiar red. The Boston battery consisted of Nichols in the box and Charlie Bennett behind the plate. The Cleveland battery comprised Nig Cuppy pitching and Zimmer once again behind home base.

Cupid Childs walked to open the match, but failed to reach second. In the Boston half of the first, Cuppy gave up one-out walks to McCarthy and Duffy without any damage. The Beaneaters scored in the third inning when McCarthy walked for the second time and Duffy hit the first offering over the right-field fence, much to the delight of the home crowd. Nichols continued to hold the Spiders scoreless with a couple of key strikeouts, backed by some fine fielding, especially by Billy Nash at the hot corner. In the sixth inning, Boston rallied for two more runs. Duffy opened with a single but was cut down by Zimmer trying to steal. Nash got to first on an error by first baseman Jake Virtue, who dropped shortstop Ed McKean's wide throw. Nash stole second, and went to third on a safe bunt hit by Lowe, who then stole second. Light-hitting Quinn brought both runners in with a sharp hit up the middle. The final score was 4-0, as Boston won its third game without a loss.[39]

The fifth game of the championship series was played on Saturday, October 22, in the presence of 8,486 recorded fans at the South End. Cy Young complained of a lame arm and was replaced in the box by John Clarkson for his fifth attempt to defeat his former teammates.

The Cleveland devotees became jubilant after the Spiders scored six times off Harry Staley in the second inning. With two away, Chief Zimmer singled. The next batter was manager Patsy Tebeau, who gained first base on Herman Long's fumble. Clarkson then cracked a homer over the right-field fence for a 3-0 lead, but the visitors were not finished. Another two runs were scored after a single by Childs and another error by Long allowing Burkett to reach first, and a walk to Virtue to load the bases. Shortstop Ed McKean drove in Zimmer and Tebeau with a blast off the top board of the right-field fence. Virtue scored the sixth run while catcher Ganzel tried to throw out McKean trying to steal second base.

The score stood at 6-0 until the fourth inning when the Beaneaters began to pound what were described as Clarkson's dewdrops and cut the deficit in half with three runs on four singles and two sacrifice hits. In the top of the fifth Cleveland scored one run when McKean singled, McAleer sacrificed, and Zimmer got a base hit to drive McKean in. With the score 7-3, Boston answered in its half of the fifth with two more runs. Herman Long reached first on an error by third baseman Tebeau and scored on McCarthy's double to right. Duffy sacrificed him to third and McCarthy scored on Billy Nash's fly ball to deep left, making the score 7-5. In the last of the sixth, Boston scored four more runs to take the lead on a single by Quinn, a triple by Stivetts, a single by Long to tie the score, and a wild throw by Tebeau to put McCarthy on second. On the play, Childs threw out Long trying to score. Duffy's double to right scored McCarthy for the go-ahead and eventual winning run, and a single by Ganzel drove in the ninth run. Three more insurance runs were tallied in the last of the seventh, the big blow being Tucker's home run over the right-field fence. Jack Stivetts allowed just one man to reach first over the final three innings. The final score was an extraordinary come-from-behind 12-7 victory.[40]

Selee's nine needed just one more victory to capture the championship. With the series outcome nearly assured, the turnout for the finale on October 24 was only about a third of the South End capacity.[41] It didn't help that the fair weather was in the 50s.

Once again Kid Nichols battled Cy Young. The umpires were Jack McQuaid on the bases and John Gaffney behind the plate. The Spiders grabbed a 3-0 lead in the third inning with singles by Young, Childs, and Burkett, who stole second base, and a wild throw. In the Boston half, however, the locals fought back with two runs as Nichols scored on Virtue's error and McCarthy scored on Duffy's double to left. In the fourth inning Boston teed off on Young's curves, scoring two more runs as Tucker, Bennett, and Nichols all singled, giving the Beaneaters a 4-3 lead. They added a run in the fifth when McCarthy doubled, moved to third on Duffy's hit, and scored on Tucker's grounder. In the sixth inning, Bennett smashed a home run over the right-field fence, improving the lead to 6-3.[42] Boston scored one run each in the seventh and eighth innings. The final score was 8-3 and Boston won the World's Flag for 1892 and their ninth pennant in what was described as a "Blooming Walk."[43]

When the final out was recorded, friends and fans of the team took to the field to congratulate their Beaneaters. Arthur Soden presented Frank Selee with a $1,000 check to be disbursed among the 13 players, about $76.92 per man.[44]

Not everyone was pleased. Had Cleveland won the fifth game, the series would have resumed in New York, where greater crowds meant more money, something the League's magnates were quietly wishing for. In fact, the feeling in the baseball world was that the double season was doomed. On the other hand, the 12-team league was simply too large for a practical or interesting race.

Although he was well back of Cupid Childs (.3351) and Dan Brouthers (.335) in the batting race, Hugh Duffy, who led his team during the regular season with a revised .301 average [an original average of .302] became the pre-eminent hitting star of the series with 12 hits, two doubles, two triples, and one homer, stamping him "as a man for an emergency."[45]

On October 27, 1,200 spectators attended a benefit in honor of the champs. The attractions included races and throwing competitions plus a five-inning match between a picked nine and the regulars that the Beaneaters lost through carelessness. The Beaneaters' longtime booster, General Arthur Dixwell, awarded each member of the Boston club a scarf pin.[46]

After the benefit, the players left for their homes, although some, like King Kelly, appeared on stage with Tony Lions in a performance of *We Never Strike Out*.[47] Kelly, along with Duffy and McCarthy, could be seen refereeing New England Polo League matches until winter set in. Bobby Lowe left for California after a stint with Uncle Billy Marshall's billiard parlor, and manager Frank Selee left for Melrose, about eight miles north of Boston, to build a house.[48]

NOTES

1 "The Real Situation," *The Sporting News*, December 12, 1891: 1.

2 In 1958 the Dodgers and the Giants moved to the West Coast.

3 The 15-player limit is noted by Harold Seymour in *Baseball: The Early Years* (New York: Oxford University Press, 1989), 266.

4 George V. Tuohey, *A History of the Boston Baseball Club* (Boston: M.F. Quinn & Co., 1897), 106.

5 "Unworthy a Magnate," *Sporting Life*, May 7, 1892: 1; "The Browns' Work, Tommy McCarthy's Case," *The Sporting News*, May 14, 1892: 1.

6 A.D. Suehsdorf, "Frank Selee, Dynasty Builder," *The National Pastime*, 1987: 330.

7 *Boston Globe*, February 22, 1892: 9; Jacob B. Morse, Hub Happenings, "That Cracking Outfield," *Sporting Life*, March 26, 1892: 15.

8 Donald Hubbard *The Heavenly Twins of Boston Baseball* (Jefferson, North Carolina: McFarland & Company, Inc., 2008).

9 In 1892 the postseason series was normally called the World's Championship and the Championship Series, and the World's Championship series.

10 Jacob B. Morse, "Hub Happenings," *Sporting Life*, March 26, 1892: 15.

11 Boundary Field was identified as National Park in *The Sporting News*, April 30, 1892: 1.

12 Duffy, McCarthy, Kelly, and Clarkson, as well as Selee himself were eventually enshrined in the National Baseball Hall of Fame.

13 National League "Games Played Friday, May 6," *Sporting Life*, May 14, 1892: 8.

14 "Decoration Day Attendance," *Sporting Life*, June 4, 1892: 2.

15 "Games Played Monday, May 30," *Sporting Life*, June 4, 1892: 3.

16 "The Big League Averages," *The Sporting News*, June 18, 1892: 4.

17 "Boston Ways," *Sporting Life*, July 16, 1892: 1.

18 T.H. Murnane, "Pretty Finish," *Boston Daily Globe*, June 21, 1892: 12.

19 "New York Wants Stovey," *The Sporting News*, May 7, 1892: 1; "Base Ball, Caught on the Fly," *The Sporting News*, May 21, 1892: 3; T.H.M., "Boston Releases Stovey," *The Sporting News*, June 25, 1892: 1; "Keeps the Boys Guessing," *Boston Globe*, May 10, 1892: 21; and various other sources.

20 Harold Kaese, *The Boston Braves* (Boston: Northeastern University Press, 2004), 60.

21 T.H. Murnane, "Cannot Lose It," *Boston Globe*, July 9, 1892: 5.

22 *Sporting Life*, August 13, 1892: 9; T.H. Murnane, "Awake at Last," *Boston Globe*, July 21, 1892: 5.

23 W.H.K., "Kelly's Little Joke," *The Sporting News*, July 16, 1892: 1; Base Ball, "Caught on the Fly," July 23, 1892: 3.

24 "Work of League Players," *Sporting Life*, July 23, 1892: 4. The author used original statistics.

25 Jacob C. Morse, "Hub Happenings," *Sporting Life*, July 30, 1892: 9.

26 "National League," *Sporting Life*, August 13, 1892: 3.

27 T.H. Murnane, "Shut Out," *Boston Daily Globe*, August 27, 1892: 5.

28 National League, "Games Played Saturday, August 13," *Sporting Life*, August 20, 1892: 3.

29 *The World*, August 28, 1892: 8; *Logansport* (Indiana) *Chronicle*, September 15, 1906: 6.

30 "League Leaders," *Sporting Life*, August 20, 1892: 3.

31 Jacob C. Morse, "Hub Happenings," *Sporting Life*, October 15, 1892: 9.

32 National League, "Games Played Saturday, October 1," *Sporting Life*, October 8, 1892: 4.

33 *Boston Evening Transcript*, October 17. 1892: 7.

34 According to various sources, the park had a capacity of 9,000 or 10,000.

35 Bob Emslie and Pop Snyder were the umpires, according to *The Sporting News* box score.

36 *Logansport* (Indiana) *Daily Pharos-Tribune*, October 18, 1892: 1; "For the Big Pennant, the Good Work Continues," *The Sporting News*, October 22, 1892: 3.

37 George Davis, who didn't finish the first game due to a sprained tendon in his heel, was unavailable for pinch-hitting.

38 "For the Big Pennant," *The Sporting News*, October 22, 1892: 3.

39 T.H. Murnane, "Duffy Again," *Boston Daily Globe*, October 22, 1892: 11.

40 The facts for the fifth game were drawn from the October 25 issue of the *Boston Globe* and the October 29 issue of *The Sporting News*.

41 Two references reported a crowd of 2,000. The park's capacity in 1888 was 6,800.

42 Cy Young thus became the last pitcher to serve up a home run from the pitcher's box in a major-league game. The box was 5½ feet long and Young was required to place one foot on the back line before his delivery, a distance of 55½ feet from the four-sided home plate.

43 Bean Blower, "In a Blooming Walk," *The Sporting News*, October 29, 1892: 3.

44 T.H. Murnane, "Five Straight," *Boston Globe*, October 25, 1892: 5.

45 Duffy's original average was .302 per *Reach's Official 1893 Base Ball Guide*; also .319 per Clarence Dow, "Cold Numerals," *Boston Globe*, October 19, 1892: 5. See also "The World's Series, Review of the Series," *Sporting Life*, October 29, 1892: 3.

46 "Picked Team Won," *Boston Globe*, October 28, 1892: 3; *Boston Evening Transcript*, October 28. 1892: 10.

47 "Kelly's Future," *The Sporting News*, October 29, 1892: 3.

48 For Kelly, Duffy, and McCarthy, see *Boston Post,* November 5, 1892: 5; and various other sources. For Lowe, see *Boston Post,* December 1, 1892: 3; and for Selee, see "Personals," *Sporting Life*, November 12, 1892: 3.

1893: SUMMER 35-5 STRETCH GARNERS THIRD STRAIGHT FLAG

BY RICHARD "DIXIE" TOURANGEAU

"It was the best of times, it was the worst of times, it was the age of wisdom, it was the age of foolishness …"

Novelist supreme Charles John Dickens was not a sportswriter and died (1870) 23 years before the 1893 Beaneaters season began, but the opening lines of his 1849 famed epic, *A Tale of Two Cities*, are perfect to describe the situation base ball found itself in by May 1893. Former player and Philadelphia sporting-goods entrepreneur A.J. Reach's *Official Base Ball Guide* was on the stands by late March and told of how 1892 had been a disappointment to fans, players, and owners, but that 1893 would likely be better. There would be no competitors to the 12-team National League and the NL schedule was cut back to 132 games from 154. Opening days were in late April, the pitcher's mound was moved back essentially 5 or 10 feet to facilitate more offense, owners had colluded and cut the largest player salaries (abhorrent to them and investors), and, finally, the split-season champion gimmick of 1892 was abolished. Because of these changes, there was springtime hope.[1]

Outside of baseball circles appeared the daily newspaper promotional reminders of mankind's self-backslap of great achievements, in the form of the wondrous Chicago Columbian Exposition, the World's Fair, within the spectacular 640-acre "White City," a nineteenth-century Disneyland, which included the first (specially constructed) Ferris wheel as one of many attractions. Baseball would open on April 27, and the fair would commence entertaining the world on May 1. Unfortunately, few saw the national doom of May 4 on the horizon. On that day the National Cordage Company, based in New Jersey but with tentacles all over the East Coast, went into receivership as it neared bankruptcy. NCC manufactured rope and had tried to corner the hemp market.[2] Overspending, wild speculation, and other reckless misdeeds by out-of-control businessmen combined to ignite the Panic of 1893, much larger in scope than the disastrous Panic of 1873. The NCC fiasco followed the "red flag" bankruptcy of the Pennsylvania and Reading Railroad (February 20) due to much the same policies. Even the nation's gold reserves almost disappeared because of bank runs caused by these developments. The economic catastrophe brought about became national as eventually 500 banks closed, 15,000 businesses collapsed, and unemployment soared to 20 percent by the summer. Within a week's time, what should have been a pleasant start to the baseball campaign instead found the sport merely hoping to survive a huge problem it had no part in creating. Hindsight analysis of the Panic explains that it took nearly four years for things to crawl back to normal thanks in part to clever financier J.P. Morgan, who loaned the government millions to help restore order. The daily life atmosphere was treacherous, but it didn't stop the World's Fair crowds or enthusiasm for baseball.

Reach's *Guide* had interesting news specifically for Boston's fan base. "The great slump in base ball interest in Boston has puzzled students of the game everywhere. Up to 1890 Boston bore the deserved reputation of being the best base ball city in the country. No other city could make a pretense of disputing that claim with her. Last year (1892) with a winning team, the club could scarcely draw patronage to pay expenses. This year, it is expected, will see Boston return to the old crowds."[3] The *Guide*'s attendance stats showed that the South End Grounds drew just under 124,000 fans, placing ninth in the 12-team League (total draw was 1.67 million).

In October 1892 the game had a lucrative "World's Championship Series" between Boston and Cleveland. It drew more than 20,000 in Cleveland's three games and almost 12,000 in Boston for three more. The Spiders and Beaneaters played a 0-0 tie in the first game and then Boston won the next five, making a joke of the best-of-nine event. Even winning the championship at home didn't bring out as many Boston fans as expected. The Beaneaters had now won two consecutive pennants and looked to equal the Chicago White Stockings of 1880-81-82 as three-time NL champs. Only its ancestral National Association Red Stockings of 1872-73-74-75 had won four straight along with the American Association ("Beer and Whiskey League") St. Louis Browns of the mid-1880s.

Arthur Soden's Beaneaters were a solid bunch and were kept hustling under the watchful eye of manager Frank Selee, then in his fourth season. The only changes made from 1892 were the release of aging stars, now deadweights, John Clarkson (p), Joe Quinn (2b), Mike King Kelly (c), and slugger Harry Stovey (of). Their slots were filled by younger teammates. Utilityman Bobby Lowe settled in at second base and Charlie Bennett and Charlie Ganzel formed the best catching tandem in the game. Cliff Carroll (of) was obtained from St. Louis and pitcher Hank Gastright arrived from Pittsburgh in July to round out the defending champions' roster. The pitching core of Charlie "Kid" Nichols, "Happy Jack" Stivetts, Harry Staley, and Gastright threw all but 36 innings for the year. With the expanded schedule in 1892, both Nichols and Stivetts had won 35 games. The infield of Billy Nash (3b), Herman Long (ss), Lowe, and Tommy Tucker (1b) was superb while flychasers Hugh Duffy and Tommy McCarthy could hit, run, and field with any opponent.

Starting sluggishly, the Beaneaters were 12-11 in late May but that changed during their decade-longest 34-game homestand (24-10), which included an eight-game winning streak. Later three nine-game streaks helped them into first place to stay by July 28. The "friendly and beautiful confines" of the South End Grounds were always helpful to the Beaneaters (49-15). Only Nichols, Stivetts, and Staley pitched in the first 58 games, but in July Gastright was bought from Pittsburgh and went 12-4. His acquisition is notable because Pittsburgh finished second to Boston that year. It was the only season of the 1890s when the Pirates sniffed the pennant, yet they parted with a good pitcher. Pittsburgh finished second in pitching (4.08 ERA) to St. Louis (4.06) and third in batting average, .299 to Philadelphia's .301. The Smoky City stars were Jake Beckley (.303), Denny Lyons (.306), Jack Glasscock (.341), Jake Stenzel (.362), Mike Smith (.346), George Van Haltren (.338), Connie Mack (.286), and pitcher Frank Killen (36-14). The Pirates beat Boston in the season's series 6-4-1, with one postponed game not played, but they still finished five games out.

Despite being fifth in both ERA (4.43) and batting average (.290), the Beaneaters raised the pennant. They were second in runs, 1,008, to Philly's 1,011 (played two more games). Boston finished 30-6 against Baltimore, St. Louis, and Louisville to gain their edge. Leading the club were Duffy (.363, fourth) and McCarthy (.346), while reserve catcher Bill Merritt hit .348 in 39 games. Long topped the circuit in runs scored (149), with Duffy close behind with 147. Billy Nash knocked home 123 mates (NL fourth). Lowe scored 130 runs and was tied for third in home runs with 14 to Ed Delahanty's 19, two guys who were later etched together forever in the record books. Nichols finished 34-14, second in wins to Pirate Killen (36) and tied with Cy Young of Cleveland. Head to head, Kid and Killen split two games in September. Staley surrendered the most home runs in the League, 22, of Boston's 66 total, topping the circuit. Offensively, Beaneater bats whacked 65 round-trippers, second to Philadelphia's 80.

The most noteworthy personal mark of the Beaneaters season belongs to veteran Staley (18-10) because it still lingers, more than 125 years later. On June 1 at the South End Grounds vs. Louisville's Hal Rhines, Harry belted two of his seven career home runs in a 15-4 win, plating nine runs in the process. It remains the Boston-Milwaukee-Atlanta franchise RBI record. It was equaled by Atlanta pitcher Tony Cloninger (two slams) on July 3, 1966. Stivetts (20-12) had the honor of tossing the only shutout at the South End Grounds all season when he blanked Chicago, 7-0, on August 31. On the opposite side of things, Cincinnati hurler Elton "Icebox" Chamberlain no-hit the champs on September 23 in Cincy, 6-0, in seven innings before the game was called due to darkness.

Of the players who made their first appearance in that NL season, the best careers belonged to Jimmy Bannon (he joined the Beaneaters in 1894), Bill Lange, Bill "Boileryard" Clarke, Heinie Reitz, George "Candy" LaChance (of the 1902-05 AL Bostons), and George "Tuck" Turner. Ending their careers were Clarkson, Quinn, King Kelly, Cliff Carroll (pickup who hit .224), Parisian Bob Caruthers, Smiling Tim Keefe (342 wins), four-time home-run champ Stovey, Sam Wise of the 1880s Bostons, Ed "Cannonball" Crane, and Boston catcher Charlie Bennett, who lost parts of both legs in a train accident in January 1894. He is often cited as the best catcher of the nineteenth century.

Among those notables who passed away were 1870s batting star Lipman Pike (.322), one of the first players paid for his talents; Elmer Sy Sutcliffe (.288), William Darby O'Brien (.282), John J. Fox (13-28), and Clarence G. Dow, 2-for-6 for the Boston Unions in September 1884. At his death the *Boston Globe*, *Boston Post*, and *Sporting Life* claimed Dow was thought of as the most reliable baseball statistician in the country.

In Reach's 10-cent, 150-page publication for 1894, the 1893 campaign was declared a financial success despite the economic woes of the country. Attendance swelled and helped pay off a huge debt the League had incurred a few years before. Reach thought the reason the number of .300 hitters grew from a dozen in 1892 to more than 60 in 1893 was in great part the mound distance change. He claimed, "The Public interest in the game was thereby most certainly stimulated. The more uncertain quantity in games under the increased batting gave fascination to the sport and the crowds which filled the grounds of the various clubs attested to the popularity of the new rule and its workings."[4] According to Baseball-Reference.com, 193,000 saw games at the South End Grounds, ranking seventh of the 12 teams.

SOURCES

In addition to the sources cited in the Notes, the author relied on Retrosheet.org, Baseball-Refrence.com, and the following:

Appleton's Annual Cyclopedia and Register of Important Events for the Year (annual 1893-1897). (New York: D. Appleton & Company, annuals 1893-1897).

Stevens, Albert Clark. "An Analysis of the Phenomena of the Panic in the United States in 1893," *Quarterly Journal of Economics* 8 (January 1894): 117-48. (Oxford University Press). jstor.org/stable/1883708.

NOTES

1. Before 1893 the pitcher's "box" was a five-foot area beginning 50 feet from home plate. The back boundary line was therefore 55 feet away but the hurler had the right to move around in his box to deliver a pitch. For 1893, new Rule 5 decreed: *The pitcher's boundary should be marked by a white rubber plate, twelve inches long and four inches wide, so fixed in the ground as to be even with the surface, at the distance of sixty feet and six inches from the outer corner of the home plate, so that a line drawn from the center of Home Base to the center of Second Base will give six inches on either side.*

2. "Cordage Trust Goes Under," *New York Times*, Friday, May 5, 1893: 1.

3. *Reach Official Base Ball Guide* (Philadelphia: A.J. Reach Co., Philadelphia, 1893), 44-45.

4. *Reach Official Base Ball Guide* (Philadelphia: A.J. Reach Co., Philadelphia, 1894), 10.

THE 1894 SEASON: NO FOUR-PEAT FOR BOSTON

BY CHARLIE BEVIS

After winning three pennants in a row from 1891 to 1893, the Boston Beaneaters were denied a fourth consecutive championship during the 1894 season when the brawling Baltimore Orioles earned their first National League title.

The team's prospects for 1894 were derailed early that January when veteran catcher Charlie Bennett lost both of his legs in a train accident. Bennett's work with the Boston pitching staff, particularly with ace Kid Nichols, had been a significant factor in the team's pennant streak. He was also a steadying influence in the clubhouse, where his presence was decidedly missed during the 1894 season.

For the 1894 season, manager Frank Selee had a veteran, battle-hardened team. The entire infield returned from 1893, with Tommy Tucker at first base, Bobby Lowe at second base, Herman Long at shortstop, and Billy Nash at third base. Hugh Duffy and Tommy McCarthy continued to anchor the outfield, with newcomer Jimmy Bannon taking over right field. The team's top three pitchers – Nichols, Jack Stivetts, and Harry Staley – returned as well, with Tom Lovett coming aboard as the fourth hurler. At catcher, Jack Ryan took Bennett's spot in Boston's three-man backstop corps, joining holdovers Charlie Ganzel and Bill Merritt.

In March 1894 a significant change occurred in the three-man ownership group of the Boston ballclub. Among the triumvirate, Arthur Soden and William Conant now controlled club policy, since James Billings was no longer a co-equal owner. Billings transferred to Soden and Conant all but one share of his stock in the ballclub in order to raise enough money to pay off the creditors of his bankrupt shoe factory.[1] Now a minority owner, Billings, who had a more temperate attitude toward the ballplayers, had little voice in ballclub affairs. During the 1894 season, ownership decisions increasingly spiraled from frugal to downright penny-pinching, resulting in an under-insured ballpark and a more rampant discord among the players than in the previous two seasons

Several players staged holdouts into April, including Nichols, who later said he finally reached an agreement with Soden "to pitch two games a week and receive extra salary for extra games."[2] Early in the season, the disgruntled Boston players openly complained that they "ought to get better pay, because the team was playing good ball and the management was making money."[3] Ultimately, this "simmering discontent on the team" deflated the motivation of the players and thwarted Boston's chance to repeat as league champion during the 1894 season.[4]

On April 19 Boston opened the 1894 season at the South End Grounds against Brooklyn to christen the new state holiday of Patriots Day. Replacing Fast Day, which had been held earlier in the month, Patriots Day celebrated the start of the American Revolution.[5] The new holiday made an apt date for the opening battle of the baseball season in Boston for many years. Before a crowd of 8,000 for the holiday season-opener, Boston defeated Brooklyn, 13-2, to commence the season atop the National League standings.

During the ensuing three-week road trip, the Beaneaters played inconsistently and returned to Boston in fourth place. The player discontent became public. The *Brooklyn Eagle* reported, "There is promise of a tall rumpus over the salary question between the Boston players and management."[6] The *New York Sun* anonymously quoted one Boston player, reputedly McCarthy, who said, "To tell you the truth, the gang doesn't care whether Boston wins or loses. You see, Soden and Conant cut all of our salaries down this spring, in spite of the fact that we won the championship three times in succession."[7] Once back in Boston, though, a second team-related adversity just four months after Bennett's disabling accident provided the impetus for the disgruntled players to put aside their conflict with ownership (for a few months) and focus on winning ballgames.

On May 15 in the third inning of the game between Boston and Baltimore, fire broke out in the right-field bleachers at the South End Grounds. The Great Roxbury Fire not only destroyed the ballpark but also burned down 200 buildings in a 12-acre section of the adjacent neighborhood, leaving 1,900 people homeless. One of the homeless was John Haggerty, the groundskeeper at the South End Grounds, who had run to sound the alarm at the local firehouse. "When John got back to the grounds," the *Boston Globe* reported, "the whole grand stand was afire, as well as his own little house close by on Walpole St."[8]

Despite the personal adversity, Haggerty went to work to shape up the Congress Street Grounds, which the ballclub quickly leased to continue playing the team's home games.[9] However, the old ballpark, last used by a minor-league team in 1893, was in deplorable condition. Besides improving the field conditions, Haggerty had to borrow hundreds of chairs to put in the grandstand, since the ballpark seats had been sold earlier that spring.[10]

On May 16 Boston defeated Baltimore on the rough playing conditions at the Congress Street Grounds. Boston then moved its home series with Philadelphia to the City of Brotherly Love, to give Haggerty more time to get the grounds into better shape for the remainder of the six-week homestand, which reconvened on May 21. After the homestand ended on June 20, when Duffy poked a three-run walk-off homer to propel Boston to a 13-12 come-from-behind victory over Baltimore, Boston was in second place, a game and a half behind the first-place Orioles.

Home runs were hit unusually often at the Congress Street Grounds. In the renovation of the ballpark, the playing field likely was reoriented, resulting in an incredibly short 225-foot distance from home plate to the left-field fence.[11] During the 27 games played at the Congress Street Grounds, players hit 86 home runs. This volume of four-baggers represented 14 percent of the league's total of 629 home runs stroked in the 799 games played by all 12 teams that season. On May 30, 1894, Boston second baseman Lowe became the first major leaguer to hit four home runs in one game.

High-scoring games were also the norm at the Congress Street Grounds. For example, in the Decoration Day twin bill on May 30, Boston won the first game, 13-10, and, when Lowe hit his four home runs, won the second game, 20-11. In the Bunker Hill Day holiday twin bill on June 18 (the holiday, normally June 17, fell on a Sunday in 1894), Boston scored 16 runs in the first inning.

During the entire 1894 season, Boston scored 1,220 runs, which today remains the major-league record for the most runs scored by a team in a season. The Beaneaters averaged 9.2 runs per game over the 132-game season, averaging 10.6 runs at home and 7.9 runs on the road. Boston exploited a home-field advantage because visiting teams were unfamiliar with the Congress Street Grounds as well as the rebuilt South End Grounds (where Boston won an August doubleheader by the scores of 18-3 and 25-8). The Beaneaters also exploited the sore arms of the league's pitchers that season.

The standard explanation for 1894 being a big-hitting year was that batters took advantage of the poor adaptability by pitchers to the longer pitching distance instituted in 1893 (from 55 feet to 60 feet 6 inches), since there were no major changes to the batting rules in 1894 (the infield-fly rule being the most significant change). "Pitchers, in exploring how to adjust to the new circumstances, exhausted their arms in 1893 by trying to sustain the customary pitching loads of the past," one historian explained. "They then found themselves in 1894 not only struggling with the greater distance but also toiling with throwing arms made lame by the overwork of the previous year."[12]

Nichols, Boston's ace pitcher, was one of the few pitchers unaffected by the 1893 pitching-distance change.[13] He led the 1894 Boston staff with a won-lost record of 32-13, his fourth consecutive season of 30 or more victories. This consistency before and after the rule change was the direct opposite of the experience of most pre-1893 star pitchers. Nichols made the adjustment in his delivery to maintain the speed of his fastball and the break of his curveball, so his arm was better conditioned to the longer distance.

Despite the success of Nichols, pitching scuttled the pennant chances for Boston in 1894. While Stivetts proved to be a capable number-two pitcher (26-14), Staley (12-10) was inconsistent and Lovett was released in early July, replaced by George Hodson in August. Selee tried out a half-dozen recruit pitchers, to no avail. Catching also presented complications. In mid-June Boston signed Fred Tenney, a left-handed catcher, to try to compensate for Bennett's absence.

Hitting, on the other hand, was exceptional in 1894. During Boston's four-week road trip, from June 21 to July 18, Duffy raised his batting average nearly 50 points, from .375 to .422, to solidify his stake as one of the league's top batters in 1894.[14] "Mr. Duffy has grown to be a full blown sunflower in the batting department of the game since the champions started out in dead earnest for that piece of [pennant] bunting," the *Boston Globe* remarked.[15] Duffy went on to lead the league with a .440 average, which remains the high-water mark for a single-season batting average in the major leagues.[16] Five other Boston players hit over .300: McCarthy (.349), Lowe (.346), Bannon (.336), Tucker (.330), and Long (.324), as the Beaneaters compiled an eye-popping .331 team batting average.

Bennett, recovering from his leg amputations, attended Boston's game in Pittsburgh on July 2 as well as the exhibition game the next day in Sharon, Pennsylvania, a few miles from Bennett's hometown. Bennett's presence seemed to inspire the Beaneaters. After splitting the Independence Day twin bill in Pittsburgh, Boston obliterated Cleveland, 22-7, on July 5 to move into a virtual tie for first place with Baltimore. Duffy had a 5-for-5 day and another four players garnered four hits apiece. "From the very start, the batters at the top of Boston's list began to hit the ball," the *Boston Globe* reported. "They kept it going until the tongues of the Cleveland fielders were hanging out from exhaustion."[17]

Boston held first place for 10 days in July during the road trip before dropping back to second place at the trip's conclusion, just one game behind Baltimore. On July 20 the Beaneaters returned to play in the rebuilt, now fireproof, South End Grounds. Because the former ballpark was not fully insured, the new structure was less grandiose than the previous facility and had just a one-story grandstand to replace the more regal double deck. For 1894, only one of three grandstand sections was completed, but there was ample bleacher seating.[18]

On July 21 Boston returned to first place as Nichols defeated third-place New York. After defeating Baltimore in three straight games at Baltimore in late July (taking the season series eight games to four), Boston was in first place with a five-game lead, its largest lead of the season. Boston seemed headed to its fourth consecutive pennant, but not everyone in the league agreed with that prognostication.

"They are all picking Boston to win the pennant. I don't know about that," Brooklyn team president Charlie Byrne commented in mid-July. "Outside of the wonderful playing of four members of the Boston team, who have been playing lucky as well as brainy ball, I can't see wherein they have a 'cinch' on the pennant. The showing of the Baltimores in the race is more clear cut than of Boston for Manager Hanlon's men have hit the ball as well as fielded it, and hitting the ball is the thing after all."[19] Byrne turned out to be very prescient.

Boston merely chugged along in first place, maintaining just a slim lead during the first four weeks of August. Nichols began to falter on the pitching rubber during the dog days of August, but luckily Stivetts became a steadying force and newcomer Hodson helped to plug the gap. And Duffy continued to lead Boston's hit parade. What little momentum Boston had in first place stalled after the August 25 game, an 8-3 victory over Cleveland, when a disappointingly small crowd of "3773 spectators were full of enthusiasm, and applauded the good plays of the game liberally and in a non-partisan manner, such as Boston is noted for throughout the country."[20] Despite the team contending for a pennant, home attendance was dismal all season.

Total attendance for the 1894 season was just 152,000 people, down substantially from 193,000 in 1893 and nearly half of the 283,000 drawn back in 1889. The economic depression was one reason for the tepid attendance. Another was the beginning of a shift in spectator composition at the ballpark. Businessmen, the primary spectator base, were moving their residences out to the streetcar suburbs that were far from the ballpark. They were slowly replaced by emerging middle-class Irish-Americans, who lived within a short trolley ride of the ballpark.[21] Simply put, 1894 was a transition year for attendance, as the rowdier Royal Rooters began to attend games at the South End Grounds and would soon emerge at the dominant base of spectators during the next few years.

President Soden blamed attendance for the team's failure to repeat as champions. "I attribute the loss of the championship very largely to the apathy of the home crowds toward the home team. Time and again I have heard complaints from our players about this fact," Soden said after the season ended. "If our people rooted as hard for their own players as the crowds do in Baltimore and Pittsburg[h], the club would undoubtedly have more [winning] games to its credit."[22]

The largest crowd of the 1894 season at the South End Grounds attended on August 27 at the benefit game for Bennett, when 9,000 people bought tickets to generate a $6,000 donation to the double-amputee.[23] However, the emotion of the benefit game appears to have negatively impacted the psyche of the Boston ballplayers, resuscitating their latent disgruntlement, as the team went into an immediate tailspin.

On August 28 Nichols surrendered four runs in the seventh inning as St. Louis broke a 5-5 tie and went on to defeat Boston, 9-5. Boston lost two of the three games with the lowly St. Louis Browns, which dropped the Beaneaters into a first-place tie with Baltimore on August 30. On August 31 the Beaneaters faded to second place when the New York Giants defeated them, 5-1, as Nichols lost his second straight game. On September 6, after losing to last-place Louisville in the season's final home game, Boston fell to third place as the *Boston Globe* reported the obvious fact that "the outlook for the pennant is very doubtful."[24]

During the season-ending three-week road trip, the energy was zapped from the Beaneaters as they played moribund .500 ball against weak opponents. Even the reward of postseason cash from the newly instituted Temple Cup series, to be contested by the top two teams in the league standings with the net proceeds going to the ballplayers, failed to motivate the Boston team. There was really no fight for second place between New York and Boston, as Boston finished the 1894 season in third place with an 83-49 record, eight games behind pennant-winning Baltimore.

In mid-September, Jake Morse, baseball writer for the *Boston Herald*, blamed the pennant derailment on the loss of Bennett. "Game after game has been lost to the champions this year by the poor work of the catchers," Morse wrote, then blandly added that "a club which has won the pennant three years in succession is not likely to play the ball that a club will which is after the pennant for the first time."[25]

During the season finale in Pittsburgh, Tim Murnane, baseball writer for the *Boston Globe*, explained a more sinister reason for the team's collapse in 1894. "Nearly every one of the old men is anxious to get away from Boston," Murnane wrote about the undercurrent of dissension on the team. "Several of the boys claim they have grievances against the owners of the club."[26]

Boston barnstormed its way home from Pittsburgh by playing exhibition matches in Pennsylvania and New Jersey, as New York swept Baltimore in the inaugural Temple Cup series. Upon the team's return to Boston, Duffy, the league batting champion, was feted at a banquet and opened a bowling alley in partnership with fellow outfielder McCarthy.[27] Nichols returned to his home in Kansas City, where he kept his right arm limber by competing in a bowling league.[28]

During the fall of 1894, both ownership and the ballplayers hoped to make more money in 1895. After producing an estimated $30,000 profit in 1894, the triumvirate looked forward to the completion of the rebuilt South End Grounds, which would encourage a greater number of spectators to make the trek to the ballpark.[29] Talk of reviving the American Association to compete with the National League raised player hopes for higher salaries, but these expectations were dashed when that movement collapsed by year-end. The tussle over money would continue into the 1895 season.

NOTES

1. "Business Failures," *Boston Globe*, March 22, 1894: 7; "Treasurer Billings Fails in Business," *The Sporting News*, March 17, 1894: 1; "Broken at Last: The Famous Boston Triumvirate Now Dissolved," *Sporting Life*, March 17, 1894: 4.

2. Richard Bogovich, *Kid Nichols: A Biography of the Hall of Fame Pitcher* (Jefferson, North Carolina: McFarland, 2012), 79.

3. "The Boston Row: The Triumvirs Do Not Relish the Floating Talk," *Sporting Life*, May 19, 1894: 8.

4. Donald Hubbard, *The Heavenly Twins of Boston Baseball: A Dual Biography of Hugh Duffy and Tommy McCarthy* (Jefferson, North Carolina: McFarland, 2008), 108.

5. "Fast Day Goes: House Votes to Abolish Historic Holiday: April 19 Takes Its Place on the State's Calendar," *Boston Globe*, February 17, 1894: 10; "League Schedule: Season Opens in Boston on April 19," *Boston Globe*, February 28, 1894: 2.

6. "Byrne Calls on Keefe," *Brooklyn Eagle*, May 12, 1894: 2.

7. "Trouble Among the Champions," *New York Sun*, May 10, 1894: 4.

8. "1900 Persons Homeless," *Boston Globe*, May 16, 1894: 4.

9. "Grounds for the Present," *Boston Post*, May 16, 1894: 5.

10. "The Boston Fire," *Sporting Life*, May 26, 1894: 3.

11. Correspondence dated July 13, 2015, with Ron Selter, an expert in re-creating ballpark dimensions. The distance to left field in 1894 was shorter by 15 feet from the distance in 1890 and 1891 when the ballpark was used for games in the Players League and American Association.

12. Reed Browning, *Cy Young: A Baseball Life* (Amherst: University of Massachusetts Press, 2000), 35.

13. Browning, *Cy Young*, 36. Two other successful converts were Amos Rusie and Cy Young.

14. Averages are from the estimated statistics published every Monday in the *Boston Globe*.

15. "Fine Stick Work," *Boston Globe*, July 22, 1894: 7.

16. "Duffy Heads the List," *New York Clipper*, October 27, 1894: 543. At the time, Duffy had a recorded .438 average, which has since been adjusted to .440 under modern rules.

17. "Poor Old John," *Boston Globe*, July 6, 1894: 2.

18. "New Grand Stand, South End Ball Grounds," *Boston Globe*, June 24, 1894: 16; "Must Be a Brick Stand," *Boston Globe*, June 13, 1894: 4.

19. "Diamond Field Gossip," *New York Clipper*, July 21, 1894: 312.

20. "Clever Hodson," *Boston Globe*, August 26, 1894: 2.

21. Charlie Bevis, *Red Sox vs. Braves in Boston: The Battle for Fans' Hearts, 1901-1952* (Jefferson, North Carolina: McFarland, 2017), 46-47.

22. "Diamond Field Gossip," *New York Clipper*, October 13, 1894: 511.

23. "Benefit to Bennett Was a Grand Success," *Boston Globe*, August 28, 1894: 1.

24. "Champions Fall Before Battered Colonels," *Boston Globe*, September 7, 1894: 2.

25. Jake Morse, "Reconciled to the Loss of the Pennant," *Sporting Life*, September 22, 1894: 6.

26. Tim Murnane, "They May Quit: Boston Ball Players Are Not Satisfied," *Boston Globe*, September 29, 1894: 1.

27. Hubbard, *Heavenly Twins*, 119.

28. Bogovich, *Kid Nichols*, 76.

29. Morse, "Reconciled to the Loss of the Pennant."

THE 1895 SEASON: STRICTLY FOR THE BIRDS, AGAIN.

BY BOB LEMOINE

The Boston Beaneaters were coming off a disappointing third-place finish in 1894 at 78-54. If that doesn't sound disappointing, take into account that the team had won three straight National League pennants (1891-1893) and set the bar and the expectations of Boston fans high. In 1894 the Beaneaters didn't have a losing month or even a losing streak of over three games, but simply were outplayed by both New York and pennant winner Baltimore. After beating Baltimore on July 30, Frank Selee's Beaneaters led the Orioles and New York Giants by five games. While finishing a strong 29-22, Boston was no match for Ned Hanlon's Baltimore team, which went 43-10 from that point on and the Giants, who were 40-13. Baltimore won 18 in a row from late August to mid-September and outlasted the Giants by three games. Baltimore, 60-70 in 1893 and a perennial second-division club since its days in the American Association, was now on the baseball map as it began its own dynasty.

Boston made very few acquisitions during the offseason, and the starting nine was exactly the same as in 1894. The only move of significance was the purchase of third baseman Jimmy Collins from Buffalo. The future Boston star and Hall of Famer played in only 11 games in 1895 before being farmed out to Louisville as Beaneaters veteran Billy Nash was still in charge of the hot corner.

Baltimore made no significant changes in the offseason, although the club had to rebuild the Union Grounds grandstands and clubhouses after a fire on January 14, 1895. The entire ballpark could have been gone had it not been for the groundskeeper, who lived on the grounds in a small cottage near the ticket office.[1] Iron pillars were installed to support the grandstand, instead of wood.

There were more significant changes in the rules of baseball during the offseason. Baseball magnates ruled that only catcher's mitts and first basemen's gloves could be larger than 14 inches in circumference or weigh over 10 ounces. Tim Murnane of the *Boston Globe* was opposed to any "big glove rule," calling the mitt "a detriment to the sport." He asserted that all but two magnates agreed with him, and the two, Al Spalding and Al Reach, were in the sporting-goods business. The size of the rubber on the pitcher's mound was doubled to 24 by 6 inches. The infield-fly rule was put into place, and a held foul tip was ruled to be a strike. Players were also not allowed to coach first or third base after being replaced during the game.[2] Murnane reported that 20 men on the Boston payroll traveled to Charlestown, South Carolina, for spring training. Perhaps they discussed the rule changes on the train ride down, or maybe the authority given to umpires to levy heavier fines for player rowdiness.

Twenty-five spring exhibition games were planned from March 20 to April 18, the last six of them in the Northeast.[3] The Beaneaters returned home for Opening Day on Patriots Day, April 19. Many events were going on throughout the city, including a commemoration at Old North Church of Paul Revere's ride. At 2:30 P.M., Boston took on Washington at the South End Grounds.[4]

Boston fell behind 4-1, but poured on seven runs in the seventh, including a bases-loaded double by Tommy McCarthy, leading to an 11-6 win. Boston took two out of three from Washington, then lost two of three at New York, as Zeke Wilson, one of the Beaneaters' new starting pitchers, was hammered for nine runs in three innings.[5] Zeke and his 5.20 ERA didn't last beyond June.

Baltimore opened its rebuilt park to a crowd of 15,000, which saw the 1894 pennant raised to the flagpole. But the Orioles got a taste of their own rowdy medicine as the Phillies staged a comeback in the ninth after being down 6-2. Hughie Jennings, Baltimore third baseman, used his usual tactics in trying to block the go-ahead run from scoring on a fly out. Jack Taylor would have none of it, however, and gifted Jennings with a knuckle sandwich on the way by. The game was tied, and Philadelphia would go on to spoil the Orioles' home opener.

Boston hung around .500 for much of May, losing its fifth in a row on May 25 to close a Western road trip in a 1-0 classic as Kid Nichols was outdueled by Pittsburgh's Pink Hawley.[6] The Beaneaters were already in seventh place in the 12-team league, albeit only six games behind the first-place Pirates. But back home, Boston won 12 of its next 13, over those same Western clubs, including a 20-3 shellacking of Chicago on June 13. Jimmy Bannon, Hugh Duffy, and McCarthy each had three hits in the onslaught, and Boston now trailed Pittsburgh by a mere half-game at 24-13.[7] A 15-5 domination of Philadelphia on June 26 propelled Boston to 2½ games ahead in first place, but July saw a step backward as they went 10-15 in the month. Boston was five games back as the dog days of August began.

The Beaneaters could make up ground when they traveled to Baltimore for a four-game series August 13-15 (including a doubleheader), trailing by only 4½ games. In the twin bill Boston's pitchers were clobbered for 29 hits and 21 runs, losing 8-3 and 13-8. "Spy glass now needed to see pennant," wrote the *Globe*.[8] The third game was no better as they suffered a lackluster 9-2 loss. Desperately trying to salvage the final game of the series, the Beaneaters went into the 15th inning tied 10-10 with the Orioles. Baltimore's Wee Willie Keeler reached on Bannon's error, and scored on Hughie Jennings's single for the 11-10 win. Boston's season was essentially over, even if you asked Frank Selee: "Because they were the best club last year they won the pennant, and because they are the best club this year I believe they will fly the flag again. I am willing to back my opinion at even money, too."[9] By the end of August, Boston was hopelessly nine games back and far out of the pennant race.

Despite never having a lead larger than four games, Baltimore nevertheless was unstoppable in August (23-5) and September (20-7). The Orioles had to make many changes to their 1894 roster, often due to injuries. Their ace pitcher, Sadie McMahon, was plagued with arm troubles but Ned Hanlon pulled the right strings in bringing in rookie Bill Hoffer, who amazed with a 31-6 record. Second baseman Heinie Reitz also went down and one-time pitching legend Kid Gleason found new life in the field, where he batted .309. Boileryard Clarke filled in behind the plate and batted a solid .290 when future Hall of Famer Wilbert Robinson went down. The pitching was bolstered by Dad Clarkson, picked up in a late-season trade, and he went 12-3 down the stretch.

The surprising Cleveland Spiders were Baltimore's biggest threat, creeping near first place in early September. With the Orioles ahead by just two games on September 7, Cleveland came to Baltimore for a three-game series. The Orioles won two out of three to increase their lead to three games. The Beaneaters themselves tried to play spoiler by beating the Orioles twice and Baltimore saw its lead slip to a half-game on September 20. But the Orioles held off the Spiders, going 7-1-1 over the final eight days. On September 28 they held a 5-2 lead over the Giants in the eighth inning. The Giants had two runners on with one out and darkness settling in. Hughie Jennings snagged a line drive from Larry Battam and doubled off George Van Haltren at second. The *Baltimore Sun* described the dramatic scene:

> These faithful few who had been rooting until they could scarcely keep their seats from pure nervousness, whose faces had a moment before been blanched and drawn by apprehension, poured over the railing of the grand stand in a frenzy of delight, embraced and hugged any one of the Oriole players they happened to run against, and finally, laying violent hands upon the hero of the hour, the good-natured, auburn-haired shortstop, lifted him upon their shoulders and bore him across the field to the clubhouse.[10]

The second annual Temple Cup, by far an anticlimactic affair since, in the minds of players and fans, the tournament was a mere exhibition, began two days later. Baltimore traveled to Cleveland and lost Game One to Cy Young, prompting Cleveland fans to carry Spiders players off in their celebration. In Game Two they threw pop bottles and trash at the Orioles and set off firecrackers. The Spiders prevailed again, 7-2, behind Nig Cuppy, and then took Game Three, 7-1, with Young dominating again. Back at Baltimore in Game Four, the uninspired Orioles saw their own fans throw rotten eggs and potatoes at the Spiders, and the Orioles won, 5-0, behind Duke Esper. Cleveland players needed a police escort to leave the ballpark in one piece. Game Five saw Cleveland take the series with a 5-2 win.

Off the field, one of baseball's classiest legends, Harry Wright, died. Wright had formed the original Cincinnati Red Stockings in 1868 and was part of Boston's early days of professional baseball. An era had passed.

Baltimore exhibited sterling defense. Robinson (.979), first baseman Scoops Carey (.987), and Jennings (.940) had the best fielding percentages in the league at their positions. Besides Gleason (.309), the Orioles lineup boasted five others who batted .300 or better: Joe Kelley (.365), Steve Brodie (.348), Keeler (.377), John McGraw (.369), and Jennings (.386). On the basepaths, the Orioles were the masters of nineteenth-century "small ball" as their 310 stolen bases were second in the NL with five players swiping 35-plus, and their 125 sacrifices trailed only Boston. On the mound, besides Hoffer's league-leading 31 wins and Clarkson's unexpected 12, George Hemming won 20, and McMahon returned late to win 10.

Already known as a bunch of players who weren't afraid to break a rule or throw a fist to win a game, the Orioles would get even more of a rugged reputation as in the offseason. They traded

Gleason to the St. Louis Browns for first baseman Dirty Jack Doyle.

Boston's club was shaken up for 1896 as well. Collins now had a spot on the roster after Nash was traded to Philadelphia for Sliding Billy Hamilton, the fastest man in the game, in the hopes that they could keep up with the swift birds. McCarthy, who spent part of 1895 injured and replaced by Fred Tenney, was sold to Brooklyn for cash. The seldom-used utilityman Frank Connaughton was sold to Kansas City of the Western League for catcher Marty Bergen.

"Clubs which have pennant-winning aspirations must depend on thorough team-work – alike in batting as in fielding and base running – for success in winning championship honors," wrote the *Spalding Guide* in 1896, referring to the Orioles' 1895 triumph.[11] They indeed had all of those ingredients, and would be favored again for the pennant, while Boston tried to figure out how to stop them and build another dynasty of its own.

NOTES

1. "Fire at the Union Park Ball Grounds," *Baltimore Sun*, January 15, 1895: 8.
2. T.H. Murnane, "Change in Rules," *Boston Globe*, February 28, 1895: 4; David Nemec. *The Great Encyclopedia of 19th Century Major League Baseball* (New York: Donald I. Fine, 1997), 536.
3. T.H. Murnane, "Boston's Ball Players," *Boston Globe*, March 17, 1895: 3.
4. "First Day," *Boston Globe*, April 19, 1895: 12.
5. T.H. Murnane, "Wipe Out Wilson," *Boston Globe*, April 27, 1895: 5.
6. "Errorless Fight," *Boston Globe*, May 26, 1895: 4.
7. T.H. Murnane, "Hog Killing," *Boston Globe*, June 14, 1895: 5.
8. "Hopes Dashed," *Boston Globe*, August 14, 1895: 1.
9. "Selee on the Outlook," *Boston Globe*, August 16, 1895: 1.
10. "The Orioles' Pennant," *Baltimore Sun*, September 30, 1895: 7.
11. Henry Chadwick, ed., *Spalding's Base Ball Guide and Official League Book for 1896* (New York: American Sports Publishing Company, 1996), 18.

SOURCES

In addition to the sources cited in the Notes, the author also consulted:

Arnold, Teddie. "Union Park (Baltimore)," SABR BioProject. Retrieved May 27, 2018. sabr.org/bioproj/park/union-park-baltimore.

Lansche, Jerry. *Glory Fades Away: The Nineteenth-Century World Series Rediscovered* (Dallas: Taylor Publishing, 1991), 255-272.

1896 SEASON: ANOTHER PENNANT FROM A BIRDS-EYE VIEW

BY BOB LEMOINE

The Boston Beaneaters dominated the beginning of the 1890s, winning three straight pennants from 1891 to 1893. The Baltimore Orioles, continual also-rans in the second division, came out of nowhere to win the 1894 pennant, and then followed that up with another title in 1895. Both clubs could boast of being the dynasty of the decade, and except for Brooklyn (1890, 1899), these two powerhouses would continue to dominate the decade. The Orioles matched the Boston three-peat with one of their own, as 1896 would be another strong year for the Birds.

Baltimore traded away two role players who had helped their pennant run in 1895. Rookie Scoops Carey had done a solid job at first base for Ned Hanlon's crew, but he was sold. Kid Gleason, one-time pitching ace who had reinvented himself as a second baseman and batted .309, was traded away for the much more experienced, and appropriately dubbed, "Dirty Jack" Doyle. Doyle manned first base and batted .339 for the season with a steady .400 OBP and 73 stolen bases. Reserve man Heinie Reitz took over at second base and batted a solid .287, yet was the worst-hitting starter on the team. Steve Brodie (.297) was the only other starter who batted under .300, understandable when you are surrounded by future Hall of Famers like outfielders Joe Kelley (.364) and Wee Willie Keeler (.386), catcher Wilbert Robinson (.347), and shortstop Hughie Jennings (.401), and a non-Hall of Famer who nevertheless batted .328 that year, third baseman Jim Donnelly. Donnelly, a longtime minor leaguer, was actually only on the field because another future Hall of Famer, John McGraw, was limited to 23 games after contracting typhoid fever in spring training. No surprise that the Orioles batted .328 as a team and blew everybody away with 441 stolen bases, a .393 OBP, and 995 runs.

On the mound the Orioles tied for second in ERA (3.67) and were third in defensive efficiency (.666).[1] Bill Hoffer was the ace of the staff (25-7, 3.38), but was backed up with solid starters Arlie Pond (16-8, 3.49), George Hemming (15-6, 4.19), and Duke Esper (14-5, 3.58). In modern sports lingo, one might say this team was stacked.

The Boston Beaneaters were not able to compete with the Baltimore greatness for the long haul, yet still hung around close to first place through the end of June. Boston made some key offseason moves that would pay dividends in the future. Veteran team captain Billy Nash was traded to Philadelphia for the blazing speed of outfielder Billy Hamilton. Sliding Billy hit the ground running from day one. His .478 OBP led the league, and in a nod to baseball statistical gurus over a century later, his league-best 110 walks with a .366 batting average gave headaches to opposing pitchers. Nash's third-base spot was filled by young Jimmy Collins, who had spent much of 1895 in the minors and would one day find himself in the Baseball Hall of Fame. Tommy McCarthy was sold to Brooklyn, opening the outfield spot for Hamilton. Rookie Marty Bergen began his colorful yet tragic career as Boston's catcher, while the Beaneaters had their reliable four veterans who hit .300 or better: 1B Tommy Tucker (.304), 2B Bobby Lowe (.320), SS Herman Long (.345), and outfielder

Hugh Duffy (.300). The pitching staff was led by the ever-dependable Kid Nichols, who reached 30 wins again (30-14, 2.83), and veteran Jack Stivetts, who threw in another 22 victories. Two other pitchers were signed during the season and would pay dividends in later Beaneaters championships. Ted Lewis was fresh out of college and Fred Klobedanz had been in the minors.

"Over 23,000 Overlook the Calamity" was the headline of the *Philadelphia Inquirer* as Boston came in on Opening Day, April 16, and beat the home club, which lost "because the other fellows play better ball."[2] Nichols allowed only seven hits in the 7-3 victory. But the Beaneaters lost the next two in Philadelphia before coming home.

Boston's home opener drew 18,033, reported by Tim Murnane in the *Boston Globe* as the third highest attendance in Boston's baseball history. Thousands more were left outside when the gates were closed. "If all who wanted to get in had been admitted," Murnane speculated, "the crowd would have been by far the largest ever known in this city."[3] The Beaneaters sliced up 27 hits while putting up some crooked numbers on the scoreboard for a 21-6 whitewash. A 7-4 April had the Beaneaters just 1½ games behind surprising Pittsburgh.

A surge in May saw the Beaneaters sweep at Louisville, outscoring the Colonels 31-11 in three games, then beating Pittsburgh and St. Louis amid a four-game winning streak in which they were tied for first with Cincinnati and Cleveland on May 18, with Baltimore one game back. The two-time defending champions had played mediocre ball to begin the year and were 3½ games back on May 22. That was when they went on a 10-game winning streak, sweeping home games against St. Louis, Cincinnati, and Pittsburgh to put themselves 1½ games in front. Boston had a 14-8 June; Baltimore went 15-6, but both were superseded by the surprising Cincinnati Reds, who went 18-8 in the month and tied with Baltimore, a half-game ahead of Cleveland.

If this were a horse race, we would say other teams were sprinting to the finish in July: Baltimore (18-8 in the month), Cincinnati (21-7), and Cleveland (20-12), while Boston fell behind with a 10-17 month. The *Globe* headline simply stated the obvious: "Not Coming Here" – in regard to the pennant.[4] The Beaneaters pulled out a 3-2 win over the Orioles on July 28. It meant little to Boston, which was 14½ games behind. The loss knocked Baltimore back five games from Cincinnati, but fortunes would change from that day on. The Orioles began a 10-game winning streak, which ended on August 12. At that point, the Orioles were in a virtual tie with Cincinnati, with Baltimore 63-28 and Cincinnati 65-30.

Who were these Reds and how did they surprise the baseball world? Buck Ewing, at the end of his long career as a player, also led this group of overachievers as manager. They had finished eighth in 1895. Ewing had three speedy outfielders who could hit and steal: Eddie Burke (.340, 53 SB), Dusty Miller (.321, 76), and Dummy Hoy (.298, 50), while Hoy also led the team in on-base percentage (.403). The Reds were second in stolen bases and ERA. Frank Dwyer and Red Ehret won 24 and 18 games, respectively. The Reds were a half-game up on the Orioles after winning, 9-7, in Boston on August 19. It was the beginning of a 21-game road trip, and it was off to a good start. But then the bottom fell out, as the Reds lost their next 11 in a row to fall 6½ back on September 1. It was indicative of the Reds' season, as they went 51-15 at home but only 26-35 on the road. The Orioles streaked to 38-12 overall to finish the season, while Cincinnati, the oldest team in the league, flopped at 16-24.

The Cleveland Spiders were a much more balanced team than the Reds were. The Spiders had time for a few cups of coffee while in first place, falling no more than four games out of first but never leading by more than a half-game through June. With Cy Young (28-15, 3.24) and Nig Cuppy (25-14, 3.12) anchoring the pitching staff, Cleveland had the best ERA in the NL, allowed the fewest walks, and had the best strikeout-to-walk ratio (1.20). Unlike Cincinnati, the Spiders were built not on legs but on bats; their .301 batting average was tied for second with Boston behind Baltimore's .328. Their hits (1,463) were also second to Baltimore, led by Jesse Burkett's league-best .410 batting with a .461 OBP and 1.002 OPS. Cupid Childs batted a forceful .355, while Ed McKean chipped in a .338 BA. After a 2-0 victory over Philadelphia on July 23, the Spiders trailed the Reds by a mere game. They lost their next five in a row, however, with three of them to the Reds, then slumped to 10-12 in August. A few wins here and there could have paid dividends, as the Spiders had one of their best months in September at 15-6, but the race had been decided by that point.

Neither Cincinnati nor Cleveland would have a season like this again in this era. The Spiders would become one of worst clubs in baseball history, going 20-134 in 1899 before folding from existence. While not matching that extreme futility, Cincinnati wouldn't have a better team until the Black Sox season in 1919.

Baltimore started slowly, to everyone's surprise. The Orioles were 5-7 at the end of April, and traveling logistics contributed to their frustrations, the *Baltimore Sun* reported. A game with Boston ran long so that the team missed its boat to New York. They caught the midnight train, getting into the city in the early morning. The players waited four hours for a train to Baltimore. Home just a few hours, they then caught a train for Pittsburgh.[5] They found the energy to jump over .500, finishing 17-7 in May and 15-6 in June. The champion Orioles were back, and they hung within a few games of first place through July, falling no further than five games back. One amazing victory at Philadelphia on August 17 saw the Orioles score eight runs in the ninth to come from behind, 16-15. "Not a man could be found on either team or among the spectators so sanguine as to suppose such a consummation possible," the *Baltimore Sun* wrote, "but the Orioles went to work with a will nevertheless."[6]

Baltimore won the pennant by 9½ games over Cleveland and again played the Spiders in the Temple Cup postseason series. Public perception was such that, despite winning three pennants, Baltimore had yet to win a Temple Cup, so those titles were tainted, even though the tournament was mere exhibition.[7] Diminished by poor attendance (fewer than 13,000 turned out for the entire series), the Orioles finally got the monkey off their back as they proved without a doubt who the superior team was. In Game One, Hoffer shut down the Spiders and the Orioles battered Cy Young in the 7-1 win. In Game Two, Baltimore jumped out to a 6-0 lead and cruised for the 7-2 win. In Game Three, it was Hoffer beating Cuppy, 6-2. Only 1,200 turned out for what would be Cleveland's only home game, and they had little to cheer about as 20-year-old Joe Corbett was the pitching hero of the day with a 5-0 shutout.

"The Orioles have made an exceptionally brilliant finish this year," wrote the *Baltimore Sun*, "carrying off the pennant and the Temple Cup with an ease that is astonishing when the discouraging way in which they began the season seemed to indicate that they were not in the contest for either honor."[8] This championship club was their best of the decade, based on their season-best .698 winning percentage and the fact that they won the 1896 pennant by 9½ games. But the legacy the Orioles are remembered for today ended in 1896.

Frank Selee's crew went to Hot Springs, Arkansas, for spring training in 1897, the first such trip for the Beaneaters. They did so with a few new faces who would be key members of their next championship run.

"I discovered," wrote baseball historian Robert Creamer, "that the Old Orioles were not a dynasty at all but a nova, a sudden manifestation in the baseball skies that flared brilliantly for a very short time and then disappeared."[9]

The Orioles' reign may have ended in 1896, but it ended in a blaze of glory.

SOURCES

Baseball-reference.com.

Lansche, Jerry. *Glory Fades Away: The Nineteenth-Century World Series Rediscovered* (Dallas: Taylor Publishing, 1991).

Nemec, David. *The Great Encyclopedia of 19th Century Major League Baseball* (New York: David I. Fine, 1997).

NOTES

1 The defensive efficiency ratio is a statistic seeking to evaluate team defense by determining the rate of times a team allows batters to reach base on balls put in play.

2 "We've Met the Enemy and We're Therein," *Philadelphia Inquirer*, April 17, 1896: 1.

3 T.H. Murnane, "Out in Batting Togs," *Boston Globe*, April 21, 1896: 1.

4 *Boston Globe*, July 11, 1896: 2.

5 "Orioles Stop in Baltimore," *Baltimore Sun*, May 4, 1896: 7.

6 "Two Great Finishes," *Baltimore Sun*, August 18, 1896: 6.

7 "Baltimore Is Used to it," *Boston Globe*, September 19, 1896: 3.

8 "The Temple Cup With the Pennant," *Baltimore Sun*, October 9, 1896: 4.

9 Robert W. Creamer, "Team: The Old Orioles," in Daniel Okrent and Harris Lewine, eds., *The Ultimate Baseball Book* (Boston: Houghton Mifflin, 1981), 34.

1897: BOSTON'S CRUSADE

BY BILL FELBER

THE WAR FOR THE PENNANT

The 1897 Beaneaters opened spring training in Macon, Georgia, with optimism that may have been out of proportion to their 74-47 fourth-place finish, 17 games behind the champion Baltimore Orioles, a year earlier. The core of the team was familiar: Tommy Tucker, Bobby Lowe, Herman Long, and Jimmy Collins across the infield, Hugh Duffy and Billy Hamilton forming two-thirds of the outfield, and Kid Nichols leading the pitching staff. Fred Tenney, who had inherited the right-field job when Jimmy Bannon was released late in the 1896 season, prepared to assume that duty full time. Reliable Jack Stivetts and youngsters Fred Klobedanz and Ted Lewis appeared ready to support Nichols as needed on the mound.

However high the Beaneaters' hopes were, the schedule maker could not have created a more imposing start to the season. It began with a thoroughly disappointing April 19 Patriots Day home opener against Philadelphia marred by the club's inability to touch Phillies ace Al Orth and by Nap Lajoie's three-run eighth-inning home run that gave the visitors a 6-0 advantage. A desperate two-out ninth-inning rally produced two runs and loaded the bases for Tucker, who drove an Orth pitch high off the wall in the recesses of right field for a three-run double. The shot barely missed leaving the playing area for a game-tying grand slam; in fact, witnesses agreed it would have gone out had not Beaneaters management raised the fence by a few feet during the offseason. As it was, Tucker stopped at second and he died there when Orth retired Charles Ganzel on a game-ending infield grounder.

The opening road trip, a three-city, eight-game swing, began three days later in Baltimore, where that city celebrated its three-time defending champions on April 22 with a parade from the Eutaw House downtown to the ballpark, 2½ miles away. The city virtually closed for the occasion, an estimated 1,000 bankers and merchants opting to hail their heroes rather than work. While players were the main attractions, one of the attention-getting floats featured the 1894, 1895, and 1896 championship trophies as well as the 1896 Temple Cup, which the Orioles had won the previous October by beating the Cleveland Spiders.

Once at the park, the entire parade order was reassembled inside the gates for a march to the center-field flagpole, where the three pennants were unfurled and raised.

The Beaneaters, whose role through all of this was accoutremental, seized their chance to actually do something once play began. Halfway through the contest, they led 5-4. But Stivetts, the starting pitcher, complained to manager Frank Selee about a sore arm and the Orioles tore into Klobedanz, his replacement for the sixth. It was the kind of ethically questionable rally the Orioles had become famous for, beginning when Hughie Jennings leaned into a pitch that hit him. Umpire Tom Lynch ignored Beaneater protests that Jennings should have been denied his base for failure to make an effort to get out of the way, and moments later

Jack Doyle drove a pitch over Hamilton's head in center, producing three game-changing runs. The Orioles won, 10-5.

The series' second game was more of the same. Nichols protected a 5-4 lead into the eighth inning when Willie Keeler slapped a single past Lowe. Jennings followed with a hit that sent Keeler to third, and when Jennings' successful attempt to steal second drew Doc Yeager's throw, Keeler trotted home with the tying run. A Collins error and two hits later, the Orioles led by their eventual winning score, 7-5.

In the third game, Joe Corbett – brother of former heavyweight champion James J. Corbett and a lightly used member of the Orioles 1896 staff – announced his presence for 1897 by stifling the Beaneaters' bats, 7-1, to complete the series sweep. The Orioles' most pleasant mound surprise, Corbett – who had made just six career starts to that point – would win 24 times for the Orioles in 37 appearances.

The train ride to Philadelphia provided Selee a chance to ponder a quick makeover. Tucker, showing the effects of age both at bat and at first base, was benched, to be succeeded by Tenney. (Tucker would be sold to Washington in June.) The latter's place in right field was given over to rookie Chick Stahl. But the revised lineup managed just one win and two ties in the trip's remaining five games in Philadelphia and Washington, outcomes made more depressing by Collins and Long errors undermining Lewis's work in a 5-3 loss to the Senators. "Put that mob in cotton and ship them to Oshkosh," a fan wired Selee of his 1-6 team.[1]

EQUILIBRIUM

The Beaneaters could not have sensed it at that moment, but less than two weeks into the season they had already weathered their stormiest stretch of play. Yet the coming together was less an epiphany than a gradual process of talented players gradually rising to their level. They were .500 (9-9) after defeating Cleveland on May 15, and two days later launched a six-game winning streak, outlasting the Chicago White Stockings 7-6 in 10 innings. Their first visit to St. Louis for a series against the woeful Browns produced three wins, scoring 11 runs in each of the three games while the Browns scored a total of nine. On the Western swing that concluded on May 29, they had gone 12-5 and lifted themselves from eighth place to fourth, five games behind the Orioles.

Even better, the schedule called for the same Western teams the Beaneaters had just collectively dispatched to visit Boston during most of the month of June. "I fully believe the home team will pass all the teams higher up in the standings before long and be in position to fight Baltimore for the lead when that team arrives here late in the month (June 24-26)," predicted Tim Murnane, the best-known sports reporter of the era.[2] He was right: The Beaneaters launched a 17-game winning streak. It began with a crushing 25-5 dispatch of the hapless Browns May 31 and a doubleheader sweep of the Browns the next day, this time by scores of 14-6 and 12-3. In six games against St. Louis over the previous 10 days, the Beaneaters had scored 84 runs, the Browns 23. The Spiders and Louisville Colonels were both dispatched twice, the Pirates, Reds and Cubs three times, and the Dodgers once. Between May 20 and June 25, the Beaneaters played 29 games, winning all but three by an average margin of five runs and scoring in double digits 16 times. Aside from Marty Bergen, every Beaneaters regular was hitting above .300, and Duffy was pushing .400. When the Giants swept a doubleheader from Baltimore on June 21, the streaking Beaneaters completed their ascent in the standings, jumping a half-game ahead of the Orioles. Coming off a 1-6 month of April, they had won 17 of 23 in May and 22 of 24 in June.

The momentum was undeniable, even to Selee. "I have managed three champion league teams for Boston," he said, "but the team I have this year is stronger than any I ever managed before."[3]

TURBULENCE

The Beaneaters' 5-1 victory over Cincinnati on June 12, in the midst of the streak, provided a glimpse into one of those moments that makes 1890s baseball deliciously larcenous. In the sixth inning, with Nichols working on a 3-0 shutout, Tommy Corcoran stood at third and Jake Beckley at second when Claude Ritchey rolled a one-out grounder to Bobby Lowe. Corcoran scored and Beckley followed him around seconds later, only to be called out by umpire Tim Hurst for failing to touch third base even though Hurst's attention had been focused on the play at first. Witnesses later said Beckley had actually cut the bag by 20 feet, trying to take advantage of the fact that Hurst could not see him. But Hurst knew it would have been impossible for Beckley to score as quickly as he did by legitimate means. "As I saw him coming I said to myself, 'O, what a bluff, but I've got you this trip,'" Hurst said after the game.[4]

Seventeen-game winning streaks ought to go a long way to promoting team unity, but that was not always the case among the Beaneaters, and particularly as it involved Bergen. A troubled individual who would 2½ years later murder his wife and children, then kill himself, he was probably schizophrenic, although such a diagnosis did not exist in those days. Certainly he was prone to periodic fits of imagined wrongs at the hands of his teammates. During one of the June games against the White Stockings, he lashed out at teammates he imagined were talking disparagingly of him behind his back, leaving the team for several days and returning home. Yet as much as Bergen agitated Selee's life needlessly, the Beaneaters manager needed his arm and field generalship behind the plate. When the Dodgers finally snapped Boston's winning streak on June 22, they stole three bases in key situations off backup Charlie Ganzel. So it was with a mixture of trepidation and relief that his teammates welcomed Bergen back to the clubhouse before the start of the Orioles series, with the Beaneaters clinging to their half-game lead.

A local cigar company offered Boston players a free box of cigars in exchange for a hit in that opener, which pitted Nichols against Jerry Nops. The cigar tab went up drastically when fans stormed the South End Grounds, hundreds of them penned behind outfield ropes that shrunk the playing surface to something approaching youth league dimensions. "The game was a pure farce … (the field) not much larger than a tennis court," the *Baltimore Sun*'s correspondent complained.[5] Taking full advantage of the confines, Beaneaters batters pounded out 19 or 20 hits (accounts differ), five by Duffy alone, while Nichols held the Orioles relatively in check for a 12-5 win. "Next to winning a game of ball, the thing that pleases me the most is a quiet half hour with one of these cigars," Duffy told a reporter afterward.[6] The most disquieting moment for Beaneaters partisans was a foul tip that fractured one of Bergen's fingers, sidelining him again, this time for physical reasons.

Baltimore led the next day's game, 9-8, with two out in the ninth when Bill Hoffer, the starting pitcher, began to wobble. Collins rolled a single through an opening on the right side, then Hoffer walked Ganzel and Stahl, filling the bases. Tenney took two strikes and smacked a line drive into the gap between Keeler and Jake Stenzel in right-center, a game-winning hit that touched off the type of walk-off celebration that is common today, but which was rare in the 1890s. The crowd burst on the field, swept Tenney off his feet, and carried him to the grandstand to receive its tribute. He emerged literally bruised for the experience, and hobbled through the series' final game, a 1-0 Oriole victory with Corbett bettering Nichols before a crowd estimated at 17,000. For the record, the park's listed capacity was 6,800.

BIRTH OF THE ROOTERS

In the afterglow of the enthusiasm sweeping through the city emerged an entity unique for its time, an organized fan club. The Royal Rooters were a semi-organized collection of fans that coalesced in June and July to celebrate and revel in the achievements of their Beaneaters. It was, by the standards of baseball fandom, a noteworthy assemblage, featuring – among others – Congressman John "Honey Fitz" Fitzgerald, the future grandfather of President John F. Kennedy. As a group, the Rooters divided their time between two sites. The first was South End Grounds itself, where they established a more or less permanent presence in the seats adjacent to the Boston bench. The second was 3rd Base, a tavern owned by Rooter Michael "Nuf Ced" McGreevy,[7] whose nickname derived from his habit of ending all baseball-related disputes with the declaration "Nuf Ced." McGreevy outfitted his business with décor designed to celebrate the group's heroes, including dozens of photos as well as chandeliers made of old Beaneater bats.

Having seized first place just prior to the Baltimore series, the Beaneaters spent the next several weeks methodically fortifying their advantage. After the series-ending 1-0 loss to Corbett, they reeled off eight more wins in succession, leading by 5½ games. It was all too efficient to be maintained; in Chicago the Beaneaters lost three straight one-run decisions, touching off a 2-6 stretch that reduced their advantage over the Oriole to 2½ games. Among those losses was a contentious one in Pittsburgh whose resolution illustrated several of the rough-and-tumble idiosyncrasies of 1890s baseball.

The Pirates, who had chosen to bat first, led by the eventual final score of 5-4 when Lowe drew a one-out base on balls and Bergen followed with a single in the bottom of the ninth. The afternoon had been rife with vulgar bench jockeying involving exchanges between Duffy, Pittsburgh pitcher Frank Killen, and fans. There were two out with Lowe at third and Bob Allen at second when Hamilton slipped a slow bounder toward second baseman Dick Padden and sped off toward first. Observers agreed that Hamilton arrived at the base simultaneously with Padden's throw to first baseman Denny Lyons; in fact, the throw pulled Lyons into Hamilton's path and the collision sent both players sprawling. Lowe, of course, crossed home plate easily and Allen, with no reason to stop running, also touched home before Lyons could recover his equilibrium. But did either of the runs count, or had Hamilton been retired at first, ending the game? Initially, umpire Bob Emslie made no clear signal, bringing both teams onto the field to celebrate their victory. Finally, Emslie signaled that Hamilton had been out at first, neither run counted, and Pittsburgh had won.

THE PENNANT FIGHT

The Beaneaters lead was three games when the Orioles made their final trip into Boston for the start of a three-game series on August 5. Aside from the decisive final-week series in Baltimore, these contests may have been the most contentious and most closely watched in baseball history to that point. It caught the attention of much of the sporting nation, which viewed it in terms that touched a national sense of right and wrong. There was not much question which side the three-time defending champions represented. Known for their cutthroat, brawling, and often under-handed methods of play, the Orioles had made enemies almost everywhere they played. The Beaneaters were no saints, but compared with their foes they inherited that image by default and wore it proudly. An editorial in the *Pittsburgh Dispatch* summed up the mood. "The most important point … is the superiority of the Bostons over the Baltimores as gentlemen. The latter have degenerated into a set of rowdies who resort to the smallest and dirtiest tricks ever seen on the ball field. How different it is with the Boston team."[8]

League President Nick Young decided the games were of such importance that he should assign two umpires, not just one, to work them. The league's senior umpire, Thomas Lynch, was an obvious choice, and Lynch's second pick was Tommy Connolly, a future Hall of Famer at the time working in a regional minor league. Young was stunned, however, when Connolly declined the offer to work such highly visible major-league games, citing prior commitments to his minor league. The real reason for Connolly's hesitation was the fetid atmosphere surrounding the games. He did not want to be a part of the antics he thought likely to ensue.

Whatever one thinks of Connolly's action, his instincts proved solid. During the first few innings of the opening game, Beaneaters players and fans continuously berated Lynch for what they saw as his failure to prevent Orioles starter Joe Corbett from cheating forward off the pitching rubber. When Lynch finally did issue a warning, Doyle, Jennings, and John McGraw took up Corbett's cause. The game was Baltimore's pretty much from the start, the Orioles pushing four first-inning runs across against Nichols and coasting from there.

Baltimore again seized an early lead in the series' second game, but this time the Beaneaters rallied … and that rally set off a chain of events that rocked the baseball world. In the top of the eighth inning, Lowe drove a triple over Stenzel's head to the wall in center and Bergen rifled a single to right, giving Boston a 6-5 lead. In the bottom of the inning, Doyle, whose nickname of Dirty Jack betrayed his reputation as the Orioles' most tempestuous player, popped an easy foul to Bergen, then unleashed a string of epithets toward Lynch. When the Orioles took the field for the top of the ninth, Doyle repeated his verbal assault and Lynch ejected him. Now teammates joined Doyle in surrounding Lynch, each of them verbally assaulting the umpire, and Lynch returning insult for insult. It's not clear who threw the first actual punch, but Doyle punched Lynch in the eye, blackening it, and Lynch sent Doyle sprawling with a full left to the player's neck. Kelley and Corbett raced to separate the combatants, and their presence brought fans streaming from the stands onto the field. "The cry was to mob the Baltimore players and it doubtless would have been done" had not Boston players and police jumped in to calm the fans. It took 10 minutes before the scene could be cleared sufficiently for play to resume.[9]

Compared with what had preceded, the game's conclusion was uneventful. All it featured was some bottles thrown Kelley's way, blatant interference and a disputed game-saving play. McGraw had reached second on Long's one-out error, slightly wrenching his knee when he bowled over Tenney, who was blocking his way around first base. The injured McGraw left, replaced by the slower Joe Quinn. With two out, Jennings singled cleanly to Duffy in left and he fired home in time, Lynch said, to retire Quinn. "That Quinn was clearly safe was frankly admitted by some of the Boston writers," the *Baltimore Sun*'s correspondent declared the following morning. Hanlon virtually accused Lynch of throwing the game, calling the umpire "at heart a Boston man and I know it." He added that he knew "pretty well when a man makes an honest mistake."[10]

Boston partisans told a far different story: The abusive Orioles were reaping their just rewards. "Numbers will be found who will excuse anybody for acting as Lynch did under … such provocation," argued the *Boston Journal*'s J.C. Morse.[11]

Lynch notified Young that he would remain in his hotel room to nurse his injuries rather than umpire the Saturday game, forcing the league president to scramble for a replacement. Given the short notice, the best Young could find was Bill Carpenter, a rookie he had hired only a few weeks earlier. Boston city officials took it upon themselves to provide backup, assigning two members of the city's police department to duty on the field, and 40 more to the grandstands. The officers were needed. In the first, Keeler loudly protested Carpenter's ruling that he had been picked off first, and Carpenter promptly summoned the officers to restrain the player. Lewis did the rest, limiting the Orioles to five hits in a 4-2 Boston victory.

ROAD TRIP

The Beaneaters bade farewell to the Orioles in front by three games, a margin the Orioles reduced to a half-game over the ensuing several weeks. More significantly, the National League race had functionally been reduced to two combatants, with the third-place Giants 5½ games further back. Then, like twin comets streaking across the late-summer sky, they jointly spent the next month distancing themselves from the terrestrial portion of the league while never losing touch with one another. Between August 28 and September 22, the Beaneaters won 17 of their 21 decisions, the Orioles won 18 of 24, and neither team managed to open up a lead over the other that was larger than 10 percentage points.

The closeness of the race, overlaid by the ethical patina attached at that time to any challenge to the supremacy of the hated Orioles, ensured a steady buildup of interest, nationally as well as regionally, as a final-week series approached in Baltimore for September 24-27. Nowhere was this buildup more noticeable than in and around McGreevy's 3rd Base Saloon, where the Royal Rooters conceived the idea of something unprecedented in sports at the time: A large-scale fan invasion of the other team's home turf. At a cost of $25 apiece, more than 125 Rooters purchased a package that included steamship and rail travel, overnight accommodations, plus grandstand tickets to all three of the games. In Baltimore, fans lined up in rainy weather across several city blocks to get the tickets, and scammers hired women to pose as pregnant in order to be moved to the front of the line.

Ensconced at the Eutaw House the evening before the first game, the Beaneaters did something unexpected: They socialized with the Orioles. Proprietors of Ford's Theater presented players on both sides with complimentary tickets to that evening's presentation of *A Man From Mexico*, and the players who had fought so bitterly as recently as early August freely intermingled while enjoying the performance.

For Selee, there was but one problem: Bergen was not in town. The unreliable catcher had disappeared while the team passed through New York City on September 23, and his whereabouts was temporarily unknown. The matter resolved itself the morning of September 24, when Bergen showed up and blamed Selee for his absence. Several weeks earlier, the manager had scheduled an exhibition game against a local team in Jersey City for September 23 as a means of picking up a few extra dollars … a common activity at the time. As the importance of the Baltimore series grew, Selee canceled the exhibition … but nobody told Bergen, who that afternoon had been surprised to find himself the only person at the field.

Rooters who were unable to make the trip gathered Friday morning at the Music Hall, or in front of Boston's several newspaper offices, to watch re-creations of the play-by-play. At the Union Street Grounds, the old wooden ballpark groaned beneath the weight of the estimated 13,000 who paid for entry, many standing in roped areas in the outfield. Thousands more perched atop the fence, or on rooftops across the streets, to peer in. The Royal Rooters huddled en masse behind the Boston bench, waving banners and raising what Orioles partisans described as an "unearthly din."

THE SERIES ON THE FIELD

Both managers sent their aces, Nichols (29-12) and Corbett (24-6), to the mound. The home team struck first, McGraw opening the game with a walk, stealing second, and scoring on Jennings' single. Joe Kelley's double between Duffy and Hamilton plated Jennings with a second run.

Through three innings Corbett was perfect. In the fourth, however, Doyle's error allowed Tenney to score his team's first run. In the fifth Long singled and Bergen doubled, tying the game. Lowe's two-out hit a few moments later gave Boston its first lead, 3-2.

The Orioles repeatedly fell back on their "inside baseball" tactics, only to see the Beaneaters' skill or their own errors of execution undermine them. In the third Collins raced in to field Keeler's bunt attempt and threw him out. In the fourth, Stenzel was thrown out by Collins trying to score. Doyle attempted to steal second, only to have Bergen throw him out. Again in the fifth, McGraw tried to bunt but popped up to Nichols. In the sixth Bergen threw out Keeler attempting to steal second. It marked the fifth time that an Oriole had been retired on the bases.

Corbett's errors helped the visitors break the game open in the seventh. With Nichols on first, he threw Hamilton's easy grounder past Doyle into short right, allowing the runners to take second and third. Then he wild-pitched Nichols across. Tenney's bunt single made the score 5-2. The Beaneaters added a sixth run in the eighth on Long's double with Duffy at second.

A contributor for his offense, Long would soon become a hero for his defense. In the bottom of the inning, two walks and an infield hit filled the bases for Stenzel, who rocketed a shot toward left. Long leaped and snared the ball, ending the inning. "It was one of the greatest catches ever seen on the ballground," asserted the *Boston Globe*'s Tim Murnane.[12] The Rooters rewarded Long in the most meaningful way possible, by showering him with silver coins in such volume that his teammates had to help the player collect them.

It was Long's richest moment, but hardly his last. The Orioles mounted a ninth-inning rally that produced two runs and found runners at first and second with just one out for Keeler. He punched a line drive past the pitcher, but Long intercepted it and tossed to Lowe at second, doubling off Wilbert Robinson, the Orioles captain and lead runner, for a game-ending double play.

That evening at the Eutaw House, Selee held an impromptu press conference for the Rooters, at which he essentially guaranteed them the pennant. Congressman Fitzgerald, in a celebratory mood, hired a band, which played well into the night, ensuring that the inn's guests – mostly the Boston players and delegation – would get little if any sleep. This was a particular concern for Collins, who had taken a foul ball off his face, swelling an eye shut. To address that concern, the Beaneaters applied the standard remedy of the day to Collins's face: leeches.

The bleary-eyed players and fans awoke the next morning in time to pose for a group photo outside the hotel, then departed for the ballpark, where Klobedanz prepared to battle Bill Hoffer. The crowd was, if anything, even larger, and this time the home faithful were rewarded. In the first inning Keeler beat out a disputed infield hit and Kelley's double scored him. In the second Collins botched McGraw's bunt with runners at second and third, permitting both runs to come across. The Orioles led, 3-0. Boston rallied in the seventh, scoring two runs with Hamilton at third and Lowe at first after two were out. Lowe chose that moment to turn Baltimore's gambling style of ball against the Orioles, breaking for second in the hope of drawing a throw that would enable Hamilton to score. He drew Robinson's throw, all right, but Hamilton failed to break, prompting Lowe to retreat.

When Jennings fired back to Doyle, Hamilton finally took off for home, but Doyle's throw beat him for the third out.

The home team put the game out of reach moments later. Keeler singled, Jennings doubled, and Kelley drove them both across. The 6-3 final moved Baltimore back within a half-game of the Beaneaters. The result seemed to put the home fans in a mood the Royal Rooters described as puzzlingly friendly. "Someone yelled, "Three cheers for the Boston Rooters" and that's what they were given … several times over. "We expected to be obnoxious to the crowd here," one Rooter lamented of the cheerful reception.[13]

Sunday baseball being illegal in Maryland, many of the Rooters enjoyed a side trip to the nation's capital. Collins, Tenney, and a few other players dined that evening at Baltimore's Diamond Café, whose proprietors were McGraw and Robinson.

It did not take long on Monday morning for Baltimore team and city officials to realize that the decisive game was an event beyond their control. Orioles owner Harry von der Horst tried to shore up his undermanned staff of ticket-takers by joining them at the turnstiles, only to see those same turnstiles literally uprooted by late morning. Outside the ballpark, speculators commanded six to ten times the face value for tickets. The trolley line required 10 minutes to traverse the few patron-thick blocks in front of the ballpark. The ropes that had been strung across the outfield to handle the first two days' overflows were now extended, virtually eliminating foul territory beyond the bases and shrinking the playing surface substantially. By the time players arrived for warm-ups, estimates put the throng inside the gates at 20,000. Then, quickly, the crowd burst through the left-field gate itself, creating a gap through which hundreds more poured freely. By game time an estimated 30,000 were on hand, with thousands more clinging from telegraph poles or atop nearby rooftops. Although the precise number in attendance remains impossible to determine, it was almost certainly the largest crowd to watch a team sporting event in America to that date.

The outcome may have turned in the first inning when Chick Stahl's line drive caromed off Corbett's pitching hand, jamming several fingers and forcing him from the game. Boston took full advantage, scoring eight times by the end of the fourth inning. For Baltimore fans, the only saving grace was that the visitors and Nichols particularly were also off their game, Boston holding only an 8-5 lead entering the seventh.

That's when the issue turned permanently. Hoffer, worn down by the combination of his Saturday effort plus his relief work to that moment, allowed consecutive hits to Duffy, Collins, Long, Bergen, Nichols, and Hamilton, two of them reaching the overflow crowd on the field for doubles. By the time Robinson cut down Long attempting to steal for the third out, the Beaneaters had touched the frazzled Orioles for nine runs on 11 hits. A half-hour later, the Royal Rooters celebrated a 19-10 Beaneaters victory.

The outcome left Boston 1½ games ahead of Baltimore and all but clinched the pennant, which was formalized three days later when they beat the Dodgers, 12-3, while Washington defeated the Orioles, 9-3. The Orioles and Beaneaters met a week later in the Temple Cup series, Baltimore gaining whatever consolation there was to be derived from their four-games-to-one victory.

To the Beaneaters, the Royal Rooters, and also to the broader baseball world, that outcome was anticlimactic. What mattered was that Boston had ended the roughians' three-year siege of the National League pennant and restored the franchise to its place at the forefront of the baseball world.

SOURCES

In addition to the sources cited in the Notes, the author relied heavily on his book *A Game of Brawl: The Orioles, the Beaneaters, and the Battle for the 1897 Pennant* (Lincoln: University of Nebraska Press, 2007).

NOTES

1. T.H. Murnane, "Can't Tell Why," *Boston Globe*, April 30, 1897: 4.
2. T.H. Murnane, "Welcome the Team Today," *Boston Globe*, May 31, 1897: 4.
3. Ibid.
4. T.H. Murnane, "Path to Pennant," *Boston Globe*, June 14, 1897: 3.
5. "Orioles Were Too Easy," *Baltimore Sun*, June 25, 1897: 6.
6. "Boston Wins," *Boston Globe*, June 26, 1897: 7.
7. In records, the name is variously spelled as McGreevey; he spelled it both ways.
8. As printed in "Unjust Criticism," *Baltimore American*, July 27, 1897. The *American* said the *Dispatch* article was "as unjust as it is uncalled for, and so far as the Baltimore club is concerned is not true."
9. "Fight on the Diamond," *Baltimore Sun*, August 7, 1897: 6.
10. Ibid.
11. "Hub Happenings," *Sporting Life*, August 14, 1897: 9.
12. "They're in the Lead," *Boston Globe*, September 25, 1897: 1.
13. 'Pennant Hopes," *Boston Herald*, September 27, 1897: 1.

1898: A VERY LONG SEASON ENDS WITH ANOTHER FLAG

BY RICHARD RIIS

Coming off their fourth National League pennant of the decade and seventh overall, the Boston Beaneaters were not considered a lock for the 1898 championship. Baseball touts and prognosticators were divided as to whether the club was up to a repeat, or if Baltimore, which had upset Boston in the Temple Cup, or New York, with a pitching staff perceived by many as the league's best, might snatch the flag from manager Frank Selee's men.

Some of the uncertainty centered on Selee himself. The highly-regarded leader had given notice to the club in the offseason that he wished to be released from a verbal commitment to manage Boston again to assume ownership of a new Western League franchise in Omaha. Boston President Arthur Soden publicly dismissed questions about Selee with a statement to a reporter on January 22, saying that his manager "remarked that he would like nothing better than to have the Omaha franchise in the Western League, if he could get away from Boston, and his interviewer construed that to mean that he wanted to get away. He added, "Mr. Selee has said nothing to me about wanting a change. We are satisfied with him, and he seems satisfied here."[1]

Nevertheless, the question of Selee's status with the Beaneaters would continue to crop up throughout the season.

Other questions were fueled by the holdouts of two of Boston's most gifted players, pitcher Charles "Kid" Nichols and third baseman Jimmy Collins. League owners voted in February to extend the season from 132 to 154 games with no discussion of additional compensation for players. A handful of players held out for more pay, including Nichols, the NL leader two years running with 30 and 31 wins, and Collins, while others revived talk of the organization of a players labor union.

"The shabby treatment accorded Nichols by the Boston Club, for whom he virtually won the championship last year, and other things, have spurred the players on to form an organization for their self-protection," said the *St. Louis Post-Dispatch*. "The demands of the players will be for increased pay, corresponding to the lengthened season, compensation for the weeks spent in spring training, and abolition of the current farming system."[2]

Nichols arrived at training camp in Greensboro, North Carolina, without a contract, but Collins was conspicuously absent. Collins had emerged as a star in his third season in Boston, batting .346 with 132 RBIs, second most in the league, and 14 stolen bases. He excelled in the field as well, acquiring a reputation as the circuit's premier third baseman as he led his peers in putouts and assists. Without Collins, the Beaneaters would find it difficult to repeat their 93-39 record of the previous season.

There were three changes on the Boston roster coming into training camp. Gone was catcher Charlie Ganzel, who, having lost his starting job in 1896 to Marty Bergen, was given his unconditional release in February. Added were two promising players, infielder Bill Keister and pitcher Vic Willis.

The left-handed-hitting Keister, 26, had played in 15 games at second and third for Baltimore in 1896 before hitting .334 in 1897 as the shortstop for Paterson of the Atlantic League. It was hoped Keister would provide the club with a solid utilityman to spell veterans Bobby Lowe and Herman Long at second and short. Neither Lowe nor Long seemed to need much rest in 1898 and Keister would see little action before being loaned to Rochester of the Eastern League for six weeks in June and July, then returned to Boston and released.

Willis, on the other hand, arrived on the club with considerable fanfare and an $1,800 contract,[3] and was expected to join Nichols, Fred Klobedanz, and Ted Lewis in Frank Selee's four-man pitching rotation. Willis, 22, was a tall right-hander acquired from Syracuse of the Eastern League for $1,000 and catcher Fred Lake after going 21-17 with a 1.16 ERA in 1897. Sportswriter H.G. Merrill, who covered the Eastern League for the *Wilkes-Barre Record*, wrote, "While I am one of the few writers who give the laugh to the chap who talks about strike-out records being a sure criterion of a pitcher's ability, in the case of Willis, it is something worth considering, and is a criterion. … [W]ith the Boston team behind him, Willis ought to be a terror."[4]

"My men are all little fellows," explained Selee in justifying the club's brief, two-week training camp, "and they do not need very much work to put them in good condition."[5] Breaking camp, the Beaneaters hit the road for exhibition games against Eastern League clubs in Lancaster, York, Reading, and Allentown, Pennsylvania, playing their way north to New York for the season opener vs. the Giants. Their outlook improved when Collins signed for the league's unofficial maximum of $2,400[6] and reported to the team on the road at the end of March.

Opening Day was scheduled for April 15. Selee pitted left-hander Klobedanz, 26-7 in 1897, against the Giants' Ed Doheny. As both clubs marched ceremoniously onto the field behind a military band, a drizzling rain set in. With Boston ahead 3-2 in the third, the drizzle turned into a downpour, and the game was called.

The Beaneaters bested the Giants, 4-2, the next day in the official opener behind the pitching of Kid Nichols, in a game marred by confrontations on and off the field. "The enthusiasm was intense"[7] as Boston rallied for two runs in the seventh inning to tie the game at 2-2. In the eighth, speedy Billy Hamilton reached on a groundball fumbled by third baseman Fred Hartman and advanced to second on a single by Fred Tenney. A throw by catcher Jack Warner to catch Hamilton off the bag went over shortstop George Davis's head, and Hamilton took off for third. George Van Haltren scooped up the ball in left field and threw to Hartman, who, according to some, tagged Hamilton a foot from the bag. Umpire Charles "Pop" Snyder, however, ruled Hamilton safe. The crowd howled their disapproval, and Giants player-manager Bill Joyce ran in from second base to argue. Second baseman Kid Gleason threw his glove down and kicked it, earning himself an ejection under the season's tightened rules about on-field displays. A subsequent grounder to Gleason's replacement, Charlie Gettig, was fired to the plate, but Hamilton, running at full bore, was called safe with the go-ahead run. When Boston followed up with another run, the crowd became unruly.

Approaching the grandstand to confront one egregiously abusive fan, umpire Snyder found himself pelted with a barrage of seat cushions and garbage, forcing Giants officials and police to take the field to quiet the crowd. After the game, fans clambered from the stands to confront Snyder, and the arbiter had to be escorted to the clubhouse by police. The Giants got their revenge against the "lucky" Bostons the following day, hitting Klobedanz freely for an 8-2 win.

The two clubs traveled to Boston for the opener at South End Grounds on April 19, where turnabout was again fair play, the Beaneaters bludgeoning the Giants for 18 hits and a 14-2 victory. Nichols gave up two runs on four hits in the first inning, then held the Giants hitless until he was relieved after seven innings by Lewis, who likewise kept the Giants off the basepaths. Lowe collected four hits and Nichols added a home run. After the game Nichols reportedly met with Arthur Soden and reached an undisclosed settlement on his contract.[8]

The the team left for an 11-game East Coast road trip. Vic Willis saw his first action on April 20, pitching three innings in relief of Jim Sullivan in an 18-3 drubbing at Union Park in Baltimore. Willis was "perceptibly nervous and unsteady,"[9] hitting the first two batters he faced before being tagged for eight runs on six hits, three walks, and a wild pitch.

Boston topped Baltimore 10-5 the following day, but on April 22, the Orioles again embarrassed the Beaneaters, and then some. Jay Hughes, a young hurler from California who impressed Orioles manager Ned Hanlon into signing him after he whitewashed Hanlon's men on three hits in a postseason West Coast exhibition, tossed an 8-0 no-hitter against Boston in only the second start of his major-league career. (Cincinnati's Ted Breitenstein pitched a no-hitter against Pittsburgh the same afternoon. This was the first time two no-hitters were thrown on the same day in the major leagues, a feat that wasn't duplicated for almost a century": The Oakland A's Dave Stewart and the Los Angeles Dodgers' Fernando Valenzuela turned the trick on June 29, 1990.)

Hughes's gem was a particularly painful one for Long, who was plunked on the basepaths by a thrown ball and spiked in the foot and leg in a baserunning collision with Hughie Jennings and Dan McGann. Long nursed his wounds on the bench for the rest of the afternoon.

Making his first start on April 29, a settled-down Willis scattered 10 hits and struck out five in pitching all nine innings of an 11-4 victory at Washington. Klobedanz lost to the Senators the next day, and Boston finished April in a disappointing sixth place with six victories and five losses.

Returning home on May 5, the Beaneaters dropped three of four to the Giants, then righted themselves, taking three of four from the Orioles and sweeping three from Brooklyn. As the team departed Boston for their first Western trip of the season, they had moved into third place behind Cincinnati and Cleveland.

Kid Nichols took a 5-4 loss in the opening match of a three-game series in Cincinnati on May 19, but Vic Willis, despite obvious wildness in hitting two batters and walking eight, pitched well enough the next day to beat the Reds, 5-4, for his fifth win in as many starts. In the final matchup, on May 21, Lewis, saved by center fielder Billy Hamilton's "wonderful catch"[10] of a long drive by the Reds' Jake Beckley with two men on, pulled out a 4-3 victory.

The press was impressed with Boston's spirited play, even in pregame practice.

"What a snappy game of ball the champions put up at all stages! Even in their practice they are a revelation," wrote the *Cincinnati Enquirer*. "Especially is this the case with Tenney, the collegiate first baseman. He never wearies, apparently, and is running and jumping about all the time. His practice shows up in the game, for circus stops and sensational pick-ups are 'ready money' for him. Herman Long is another of the Bostons who is doing 'stunts' half the time. The champs tackle their work with a vim and vigor that unquestionably presages the addition later on of another victory."[11]

Boston's hitting prowess drew sharp attention as well. "Billy Hamilton and Capt. Hugh Duffy came close to being the whole thing for Boston in the Cincinnati series," said the *Pittsburgh Press*. "Their batting average off the Reds' pitchers were .555 and .416 respectively. Herman Long rapped out .463."[12]

"Take him day in and day out," wrote another journalist about Billy Hamilton, "count what he does on the 'inside' as well as the outside, consider the clever manner in which he can wait out a pitcher, his wonderful batting eye, his skill in getting around the circuit, and I think I am justified in saying that if there is an individual entitled to be the best ball player in the world, it is Billy Hamilton."[13] Through May, Hamilton topped the league in hitting, with an average as high as .425.[14]

The Beaneaters experienced their most unusual loss of the season on May 28 in Louisville. Both teams had agreed to have the day's game called at 5 P.M. to allow them to catch a train for the East. Trailing 7-5 after eight innings, Boston scored five runs with only one out in the ninth when umpire Hank O'Day called the game. To the Beaneaters' disgust and the Colonels' delight, the score reverted to the last completed inning, giving Louisville the victory.

From May 30 through June 1, the Beaneaters took four straight at home from Chicago to find themselves in second place, four games behind red-hot Cincinnati.

On June 7, Boston, 4½ games behind Cincinnati, hosted the Reds in the first of a four-game series. Three hits, including a home run by Hamilton, and effective pitching by Nichols gave Boston a 9-2 victory and, coupled with a Brooklyn win over Cleveland, moved the Beaneaters into a second-place tie with the Spiders.

The next day Willis, struggling with his control, walked eight but managed to beat the Reds, 8-1. Cleveland downed Brooklyn 8-2.

After Cincinnati tied the game of June 9 in the top of the ninth, Jack Stivetts, batting for Klobedanz in the bottom of the inning, connected for a solo home run to give Boston a 6-5 victory. It was his third pinch-hit home run and the last of his 35 homers in the major leagues.[15]

Boston failed to complete the sweep, though, falling on June 10 to the Reds, 4-3, on a home run by Dusty Miller, while the Spiders won their third straight to push the Beaneaters back into third place.

Back-to-back wins against the Phillies on June 12-13 put Boston back into a tie for second place. On June 14 Willis struck out 11, only to lose to Philadelphia 9-0.

Despite the absence of Hamilton and Long with minor injuries, Boston collected 17 hits in beating Philadelphia 12-6 on June 15 to take sole possession of second place, 2½ games behind Cincinnati. By June 20 Boston had cut Cincinnati's lead to a single game; a week later, they were only a half-game out of first place. Boston's hitting, while somewhat weaker than the previous season's, still impressed, with Hamilton topping his teammates at .386, followed by Collins at .319, Jake Stahl and Bergen at .314, Tenney at .313, and Hugh Duffy at .299 through June 25.[16]

The Beaneaters had begun playing mediocre ball, though. From June 20 through July 2, they were 5-7. On July 1 Cincinnati began an eight-game winning streak that put them up five games on Boston.

On a sweltering day in Philadelphia, the Beaneaters failed to come up with as much as a hit on July 8 for the second time in the season, Red Donahue issued only two walks in taming Boston, 5-0. "[Donahue] gave the most brilliant exhibition of twisting the sphere that has been seen on the local grounds this season," noted the *Philadelphia Times*. "Not a Champion got beyond second base during the entire nine innings, and not a single Champion got a safe hit during the entire nine innings."[17] Willis, on the other hand, was wild again, walking eight and hitting two batters.

Starting with a Fourth of July doubleheader sweep of the Giants at New York, Boston caught fire again, winning four straight, losing two, then winning 15 of 18. An equally torrid streak by Cincinnati, which won 18 of 24 with one tie over the same span, kept the Bostons from gaining much ground on the Reds.

The status of Selee's job as manager was raised again in July, with considerable doubt raised by Selee himself. "I expect to own a club next year," he told a reporter in Pittsburgh, adding that he'd remained with Boston this season only because he'd given his word to the owners.[18]

While still winning games, the Beaneaters were beginning to show some wear and tear. Hamilton and Stahl were both felled by serious knee injuries, and Tenney was laid low by a serious stomach ailment. With all three regulars expected to be out for a lengthy stretch and pitcher-outfielder Stivetts banged up with a split thumb, on July 25 the Beaneaters signed utilityman Jim "General" Stafford, recently released by Louisville, to play right field in place of Stahl. Backup receiver George Yeager assumed Tenney's duties at first base.

On July 25, in a game at New York's Polo Grounds, Orioles left fielder James "Ducky" Holmes struck out. On his way back to the bench, he responded to the heckling of fans by referring to

Giants team owner Andrew Freedman with an anti-Semitic slur. Freedman, seated within earshot, demanded that Holmes be removed from the game. Orioles manager Ned Hanlon refused, whereupon Freedman ordered Giants skipper Bill Joyce to keep his players on the bench. The game was forfeited to Baltimore.

The incident left league officials in a quandary. Freedman demanded disciplinary action against Holmes, while Hanlon demanded punitive sanctions against Freedman for causing the game forfeiture and for withholding Baltimore's share of the gate for the game. Trying to placate both sides, the NL Board of Discipline fined Freedman $1,000 and imposed a season-long suspension on Holmes. The Orioles were given until August 24 to comply with the ruling.

Deeming Holmes's suspension illegal because it had been imposed without affording the player a hearing, NL players urged that it be lifted. The Beaneaters passed a collective resolution condemning Holmes' suspension, calling the verdict "extremely erroneous and such arbitrary use of power extremely unjust," and criticizing the autocratic and abrasive Freedman for manifesting "a spirit of impatience, intolerance, arrogance, and prejudice against players, a spirit inimical to the best interest of the game and the public."[19] The resolution was signed by all 15 Beaneaters and sent to newspapers and the Board of Directors of the National League. On August 25, with the support of nine of the league's owners, the order of suspension against Holmes was lifted.

Of likely greater concern to Boston's players was a growing problem with one of their own, Marty Bergen. Considered by many as the league's most gifted backstop, Bergen had been regarded by his teammates as eccentric, but his disposition over the course of the season had taken a turn for the worse, bringing discord to the tight-knit club. "Backstop Marty Bergen," wrote one journalist, "with all his talents as a catcher, is an odd specimen with a grievance continually concealed in his craw."[20]

There was an incident between Bergen and Vic Willis in the dining room of a St. Louis hotel on July 28 that went unreported in the press until after the season. Willis, Bergen, and other players were kidding one another on the train from Brooklyn the previous night. Suddenly, Bergen grew morose and withdrawn. The next morning, as teammate Ted Lewis later recalled, "(Bergen) was talking in an apparently friendly way with Willis, who sat down in a chair next to him, but in an instant, however, he drew back his arm and struck Willis in the face."[21] Intervening Boston players led Willis from the room to avoid escalating the situation.

"Bergen, often surly, lets his temper get away with him," observed one sportswriter, "and makes breaks for which there is no provocation."[22] Relations between Bergen and his teammates were seriously strained after the incident.

Despite the off-field distractions, Boston played at a .720 clip in July, winning 18 of 25, to remain in second place, 3½ games behind Cincinnati, and 2½ games ahead of Cleveland.

The Beaneaters beat St. Louis 4-3 in the first game of a doubleheader on August 1, then entered into a collective slump, losing five of six with one tie, scoring only one run in four of the six. In the 12-inning tie game, played in Louisville, Boston went into the ninth with a 1-0 lead, but a walk, stolen base, error, and a groundout produced the tying run and sent the game into extra innings. Nichols and Louisville's Bill Magee both pitched all 12 innings, surrendering but six and seven hits, respectively.

Less than a month after Selee called him "one of the prettiest batters in the league" and "one of the best utility men in the business,"[23] the Beaneaters made a deal with the Browns to swap Jack Stivetts for Kid Carsey, a washed-up pitcher already past his prime at 25, and cash. The trade, though, was made contingent on Stivetts's consent to go to St. Louis, whereupon Stivetts declined, prompting Boston to send him home to think it over. For a while the deal hung in limbo, until Browns owner Chris von der Ahe came back on August 14 with a straight cash offer of $2,000, which Boston accepted.[24] Stivetts refused to report to St. Louis and was sold by the Browns to Cleveland for the 1899 season.

Stivetts's spot on the roster was filled with a catcher-outfielder signed from the semipro leagues of Worcester, Massachusetts. William "Kitty" Bransfield, 23, played in only five games before being released to Brockton of the Eastern League. He returned to the major leagues later and enjoyed a respectable career as a first baseman for the Pirates and Phillies.

Boston realized its longest winning streak of the season, 11 games, beginning with an 8-0 whitewash of the Reds at Cincinnati on August 9, and concluding with a 2-1 victory over the Reds at home on August 20. Behind superb pitching that surrendered only 23 runs in those 11 games, including shutouts by Nichols, Willis, and the tandem of Lewis and Charlie Hickman. Hickman and Jim Stafford enjoyed a stellar outing in Boston's 10-0 rout of Chicago on August 18. Stafford, playing right field in place of an again-injured Stahl, collected four hits in four at-bats, including his only home run of the season. Hickman, sent in to give Lewis the rest of the afternoon off after the starter had given up but one hit in five innings, hurled four innings of one-hit ball and hit a double. (He eventually transitioned from pitching to playing first base and enjoyed some solid seasons with the Giants and future American League teams in Cleveland, Detroit, and Washington.)

With Boston in first by 3½ games, the Beaneaters drew their largest crowd of the season, 12,000, for an August 22 doubleheader against second-place Cincinnati. The crowd was so large that ropes were put around the field to keep them back, but several times they pushed their way onto the field of play and in the way of the fielders. A ground rule was established that a ball hit into the crowd was a double. Stahl sat out both games with a sore knee, and Tenney also withdrew, complaining of stiffness in his leg.

Nichols was ineffective in the opener, pitching only seven innings in a 7-2 loss. Controversy arose when in the third inning Heine Peitz opened for the Reds with a single, advanced to second on a passed ball, and, with one out, scored on a single by Mike Smith. Smith took second on the second out of the inning, and trotted home on a groundball by Bid McPhee to Collins, who threw to first for the third out. The Beaneaters had come in from when the field when umpire Tom Brown ruled that George Yeager had his foot off the bag when he caught the throw, McPhee was safe, and Smith's run counted. The Beaneaters charged back onto the field to object, and Yeager wound up ejected, with Kitty Bransfield, making his major-league debut, replacing him at first for the remainder of the game.

The second game began with the understanding that the game would be called at 5:45 P.M. In the sixth inning, with Boston up, 5-3, McPhee homered, and singles by Jake Beckley and Charlie Irwin brought Dusty Miller to the plate. On Lewis's first pitch, Miller hit a line drive to center field. Hamilton took off after the ball, racing toward the fence, when he hit the rope holding back the crowd and was flipped onto his back. While Hamilton lay dazed on the field, the umpire called a ground-rule double, and Beckley scored to tie the game. Hamilton was several minutes in recovering,[25] and after the Reds were finally retired, Boston came to bat with only 10 minutes left.

If Boston was still at bat when the game was called at 5:45, the score would revert to that of the last completed inning, giving the Beaneaters the victory, but Yeager struck out, and after Long singled, Duffy and Collins each drove the ball deep to left field, only to have them hauled in by Mike Smith. The game was called, and a 5-5 tie entered into the books.

Fred Tenney, his leg still stiff, was left behind as Boston headed west on a road trip on August 24. With Tenney out, Boston won but three of 12 games, allowing Cincinnati to slip past Boston and back into the lead on September 1. A 6-6 tie with Cleveland on September 2, called after 10 innings because of darkness, found Boston looking distracted and listless. "The game should have been won by the Boston," according to one account, "but poor running, weird fielding, and Lewis' lack of control and speed all but lost it."[26] Club President Soden was disgusted. "The playing of the team the last two weeks is the worst it's been in years," he said.[27]

Bergen abruptly took unauthorized leave of the club for a trip to his home in North Brookfield, Massachusetts. With Bergen missing for two days (and subsequently fined), Yeager, who had been substituting for Tenney at first base, had to catch, and when Boston took the field against New York on September 3, Kid Nichols was at first. The Beaneaters beat the Giants, 6-5, with Nichols batting ninth behind pitcher Lewis. "Manager Selee was responsible for as poor a piece of judgment as ever befell the lot of a baseball manager," wrote a baffled Boston sportswriter, Tim Murnane, a former major leaguer. "The idea of using a great pitcher at first base, taking chances of having him put out of the game for the rest of the season was enough to make the directors of the Boston club wonder if their manager was in his right mind when he made out the batting order."[28] For the next game, and every other until Tenney returned to the lineup, Hickman, a less valuable pitcher than Nichols, substituted at first base. The slow return of Tenney prompted Captain Duffy to gripe about contemporary players getting soft. Speaking to a reporter, he said, "There are too many doctors in the game now."[29]

No sooner had Tenney returned to the lineup than Hamilton, batting .369, close behind the Orioles' Willie Keeler atop the list of NL hitters, went down again with his nagging knee injury. Duffy was moved to center field and Stafford took over in left. As Cincinnati faded, Boston went on a nine-game winning streak beginning September 3.

Coming into the pennant stretch, newspapers once again reported that "Frank Selee, the highly successful and rightfully popular manager of the Boston team, will quit the city of beans and crooked streets at the end of the pennant season."[30] This time Selee remained silent, even as many speculated that Hugh Duffy would succeed Selee.

Despite an exciting pennant race, attendance around the league was lagging, and Nick Young, president of the National League, said near season's end that seven of the league's 12 clubs – St. Louis, Cleveland, Pittsburgh, Washington, New York, Brooklyn, and even perennial contender Baltimore – were losing money.[31] Most, including Young, ascribed the decline in attendance to fans' preoccupation with the Spanish-American War. On April 25 the United States had declared war on Spain after the explosion aboard the battleship *Maine* in Havana harbor on February 15, and war news dominated the newspapers and the national conversation. Perhaps that was the case when Boston reclaimed first place with a pair of Labor Day victories over Washington on September 5. In the morning game, Willis won 2-1 before 2,200 fans; in the afternoon, Nichols stopped the Senators 6-2 before 6,500. A year before, a Labor Day doubleheader in Boston had drawn 6,500 and 12,000.

The Orioles, still very much in the chase, reeled off 12 straight victories, cutting Boston's lead to 2½ games on September 22, but fell back when Chicago snapped their winning streak. That same day, Willis beat Philadelphia, 2-1, with a double by Duffy winning the game in the ninth.

The Beaneaters drew within grasp of the pennant by taking a pair from Brooklyn on September 26 for their seventh and eighth wins in a row, while Washington was beating Baltimore. Selee then made a curious choice by starting Willis two games in a row. Willis beat Brooklyn, 3-1, on September 27, but was frequently in trouble. The next day Brooklyn battered Willis, Duffy was tossed from the game for arguing with the umpire, and Boston's win streak was snapped at eight.

No matter. The Beaneaters toppled Philadelphia 11-10 on September 29 with a six-run rally in the ninth inning, highlighted by a three-run home run by Collins that tied the score, and Stahl's sprint home after Lewis's fly fell between three Phillies in left field.

On October 3, in what the *Boston Globe* called the "most curious game of the season,"[32] the Beaneaters seemed to do everything within their power to hand the game to the visiting Orioles, making 10 errors in the first four innings, "misplays that brought tears of laughter to the Oriole players and long looks of disgust from manager Frank Selee."[33] Four errors were made in the first inning, and four more in the third, as the Orioles took a 6-3 lead. Boston then batted around in the fourth, with two hits in the inning by Willis and a home run by Bergen netting six runs, to pull ahead, 9-6. The Orioles answered with four runs in the bottom of the inning to retake the lead, 10-9, before Boston plated three more runs in the fifth. Adding another run in the sixth, the Beaneaters pulled out an abbreviated 13-10 win when umpire John Gaffney ruled it too dark to continue play.

Having won four in a row, the Beaneaters ran the streak up to nine before dropping two of three to complete the schedule. When the season ended October 15, Boston's record stood at 102-47, six games ahead of Baltimore and 11½ up on Cincinnati, in capturing the NL pennant for the second straight year.

Several Beaneaters enjoyed fine seasons. Hamilton finished second in the batting race at .369 and in stolen bases (54), and was first in on-base percentage (.480). Limited by his knee injuries to 110 games, he nevertheless scored 110 runs. Collins hit .328, led the NL in home runs with 15 and in total bases with 286, and was second in RBIs (111) and slugging percentage (.479). Tenney hit .328. Although Duffy's batting average slumped from .340 to .298, he drove in 108 runs, fourth-best in the league. Among the league's hurlers, Kid Nichols was the winningest pitcher for the third consecutive year with a 31-12 won-lost record, his third and last season with 30 or more victories. He was third in ERA (2.13) and fourth in strikeouts (138). Rookie Willis went 25-13 to launch a Hall of Fame career and finished third in the league with 160 strikeouts. Lewis, 26-8, topped NL hurlers with a .765 won-lost percentage. Klobedanz logged 19 wins against 10 losses. Willis, Collins, Duffy, Hamilton, and Nichols are in the Hall of Fame. Boston's dynasty was coming to a close in 1898, but such stars made this team, in the words of historian David Nemec, "the greatest team of the 1890s."[34]

On a more ominous note, there were reports that Marty Bergen, after an altercation on the bench in one of the season's final games, had grabbed a bat and threatened to club a few of the Beaneaters. He didn't, but Bergen had worn out his welcome with his teammates. The effects would carry over into the 1899 season.

With the war on Americans' minds and public interest in the Temple Cup diminished by second-place teams winning three of the four series, there was little interest in postseason play. Both the Orioles and the Reds rejected Selee's challenge to play a nine-game exhibition series. Most players seemed to agree that the new, longer season was just too long.

SOURCES

In addition to the sources listed in the notes, the author also consulted a number of newspapers and the following:

Caruso, Gary. *The Braves Encyclopedia* (Philadelphia: *Temple University Press*, 1995).

NOTES

1. "Soden and Selee," *Buffalo Morning Express and Illustrated Buffalo Express*, January 23, 1898: 18.
2. "A New Brotherhood," *St. Louis Post-Dispatch*, April 6, 1898: 6.
3. David L. Fleitz, *Ghosts in the Gallery at Cooperstown: Sixteen Little-Known Members of the Hall of Fame* (Jefferson, North Carolina: McFarland & Company, 2004), 178.
4. "Boston's New Pitcher," *Bryan* (Texas) *Daily Eagle*, April 13, 1898: 2.
5. "The National Game," *Dollar Weekly News* (Wilkes-Barre, Pennsylvania), January 8, 1898: 6.
6. "Sporting Notes," *Fort Wayne* (Indiana) *News*, April 2, 1898: 3.
7. "Disgraceful Conduct of the Crowd at the Polo Grounds," *Brooklyn Daily Eagle*, April 17, 1898: 31.
8. "Sporting Notes," *Pittsburgh Post-Gazette*, April 20, 1898: 6.
9. "Baltimore 18, Boston 3," *Kansas City Journal*, April 21, 1898: 5.
10. "Boston Wins Two Out of Three," *Sandusky* (Ohio) *Star-Journal*, May 22, 1898: 4.
11. "Baseball Gossip," *Cincinnati Enquirer*, May 22, 1898: 30.
12. "Baseball Brevities," *Pittsburgh Press*, May 24, 1898: 5.
13. "All Sorts," *Cincinnati Enquirer*, May 29, 1898: 18.
14. "Diamond Dust," *Washington Evening Times*, May 12, 1898: 6.
15. L. Robert Davids, ed., *Great Hitting Pitchers* (Phoenix: Society for American Baseball Research, second edition, 2012), 60.
16. "The League Batsmen," *St. Louis Post-Dispatch*, June 25, 1898: 5.
17. "Boston Did Not Make Hit or Run," *Philadelphia Times*, July 9, 1898: 6.
18. "Frank Selee's Views," *Wilkes-Barre Record*, July 6, 1898: 3.
19. "Boston Protests," *Buffalo Morning Express and Illustrated Buffalo Express*, August 21, 1898: 18.
20. "Base Ball Notes," *Scranton Republican*, September 17, 1898: 3.
21. Patrick R. Redmond, *The Irish and the Making of American Sport* (Jefferson, North Carolina: McFarland & Company, 2014), 209.
22. "Base Ball Briefs," *Nebraska State Journal* (Lincoln), October 30, 1898: 14.
23. "Happy Jack Stivetts," *Buffalo Enquirer*, July 1, 1898: 6.
24. "Base Ball Notes," *Washington Evening Star*, August 19, 1898: 9.
25. "Grand Baseball at Boston," *Cincinnati Enquirer*, August 23, 1898: 4.
26. "Tied in the Tenth," *North Adams* (Massachusetts) *Transcript*, September 3, 1898: 4.
27. Harold Kaese, *The Boston Braves, 1871-1953* (Boston: Northeastern University Press, 2004), 94.
28. T.H. Murnane, "Rough Going," *Boston Globe*, September 5, 1898: 5.
29. Ibid.
30. "Baseball Gossip," *Cincinnati Enquirer*, September 12, 1898: 3.
31. "Seven Lost Money," *Buffalo Morning Express and Illustrated Buffalo Express*, October 1, 1898: 10.
32. "Chalk Up One," *Boston Globe*, October 4, 1898: 9.
33. Ibid.
34. David Nemec, *The Great Encyclopedia of 19th Century Major League Baseball* (New York: Donald I. Fine Books, 1997), 606.

1899: THE CRACKS BEGIN TO SHOW

BY RICHARD RIIS

With a little luck and considerable pluck, the 1898 Boston Beaneaters were able to overcome injuries to three of their regulars to capture the National League pennant. While injuries would figure in 1899 as well, none matched the far-reaching consequences of the deteriorating mental health of one of the team's most popular players.

During the offseason, a bruise on Marty Bergen's right hip, the result of sliding into home in one of the final games of the 1898 season, developed into an abscess, necessitating surgery on January 21, 1899. Although the surgery went well and Bergen quickly recovered, Boston manager Frank Selee sought to secure insurance behind the plate. On March 2 the club purchased Bill "Boileryard" Clarke from Baltimore. Clarke, a solid receiver and a six-year veteran, had been deemed expendable by the Orioles and their new player-manager, John McGraw, after Clarke objected to a proposed salary cut. Although Bergen remained Boston's first-string catcher, the presence of Clarke may have only exacerbated his growing feelings of paranoia and antipathy toward his teammates and Selee.

With the Beaneaters scheduled to begin training in Durham, North Carolina, on March 24, expectations ran high for the new campaign. "The Bostons," wrote one prognosticator, "are practically the same team as last season. … This team has played for a number of years together and understand each other thoroughly. Their team work is perfection, and none excel them in batting, fielding, and base running. Nicol [sic], their pitcher, is king of them all, and will be ably assisted by Klobedanz and Willis. From the lights seen at the present writing, it looks as if Boston would be the champion of 1899."[1] Lauded another, "Here is a magnificent aggregation of talent, containing as it does the best infield in the league, a grand outfield, and splendid batteries. In brief, the team that beats Boston out this year will be entitled to championship honors."[2] That the team failed to arrive at camp intact might have been taken as an omen. Center fielder Billy Hamilton begged off to stay home with his sick wife; first baseman Fred Tenney, second baseman Bobby Lowe, and pitching ace Charles "Kid" Nichols delayed their arrival to attend to personal matters; and shortstop Herman Long and new Beaneater Clarke received permission to skip training camp altogether and join the team for the opening game. Marty Bergen was, to no one's great surprise, a no-show.[3]

Boston broke camp with one rookie, pitcher, Oscar Streit, on the roster. The 25-year-old left-hander, who had won 22 games the previous season between the Western League's Columbus Buckeyes and Dayton of the Interstate League, was expected to help pick up the slack in the absence of starting pitcher Ted Lewis, felled by illness just before the start of the season and expected to miss the remainder of April.

The Beaneaters began the work of defending their championship at Washington Park in Brooklyn. During the offseason the Brooklyn and Baltimore teams had merged ownership groups, with Orioles owner Harry von der Horst and manager Ned Hanlon becoming part-owners of the Brooklyn club. Von der Horst appointed Hanlon manager of the rechristened Superbas, and shifted several of the Orioles' best players, including first baseman Dan McGann, shortstop Hughie Jennings, pitcher Jay Hughes, and outfielders Willie Keeler and Joe Kelley, to Brooklyn. Veteran shortstop Bill Dahlen, acquired by the Orioles from Chicago in January in a trade for second baseman Gene DeMontreville, was also transferred to Brooklyn.

Amid festive bunting and the music of the 23rd Regimental Band, the Beaneaters and Superbas paraded onto the field on April 15 before an overflow crowd of more than 21,000. Billy Hamilton, leading off for Boston against William "Brickyard" Kennedy, singled just out reach of Jennings, and had advanced to third when Long hit a long fly to left-center. Upon the catch by Kelley, Hamilton took off for home. "But Captain Kelley was out to show a fast pace and the ball hardly touched his hands before his arm flew back and it came flying toward the plate. Hamilton was moving fast, but the relentless sphere was faster, and it came into Alex Smith's hands as perfectly placed as would have been possible had the thrower walked in and handed the ball to his catcher instead. The run was not only cut off, but Hamilton was out, and the team was retired in a manner to suit the most exacting critic."[4] Kelley's crowd-pleasing throw, and another a few innings later that beat Hugh Duffy by a step as he tried trying to take two bases on an error, proved crucial as the game remained scoreless through nine innings.

The winning run was achieved by Boston in the 11th, when Bergen hit to Jennings, who threw past McGann, allowing Bergen to take second. Nichols advanced the runner to third on a groundout and Tenney tripled to deep center, scoring Bergen. Brooklyn was retired easily in the bottom of the inning to secure a 1-0 victory for Boston and a shutout for Nichols.

Boston dropped the next two games to Brooklyn before both teams traveled to the South End Grounds for the Beaneaters' home opener on April 19. With an overflow crowd finding spectators encircling the field, ground rules were enforced, each batter being allowed a base for a hit into the crowd. Brooklyn failed to capitalize, and Nichols hurled his second straight shutout, winning 7-0.

An outpouring of hitting by Boston and splendid pitching by Vic Willis the next day in Washington was too much for the Senators, Boston winning 17-1, on 21 hits, 19 of them singles, including four by Tenney. On April 21 Oscar Streit made his major-league debut, defeating Washington 7-3 despite issuing seven bases on balls.

Boston took its fifth straight with a 10-1 victory in Washington on April 24. The six-hit pitching of Klobedanz, who contributed a home run to the scoring, came as a welcome relief after he'd been shelled for 15 hits in an 11-7 loss to Brooklyn in his first start of the season. With a record of 6-2, the Beaneaters were in second place, a game behind the surprising 6-0 St. Louis Browns.

None of this could have mattered to Marty Bergen, who received a telegram that day that his four-year-old son had been taken critically ill. Bergen left the club to head home, but little Willie Bergen died of diphtheria before his father could reach his side. "It's pretty tough that my boy should be taken away," Bergen lamented to neighbors, "but it seems a great deal harder still to think that I should just get home in time to see him being taken out of the door in a box."[5] Until Bergen rejoined the club on May 6, Clarke assumed the catching duties and George Yeager, the prior season's backup receiver, was recalled from Worcester.

Kolbedanz was knocked out of the box in the first inning of his next start, in Philadelphia on April 27. Streit pitched poorly in five-plus innings of relief, and right fielder Chick Stahl pitched the final two innings. The Phillies capitalized on 14 walks given up by Boston's pitchers in winning 20-3, handing the Beaneaters their most decisive loss of the season. The loser of four in a row as April turned to May, Boston slumped to 7-7 and seventh place.

A serious blow was dealt to the club on May 2 when Billy Hamilton, batting over .400 at the time, wrenched his knee sliding home with a run in a 9-2 win at Baltimore. He was initially out for two weeks, and a strained tendon plagued the aging star for the remainder of the season, limiting his playing time to 84 games and reducing his speed and agility on the basepaths. Chick Stahl was moved to the top of the batting order, and utilityman Jimmy "General" Stafford was pressed into duty as the center fielder in Hamilton's absence.

Barely a month into the season, it was apparent that outside of Nichols and Willis, Boston's pitching was not performing up to snuff. Klobedanz, 19-10 in 1898, had struggled in winning once in five decisions, and the rookie Streit had not impressed enough to pitch in more than two games. On May 11, with the Boston club hovering just over .500 in sixth place, Selee released Klobedanz and Streit and signed veteran southpaw Frank Killen. Killen had topped NL pitchers in victories in 1893 and 1896 with Pittsburgh, but had started the 1899 season 0-2 with the hapless Senators and been released.

"The champions are handicapped in the box," observed one journalist. "Nichols and Willis are in good shape. [Charlie] Hickman, Lewis, and Killen are not to be depended upon, and the members of the team have little confidence in any of these men at the present time."[6] But Killen made an impressive debut with the club, limiting Louisville to five hits in a 13-4 win on May 19. "This is the left-hander we have been looking for a long time," someone on the Boston squad was quoted as saying, "and now that we have him there is no way on earth to keep us from winning the pennant again."[7]

In an otherwise dreary 5-2 loss at Washington on May 15, Marty Bergen demonstrated why he was considered the circuit's best defensive catcher when he threw out five runners attempting to steal.

Bergen, though, was struggling in his mind. After his son died in April, Bergen began to imagine that his teammates were making light of the boy's death and joking about it behind his back. His teammates, in turn, would later confess they felt "an indescribable fear"[8] whenever they were in his company.

On June 20, in one of the hardest-fought contests of the season, Kid Nichols matched Chicago's Clark Griffith inning for inning, each giving up a single run in the fourth and nothing thereafter, and carrying the game into extra innings. Finally, in the 13th, with two men on and two outs, Chicago second baseman Barry McCormick fumbled what ought to have been the third out, loading the bases. Griffith, perhaps rattled, walked in a run before giving up a bases-clearing double to Jimmy Collins. Nichols went the distance in the 5-1 victory.

Collins, the league's premier third baseman in only his third season, put together a string of 18 straight games without an error, ending on June 3.

On June 21 Charlie Frisbee, "crack outfielder of the Western League,"[9] a .316 hitter over four minor-league seasons, was plucked from the Worcester roster to be Hamilton's on-again, off-again replacement in center field. Although no match for Hamilton's skill at the bat and on the basepaths, Frisbee would prove an adequate substitute, stroking the ball at a better-than-.300 clip all season.

Still looking to bolster the pitching staff, Boston signed Harvey Bailey, a 22-year-old left-handed pitcher for the independent South Bend club, on June 29, and put him in the pitcher's box the next day. Bailey looked sharp in his major-league debut, scattering seven hits and one walk in nine innings in beating Cleveland 3-1.

"When a team begins to lose," observed the *Pittsburgh Press*, "all kinds of stories are put into circulation. The latest report is to the effect that the Boston players are fighting among themselves. The fact that Ted Lewis … threatened to leave the team the other day and go home would indicate that there is not the best of feeling among the players. Lewis is one of the nicest players in the business, and would not make such a declaration unless there were some reason for it."[10]

The Beaneaters were suffering internal unrest, but they were hardly losing. From May 11 through June 15, they had won 23 of 28, mostly on the strength of hitting by Tenney and Stahl, both batting over .350, and had climbed into second place behind Brooklyn. The Superbas, though, were all but uncatchable, winning games at an astonishing pace, including 12 in a row from May 28 through June 9, and 20 of 21 through June 22. As June came to a close, Brooklyn sat atop the NL at 45-18, a .714 percentage, with Boston five games back at 39-22 (.639).

On July 1 Boston took on the Cleveland Spiders, 11-48 and on their way to an abominable 20-134 won-lost record for the season, in a doubleheader at League Park. In the opener Boston, behind the splendid three-hit pitching of Willis, led 7-0 going into the ninth inning when Cleveland, "by a batting streak such as they have seldom developed, sent seven men across the plate and tied the score." In the 11th, after Boston had scored twice to regain the lead, Cleveland, having driven Willis from the box, rallied for three runs off Ted Lewis to pull out an exciting victory and send the disbelieving crowd into a celebratory frenzy. In the six-inning second game, the Beaneaters pulled themselves together and, in support of a two-hit, scoreless performance by seldom-used starter Charlie Hickman, pounded Cleveland's Fred "Crazy" Schmit and Harry Maupin for 14 runs on 17 hits.

Boston was, in its next game, on July 3, on the receiving end of a 15-2 pounding from Washington, loser of 18 of its last 19. Killen was driven from the box in a nine-run explosion by the ordinarily woeful Senators in the third. An unusual play unfolded in the eighth inning when with two on, Washington's Shad Barry hit a fly that landed safely in deep center. After racing around the bases with what appeared to be a home run, Barry was called out for failing to touch first base, depriving him of even a base hit.

A stripped but still competitive Orioles team hosted the Beaneaters in a July 4 morning-afternoon doubleheader at Baltimore's Union Park. After taking the morning game 2-1 when Ted Lewis walked the bases full in the sixth and allowed the Orioles' Jimmy Sheckard to drive in the winning run on a sacrifice fly, the Orioles stole another close one in the afternoon, 5-4, from Nichols. Steal, indeed – with two out in the fourth inning, John McGraw reached on a bunt single, then stole second, then third. Nichols walked Ducky Holmes, who became "engaged in dodging up and down the base lines."[11] While Nichols was distracted, McGraw took off for home and got his third stolen base of the inning. In doing so, McGraw became the first player in history to steal second, third, and home in the same inning. (Louisville's Honus Wagner duplicated McGraw's feat less than a month later, on August 1. Wagner today shares a record with Ty Cobb, each having accomplished the feat four times.)

The pair of losses dropped the Beaneaters into fourth place behind Brooklyn, Philadelphia, and Chicago. A turnabout in fortune gave Boston four straight victories and returned the team to second place.

On July 9 the Grand Rapids Cabinet Makers of the Interstate League filed a protest with the national board claiming that Harvey Bailey had signed with the team before jumping to Boston. Bailey denied accepting terms with Grand Rapids, but the board upheld the team's claim, and Boston was forced to turn over $300 to buy Bailey's contract.[12] Opting for the younger Bailey, Selee released Killen on July 28, despite the veteran's 7-5 won-lost record. The gamble worked for Boston, as Bailey went 6-4 before season's end.

Batting records through July 12 showed Philadelphia's Ed Delahanty leading the NL at .421, with Boston's Fred Tenney fourth at .394. Despite distractions, Bergen topped the league's catchers in fielding percentage.[13]

On July 21, on the way to Cincinnati with the team to begin a long Western road trip, Bergen, suitcase in hand, stepped off the train in Washington, and caught another train for home. Bergen "has melancholia at times," one of his teammates told *The Sporting News*. "When he has one of his spells he talks of nothing but his children and home and usually jumps a train and goes to them."[14] Selee fined Bergen $25.

"[Bergen] says that last season he had trouble with one of the players, which was magnified. He claims he could not get a day off to see his family, and that Selee would not listen to his excuses for going home; that at Chicago, at least four members of the team went out of the way to abuse him every time he went to bat, and would call out 'Strike him out'; that one player, after the loss of [Bergen's] child, continually reminded him of his trouble.

"He says he left the team at Washington because he found that Selee and most of the players were avoiding him. He is in good condition, with the exception of his nerves, which he says will be all right 'if the boys play ball and let up aggravating me while manager Selee sits silently by.'"15

While observers weighed Boston's chances at the pennant without their star backstop, Boston players were irritated at Bergen's allegations. Meanwhile, Clarke was catching every inning of every game in Bergen's absence.

Selee wired Bergen to return at once or not at all. Bergen tore up the telegram. On July 28 he met with club President Arthur Soden, telling him he was "subject to a nervous trouble, and when he was attacked he had no control over himself but to get away from the team as rapidly as possible."16 Soden advised Bergen to rejoin the team when they returned from their road trip.

The prodigal catcher's return turned out to be one of the finest games of his career. Against the Washington Senators at Boston on August 4, Bergen threw out all three runners who tried to steal. The fans at the South End Grounds cheered Bergen like a returning hero each time he came to bat. In the ninth inning, with two out, Boston down 3-2 and men on second and third, Bergen drove a single to left that scored both runners and won the game. "After the game Bergen was a mark for the crowd, who cheered him until he went out of sight."17

His teammates, still riled over what Bergen had said about them in the newspapers, bristled at the cheers for Bergen, believing that the public had taken Bergen's side. Before the game the next day, the Boston players demanded that Bergen retract his allegations, but he refused. Threatening to strike and delaying the start of the game by 15 minutes, they took the field only after Bergen alleged that he had been "incorrectly quoted."18

Boston enjoyed its biggest offensive afternoon of the year at home against the Cleveland Spiders on August 8. The Beaneaters teed off on Frank Bates, scoring four runs in the first, another in the third, and five more in the fourth to take a 10-1 lead. Harvey Bailey faltered in the fifth, with Cleveland scoring four runs on four singles and a home run by center fielder Tommy Dowd. Hickman replaced Bailey for the final four innings, as Boston added three more runs in the seventh, and another five in the eighth. In all, the Beaneaters tallied 20 hits, including home runs by General Stafford and Hugh Duffy, winning 18-8.

One game behind the first-place Brooklyn squad on August 10, Boston began to shake up the roster. Jouett Meekin, 5-11 as a starting pitcher with the New York Giants, was purchased for $5,000 on August 11. Meekin posted a 7-6 won-lost record and a fine 2.83 ERA over the remaining two months of the season. The next day, despite batting .302 in 55 games, utilityman Stafford was released. None of Boston's moves would make a difference in trying to catch the Superbas, who were busy winning 26 of 30 games between August 11 and September 14.

Batting above .310 through most of the summer, third baseman Jimmy Collins twisted his ankle while sliding in a game against Baltimore on August 19, and although he remained in the lineup, his hitting suffered, and his average fell more than 30 points by season's end.

Making more roster moves, Selee gave second baseman Mike Hickey and pitcher Billy Ging each a one-game trial. Hickey went 1-for-3 on September 14, but his defensive play showed "poor form."19 Ging's outing, on the other hand, was a good one; he tossed eight innings of five-hit, one-run ball on September 25 in beating the New York Giants, 2-1. Curiously, Ging never appeared in another major-league game.

Another young player, 24-year-old Billy Sullivan, later an outstanding defensive receiver for the American League's Chicago White Stockings, was purchased in September from the Western League's Grand Rapids Furniture Makers. Sullivan made his debut behind the plate on September 13, ultimately getting into 22 games as Bergen's erratic behavior increasingly cost him playing time.

A Boston loss to Baltimore on September 5, in the middle of a 3-6 slide, allowed the Philadelphia Phillies to slip past the Beaneaters into second place. Held scoreless in consecutive games, September 8-9, by Brooklyn's all-star aggregation, Boston fell behind in the standings by double digits.

On September 25 Bergen again went home after splitting his finger in a game in New York against the Giants, leaving only a note for Frank Selee.20 He returned unannounced a week later, showing up in Boston, where the Beaneaters were again to take on the Giants, and suiting up for the game without speaking to anyone, not even Selee.

Finally, on October 9, Bergen appeared to suffer a mental breakdown during a game against Philadelphia. Imagining someone was trying to stab him with a knife,21 Bergen leapt out of the way of several pitches, letting the ball fly by. One of these dodged pitches was a third strike to Ed Delahanty with two men out, allowing him to reach first base.22 Selee removed Bergen from the game. "Bergen Makes a Farce of His Position," remarked a headline in the *Boston Globe*.23

Boston won 13 of 18, including one tie, down the stretch, including three shutouts – by Lewis, Willis, and Nichols – in four games against Philadelphia. They had reclaimed second place on October 2, but were unable to gain further ground on the Superbas, who captured the pennant with a 101-47 record, eight games ahead of the Beaneaters.

Bergen, playing in only 72 games in 1899, caused considerable tension and disruption for the rest of the team. "Mr. Soden makes no bones in asserting that his club has lost the pennant on account of the Bergen trouble," a newspaper said. "This created a bad feeling on the team, on account of which the men did not play the ball of which they were capable."24

No doubt. But Bergen hadn't sidelined Billy Hamilton, whose strained tendon cost him 64 games and contributed to a sharp decline in his batting average. from .369 in 1898 to .310, and his stolen-base total from 54 to 19. Jimmy Collins's slump in the second half of the season hurt, too, his totals dropping from .328 with 15 home runs in 1898 to just .277 with 5 four-baggers. Fred Tenney and Chick Stahl batted .347 and .351, respectively, and Hamilton's frequent stand-in Charlie Frisbee hit .329 in 42 games. Vic Willis enjoyed a superb sophomore season, winning 27 against only 8 losses, with a league-leading 2.50 ERA, but staff ace Kid Nichols, after three straight seasons with 30 or more wins, turned in a disappointing 21-19 won-lost record, and Ted Lewis dropped to 17-11 after going 26-8 for the pennant-winning club of 1898. The generally overlooked Charlie Hickman was a perfect 6-0 with a pair of shutouts in nine starts out of 11 appearances in the pitcher's box, and added eight more games as an outfielder-first baseman, batting an impressive .397 with seven triples in only 63 at-bats; next season would find him playing regularly at first base for the New York Giants.

The postscript to Boston's 1899 season is a tragic one. On the morning of January 19, 1900, Marty Bergen surrendered to the demons in his mind. Rising early, he took an axe and murdered his wife, Hattie, 3-year-old son, Joe, and 6-year-old daughter, Florence. Standing before a mirror, he then took his own life by slashing his throat with a razor.[25] The next day, 800 mourners gathered at St. Joseph's Church in North Brookfield. Only one member of the Boston club – Billy Hamilton, Bergen's roommate on the road – attended the funeral. Frank Selee sent flowers.

The era of Boston's baseball greatness had also come to an end. After winning five pennants in the 1890s, the club managed one only winning season in the next 14, losing 100 or more games five times. By the time the team hoisted another pennant, it was 1914 and they had been rechristened the Braves. Meanwhile, a new Boston team, a charter member of the rival American League, had opened for business at a ballpark across the railroad tracks from the South End Grounds. As one dynasty ended, another was about to begin.

SOURCES

In addition to the sources listed in the notes, the author also consulted:

Caruso, Gary. *The Braves Encyclopedia* (Philadelphia: Temple University Press, 1995).

Kaese, Harold. *The Boston Braves, 1871-1953* (Boston: Northeastern University Press, 2004).

NOTES

1 "Leaders of the National League," *Nashville American*, March 6, 1899: 6.
2 "Promise Good Sport," *Daily Inter Ocean* (Chicago), March 7, 1899: 8.
3 "Players Were Scarce," *Baltimore Sun*, March 22, 1899: 6.
4 "Brilliant Base Ball Opens the Season," *Brooklyn Daily Eagle*, April 16, 1899: 10.
5 William Nack, "Collison at Home," *Sports Illustrated*, June 4, 2001: 71.
6 "Must Play Faster," *Pittsburgh Press*, May 17, 1899: 5.
7 "Made Scores in Bunches," *North Adams* (Massachusetts) *Transcript*, May 20, 1899: 6.
8 "Tragedy on Heels of Romance," *Cincinnati Post*, January 23, 1900: 2.
9 "Baseball Briefs," *Buffalo Evening News*, March 7, 1899: 14.
10 "Plays and Players," *Pittsburgh Press*, July 3, 1899: 5.
11 "Orioles on Top," *Baltimore Sun*, July 5, 1899: 6.
12 "World of Sport," *Buffalo Commercial*, July 25, 1899: 7.
13 "Baseball Briefs," *Washington Evening Star*, July 17, 1899: 9.
14 "Selee Reinstates Bergen," *The Sporting News*, July 29, 1899: 5.
15 "Bergen's Tale," *Cincinnati Post*, July 26, 1899: 5.
16 "Bergen Is Penitent," *Philadelphia Times*, July 29, 1899: 11.
17 "Bergen's Triumph," *Boston Globe*, August 5, 1899: 1.
18 "Brooklyn Sends Meekin in Air," *Deseret Evening News* (Salt Lake City), August 23, 1899: 5.
19 "St. Louis 11-7, Boston 1-4," *Kansas City Journal*, September 15, 1899: 5.
20 "Baseball Gossip," *Detroit Free Press*, September 27, 1899: 6.
21 William Nack, "Collison at Home," *Sports Illustrated*, June 4, 2001: 80.
22 "The Phillies Play Fast Ball and Defeat Boston in the Second Game," *Philadelphia Times*, October 10, 1899: 10.
23 "Tie for Second," *Boston Globe*, October 10, 1899: 3.
24 "Recent Peace Conference," *Washington Evening Star*, October 13, 1899: 8.
25 "Bergen's Awful Deed," *Illustrated Buffalo Express*, January 21, 1900: 14.

Contributors

We're the glorious Beaneaters,

Who've won the championship!

We've had baked beans for supper

And we're happy, hip, hip, hip!

(Anonymous, 1897)

MATT ALBERTSON resides in Havertown, Pennsylvania with his wife Jess with whom he attends many Phillies games throughout the year. He joined SABR in 2015 and in 2018 was named the recipient of the SABR 19th Century Committee's Chairman's Award. Matt concentrated on public history in graduate school and continues that passion through baseball research and activity in vintage baseball. He dedicated a Pennsylvania Historical Marker to the Jefferson Street Ballparks in Philadelphia in 2017 and in the same year joined the Athletic Base Ball Club of Philadelphia. Matt is also the historical columnist for SportsTalkPhilly.com.

DENNIS AUGER was born and raised in New Hampshire and now resides in Massachusetts with his wife Elaine. A lifelong Yankee fan and a SABR member since 2000, he is now retired from providing services in the substance abuse field. He has written several SABR articles focusing on the Deadball Era. A present interest is researching the history of baseball mill teams in the Granite State textile industry.

JOHN BAUER resides with his wife and two children in Bedford, New Hampshire, having recently relocated from Kansas City. By day, he is an attorney specializing in insurance regulatory law and corporate law. By night, he spends many spring and summer evenings cheering for the San Francisco Giants and many fall and winter evenings reading history. He is a past and ongoing contributor to other SABR projects.

CHARLIE BEVIS is the author of seven books on baseball history, most recently *Red Sox vs. Braves in Boston: The Battle for Fans' Hearts, 1901–1952*. A member of SABR since 1984, he has contributed more than four dozen biographies to the SABR BioProject as well as several to SABR books, including *The 1967 Impossible Dream Red Sox*. He is an adjunct professor of English at Rivier University in Nashua, New Hampshire, and lives in Chelmsford, Massachusetts.

RICHARD BOGOVICH is the author of *Kid Nichols: A Biography of the Hall of Fame Pitcher* and *The Who: A Who's Who*, both published by McFarland & Co. He has contributed to such SABR books as *The 1986 Boston Red Sox: There Was More Than Game Six*. He works for the Wendland Utz law firm in Rochester, Minnesota.

THOMAS J. BROWN JR. is a lifelong Mets fan who became a Durham Bulls fan after moving to North Carolina in the early 1980s. He was a national board certified high school science teacher for 34 years before retiring in 2016. Tom still volunteers with the ELL students at his former high school, serving as a mentor to those students and the teachers who are now working with them. He also provides support and guidance for his former ELL students when they embark on different career paths after graduation. Tom has been a member of S.A.B.R. since 1995 when he learned about the organization during a visit to Cooperstown on his honeymoon. He has become active in the organization since his retirement and has written numerous biographies and game stories, mostly about the NY Mets. Tom also enjoys traveling as much as possible with his wife and has visited major league and minor league baseball parks across the country on his many trips. He also loves to cook and makes all the meals for at his house while writing about those meals on his blog, Cooking and My Family.

JEAN-PIERRE CAILLAULT has been a Professor of Astronomy at the University of Georgia for 32 years. He joined SABR in 1984, when, as a PhD student at Columbia University, he made his first SABR presentation to the Casey Stengel Chapter (NYC) at the Shea Stadium Diamond Club. He has since written articles for *Baseball Digest* and SABR's *Baseball Research Journal*, a chapter for *Inventing Baseball: The 100 Greatest Games of the 19th Century* (SABR 2013), and two books on 19th-century baseball: *A Tale of Four Cities* (McFarland & Co., 2003) and *The Complete New York Clipper Biographies* (McFarland & Co., 2009). His presentation at the 2010 SABR National Convention in Atlanta was awarded the USA Today Sports Weekly Award for Best Poster Presentation. He is an avid collector of baseball cards, owning the complete set of Topps cards for every season dating back to 1957.

Since 1993, not a day has passed on which **MATT CLEVER** did not watch, read about, or dream about baseball. Growing up in eastern Pennsylvania, his heart was captured that summer by an unforgettable Phillies squad that came up just short in October. Matt is a land surveyor, and also works part-time as a scorekeeper at the Phillies' Double-A affiliate in Reading, Pennsylvania. This is his first contribution to a SABR publication.

ALAN COHEN serves as Vice President-Treasurer of the Connecticut Smoky Joe Wood Chapter, and is datacaster for the Hartford Yard Goats, the Double-A affiliate of the Rockies. He has written more than 50 biographies for SABR's bio-project. His work on ballplayers who homered in the same ballparks in the minors and majors led him to this interest in the story of Cliff Carroll. Alan has continued to expand his research into the Hearst Sandlot Classic (1946-1965), which launched the careers of 88 major-league players. He has four children and six grandchildren and resides in Connecticut with wife Frances and their cat Morty, and their dog Buddy.

RORY COSTELLO is an alumnus of Williams College and was thus drawn to write about Ted Lewis, as well as all the other Ephmen in the majors. Alas, there hasn't been one since 1934. Rory lives in Brooklyn, New York with his wife Noriko and son Kai.

JERROD COTOSMAN is a CPA who oversees the State of Colorado's Medicaid accounting. He became a Red Sox fan at age 7 in the summer of 1978 after reading a book about Fred Lynn. He has contributed to a variety of SABR projects and has written a novel and an anthology of short stories. He lives in Denver with his wife and daughter.

RICHARD CUICCHI joined SABR in 1983 and is an active member of the Schott-Pelican Chapter. Since his retirement as an information technology executive, Richard authored *Family Ties: A Comprehensive Collection of Facts and Trivia about Baseball's Relatives*. He has contributed to numerous SABR BioProject and Games publications. He does freelance writing and blogging about a variety of baseball topics on his website TheTenthInning.com. Richard lives in New Orleans with his wife, Mary.

CHARLES F. FABER was a native of Iowa who lived in Lexington, Kentucky, until his passing in August 2016. He held degrees from Coe College, Columbia University, and the University of Chicago. A retired public school and university teacher and administrator, he contributed to numerous SABR projects, including editing *The 1934 St. Louis Cardinals: The World Champion Gas House Gang*. Among his publications are dozens of professional journal articles, encyclopedia entries, and research reports in fields such as school administration, education law, and country music. In addition to textbooks, he wrote 10 books (mostly on baseball) published by McFarland. His last book, co-authored with his grandson Zachariah Webb, was *The Hunt for a Reds October*, published by McFarland in 2015.

BILL FELBER is a retired newspaper editor. He is the author of numerous books on baseball, golf and the cavalry, among them *A Game of Brawl: The Orioles, the Beaneaters and the Battle for the 1897 Pennant*. He is a regular contributor to calltothepen.com.

DAVID FLEITZ, a web developer and SABR member from Troy, Michigan, has written nine well-received books on baseball history, including biographies of Shoeless Joe Jackson, Louis Sockalexis, and Cap Anson. David is a graduate of Bowling Green State University and is a lifelong Detroit Tigers fan. David's next work, a biography of Chicago White Sox pitcher Eddie Cicotte, one of the key figures in the Black Sox Scandal of 1919, will be published by McFarland and Company in 2020. David is also a trivia expert, having won the individual trivia competition at three consecutive SABR conventions.

BRIAN FRANK is passionate about documenting the history of major and minor-league baseball. He is the creator of the website The Herd Chronicles (www.herdchronicles.com), which is dedicated to preserving the history of the Buffalo Bisons. His articles can also be read on the official website of the Bisons. He was a contributor to and assistant editor of the book *Seasons of Buffalo Baseball, 1857-2019*, and he's a frequent contributor to SABR publications. Brian and his wife Jenny enjoy traveling around the country in their camper to major and minor-league ballparks and taking an annual trip to Europe. Brian was a history major at Canisius College where he earned a Bachelor of Arts. He also received a Juris Doctor from the University at Buffalo School of Law.

PETER M. GORDON is a long-time member of SABR who›s written articles for 16 of our published books, including the history of the Tampa Bay Rays› first year for 2018›s *Time for Expansion Baseball*. He's an award-winning poet with more than 100 poems published, including his Amazon best-selling collection of baseball poems, *Let's Play Two*. After a 40-year career creating and curating content for platforms from live theatre to digital television, he lives in Orlando, Florida where he teaches Business of Film in Full Sail University's Film Production MFA program.

TERRY GOTTSCHALL teaches recent European history at Walla Walla University. His research interests alternate between 19th-century townball in the interior Pacific Northwest and Imperial German naval operations in East Asian waters. He has yet to reconcile the two interests into a single subject.

GERARD R. (GERRY) GOULET, of Warwick, Rhode Island, is now semi-retired after more than forty years in health care regulation as an analyst and attorney. A lifetime Red Sox fan, this is his second contribution to books about nineteenth-century baseball history in Boston. His game summaries in this volume are dedicated to the memory of Ray Peters, college classmate and friend, who pitched briefly for the Milwaukee Brewers in 1970 and recently passed away on May 4, 2019.

STEVE HATCHER has been a member of SABR since 1988, and has been a loyal fan of the Braves from the Milwaukee years on through the Atlanta years. He and his wife are retired and living in North Idaho, having the interest and time to write biographical contributions for SABR with a focus on the Nineteenth Century.

PAUL HOFMANN, a SABR member since 2002, is the Associate Vice President for International Programs at Sacramento State University. He is a native of Detroit, Michigan and lifelong Detroit Tigers fan. Paul currently resides in Folsom, California.

MIKE HUBER is a Professor of Mathematics at Muhlenberg College in Allentown, Pennsylvania. He is the Chair of SABR's Games Project Committee and enjoys researching and writing about baseball games from the nineteenth century.

JOANNE HULBERT. Co-chair of the Boston Chapter and of SABR's Baseball Arts Committee, spends long hours gathering baseball poetry and other unique history related to baseball. A resident of Mudville, a village of Holliston, Massachusetts she proudly and unabashedly admits to having been nurtured on countless Saturday night suppers that included Boston Baked Beans, cuisine that eminently prepared her to take on a bit of Beaneater history. She offers the following recipe from *Fanny Farmer's 1896 Boston Cooking School Cook Book*: "Pick over one quart pea beans, cover with cold water, and soak over night. In morning, drain, cover with fresh water, heat slowly (keeping water below boiling point), and cook until skins will burst, which is best determined by taking a few beans on the tip of a spoon and blowing on them, when skins will burst if sufficiently cooked. Beans thus tested [and fail] must, of course, be thrown away. Drain beans, throwing bean-water out of doors, not in sink. Scald rind of one-half pound fat salt pork, scrape, remove one-fourth rind of remaining pork every one-half inch, making cuts one inch deep. Put beans in pot and bury pork in beans, leaving rind exposed. Mix one tablespoon salt, one tablespoon molasses, and 3 tablespoons sugar; add one cup boiling water to cover beans. Cover bean-pot, put in oven, and bake slowly 6 or 8 hours, uncovering the last hour of cooking, that rind may become brown and crisp. Add water as needed. Many feel sure that by adding with seasonings one-half tablespoon mustard, the beans are more easily digested. If pork mixed with lean is preferred, use less salt. The fine reputation which Boston Baked Beans have gained, has been attributed to the earthen bean-pot with small top and bulging sides in which they are supposed to be cooked. Equally good beans have often been eaten where a five-pound lard pail was substituted for the broken bean-pot."

Ah! A supper fit for a Beaneater.

BILL LAMB is the editor of *The Inside Game*, the newsletter of the Deadball Era Committee, and the author of *Black Sox in the Courtroom: The Grand Jury, Criminal Trial and Civil Litigation* (McFarland, 2013). Prior to his retirement, he spent more than 30 years as a state/county prosecutor in New Jersey.

KEVIN LARKIN retired after 24 years as a police officer in his hometown of Great Barrington Massachusetts. He has always been a baseball fan and has been going to minor league and major league baseball games since he was five years old. He has authored two books on baseball: *Baseball in the BayState* (a history of baseball in the Commonwealth of Massachusetts) and *Gehrig: Game by Game* (an account of all of the major-league baseball games played by his hero, Lou Gehrig. He has also co-authored *Baseball in the Berkshires: A County's Common Bond* along with James Tom Daly, James Overmyer and Larry Moore. The book details a history of baseball in Berkshire County where Larkin grew up. He has authored numerous articles for SABR and also recently had published on Legends On Deck, a list of who Larkin thinks are the top 100 Black Baseball/Negro League baseball players. He does fact checking and hyperlinking for SABR, as well as writing biographies and game accounts, and according to him, is living the dream of writing and researching about the great sport of baseball.

BOB LEMOINE was previously co-editor of *Boston's First Nine: The 1871-75 Boston Red Stockings* (SABR, 2016). He has specific interests in Boston's baseball history, the 19th Century, and the Negro Leagues, but he often jumps into any SABR project. Bob lives in New Hampshire and works as a high school librarian and adjunct professor.

LEN LEVIN is sure that if the Beaneaters were still around today he'd root for them. An ardent fan of the Boston Red Sox, he is a retired newspaper editor in Providence who now edits the decisions of the Rhode Island Supreme Court and also copyedits many of SABR's publications, including this one.

DAN LEVITT is the author of several baseball books and numerous essays. He is a longtime SABR member and a recipient of the Davids Award and the Chadwick Award. His books have won the Larry Ritter Book Award, the Sporting News-SABR Baseball Research Award, and have twice been finalists for the Seymour Medal.

WILLIAM H. LYONS has been a SABR member since 1995 and is a member of the Boston Braves Historical Association. He grew up in Fitchburg, Massachusetts, graduated from Colby College and Boston College Law School, and practiced law in Bangor, Maine. He taught at the University of Nebraska College of Law for 35 years before retiring in 2016 and returning home to New England. He now lives in Castine, Maine. He was a fan of the Boston Braves for a year (1952), then followed the team in Milwaukee and Atlanta. He is a Red Sox fan, although he wishes that Boston still had a National League team. He enjoys researching and writing about baseball history and has just joined a SABR group working on the origins of baseball in New England.

MIKE MCAVOY is a member in the Cliff Kachline chapter of SABR and attends most of its excellent meetings. He earned a Ph.D. from the University of Illinois at Urbana-Champaign, and he teaches courses in economics at Oneonta State. He comes from a long line of Cub fans, although when younger and more foolish, he shared his loyalties briefly to closely follow the South Side Hitmen and cheered the Winning Ugly team. These days, when he has time, he thinks about the business of organizing a sports league and how early sport capitalists protected their property from entrants.

BRIAN MCKENNA has been a member of SABR since 1991. He lives in Baltimore and works as a retail manager. He has written nearly 60 biographies for SABR's BioProject.

ERIC MIKLICH has contributed to numerous SABR publication contributions and is the co-author with David Nemec of *Forfeits and Successfully Protested Games in Major League Baseball*, published by McFarland & Co. He is the founder and owner of 19C Base Ball Inc., and maintains its 500 plus page web site, www.19cbaseball.com. 19C Base Ball continues to be the baseball supplier to many clubs and festivals each year. Eric was the Volunteer 19th Century Base Ball Coordinator at Old Bethpage Village Restoration, on Long Island, from 2000-2009. Miklich has appeared in over 900 19th century base ball matches since 1998, is just shy of 400 wins and currently pitches for the Eckford of Brooklyn BBC. He spent 7 seasons with the New York Islanders as the Assistant Equipment Manager and practice goalie and with Team USA at the 1997 World Championships in Finland. Eric is currently the Goaltending Coach for three East Islip High School Freshman ice hockey teams. Miklich has a daughter, Christina and resides in Islip, New York.

SETH MOLAND-KOVASH is a lifelong passionate baseball fan and amateur historian. He grew up in Minnesota and his love of the game and the Twins has carried through many years, many moves, and many Twins eras. During the day, Seth is a Lutheran pastor in suburban Chicago where he lives with his wife Jennifer and their son Carl. Carl has also inherited the love of baseball and plays whenever the fields are not covered by snow. Seth›s favorite teams are the Twins and whatever team Carl is on.

CHAD MOODY is a nearly lifelong resident of suburban Detroit, where he has been a fan of the Detroit Tigers from birth. An alumnus of both the University of Michigan and Michigan State University, he has spent 25 years working in the automotive industry. Chad's first foray into formal baseball research occurred as a teenager, when he had a letter published in *Baseball Digest*. From that humble beginning, he has since frequently contributed to SABR's BioProject and Games Project. Chad and his wife, Lisa, live in Northville, Michigan, with their children, Jacob and Jessica, and dog, Daisy.

BILL MORTELL has been a SABR member since 1977. For 35 years he worked for the U.S. Department of Defense, from which he retired in 1987. A Chicago native, he lived in various cities in Japan (Kyoto, Nara, and Tokyo area) for 13 years and once saw both Frank and Brooks Robinson homer in the same Tokyo game against a Japanese all-star team. His current interests include family genealogy, and watching MLB, particularly Cubs and White Sox. He provides occasional research assistance to SABR members who are engaged in writing biographies of major-league players.

ROB NEE grew up in Norwood, Massachusetts and is consequently an avid Red Sox fan. He is a Special Education teacher at Weymouth High School with an affinity for local history. Rob's interest in the Beaneaters began after attending a Cemetery Walk organized by the Boston SABR Chapter which included a visit to the grave of Mike "King" Kelly. When not watching baseball, Rob enjoys playing the game with his sons Colman and Luke. This is his first contribution to a SABR publication.

DAVID NEMEC is a novelist and baseball historian. He has written *The Great Encyclopedia of Nineteenth Century Major League Baseball*; *The Beer and Whisky League,* a history of the American Association's 10-year sojourn as a rebel major league; *Major League Baseball Profiles: 1871-1900*; and many other baseball history and memorabilia books. His novel *The Picture Maker* was translated into Czech and published in April 2016 in the Czech Republic under the title *Zajatec Predstav*.

ROCHELLE LLEWELYN NICHOLLS has worked as a medical researcher and sports scientist in Australia, the USA, and Europe. She is Australian by birth and her home country's silver medal in baseball at the 2004 Athens Olympic Games remains her favourite sporting moment.

BILL NOWLIN has been eating Boston baked beans ever since he can remember. It's still a frequent staple with home-grilled hot dogs. His preferred brand is B&M, from the can. A native of Boston, living in Cambridge, he is one of the founders of Rounder Records and has also written or edited numerous books about baseball. He has been on the Board of Directors of SABR since 2004.

RALPH PELUSO born in New York City, and remains a loyal Yankees fan. Since becoming a member of SABR in 2009, he has been a contributing member of the Overlooked Legends committee. Ralph holds an MBA in finance from Bernard Baruch College and is now retired after 45 years in corporate finance and management consulting. His book *512*, a fictional re-imagination based on Babe Ruth, was published in 2014. He has had several short stories published, but this is first effort for a SABR project. Ralph recently returned from a trek to Mt. Everest base camp and is planning his next adventure. He serves as the literary editor for the Zebra Press, a monthly newspaper serving Northern Virginia, and writes the monthly book reviews. Ralph and his spouse Janet enjoy life in an active 55+ community near the beaches of Delaware.

MARK PESTANA has been a SABR member since 1990, and a baseball fan since 1967 when he moved to the Boston area during the summer of the Impossible Dream Red Sox. He currently lives in rural Dunstable, Massachusetts, and his focus is on 19th Century baseball history. He has contributed to the SABR publications *Inventing Baseball: The 100 Greatest Games of the 19th Century, Boston's First Nine: The 1871-75 Boston Red Stockings, Base Ball's 19th Century Winter Meetings 1857-1900, The World Series in the Deadball Era, Braves Field: Memorable Moments at Boston's Lost Diamond*, and *From the Braves to the Brewers: Great Games & Exciting History at Milwaukee's County Stadium*.

RICHARD RIIS is a writer, researcher, and genealogist with an abiding interest in baseball since he beheld his first baseball card in 1964. In addition to contributing to the SABR BioProject and 10 SABR books, he has been a contributing editor for a popular music magazine and is presently working with his friend and former child star Pamelyn Ferdin on her memoirs. He lives in South Setauket, New York.

JOEL RIPPEL, a Minnesota native and graduate of the University of Minnesota, is the author or co-author of 10 books on Minnesota sports history and has contributed as a writer to several books published by SABR.

BOB RUZZO is the Chief Operating Officer of Mass-Development, a quasi-governmental authority that finances and supports economic development initiatives of all kinds throughout the Commonwealth of Massachusetts. Before becoming a Red Sox fan, his father rooted for the Boston Braves, and so the spirit lives on. Bob's articles about Braves Field and the Federal League have appeared in SABR's *Baseball Research Journal*. Bob lives in Melrose with his wife Susan and his son Patrick, who inspires him every day as he continues to push past the limits autism tries to impose.

MARK SOUDER served as the U.S. Congressman for northeastern Indiana from 1995-2010. He was a senior staff member in the U.S. House and Senate for a decade prior to being elected to Congress. Souder was one of the primary leaders of the hearings on steroid abuse in baseball. He has contributed articles to *The National Pastime* for the Chicago, New York, Pittsburgh, and San Diego issues. He has also contributed to four previous SABR books on the Boston Red Stockings, Puerto Rico, ballplayers and the movies, and the San Diego Padres. He also wrote the 2019 spring issue of *Old Fort News* on the history of professional baseball in Fort Wayne, the official publication of the Fort Wayne, Indiana Historical Society. He is retired, and lives in Fort Wayne with his wife and his books.

GLEN SPARKS looks forward to the day the Dodgers finally win another World Series. He has contributed to several SABR books and is at work on a full-length biography of Hall of Fame shortstop Pee Wee Reese. Sparks grew up in Santa Monica, California, and lives with his wife, Pam, in Cardinals country.

LYLE SPATZ joined SABR in 1973. He was chairman of the Baseball Records Committee from 1991 to 2016. Although currently living in Florida, his heart remains in Maryland.

MARK S. STERNMAN has written profiles of several Boston NL players (Tommy Beals, Buster Brown, Jack Burdock, Ben Cardoni, Scotty Ingerton, Fred Tenney, and Sam Wise) and recaps of some of the team's most memorable games (including all four 1914 World Series contests). He works at the Massachusetts State House and wishes he could make the hour-long walk to Braves Field to see a major league game.

JW STEWART is an associate professor at Collin College in Frisco, TX teaching American History. In addition to contributing to several SABR book projects, he also published a history of 19th century mascots and bat boys in *Base Ball: New Research in the Early Game*. He is a dedicated fan of the AA Frisco RoughRiders and is working on his PhD in English at the University of North Texas.

TREY STRECKER teaches English and sport studies at Ball State University. He is the editor of *Dead Balls and Double Curves: An Anthology of Early Baseball Fiction* (Southern Illinois University Press, 2004) and *The Collected Baseball Stories of Charles Van Loan* (McFarland, 2004), and he edits the book review section of *NINE: A Journal of Baseball History & Culture*.

ANDY TERRICK is a native of Pittsburgh and a member of SABR's Forbes Field chapter. His obsession in digging up information about local 19th century ballparks has likely alienated many friends and family, but has also proven fulfilling in numerous ways. His contributions to this volume will be the first of, hopefully, many SABR-published game accounts, most of which will involve a player with the last name Wagner, Beckley, or Galvin.

STEW THORNLEY has been a member of SABR since 1979. He has written or edited two books on the Polo Grounds.

RICHARD "DIXIE" TOURANGEAU is a retired (2012) National Park Service ranger who has lived in his Boston triple-decker since 1974. It is one mile from the Beaneaters South End Grounds home, now part of his Northeastern University alma mater's campus. He joined SABR in 1980 after being recruited by head Hall of Fame librarian Cliff Kachline. That same year he edited, then authored the *Play Ball!!* baseball calendar for Tide-Mark Press, of West Hartford, Connecticut. That research/writing task lasted 25 years through 2005's issue. Just before this century began, Dixie decided it was time know "a little bit more" about 19th century base ball and took the plunge. Still immersed, he is trying to get a commemorative location sign for the iconic South End ballyard and a bronze plaque in Cooperstown for shortstop Herman Long. He roots mostly for the Rockies and Astros while petting four kitties. After 30 seasons, he gave up his Red Sox season tickets after 2017. As a volunteer guide, he gives tours on the museum ship, *USS Cassin Young* (DD793), at the old Charlestown Navy Yard, now Boston National Historical Park.

GREGORY H. WOLF was born in Pittsburgh, but now resides in the Chicagoland area with his wife, Margaret, and daughter, Gabriela. A professor of German studies and holder of the Dennis and Jean Bauman Endowed Chair in the Humanities at North Central College in Naperville, Illinois, he has edited 10 books for SABR. He is currently working on projects about Griffith Stadium in Washington, Shibe Park in Philadelphia, and the 1982 Milwaukee Brewers. Since January 2017 he has been co-director of SABR's BioProject, which you can follow on Facebook and Twitter.

JOHN ZINN is a graduate of Rutgers University and a Vietnam veteran. He is the chairman of the board of the New Jersey Historical Society. John is the author of five books including the first full length biography of Brooklyn Dodgers owner Charles Ebbets and a history of early New Jersey baseball. He also writes a blog on baseball history entitled "A Manly Pastime" and is the score keeper for the Flemington Neshanock vintage baseball team.

www.ingramcontent.com/pod-product-compliance
Lightning Source LLC
Chambersburg PA
CBHW081352070526
44583CB00020B/2527